EU Law

EU Law

Tenth Edition

Josephine Steiner and Lorna Woods

OXFORD
UNIVERSITY PRESS

OXFORD

UNIVERSITY PRESS

Great Clarendon Street, Oxford ox2 6dp

Oxford University Press is a department of the University of Oxford.
It furthers the University's objective of excellence in research, scholarship,
and education by publishing worldwide in

Oxford New York

Auckland Cape Town Dar es Salaam Hong Kong Karachi
Kuala Lumpur Madrid Melbourne Mexico City Nairobi
New Delhi Shanghai Taipei Toronto

With offices in

Argentina Austria Brazil Chile Czech Republic France Greece
Guatemala Hungary Italy Japan Poland Portugal Singapore
South Korea Switzerland Thailand Turkey Ukraine Vietnam

Oxford is a registered trade mark of Oxford University Press
in the UK and in certain other countries

Published in the United States
by Oxford University Press Inc., New York

© Josephine Steiner and Lorna Woods, 2009

The moral rights of the authors have been asserted
Database right Oxford University Press (maker)

Crown copyright material is reproduced under Class Licence
Number C01P0000148 with the permission of OPSI
and the Queen's Printer for Scotland

Tenth edition 2009

British Library Cataloguing in Publication Data
Data available

Library of Congress Cataloging in Publication Data
Data available

Typeset by MacMillan Publishing Solutions
Printed in Great Britain
on acid-free paper by
Ashford Colour Press Ltd, Gosport, Hants

ISBN 978–0–19–921907–0

3 5 7 9 10 8 6 4 2

GUIDE TO USING THE ONLINE RESOURCE CENTRE

The Online Resource Centre that accompanies this book provides students and lecturers with ready to use teaching and learning resources.

www.oxfordtextbooks.co.uk/orc/steiner_woods10e

For Students

Freely available to all with no registration or password required.

Regular updates
A vital resource allowing you to follow the changes and developments to EU law that have occurred since publication.

Interactive timeline
Allows you to trace the developments in EU legal history from the birth of the EU through to the present day. Ideal for students new to the subject and as a source of revision.

Interactive map of Europe
Provides a useful summary of each of the Member States including essential facts and figures.

Video clips
Archive footage from the European Commission showing key moments in the development of the EU.

Web links
An guide to EU material on the internet allows you to take your learning further and research those important topics of particular interest.

Lisbon Treaty ratification monitor
Produced by the Bertelsmann Foundation, the Lisbon Treaty ratification monitor allows you to explore the background to this potentially vital new reform of EU law and follow its ratification process.

Flashcard glossary
Interactive flashcards containing key words and terms allow you to test your knowledge and understanding.

For Lecturers

Password protected to ensure only lecturers can access these resources; each registration is personally checked to ensure security of the site.

Registration is straightforward: click on 'Lecturer Resources' on the Online Resource Centre, complete a simple registration form which allows you to choose your own username and password, and access will be granted within 48 hours (subject to verification).

Test bank
A fully customisable resource containing ready-made assessments with which to test your students. Offers versatile testing tailored to the contents of the textbook.

Figures and diagrams
Electronic copies of the figures from the book are available for use in lectures and handouts.

OUTLINE CONTENTS

DETAILED CONTENTS

PREFACE

Many important changes have occurred in the European Union since this book was first published in 1988. Membership of the Union, originally called the European Economic Community, has risen to 27 and may increase still further. The goal of the internal market, set down in the 1986 Single European Act, has been largely achieved. 1992 saw the signing at Maastricht of the Treaty on European Union, committing members to new goals, not least to economic and monetary union, and increasing governmental cooperation in the fields of foreign and security policy and justice and home affairs: the concept of citizenship of the Union was born. The first stage of economic and monetary union came into effect in 1992; the final stage for participating Member States occurred on 1 January 1999. The Treaty of Amsterdam, signed in 1997, added significantly to the EC Treaty, renumbering most of its articles, and together with the Treaty of Nice effected radical changes to the institutional structures and decision-making processes of the Union, paving the way for a larger, more flexible Union. Whilst the Maastricht Treaty ran into constitutional difficulties as Member States sought to ratify it, it eventually came into force. Resistance to what is perceived as continued transfer of power to the Union is increasing and, the Treaty establishing a Constitution for Europe sank on the rocks of public opinion. The Constitution was, on the one hand, significant as it would have completely replaced the existing treaty structure and would have made express a number of key principles of constitutional law. On the other hand, in terms of new developments, the Constitution would have changed little. As we will see, France and the Netherlands voted 'no' on their respective referenda. The response of the Member States to the failure of the Constitutional Treaty was to produce, after some deliberation, a new treaty, the Lisbon Treaty, which did not attempt the grand structural changes of the Constitution; nor did it use the state-like language which had, seemingly, incensed so many. In many respects, however, the detailed changes from the Constitution can be found in Lisbon, and for this, some have criticised it as an illegitimate attempt to circumvent the 'no' vote to the Constitution. The Irish have again voted no, and there is ambivalence in a number of Member States despite the fact that the changes proposed by Lisbon may improve the workings of the institutions and make clear the limited power of the Union. At the time of writing, the outcome of the Lisbon process is still not clear. Nonetheless, despite disagreement both within and between Member States over the nature and pace of future developments, there are no doubts as to the need for the Union's continued existence.

The purpose of this tenth edition is not to chart the political developments in the Union and its relationship with Member States and would-be Member States, except in outline. Instead, it aims to continue the approach adopted in previous editions of providing an accurate and succinct account of the present state of European law. There is still a need for a single textbook of manageable size, concise but not simplistic, covering the major areas of EU law—constitutional, institutional and administrative as well as substantive—to cater for the growing body of students (and not only lawyers) from around the world who wish to study EU law, and for practitioners who realise that they can no longer afford to ignore it. The advent of the internal market and the continuing expansion of the Union has simply reinforced that need.

A book of this type cannot of necessity provide an in-depth account of the EU institutions (although this section has been expanded over previous editions), nor can it cover all areas of substantive law. Much EU law, for example in the field of company or commercial or environmental law, or the law relating to employment or consumer protection, is increasingly, and more appropriately, incorporated into the general textbooks on these subjects. Some topics, such as agriculture or monetary union are too large or too specialised for inclusion. Others, such as transport, are still in the process of development. The book continues to concentrate on the more highly developed areas of EU law, what one might describe as fundamental Community law—the law relating to the free movement of goods, persons, and services; competition law; and discrimination—and on the remedies available for breaches of Community law.

There are a number of changes to this edition. All chapters have been revised in the light of the possible impact of the Treaty of Lisbon, should it come into force. This affects the chapters on the Union's development (Chapter 1), that on the institutions (Chapter 2), and on lawmaking (Chapter 3) the most. This edition also includes a chapter on the area of freedom and security. In the light of this, and the fact that the separate pillar structure is likely to be abandoned, more detail on the second and third pillars has been included in a number of constitutional and administrative chapters. The chapters on the free movement of persons have been completely reworked in the light of the ECJ's approach based on citizenship. Given that many points of law apply in parallel across the free movement rights, it seemed more appropriate to adopt a horizontal approach across the freedoms, dealing with different aspects of the right together. Because of the distinct issues that it raises, there is a separate chapter on the right to receive services and public services. Given that many institutions now have separate courses on competition law, with specialist books on the subject, the material on competition law and policy has been condensed.

As before, the book aims to provide sufficient insight into the principles of EU law, including its current difficulties, and the processes of the European institutions, to enable the reader to pursue studies, resolve problems, and enforce rights in areas of law whether or not covered by the book, as and when the need arises. The principal sources of EU law and a selection of textbooks are listed at the end of the book. Each chapter provides a list of further reading.

As with the eighth and ninth editions, Jo Steiner, who wrote the original Textbook in 1988, has had no involvement with this edition. She continues to enjoy a well-earned retirement. Lorna Woods joined Jo Steiner in 1996 for the fifth and subsequent editions. Although she has in the previous edition been assisted in this task by Christian Twigg-Flesner, he was unable to participate fully in this edition. He worked on two chapters, state liability and competition. Lorna Woods was greatly helped out by two colleagues, Dan Wilsher and Nick Hatzis, who contributed to the chapters on the area of freedom, security and justice, and preliminary rulings; and discrimination respectively. Without their willingness to participate under considerable time constraints, this edition of the book would have been unlikely to have seen the light of day.

My thanks go to all of those who helped in the preparation of this book: to colleagues in respective institutions for their helpful comments and suggestions, and to my family and friends for their unflinching support and encouragement, and for providing a welcome distraction from the demands of academic research.

Lorna Woods
April 2009

ABBREVIATIONS

Bull.EC	*Bulletin of the European Communities*
CAP	Common Agricultural Policy
CCT	Common Customs Tariff
CDE	*Cahiers de Droit Enropéen*
CET	Common External Tariff
CFI	Court of First Instance
CFSP	common foreign and security policy
CMLR	*Common Market Law Reports*
CML Rev	*Common Market Law Review*
COREPER	Committee of Permanent Representatives
D/G	Directorate-General
EAGGE	European Agriculture Guidance and Guarantee Fund
EC	European Community/Communities, Treaty Establishing the European Community
ECB	European Central Bank
EC Bull	*Bulletin of the European Communities*
ECHR	European Convention for the Protection of Human Rights and Fundamental Freedoms 1950
ECJ	European Court of Justice
ECLR	*European Competition Law Review*
ECR	*European Court Reports* (official reports of the judgments of the European Court, English version)
ECSC	European Coal and Steel Community
ECtHR	European Court of Human Rights
EEA	European Economic Area
EEC	European Economic Community
EFTA	European Free Trade Association
EIPR	*European Intellectual Property Review*
EL Rev	*European Law Review*
EMU	Economic and Monetary Union
EPL	*European Public Law*
ESCB	European System of Central Banks
EUCFR	European Charter of Fundamental Rights
Euratom	European Atomic Energy Community
FSP	foreign and security policy
FYR	Former Yugoslav Republic
GATT	General Agreement on Tariffs and Trade
GG	Grundgesetz (Basic Law for the Federal Republic of Germany)
Harv Int'l LJ	*Harvard International Law Journal*
ICLQ	*International and Comparative Law Quarterly*
ICTY	International Criminal Tribunal for the former Yugoslavia
IGC	Intergovernmental Conference
JHA	justice and home affairs
JO	*Journal Officiel* (French version of OJ)
LIEI	*Legal Issues of European Integration*
LQR	*Law Quarterly Review*
MCA	Monetary Compensatory Amount
MEQR	measure having equivalent effect to quantitative restrictions
MLR	*Modern Law Review*
OJ	*Official Journal* (of the European Communities)
OMC	Open Method of Co-ordination
PL	*Public Law*

qmv	qualified majority voting
RPM	relevant product market
SEA	Single European Act
SGP	Stability and Growth Pact
SME	small and medium-sized enterprises
SSNIP	small but significant and non-transitory increase in prices
TCN	third country national
TEU	Treaty on European Union
TFEU	Treaty on the Functioning of the European Union
ToA	Treaty of Amsterdam
UNICE	Union des industries de la communauté européenne (federation of European employers' groups)
WashLRev	*Washington Law Review*
WTO	World Trade Organization
YEL	*Yearbook of European Law*

Unless otherwise stated, cases cited were decided by the ECJ and Articles cited are Articles of the EC Treaty.

TABLE OF CASES

Court of Justice of the European Communities–Chronological List

Cases have been arranged in chronological order by case number and year. See page ... for alphabetical list of Court of Justice of the European Communities cases.

TABLE OF CASES

Court of Justice of the European Communities–Alphabetical List

Cases have been arranged in alphabetical order. See page ... for chronological list of Court of Justice of the European Communities cases.

Belgian Courts

Dutch Courts

French Courts

German Courts

Italian Courts

TABLE OF COMMISSION DECISIONS

TABLE OF UK STATUTES

*Page references in **bold** indicate that the text is reproduced in full*

TABLE OF EUROPEAN COMMUNITY TREATIES

*Page references in **bold** indicate that the text is reproduced in full*

TABLE OF EU SECONDARY LEGISLATION

TABLE OF EQUIVALENCES

Previous numbering of the Treaty on European Union	Current numbering of the Treaty on European Union	New numbering of the Treaty on European Union (as amended by the Treaty of Lisbon)
Title I	**Title I**	**Title I**
Article A	Article 1	Article 1
		Article 2
Article B	Article 2	Article 3
Article C	Article 3 (repealed)[(1)]	
		Article 4
		Article 5[(2)]
Article D	Article 4 (repealed)[(3)]	
Article E	Article 5 (repealed)[(4)]	
Article F	Article 6	Article 6
Article F.1(*)	Article 7	Article 7
		Article 8
Title II	**Title II**	**Title II**
Article G	Article 8 (repealed)[(5)]	Article 9
		Article 10[(6)]
		Article 11
		Article 12
Title III	**Title III**	**Title III**
Article H	Article 9 (repealed)[(7)]	Article 13
		Article 14[(8)]
		Article 15[(9)]
		Article 16[(10)]
		Article 17[(11)]
		Article 18
		Article 19[(12)]
Title IV	**Title IV**	**Title IV**
Article I	Article 10 (repealed)[(13)]	Article 20[(14)]
	Articles 27a to 27e (replaced)	
	Articles 40 to 40b (replaced)	
	Articles 43 to 45 (replaced)	
Title V(***)	**Title V**	**Title V**
		Chapter 1 — General provisions on the Union's external action
		Article 21
		Article 22

Previous numbering of the Treaty on European Union	Current numbering of the Treaty on European Union	New numbering of the Treaty on European Union (as amended by the Treaty of Lisbon)
		Chapter 2 — Specific provisions on the common foreign and security policy
		Section 1 - common provisions
		Article 23
Article J.1	Article 11	Article 24
Article J.2	Article 12	Article 25
Article J.3	Article 13	Article 26
		Article 27
Article J.4	Article 14	Article 28
Article J.5	Article 15	Article 29
	Article 22 (moved)	Article 30
	Article 23 (moved)	Article 31
Article J.6	Article 16	Article 32
Article J.7	Article 17 (moved)	Article 42
Article J.8	Article 18	Article 33
Article J.9	Article 19	Article 34
Article J.10	Article 20	Article 35
Article J.11	Article 21	Article 36
Article J.12	Article 22 (moved)	*Article 30*
Article J.13	Article 23 (moved)	*Article 31*
Article J.14	Article 24	Article 37
Article J.15	Article 25	Article 38
		Article 39
	Article 47 (moved)	Article 40
Article J.16	Article 26 (repealed)	
Article J.17	Article 27 (replealed)	
	Article 27a (replaced)[15]	*Article 20*
	Article 27b (replaced)[15]	*Article 20*
	Article 27c (replaced)[15]	*Article 20*
	Article 27d (replaced)[15]	*Article 20*
	Article 27e (replaced)[15]	*Article 20*
Article J.18	Article 28	Article 41
		Section 2 — Provisions on the common security and defence policy
Article J.7	*Article 17 (moved)*	Article 42
		Article 43
		Article 44
		Article 45
		Article 46
Title VI(***)	**Title VI[16]**	
Article K.1	Article 29 (replaced)[17]	
Article K.2	Article 30 (replaced)[18]	

Previous numbering of the Treaty on European Union	Current numbering of the Treaty on European Union	New numbering of the Treaty on European Union (as amended by the Treaty of Lisbon)
Article K.3	Article 31 (replaced)[19]	
Article K.4	Article 32 (replaced)[20]	
Article K.5	Article 33 (replaced)[21]	
Article K.6	Article 34 (repealed)	
Article K.7	Article 35 (repealed)	
Article K.8	Article 36 (replaced)[22]	
Article K.9	Article 37 (repealed)	
Article K.10	Article 38 (repealed)	
Article K.11	Article 39 (repealed)	
Article K.12	Article 40 (replaced)[23]	*Article 20*
	Article 40 A (replaced)[23]	*Article 20*
	Article 40 B (replaced)[23]	*Article 20*
Article K.13	Article 41 (repealed)	
Article K.14	Article 42 (repealed)	
Title VIa(**)	**Title VII** [24]	**Title VII**
Article K.15(*)	Article 43 (replaced)[24]	*Article 20*
	Article 43 A (replaced)[24]	*Article 20*
	Article 43 B (replaced)[24]	*Article 20*
	Article 44[24]	*Article 20*
Article K.16(*)	Article 44 A (replaced)[24]	*Article 20*
Article K.17(*)	Article 45 (replaced)[24]	*Article 20*
Title VII	**Title VIII**	**Title VIII**
Article L	Article 46	
		Article 47
Article M	Article 47 (replaced)	*Article 40*
Article N	Article 48	Article 48
Article O	Article 49	Article 49
		Article 50
		Article 51
		Article 52
Article P	Article 50 (repealed)	
Article Q	Article 51	Article 53
Article R	Article 52	Article 54
Article S	Article 53	Article 55

(*) New Article introduced by the Treaty of Amsterdam.

(**) New Title introduced by the Treaty of Amsterdam.

(***) Title restructured by the Treaty of Amsterdam.

(1) Replaced, in substance, by Article 7 of the Treaty on the Functioning of the European Union ('TFEU') and by Articles 13(1) and 21, paragraph 3, second subparagraph of the Treaty on European Union ('TEU').

(2) Replaces Article 5 of the Treaty establishing the European Community ('TEC').

(3) Replaced, in substance, by Article 15.

(4) Replaced, in substance, by Article 13, paragraph 2.

(5) Article 8 TEU, which was in force until the entry into force of the Treaty of Lisbon (hereinafter 'current'), amended the TEC. Those amendments are incorporated into the latter Treaty and Article 8 is repealed. Itsnumber is used to insert a new provision.

(6) Paragraph 4 replaces, in substance, the first subparagraph of Article 191 TEC.

9.5.2008 EN Official Journal of the European Union C 115/361

(1) Tables of equivalences as referred to in Article 5 of the Treaty of Lisbon. The original centre column, which set out the intermediate numbering as used in that Treaty, has been omitted.

(7) The current Article 9 TEU amended the Treaty establishing the European Coal and Steel Community. This latter expired on 23 July 2002. Article 9 is repealed and the number thereof is used to insert another provision.

(8) — Paragraphs 1 and 2 replace, in substance, Article 189 TEC;

— paragraphs 1 to 3 replace, in substance, paragraphs 1 to 3 of Article 190 TEC;

— paragraph 1 replaces, in substance, the first subparagraph of Article 192 TEC;

— paragraph 4 replaces, in substance, the first subparagraph of Article 197 TEC.

(9) Replaces, in substance, Article 4.

(10) — Paragraph 1 replaces, in substance, the first and second indents of Article 202 TEC;

— paragraphs 2 and 9 replace, in substance, Article 203 TEC;

— paragraphs 4 and 5 replace, in substance, paragraphs 2 and 4 of Article 205 TEC.

(11) — Paragraph 1 replaces, in substance, Article 211 TEC;

— paragraphs 3 and 7 replace, in substance, Article 214 TEC.

— paragraph 6 replaces, in substance, paragraphs 1, 3 and 4 of Article 217 TEC.

(12) — Replaces, in substance, Article 220 TEC.

— the second subparagraph of paragraph 2 replaces, in substance, the first subparagraph of Article 221 TEC.

(13) The current Article 10 TEU amended the Treaty establishing the European Atomic Energy Community. Those amendments are incorporated into the Treaty of Lisbon. Article 10 is repealed and the number thereof is used to insert another provision.

(14) Also replaces Articles 11 and 11a TEC.

(15) The current Articles 27a to 27e, on enhanced cooperation, are also replaced by Articles 326 to 334 TFEU.

(16) The current provisions of Title VI of the TEU, on police and judicial cooperation in criminal matters, are replaced by the provisions of Chapters 1, 5 and 5 of Title IV of Part Three of the TFEU.

(17) Replaced by Article 67 TFEU.

(18) Replaced by Articles 87 and 88 TFEU.

(19) Replaced by Articles 82, 83 and 85 TFEU.

(20) Replaced by Article 89 TFEU.

(21) Replaced by Article 72 TFEU.

(22) Replaced by Article 71 TFEU.

(23) The current Articles 40 to 40 B TEU, on enhanced cooperation, are also replaced by Articles 326 to 334 TFEU.

(24) The current Articles 43 to 45 and Title VII of the TEU, on enhanced cooperation, are also replaced by Articles 326 to 334 TFEU.

Previous numbering	Current numbering of the Treaty establishing the European Community	New numbering of the Treaty on the Functioning of the European Union (as amended by the Treaty of Lisbon)
PART ONE	PART ONE — PRINCIPLES	PART ONE — PRINCIPLES
Article 1	Article 1 (repealed)	
		Article 1
Article 2	Article 2 (repealed)[(25)]	
		Title I — Categories and areas of union competence
		Article 2
		Article 3
		Article 4
		Article 5
		Article 6
		Title II — Provisions having general application
		Article 7
Article 3	Article 3, paragraph 1 (repealed)[(26)]	
Article 3	Article 3, paragraph 2	Article 8
Article 3a	Article 4 (moved)	*Article 119*
Article 3b	Article 5 (replaced)[(27)]	
		Article 9
		Article 10
Article 3c(*)	Article 6	Article 11
	Article 153, paragraph 2 (moved)	Article 12
		Article 13[(28)]
Article 4	Article 7 (repealed)[(29)]	
Article 4a	Article 8 (repealed)[(30)]	
Article 4b	Article 9 (repealed)	
Article 5	Article 10 (repealed)[(31)]	
Article 5a(*)	Article 11 (replaced)[(32)]	*Articles 326 to 334*
	Article 11a (replaced)[(32)]	*Articles 326 to 334*
Article 6	Article 12 (repealed)	*Article 18*
Article 6a(*)	Article 13 (moved)	*Article 19*
Article 7 (repealed)		
Article 7a	Article 14 (moved)	*Article 26*
Article 7b (repealed)		
Article 7c	Article 15 (moved)	*Article 27*
Article 7d(*)	Article 16	Article 14
	Article 255 (moved)	Article 15
	Article 286 (moved)	Article 16
		Article 17
PART TWO	PART TWO — CITIZENSHIP OF THE UNION	PART TWO — NON-DISCRIMINATION AND CITIZENSHIP OF THE UNION

Previous numbering	Current numbering of the Treaty establishing the European Community	New numbering of the Treaty on the Functioning of the European Union (as amended by the Treaty of Lisbon)
	Article 12 (moved)	Article 18
	Article 13 (moved)	Article 19
Article 8	Article 17	Article 20
Article 8a	Article 18	Article 21
Article 8b	Article 19	Article 22
Article 8c	Article 20	Article 23
Article 8d	Article 21	Article 24
Article 8e	Article 22	Article 25
PART THREE	PART THREE — COMMUNITY POLICIES	PART THREE — POLICIES AND INTERNAL ACTIONS OF THE UNION
		Title I — The internal market
	Article 14 (moved)	Article 26
	Article 15 (moved)	Article 27
Title 1	Title I — Free movement of goods	Title II — Free movement of goods
Article 9	Article 23	Article 28
Article 10	Article 24	Article 29
Article 11 (repealed)		
Chapter 1	Chapter 1 — The customs union	Chapter 1 — The customs union
Section 1 (deleted)		
Article 12	Article 25	Article 30
Articles 13-26 (repealed)		
Article 27 (repealed)	Article 26	Article 31
Article 28	Article 27	Article 32
	Part Three, Title X, Customs cooperation (moved)	Chapter 2 — Customs cooperation
Article 29	Article 135 (moved)	Article 33
	Chapter 2 — Prohibition of quantitative restrictions between Member States	Chapter 3 — Prohibition of quantitative restrictions between Member States
Article 30	Article 28	Article 34
Articles 31-33 (repealed)		
Article 34	Article 29	Article 35
Article 35		
Article 36	Article 30	Article 36
Article 37	Article 31	Article 37
Title II	Title II — Agriculture	Title III — Agriculture and fisheries
Article 38	Article 32	Article 38
Article 39	Article 33	Article 39

Previous numbering	Current numbering of the Treaty establishing the European Community	New numbering of the Treaty on the Functioning of the European Union (as amended by the Treaty of Lisbon)
Article 40	Article 34	Article 40
Article 41	Article 35	Article 41
Article 42	Article 36	Article 42
Article 43	Article 37	Article 43
Articles 44-45 (repealed)		
Article 46	Article 38	Article 44
Article 47 repealed		
Title II	Title III — Free movement of persons, services and capital	Title IV — Free movement of persons, services and capital
Chapter 1	Chapter 1 — Workers	Chapter 1 — Workers
Article 48	Article 39	Article 45
Article 49	Article 40	Article 46
Article 50	Article 41	Article 47
Article 51	Article 42	Article 48
Chapter 2	Chapter 2 — Right of establishment	Chapter 2 — Right of establishment
Article 52	Article 43	Article 49
Article 53 (repealed)		
Article 54	Article 44	Article 50
Article 55	Article 45	Article 51
Article 56	Article 46	Article 52
Article 57	Article 47	Article 53
Article 58	Article 48	Article 54
	Article 294 (moved)	Article 55
Chapter 3	Chapter 3 — Services	Chapter 3 — Services
Article 59	Article 49	Article 56
Article 60	Article 50	Article 57
Article 61	Article 51	Article 58
Article 62 (repealed)		
Article 63	Article 52	Article 59
Article 64	Article 53	Article 60
Article 65	Article 54	Article 61
Article 66	Article 55	Article 62
Chapter 4	Chapter 4 — Capital and payments	Chapter 4 — Capital and payments
Articles 67-73a (repealed)		
Article 73b	Article 56	Article 63
Article 73c	Article 57	Article 64
Article 73d	Article 58	Article 65
Article 73e (repealed)		

Previous numbering	Current numbering of the Treaty establishing the European Community	New numbering of the Treaty on the Functioning of the European Union (as amended by the Treaty of Lisbon)
Article 73f	Article 59	Article 66
Article 73h (repealed)		
	Article 60 (moved)	*Article 75*
Title IIIa(**)	Title IV — Visas, asylum, immigration and other policies related to free movement of persons	Title V — Area of freedom, security and justice
		Chapter 1 — General provisions
Article 73i(*)	Article 61	Article 67[33]
		Article 68
		Article 69
		Article 70
		Article 71[34]
	Article 64, paragraph 1 (replaced)	Article 72[35]
		Article 73
	Article 66 (replaced)	Article 74
	Article 60 (moved)	Article 75
		Article 76
		Chapter 2 — Policies on border checks, asylum and immigration
Article 73j(*)	Article 62	Article 77
Article 73k(*)	Article 63, points 1 et 2, and Article 64, paragraph 2[36]	Article 78
Article 73k(*)	Article 63, points 3 and 4	Article 79
		Article 80
Article 73l(*)	Article 64, paragraph 1 (replaced)	*Article 72*
		Chapter 3 — Judicial cooperation in civil matters
Article 73m(*)	Article 65	Article 81
Article 73n(*)	Article 66 (replaced)	Article 74
Article 73o(*)	Article 67 (repealed)	
Article 73p(*)	Article 68 (repealed)	
Article 73q (*)	Article 69 (repealed)	
		Chapter 4 — Judicial cooperation in criminal matters
		Article 82[37]
		Article 83[37]
		Article 84
		Article 85[37]
		Article 86

Previous numbering	Current numbering of the Treaty establishing the European Community	New numbering of the Treaty on the Functioning of the European Union (as amended by the Treaty of Lisbon)
		Chapter 5 — Police cooperation
		Article 87[38]
		Article 88[38]
		Article 89[39]
Title IV	Title V — Transport	Title VI — Transport
Article 74	Article 70	Article 90
Article 75	Article 71	Article 91
Article 76	Article 72	Article 92
Article 77	Article 73	Article 93
Article 78	Article 74	Article 94
Article 79	Article 75	Article 95
Article 80	Article 76	Article 96
Article 81	Article 77	Article 97
Article 82	Article 78	Article 98
Article 83	Article 79	Article 99
Article 84	Article 80	Article 100
Title V	Title VI — Common rules on competition, taxation and approximation of laws	Title VII — Common rules on competition, taxation and approximation of laws
Chapter 1	Chapter 1 — Rules on competition	Chapter 1 — Rules on competition
Section 1	Section 1 — Rules applying to undertakings	Section 1 — Rules applying to undertakings
Article 85	Article 81	Article 101
Article 86	Article 82	Article 102
Article 87	Article 83	Article 103
Article 88	Article 84	Article 104
Article 89	Article 85	Article 105
Article 90	Article 86	Article 106
Section 2 (deleted)		
Article 91 (repealed)		
Section 3	Section 2 — Aids granted by States	Section 2 — Aids granted by States
Article 92	Article 87	Article 107
Article 93	Article 88	Article 108
Article 94	Article 89	Article 109
	Chapter 2 — Tax provisions	Chapter 2 — Tax provisions
Article 95	Article 90	Article 110
Article 96	Article 91	Article 111
Article 97 (repealed)		
Article 98	Article 92	Article 112
Article 99	Article 93	Article 113

Previous numbering	Current numbering of the Treaty establishing the European Community	New numbering of the Treaty on the Functioning of the European Union (as amended by the Treaty of Lisbon)
	Chapter 3 — Approximation of laws	Chapter 3 — Approximation of laws
Article 100a	*Article 95 (moved)*	Article 114
Article 100	*Article 94 (moved)*	Article 115
Articles 100b-d (repealed)		
Article 101	Article 96	Article 116
Article 102	Article 97	Article 117
		Article 118
	Title VII — Economic and monetary policy	Title VIII — Economic and monetary policy
	Article 4 (moved)	Article 119
	Chapter 1 — Economic policy	Chapter 1 — Economic policy
Article 102a	Article 98	Article 120
Article 103	Article 99	Article 121
Article 103a	Article 100	Article 122
Article 104	Article 101	Article 123
Article 104a	Article 102	Article 124
Article 104b	Article 103	Article 125
Article 104c	Article 104	Article 126
Chapter 2	Chapter 2 — monetary policy	Chapter 2 — monetary policy
Article 105	Article 105	Article 127
Article 105a	Article 106	Article 128
Article 106	Article 107	Article 128
Article 107	Article 108	Article 130
Article 108	Article 109	Article 131
Article 108a	Article 110	Article 132
Article 109	Article 111, paragraphs 1 to 3 and 5 (moved)	*Article 219*
Article 109	Article 111, paragraph 4 (moved)	*Article 138*
		Article 133
Chapter 3	Chapter 3 — Institutional provisions	Chapter 3 — Institutional provisions
Article 109a	Article 112 (moved)	Article 283
Article 109b	Article 113 (moved)	Article 284
Article 109c	Article 114	Article 134
Article 109d	Article 115	Article 135
		Chapter 4 — Provisions specific to Member States whose currency is the euro
		Article 136
		Article 137
	Article 111, paragraph 4 (moved)	Article 138

Previous numbering	Current numbering of the Treaty establishing the European Community	New numbering of the Treaty on the Functioning of the European Union (as amended by the Treaty of Lisbon)
	Chapter 4 — Transitional provisions	Chapter 5 — Transitional provisions
Article 109e	Article 116 (repealed)	
		Article 139
Article 109f	Article 117, paragraphs 1, 2, sixth indent, and 3 to 9 (repealed)	
Article 109f	Article 117, paragraph 2, first five indents (moved)	*Article 141, paragraph 2*
	Article 121, paragraph 1 (moved)	
	Article 122, paragraph 2, second sentence (moved)	
	Article 123, paragraph 5 (moved)	Article 140[40]
Article 109g	Article 118 (repealed)	
	Article 123, paragraph 3 (moved)	
	Article 117, paragraph 2, first five indents (moved)	Article 141[41]
	Article 124, paragraph 1 (moved)	Article 142
Article 109h	Article 119	Article 143
Article 109i	Article 120	Article 144
Article 109j	Article 121, paragraph 1 (moved)	*Article 140, paragraph 1*
Article 109j	Article 121, paragraphs 2 to 4 (repealed)	
Article 109k	Article 122, paragraphs 1, 2, first sentence, 3, 4, 5 and 6 (repealed)	
Article 109k	Article 122, paragraph 2, second sentence (moved)	*Article 140, paragraph 2, first subparagraph*
Article 109l	Article 123, paragraphs 1, 2 and 4 (repealed)	
Article 109l	Article 123, paragraph 3 (moved)	*Article 141, paragraph 1*
Article 109l	Article 123, paragraph 5 (moved)	*Article 140, paragraph 3*
Article 109m	Article 124, paragraph 1 (moved)	Article 142
Article 109m	Article 124, paragraph 2 (repealed)	
Title VIa(**)	Title VIII — Employment	Title IX — Employment
Article 109n(*)	Article 125	Article 145
Article 109o(*)	Article 126	Article 146
Article 109p(*)	Article 127	Article 147
Article 109q(*)	Article 128	Article 148

Previous numbering	Current numbering of the Treaty establishing the European Community	New numbering of the Treaty on the Functioning of the European Union (as amended by the Treaty of Lisbon)
Article 109r(*)	Article 129	Article 149
Article 109s(*)	Article 130	Article 150
Title VIII	Title IX — Common commercial policy (moved)	Part Five, Title II, common commercial policy
Article 110	Article 131 (moved)	*Article 206*
Article 111 (repealed)		
Article 112	Article 132 (repealed)	
	Article 133 (moved)	Article 207
	Article 134 (repealed)	
Title VIIa(**)	Title X — Customs cooperation (moved)	Part Three, Title II, Chapter 2, Customs cooperation
Article 116(*)	Article 135 (moved)	Article 33
Title VIII	Title XI — Social policy, education, vocational training and youth	Title X — Social policy
Chapter 1(***)	Chapter 1 — social provisions (repealed)	
Article 117	Article 136	Article 151
		Article 152
Article 118	Article 137	Article 153
Article 118a	Article 138	Article 154
Article 118b	Article 139	Article 155
Article 118c	Article 140	Article 156
Article 119	Article 141	Article 157
Article 119a	Article 142	Article 158
Article 120	Article 143	Article 159
Article 121	Article 144	Article 160
Article 122	Article 145	Article 161
Chapter 2	Chapter 2 — The European Social Fund	Title XI — The European Social Fund
Article 123	Article 146	Article 162
Article 124	Article 147	Article 163
Article 125	Article 148	Article 164
Chapter 3	Chapter 3 — Education, vocational training and youth	Title XII — Education, vocational training, youth and sport
Article 126	Article 149	Article 165
Article 127	Article 150	Article 166
Title IX	Title XII — Culture	Title XIII — Culture
Article 128	Article 151	Article 167
Title X	Title XIII — Public health Title	XIV — Public health
Article 129	Article 152	Article 168
Title XI	Title XIV — Consumer protection	Title XV — Consumer protection

Previous numbering	Current numbering of the Treaty establishing the European Community	New numbering of the Treaty on the Functioning of the European Union (as amended by the Treaty of Lisbon)
Article 129a	Article 153, paragraphs 1, 3, 4 and 5	Article 169
	Article 153, paragraph 2 (moved)	*Article 12*
Title XII	Title XV — Trans- European networks Title XVI — Trans-European networks	
Article 129b	Article 154	Article 170
Article 129c	Article 155	Article 171
Article 129d	Article 156	Article 172
Title XIII	Title XVI — Industry Title XVII — Industry	
Article 130	Article 157	Article 173
Title XIV	Title XVII — Economic and social cohesion	Title XVIII — Economic, social and territorial cohesion
Article 130a	Article 158	Article 174
Article 130b	Article 159	Article 175
Article 130c	Article 160	Article 176
Article 130d	Article 161	Article 177
Article 130e	Article 162	Article 178
Title XV	Title XVIII — Research and technological development	Title XIX — Research and technological development and space
Article 130f	Article 163	Article 179
Article 130g	Article 164	Article 180
Article 130h	Article 165	Article 181
Article 130i	Article 166	Article 182
Article 130j	Article 167	Article 183
Article 130k	Article 168	Article 184
Article 130l	Article 169	Article 185
Article 130m	Article 170	Article 186
Article 130n	Article 171	Article 187
Article 130o	Article 172	Article 188
		Article 189
Article 130p	Article 173	Article 190
Article 130q (repealed)		
Title XVI	Title XIX — Environment	Title XX — Environment
Article 130r	Article 174	Article 191
Article 130s	Article 175	Article 192
Article 130t	Article 176	Article 193
		Titre XXI — Energy
		Article 194
		Title XXII — Tourism

Previous numbering	Current numbering of the Treaty establishing the European Community	New numbering of the Treaty on the Functioning of the European Union (as amended by the Treaty of Lisbon)
		Article 195
		Title XXIII — Civil protection
		Article 196
		Title XXIV — Administrative cooperation
		Article 197
Title XVII	Title XX — Development cooperation (moved)	Part Five, Title III, Chapter 1, Development cooperation
Article 130u	Article 177 (moved)	*Article 208*
Article 130v	Article 178 (repealed)(42)	
Article 130w	Article 179 (moved)	*Article 209*
Article 130x	Article 180 (moved)	*Article 210*
Article 130y	Article 181 (moved)	*Article 211*
	Title XXI — Economic, financial and technical cooperation with third countries (moved)	*Part Five, Title III, Chapter 2, Economic, financial and technical cooperation with third countries*
	Article 181a (moved)	*Article 212*
PART FOUR	**PART FOUR — ASSOCIATION OF THE OVERSEAS COUNTRIES AND TERRITORIES**	**PART FOUR — ASSOCIATION OF THE OVERSEAS COUNTRIES AND TERRITORIES**
Article 131	Article 182	Article 198
Article 132	Article 183	Article 199
Article 133	Article 184	Article 200
Article 134	Article 185	Article 201
Article 135	Article 186	Article 202
Article 136	Article 187	Article 203
Article 136a	Article 188	Article 204
		PART FIVE — EXTERNAL ACTION BY THE UNION
		Title I — General provisions on the union's external action
		Article 205
	Part Three, Title IX, Common commercial policy (moved)	Title II — Common commercial policy
	Article 131 (moved)	Article 206
	Article 133 (moved)	Article 207
		Title III — Cooperation with third countries and humanitarian aid
	Part Three, Title XX, Development cooperation (moved)	Chapter 1 — development cooperation
	Article 177 (moved)	Article 208(43)
	Article 179 (moved)	Article 209

Previous numbering	Current numbering of the Treaty establishing the European Community	New numbering of the Treaty on the Functioning of the European Union (as amended by the Treaty of Lisbon)
	Article 180 (moved)	Article 210
	Article 181 (moved)	Article 211
	Part Three, Title XXI, Economic, financial and technical cooperation with third countries (moved)	Chapter 2 — Economic, financial and technical cooperation with third countries
	Article 181a (moved)	Article 212
		Article 213
		Chapter 3 — Humanitarian aid
		Article 214
		Title IV — Restrictive measures
	Article 301 (replaced)	Article 215
		Title V — International agreements
		Article 216
	Article 310 (moved)	Article 217
	Article 300 (replaced)	Article 218
	Article 111, paragraphs 1 to 3 and 5 (moved)	Article 219
		Title VI — The Union's relations with international organisations and third countries and the Union delegations
	Articles 302 to 304 (replaced)	Article 220
		Article 221
		Title VII — Solidarity clause
		Article 222
PART FIVE	PART FIVE — INSTITUTIONS OF THE COMMUNITY	PART SIX — INSTITUTIONAL AND FINANCIAL PROVISIONS
Title I	Title I — Institutional provisions	Title I — Institutional provisions
Chapter 1	Chapter 1 — The institutions	Chapter 1 — The institutions
Section 1	Section 1 — The European Parliament	Section 1 — The European Parliament
Article 137	Article 189 (repealed)[44]	
Article 138	Article 190, paragraphs 1 to 3 (repealed)[45]	
Article 138	Article 190, paragraphs 4 and 5	Article 223
Article 138a	Article 191, first paragraph (repealed)[46]	
Article 138a	Article 191, second paragraph	Article 224

Previous numbering	Current numbering of the Treaty establishing the European Community	New numbering of the Treaty on the Functioning of the European Union (as amended by the Treaty of Lisbon)
Article 138b	Article 192, first paragraph (repealed)[47]	
Article 138b	Article 192, second paragraph	Article 225
Article 138c	Article 193	Article 226
Article 138d	Article 194	Article 227
Article 138e	Article 195	Article 228
Article 139	Article 196 Article 229	Article 229
Article 140	Article 197, first paragraph (repealed)[48]	
Article 140	Article 197, second, third and fourth paragraphs	Article 230
Article 141	Article 198	Article 231
Article 142	Article 199	Article 232
Article 143	Article 200	Article 233
Article 144	Article 201	Article 234
		Section 2 — The European Council
		Article 235
		Article 236
Section 2	Section 2 — The Council	Section 3 — The Council
Article 145	Article 202 (repealed)[49]	
Article 146	Article 203 (repealed)[50]	
Article 147	Article 204 Article 237	
Article 148	Article 205, paragraphs 2 and 4 (repealed)[51]	
Article 148	Article 205, paragraphs 1 and 3	Article 238
Article 149 (repealed)		
Article 150	Article 206	Article 239
Article 151	Article 207	Article 240
Article 152	Article 208	Article 241
Article 153	Article 209	Article 242
Article 154	Article 210	Article 243
Section 3	Section 3 — The Commission	Section 4 — The Commission
Article 155	Article 211 (repealed)[53]	
		Article 244
Article 156	Article 212 (moved)	*Article 249, paragraph 2*
Article 157	Article 213	Article 245
Article 158	Article 214 (repealed)[55]	
Article 159	Article 215	Article 246
Article 160	Article 216	Article 247
Article 161	Article 217, paragraphs 1, 3 and 4 (repealed)[56]	
Article 161	Article 217, paragraph 2	Article 248

Previous numbering	Current numbering of the Treaty establishing the European Community	New numbering of the Treaty on the Functioning of the European Union (as amended by the Treaty of Lisbon)
Article 162	Article 218, paragraph 1 (repealed)[57]	
Article 162	Article 218, paragraph 2	Article 249
Article 163	Article 219	Article 250
Section 4	Section 4 — The Court of Justice	Section 5 — The Court of Justice of the European Union
Article 164	Article 220 (repealed)[58]	
Article 165	Article 221, first paragraph (repealed)[59]	
Article 165	Article 221, second and third paragraphs Article 251	
Article 166	Article 222	Article 252
Article 167	Article 223	Article 253
Article 168	Article 224[60]	Article 254
		Article 255
Article 168a	Article 225	Article 256
	Article 225a	Article 257
Article 169	Article 226	Article 258
Article 170	Article 227	Article 259
Article 171	Article 228	Article 260
Article 172	Article 229	Article 261
	Article 229a	Article 262
Article 173	Article 230	Article 263
Article 174	Article 231	Article 264
Article 175	Article 232	Article 265
Article 176	Article 233	Article 266
Article 177	Article 234	Article 267
Article 178	Article 235	Article 268
		Article 269
Article 179	Article 236	Article 270
Article 180	Article 237	Article 271
Article 181	Article 238	Article 272
Article 182	Article 239	Article 273
Article 183	Article 240	Article 274
		Article 275
		Article 276
Article 184	Article 241	Article 277
Article 185	Article 242	Article 278
Article 186	Article 243	Article 279
Article 187	Article 244	Article 280
Article 188	Article 245	Article 281
		Section 6 — The European Central Bank
		Article 282
	Article 112 (moved)	Article 283
	Article 113 (moved)	Article 284

Previous numbering	Current numbering of the Treaty establishing the European Community	New numbering of the Treaty on the Functioning of the European Union (as amended by the Treaty of Lisbon)
Section 5	Section 5 — The Court of Auditors	Section 7 — The Court of Auditors
Article 188a	Article 246	Article 285
Article 188b	Article 247	Article 286
Article 188c	Article 248	Article 287
Chapter 2	Chapter 2 — Provisions common to several institutions	Chapter 2 — Legal acts of the Union, adoption procedures and other provisions
		Section 1 — The legal acts of the Union
Article 189	Article 249	Article 288
		Article 289
		Article 290[61]
		Article 291[61]
		Article 292
		Section 2 — Procedures for the adoption of acts and other provisions
Article 189a	Article 250	Article 293
Article 189b	Article 251	Article 294
Article 189c	Article 252 (repealed)	
		Article 295
Article 190	Article 253	Article 296
Article 191	Article 254	Article 297
		Article 298
Article 191a(*)	Article 255 (moved)	*Article 15*
Article 192	Article 256	Article 299
		Chapter 3 — The Union's advisory bodies
		Article 300
Chapter 3	Chapter 3 — The Economic and Social Committee	Section 1 — The Economic and Social Committee
Article 193	Article 257 (repealed)[62]	
Article 194	Article 258, first, second and fourth paragraphs	Article 301
Article 195	Article 258, third paragraph (repealed)[63]	
Article 196	Article 259	Article 302
Article 197	Article 260	Article 303
Article 198	Article 261 (repealed)	
	Article 262	Article 304
Chapter 4	Chapter 4 — The Committee of the Regions	Section 2 — The Committee of the Regions
Article 198a	Article 263, first and fifth paragraphs (repealed)[64]	

Previous numbering	Current numbering of the Treaty establishing the European Community	New numbering of the Treaty on the Functioning of the European Union (as amended by the Treaty of Lisbon)
Article 198a	Article 263, second to fourth paragraphs	Article 305
Article 198b	Article 264	Article 306
Article 198c	Article 265	Article 307
Chapter 5	Chapter 5 — The European Investment Bank	Chapter 4 — The European Investment Bank
Article 198d	Article 266	Article 308
Article 198e	Article 267	Article 309
Title II	Title II — Financial provisions	Title II — Financial provisions
Article 199	Article 268	Article 310
Article 200 (repealed)		
		Chapter 1 — The Union's own resources
Article 201	Article 269	Article 311
Article 201a	Article 270 (repealed)[(65)]	
		Chapter 2 — The multiannual financial framework
		Article 312
		Chapter 3 — The Union's annual budget
Article 203	*Article 272, paragraph 1 (moved)*	Article 313
Article 202	Article 271 (moved)	*Article 316*
Article 203	Article 272, paragraph 1 (moved)	*Article 313*
Article 203	Article 272, paragraphs 2 to 10	Article 314
Article 204	Article 273	Article 315
Article 202	*Article 271 (moved)*	Article 316
		Chapter 4 — Implementation of the budget and discharge
Article 205	Article 274	Article 317
Article 205a	Article 275	Article 318
Article 206	Article 276	Article 319
Article 206a (repealed)		
		Chapter 5 — Common provisions
Article 207	Article 277	Article 320
Article 208	Article 278	Article 321
Article 209	Article 279	Article 322
		Article 323
		Article 324
		Chapter 6 — Combating fraud

Previous numbering	Current numbering of the Treaty establishing the European Community	New numbering of the Treaty on the Functioning of the European Union (as amended by the Treaty of Lisbon)
Article 209a	Article 280	Article 325
		Title III — Enhanced cooperation
	Articles 11 and 11a (replaced)	Article 326[66]
	Articles 11 and 11a (replaced)	Article 327[66]
	Articles 11 and 11a (replaced)	Article 328[66]
	Articles 11 and 11a (replaced)	Article 329[66]
	Articles 11 and 11a (replaced)	Article 330[66]
	Articles 11 and 11a (replaced)	Article 331[66]
	Articles 11 and 11a (replaced)	Article 332[66]
	Articles 11 and 11a (replaced)	Article 333[66]
	Articles 11 and 11a (replaced)	Article 334[66]
PART SIX	**PART SIX — GENERAL AND FINAL PROVISIONS**	**PART SEVEN — GENERAL AND FINAL PROVISIONS**
Article 210	Article 281 (repealed)[67]	
Article 211	Article 282	Article 335
Article 212(*)	Article 283	Article 336
Article 213	Article 284	Article 337
Article 213a(*)	Article 285	Article 338
Article 213b(*)	Article 286 (replaced)	*Article 16*
Article 214	Article 287	Article 339
Article 215	Article 288	Article 340
Article 216	Article 289	Article 341
Article 217	Article 290	Article 342
Article 218(*)	Article 291	Article 343
Artilce 219	Article 292	Article 344
Article 220	Article 293 (repealed)	
Article 221	Article 294 (moved)	Article 55
Article 222	Article 295	Article 345
Article 223	Article 296	Article 346
Article 224	Article 297	Article 347
Article 225	Article 298	Article 348
Article 226 (repealed)		
Article 227	Article 299, paragraph 1 (repealed)[68]	
Article 227	Article 299, paragraph 2, second, third and fourth subparagraphs	Article 349
Article 227	Article 299, paragraph 2, first subparagraph, and paragraphs 3 to 6 (moved)	*Article 355*
Article 228	Article 300 (replaced)	*Article 218*
Article 228a	Article 301 (replaced)	*Article 215*
Article 229	Article 302 (replaced)	*Article 220*
Article 230	Article 303 (replaced)	*Article 220*

Previous numbering	Current numbering of the Treaty establishing the European Community	New numbering of the Treaty on the Functioning of the European Union (as amended by the Treaty of Lisbon)
Article 231	Article 304 (replaced)	*Article 220*
Article 232	Article 305 (repealed)	
Article 233	Article 306	Article 350
Article 234	Article 307	Article 351
Article 235	Article 308	Article 352
		Article 353
Article 236(*)	Article 309	Article 354
Article 237 (repealed)		
Article 238	Article 310 (moved)	Article 217
Article 239	Article 311 (repealed)[69]	
	Article 299, paragraph 2, first subparagraph, and paragraphs 3 to 6 (moved)	Article 355
Article 240	Article 312 Article 356	
Articles 241-246 (repealed)		
Final Provisions	Final Provisions	
Article 247	Article 313	Article 357
		Article 358
Article 248	Article 314 (repealed)[70]	

(*) New Article introduced by the Treaty of Amsterdam.

(**) New Title introduced by the Treaty of Amsterdam.

(***) Chapter 1 restructured by the Treaty of Amsterdam.

(25) Replaced, in substance, by Article 3 TEU.

(26) Replaced, in substance, by Articles 3 to 6 TFEU.

(27) Replaced, in substance, by Article 5 TEU.

(28) Insertion of the operative part of the protocol on protection and welfare of animals.

(29) Replaced, in substance, by Article 13 TEU.

(30) Replaced, in substance, by Article 13 TEU and Article 282, paragraph 1, TFEU.

(31) Replaced, in substance, by Article 4, paragraph 3, TEU.

(32) Also replaced by Article 20 TEU.

(33) Also replaces the current Article 29 TEU.

(34) Also replaces the current Article 36 TEU.

(35) Also replaces the current Article 33 TEU.

(36) Points 1 and 2 of Article 63 EC are replaced by paragraphs 1 and 2 of Article 78 TFEU, and paragraph 2 of Article 64 is replaced by paragraph 3 of Article 78 TFEU.

(37) Replaces the current Article 31 TEU.

(38) Replaces the current Article 30 TEU.

(39) Replaces the current Article 32 TEU.

(40) — Article 140, paragraph 1 takes over the wording of paragraph 1 of Article 121.

    — Article 140, paragraph 2 takes over the second sentence of paragraph 2 of Article 122.

    — Article 140, paragraph 3 takes over paragraph 5 of Article 123.

(41) — Article 141, paragraph 1 takes over paragraph 3 of Article 123.

— Article 141, paragraph 2 takes over the first five indents of paragraph 2 of Article 117.

(42) Replaced, in substance, by the second sentence of the second subparagraph of paragraph 1 of Article 208 TFUE.

(43) The second sentence of the second subparagraph of paragraph 1 replaces, in substance, Article 178 TEC.

(44) Replaced, in substance, by Article 14, paragraphs 1 and 2, TEU.

(45) Replaced, in substance, by Article 14, paragraphs 1 to 3, TEU.

(46) Replaced, in substance, by Article 11, paragraph 4, TEU.

(47) Replaced, in substance, by Article 14, paragraph 1, TEU.

(48) Replaced, in substance, by Article 14, paragraph 4, TEU.

(49) Replaced, in substance, by Article 16, paragraph 1, TEU and by Articles 290 and 291 TFEU.

(50) Replaced, in substance, by Article 16, paragraphs 2 and 9 TEU.

(51) Replaced, in substance, by Article 16, paragraphs 4 and 5 TEU.

(53) Replaced, in substance, by Article 17, paragraph 1 TEU.

(55) Replaced, in substance, by Article 17, paragraphs 3 and 7 TEU.

(56) Replaced, in substance, by Article 17, paragraph 6, TEU.

(57) Replaced, in substance, by Article 295 TFEU.

(58) Replaced, in substance, by Article 19 TEU.

(59) Replaced, in substance, by Article 19, paragraph 2, first subparagraph, of the TEU.

(60) The first sentence of the first subparagraph is replaced, in substance, by Article 19, paragraph 2, second subparagraph of the TEU.

(61) Replaces, in substance, the third indent of Article 202 TEC.

(62) Replaced, in substance, by Article 300, paragraph 2 of the TFEU.

(63) Replaced, in substance, by Article 300, paragraph 4 of the TFEU.

(64) Replaced, in substance, by Article 300, paragraphs 3 and 4, TFEU.

(65) Replaced, in substance, by Article 310, paragraph 4, TFEU.

(66) Also replaces the current Articles 27a to 27e, 40 to 40b, and 43 to 45 TEU.

(66) Also replaces the current Articles 27a to 27e, 40 to 40b, and 43 to 45 TEU.

(67) Replaced, in substance, by Article 47 TEU.

(68) Replaced, in substance by Article 52 TEU.

(69) Replaced, in substance by Article 51 TEU.

(70) Replaced, in substance by Article 55 TEU.

PART I

1

From EEC to EU: A brief history of the development of the Union

1.1 Introduction

The purpose of this chapter is to provide a brief overview of the development of the European Economic Community into the European Union. The development of the organisation will be traced chronologically and certain underlying themes and tensions will be identified, as well as the theories that have been used to explain the development of the EU. It is these perennial issues, or the way the Community institutions and the Member States choose to deal with them, that have shaped the way the EU works and, indeed, will shape the future of the EU.

1.2 Development prior to the Single European Act

The European Economic Community (EEC) came into existence following the signing of the Treaty of Rome in 1957 by the six original Member States, France, Germany, Italy, Belgium, The Netherlands, and Luxembourg. A second Rome Treaty signed by the same six states created Euratom (the European Atomic Energy Community) on the same day. These treaties, but particularly the EEC Treaty, represented the culmination of a movement towards international cooperation which had been growing throughout the twentieth century, and which was given particular impetus in Europe following the devastation inflicted by the Second World War.

The institutional model for the EEC had already been provided by the European Coal and Steel Community (ECSC) set up in 1951 with the Treaty of Paris by the same six states. However, the scope of the EEC was altogether wider. The ECSC was concerned only with creating a single market in coal and steel; the EEC was designed to create an economic community. Although its aims were primarily economic, to create a single 'common' market in Europe, they were not exclusively so. The founder members of the EEC were fired by ideals as well as economic practicalities. As stated in the preamble to the EEC Treaty, its signatories were 'Determined to lay the foundations of an ever closer union among the peoples of Europe', 'Resolved by thus pooling their resources to preserve and strengthen peace and liberty'.

Although the institutional framework of the EEC, as of Euratom, was modelled on that of the ECSC, the three communities at the outset held only two institutions in common, the Assembly (subsequently renamed the Parliament) and the European Court of Justice (ECJ). It was not until the Merger Treaty 1965 that the other two main institutions merged. The High Authority, the executive body of the ECSC, merged with the EEC and Euratom Commission to form what is now the Commission, and the Council of Ministers of the ECSC with that of the EEC and Euratom to become a single Council. Henceforth the three communities continued to function as separate entities, but with shared institutions.

1.3 Enlargement

The United Kingdom, together with Denmark and the Republic of Ireland, finally joined the Communities in 1973 with the Treaty of Accession under a Conservative government led by Edward Heath. Incorporation of the Treaties into UK law was achieved by the European Communities Act 1972. (Norway joined at the same time but subsequently withdrew following a referendum which came out against membership.)

There were many reasons for the UK remaining outside the EEC for so long. The UK was reluctant to loosen its existing ties with the Commonwealth, which membership of the EEC would clearly entail; it wished to retain its (perceived) 'special relationship' with the USA; and, as an island nation which had not been subject to enemy occupation during the First and Second World Wars, it no doubt lacked the sense of urgency which inspired the original Member States. Suspicious that membership of the EEC would involve an unacceptable loss of sovereignty, the UK preferred the looser ties of the European Free Trade Association (EFTA) which it entered on its creation in 1959. When the UK did seek to join the EEC, persuaded by its clear economic success, its entry was blocked for some years, largely due to the efforts of the French president, General de Gaulle. Even after accession in 1973 public opinion in the UK was divided; it was only following a referendum in favour of membership conducted in 1975 under the government of the Labour Party that the UK's membership was fully and finally confirmed.

In 1979 Greece, and in 1986 Spain and Portugal, signed acts of accession to join the EEC, bringing the then total membership to 12. Membership increased again with the accession of Austria, Finland and Sweden on 1 January 1995. Norway held a referendum which again resulted in a vote against membership. Expansion continued with the largest number of countries joining what had become the EU in one go, ten, acceding in 2004. These new Member States, sometimes referred to as the EU10, are, in alphabetical order, Cyprus, Czech Republic, Estonia, Hungary, Latvia, Lithuania, Malta, Poland, Slovakia, and Slovenia, resulting in an EU of 25. Two more Member States joined on 1 January 2007: Bulgaria and Romania despite some concerns about compliance with the Community *acquis* (see COM (2006) 549 final). Further expansion is planned.

The process of joining the EU involves several stages. A country must first of all apply, then be recognised as a candidate country, at which point formal negotiations are opened between the candidate country and the EU. The negotiations have the aim of concluding an accession treaty. After the signing of the accession treaty, there is usually a period before the treaty comes into force. Before a country can accede to the EU, it must satisfy the terms of Article 49 of the Treaty on European Union (TEU), Article 6 TEU, and three additional criteria: the Copenhagen Criteria.

Article 49 requires that a state be European, Article 6 requires respect for democracy, the rule of law, and respect for human rights. The Copenhagen criteria are:

- the political criterion (respect for democracy and human rights)
- the economic criterion (the need for viable market economies and the capacity to cope with competitive pressure and market forces within the EU)
- the ability to adopt the Community *acquis*.

During the accession period, the Commission will review progress of the country and publish its views.

Croatia (application submitted 21 February 2003), Turkey (application submitted 14 April 1987) and the Former Yugoslav Republic of Macedonia (application submitted 22 March 2004) have all applied to join the Union. More recently, Montenegro including Kosovo (as defined by the United Nations Security Council Resolution 1244 of 10 June 1999) (application submittted 16 December 2008) and Albania (application submitted 10 March 2009) have also applied to join, though there have been concerns about Albania's electoral processes. Additionally, the EU has established European partnerships with Bosnia–Herzegovina and Serbia, as they have been recognised as potential candidate countries. Croatia and the former Yugoslav Republic of Macedonia likewise entered into European partnerships, the purpose of which is to assist countries in preparing for membership of the EU. The position as regards these four countries has, to varying degrees, been contentious.

The Commission Communication (COM (2004) 656 final) stated that in the Commission's opinion Turkey satisfied the Copenhagen Criteria. The Commission additionally suggested using a three-tier strategy for the negotiations, to ensure that the reform process in Turkey continues, with particular regard to the zero-tolerance policy towards torture and ill-treatment. The first pillar of the strategy deals with the political criterion and seeks to support the reform process. The EU will monitor the political reforms on an annual basis, and the Commission may suspend negotiations if there is a serious and persistent breach of the principles of liberty, democracy, respect for human rights and fundamental freedoms or the rule of law on which the Union is founded. If such a recommendation is made, the Council may, by a qualified majority, decide to suspend negotiations. This wording mirrors the wording found in the TEU regarding Member States' obligations to comply with human-rights obligations. The second pillar introduces an intergovernmental conference within which the negotiation process will be held. The Commission notes that amongst other factors, the EU will have to consider its financial position before negotiations can be concluded. The third pillar concerns cultural dialogue and dealing with differences in society and specifically the rights of minorities. The Commission aims to facilitate dialogue involving civil society. Finally, the Commission in its Communication emphasised that Turkey's accession could not take place before 2014. In November 2005, the Council agreed to start negotiations, the process actually starting in Spring 2006. The Commission published a report on Turkey's progress towards accession to the EU (SEC (2007) 1436 and 'Enlargement Strategies and Main Challenges 2007–2008' (COM (2007) 663 final)). Although economic progress has been good, more is required, particularly in the labour market, social security, and the energy sector. Significantly, problems remain with Turkey's human-rights record, particularly its record regarding investigation of claims of abuse.

Croatia has been officially recognised as a candidate country and the Commission, in November 2004, recommended opening negotiations. The December 2004 European Council envisaged commencing negotiations the following March, provided Croatia fully cooperated with the International Criminal Tribunal for the former Yugoslavia. On the day before negotiations were due to start, the European Council found that Croatia had not so cooperated and the Council of Ministers decided to postpone the commencement of accession negotiations with Croatia indefinitely. In November 2005, the European Council agreed to start the negotiation process. The Commission published a progress report in 2007, highlighting potential problems with corruption (SEC (2007) 1431). Nonetheless, it was envisaged that Croatia would join the EU in 2009. At the time of writing, the process has run into difficulty, due to a border dispute with Slovenia, in the resolution of which the EU is involved.

FYR Macedonia has also been recognised as an official candidate country. In 2007, the Commission reported on progress (SEC (2007) 1432). According to the Commission, FYR Macedonia saw excellent economic growth, but unemployment was very high and the market economy was still struggling. In the political arena, concerns were raised about non-cooperation between the different political parties, which impeded the reforms, but improvements were made in respect of human rights and the protection of minorities. Nonetheless, three years after FYR Macedonia was granted candidate status, negotiations for accession have not started: the key outstanding condition is the ability to meet international standards for the conduct of free and fair elections, which is a core requirement to comply with the Copenhagen political criteria.

Despite these difficulties, and the current economic difficulties, the intention of the EU is to continue to work towards further enlargement, and perhaps to take the EU further. The Commission launched in late 2008 the Eastern Partnership which aims to facilitate travel; proposes cooperation on energy security; aims for better institution building by borrowing instruments from the EU's enlargement policy; and puts a new emphasis on social and economic development. Further, if the Treaty of Lisbon comes into force, the TEU will contain a new provision on the EU's relationship with neighbouring countries, aiming to establish an area of prosperity and good neighbourliness (Article 8 TEU, as amended by Lisbon).

1.4 The Single European Act

An important development in 1986 was the signing by the then 12 Member States of the Single European Act (SEA). A White Paper issued by the Commission in 1985 had revealed that despite the Community's long existence, many barriers still existed to the achievement of the single internal market. The result was a new treaty, the SEA. The principal purpose of the SEA was to eliminate the remaining barriers to the single internal market within the deadline of 31 December 1992, to be achieved by a massive programme of harmonisation (see Chapter 16). In addition, the SEA extended the sphere of Community competence and introduced a number of procedural changes designed to accelerate the Community decision-making process (see Chapter 3). The SEA undoubtedly injected a new dynamism into Community affairs. By February 1992, 218 of the 282 proposals forming the complete programme for the completion of the internal market had been adopted. Although the 1992 programme reached its termination date, it is important to remember that the provisions the SEA introduced remain and are still used as a basis for legislation (see Chapter 16), as barriers to the internal remain even now (see eg the Services Directive, discussed in Chapter 22). Note also that legislation may be enacted but, to a large extent is dependent on Member States for implementation, and that this may be where the real difficulty lies (see Chapters 5 and 16).

1.5 Treaty on European Union

The late 1980s saw a growing movement within the Community towards closer European union. In December 1989, two intergovermental conferences were convened pursuant to cooperation procedures introduced by the SEA to consider the questions of (a) economic and monetary union and (b) political union. The conferences, which lasted for a year, resulted in the signing, at Maastricht, on 7 February 1992, of the TEU.

The TEU comprised two distinct parts. One part (Article G, renumbered Article 8 following the ratification of the 1997 Amsterdam Treaty ('ToA') which, in pursuit of greater coherence, renumbered most of the articles of both the EC Treaty and the TEU), consisting of 86 paragraphs, introduced substantial amendments to the EEC Treaty, and renamed it the European Community (EC) Treaty, reflecting its wider purposes.

The second part of the TEU (Articles 1–7 and 9–53: Articles A–F and H–S respectively as originally provided in the TEU), representing the political pillar of the treaty, stood as a separate treaty establishing the European Union (Article 1 (ex A)). It set out a number of general principles (Articles 1–7 (ex A–F)) and provided specifically for cooperation, with a view to adopting joint action, in the field of foreign and security policy (FSP), and eventually defence (Articles 11–28 (ex J)) and for cooperation and the framing of common policies in justice and home affairs (JHA) (Articles 29–45 (ex K)). These two areas of cooperation came to be referred to as the second and third pillars respectively of the European Union. The remaining pillar is the EC, together with Euratom and, prior to its expiry in 2002, ECSC. The communities comprising this pillar, referred to as the first pillar of the Union, are together called the European Communities.

The TEU was due to come into effect on 1 January 1993, following ratification as required by all Member States. As a result of difficulties, political and legal, causing delay in ratification in some Member States (notably the UK, Denmark, and Germany), the treaty did not enter into force until 1 November 1993. From that date the EEC Treaty became the EC Treaty, and will henceforth be referred to as such in this book, except where the term EEC is needed for reasons of historical accuracy (note also impact of Lisbon Treaty—see below). The term European Union (EU), introduced in Article 1 (ex A) of the TEU to describe the union of Member States as comprised under the European Community treaties and the TEU, is not strictly applicable to matters of law relating to the EC Treaty, although it is widely used in that context. The law emanating from JHA and common foreign and security policy (CFSP) may be referred to as EU law. For the most part, these areas fall outside the scope of this book. Nonetheless, although there are occasions when we might properly continue to distinguish between the EU and the EC, given the intention to remove the distinction evidenced by first the Constitutional Treaty (see 1.8) and the Treaty of Lisbon (see 1.9), the term EC will be replaced throughout this book to avoid confusion. There are two exceptions to this approach: first, references to the Treaty of Rome (as amended) will continue to be to the EC Treaty (except where we are discussing proposals made by Lisbon); and, secondly, where context (for example historical accuracy), requires a distinction to be made between EC and EU.

1.5.1 Monetary union

Like the SEA, the TEU extended the scope of Community competence and strengthened its institutional machinery; in particular, the powers of the European Parliament (see Chapter 2). Perhaps one of the most politically sensitive issues was the introduction of provisions designed to lead to full economic and monetary union by 1999. The fact that of the then Member States both Britain and Denmark negotiated provisions allowing them to opt out of this process indicates the importance of this issue. Even Germany, one of the driving forces behind monetary union, experienced difficulties: the validity of Germany's entry into the single currency was challenged, albeit unsuccessfully, before the German constitutional court.

The road to monetary union fell into three stages (Articles 98–124 (ex 102a–9m) EC). Stage one consisted of the completion of the internal market and the removal of controls on the movement of capital. This stage has been completed. Stage two began on 1 January 1994. It aimed to ensure the convergence of the economies of the Member States, measured by criteria set out in the EC Treaty. These are commonly referred to as the 'convergence criteria'. Only countries which satisfy the convergence criteria will be able to join the single currency. A two-year membership of the exchange rate mechanism (ERM) is also a prerequisite to demonstrate monetary stability before a country can join the euro. The final stage was the irrevocable locking of the exchange rates of the Member States' currencies and the introduction of a common currency, the euro. The date set for the introduction of the single currency was 1 January 1999, although euro coins and notes were not issued in all the participating states until 2002. Following the introduction of the single currency, a new ERM was introduced between the euro and the currencies of those Member States that have not yet joined the single currency. In addition to this, the treaty contains provisions detailing the institutions necessary to run the single currency (Articles 112–15 (ex 109a–d) EC). These are the European Central Bank (ECB) and a committee to determine economic policy, the Council of Economic and Finance Ministers (ECOFIN). Member States, including those which have not adopted the euro, are supposed to run their economies in line with the Stability and Growth Pact (SGP), though difficulties in practice lead to its revision in 2005 so as to allow greater flexibility in national responses to difficult economic times.

The Member States joining economic and monetary union in the first wave were identified in a Commission recommendation based on its Convergence Report of 25 March 1998 on the state of the Member States' economies. Eleven states were identified as having satisfied the convergence criteria: Belgium, Germany, Spain, France, Ireland, Italy, Luxembourg, The Netherlands, Austria, Portugal, and Finland (the UK, Denmark, and Sweden having, for the time being, opted out of monetary union). This recommendation was confirmed by the European Council meeting in May 1998. Subsequently, Greece became the twelfth Member State to join the Eurozone, on 1 January 2002. All the new Member States are entitled to join the euro if they meet the criteria. Estonia, Latvia, and Lithuania have joined the ERM as a preliminary step. Slovenia joined the Eurozone in January 2007; Malta and Cyprus joined in January 2008. The most recent entrant is Slovakia; with official adoption of the euro on 1 January 2009. Slovakia's entry was approved notwithstanding the ECB's concerns about the country's inflation. Enthusiasm for early adoption of the euro has faded somewhat due to the current economic situation, and most countries in ERM have dropped specific target dates for its adoption.

1.5.2 Union citizenship

The TEU also introduced the notion of citizenship of the Union (Article 17 (ex 8)). On the face of it, citizenship seems a relatively straightforward notion. It entitles EU nationals to certain rights such as freedom of movement throughout the Union (see Chapters 21–25) and the right to vote and to stand in municipal elections or elections to the European Parliament in any Member State in which they are resident. The precise extent of the rights to be granted to citizens, however, is not clear. Will citizenship incorporate rights contained elsewhere in the EC Treaty hitherto granted to EC workers, the self-employed and their families (see Chapters 21 and 23)? Does it include rights and duties found in the TEU provisions relating to the other pillars (eg, Article 6(2) TEU)? There has been much debate about the significance of European citizenship. Some see it as the beginning of the development of a common European identity or as a means to ameliorate the democratic deficit (see Chapter 3) within the Union. Others have criticised it for being no more than a label for the rights of free movement already incorporated in the EC Treaty. The treaty does allow the Member States to increase the rights attaching to the notion of citizenship, but more than ten years on, it is still too early to tell how citizenship will fully develop. Recent secondary legislation is based in part on Article 18, though the legislation in question is in part a codification of existing secondary legislation and ECJ jurisprudence in the context of free movement of people (see further Chapters XX and XX). Whilst the jurisprudence of the ECJ has done much to enhance the rights available to migrant EU citizens, in the eyes of some commentators, there is no real European citizenship, but rather the links of nationality to individual Member States remain strong.

1.5.3 The other two pillars of the Union

Articles 11–28 (FSP) and 29–42 (JHA) of the TEU constitute the second and third pillars respectively of the European Union. Although they can be seen as extending the powers transferred to the European level, they can also be seen as maintaining the autonomy of the nation state. Decision-making within these pillars was, under the TEU, predominantly in the hands of the Council representing the Member States, and, although these two pillars share the institutions of the EC, the other Community institutions were limited in the role they played in both policymaking and enforcement. In addition, all decisions were required to be made unanimously and consequently progress towards effective policies within these areas would inevitably be slow. The TEU contained provisions whereby some of the policies in JHA could be transferred to the EC (former Article K.9 TEU). A comparison between the decision-making processes within these two pillars and those of the EC (Chapter 3) would suggest that such a transfer must surely increase the speed of common policymaking in those areas. This was recognised and, following the ratification of the ToA, several policy areas originally dealt with under JHA (eg, immigration and asylum of third-country (non-EU) nationals) are now dealt with under the EC Treaty (see further 1.6 below and Chapter 26). The decision-making procedures under JHA have also been amended following Amsterdam, specifying in limited circumstances the use of qualified majority voting (QMV).

1.6 Impact of the Treaty of Amsterdam

Former Article N(2) TEU provided that an intergovernmental conference (IGC) should be held in 1996 to examine the provisions which the TEU required to be reviewed. Other issues could also be included on the agenda (Article N(1) TEU). The purpose of the review was to revise the policies and institutional structure of the Union to ensure its effectiveness (Article 2 TEU). This was an issue gaining ever-more relevance with the increase of Union competence under the TEU and the further expansion of Union membership. As the IGC discussions progressed, it became clear that the issues to be decided coalesced round three broad, interlinked themes: democracy, transparency, and efficiency (discussed further in Chapters 2 and 3). The review process continued into June 1997, when a draft treaty was agreed at Amsterdam. This treaty, the ToA, was signed on 2 October 1997 and came into force on 1 May 1999. Since the ToA renumbered all treaty articles, the new numbers of the treaty articles will henceforth throughout this book be used, with the former numbers bracketed alongside them where necessary to clarify the meaning (eg, Article 30 (ex Article 36) EC), save where reasons of historical accuracy (such as articles cited in the context of cases) dictate that the original article number be shown. Discussions of changes introduced by the Treaty of Lisbon, which if it comes into force will again renumber the Treaties, will refer to post-Lisbon Treaty numbering.

1.6.1 Strengthening the EC pillar

The ToA, when compared with the ambitious TEU, may seem to achieve little; indeed, when one considers the stresses to which the EU will increasingly find its decision-making subject in an EU of 27 or more, the ToA could be criticised for failing to deal adequately with the difficult institutional questions involved. Nonetheless, the ToA can still be seen as constituting a cautious but significant expansion of the Union's scope. The first (EC) pillar was strengthened by streamlining its decision-making powers and by the allocation of new competences (see Chapter 3). Certain provisions, for example those relating to the admission of third-country nationals, have been moved from the third pillar (JHA) to the EC pillar. In addition, the Schengen Agreement which dealt with controls at internal borders (an agreement outside the EC/EU framework between a number of the EU

Member States) and its associated decisions have, in effect, been incorporated into the EC Treaty. All of these have been combined to form a Title in Part Three of the EC Treaty, Title IV. These are discussed further in Chapter 26. Some completely new provisions were also introduced into the EC Treaty, such as those relating to unemployment. The Protocol on Social Policy, originally annexed to the EC Treaty by the TEU, has now been incorporated into the main body of the EC Treaty, replacing the existing social-policy provisions.

1.6.2 Equality and fundamental rights

These changes reflect a shift of emphasis away from the mainly economic conception of the EC to a more political idea, founded on fundamental rights and principles. In particular, the provision prohibiting discrimination on grounds of nationality (Article 12 EC) has been developed by the insertion of a new clause (Article 13 EC) authorising the Council to 'take appropriate action to combat discrimination based on sex, racial or ethnic origin, religion or belief, disability, age or sexual orientation'.

Although not phrased in the absolute terms of Article 12 EC, it reinforces the idea of non-discrimination as a fundamental principle which the ECJ has invoked and used to significant effect in its case law. Further, the promotion of the equality of men and women is now identified in Article 2 EC as a task of the Community. Note that should Lisbon come into force, this requirement would be strengthened as Article 10 TFEU requires the Union, in defining all its policies, to combat discrimination whether based on sex, racial or ethnic origin, religion or belief, disability, age, or sexual orientation.

This concern with fundamental principles is also evidenced by amended Article 7 TEU. This provides that any Member State found to have committed a persistent and serious breach of the fundamental principles listed in Article 6 TEU may be suspended from voting in the Council of Ministers, although it will remain subject to obligations arising out of the Union membership, such as compliance with EC legislation. The principles listed in Article 6 TEU are: liberty, democracy, respect for human rights and fundamental freedoms, and the rule of law. Respect for the rule of law, in particular, is evidenced by the expansion of the ECJ's jurisdiction in relation to Part Three Title IV of the EC Treaty and to the JHA provisions remaining in the TEU. In both these cases, however, the jurisdiction of the ECJ is subject to serious limitations (discussed further in Chapters 10 and 26). Nevertheless, the ToA extended the scope of Union competence under the EC Treaty and effected significant changes in the TEU (Chapter 3).

1.6.3 Closer cooperation

The last main change introduced by the ToA was the introduction of provisions allowing for 'closer cooperation' by Member States. This is often referred to as an example of the principle of 'flexibility', described as the leitmotif of the ToA. It allows differing conceptions of the European ideal and different degrees of commitment to coexist within the Union framework. As such, it is a variant of the concepts variously described as 'multi-speed Europe', 'Europe of variable geometry' and 'Europe of concentric circles' prior to the 1996 IGC. The ToA allows Member States that wish to cooperate more closely in specific areas within the general scope of the treaties, but which are not yet subject to Community legislation, to do so. Although the Union had, in effect, accepted this approach in specific policy areas, for example, the UK and Danish opt-out of monetary union under the TEU and the UK opt-out of the Protocol on Social Policy in the TEU, this is the first time that a *general* provision (Article 11 EC and, in respect of JHA, Article 40, subject in both cases to Articles 43–4 TEU) allowing for such separate development within the Union framework, has been incorporated.

Cooperation is limited to the matters within the scope of the treaties and cannot in any way conflict with Community law (see Article 11 EC as inserted by ToA). Article 11 limits the circumstances in which closer cooperation may operate; in particular, a majority of the Member States must be involved, the action must be in the furtherance of the Union's objectives and closer cooperation must not affect the rights and obligations of Member States not involved. The provisions in relation to closer cooperation within the JHA provisions of the TEU are couched in similar terms (Article 43 TEU). Note that these provisions have been amended by Nice (see below at 1.7.1) and would have been amended by the Constitution (see below at 1.8) and will be affected by Lisbon if it comes into force (see 1.9).

This provision for closer cooperation may bring some advantages, notably by preventing the frustration of the integrationist aims of the majority of Member States by the minority, thus relieving the tensions between the Member States which disagree about the depth of European integration and allowing compromise within the Union. It also carries disadvantages. In particular, the boundary between matters falling only within the sphere of EC law proper and areas permitting closer cooperation may be unclear. Furthermore, is it possible in the context of the internal market for some Member States to become involved in closer cooperation without affecting the position of other Member States? In which case, should the other Member States be involved in the discussions leading to the adoption of closer cooperation measures even though they will not be bound by them? This problem has already surfaced in the context of the UK's role in the introduction of monetary union. On the other hand, if the ECJ interprets the provisions set out in new Article 11 EC strictly so as to preserve and even stretch the boundaries of Community law, then the opportunities for such cooperation will be severely curtailed. In any event, the very fact that the Union contemplates an approach where some Member States go ahead regardless of the wishes of others will undermine the ideas of community and solidarity which are fundamental to the creation of both the internal market and an ever closer union. Unless benefits and burdens are equally shared, there is a danger that the achievements of the past 49 years could be undone. It seems, however, that 'flexibility' is now an unavoidable part of ensuring agreement within the Union and allowing it to develop.

1.7 Treaty of Nice

It has been suggested that the ToA failed to deal with one of the main issues identified by the 1996 IGC—that of preparing the EU for enlargement. On that basis, the swift progression from treaty negotiation (in respect of the ToA) to treaty negotiation (regarding the Treaty of Nice) is not that surprising. Just two months after the ToA was signed, the European Council at the Cologne Summit in 1999 called for an IGC with a mandate to address certain unresolved issues: size and composition of the Commission; the weighting of votes in Council; and the extension of QMV. At the same time, wider discussions were taking place about the legitimacy of the Union and the scope of its powers. There was consequently a debate as to whether the issues to be dealt with by the Nice Treaty should be broadened. In the event, the treaty remained relatively narrowly focused, although following the 2000 Feira European Council, it also dealt with 'enhanced cooperation'. Difficult constitutional questions, including the status of the Charter of Fundamental Rights, the form of which had been agreed prior to Nice, were deferred until the 2004 IGC. The Treaty of Nice then might well be described as dealing with the leftovers of the ToA but going no further.

1.7.1 Changes to the TEU: Enhanced cooperation

The main changes to CFSP and JHA pillars relate to the provisions on closer cooperation, now called in what seems like a symbolic change, 'enhanced cooperation'. Article 43 TEU, which introduced closer cooperation, has been replaced by a revised version of that provision and new Article 43a–b. Significantly, following Nice, enhanced cooperation may take place with only eight Member States. Under the ToA version 'a majority of Member States' was required. Although 8 out of 15 Member States would constitute a majority of Member States at that time, post enlargement this is no longer the case. In a EU of 27 members (or perhaps more), the number of participating Member States required to make a majority has increased. Article 43 EC following Nice is less strict in other aspects too, particularly as regards the level of impact 'enhanced cooperation' is permitted to have on non-participating Member States. Article 43(1)(f) in its original form required that any closer cooperation 'does not affect the competences, rights, obligations and interests of those Member States which do not participate therein', whilst the post-Nice version requires that the competences, rights, and obligations of such Member States be respected. Similarly post Nice, the *acquis communautaire* is to be 'respected' rather than to be unaffected by the cooperation, as had been the requirement following ToA. In both instances, it will be easier to satisfy the tests in the post-Nice version of Article 43 than it would have been under the version inserted by ToA. It would seem that the intention is to make the enhanced cooperation provisions more workable, though if Lisbon comes into force there will be yet more changes to these provisions.

1.7.2 Changes to the EC pillar

As already noted, certain institutional changes were included in Nice: these are discussed further in Chapter 2. Changes were also made to the court structure, significantly strengthening the role of the Court of First Instance which gained the right to hear some preliminary rulings procedures. (See Part II.) The closer cooperation provisions in Article 11 EC have been amended and renamed 'enhanced cooperation' in line with the amendments to Article 43 EC. Further, co-decision and QMV are extended to a wider range of substantive provisions. Certain sensitive areas, such as taxation, still remain outside QMV.

1.7.3 **Ratification of the Treaty of Nice**

Although it may not have had the great ambitions of TEU, Nice ran into difficulties when the Member States sought the approval of the treaty within their own legal orders. Surprisingly, perhaps, the Irish voted 'no' to the Nice Treaty in June 2001. This was an embarrassing result, as the institutional rebalancing contained in Nice was viewed as the necessary precursor to further enlargement, which was already being negotiated. It was only in October 2002 that a second Irish referendum accepted the Treaty of Nice. Ireland finally lodged its instrument of ratification on 18 December 2002. As provided in the Nice Treaty, it came into force on 1 February 2003.

1.8 **Treaty establishing a Constitution for Europe**

Although the Declaration on the Future of Europe attached to the Treaty of Nice identified specific issues that would need to be addressed: the delimitation of powers between the EU and the Member States; the simplification of the Treaties; and the role of the national parliaments within the EU, it also called for 'a wider and deeper debate about the future of the European Union'. The Laeken Declaration confirmed the issues to be addressed by the next round of treaty negotiations. It confirmed the points identified in the Nice Declaration and emphasised the importance of bringing Europe closer to its citizens. In doing so, however, it raised the possibility of reorganising the Treaties so as to introduce a constitutional text for the EU. Such a text would be important for setting down the future characteristics of the Union; indeed the fact that the word 'constitutional' was introduced was seen by some as significant. Unusually by comparison with the intergovernmental nature of previous treaty revisions, the Laeken Declaration provided for the establishment of a Convention on the Future of Europe. Its function was to identify and discuss the relevant issues before drawing up a final document containing the possible options for the Union's future development to form a starting point for the ICC's discussions.

The resulting treaty, the Treaty establishing a Constitution for Europe (the Constitution), was signed on 29 October 2004. Significantly, referenda held in France and the Netherlands produced a 'no' vote, and the governments of both countries accepted this outcome. Nonetheless, 13 Member States ratified it. As a result, the Union entered a period of reflection to consider how to proceed. The outcome was the Treaty of Lisbon, discussed at 1.9. Before we consider Lisbon, a few points about the Constitution should be noted.

Despite the grand title, the Constitution can be seen as reordering, clarifying and simplifying, and making existing principles express rather than adding much that is totally new.

Although the Constitution may have been a consolidating act, it would have introduced some changes, some of which, though small, are significant. Crucially, it would have repealed all existing treaties and the current pillar structure, thus removing the distinction between Community and Union. It also identified the powers, or competence, of the Union and the Member States expressly (discussed

Chapters 3 and 16), and would have formally incorporated the doctrine of primacy of Union law (discussed Chapter 4). Some changes were proposed to the operation of the institutions, mainly to improve efficiency of decision-making (see Chapter 2) and to contain the size of the institutions with the increased size of the Union. Particular controversy surrounded the introduction of a formal president of the Council as well as a foreign minister. Some limited areas of Union competence were to be added and the scope of some areas amended. Thus we saw references to space, energy, humanitarian aid, and territorial cohesion. Although not hitherto mentioned in the Treaties, the introduction of these areas would have reflected existing Union practice. Similarly, areas such as sport have been the subject of declarations attached to treaties, if not part of the formal Union competence. Article I–44 dealt with enhanced cooperation. A minimum of one third of the Member States were required to participate, a lower percentage than currently, but enhanced cooperation was expressed to be used only as a last resort and within the framework of Union non-exclusive competence. Finally, there were changes to the types of Union legislation and their terminology, discussed further in Chapter 3.

How do we assess the impact of the Constitution? On the one hand it sought formally introduce the notion of constitution, with all its implications of statehood. On the other, the word constitution has been used in the context of the Community and the Union for some considerable time: the ECJ in its judgment in *Parti Ecologiste 'Les Verts' v European Parliament* (case 294/83) referred to the EC Treaty as a constitutional document and the debates about statehood of the Union arose in the context of European citizenship, introduced by TEU. In terms of the text itself, the Constitution did not constitute a huge turning point. As with many of the previous treaties, it is a reaction to the current concerns afflicting the EU. In this case, the triggers seem to have been the need to 'tidy up' the Union's procedures in the face of the expansion in membership and, importantly, to try to deal with the increased public disaffection with the EU. Thus we see an increased emphasis on democracy, participation, the rights of individuals and the values of the Union. Vaclav Havel, President of the Czech Republic, sought a:

> concise, clearly formulated and universally understandable constitution [which] would simply make it easier for the citizens of an integrating Europe to recognize what the European Union stands for; to understand it better; and, consequently, to identify with it.

With the abandonment of the Constitution, this task falls to Lisbon. Whether this aim has been achieved is another matter.

1.9 Treaty of Lisbon

In June 2007, the EU summit agreed a new IGC mandate for institutional reform. A new Reform Treaty was agreed and signed at a special summit in Lisbon on 13 December 2007. This is the Treaty of Lisbon. It was due to come into force on 1 January 2009, provided all Member States ratified it. There has been intense debate, both academic and political, about the impact of the Treaty of Lisbon. It is clear that the treaty comprises much of what was contained in the Constitution; indeed the starting point for discussions on the Lisbon Treaty was the Constitution. In the UK particularly, there was political debate as to whether the treaty should attract a referendum, however the government pressed ahead without, and the UK officially ratified the Treaty of Lisbon on 16 July 2008. An attempt to challenge the decision, on the basis of legitimate expectations was unsuccessful (*R, on the application of Wheeler v Office of the Prime Minister, Secretary of State for Foreign and Commonwealth Affairs and Speaker of the House of Commons* [2008] EWHC 1409 (Admin)). Ratification has been fairly smooth in almost all of the Member States, however in a case of history repeating itself, the Irish—after a poorly orchestrated 'yes' campaign—voted no, apparently due to concerns about the right to mandate a commissioner, taxation, military neutrality and abortion. Its seems concessions—or clarifications—have been given on these points. Notably, all Member States will be able to nominate a Commissioner. Ireland has agreed to organise another referendum by November 2009. The Polish president has announced that he will only formally approve the Lisbon Treaty if the Irish vote 'yes'. Despite these difficulties, most other Member States have ratified the treaty; most recently the Swedes and, subject to the approval of Senate, the Czechs. The Czechs had to wait until a decision of their constitutional court on the subject. Whilst that court approved ratification, the Czech implementing legislation is to contain a provision that no further transfer of power to the EU may take place without the express permission of the Czech parliament. Although the German parliament approved Lisbon, the treaty has not yet been formally ratified as President Horst Köhler, withheld his signature pending legal challenges filed by a number of appellants. The Federal Constitutional Court gave a conditional approval to the Lisbon Treaty. While the treaty itself is compatible with the German constitution, ratification cannot proceed until an accompanying law dealing with 'bridging clauses' (which allow for an extension of Union competence) have been amended so as to ensure democratic control of the process, potentially limiting further integration. The court also held that Union law deemed to violate requirements of the judgment could be declared inapplicable in Germany. In a return to *Brunner* language the court emphasised its place in the legal hierarchy as final arbiter of any disputes between German and EU legal orders. A brief overview of Lisbon follows.

1.9.1 Constitutional issues

Like the Constitution, Lisbon disposes of the pillar structure. There remains a distinction between JHA and CFSP. The first and third pillars of the EU will in effect be merged into a single system, what is currently the EC Treaty (and will become TFEU, see below). CFSP will remain in the EU Treaty, with a different institutional structure. So whilst JHA will become subject to the greater involvement of the Union institutions, with presumably greater scrutiny of actions at Union level, the CFSP will remain essentially intergovernmental in form. Whilst the ECJ's jurisdiction is extended as regards JHA subject to some limitations, it will remain largely excluded as regards CFSP. We shall see later (Chapter 3) that the ECJ has interpreted Article 47 TEU, which preserves the EC pillar against encroachment by the other pillars, so as to create a hierarchy between the pillars, with the EC pillar taking primacy (see eg *Commission v Council* (ship source pollution) (case C–440/05) regarding the current JHA; and *Commission v Council* (moratorium on small arms and light weapons) (case C–91/05) regarding the CFSP). Significantly, Article 40 TEU (as amended by Lisbon) specifies that both the TFEU pillar (containing the EC and JHA) and the EU pillar (containing CFSP) are equal; neither one shall affect the operation of the other. It remains to be seen whether this will change the approach of the ECJ to future disputes.

As part of this change, the EC Treaty will be renamed the Treaty on the Functioning of the Union (TFEU), another classic in the Union tendency to pick 'un-user friendly' terminology, and references to the 'Community' will become references to the 'Union'. Further, the EU will be given a single legal personality; currently the Union has no legal personality although the Community does. The inclusion of JHA within what is currently the EC pillar will mean that some case law, emphasising the culturally specific nature of criminal sanctions (eg *Commission v Council* (case C–176/03)), will be consigned to history by Lisbon, even taking into account the 'brake-accelerator' mechanism on legislation in this field (Article 88).

The Charter does not have legal status at the moment, though the ECJ has referred to it in some judgments (see eg *Parliament v Council* (case C–540/03)). The Constitution envisaged including the Charter of Fundamental Rights in the constitutional treaties themselves. Lisbon abandons this format, though the Charter will be given the same status as the treaties. This is achieving effectively the same end by a different route. The precise impact of this change is hard to assess, though some have suggested that if the scope of application of the Charter is understood in the light of European citizenship, it will be very broad indeed. The British have negotiated an opt-out, as they have in relation to some of the JHA provisions, and the Poles have also opted out of the Charter provision. Like the Constitution, Lisbon envisages accession to the European Convention on Human Rights. Finally, and with great symbolic significance, an exit clause has been introduced; hitherto the possibility of a member State leaving the EU was not envisaged in the treaties. Now, a mechanism has been introduced for that to happen.

Lisbon emphasises the division of competence between the EU and the Member States, re-emphasising the competence is granted to the EU on a limited basis and residual power remains with the Member States. The current Article 5 EC, which sets out the principle of subsidiarity (see Chapter 3) will be reformulated in the EU Treaty. A new Title (Title I) in the TFEU on *Categories and areas of Union competence* reflects the ambition to provide a more transparent and better organised catalogue than the current Treaties. In this, there are similarities to the approach adopted in the Constitution. Another point of similarity to the Constitution is the approach taken to enhance cooperation. Should Lisbon come into force, the amendments inserted by Nice would be removed. The criteria for permission to use enhanced cooperation is that nine Member States (currently one-third of Member States) will participate and that this is a 'last resort'.

1.9.2 Institutional matters

The main impetus for reform was a desire to make the EU function more effectively. Although there are differences between Lisbon and the Constitution, there are also marked similarities in approach. Lisbon will introduce a permanent Council president and a High Representative of the EU for foreign affairs (see Chapter 2). The number of Commissioners and MEPs was reduced, though note the concession to

Ireland in this regard. A 'double majority' rule for Council decisions made by QMV will be introduced (see Chapter 3), but due to Polish opposition, will not come in to force immediately (the Ioannina Clause). In terms of seeking to prevent further 'mission creep' on the part of the EU institutions, the role of national parliaments will be strengthened (Article 12 TEU, as amended by Lisbon). The so-called 'orange-card' system will allow national parliaments to review legislative proposals for compliance with the subsidiarity principle, thus introducing a political solution to an essentially political question about the appropriate boundaries of EU competence. This is linked to the approach which is a theme of the Lisbon Treaty; that competence granted to the EU is limited, as we can see in what will become Articles 4 and 5 EU if Lisbon enters force.

1.9.3 Policy matters

We have noted the change consequent to the proposed abolition of the pillar structure. Linked to this development and reflecting a changing approach to these policy areas, is the extension of QMV to approximately 40 policy areas, including asylum, immigration, police cooperation and judicial cooperation in criminal matters. A significant change arises from the inclusion of matters formerly dealt with under the third pillar by the 'Community method'. New areas, such as climate change and energy solidarity, have also been introduced in to Lisbon and, at the request of the French, a reference to 'free and undistorted competition', found in the Constitution, has been removed as an objective of the Union. This change is unlikely to undermine competition policy with has been central to the common market project for the last half-century. Its downgrading perhaps reflects the wider aims of the Union.

1.9.4 Key differences from the Constitution

Whilst the issues that were addressed in the Constitution still needed addressing, it was equally obvious that a treaty that was exactly the same as that that had been rejected by the voters of two Member States could not be put forward with any degree of legitimacy. Lisbon therefore needed to fulfil some symbolic, as well as practical, functions. Crucially, it was needed to put an end to the process of reform started by the Laeken Declaration; essentially saying the EU has now been reformed and thus bring an end to discussions about the nature of the EU and how to improve it. Bringing these debates to an end would allow the institutions of the EU freedom to concentrate on their mission, rather than justifying their very existence. With the impact of economic downturn, refocusing the Union on problem solving becomes increasingly important. The key differences follow.

(a) Arguably the most notable difference is the change in format of implementation. The Constitution was to re-establish the EU in a new treaty which would have replaced all of the old treaties; the Treaty of Lisbon on the other hand will amend the existing EU treaties, even though the EC Treaty will be renamed as part of this process. Whilst the Lisbon proposals are less radical, they leave the existing treaties as a rather untidy bundle of provisions. Certainly in approach then, Lisbon is significantly less far-reaching than the grand recasting of the treaties envisaged by the Constitution. Like the previous treaties, with the exception of the Constitution, Lisbon is an amending treaty and, read on its own, makes little sense as it contains only amendments. Whilst an attempt is made to impose a certain order through renumbering, this is of dubious helpfulness as the net result is that anyone reading materials has to be familiar with the numbering which will be introduced by Lisbon, the post-ToA numbers and the original numbers. This edition of the textbook will remain with the ToA numbering, as the Lisbon Treaty is not yet in force and, indeed, may not come into force. Lisbon numbering will be identified were relevant.

(b) Under the Constitution, primacy of the EU treaties and EU law was to be given explicit recognition; under the Lisbon Treaty, primacy will be recognised in an annexed declaration. This is another example of the softening in approach between the Constitutional Treaty and Lisbon, and may reflect a pragmatic desire not to destabilise the relationship between the Union legal order and those of Member States, by removing the principle of supremacy from its case law basis in to the form of a treaty provision. Note that one consequence of the structural changes (and 'horizontal' amendments) is that it would appear to be EU law rather than EC law, which is supreme.

(c) The various symbols and terminology, which were criticised for carrying overtones of statehood, such as the European flag, anthem, and motto have been abandoned.

(d) Under the Constitution the office of the 'minister for foreign affairs' was to be created, again a term with state like overtones. As already noted at 1.9.1 above, Lisbon creates a 'High Representative of the Union for Foreign Affairs and Security Policy', a much less contentious name for what might be the same job.

(e) The change in approach to fundamental rights; whilst the Constitution highlighted the significance of the Charter of Fundamental Rights, in Lisbon it is dealt with by a cross-reference and is not incorporated in to the treaty structure itself. This distinction may have a symbolic significance, though the Charter will, post Lisbon, have a similar effect.

This leaves us with the question of whether Lisbon is merely the Constitution repackaged. As we shall see in Chapters 2 and 3, there are many areas in which the Lisbon Treaty takes the same approach as the Constitution would have done, using the same provisions almost word-for-word. Like the Constitution, Lisbon makes little change to the substantive policies at the heart of the common market. There are significant differences, however, in the way Lisbon achieves its aims and, crucially, many of the controversial elements relating to the statist overtones in the Constitution have been removed. It is not the same treaty; it is, however, very similar.

1.10 Theories of integration

Although the development of the Union is usually described as a linear progression towards a specified goal, it has also been argued that the integration process has actually fallen into different phases with key characteristics. These phases may even suggest that, despite the rhetoric of an 'ever-closer Union', the end goal of the Union is not well defined or even necessarily agreed upon. Different theories have been put forward to describe and explain these different phases, though the degree to which it is possible to describe each such phase only by reference to an individual theory is debatable. The main schools of thought follow.

1.10.1 Functionalism

Functionalism was a theory which was popular during the Community's early years. As its name implies, it is based on identifying specific, discrete economic areas, usually those perceived as 'non-contentious', in which Member States are encouraged to cooperate. Technocrats (technical experts in the relevant field) would manage these fields in the interests of the Community as a whole. Unlike politicians, they would not be influenced by the need to retain power. Instead, technocrats were perceived as making rational choices. Functionalism can be used to describe the ECSC prior to its demise.

1.10.2 Neofunctionalism

What is currently the European Community is much broader than the ECSC. Neofunctionalism developed as a way of describing this endeavour. It has similarities to functionalism in that it, too, is based on cooperation in specific areas. Neofunctionalism argues, however, that those involved in the process became key players to whom allegiance may be transferred; thus it accepts that the state is not a single unified actor and, indeed, that states are not the only players on the international stage. In this, it was an appropriate theory of European integration and some have described it as the dominant ideology of the early years. Central to neofunctionalism is 'spill-over' which has both a functional and political aspect. The functional aspect was based on the idea that elements of the economy do not exist in isolation and that integration in one area would lead to pressure in other areas. Integration in non-contentious areas spills over into other, more sensitive areas. As regards the political aspect, the theory was that in areas which had been integrated, interest groups would be expected to focus their attention on the Community level, as that was where the regulatory power lay and would also add to pressure for further integration. The process results in a diminution of national governmental power and a matching increase in the power of the technocratic level to deal with sensitive issues. Whilst attractive at a superficial level, the theory was criticised as it did not describe the reality of later Community development.

1.10.3 Intergovernmentalism

Both of the above theories can be described as forms of supranationalism. Supranationalism argues that power is located above the nation state. This view is challenged by intergovernmentalism which means literally between governments. It assumes that the central actors are the states themselves, which essentially act to protect their own interests and power base. On this view, integration occurs because such behaviour is in the rational best interests of the states, as they seek to acquire and maintain the support of domestic interest groups by promising to attain the preferences which those interest groups have articulated. Underlying this is the assumption that groups in society recognise that increasing the flow of goods, services, etc gives rise to benefits, which leads to the policy coordination in the sphere of economic policy.

The Union can be seen as containing elements that illustrate a supranational aspect, but also intergovernmental elements. Intergovernmentalism can be seen in the Luxembourg Accords, in which the then Member States agreed that one Member State could effectively veto a measure in its national interest. The sections of the Union Treaty which deal with JHA and CFSP vest most power in the Council, made up of representatives of the Member States' governments. Agreement in these spheres was by agreement of all Member States. In contrast, the powers of the institutions are unusual in their scope and their independence from the Member States (see further Chapter 2). The use of QMV in Council (see Chapter 3) introduces the possibility of Member States being outvoted with the consequence that a Member State may be obliged to implement policies with which it might not agree. This is not easily compatible with a view of Member States each acting in their own interest unless membership of the Community itself is taken into account.

1.10.4 Multi-level governance

To some extent the discussion in academic writing about the tension between supranationalism and intergovernmentalism has been replaced during the 1990s with writings on the subject of multi-level governance. Certainly intergovernmentalism has been criticised as being very state-centric. Multi-level governance seeks to explain how the Union is governed rather than focusing on the nature of the integration process. Theories in this school of thought allow a broader range of actors to appear in the discussion of EU governance, important with the introduction of new methods of governance such as open method coordination (see Chapter 3). Thus states do not have a monopoly of control, and in particular do not monopolise the links between sub-state actors and the Community level. This results in a picture which is not just based on a conception of the EU as driven by the Member States or by the actions of the EU institutions and may be more relevant given the dual sources of legitimacy of the EU (the states and their peoples); the tendency to technocratic solutions (involving 'experts' of various sources); the move towards different regulatory solutions, which involve other actors in setting and enforcing standards; and de-centralised enforcement through national courts and regulatory authorities.

1.11 Conflicting attitudes towards the Union

It should be noted that the frequency of treaty revision has increased dramatically during the 1990s. While the EEC Treaty survived from 1957 to the SEA of 1986 relatively unchanged: since then there have been three treaty revisions that have been brought into force: TEU, ToA and Nice, as well as the proposed revisions contained in the Constitution and Lisbon. The significance of this development is unclear. One might suggest that it reflects the political changes occurring during the 1990s, particularly in Europe. Alternatively, the change could reflect the dissatisfaction of the Member States (and their population) with the current EU. The difference between the European Communities and the other two pillars created by the TEU and largely retained by the ToA is illustrative of the conflicting attitudes held by Member States and individuals towards the Community (and now the Union) since its inception, as exemplified by the divergent views expressed by politicians. Although academic literature may now focus on the way the EU operates, within political debate, tensions remain as to the nature of the EU and its future. These tensions seemed particularly apparent during the negotiation and ratification of the TEU although, as noted at 1.7.3 above, this issue is not new, nor has it gone away . The problem is that there are two main competing visions of Europe: the intergovernmental and the federal. In *Brunner v European Union Treaty* ([1994] 1 CMLR 57) Germany's power to ratify the TEU was challenged as being contrary to the German constitution. It was argued that in transferring further powers and competence to the EC institutions, the TEU was seeking to create a Euro-state. The German constitutional court found, it is submitted correctly, that the EC was a federation of states not a Euro-state. Nevertheless, the loss of autonomy of action of the Member States consequent on membership of the EC has certainly been considerable. This has increased during the life of the EC as more and more powers have been transferred to the Community in the SEA, the TEU, and the ToA. This process has been emphasised by the increased use of both QMV and co-decision. Some integrationists approve of this as part of the process of achieving an 'ever-closer union'. Others fear the loss of sovereignty and see the EC as having grown beyond the loose association of states within a free trade area that the EC was intended to be. The concern about controlling EU competence permeates the approach to the treaty revision at Lisbon, the response in Germany, where two challenges have been brought before the German constitutional court, suggests that the proposals are not enough. According to a press release from the second challenger, EU integration has been characterised by 'continuous breaches of the stability pact, a presumptuous over-stepping of power by the European Commission, unaccountable leadership and dissolution of the separation of powers' (*Frankfurter Allgemeine Zeitung*, 26 January 2009).

Sometimes these differing views of the EU result in Member States being characterised as either Euro-sceptic or pro-Europe, but a degree of caution must be exercised about such generalisations. There is a difference between political rhetoric and legal reality. Out of the group of 27 member states, it is perhaps surprising that Italy and France, both original member states, had a much less impressive record of compliance than Denmark, which is often perceived as more Euro-sceptic. According to the 2004 Commission *Review on Implementation of Community Law* (COM (2005) 570), all the EU-15 states had a much less impressive implementation record than the new Member States, though this may be due to the pressures of proving compliance with the Copenhagen criteria and acceding to the EU, than evidence of a long-term political intention to ensure prompt implementation of all Community legislation. Furthermore, there is a tendency for Member States' representatives to put national interest—or national political pressures—over the Community interest. This is not just the case with France (see its ban on British beef in defiance of the Community position) or the UK (veto on introduction of Community tax on interest income, thought to threaten the UK bond market), but with all Member States (see the impact of the Greek position on the accession of Turkey, or Portugal on the diversion of Community funding to new Member States).

With the introduction of monetary union, the transfer of further competence to the EU and the proposed expansion in membership the question, 'where next?' assumes a new significance as Member States try to fight for their own view on the future of Europe. The ToA, re-emphasised by Nice, sought to solve the problem by the principle of 'flexibility'; opt-outs have become common in the treaty-revision process. The danger is that a flexible Europe could become a fragmented Europe. Arguably, any risk of fragmentation could increase with further expansion, as the Union will have not just more voices, but a greater variety of interests to satisfy.

1.12 The future

With the future of the Lisbon Treaty uncertain, the future of the EU likewise remains in doubt. As the European Parliament noted in its December 2005 Resolution, the discussions have so far focused on the context of the treaty, rather than the actual legal text, thus reaffirming the idea that the development of the Union has resulted from responses to external pressures rather than developing in a legal vacuum according to a grand plan laid down in advance. At the moment, it seems that the EU is under pressure as a result of the economic downturn, which is causing instability in the economies of Member States. It has also been suggested that successful federal structures are those which respond to an external threat, often war. It could be argued that the Union is no longer threatened, and that it has, to a large extent, achieved its purpose and that its time is therefore over. On this view the problems of the Constitutional Treaty and Lisbon are signs of the fact that the Union has outlived its usefulness. Equally, it could be, if the Union manages to get beyond the current phase of institutional doubt and questioning, that it may become stronger in terms of responding to global challenges, such as economic problems, climate change, and even the threats perceived to be posed by terrorism. The Union has therefore the opportunity to redefine its role through responding to such challenges. Whether it can do so, is a question history will answer.

In view of the disputes and reservations within the Union about its future, and the current economic problems, the continuing enthusiasm for membership may seem surprising, but it cannot be denied that the EU has achieved a great deal, both economically and beyond. It is an important market. The figures for the EU-15 in 2001 show that the Union was responsible for just under of 20 per cent of world trade in goods and approximately 25 per cent of trade in services. Especially given its expansion in membership, it thus constitutes a trading block which has the potential to influence world affairs significantly. Membership of the EU gives states the opportunity to be part of this. Also, for some countries, because of the criteria for membership, it will indicate that they have achieved democratic respectability in the eyes of other nations. Last, but by no means least, during the past 50 years the EC has enjoyed an era of unprecedented peace; and the expansion of peace, stability, freedom, and prosperity has been—and continues to be—an underlying aim of the eastward enlargement of the Union. It is easy to overlook the fact that one of the underlying objectives of the European communities was, in the words of the preamble to the ECSC Treaty 'to substitute for age-old rivalries the merging of their essential interests; to create . . . the basis for a broader and deeper community among peoples long divided by bloody conflicts'.

FURTHER READING

Birkinshaw, P, 'A constitution for the EU?' (2004) 10(1) EPL 57.

Bradley, K, 'Institutional design in the Treaty of Nice' (2001) 38 CML Rev 1095.

Church, CH, and Phinnemore, D, *Understanding the European Constitution: An introduction to the EU Constitutional Treaty* (Routledge, 2006).

Craig, P, 'Constitutions, constitutionalism and the European Union' (2001) 7(2) EL Rev, 125.

——, 'The Lisbon Treaty: Process, architecture and substance' (2008) 33 EL Rev 137.

Curtin, D, 'The constitutional structure of the Union: A Europe of bits and pieces' (1993) 30 CML Rev 17.

De Burca, G, 'The institutional development of the EC: A constitutional analysis' in P Craig and G de Burca (eds), *The Evolution of EU Law* (Oxford University Press, 1999).

Delacourt, C, 'The *Acquis Communautaire*: Has the concept had its day?' (2001) 38 CML Rev 829.

de Witte, B, 'The closest thing to a constitutional conversation in Euorpe: The semi-permanent treaty revision process' in P Beaumont, C Lyons, and N Walker (eds), *Convergence and Divergence in European Public Law* (Hart Publishing, 2002).

Dougan, M, 'The Treaty of Lisbon 2007: Winning minds, not hearts' (2008) 45(3) CML Rev 609–15.

Douglas-Scott, S, 'In Search of Union Citizenship' (1998) 18 YEL 29.

Edwards, D, 'The impact of the single market' (1987) 24 CML Rev 19.

Ehlermann, CD, 'Differentiation, flexibility, closer cooperation: The new provisions of the Amsterdam Treaty' (1998) 4 ELJ 246.

Gormley, L, 'Reflection on the architecture of the EU after the Treaty of Amsterdam' in D O'Keeffe and P Twomey (eds), *Legal Issues of the Amsterdam Treaty* (Hart Publishing, 1999).

Harmser, R, 'A European Union of Variable Geometry' (1994) 45 NILQ 109.

Meyring, B, 'Intergovernmentalism and supranationality: Two stereotypes of a complex reality' (1997) 22 EL Rev 221.

Schilling, T, 'The autonomy of the Community legal order: An analysis of possible foundations' (1996) 37 Hav Int'l LJ 307.

Shaw, J et al (eds), *The Convention on the Future of Europe: Working towards an EU Constitution* (Federal Trust, 2003).

Somek, A, 'Postconstitutional Treaty' [2007] German Law Journal 1121.

Usher, J, 'Variable geometry or concentric circles: Patterns for the European Union' (1997) 46 ICLQ 243.

Weiler, JHH, 'The transformation of Europe' (1991) 100 Yale LJ 2403.

—— and Haltern, UR, 'Response: The autonomy of the Community legal order—Through the looking glass' (1996) 37 Harv Int'l LJ 411.

2

Institutions of the Union: Composition and powers

2.1 Introduction

One of the defining features of the Community and, to a certain extent the Union, is the scope and level of power given to its institutions. This chapter outlines the composition and powers of the institutions and the relationship between them. Where appropriate, the main changes that would be introduced by the Lisbon Treaty, should it come into force, will be outlined.

The relationship between the institutions is important, because it is the different powers ascribed to the institutions and the way they have to work together that provide the 'checks and balances' within the Union legal order. It is important to note that we should not approach a review of the institutions from the perspective of traditional notions of governmental functions: legislative, executive, administrative and judicial. It is the institutional balance that prevents one institutional actor from becoming too powerful, rather than the more traditional notion of 'separation of the powers'. Another key point in this area is that the powers of the respective institutions have evolved over time. The institutional balance is not a static notion, reflecting the development of the Union—and our expectations of it in terms of effectiveness, responsibility, and accountability. The institutional balance is not just about limiting the power of the institutions, but has a positive side in that the political institutions at least must cooperate to achieve anything at all, though the nature of the relationship between the individual institutions has varied. It is possible to see some of the institutions representing various interests: the Commission as supranational and integrationist, the Council as intergovernmental and incorporating the individual state interests. The institutional balance has also been affected by the emergence of other actors of various sorts which do not fall within the definition of 'institution' for the purposes of the treaty, yet these bodies also have a role in policymaking and its implementation and enforcement. Finally, we should note that the powers of the institutions vary depending on the different areas of competence; the ways in which these different fields of competence interrelate also affect the institutional balance. This latter issue is discussed further in Chapter 3.

2.2 The institutions

A preliminary question, however, is 'What are the institutions?' While the term can be used generically to refer to bodies involved generally in the governance of the EU, it has a specific meaning within the treaty.

The principal institutions set up by the original EEC Treaty (now Article 7 (ex 4) EC) to carry out the Community's tasks comprised:

(a) the Assembly or Parliament

(b) the Council

(c) the Commission

(d) the Court of Justice.

In addition, Article 7 (ex 4) provided for the setting up of a Court of Auditors and an Economic and Social Committee, and the Merger Treaty 1965 (Article 4) for the creation of a Committee of Permanent Representatives of the Member States (COREPER). Following the SEA, the Court of First Instance (CFI) was set up in October 1988 (Decision 88/591 [1989] OJ C215/1). Under the Treaty on European Union (TEU), the Court of Auditors was added to the institutions listed in Article 7, and the various treaties, as well as ECJ case law, have affected its evolution. Both COREPER and the Committee of the Regions are now based on Article 7(2) EC. In addition, a European Investment Bank has been created (Article 9 (ex 4b) EC), and provision made for setting up of the European System of Central Banks (ESCB) and a European Central Bank (ECB) (Article 8 (ex 4a) EC). This chapter focuses on the institutions that have general roles in the Community and so will not deal with bodies like the ECB, whose function is more specific.

It should also be noted that the TEU provides for institutional unity within the Union. This means that the same institutions have roles not only within the EC but within the other two pillars. Should the Lisbon Treaty enter into force (see Chapter 1), the three-pillar structure would be abandoned and there would be a single Union. The EU Treaty would be amended to include a new Title III, entitled 'Provisions on the Institutions' which contains the list of institutions currently found in Article 7 EC (see Article 13(1) EU as amended and renumbered by Lisbon); ECOSOC and COREPER find mention in Article 9(4) EU. In new provisions, the main responsibilities of the various institutions will be set out in Articles 14–19 EU. Crucially, it is in the post-Lisbon TEU that we find the first express reference to the European Council, and its main function is identified in Article 15 EU. The significance of the abandonment of the pillar structure is that the institutional differences that that structure created will, to a large extent, cease to exist.

2.3 Parliament (Articles 189–201 (ex 137–44) EC)

2.3.1 Appointment

As created by the Treaty of Rome in 1957, the European Parliament, called in that treaty the Assembly (but since called by the SEA the Parliament), was not a democratic body, although the treaty provided for the eventual introduction of direct elections. It consisted of representatives of Member States who were required to be members of a national parliament. The introduction of direct elections, which occurred in 1979, resulted in increased democracy and increased concentration and expertise, since members are responsible to their electorate, and, as anyone is now eligible to stand, many are no longer subject to the rigorous demands of the 'dual mandate' at home and in Europe. MEPs are elected for five years (Article 190(3); post Lisbon, Article 11 TEU). The significance of the European Parliament, and particularly its manner of appointment, is that it creates a direct link between the national electorates and the Union political institutions. There are limits to seeing the Parliament as the creature of a pan-European democracy. Constituencies are still organised on a national basis. A perennial complaint is that, despite the introduction of direct elections, the uniform system of election envisaged by Article 190(3) (ex 138(3) EC has not yet been introduced. This particular provision would be repealed by the Lisbon Treaty and replaced, in broadly the same terms, by Article 14 TEU. It should also be noted that recent elections have revealed a low voter turnout, which may cast doubt on the claims of the European Parliament to legitimacy on the basis of the direct election of its members.

2.3.2 Composition

Following enlargement in 2004, Parliament consisted of 732 members, with Germany having 99; France, Great Britain, and Italy each having 78 representatives; Poland and Spain 54; The Netherlands 27; Belgium, the Czech Republic, Greece, Hungary, and Portugal 24; Sweden 19; Austria 18; Denmark, Finland, and Slovakia 14; Ireland and Lithuania 13; Latvia 9; Slovenia 7; Cyprus, Estonia, and Luxembourg 6; and Malta 5. The Treaty of Nice fixed the maximum number of MEPs at 732 (Article 189 EC), but with a temporary exception in the event of new accessions between 2004 and 2009 (Treaty of Nice, Protocol on Enlargement, Article 2(4)). The total number of representatives of the Parliament has increased to 785, with Bulgaria being granted 18 representatives and Romania being granted 35.

Article 190(2) EC specifies the number of representatives. The division of MEPs among the Member States has always been subject to criticism: Germany has fewest representatives per head of population, whilst Luxembourg has a disproportionately high number of representatives given its size. The Treaty of Amsterdam sought to improve the position, as Article 190 EC was amended to state that 'the number of representatives elected in each Member State must ensure appropriate representation'. The post-Nice position, however, may still be seen as unfair in some regards: for example, the Czech Republic and Hungary are, arguably, underrepresented. Again, this may cast doubt on the representative nature of democracy in the European Parliament. Lisbon specifies that the maximum number of MEPs shall be 750 (Article 14(2) EU, as amended by Lisbon) and that representation shall be degressively proportional, with a minimum number of 6 MEPs and a maximum of 96.

Members meet in plenary sessions of approximately one week per month in Strasbourg, although the majority of Parliament's Committee meetings, where much important work is done, are held in Brussels. The rest take place in Strasbourg or, occasionally, Luxembourg. Members, who are drawn from 75 political parties, sit in 11 broad, multinational political groupings, the largest being the Socialist group; they are required to vote 'on an individual and personal basis' and 'they shall not be bound by any instructions and shall not receive a binding mandate' (Act Concerning Direct Elections, Article 4(1)). Although the fact that MEPs do not sit in national groupings might indicate that the European Parliament has supranational characteristics, it should not be forgotten that MEPs are still elected within national systems along national-party lines. The European Parliament does not have what might be termed a 'European political consciousness'. Article 191 EC, however, contains an expression of the importance of political parties at the European level for the formation of 'a European awareness' and the expression of 'the political will of the citizens of the Union'. The Treaty of Nice supplemented this provision by the insertion of a second paragraph which gives the Council the power to lay down regulations governing such parties and their funding. This was done with Regulation 2004/2003 on the regulations governing political parties at European level and the rules regarding their funding ([2003] OJ L297/1), which provides the criteria for allocating funding, with the main role given to the European Parliament. This provision would be moved by Lisbon to the TEU (Article 10(4) TEU, as amended by Lisbon).

The Parliament has a president, elected by the Parliament for a two-and-a-half-year term (see Article 14(4) EU, as amended by Lisbon). There are also 14 vice-presidents. Together the presidents and vice-presidents constitute the Bureau of the Parliament, which is the body responsible for the Parliament's administrative, organisational and staff matters, as well as for budgetary matters. The agenda of the Parliament is set by the 'Conference of Presidents', a group made up of the president and the leaders of the various political groups in the Parliament; it also establishes the terms of reference for the various Parliamentary committees, of which the Parliament has 20 standing committees. Subcommittees and temporary committees can also be established. These committees fulfil a vital role in the functioning of the Parliament, as they comment on the legislative proposals put forward by the Commission in their respective areas of expertise and can also produce own initiative reports (Rule 45, Rules of Procedure of the European Parliament, 16th edition, Oct 2008). For example, the Committee on Foreign Affairs put forward a report with a proposal for a European Parliament recommendation to the Council on the mandate of the International Criminal Tribunal for the former Yugoslavia (A6-0112/2009).

2.3.3 Functions

As befitted a non-elected body, the original Parliament had few powers. Its functions were advisory and supervisory. It was not intended as a legislative body. Following the introduction of direct elections, Parliament has played an increasingly important consultative role in the legislative process and has been given the final say over certain aspects of the budget. Budgetary procedure will be discussed further below. The TEU, ToA, and Nice have further and substantially increased its powers, so that it is no longer limited to the merely consultative but may be said to have a legislative role. This development is linked to the wider role of the Union and the need to ensure its democratic legitimacy. Should Lisbon come into force, the EU Treaty will describe the Parliament's functions in Article 14 TEU (as amended by Lisbon) as follows:

> The European Parliament shall, jointly with the Council, exercise legislative and budgetary functions. It shall exercise functions of political control and consultation as laid down in the Treaties. It shall elect the President of the Commission.

2.3.3.1 *Consultative and advisory role*

In its advisory role, Parliament was originally required by the EC Treaty to be consulted by the Council of Ministers where legislation is proposed in a number of specific (and important) areas, eg Articles 52, 83, and 308 (ex 63, 87, and 235 EC respectively), but contrast Article 40 (ex 49) (workers). In these areas the Council must seek, and is obliged to consider, Parliament's opinion, although there is no obligation on the Council to follow it. This is an essential procedural requirement. Legislation has been successfully challenged when, although the Parliament had been consulted on an initial draft of the legislation, it was not consulted following substantial amendment to the draft (*Parliament v Council* (case C–21/94) (road taxes); by contrast *Germany v Council* (case C–280/93) (banana quotas) was unsuccessful. In *Roquette Frères SA v Council* (case 138/79) and *Maizena GmbH v Council* (case 139/79) a regulation of the Council was annulled because, although Parliament's opinion had been sought, the regulation had been passed by the Council before that opinion had been obtained. Nonetheless, in *Parliament v Council* (case C–65/93), where the Parliament's opinion was clearly required as a matter of some urgency, the Council made all efforts to obtain that opinion in time. In failing to meet the deadline, the Parliament, according to the Court, had failed in its duty of cooperation. The Court, as a consequence, refused to annul the regulation. How far the Parliament's duty of cooperation extends is not clear. The Advocate-General in this case was clearly unhappy about the effect such a decision would have on the institutional balance and thought that any changes to it would be more appropriately dealt with by treaty amendment.

The requirement for consultation and cooperation by Parliament, and consequently Parliament's influence, was strengthened by the introduction of conciliation procedures in 1977 (Joint Declaration of the European Parliament, the Council and the Commission, [1975] OJ C89/1) and the cooperation procedures introduced by the SEA. The SEA also greatly extended the range of matters on which Parliament had to be consulted. The SEA also gave Parliament the power of (final) assent in respect of the admission of new members and the conclusion of association agreements with non-member countries. The TEU gave Parliament certain rights to be consulted in respect of the justice and home affairs (JHA) and common foreign and security policy (CFSP) provisions. What was then Article K.6 (now Article 34) TEU provided that Parliament was to be consulted on the principal aspects of activities within JHA provisions. This provision also ensured that the Parliament's views were duly to be taken into consideration. Similar provisions existed in respect of the CFSP provisions (Article 21 (ex J.7) TEU). Parliament's right to be consulted and informed has increased under the ToA and Nice, but it still has no real powers over the second and third pillars of the TEU. Although there would no longer be separate pillars if the Lisbon Treaty were to enter into force, Parliament's role would remain confined to a consultative role regarding the CFSP. It would have greater powers with regard to JHA, which under the Lisbon Treaty would be integrated within what would be the Treaty on the Functioning of the European Union (TFEU) (the EC Treaty as amended by Lisbon).

2.3.3.2 *Legislative role*

The power of the European Parliament has increased over time, reflecting the dual source of the Union's legitimacy—not only the Member States, but also the citizens of those states. As well as a right to be *consulted*, and to participate in *conciliation* and *cooperation* procedures, the TEU introduced for Parliament, in Article 251 (ex 189b) EC, a right of *co-decision* with the Council in certain defined areas. Thus, under this procedure, the European Parliament now has a significant power of veto in matters subject to the new procedures; effectively the Parliament is an equal partner in the legislative process using this procedure. The co-decision procedure was to apply in a number of areas previously governed by the less onerous coopera- tion procedures (eg, Articles 40, 44, 46, and 94 (ex 49, 54(2), 56(2), 100a) EC) and in some new spheres of activity (eg, health, consumer protection). In other areas, the consultation or cooperation procedures (the latter now laid down in Article 252 (ex 189c) EC) were to continue to apply. In cases of doubt it will be necessary to consult the treaty to ascertain which procedure is applicable, although the ToA and subsequent treaties have greatly extended the areas to which co-decision ap- plies with the result that the cooperation procedures in future will largely disappear. Further, should Lisbon come into effect, there would be an 'ordinary legislative procedure', which is, in essence, the present co-decision procedure (see Article 289 TFEU). Significantly, this would form the default legislative procedure in the Union, reaffirming the strength of the Parliament's involvement. These procedures will be examined further in Chapter 3.

Despite the increase in areas in which the co-decision procedure is used already, the European Parliament is still limited to a subordinate role in certain key areas, such as agriculture, and what are currently the JHA and CFSP pillars. We have noted the changes that Lisbon might introduce (see 2.3.3.1 above).

Parliament was also given a new power of initiative by the TEU. Under Article 192 (ex 138b) EC it may, acting by a majority of its members, request the Commission to submit any appropriate proposals on matters on which it considers that a Community act is required for the purpose of implementing the treaty. This provi- sion will be renumbered as Article 225 TFEU should the Lisbon Treaty come into force (and terminology will change to reflect amendments to the treaty structure). It has been suggested that, provided Parliament stays within the guidelines set out in its rules of procedure, these requests are likely to be considered sympathetically by the Commission. To date, Parliament has exercised these rights sparingly.

Although the European Parliament's powers have been increased, there are weak- nesses in the ways it fulfils its responsibilities. The European Parliament does not have great expertise in highly technical areas. Further, under Article 192 it may *request* policy initiatives; it does not have the *right* of policy initiative. This would remain the case if Lisbon were to come into effect in its present form, although the Commission would, if it chose not to respond, give reasons why.

2.3.3.3 *Supervisory role*

In its supervisory role, Parliament exercises direct political control over the Commission. Commissioners must reply orally or in writing to its questions. The Commission must publish a general report which is discussed in Parliament in open session. Parliament meets members of the Commission in committees, and in practice, though this is not required by law, members of Parliament are consulted by the Commission at the pre-legislative stage. Parliament also has the power to dismiss the Commission, by passing a vote of censure (Article 201 (ex 144) EC). The provision would be renumbered as Art 234 TFEU should Lisbon come into force. Such a motion must be carried by a two-thirds majority of the votes cast, which must represent a majority of the members of Parliament. A particular weakness of this sanction is the fact that the existing Commissioners will remain in office until their replacements are appointed. There is nothing to prevent the Member States from suggesting the same Commissioners be reappointed. Nonetheless, it was the Parliament's dissatisfaction with the conduct of the Commission that resulted in the Commissioners resigning in 1999. Some, but not all, of the Commissioners were reappointed. Prior to Maastricht, Parliament had no say in the appointment of new Commissioners. This has now been remedied; under Article 214(2) (ex 158(2)) EC, Parliament must be consulted on the nomination of the president and the appointment of Commissioners and the Commission as a whole has to be approved by Parliament. Parliament approves the appointment of the president individually and then the president and the other Commissioners together as a group. This procedure would, in essence, remain under the Lisbon (Article 17(7) TEU, as amended by Lisbon).

The Council is not subject to the control of Parliament, but is subject to extensive supervision. Parliament reports on the activities of the Council three times a year, and the president of the Council must present an address to Parliament at the beginning of every year. This is followed by a general debate. The incoming president also presents a survey of the previous six months' presidency, and the chairman of the conference of foreign ministers reports to Parliament once a year on the progress of European political cooperation. Under the Constitution, there would have been a new role of 'European Council President' (see Article I–22), who would have been required to report to Parliament after each meeting of the European Council. Unlike proceedings in the Council and the Commission, proceedings in Parliament are published in the *Official Journal* (see the discussion on transparency in Chapter 3). The post of president of the Council has been retained by Lisbon (see 2.11.1 below).

Parliament also has standing to challenge the legality of acts adopted by the other institutions in accordance with Article 230 (ex 173) EC (see Chapter 12). It is through such challenges that Parliament enforces its rights and seeks to ensure that the correct treaty base is used for legislative measures. This is important because the treaty base affects the degree of parliamentary involvement in the legislative process. Judicial review under Article 230 EC has been used vigorously for these purposes. In passing, it should be noted that the Parliament's power in this regard was extended under the Treaty of Nice and it now also has the power to request advisory opinions under Article 300(6) from the European Court of Justice (ECJ). (See Article 218 TFEU.)

To broaden Parliament's role it was given power under the TEU to set up a temporary committee of inquiry to investigate alleged contraventions or maladministration in the implementation of Community law (except where the alleged facts are being examined before a court or subject to legal proceedings) (Article 193 (ex 138c) EC) and has been required to appoint an Ombudsman to receive and enquire into complaints of maladministration in the activities of the EC institutions or bodies (with the exception of the ECJ and the CFI acting in their judicial capacity) (Article 195 (ex 138e) EC). At the end of an investigation, the Ombudsman is under an obligation to produce a report to the Parliament and to the institution under investigation. The original complainant is also notified of the result. The Ombudsman has also to produce an annual report to Parliament. In addition, any natural or legal person residing or having its registered office in a Member State is to be given the right to address a petition to the European Parliament on a matter which comes within the Community's fields of activity, and which affects him, her or it directly (Article 194 (ex 138d) EC). These provisions would remain essentially unaltered, should Lisbon become effective in its present form (see Articles 226–8 TFEU).

One area of the Parliament's activities which is sometimes overlooked is the work that it does in promoting human rights. We will see when looking at the role of general principles of Community law (Chapter 6) that the Parliament was instrumental in persuading the other institutions to recognise the importance of human rights and, in particular, the European Convention on the Protection of Human Rights. The Parliament is not concerned only with human-rights protection within the Union. The European Parliament also established a subcommittee to identify urgent cases of human-rights abuse throughout the world, and the facts surrounding each case. In appropriate circumstances it will put forward resolutions on specific cases to the whole Parliament. The passing of such resolutions can raise the profile of certain issues and can therefore play a useful role in generating pressure to remedy the problem. The subcommittee also produces an annual report and the degree of reaction that it provokes in countries criticised by it is indicative of its influence.

2.4 Council (Articles 202–10 (ex 145–54) EC)

2.4.1 Appointment

The Council, following the TEU now called 'The Council of the European Union', consists of representatives of the Member States, one from each Member State, who must be 'at ministerial level, authorised to commit the government of that Member State' (Article 203 (ex 146) EC). If Lisbon comes into force, this provision will be moved from the EC Treaty, to form Article 16(2) TEU. Ministerial representatives tend not to be appointed specifically for their role within the Council; appointment is a consequence of their appointment within the domestic system. A common concern about the Council is that it represents the views of the Member States and the individual members of the Council look to the national interest, rather than the Union common interest when making their decisions. This presumably is the case because members of the Council hold their respective posts as part of their responsibilities within the national political system. Although ministerial representatives may be accountable as part of an individual Member State's government through that Member State's parliamentary system, there is no body, at European or national level, to hold the Council itself accountable.

2.4.2 Composition

The Council is not a fixed body. Although it is limited to one voting delegate from each state, membership may fluctuate depending on the topic under discussion. For example, where matters of agriculture are at stake, the ministers of agriculture will normally participate; if the matters relate to general economic policy the finance ministers may be present; where high-level policy matters are to be discussed, the Council may consist of heads of state.

Where heads of state come together in a specially constituted body, acting on matters of both EC law and political cooperation, the body is termed the European Council. Although it had been in existence since 1974 it was not recognised in the EC Treaty until the Single European Act (SEA). Article 2 SEA provided:

> The European Council shall bring together Heads of State or of government of the Member States and the President of the Commission of the European Communities. They shall be assisted by a Minister for Foreign Affairs and by a member of the Commission. They shall meet at least twice a year.

This provision has been further amplified by Article 4 (ex D) TEU. If Lisbon comes into force, the European Council will be recognised as an institution of the EU (Article 13(1) TEU). The changing level of recognition awarded to the European Council is an example of the changing relationships between the institutions and also an example of the way that the institutional set-up can respond and accept political reality. Despite the relatively few references in the Treaties to the European Council, it does not do to underestimate its importance; its membership is the leaders of the Member States and it serves to set the general direction of the EU itself.

Specific configurations based on subject matter have been identified. This varying membership has led to criticism that the Council of Ministers lacks coherency: there is no one who is responsible for coordinating policies. This approach means that the role of bodies assisting the Council, notably COREPER (discussed further at 2.4.5 below) is crucial in the legislative process. It has been suggested that to improve coherency the different configurations of the Council should be reduced.

The fact that different 'configurations' exist is recognised in the Treaties (see post-Lisbon amendments, Article 16(6) and (9) TEU, Article 236 TFEU). The Lisbon Treaty, should it enter into force, would not impose a restriction on the number of different configurations. Two improvements would be made, however: there would be a 'General Affairs Council' responsible for ensuring consistency in the work of the different Council configurations (Article 16(6) TEU). Moreover, the European Council would be given the power to specify, by qualified majority, the various configurations of the Council of Ministers (Article 236 TFEU). Two exceptions are the 'General Affairs Council' and a 'Foreign Affairs Council', both of which would be identified in Article 16 EU. In adopting this approach, Lisbon is similar to what was proposed by the Constitution and constitutes the major significance of the treaty amendments to the workings of the Council.

Under Lisbon, as was proposed in the Constitution, there would be a more formal separation between the European Council (Article 15 TEU) and the Council of Ministers (as it would be called again; see Article 16 TEU). The European Council would comprise the heads of state or government for the Member States, together with the president of the European Council and the president of the Commission. The High Representative of the Union for Foreign Affairs (a post which will be introduced by Lisbon)would also participate (see further 2.11.2 below).

2.4.3 **Functions**

Currently, the Council's task is 'to ensure that the objectives set out in this Treaty are attained' (Article 202 (ex 145) EC). To this end it:

> shall . . . ensure coordination of the general economic policies of the Member States; have power to take decisions . . . and confer on the Commission, in the acts which the Council adopts, powers for the implementation of those rules which the Council lays down.

The degree to which ministers can comply with this requirement and satisfy their domestic obligations is, however, debatable.

Since the Council has the final power of decision on most secondary legislation some control by the Member States is thus assured. However, in most cases it can only act on the basis of a proposal from the Commission. Furthermore, other institutions are involved in the decision-making process to an increasing degree. Nonetheless, since legislation (even under the co-decision procedure) cannot be enacted without the consent of the Council, its methods of voting are crucial. The treaty (Article 205 (ex 148) EC as amended) provides that voting may be by a simple majority (which is rare), by qualified majority or by unanimity. Under Lisbon (as would have been the case under the Constitution), voting by qualified majority would be the default position for the Council of Ministers, except where the treaties provide that a different majority would be required (Article 16(3) TEU). The European Council (see 2.4.2 above), however, would generally be required to act by consensus (Article 15(4) TEU).

Perhaps in recognition of changing circumstances, Lisbon—should it come into force—redefines the functions of all the institutions. The function of the European Council is defined at Article 15(1) TEU as:

> provid[ing] the Union with the necessary impetus for its development and . . . defin[ing] the general political directions and priorities thereof. It shall not exercise legislative functions.

The role of the Council is found in Article 16(1) TEU (post Lisbon).

> The Council shall, jointly with the European Parliament, exercise legislative and budgetary functions. It shall carry out policy-making and coordinating functions as laid down in the Treaties.

2.4.4 **The emergence of qualified majority voting**

It is generally the case today that most decisions by the Council are taken by qualified majority voting (QMV). However, this has not always been the case. The existence of QMV is one of the more unusual, and perhaps controversial, aspects of EC law—whenever a new area is opened up to QMV, objections are raised against 'giving up the veto' in respect of that area. Yet, there are good reasons for having this form of majority.

Historically, some more sensitive areas of the treaty were required to be implemented only by unanimous vote (eg, Article 94 (ex 100) EC on the approximation of laws). It was, however, intended that once the period of adjustment to membership, known as the transitional period, provided by the EC Treaty had expired, Member States would be required to move towards QMV. This did not happen. A crisis in the Council in 1962 resulted, at the insistence of the French, in the Luxembourg Accords (1966). Under the Accords, where vital national interests are at stake, Member States may insist on a unanimous vote. The Accords noted 'a divergence of views on what should be done in the event of a failure to reach agreement'. It has been suggested that this approach is partly a reaction against the judicial activism of the time.

The Luxembourg Accords did not have the force of law, but they were followed in practice, with the result that in many cases the Council sought unanimity where the treaty would not have required it. In only one case, in 1982, was a measure passed by the Council by QMV against the wishes of the UK government, in a situation in which it was suggested that the UK was abusing its veto by attempting to force the Council's hand in a matter unrelated to the measure under discussion.

QMV is a system of weighted voting. Clearly, from the Community standpoint it makes for more rapid and effective decision-making than unanimity as the consent of all parties is not required. It is, however, controversial because it runs contrary to the idea that a nation state is a sovereign entity and the government (or ruler) of that entity has freedom to choose which policies to implement within that state. With QMV (and also with simple majority voting) a Member State could be put in the position of being under a treaty obligation to put in place a policy for which it had not voted. Though this is true, there is a positive side to the loss of veto, in that Member States 'in the minority' on a given issue now have an incentive to negotiate positively to try to arrive at an outcome which is more acceptable to them than perhaps the original proposal had been. This perhaps introduces a more supranational—or Union focused—element to the Council than might at first appear.

Perhaps the most significant innovation of the SEA was to increase the number of areas in which voting was to be by qualified majority. The majority of legislation required to complete the internal market was enacted by qualified majority. Only fiscal measures, measures relating to the free movement of persons and to the rights and interests of employed persons (Article 95(2) (ex 100a(2)) and measures relating to professional training and standards (Article 47(2) (ex 57(2)) require a unanimous vote. The TEU, ToA, and Nice all further increased the scope for QMV, introducing QMV into Article 175 (ex 130s) (environment), Article 141(3) (ex 119(3)) (equal pay) and Article 100 (ex 103) (difficulties in economic situation), respectively. More sensitive areas however remain subject to unanimous approval. Lisbon would broaden the use of QMV further still (although some, such as the provisions on social security coordination are subject to an 'emergency brake' procedure), but there would remain some areas where unanimity would continue to be required. Member States have so far been prepared to accede to QMV in the areas in which it has been required, although in some cases they have challenged the appropriateness of the legal basis of a measure demanding such a vote.

Furthermore, the procedure has been reinforced in the ToA in respect of the 'flexibility' provisions of both the EC and EU Treaties (Articles 11 EC and 43 TEU, as amended by Nice).

A difficulty with QMV is to determine the respective strength of each Member State's vote, an issue which gains in complexity whenever new countries join the existing Member States. Prior to the succession of Finland, Sweden, and Austria, which joined in 1995, concern was expressed that the number of votes required to block a proposal would increase. Eventually, the Ioannina Compromise (1994) was agreed with the result that the blocking minority increased to 71 per cent of the new total, but if states carrying together 23 to 25 votes intended to vote against the proposal then negotiations would continue in an attempt to satisfy their concerns.

The Ioannina Compromise raised concerns that the attitudes of Member States had not changed since the Luxembourg Accords. A contrary view has also been suggested. Although clearly there are difficulties, the Ioannina Compromise does represent some progress because under its terms the Member States are committed to trying to come to some form of compromise acceptable to all. Contrast this with the Luxembourg Accords, where Member States merely agreed to disagree.

Further attempts were made to improve the system of qualified majority voting in the ToA, and then by the Treaty of Nice. The position (in Article 205(2) EC) was that a minimum of 232 votes (out of a total of 321) must be in favour of a proposal for it to be adopted (72.3 per cent of the share, a slight increase from 71 per cent prior to the 2004 enlargement), provided that a majority of Member States have voted in favour too (a two-thirds majority may be required where the vote is not based on a proposal by the Commission). But even then, a Member State may request confirmation that the votes in favour represent at least 62 per cent of the total population of the Union; where that is not the case, the vote will still fail (Article 205(4)). The total number of votes in the Council has increased to 345, with the accession of Bulgaria and Romania.

The distribution of votes in Council is as follows:

Germany, France, Italy, UK	29
Spain, Poland	27
Romania	14
Netherlands	13
Belgium, Czech Republic, Greece, Hungary, Portugal	12
Austria, Sweden, Bulgaria	10
Denmark, Ireland, Lithuania, Slovakia, Finland	7
Cyprus, Estonia, Latvia, Luxembourg, Slovenia	4
Malta	3
TOTAL	**345**

The Lisbon Treaty, like the Constitution, tried to make the system a little more transparent. Following strong Polish lobbying, a long transitional period has been included in the treaties, with a two transitional periods (one until 31 October 2014, and the second from 1 November 2014 until 31 March 2017) being laid out in the Protocol on Transitional Provisions. Essentially, it seeks to maintain the status quo.

The end point aimed for in the Lisbon Treaty reflected that adopted in The Constitution which, in recognition of the dual source of legitimacy in the EU, sought to impose a system of majority which would reflect those two sources. Thus

Article 16(4) TEU (as amended by Lisbon) provides that a qualified majority comprises two elements:

(e) at least 55 per cent of the Members of Council comprising at least 15 of them (thus representing the interests of the states)

(f) states representing at least 65 per cent of the population of the Union.

Moreover, a blocking minority would have to comprise at least four Council members, or the qualified majority would be deemed to have been attained. Further, should Lisbon come into force, from 1 November 2014, where the Council is not acting on a proposal from the Commission, the qualified majority would be at least 72 per cent of the members of the Council, representing at least 65 per cent of the Union's population. There are also special provisions relating to areas of policy where Member States have negotiated an opt-out (Article 238 TFEU). The intention is clearly to simplify the concept of a 'qualified majority', but only practical experience would demonstrate if that would be the effect of this provision. The complexity attendant on the transitional period is not an auspicious start.

2.4.5 COREPER

Since the Council is not a permanent body, meeting only a few days a month, and its members have full-time responsibilities at home, either as ministers or civil servants (civil servants have no power to vote), much of its work has been taken over by the Committee of Permanent Representatives (COREPER) (see Article 207 (ex 151) EC). COREPER is a permanent and full-time body, also consisting of representatives of Member States, whose main task is to scrutinise and sift proposals coming from the Commission prior to a final decision being made by the Council. COREPER is assisted in turn by a number of working groups, similarly represented, operating at different levels and in specialised areas. This sifting process, from working group to COREPER to Council, enables the more straightforward issues to be decided at the appropriate level, leaving the Council to focus on the more difficult or controversial decisions. Indeed, the amendments inserted by the ToA expressly recognise the power of COREPER to make procedural decisions where provided for by the Council's Rules of Procedure (see new Article 207(1) EC). Although COREPER and the working groups might be crucial in ensuring the Council can operate as a decision making body, their use is problematic in terms of transparency and accountability. The Lisbon Treaty would retain the function of COREPER (Article 240 TFEU) (see also Chapter 3).

2.5 Commission (Articles 211–19 (ex 155–63) EC)

2.5.1 Appointment

Note that the term 'Commission' is used in two ways: first to describe the high-level political appointments constituting the 'College of Commissioners' and, secondly, the permanent bureaucracy in Brussels. Whilst the staff members of the bureaucracy apply for jobs (after having passed an entrance examination), the Commissioners themselves are nominated by individual Member States, and agreed amongst the Member States. Since the TEU, they are appointed for a period of five years (Article 214 (ex 158) EC), and may be reappointed. Following the entry into force of Nice, voting on this point is by QMV. Since the TEU, the Parliament has been given an increasing role in the appointment process (see 2.2.3 above), lending the Commissioners and especially the president of the Commission, a greater degree of legitimacy. This will basically remain the same should the Lisbon Treaty come into force, although some of the provisions relating to the institutions will be relocated to the TEU.

At the moment, all the Member States have one Commissioner (Article 213(1), as of 1 January 2005). Although Commissioners are not supposed to represent the national interest of the Member State of origin, it is felt that Member States accept policies more readily where they have a voice in the discussions forming that policy. With each wave of enlargement, the Commission has adhered to the principle of one Commissioner per Member State. Continuing with this would have made the Commission unwieldy and would also have made it difficult for it to continue to function as it currently does. The Treaty of Nice accepted that it will no longer work on the basis that each Member State will have a Commissioner. According to a protocol adopted at Nice, once there are 27 Commissioners the Council will determine the number of Commissioners and the mechanism by which they are to be selected. Some form of rotation is envisaged based on the principle of 'equality' and reflecting 'satisfactorily the demographic and geographical range of all the Member States'. This principle found its way into Lisbon where it was envisaged that, after the expiry of a transitional period on 31 October 2014, the number of Commissioners would be limited to a number equal to two-thirds the number of Member States, commissioner posts rotating on a system (to be determined by Council) 'reflecting the demographic and geographical range of all the Member States'(Article 17(5) TEU, as amended by Lisbon). Following the Irish 'no' vote, it seems that the one Commissioner per Member State system will continue.

2.5.2 Composition

The present Commission consists of 27 members (one from each Member State), chosen on the grounds of their general competence and 'whose independence is beyond doubt' (Article 213 (ex 157) EC). Although appointees of the Member States, they must, in the performance of their duties, 'neither seek nor take instructions from any government or from any other body' (Article 213(2) (ex 157(2)) EC). Of late, the probity of some Commissioners has been the subject of adverse comment (see 2.5.3 below). The Commission is headed by a president appointed from among the Commissioners.

The Commission is divided into directorates-general, each one responsible for certain aspects of Community policy (eg, D-G competition), and headed by a director-general. Commissioners are given responsibility for particular directorates (a 'portfolio'). Portfolios vary considerably in size and prestige. Although Commissioners are supposed to be generally competent, whether they have any particular expertise in the portfolio allocated to them is a matter of luck rather than judgement, as individual Member States seek to ensure that its commissioner has the most prestigious portfolio possible. One might argue that, as a result, the interests (or prestige) of individual Member States take priority over the interests of the Union.

2.5.3 Probity

As noted at 2.5.2 above, Commissioners are expected to carry out their functions with a high degree of probity; it is a term of their appointment that they be independent. Article 216 EC allows a Commissioner who fails in his or her duties to be retired compulsorily or deprived of his right to a pension or other benefits. It was concerns about fraud and mismanagement that led to the setting-up of a Committee of Independent Experts, which delivered a damning report in 1999. This led to the resignation of all Commissioners, en bloc; the principle problem was not necessarily the Commissioners themselves, but the persons to whom responsibility had been contracted out. This led to a process of review and reform under the leadership of Prodi, the new Commission president, which led to a greater system of accountability, including over contracted-out functions, and to the changes in management powers noted at 2.5.4 below.

In this context we should note *Commission v Edith Cresson* (case C–432/04), a case which concerns a member of the Commission who was part of the Commission that had resigned en bloc. She had wanted to appoint an acquaintance as a personal advisor despite being told that the rules did not allow for this appointment. Nonetheless, he worked for Cresson for two years. It was discovered that he had been paid for numerous tasks which were fictitious. The Commission sought a declaration that Mrs Cresson had breached the obligations arising from her status as a Commissioner and that she be deprived of her right to a pension or other benefits. Whilst Cresson had no knowledge of the fictitious tasks, the appointment was in clear breach of Commission rules. The ECJ determined that the finding of breach was sufficient and therefore did not deprive her of her pension.

2.5.4 Management powers of the Commission president

In addition to the changes noted at 2.5.1 above relating to appointment, the Nice Treaty gave more power to the president regarding the management of the Commissioners (Article 217), although these changes substantially reflect changes introduced by the working rules of the Prodi Commission (OJ [2000] L308/26). In particular, Prodi suggested that the portfolios of the commissioners should be allocated on a more rational basis rather than as a matter of horse trading between the various Member States. Although the Commission acts collectively, Article 217(4) as inserted by Nice allows individual commissioners to be impugned, again reflecting the Prodi working practice. The Lisbon Treaty, if it were to enter into force, would confirm the management powers of the Commission president (Article 17(6) TEU as amended by Lisbon).

2.5.5 Functions

The functions of the Commission are threefold. First, it acts as initiator or 'motor' of Community action. It has described itself as 'the driving force behind European integration' ((2000) COM 34), although some commentators have criticised this view of the Commission as having a unitary goal, since its policies are fragmented and sometimes conflict with each other. Nonetheless, all important decisions made by the Council must be made on the basis of proposals from the Commission (subject to the Council's power to 'request the Commission to undertake any studies which the Council considers desirable for the attainment of the common objectives, and to submit to it any appropriate proposals' (Article 208 (ex 152) EC—see Article 241 TFEU) and the Parliament's powers to request the Commission to submit proposals (Article 192 (ex 138b) EC). Using the EC Treaty as its brief, the Commission may formulate proposals on any matter provided for under the treaty, either where the power is specifically granted or under the more general power provided by Article 308 (ex 235) EC. Clearly, as long as a policy of unanimous voting was pursued by the Council the Commission's power of initiative was limited to what was politically acceptable; measures must, of necessity, be diluted for common consumption. Nevertheless, although the Council may limit the Commission's power of initiative, the importance of this power should not be underestimated. The power of initiative allows the Commission to frame the terms of the debate in Council and Parliament through the way it drafts the proposals. Furthermore, the Commission has responsibilities which also give it control: it sets the legislative timetable for the year; and it formulates more general policy guidance through its white papers. A novel proposal found in the Treaty of Lisbon is the provision which allows a group of citizens to invite the European Commission to submit a proposal (Article 11(4) TEU, after amendment by Lisbon). To take advantage of this opportunity there must be more than one million citizens who make the request and they must be nationals of 'a significant number of Member States'. Given that it will be logistically difficult to coordinate such a request, it seems unlikely that this procedure would be much used. The procedural requirements are set out in Art 21 TFEU.

Secondly, the Commission acts as the Community watchdog: it has been described as the guardian of the treaties. Member States are obliged under Article 10 (ex 5) EC to:

> take all appropriate measures . . . to ensure fulfilment of the obligations arising out of this Treaty or resulting from action taken by the institutions of the Community. . . . They shall abstain from any measure which could jeopardise the attainment of the objectives of this Treaty.

It is the Commission's task to seek out and bring to an end any infringements of EC law by Member States, if necessary by proceedings under Article 226 (ex 169) EC (see Chapter 11) before the ECJ. (See also similar provisions for the enforcement of the law relating to state aids, Article 88 (ex 93) EC.) The Commission has complete discretion in this matter (see *Alfons Lütticke GmbH v Commission* (case 48/65) noted in Chapter 11).

Thirdly, the Commission functions as the executive of the Community. Once a policy decision has been taken by the Council, the detailed implementation of that policy, often requiring further legislation, falls to the Commission, acting under powers delegated by the Council. In exercising its powers of implementation the Commission is subject to the supervision of a range of advisory, management, and regulatory committees, comprising national civil servants and appointed by the Council for that purpose. This process is referred to as 'comitology'. It has been suggested that this system, together with the Council's power under Article 202 (ex 145) (3rd indent) to reserve the right 'to exercise directly implementing powers itself' alone, or on the advice of its committees, tends to undermine the Commission's authority. Comitology has also been criticised for adding to the lack of transparency over democratic accountability in the decision-making process (see Chapter 3).

The Commission has in addition 'its (own) power of decision' (Article 211 (ex 155) EC). Regulations enacted, for example in the field of agriculture, to implement Community rules may provide for decisions of an executive nature to be taken by the Commission alone.

Finally, in pursuit of the Community's external policies, the Commission is required to act as negotiator, leaving agreements to be concluded by the Council (Articles 300 and 133 (ex 228 and 113) EC). Certain agreements can only be concluded after the assent of the European Parliament has been obtained (Article 300(3) (ex 228(3)). It has been suggested that the role of the Council under the FSP provisions may in time overshadow this aspect of the Commission's role. Articles 300 and 133 would be re-numbered 218 and 207 TFEU respectively should Lisbon come into force.

The functions of the Commission would essentially remain the same if the Lisbon Treaty enters into force, although there have been changes to the wording of the relevant provisions to reflect the general changes that would be introduced (see, eg, Article 17 TEU, as amended by Lisbon).

2.6 Economic and Social Committee (Articles 257–62 (ex 193–8) EC)

The Economic and Social Committee plays a consultative role in the Community decision-making process. Its members are appointed by the Council in their personal capacity, and represent a variety of sectional interests such as farmers, workers, trade unionists, or merely members of the general public. Where consultation is provided for by the treaty this is an essential procedural requirement: such consultation must also be referred to in any resulting legislation. The Committee may also be consulted by the Council and the Commission, and—if the Treaty of Lisbon comes into force—by the European Parliament whenever they consider it appropriate. In addition, it is entitled to advise the institutions on its own initiative on all questions affecting Union law. The Lisbon Treaty would re-enact this position (see Articles 13(4) TEU and Articles 300–4 TFEU), save that the term of appointment would be five years rather than the current four.

2.7 Committee of the Regions

This committee was established by the TEU to represent regional interests, and to act (like the Economic and Social Committee) in an advisory capacity in specified circumstances, as provided by the EC Treaty (eg, Article 149(4) (ex 126(4)) education; 151(5) (ex 128(5)) culture; 161 (ex 130d) and 162 (ex 130e) regional development). The Treaty of Nice introduced a limit of 350 on its total membership (see Article 263 EC, as amended by Nice). Although the committee is supposed to represent the regions, Member States take a different approach to whether representatives should be determined regionally or centrally. Should Lisbon come into force, the composition of the Committee of the Regions shall be decided by the Council, acting unanimously on a proposal from the Commission. The committee does not represent one particular set of interests and so its members may be pursuing divergent if not conflicting goals. In any event its powers are weak: the treaty only requires that it be consulted and, unlike the Parliament, it cannot rely on the judicial review mechanism in Article 230 to ensure its powers are respected.

2.8 Budgetary procedures

These are laid down by Article 272 (ex 203) EC. As might be expected, the Commission is responsible for drawing up a preliminary draft budget. The Commission thus sets the parameters, and fixes the 'maximum rate of increase' for 'non-compulsory items' of expenditure, which neither the Council nor the Parliament is free to exceed. The preliminary draft is forwarded to the Council, which establishes the draft budget and forwards it to Parliament. At this stage Parliament may approve the budget within 45 days, in which case it stands adopted. Alternatively, Parliament may suggest 'modifications' or 'amendments'. 'Modifications' may be proposed to items of 'compulsory' expenditure—expenditure already accounted for by Community rules, principally the amount (approximately half) allocated to the common agricultural policy. 'Amendments' refer to non-compulsory expenditure, principally concerned with regional or social policy. In this case the draft is returned to the Council and Parliament's 'modifications' may then be rejected by the Council acting by a qualified majority. Its 'amendments' too may be subject to 'modification' by the Council within a 15-day time limit. However, on return to Parliament that body may reject the Council's 'modifications' within a 15-day time limit, acting by a majority of its members and three-fifths of the votes cast. Parliament may then adopt the budget.

Thus Parliament is responsible for adopting the budget and has the final say over 'non-compulsory' expenditure. It also has one further weapon. If it is not satisfied with the budget overall it may reject it, and in 1979 and 1984 it did not hesitate to do so. The Treaty of Lisbon introduces a new special legislative procedure whereby in the case of a failure to agree the budget, a Conciliation Committee is to be convened to agree a joint text. Ultimately, either the Council or the Parliament may reject the budget or fail to agree a joint text, in which case a new budget must be submitted by the Commission. After Lisbon the relevant provisions will be found at Articles 313–16 TFEU.

2.9 Court of Auditors

The Court of Auditors was established in 1975 under the Budgetary Powers Treaty ([1977] OJ L359/1). Article 247 EC provides that the Court of Auditors comprises one member from each of the Member States and its members shall be completely independent in the performance of their duties. Appointment is by the Council of Ministers after consultation with Parliament. Following Nice, the term of office is six years. Its function is to exercise control and supervision over the implementation of the budget by carrying out an audit. Its creation represents an important step forward in the accountability of the institutions, particularly the Commission. Its annual report is published in the *Official Journal*. As a sign of its importance it was added to the list of Community institutions in Article 7 (ex 4) of the EC Treaty by the TEU (although it would be relegated from this position under the Lisbon Treaty). This change may be seen as purely symbolic. A more concrete change is the requirement that it must provide both the Parliament and the Council with a statement of assurance as to the reliability of the Community accounts and the legality of the underlying transactions (Article 248 (ex 188c(1)) EC) which, following the ToA, will be published in the *Official Journal*. Article 248 EC also requires the Court of Auditors to report any cases of irregularity. It is, however, limited in its effectiveness because there seems to be no one conception amongst the Member States of what it is intended to do. Secondly, there is no one body to respond to the Court of Auditors' reports to ensure that the Community is getting value for the money it spends. This is worrying in a time where there is increased public concern about the amounts of public spending and potential fraud within the Community. Indeed, the Court of Auditors has refused to sign off the budget for the past 11 years although, in what was the most recent instance at the time of writing, 'significant improvements' in budgetary controls compared to previous years were noticed. If Lisbon comes into force the provisions relating to the Court of Auditors will be found at Article 285 TFEU *et seq*.

2.10 Court of Justice (Articles 220–45 (ex 164–88) EC)

2.10.1 Appointment

There is currently one judge from each Member State (Article 220), chosen 'by common accord of the governments of the Member States' (Article 233 EC). The Lisbon Treaty would maintain the position that there would be one judge from each Member State for the ECJ, and at least one from each Member State for the 'General Court' (the current CFI) (Article 19(2) TEU, as amended by Lisbon). The inclusion of judges from all the Member States allows the national legal traditions to be reflected (Articles 235 and 255 EC). The judges have a variety of backgrounds within the legal sphere, but are not appointed to represent the political interests of their 'home' Member State. All must be 'persons whose independence is beyond doubt' (Article 223 (ex 167) EC).

Judges are appointed for a six-year term, as are the judges of the CFI. They are eligible for reappointment, but there is no express guarantee that they could not be removed during their term. Appointments are staggered so that not all judges are replaced at the same time. In practice, some of the judges and Advocates-General have had a long term of office: Jacobs, a former British Advocate-General, was at the Court from 1988–2006.

The judges of the ECJ are assisted by eight Advocates-General. Should the Lisbon Treaty come into force, a seven-strong panel drawn from former members of the Court, national supreme courts and 'lawyers of recognised competence' would give their opinion on candidates for appointment as judges or Advocates-General before the Member States would make their appointments (Article 255 TFEU). In this, the Lisbon Treaty follows a proposal in the Constitution.

2.10.2 Composition

There are currently 27 judges and eight Advocates-General. Although it could sit with all 27 members, given its increasing workload, the court may sit in chambers of three or five judges, or a Grand Chamber of 13 judges (Article 16 of the Statute of the Court of Justice, based on Article 221 EC, as amended by the Treaty of Nice). The ECJ will now only sit with all members in the small instances specified in Article 16 of its Statute. Whereas a Member State could previously request a hearing before a full court, it will now only be possible to insist on a hearing before the Grand Chamber. Grand Chamber hearings are also held when an institution is a party to the proceedings or when the matter is particularly important or complex.

The ECJ may face further reform due to the pressures of enlargement. More Member States mean more judges, more different languages and a wider range of legal traditions. It remains to be seen how the Court will cope with these pressures in terms of working method and how much the changes introduced by Nice will ameliorate problems of delay. The ECJ has commented that enlargement would mean the ECJ 'would cross the invisible boundary between a collegiate court and a deliberative assembly'. The use of chambers or a devolved system of justice, however, may cause problems in ensuring uniformity between the different chambers, especially given the different legal traditions in which each judge will be grounded.

All cases before the ECJ are allocated a number, the last two digits of which refer to the year in which the action was started. Since the setting up of the CFI in 1988, all ECJ cases start with the letter 'C'. Cases with the suffix 'P' are appeals from the CFI, and those followed by 'R' are applications for interim relief.

2.10.3 Functions

The task of the ECJ is to 'ensure that in the interpretation and application of this Treaty the law is observed' (Article 220 (ex 164) EC; if Lisbon comes into force this provision will be found at Article 19(1) TEU). It is the supreme authority on all matters of Community law, and in this capacity may be required to decide matters of constitutional law (see eg, Chapters 4 and 6), administrative law (see Chapters 12 and 13), social law (Chapter 27) and economic law (Chapters 29 and 31) in matters brought directly before it or on application from national courts. Its jurisdiction is principally over the acts of the institutions and Member States within the Communities' sphere of activity. It thus does not have jurisdiction over the actions of the European Council (*Roujansky v Council* (case T–584/93) and Article 46 (ex L) TEU excluded the ECJ's jurisidiction as regards the majority of the TEU provisions (see also *Grau Gomis* (case C–167/94)). This provision will be repealed should Lisbon come into force. Post Lisbon, the ECJ will still not have jurisdiction with regard to the CFSP provisions however (Article 275 TFEU). The ECJ may rule on the boundary between Community law and the other pillars, (Article 47 TEU) to ensure that there is no encroachment upon the *acquis communautaire*; in practice the ECJ has given a wide scope to the needs of the *acquis communautaire*, effectively giving the EC pillar primacy and retaining its jurisdiction to interpret or to rule on the validity of certain provisions (see further Chapter 3); this power in an amended form remains following the Lisbon Treaty (Article 40 TEU). As noted in Chapter 1, if Lisbon comes into force, the current pillar structure will be abolished, and the remaining distinction between what is now the EC Treaty (to become TFEU) and the TEU will be redefined. Article 1 TEU states that the two Treaties 'shall have the same legal value'.

The ECJ's jurisdiction in relation to instruments made under the JHA has been extended under the ToA: new Article 35 TEU provides that the ECJ may have jurisdiction in this area subject to the agreement of the Member States (discussed further below).

An Advocate-General's function is to assist the Court by presenting his 'submissions'—a detailed analysis of all the relevant issues of fact and law together with his recommendations to the Court. Under the new Statute of the Court, Article 20 permits the Court to decide not to have a submission from the Advocate-General if the case raises no new point of law. This possibility has already been used extensively.

Although the Advocate-General's recommendations are not always followed, where they are they are useful as a means of ascertaining the reasoning behind the Court's decision. The judgment itself, which is a single collegiate decision, is, to English eyes, terse, cryptic, with little indication of the reasoning on which it is based. Even where the Advocate-General's recommendations are not followed they may still be invoked as persuasive authority in a subsequent case.

In its practices and procedures the ECJ draws on continental models; in developing the substantive law it draws on principles and traditions from all the Member States. Although the ECJ seeks to achieve consistency in its judgments, its precedents are not binding in the English sense; it always remains free to depart from previous decisions in the light of new facts. An example of the Court expressly, and somewhat abruptly, departing from previous jurisprudence on the scope of Article 28 (ex 30) can be found in the infamous case of *Keck* (case C–267/91), in which the ECJ stated 'contrary to what has previously been decided'. This judgment has been the subject of some criticism, as the ECJ never precisely identified which previous case law it overturned (see further Chapter 19). More recently, the judgment of the ECJ in *Mettock* (case C–127/08) suggested that *Akrich* (Case C-109/01) should be 'reconsidered'.

As the EC Treaty is a framework treaty the ECJ has been extremely influential in 'filling the gaps', and in doing so has created law in bold, and, to those accustomed to English methods of interpretation, often surprising ways. As Lord Diplock pointed out in *R v Henn* [1981] AC 850:

> The European Court, in contrast to English courts, applies teleological rather than historical methods to the interpretation of the Treaties and other Community legislation. It seeks to give effect to what it conceives to be the spirit rather than the letter of the Treaties; sometimes, indeed, to an English judge, it may seem to the exclusion of the letter. It views the Communities as living and expanding organisms and the interpretation of the provisions of the Treaties as changing to match their growth.

The Court has, on occasion, been criticised for its activism. Others have argued that such boldness was necessary to carry the Community forward at a time, during the 1970s and early 1980s, when progress was blocked by political inertia. Whether in response to criticism, or as a result of the increased dynamism of the other institutions following the SEA, some judgments of the Court showed signs of a new conservatism, although in certain areas, for example the imposition of penalties on the Member States for non-compliances with EC law under Article 228, it continues to surprise (see, eg, *Commission v France* (case C–304/02) and Chapter 11). Most recently, it has given a wide scope to the right of citizens to claim benefits from host Member States and even to travel in search of medical treatment paid for by the home Member State. It has been this dynamism, or the consequences thereof, which led to the suggestion that the jurisdiction of the Court be limited by the 1996 IGC. This suggestion was not taken up in the ToA. Indeed following the ToA, it is possible that the ECJ's jurisdiction was extended. Prior to the ToA, it had no power to rule on matters under the TEU. Following the ToA, it has the power to rule on decisions made under JHA provisions of the TEU, subject to agreement by individual Member States. Also, the transfer of competence over some of the JHA provisions to the EC Treaty will bring more policy areas under the ECJ's jurisdiction: it is here, however, that we find some limitations creeping in. Within these policy areas, only the courts of last instance may make a reference to the ECJ (new Article 68 EC), compared with the usual 'any court or tribunal' empowered to refer under Article 234 (ex 177) EC in respect of all other areas of the EC Treaty (see Chapter 10). Furthermore, there are significant exceptions to the jurisdiction of the ECJ where a measure concerns national security (Article 68(2) EC).

These latter developments undermine the homogeneity of the ECJ's jurisdiction and reduce protection of individuals. The Treaty of Lisbon would introduce further changes, with the abolition of the pillar structure; notably Article 68 EC, which limits the jurisdiction of the ECJ will be repealed, reintroducing some homogeneity. Limitations remain with regard to law enforcement and national security (Article 276 TFEU). Likewise, Article 46, which limited the scope of the ECJ's jurisdiction with regard to the other two pillars, will be repealed, although the ECJ will continue to have a limited role with regard to CFSP matters (Article 275 TFEU).

2.10.4 Court of First Instance

In 1986 the SEA provided for the setting up of a new CFI. Approval for this court was obtained in October 1988 ([1989] OJ C215/1). The court commenced proceedings on 1 September 1989. There are now 15 judges who, as in the ECJ, may sit in chambers. Its jurisdiction includes disputes between the Community and its servants ('staff cases'), and applications for judicial review and damages by 'natural and legal persons', under Articles 230 and 232, respectively). There is a right of appeal on matters of law from this court to the ECJ. An applicant cannot appeal against a decision of the ECJ unless new facts come to light (*ISAE/VP v Commission* (case C–130/91); see further Chapters 7 and 11).

The CFI's jurisdiction can be extended under provisions introduced by the Treaty of Nice has entered into force. Crucially, it will have jurisdiction to hear preliminary references 'in specific areas laid down by the Statute [of the Court]' (Article 225(3) as amended by Nice), although to date, no areas have been allocated to the CFI. Article 225a, introduced by Nice, creates the possibility for some areas, such as staff cases, that are currently the responsibility of the CFI to be dealt with by judicial panel (Article 225a EC). The Civil Service Tribunal was set up by Council decision in November 2004 (2004/752/EC, Euratom, [2004] OJ L333/7) and is a judicial panel attached to the CFI. Until the Tribunal has established its own rules of procedure, it will continue to operate under the CFI's rules. It has, in essence, been set up to deal with staff cases between the Community and its officials.

Under Lisbon, like the Constitution, the present position of the courts would, in essence, remain. However, the CFI would, perhaps confusingly, be renamed the 'General Court'. This may reflect the intention to deal with a greater number of cases which are not raising difficult new issues of law at first instance, and reserving the ECJ itself for more complex cases.

2.11 Lisbon Treaty

In the preceding sections, we have already set out the impact of the Lisbon Treaty on the institutions, should it enter into force. In addition, there would be two further significant developments: the creation of the separate office of 'European Council President', and the establishment of a 'High Representative of the Union for Foreign Affairs and Security Policy'. Both developments have parallels with similar proposals found in the Constitution which sparked considerable controversy, because the existence of a political figurehead and of a foreign minister might be seen as a further step towards a European state. However, on closer examination, these fears are overstated, and both positions would be a development of existing roles.

2.11.1 Council president

Article 15(5) TEU would establish a European Council president, elected by the European Council, for a period of two and a half years, renewable once. The Council president would not be a current head of state or government, or be entitled to hold any other national office (Article 15(6)). He or she would be responsible for chairing the European Council and managing its work, endeavour to facilitate cohesion and consensus within the European Council and represent the Union externally on matters falling within the CFSP, although this must be without prejudice to the powers of the High Representative.

2.11.2 High Representative for Foreign Affairs and Security Policy

The High Representative for Foreign Affairs and Security is a member of the Commission and constitutes one of the vice-presidents; as such he or she would be subject to the approval of the European Parliament on appointment. The High Representative will be appointed by the European Council, acting by a qualified majority (Article 18 TEU). The European Council may terminate the appointment using the same procedure. The High Representative is responsible for conducting the Union's CFSP and the common security and defence policy. As such, he would preside over the Foreign Affairs Council (Article 18(3) TEU), Within the Commission, the High Representative would be responsible for coordinating external actions within the Commission to ensure its consistency. Some commentators have expressed concern about the hybrid nature of this role; somewhere between

Commission and Council. In particular, some feel that the post may disturb the institutional balance between institutions, as this role seems almost to be part of two of them.

2.12 Conclusions

When looking at the institutions, it is important to remember that they operate as a system, and individual institutions should not be seen in isolation; what is crucial is the relationship between them, and the other actors that increasingly play a role in Union policymaking. It is tempting to see different institutions as representatives for different ideas—supranationalism versus intergovernmentalism, and democracy versus a technocratic or interstate method. The shifting relationships and relative strengths of the institutions on this basis reflect the approach of the Union. In many respects, this is an oversimplification; even the Council can be seen to have some integrationist tendencies and the Parliament cannot be considered an ideal of democracy. In practice then, the institutions have had to learn to cooperate and to negotiate the hard points to permit any actions to be taken. This complicity of all institutions in the process is the basis of policymaking and the way in which over-ambitious or over-mighty institutions are, on the whole, controlled. This works for an assessment of the relationship between the institutions; what of the way the institutions work within themselves?

The current institutional structure of the Union was established for a system with a more limited membership and substantive scope. Since then there has been enlargement so that membership of the Union has more than quadrupled. It became accepted that what was in essence the original institutional structure was unable to function effectively in the modern Union and that institutional problems would only be exacerbated by further enlargement. Not only is it more difficult to reach agreement between a greater number of representatives, but with eastward expansion the Member States reflect a greater diversity of interests, traditions and languages. In addition to the sheer weight of numbers, there will be a risk of fragmentation as the Union becomes less cohesive. The current Member States were aware of this problem even before the ToA, resulting in a protocol being annexed to the ToA regarding proposed institutional reform. Although this document envisaged a two-stage approach to reform, to commence negotiations with more than ten candidate countries, it was decided to commence full-scale institutional reform foreseen by the second stage of the ToA protocol. The result was the Treaty of Nice.

In contrast to the TEU, Nice was not a treaty of grand constitutional plans. Instead, it aimed to revise the way the institutions worked, to prepare the Union for enlargement. On one level the treaty can be seen as successful: difficult points of principle, such as the composition of the Commission and the issue of qualified majority voting in Council, were agreed but perhaps not to the satisfaction of all. Given the tension between the large and small nations, it is commendable that any balance between these different interests was found. Nonetheless, the process of refining the institutional workings continued, with some of the same items (QMV for example) on the agenda. Despite its magniloquent title, the Constitution was much in the same vein as Nice.

The Constitution would have changed the institutional structure to an extent, but it would not produce a complete overhaul. The main institutions would have remained, although their organisation and voting arrangements would be streamlined and most of these developments have been incorporated into Lisbon. Most of the changes are benign, or even mildly positive. Perhaps the most significant development would be the departure of the 'one Commissioner per Member State' approach, although the future of this, after the Irish 'no' vote, is in doubt. In any event, it remains to be seen whether these provisions will appear in a new treaty, whichever form it might take.

FURTHER READING

Arnull, A, 'The European Court and judicial objectivity: a reply to Professor Hartley' (1996) 112 LQR 411.

——, 'Taming the beast? The Treaty of Amsterdam and the Court of Justice' in D O'Keeffe and P Twomey (eds), *Legal Issues of the Amsterdam Treaty* (Hart Publishing, 1999).

Bradley, K, 'The European Parliament and treaty reform: Building blocks and stumbling blocks' in D O'Keeffe and P Twomey (eds), *Legal Issues of the Amsterdam Treaty* (Hart Publishing, 1999).

Capelletti, M, *The Judicial Process in Comparative Perspective* (Clarendon Press, 1989).

Craig, P, 'The Treaty of Lisbon: Process, architecture and substance'(2008) EL Rev 137–66.

Dashwood, A and Johnson, A, 'The institutions of the enlarged EU under the regime of the Constitutional Treaty' (2004) 41 CML Rev 1481.

Dehousse, R, 'European institutional architecture after Amsterdam: Parliamentary system or regulatory structure?' (1998) 35 CML Rev 595.

Dinan, D, 'Governance and institutions: A new constitution and a new Commission' (2005) 43 *JCMS Supp* 37–54.

European Parliament, 'Co-governing after Maastricht', Working Paper POLI 104/rev EN.

Fennelly, N, 'The area of "freedom, security and justice" and the European Court of Justice: A personal view' (2000) 29 ICLQ 1.

Harden, I and Donnelly, K, 'The Court of Auditors and financial control and accountability in the European Community' [1995] EPL 599.

Hartley, T, 'Constitutional and institutional aspects of the Maastricht Treaty' (1993) 42 ICLQ 213.

——, 'Federalism, courts and legal systems: The emerging constitutions of the European Community' (1986) 34 Am J Comp L 229.

Hartley, TC, 'The European Court, judicial objectivity and the constitution of the European Union' (1996) 112 LQR 95.

Laffan, B., 'Becoming a "living institution": The evolution of the European Court of Auditors' (1999) 37 JCMS 252.

Lang, JT, 'Checks and balances in the European Union: The institutional structure and the "community method"' (2006) 12 European Public Law 127–54.

Lefevre, S, 'Rules of procedure do matter: The legal status of the institutions' power of self-organisation' (2005) 30 EL Rev 802–20.

Petersen, J, and Bomberg, E, *Decision-Making with European Union* (MacMillan, 1999).

Rasmussen, H., 'Between self-restraint and activism: A judicial policy for the European Court' (1988) 13 EL Rev 28.

Skiadis, DV, 'European Court of Auditors and European Investment Bank: An uneasy relationship' (1999) 5 EPL 215.

Slynn, G, 'The Court of Justice of the European Communities' (1984) 33 ICLQ 409.

Tridimas, T, 'The Court of Justice and judicial activism' (1996) 21 EL Rev 199.

Usher, J, 'Institutional aspects of the Constitutional Treaty: Which way does it go?' (2005) 37 Bracton Law Journal 30.

3

Scope of the EC Treaty: Laws and lawmaking

3.1 Introduction

The purpose of this chapter is to outline the main tasks of the Union and the mechanisms by which the institutions carry out their tasks. This chapter looks at the provisions setting down the general objectives of the treaties and their relationship to more specific policy areas. It then goes on to consider matters such as treaty base for legislative action, legislative procedures, and subsidiarity, before looking at difficulties in this area. It also develops a couple of points touched on in Chapter 2: the institutional balance and the democratic legitimacy—or lack of it—of the European Union. Note that the main focus of this chapter is the lawmaking powers of the institutions as they relate to the current EC Treaty; the separate systems under the second and third pillars, such as justice and home affairs (JHA), will be discussed only briefly. The main changes that would be introduced by the Lisbon Treaty should it come into force are briefly discussed where relevant.

3.2 Scope of the EC Treaty

Although primarily an economic treaty, concerned with creating a single market in Europe, the original EEC Treaty extended far beyond the traditional free-trading agreement such as we find in GATT and EFTA, to cover a wide range of matters only peripherally economic, and expressly included a number of purely social goals. The Single European Act (SEA) further extended the scope of Community competence into new areas which had hitherto been dealt with only on a piecemeal basis. It also provided a formal framework for political cooperation by Member States which was absent from the original treaty. At Maastricht, and to a lesser extent in Amsterdam and Nice, this led to a further and significant extension of Community (and Union) goals. Neither the Constitution nor Lisbon, should it come into force, would extend Union competence significantly, though Lisbon (like the intention in the Constitution) will remove the structural distinction between Community and Union competence. Thus, Lisbon subsumes the EC into the EU (See Article 1(3) of the Treaty on European Union (TEU), as amended by Lisbon).

Although some provisions do not require further implementation, the EC Treaty is essentially a 'framework' treaty (*traité cadre*). It sets out as broad general principles the aims to be achieved, leaving its institutions, where necessary, to fill the gaps by means of secondary legislation.

The general aims of the EC Treaty, as variously amended, are set out in Article 2:

The Community shall have as its task, by establishing a common market and an economic and monetary union and by implementing policies or activities referred to in Articles 3–4, the promotion throughout the Community of a harmonious, balanced and sustainable development of economic activities, *a high level of employment and of social protection*, equality between men and women, sustainable and non-inflationary growth, a high degree of competitiveness and convergence of economic performance, *a high level of protection and improvement of the quality of the environment*, the raising of the standard of living and quality of life, and economic and social cohesion and solidarity among Member States.

Article 3 provides:

For the purposes set out in Article 2, the activities of the Community shall include, as provided by this Treaty and in accordance with the timetable set out therein:

(a) the prohibition as between Member States, of customs duties and quantitative restrictions on the import and export of goods, and of all other measures having equivalent effect;

(b) a common commercial policy;

(c) an internal market characterised by the abolition, as between Member States, of obstacles to the free movement of goods, persons, services and capital;

(d) measures concerning the entry and movement of persons as provided for in Title IV;

(e) a common policy in the sphere of agriculture and fisheries;

(f) a common policy in the sphere of transport;

(g) a system ensuring that competition in the common market is not distorted;

(h) the approximation of the laws of the Member States to the extent required for the functioning of the common market;

(i) the promotion of coordination between employment policies of the Member States with a view to enhancing their effectiveness by developing a coordinated strategy for employment;

(j) a policy in the social sphere comprising the creation of a European Social Fund;

(k) the strengthening of economic and social cohesion;

(l) a policy in the sphere of the environment;

(m) the strengthening of the competitiveness of Community industry;

(n) the promotion of research and technology development;

(o) encouragement for the establishment and development of trans-European networks;

(p) a contribution to the attainment of a high level of health protection;

(q) a contribution to education and training of quality and to the flowering of the cultures of the Member States;

(r) a policy in the sphere of development cooperation;

(s) the association of the overseas countries and territories in order to increase trade and promote jointly economic and social development;

(t) a contribution to the strengthening of consumer protection;

(u) measures in the spheres of energy, civil protection and tourism.

Article 4 (ex 3a), introduced by the TEU, sets out the Community's policies in the field of economic and monetary union, including the creation of the single currency.

Although Article 3 was greatly extended by the TEU, it must be noted that Article 3(a)–(h), (j), and (s) as currently numbered were all present in the original EEC Treaty, albeit differently numbered and with some differences in wording. The remaining provisions were new to Article 3, but most of the activities listed had already been subject to some Community legislation, even before the SEA, and a number of these (Article 3(k), (l), and (n)) had been incorporated into the treaty by the SEA, if not in Article 3. Their incorporation into Article 3 thus merely reflected, and gave greater legitimacy to, existing practice. Only the provision for economic and monetary union in Article 4 (ex 3A) represented a genuine new departure for the EC. The Treaty of Amsterdam (ToA) further amended Articles 2–3 EC, reflecting the increased emphasis to be put on both employment and environmental concerns (see italicised provisions of Article 2).

These provisions would be replaced were Lisbon to come into force, Articles 1 and 2 EC being repealed, along with para 1 of Article 3. Instead, Article 3 TEU (after amendment by Lisbon) will enumerate the Union's aims and tasks. The terms of current Articles 2 and 3(1) EC subsumed within this provision. There would be some changes in emphasis. Thus, the Union's primary aim is to promote peace, its values, and the well-being of its peoples. The reference to the internal market (rather than common market) comes further down the list of objectives than it does currently in the EC Treaty. Article 3(2) TEU provides that the 'Union shall offer its citizens an area of freedom, security and justice without internal frontiers, and an internal market where competition is free and undistorted'. Article 3(3) lists the more specific tasks of the Union, which reflect the current Article 2 EC. Again there are differences between the current format and that proposed by Lisbon. Notably, the provision commences by referring to Europe's sustainable development and, although there are references to a competitive economy, the provision also makes clear that one of the elements on which this development is to be based is a social market economy, not just a market economy, a point implicit in the current EC Treaty. Interestingly, there is no mention of free competition as a goal, though the main provisions in the treaty providing for competition policy have not been amended. According to the French government, who requested the change, competition is a means, not an end.

3.2.1 Relationship between Articles 2–3 EC and other Treaty Articles

Articles 2–3 describe the main objectives of the Community and identify the means by which they are to be attained. They do not themselves impose specific legal obligations on the Member States. The detailed obligations are spelled out in specific provisions in subsequent parts of the treaty. Articles 2–3 nonetheless have interpretive value; they may be used to clarify the scope of the more precise treaty provisions. A similar relationship was discernable between Parts I and III of the Constitution. Presumably, should Lisbon come into force, that relationship will arise between Article 3 EU and the substantive provisions in the Treaty on the Functioning of the European Union (TFEU) (as the EC Treaty will be renamed).

3.2.2 General principles

In addition to the goals and tasks enunciated in Articles 2–3, the EC Treaty contains other provisions laying down principles underlying the Community. This list of principles has been expanded by the successive treaty amendments. The EC Treaty always did contain a provision prohibiting discrimination on the grounds of nationality (current Article 12 EC) and the principle of cooperation by the Member States (Article 10 EC). The SEA introduced the notion of the internal market. The TEU introduced concepts as varied as the introduction of monetary union as a goal of the Community (Article 4 EC) and the principle of subsidiarity (Article 5 EC). The ToA continued this trend by highlighting the importance of environmental protection (Article 6), introducing closer cooperation (Article 11) and a provision on the importance of services of general economic interest (Article 16). As noted in Chapter 1, the principle of non-discrimination has been extended by the ToA with the insertion of a new article (Article 13 EC) to cover discrimination on grounds of sex, race and ethnic origin, religion or belief, disability, age, or sexual orientation. Unlike the provision on discrimination on grounds of nationality, the treaty does not expressly state that such discrimination is prohibited; instead it merely permits the Member States, acting unanimously, to take action to combat such discrimination. For example, a directive prohibiting discrimination on grounds of race has already been enacted (Directive 2000/43/EC OJ L180/22 2000). As has been suggested, these principles vary considerably in subject matter and in form, so some, such as Articles 6, 12, and 13, may have a greater impact on the interpretation of provisions comprising the Community policies than others. Lisbon includes a title called 'provisions having general application' which covers some of the provisions formally included in the 'Principles' title. The provisions identify principles which should inform the Union (and the institutions) in carrying out its activities and policies and in this similar concerns can be seen to reoccur (non-discrimination, for example—Article 10 TFEU). Where a policy is required to be taken into account by the Union in all its policies, this is called 'mainstreaming'; another example is environmental policy. The provision ensuring respect for human rights remains in the TEU; interestingly post Lisbon, the TEU would also include a provision requiring respect for the principles of the UN Charter (Article 3(5) TEU, as amended by Lisbon). There is a new article, having general application emphasising the need for open government (Article 15 TFEU). Note that the attempt found in the Constitution to include the supremacy of Union law, which is part of the jurisprudence of the European Court of Justice (ECJ), has been abandoned. Supremacy remains a creature of case law not expressly mentioned in the EC Treaty, although there is attached to the Lisbon Treaty a protocol on the subject (see further below and Chapter 4).

3.2.3 Community policies

Seeing as the status of Lisbon is in doubt, we will focus on the policies as currently found in the EC Treaty. We have already noted the introduction of provisions relating to monetary union (Chapter 1). In addition, and as a supplement to the activities listed in Article 3, the EC Treaty provided for the harmonisation of indirect taxation (Articles 90–3 (ex 95–9) EC).

Central to the creation of both the common and the internal market are the four freedoms: the free movement of goods, services, persons, and capital (Article 14(2) EC). These are elaborated in Titles 1 and 3 of Part III to the treaty. A more detailed discussion of these freedoms forms Part Three of this book.

The EC Treaty also provided for action in the field of social policy, requiring Member States to promote improved working conditions and living standards

(Article 136 (ex 117)) and to harmonise conditions of health and safety (Article 138 (ex 118a)) for workers, and to observe a principle of equal pay for equal work for men and women (Article 139 (ex 119)). A protocol on social policy was attached to the TEU. It further committed all Member States except the UK to a range of actions designed to protect the interests of workers. The social policy provisions in the EC Treaty were substantially amended as the ToA incorporated this protocol on social policy into the main body of the treaty (new Articles 136–45 EC), replacing and augmenting the existing provisions. This had the advantage of removing the potential for disputes over the borderline between social measures permissible under the EC Treaty and those which, hitherto, should have been made under the protocol. In addition, following the ToA, the EC Treaty also includes a new chapter on employment (Articles 125–30 EC). These provisions are not aimed at giving individuals rights to a job; rather, they aim at coordinating the Member States' employment policies so as to reduce unemployment. These policies may be seen as a form of economic management, an approach which is reinforced by these provisions' location within the treaty, which is between monetary union and common commercial policy, rather than next to social policy. Should Lisbon come into force, these provisions will be found in Title IX TFEU, at Articles 145–50.

Following the ToA, the treaty also incorporated new measures (Part III Title IV, Articles 61–9 EC) to attain the free movement of individuals within the EC (see Chapter 26). These have been broadly based on the measures taken under the 1990 Schengen Agreement on the abolition of frontier controls between the signatory States, an agreement outside the Union framework but which most of the EU Member States have joined. A protocol annexed to the ToA stated that on ratification of the ToA, the Schengen *acquis* (that is, all binding decisions made under the Schengen Agreement) would apply to the Member States and that these decisions would be treated as though they were measures made in accordance with procedures of the EC Treaty. The UK and Ireland have opted out of this chapter of the treaty (although either of them may opt in to individual measures), and consequently the Schengen *acquis* and measures made under the new chapter in the EC Treaty will not necessarily apply to them. Denmark has also expressed reservations about these provisions. Although the inequalities and the uncertainties concerning the scope of the social policy provisions of the EC Treaty have been removed by the ToA, similar problems replaced them in relation to the free movement of persons. Should Lisbon come into force, these provisions will be found in Title V TFEU, Articles 67–81.

It should be noted that although Community competence has been expanded, the level of Community activity in different policy areas varies. Articles 94–5 EC (discussed below at 3.3.1 and in Chapter 16) authorise the institutions to take harmonising action in the area of the common and internal market. Article 47 also authorises this for the mutual recognition of qualifications and the cross-border provision of services. In other areas, Community action is constrained. Article 152, for example, which relates to public health, expresses Community action as complementing, rather than replacing, national action (see Article 168 TFEU). Community involvement tends to be limited in this way in flanking policy areas. One innovation from the Constitution and carried over into Lisbon is that the treaty tries to identify more clearly the different levels of power to act ascribed to the Union in the various different fields. New provisions would be inserted into TFEU to recognise this (see further below at 3.5.5).

3.2.4 **External competence**

To enable the Community to carry out its policies towards third countries, the EC Treaty provides that 'The Community shall have legal personality' (Article 281 (ex 210) EC). Note that the Union currently does not enjoy legal personality, although this would change should the Lisbon Treaty come into force. Article 300 (ex 228) EC empowers the Commission to negotiate, and the Council to conclude (in most cases following consultation with Parliament) agreements between the Community and one or more states or an international organisation. (This provision will be replaced, should Lisbon come in to force, by Article 218 TFEU). The EC Treaty also contains a provision (Article 310 (ex 238) EC) allowing the Community to conclude association agreements. Many agreements have been concluded in the field of trade and aid under these provisions (Article 217 TFEU).

Article 133 (ex 113) EC also allows the Commission, under the guidance of the Council, to enter into negotiations to make agreements necessary to implement the Common Commercial Policy (Art 207 TFEU). It was on this basis that representation for Member States at GATT meetings was developed. The line between Community competence and that of the Member States is not, however, clear-cut as *Opinion 1/94* shows. The Court in this opinion determined that not all the issues covered by the WTO fall within Community competence and therefore not only must the EC be a member of the WTO, but so must the Member States. This may lead to difficulties in the administration of the WTO as far as the Member States are concerned, as their membership, to a certain extent, is duplicated. By contrast, the negotiation of the Lugano Convention dealing with conflicts of national jurisdiction and enforcement of judgments in civil and commercial matters was held to fall within the exclusive competence of the Community. The ECJ in its opinion on Community competence in this area (*Opinion 1/03*) emphasised that the Lugano Convention would affect the uniform and consistent application of Community rules. Post-Lisbon, the customs union falls within exclusive Union competence.

Article 3(5) TEU (as amended by Lisbon) would specifically refer to the Union's external competence, stating that 'in its relations with the wider world, the Union shall uphold and promote its values and interests', specifically contributing to 'peace, security and sustainable development of the earth, solidarity and mutual respect among peoples, free and fair trade, eradication of poverty and protection of human rights'. Whether these aims would limit the Union's external competence, should the treaty come into force, is far from clear, as is the question of how this interrelates with the provisions in TFEU. Given that the Union's activities should already take at least some of these concerns into account, arguably there would not be much difference in substantive approach. A more detailed discussion of the Union's external policies falls outside the scope of this book.

3.3 **Basis for legislative action**

As we have noted in Chapter 2, the three main institutions of the Community—the Commission, the Council, and the European Parliament—are empowered to legislate (subject to review by the European Courts) on any of the matters within the framework. Many of the treaty provisions, for example, the articles relating to free movement of goods and workers (Articles 25, 28, and 39 (ex 12, 30, and 48) respectively) contain obligations which are sufficiently precise to be applicable as they stand (see further Chapter 5). Others provide for, and often require, further measures of implementation before they can take full legal effect. Note that currently, different provisions apply to the other two pillars; should Lisbon come into force, the JHA matters will be dealt with within the amendment EC Treaty (TFEU); common foreign and security policy (CFSP) will continue to be subject to a separate regime.

3.3.1 Broad provisions for action

Article 94 (ex 100) EC provides for the 'approximation' (ie, harmonisation) of such laws as directly affect the establishment or functioning of the common market by unanimous vote. Article 95 (ex 100a) makes similar provision for measures which have as their object the establishing or functioning of the internal market, in most cases, by qualified majority vote (QMV) (see Article 95(4) and Chapter 16). Both these provisions are broad and their precise extent and relationship to each other and to other treaty provisions is sometimes open to discussion (see discussion of the Tobacco Advertising Directive case (*Germany v Parliament and Council* (case C–376/98) at 16.4.1). Should the Lisbon Treaty come into force Article 94 EC will become Article 115 TFEU, and in a reversal of their order of appearance, Article 95 EC will become Article 114 TFEU. This change reflects their actual level of importance, and the phrase currently included in the text of Article 95 EC, 'by way of derogation from Article 94' is to be deleted. In practice, the treaty base of choice is Article 95; it is not limited to a role as exception; that, rather, seems to be the role of Article 94 EC.

Even where the institutions are not specifically empowered to act, Article 308 (ex 235) provides:

> If action by the Community should prove necessary to attain, in the course of the operation of the common market, one of the objectives of the Community and this Treaty has not provided the necessary powers, the Council shall, acting unanimously on a proposal from the Commission and after consulting the European Parliament, take the appropriate measures.

This blanket power has been used as a basis for legislation on matters of regional or social policy (eg, equal treatment for men and women) which fell within the broad aims of the Community, as expressed in the preamble, but which were not spelt out specifically in the treaty. Many of these matters have now been incorporated expressly into the EC Treaty by subsequent treaty amendments. Although this provision is potentially wide, concerns about its use to extend treaty competence by the back door are limited by the fact that the consent of all Member States to any proposed measure is required under Article 308. This point does not, however, recognise that Article 308 permits the European Parliament a very limited role; it also excludes the national parliaments. Both sets of institutions have a much more limited role than that they would have if Community competence was to be expanded by formal treaty amendment. Given the breadth of Articles 94–5, recourse to Article 308 seems to have become less frequent. The expansion of ex-press Community competence by various treaties and the related political tensions (discussed at 3.3.2 below) render it less likely that Article 308 EC will be used as extensively as hitherto.

During the deliberations on the Future of Europe it was suggested that Article 308 be removed to prevent further 'competence creep'—that is, an expansion of the Union's competence. Although the 'flexibility clause' (Article I–17), as it came to be known, survived, national parliaments were given an increased role in determining the circumstances in which this provision could be used. Should the Constitution have come into force, under Article I–17(2) the Commission would have been re-quired to solicit the views of national parliaments on the compliance with the prin-ciple of subsidiarity (discussed at 3.5 below) of any measure put forward under this provision. In Lisbon, the provision remains where it is, but amended to extend the power of using the flexibility clause to objectives defined in either of the treaties, but it cannot be used either for circumventing any prohibition on harmonisation found in the treaty or as a basis for attaining objectives pertaining to the CFSP. Should Lisbon come into force, this provision will be renumbered as Article 352 TFEU.

3.3.2 Implied powers

The Court has also determined that the Community has implied powers, so that when powers which are not specifically enumerated in the treaty are required to achieve a Community goal, the Community is deemed to have the neces-sary powers. There are two possible formulations of this doctrine. The narrow approach states that the existence of a power implies the existence of any other power that is reasonably necessary for the exercise of the original power. This was the approach taken by the Court in *Fédération Charbonnière de Belgique v High Authority* (case 8/55). A wider approach was taken in *Germany v Commission* (cases 281, 283–5 and 287/85) where the powers of the Commission arising out of ori-ginal Article 118 (which has been amended significantly and renumbered as 137 EC by the ToA) were the subject of dispute. The article provided the Commission with a task—that of promoting close cooperation between Member States in the social field—but did not give the Commission any specific legislative powers. Germany therefore argued that the proposed legislative act of the Commission was outside the treaty. The Court commented that to avoid rendering provisions such as the then Article 118 totally ineffective, the powers necessary for carrying out the task must be inferred. This is a significant decision because there are many instances where the Commission has been allocated a task but not been given legislative power.

It is not just internally that the Court has deduced Community competence. Following *Commission v Council* (case 22/70) (the *ERTA* case) and *Opinion 1/76* it was thought that the EC would have implied powers to act in the international sphere in relation to matters with respect to which the EC has power to act within the Union under the EC Treaty. In addition, the *ERTA* case appeared to suggest that the competence of the Community, in this regard, was exclusive: Member States were precluded from acting. The degree, however, to which this is still the case is now unclear following *Opinion 1/94*, in which the Court held that, although the

EC had exclusive competence under Article 113 (now Article 133) to act in some spheres, with respect to other areas (such as intellectual property) the Member States also have competence. In more and more spheres the Court has acknowledged that Member States and the Community have concurrent competence (eg, *Commission v Council* (case C–25/94) (FAO Fishery Agreement), but compare the approach in the *Lugano Convention* case: *Opinion 1/03*). Following the German constitutional court's decision in *Brunner v European Union Treaty* (see also Czech and German Lisbon Treaty decisions) (see further below at 3.4 and Chapter 4), it is likely that the national courts will keep a watchful eye on all Community activities in the internal and external field to ensure that the Community institutions do not exceed their powers.

3.4 Expansion of Union competence

The degree to which the framework provided by the treaty has been filled in will form the subject matter of later chapters of this book. Suffice it to say that all the main areas of activity outlined above, in both the internal and external fields, have been subject to some measures of implementation. In some cases, such as agriculture and competition policy, implementation has been extensive. In others, such as the free movement of capital, transport, and freedom to provide services, progress was, initially, slow. As a result of the SEA there was substantial progress, although some barriers to trade still exist, as well as in the 'new' areas of health and safety, environmental and consumer protection and research and technological development. The TEU ensured continuing activity in these fields as well as in the newer field of education and training, culture and the development of trans-European networks and tourism. As noted above, the changes introduced by the ToA, especially to Articles 2–3, indicate an increased emphasis to be placed on environmental and employment policies.

From the foregoing outline two matters will be clear:

(a) The framework provided by the treaty, both originally and as amended by subsequent treaties (SEA, TEU, ToA, and Nice), is extremely broad, embracing many areas of economic and social activity which had hitherto been within the sole competence of Member States.

(b) Within that framework there is almost unlimited (though not uncontrolled) scope for legislation by the Community institutions.

Since, under Article 10 (ex 5) EC, Member States are required to 'take all appropriate measures, whether general or particular, to ensure fulfilment of the obligations arising out of this treaty or resulting from action taken by the institutions of the Community' and 'shall abstain from any measure which could jeopardise the attainment of the objectives of this Treaty', perhaps it is not surprising that Lord Denning MR was moved to say, in *HP Bulmer Ltd v J Bollinger SA* [1974] Ch 401: 'the Treaty is like an incoming tide. It flows into the estuaries and up the rivers. It cannot be held back'.

It is no doubt to stem that tide that the principle of subsidiarity was incorporated as a general principle into the EC Treaty by the TEU, in Article 5 (ex 3b) EC.

It is with subsidiarity in mind that the German constitutional court delivered its landmark judgment in *Brunner v European Union Treaty* [1994] 1 CMLR 57. In upholding the powers of the German Parliament to ratify the Maastricht Treaty, it sounded a number of warnings about the extent of the powers of the Community and its institutions. Any further transfer of powers to Community level will need express democratic approval to be binding. As it commented in the judgment (at para 33):

> because the principle of limited powers is adhered to, no power to extend its powers is conferred on the European Union, and the claiming of further functions and powers by the European Union and the Communities is made dependent on supplementation and amendment of the Treaty and is therefore subject to the affirmative decision of the national parliaments.

The Member States' status as 'masters of the treaty' would, to some extent, have been reinforced in the Constitution. The Constitution made express the principle of primacy of Union law, but primacy is limited to the Union operating within the sphere of competence conferred on it by the Member States. The use of the word 'conferred' seems to suggest that the relationship between the Member States and the Union is one of delegated powers (see Articles I–6 and I–11(1)–(2)). This is a theme that returns in the Lisbon Treaty. In a number of provisions, both the EU and EC treaties are amended to emphasise that the Union is a creature of conferred powers. Thus, for example, Article 1 TEU which is a fundamental provision establishing the Union, is amended to read:

> By this Treaty, the HIGH CONTRACTING PARTIES establish among themselves a EUROPEAN UNION, hereinafter called 'the Union', *on which the Member States confer competences to attain objectives they have in common.* [Words in italics added by Lisbon.]

Likewise, the replacement provision for the current Article 1 EC specifies that:

> This Treaty organises the functioning of the Union and determines the areas of, delimitation of, and arrangements for exercising its competences.

New provisions are also inserted to identify and categorise areas of Union competence. This suggests that there is an intention on the part of the Member States to limit competence creep. Whether it is enough or whether the judicial and political views of the scope of the treaties will continue to diverge is another question. As noted in Chapter 1, both the Czech Republic and Germany have had questions referred to their respective constitutional courts about the acceptability of the Lisbon Treaty. The Czech court ruled in favour of the treaty but the enabling legislation is subject to a requirement that no further competence may be transferred without express consent of the Czech Parliament. The German court made a similar point. It emphasised the principle of 'conferral' and the obligation in EU law 'to respect the constituent power of the Member States as the masters of the Treaties', which respect it has the power to review.

3.5 Competence and subsidiarity

3.5.1 Principle of attributed powers

Subsidiarity is, following the Maastricht Treaty, a well-known word. Its meaning is, however, not clear. The first paragraph of Article 5 EC is not contentious: it merely restates what was common ground, namely that the Community can only act within the powers conferred on it by the treaty. Lisbon, if it comes into force, would repeal Article 5, but the ideas would be restated in a new Article 5 TEU; that is, the provision would be moved from the EC Treaty to the TEU, which re-emphasises the principle of conferral and makes express the point that was always implicit, that the Union can only act 'within the limits of the competences conferred upon it by the Member States in the treaties to attain the objectives set out therein' (Article 5(2) TEU, as amended by Lisbon). Article 5(1) TEU (as amended by Lisbon) also highlights the fact that not only are the Union's actions limited by subsidiarity, but also by proportionality. Under new Article 12 TEU (as amended by Lisbon) national parliaments would also have a role in ensuring that proposed EU legislation complies with the principle of subsidiarity.

3.5.2 Principle of subsidiarity

The difficulties start with the second paragraph of current Article 5 EC. This states that:

> In areas which do not fall within its exclusive competence, the Community shall take action, in accordance with the principle of subsidiarity, only if and insofar as the objectives of the proposed action cannot be sufficiently achieved by the Member States and can therefore, by reason of the scale or effects of the proposed action, be better achieved by the Community.

Clearly, subsidiarity will not apply where the Community has exclusive competence. Therefore, to determine whether subsidiarity applies, we must distinguish between areas where the Community has exclusive competence and areas where it does not. The boundary between exclusive Community competence and shared competence has not been clear: there are no provisions in the EC Treaty or TEU which identify the exclusive (or non-exclusive) powers of the Community (or the Union). Although the ToA has a protocol on subsidiarity annexed to it, the protocol does not clarify where the boundary of exclusive Community competence lies. This issue was discussed by the Convention on the Future of Europe, and a group of provisions would have been introduced in the Constitution that would have addressed the issue of Union competence in its various types. This idea is found also in the Lisbon Treaty, which restates the same principle found in current Article 5 EC in broadly similar terms. These articles are discussed below at 3.5.5.

3.5.3 Test for the exercise of concurrent powers

Looking now at the principle of subsidiarity itself, it can be seen that the idea in the second paragraph of Article 5 can be broken down into two further blocks:

(a) that no Community action should be taken unless the action cannot be sufficiently achieved by the Member States

(b) that because of the proposed scale or effects of the measure, the Community can better achieve the end result desired.

This test raises several issues: it is a test of comparative efficiency ('Commission Communication to the Council and the European Parliament', Bull EC 10-1992, 116) which might, in the context of achieving goals such as common trading rules throughout the Union, be seen to favour action at Community level. How this fits in with the definition of subsidiarity given in the preamble to the TEU (which, therefore, is of interpretative value) is not clear, as that version states that the principle of subsidiarity requires that decision-making should be made as close to the citizen as possible. Note that the Lisbon Treaty would introduce a provision which states that decisions are to be taken as closely as possible to the citizen, re-emphasising this point (Art 10(3) TEU, as amended by Lisbon), together with the possibility of decision-making at a sub-national level. Further, when will 'sufficiently' be satisfied? Will these questions relate to the scale or the effect of the proposed action? Although the protocol annexed to the ToA is aimed at clarifying the meaning of subsidiarity it does not answer these questions. It puts forward three criteria which reflect the two-stage test above:

(a) the issue has transnational aspects which cannot be satisfactorily regulated by other Member States

(b) actions by Member States alone would conflict with requirements of the treaty such as the internal market provisions

(c) action at Community level would produce clear benefits by reason of its scale or effects.

It is submitted that these criteria do no more than restate the problem; indeed they may even add to the difficulties because it is not even clear whether these criteria are cumulative or alternative. These problems could lead to litigation to obtain clarification of these points. Some writers have suggested that, in any event, these issues are not appropriately decided by the Court because of their political nature. In view of the fact that a number of cases have already raised this issue (eg, *UK v Council* (case C–84/94) and *Germany v Parliament* (case C–233/94)), it seems that the Court has not, so far, refused jurisdiction and is now unlikely to do so. It has been reluctant to exercise a high level of review, however. Note also that annexed to the Lisbon Treaty is a protocol on subsidiarity and proportionality; this seems more focused on ensuring the implementation of the principles than in clarifying the meaning of either subsidiarity or proportionality.

3.5.4 **Principle of proportionality**

The final element of subsidiarity is that contained in the third paragraph of Article 5. It states: 'Any action by the Community shall not go beyond what is necessary to achieve the objective of this Treaty'.

This requirement, an expression of the proportionality principle which permeates EC law, and which is restated in the Lisbon Treaty, may have an impact on the type of action proposed by the Community (and post Lisbon, the Union). Rather than adopting an approach which prescribes the obligations of the Member States in minute detail, this would require the Community simply to provide the outline, leaving the Member States to fill in the detail. This would follow the 'new' approach to harmonisation already adopted by the institutions to ensure the completion of the internal market. Article 149 (ex 126) EC, for example, also embodies this approach which requires the Community to support and supplement Member State action rather than prescribing rules with which Member States must comply. The Lisbon Treaty rephrased the proportionality provision, but to the same effect (Article 5(4) TEU, as amended by Lisbon).

3.5.5 Impact of proposed treaty reform: Different types of Union competence

We have seen that the distinction between exclusive and concurrent competence is key to the operation of subsidiarity but that there has been little clarity about the scope of the two groups of competence. The Commission has tended to take a broad view; individual Member States a narrower view. The Constitution addressed the matter, though whether it would have solved all the problems in this area is unlikely. It identified three main categories of competence: exclusive Union competence; competence shared between the Union and the Member States; and supporting, coordinating and supplementing competence. This approach would similarly be introduced by the Treaty of Lisbon (see Article 2 TFEU), as the relevant provisions in that treaty were based on Article I–12 of the Constitution. Note, however, that Lisbon (by contrast to the Constitution) makes express the point that Member States 'regain their competence to the extent that the Union has decided to cease exercising its competence' (Article 2(2) TFEU). Additionally (and as there were in the Constitution), there are specific provisions dealing with the coordination of economic and employment policies and the CFSP. One can thus suggest that although the three-pillar system will be abolished by the Treaty of Lisbon coming into force, the approach here re-emphasises that CFSP would still be a special case. There is no category of exclusive Member State competence, although Lisbon also makes express the point that competences not conferred upon the Union remain with the Member States (Article 4(1) TEU, as amended by Lisbon).

The Treaty of Lisbon then goes on to identify the policy areas which fall within two of the three categories of competence. Thus, according to Article 3 TFEU, exclusive competence comprises the customs union; the establishment of the competition rules necessary for the functioning of the internal market; monetary policy, for the Member States whose currency is currently the Euro; the conservation of marine biological resources under the common fisheries policy (presumably this means more than the conservation of fish stocks); and common commercial policy. Additionally, the Union would have exclusive competence for the conclusion of international agreements where such an agreement is provided for in a Union legislative act, or is necessary to enable the Union to exercise its internal competence. The wording of Lisbon in this regard has clear links to the jurisprudential position discussed at 3.2.4 above. The coordination competence concerns action in the areas of the protection and improvement of human health; industry; culture; tourism; education, youth, sport, and vocational training; civil protection; and administrative cooperation. Again this provision reflects the terms of the Constitution. Shared or joint competence is not listed exhaustively, probably because it seems the intention of the treaty is that this category of competence would be the default or fall-back position. The Constitution gives examples of shared competence, which includes the internal market and the area of freedom, security and justice. Interestingly, the Union has not been granted exclusive competence in areas relating to the creation of the internal market, for example, in free movement of goods, persons and services, although the Commission had argued for this position, presumably because of the potential breadth of internal market measures. Although these provisions have the advantage of relative brevity and simplicity, the real test would be likely to arise in the application of the provisions and the determination in individual cases of where the boundaries lie between the different types of competence. Note also that Lisbon specifies that the scope of the Union's respective competences is to be determined by the provisions specific to each area (Article 2(6) TFEU), that is the provisions which, inter alia, reflect the substantive provisions of the EC Treaty. In this, again, it reflects the approach taken by the Constitution. It may be that Lisbon would not solve difficult boundary problems; it would merely relocate them to a different part of the treaty.

3.6 Lawmaking process

As we have seen in Chapter 2, the legislative process involves three out of the five institutions: the Commission as initiator, the Council, and the Parliament. The relative importance of the Parliament's role varies according to the nature of the legislation and whether the legislation is to be made according to the consultation, the cooperation or the co-decision procedure.

3.6.1 Consultation procedure

This procedure requires that the Council consult the European Parliament before it adopts an act. Parliament's views must be considered but have no binding effect on the Council (see *Roquette Frères SA v Council* (case 138/79) discussed in Chapter 2). Indeed, the Council need give no reasons for its disregard of the Parliament's views. Until the SEA, consultation was the usual form of legislative process. It is still used in some areas, such as agriculture, and it has also been introduced into new areas in the TEU, ToA and even by Nice. Examples of these areas are economic and social cohesion (Article 159 EC) and economic and monetary policy (Articles 104 (14), 107 (6) and 117 EC). Some of these 'new' areas, such as Article 13 EC regarding non-discrimination, have now been amended so that they fall under the co-decision procedures. As noted, consultation now seems to be the exception, rather than the rule.

3.6.2 Cooperation procedure (Article 252 (ex 189c) EC)

This requires that the European Parliament be given the opportunity to propose amendments to the draft legislation.

First, the proposal is sent to both the Parliament and the Council. The Council agrees a common position on the proposal, after taking into account the opinion of the Parliament. Parliament then has a second opportunity to consider the draft proposal. It may agree with the common position of the Council. If this is the case, the Council may adopt the common position acting by QMV.

Alternatively, Parliament may propose amendments to the common position or reject it. Either way, the proposal is then returned to the Commission, to re-examine. The Commission produces a new draft adopting all, some, or none of Parliament's proposed amendments. The document is then sent to the Council. If the Council wishes to adopt the proposal in its new form, it may do so by QMV. If, however, it wishes to amend the proposal further (or even adopt the original agreed common position), it needs to act by unanimity. Although the Council ultimately has the final say, it can only overrule Parliament (and the Commission) if it acts unanimously. This procedure, which gave only limited powers to the Parliament, was criticised. The Council could still overrule Parliament; all Parliament could do, in the absence of agreement, was hinder the legislative process. Nonetheless, the procedure did result in changes in the way in which institutions operate, stimulating a greater dialogue, for example, between the Parliament on the one hand and the Commission and the Council on the other.

The cooperation procedure was introduced in limited but important areas, such as the single market provisions. TEU expanded the areas in which it was used, mainly by virtue of the introduction of new areas of Community competence. Post ToA and Nice, however, the cooperation has virtually disappeared, being virtually limited to certain aspects of monetary policy (eg, Article 102). Should Lisbon come into force, this procedure will effectively be abolished (monetary union becoming subject to co-decision procedure) and the current Article 252 will be repealed. In its place will be a general power for the institutions to cooperate, as apart of which they may conclude inter-institutional agreements.

3.6.3 Co-decision procedure (Article 251 (ex 189b) EC)

This procedure, which was introduced by the TEU and amended by ToA, improved the bargaining power of Parliament. Here, Parliament, as with the cooperation procedure, has two opportunities to view the proposal. At its simplest, both institutions can adopt the Commission's proposal unamended (see Fig 3.1). If Parliament approves the common position, the act is adopted (usually by QMV in the Council). The treaty does not expressly deal with the possibility of the Parliament rejecting a proposal at this stage, though the Parliament's internal rules envisage that possibility; in that case, the Parliament would ask the Commission to withdraw its proposal, though the Commission may refuse to do so.

The Parliament may propose amendments. The document is re-examined by the Commission, which may include or reject any or all of the Parliament's amendments in a new draft. The Council finalises its common position on the basis of the Commission's proposal. It may accept the new form of document acting by qualified majority (see Fig 3.2); if it does not act with the support of the Commission, unanimity is required. If is thus easier for the Council to adopt the suggestions of the Parliament than to agree its own proposals. If it does not accept the proposal it will adopt a common position, which is then sent to the Parliament for consideration. The Parliament may accept, reject, or propose amendments. In the case of amendments, these plus a Commission opinion come before the Council for second reading.

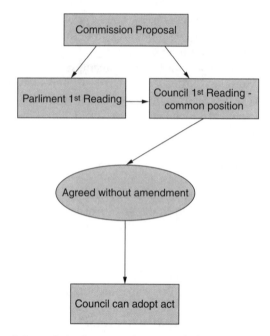

Fig 3.1 Adoption of Commission's proposal unamended

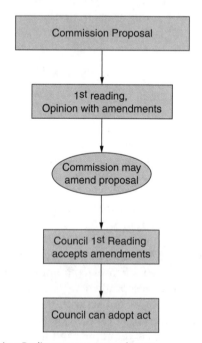

Fig 3.2 Adoption following Parliamentary amendment

If the Council does not adopt the new form of the proposal then the Conciliation Committee, made up of the members of the Council or their representatives and

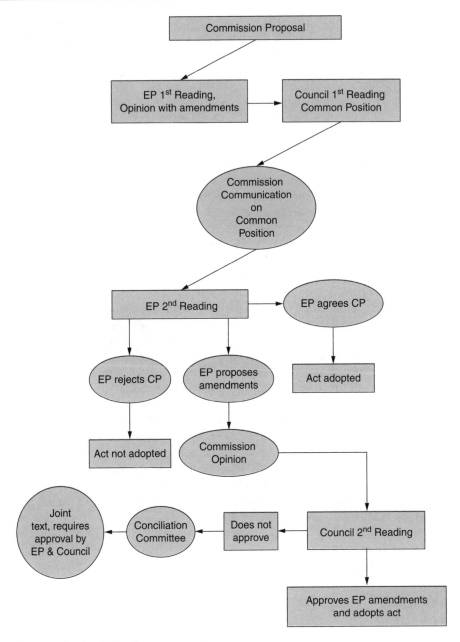

Fig 3.3 Adoption following compromise

an equal number of representatives of the Parliament, meets to try to reach a compromise (see Fig 3.3). If the Conciliation Committee approves a joint text, it is then sent to the Council and the Parliament. Both institutions must approve the text for it to be adopted; either (or both) may reject it. This is more problematic for the European Parliament than the Council as the representatives in the Conciliation Committee may not be representative of the Parliament as a whole.

Although the Council's common position may be affirmed, ultimately Parliament may veto a piece of legislation. It is also more difficult to ignore the Commission's views on the form of the amended proposal; if it wishes to do so, the Council must act unanimously. In giving the Parliament more power, the procedure might be seen as improving the democratic credentials of the Community but, post TEU, the procedure was not only long-winded and complex, it also only applied within specified policy areas.

The amendments introduced by the ToA went some way to improving this situation. The list of areas in which co-decision may be used have been increased; indeed, the cooperation procedure has virtually ceased to exist, a process taken further by Nice. Should the Lisbon Treaty come into force more areas will be dealt with by co-decision, renamed the 'ordinary legislative procedure'. Perhaps more importantly, the co-decision procedure was streamlined by the ToA and in such a way as to tilt the balance of power a little more in the direction of the Parliament. Prior to the ToA, in the event of the Parliament rejecting the Council's common position entirely at its second reading, the Conciliation Committee was convened at that stage to try to reach a solution. Now, in such an event, the act shall be deemed not to be adopted. The power of the Council to reaffirm its common position in the absence of agreement in the Conciliation Committee (albeit subject to rejection by Parliament), originally granted under TEU, was removed by the ToA. If the institutions fail to reach an agreement through the Conciliation Committee, the proposed legislation will fall.

Co-decision now seems to have given the Parliament real power within the legislative process, and in this it is not necessarily the impact of the use of the veto that is key, but the threat of the use of the veto. Thus representatives from the European Parliament can be involved in 'trialogues', which occur outside the formal treaty provisions whereby the three institutions try to negotiate an acceptable compromise before the Commission proposes a redraft. This occurred, for example, in the process of amending the Television without Frontiers Directive for the second time (now, the Audiovisual Media Services Directive). In being able to introduce amendments to the draft legislation, the Parliament has to some degree an agenda-setting role too; these amendments can also form part of the basis of discussions in the Conciliation Committee. Nonetheless, it is not without its critics. Even after the ToA changes, the procedure is complex. Co-decision, especially when the Conciliation Committee procedure is activated, adds to the length and complexity of the legislative process. The proceedings of the Conciliation Committee are not open to the public, which leads to questions as to how transparent and democratic the process actually is.

3.6.4 Assent

The assent procedure was also introduced by the SEA. As the name suggests, a measure to be adopted by the assent procedure may only be so adopted if the Parliament gives its consent. This procedure gives the Parliament considerable power and is used only in limited circumstances such as external relations (Article 300 EC; post Lisbon, 218 TFEU) and, post Nice, with the finding regarding the right to reject association agreements of a serious and persistent breach of fundamental rights by a Member State (Article 7 TEU). The disadvantage with this procedure is that there is no mechanism by which the Council and Parliament might resolve their differences: the only option for Parliament is to agree or block the proposal entirely.

3.6.5 **Delegation**

As noted in Chapter 2, Article 202 EC gives the Council the power to delegate 'powers for the implementation of the rules which the Council lays down' which Article 211 EC requires the Commission to so exercise. On one level this is relatively unproblematic. Many legal systems allow the delegation of powers to prevent the entire legislative process from being clogged up with matters of detail; such delegation also permits issues to be dealt with by experts. The current system often involves supervision of the Commission decisions in these areas by committees of national experts. This system is referred to as comitology (see Comitology Decision 1999/468/EC, [1999] OJ L184). The Commission has not appeared particularly happy with such oversight, suggesting in its White Paper on Governance (COM (2001) 428 final) that comitology committees should be removed. The difficulty is that the Community practice is not transparent and is problematic from a democratic perspective. Nonetheless, dispensing with the comitology committees, which allow some level of supervision by the Member States, albeit themselves unelected and non-accountable, would arguably remove whatever level of national or Council-based oversight there currently is. It is important to note that members of the committees of national experts see themselves as experts and not as national representatives. This can bring its own problems, as science and its interpretation is not neutral, notwithstanding claims of scientific objectivity. Despite these difficulties, the ECJ has confirmed that delegation to the Committee is permissible if the matter is one of implementation rather than determining general policy (case 25/70 *Koster*). Some of the difficulties about transparency and access were alleviated by reforms in 1999 which, inter alia, allowed for greater involvement by the European Parliament and, as we shall see below at 3.9.2, comitology committees are subject to the right of access to documents.

The Council may delegate powers to itself, to Member States, and to outside agencies. In such agencies, the Court has reviewed the permitted scope of the delegation closely, presumably to ensure that the institutional balance in the Community legal order is not affected. Delegation in these circumstances raises similar problems regarding democracy as delegation to the Commission.

3.6.6 **Matters of procedure**

In each case where the institutions have the power to enact legislation, the treaty specifies the type of legislation to be made and the procedures to be used. The treaty provision itself, or the procedure chosen, will specify whether the Council must act unanimously, by QMV, or by simple majority voting. Failure to abide by such requirements may give rise to an action for the annulment of the measure. The various combinations arising out of the possible permutations of the different voting procedures in Council, types of Community act and degrees of involvement of Parliament make the legislative process very complex. Despite attempts to do so, the various treaties have done little to improve this situation. In addition to encouraging judicial challenges, this complexity has been criticised as making the Union legal order impenetrable to the average lay person. The complexity is compounded by the fact the JHA and CFSP pillars use different procedures and different forms of legislation (see 3.7.9 below).

There are further restrictions on the making of Community acts. As noted at 3.5.1 above, the institutions can only act within the scope of the powers conferred on them. Community acts must make their legal basis within the treaty clear. They must 'state the reasons on which they are based and shall refer to any proposals or opinions which were required to be obtained pursuant to this Treaty' (Article 253 (ex 190) EC). This is done in the preamble to the legislation. It is an essential procedural requirement. Any act which does not comply will be subject to annulment (see Chapter 11, Article 230 (ex 173) EC, Chapter 10, Article 234 (ex 177) EC). Further, the freedom of the institutions to legislate is now counterbalanced by the notion of subsidiarity (Article 5 EC) (see 3.5.2 above). According to the protocol on subsidiarity annexed to the Lisbon Treaty, draft legislative acts should contain a detailed statement making it possible to appraise compliance with the principles of subsidiarity and proportionality. Acts will further be reviewed by national parliaments.

3.7 Legislative acts

The legislative powers of the Community institutions are laid down in Article 249 (ex 189) EC: 'In order to carry out their task the Council and the Commission shall, in accordance with the provisions of this Treaty, make regulations, issue directives, take decisions, make recommendations or deliver opinions'.

Article 249 EC was amended by the TEU to take into account Parliament's power of co-decision. Note that the other two pillars of the Union used different legal instruments to give effect to policy decisions. For example, under CFSP we see references to common positions and joint actions; under the JHA we see not only common positions but also framework decisions and conventions. Should the Lisbon Treaty come into force, the abolition of the pillar system will mean that in principle the types of legal act in use will be common to all areas of policy.

The measures in Article 249, described as 'acts', are defined as follows:

> A regulation shall have general application. It shall be binding in its entirety and directly applicable in all Member States.
>
> A directive shall be binding, as to the result to be achieved, upon each Member State to which it is addressed, but shall leave to the national authorities the choice of form and methods.
>
> A decision shall be binding in its entirety upon those to whom it is addressed.
> Recommendations and opinions shall have no binding force.

There is a division between binding and non-binding acts. Only the first three are binding. Non-binding acts can be seen as a form of soft law. Article 249 is open to criticism because, beyond this basic division, it does not provide a clear definition of each of the types of act. Nor does it distinguish between legislation and administrative acts, which most Member States' legal systems do. To a certain extent, it has fallen to the ECJ to fill in some of the detail. The Constitution proposed to change the types of act; this has been abandoned by the Lisbon Treaty, there being only a clarification of the definition of a decision.

3.7.1 Regulations

The principal feature of a regulation is its general application: it is a normative rather than an individual act, designed to apply to situations in the abstract. The ECJ has held that 'the Regulation, being of an essentially normative character, is applicable not to a limited identifiable number of persons but rather to categories of persons envisaged both in the abstract and as a whole' (joined cases 16 and 17/62 *Confédération Nationale des Producteurs de Fruits et Légumes v Council*). Since it is 'binding in its entirety and directly applicable in all Member States' it does not require further implementation to take effect. It may give rise to rights and obligations for states and individuals as it stands. Indeed, it has been held (*Leonesio v Ministero dell' Agricoltura e delle Foreste* (case 93/71)) that the rights bestowed by a regulation cannot be subjected, at the national level, to implementing provisions diverging from those laid down by the regulation itself.

3.7.2 Directives

A directive is binding 'as to the result to be achieved, upon each Member State to which it is addressed', but allows Member States a discretion as to the form and method of implementation. Thus it is a measure intended to be addressed to, and binding on states, either individually or collectively, but apparently requiring implementation by states before it can be fully effective in law. Indeed it seems that Member States are obliged to enact implementing measures rather than rely on the fact that pre-existing law or administrative practice complied with the requirements of the directive.

3.7.3 Decisions

A decision is an individual act designed to be addressed to a specified person or persons. As a 'binding' act it has the force of law and does not therefore require implementation in order to take effect. Decisions may be addressed to states or individuals.

3.7.4 Recommendations and opinions

Since they have no binding force, they are ineffective in law, although clearly of persuasive authority (see *Grimaldi* (case C–322/88) noted in Chapter 5).

3.7.5 Acts *sui generis*

Article 249 does not provide an exhaustive list of legal acts and the Court has recognised acts not identified by Article 249. These are usually described as *sui generis* acts and include rules relating to the internal management of the Community, such as rules of procedure.

3.7.6 Boundary between different types of act

The line between these acts is not as clear-cut as Article 249 would suggest. It was held in *Confédération Nationale des Producteurs de Fruits et Légumes v Council* (cases 16 and 17/62) that the true nature of an act is determined not by its form but by its content and object. The label attached to the measure is not decisive, and in the case of *International Fruit Co NV v Commission (No 1)* (cases 41–4/70) what was termed a regulation was found to comprise a 'bundle of decisions'. Measures have been found to be hybrid—to contain some parts in the nature of a regulation, and other parts in the nature of decisions (see Advocate-General Warner's submissions in *NTN Toyo Bearing Co Ltd v Council* (case 113/77)). In ascertaining the true nature of the act, the essential distinction seems to be between a regulation, which is nor-mative, applicable not to a limited identifiable number of designees but rather to categories of persons envisaged both in the abstract and as a whole, and a deci-sion, which concerns designated persons individually (*Confédération Nationale des Producteurs de Fruits et Légumes v Council*). The nature of a directive has not been called into question, but considerable controversy has arisen over its effects. These will be discussed in Chapter 5.

3.7.7 Publication

With regard to publication, Article 254 (ex 191) EC provides:

1. Regulations, directives and decisions adopted in accordance with the procedure re-ferred to in Article 251 [ex 189b] shall be signed by the President of the European Parliament and by the President of the Council and shall be published in the *Official Journal* of the Community. They shall enter into force on the date specified in them or, in the absence thereof, on the twentieth day following that of their publication.
2. Regulations of the Council and of the Commission, as well as directives of those in-stitutions which are addressed to all Member States shall be published in the *Official Journal* of the Community. They shall enter into force on the date specified in them or, in the absence thereof, on the twentieth day following that of their publication.
3. Other directives and decisions shall be notified to those to whom they are addressed and shall take effect upon such notification.

The majority of EC legislation must be published in the *Official Journal*.

3.7.8 Soft law

In addition to the above types of law specified in Article 249 (ex 189) EC, the Commission has, in recent years, used new ways of developing policy, for example, by issuing guidelines (for example, in the state-aid field—see Chapter 31). In the area of competition law, the Commission has issued notices. A notice provides guid-ance on the Commission's policy in particular fields but is non-binding. Therein lies the difficulty: while these documents are often of great importance and are re-lied on by individuals, as non-binding instruments they are not open to challenge before the Court of First Instance (CFI), although they have been challenged before national courts. Their creation is informal and ad hoc and not subject to the rules laid down in the treaty for the enactment of other forms of Community legislation. It is difficult to hold the policymakers to account and this has further implications for democracy.

Despite possible problems with informal approaches to lawmaking, a further move towards the use of soft-law methods can be seen following the conclusions of the Lisbon Council Summit (European Council 2002). There the European

Council formally established its Open Method of Coordination (OMC). This is a method of rule-making which allows for the agreement of policy guidelines through exchanges of information on best practice, benchmarking, monitoring, target-setting, and peer review. This approach potentially allows discretion on best practice to be exercised by national regulatory bodies. It has the disadvantage of other soft-law methods: OMC allows the democratic structures of the European Parliament to be bypassed, increasing concerns about any democratic deficit in policymaking.

Another change in the approach to regulation, perhaps in line with concerns about proportionality is the move towards co-regulation and self-regulation found the institutions' documents on better governance. This, too, raises concerns about who is making decisions about standards, on what basis and in whose interests.

3.7.9 Decision-making under JHA and CFSP

This book focuses mainly on the activities within the Community pillar. It is nonetheless important to have a understanding of the main points pertaining to the other pillars, especially given the increasing degree of cross-pillar policymaking and the proposed changes incorporated in the Lisbon Treaty. As noted in Chapter 1, the approach under pillars two and three is much more intergovernmental, particularly as regards CFSP.

3.7.9.1 *CFSP*

The European Council and the Council are the key players in CFSP, which is largely intergovernmental in approach; the role of the European Council is to identify the principles and general guidelines for the approach to be adopted in regard to relevant policies; the Council takes the decisions for defining and implementing the policy based on those guidelines (Article 13 TEU). Essentially, the role of the other institutions is that of observers. Article 21 TEU provides that the presidency shall consult the Parliament, and indeed, take its views into consideration. The European Parliament may also ask question or make recommendations (see also Article 22 TEU regarding the Commission). It has no legal power to change the outcome of Council choices though.

The mechanisms for pursuing the objectives of the CFSP are found in Article 12, which, in addition to noting the guidelines, lists common strategies, the adoption of joint actions, common positions, and the strengthening of systematic cooperation between the Member States in the conduct of policy. Although it is clear that legally binding instruments may be enacted as a result of Union action, their nature is not entirely clear; it is often suggested that they are best regarded as a form of international law, binding on the Member States and the institutions.

3.7.9.2 *JHA*

JHA is likewise more intergovernmental in form than the EC pillar with the main actor being the Council. Nonetheless, the other institutions do have a limited role; the Commission (under Article 34(2) TEU) has a right of initiative (as do individual Member States). The Council is required to consult the Parliament before adopting any measures (other than common positions) and, as under CFSP, the Parliament may ask questions and shall hold an annual debate on progress made. Article 34 identifies the types of measure which may be taken under this pillar:

- common positions
- framework decisions
- decisions
- conventions.

Framework decisions are similar to directives; they are binding as to the result but leave the means to the choice of the Member States. Unlike directives they are expressed not to have direct effect; indeed none of the measures can have direct effect, although the ECJ held that the principle of indirect effect might apply (*Pupino* (case C–105/03)—see Chapter 5). Decisions are also binding. Conventions are measures the Member States adopt in accordance with their respective national constitutions. The ECJ has jurisdiction to interpret and give rulings on the validity of framework decisions, decisions, and conventions, and on the measures implementing them, where Member States have accepted its jurisdiction in this regard. Article 34 would be repealed by Lisbon, and acts described in what is currently Art 249 EC would be used instead.

3.7.9.3 *Boundary between the pillars*

The boundary between the pillars is not clear cut, particularly with regard to the boundary between Title IV EC (Visas, asylum, immigration) and the JHA pillar. There are indeed provisions which allow for bridging between the two pillars (Article 42 TEU and Article 67(2) EC). Given the different powers of the various institutions under the different pillars, there has sometimes been dispute as to whether an action should properly be made under the EC Treaty or one of the other two pillars, the Commission in particular being keen to see matters being dealt with by the Community method. Although the ECJ does not have jurisdiction in the other two pillars, under Article 47 TEU it has jurisdiction to ensure that nothing in the TEU affects the EC Treaties, as variously amended. The ECJ has given a broad interpretation to the needs of the EC Treaties as can be seen by the following example.

In *Commission v Council* (moratorium on small arms) (case C–91/05), the Commission argued that both a decision and a joint action made under CFSP aimed at stopping the spread of small arms should be annulled on the basis that they encroached upon Community competence and therefore infringed Article 47 TEU. Although the Member States argued the ECJ had no jurisdiction to rule on the joint action, the ECJ maintained that Article 47 TEU covers any act with the potential to have legal effects which affects the EC Treaty. According to the ECJ, a measure so affects the EC Treaty whenever it could have been adopted under the EC Treaty, and it is irrelevant whether the Community has exclusive or shared competence in that area. Here, the Commission argued that the measure could have been adopted under development policy. The ECJ noted that, to fall within these provisions, it is necessary that the measure can contribute to the aims of the policy: the elimination or reduction of obstacles to the economic and social development objectives. It is also necessary that its main aims should not be the pursuit of the objectives of CFSP. The ECJ concluded that the decision aimed at objectives which fell within both CFSP and the EC, as proliferation of small arms is inimical to sustainable development. Although the CFSP element was legitimate, as there was a valid EC claim, Article 47 TEU was violated and the decision was annulled. This seems to be a very broad interpretation of the scope of EC powers. A similarly broad approach to Article 47 TEU has been taken with regard to the boundary between EC and JHA pillars. Perhaps in response to the ECJ's jurisprudence, which does not seem to place much emphasis on the structural differences between the policy areas arising from the pillar structure, the Lisbon Treaty specifically states that the treaties in the new unified structure are to be of equal value; currently, the position of the EC seems to be given priority by the ECJ's interpretation of Article 47 TEU.

3.8 Sources of EC law

The sources of EC law comprise the following:

(a) The EC Treaty and protocols, as amended by the succeeding treaties: Merger Treaty 1965; Acts of Accession 1972 (UK, Ireland, Denmark), 1979 (Greece), 1985 (Spain, Portugal), 1995 (Austria, Finland, Sweden); Budgetary Treaties 1970, 1975; SEA 1986; TEU 1992; ToA 1998; Treaty of Nice 2001; and Treaty of Accession 2003. Should the Lisbon Treaty come into force, it too will constitute a source of law via its amendment to the EC Treaty.

(b) EC secondary legislation in the form of regulations, directives, and decisions. Recommendations and opinions are of persuasive force only.

(c) Such international agreements as are entered into by Community institutions on behalf of the Community pursuant to their powers under the EC Treaty. These agreements may result from accession by the Community to existing agreements, such as GATT, or from new agreements such as the Lomé Convention. Conventions entered into by Member States, on the other hand, even though entered into pursuant to the EC Treaty, Article 293 (ex 220) EC, cannot be considered as forming part of Community law. Despite the apparent clarity of the provision, there has been some erosion of this principle. Note that some international human-rights treaties have been found to inspire principles of Community law (see further Chapter 6). Further, the Commission has suggested that the UN Convention on the International Sale of Goods, to which some but not all Member States are parties, should be viewed as Community law.

(d) Judicial legislation. This comprises the entire jurisprudence of the European Courts, embracing not only decisions, but general principles and even expressions of opinion, provided they concern matters of *Community law* and now, to a limited extent, some aspects of Union law. The importance and the extent of the Court of Justice's contribution to the corpus of EC law will become apparent in the course of this book. This jurisprudence on the interpretation of treaty provisions will remain good law should the Lisbon Treaty come into force in respect of the interpretation of the comparable provisions of that treaty.

As a matter of international law, the law arising from all these sources is binding on Member States, which are obliged under Article 10 (ex 5) EC to 'take all appropriate measures, whether general or particular, to ensure fulfilment' of all these obligations. Special provision was made for certain provisions of the EC Treaty to apply to countries linked to Member States by particular association agreements (Article 229 and Annex II (ex 227 and Annex IV)).

Since the UK is dualist in its approach to international law—that is, it does not regard international law as part of its domestic legal system unless it is incorporated by an Act of Parliament—EC law did not become binding in the UK as a matter of *internal* law until incorporated by the European Communities Act 1972.

3.9 Problems in the lawmaking process

Prior to the 1996 IGC leading to the ToA, a reflection group was established to consider the issues that needed addressing. Its reports revealed that the central issues which the IGC had to tackle were democracy, transparency and, as already discussed in Chapter 2, efficiency. We will look mainly at the first two of these issues, identifying the problem as presented at the IGC and then assessing what not only the ToA has done to improve the position, but also the impact of the Nice Treaty. The significance of both the Constitution and the Treaty of Lisbon will be briefly reviewed where relevant.

3.9.1 Democracy

The EC decision-making process has often been criticised for its lack of democratic legitimacy. This is frequently referred to as the 'democratic deficit'. Before we go on to look at some specific issues, some have suggested that this criticism, in fact, is misplaced. On this basis the European constitutional settlement is focused on the limited powers of the EU both in terms of the type of power exercised and the salience of those powers. The first aspect concerns the argument that the EU policies are focused on regulatory aspects, which are efficiency-enhancing and therefore wealth-creating, rather than redistributive. Greater legitimacy is required for the latter type of policy because in redistribution one group loses out to the benefit of another; with efficiency-enhancing policies, in theory, everyone benefits. This gives efficiency-enhancing policies output legitimacy. The salience argument states that the policies dealt with by the EU are of low interest to voters and therefore it makes sense to leave such issues to the technocratic approach. Unfortunately, these arguments are based on an assumption of limited competence which does not reflect the growth of Union powers. Criminal law, for example, a matter of great concern to the general populace, falls within Union competence; public services are likewise affected by internal market and competition provisions. This theory has therefore been much criticised.

The problem of democratic legitimacy has bedevilled the Community (and the Union) for some time. One of the reasons for the introduction of European citizenship, it seems, was a desire to create a greater connection between individuals and the Community/Union. This developed the direct link between individual and Community introduced with direct elections to the Parliament. Nonetheless, concerns—and the attempts to address them—remained, and the democratic legitimacy of the Union was one of the central themes of the Constitution. Not only was one of the Union's values expressed to be a respect for democracy (Article I–2), which was not new, but a separate title, Title VI, in Part I of the Constitution was entitled 'The Democratic Life of the Union', emphasising the significance of democracy within the Union order. This has been reformulated in the Lisbon Treaty as a new title, 'Provisions on Democratic Principles'. In particular, Article I–46(1) stated that 'the functioning of the Union shall be founded on representative democracy', and this is now found, word for word, in Article 19(1) TEU (as amended by Lisbon) though the obligation on the institutions is stated to be to involve citizens by 'appropriate means' (Article I–47(1) of the Constitution, restated by Lisbon at Article 11(1) TEU), without specifying those means. The issues to be addressed are whether Lisbon adds anything new and the effect of new provisions; are they merely words with little impact?

One of the main concerns is the lack of democratic accountability of the institutions. The Commission is not elected at all, the Commissioners being political appointments by individual Member States. As we have seen in Chapter 2, however, changes have been made to increase the European Parliament's control over the appointment process. Although the Council of Ministers usually constitutes members of the national parliaments, those members tend not to have been elected for the purpose of serving as a member of the Council of Ministers. As noted in Chapter 2, any control is therefore indirect and only over the individual members rather than the Council as a body. The Belgian people will only have control over the Belgian ministers but not, for example, the Danish ministers. Ministers can avoid taking responsibility for a decision by passing it on to ministers of the other Member States. The quality of democratic control will rest with each of the national parliaments, so its standard may well vary throughout the Union.

Another concern is the use of non-elected bodies in the decision-making process. There are many of these, for example ECOSOC and the Committee of the Regions. These fulfil an advisory role only. Of more concern here is COREPER, which plays an important role in filtering out the non-contentious issues. It has been argued that in so doing, although technically the final decision is the Council's, in effect COREPER is functioning as a decision-making body. In deciding whether issues are contentious or not, COREPER frames the terms of the debate in Council, potentially having the effect of discouraging debate on certain issues. The role of COREPER is likely to remain strong.

The only directly elected body, the Parliament, has historically been the weakest of the institutions involved in the decision-making process. Admittedly, the TEU improved the position by increasing the control of Parliament over the Commission, introducing the Ombudsman and introducing the co-decision procedure. This latter, however, operated only in limited areas. We have seen that the ToA and Nice increased the areas in which co-decision is used and that the ToA amended the procedure so as to limit further the Council's power under this procedure. Both of these moves can be seen as improving the democratic legitimacy of the Community, though, of course, problems have been noted regarding the operation of the conciliation committee. The Treaty of Lisbon would bring a further shift in the areas in which co-decision is be used. Significantly, the co-decision procedure would also be renamed, 'ordinary legislative procedure'. This change in terminology re-emphasises the fact that it is this procedure, which requires the greatest level of involvement of the European Parliament, that should be the normal or default form of lawmaking in the Union.

Further increases in powers relate to the appointment of the Commission (discussed in Chapter 2). Although the Parliament's powers in the second and third pillars remain limited, the transfer of the powers formerly contained in the TEU or the Schengen Agreement to the Community also brought issues which were dealt with in an intergovernmental and therefore undemocratic manner within the comparatively democratic system of the EC. The incorporation of Schengen brought its own problems, however. The protocol incorporating the Schengen *acquis* gave the force of law to decisions made under Schengen. Not only does the protocol not identify a full list of such texts, but also some of these decisions were made, following the old Schengen procedures, in secret by unelected bureaucrats rather than by politicians. This gives rise to concerns about the democratic accountability of the people who made these decisions; it also raises questions about respect for the rule of law within the Union. Comitology, as noted at 3.6.5 above and in Chapter 2, continues to give rise to similar concerns. Similarly, the changes to the articles relating to COREPER confirmed that it may make procedural decisions, although it remains unaccountable. The ECJ has no jurisdiction to review acts of COREPER. Furthermore, its jurisdiction in relation to the new free-movement-of-persons provision is limited and is subject to an exception in the interests of 'national security'. We have seen that the Treaty of Lisbon proposes changes in this area, providing at least a constitutional framework for the exercise of delegated powers even if there are some concerns about where the boundary between legislative and executive acts lies.

One problem with relying on the European Parliament to assuage democratic concerns is the 'no demos' theory. This posits that, for democracy to work, there needs to be a 'demos', or a group of people. The common membership of the group is such that members of that group allow their own interests sometimes to be outweighed by the interests of others. It is suggested that what we have within the EU is actually a multitude of groups of people—so we see the crucial plural in the phrase 'peoples of the Union' and on this basis there is no common demos across the EU which the institutions, particularly, the European Parliament might represent. This is a theoretical criticism which no amount of tinkering with the powers of the European Parliament can solve.

One might suggest that the national parliaments could compensate for some of the European Parliament's weaknesses. There are difficulties with this suggestion. The main problem is that, at the level of individual pieces of legislation, national parliaments became involved in the process too late to have any real impact on the outcome, and the level of control exercised by the individual national parliaments may vary significantly between Member States. The problems in this context were apparent even at the time of the TEU: a declaration (No 13) which was attached to that treaty emphasised the importance of giving a greater role to the national parliaments. The ToA took this point up with a protocol, which provided that draft legislation must be circulated to each national parliament at least six weeks before it can be considered by the Council. The position was still clearly unsatisfactory and the role of the national parliaments continued to be a subject of debate in the

Convention on the Future of Europe. As noted in the discussion of subsidiarity, the Treaty of Lisbon envisages a greater role for the involvement of national parliaments prior to the enactment of European legislation, with the introduction of the 'yellow card' system. Although we might still comment that there could be variation in the level of oversight, with national parliaments perhaps having neither the time nor the inclination to review Union legislation thoroughly, at least in Lisbon's framework national parliaments would have the possibility of having a voice in the legislative process.

3.9.2 Transparency

The complexity of the legislative procedures means that decision-making is not transparent. Consequently, it is difficult for individuals to become involved in the process and to hold the decision-makers accountable. The suggestion was to simplify these procedures, without altering the institutional balance. Similarly, improvements could be made in the way documents are drafted and made available. A Council resolution on plain language was passed in 1993 ([1993] OJ C166), but the position did not improve much. ECOSOC subsequently made an own-initiative resolution on plain language, requesting that the Commission make attempts actually to comply with the 1993 Council resolution on the same subject, arguably to as little effect. The Commission has also been aware of the concern, producing annual reports on 'Better Lawmaking' together with various initiatives on simplifying legislation in specific areas. In this context, subsidiarity and proportionality may also have a role to play in determining the scope and style of legislation. The need to take action was re-emphasised by the *White Paper on Governance* (COM (2001) 428 final).

The availability of documents is another part of the overall problem revolving round the way the decision-making process, particularly at Council level, operates. The complaint is that, because the Council operated behind closed doors, it was not possible for the citizen to identify who is agreeing to which proposals or the basis on which this is done. The counter-argument that has always been raised is that if Council meetings were completely open to the public gaze, it would make it difficult for the ministers to reach decisions as many of the compromises made are politically sensitive. However, some changes have been made.

In 1993, a Code of Conduct regarding public access to Council and Commission documents was published (93/730/EC; see also Council Decision 93/731/EC, [1993] OJ L340). The significance of this was emphasised by *Carvel v Council* (case T–194/94). This case relied on the Code of Practice to seek the annulment of a Council decision refusing to reveal Council meeting minutes to the applicant. The CFI held that although the Code might permit the withholding of documents when certain specified interests would be threatened by their disclosure, this is not automatic. The rights of citizens to see documents must be balanced against the other interests. In this case the Council had *automatically* refused to reveal the minutes on the basis that all minutes are confidential. Since there was no attempt to take the claims of the applicant into account, the Council was therefore held to be in breach of the Code. Although this did not mean that citizens have an automatic right to see all documents, it was a step forward in that the Council has to consider whether it is proper to refuse access, arguably changing the attitude of ministers towards the release of non-controversial information. In addition, the Council agreed, amongst other points, that the outcome of votes on legislative acts should be made public, that debates on issues of public significance will be broadcast, and that access to the minutes of meetings will be facilitated (Bull 5-1995, 1.9.5). Subsequent case law has made it clear that exceptions to the rights are to be construed narrowly, a point made expressly in *WWF* (case T–105/95), and clarified certain points not covered by Council Decision 93/731 and Commission Decision 94/90. For example, in *Rothmans* (case T–188/97), the CFI held that comitology committees were covered by the right of access to documents. Further, institutions should consider whether partial access to documents is possible where full disclosure is not (*Mattila* (case C–353/01P).

Again, there has been some progress in attempting to ensure transparency of following the ToA, but equally, some difficulties arise. Looking at the progress first, the streamlining of the co-decision procedure and the virtual removal of the cooperation procedure (this remains in monetary policy areas only) makes the legislative process simpler and, as a consequence, more transparent. A declaration annexed to ToA re-emphasises the points made in the Council resolution on plain language referred to above. It goes on to state that the institutions ought to establish by common accord guidelines for improving the drafting of Community legislation. Whether such guidelines will have much impact in practice is another question, although the declaration also obliges the institutions to take the internal organisational measures necessary to make sure the guidelines are properly carried out. Clarifying and codifying Community legislation will, it is to be hoped, improve transparency. Additionally, we have already noted the impact of other initiatives regarding the approach to drafting and legislation in relation to the types of legal act available should the Constitution come into force, and the use of soft law.

Article 255 EC provides that 'any citizen, and any natural or legal person residing or having its registered office in a Member State, shall have a right of access to European Parliament, Council and Commission documents'. Thus, all the institutions must amend their own rules of procedure to allow access to documents. Access to Council documents is particularly important. Article 207 EC provides that, within the limits set down by the needs of efficient decision-making, documents involved in the legislative process should be accessible to the public and that, in any event, the results of the vote, explanations of the vote, together with any statements in the minutes, shall be made public. Although it does not clarify what the needs of 'efficient decision-making' are, it is still to be hoped that this provision will increase the accountability of the ministers in the Council to their national parliaments, as individuals will be able to identify how the individual representatives of the Member States voted. The right to access documents is, however, subject to limitation in the public or private interest (Article 255(2) EC).

Article 255(2) EC specified that a legal instrument was to be enacted under the co-decision procedure to give effect to the principle in Article 255(1). Regulation 1049/2001 on Access to Information was finally adopted on 30 May 2001 after a troubled negotiation period, which included the proposal by the Commission of a draft regulation without any public consultation and the amendment of the Council's earlier decision on access to documents by the introduction of further categories of mandatory public-interest exception.

Nonetheless, agreement on a form of regulation has been reached, even if there is some dissent on an assessment of its usefulness. Article 2(3) of the regulation provides that public access will apply to all documents *held* by an institution and not just those which it drafted. This principle applies not just to the EC, but also to the other two pillars. Article 11 obliged the institutions to draw up a public register of documents by 3 June 2002. Article 4 contains a list of exceptions, comprising nine different categories divided into three groups.

The first group consists of public security; defence and military matters; international relations; financial, economic, or monetary policy of the Community or a Member State; and privacy and integrity of an individual (especially regarding personal data). Article 4(1) specifies that the appropriate test for determining whether access should be allowed to documents in any of these categories is whether public access would undermine the protection of the public interest. Article 9 provides for extra protection of the public interest in relation to 'sensitive documents' dealing with issues falling in Article 4(1)(a).

The second group of concerns (Article 4(2)) comprises the commercial interests of private persons; court proceedings and legal advice; and inspections, investigations and audits. The test here is whether public access would undermine the protection of one of these interests themselves.

Finally, Article 4(3) provides that documents relating to a matter on which a decision has not yet been taken 'shall be refused if the disclosure of the document would seriously undermine the institution's decision-making process, unless there is an overriding public interest in disclosure'. It is still too early to tell what impact this regulation will have in practice. The ECJ has regularly ruled in cases involving the interpretation of this regulation that exceptions to the right of access to documents must be interpreted strictly, and the assessment must be made on the facts of each individual case. Thus the fact that a document falls into a particular category of document cannot of itself trigger the application of the claimed exception (*Sweden v Commission* (case C–65/05 P)). Thus the fact that a document is entitled 'legal advice' does not automatically bring it within the exception in Article 4(2). In this case (*Sweden and Turco v Council* (joined cases C–39/05 P and C–52/05 P)), the Council argued that a refusal to disclose an opinion from the legal service on the legality of a proposed legislative measure was justified, as otherwise there would remain lingering uncertainty as to the legality of that measure. The CFI accepted this reasoning, but the ECJ did not. The ECJ emphasised that access of documents was necessary for the conferring of legitimacy on the institutions and their workings in the eyes of European citizens; it is a lack of information and of debate which is contributing to the perceived lack of legitimacy of the decision-making process overall. Even though Article 4(2) accepted that the institutions needed to be able to access frank legal advice, the institutions may not rely on the exception by making broad assertions without more evidence. In coming to its decision, the ECJ re-emphasised the three stage approach for assessing disclosure: (1) identify which documents are covered by the exception; (2) identify the relevant Community interest; and (3) balance the right of access against the Community interest. Crucially, a reasoned decision must be given. The problem here is in the approach to balancing; the ECJ in adopting its balancing text in this context is neutral; the problem is the initial decision is made by an institution that has an interest in the outcome, and whose perception of the relevant weighting of interests may be affected by that fact. As well as emphasising the links between transparency and democracy, this case illustrates the differences in approaches between the institutions and some of the Member States. The regulation is currently under review and again progress has not been straightforward as there are tensions within the Council and between the Council and the Parliament.

It is questionable whether transparency is a general principle of Union law. The Advocate-General suggested it should be viewed as such in *Hautala v Council* (case C–353/99P), but the ECJ expressly rejected this idea. This is surprising as the right of access is found in the European Charter. The significance of transparency has been highlighted again more recently (see, eg, *Sweden v Council* (cases C–39 and 52/05 P)). Further, the Constitution emphasised transparency as part of its title on democracy. The institutions in general are under an obligation to 'conduct their work as openly as possible' and this has been retained by the Treaty of Lisbon in Article 24 TFEU in line with the stated intention to extend openness and transparency. Although we might suggest that the use of the proviso, 'as possible', undercuts the obligation considerably, Article 24(2) TFEU specifies that the European Parliament should meet in public, as should the Council when considering and voting on a draft legislative act. Article 24(3) TFEU embodies the right of access to information introduced by Article 255. In practice, most bodies have already adopted rules on access to documents, with the exception of the ECJ and the European Council.

3.9.3 Efficiency

The institutions have also been criticised for being inefficient, especially as regards the time-consuming need to reach unanimity. This problem can only get worse with enlargement of the Union. QMV was extended to new policy areas by both ToA and Nice and Lisbon continues this trend. Notwithstanding this development, difficulties remain. Notably, the Community lawmaking processes remain extremely complex, inevitably taking considerable time to reach agreement. This is compounded by the need to work in all official languages. The number of languages has risen and will rise again with enlargement and, although it is likely that not all documents will be translated into all languages, all legally binding documents of general application, as the situation currently stands, will be. In addition to problems relating to efficiency, the need to translate into all official languages increases the risk of small differences in meaning of key terms between the different language versions. (See also Chapter 10.)

3.10 Conclusions

The Community has the competence to make law in a broad range of areas, albeit constrained by a procedural framework. It is perhaps this breadth of scope that has led to concern about the law-making procedures. As a result of this, successive treaty revisions have amended the lawmaking procedures, which have affected the institutional balance. Over the years, the role of the European Parliament has increased, arguably increasing the Community's democratic credentials, if not those of the Union, as a result. Whether the increase in power of the European Parliament is sufficient to assuage concerns about mission creep is debatable; within the Treaty of Lisbon there is a clear endeavour to ensure that the Union is understood to be a creature of conferred powers. Nonetheless, problems with the efficiency, democratic accountability and transparency of the procedures remain, as a glance at the issues dealt with by the Convention on the Future of Europe and the resulting Constitution and its successor, the Lisbon Treaty, illustrate. There are, however, other concerns: in particular, the vexed question of the proper scope of Community competence. There are two main aspects to this issue. The first is the identification of exclusive and concurrent competence, particularly important in the context of subsidiarity. The second is the question of how 'complementary competence'—those additional areas of Community competence in which the Community's role is to support the activities of Member States—should be dealt with. Although Lisbon attempts to deal with these, even if it comes into force, it is unlikely to solve all these difficulties that have dogged the Community for some period, especially given the fact that the Community (and Union) legal order has changed and continues to change over time. It is to be hoped, however, that some of these problems will be ameliorated.

FURTHER READING

Bradley, K St Clair, 'Comitology and the law: Through a glass darkly' (1992) 29 CML Rev 693.

Craig, P, 'The hierarchy of norms' in T Tridimas and P Nebbia (eds), *European Law for the Twenty-first Century* (Hart Publishing, 2004).

Curtin, D, 'The constitutional structure of the Union: A Europe of bits and pieces' (1993) 30 CML Rev 170.

Dashwood, A, 'The limits of European Community powers' (1996) 21 EL Rev 113.

——, 'States in the European Union' (1998) 23 EL Rev 201.

Davies, G, 'Subsidiarity: The wrong idea, in the wrong place, at the wrong time' (2006) 43 CMLRev 63.

De Burca, G, 'The quest for legitimacy in the European Union' (1996) 59 MLR 349.

De Burca, G, and Scott, J (eds), *Law and New Governance in the EU and US* (Hart, 2006).

Dryberg, P, 'Current issues in the debate on public access to documents' (1999) 24 EL Rev 3.

Emilou, N, 'Subsidiarity: An effective barrier against enterprises of ambition' (1992) 29 CML Rev 383.

Follesdal, A and Hix, S, 'Why there is a democratic deficit in the EU: A response to Majone and Moravcsik' (2006) 44 JCMS 533

Klabbers J, 'Informal instruments before the European Court of Justice' (1994) 31 CML Rev 997

Koopmans, T, 'The role of law in the next stage of European integration' (1986) 35 ICLQ 925.

Lane, R, 'New competences and the Maastricht Treaty' (1993) 30 CML Rev 939.

Lenaerts, K and Verhoeven, A, 'Towards a legal framework for executive rule-making in the EU' (2000) 37 CML Rev 645.

Majone, G, 'Unity in diversity: European integration and the enlargement process' (2008) 33 EL Rev 457.

Mancini, GF, 'The making of a constitution for Europe' (1989) 26 CML Rev 594.

Obradovic, D, 'Repatriation of powers in the European Community' (1997) 34 CML Rev 59.

O'Keeffe, D and Twomey, P (eds), *Legal Issues of the Maastricht Treaty* (Wiley Chancery Law, 1994).

Peers, S, 'Justice and home affairs: Decision-making after Amsterdam' (2000) 23 EL Rev 183.

Peers, S, *EU Justice and Home Affairs*, 2nd edn (OUP, 2006), Ch 2.

Rasmussen, H, *On Law and Policy-making in the European Communities* (1986) Nijhoff Publications, 1986.

Scott, J and Trubeck, D, 'Mind the gap: Law and new approaches to governance in the European Union' (2002) 8 ELJ 1.

Swaine, ET, 'Subsidiarity and self interest: Federalism at the European Court of Justice' (2000) 41 Harv Int'l LJ 1.

Usher, J, 'Variable geometry or concentric circles: Patterns for the European Union' (1997) 46 ICLQ 243.

Zuleeg, M, 'Cohesion and democracy in the US and EC' (1997) 45 Am J Comp L 505.

4

Principle of supremacy of EC law

4.1 Introduction

The wide scope of the EC Treaty, covering a number of areas normally reserved to national law alone, coupled with the extended application by the European Court of Justice (ECJ) of the principle of direct effects (discussed in Chapter 5), led inevitably to a situation of conflict between national and EC law. In such a case, which law was to prevail? The way in which that conflict was resolved was of crucial importance to the Community legal order; it was a constitutional problem of some magnitude for Member States as it affects our understanding not only of the relationship between Member States and what is now the Union, but also their respective autonomy and sovereignty. In one sense, this is a tale of a power struggle or the story of the birth of a new form of legal order. After considering the position in traditional international law, this chapter will review the development of the ECJ's case law on supremacy of Community law and identify the problems from the perspective of the national courts. Finally, we will consider the potential impact of the Constitution and of the Lisbon Treaty, should that treaty come into force and ask the question of whether in future we should talk of the supremacy of EU law.

4.2 The problem of priorities

The EC Treaty (and the Treaty on European Union (TEU)) is silent on the issue of which law should in the case of conflict take priority, and always has been. Perhaps this was a diplomatic omission; perhaps it was not thought necessary to make the matter explicit, since the extent to which Community law might be directly effective was not envisaged at the time of signing the treaty. In the absence of guidance, the matter was left to be decided by the courts of Member States, assisted by the ECJ in its jurisdiction under Article 234 EC (ex 177; post Lisbon, Article 254 TFEU) (see Chapter 10). As with the concept of direct effects, the ECJ has proved extremely influential in developing the law.

The question of priorities between directly effective international law and domestic law is normally seen as a matter of national law, to be determined according to the constitutional rules of the state concerned. It will depend on a number of factors. Primarily it will depend on the terms on which international law has been incorporated into domestic law, which in turn will depend on whether the state is monist or dualist in its approach to international law. If monist, it will be received automatically into national law from the moment of its ratification, without the need for further measures of incorporation. If dualist, international law will not become binding internally, as part of domestic law, until it is incorporated by a domestic statute. In the EU, France, for example, is monist; Germany, Belgium, Italy, and the UK are dualist. But whether received automatically, by process of 'adoption', or incorporated by statute, by way of 'transformation', the incorporation of international law does not itself settle the question of priorities. The status accorded to international law will depend, in the case of each state, on the extent to which that state has provided for this, either in its constitution, where it has a written constitution, or, where it has no written constitution, in its statute of incorporation.

There is wide variation in the way in which, and the extent to which, Member States of the Union have provided for this question of priorities. Where states have a written constitution, there will be express provision for this issue. At the time of their accession, it ranged from the wholehearted acceptance of international law of the Dutch Constitution (Article 66), which accords supremacy to *all* forms of international law, whether prior or subsequent to domestic law, to Article 55 of the French Constitution, which, at that time, provided that treaties or agreements duly ratified 'have authority superior to that of laws' (thus leaving open the question of secondary legislation), to Article 24 of the German Constitution (Grundgesetz (GG)), which provided, rather loosely, that the state 'may transfer sovereign powers' to international organisations (although Article 23 GG has been introduced to deal specifically with the EU); or Article 11 of the Italian Constitution whereby the state 'consents, on conditions of reciprocity with other States, to limitations of sovereignty necessary for an arrangement which may ensure peace and justice between the nations'. (Under the principle of reciprocity, if one party to an agreement breaches his obligations, the other contracting parties may regard themselves as entitled to be relieved of theirs.)

A state which does not have a written constitution, and which is dualist, such as the UK, must provide for priorities in the statute of incorporation itself. This statute will have the same status as any other statute. As such it will be vulnerable to the doctrine of implied repeal, or *lex posterior derogat priori*, whereby any inconsistency between an earlier and a later statute is resolved in favour of the latter. The later statute is deemed to have impliedly repealed the earlier one (see *Ellen Street Estates Ltd v Minister of Health* [1934] 1 KB 590). On a strict application of this doctrine, any provision of a domestic statute passed subsequent to the statute incorporating EC law, in the British case the European Communities Act 1972, which was inconsistent with EC law, would take priority (see further 4.4.1. below). The British courts have, however, come up with their own solutions to this problem, involving the introduction of a distinction between different types of statute, whereby 'constitutional' Acts will not be repealed by subsequent statutes unless that is express in the terms of the subsequent statute (*Metric Martyrs* case, *Thoburn v Sunderland CC* [2003] QB 151, QBD, see further 4.4.2. below.)

Given the differences from state to state it is clear that if national courts were to apply their own constitutional rules to the question of priorities between domestic law and EC law, there would be no uniformity of application, and the primacy of EC law could not be guaranteed throughout the Community. This was the principal reason advanced by Advocate-General Roemer in *Van Gend en Loos* (case 26/62) for denying the direct effects of what was then Article 12 EEC (now 25 EC; post Lisbon, Article 30 TFEU). Not only would this weaken the effect of Community law, it would undermine solidarity among the Member States, and in the end threaten the Community itself.

Thus, for the EC supremacy was central its effectiveness, if not its existence. It is no doubt reasons such as these which led the ECJ to develop its own constitutional rules to deal with the problem, in particular the principle of supremacy, or primacy, of EC law.

4.3 The Court of Justice's contribution

4.3.1 Development of the principle of supremacy

The first cautious statement of the principle of supremacy of EC law came in the case of *Van Gend en Loos* (case 26/62). The principal question in the case was the question of the direct effects of Article 25 (ex 12) EC. The conflict, assuming that article were found directly effective, was between Article 25 and an *earlier* Dutch law. Under Dutch law, if Article 25 were directly effective it would, under the Dutch Constitution, take precedence over domestic law. So the questions referred to the ECJ under Article 234 did not raise the issue of sovereignty directly. Nevertheless, in addition to declaring that what is now Article 25 was directly effective, the Court went on to say that 'the Community constitutes a new legal order in international law, for whose benefit the States have limited their sovereign rights, albeit within limited fields'.

Although the main emphasis of the judgment relates to the doctrine of direct effect, it is also significant because, by referring to the 'new legal order', the ECJ indicated that the Community was not just a 'normal' international law organisation. In particular, the Community had an independent status as well as, arguably, greater impact on the national legal systems of the Member States. It is difficult to overstate the importance of this step from treaty organisation to independent legal order.

The conflict in *Costa v ENEL* (case 6/64) posed a more difficult problem for the Italian courts. This case too involved an alleged conflict between a number of treaty provisions and an Italian statute nationalising the electricity company of which the defendant, Signor Costa, was a shareholder, but here the Italian law was later in time than the treaty provision. On being brought before the Milan *tribunale* for refusing to pay his bill (the princely sum of L1,925, or approximately £1.10), Signor Costa argued that the company was in breach of EC law. The defendants argued *lex posterior*; the Italian Act nationalising the electricity company was later in time than the Italian Ratification Act, the Act incorporating EC law, and therefore took priority. The Italian court referred this question of priorities to the ECJ. It also referred the matter to its own constitutional court. This time the principle of supremacy was clearly affirmed by the Court. It cited *Van Gend*; the Member States had 'limited their sovereign rights'. It went further. It looked to the treaty and noted that Article 249 (ex 189; post Lisbon, Article 288 TFEU) indicated that there had been a transfer of powers to the Community institutions; Article 10 (ex 5; post Lisbon, Article 4 TFEU) underlined Member States' commitment to observe Community law. The Court concluded:

> The reception, within the laws of each Member State, of provisions having a Community source, and more particularly of the terms and of the spirit of the Treaty, has as a corollary the impossibility, for the Member State, to give preference to a unilateral and *subsequent* measure against a legal order accepted by them on a basis of reciprocity . . .

Such a measure cannot be inconsistent with that legal system. The executive force of Community law cannot vary from one State to another in deference to subsequent domestic laws, without jeopardizing the attainment of the objectives of the Treaty . . .

The obligations undertaken under the Treaty establishing the Community would not be unconditional, but merely contingent, if they could be called into question by subsequent legislative acts of the signatories . . .

It follows from all these observations that the law stemming from the Treaty, an independent source of law, could not, because of its special and original nature, be overridden by domestic legal provisions, however framed, without being deprived of its character as Community law and without the legal basis of the Community itself being called into question.

The transfer, by Member States, from their national orders in favour of the Community order of the rights and obligations arising from the Treaty, carries with it a clear limitation of their sovereign right upon which a *subsequent* unilateral law, incompatible with the aims of the Community, cannot prevail. [Emphasis added.]

The reasoning used by the ECJ is worthy of note as, in developing its argument, the ECJ uses a teleological—or purposive—approach that is not tied in particularly closely to the actual wording of the treaty. The ECJ's substantive arguments can be divided into two main groups:

(a) those relating to the *nature* of the Community

(b) those relating to the *purposes* of the Community.

The first category comprises the ECJ's assertion about the independent nature of the new Community legal order and the mechanism by which this legal order was created: the permanent limitation of Member States' sovereign rights. There is no express basis in the treaty for either of these points. The other arguments, referring to the aims of the treaty, are more practical. They look to the purpose of the Community and the need to ensure that those goals are not undermined. These arguments are based on the need to make Community law effective. Effectiveness itself becomes a leitmotif of the ECJ's judgments in many areas and while it might sound merely pragmatic, it has had a huge influence on the development of Community law (see further Chapter 8).

In the case of *Internationale Handelsgesellschaft mbH* (case 11/70) the Court went even further. Here, the conflict was between not a treaty provision and a domestic statute, but between an EC regulation and provisions of the German Constitution. The claimant argued that the regulation infringed, inter alia, the principle of proportionality enshrined in the German Constitution and sought to nullify the regulation on those grounds. Normally, any ordinary law in breach of the constitution is invalid, since the constitution is superior in the hierarchy of legal rules to statute law. EC law had been incorporated into German law by statute, the Act of Ratification. There was no provision in the constitution that the constitution could be overridden by EC law. Article 24 GG merely provided for 'the transfer of sovereign powers to intergovernmental institutions'. So the question before the German Administrative Court (Verwaltungsgericht, Frankfurt) was: if there were a conflict between the regulation and the German Constitution, which law should prevail? As in *Costa*, the German judge referred the question to the ECJ and his own federal constitutional court (Bundesverfassungsgericht).

The ruling from the ECJ was in the strongest terms. The legality of a Community act cannot be judged in the light of national law:

> the law born from the Treaty [cannot] have the courts opposing to it rules of national law *of any nature whatever* . . . the validity of a Community instrument or its effect within a Member State cannot be affected by allegations that it strikes at either the fundamental rights as formulated in that State's constitution or the principles of a national constitutional structure. [Emphasis added.]

Underlying this judgment one can see concerns similar to those expressed in *Costa*: the need to ensure the effectiveness of Community law, whatever the cost to the national legal order. If the Court's ruling seems harsh in the light of the importance of the rights protected in a state's constitution, many of which are regarded as fundamental human rights, it is worth adding that the Court went on to say that respect for such rights was one of the principal aims of the Community and as such it was part of its own (albeit unwritten) law (see Chapter 6).

The principle of supremacy of Community law applies not only to internal domestic laws, but also to obligations entered into with third countries, that is, countries outside the EU. In the *ERTA* case (case 22/70) the ECJ held, in the context of a challenge to an international road transport agreement to which the Community was a party, that once the Community, in implementing a common policy, lays down common rules, Member States no longer have the right, individually or collectively, to contract obligations towards non-Member States affecting these common rules. And where the Community concludes a treaty in pursuance of a common policy, this excludes the possibility of a concurrent authority on the part of the Member States. This means that where a state attempts to exercise concurrent authority it will be overridden to the extent that it conflicts with Community law. This principle does not, however, appear to apply to Member States' pre-accession agreements with third countries. Where such agreements are 'not compatible' with the EC Treaty, Member States are required to 'take all appropriate steps to eliminate the incompatibilities established' (Article 307 EC (ex 234; post Lisbon, Article 351 TFEU)). In *R v Secretary of State for the Home Department, ex parte Evans Medical Ltd* (case C–324/93), the Court conceded that provisions of such an agreement contrary to Community law may continue to be applied where the performance of that agreement may still be required by non-Member States which are parties to it. The Court has, however, urged national courts to give effect to such provisions only to the extent that it is necessary to meet the demands of that agreement (*Minne* (case C–13/93)).

The case of *Kadi v Council* (joined cases C–402 and 415/05 P) shows a further development in this area. The background to this case is the fight against terrorism, according to which the UN Security Council adopted a number of resolutions for the freezing of assets of people thought to be involved in terrorism. All Member States are members of the UN, and as a prior agreement, must be respected by the Union. The Council adopted two common positions under the common foreign and security policy (CFSP), which were then implemented by regulations to which a list was attached, updated in accordance with decisions made at UN level, as to whose assets should be frozen. Kadi was one such and he sought to challenge the legality of the EU action on the basis, inter alia, of human-rights concerns. The ECJ (overruling a decision of the Court of First Instance) emphasised the autonomy of the EC and its constitutional status as a legal order based on the rule of law. On this reasoning, the obligations imposed on the Member States and the relationship between them and the EC were unaffected by any international agreement whatsoever its nature. In reaching this conclusion, the ECJ distinguished between the international obligations of the EC and the effect of Community norms, regardless of their source. On this basis, the ECJ was able to review the Union measures implementing the UN Resolutions. The impact of this judgment was to reassert the coherence and autonomy of the *Community* legal order, and to re-emphasise its constitutional basis. As regards the relationship of the EU and other international organisations, it suggests that the EC, if not the EU constitutes an impermeable layer protecting its own inner organisational structure; it also reminds us that to the extent that the EU is still an international law body, it sees itself in a different light from other such bodies.

Thus, subject to the narrow exception in *Evans*, as far as the ECJ is concerned *all* EC law, whatever its nature, must take priority over *all* conflicting domestic law, whether it be prior or subsequent to Community law. Given the fact that the Court was approaching the matter *tabula rasa*, there being no provision in the treaty to this effect, on what basis did the Court justify its position?

All these cases show a common theme in the ECJ's approach: the need to ensure the effectiveness of Community law. The position can be summarised as follows. The Court's reasoning is pragmatic, based on the purpose, the general aims and spirit of the treaty. States freely signed the treaty; they agreed to take all appropriate measures to comply with EC law (Article 10 EC); the treaty created its own institutions, and gave those institutions power to make laws binding on Member States (Article 249 EC). They agreed to set up an institutionalised form of control by the Commission (under Article 226 (ex 169; post Lisbon Art 258 TFEU)—see Chapter 11) and the Court. The Community would not survive if states were free to act unilaterally in breach of their obligations. If the aims of the Community are to be achieved, there must be uniformity of application. This will not occur unless all states accord priority to EC law; can we apply the same reasoning to EU law? This issue is discussed at 4.3.4 below.

4.3.2 Problems for the national courts

National courts were understandably reluctant to disregard their own constitutional rules and the Italian and German constitutional courts in *Costa v ENEL* ([1964] CMLR 425 at 430) and *Internationale Handelsgesellschaft mbH (Solange I)* ([1974] 2 CMLR 540), adhering to their own traditional view, refused to acknowledge the absolute supremacy of EC law.

There were other problems too for national courts—problems of application. Even if the principle of primacy of EC law were accepted in theory, what was a national judge to do in practice when faced with a conflict? No English judge can declare a statute void or unlawful (subject to limited powers in respect of the Human Rights Act); in most countries with a written constitution only the constitutional court has power to declare a domestic law invalid for breach of the constitution, if it has such a power at all. Must the national judge wait for the offending national law to be repealed or legally annulled before he can give precedence to EC law?

The ECJ suggested a solution to this problem in *Simmenthal SpA* (case 106/77). This case involved a conflict between a treaty provision, the then Article 30 (now 28) EC on the free movement of goods, and an Italian law passed *subsequent* to the

Italian Act incorporating EC law, a similar clash to the one in *Costa v ENEL* (case 6/64). Following *Costa*, the Italian constitutional court had revised its view and declared that it would be prepared to declare any national law conflicting with EC law invalid. When the problem arose in *Simmenthal* the Italian judge, the Pretore di Susa, was perplexed. Should he apply EC law at once to the case before him, or should he wait until his own constitutional court had declared the national law invalid? He referred this question to the ECJ. The Court's reply was predictable:

> any recognition that national legislative measures which encroach upon the field within which the Community exercises its legislative power or which are otherwise incompatible with the provisions of Community law had any legal effect would amount to a corresponding denial of the effectiveness of obligations undertaken unconditionally and irrevocably by Member States pursuant to the Treaty and would thus imperil the very foundations of the Community. [Para 18.]
>
> . . . a national court which is called upon . . . to apply provisions of Community law is under a duty to give full effect to those provisions, if necessary refusing . . . to apply any conflicting provision of national legislation, even if adopted subsequently, and it is not necessary for the court to request or await the prior setting aside of such provision by legislative or other constitutional means. [Para 24.]

The reasoning behind the judgment is clear. Unless Community law is given priority over conflicting national law at once, from the moment of its entry into force, there can be no uniformity of application throughout the Community. Community law will be ineffective. According to the ECJ, national judges faced with a conflict between national law, whatever its nature, and Community law, must ignore, must shut their eyes to national law; they need not, indeed must not, wait for the law to be changed. Any incompatible national law is automatically inapplicable.

The principles expressed in *Simmenthal SpA* were applied by the Court in *R v Secretary of State for Transport, ex parte Factortame Ltd* (case C–213/89), in the context of a claim before the English courts by a group of Spanish fishermen for an interim injunction to prevent the application of certain sections of the Merchant Shipping Act 1988, which denied them the right to register their boats in the UK, and which the claimants alleged were in breach of EC law. The question of the 'legality' of the British provisions under Community law had yet to be decided, following a separate reference to the ECJ. The British courts were being asked to give primacy to a *putative* Community right over an allegedly conflicting national law, and to grant an interim injunction against the Crown, something which they considered they were not permitted to do under national law. Following a reference by the House of Lords asking whether they were obliged to grant the relief in question as a matter of Community law, the ECJ pointed out that national courts were obliged, by Article 10 EC, to ensure the legal protection which persons derive from the direct effect of provisions of Community law. Moreover:

> The full effectiveness of Community law would be . . . impaired if a rule of national law could prevent a court seised of a dispute governed by Community law from granting interim relief in order to ensure the full effectiveness of the judgment to be given on the existence of the rights claimed under Community law. It follows that a court which in those circumstances would grant interim relief, if it were not for a rule of national law, is obliged to set aside that rule. [Para 21.]

The obligation on Member States to ensure the full effectiveness of Community law requires national courts not only to 'disapply' the offending national law but also to supply a remedy which is not available under national law (see more recently *Unibet* (case C–432/05)). It now seems that the obligation to disapply inconsistent national law extends beyond the courts to administrative agencies. In *Larsy* (case C–118/00), reasoning from its judgments in *Simmenthal* and *Factortame* (case C–213/89), the ECJ held that the national social security institution, INASTI, should disapply national laws that precluded effective protection of Larsy's Community law rights (para 53). (See also *CIF v Autorita* (case C–198/01): disapplication of national legislation incompatible with the competition provisions.) The issue of procedural rules and remedies is discussed further in Chapter 8.

A finding that a provision of national law is 'inapplicable' because of its incompatibility with Community law does not, however, result in its annulment, or even prevent its application in situations falling outside the scope of Community law. In *IN.CO.GE. '90* (cases C–10 and 22/97) the Court held that:

> it does not follow from *Simmenthal* that a domestic rule which is incompatible with EC law is non-existent.

Similarly in *Arcaro* (case C–168/95) it made it clear that there was:

> no method or procedure in Community law allowing national courts to eliminate national provisions contrary to a directive which has not been transposed where that provision may not be relied on before the national court.

In *ICI v Colmer* (case C–264/96) the ECJ found a system of tax relief for holding companies with a seat in the EU discriminatory, and therefore contrary to EC law, when applied to subsidiary companies in other Member States, but lawful in a situation where holding companies control subsidiaries in non-Member States. Despite its inapplicability in the former context, the national court was under no obligation to disapply national law in the latter situation, since that lay outside the scope of Community law. However:

> Where the same legislation must be disapplied as contrary to EC law in a situation covered by Community law it is for the competent body of the Member State concerned to remove that legal uncertainty insofar as it might affect rights deriving from Community rules.

The case of *Kapferer v Schlank and Schick* (case C–234/04) concerned the principle of *res judicata*, whereby judicial decisions which have become final can no longer be called in to question. Referring to *res judicata*, the ECJ held that, subject to the rules of equivalence and effectiveness (see Chapter 8), a national court did not have to disapply procedural rules which enshrined this principle, even if disapplying those rules would allow it to end an infringement of Community law caused by an ruling inconsistent with Community law. The ECJ, however, ruled to the contrary in *Lucchini Siderurgica* (case C–119/05), where it held that the national law upholding the principle of *res judicata* should be disapplied. This case, which goes against the run of authorities, should perhaps be regarded as exceptional rather than implying a new disregard for *res judicata,* which the ECJ has recognised as being a general principle of law (see Chapter 6).

4.3.3 EC rules which do not have direct effect

It may be noted that all the earlier landmark rulings of the Court, up to and including *Simmenthal* (case C–106/77), were expressed in terms of directly effective Community law, that is, rules that gave rise to rights that could be relied on within the national legal system. Until the Court introduced the principle of indirect effects in *von Colson* (case 14/83) (see Chapter 5) and the principle of state liability in *Francovich* (cases C–6 and 9/90) (see Chapter 9), it was thought that national courts would only be required to apply, and give priority to, EC law which was directly effective. This proved not to be the case. The obligation on national courts to interpret domestic law to comply with EC directives which are not directly effective (because invoked horizontally), as extended in *Marleasing,* impliedly requires those courts to give priority to EC law. Similarly, although the granting of a remedy in damages against the state under *Francovich* does not require the *application* of Community law, the remedy, based on Member States' obligation to guarantee full and effective protection for individuals' rights under Community law, is premised on the supremacy of EC law. This obligation was held in *Francovich* (at para 42) to apply to all rights 'which parties enjoy under Community law'. That protection cannot be achieved unless those rights prevail over conflicting provisions of national law. As *Brasserie du Pêcheur* and *R v Secretary of State for Transport, ex parte Factortame* (cases C–46 and 48/93) subsequently made clear, individuals' Community rights, including the right to damages, must prevail over *all* acts of Member States, legislative, executive, or judicial, which are contrary to Community law.

4.3.4 Supremacy in JHA and CFSP

Much of the case law discussed above pre-dates the TEU and the creation of the EU. It was therefore an open question as to whether supremacy was limited to the EC pillar, or applied to all three pillars of the EU. The exclusion of direct effect in the second and third pillars could be seen as an indication that these two pillars are different from the EC pillar. Conversely, direct effect is not a condition for supremacy and the reasoning the ECJ used in *Costa* can be just as much used in the context of the other pillars, a point re-emphasised by the fact that the ECJ held in *Pupino* (case C–105/03) that the Member States' duty of loyalty applied in the context of the third pillar, as did the obligation to interpret national law consistently with third pillar measures (see further 26.4.3, for impact of Lisbon treaty see 4.5 below).

4.4 The Member States' response

Although the ECJ might rule that Community law is supreme, this principle requires acceptance by the courts of the Member States if it is to have any real effect. After a shaky start (we have already noted the Italian and German constitutional courts' response in *Costa* and *Internationale Handelsgesellschaft mbH*), the courts of Member States have now broadly accepted the principle of supremacy of EC law *provided they regard it as directly effective*. They have done so in a variety of ways: by bending and adapting their own constitutional rules; by devising new constitutional rules to meet the new situation. Different Member States have shown different degrees of deference. The point here is that in each system it seems that the national courts have accepted supremacy on the terms of their constitutional system. That is, they have argued for the supremacy of Community law on the basis of national legal provisions, not the provisions of Community law itself. Their acceptance of supremacy is thus conditional. There is consequently the potential for conflict on specific issues, as the human-rights cases illustrate (see Chapter 6). Given the expanded membership of the Union, for reasons of space alone it is not possible to discuss the response of each of the Member States; further, for the newest Member States, it may well still be too soon for problems to work their way through the judicial system. It would be naive to suggest that the newer Member States would have no difficulties absorbing the doctrine of primacy, as they should have been aware of it on entry. As illustrated by the UK, whose politicians knew of the doctrine at the time of accession, legal reality is often different from political aspirations. Indeed, the Polish and Czech constitutional Courts have already faced questions on this issue. The response of national courts to the possible supremacy of EU law is also uncertain (see 26.4.3.1). What follows is a discussion of the response of the British and German courts; a full comparative survey of the position in other Member States must fall outside this book.

4.4.1 Great Britain

The status of Community law in the UK derives from the European Communities Act 1972. To what extent does that Act enable the British courts to give effect to the principle of supremacy of EC law?

The most important provisions are ss 2 and 3. Section 2(1) provides for the direct applicability of EC law in the UK:

> All such rights, powers, liabilities, obligations and restrictions from time to time created or arising by or under the Treaties, and all such remedies and procedures from time to time provided for by or under the Treaties, as in accordance with the Treaties are without further enactment to be given legal effect or used in the United Kingdom shall be recognised and available in law, and be enforced, allowed and followed accordingly; and the expression 'enforceable Community right' and similar expressions shall be read as referring to one to which this subsection applies.

Section 2(2) provides a general power for the further implementation of Community obligations by means of secondary legislation.

This is subject to Schedule 2, which lists the 'forbidden' areas, such as the power to increase taxation, to introduce retrospective measures or to create new criminal offences. These areas apart, s 2(2) thus allows for ongoing domestic legislation over the whole field of objectives of the treaty.

Section 2(4) is the section relevant to the question of primacy. It does not expressly say EC law is supreme. Section 2(4) provides (emphasis added):

> The provision that may be made under subsection (2) above includes, subject to schedule 2 to this Act, any such provision (of any such extent) as might be made by Act of Parliament, and *any enactment passed or to be passed*, other than one contained in this part of this Act [ie, an enactment of a non-Community nature], *shall be construed and have effect subject to the foregoing provisions of this section* [ie, obligations of a Community nature].

4.4.2 Effect of the European Communities Act 1972, s 2(1) and (4)

4.4.2.1 *Directly effective EC law*

The first question to arise is whether the combined effect of s 2(1) and (particularly) s 2(4) of the European Communities Act 1972 is sufficient to enable the British courts to give priority to EC law, on *Simmenthal* (case 106/77) principles, as the ECJ would require. Or does it merely lay down a rule of construction, whereby domestic law must be *construed*, so far as possible, to conform with EC law? The traditional constitutional view is that the doctrine of parliamentary sovereignty, and particularly the principle of implied repeal, makes entrenchment of EC law impossible. Parliament is not free to bind its successors. Therefore priority for EC law cannot be guaranteed, and s 2(4) can only provide a rule of construction.

An approach based on the jurisprudence of the ECJ, particularly *Simmenthal*, would involve a departure from that view.

There was considerable wavering in the early years on the question of primacy, but in 1979 the Court of Appeal in *Macarthys Ltd v Smith* ([1979] ICR 785), a landmark case, took the 'European' view. Cumming-Bruce and Lawton LJJ, invoking the ECJ in *Costa* (case 6/64) and *Simmenthal* (case 106/77), were prepared, on the basis of the European Communities Act 1972, s 2(4), to give European law 'priority'. Lord Denning MR preferred to use s 2(4) as a rule of construction and construed the relevant English legislation (Equal Pay Act 1970) to conform with the principle of equal pay for equal work in what was then Article 119 (now, as amended, 141) EC. However, in doing so he took a rather broader view of 'construction' than is usually taken in construing international agreements. In construing the English statutes, he said, 'we are entitled to look to the treaty as an aid to its construction: and even more, not only as an aid but as an overriding force'. He went on to say that 'If . . . our legislation is deficient—or is inconsistent with Community law . . . then it is our bounden duty to give priority to Community law.'

The current British position is found in the ruling of the House of Lords in *Factortame Ltd v Secretary of State for Transport* ([1990] 2 AC 85). Lord Bridge suggested that the combined effect of sub-ss (1) and (4) of the European Communities Act 1972, s 2, was:

> as if a section were incorporated in Part II [the impugned part] of the Merchant Shipping Act 1988 which in terms enacted that the provisions with respect to registration of British fishing vessels were to be without prejudice to the directly enforceable Community rights of nationals of any Member State of the EEC.

He suggested that if it were to be found that the British Act was in breach of the claimants' directly effective Community rights the latter rights would 'prevail' over the contrary provisions of the 1988 Act.

Subsequently, in applying the ECJ's ruling (in case C–213/89 noted above) that national courts must grant interim relief against the Crown where this was necessary to protect individuals' Community rights, the House of Lords, unanimously, granted that relief (*R v Secretary of State for Transport, ex parte Factortame Ltd* [1991] 1 AC 603 at 645). Here clearly no question of 'interpretation' of national law was possible; the House simply gave 'priority' to Community law. In justification, Lord Bridge pointed out that the principle of supremacy of Community law, if it was not always inherent in the treaty, was 'well established in the jurisprudence of the Court long before the United Kingdom joined the Community. Whatever limitation of its sovereignty Parliament accepted when it enacted the European Communities Act was entirely voluntary'. As a corollary, it seems that the doctrine of implied repeal, discussed at 4.2 above, has changed. In the context of 'constitutional' Acts of Parliament, such as the European Communities Act (and the Human Rights Act), express intention to repeal the Act is required. Such Acts will not be repealed through inconsistency with a later act. (See *Metric Martyrs* case, *Thoburn v Sunderland CC* [2003] QB 151, QBD.)

Primacy of Community law, together with the obligation imposed by Article 10 EC on national courts to provide effective protection for individuals' Community rights (the 'effectiveness' principle), has resulted in remedies being granted which were not at the time available under national law (see Chapter 8).

4.4.2.2 *The limits of primacy*

Thus the British courts have been willing to accord supremacy to directly effective Community law, either by a (fictional) 'construction' of domestic law, or, where necessary, by applying EC law directly, in priority over national law. As suggested by Lord Bridge in *Factortame*, this appears to rest on the implied intentions of Parliament. However, both Lord Denning in *Macarthys Ltd v Smith* and Lord Diplock in *Garland* have made it clear that should Parliament expressly attempt to repudiate its EC obligations the courts would be obliged to give effect to its wishes:

> If the time should come when our Parliament deliberately passes an Act—with the intention of repudiating the Treaty or any provision in it—or intentionally of acting inconsistently with it—and says so in express terms—then . . . it would be the duty of our courts to follow the statute of our Parliament. [Per Lord Denning in *Macarthys Ltd v Smith* [1979] ICR 785 at 789.]

While this is unlikely to happen as long as the UK remains a member of the Union, it was perhaps seen as important that it should remain a theoretical possibility. As Laws LJ noted in the *Metric Martyrs* case, any changes have been introduced as a matter of English law, not as a direct requirement of Community law. If the British courts have changed in their approach to statutory interpretation in the context of Community law, the principle of parliamentary sovereignty remains intact.

4.4.2.3 *EC law which is not directly effective*

In *Factortame* their Lordships' views on the European Communities Act 1972, s 2(4), were expressed in the context of a conflict between domestic law and *directly effective* Community law. Is it possible to achieve primacy for EC law for provisions of EC directives which, although sufficiently clear and precise for direct effects, are not directly effective because they are being invoked against a private party? In other words, does s 2(4) of the Act enable the British courts to follow *von Colson* (case 14/83) and *Marleasing* (case C–106/89) (see Chapter 5) and interpret domestic law to comply with EC law, even when it is not directly effective? In *Duke v GEC Reliance Ltd* ([1988] AC 618) the House of Lords thought not. The European Communities Act 1972, s 2(1) and (4), said Lord Templeman, applied, and only applied, to EC law which was directly effective:

> Section 2(4) of the European Communities Act 1972 does not . . . enable or constrain a British court to distort the meaning of a British statute in order to enforce against an individual a Community Directive which has no direct effect between individuals.

This reasoning may have been understandable on the particular facts of the case. In *Litster v Forth Dry Dock & Engineering Co. Ltd* ([1990] 1 AC 546), in the context of a claim against a 'private' party, the House of Lords interpreted certain UK regulations to comply with EC Directive 80/777, suggesting that where legislation had been introduced specifically in order to implement an EC directive, UK courts must interpret domestic law to comply with the directive, if necessary 'supplying the necessary words by implication' in order to achieve a result compatible with EC law. No reference was made to *Duke v GEC Reliance Ltd*, nor to the fact that the directive in question was not directly effective.

Thus, in the absence of evidence, such as was adduced in *Duke v GEC Reliance Ltd*, that Parliament did not intend to comply with Community law, *Litster* suggests that even where EC law is not directly effective, 'priority' for EC law should be ensured by way of interpretation of national law. However, there is no guarantee that *Litster* will be followed. In *Webb v EMO Air Cargo (UK) Ltd* ([1992] 2 All ER 43) Lord Templeman's dicta in *Duke v GEC Reliance Ltd* were cited by the Court of Appeal and the House of Lords ([1993] 1 WLR 49). However, following a ruling from the ECJ on the interpretation of Directive 76/207, the House of Lords found that it was possible to construe s 5(3) of the Sex Discrimination Act 1975 to comply with the Court's ruling without 'distorting' the meaning of the section. The Court of Appeal's decision had been based on a different, if equally legitimate, interpretation of s 5(3), and past case law. On the other hand, in *R v British Coal Corporation, ex parte Vardy* ([1993] ICR 720), Glidewell J found that it was 'not possible' to follow the House of Lords' example in *Litster* and interpret certain provisions of the Trade Union and Labour Relations Act 1992 to comply with EC (Collective Redundancies) Directive 75/129 since they were clearly at odds with the directive. Thus in the absence of ambiguity or evidence that Parliament intended UK law to have the meaning contended for or where there is a clear conflict between domestic and EC law, it seems that the British courts will be reluctant to apply the *von Colson* principle, particularly as extended by the ECJ in *Marleasing*. This appears to have been acknowledged by the ECJ in *Wagner Miret* (case C–334/92). Arguably this approach, which respects the principles of legal certainty and non-retroactivity, is consistent with the principles of EC law expressed by the ECJ in *Officier van Justitie v Kolpinghuis Nijmegen* (case 80/86, noted Chapter 5). Where it is not possible for national courts to give indirect effect to Community directives, enforcement of EC law should perhaps be left to the Commission under Article 226, or, now, to an action against the state under *Francovich* (cases C–6 and 9/90), as suggested by the Court in *Dori* (case C–91/92) and *Wagner Miret*. Note, however, the possibility for an action against the state for judicial failure to apply Community law (see Chapter 9). The reaction of the English courts will be discussed in more detail there; suffice it to note here that they have accepted the principle of state liability and domestic law has been developed accordingly (*R v Secretary of State for the Home Department, ex parte Gallagher* ([1996] 2 CMLR 951)).

It interesting to note that the courts' decisions in all of the cases were state liability has been raised were based on the ECJ's jurisprudence: they did not seek to justify their decisions on the basis of the European Communities Act 1972.

4.4.3 *Germany*

The German federal constitutional court modified its original view in *Internationale Handelsgesellschaft (Solange I)* ([1974] 2 CMLR 540). In *Steinike und Weinleg* ([1980] 2 CMLR 531) it suggested that any challenge to the constitutionality under German law of EC law could only be brought by way of challenge to the German Act of Ratification itself, and in October 1986, in *Application of Wünsche Handelsgesellschaft (Solange II)* ([1987] 3 CMLR 225), its position in *Internationale Handelsgesellschaft* was finally reversed. As long as EC law itself ensured the effective protection of fundamental rights, a ruling from the ECJ under Article 234 would not, the court held, be subject to review. Similarly, in *Re Kloppenberg* ([1988] 3 CMLR 1), in the context of a successful challenge to the Bundesfinanzhof's decision on the direct effect of directives (see *Re VAT Directives* [1982] 1 CMLR 527, noted in Chapter 5), it affirmed the principle of the supremacy of Community law in the strongest terms. In 1992, as in France, the constitution was amended to provide specifically for the transfer of sovereign powers to the EU (see new Article 23 GG).

However, the case of *Brunner v The European Union Treaty* ([1994] 1 CMLR 57) indicates that the German federal constitutional court (Bundesverfassungsgericht), while respecting the supremacy of Community law in matters within the sphere of Community competence, will itself reserve the right:

(a) to ensure the protection of fundamental human rights guaranteed under the German Constitution
(b) to decide whether the Union institutions have acted within their powers under the EC and EU Treaties.

The case involved a challenge to the German Federal Parliament's power to ratify the TEU. It was argued that the transfer via the proposed Act of Ratification of further powers and competences to the European Union would threaten human rights and democratic principles protected under the German Constitution. The Bundesverfassungsgericht found these allegations unfounded. The TEU did not, as was suggested, establish a European state but a federation of states. It equipped the Union only with specific competences and powers in accordance with the

principle of limited individual competences and established a principle of subsidiarity for the Union. It would permit no further extension of Community competence under Article 308 (ex 235—see Chapter 3). If the Union institutions or
organisations were to develop the treaty in a way not covered by the treaty in the
form that was the basis for the Act of Accession the resultant legislative instruments would not be binding within the sphere of German sovereignty. If parts of
the Community legal order were to breach fundamental rights protected under the
German Constitution it would declare those provisions inapplicable. Accordingly,
the court would review legal instruments of European institutions and agencies
to see whether they remained within the sovereign rights conferred on them or
transgressed them. Germany was one of the masters of the treaty with the intention of long-term membership: but it could ultimately revoke its adherence by a
contrary act.

According to the federal constitutional court, German sovereignty remains intact, and that court will itself decide whether the institutions of the Union have
acted within their powers under the EC and EU Treaties.

The unequivocal stance of the federal constitutional court in *Brunner* emboldened
the German courts to take a stand in a series of cases concerning the Community's
banana regime. The regime, which was set up in 1993 by EC Regulation 404/93,
and which operated to the serious disadvantage of German importers, was challenged by Germany on the grounds that it breached the Community's international obligations (inter alia GATT) and violated vested property rights protected under
the German Constitution. Despite strong arguments, acknowledged by Advocate-
General Gulmann, that there were 'circumstances which might provide a basis for
a finding that the Regulation was invalid' the ECJ found that there was no illegality in the Community's market organisation of bananas (*Germany v Council* (case
C–280/93); see further Chapter 12).

This case, which was extremely thin in its reasoning, for which it was round-
ly criticised, even by a former judge of the ECJ (see article by Everling noted
below), did little to stem the flood of actions before the German (and not only
German) courts seeking to suspend the application of the contested regulation
and/or to obtain compensation for damage suffered as a result of its application.
Following *Germany v Council* the legality of the Banana regulation was again
questioned before the Frankfurt Administrative Court (Verwaltungsgericht), and
further questions referred to the ECJ (*Atlanta* (case C–465/93)). While affirming
national courts' power to award interim relief, even positive relief in the form
of the grant of import licences, pending a ruling from the ECJ on validity, the
ECJ confirmed its finding in *Germany v Council* on the legality of the regulation,
pointing out that in deciding whether or not to grant interim relief national
courts were 'obliged to respect what the Community Court has decided on this
issue' (*Atlanta* (case C–465/93)). This did not prevent further claims before the
German courts raising the issue of the compatibility of the regulation with the
German Constitution, and questioning its applicability in Germany on the basis
of *Brunner*. In one case, following rejection of the claimants' application for relief
by the Kassel Verwaltungsgerichtshof, which followed the ECJ's ruling in *Germany
v Council*, the claimants took their case to the federal constitutional court, which
ordered a re-examination of the case, basing its decision on Article 19(4) of the
German Basic Law. Article 19(4) enshrines the right to effective judicial protection.

Significantly the constitutional court did not seek a ruling from the ECJ. On re-examination, the referring court granted the requested interim relief and referred further questions to the ECJ on the interpretation and validity of the regulation. In another case, the federal finance court (Bundesfinanzhof) accepted the finding of the Finanzgericht Hamburg that parts of the Banana regulation might be incompatible with GATT, and suggested that if they were, the German courts might be prevented from applying them following principles established in *Brunner*. Again further questions on the compatibility of the regulation with GATT were referred to the ECJ (*T Port GmbH & Co v Hauptzollamt Hamburg-Jonas* (cases C–364 and 365/95)).

Although the courts have not openly contradicted the ECJ's judgment in *Germany v Council* (case C–280/93) they have been prepared to question its applicability and even refrain from applying it. As Everling pointed out, the German courts 'are deeply concerned about the extremely unjust effects of the Banana Regulation and insufficiency of the judicial control by the ECJ in this case'. So far they have avoided open conflict by awarding provisional relief and submitting further questions to the ECJ in the hope that the Court will reconsider its decision in case C–280/93. It appeared to have done so (albeit to a limited extent) in *T Port GmbH & Co v Hauptzollamt Hamburg-Jonas* (cases C–364 and 365/95) when it found that certain aspects of the banana regime were invalid for breach of the principle of non-discrimination. However, it has denied national courts' power to award interim relief in the context of the EC institutions' (allegedly unlawful) *failure to act*, holding that any challenge to such a failure could only be brought before the ECJ under Articles 230 and 232 (ex 173 and 175, respectively) (*T Port GmbH & Co KG* (case C–68/95). As will be seen in Chapters 12 and 13, this represents a weakness in the system of judicial control of the EC institutions.

The Administrative Court which had made the reference in *Atlanta* (case C–465/93) was still not satisfied by the ECJ's response and referred the question back to the German constitutional court. It was only in 2000, four years later, that that court delivered its ruling, declaring in a much criticised judgment that the Administrative Court's application was inadmissible. The constitutional court argued that in *Solange II* and *Brunner* it had found the level of human-rights protection in Germany and within the EC legal order to be comparable. To succeed in a challenge against Community law, it would be necessary to show that the level of protection guaranteed by the ECJ fell below the German level of protection. In the case in issue, the referring Administrative Court had not pointed to any decline in human-rights standards since *Solange*. Some commentators have suggested that this ruling constituted evidence of renewed cooperation between the constitutional court and the ECJ. Indeed, some have also suggested that in the light of this judgment and *Alcan* (BVerf G judgment 17 February 2000) the threat to supremacy suggested by *Brunner* has been dispersed and even that *Brunner* has partially been repealed. The political unease regarding the Treaty of Lisbon has reawakened old concerns resulting in references to the constitutional court including the question of whether the '*Brunner* test' is satisfied by the guarantees in Lisbon. While the court approved Lisbon, it broadly reiterated its approach in *Brunner* and emphasised that the EU has 'an autonomy to rule which is independent but derived' and ultimately subject to review by the Member States to ensure their constitutional identities are respected.

Nonetheless, it seems that as long as Community law does not threaten German constitutional rights or make unwarranted intrusions into areas within the legislative jurisdiction of Member States, the German courts are prepared fully to comply with the principle of primacy of EC law. In applying the ECJ's ruling in *Brasserie du Pêcheur SA v Germany* ([1997] 1 CMLR 971), the German Federal Supreme Court held that, even though there was no basis for the applicants' claim for damages in these circumstances for legislative breaches of Community law under German law, liability in respect of such breaches 'flowed directly from that [Community] law itself'. Nevertheless, although the state might be liable in principle for such breaches, Germany was found on the facts not to be liable, since the breach of Community law which caused the applicants' damage (the prohibition on the use of additives in the manufacture of beer) was, as the ECJ itself had suggested, not sufficiently serious to give rise to liability.

Like the UK courts, the German courts have had difficulty with the principle of direct effects, and particularly indirect effects, in the context of the application of EC directives. In *Re v Rehabilitation Centre* ([1992] 2 CMLR 21) the German Federal Supreme Court refused to 'interpret' the German Legal Code against its clear meaning, to comply with EC Equal Treatment Directive 76/207. The court held:

> even an interpretation of statutes by reference to conformity with the constitution reaches its limits when it comes into conflict with the wording and evident intention of the legislature. The position can be no different as regards the interpretation of national law in the light of the wording and purpose of a Directive.

As is suggested in Chapter 5 it is likely that these difficulties and this resistance caused the ECJ to turn to the alternative remedy of state liability in damages in *Francovich v Italy* (case 9/90).

4.5 Supremacy, the Constitution, and Lisbon

The Constitution provided, in Article I–6, that 'The Constitution and law adopted by the institutions of the Union in exercising competences conferred on it shall have primacy over the law of the Member States'.

Despite the extensive and well-established jurisprudence on this point, Article I–6 constituted the first express treaty reference to primacy of Community, and Union, law, causing some consternation in those who would seem not to have included Union law textbooks in their reading. The provision was straightforward and a protocol attached to the treaty establishing a Constitution for Europe clarified that the provision was intended only to codify the existing law. Nonetheless, some commentators questioned whether Article I–6 was merely a codification. They argue that it implicitly would have given the ECJ the power to review matters in *all* areas covered by the Constitution, an extension of its current jurisdiction. Equally, others have pointed out that Article I–6 reaffirmed the limitation on the Union's powers, as primacy occurs only within the scope of attributed powers (see Chapter 3). Perhaps due to the excessive reaction to this provision, the Lisbon Treaty contains no such reference to supremacy maintaining, with the exception of a declaration, a tactful silence on the issue. The declaration, which does not have binding legal effect, states that:

> [t]he conference recalls that, in accordance with well settled case law of the EU Court of Justice, the Treaties and the law adopted by the Union on the basis of the Treaties have primacy over the law of Member States, under the conditions laid down by the said case law.

This is rather non-contentious. Interestingly, the declaration also contains a reference to a legal opinion of the Council Legal Service, which states that, '[t]he fact that the principle of primacy will not be included in the future treaty shall not in any way change the existence of the principle and the existing case-law of the Court of Justice', though quite on what basis it draws this conclusion is not made clear. It is perhaps an attempt to pretend that the Constitution, and particularly Article I-6, never happened. Nonetheless, the abolition of the pillar structure raises the question of whether supremacy will extend to all Union law and not just what is currently Community law. Whilst the integration of JHA matters into what will become the TFEU may make it difficult to argue that there is a difference between those provisions and Community law, even after Lisbon, the CFSP provisions remain separate, in the TEU.

4.6 Conclusions

The ECJ, in introducing the notion of supremacy, was instrumental in providing a view of the Community as a body that went beyond what was normal for an international law organisation. In a number of key judgments it identified the Community as an independent legal order, supreme over the national legal systems. One of the mechanisms used to justify this was the effectiveness of Community law, a doctrine that the ECJ has used again and again in different contexts to justify the development of Community law in a particular direction. As has been noted, however, the success of this project cannot be ascribed entirely to the ECJ. To a large part, it has been dependent on the cooperation of the Member States, particularly their courts. In a relatively short space of time the courts of Member States, despite their different constitutional rules and traditions, have adapted to the principle of supremacy of EC law where it is found to be directly effective. Their application of directives, particularly their indirect application, remains uncertain. Their reaction to *Francovich*, as refined in *Brasserie du Pêcheur* (cases C–46 and 48/93) has been positive. Credit for national courts' acceptance of the principle of supremacy of EC law must go to the ECJ, which has supplied persuasive reasons for doing so. However, equal credit must go to the courts of Member States, which have contrived to embrace the principle of primacy of Community law while at the same time insisting that ultimate political and judicial control remains within the Member States. As *Brunner* indicates, the courts of Member States, particularly their supreme courts, will be vigilant, and use all the means at their disposal, to ensure that the EU institutions do not exceed their powers or transgress fundamental constitutional rights, particularly in the post-Maastricht political climate, with its emphasis on subsidiarity. As Kumm suggests, 'they need to keep a handle on the emergency brake'; but they would disapply a Community act or a ruling from the ECJ only where that act or that ruling was manifestly and gravely erroneous. So far they have stopped short of outright defiance, despite the occasional errors of understanding the scope of Community law. Note, however, that when an individual seeks to rely on Community law rights, the ECJ has not shied away from the ultimate step: a claim for damages against the state in respect of judicial breaches of Community law (see *Kobler* (case C–224/01), and *Traghetti* (case C–173/03) discussed Chapter 9).

FURTHER READING

See also the reading list at the end of Chapter 5.

Bebr, G, 'Agreements concluded by the Community and their possible direct effects: from International Fruit Company to Kupferberg' (1983) 20 CML Rev 35.

Bonnie, A, 'The constitutionality of transfers of sovereignty: The French approach' (1998) 4 EPL 517.

Coppel, J and O'Neill, A, 'The European Court of Justice: Taking rights seriously?' (1992) 29 CML Rev 669.

Craig, P, 'UK sovereignty after *Factortame*' (1991) 11 YEL 221.

de Noriega, E, 'A dissident voice: The Spanish constitutional case law on European integration' (1999) 5 EPL 269.

De Witte, B, 'Community law and national constitutional values' (1991) 2 LIEI 1.

Elbers, U and Urban, N, 'The order of German federal constitutional court of 7 June 2000 and the Kompetenz-Kompetenz in the European judicial system' (2001) 7 EPL 21.

Everling, U, 'Will Europe slip on bananas? The bananas judgment of the European Court and national courts' (1996) 33 CML Rev 401.

Gaja, G, 'New developments in a continuing story: The relationship between EEC law and Italian law' (1990) 27 CML Rev 83.

Granger, M-PF, 'National applications of *Francovich* and the construction of a European administrative *ius commune*' (2007) 32(5) EL Rev 157.

Green, N, 'Directives, equity and the protection of individual rights' (1984) 9 EL Rev 295.

Hartley, T, 'International agreements and the Community legal system: Some recent developments' (1983) 8 EL Rev 383.

Herdegen, M, 'Maastricht and the German constitutional court: Constitutional restraints for an ever closer union' (1994) 31 CML Rev 235.

Hoskins, M, 'Tilting the balance: Supremacy and national procedural rules' (1996) 21 EL Rev 365.

Kumm, M, 'Who is the arbiter of constitutionality in Europe?' (1999) 36 CML Rev 351.

Marshall, G, 'Parliamentary sovereignty: The new horizons' [1997] PL 1.

Obradovic, D, 'Aspects of European constitutionalism' (1996) 21 EL Rev 32.

——, 'Repatriation of powers in the European Community' (1997) 34 CML Rev 59.

Oliver, P, 'The French Constitution and the Treaty of Maastricht' (1994) 43 ICLQ 1.

Peers, S., 'Taking supremacy seriously' (1998) 23 EL Rev 146.

Pescatore, P, 'The doctrine of direct effect: An infant disease of Community Law' (1983) 8 EL Rev 155.

Peters, A, 'The Bananas Decision 2000 of the German federal constitutional court: Towards reconciliation with the ECJ as regards fundamental rights protection in Europe' (2000) 43 German Yearbook of International Law 276.

Pollard, D, 'The Conseil d'État is European: Official' (1990) 15 EL Rev 267.

Reich, N, 'Judge-made Europe à la carte: Some remarks on recent conflicts between European and German Constitutional Law provoked by the bananas litigation' (1996) 7 EJIL 103.

Schermans, H, 'The scales in balance: National constitutional court v Court of Justice' (1990) 27 CML Rev 97.

Schmid, C, 'All bark and no bite: Notes on the federal constitutional court's "Banana Decision"' (2001) 7 *ELJ* 95.

Steiner, J, 'Coming to terms with EEC directives' (1990) 106 LQR 144.

Weiler, J, 'The Community system: The dual character of supranationalism' (1981) 1 YEL 267.

——, 'The transformation of Europe' (1991) 100 Yale Law Journal 2403.

——, 'The reformulation of German constitutionalism' (1997) 35 JCMS 597.

Weiler, J and Lockhart, N, '"Taking rights seriously" seriously' ? (1995) 32 CML Rev 51 and 579.

Wyatt, D, 'Direct effects of Community law, not forgetting directives' (1983) 8 EL Rev 241.

Zuleeg, M, 'The European Constitution under European constraints: The German scenario' (1997) 22 EL Rev 19.

5

Principles of direct applicability and direct effects

5.1 Introduction

It has already been seen that EC law, if not EU law, is supreme to national law and that domestic courts are under an obligation to give full effect to EC law (see Chapter 4). With this in mind, the question then arises to what extent individuals can rely on EC law before the national courts, particularly where a Member State has failed to implement a particular measure, or where the implementation is in some way defective and does not provide the full extent of the rights an individual should enjoy by virtue of the relevant EC measure. To deal with this question, and very much in accordance with the principle of supremacy, the European Court of Justice (ECJ) has developed three interrelated doctrines: direct effect, indirect effect, and state liability. Taken together, these seek to ensure that individuals are given the greatest possible level of protection before their national courts. This chapter considers the scope of the doctrines of direct and indirect effect, as well as identifying difficulties in the jurisprudence. One particular area in which problems arise is that of ensuring the enforceability of directives. This chapter will look at this issue and the various approaches that the ECJ has developed with regard to it. Chapter 9 will examine the jurisprudence in the field of state liability.

5.2 Doctrine of direct effects

5.2.1 Direct applicability

As was noted in Chapter 4, the European Community Treaties were incorporated into UK law by the European Communities Act 1972. With the passing of this Act all Community law became, in the language of international law, directly applicable, that is, applicable as part of the British internal legal system. Henceforth, 'Any rights or obligations created by the Treaty are to be given legal effect in England without more ado' (per Lord Denning MR in *HP Bulmer Ltd v J Bollinger SA* [1974] Ch 401). As directly applicable law, EC law thus became capable of forming the basis of rights and obligations enforceable by individuals before their national courts.

Provisions of international law which are found to be capable of application by national courts *at the suit of individuals* are also termed 'directly applicable'. This ambiguity (the same ambiguity is found in the alternative expression 'self-executing') has given rise to much uncertainty in the context of EC law. For this reason it was suggested by Winter that the term 'directly effective' be used to convey this secondary meaning. Although this term has generally found favour amongst British academic writers, the ECJ as well as the British courts tend to use the two concepts of direct applicability and direct effects interchangeably. However, for purposes of clarity it is proposed to use the term 'directly effective' or 'capable of direct effects' in this secondary meaning, to denote those provisions of EC law which give rise to rights or obligations which individuals may enforce before their national courts.

Not all provisions of directly applicable international law are capable of direct effects. Some provisions are regarded as binding on, and enforceable by states alone; others are too vague to form the basis of rights or obligations for individuals; others are too incomplete and require further measures of implementation before they can be fully effective in law. Whether a particular provision is directly effective is a matter of construction, depending on its language and purpose as well as the terms on which the treaty has been incorporated into domestic law. Although most states apply similar criteria of clarity and completeness, specific rules and attitudes inevitably differ, and since the application of the criteria often conceals an underlying policy decision, the results are by no means uniform from state to state.

5.2.2 Relevance of direct effect in EC law

The question of the direct effects of Community law is of paramount concern to EC lawyers. If a provision of EC law is directly effective, domestic courts must not only apply it but, following the principle of primacy of EC law (discussed in Chapter 4), must do so in priority over any conflicting provisions of national law. Since the scope of the EC Treaty is wide, the more generous the approach to the question of direct effects, the greater the potential for conflict.

Which provisions of EC law will then be capable of direct effect? The EC Treaty merely provides in Article 249 (ex 189; post Lisbon, Article 288 TFEU) that regulations (but only regulations) are 'directly applicable'. Since, as has been suggested, direct applicability is a necessary precondition for direct effects, this would seem to imply that only regulations are capable of direct effects.

This has not proved to be the case. In a series of landmark decisions, the ECJ, principally in its jurisdiction under Article 234 EC (ex 177; post Lisbon, Article 267 TFEU) to give preliminary rulings on matters of interpretation of EC law on reference from national courts, has extended the principle of direct effects to treaty articles, directives, decisions, and even to provisions of international agreements to which the EC is a party.

5.2.3 Treaty articles

5.2.3.1 The Starting Point: Van Gend en Loos

The question of the direct effect of a treaty article was first raised in *Van Gend en Loos v Nederlandse Administratie der Belastingen* (case 26/62). The Dutch administrative tribunal, in a reference under Article 234, asked the ECJ 'Whether Article 12 of the EEC Treaty [now 25 EC] has an internal effect . . . in other words, whether the nationals of Member States may, on the basis of the Article in question, enforce rights which the judge should protect?'

Article 25 (ex 12) EC (Article 30 TFEU) prohibits states from 'introducing between themselves any new customs duties on imports or exports or any charges having equivalent effect'.

It was argued on behalf of the defendant customs authorities that the obligation in Article 25 was addressed to states and was intended to govern rights and obligations between states. Such obligations were not normally enforceable at the suit of individuals. Moreover the treaty had expressly provided enforcement procedures under what are now Articles 226–7 EC (ex 169–70; post Lisbon, Articles 258–9 TFEU) (see Chapter 11) at the suit of the Commission or Member States, respectively. Advocate-General Roemer suggested that Article 25 was too complex to be enforced by national courts; if such courts were to enforce Article 25 directly there would be no uniformity of application.

Despite these persuasive arguments the ECJ held that Article 25 was directly effective. The Court stated that 'this Treaty is more than an agreement creating only mutual obligations between the contracting parties . . . Community law . . . not only imposes obligations on individuals but also confers on them legal rights'. These rights would arise:

> not only when an explicit grant is made by the Treaty, but also through obligations imposed, in a clearly defined manner, by the Treaty on individuals as well as on Member States and the Community institutions.
> . . . The text of Article 12 [now 25] sets out a clear and unconditional prohibition, which is not a duty to act but a duty not to act. This duty is imposed without any power in the States to subordinate its application to a positive act of internal law. The prohibition is perfectly suited by its nature to produce direct effects in the legal relations between the Member States and their citizens.

And further:

> The vigilance of individuals interested in protecting their rights creates an effective control additional to that entrusted by Articles 169–70 [now 226–7] to the diligence of the Commission and the Member States.

Apart from its desire to enable individuals to invoke the protection of EC law the Court clearly saw the principle of direct effects as a valuable means of ensuring that EC law was enforced uniformly in all Member States, even when states had not themselves complied with their obligations.

5.2.3.2 *Subsequent developments*

It was originally thought that, as the Court suggested in *Van Gend*, only prohibitions such as (the then) Article 25 ('standstill' provisions) would qualify for direct effects; this was found in *Alfons Lütticke GmbH v Hauptzollamt Saarlouis* (case 57/65) not to be so. The article under consideration in this case was Article 95(1) and (3) (now 90; post Lisbon, Article 110 TFEU); this article contains a prohibition on states introducing discriminatory taxation; the then Article 95(3) contained a positive obligation that 'Member States shall, not later than at the beginning of the second stage, repeal or amend any provisions existing when this Treaty enters into force which conflict with the preceding rules'.

The ECJ found that the then Article 95(1) was directly effective; what was Article 95(3), which was subject to compliance within a specified time limit, would, the Court implied, become directly effective once that time limit had expired.

The Court has subsequently found a large number of treaty provisions to be directly effective. All the basic principles relating to free movement of goods and persons, competition law, and discrimination on the grounds of sex and nationality may now be invoked by individuals before their national courts.

5.2.3.3 *Criteria for direct effect*

In deciding whether a particular provision is directly effective certain criteria are applied: the provision must be sufficiently clear and precise; it must be unconditional, and leave no room for the exercise of discretion in implementation by Member States or Community institutions. The criteria are, however, applied generously, with the result that many provisions which are not particularly clear or precise, especially with regard to their scope and application, have been found to produce direct effects. Even where they are conditional and subject to further implementation they have been held to be directly effective once the date for implementation is past. The Court reasons that while there may be discretion as to the means of implementation, there is no discretion as to ends.

5.2.3.4 *Vertical and horizontal effect of treaty provisions*

In *Van Gend* the principle of direct effects operated to confer rights on Van Gend exercisable against the Dutch customs authorities. Thus the obligation fell on an organ of the state, to whom Article 25 was addressed. (This is known as a 'vertical' direct effect, reflecting the relationship between individual and state.) But treaty obligations, even when addressed to states, may fall on individuals too. May they be invoked by individuals against individuals? (This is known as a 'horizontal effect', reflecting the relationship between individual and individual.)

Van Gend implies so, and this was confirmed in *Defrenne v Sabena (No 2)* (case 43/75). Ms Defrenne was an air hostess employed by Sabena, a Belgian airline company. She brought an action against Sabena based on what was then Article 119 of the EEC Treaty (now 141 EC; post Lisbon Article 157 TFEU). It provided that 'Each Member State shall during the first stage ensure and subsequently maintain the application of the principle that men and women should receive equal pay for equal work'.

Ms Defrenne claimed, inter alia, that in paying their male stewards more than their air hostesses, when they performed identical tasks, Sabena was in breach of the then Article 119. The gist of the questions referred to the ECJ was whether, and in what context, that provision was directly effective. Sabena argued that the treaty articles so far found directly effective, such as Article 25, concerned the relationship between the State and its subjects, whereas former Article 119 was primarily concerned with relationships between individuals. It was thus not suited to produce direct effects. The Court, following Advocate-General Trabucci, disagreed, holding that 'the prohibition on discrimination between men and women applies not only to the action of public authorities, but also extends to all agreements which are intended to regulate paid labour collectively, as well as to contracts between individuals'.

This same principle was applied in *Walrave v Association Union Cycliste Internationale* (case 36/74) to Article 12 (ex 6, originally 7) EC which provides that 'Within the scope of application of this Treaty, and without prejudice to any special provisions contained therein, any discrimination on grounds of nationality shall be prohibited'.

The claimants, Walrave and Koch, sought to invoke Article 12 (post Lisbon, Article 18 TFEU) in order to challenge the rules of the defendant association which they claimed were discriminatory.

The ECJ held that the prohibition of any discrimination on grounds of nationality 'does not only apply to the action of public authorities but extends likewise to rules of any other nature aimed at regulating in a collective manner gainful employment and the provision of services'.

To limit the prohibition in question to acts of a public authority would risk creating inequality in their application. Even now, the precise scope of the horizontal nature of the provisions relating to free movement of individuals (Articles 39, 43, and 49; post Lisbon Articles 45, 49 and 56 TFEU respectively) is not clear. Whilst the judgment in *Walrave* can be read as a form of effectiveness, which could then extend the scope of the provisions to all non-state actors, it can equally be read as relating to collective agreements, or to situations where there is a violation of the principle of non-discrimination. Subsequent cases have not cleared up this ambiguity (see Chapter 21). It is generally accepted that the provisions on the free movement of goods (Articles 28–9 EC; post Lisbon Articles 34–5 TFEU) do not have horizontal direct effect, although the ECJ's jurisprudence has operated to compensate for this limitation (see Chapter 20). Nonetheless, many treaty provisions have now been successfully invoked vertically and horizontally. The fact of their being addressed to, and imposing obligations on, states has been no bar to their horizontal effect.

5.2.4 **Regulations**

A regulation is described in Article 249 EC as of 'general application . . . binding in its entirety and directly applicable in all Member States'. It is clearly intended to take immediate effect without the need for further implementation.

Regulations are thus by their very nature apt to produce direct effects. However, even for regulations direct effects are not automatic. There may be cases where a provision in a regulation is conditional, or insufficiently precise, or requires further implementation before it can take full legal effect. But since a regulation is of 'general application', where the criteria for direct effects are satisfied, it may be invoked vertically or horizontally.

In *Antonio Munoz Cia SA v Frumar Ltd* (case C–253/00), the ECJ confirmed that regulations by their very nature operate to confer rights on individuals which must be protected by the national courts. In this case, Regulation 2200/96 ([1996] OJ L 297/1) laid down the standards by which grapes are classified. Munoz brought civil proceedings against Frumar who had sold grapes under particular labels which did not comply with the corresponding standard. The relevant provision in the regulation did not confer rights specifically on Munoz, but applied to all operators in the market. A failure by one operator to comply with the provision could have adverse consequences for other operators. The ECJ held that, since the purpose of the regulation was to keep products of unsatisfactory quality off the market, and to ensure the full effectiveness of the regulation, it must be possible for a trader to bring civil proceedings against a competitor to enforce the regulation. This decision is noteworthy for several reasons. As with the early case law on the treaty articles, it reasons from the need to ensure the effectiveness of Community law. It also confirms that, as directly applicable measures, regulations can apply horizontally between private parties as well as vertically against public bodies. In terms of enforcement, it also seems to suggest that it is not necessary that rights be conferred expressly on the claimant before that individual may rely on the sufficiently clear and unconditional provisions of a regulation. Insofar as the ECJ's jurisprudence requires individuals seeking to rely on a directive to have received rights under that directive (see 5.2.5.3 below), there seems to be the beginning of a divergence between the jurisprudence on regulations and that on directives.

5.2.5 **Directives**

5.2.5.1 *The problem of the direct effect of directives*

A directive is (Article 249 EC) 'binding, as to the result to be achieved, upon each Member State to which it is addressed, but shall leave to the national authorities the choice of form and methods'.

Because directives are not described as 'directly applicable' it was originally thought that they could not produce direct effects. Moreover the obligation in a directive is addressed to states, and gives the state some discretion as to the form and method of implementation; its effect thus appeared to be conditional on the implementation by the state.

5.2.5.2 *The principle of direct effect of directives*

This was not the conclusion reached by the ECJ, which found, in *Grad v Finanzamt Traunstein* (case 9/70) that a directive could be directly effective. The claimant in *Grad* was a haulage company seeking to challenge a tax levied by the German authorities that the claimant claimed was in breach of an EC directive and decision. The directive required states to amend their VAT systems to comply with a common EC system and to apply this new VAT system to, inter alia, freight transport from the date of the directive's entry into force. The German government argued that only regulations were directly applicable. Directives and decisions took effect internally only via national implementing measures. As evidence they pointed out that only regulations were required to be published in the *Official Journal*. The ECJ disagreed. The fact that only regulations were described as directly applicable did not mean that other binding acts were incapable of such effects:

> It would be incompatible with the binding effect attributed to Decisions by Article 189 [now 249] to exclude in principle the possibility that persons affected may invoke the obligation imposed by a Decision . . . the effectiveness of such a measure would be weakened if the nationals of that State could not invoke it in the courts and the national courts could not take it into consideration as part of Community law.

Although expressed in terms of a decision, it was implied in the judgment that the same principle applied in the case of directives. The direct effect of directives was established beyond doubt in a claim based on a free-standing directive in *Van Duyn v Home Office* (case 41/74). Here the claimant sought to invoke Article 3 of Directive 64/221 to challenge the Home Office's refusal to allow her to enter to take up work with the Church of Scientology. Under EC law Member States are allowed to deny EC nationals rights of entry and residence only on the grounds of public policy, public security and public health (see Chapter 25). Article 3 of Directive 64/221 provided that measures taken on the grounds of public policy must be based exclusively on the personal conduct of the person concerned. Despite the lack of clarity as to the scope of the concept of 'personal conduct' the ECJ held that Mrs Van Duyn was entitled to invoke the directive directly before her national court. It suggested that even if the provision in question was not clear the matter could be referred to the ECJ for interpretation under Article 234 EC.

So both directives and decisions may be directly effective. Whether they will in fact be so will depend on whether they satisfy the criteria for direct effects—they must be sufficiently clear and precise, unconditional, leaving no room for discretion in implementation. These conditions were satisfied in *Grad*. Although the directive was not unconditional in that it required action to be taken by the state, and gave a time limit for implementation, once the time limit expired the obligation became absolute. At this stage there was no discretion left. *Van Duyn* demonstrates that it is not necessary for a provision to be particularly precise for it to be deemed 'sufficiently' clear. Significantly, the ECJ held in *Riksskatterverket v Soghra Gharehveran* (case C–441/99) that a provision in a directive could be directly effective where it contained a discretionary element if the Member State had already exercised that discretion. The reason for this was that it could then no longer be argued that the Member State still had to take measures to implement the provision.

The reasoning in *Grad* was followed in *Van Duyn* and has been repeated on many occasions to justify the direct effect of directives once the time limit for implementation has expired. A more recent formulation of the test for direct effects, and one that is generally used, is that the provision in question should be 'sufficiently clear and precise and unconditional'.

A directive cannot, however, be directly effective before the time limit for implementation has expired. It was tried unsuccessfully in the case of *Pubblico Ministero v Ratti* (case 148/78). Mr Ratti, a solvent manufacturer, sought to invoke two EC harmonisation directives on the labelling of dangerous preparations to defend a criminal charge based on his own labelling practices. These practices, he claimed, were not illegal according to the directive. The ECJ held that since the time limit for the implementation of one of the directives had not expired it was not directly effective. He could, however, rely on the other directive for which the implementation date had passed.

Even when a state has implemented a directive it may still be directly effective. The ECJ held this to be the case in *Verbond van Nederlandse Ondernemingen (VNO) v Inspecteur der Invoerrechten en Accijnzen* (case 51/76), thereby allowing the Federation of Dutch Manufacturers to invoke the Second VAT Directive despite implementation of the provision by the Dutch authorities. The grounds for the decision were that the useful effect of the directive would be weakened if individuals could not invoke it before national courts. By allowing individuals to invoke the directive the Union can ensure that national authorities have kept within the limits of their discretion. Indeed, it seems possible to rely on even a properly implemented directive if it is not properly applied in practice (*Marks and Spencer* (case C–62/00)). Arguably, the principle in *VNO* could apply to enable an individual to invoke a 'parent' directive even before the expiry of the time limit, where domestic measures have been introduced for the purpose of complying with the directive (see *Officier van Justitie v Kolpinghuis Nijmegen* (case 80/86)). This view gains some support from the case of *Inter-Environment Wallonie ASBL v Region Wallonie* (case C–129/96). Here the ECJ held that even within the implementation period Member States are not entitled to take any measures which could seriously compromise the result required by the directive. This applies irrespective of whether the domestic measure which conflicts with a directive was adopted to implement that directive (case C–14/02 *ATRAL*). In *Mangold* (case C–144/04, see further below), the ECJ strengthened this view. According to its ruling, the obligation on a national court to set aside domestic law in conflict with a directive before its period for implementation has expired appears to be even stronger where the directive in question merely aims to provide a framework for ensuring compliance with a general principle of Community law, such as non-discrimination on the grounds of age (see Chapter 6). Note also the approach in regards to the obligation for consistent interpretation (see, eg, *Adeneler v ELOG* (case C-212/04) below).

5.2.5.3 *Must rights be conferred by the directive?*

The ECJ's test for direct effects (the provision must be sufficiently clear, precise, and unconditional) has never expressly included a requirement that the directive should be intended to give rise to rights for the individual seeking to invoke its provisions. However, the justification for giving direct effect to EC law has always been the need to ensure effective protection for individuals' Community rights. Furthermore, the ECJ has, in a number of recent cases, suggested that an individual's right to invoke a directive may be confined to situations in which he can show a particular interest in that directive. In *Becker v Finanzamt Munster-Innenstadt* (case 8/81), in confirming and clarifying the principle of direct effect as applied to directives, the Court held that 'provisions of Directives can be invoked by individuals *insofar as they define rights which individuals are able to assert against the state*' (emphasis added).

Drawing on this statement in *Verholen* (cases C–87 to C–89/90), the Court suggested that only a person with a direct interest in the application of the directive could invoke its provisions: this was held in *Verholen* to include a third party who was directly affected by the directive. In *Verholen*, the husband of a woman suffering sex discrimination as regards the granting of a social security benefit, contrary to Directive 79/7, was able to bring a claim based on the directive in respect of disadvantage to himself consequential on the discriminatory treatment of his wife.

In most recent cases in which an individual seeks to invoke a directive directly, the existence of a direct interest is clear. The question of his or her standing has not therefore been in issue. Normally the rights he or she seeks to invoke, be it for example a right to equal treatment or to employment protection, are contained in the directive. Its provisions are clearly, if not explicitly, designed to benefit persons such as the individual. There are circumstances, however, where this is not so.

5.2.5.4 *Member States' initial response*

Initially national courts were reluctant to concede that directives could be directly effective. The Conseil d'État, the supreme French administrative court, in *Minister of the Interior v Cohn-Bendit* ([1980] 1 CMLR 543), refused to follow *Van Duyn v Home Office* and allow the claimant to invoke Directive 64/221. The English Court of Appeal in *O'Brien v Sim-Chem Ltd* ([1980] ICR 429) found the Equal Pay Directive (75/117) not to be directly effective on the grounds that it had purportedly been implemented in the Equal Pay Act 1970 (as amended 1975). *VNO* was apparently not cited before the court. The German Federal Tax Court, the Bundesfinanzhof, in *Re VAT Directives* ([1982] 1 CMLR 527) took the same view on the direct effects of the Sixth VAT Directive, despite the fact that the time limit for implementation had expired and existing German law appeared to run counter to the directive. The courts' reasoning in all these cases ran on similar lines. Article 249 expressly distinguishes regulations and directives; only regulations are described as 'directly applicable'; directives are intended to take effect within the national order via national implementing measures.

On a strict interpretation of Article 249 EC this is no doubt correct. On the other hand the reasoning advanced by the ECJ is compelling. The obligation in a directive is 'binding "on Member States" as to the result to be achieved'; the useful effects of directives would be weakened if states were free to ignore their obligations and enforcement of EC law were left to direct action by the Commission or Member States under Articles 226 or 227. Moreover states are obliged under Article 10 (post Lisbon, Article 4 of the Treaty on European Union (TEU)) to 'take all appropriate measures . . . to ensure fulfilment of the obligations arising out of this Treaty or resulting from action taken by the institutions of the Community'. If they have failed in these obligations why should they not be answerable to individual litigants?

5.2.5.5 *Vertical and horizontal direct effects: A necessary distinction*

The reasoning of the ECJ is persuasive where an individual seeks to invoke a directive against the state on which the obligation to achieve the desired results has been imposed. In cases such as *VNO*, *Van Duyn*, and *Ratti*, the claimant sought to invoke a directive against a public body, an arm of the state. This is known as *vertical* direct effect, reflecting the relationship between the individual and the state. Yet as with treaty articles, there are a number of directives, impinging on labour, company or consumer law for example, which a claimant may wish to invoke against a private person. Is the Court's reasoning in favour of direct effects adequate as a basis for the enforcement of directives against individuals? This is known as *horizontal* direct effect, reflecting the relationship between individuals.

The arguments for and against horizontal effects are finely balanced. Against horizontal effects is the fact of uncertainty. Prior to the entry into force of the TEU, directives were not required to be published. More compelling, the obligation in a directive is addressed to the state. In *Becker v Finanzamt Münster-Innenstadt* (case 8/81) the Court, following dicta in *Pubblico Ministero v Ratti* (case 148/78), had justified the direct application of the Sixth VAT Directive against the German tax authorities on the grounds that the obligation to implement the directive had been placed on the state. It followed that:

> a Member State which has not adopted, within the specified time limit, the implementing measures prescribed in the Directive, cannot raise the objection, as against individuals, that it has not fulfilled the obligations arising from the Directive.

This reasoning is clearly inapplicable in the case of an action against a private person. In favour of horizontal effects is the fact that directives have always in fact been published; that treaty provisions addressed to, and imposing obligations on, Member States have been held to be horizontally effective; that it would be anomalous, and offend against the principles of equality, if an individual's rights to invoke a directive were to depend on the status, public or private, of the party against whom he wished to invoke it; and that the useful effect of Community law would be weakened if individuals were not free to invoke the protection of Community law against *all* parties.

Although a number of references were made in which the issue of the horizontal effects of directives was raised, the ECJ for many years avoided the question, either by declaring that the claimant's action lay outside the scope of the directive, as in *Burton v British Railways Board* (case 19/81) (Equal Treatment Directive 76/207) or by falling back on a directly effective treaty provision, as in *Worringham v Lloyds Bank Ltd* (case 69/80) in which the then Article 119 (now 141) was applied instead of Directive 75/117, the Equal Pay Directive.

The nettle was finally grasped in *Marshall v Southampton & South West Hampshire Area Health Authority (Teaching)* (case 152/84). Here Mrs Marshall was seeking to challenge the health authority's compulsory retirement age of 65 for men and 60 for women as discriminatory, in breach of the Equal Treatment Directive 76/207. The difference in age was permissible under the Sex Discrimination Act 1975, which expressly excludes 'provisions relating to death or retirement' from its ambit. The Court of Appeal referred two questions to the ECJ:

(a) Was a different retirement age for men and women in breach of Directive 76/207?

(b) If so, was Directive 76/207 to be relied on by Mrs Marshall in the circumstances of the case?

The relevant circumstances were that the area health authority, though a 'public' body, was acting in its capacity as employer.

The question of vertical and horizontal effects was fully argued. The Court, following a strong submission from Advocate-General Slynn, held that the compulsory different retirement age was in breach of Directive 76/207 and could be invoked against a public body such as the health authority. Moreover 'where a person involved in legal proceedings is able to rely on a Directive as against the State he may do so regardless of the capacity in which the latter is acting, whether employer or public authority'.

On the other hand, following the reasoning of *Becker*, since a directive is, according to Article 249, binding only on 'each Member State to which it is addressed':

It follows that a Directive may not of itself impose obligations on an individual and that a provision of a Directive may not be relied upon as such against such a person.

If this distinction was arbitrary and unfair:

Such a distinction may easily be avoided if the Member State concerned has correctly implemented the Directive in national law.

So, with *Marshall v Southampton & South West Hampshire Area Health Authority (Teaching)* the issue of the horizontal effect of directives was, it seemed, finally laid to rest (albeit in an *obiter* statement, since the health authority was arguably a public body at the time). By denying their horizontal effect on the basis of Article 249 the Court strengthened the case for their vertical effect. The decision undoubtedly served to gain acceptance for the principle of vertical direct effects by national courts (see, eg, *R v London Boroughs Transport Committee, ex parte Freight Transport Association Ltd* [1990] 3 CMLR 495). But problems remain, both with respect to vertical and horizontal direct effects.

5.2.5.6 *Vertical direct effects: Reliance against public body*

First, the concept of a 'public' body, or an 'agency of the State', against whom a directive may be invoked, is unclear. In *Fratelli Costanzo SPA v Comune di Milano* (case 103/88), in a claim against the Comune di Milano based on the Comune's alleged breach of Public Procurement Directive 71/305, the Court held that since the reason for which an individual may rely on the provisions of a directive in proceedings before the national courts is that the obligation is binding on all the authorities of the Member States, where the conditions for direct effect were met, 'all organs of the administration, including decentralised authorities such as municipalities, are obliged to apply these provisions'. The area health authority in *Marshall* was deemed a 'public' body, as was the Royal Ulster Constabulary in *Johnston v RUC* (case 222/84). But what of the status of publicly owned or publicly run enterprises such as the former British Rail or British Coal? Or semi-public bodies? Are universities 'public' bodies and what is the position of privatised utility companies, or banks, which are in the main owned by the taxpayer?

These issues arose for consideration in *Foster v British Gas plc* (case C–188/89). In a claim against the British Gas Corporation in respect of different retirement ages for men and women, based on Equal Treatment Directive 76/207, the English Court of Appeal had held that British Gas, a statutory corporation carrying out statutory duties under the Gas Act 1972 at the relevant time, was not a public body against which the directive could be enforced. On appeal the House of Lords sought clarification on this issue from the ECJ. That court refused to accept British Gas's argument that there was a distinction between a nationalised undertaking and a state agency and ruled (at para 18) that a directive might be relied on against organisations or bodies which were 'subject to the authority or control of the State or had special powers beyond those which result from the normal relations between individuals'.

Applying this principle to the specific facts of *Foster v British Gas plc* it ruled (at para 20) that a directive might be invoked against:

> a body, whatever its legal form, which has been made responsible, pursuant to a measure adopted by the State, for providing a public service under the control of the State and has for that purpose special powers beyond those which result from the normal rules applicable in relations between individuals.

On this interpretation a nationalised undertaking such as the then British Gas would be a 'public' body against which a directive might be enforced, as the House of Lords subsequently decided in *Foster v British Gas plc* ([1991] 2 AC 306).

It may be noted that the principle expressed in para 18 is wider than that of para 20, the criteria of 'control' and 'powers' being expressed as alternative, not cumulative; as such it is wide enough to embrace any nationalised undertaking, and even bodies such as universities with a more tenuous public element, but which are subject to *some* state authority or control. However, in *Rolls-Royce plc v Doughty* ([1992] ICR 538), the English Court of Appeal, applying the 'formal ruling' of para 20 of *Foster*, found that Rolls-Royce, a nationalised undertaking at the relevant time, although 'under the control of the State', had not been 'made responsible pursuant to a measure adopted by the State for providing a public service'. The public services which it provided, for example, in the defence of the realm, were provided to the *state* and not to the *public* for the purposes of benefit to the state: nor did the company possess or exercise any special powers of the type enjoyed by British Gas. Mustill LJ suggested that the test provided in para 18 was 'not an authoritative exposition of the way in which cases like *Foster* should be approached': it simply represented a 'summary of the (Court's) jurisprudence to date'.

There is little evidence to support such a conclusion. The Court has never distinguished between its 'formal' rulings (ie, on the specific issue raised) and its more general statements of principle. Indeed such general statements often provide a basis for future rulings in different factual situations. A restrictive approach to the Court's rulings, as taken in *Rolls-Royce plc v Doughty*, is inconsistent with the purpose of the ECJ, namely to ensure the effective implementation of Community law and the protection of individuals' rights under that law by giving the concept of a public body the widest possible scope. This was acknowledged by the Court of Appeal in *National Union of Teachers v Governing Body of St Mary's Church of England (Aided) Junior School* ([1997] 3 CMLR 630) when it suggested that the concept of an emanation of the state should be a 'broad one'. The definition provided in para 20 of *Foster* should not be regarded as a statutory definition: it was, in the words of para 20, simply '*included among* those bodies against which the provisions of a Directive can be applied'.

The English courts' approach to whether a particular body is an 'emanation of the state' for the purpose of enforcement of EC directives is unpredictable. It is not altogether surprising that they fail to take a generous view when the result would be to impose liability on bodies which are in no way responsible for the non-implementation of directives, a factor which was undoubtedly influential in *Rolls-Royce plc v Doughty*. But even if national courts were to adopt a generous approach, no matter how generously the concept of a 'public' body is defined, as long as the public/private distinction exists there can be no uniformity in the application of directives as between one state and another. Neither will it remove the anomaly as between individuals. Where a state has failed to fulfil its obligations in regard to directives, whether by non-implementation or inadequate implementation, an individual would, it appeared, following *Marshall*, be powerless to invoke a directive in the context of a 'private' claim.

5.2.5.7 *Horizontal direct effects*

In 1993, in the case of *Dori v Recreb Srl* (case C–91/92), the Court was invited to change its mind on the issue of horizontal direct effects in a claim based on EC Directive 85/577 on Door-step Selling, which had not at the time been implemented by the Italian authorities, against a private party. Advocate-General Lenz urged the Court to reconsider its position in *Marshall* and extend the principle of direct effects to allow for the enforcement of directives against *all* parties, public and private, in the interest of the uniform and effective application of Community law. This departure from its previous case law was, he suggested, justified in the light of the completion of the internal market and the entry into force of the Treaty on European Union, in order to meet the legitimate expectations of citizens of the Union seeking to rely on Community law. In the interests of legal certainty such a ruling should however not be retrospective in its effect (on the effect of Article 234 rulings—see Chapter 10).

The Court, no doubt mindful of national courts' past resistance to the principle of direct effects, and the reasons for that resistance, declined to follow the Advocate-General's advice and affirmed its position in *Marshall*: Article 249 distinguished between regulations and directives; the case law establishing vertical direct effects was based on the need to prevent states from taking advantage of their own wrong; to extend this case law and allow directives to be enforced against individuals 'would be to recognise a power to enact obligations for individuals with immediate effect, whereas (the Community) has competence to do so only where it is empowered to adopt Regulations'. This decision was confirmed in subsequent cases, such as *El Corte Inglés SA v Rivero* (case C–192/94) *Arcaro* (case C–168/95), and more recently in *Carp v Ecorad* (case C-80/06).

However, in denying horizontal effects to directives in *Dori*, the Court was at pains to point out that alternative remedies might be available based on principles introduced by the Court prior to *Dori*, namely the principle of indirect effects and the principle of State liability introduced in *Francovich v Italy* (cases C–6 and 9/90—see Chapter 9). *Francovich* was also suggested as providing an alternative remedy in *El Corte Inglés SA v Rivero*. *Pfeiffer* (joined cases C–397/01 to 403/01) confirmed that directives could not have horizontal direct effect, but it emphasised, in the strongest possible terms, that a court was obliged to interpret domestic law in so far as possible in accordance with a directive (see 5.3, below). In the circumstances of that case, the practical outcome would have been akin to admitting horizontal direct effect, albeit by following the 'indirect effect' route. It must be borne in mind that one of the principal justifications for rejecting 'horizontal direct effect' has been that directives cannot, of themselves, impose obligations on individuals. In two-party situations, this reasoning is straightforward. It is less so in a three-party situation where an individual is seeking to enforce a right under a directive against the Member State where this would have an impact on a third party. This issue arose in *Wells v SoS for Transport, Local Government and the Regions* (case C–201/02), where Mrs Wells challenged the government's failure to carry out an environmental impact assessment (as required under Directive 85/337/EEC, [1985] OJ L175/40) when authorising the recommencement of quarrying works. The UK government argued that to accept that the relevant provisions of the directive had direct effect would result in 'inverse direct effect' in that UK government would be obliged to deprive another individual (the quarry owners) of their rights. The ECJ dismissed this, holding that permitting an individual to hold the Member State to its obligations was not linked to the performance of any obligation which would fall on the third party (at para 58), although there would be consequences for the third party as a result. It would be for the national courts to consider whether to require compliance with the directive in the particular case, or whether to compensate the individual for any harm suffered. A similar approach can be seen in *Arcor* (case C–152–4/07). The case concerned a decision by the German telecommunications authority, approving a connection charge for calls from Deutsche Telekom's national network to a connection partner to cover the costs of maintaining the local telecommunications infrastructure. Third-party telecommunications operators sought to challenge that decision and it was this challenge that formed the basis of the reference. The ECJ held that the decision was incompatible with the directives regulating the area. The ECJ then referred to its decision in *Wells,* although the referring court had not raised the question in these terms, and re-emphasised that 'mere adverse repercussions on the rights of third parties, even if the repercussions are certain, do not justify preventing an individual from relying on the provisions of a directive against the Member State concerned' (para 36). In coming to its conclusion in *Wells,* the ECJ relied, in part, on case law developed in the context of Directive 83/189/EEC on the enforceability of technical standards which have not been notified in accordance with the requirements of that directive. It had been suggested that these cases create something akin to 'incidental' horizontal effect, and it is therefore necessary to examine these in more detail.

5.2.5.8 *'Incidental' horizontal effect*

There have been cases in which individuals have sought to exploit the principle of direct effects not for the purposes of claiming Community rights denied them under national law, but simply in order to establish the illegality of a national law and thereby prevent its application to them. This may occur in a two-party situation, in which an individual is seeking to invoke a directive, whether as a sword or a shield, against the state. It presents particular problems in a three-cornered situation, in which a successful challenge based on an EC directive by an individual to a domestic law or practice, although directed at action by the state, may adversely affect third parties. In this case the effect of the directive would be felt horizontally. To give the directive direct effects in these cases would seem to go against the Court's stance on horizontal direct effects in the line of cases beginning with *Dori v Recreb Srl,* and the reasoning in these cases. Two cases, with contrasting outcomes, *CIA Security International SA v Signalson SA* (case C–194/94) and *Lemmens* (case C–226/97), illustrate the difficulty. Both cases involve Directive 83/189 (Directive 83/189 has been replaced and extended, by Directive 98/34 ([1998] OJ L204/37, amended by Directive 98/44, OJ L217/18), see 16.3.6). The directive, which is designed to facilitate the operation of the single market, lays down procedures for the provision of information by Member States to the Commission in the field of technical standards and regulations. Article 8 prescribes detailed procedures requiring Member States to notify, and obtain clearance from, the Commission for any proposed regulatory measures in the areas covered by the directive. In *CIA Security International SA v Signalson SA*, the defendants, CIA Security, sought to rely on Article 8 of Directive 83/189 as a defence to an action, brought by Signalson, a competitor, for unfair trading practices in the marketing of security systems. The defendants claimed that the Belgian regulations governing security, which the defendants had allegedly breached, had not been notified as required by the directive: they were therefore inapplicable. Contrary to its finding in the earlier case of *Enichem Base v Comune di Cinsello Balsamo* (case C–380/87), involving very similar facts and the same directive, the ECJ accepted this argument, distinguishing *Enichem* on the slenderest of grounds. Thus the effects of the directive fell horizontally on the claimant, whose actions, based on national law, failed.

Article 8 of Directive 83/189 was again invoked as a defence in *Lemmens* (case C–226/97). Lemmens was charged in Belgium with driving above the alcohol limit. Evidence as to his alcohol level at the relevant time had been provided by a breath analysis machine. Invoking *CIA Security International SA v Signalson SA*, he argued that the Belgian regulations with which breath analysis machines in Belgium were required to conform had not been notified to the Commission, as required by Article 8 of Directive 83/189. He argued that the consequent inapplicability of the Belgian regulations regarding breath analysis machines impinged on the evidence obtained by using those machines; it could not be used in a case against him. The ECJ refused to accept this argument. It looked to the purpose of the directive, which was designed to protect the interest of free movement of goods. The Court concluded:

> Although breach of an obligation (contained in the Directive) rendered (domestic) regulations inapplicable inasmuch as they hindered the marketing of a product which did not conform with its provisions, it did not have the effect of rendering unlawful any use of the product which conformed with the unnotified regulations. Thus the breach (of Article 8) did not make it impossible for evidence obtained by means of such regulations, authorized in accordance with the regulations, to be relied on against an individual.

This distinction, between a breach affecting the marketing of a product, as in *CIA Security International SA v Signalson SA*, and one affecting its use, as in *Lemmens*, is fine, and hardly satisfactory. The decision in *CIA Security International SA v Signalson SA* had been criticised because the burden imposed by the breach (by the state) of Article 8, the non-application of the state's unfair practice laws, would have fallen on an individual, in this case the claimant. This was seen as a horizontal application in all but name. In two other cases decided, like *CIA Security International SA v Signalson SA*, in 1996, *Ruiz Bernaldez* (case C–129/94) and *Panagis Parfitis* (case C–441/93), individuals were permitted to invoke directives to challenge national law, despite their adverse impact on third parties.

Lemmens, on the other hand, did not involve a third-party situation. The invocation by the defendant of Article 8 of Directive 83/189 did, however, smack of abuse. The refinement introduced in *Lemmens* may thus be seen as an attempt by the ECJ to impose some limits on the principle of direct effects as affected by *CIA Security* and as applied to directives.

The *CIA Security* principle was, however, confirmed and extended to a contractual relationship between two companies in *Unilever Italia SpA v Central Food SpA* (case C–443/98). Italy planned to introduce legislation on the geographical origins of various kinds of olive oil and notified this in accordance with Article 8 of the directive after the Commission requested that this be done. The Commission subsequently decided to adopt a Community-wide measure and invoked the 'standstill' procedure in Article 9 of the directive, which requires a Member State to delay adoption of a technical regulation for 12 months if the Commission intends to legislate in the relevant field. Italy nevertheless adopted its measure before the 12-month period had expired. The dispute leading to the Article 234 reference arose when Unilever supplied Central Foods with olive oil which had not been labelled in accordance with Italian law. Unilever argued that Italian legislation should not be applied because it had been adopted in breach of Article 9 of the directive. Advocate-General Jacobs argued that the *CIA* principle could not affect contractual relations between individuals, primarily because to hold otherwise would infringe the principle of legal certainty. The Court disagreed and held that the national court should refuse to apply the Italian legislation. It noted that there was no reason to treat the dispute relating to unfair competition in *CIA Security* differently from the contractual dispute in *Unilever*. The Court acknowledged the established position that directives cannot have horizontal direct effect, but went on to say that this did not apply in relation to Articles 8–9 of Directive 83/189. The Court did not feel that the case law on horizontal direct effect and the case law under Directive 83/189 were in conflict, because the latter directive does not seek to create rights or obligations for individuals.

The initial reaction to *CIA Security* was that the Court appeared to accept that directives could have horizontal direct effect. But after *Unilever*, it is clear that this has not been its intention. However, this area remains one of some uncertainty. The position now seems to be that private parties to a contract for the sale or supply of goods need to investigate whether any relevant technical regulations have been notified in accordance with the directive. There may then be a question of whether the limitation introduced by *Lemmens* comes into play. The end result appears to be the imposition on private parties of rights and obligations of which they could not have been aware—this was the main reason *against* the acceptance of horizontal direct effect in the case of directives. Although the Court in *Unilever* was at pains to restrict this line of cases to Directive 83/189 (and its replacement, Directive 98/34), this is not convincing. Nevertheless, the ECJ has maintained its approach under this Directive (see, eg, *Lidl Italia Srl v Comune di Stradella* (case C–303/04)), and it would appear to be best to regard the case law under Directive 98/34 (and its predecessor) as being confined to the context of that and similar directives (see also, eg, *R v Medicines Control Agency ex parte Smith & Nephew Ltd* (case C–201/94) in the context of the authorisation of medicinal products under Directive 65/65/EEC (superseded by 1993 measures), permitting the holder of a marketing authorisation to rely on Article 5 of that directive in challenging the grant of an authorisation to a competitor). It should also be noted that the ECJ has not adopted this approach in analogous situations involving decisions (*Carp v Ecorad* (case C–80/06)). Such a view should, of course, not be understood as reducing the significance of these cases in the context of an important field of EC law, and *Wells* (case C–201/02) and *Arcor* (case C–152–4/07) have taken this approach into the field of direct effect generally.

5.2.5.9 No direct effect to impose criminal liability

One important limitation to the direct effect principle was confirmed in *Berlusconi and others* (joined cases C–387/02, C–391/02, and C–403/02). Here, Italian company legislation had been amended after proceedings against Mr Berlusconi and others had been commenced to make the submission of incorrect accounting information a summary offence, rather than an indictable offence. The Italian criminal code provides that a more lenient penalty introduced after proceedings have been commenced but prior to judgment should be imposed, and in the instant cases, proceedings would therefore have to be terminated as the limitation period for summary offences had expired. The ECJ was asked (in Article 234 proceedings) if Article 6 of the First Company Law Directive (68/151/EEC) could be relied upon directly against the defendants. Having observed that the directive required an appropriate penalty and that it was for the national court to consider whether the revised provisions of Italian law were appropriate, the Court confirmed that it is not permissible to rely on the direct effect of a directive to determine the criminal liability of an individual (paras 73–8). In so holding, the ECJ followed the principles developed in the context of indirect effect (5.3.2, below) and reflects general principles of law (see Chapter 6).

5.2.5.10 *Direct effect of directives: Conclusions*

The jurisprudence of the ECJ in this area has matured sufficiently to permit the conclusion that, as a general rule, directives cannot take direct effect in the context of a two-party situation where both parties are individuals. Directives can only be relied upon against a Member State (in a broad sense) by an individual (on limitations on the obligations an individual can enforce, note *Verholen* (case C–87/90)). A directive cannot impose an obligation on an individual of itself; it needs to be implemented to have this consequence. Nevertheless, it is apparent that the clear-cut distinction between vertical and horizontal direct effect in two-party situations becomes blurred when transposed into a tripartite context. The enforcement by an individual of an obligation on the Member State may affect the rights of other individuals, which, according to *Wells* (case C–201/02), is a consequence of applying direct effect, but does not appear to change its vertical nature. The rather specific context of notification and authorisation directives, which may also have an effect on relationships not involving Member States, adds to the uncertainty. But whilst the case law may seem settled, the debate as to whether directives *should* have horizontal direct effect is one that is unlikely to go away soon.

5.2.6 **Decisions**

A decision is 'binding in its entirety upon those to whom it is addressed' (Article 249 EC).

Decisions may be addressed to Member States, singly or collectively, or to individuals. Although, like directives, they are not described as 'directly applicable', they may, as was established in *Grad v Finanzamt Traustein* (case 9/70), be directly effective provided the criteria for direct effects are satisfied. The direct application of decisions does not pose the same theoretical problems as directives, since they will only be invoked against the addressee of the decision. If the obligation has been addressed to him and is 'binding in its entirety', there seems no reason why it should not be invoked against him, providing, of course, that it satisfies the test of being sufficiently clear precise and unconditional. In the recent case of *Fosele v Sud-Ouest-Sarl* (case C–18/08), which concerned a decision which permitted the state to exempt certain vehicles from motor tax, the ECJ held that due to the element of choice left to the Member State, the individual could not rely on the decision to obtain such an exemption. An individual may seek to rely on a decision addressed to a Member State against that Member State (eg, recently, *Fosele v Sud-Ouest-Sarl* (case C–18/08)). In *Ecorad* (case C–80/60), Ecorad sought to rely on the contents of a decision, adopted according to the terms of a directive, addressed to a Member State in the context of a contractual dispute with Carp. Carp claimed it was not bound by the decision. The ECJ reviewed the cases on the horizontal application of directives and concluded that:

> the considerations underpinning the case-law referred to in the preceding paragraph with regard to directives apply *mutatis mutandis* to the question whether Decision 1999/93 may be relied upon as against an individual. [Para 21.]

5.2.7 Recommendations and opinions

Since recommendations and opinions have no binding force it would appear that they cannot be invoked by individuals, directly or indirectly, before national courts. However, in *Grimaldi v Fonds des Maladies Professionnelles* (case C–322/88), in the context of a claim by a migrant worker for benefit in respect of occupational diseases, in which he sought to invoke a Commission recommendation concerning the conditions for granting such benefit, the ECJ held that national courts were:

> bound to take Community recommendations into consideration in deciding disputes submitted to them, in particular where they clarify the interpretation of national provisions adopted in order to implement them or where they are designed to supplement binding EEC measures.

Such a view is open to question. It may be argued that recommendations, as non-binding measures, can at the most only be taken into account in order to resolve ambiguities in domestic law.

5.2.8 International agreements to which the EC is a party

There are three types of international agreements capable of being invoked in the context of EC law arising from the Community's powers under Articles 281, 300, 133, and 310 (ex 210, 228, 113 and 238 EC, post Lisbon, Articles 243, 260, 294, and 272 TFEU respectively—see Chapter 3). First, agreements concluded by the Community institutions falling within the treaty-making jurisdiction of the EC; secondly, 'hybrid' agreements, such as the WTO agreements, in which the subject matter lies partly within the jurisdiction of Member States and partly within that of the EC; and thirdly, agreements concluded prior to the EC Treaty, such as GATT, which the EC has assumed as being within its jurisdiction, by way of succession. There is no indication in the EC Treaty that such agreements may be directly effective.

The ECJ's case law on the direct effect of these agreements has not been wholly consistent. It purports to apply similar principles to those which it applies in matters of 'internal' law. A provision of an association agreement will be directly effective when 'having regard to its wording and the purpose and nature of the agreement itself, the provision contains a clear and precise obligation which is not subject, in its implementation or effects, to the adoption of any subsequent measure'. Applying these principles in some cases, such as *International Fruit Co NV v Produktschap voor Groenten en Fruit (No 3)* (cases 21 and 22/72), the Court, in response to an enquiry as to the direct effects of Article XI of GATT, held, following an examination of the agreement as a whole, that the Article was not directly effective.

In others, such as *Bresciani* (case 87/75) and *Kupferberg* (case 104/81), Article 2(1) of the Yaoundé Convention and Article 21 of the EC–Portugal trade agreement were examined respectively on their individual merits and found to be directly effective. The reasons for these differences are at not at first sight obvious, particularly since the provisions in all three cases were almost identical in wording to EC Treaty articles already found directly effective. The suggested reason (see Hartley (1983) 8 EL Rev 383) for this inconsistency is the conflict between the ECJ's desire to provide an effective means of enforcement of international agreements against Member States and the lack of a solid legal basis on which to do so. The Court justifies divergences in interpretation by reference to the scope and purpose of the agreement in question, which are clearly different from, and less ambitious than, those of the EC Treaty (*Opinion 1/91* (on the draft EEA Treaty)). As a result, the criteria for direct effects tend to be applied more strictly in the context of international agreements entered into by the EC.

Since the *International Fruit Co* cases the Court has maintained consistently that GATT rules cannot be relied upon to challenge the lawfulness of a Community act except in the special case where the Community provisions have been adopted to implement obligations entered into within the framework of GATT. Because GATT rules are not unconditional, and are characterised by 'great flexibility', direct effects cannot be inferred from the 'spirit, general scheme and wording of the Treaty'. This principle was held in *Germany v Council* (case C–280/93) to apply not only to claims by individuals but also to actions brought by Member States. As a result the opportunity to challenge Community law for infringement of GATT rules is seriously curtailed. Despite strong arguments in favour of the direct applicability of WTO provisions from Advocate-General Tesauro in *T Hermes International v FH Marketing Choice BV* (case C–53/96), the Court has not been willing to change its mind. It appears that there is near-unanimous political opposition to the direct application of WTO. (See recently *Merck Genéricos–Produtos Farmacêuticos Lda v Merck & Co Inc, and Merck Sharp & Dohme Lda* (case C–431/05)).

However, where the agreement or legislation issued under the agreement confers clear rights on *individuals* the ECJ has not hesitated to find direct effects (eg, *Sevince* (case C–192/89); *Bahia Kziber* (case C–18/90)).

Thus, paradoxically, an individual in a dualist state such as the UK will be in a stronger position than he would normally be vis-à-vis international law, which is not as a rule incorporated into domestic law.

5.2.9 Exclusions from the principle of direct effects

In extending the jurisdiction of the ECJ to matters within the third—justice and home affairs (JHA)—pillar of the TEU to encompass decisions and framework decisions in the field of political and judicial cooperation in criminal matters taken under Title VI TEU, the Treaty of Amsterdam (ToA) expressly denied direct effects to these provisions (Article 34(2) TEU). Similarly, although areas within the third pillar of the TEU, relating to visas, asylum, immigration, and judicial cooperation in civil matters, were incorporated into the EC Treaty (new Title IV), the ToA excluded the ECJ's jurisdiction to rule on any measure or decision taken pursuant to Article 62(1) 'relating to the maintenance of law and order and the safeguarding of internal security' (Article 68(2) EC); thus access to the ECJ via a claim before their national court was denied to individuals in areas in which they may be significantly and adversely affected. It should be noted that if the Treaty of Lisbon comes into force, Article 34 TEU would be deleted, all the provisions relating to judicial cooperation in criminal matters and to police cooperation being relocated to the TFEU (the EC Treaty after Lisbon comes into effect) as part of the area of freedom security and justice provisions. With the unitary structure, it will no longer be possible to distinguish between the policy areas in the current manner and thus these areas would seem to have the potential to become directly effective, though it should be noted that the CFSP provisions will remain in the TEU and therefore structurally separate. Arguably, distinctions may continue to be made here.

Although not an express exclusion from the principle of direct effects, a situation in which an individual was not be able to rely on Community law arose in the case of *Rechberger and Greindle v Austria* (case C–140/97). The case, a claim based on *Francovich*, concerned Austria's alleged breaches of Directive 90/134 on package travel both before Austria's accession, under the EEA Agreement, and, following accession, under the EC Treaty. The ECJ held that where the obligation to implement the directive arose under the EEA Agreement, it had no jurisdiction to rule on whether a Member State was liable under that agreement prior to its accession to the European Union (see also *Ulla-Brith Andersson v Swedish State* (case C–321/97)).

5.3 Principle of indirect effects

Although the ECJ has not shown willing to allow horizontal direct effect of directives, it has developed an alternative tool by which individuals may rely on directives against another individual. This tool is known as the principle of 'indirect effect', which is an interpretative tool to be applied by domestic courts interpreting national legislation which conflicts with a directive in the same area. It is sometimes also called the principle of consistent interpretation.

The principle of indirect effects was introduced in a pair of cases decided shortly before *Marshall*, namely: *von Colson v Land Nordrhein-Westfalen* (case 14/83) and *Harz v Deutsche Tradax GmbH* (case 79/83). Both cases were based on Article 6 of Equal Treatment Directive 76/207. Article 6 provides that:

> Member States shall introduce into their national legal systems such measures as are necessary to enable all persons who consider themselves wronged by failure to apply to them the principle of equal treatment . . . to pursue their claims by judicial process after possible recourse to other competent authorities.

The claimants had applied for jobs with their respective defendants. Both had been rejected. It was found by the German court that the rejection had been based on their sex, but it was justifiable. Under German law they were entitled to compensation only in the form of travelling expenses. This they claimed did not meet the requirements of Article 6. Ms von Colson was claiming against the prison service; Ms Harz against Deutsche Tradax GmbH, a private company. So the vertical/horizontal, public/private anomaly was openly raised and argued in Article 234 proceedings before the ECJ.

The Court's solution was ingenious. Instead of focusing on the vertical or horizontal effects of the directive it turned to Article 10 of the EC Treaty. Article 10 requires states to 'take all appropriate measures' to ensure fulfilment of their Community obligations.

This obligation, the Court said, applies to *all* the authorities of Member States, including the courts. It thus falls on the courts of the Member States to interpret national law in such a way as to ensure that the objectives of the directive are achieved. It was for the German courts to interpret German law in such a way as to ensure an effective remedy as required by Article 6 of the directive. The result of this approach is that although Community law is not applied directly—it is not 'directly effective'—it may still be applied indirectly as domestic law by means of interpretation.

The success of the *von Colson* principle of indirect effect depended on the extent to which national courts perceived themselves as having a discretion, under their own constitutional rules, to interpret domestic law to comply with Community law. Although the courts in the UK showed some reluctance initially to apply this principle, relying on a strict interpretation of s 2(1) of European Communities Act 1972 as applying only to directly effective Community law (see the House of Lords in *Duke v GEC Reliance Ltd* ([1988] AC 618)), the position soon changed (*Litster v Forth Dry Dock & Engineering Co Ltd* ([1990] 1 AC 546). Occasional 'hiccups' still occurred, however, and may still do so today. In *Finnegan v Clowney Youth Training Programme Ltd* ([1990] 2 AC 407) the House of Lords had refused to interpret Article 8(4) of the Sex Discrimination (Northern Ireland) Order 1976 (SI 1976/1042) in line with *Marshall*, even though the order had been made after the ECJ's decision in *Marshall*. This was because that provision was enacted in terms identical to the parallel provision considered in *Duke v GEC Reliance Ltd*, and 'must have been intended to' have the same meaning as in that Act. In the light of *Marleasing* (case 106/89, see below), such a decision would be unsustainable now, and today, the UK courts are taking their obligation seriously (see, eg, *Braymist Ltd v Wise Finance Co Ltd* [2002] Ch 273; *Director-General of Fair Trading v First National Bank* [2002] 1 AC 481).

5.3.1 The scope of the doctrine: *Marleasing*

The ECJ considered the scope of the 'indirect effect' doctrine in some depth in *Marleasing SA v La Comercial Internacional de Alimentación SA* (case C–106/89). In this case, which was referred to the ECJ by the Court of First Instance, Oviedo, the claimant company was seeking a declaration that the contracts setting up the defendant companies were void on the grounds of 'lack of cause', the contracts being a sham transaction carried out in order to defraud their creditors. This was a valid basis for nullity under Spanish law. The defendants argued that this question was now governed by EC Directive 68/151. The purpose of Directive 68/151 was to protect the members of a company and third parties from, inter alia, the adverse effects of the doctrine of nullity. Article 11 of the directive provides an exhaustive list of situations in which nullity may be invoked. It does not include 'lack of cause'. The directive should have been in force in Spain from the date of accession in 1986, but it had not been implemented. The Spanish judge sought a ruling from the ECJ on whether, in these circumstances, Article 11 of the directive was directly effective.

The ECJ reiterated the view it expressed in *Marshall* that a directive cannot of itself 'impose obligations on private parties'. It reaffirmed its position in *von Colson* that national courts must *as far as possible* interpret national law in the light of the wording and purpose of the directive in order to achieve the result pursued by the directive (para 8). And it added that this obligation applied *whether the national provisions in question were adopted before or after the directive*. It concluded by ruling specifically, and without qualification, that national courts were 'required' to interpret domestic law in such a way as to ensure that the objectives of the directive were achieved (para 13).

Given that in *Marleasing* no legislation had been passed, either before or after the issuing of the directive, to comply with the directive, and given the ECJ's suggestion that the Spanish court must nonetheless strive to interpret domestic law to comply with the directive, it seems that, according to the ECJ, it is not necessary to the application of the *von Colson* principle that the relevant national measure should have been introduced for the purpose of complying with the directive, nor even that a national measure should have been specifically introduced at all.

5.3.2 **The limits of** *Marleasing*

The strict line taken in *Marleasing* was modified in *Wagner Miret v Fondo de Garantira Salaria* (case C–334/92), in a claim against a private party based on Directive 80/987. This directive is an employee protection measure designed, inter alia, to guarantee employees arrears of pay in the event of their employer's insolvency. Citing its ruling in *Marleasing* the Court suggested that, in interpreting national law to conform with the objectives of a directive, national courts must *presume* that the state intended to comply with Community law. They must strive 'as far as possible' to interpret domestic law to achieve the result pursued by the directive. But if the provisions of domestic law cannot be interpreted in such a way (as was found to be the case in *Wagner Miret*) the state may be obliged to make good the claimant's loss on the principles of state liability laid down in *Francovich v Italy* (cases 6 and 9/90).

Wagner Miret thus represents a tacit acknowledgment on the part of the Court that national courts will not always feel able to 'construe' domestic law to comply with an EC directive, particularly when the provisions of domestic law are clearly at odds with an EC directive, and there is no evidence that the national legislature intended national law to comply with its provisions, or with a ruling on its provisions by the ECJ. This limitation proved useful for courts which were unwilling to follow *Marleasing*. Thus, in *R v British Coal Corporation, ex parte Vardy* ([1993] ICR 720), a case decided after, but without reference to, *Marleasing*, the English High Court adverted to the House of Lords judgment in *Litster* but found that it was 'not possible' to interpret a particular provision of the Trade Union and Labour Relations Act 1992 to produce the same meaning as was required by the relevant EC directive (see also *Re Hartlebury Printers Ltd* [1993] 1 All ER 470 at 478b, ChD).

Thus the indirect application of EC directives by national courts cannot be guaranteed. Some reluctance on the part of national courts to comply with the *von Colson* principle, particularly as applied in *Marleasing*, is hardly surprising. It may be argued that in extending the principle of indirect effect in this way the ECJ is attempting to give horizontal effect to directives by the back door, and impose obligations, addressed to Member States, on private parties, contrary to their understanding of domestic law. Where such is the case, as the House of Lords remarked in *Duke v GEC Reliance Ltd* (see also *Finnegan v Clowney Youth Training Programme Ltd*), this could be 'most unfair'. Indeed, the dividing line between giving 'horizontal direct effect' to a directive and merely relying on the interpretative obligation under the doctrine of 'indirect effect' can be a very fine and technical one in the circumstances of a particular case, as evidenced by *Mangold* (case C–144/04). This case involved an interpretation of the notion of 'working time' in the context of the Working Time Directive (93/104/EC [1993] OJ L307/18). German case law had developed a distinction between duty time, on-call time and stand-by time, with only the first being regarded as 'working time'. Emergency workers employed by the German Red Cross had challenged a provision in their collective labour agreement which, they argued, extended their working time beyond the prescribed 48-hour limit. The Court suggested that this agreement may be in breach of the directive, but that the claimants could not rely on the directive itself as against their employer. Having restated the basic principle that national law must be interpreted in accordance with the treaty, in particular where this has been enacted to implement a directive, the Court went on to say that this obligation was not restricted to the provisions themselves, but extended to 'national law as a whole in order to assess to what extent it may be applied so as not to produce a result contrary to that sought by the directive' (para 115).

A national court must do 'whatever lies within its jurisdiction' to ensure compliance with EC law. The ECJ did not go so far as to state expressly that existing case law might have to be reviewed to ensure such compliance, but the force of its reasoning appears to point in that direction. On the facts of the case, the outcome would be very close to allowing the individuals to invoke the direct effect of the directive against their employer.

The ECJ in *Adeneler* (case C–212/04) referred to another limitation on indirect effect, legal certainty and non-retroactivity. This line of reasoning finds its basis in the case of *Kolpinghuis Nijmegen* (case 80/86). Here, in the context of criminal proceedings against Kolpinghuis for breach of EC Directive 80/777 on water purity, which at the relevant time had not been implemented by the Dutch authorities, the Court held that national courts' obligation to interpret domestic law to comply with EC law was 'limited by the general principles of law which form part of Community law [see Chapter 6] and in particular the principles of legal certainty and non-retroactivity'.

Although expressed in the context of criminal liability, to which these principles were 'especially applicable', it was not suggested that the limitation should be confined to such situations. Where an interpretation of domestic law would run counter to the legitimate expectations of individuals *a fortiori* where the state is seeking to invoke a directive against an individual to determine or aggravate his criminal liability, as was the case in *Arcaro* (case C–168/95, see further below), the doctrine will not apply. Where domestic legislation has been introduced to comply with a Community directive, it is legitimate to expect that domestic law will be interpreted in conformity with Community law, provided that it is capable of such an interpretation (cf *Mangold*, case C–144/04, above). Where legislation has not been introduced with a view to compliance domestic law may still be interpreted in the light of the aims of the directive as long as the domestic provision is reasonably capable of the meaning contended for. But in either case an interpretation which conflicts with the clear words and intentions of domestic law is unlikely to be acceptable to national courts. This has repeatedly been acknowledged by the Court (*Wagner Miret* (case C–334/92) and *Arcaro* (case C–168/95)).

Mangold could, however, be seen as a more unsympathetic approach to the limits of interpretation. A similarly unsympathetic approach to the difficulties of the national court can be seen in *Quelle AG v Bundesverband der Verbraucherzentralen und Verbraucherverbände* (case C-404/06), where it was argued that, as the national court had ruled that there was only one possible interpretation and it was prohibited under national law from making a ruling *contra legem*, the reference should be declared inadmissible as the referring court would not be able to take account of any differing interpretation from the ECJ. The ECJ rejected the argument, on the basis of the separation of functions between the ECJ and the national court (see Chapter 10). It continued:

> The uncertainty as to whether the national court—following an answer given by the Court of Justice to a question referred for a preliminary ruling relating to interpretation of a directive—may, in compliance with the principles laid down by the Court . . . interpret national law in the light of that answer cannot affect the Court's obligation to rule on that question. [Para 22.]

In effect, the ECJ held here that the problems of dealing with the doctrine of indirect effect are for the national court. It should not be thought that *Quelle* signals an end to the *contra legem* principle. It was a ruling of one of the chambers. The Grand Chamber shortly before *Quelle* in *Impact v Minister for Agriculture and Food and others* (case C–268/06) reaffirmed the principle, holding that the national court's duty under indirect effect is 'limited by general principles of law, particularly those of legal certainty and non-retroactivity' and therefore indirect effect 'cannot serve as the basis for an interpretation of national law *contra legem*' (para 100). *Quelle* and *Mangold* seem then to be exceptions, but the uncertainty they introduced is not helpful.

Arcaro (case C–168/95) could also be seen as introducing further limitations on the scope of indirect effect. There, the ECJ held that the:

> obligation of the national court to refer to the content of the directive when interpreting the relevant rules of its own national law *reaches a limit where such an interpretation leads to the imposition on an individual of an obligation laid down by a directive which has not been transposed* or, more especially, where it has the effect of determining or aggravating, on the basis of the directive and in the absence of a law enacted for its implementation, the liability in criminal law of persons who act in contravention of that directive's provisions.

The Court has subsequently affirmed that the obligation to interpret domestic law in accordance with EC law cannot result in criminal liability independent of a national law adopted to implement an EC measure, particularly in light of the principle of non-retroactivity of criminal penalties in Article 7 of the European Convention on Human Rights (case C–60/02 *Criminal Proceedings against X ('Rolex')*). This reasoning has also been applied in the context of direct effect (see *Berlusconi and others* (joined cases C–387/02, C–391/02 and C–403/02)).

The phrase 'imposition on an individual of an obligation' in *Arcaro* could be interpreted to mean that indirect effect could never require national law to be interpreted so as to impose obligations on individuals not apparent on the face of the relevant national provisions. It is submitted, however, that the ECJ's view in *Arcaro* is limited to the context of criminal proceedings, and that the application of the doctrine of indirect effect can result in the imposition of civil liability not found in domestic law (see also Advocate-General Jacobs in *Centrosteel Srl v Adipol GmbH* (case C–456/98), paras 31–5).

This seems to be the result of *Oceano Grupo Editorial v Rocio Murciano Quintero* (case C–240/98). Here, Oceano had brought a claim in a Barcelona court for payment under a contract of sale for encyclopaedias. The contract contained a term which gave jurisdiction to the Barcelona court rather than a court located near the consumer's home. That court had doubts regarding the fairness of the jurisdiction clause. The Unfair Contract Terms Directive (93/13/EEC) requires that public bodies be able to take steps to prevent the continued use of unfair terms. It also contains a list of unfair terms, including a jurisdiction clause, but this only became effective in Spanish law *after* Oceano's claim arose. Spanish law did contain a general prohibition on unfair terms which could have encompassed the jurisdiction clause, but the scope of the relevant Spanish law was unclear. The question arose whether the Barcelona court should interpret Spanish legislation in accordance with the Unfair Contract Terms Directive. The ECJ reaffirmed the established position that a 'national court is obliged, when it applies national law provisions predating or postdating [a directive], to interpret those provisions, so far as possible, in the light of the wording of the directive' (para 32).

The Court went on to say that in light of the emphasis on public enforcement in the Unfair Contract Terms Directive, the national court may be required to decline of its own motion the jurisdiction conferred on it by an unfair term. As a consequence, Oceano would be deprived of a right which it might otherwise have enjoyed under existing Spanish law. This latter consideration should not prevent the national court from interpreting domestic law in light of the directive. In terms of the scope of the doctrine of indirect effect, it would be nonsensical to distinguish between cases which involve the imposition of obligations and those which concern restrictions on rights. Often, in a relationship between individuals, one individual's right is an obligation placed on another individual. The reasoning in *Arcaro* is best confined to the narrow context of criminal penalties.

Some questions have arisen as to when the obligation to use a consistent interpretation arises and in particular should it be the date the directive is enacted, or the date by which it must be implemented. This question came before the ECJ in *Adeneler*. The ECJ distinguished a positive and a negative duty for the courts of Member States. The positive aspect is the obligation to interpret all national law in line with the directive; that arises from the date by which the directive must be transposed. The negative aspect is based on the ECJ's reasoning in *Inter-Environnement Wallonie* (see 5.2.5.2 above). According to this line of reasoning, the national courts must, once the directive is in force (but before it is due to be transposed), refrain from interpreting national law in a way liable seriously to compromise the attainment of the result prescribed by the directive.

It may therefore be stated that the doctrine of indirect effect continues to be significant. However, there will be circumstances when it will not be possible to apply it. In such a situation, as the Court suggested in *Wagner Miret*, it will be necessary to pursue the alternative remedy of a claim in damages against the state under the principles laid down in *Francovich v Italy* (cases C–6 and 9/90—see Chapter 9).

It may be significant that in *El Corte Inglés SA v Rivero* (case C–192/94) the Court, in following the *Dori* ruling that a directive could not be invoked directly against private parties, did not suggest a remedy based on indirect effect, as it had in *Dori*, but focused only on the possibility of a claim against the state under *Francovich*.

5.3.3 Indirect effect in other contexts

The discussion has, so far, concentrated on the application of this principle in the context of directives. However, in *Maria Pupino* (case C–105/03), the ECJ held that the obligation to interpret national law in accordance with European rules can extend to framework decisions adopted under Article 34(2) TEU, and that a national court is required to interpret domestic law, in so far as possible, in accordance with the wording and purpose of a corresponding framework decision. The decision is controversial, because it extends the notion of indirect effect into the domain of criminal law, an area in respect of which the Community has no competence to act and seems also to circumvent the limitation on the direct effect of JHA provisions noted at 5.2.9.

5.4 Conclusions

The principle of direct effects, together with its twin principle of supremacy of EC law, discussed in Chapter 4, has played a crucial part in securing the application and integration of Community law within national legal systems. By giving individuals and national courts a role in the enforcement of Community law it has ensured that EC law is applied, and Community rights enforced, even though Member States have failed, deliberately or inadvertently, to bring national law and practice into line with Community law. Thus, as the Court suggested in *Van Gend* (case 26/62), the principle of direct effects has provided a means of control over Member States additional to that entrusted to the Commission under Article 226 and Member States under Article 227 (see further Chapter 11). But there is no doubt that the ECJ has extended the concept of direct effects well beyond its apparent scope as envisaged by the EC Treaty. Furthermore, although the criteria applied by the ECJ for assessing the question of direct effects appear straightforward, in reality they have in the past been applied loosely, and any provision which is justiciable has, until recently, been found to be directly effective, no matter what difficulties may be faced by national courts in its application, or what impact it may have on the parties, public or private, against whom it is enforced. Thus the principle of direct effects created problems for national courts, particularly in its application to directives.

In recent years there have been signs that the ECJ, having, with a few exceptions, won acceptance from Member States of the principle of direct effects, or at least—in the case of directives—of vertical effects, had become aware of the problems faced by national courts and was prepared to apply the principles of direct and indirect effect with greater caution. Its more cautious approach to the question of standing, demonstrated in *Lemmens* (case C–226/97), has been noted above. In *Comitato di Coordinamento per la Difesa della Cava v Regione Lombardia* (case C–236/92), the Court found that Article 4 of Directive 75/442 on the Disposal of Waste, which required states to 'take the necessary measures to ensure that waste is disposed of without endangering human health and without harming the environment', was not unconditional or sufficiently precise to be relied on by individuals before their national courts. It 'merely indicated a programme to be followed and provided a framework for action' by the Member States. The Court suggested that in order to be directly effective the obligation imposed by the directive must be 'set out in unequivocal terms'. In *R v Secretary of State for Social Security, ex parte Sutton* (case C–66/95) the Court refused to admit a claim for the award of interest on arrears of social security benefit on the basis of Article 6 of EC Directive 79/7 on Equal Treatment for Men and Women in Social Security, although in *Marshall (No 2)* (case C–271/91) it had upheld a claim for compensation for discriminatory treatment based on an identically worded Article 6 of Equal Treatment Directive 76/207. The Court's attempts to distinguish between the two claims ('amounts payable by way of social security are not compensatory') were unconvincing. In *El Corte Inglés SA v Rivero* (case C–192/94) it found the then Article 129a (now 153) of the EC Treaty requiring the Community to take action to achieve a high level of consumer protection insufficiently clear and precise and unconditional to be relied on as between individuals. This may be contrasted with its earlier approach to the former Article 128 EC, which required the Community institutions to lay down general principles for the implementation of a vocational training policy, which was found, albeit together with the non-discrimination principle of (the then) Article 7 EEC, to be directly effective (see *Gravier v City of Liège* (case 293/83)). Thus, a directive may be denied direct effects on any of the following the grounds:

(a) the right or interest claimed in the directive is not sufficiently clear, precise and unconditional

(b) the individual seeking to invoke the directive did not have a direct interest in the provisions invoked (*Verholen*, cases C–87–9/90)

(c) the obligation allegedly breached was not intended for the benefit of the individual seeking to invoke its provisions (*Lemmens*).

In the area of indirect effects, in *Dori v Recreb Srl* (case C–91/92), the ECJ, following its lead in *Marshall* (case 152/84), declared unequivocally that directives could not be invoked horizontally. This view was endorsed in *El Corte Inglés SA v Rivero*, *Arcaro* (case C–168/95) and, most recently, in *Pfeiffer* (joined cases C–397/01 to C–403/01). In *Wagner Miret* (case C–334/92) the ECJ acknowledged that national courts might not feel able to give indirect effect to Community directives by means of 'interpretation' of domestic law. This was also approved in *Arcaro*. In almost all of these cases, decided after *Francovich*, the Court pointed out the possibility of an alternative remedy based on *Francovich*, discussed in Chapter 9.

FURTHER READING

Amstutz, M, 'In-between worlds: *Marleasing* and the emergence of interlegality in legal reasoning' (2005) 11 European Law Journal 766.

Bebr, G, 'Agreements concluded by the Community and their possible direct effects: From International Fruit Company to Kupferberg' (1983) 20 CML Rev 35.

Bronckers, M, 'From "direct effect" to "muted dialogue": Recent developments in the European courts' case law on the WTO and beyond' (2008) 11(4) JIEL 885.

Coppel, J, 'Rights, duties and the end of *Marshall*' (1994) 57 MLR 859.

Craig, P, 'Directives: Direct effect, indirect effect and the construction of national legislation' (1997) 22 EL Rev 519.

Curtin, D, 'The province of government: Delimiting the direct effect of directives' (1990) 15 EL Rev 195.

—— 'The effectiveness of judicial protection of individual rights' (1990) 27 CML Rev 209.

de Burca, G, 'Giving effect to European Community directives' (1992) 55 MLR 215.

Green, N, 'Directives, equity and the protection of individual rights' (1984) 9 EL Rev 295.

Hartley, T, 'International agreements and the Community legal system: Some recent developments' (1983) 8 EL Rev 383.

Lackoff, K and Nyssens, H, 'Direct effect of directives in triangular situations' (1998) 23 EL Rev 397.

Lenz, M, 'Horizontal what? Back to basics' (2000) 25 EL Rev 502.

Lewis, C, and Moore, S, 'Duties, directives and damages in European Community Law' [1993] PL 151.

Mastoianni, R, 'On the distinction between vertical and horizontal direct effects of community directives: What role for the principle of equality?' (1999) 5 EPL 417.

Prechal, S, 'Remedies after *Marshall*' (1990) 27 CML Rev 451.

—— *Directives in European Community Law*, 2nd edn (Oxford University Press, 2005), Ch 9.

Prechal, S, and De Vries, S, 'Seamless web of judicial protection in the internal market?' (2009) 34(1) EL Rev 5.

Ruffert, M, 'Rights and remedies: European Community Law: A comparative view' (1997) 34 CML Rev 307.

Steiner, J, 'Coming to terms with EEC directives' (1990) 106 LQR 144.

Szyczak, E, 'Making Europe more relevant to its citizens' (1996) 21 EL Rev 351.

Van Gerven, W, 'The horizontal effect of directive provisions revisited: The reality of catch-words', Institute of European Public Law Lecture Series, University of Hull (1993).

Von Bogdandy, A, 'Pluralism, direct effect, and the ultimate say: On the relationship between international and domestic law' (2008) 6(3–4) International Journal of Constitutional Law 397.

Winter, TA, 'Direct applicability and direct effects' (1972) 9 CML Rev 425.

Wyatt, D, 'Direct effects of Community law, not forgetting directives' (1983) 8 EL Rev 241.

6

General principles of law

Introduction

6.1.1 **The relevance of general principles**

After the concept of direct effects and the principle of supremacy of EC law the third major contribution of the European Court of Justice (ECJ) has been the introduction of general principles of law into the corpus of EU law. Although primarily relevant to the question of remedies and enforcement of EC law, a discussion of the role of general principles of law is appropriate at this stage in view of their fundamental importance in the jurisprudence of the ECJ.

General principles of law are relevant in the context of EU law in a number of ways. First, they may be invoked as an aid to interpretation: EU law, including domestic law implementing EC law obligations, must be interpreted in such a way as not to conflict with general principles of law. Secondly, general principles of law may be invoked by both states and individuals to challenge Community action, either to annul or invalidate acts of the institutions (under Articles 230, 234, 236, and 241 (ex 173, 177, 179, and 184) EC post Lisbon 263, 267, 270 and 277 TFEU), or to challenge inaction on the part of these institutions (under Articles 232 or 236 (ex 175 and 179) EC post Lisbon 265 and 270 TFEU). Thirdly, as a logical consequence of its second role, but less generally acknowledged, general principles may also be invoked as a means of challenging action by a Member State, whether in the form of a legal or an administrative act, where the action is performed in the context of a right or obligation arising from Community law (see *Klensch* (cases 201 and 202/85); *Wachauf v Germany* (case 5/88); *Lageder v Amministrazione delle Finanze dello Stato* (case C–31/91); but cf *R v Ministry of Agriculture, Fisheries and Food, ex parte Bostock* (case C–2/93)). The degree to which general principles of law affect actions by Member States will be discussed in more detail later in this chapter. General principles of law may be invoked to support a claim for damages against the Community, under Article 288(2) (ex 215(2) post Lisbon Article 340 TFEU) (see Chapter 14).

These reasons are all practical reasons, based in the arena of legal action. There are other reasons, too, which relate to how the Union is seen; what sort of values it has. The jurisprudence in this area expands the rights of individuals beyond the economic rights found in the original treaty. In parallel with the concept of citizenship, the protection of such rights suggests the Union itself has greater links with the individuals and is, itself, obtaining greater legitimacy.

This area has become a steadily evolving aspect of Union law. This chapter examines the general historical development of the Court's jurisprudence to explain how general principles have been received into Union law. It will be seen that general principles, in particular fundamental rights, are invoked with increasing frequency before the European courts. Some of these general principles are examined in more detail. However, this chapter does not provide a full survey of the substantive rights which are now recognised in Union law. Such a discussion is beyond the scope of this book and readers should refer to the specialist texts which are now available.

6.1.2 Fundamental principles

General principles of law are not to be confused with the fundamental principles of Community law, as expressed in the EC Treaty, for example, the principles of free movement of goods and persons, of non-discrimination on the grounds of sex (Article 141 (ex 119, as amended) EC) or nationality (Article 12 (ex 6) EC), although there may be some overlap or commonality between the two. General principles of law constitute the 'unwritten' law of the Union and they have been developed—or discovered—over time by the ECJ.

6.2 Rationale for the introduction of general principles of law

The original legal basis for the incorporation of general principles into Union law was slim, resting precariously on three articles. Article 230 gives the ECJ power to review the legality of Community acts on the basis of, inter alia, 'infringement of this Treaty', or 'any rule of law relating to its application'. Article 288(2), which governs Community liability in tort, provides that liability is to be determined 'in accordance with the general principles common to the laws of the Member States'. And Article 220, governing the role of the ECJ, provides that the Court 'shall ensure that in the interpretation and application of this Treaty the law is observed'.

In the absence of any indication as to the scope or content of these general principles, it has been left to the ECJ to put flesh on the bones provided by the treaty. This function the Court has amply fulfilled, to the extent that general principles now form an important element of EU law.

One of the reasons for what has been described as the Court's 'naked law-making' in this area is best illustrated by the case of *Internationale Handelsgesellschaft mbH* (case 11/70). There the German courts were faced with a conflict between an EC regulation requiring the forfeiture of deposits by exporters if export was not completed within an agreed time, and a number of principles of the German constitution, in particular, the principle of proportionality. It is in the nature of constitutional law that it embodies a state's most sacred and fundamental principles. Although these principles were of particular importance, for obvious reasons in post-war Germany, other Member States also had written constitutions embodying similar principles and rights. Clearly it would not have done for EC law to conflict with such principles. Indeed, as the German constitutional court made clear ([1974] 2 CMLR 540), were such a conflict to exist, national constitutional law would take precedence over EC law. This would have jeopardised not only the principle of primacy of EC law but also the uniformity of application so necessary to the success of the new legal order. So while the ECJ asserted the principle of primacy of EC law in *Internationale Handelsgesellschaft*, it was quick to point out that respect for fundamental rights was in any case part of EC law.

Another reason now given to justify the need for general principles is that the Community's powers—and now those of the Union—have expanded to such a degree that some check on the exercise of the institutions' powers is needed. Furthermore, the expansion of Union competence means that the institutions' powers are now more likely to operate in policy areas in which human rights have an influence. Although those who wish to see sovereignty retained by the nation state may originally have been pleased to see the limitation of the institutions' powers, the development of human-rights jurisprudence in this context can be seen as a double-edged sword, giving the ECJ increased power to impugn both acts of the Union institutions and implementing measures taken by Member States on grounds of infringement of general principles.

6.3 Development of general principles

6.3.1 Fundamental human rights

The Court's first tentative recognition of fundamental human rights was prior to *Internationale Handelsgesellschaft*, in the case of *Stauder v City of Ulm* (case 29/69). Here the applicant was claiming entitlement to cheap butter provided under a Community scheme to persons in receipt of welfare benefits. He was required under German law to divulge his name and address on the coupon which he had to present to obtain the butter. He challenged this law as representing a violation of his fundamental human rights (namely, equality of treatment). The ECJ, on reference from the German court on the validity of the relevant Community decision, held that, on a proper interpretation, the Community measure did not require the recipient's name to appear on the coupon. This interpretation, the Court held, contained nothing capable of prejudicing the fundamental human rights enshrined in the general principles of law and protected by the Court.

The ECJ went further in *Internationale Handelsgesellschaft*. There it asserted that respect for fundamental rights forms an integral part of the general principles of law protected by the Court—such rights are inspired by the constitutional traditions common to the Member States. One point to note here is that the ECJ was not comparing EC law with *national* law but with the principles of *international* law which are embodied in varying degrees in the national constitutions of Member States. A failure to make the distinction between general principles of international law (even if embodied in national laws) which the Community legal order respects and national law proper could erode the doctrine of supremacy of Community law vis-à-vis national laws.

The *International Handelsgesellschaft* judgment can be taken as implying that only rights arising from traditions common to Member States can constitute part of EC law (a 'minimalist' approach). It may be argued that if the problem of conflict between Community law and national law is to be avoided in *all* Member States it is necessary for *any* human right upheld in the constitution of *any*

Member State to be protected under EU law (a 'maximalist' approach). In *Hoechst v Commission* (cases 46/87 and 227/88), in the context of a claim based on the fundamental right to the inviolability of the home, the Court, following a comprehensive review by Advocate-General Mischo of the laws of all the Member States on this question, distinguished between this right as applied to the 'private dwelling of physical persons', which was common to all Member States (and which would by implication be protected as part of Community law), and the protection offered to commercial premises against intervention by public authorities, which was subject to 'significant differences' in different Member States. In the latter case the only common protection, provided under various forms, was protection against arbitrary or disproportionate intervention on the part of public authorities. Similarly, but dealing with administrative law, in *Australian Mining & Smelting Europe Ltd v Commission* (case 155/79), in considering the principle of professional privilege, the Court found that the scope of protection for confidentiality for written communications between lawyers and their clients varied from state to state; only privilege as between independent (as opposed to in-house) lawyers and their clients was generally accepted, and would be upheld as a general principle of Community law.

These cases suggest that where certain rights are protected to differing degrees and in different ways in Member States, the Court will look for some *common* underlying principle to uphold as part of Union law. Even if a particular right protected in a Member State is not universally protected, where there is an apparent conflict between that right and EU law, the Court will strive to interpret Union law so as to ensure that the substance of that right is not infringed. An exception to this approach can be seen in *Society for the Protection of the Unborn Child v Grogan* (case 159/90). This case concerned the officers of a students' union who provided information in Ireland about the availability of legal abortion in the UK. SPUC brought an action alleging that this was contrary to the Irish constitution. The officers' defence was based on the freedom to provide services within the Community and on the freedom of expression contained in the ECHR which also forms part of Community law as a general principle (see further below). The ECJ evaded this issue. Since the students' union did not have an economic link with the clinics whose services they advertised, the provision of information about the clinics was not an economic activity within the treaty. As the issues fell outside the scope of EC law, the officers could not rely on either the provisions on freedom to provide services in the treaty or on general principles of law. (See further Chapter 21.)

6.3.2 Role of international human-rights treaties

Following *Internationale Handelsgesellschaft* the scope for human-rights protection was further extended in the case of *J Nold KG v Commission* (case 4/73). In this case J Nold KG, a coal wholesaler, was seeking to challenge a decision taken under the ECSC as being in breach of the company's fundamental right to the free pursuit of business activity. While the Court did not find for the company on the merits of the case, it asserted its commitment to fundamental rights in the strongest terms. As well as stating that fundamental rights form an integral part of the general principles of law, the observance of which it ensures, it went on to say:

> In safeguarding these rights, the Court is bound to draw inspiration from constitutional traditions common to the Member States, and it cannot therefore uphold measures which are incompatible with fundamental rights recognised and protected by the constitutions of those States.
>
> Similarly, international treaties for the protection of human rights on which the Member States have collaborated or of which they are signatories, can supply guidelines which should be followed within the framework of Community law.

The reasons for this inclusion of principles of certain international treaties as part of EU law are clearly the same as those upholding fundamental constitutional rights; it is the one certain way to guarantee the avoidance of conflict.

In this context, the most important international treaty concerned with the protection of human rights is the European Convention for the Protection of Human Rights and Fundamental Freedoms 1950 (ECHR), to which all Member States are now signatories. The Court has on a number of occasions confirmed its adherence to the rights protected therein, an approach to which the other institutions gave their support (Joint Declaration, [1977] OJ C103/1). In *R v Kirk* (case 63/83), in the context of criminal proceedings against Kirk, the captain of a Danish fishing vessel, for fishing in British waters (a matter subsequently covered by EC regulations), the principle of non-retroactivity of penal measures, enshrined in Article 7 of the ECHR, was invoked by the Court and applied in Captain Kirk's favour. The EC regulation, which would have legitimised the British rules under which Captain Kirk was charged, could not be applied to penalise him retrospectively. (See also *Johnston v Chief Constable of the Royal Ulster Constabulary* (case 222/84) (ECHR, Article 6, right to judicial process); *Hoechst* (cases 46/87, 227/88) contrast substantive ruling in *Roquette Frères* (case C–94/00); *National Panasonic v Commission* (case 136/79) (ECHR Article 8, right to respect for private and family life, home and correspondence—not infringed).) The impact of Article 8 ECHR can be seen clearly in the case law on free movement of people (see Chapter 25).

Thus, it seems that any provision in the ECHR may be invoked, provided it is done in the context of a matter of EU law. In *Kaur v Lord Advocate* ([1980] 3 CMLR 79), an attempt was made to invoke the Convention (Article 8 'respect for family life') by an Indian immigrant seeking to challenge a deportation order made under the Immigration Act 1971. She failed on the grounds that the Convention had not been incorporated into British law. Its alleged incorporation via the European Communities Act 1972 did not enable a party to invoke the Convention before a Scottish court in a matter wholly unrelated to EU law (see also *SPUC v Grogan* (case 159/90) and *Kremzow v Austria* (case C–299/95)). In *Mannesmannröhren-Werke AG v Commission* (Case T–112/98), the Court of First Instance (CFI) emphasised that although the ECHR has special significance in defining the scope of fundamental rights recognised by the Community, because it reflects the constitutional traditions common to the Member States, the Court has no jurisdiction to apply the ECHR itself. The CFI therefore rejected arguments based directly on Article 6 ECHR in relation to an application to annul a Commission decision, but allowed the application on other grounds (see 6.6.7). The CFI's view with regard to invoking ECHR articles may be technically correct, but it sits somewhat uneasily with other judgments both by the CFI and the ECJ in which the courts appeared more willing to refer directly to ECHR provisions, and even to the jurisprudence of the European

Court of Human Rights itself (see, eg, *Roquette Frères* (case C–94/00); *Orfanopoulos* (case C–482/01), citing *Boultif v Switzerland* concerning right to family life; *Connolly v Commission* (case C–274/99P): civil servants' freedom of expression under Article 10 ECHR).

Other international treaties concerned with human rights referred to by the Court as constituting a possible source of general principles are the European Social Charter (1971) and Convention 111 of the International Labour Organisation (1958) (*Defrenne v Sabena (No 3)* (case 149/77)). In *Ministère Public v Levy* (case C–158/91) the Court suggested that a Member State might even be obliged to apply a national law which conflicted with a ruling of its own on the interpretation of EC Directive 76/207 where this was necessary to ensure compliance with an international convention (in this case ILO Convention 89, 1948) concluded prior to that state's entry into the EC. The list has grown over the years, with the ECJ adding recently, for example, Convention on the Protection and Promotion of the Diversity of Cultural Expressions (*UTECA v Administración General del Estado* (case C–222/07)) and the UN Convention on the Rights of the Child (*Dynamic Medien* (case C–244/06)).

6.3.3 Relationship between different legal systems protecting human rights

6.3.3.1 *Relationship with national constitutions*

We saw at the beginning of this chapter that one of the central reasons for the introduction of fundamental rights into EU law was the resistance of some of the constitutional courts to giving effect to Community rules which conflicted with national constitutional principles. The ECJ's tactics to incorporate these principles and stave off rebellion were undoubtedly successful as exemplified by the *Wünsche* case ([1987] 3 CMLR 225), in which the German constitutional court resiled from its position in *Internationale Handelsgesellschaft* ([1974] 2 CMLR 540) (see Chapter 4). This does not, however, mean that the ECJ can rest on its laurels in this regard. The Italian constitutional court in Fragd (*SpA Fragd v Amministrazione delle Finanze* Decision No 232 of 21 April 1989) reaffirmed its right to test Community rules against national constitutional rules and stated that Community rules that, in its view, were incompatible with the Italian constitution would not be applied. Similarly, the German constitutional courts have reasserted the right to challenge Community legislation that is inconsistent with the German constitution (see, eg, *Brunner v European Union Treaty* [1994] 1 CMLR 57; *M GmbH v Bundesregierung* (case 2 BvQ 3/89) [1990] 1 CMLR 570 (an earlier tobacco-advertising case) and the bananas cases—*Germany v Council (Re Banana Regime)* (case C–280/93), *Germany v Council (Bananas II)* (case C–122/95) and *T Port GmbH v Hauptzollamt Hamburg-Jonas* (cases C–364 and 365/95)—discussed further in Chapter 4). Although the supremacy of Community law vis-à-vis national law might not be threatened by the possibility of its review in accordance with provisions of national constitutions embodying general principles of international law, its uniformity and the supremacy of the ECJ might well be eroded if national courts seek themselves to interpret these broad and flexible principles, rather than referring for a ruling on these matters from the ECJ. Equally, a failure on the part of national courts to recognise fundamental principles, in conjunction with a failure to refer, may have a similar effect.

6.3.3.2 *Accession to the ECHR*

Deferring to the ECJ does, however, concentrate a significant degree of power in that court, against whose rulings there is no appeal. One suggested safeguard for fundamental rights would be for the Community to accede to the ECHR. Questions of human rights and, in particular, interpretation of the ECHR, could then be taken to the European Court of Human Rights, a court which specialises in these issues. This would minimise the risk of the ECJ misinterpreting the ECHR and avoid the possibility of two conflicting lines of case law developing (eg, *Orkem* (case 374/87) and *Funke v France* (case SA 256A)). The ECJ, however, has ruled that accession to the ECHR would not be within the present powers of the Community: treaty amendment would be required before the Community could take this step (*Opinion 2/94 on the Accession by the Community to the European Convention on Human Rights*).

This was one of the issues discussed by the Convention on the Future of Europe preparing for the 2004 IGC. The treaty establishing a Constitution would not only have incorporated the EU Charter of Fundamental Rights (a separate document, not to be confused with the ECHR) into the Constitution (see further below), but would also have included an article in Part I which provided that the Union 'shall accede to the European Convention for the Protection of Human Rights and Fundamental Freedoms'. A further declaration provided for cooperation between the ECHR and the ECJ. As we know, the Constitution has been abandoned and replaced by the Lisbon Treaty. Although Lisbon does not incorporate the charter, it continues the intention to accede to the ECHR (Article 6(2) TEU), but the status of the Lisbon Treaty is, like the Constitution before it, in doubt (see Chapter 1). Even if it were in force, the details of timing and other practicalities of accession remain to be worked out. The Treaty on European Union (TEU) (as amended by Lisbon) also specifies that accession would not affect the Union's competence as defined in the treaties. Yet, this remains a significant step forward. It also follows the line established by recent treaty amendments, which have seen a progressive raising of the profile of human-rights protection within the Community and, indeed, the Union.

6.3.3.3 *Enforcing respect for the ECHR within the EU structure*

The TEU had included in the Union general provisions a reference to the ECHR to the effect that:

> The Union shall respect fundamental rights, as guaranteed by the European Convention for the Protection of Human Rights and Fundamental Freedoms . . . and as they result from the constitutional tradition common to the Member States, as general principles of Community law. [Article 6(2) (ex F(2) TEU).]

The Constitution provided, to a similar effect, that:

> Fundamental Rights, as guaranteed by the European Convention for the Protection of Human Rights and Fundamental Freedoms and as they result from the constitutional traditions common to the Member States, shall constitute general principles of the Union's law. [Article I–9(3).]

This wording has been reproduced by the Lisbon Treaty at Article 6(3) TEU.

Additionally, Article 6(1) (ex F(1)) TEU stated that the Union was founded on respect for 'liberty, democracy and respect for human rights'. However, by Article L TEU, as it then was (now amended and renumbered as Article 46 TEU), the ECJ's jurisdiction as regards the general Union provisions was excluded. The Treaty of Amsterdam (ToA) amended Article 46 TEU to give the ECJ express competence in respect of Article 6(2) TEU with regard to action of the institutions 'insofar as the ECJ has jurisdiction either under the treaties establishing the Communities or under the TEU'. This would seem to be little more than a confirmation of the existing position, at least as far as the EC Treaty is concerned, though it might have some significance in respect of the ECJ's (limited) jurisdiction regarding justice and home affairs (JHA). Article 46 TEU will be repealed should the Lisbon Treaty come in to force.

The ToA inserted Article 7 into the TEU. This provided that where there has been a persistent and serious breach of a principle mentioned in Article 6(1) TEU, the Council may suspend certain of the rights of the offending Member State, including its voting rights. Were this provision used, it could have serious consequences for the Member State in question; such a Member State would lose its opportunity to influence the content of Union legislation by which it would be bound, even in sensitive areas where otherwise it could have vetoed legislation. Thus, one might suggest that the need to comply with fundamental principles is being taken seriously indeed. It is likely, though, that this provision will be used only rarely given the severity of the breach needed to trigger the procedure, which itself is long-winded, requiring unanimity (excluding the offending Member State) in the first instance. Given the potential consequences for Member States, however, the complexity of the procedure is perhaps appropriate. The Lisbon Treaty contains a new provision, Article 269 TFEU, which gives the ECJ the jurisdiction to decide on the legality of such a decision on procedural grounds only.

6.3.3.4 *Relationship with international law*

The relationship between EU and international law has been the subject of consideration recently. The factual backdrop concerned Union measures implementing UN Resolutions on economic sanctions. Effectively, these measures allowed for the freezing of individuals' assets, without prior warning. The matter came before the CFI, as an action for annulment. It held that the courts are not empowered to review decisions of the UN, including the Security Council, even in the light of Community law or the fundamental rights recognised by Union law (*Ahmed Ali Yusuf and Others v Council of the European Union* (cases T–306 and 315/01), known as *Kadi*). The CFI based this decision on the fact that, according to its interpretation of the requirements of international law, the obligations of the Member States of the United Nations prevail over any other obligation. The Community, although not itself a member of the UN, must, in the CFI's opinion, be bound by the obligations flowing from the Charter of the United Nations. Nonetheless, the CFI reserved the rights of the Community courts to check the lawfulness of the Council Regulation (which implemented the UN Security Council Resolution and was under challenge in this case), and therefore implicitly the underlying resolution, by reference to the higher rules of international law (*jus cogens*), from which neither the Member States nor the bodies of the Union should, under international law, be able to derogate. This includes provisions intended to secure universal protection of fundamental human rights. On the facts, the CFI found the application unfounded.

The ECJ heard the appeal in *Kadi* (joined cases C–402 and 415/05 P) and approached the matter in a completely different way, overturning the CFI's internationalist approach. While the ECJ accepted that the EU (and its Member States) were subject to international obligations, such as those contained in the UN, this does not change the allocation of powers within the EU. Furthermore, the EU was characterised by the ECJ, drawing on its previous jurisprudence, as an autonomous legal order built on the rule of law and respect for fundamental human rights. Thus there is a distinction between international obligations and the effect of Community norms, and the fact that Community measures might arise from those international obligations does not affect the fact that Union law must comply with human rights, as recognised by the EU. On this basis, the ECJ reviewed whether the EU implementing measures (not the UN Resolutions) complied with a number of procedural rights and the right to respect for property, and in this, it is arguable that the ECJ was taking a stronger line that had the European Court of Human Rights. This is a significant judgment, which re-emphasises the centrality of the rule of law and the protection of human rights within the EU.

6.4 Relationship between the EC/EU and the ECHR in the protection of human rights: View from the ECHR

All Member States of the EU have signed the ECHR, and in most Member States, the Convention has been incorporated into domestic law. (It was incorporated in the UK by the Human Rights Act 1998, which came into force in October 2000.) When it is so incorporated, the Convention's provisions may be invoked before the domestic courts in order to challenge *national* rules or procedures which infringe the rights protected by the Convention. Even without the Convention being incorporated into domestic law, the Member States are bound by its terms and individuals, after they have exhausted national remedies, have a right of appeal under the Convention to the European Court of Human Rights.

The ECJ has done a great deal to ensure the protection of human rights within the context of the application of Community law, whether by Community institutions or by Member States. But, as the ECHR has not so far been incorporated into *Community* law, its scope has been limited and the relationship between the ECHR and the Union legal system is somewhat unclear. The difficulties are illustrated by the decision of the European Court of Human Rights in the *Matthews* case (European Court of Human Rights judgment, 18 February 1999).

Matthews concerned the rights of UK nationals resident in Gibraltar to vote in European Parliamentary elections. They were excluded from participating in the elections as a result of the 1979 agreement between the Member States which established direct elections in respect of the European Parliament. The applicants argued that this was contrary to Protocol 1, Article 3 of the ECHR, which provides that signatory States to the Convention are under an obligation 'to hold free elections at reasonable intervals by secret ballot, under conditions which will ensure the free expression of the opinion of the people in the choice of the legislature'. The British government argued that not only was Community law not within the jurisdiction of the ECHR (as the Community had not acceded to the Convention), but also that the UK government could not be held responsible for joint acts of the Member States. The European Court of Human Rights found, however, that there had been a violation of the Convention.

The Court held that States which are party to the ECHR retain residual obligations in respect of the rights protected by the Convention, even as regards areas of lawmaking which had been transferred to the Union. Such a transfer of power is permissible, provided Convention rights continue to be secured within the Community framework. In this context the Court of Human Rights noted the ECJ's jurisprudence in which the ECJ recognised and protected Convention rights. In this case, however, the existence of the direct elections was based on a *sui generis* international instrument entered into by the UK and the other Member States which could not be challenged before the ECJ, as it was not a normal Community act. Furthermore, the TEU, which extended the European Parliament's powers to include the right to co-decision thereby increasing the Parliament's claim to be considered a legislature and taking it within the terms of Protocol 1, Article 3 of the ECHR, was equally an act which could not be challenged before the ECJ. There could therefore be no protection of Convention rights in this regard by the ECJ. Arguing that the Convention is intended to guarantee rights that are not theoretical or illusory, the Court of Human Rights held that:

> The United Kingdom, together with all other parties to the Maastricht Treaty, is responsible *ratione materiae* under Article 1 of the Convention and, in particular, under Article 3 of Protocol 1, for the consequences of that Treaty. [Para 33.]

It may be noted that it is implicit in the reasoning in this judgment that the EU is regarded by the Court of Human Rights as being the creature of the Member States, which remain fundamentally responsible for the Community's actions—and for those of the Union. This corresponds with the conception of the EU expressed by some of the Member States' constitutional courts (eg, see the German constitutional court's reasoning in *Brunner* [1994] 1 CMLR 57).

Arguably, this judgment opens the way for the Member States to be held jointly responsible for those Community (or Union) acts that currently fall outside the jurisdiction of the ECJ, sealing lacunae in the protection offered to individual human rights within the Community legal order. The difficulty is, of course, that in this case only the UK was the defendant. The British government is dependent on the cooperation of the other Member States to enable it to fulfil its own obligations under the ECHR. It is possible that a case could be brought under the ECHR against all Member States jointly. (See, eg, *Société Guerin Automobiles* (Application No 51717/99), inadmissible on other grounds; *DSR Senator Lines*, (Application No 56672/00) (Grand Chamber), dismissed as the applicant could not claim on the facts to be a victim, though note third-party representations, including that of the ICJ.) Although this would not obviate the need for cooperation to remedy any violation found, it would avoid the situation where one Member State alone was carrying the responsibility for Union measures that were the choice of all (or most) Member States. The implication that the European Court of Human Rights will step in only where there is no effective means of securing human-rights protection within an existing international body (ie, that the ECJ has primary responsibility for these issues in the EU) is underlined by its approach in another case involving another European supranational organisation, Euratom (*Waite and Kennedy v Germany*, European Court of Human Rights judgment, 18 February 1999). There the Court emphasised the necessity for an independent review board which is capable of protecting fundamental rights to exist within the organisational structure. More recently, we can see this approach in *Bosphorus Airways v Ireland* (European Court of Human Rights judgment, 30 June 2005 (GC)), which concerned alleged human-rights violations resulting from Community secondary legislation which the ECJ had upheld. There the European Court of Human Rights held that it would not interfere provided the rights protection awarded by the ECJ was equal to that under the ECHR, noting that in this context, 'equal' means equivalent or comparable rather than identical (para 155). It should be noted that in a concurring judgment, one of the European Court of Human Rights judges did make the point that, although there have been reviews of ECJ jurisprudence, they have looked at the level of protection in a general or formal way, rather than looking at the substance of a right in an individual case (Concurring Opinion of Judge Ress, para 2), highlighting a potential weakness in the system of protection awarded to individuals. Of course, this may all change should the EU accede to the ECHR.

6.5 The EU Charter of Fundamental Rights

6.5.1 Background

We have already seen that there has been a debate about whether the EC/EU should accede to the ECHR. In 1999, the Cologne European Council set up a Convention, under the chairmanship of Roman Herzog (a former German federal president), to produce a draft Union charter as an alternative mechanism to ensure the protection of fundamental rights. This was completed in time for the 2000 European Council meeting at Nice, where the European institutions solemnly proclaimed the charter (published at [2000] OJ C364/1—hereinafter EUCFR). At the present time, the EUCFR does not have legal effect. As with the Constitution, the Lisbon Treaty proposes to give legal effect to the Charter. It does so by a different route, though. The Constitution would have incorporated the Charter as Part II and Article I–9(1) specified that 'the Union shall recognize the rights, freedoms and principles set out in the Charter of Fundamental Rights'. Lisbon instead refers to the Charter rather than incorporating it. Thus, Article 6(1) TEU (as amended by Lisbon) states:

> the Union recognises the rights, freedoms and principles set out in the Charter of Fundamental Rights . . . which shall have the same legal value as the Treaties.

Nonetheless the scope of the rights granted is as limited as it was under the Charter (see 6.5.2). Further provisions clarify that the reference to the Charter does not create any new rights or extend the Union's competence.

Despite some contention about the status and impact of the Charter, the ECJ has already mentioned the EUCFR in a number of judgments by way of reference in confirming that the European legal order recognises particular fundamental rights (see, eg, *R v SoS ex parte BAT* (Case C–491/01), where the Court observed that 'the right to property . . . is recognised to be a fundamental human right in the Community legal order, protected by the first subparagraph of Article 1 of the First Protocol to the European Convention on Human Rights ("ECHR") and *enshrined in Article 17 of the Charter of Fundamental Rights of the European Union*' (para 144, emphasis added). See also *Jego-Quere et Cie v Commission* (case T–177/01 para 42; see further Chapter 12 and *Mannesmannröhren-Werke AG v Commission* (case T–112/98) paras 15 and 76). These have begun to cover a wide range of rights: we have already noted the *Kadi* judgment. In *Dynamic Medien,* the ECJ referred to the rights of the child protected by the Charter and in *Varec v Belgian State* (case C–450/06), the ECJ refers to the right to private life. However, there has been no judgment to date in which the ECJ has *based* its judgment on the EUCFR.

6.5.2 Scope

By virtue of Article 51(1) EUCFR, its provisions are addressed to the institutions and bodies of the Union and to the Member States only when they are implementing Union law. As far as the institutions and bodies of the Union are concerned, due regard is to be had to the principle of subsidiarity. It is not entirely clear what the significance of this reference is, other than perhaps to confirm that the Union must always act in accordance with the principle of subsidiarity. With regard to the Member States, Article 51(1) EUCFR confirms existing case law which has held that there is only an obligation on the Member States to respect fundamental rights under EU law when they are acting in the context of Community law (see *Karlsson and ors* (case C–292/97), para 37). Outside this context, Member States are, of course, obliged to respect fundamental rights under the ECHR (see above, on 'residual obligations').

Article 52(1) EUCFR provides that limitations on the exercise of the rights and freedoms guaranteed by the EUCFR must be provided by law. Any such limitations must be proportionate and are only permitted if they are necessary and genuinely meet objectives recognised by the EU. In this, there are similarities to the approach taken with regard to the derogation provisions in the ECHR. Article 52(2) EUCFR further confirms that those rights which derive from the treaties are subject to the conditions and limitations that apply to the corresponding treaty provisions.

6.5.3 Substance

The EUCFR is divided into six substantive chapters. Chapter I, Dignity, includes:

(a) human dignity

(b) the right to life

(c) the right to the integrity of the person

(d) prohibitions on torture, inhuman or degrading treatment or punishment, slavery and forced labour.

Chapter II, Freedoms, provides for:

(a) right to liberty and security

(b) respect for private and family life

    (c) protection of personal data

    (d) right to marry and found a family

    (e) freedom of:

        (i) thought, conscience and religion

        (ii) expression and information

        (iii) assembly and association

        (iv) the arts and sciences

        (v) a right to education;

        (vi) choice in an occupation and a right to engage in work;

        (vii) ability to conduct a business, right to property, right to asylum, and protection in the event of removal, expulsion or deportation.

Chapter III, Equality, guarantees:

    (a) equality before the law, non-discrimination, cultural, religious and linguistic diversity

    (b) equality between men and women

    (c) the rights of the child and the elderly

    (d) the integration of persons with disabilities.

The solidarity rights in Chapter IV are:

    (a) the workers' right to information and consultation with the right of collective bargaining and action

    (b) right of access to placement services

    (c) protection in the event of unjustified dismissal

    (d) fair and just working conditions

    (e) prohibition of child labour and protection of young people at work

    (f) family and professional life

    (g) social security and social assistance

    (h) health care

    (i) access to services of general economic interest

    (j) environmental protection

    (k) consumer protection.

Chapter V provides for citizenship rights (see also Chapter 24), which are the right to:

    (a) vote and stand as candidate at elections to the European Parliament and at municipal elections

    (b) good administration

    (c) access to documents

    (d) access to the Ombudsman

    (e) petition the European Parliament

    (f) have freedom of movement and residence

    (g) diplomatic and consular protection.

Finally, Chapter VI, Justice, guarantees a right to:

(a) effective remedy and to a fair trial

(b) presumption of innocence and right of defence

(c) principles of legality and proportionality of criminal offences and penalties;

(d) not to be tried or punished twice in criminal proceedings for the same criminal offence.

The preceding enumeration of all the rights contained in the EUCFR demonstrates that the Charter consists of a mixture of human rights found in the ECHR, rights derived from other international conventions and provisions of the EC Treaty. The Council of the European Union has published a booklet which explains the origin of each of the rights contained in the EUCFR (see 'Further Reading' at the end of this chapter).

6.5.4 Overlap between the Charter and the ECHR

Article 52(3) deals with the complex problem of overlap between the ECHR and the EUCFR. It specifies that those rights in the EUCFR which correspond with ECHR rights must be given the same meaning and scope as the ECHR rights. EU law may provide more generous protection, but not a lower level of protection than guaranteed under the ECHR and other international instruments (Article 53).

At present, the question of overlap is not a cause for concern, because the EUCFR has no legal status. However, if the Lisbon Treaty comes into force, it will be necessary to determine to what extent the ECJ has jurisdiction to enforce the Charter. Presumably, Article 51 would mean that the EUCFR rights are not free-standing rights, but are only relevant in matters of European law. In that case, the position would probably not be any different from the current situation.

If, however, certain EUCFR rights (such as those based on the ECHR) are regarded as free-standing rights, then the ECJ may be in danger of 'competing' with the European Court of Human Rights. The ECJ would be obliged to interpret EUCFR rights in accordance with the ECHR, but a difficulty may arise if the ECJ interprets an ECHR-based right in one way and the Court of Human Rights subsequently takes a different view. Member States may then face a conflict between complying with their obligations under European law, in particular the doctrine of supremacy (see Chapter 4) and under the ECHR, respectively. It is submitted that in such a case, the ECHR should prevail. This seems to be the current position under the ECJ's case law. In *Roquette Frères* (case C–94/00), the question arose whether business premises could be protected under Article 8 ECHR against 'dawn raids' by the Commission under Regulation 17 (now replaced by Regulation 1/2003). In its earlier decision in *Hoechst* (case C–46/87), the ECJ had held that Article 8 required no such protection. However, subsequent ECHR case law has extended the scope of Article 8 to cover business premises. In *Roquette*, the ECJ held that the case law under the ECHR must be taken into account in applying the *Hoechst* decision. The ECJ therefore appears to recognise that ECHR case law can have an impact on the scope of fundamental rights guaranteed by Union law. Interestingly, it has been noted the Court of Human Rights has likewise taken account of relevant case law of the ECJ. It seems that in their respective jurisdictions the two courts are endeavouring to minimise conflict. Whilst this is good practice, the risk of inconsistency remains.

6.5.5 **Conclusion on EUCFR**

Currently, the EUCFR has only declaratory status and it remains to be seen whether it will become legally binding. If this were to happen, some thought would need to be given to the relationship between the ECHR and the EUCFR and the role of the ECJ in interpreting the fundamental rights contained in the EUCFR. The potential accession of the EU to the ECHR, which would be possible if the Lisbon Treaty became effective in its current form, would acknowledge the supremacy of the Convention and the European Court of Human Rights.

The general principles of Union law have been expanded through the case law of the ECJ to cover a wide variety of rights and principles developed from many sources. We will now look at some specific examples of those rights. The following is not, however, an exhaustive list, and there may be degrees of overlap between the categories mentioned.

6.6 **Rules of administrative justice**

6.6.1 **Proportionality**

This was the principle invoked in *Internationale Handelsgesellschaft mbH* (case 11/70). It is now enshrined in Article 5 (ex 3b) EC (see 6.8 below). The principle, applied in the context of administrative law, requires that the means used to achieve a given end must be no more than that which is appropriate and necessary to achieve that end. The test thus puts the burden on an administrative authority to justify its actions and requires some consideration of possible alternatives. In this respect it is a more rigorous test than one based on reasonableness.

The principle has been invoked on many occasions as a basis of challenge to EC secondary legislation, often successfully (eg, *Werner A Bock KG v Commission* (case 62/70); *Bela-Mühle Josef Bergmann KG v Grows-Farm GmbH & Co KG* (case 114/76). It was applied in *R v Intervention Board for Agricultural Produce, ex parte ED & F Man (Sugar) Ltd* (case 181/84) in the context of a claim by ED & F Man (Sugar) Ltd before the English Divisional Court, on facts very similar to *Internationale Handelsgesellschaft*. Here the claimant, ED & F Man (Sugar) Ltd, was seeking repayment of a security of £1,670,370 forfeited when it failed to comply with an obligation to submit licence applications to the Board within a specified time limit. Due to an oversight they were a few hours late. The claimant's claim rested on the alleged illegality of the EC regulations governing the common organisation of the sugar market. The regulations appeared to require the full forfeiture of the deposit (lodged by the exporter at the time of the initial offer to export) in the event of a breach of both a *primary* obligation to export goods as agreed with the Commission and a *secondary* obligation to submit a licence application following the initial offer within a specified time limit. The ECJ held, on a reference from the Divisional Court on the validity of the regulations, that to require the same forfeiture for breach of the secondary obligation as for the primary obligation was disproportionate, and to the extent that the regulation required such forfeiture, it was invalid. As a result of this ruling, the claimant was held entitled in the Divisional Court to a declaration that the forfeiture of its security was unlawful: a significant victory for the claimant.

The proportionality principle has also been applied in the context of the EC Treaty, for example, in the application of the provisions relating to freedom of movement for goods and persons. Under these provisions States are allowed some scope for derogation from the principle of free movement, but derogations must be 'justified' on one of the grounds provided (Articles 30 (ex 36) and 39(3) (ex 48(3) post Lisbon Articles 36 and 45(3) TFEU). This has been interpreted by the ECJ as meaning that the measure must be *no more than is necessary* to achieve the desired objective (see Chapters 20 (goods), and 25 (persons)).

In *Watson* (case 118/75) the proportionality principle was invoked in the sphere of the free movement of persons to challenge the legality of certain action by the Italian authorities. One of the defendants, Ms Watson, was claiming rights of residence in Italy. The right of free movement of workers expressed in Article 39 EC is regarded as a fundamental Community right, subject only to 'limitations' which are 'justified' on the grounds of public policy, public security or public health (Article 39(3)). The Italian authorities sought to invoke this derogation to expel Ms Watson from Italy. The reason for the defendants' expulsion was that they had failed to comply with certain administrative procedures, required under Italian law, to record and monitor their movements in Italy. The ECJ, on reference from the Italian court, held that, while states were entitled to impose penalties for non-compliance with their administrative formalities, these must not be disproportionate; and they must never provide a ground for deportation. Here, it is worth noting, it is a Member State's action which was deemed to be illegal for breach of the proportionality principle. Likewise, in *Wijsenbeek* (case C–378/97) the ECJ held that, although Member States were still entitled to check the documentation of EC nationals moving from one Member State to another, any penalties imposed on those whose documentation was unsatisfactory must be proportionate: in this case, imprisonment for failure to carry a passport was disproportionate. (See further Chapter 25.)

Similarly, in the context of goods, in a case brought against Germany in respect of its beer purity laws (case 178/84), a German law imposing an absolute ban on additives was found in breach of EC law (Article 28 EC) and not 'justified' on public-health grounds under Article 30. Since the same (public health) objective could have been achieved by other less restrictive means, the ban was not 'necessary'; it was disproportionate.

More recently, however, there seems to have been a refinement of the principle of proportionality. In the case of *Südzucker Mannheim/Ochsenfurt AG v Hauptzollamt Mannheim* (case C–161/96) the ECJ confirmed the distinction between primary and secondary (or administrative) obligations made in *R v Intervention Board for Agricultural Produce* (case 181/84). The breach of a secondary obligation should not be punished as severely as a breach of a primary obligation. On the facts of the case, the ECJ held that a failure to comply with customs formalities by not producing an export licence was a breach of a primary and not a secondary obligation. The ECJ stated that the production of the export licence was necessary to ensure compliance with export requirements and thus the production of the export licence was part of the primary obligation. On this reasoning, it may be difficult to distinguish between primary and secondary obligations.

Further, the ECJ has held that, where an institution has significant discretion in the implementation of policies, such as in CAP, the ECJ may only interfere if the 'measure is manifestly inappropriate having regard to the objectives which the competent institution is seeking to pursue' (*Germany v Council (Re Banana Regime)* (case C–280/93), para 90). The same is also true of actions of Member States where they have a broad discretion in the implementation of Community policy (see *R v Minister of Agriculture, Fisheries and Food*, ex parte *National Federation of Fishermen's Organisations* (case C–44/94)). In these circumstances, the distinction between proportionality and *Wednesbury* reasonableness is not great.

6.6.2 Legal certainty

The principle of legal certainty was invoked by the ECJ in *Defrenne v Sabena (No 2)* (case 43/75). The principle, which is one of the widest generality, has been applied in more specific terms as:

(a) the principle of legitimate expectations

(b) the principle of non-retroactivity

(c) the principle of *res judicata*.

The principle of legitimate expectations, derived from German law, means that, in the absence of an overriding matter of public interest, Community measures must not violate the legitimate expectations of the parties concerned. A legitimate expectation is one which might be held by a reasonable person as to matters likely to occur in the normal course of his affairs. It does not extend to anticipated windfalls or speculative profits. In *Efisol SA v Commission* (case T–336/94) the CFI commented that an individual would have no legitimate expectations of a particular state of affairs existing where a 'prudent and discriminating' trader would have foreseen the development in question. Furthermore, in *Germany v Council* (case C–280/93), the ECJ held that no trader may have a legitimate expectation that an existing Community regime will be maintained. In that the principle requires the encouragement of a reasonable expectation, a reliance on that expectation, and some loss resulting from the breach of that expectation, it is similar to the principle of estoppel in English law.

The principle was applied in *August Töpfer & Co GmbH v Commission* (case 112/77) (see Chapter 2). August Töpfer & Co GmbH was an exporter which had applied for, and been granted, a number of export licences for sugar. Under Community law, as part of the common organisation of the sugar market, certain refunds were to be payable on export, the amount of the refunds being fixed in advance. If the value of the refund fell, due to currency fluctuations, the licence holder could apply to have his licence cancelled. This scheme was suddenly altered by an EC regulation, and the right to cancellation withdrawn, being substituted by provision for compensation. This operated to Töpfer's disadvantage, and it sought to have the regulation annulled, for breach, inter alia, of the principle of legitimate expectations. Although it did not succeed on the merits, the principle of legitimate expectations was upheld by the Court. (See also *CNTA SA v Commission* (case 74/74), monetary compensation scheme ended suddenly and without warning: Chapter 14.) In *Opel Austria GmbH v Council* (case T–115/94) the Court held that the principle of legitimate expectations was the corollary of the principle of good faith in public international law. Thus, where the Community had entered into an obligation and the date of entry into force of that obligation is known to traders, such traders may use the principle of legitimate expectations to challenge measures contrary to any provision of the international agreement having direct effect.

The principle of non-retroactivity, applied to Community secondary legislation, precludes a measure from taking effect before its publication. Retrospective application will only be permitted in exceptional circumstances, where it is necessary to achieve particular objectives and will not breach individuals' legitimate expectations. Such measures must also contain a statement of the reasons justifying the retroactive effect (*Diversinte SA v Administración Principal de Aduanos e Impuestos Especiales de la Junqueros* (case C–260/91)).

In *R v Kirk* (case 63/83) the principle of non-retroactivity of penal provisions (activated in this case by a Community regulation) was invoked successfully. However, retroactivity may be acceptable where the retroactive operation of the rule in question improves an individual's position (see, for example, *Road Air BV v Inspecteur der Invoerrechten en Accijnzen* (case C–310/95)).

This principle also has relevance in the context of national courts' obligation to interpret domestic law to comply with Union law when it is not directly effective (the *Von Colson* principle, see Chapter 5). In *Pretore di Salò v Persons Unknown* (case 14/86) in a reference from the Salò magistrates' court on the compatibility of certain Italian laws with EEC Water Purity Directive 78/659, which had been invoked against the defendants in criminal proceedings, the Court held that:

> A Directive cannot of itself have the effect of determining or aggravating the liability in criminal law of persons who act in contravention of the provisions of the Directive.

The Court went further in *Officier van Justitie v Kolpinghuis Nijmegen* (case 80/86). Here, in response to a question concerning the scope of national courts' obligation of interpretation under the *von Colson* principle, the Court held that that obligation was 'limited by the general principles of law which form part of Community law and in particular the principles of legal certainty and non-retroactivity'. Thus national courts are not required to interpret domestic law to comply with EC law in violation of these principles. This would appear to apply even where the EC law in question has direct effects, at least where criminal proceedings are in issue (see *Berlusconi* (joined cases C–387/02, C–391/02 and C–403/02), discussed in Chapter 5).

Problems also arise over the temporal effects of ECJ rulings under Article 234. In *Defrenne v Sabena (No 2)* (case 43/75) the Court held that, given the exceptional circumstances, 'important considerations of legal certainty' required that its ruling on the direct effects of the then Article 119 (now 141 post Lisbon, 157 TFEU) should apply prospectively only. It could not be relied on to support claims concerning pay periods prior to the date of judgment, except as regards workers who had already brought legal proceedings or made an equivalent claim. However, in *Ariete SpA* (case 811/79) and *Meridionale Industria Salumi Srl* (cases 66, 127 and 128/79) the Court affirmed that *Defrenne* was an exceptional case. In a 'normal' case a ruling from the ECJ was retroactive; the Court merely declared the law as it always was. This view was approved in *Barra* (case 309/85). However, in *Blaizot* (case 24/86), a case decided the same day as *Barra*, 'important considerations of legal certainty' again led the Court to limit the effects of its judgment on the lines of *Defrenne*. It came to the same conclusion in *Barber v Guardian Royal Exchange Assurance Group* (case 262/88). These cases indicate that in exceptional cases, where the Court introduces some new principle, or where the judgment may have serious effects as regards the past, the Court will be prepared to limit the effects of its rulings. *Kolpinghuis Nijmegen* may now be invoked to support such a view. Nevertheless, the Court did not limit the effect of its judgment in *Francovich* (cases C–6 and 9/90) contrary to Advocate-General Mischo's advice, despite the unexpectedness of the ruling and its 'extremely serious financial consequences' for Member States. Nor did it do so in *Marshall (No 2)* (case C–271/91) when it declared that national courts were obliged, by Article 5 of Directive 76/207 and their general obligation under Article 10 (ex 5) EC to ensure that the objectives of the directives might be achieved, to provide full compensation to persons suffering loss as a result of infringements of the directive, a matter which could not have been deduced either from the ECJ's case law or from the actual wording of the directive (see further Chapter 8).

The question of the temporal effect of a ruling from the ECJ under Article 234 EC was considered by the Italian constitutional court in *Fragd (SpA Fragd v Amministrazione delle Finanze* Decision No 232 of 21 April 1989) in the light of another general principle. Although the point did not arise out of the reference in question, the Italian court considered the effect that a ruling under Article 234 holding a Community measure void should have on the referring court if the ECJ had held that the ruling would apply for future cases only, excluding the judgment in which it was given. The Italian constitutional court suggested that in the light of the right to judicial protection given under the Italian constitution, such a holding should have effect in the case in which the reference was made. A finding of invalidity with purely prospective effect would offend against this principle and would therefore be unacceptable.

Res judicata is a principle accepted in both the civil- and common-law traditions; its significance has been recognised also by the Human Rights Court in Strasbourg (see eg *Brumarescu* v *Romania* (28342/05)). Essentially it operates to respect the binding force of a final judgment in a matter; once any relevant time limits for appeal have expired, the judgment cannot be challenged. The ECJ has recognised this principle in many cases. In *Köbler* (case C–224/01), the ECJ held that:

> attention should be drawn to the importance, both for the Community legal order and national legal systems, of the principle of *res judicata*. In order to ensure both stability of the law and legal relations and the sound administration of justice, it is important that judicial decisions which have become definitive after all rights of appeal have been exhausted or after expiry of the time-limits provided for in that connection can no longer be called into question. [Para 38.]

Applying this in *Kapferer* (case C–234/04) the ECJ ruled that in the light of *res judicata*, a national court does not have to disapply domestic rules of procedure conferring finality on a decision, even though doing so would enable it to remedy an infringement of Community law by the decision at issue. Surprisingly, in *Lucchini Siderurgica* (case C–119/05), the ECJ came to the opposite conclusion. An undertaking was seeking to claim state aid, which had been granted by the Italian government in breach of the state aid rules. The undertaking had a decision of an Italian court to this effect, whose judgment was protected by the principle of *res judicata*.

In proceedings to challenge this decision, the ECJ addressed the question of wheth-er Community law precluded the appplication of *res judicata*. The ECJ concluded that it did. The Advocate-General in *Lucchini* pointed out that the principle is not absolute; the systems of the various Member States allow exceptions under cer-tain strict conditions and the ECtHR has accepted this. Some commentators have questioned whether the circumstances in *Lucchini* come within the ECHR case law, however. Certainly, *Lucchini* is best regarded as an isolated case on exceptional facts.

6.6.3 Procedural rights

Where a person's rights are likely to be affected by EC law, EC secondary legislation normally provides for procedural safeguards (eg, Regulation 1/2003, competition law; and Directive 2004/38/EC, free movement of workers, Chapter 25). However, where such provision does not exist, or where there are lacunae, general principles of law may be invoked to fill those gaps.

6.6.4 Natural justice: The right to a hearing

The right to natural justice, and in particular the right to a fair hearing, was invoked, this time from English law, in *Transocean Marine Paint Association v Commission* (case 17/74) by Advocate-General Warner. The case, which arose in the context of competition law, was an action for annulment of the Commission's decision, addressed to the claimant association, that their agreements were in breach of EC law. The Court, following Advocate-General Warner's submissions, asserted a gen-eral rule that a person whose interests are perceptibly affected by a decision taken by a public authority must be given the opportunity to make his views known. Since the Commission had failed to comply with this obligation its decision was annulled. The principle was affirmed in *Hoffman-La Roche & Co AG v Commission* (case 85/76), in which the Court held that observance of the right to be heard is, in all proceedings in which sanctions, in particular fines and periodic payments, may be imposed, a fundamental principle of law which must be respected even if the proceedings in question are administrative proceedings.

Another aspect of the right to a fair hearing is the notion of 'equality of arms'. This is exemplified in a series of cases against the Commission following a Commission investigation into alleged anti-competitive behaviour on the part of ICI and an-other company, Solvay. In the *Solvay* case (case T–30/91) the Court stated that the principle of equality of arms presupposed that both the Commission and the de-fendant company had equal knowledge of the files used in the proceeding. That was not the case here, as the Commission had not informed Solvay of the existence of certain documents. The Commission argued that this did not affect the proceed-ings because the documents would not be used in the company's defence. The Court took the view that this point was not for the Commission to decide, as this would give the Commission more power vis-à-vis the defendant company because it had full knowledge of the file whereas the defendant did not. Equally, in the *ICI* cases (T–36 and 37/91) the Commission's refusal to grant ICI access to the file was deemed to infringe the rights of the defence.

There are, however, limits to the rights of the defence: in *Descom Scales Manufacturing Co Ltd v Council* (case T–171/94), the ECJ held that the rights of the defence do not require the Commission to provide a written record of every stage of the investigation detailing information which needed still to be verified. In this case, the Commission had notified the defendant company of the position although it had not provided a written record and the ECJ held that this was sufficient.

The right to a hearing within Article 6 ECHR also includes the right to a hearing within a reasonable period of time. The ECJ, basing its reasoning on Article 6 ECHR, thus held that, in respect of a case that had been pending before the CFI for five years and six months, the CFI had been in violation of its obligation to dispose of cases within a reasonable time (*Baustahlgewerbe v Commission* (case C–185/95 P)).

The right to a hearing has arisen in more difficult circumstances, that of the freezing of assets of persons thought to be involved in or supporting terrorism. Even in these circumstances, the European courts have reiterated the principle of the right to be heard (*OMPI v Council (OMPI I)* (case T–228/02). Nonetheless, the CFI recognised that this right is subject to broad limitations in the interests of the overriding requirement of public security, which relate to all aspects of procedural justice rights, including the hearing of certain types of evidence, It seems in these circumstances the right to a hearing is limited to a right to be notified as soon as possible as to the adoption of an economic sanction; given this finding, the duty to state reasons has a still greater significance than it usually would have. The rule of law is protected by the right to seek a review of the decision-making process subsequently. In *OMPI II* (case T-256/07) the CFI clarified that the right to a hearing does not necessitate a formal hearing if the relevant legislation does not provide for it; nor is there a right to continuous conversation. Rather, it suffices if the persons involved have the right to make their views known to the competent authorities (See *OMPI II*, para 93; see also *Common Market Fertilisers v Commission* (cases T–134–5/03, para 108)).

6.6.5 The duty to give reasons

The duty was affirmed in *Union Nationale des Entraîneurs et Cadres Techniques Professionels du Football (UNECTEF) v Heylens* (case 222/86). In this case, M Heylens, a Belgian and a professional football trainer, was the defendant in a criminal action brought by the French football trainers' union, UNECTEF, as a result of his practising in Lille as a professional trainer without the necessary French diploma, or any qualifications recognised by the French government as equivalent. M Heylens held a Belgian football trainers' diploma, but his application for recognition of this diploma by the French authorities had been rejected on the basis of an adverse opinion from a special committee, which gave no reasons for its decision. The ECJ, on a reference from the Tribunal de Grande Instance, Lille, held that the right of free movement of workers, granted by Article 39 EC, required that a decision refusing to recognise the equivalence of a qualification issued in another Member State should be subject to legal redress which would enable the legality of that decision to be established with regard to Community law, and that the person concerned should be informed of the reasons upon which the decision was based.

Similarly in *Al-Jubail Fertiliser Company (SAMAD) v Council* (case C–49/88) in the context of a challenge to a Council regulation imposing antidumping duties on the import of products manufactured by the applicants, the Court held that since the applicants had a right to a fair hearing the institutions were under a duty to supply them with all the information which would enable them effectively to defend their interests. Moreover if the information is supplied orally, as it may be, the Commission must be able to prove that it was in fact supplied.

The duty to give reasons was considered in the OMPI cases. These have a greater significance due to the potential for a limited right to a hearing. In *OMPI II*, the CFI emphasised that the Council was under an obligation to provide actual and specific reasons justifying the inclusion of a person on a sanctions list. This requires the Council not only to identify the legal conditions found in the underlying regulation, but why the Council considered that they applied to the particular person, justifying their inclusion on the sanctions list. The duty to give reasons does not, however, include the obligation to respond to all points made by the applicant.

6.6.6 The right to due process

As a corollary to the right to be informed of the reasons for a decision is the right, alluded to in *UNECTEF v Heylens* (case 222/86), to legal redress to enable such decisions and reasons to be challenged. This right was established in *Johnston v Chief Constable of the Royal Ulster Constabulary* (case 222/84). The case arose from a refusal by the RUC (now the Police Service of Northern Ireland) to renew its contracts with women members of the RUC Reserve. This decision had been taken as a result of a policy decision taken in 1980 that henceforth full-time RUC Reserve members engaged on general police duties should be fully armed. For some years women had not been issued with firearms nor trained in their use. Ms Johnston, who had been a full-time member of the Reserve for some years and wished to renew her contract, challenged the decision as discriminatory, in breach of EC Directive 76/207, which provides for equal treatment for men and women in all matters relating to employment. Although the measure was admittedly discriminatory, since it was taken solely on the grounds of sex, the Chief Constable claimed that it was justified, arguing from the 'public policy and public security' derogation of Articles 30 (goods, see Chapter 20) and 39 (workers, see Chapter 25), and from Article 297, which provides for the taking of measures in the event of, inter alia, 'serious internal disturbances affecting the maintenance of law and order'. As evidence that these grounds were made out the Chief Constable produced before the industrial tribunal a certificate issued by the Secretary of State certifying that the act refusing to offer Ms Johnston further employment in the RUC Reserve was done for the purpose of safeguarding national security and safeguarding public order. Under Article 53(2) of the Sex Discrimination (Northern Ireland) Order 1976 (SI 1976/1042) a certificate that an act was done for that purpose was 'conclusive evidence' that it was so done. A number of questions were referred to the ECJ by the industrial tribunal on the scope of the public order derogation and the compatibility of the Chief Constable's decision with Directive 76/207. The question of the Secretary of State's certificate and the possibility of judicial review were not directly raised. Nevertheless this was the first matter seized upon by the Court. The Court considered the requirement of judicial control, provided by Article 6 of Directive 76/207, which requires states to enable persons who 'consider themselves wronged' to 'pursue their claims by judicial process after possible recourse to the competent authorities'. This provision, the Court said, reflected:

> a general principle of law which underlies the constitutional traditions common to the Member States. That principle is also laid down in Articles 6 and 13 of the European Convention for the Protection of Human Rights and Fundamental Freedoms . . .
>
> It is for the Member States to ensure effective judicial control as regards compliance with the applicable provisions of Community law and of national legislation intended to give effect to the rights for which the Directive provides.

The Court went on to say that Article 53(2) of the Sex Discrimination (Northern Ireland) Order 1976, in requiring the Secretary of State's certificate to be treated as conclusive evidence that the conditions for derogation are fulfilled, allowed the competent authority to deprive an individual of the possibility of asserting by judicial process the rights conferred by the directive. Such a provision was contrary to the principle of effective judicial control laid down in Article 6 of the directive. A similar approach has, in fact, been taken by the European Court of Human Rights in relation to such certificates issued in relation to a variety of substantive issues (eg, *Tinnelly and ors v UK*, ECHR judgment, 10 July 1998).

Although the ECJ's decision was taken in the context of a right provided by the directive it is submitted that the right to effective judicial control enshrined in the European Convention on Human Rights and endorsed in this case could be invoked in any case in which a person's Community rights have been infringed. The case of *UNECTEF v Heylens* (case 222/86) would serve to support this proposition. Further, the CFI has held that the Commission, in exercising its competition-policy powers, must give reasons sufficient to allow the Court's review of the Commission's decision-making process, if that decision is challenged (eg, *Ufex v Commission* (case C–119/97P)).

In the *OMPI* cases, the CFI made clear that reasons of public security could not remove the decisions and the decision making processes at issue from the scope of judicial review (see also *Kadi*, para 344 and see comments of Advocate-General at para 45), although that review may necessarily be limited. In *OMPI II*, the CFI clarified (at paras 138–41) the scope and standard of review, at least as regards decisions concerning economic sanctions. While the Council has broad discretion as to whether to impose sanctions, the CFI must ensure that a threefold test is satisfied: whether the requirements of the applicable law are fulfilled; whether the evidence contains all information necessary to assess the situation and whether it is capable of supporting the inferences drawn from it; and whether essential procedural guarantees have been satisfied. The CFI seems to have taken a surprisingly tough stance in favour of the protection of procedural rights here.

Thus general principles of law act as a curb not only on the institutions of the Union but also on Member States, which are required, in the context of EU law, to accommodate these principles alongside existing remedies and procedures within their own domestic systems of administrative law and may result eventually in some modification in national law itself. There are, in any event, problems in determining the boundaries between matters of purely national law and matters of Union law (see 6.9 below).

6.6.7 Right to protection against self-incrimination

The right to a fair trial and the presumption of innocence of 'persons charged with a criminal offence' contained in Article 6 ECHR are undoubtedly rights which will be protected as general principles of law under Community law. However, in *Orkem* (case 374/87) and *Solvay* (case 27/88) the ECJ held that the right under Article 6 not to give evidence against oneself applied only to persons charged with an offence in criminal proceedings; it was not a principle which could be relied on in relation to infringements in the economic sphere, in order to resist a demand for information such as may be made by the Commission to establish a breach of EC competition law. This view was placed in doubt following a ruling from the Court of Human Rights in the case of *Funke v France* (case SA 256A) ([1993] 1 CMLR 897) and has been the subject of some academic criticism.

Funke involved a claim, for breach of Article 6 ECHR, in respect of a demand by the French customs' authorities for information designed to obtain evidence of currency and capital transfer offences. Following the applicant's refusal to hand over such information fines and penalties were imposed. The Court of Human Rights held that such action, undertaken as a 'fishing expedition' in order to obtain documents which, if found, might produce evidence for a prosecution, infringed the right, protected by Article 6(1) ECHR, of anyone charged with a criminal offence (within the autonomous meaning of that phrase in Article 6 ECHR), to remain silent and not incriminate himself. It appears that Article 6, according to its 'autonomous meaning', is wide enough to apply to investigations conducted under the Commission's search-and-seizure powers under competition law, and that *Orkem* and *Solvay* may no longer be regarded as good law. This view, assimilating administrative penalties to criminal penalties, appears to have been taken by the ECJ in *Otto BV v Postbank NV* (case C–60/92). Moreover, in *Mannesmannröhren-Werke AG v Commission* (case T–112/98), also a case involving a request for information about an investigation into anti-competitive agreements, the CFI held that although Article 6 ECHR could not be invoked directly before the Court, Community law offered 'protection equivalent to that guaranteed by Article 6 of the Convention' (para 77). A party subject to a Commission investigation could not be required to answer questions that might involve an admission of involvement in an anti-competitive agreement, although it would have to respond to requests for general information.

6.7 Equality

The principle of equality means, in its broadest sense, that persons in similar situations are not to be treated differently unless the difference in treatment is objectively justified. This, of course, gives rise to the question of what are similar situations. Discrimination can only exist within a framework in which it is possible to draw comparisons, for example, the framework of race, sex, nationality, colour, religion. The equality principle will not apply in situations which are deemed to be 'objectively different' (see *Les Assurances du Crédit SA v Council* (case C–63/89), public export credit insurance operations different from other export credit insurance operations). What situations are regarded as comparable, subject to the equality principle, is clearly a matter of political judgement. The EC Treaty expressly prohibits discrimination on the grounds of nationality (Article 12 (ex 6) EC) and, to a limited extent, sex (Article 141 (ex 119) EC provides for equal *pay* for men and women for equal work). In the field of agricultural policy, Article 34(3) (ex 40(3)) prohibits 'discrimination between producers or consumers within the Community'. The ToA introduced further provisions, giving the EC powers to regulate against discrimination on grounds of race, religion, sexual orientation or disability (Article 13 EC). There has been some discussion as to whether these aspects of discrimination constitute separate general principles of law, as seemed to be suggested by the ECJ in *Mangold* (Case C–144/04). Although a number of Advocates-General have discussed the issue, it is indicative of the matter's sensitive nature that in each of the cases, the ECJ has handed down rulings without addressing the *Mangold* point. (See, eg, *Chacon Navas* (case C–13/05) concerning disability discrimination and see Opinion of Advocate-General at paras 46–56; *Lindorfer* (case C–227/04) and the Opinion of the Advocate-General at paras 87–97 and 132–8; *Palacios de la Villa* (case C–411/05) and *Maruko* (case C–267/06) on discrimination based on sexual orientation—see Opinion of Advocate-General at para 78; *The Queen, on the application of The Incorporated Trustees of the National Council on Ageing (Age Concern England) v Secretary of State for BERR* (case C–388/07) and *Bartsch v Bosch und Siemens Hausgeräte (BSH) Altersfürsorge GmbH* (case C–427/06).) Directive 2000/43/EC ([2000] OJ L180, p 22) has been adopted to combat discrimination, both direct and indirect, on grounds of racial or ethnic origin, in relation to employment matters, social protection, education, and access to public goods and services (see, eg, *Centrum voor gelijkheid van kansen en voor racismebestrijding v Feryn* (case C–54/07)). Directive 2000/78/EC ([2000] OJ L303, p 16) has been adopted to combat discrimination on the grounds of religion or belief, disability, age, or sexual orientation with regard to employment and occupation. These directives are discussed further in Chapter 27.

However, a general principle of equality is clearly wider in scope than these provisions. In the first isoglucose case, *Royal Scholten-Honig (Holdings) Ltd v Intervention Board for Agricultural Produce* (cases 103 and 145/77), the claimants, who were glucose producers, together with other glucose producers, sought to challenge the legality of a system of production subsidies whereby sugar producers were receiving subsidies financed in part by levies on the production of glucose. Since glucose and sugar producers were in competition with each other the claimants argued that the regulations implementing the system were discriminatory, ie in breach of the general principle of equality, and therefore invalid. The ECJ, on a reference on the validity of the regulations from the English court, agreed. The regulations were held invalid. (See also *Ruckdeschel* (case 117/76); *Pont-à-Mousson* (cases 124/76 and 20/77).)

Similarly, the principle of equality was invoked in the case of *Airola* (case 21/74) to challenge a rule which was discriminatory on grounds of sex (but not pay), and in *Prais* (case 130/75) to challenge alleged discrimination on the grounds of religion. Neither case at the time fell within the more specific provisions of Community law, although would now fall within the scope of Directive 2000/78/EC (see above).

6.8 Subsidiarity

The principle of subsidiarity in its original philosophical meaning, as expressed by Pope Pius XI (Encyclical letter, 1931), is that:

> It is an injustice, a grave evil and disturbance of right order for a larger and higher association to arrogate to itself functions which can be performed efficiently by smaller and lower societies.

It was invoked in the Community context during the 1980s when the Community's competence was extended under the Single European Act. It was incorporated into that Act, in respect of environmental measures, in the then Article 130r (now 174) EC (post Lisbon Article 191 TFEU), and introduced into the EC Treaty in Article 5 (ex 3b) by the TEU. Article 5 EC requires the Community to act 'only if and so far as the objectives of the proposed action cannot be sufficiently achieved by the Member States, and can therefore, by reason of the scale or the effects of the proposed action, be better achieved by the Community'. Article 5 EC will, should Lisbon come into force, be replaced in substance by Article 5 TEU.

As expressed in Article 5 EC, subsidiarity appears to be a test of comparative efficiency; as such it lacks its original philosophical meaning, concerned with fostering social responsibility. This latter meaning has however been retained in Article 1 (ex A) TEU, which provides that decisions of the European Union 'be taken as closely as possible to the people'. Although it has not been incorporated into the EC Treaty it is submitted that this version of the principle of subsidiarity could be invoked as a general principle of law if not as a basis to challenge EC law then at least as an aid to the interpretation of Article 5 EC (see Chapter 3). The principle of subsidiarity in its narrow form in Article 5 has, on occasion, been referred to as a ground for challenge of EC legislation (*R v Secretary of State for Health, ex parte British American Tobacco and others* (case C–491/01); *R v SoS for Health ex parte Swedish Match* (case C–210/03)), but this has never succeeded.

6.9 Effectiveness

The doctrine of effectiveness is not usually recognised as a general principle of Union law, save—perhaps—when it is equated with the idea of effective judicial protection. Nonetheless, the principle is ubiquitous and has had a significant effect on the development of Union law. Notably, it was an effectiveness argument that was used to develop the doctrine of supremacy, direct effect (*Van Gend en Loos* (case 26/62) and *Costa v ENEL* (case 6/64), and state liability (*Francovich and Bonifaci v Italy* (joined cases C–6 and 9/90), and was used to extend the loyalty principle found in Article 10 EC to the third pillar (*Pupino* (case C–105/03)). As we shall see in Chapter 8, it has been used to ensure effective protection for EC law, and for individuals' rights; indeed sometimes the ECJ seems to blur the boundaries between the two (eg *Courage v Creehan* (case C–453/99)). Should the Lisbon Treaty come into force, Article 19 TEU (as amended by Lisbon) expressly requires Member States to provide remedies so as to ensure effective legal protection of Union law rights. The concept is a somewhat slippery one, used in different contexts for different purposes. Crucially, it can operate both to determine the scope of Union law (identifying the boundary between national and EU law) and to determine the scope of any remedial action needed within the national legal system. While it may be argued that fundamental rights arguments may be used on both these ways (see below), the broad and amorphous nature of the effectiveness principle(s) make it particularly difficult to determine its proper scope and appropriate use.

6.10   General principles applied to national legislation

It has been suggested that general principles of law, incorporated by the ECJ as part of Union law, also affect certain acts of the Member States. These fall into three broad categories:

(a) when EC rights are enforced within national courts

(b) when the rules of a Member State are in (permitted) derogation from a fundamental principle of Community law, such as free movement of goods (Articles 25 and 28 EC) or persons (Articles 39 and 49)

(c) when the Member State is acting as an agent of the Community in implementing Community law (eg, *Klensch v Secrétaire d'État à l'Agriculture et à la Viticulture* (cases 201 and 202/85)).

6.10.1 Enforcement of Community law in national courts

The ECJ has repeatedly held that, in enforcing Community rights, national courts must respect procedural rights guaranteed in international law; for example, individuals must have a right of access to the appropriate court and the right to a fair hearing (see, eg, *Johnston v RUC* (case 222/84) and *UNECTEF v Heylens* (case 222/86)). This applies, however, only where the rights which the individual seeks to enforce are derived from *Community* sources: Ms Johnston relied on the Equal Treatment Directive (Directive 76/207); M Heylens on the right of freedom of movement for workers enshrined in Article 39 EC. In *Konstantinidis* (case C–168/91), a case concerning the rules governing the transliteration of Greek names, the ECJ handed down a judgment which did not follow the Opinion of the Advocate-General. The Advocate-General suggested that such rules, which resulted in a change in a person's name as a result of the way the transliteration was carried out, could constitute an interference with the rights protected by Article 8 ECHR. Although the ECJ agreed that this could be the case, it held that such rules would only be contrary to EC law where their application causes such inconvenience as to interfere with a person's right to free movement.

The constraints implied by this case seem to have been undermined. *Carlos Garcia Avello* (case C–148/02) concerned a Spanish national's right to register his children's names in the Spanish style in Belgium, where they were born. The case is based not on free-movement rights, but on European citizenship, a factor which both the European Commission and the Advocate-General agree allows a broader scope to EC protection of human rights. The ECJ agreed with the outcome without expressly considering human rights. The decision seems to limit the notion of the internal situation seen in *Kaur* (discussed above) and *Uecker and Jacquet* (joined cases C–64/96 and C–65/96, discussed in Chapter 21) and to extend the scope of circumstances in which the ECJ would be required to respect ECHR rights (see 6.10.4 below). A similar extension can be seen in *Chen* (case C–200/02), in which a baby holding Irish nationality but born in the UK was deemed to have rights to have her mother, a Chinese national, remain in the UK with her (see further Chapter 21).

The extension of human-rights protection is not limited to circumstances in which citizenship is in issue, but arises in the context of any of the treaty freedoms. In *Karner* (case C–71/02), a case concerning advertising on the Internet, the ECJ held that the national rules complained of were not selling arrangements and therefore they would not fall within Article 28 EC (see Chapter 19). In this aspect, the case is different from the preceding cases, as those cases concerned situations where the national legislation fell within the relevant treaty provision. Despite the fact that the situation seemed to lie outside the prohibition in Article 28 (thus rendering a consideration of a derogation, discussed at 5.9.2, unnecessary), the ECJ then went on to give the national court 'guidance as to interpretation necessary to enable it to assess the compatibility of that legislation with the fundamental rights whose observance the Court ensures' (para 49). According to the ECJ, in this case the national legislation fell within the scope of application of EC law (see further 6.10.4 below).

Finally, any penalties imposed by national judicial bodies must be proportionate (eg, *Watson and Belmann* (case 118/75)).

6.10.2 Derogation from fundamental principles

Most treaty rules provide for some derogation in order to protect important public interests (eg, Articles 30 and 39(3)). The ECJ has insisted that any derogation from the fundamental principles of Community law must be narrowly construed. When Member States do derogate, their rules may be reviewed in the light of general principles, as the question of whether the derogation is within permitted limits is one of Community law. Most, if not all, derogations are subject to the principle of proportionality (eg, *Watson* (case 118/75)). The *ERT* case (*Elliniki Radiophonia Tileorassi AE v Dimotiki Etairia Pliroforissis* (case C–260/89)) concerned the establishment by the Greek government of a monopoly broadcaster. The ECJ held that this would be contrary to Article 49 (ex 59) regarding the freedom to provide services. Although the treaty provides for derogation from Article 49 in Articles 46 and 55 (ex 56 and 66), any justification provided for by Community law must be interpreted in the light of fundamental rights, in this case the principle of freedom of expression embodied in Article 10 ECHR. Similarly, in *Vereinigte Familiapress Zeitungsverlags- und vertriebs GmbH v Heinrich Bauer Verlag* (case C–368/95), the need to ensure plurality of the media (based on Article 10 ECHR) was accepted as a possible reason justifying a measure (the prohibition of prize games and lotteries in magazines) which would otherwise breach Article 28 EC. More recently, in *Schmidberger* (C–112/00), Advocate-General Jacobs argued that the right to freedom of expression and assembly permits a derogation from the free movement of goods (Article 28 EC)) in a context where the main transit route across the Alps was blocked for a period of 28 hours on a single occasion and steps were taken to ensure that the disruption to the free movement of goods was not excessive. The ECJ came to the same end conclusion, noting the wide margin of discretion given to the national authorities in striking a balance between fundamental rights and treaty obligations (and contrast *Commission v France* (case C–265/95)). (See also on Article 8 ECHR, *Mary Carpenter v SoS for the Home Department* (case C–60/00).)

One issue in this context is whether fundamental human rights should properly be seen as a derogation from treaty freedoms, perhaps falling within the scope of the public-policy objection, or whether they should be seen as operating to limit treaty freedoms at an earlier point in the legal analysis. In *Omega Spielhallen* (case C–36/02), human dignity was seen as forming part of the public-policy grounds of derogation. In her Opinion in this case, Advocate-General Stickx-Hackl emphasised, the importance of the protection of human dignity, and suggested that public policy should be interpreted in the light of the Community-law requirement that human dignity should be protected. Nonetheless, this still leaves human-rights protection with the status of an exception to EC Treaty freedoms rather than constraining the scope of those rights in the first place. Recognition that human-rights protection forms part of the public-policy exception can be seen in *Dynamic Medien Vertriebs GmbH v Avides Media AG* (C–244/06). The potential problem with this approach is that exceptions to the treaty freedoms are normally narrowly construed and subject to the proportionality test, which hardly puts them on the same footing as the economic treaty freedom. In *Schmidberger* (case C-112/00), the ECJ suggested that rather than the usual proportionality test, in such cases the different interests should be balanced; whether this approach is consistently adopted in cases concerning fundamental rights, remains to be seen.

6.10.3 State acting as agent

When Member States implement Union rules, either by legislative act or as administrators for the Union, they must not infringe fundamental rights. National rules may be challenged on this basis: for example, in *Commission v Germany* (case 249/86), the Commission challenged Germany's rules enforcing Regulation 1612/86 which permitted the family of a migrant worker to install themselves with the worker in a host country provided that the worker has housing available for the family of a standard comparable with that of similarly employed national workers. Germany enforced this in such a way as to make the residence permit of the family conditional on the existence of appropriate housing for the duration of the stay. The ECJ interpreted the regulation as requiring this only in respect of the beginning of their period of residence. Since the regulation had to be interpreted in the light of Article 8 ECHR concerning respect for family life, a fundamental principle recognised by Community law, German law was incompatible with Community law. When Member States are implementing obligations contained in Union law, they must do so without offending against any fundamental rights recognised by the Union. In *Wachauf v Germany* (case 5/88)) the ECJ held that 'Since those requirements are also binding on the Member States when they implement Community rules, the Member States must, as far as possible, apply those rules in accordance with those requirements' (para 19).

6.10.4 Scope of Union law

In all three situations listed above, general principles have an impact because the situations fall within the scope of Union law, specifically Community law. The ECJ has no power to examine the compatibility with the ECHR of national rules which do not fall therein (*Cinéthèque SA v Fédération Nationale des Cinémas Françaises* (cases 60 and 61/84), noting the different approach of Advocate-General and Court, and contrast *Karner* (case C–71/02)). The problem lies in defining the boundary between Community law and purely domestic law, as can be seen in, for example, *Karner*. The scope of Community law could be construed very widely, as evidenced by the approach of the Advocate-General in *Konstantinidis v Stadt Altensteig-Standesamt* (case C–168/91). As noted above, he suggested that, as the applicant had exercised his right of free movement under Article 43 (ex 52) EC, national provisions affecting him fell within the scope of Community law; therefore he was entitled to the protection of his human rights by the ECJ. The Court has not expressly gone this far although some of the citizenship cases can be seen in this light (see *Garcia Avello* (case C–148/02), *Carpenter* (case C–60/00), *Chen* (case C–200/02)).

One particular problem area is where an individual seeks to extend the nature of the fundamental principles recognised in his or her home state by reference to rights protected in other Member States and recognised as such by the ECJ. This can be illustrated by contrasting two cases which arose out of similar circumstances: *Wachauf v Germany* (case 5/88) and *R v Ministry of Agriculture, Fisheries and Food, ex parte Bostock* (case C–2/93).

Wachauf was a tenant farmer who, upon the expiry of his tenancy, requested compensation arising out of the loss of 'reference quantities' on the discontinuance of milk production. When this was refused, he claimed that this was an infringement of his right to private property, protected under the German constitution. The German authorities claimed that the rules they applied were required by the Community regulation, but the ECJ held that on its proper interpretation the regulation required no such thing: although the regulation did not itself provide the right to compensation, equally it did not preclude it. The discretion thereby given to the Member States by the regulation should be exercised in accordance with fundamental rights, thus, in practice meaning that the applicant should receive the compensation.

Bostock, similarly, had been a tenant farmer. Following *Wachauf* (case 5/88) he argued that he too should be entitled to compensation for the value of the reference quantities on the expiry of his lease. Unlike the situation in Germany, though, this right was not protected by British law at the time when Bostock's lease ended. Bostock therefore sought to challenge that British law on the basis that the provisions breached general principles of non-discrimination and unjust enrichment. Despite its approach in *Wachauf*, the ECJ ruled that the right to property protected by the Community legal order did not include the right to dispose of the 'reference quantities' for profit. The ECJ held that the question of unjust enrichment, as part of the legal relations between lessor and lessee, was a matter for national law and therefore fell outside the scope of Community law.

It is difficult to reconcile these two cases if one accepts that general principles accepted by the ECJ should apply across the EU. From recent case law we can still see differences in the approach to the scope of rights deemed worthy of protection. In *Omega Spielhallen* (case C–36/02), the German authorities sought to prevent a laser-dome game operating on the basis that a game based on shooting people infringed respect for human dignity; no such problem arose in the UK where the game operator originated. One clear message seems to be that there are limits to the circumstances when general principles will operate and that a challenge to national acts for breach of a general principle is likely to be successful only when national authorities are giving effect to clear obligations of Community law. In matters falling within the discretion of Member States, national authorities are not required to recognise general principles not protected by that state's national laws.

6.11 Conclusions

This chapter illustrates the importance of general principles of law in the judicial protection of individual rights. Member States' commitment to fundamental human rights has now been acknowledged in Article 6 TEU. Nonetheless, certain points should be noted.

The fact that a particular principle is upheld by the ECJ and appears to be breached does not automatically lead to a decision in favour of the claimant. Fundamental rights are not absolute rights. As the Court pointed out in *J Nold KG v Commission* (case 4/73), rights of this nature are always subject to limitations laid down in the public interest, and, in the Community context, limits justified by the overall objectives of the Community (eg, *O'Dwyer v Council* (cases T–466, 469, 473–4 and 477/93)). The pursuit of these objectives can result in some hard decisions (eg, *Dowling v Ireland* (case C–85/90)), although the Court has held that it may not constitute a 'disproportionate and intolerable interference, impairing the very substance of those rights' (*Wachauf* (case 5/88) at para 18). This principle was applied in *Germany v Commission (Re Banana Regime)* (case C–280/93), para 78, another harsh decision.

Thus, where the objectives are seen from the Union standpoint to be essential, individual rights must yield to the common good. In *J Nold KG v Commission* the system set up under an ECSC provision, whereby Nold, as a small-scale wholesaler, would be deprived of the opportunity, previously enjoyed, to buy direct from the producer, to its commercial disadvantage, was held to be necessary in the light of the system's overall economic objectives. 'The disadvantages claimed by the applicant', held the Court, 'are in fact the result of economic change and not of the contested Decision'.

The latitude shown to the Union institutions, particularly where they are exercising discretionary powers in pursuit of common Community policies (most notably the CAP) does not always extend to Member States in their implementation of Union law. Where Member States are permitted a certain discretion in implementation (and Member States have little discretion as regards the ends to be achieved), the Court will not substitute its own evaluation for that of the Member State: it will restrict itself solely to the question of whether there was a patent error in the Member State's action (*R v Minister of Agriculture, Fisheries and Food, ex parte National Federation of Fishermen's Organisations* (case C–44/94)). Otherwise, general principles of law are strictly enforced. Thus, under the guise of the protection of individual rights, general principles of law also serve as a useful (and concealed) instrument of policy.

The adoption of the Charter of Fundamental Rights marks a significant further step. Although little more than a summary of the current level of protection recognised by the Union, it may evolve into a legally binding instrument which reaches beyond fundamental human rights to include employment and social rights and for this, we wait upon the ratification of the Lisbon Treaty. Nonetheless difficulties remain with its relationship with the ECHR, a convention to which the Union, it now seems, is intended to accede. Of crucial significance in the successful and equal protection of individuals' rights is the relationship between the European Court of Human Rights and both the CFI and, most importantly, the ECJ. This issue has yet to be fully resolved.

FURTHER READING

Alston, P, *The EU and Human Rights* (OUP, 1999).

Ashiagbor, D, 'Economic and social rights in the European Charter of Fundamental Rights' (2004) 1 EHRLR 62.

Canor, I, '*Primus inter pares*: Who is the ultimate guardian of fundamental rights in Europe?' (2000) 25 EL Rev 57.

Council of the EU, *Charter of Fundamental Rights of the European Union: Explanations relating to the complete text of the Charter* (Office for Official Publications of the European Communities, 2001).

De Burca, G, 'Fundamental human rights and the reach of EC law' (1993) 13 Oxford J Legal Stud 283.

Jowell, J and Lester, A, 'Beyond *Wednesbury*: Substantive principles of administrative law' [1987] PL 368.

Knook, A, 'The Court, the Charter, and the vertical division of powers in the European Union' (2005) 42(2) CML Rev 367.

Krogsgaard, L, 'Fundamental rights in the EC after Maastricht' [1993] LIEI 99.

Liisberg, J, 'Does the EU Charter of Fundamental Rights threaten the supremacy of Community law?' (2001) 38 CML Rev 1171.

Mancini, G F, 'The making of a constitution for Europe' (1989) 26 CML Rev 594.

McGoldrick, D, 'The European Union after Amsterdam: An organisation with general human rights competence' in D O'Keeffe and P Twomey (eds), *Legal Issues of the Amsterdam Treaty* (Hart Publishing, 1999).

Mendelson, M, 'The European Court of Justice and human rights' (1981) 1 YEL 126.

Ortega, L, 'Fundamental rights in the European Constitution' (2005) 11(3) EPL 363.

Riley, A, '*Saunders* and the power to obtain information in European Community and United Kingdom competition law' (2000) 25 EL Rev 264.

Schermers, H, 'The European Community bound by fundamental human rights' (1990) 27 CML Rev 249.

—— 'The scales in balance: National Constitutional Court *v* Court of Justice' (1990) 27 CML Rev 97.

Schermers, HG, *The Protection of Human Rights in the European Community* (Zentrum für Europäisches Wirtschaftsrecht, Vorträge und Berichte 36) (1994).

Schwarze, J, 'Tendencies towards a common administrative law in Europe' (1991) 16 EL Rev 3.

Sharpston, E, 'Legitimate expectations and economic reality' (1990) 15 EL Rev 103.

Twomey, P, 'The European Union: Three pillars without a human rights foundation' in D O'Keeffe and P Twomey (eds), *Legal Issues of the Maastricht Treaty* (Chancery Publications, 1993).

Usher, JA, *General Principles of EC Law* (Longmans, 1998).

Weiler, J, 'Eurocracy and distrust: Some questions concerning the role of the European Court of Justice in the protection of fundamental human rights within the legal order of the European Communities' (1986) 61 Wash L Rev 1103.

Weiler, JHH, 'Fundamental rights and fundamental boundaries: On standards and values in the protection of human rights' in NA Neuwahl (ed), *The European Union and Rights* (1995).

—— and Lockhart, NJS, '"Taking rights seriously" seriously?' (1995) 32 CML Rev 51, 579.

Woods, L, 'Freedom of expression in the EU' (2006) 12(3) EPL 371–401.

PART II

7

Framework for enforcement

7.1 Introduction

The discussion in Part III, which by no means covers the whole range of Union law, illustrates the extent to which EU law permeates our lives. In addition to the law stemming from the treaty, a wealth of secondary legislation has been, and is in the constant process of being, enacted, covering a wide and ever-increasing range of activities. Much of this law is directly effective (see Chapter 5), and will, under the principle of primacy of EC law (see Chapter 4), take precedence over any conflicting rules of national law. It thus forms an important source of *rights* and *obligations* for both states and individuals.

An effective system of enforcement requires that the rights arising under EC law may be enforced against three groups of people:

(a) *the institutions of the Community*, who, in their lawmaking or administrative capacity, may have acted or failed to act in breach of EU law

(b) *Member States*, which, in carrying out or failing to carry out their obligations under the treaty or secondary legislation, may have acted in breach of EC law

(c) *individuals*, who in failing to comply with their obligations under the treaty or secondary legislation may have acted in breach of EC law.

The EC Treaty itself provides an extensive range of remedies. It provides, by way of *direct* action before the European Courts—the European Court of Justice (ECJ) and the Court of First Instance (CFI)—for actions against the institutions of the Community and against Member States. Community secondary legislation may be challenged *indirectly* before the courts of Member States, and questions of validity referred to the ECJ under Article 234 (ex 177) EC (267 of the Treaty on the Functioning of the European Union (TFEU)) (see Chapter 10). Chapters 12–14 are concerned primarily with the means whereby states, and sometimes individuals, may challenge the institutions *directly* before the European Courts. The European Courts currently have no jurisdiction over acts of the European Council (*Roujansky v Council* (case T–584/93)), though this would change should the Lisbon Treaty come into force. Following the transfer by the Treaty of Amsterdam (ToA) (Article 46 of the Treaty on European Union (TEU)) to the EC Treaty (Title IV) of matters within the third pillar of the TEU relating to visas, asylum, immigration, and judicial cooperation in civil affairs, the ECJ has assumed a limited jurisdiction over these matters (Article 68 EC), as well as over framework decisions and decisions concerning police and judicial cooperation in criminal matters remaining within the third pillar of the TEU, subject to agreement, both as to the jurisdiction itself and its extent, by individual Member States (new Article 35 TEU). The ToA also gave the Court jurisdiction over the new 'flexibility' clauses providing for 'closer cooperation' agreements to be established under the new Articles 11 EC and 40 TEU and, for the first time, express power to rule on the conformity of action of the EU institutions with fundamental human rights in those areas where the Court has jurisdiction under the EU Treaties (new Article 46(1)(d) TEU). Matters within the second pillar of the TEU—common foreign and security policy (CFSP)—remain wholly outside the jurisdiction of the ECJ. As we discuss the various provisions, we will note the extent to which the Treaty of Lisbon extends the jurisdiction of the European courts; in sum, a cautious expansion.

7.2 Action before the European Courts

7.2.1 Actions against the Institutions of the Community

These comprise actions:

(a) for judicial review, in the form of actions to 'review the legality of acts of the Council and the Commission other than recommendations or opinions' (Article 230 (ex-173; post Lisbon, Article 263 TFEU)), the 'annulment action', and Article 241 (ex 184; post Lisbon, Article 277 TFEU), the 'plea of illegality'), and an action for 'failure to act' (Article 232 (ex 175; post Lisbon, 265 TFEU))

(b) for damages (Articles 235 and 288(2) (ex 178 and 215(2); post Lisbon, Articles 208 and 246 TFEU)

(c) in respect of disputes between the Community and its servants ('staff cases' Article 236 (ex 179; post Lisbon, Article 270 TFEU)).

7.2.1.1 *Significance of Judicial Review*

There are two ways in which control over the institutions needs to be exercised. First, it is necessary to ensure that the legislation issued by the institutions is valid; ie, that the institution has the power to issue the act concerned, that it has been passed according to the correct procedures, and exercised for the right purposes. This constitutes a check on the institutions' *activities*. This is provided under Article 230, and, as an adjunct to that article, Article 241. Article 234 also provides for the possibility of a similar review via the national courts and preliminary ruling mechanism, discussed further below. Secondly, there is a need to check on the institutions' *inactivity*—to ensure that the institutions do not fail to act when they are under a legal duty to do so. This is provided by Article 232.

Judicial review under Articles 230 and 232 requires an examination of three separate questions. First there is the question of *locus standi*: does this applicant have the right, personally, to bring proceedings? Secondly, has he brought his action in time? These two questions relate to admissibility. And thirdly, if the first questions are answered in the affirmative, is he entitled to succeed on the merits? Whilst in much of this book, we can see the profound influence that the actions of private actors have had on the development of the EC—if not EU—law, in this area private bodies have been restrained from playing such an extensive role by the limited *locus standi* rules. Indeed, the discussion is often as much about this issue, and how it relates to respect for fundamental rights and access to a court, as to the substance of any particular decision.

7.2.1.2 *Jurisdiction of the CFI*

All claims by natural and legal persons under (a) and (b), including the areas introduced in Regulation 139/2004 (control of concentrations between undertakings), Regulation 40/94 (Community trade mark, as amended) and Regulation 2100/94 (Community plant-variety rights) are now dealt with by the CFI, with a right of appeal to the ECJ (Article 256 (ex 168a) EC). Claims under (c) are now within the jurisdiction of the Civil Service Tribunal, which is attached to the CFI. The CFI also has jurisdiction to hear and determine actions brought by natural and legal persons relating to the European Central Bank (ECB) (see Council Decisions 93/350 ([1993] OJ L144/21) and 94/149 ([1994] OJ L66/29)).

Following the Treaty of Nice, the jurisdiction of the CFI was changed. It retained the right to hear direct action, but the amended Article 225 introduced the possibility of some specialist areas being referred to judicial panels, with the CFI hearing appeals from the decisions of those panels. As noted at 2.10.4, the first such panel is the Civil Service Tribunal. The precise boundary between the jurisdiction of these panels, the CFI, and the ECJ is to be determined in the Statute of the Court of Justice. As part of the Convention on the Future of Europe and as required by Declaration 12 of the Nice Summit, a proposal was put forward drawing the boundaries between the various judicial bodies to jurisdiction in relation to actions brought under Articles 230 and 232 EC. The Constitution, expressly referred to the possibility of specialist courts, and the Lisbon Treaty, should it come in to force, does likewise.

7.2.1.3 *Appeals to the ECJ in judicial-review cases*

Appeal is limited to points of law and must be based on the grounds of lack of competence of the CFI, breach of procedure before it which adversely affects the interests of the appellant, or infringement of Community law by the CFI (Article 58 of the Statutes of the Court of Justice). An appeal must contain the pleas in law and legal arguments relied on. It must indicate precisely the contested elements of the judgment which the appellant seeks to have set aside and also the legal arguments specifically advanced in support of the appeal. That requirement is not satisfied by an appeal confined to repeating the pleas and arguments previously submitted to the CFI. Such an approach would constitute no more than a re-examination by the ECJ of the application submitted to the CFI. The ECJ has no jurisdiction to do this. Likewise, an attempt to raise new issues falls outside the ECJ's jurisdiction as an appeal court.

In *John Deere* (case C–7/95P), on appeal from a judgment of the CFI, the ECJ started by referring to Article 255 (ex 168a) EC and what was Article 51 (now 58) of the EC Statute of the Court of Justice, which then stated that an appeal is to be limited to points of law and must be based on the grounds of lack of competence of the CFI, breach of procedure before the CFI which adversely affects the interests of the appellant, or infringement of Community law by the CFI. Furthermore, what remains Article 112(1)(c) in the current version of the Court's Rules of Procedure provided that an appeal must contain the pleas in law and the legal arguments relied on in the appeal; this means that an appeal must indicate *precisely* the contested elements of the judgment which the appellant seeks to have set aside, and also the legal arguments *specifically* advanced in support of the appeal. The ECJ also commented that this requirement, 'is not satisfied by an appeal confined to repeating or reproducing word for word pleas in law and arguments previously submitted to the Court of First Instance, including those based on facts expressly rejected by that court'.

The ECJ also has no jurisdiction to establish facts of examined evidence. The appraisal by the CFI of the evidence does not constitute a point of law which is subject to review by the ECJ, unless the evidence has been fundamentally mis-construed (see *John Deere v Commission* (case C–7/95P) and also *Hilti v Commission* (case C–53/92P), para 42). After a period when the ECJ seemed to dispose of appeals from the CFI on matters of intellectual-property law on the facts, as can be seen in *Baby Dry* (Case C–383/99 P), the ECJ has reverted to this approach. In *DKV Deutsche Krankenversicherung AG v OHIM* (case C–104/00 P), the ECJ held that the CFI has exclusive jurisdiction to find the facts and to appraise them. That assessment of the facts cannot be reviewed unless 'the clear sense of the evidence before it has been distorted' (para 22). Coming to the same conclusion, the Advocate-General in this case suggested that the role of the ECJ as 'highest interpreter of the law' was to 'lay down principles of general application' (Opinion, para 59).

These requirements clearly limit the scope for potential appeals; this does not, however, seem to have stopped some applicants from trying, especially in the competition field. Although the ECJ will refuse jurisdiction, these cases still impact on the ECJ's workload as in each case it still has to investigate the issue of the appeal's admissibility.

In addition to appeals made by the parties, where the CFI is hearing an appeal from a judicial panel within the terms of Article 225(2), and the First Advocate-General (appointed in accordance with Article 10 of the Court's Rules of Procedure) considers that there is a serious risk of the unity or consistency of Community law being affected by that case, he may propose that the ECJ review the decision of the CFI. That proposal must be made within one month of the delivery of the CFI's judgment and the ECJ then has a further month in which to decide whether or not the decision should be reviewed (Article 62 of the Statute of the Court of Justice).

7.2.2 Actions against Member States

These comprise:

(a) action by the Commission against a Member State for failure 'to fulfil an obligation under this Treaty' (Article 226 (ex 169) EC; post Lisbon, Article 258 TFEU)

(b) action by a Member State against another Member State for failure 'to fulfil an obligation under this Treaty' (Article 227 (ex 170) EC; post Lisbon, Article 259 TFEU)

(c) action by the Commission against a Member State, via accelerated procedures similar to those provided under Article 226, for breach of its obligation to notify the Commission under Article 88(2)(b) (ex 93(2)(b); post Lisbon, Article 108 TFEU) (state aids) and Article 95(4) (ex 100a(4);

post Lisbon, Article 114 TFEU) (unilateral restrictions on free movement of goods)

(d) similar accelerated proceedings brought by the Commission under Article 298 (ex 225; post Lisbon, Article 348 TFEU) where emergency measures taken by Member States distort conditions of competition within the Community.

These actions are brought directly before the ECJ. Note that indirect challenges to Member States' actions or inaction can be brought using the preliminary reference procedure. Although the ECJ is involved in such procedures the action is commenced in the national courts and discussed below.

7.2.2.1 *Right to intervene*

Member States and Union institutions have a right to intervene in cases before the Court. This right is also open to any other person establishing an interest in the result of any case submitted to the Court, except in cases between institutions of the Union or between Member States and institutions of the Union. In *British Coal Corporation v Commission* (case T–367/94), a case based on the parallel provisions of the statutes of the European Coal and Steel Community (ECSC), the Court held that an applicant must establish a 'direct, existing interest in the grant by the Court of the order as sought and not purely an interest in relation to the plea in law advanced'. The fact that representative associations have a right to intervene in order to protect their members in cases raising questions of principle liable to affect those members cannot be relied on in support of an individual application to intervene (see also *Dorsch Consult Ingenieurgesellschaft mbH v Council and Commission* (case T–184/95)).

7.2.2.2 *Interim relief*

Although actions before the Courts do not have suspensory effect, the Courts may, 'if [they] consider that the circumstances so require it, order that the application of the contested act be suspended' (Article 242 (ex 185); post Lisbon, Article 278 TFEU). They may also order 'any necessary interim measures in any of the above proceedings' (Article 243 (ex 186); post Lisbon, Article 279 TFEU). However, action under Article 242 is admissible only if the applicant is challenging that measure 'in proceedings before the Court'. Similarly action under Article 243 will be admitted only if it is made 'by a party to the case before the Court and relates to that case'. Interim measures may not be ordered 'unless there are circumstances giving rise to urgency and factual and legal grounds establishing a *prima facie* case for the measures applied for'. The urgency of the application will be assessed according to the necessity for such an order in order to prevent serious and irreparable damage. Parties wishing to establish the existence of 'serious and irreparable damage' for the purpose of obtaining the suspension of a Community act must provide documentary evidence both as regards the specific damage suffered or likely to be suffered and the causative link between that damage and the contested act (*Descom Scales Manufacturing Co Ltd v Council* (case C–6/94R), application for suspension of anti-dumping regulation rejected for lack of evidence). Purely financial damage cannot in principle be regarded as irreparable (*Cargill v Commission* (case 229/88R)). The interim measures requested must be of such a nature as to prevent the alleged damage (*Commission v United Kingdom (Re Merchant Shipping Rules)* (case 246/89R)). In such proceedings relief can be very speedy. In *Commission v Ireland (Re Dundalk Water Scheme)* (case 45/87R) an interim injunction was granted *ex parte* within three days of application.

The case of *Antonissen* (case C–393/96 P/R) concerned a claim for an interim award of damages. The case came on appeal to the president of the ECJ from the president of the CFI, who had rejected the applicant's request. The applicant sought provisional damages, pending a final ruling in a claim for compensation against the Community. The applicant, a dairy farmer, had been refused a milk quota on the basis of an allegedly invalid EC regulation. As a result he had received a request for payment of a substantial supplementary levy, threatening to cause him severe financial distress. The president of the ECJ allowed his appeal. He held that if an interim order is justified, prima facie—in law and in fact—and it is urgent, in order to avoid serious and irreparable damage, it must be made before a decision is reached in the main proceedings. An absolute prohibition on obtaining, in interim proceedings, part of the compensation claimed in the main proceedings, and seeking to protect the applicant's interest, would not be compatible with the individual's right to effective judicial protection. Such payment may be necessary to ensure the practical effect of the judgment in the main application. However, before ordering such payment the Court must examine the applicant's assets to assess whether it would be possible to recover any payment by way of advance when the final judgment is delivered. Recourse to such a remedy must be restricted to situations in which the prima facie case is strong and the urgency is undeniable.

7.2.3 Action against individuals

There is no provision in the EC Treaty for direct action before the ECJ *against individuals*. Individuals may, however, be vulnerable to fines and penalties under EC secondary legislation (eg, Regulation 17/62, now Regulation 1/2003), which may be challenged before the CFI. Under Article 229, the ECJ has unlimited jurisdiction in regard to the penalties provided in such regulations.

7.3 Action before national courts

7.3.1 Basic principles

In addition to these direct remedies before the European Courts, questions of infringement of EC law by Union institutions and Member States may also be raised before national courts. In describing regulations as 'directly applicable' (Article 249 EC) and in providing a means whereby national courts might refer questions of interpretation and validity of EC law to the ECJ (Article 234 EC) the treaty clearly envisaged a role for national courts in the enforcement of EC law. This role has been greatly enlarged by the development by the ECJ of the principle of direct effects and, more recently, the principles of indirect effects and state liability under *Francovich v Italy* (cases C–6 and 9/90) (see Chapters 5 and 9). A ruling on the interpretation of Community law may reveal that a national law or practice is inconsistent with

Community law; a ruling that a provision of an EC regulation, directive, or decision is invalid renders it unenforceable against the individual concerned. In both cases it may provide the basis for a claim in damages. With the decentralisation of enforcement under the competition and state aid rules, whereby the Union institutions encourage the national authorities (administrative as well as judicial) to become involved, in the spirit of cooperation, in the enforcement of these fundamental policies, the role of the national courts becomes ever more significant. Whilst the Commission has provided guidance to the courts as to its expectations of their role, this development reinforces the view of the national courts as courts of the Union legal order.

7.3.2 **Significance of actions before national courts**

This possibility of an alternative remedy via their national courts is of particular importance for individuals, since they have no *locus standi* to bring a direct action before the ECJ in respect of infringements of EC law by Member States, nor any power to compel the Commission to bring such an action (see *Alfons Lütticke GmbH v Commission* (case 48/65)—Chapters 12 and 13). Further, their *locus standi* in direct actions against the Union institutions for judicial review is limited. Moreover, national courts remain the only forums in which action can be brought *by* individuals in respect of infringements of EC law *against* individuals. EC law may be invoked as a defence to a criminal charge (eg, *Ratti* (case 148/78)), to resist payment of a charge exacted, or support a claim for the return of money withheld, in breach of EC law (eg, *Van Gend en Loos* (case 26/62)). It may provide a basis for an injunction, to prevent or put an end to action in breach of EC law (eg, *Garden Cottage Foods Ltd v Milk Marketing Board* [1982] QB 1114, Court of Appeal; [1984] AC 130, House of Lords) or a declaration, eg that a particular national measure is illegal, being based on an invalid EC regulation (eg, *Royal Scholten-Honig v Intervention Board for Agricultural Produce* (cases 103 and 145/77)). It may also provide the basis for a claim in damages, either on the principles of direct or indirect effect, against parties acting in breach of substantive provisions of EC law, or, under *Francovich v Italy* (cases C–6 and 9/90), against the state itself for its failure to comply with its obligation under Article 10 (ex 5) EC to 'take all appropriate measures . . . to ensure fulfilment of the obligations arising out of this treaty or resulting from action taken by the institutions of the Community'. Thus acts of Member States or of Union institutions which are illegal under EC law may be challenged, and remedies provided. While the illegal acts are not set aside as a result of the action, they cannot be enforced.

It has long been recognised that some of the key developments in the Union legal order have arisen as the result of an Article 234 reference from a national court, and that private actors consequently have a role in facilitating the enforcement of Community law as they seek the means to enforce their rights. This aspect may also have influenced the decision of the Commission with regards to decentralisation and with regard to the encouragement of class actions (eg, in consumer matters). Thus, both as regards competition law and consumer rights, the Commission is considering the advantages in facilitating class actions (see Green Paper on Consumer Collective Redress (COM (2008) 794 final; White Paper on Damages Actions for Breach of EC Antitrust Rules (COM (2008) 165). As we shall see in the context of remedies, it is far from clear whether the ECJ, in accepting this approach, is concerned more with effective judicial protection or the effective enforcement of Community law. Indeed, the Consumer Class Action Paper recognised the distortions in the market created by trader activity but which individual consumers did not have the incentive to challenge. Whilst the Commission did not expressly focus on 'effectiveness' in this paper, the shifting and multifaceted meaning of *effet utile*, or effectiveness, is one of the questions currently under discussion by legal academics.

7.3.3 Remedies in national courts

Where individuals seek to assert their Community rights before national courts or tribunals, they may do so in the context of any proceedings of national law, public or private, in which EC rights are relevant, in pursuit of any remedy, interim or final, available under national law. The issue of remedies is discussed in Chapter 8. Here it is worthwhile noting that while the Union does not have the competence to harmonise national legal systems' rules and remedies, the ECJ has introduced certain minimum requirements. They do not, however, go so far as to harmonise remedies, and it is questionable the extent to which these requirements undermine national legal systems' procedural autonomy—a matter that, in theory, lies outside Union competence.

7.3.4 Jurisdiction of the European Courts to give preliminary rulings

To assist national courts in their task of enforcing EC law, Article 234 gives the ECJ jurisdiction to give preliminary rulings concerning the interpretation of EC law and the validity of acts of the institutions at the request of national courts. The discussion in Chapter 10 will show the significance of this procedure in terms of the institutional architecture and the use to which national courts have been put in the service of the Union project. Originally, only the ECJ had the power to give preliminary rulings but, following Nice, some part of this jurisdiction will fall to the CFI, though this has not yet been made operational. According to Article 225(3), even within these limits, there will be the possibility of review of the CFI's decisions by the ECJ. Article 225(3) specifies, however, that such review will occur only in exceptional circumstances. The procedure seems not to be an appeals procedure. According to Article 62 of the Statute of the Court of Justice, the decision as to whether review is necessary is to be made by the First Advocate-General of the Court of Justice, not the parties to the case.

Although the ECJ has no power to *decide* the issue before the national court, an interpretation on the matter of Community law involved, or on the validity of the act in question, will normally be sufficient to establish whether an infringement of EC law has occurred. On this basis the national court may then supply the appropriate remedy. As noted above, the Court's jurisdiction to rule on these matters has been extended by the incorporation into the EC Treaty of areas previously governed by the TEU, and by a new jurisdiction over parts of the third pillar (police and judicial cooperation in criminal matters) remaining within the TEU, in provisions analogous to Article 234. Regrettably, these provisions are more limited in scope than Article 234 and, in allowing Member States a choice as to the extent and even the possibility of access to the ECJ, seriously undermine the uniformity of judicial protection for individuals under EU law (see further Chapter 12). As we will see, should the Lisbon Treaty come in to force, some of these limitations will be removed, though the ECJ will not have full jurisdiction with regard to CFSP.

7.4 Conclusions

The role played by the ECJ in securing the enforcement of Community law against both EU institutions and Member States cannot be overstated. Recognising and respecting the limitations of the remedies provided under the EC Treaty, it has provided, via the principles of direct effect, indirect effect, and state liability in damages, an extremely effective alternative means of enforcement of Community law by individuals, within the courts of Member States. It has insisted on the effective protection of individuals' Community rights by these courts, even when the rights have not been expressly, or even impliedly, granted to individuals. This principle of effective judicial protection has revealed the deficiencies in national legal systems and extended the scope of legal protection of individuals in matters of Community law. This has spilt, and will continue to spill, over into domestic law, raising the standard of judicial protection in matters of purely national law: national courts are rightly reluctant to apply a double standard. This process has resulted in some harmonisation of remedies in the legal systems of Member States. In this, the role of the private actor, although dependent on the rulings of the ECJ, has played an important role in bringing the cases so as to allow the ECJ the opportunity to develop the law. The dual function of effectiveness of individual rights and effective enforcement of Community law runs through this area of law. The gap between the approach to Community law and the rest of the body of Union law is striking and is based on the limited jurisdiction of the courts in those areas. It remains to be seen what the impact of the Lisbon Treaty will be, particularly on matters falling within the JHA pillar.

In contrast, the approach of the ECJ and CFI regarding challenges to the actions of the institutions, especially where the challenge comes from a non-privileged applicant, fails to protect the interests of the individual adequately. As discussed in Chapter 12, the narrow view taken of *locus standi* for non-privileged applicants by the European courts has given rise to some adverse criticism. It has made the possibility of challenging the validity of EC measures via national courts and the preliminary ruling mechanism particularly important. The jurisdiction of the Courts in the context of judicial review remains important, as it is one mechanism by which the institutional balance of the Union is maintained.

FURTHER READING

Albors-Llorens, A, 'Changes in the jurisdiction of the European Court of Justice under the Treaty of Amsterdam' (1998) 35 CML Rev 1273.

Caranta, R, 'Judicial protection against Member States: A new *Jus Commune* takes shape' (1995) 32 CML Rev 679.

Eeckhaut, P, 'The European Courts after Nice' in Andenas and Usher (eds), *The Treaty of Nice and Beyond: Enlargement and constitutional reform* (Hart Publishing, 2003).

Fennelly, N, 'The area of freedom, security and justice and the European Court of Justice' (2000) 46 ICLQ 941.

Garbagnati Ketvel, M-G, 'The jurisdiction of the European Court of Justice in respect of the common foreign and security policy' (2006) 5 ICLQ 77.

Jacque, JP, and Weiler, J, 'On the road to European Union: A new judicial architecture: An agenda for the intergovernmental conference' (1990) 27 CML Rev 185.

Lang, JT, 'The duties of national authorities under Community Law' (1998) 23 EL Rev 109.

8

Remedies in national courts

8.1 Introduction

The preceding chapters have identified that the European Court of Justice (ECJ), relying to a significant extent on the need to make EC law (and some EU law) effective, extended the possible mechanisms by which individuals could seek access to rights derived from EC law in their national courts. Even where such rights have been properly enacted, there may be problems. As the ECJ itself noted, however, extending access to substantive rights means nothing unless it is possible, in procedural terms, to access the national court system to obtain a remedy for any violation of those substantive rights. In *Heylens* (case 222/86), the Court stated:

> since free access to employment is a fundamental right which the Treaty confers individually on each worker in the Community, the existence of a remedy of a judicial nature against any decision of a national authority refusing the benefit of that right is essential in order to secure for the individual effective protection for his right. [Para 14.]

Rules relating to *locus standi*, periods of limitation, and quantum of damages can all have an effect on whether it would be possible to bring an action and if any such action would, in practice, be worth bringing before the national courts. The treaties are, however, silent on the issue of such procedural rules and it has fallen to the Court to develop the law in this area.

This chapter discusses the ECJ's approach to this problem. It outlines the ECJ's relevant jurisprudence and identifies how the ECJ has developed the principles of 'equivalence' and 'effectiveness'—key concepts underlying the Court's approach to procedure and remedies—to limit the scope of what might be termed 'national procedural autonomy'. In this area we see the use of 'effectiveness' in different contexts: as a shorthand for effective judicial protection; or meaning effective protection (and enforcement) of European rights. Intertwined in this debate are the differing elements of the right to a fair trial: access to a court is certainly central, but there are other concerns which may affect the outcome, notably legal certainty and the principle of *res judicata*. Against this background, one particular issue should be addressed: to what extent does EC law require the creation of new remedies for EC law rights? One particular example of this issue, state liability, is discussed in Chapter 9.

8.2 General principles regarding national procedural rules

8.2.1 Overview of principles

The ECJ has laid down a number of principles which must be observed by national courts in claims involving Community law. It has held consistently that:

> In the absence of Community rules it is for the domestic systems of each Member State to designate the courts having jurisdiction and the procedural conditions governing actions at law intended to ensure the protection of the rights which subjects derive from the direct effects of Community law, it being understood that such conditions cannot be less favourable than those relating to similar actions of a domestic nature nor render virtually impossible or excessively difficult the exercise of rights conferred by Community law. [See *Rewe Zentralfinanz v Landwirtschaftskammer Saarland* (case 33/76), *Peterbroeck* (case C–312/93), *Van Schijndel* (cases C–430 and C–431/93) and *Wells* (case C–201/02).]

This statement may be seen to embody three separate principles:

(a) the principle of national treatment ('it is for the domestic systems of each Member State to designate . . . effects of Community law')

(b) the principle of non-discrimination ('conditions cannot be less favourable than those . . . of a domestic nature')

(c) the principle of effectiveness ('nor render impossible or excessively difficult the exercise of rights conferred').

There is little basis in the treaty for these principles, although the principle of national procedural autonomy might seem self-evident when cases originate in national courts. An approach which starts from the presumption that national rules will, in principle, be accepted by the ECJ also respects the integrity of the national legal system. These arguments do not justify the principles of non-discrimination and effectiveness, which operate to limit the principle of national procedural autonomy. Article 10 EC (post Lisbon Article 4(3) TEU), which requires Member States to 'take all appropriate measures . . . to ensure fulfilment of the obligations arising out of this treaty or resulting from actions taken by the institutions of the Community' could be seen as providing some form of treaty basis for these principles, although this provision does not specifically address the question of procedures or remedies. Nonetheless, although established in early case law, these three principles remain central to the ECJ's jurisprudence in this area.

8.2.2 Equivalence and effectiveness

As the scope of national procedural autonomy depends on them, both of the concepts of non-discrimination (equivalence) and effectiveness deserve further explanation. A preliminary question concerns the relationship between the three principles noted above and the principles of equivalence and effectiveness. Since the national remedy provided for a claim based on domestic law may not be exactly comparable to a claim based on EC law, or, although seemingly comparable, may operate to the detriment of the party relying on EC law, commentators, and even the Court, have tended to merge the first and second principles (that is the principles of national treatment and non-discrimination) into a single principle of *equivalence* discussed at 8.4 below.

As we have seen in 8.2.1 above, the ECJ referred in a number of cases to the principle that national rules should not 'render impossible or excessively difficult the exercise of the rights conferred'. The Court has not always used this formulation of the effectiveness principle. Another version, enunciated in *Harz v Deutsche Tradax GmbH* (case 79/83) requires that the remedies and sanctions provided for breach of Community law must have a real deterrent effect and must be 'such as to guarantee full and effective protection' for individuals' Community rights. It is arguable that the two different formulations give the principle of effectiveness a different scope, the 'impossible or excessively difficult test' being narrower than the requirement for 'full and effective protection' of EC law rights. The differences between the two approaches to effectiveness are discussed further at 8.3.2 below.

There are a number of difficulties with the approach that the ECJ has adopted. One relates to the fact that procedures and remedies will not be uniform across the Member States, meaning that an individual in one Member State might be able to bring an action or be awarded a certain amount of damages that an individual in another Member State, relying on the same substantive right and factual situation, would not. The second set of problems relate to the scope of equivalence and effectiveness and their impact on the principle of national procedural autonomy.

8.2.3 Tension between national procedural autonomy and the principles of equivalence and effectiveness

A number of issues can be seen. First, it may not be easy to assess what is an 'equivalent' national remedy. EC law is *sui generis*. It cuts across the boundaries and classifications of national law. Even where domestic law provides a remedy in the context of a similar claim, for example in restitution, or in the field of employment law, such claims may be dealt with in different courts, subject to different procedures and different limitations as to time or the award of damages. Some potential remedies may be more 'effective' than others. How, then, is equivalence to be assessed? Does the principle of effectiveness require that the most generous treatment be accorded to claims based on EC law? Secondly, there are circumstances in which an equivalent domestic remedy may not exist. EC law is supreme over all national law. Where an individual seeks to invoke his Community rights in order to challenge national law, he may do so against any law, whatever its nature. In most Member States, concepts of sovereignty prohibit challenge to the legality of statute or, *a fortiori*, constitutional law. Furthermore, in most Member States there are lacunae, gaps in the legal protection of individuals, arising from traditional privileges and immunities. Sometimes these limitations are justified, sometimes they are not. What remedy or procedure is to be provided by national courts in these circumstances?

The ECJ, in its jurisdiction under Article 234, has provided guidance on these matters. Its approach to the principles of equivalence and effectiveness has developed over the years, from an absolutist, interventionist approach in cases such as *Marshall (No 2)* (case C–271/91), *Emmott* (case C–208/90) and *Factortame (Nos 1 and 2)*, towards a more 'hands-off' approach, described by Tridimas as a policy of 'selective deference to national rules of procedure'. As we shall, despite these general trends, the ECJ will still have moments of activism, particularly where areas of exclusive Union competence are concerned, and the case law is therefore somewhat uncertain. There are two main concerns. The first relates to whether, by focusing on effectiveness over equivalence, the ECJ has created a requirement for super remedies, which may then spill over into national law generally. The alternative position is that there is a distinction between rights derived from EC law and those not. The second issue relates to the competence of the Member States to maintain their own legal systems. Due to the shifting meaning of the terminology used, it is not always clear whether the ECJ is protecting enforcement or individuals' rights; or protecting the coherence of the legal system as a whole.

8.3 Meaning of 'effectiveness'

In some circumstances it will be clear that an effective remedy has not been provided. For example, rules that deny access to the courts altogether, such as a rule restricting payment of a duty held by the ECJ to be contrary to EC law to claimants who have brought an action for repayment before the delivery of that judgment, as was the situation in *Barra v Belgium* (case 309/85), will clearly be ineffective in protecting the Community rights of persons bringing their claim, based on that judgment, after the date of judgment (see also *Deville v Administration des Impôts* (case 240/87)). But there are many situations in which the position is not so clear. Many of the important cases in this area have arisen in the field of sex-discrimination legislation. Many of those cases were based on specific requirements in directives which require remedies to be provided. We might ask therefore, to what extent is that jurisprudence representative of the approach taken by the ECJ in other policy fields? We will consequently consider the jurisprudence relating to procedural rules in two segments: that relating to sex-discrimination legislation and then the more general case law.

8.3.1 Jurisprudence in the field of sex discrimination legislation

A significant number of cases in this area have arisen in the context of sex-discrimination legislation, notably—though not exclusively—Directive 76/207, the Equal Treatment Directive. Crucially, Article 6 of that directive requires Member States to provide judicial remedies for those with a substantive claim under the directive. The starting point for this line of jurisprudence was the *Von Colson* case (case 14/83), discussed in Chapter 5. *Von Colson* concerned two women who applied for jobs but who were not appointed. They claimed successfully that they had been discriminated against on the grounds of their gender. The damages in the case were assessed on the basis of the claimants' actual loss, in this case, travelling expenses. The question referred to the ECJ was whether this was sufficient, or, in the words of the ECJ's jurisprudence, 'effective'. The ECJ remarked that:

> if a Member State chooses to penalize breaches of [the prohibition on sex discrimination] by the award of compensation, then in order to ensure that it is effective and that it has a deterrent effect, that compensation must in any event be adequate in relation to the damage sustained and must therefore amount to more than purely nominal compensation such as, for example, the reimbursement only of the expenses incurred in connection with the application. [Para 26.]

This judgment can be seen to be making a number of points. It reaffirmed that remedies must be effective. This point is linked, as we have seen, to the idea that without adequate recompense from the perspective of the victim, a right has little value. Crucially, the ECJ also looked to the impact of the remedy on the body responsible for the violation of EC law: any compensation must be such as to make the violation of EC law-derived rights much less attractive.

The ECJ developed the effectiveness principle in this field significantly during the early 1990s. *Dekker* (case C–177/88) concerned a claim that the applicant had been discriminated against on the basis that she had not been employed because she was pregnant. Under national law, claims for redress could be subject to a requirement of fault on the part of the defendant, or a claim could be subjected to arguments based on justification; the right to compensation was not absolute even once discrimination had been shown. The ECJ, basing its judgment on *Von Colson*, held that, to be effective, 'any infringement of the prohibition suffices in itself to make the person guilty fully liable' (para 26). This ruling would seem to have pushed the boundaries of the effectiveness requirement wider than in *Von Colson*. In contrast to *Von Colson*, the damages that would have been awarded under national law in this case were not necessarily only nominal. In the words of the early judgments, it could not to be said that the national rules operated to make the exercise of substantive rights 'impossible in practice'.

In *Marshall (No 2)* (case C–271/91), two national rules were in issue: a statutory ceiling on the amount of damages that could be awarded for sex-discrimination claims and the jurisdictional limitation on the relevant tribunal which meant that it could not award interest on damages. Again, reasoning from *Von Colson*, the ECJ, based on Equal Treatment Directive 76/207, held that where damages were awarded for breaches of individuals' rights under the directive, national courts must provide 'full' compensation, including interest on the award from the date of judgment. A system in which compensation was subject to statutory limits, as provided under the UK Sex Discrimination Act 1975, would not be 'sufficiently effective to achieve the objectives of the Directive'. A principle of full compensation required that 'reparation be commensurate with the loss or damage sustained'. This case was a step forward from *Von Colson*, as the Court describes in more detail the requirements of an effective remedy. Rather than describing the lower end of what would be required—that is, more than nominal—the Court imposed a higher test: that the remedy be *full* compensation. This ruling, generally applied, could have had potentially far-reaching consequences.

However, in more recent years the Court has been prepared to accept some limits to the principle of full compensation. In *R v Secretary of State for Social Security, ex parte Sutton* (case C–66/95), in a claim based on EC Directive 79/7 on equal treatment for men and women in social security, it accepted a statutory bar on the payment of interest on an award of damages, even though the wording of the directive on which the applicants sought to rely, requiring Member States to ensure that persons alleging discrimination are able to 'pursue their claims by judicial process', was virtually identical to that on which the applicants based their claim in *Marshall (No 2)* (case C–271/91). *Marshall* was distinguished on the basis that there the award of interest was an 'essential component of compensation for the purpose of ensuring real equality of treatment'. In contrast, *Sutton* 'concerned social security benefits paid by the competent bodies which must . . . examine whether the conditions laid down in the relevant legislation were fulfilled'.

The amounts paid 'in no way constituted reparation for loss or damage sustained'. The distinction is fine, and may be seen as an example of the Court's more cautious approach following criticisms of its activism expressed by some Member States in the period leading up to the ToA. The Court in *Sutton* was similarly reserved in its comments on the possibility of recovery of interest on arrears of payment in an alternative claim based on *Francovich*. It enunciated the principles governing state liability in damages but insisted that it was for the national court to assess, in the light of those principles, whether the claimant was entitled to reparation for the loss she had suffered.

However, *Marshall (No 2)* was followed in *Draehmpaehl v Urania Immobilienservice OHG* (case C–180/95), a case decided on the same day as *Sutton*. Here, in a claim by a man, the Court held that a limit of three months' wages as compensation for sex discrimination as regards access to employment (the job advertisement requested female applicants), and a six-month aggregate limit where several applicants were involved, would not guarantee effective judicial protection for individuals' Community rights. A three-month limit would only be acceptable as reasonable if the employer could prove that the applicants would not have been given the job in the absence of discrimination. Clearly, if the applicant would have been given the job in the absence of discrimination, the limits on compensation in this case would not have been sufficient to compensate for the damage sustained. Although *Marshall (No 2)* may have been limited, it is not extinct.

A separate line of cases deals with the issue of time limits. In general, the ECJ had rules that a limitation of a 'reasonable' period would not make it 'impossible in practice' to exercise Community law rights. We have seen that this phrase was extended in the context of amount of damages for sex discrimination cases. How would the ECJ approach the question of time limits for sex discrimination? A case arose in respect of Directive 79/7, on equal treatment for men and women in matters of social security, *Emmott* (case C–208/90).

The case concerned a challenge to the Irish authorities' refusal to grant Ms Emmott disability benefit. She claimed that this was discriminatory, in breach of Directive 79/7 on equal treatment for men and women in matters of social security. At the time when her cause of action arose she was unaware that it was directly effective. When she became aware that it was, following a ruling from the Court in *McDermott v Minister for Social Welfare* (case 286/85), she applied to the minister for her case to be reviewed. Her application was deferred pending a ruling from the ECJ in *Cotter v Minister for Social Welfare* (case C–377/89). When she was finally granted leave to institute proceedings, she was found to be out of time. The Irish judge referred to the ECJ to ascertain whether it was contrary to Community law for the authorities of a Member State to rely on national procedural rules, in particular relating to time limits, in defending claims based on Community directives. The minister argued that, even though a directive had not been implemented, or properly implemented, the principle of direct effects enabled the individual effectively to assert his Community rights, at least against a 'public' body. The Court disagreed. It held that the principle of direct effects provided only a minimum guarantee: as long as a directive has not been properly implemented the individual is in a state of uncertainty; the individual is unaware of the full extent of his or her rights. Therefore the competent authorities of Member States cannot rely, in an action against them based on the directive, on national procedural rules relating to time limits for bringing proceedings as long as that Member State has not properly implemented that directive into national law.

One important point to note about *Emmott* is that (like *Cotter and McDermott* (case C–377/89)), the ECJ's reasoning is significantly different from that used in the damages cases. Although both sets of jurisprudence are aimed at ensuring the full effectiveness of Community law rights, *Emmott* is based on the principle of estoppel, that is, the state cannot benefit from its own wrongdoing. It has been suggested, notably by Advocate-General Jacobs, that it was because the state was in the wrong and indeed created the problem in *Emmott*, that the ECJ took such an uncompromising stance in that case.

This decision, expressed in the broadest terms, gave rise to some alarm in Member States. It might be acceptable in a case in which the State's failure to implement a Community directive is clear, or when, as in *Emmott*'s case, it was 'excessively difficult', as a result of action by the national authorities, for the claimant to enforce her rights. But it was likely to cause injustice, contrary to the principle of legal certainty, when applied in cases of inadvertent failure on the part of the state and when it exposed public bodies, acting bona fide according to their legitimate understanding of the law, to a flood of retrospective claims. It might be years before a directive was found not to have been 'properly' implemented into national law. Nor was it clear whether *Emmott* applied solely to the non- or faulty implementation of directives. The reasoning on which the decision was based might be applied to any breach of Community law, including claims under *Francovich v Italy* (cases C–6 and 9/90 (discussed in Chapter 9).

Perhaps recognising that it had gone too far, the Court distinguished *Emmott* in *Steenhorst-Neerings* (case C–338/91). Here it held that a statutory limit on the retrospective payment of invalidity benefit (not in itself a limitation period, although similar in its effect) was not contrary to EC law, being justified by the need to preserve the financial equilibrium of social security funds. There was a difference between national rules fixing time limits for bringing an action, as in *Emmott*, and rules which merely limited the retroactive effect of claims. *Steenhorst-Neerings* was followed, on similar facts, in *Johnson v Chief Adjudication Officer* (case C–410/92), in which the benefit in question was non-contributory, therefore posing no threat to the financial balance of social security funds (see also *Alonso-Pérez v Bundesanstat für Arbeit* (case C–394/93), three-month ceiling on the retrospective payment of family benefits did not render the exercise of Community rights impossible). It seems that time limits will be set aside only when they render the exercise of Community rights absolutely impossible and that *Emmott* is limited to its facts.

Similar thinking, albeit to different effect, lay behind the Court's ruling in *Magorrian v Eastern Health and Social Services Board* (case C–246/96). This case concerned a claim for the retrospective payment of certain pension benefits to which the applicant, a female part-time worker, found she was entitled under Article 119 (now 141) EC post Lisbon Article 157 TFEU following a ruling from the ECJ (see *Fisscher* (case C–128/93), Chapter 27). Her claim, which related to the period from 1976 to 1990, was subject to a two-year limitation period running from the date of commencement of her action. The defendant Board opposed her claim, relying on *Steenhorst-Neerings* and *Johnson*. The Court distinguished these cases. The claim in this case was not, it held, for the retrospective award of certain additional benefits but for the recognition of entitlement to full membership of an occupational scheme through acquisition of MHO status, which confers entitlement to the additional benefits. The two-year limitation rule prevented the entire record of service from 1976 to 1990 being taken into account for the purposes of calculating the additional benefits which would be payable even after the date of the claim. It 'struck at the very essence' of the applicant's rights and would not be permissible under Community law. The ECJ took the same view of the same rule in *Preston v Wolverhampton NHS Healthcare Trust* (case C–78/98). Although the ECJ accepts the need for limitation periods, even those imposing a short period of time in which would-be applicants must act, where the rule affects the underlying principle of non-discrimination, the substantive right in issue in these cases, the Court still seems prepared to strike down national measures.

8.3.2 Effectiveness in other circumstances

The case law in the sex-discrimination field has shown that the ECJ has been prepared to take an extensive view of what the notion of effectiveness requires, although some of the more far-reaching cases have been limited. Given that in many of the sex-discrimination directives, EC law requires that Member States provide a remedy, the question is to what extent the ECJ has taken a similar approach in other circumstances. This can be seen in some consumer-protection cases, but again, these involve Community measures which require that Member States provide remedies (see, eg, *Cofidis* (case C–473/00) concerning Directive 93/13/EEC on unfair consumer contracts). What, however, has been the ECJ's approach to effectiveness where the express provisions of EC law are silent as to the need to provide remedies?

The Court has applied the notion of effectiveness of national remedies outside the scope generally from its early jurisprudence. It is in the early 1990s (as with the sex-discrimination jurisprudence) that we see the logic of effectiveness being taken to its limits and in this context *Factortame I* (case C–213/89) is significant. The case concerned a challenge to British primary legislation and the applicants sought an interim injunction against the Crown, suspending the relevant legislation. At that point the English courts had no power to grant the relief sought. The matter was referred to the ECJ, which reasoned from the obligation of Member States under Article 10 EC to ensure the legal protection which derives from Community law, and its judgment in *Simmenthal* (case 106/77) (discussed in Chapter 4). It summarised *Simmenthal* as requiring:

> that any provision of a national legal system and any legislative, administrative or judicial practice which might impair the effectiveness of Community law . . . are incompatible with those requirements, which are the very essence of Community law.

The ECJ then held that:

> the full effectiveness of Community law would be just as much impaired if a rule of national law could prevent a court seised of a dispute governed by Community law from granting interim relief in order to ensure the full effectiveness of the judgment to be given on the existence of the rights claimed under Community law. [Paras 20–1.]

The Court here was clearly focusing on the need to ensure that Community law is respected. As with the other cases already mentioned at 8.3.1 above, note that the Court actually uses the word 'effectiveness' rather than the phraseology used in its earliest jurisprudence. There, what was prohibited was that the relevant national rule makes the application of Community law 'impossible or excessively difficult': effectiveness is arguably a harder test for national law to satisfy. National procedural autonomy is not mentioned; indeed the Court's first reference to the role of national legal systems was in the context of the obligation under Article 10 EC to ensure that Community law rights are protected. This could suggest a shift away from the presumption that national rules are the starting point for any discussion of remedies. The issue of equivalence was not discussed: the fact that cases based on domestic law rights would be similarly hindered was not considered. Arguably, the ECJ at this stage was prioritising the principle of effectiveness over the principle of autonomy. In any event, in this case we see the application of the effectiveness principle creating a form of reverse discrimination, a difference in treatment that the Court did not seem to find objectionable. Other consequences of this ruling for the domestic legal system are discussed below.

Factortame I was handed down at roughly the same time as cases such as *Marshall (No 2)* and might be thought to be part of the high-water mark of the effectiveness jurisprudence. In subsequent cases the ECJ has continued to reason from the need to ensure effectiveness, although with less spectacular effects. This point is well illustrated by *Peterbroeck* (case C–312/93) and *Van Schijndel* (cases C–430 and 431/93), both of which concerned the ability of national courts to refer questions to the ECJ on their own motion. *Van Schijndel* concerned a Dutch rule which precluded the national court from referring a question to the ECJ when the parties themselves had not raised the issue of EC law. The question of whether the Dutch rule itself was compatible with the principles of effectiveness and equivalence came before the ECJ. In contrast to its approach in *Factortame I*, the Court commenced by restating the concept of national procedural autonomy, subject—as ever—to the requirements of effectiveness and equivalence. Rather than emphasising the effectiveness of EC law as a guiding principle, it returned to its earlier formulation of 'impossible or excessively difficult', albeit with a new twist. In *Van Schijndel*, the Court held that:

> a national procedural provision [which] renders application of Community law impossible or excessively difficult must be analysed by reference to the role of that provision in the procedure, its progress and its special features, viewed as a whole, before the various national instances. In the light of that analysis the basic principles of the domestic judicial system, such as the *protection of the rights of the defence, the principle of legal certainty* and the *proper conduct of procedure must*, where appropriate, *be taken into consideration*. [Emphasis added.]

What is clear from this ruling is that the impact of the national rule must be analysed on the facts of each case, to see whether the exercise of the Community law right is rendered excessively difficult taking into account the demands of natural justice and legal certainty. The courts therefore have to balance competing interests. In *Van Schijndel*, the Court came to the conclusion that the Dutch rule was not incompatible with Community law. In *Peterbroeck* (case C–312/93), which imposed a 60-day time limit beyond which neither party to the case could raise a matter of

EC law, the ECJ using identical reasoning to that used in *Van Schijndel*, found on the facts that the exercise of the EC law right had been rendered excessively difficult. In this case it was not the limit of 60 days in itself that was the problem, but the particular circumstances of the case. *Van Schijndel*, was relied on in *der Weerd and ors v Minister van Landbouw, Natuur en Voedselkwaliteit* (joined cases C–222–5/05) to the same effect; again what was key was that the rights of the parties were not adversely affected. In coming to this conclusion, the ECJ carefully distinguished the circumstances in *Peterbroeck*.

Some difficulty is introduced into the case law by a number of rulings which seem to move away from this approach. The case of *Kühne und Hetiz* (case C–453/00) concerned the question of the extent to which national authorities are bound to reopen national administrative decisions when a subsequent decision of the ECJ proved that decision to be wrong. The ECJ here noted the importance of legal certainty and suggested that as a general rule such a body would not be required to do so. On the facts of the case, however, where four factors were satisfied, the duty of cooperation under Article 10 would require it to reconsider the matter. The four factors were that:

(a) national law confers on the administrative body competence to reopen the decision

(b) the decision became final only as a result of a judgment of a national court against whose decisions there is no judicial remedy

(c) the judgment was based on an interpretation of Community law (without a reference being made) which, in the light of a subsequent judgment of the ECJ, was incorrect

(d) the person concerned complained to the administrative body immediately after becoming aware of that judgment of the Court.

Kempter (case c–2/06) revisited the conditions in *Kühne und Hetiz,* making it easier for the conditions in that case to be satisfied and thus easier to review national administrative decisions contrary to EC law. Here Kempter was ordered to repay some agricultural subsidies. Kempter litigated the matter in the German courts but lost. Subsequently, a decision of the ECJ held that a litigant in a similar situation was entitled to keep the subsidies in issue. Kempter sought to reopen the decision in his case on the basis of the subsequent ruling. Two issues arose:

(a) Must the applicant in such a case have relied on EC law in his original proceedings?

(b) Does EC law impose a time limit in which such an action for review must be brought?

As regards the the first question, which essentially concerns the third element in *Kühne und Hetiz,*the ECJ held that it was sufficient the point of EC law on which the applicant could have based its claim was discussed, or that the court of last instance could have raised the matter of its own motion. In its reasoning, the ECJ has followed its approach in *van Schijndel* (case C–430–1/93). Although decided after *der Weerd, Kempter* did not consider the reasoning there. It seems difficult now to reconcile the case law and there is a real danger of some strange results in practice.

As regards the second question, *Kempter* softens the requirement in *Kühne und Heitz* for an immediate challenge. The ECJ held that EC law does not impose any time limit within which an application must be brought. Rather, this issue falls to be determined in accordance with national procedural rules, which must satisfy the twin tests of equivalence and effectiveness. That is, following *der Weerd* (and see also *Unibet* (case C–432/05), discussed below), the national rules must not render the exercise of rights impossible or excessively difficult.

Kühne und Heitz has also been limited in cases such as *Kapferer v Schlank & Schick GmbH* (case C–234/04) which, by relying on the principles of *res judicata,* suggested that a national court need not reopen final court decisions. In this case, the ECJ emphasised the element in *Kühne und Hetiz* that the facility for reopening such decisions exists in national law, arguably bring the focus back to the principle of equivalence, rather than on effectiveness. Similarly, the ECJ accepted in *Heemskerk BV, Firma Schaap v Productschap vee en Vlees* (case C–455/06) that if the national legal system recognised the prohibition of *reformatio in pejus* (that is, a claimant should not be made worse off by a court raising an issue of its own motion than if he had not brought the action) EU law could not require a national court to raise EU law in breach of that principle. It seems that where a general principle of law is at stake that is recognised generally within the national legal order, the ECJ will not insist on effectiveness. Conversely in *Lucchini* (case C–119/05), in a case concerning the recovery of illegal state aid, both the ECJ and the Advocate-General agreed that Community law would preclude the application of a provision of national law which attempted to lay down the principle of *res judicata*, in so far as that provision prevents the recovery of the illegal state aid. This case might perhaps be considered the exception rather than the rule, as it has long been recognised that the supervision of state aid rules is mandatory, and within the exclusive competence of the Community, through the activities of the Commission. The individual in this case has no EC law right to enforce (but contrast to the normal effectiveness situation where the individual is enforcing a Community law right). In this situation, the case is about compliance rather than protection of individual rights. This case may thus illustrate the point that the ECJ when talking about effectiveness may, depending on the circumstances, be talking about different issues; effective enforcement (see also *Munoz*, below) and effective judicial protection of rights (see also eg *Unibet* (case C–432/05)).

The case law is not in a satisfactory state. In addition to the fine distinctions in the case law discussed, *Van Schijndel* and *Peterbroeck* illustrate the consequence of the ECJ's 'balancing' approach. On the one hand, it might be suggested that this approach reconciles the tension between the principle of national autonomy and the need to ensure effective protection of EC law rights. The problem is that in emphasising the importance to be given to the particular facts in each case, the ECJ has—despite its emphasis on legal certainty—introduced a significant amount of uncertainty into this area. It is not possible to say that national courts must have the right to refer questions to the ECJ of their own motion or, on the other hand, that they need not. Instead, the answer to whether national rules limiting national courts' rights to refer questions of EC law to the ECJ of their own motion are acceptable is, 'it depends'. By introducing the balancing test, the ECJ has referred the assessment of all the facts back to the national courts, at least in most cases, which adds a further element of uncertainty in this area. This approach can be seen again, for example, in *Evans* (case C–63/01), a case involving the requirement in the Second Insurance Directive (84/5/EEC) to set up a compensation scheme for injuries caused by an unidentified vehicle. In the UK, this scheme is operated by the Motor Insurers' Bureau (MIB). Evans sought to challenge the procedural arrangements for appealing MIB decisions. Having confirmed its earlier case law, the ECJ stated that the ultimate assessment was for the national courts, although in this case, the Court also confirmed that the directive required only minimum procedural rules, and that the UK's system appeared to be compatible.

8.3.3 The creation of new remedies?

We have seen the starting point of the Court's jurisprudence being the concept of national procedural autonomy. As the ECJ confirmed in *Rewe-Handelsgesellschaft Nord mbH* (case 158/80), a Member State is not required to create new remedies for Community law rights, subject always to the principles of equivalence and effectiveness. It is the consequences of the application of effectiveness that gives rise to problems here, in a number of ways.

The first point to note is that in some instances the Court has seen the remedy as forming part of the substantive right. In cases involving repayment of charges levied in breach of Community law, the Court has held that repayment of the sums is a consequence of, and an adjunct to, the right not to pay customs duties. If there was no right to repayment, the substantive right itself would be undermined. This in practice requires a specific form of remedy to be available as a matter of EC law, although the procedural elements of such a claim will fall to be determined by national law, subject always to the principles of equivalence and effectiveness. Although the Court has not phrased this idea in terms of effectiveness itself, in other circumstances it has recognised that judicial remedies are, in principle, necessary to secure effective protection for the individual's rights.

We have also seen that in developing the notion of effectiveness, the ECJ has required that national rules which impede the effectiveness of Community law should be disapplied. In this context, there is a fine line between the disapplication of rules and the creation of new remedies. The *Factortame I* (case C–213/89) case is a good example. In that case, national rules precluded the granting of interim relief by injunction against the Crown. The ECJ held that the national courts should set aside this rule. The consequence was that the English courts were required to apply what was admittedly an existing remedy, but in an entirely novel situation. *Factortame I* had other consequences. The immediate result of the application of the ruling was that EC–derived rights would be treated more favourably than those based in domestic law. The English courts recognised that it is difficult to justify a difference in available remedies in similar situations based on whether the applicant's claim was based on EC law or not. When, in a subsequent case (*M v Home Office*), the possibility of an injunction against the Crown was raised, the House of Lords agreed that in principle such injunctions were available, despite the fact that the rights in question were based on English law, not EC law.

One might have argued that the *Factortame I* ruling was an isolated case, and, in the light of the ECJ's more cautious approach to the principle of effectiveness, it was not to be seen as suggesting that the 'no new remedies' principle had been eliminated entirely. *Francovich* (cases C–6 and 9/90) and more recent cases, however, suggest that it has again been eroded. The Court in *Francovich* introduced the notion of state liability. It can be seen as another enforcement mechanism for

EC law rights, and is discussed at 8.5.6 below and Chapter 9. As will be seen there, *Francovich* created substantive rights for individuals in certain circumstances, with national legal systems again to provide the procedural framework within which individuals can exercise those rights. Although the ECJ has provided some guidance as to the requirements to be satisfied regarding a successful claim under state liability, the remainder of the cause of action will also be determined within the national legal system. All elements determined by the national legal system are subject to the requirements of effectiveness and equivalence. The end result is that a cause of action and remedy is to be provided as a matter of EC law, requiring Member States to provide remedies should their national legal system not already provide them in those circumstances.

Palmisani v INPS (case C–261/95) concerned a claim for damages for losses suffered as a result of the belated transposition of Directive 80/987 on the protection of employees in the event of their employers' insolvency. INPS was the agency responsible for managing the fund set up to guarantee employees' arrears of wages as required by the directive. Following the ECJ's ruling in *Francovich*, the directive had finally been implemented in Italy by legislative decree. Under the decree, claims for compensation from INPS were limited to not more than one year from the date of entry into force of the decree. The claimant's claim, having been brought outside this period, had been rejected by the Italian court. He argued before the ECJ that the one-year limitation period was unlawful, being contrary to the requirement of equivalence and effectiveness. More recently, *Metallgesellschaft & Hoechst v Inland Revenue* (case C–410/98) concerned a British ruling which imposed advance corporation tax on subsidiary companies whose parents were not UK resident, a discriminatory rule. The applicants challenged the imposition of the tax, claiming the interest they would have earned had they not been subject to the advance taxation. It was far from clear under English law that restitution would be available in these circumstances. The Court ruled that it was the premature levying of the tax that created the lack of equality contrary to Article 43 EC. To protect the rights to equality guaranteed by the freedom of establishment, the lost interest could be claimed by way of restitution. The Court went further and, reasoning from *Marshall II* (paras 24–32), held that interest on the sum claimed was also due.

This case is significant in two main respects. The first is that the ECJ did not seem unduly concerned with whether the remedy claimed would have been available under national law or not. This disregard is hard to square with an approach that is based on respect for national procedural autonomy, equivalence and the notion that Member States would not be required to create new remedies. In this judgment the Court is returning to the approach that can be found in the 'repayment' cases mentioned earlier: that is, the Court has reasoned from the importance of the substantive EC law right in issue. In *Metallgesellschaft & Hoechst*, this was the principle of non-discrimination lying at the heart of the freedom of establishment in Article 43. The Court in *Metallgesellschaft & Hoechst* therefore seemed less concerned with assessing the effectiveness of national remedies and more with ensuring the effectiveness of the EC law right itself.

One might argue that *Metallgesellschaft & Hoechst* constitutes nothing more than a recent example of the early case law. The Court has however also looked to the substance of the EC law rights in other circumstances, not concerned with repayment. In *Courage* (case C–453/99), the ECJ held that a right of action in damages against another private party for breach of Article 81 (ex 85) must, in principle, be available. In reaching this conclusion, the Court argued that:

> [t]he full effectiveness of Article 85 [now 81] of the Treaty and, in particular, that practical effect of the prohibition laid down in Article 85(1) [now 81(1)] would be put at risk if it were not open to any individual to claim damages for loss caused to him by a contract or by conduct liable to restrict or distort competition. [Para 26.]

Similar trends to those identified in *Metallgesellschaft* & *Hoechst* can be seen here. Again there is an emphasis on the effectiveness of the substantive right which requires a cause of action to be provided, irrespective of the provisions of the national legal system. In this case, the Court emphasised the centrality of the competition provisions within the treaty and *Courage* might therefore be limited to competition cases or to other areas which are central to the Community project on competition law (see further Chapters 28 and 29). Note that the Commission has since issued a White Paper on Damages for Breach of Competition Law (COM (2008) 165 final). Nonetheless, in the light of these cases, it is difficult to maintain that EC law does not in some circumstances require that new remedies be provided. This was confirmed further by the decision in *Antonio Munoz Cia SA v Frumar Ltd* (case C–253/00), involving Regulation 2200/96 ([1996] OJ L297/1) on the standards for the classification of grapes. Munoz brought civil proceedings against Frumar who had sold grapes under particular labels which did not comply with the relevant standard. Although the regulation did not confer rights on individuals such as Munoz, but applied to all operators in the market, it was accepted that failing to comply with the regulation could have adverse consequences for other operators. Referring to the principle of effectiveness, the Court held that a trader must be able to bring civil proceedings against a competitor to ensure that the regulation is enforced effectively (assuming that the provisions in issue are directly applicable). This rather generous view seems to cement the position in *Courage v Crehan*, and it is now the case that, insofar as a provision of EC law is directly applicable (as opposed to directly effective—see Chapter 5), it is open to be invoked in civil proceedings even though the provision itself does not confer rights on an individual (see also Betlem in Further Reading below). More recently still, in *Unibet (London) Ltd and Unibet (International) Ltd v Justitiekanslern* (case C–432/05), the ECJ seems to require Member States to create new remedies where this is the only way to enforce Community rights, although in doing so suggests that this is the reapplication of the effectiveness principle. In one sense, this may well be true, as the ECJ has already used the principle to require national courts to use national remedies in novel circumstances and against branches of government that would normally enjoy immunity from suit. Crucially, here the ECJ investigated the possibility that a national legal system may have to develop a self-standing cause of action to challenge the compatibility of national law with Community law. On the other hand, it can be seen also that the ECJ emphasises the national-autonomy principle, as its starting point is to assess the adequacy of existing domestic arrangements and in particular the ECJ was prepared to accept that a self-standing remedy need not be provided where the same matter could be examined indirectly in the course of alternative judicial proceedings. Whilst the outcome on the facts in *Unibet* might not be startling, the implications of some of the ECJ's statements may revitalise the question of whether 'euro' remedies will be required.

8.4 Principle of 'equivalence'

Whilst much of the earlier case law considered in some detail the requirements of effectiveness, less attention was paid to the notion of 'equivalence'.

Clearly, a rule which discriminates, directly or indirectly, against claimants relying on EC law will be contrary to Community law. Such was the case in *Criminal Proceedings against Bickel and anor* (case C–274/96). Here, rules of the Trento-Alto region of Italy, which provided that the German language was to have the same status as Italian in relations between *citizens of that area* and the judicial and administrative authorities, but which did not extend to persons of Austrian and German nationality and residence, were held to be discriminatory in their effect, contrary to Article 12 EC. Since then, the ECJ has had to consider more directly the question of equivalence. On the question of equivalence in *Palmisani*, the applicant pointed to other, more generous limitation rules governing claims for damages and to the 'manifest difference' between (for example) the five-year limitation period for reparation in general claims for non-contractual liability and the one-year period allowed for claims based on *Francovich*. The Court held that to ascertain comparability, 'the essential characteristics of the domestic system of reference must be examined'. Prior to the passing of the legislative decree there was no remedy in Italy for such a claim: 'If the domestic system [was] incapable of serving as a basis for a claim under *Francovich* no other relevant comparisons [could] be made'. The Member State must therefore make reparation for the consequences of the loss or damage caused to the claimant on the basis of national rules of liability, provided that they satisfy the requirement of effectiveness.

In *Edis* (case C–231/96), national time limits were again the subject of challenge. This case concerned a shorter time limit imposed for claims for the recovery of payments made regarding charges which had not actually been due, when compared with the time limits for payments made for other sums paid but not due. The applicant had made payments for charges that had not been due; it claimed that the principle of equivalence meant that the longer of the two periods should be applied, as the charges had their basis in EC law. The matter was referred to the ECJ, which began by reiterating the principle that procedural rules must apply without distinction to actions originating in Community law and those based on national law. The Court continued, however, to make the point that this principle of equivalence did not mean that national legal systems could not distinguish between different types of action, such as making a distinction, as in this case, between rules regarding challenges to charges and levies and those relating to the recovery of sums paid in other circumstances, unless the less favourable rules applied only for actions based on Community law. The ECJ concluded that the principle of equivalence could not 'be interpreted as obliging a Member State to extend its most favourable rules governing recovery under national law to all actions for repayment of charges or dues levied in breach of Community law' (para 36). The Court continued:

> Community law does not in principle preclude the legislation of a Member State from laying down, alongside a limitation period applicable under the ordinary law to actions between individuals for the recovery of sums paid but not due, special detailed rules governing claims and legal proceedings to challenge the imposition of charges and other levies. The position would only be different if those detailed rules applied solely to actions based on community law for the repayment of such charges and levies. [Para 37.]

National rules are thus permitted to distinguish between different circumstances such as whether public bodies are parties to the action.

This passage in *EDIS* was cited verbatim in a similar claim for repayment of the Italian registration charge in *IN.CO.GE '90* (cases C–10 and 22/97). Here the Court held that 'any reclassification of the legal relationship between the tax authorities and certain companies in that state . . . in such circumstances . . . is a matter for national law'.

Similarly, in *Criminal Proceedings against Nunes* (case C–186/98) the Court upheld the right of a Member State to impose criminal penalties for the improper use of the European Social Fund, even though the regulation governing misuse of such funds provided only for civil remedies. The Court held that where a Community regulation failed to provide specifically for any penalty for an infringement of Community law, Article 10 of the EC Treaty required Member States to take all measures necessary to ensure the application and effectiveness of that law. The choice of penalties remained at Member States' discretion, provided that the penalty chosen complied with the principle of equivalence, and was 'effective, proportionate and dissuasive'.

The Court has had further opportunity to consider equivalence in a number of cases subsequently. In *Levez v TH Jennings (Harlow Pools) Ltd* (case C–326/96), in a claim for damages in respect of sex discrimination brought under Article 141 EC and Directive 75/117, the Court was asked to consider a two-year time limit on arrears of payment of damages under the UK Equal Pay Act in the light of the principles of equivalence and effectiveness. It was argued that the claim, brought before an industrial tribunal, could have been brought before a county court, by analogy with claims for unlawful deductions from wages or unlawful discrimination in terms of employment on grounds of race or disability, which were subject to more generous limitation rules. The Court held that it was 'for national courts to ascertain whether the procedural rules intended to safeguard rights derived from Community law were safeguarded under national law and complied with the principle of equivalence'. A rule of national law would be deemed equivalent 'where the purpose and cause of action are similar'. However, citing the earlier case of *EDIS v Ministero delle Finanze* (case C–231/96), it held that 'that principle is not to be interpreted as requiring Member States to extend their most favourable rules to all actions brought . . . in the field of employment law'. In assessing equivalence, the national court must consider 'the purpose and essential characteristics of allegedly similar domestic actions'. It must review the different procedures as a whole and weigh the relative advantages and disadvantages of each. On the facts it was found that the two-year period could not be enforced against the applicant, since, having been misled by her employer, she had no way of determining whether she was being discriminated against, or to what extent: 'To allow her employer to rely on the two-year rule would be to deprive his employee of the means provided by the Directive of enforcing the principle of equal pay before the court'. Thus, *in these particular circumstances* the remedy provided was ineffective. In applying the ECJ's ruling in *Levez*, the Employment Appeal Tribunal ([1999] 3 CMLR 715) found that the two-year limitation period provided under the Equal Pay Act did not satisfy the requirement of equivalence, since it had been introduced in order to give effect to Britain's EC obligations and it applied only to equal-pay claims based on sex discrimination. This is, it is submitted, a somewhat stricter line than that taken by the ECJ in *Palmisani*.

The House of Lords referred further questions to the ECJ on how to identify a 'similar' cause of action in *Preston* (case C–78/98). The ECJ re-emphasised the general balancing approach which it had taken in the effectiveness cases of *Peterbroeck* (case C–312/93) and *Van Schijndel* (cases C–430 and 431/93; see 8.3.2 above). It commented that the relevant national rules must be considered in their general context and concluded, in terms very similar to those used in *Van Schijndel*, that:

> the national court must verify objectively, in the abstract, whether the rules at issue are similar taking into account the role played by those rules in the procedure as whole, as well as the operation of that procedure and special feature of those rules . . . [Para 63.]

Whilst the ECJ in recent cases has not considered equivalence directly, in emphasising the conditions pertaining in the national system in cases such as *Heemskerk BV, Firma Schaap v Productschap vee en Vlees* (case C–455/06), there is some suggestion that there has been a move back to considering equivalence, albeit implicitly. It is suggested that this is the better option, given the potentially far-reaching impact on the national legal systems. The case law is however currently somewhat uncertain in this regard.

8.5 Impact of EC law on national remedies

Although EC law does not in principle prescribe specific remedies and procedures to be adopted by national courts in actions based on EC law, the obligation to ensure that national remedies are effective, or sufficiently effective, to protect individuals' Community rights has on occasions required the modification of national law, even the provision of new remedies. These will now be considered, bearing in mind that some of the earlier cases might be decided differently today.

8.5.1 Interim relief

In *R v Secretary of State for Transport, ex parte Factortame Ltd* (case C–213/89) the Court held that English courts were obliged to provide interim injunctions against the Crown where there was no other means of protecting individuals' Community rights, even though, as the House of Lords had found in that case ([1990] 2 AC 85), no such remedy was available as a matter of national law. Following the ECJ's ruling, the House of Lords granted the requested relief ([1991] 1 AC 603 at 645). (See also *Unibet* (case C–432/05)).

In *Zuckerfabrik Süderdithmarschen AG* (cases C–143/88 and 92/89) the ECJ laid down *Community* criteria for the granting of interim relief pending a ruling from the ECJ under Article 234 on the validity of a Community act, based on the principles applicable to the exercise of its own jurisdiction to grant such relief under Articles 242–3 (ex 185–6) EC. Relief should be granted only if the facts and legal circumstances are such as to persuade the court that:

(a) serious doubts exist about the validity of the Community measures on which the contested administrative decision is based

(b) in cases of urgency

(c) to avoid serious and irreparable damage to the party seeking the relief.

Given that the granting of interim relief pending a ruling on the *validity* of Community law involved a new situation for national courts, and that the suspension of a Community act would have serious implications for the Community legal order, it is not surprising that the Court provided a common Community solution here. However, although it might have been desirable, in the interests of the coherence of legal remedies, to require national courts to apply the same criteria in a claim for interim relief pending a ruling on the *interpretation* of Community law, the Court is not now likely to do so. Thus, in this context, national procedural rules will continue to apply. It may be noted that in *R v Secretary of State for Health, ex parte Imperial Tobacco Ltd* (*The Times*, 16 November 1999, QBD) Turner J considered it unnecessary to apply the criteria provided by the ECJ *in Zucherfabrik Süderdithmarschen AG* in a claim for an interim injunction to prevent the enactment of domestic regulations banning tobacco advertising pending a ruling from the ECJ on the validity of the directive on which the regulations were based. He preferred to apply the domestic criteria applicable to claims for interim relief, thereby 'avoiding the problem of the applicant having to prove that the damage that he would suffer in the absence of the grant of suspensory relief would be irreparable'. However, his justification, on the facts perhaps acceptable, was that in this case the date for implementation of the directive, 30 July 2001, had not yet been passed; thus an interim injunction would not have the effect of suspending the application of an *existing* EC obligation.

Zuckerfabrik Süderdithmarschen AG concerned the granting of *suspensory* measures pending a ruling on the validity of a Community measure under Article 234. In *Atlanta Fruchthandelsgesellschaft mbH* (case C–465/93) the Court held, in the context of a claim for interim relief in the form of a grant of licences to import bananas from third countries pending a ruling on the validity of a Council regulation setting up a common banana regime, that the principles laid down in *Zuckerfabrik Süderdithmarschen AG* also applied to the grant of *positive* measures. It was not possible to make a distinction between an order designed to preserve an existing position and an order intended to create a new legal position. In deciding whether to grant such relief, national courts must respect existing decisions from the ECJ on the matter in question whether under Article 234 or Article 230; they must take into account the Community interest, particularly the damage which the non-application of a Community regulation may cause to an established Community regime. National courts may also consider the repercussions which an interim order may entail on important individual interests and even on national interests, economic and social. If the grant of interim relief represents a financial risk for the Community the national court must be in a position to require the applicant to provide adequate guarantees, such as the deposit of money or other security. The decision whether or not to grant interim relief is a difficult one, not to be taken lightly, particularly when it involves the suspension of a normative act, a Community regulation, as was the case in *Atlanta Fruchthandelsgesellschaft mbH*.

Zuckerfabrik Süderdithmarschen AG and *Atlanta Fruchthandelsgesellschaft mbH* concerned the national courts' powers to grant interim relief pending a ruling from the ECJ on the validity of a Community act, a regulation. In the more recent case of *T Port GmbH & Co KG v Bundesanstalt für Landwirtschaft und Ernährung* (case C–68/95), the CFI refused to take the next logical step when it held that national courts had no power to order interim measures pending a decision on the EC institutions' *failure to act*. Indeed the national courts had no jurisdiction to refer questions concerning such alleged failures to the ECJ. Judicial review of alleged failures on the part of the institutions could only be carried out by the Community courts. Given the limited access of individuals to the Community courts under Article 232 EC this decision appears to have left a gap in the judicial protection of individuals (see further Chapter 13).

8.5.2 Challenge to statutory provisions

Claims based on Community law will often involve a challenge to legislative acts or omissions. In many cases the challenge is indirect, ancillary to the principal action based on Community law. If the national court finds the provisions of a national statute incompatible with Community law, it may grant the remedy requested and simply 'disapply' them, on the principles established in *Simmenthal SpA (No 2)* (case 106/77, see Chapter 4). The case of *R v Secretary of State for Employment, ex parte Equal Opportunities Commission* ([1993] 1 WLR 872) concerned a direct challenge to a domestic statute, something which is clearly not permitted in British law. The Equal Opportunities Commission (EOC) applied for a declaration that certain provisions of the Employment Protection (Consolidation) Act 1978 were contrary to Community sex-discrimination law and an order of mandamus requiring the Secretary of State to rectify the breach. A majority of the Court of Appeal thought that it would be 'wrong and unconstitutional for the Courts to grant a declaration or mandamus in an attempt to enforce obligations of Community law which, if they existed, did so only in international law'.

The House of Lords disagreed, and granted a declaration that the provisions in question were *incompatible* with EC law (the claim for mandamus was not pursued) ([1995] 1 AC 1). There was no need to declare that the UK or the Secretary of State were in *breach* of their obligations under Community law. A declaration of incompatibility would suffice for the purposes sought by the EOC and was capable of being granted consistently with the precedent afforded by *Factortame (No 2)* [1991] AC 603.

The question of whether free-standing remedy to challenge the compatibility of national law with Community law was raised by the Swedish courts in *Unibet*. The ECJ held that whilst it was possible to reach this route incidentally, through another legal action, there was no such need. The ECJ did seem to suggest that there might be some circumstances where this would be insufficient—for example, where criminal charges were involved.

8.5.3 Damages

As the case law discussed above illustrates, national rules limiting the amount of damages that may be awarded will not always be successful. The approach taken in *Marshall II* requiring 'full' compensation can be seen in other areas, such as the state liability cases, such as *Bonifaci* (cases C–94 and 95/95). Applying this principle in *Brasserie du Pêcheur*, (cases C–46 and 48/93) the ECJ held that a 'total exclusion' of loss of profit as a head of damage would not be permissible. Even an award of exemplary damages 'could not be ruled out' if such damages could be awarded pursuant to a similar claim or action founded on domestic law (para 89).

The case law is not entirely clear, however, as the Court has sought to distinguish the approach to whether interest should be awarded by reference to the nature of the right at stake, as the sex-discrimination cases illustrate. Article 6 of the Equal Treament Directive (76/207/EEC) was amended by Directive 2002/73/EC, and now limits the cases in which an upper limit on the amount of damages could be imposed in advance. This is, of course, of no help in other areas and the problem remains regarding the principles to be applied in determining whether limitations on damages and interest on damages are 'effective' for the purposes of EC law. In *Evans* (case 63/01), a case under the Second Insurance Directive, the ECJ held that compensation awarded under the rules implementing Article 1(4) of Directive 84/5/EEC 'must take account of the effluxion of time until actual payment of the sums awarded in order to guarantee adequate compensation for the victims', which suggests that the obligation to award interest may extend to other areas of EC law.

The issue of damages in the specific area of competition law is currently being discussed (White Paper on Damages Actions for Breach of Antitrust Rules (COM (2008) 165)).

8.5.4 Restitution

There have been many claims before national courts for the return of money paid in breach of Community law. The EC Treaty prohibits the imposition of customs duties or charges having equivalent effect, and discriminatory taxation (see Chapter 18). These charges are normally levied by national authorities. As early as 1960 the ECJ held, in the context of a claim for sums levied in breach of the ECSC Treaty, that once a Member State had been found to have breached Community law it must take the necessary measures to make good the lawful effects of the breach, making restitution for sums wrongfully levied as a result of that breach (*Humblet v Belgium* (case 6/60)). There is now a consistent line of authority to this effect (see, eg, *Express Dairy Foods Ltd v Intervention Board for Agricultural Produce* (case 130/79)). Prior to the House of Lords' decision in *Woolwich Equitable Building Society v Inland Revenue Commissioners* ([1993] AC 70), it was thought that there was no general right under English law to the recovery of money paid under a mistake of law. Since sums paid in breach of Community law would normally be paid under a mistake of law, such a rule would not have been 'sufficiently effective' to protect individuals' Community rights. This factor undoubtedly coloured the House of Lords' finding in *Woolwich Equitable Building Society v Inland Revenue Commissioners*, in the context of a claim based on domestic law, that money paid under a mistake of law was in certain circumstances recoverable as a matter of British law. 'It would be strange', said Lord Goff, 'if the right of the citizen to recover overpaid taxes were to be more restricted under domestic law than European law'. The ruling in *Metallgesellschaft* & *Hoechst* would seem to have confirmed this position.

8.5.5 Time limits

In *Express Dairy Foods Ltd v Intervention Board for Agricultural Produce* (case 130/79) the Court suggested that a 'reasonable' period of limitation would not make it 'impossible in practice' for national courts effectively to protect individuals' Community rights. This principle, consistently invoked, was put in doubt by the

Court's decision in *Emmott v Minister for Social Welfare* (case C–208/90), decided in 1991. Subsequent case law has retreated from the approach in *Emmott*. In *Palmisani*, on the question of the effectiveness of the remedy provided, with its one-year limitation rule, the Court held that although in principle reparation must be commensurate with the loss or damage sustained (see *Marshall (No 2)* (case C–271/91) and *Brasserie du Pêcheur* (cases C–46 and 48/93)), 'reparation cannot always be ensured by the retroactive and proper application in full of the measures implementing the Directive'. The setting of 'reasonable' limitation periods was permitted under EC law. A one-year limitation period such as the one in question 'cannot be regarded as making it excessively difficult or *a fortiori* impossible to lodge a claim for compensation'. Thus the one-year limitation period would not be incompatible with EC law.

In *Preston v Wolverhampton NHS Healthcare Trust* (case C–78/98), the ECJ found a six-month bar on proceedings (following termination of employment) acceptable under EC law. In *Fantask A/S v Industriministeriet* (case C–188/95) the ECJ accepted a Danish statutory five-year limitation period for the recovery of debts, running from the date on which the debt became payable, in the context of a challenge to the Ministry's refusal to reimburse company registration charges levied from the applicant in breach of EC Directive 69/335. The Court held (at para 48) that it had:

> acknowledged, in the interests of legal certainty, which protects the taxpayer and the authorities concerned, that the setting of reasonable limitation periods for bringing proceedings [was] compatible with Community law. Such periods cannot be regarded as rendering impossible or excessively difficult the exercise of rights conferred by Community law, even if the expiry of those periods necessarily entails the dismissal, in whole or in part, of the action brought.

This paragraph was cited by the Court in *Levez* (case C–326/96) and *EDIS* (case C–231/96).

The five-year limitation period was re-examined in *Fantask* and found to be neither discriminatory nor unreasonable. Distinguishing *Emmott*, the Court held that *Emmott* was 'justified on the particular facts of the case, in which the time bar had the result of *depriving the applicant of any opportunity whatsoever* to rely on her right to equal treatment under the Community Directive'.

It seems that reasonable limitation rules will be acceptable, since they do not render the exercise of Community rights impossible or excessively difficult; but where they 'deprive the applicant of any opportunity whatsoever' to rely on her rights, or 'strike at the very essence of those rights', or where the applicant has been misled as to her Community rights, as in *Levez*, they will not be permitted. These principles have been reaffirmed by the ECJ in more recent case law. In *Grundig Italiana SpA v Ministero delle Finanze* (case C–255/00), the ECJ had to deal with the national rules which shortened the period within which claims for sums paid but not due could be recovered. Crucially, the ECJ confirmed that such changes could be made, referring again to the 'practically impossible' test, but then went on to hold that such a change requires transitional arrangements to deal with the situation where such a change of time limits would have the effect of retroactively depriving individuals of rights to repayment, or of allowing such claimants too short a period in which to assert their rights. Rather than leaving this matter for the national court to assess, the ECJ determined that the 90-day transitional period allowed by the national legislation was too short to allow 'normally diligent tax payers [to] familiarise themselves with the new regime and commence proceedings in circumstances which do not compromise their chances of success' (para 40). This is a slightly more stringent approach to assessing national rules than that taken about other aspects of time limits since *Emmott*, as the ECJ did not require that there be a total bar to the exercise of the rights before the national rule is set aside. This aspect of the ruling, however, concerned only one aspect of the issue of time limits, that of the transitional arrangements. In contrast, in *Recheio-Cash & Carry SA* (case C–30/02), a 90-day limitation period for launching a claim for the repayment of charges levied in breach of Community law was held to be compatible with the principle of effectiveness. This case concerned the limitation period itself, rather than transitional arrangements, so issues about allowing time for acclimatisation to a new system do not arise. Nonetheless, it is noteworthy that the Court did not refer to *Grundig Italiana* in its judgment.

The trend of case law since *Emmott* indicates that the Court will be slow to regard Member States' limitation rules as unreasonable. Nevertheless, the acceptance of reasonable limitation rules will inevitably operate to modify the principle of full compensation, as occurred in *Fantask* (case C–188/95), in which the applicant sought, unsuccessfully, to recover company registration charges levied in breach of Community law over a nine-year period, from 1983 to 1992. The precise limits of what will be regarded as reasonable remain unclear.

8.5.6 State liability

The principle of state liability, discussed in Chapter 9, remains a hybrid: part national, part Community law. This has created problems for national courts. Prior to *Brasserie du Pêcheur* it was assumed, following *Francovich*, that a claim for damages against the state must be brought on the same basis, and according to the same rules, as the 'equivalent' claim based on national law. However, although the claim in English law would clearly be in the nature of a tort it was not clear which tort was appropriate. The nearest 'equivalent' actions available against a public authority, the torts of misfeasance in public office, of breach of statutory duty, or of negligence, were, as the Court found in *Brasserie du Pêcheur*, too restrictive to provide effective protection for individuals' Community rights under *Francovich*. A similar problem had arisen in the context of claims for damages based on the principle of direct effects (see, eg, *Garden Cottage Foods Ltd v Milk Marketing Board* [1984] AC 130 (HL); *Bourgoin SA v Ministry of Agriculture, Fisheries and Food* [1986] QB 716 (CA)). English law admitted no claim for damages in respect of legislative or judicial acts. The only way in which individuals' rights under *Francovich* might be effectively protected was either by 'modifying' (ie, reinterpreting) the existing national remedies of misfeasance or breach of statutory duty (negligence having been rejected as clearly inappropriate), resulting in the possibility of a different standard of liability, depending on whether the claim was based on national or Community law, or by admitting that the Community principle of state liability was a new principle calling for the creation of a new *sui generis* 'Francovich' tort.

In applying the ECJ's ruling in *R v Secretary of State for Transport, ex parte Factortame Ltd (No 5)* ([1998] 1 CMLR 1353) Hobhouse LJ in the English High Court adopted a compromise position. He examined the question of breach, and the seriousness of the breach, according to the principles laid down by the ECJ in *Brasserie du Pêcheur*. He concluded that 'whilst it could be said that the cause of action was *sui generis*, it was of the character of a breach of statutory duty'. He could find no similarity between the applicants' claim in respect of the UK's breach of its Community obligations and a claim in respect of tortious misfeasance. If the English courts were to follow his lead and treat claims based on *Francovich* as breaches of statutory duty, they would do so on the understanding that such claims could be subject to different principles, and a different approach to interpretation, from those which apply to similar claims based on domestic law. Given that the ECJ has now laid down a number of precise conditions for state liability, it is submitted that it would be better to acknowledge the unique nature of such a claim, based on the breach of a higher legal norm, and treat it as a *sui generis* tort. This now appears to have occurred. Both the Court of Appeal and the House of Lords in *Factortame (No 5)* dealt with the matter of liability simply by applying the principles of Community law laid down by the ECJ in *Brasserie du Pêcheur*.

However, regrettably, as noted above, the rules governing state liability laid down in *Brasserie du Pêcheur* were not comprehensive. It was left to national courts to decide, according to the principles applicable to equivalent claims based on national law, whether the Community law breached was intended to benefit persons such as the applicant (condition (a)); whether there existed the appropriate direct causal link between the state's breach and the applicant's damage (condition (c), which was raised, but not decided, in *Schmidberger* (case C–112/00)); and whether the damage suffered was of a kind in respect of which damages might be awarded.

It is a matter for regret that the ECJ, in laying down common Community rules concerning the nature of the breach required to give rise to liability, failed to provide some common rules or guidelines covering *all* aspects of liability, as, particularly in the area of non-contractual liability, the rules relating to breach and damage and causation are interrelated and operate together as control mechanisms restricting or extending liability according to perceived requirements of policy. While the overall result may not differ greatly from state to state the individual elements vary considerably. As long as the principle of national treatment applies in any of these areas there will be inequality in the application of the principle of state liability from state to state. There will also be uncertainty, as national rules are vulnerable to attack as being ineffective, or insufficiently effective, to protect individuals' rights. However, given the ECJ's unequivocal affirmation of the principle of national treatment in recent years, further judicial development of common Community rules appears unlikely.

Although a principle of state liability for executive acts, and judicial remedies in respect of such acts, already exists in all Member States, these claims will now also be subject to the rules laid down in *Brasserie du Pêcheur*. As with legislative acts, existing national remedies may need to be modified to ensure that they are effective in protecting individuals' rights; alternatively (and preferably) claims may be brought under a new *Francovich* tort.

A principle of liability for judicial acts in breach of Community law, as laid down in *Brasserie du Pêcheur*, clearly breaks new constitutional ground in most if not all Member States. If available in theory, it is unlikely to be applied freely in practice. If only for reasons of polity, neither the ECJ nor a national court is likely to find a judicial breach of Community law sufficiently serious to warrant liability.

8.6 Impact of treaty amendment

Should the Treaty of Lisbon come into force, a new provision will be inserted in to Article 19 EU. The second paragraph of Article 19(1) EU requires Member States to 'provide remedies sufficient to ensure effective legal protection in the fields covered by Union law'. Whether this is a restatement of the right found in the EU Charter to effective legal protection or is a restatement of the effectiveness requirement is not clear. Given the ECJ's extensive approach to the requirements of effectiveness, it is unlikely that it, in any event, adds much to the existing case law.

8.7 Conclusions

The law in this area divides the responsibility for procedural rules and remedies between European and national law. The underlying principle is that in the absence of harmonizing measures the national legal system should apply, subject to the EC law rules of equivalence and effectiveness. There seems to be little difference in the ECJ's approach to cases where EC law has specifically required that a remedy be provided and those areas where there is no such express requirement. The case law identified above shows clear parallels in the approach taken by the ECJ, both in its expansive phase and when it has become more cautious. The division between national rule and those of EC law reflects the division between the ECJ and the national courts shown in Article 234. There the national courts have the responsibility for hearing the case, determining the facts and making a ruling in the light of EC law requirements as interpreted by the ECJ.

The balance between the two court systems has not been static, reflecting different approaches by the ECJ. The cases of the early years show deference to the autonomy of the national legal systems. A more expansive approach to the requirements of 'effectiveness' can be seen immediately prior to the TEU. The problem with an approach which emphasises the need for remedies to be 'effective', rather than looking for equivalence, is that EC rights could end up being treated more favourably than rights deriving from national law. It seems as though the ECJ recognised this difficulty, or a least recognised that some concerns were being expressed as, subsequently, the ECJ has adopted an approach which seeks to balance the two extremes. In *Dorsch Consult* (case C–54/96) it held:

> It is for the legal system of each Member State to determine which court or tribunal has jurisdiction to hear disputes involving individual rights derived from Community law . . . It is not for the Court of Justice to involve itself in the resolution of questions of jurisdiction to which the classification of certain legal situations may give rise in the national legal system.

While in earlier judgments the Court was prepared to prescribe specific Community rules and express its views on the adequacy or effectiveness of particular domestic remedies or procedures, more recently it has emphasised that:

it is for national courts to ascertain whether the procedural rules intended to secure that the rights derived from Community law are safeguarded under national law and comply with the principle of equivalence (*Levez v Jennings (Harlow Pools) Ltd* (case C–326/96)).

This latter approach clearly recognises the importance of the national legal systems in providing the legal framework within which EC law operates and which fall to the national courts to assess. The principles of EC law do not mean that national rules will automatically fail. Nor does the new approach, however, mean that the national courts will not be required to disapply national rules or create new remedies, as can be seen from even recent examples. In each case, it will be a matter for the facts: the precise scope of the rules in question and their interplay with the substantive EC law rights.

This view is borne out in the case of *Adidas AG* (case C–223/98), decided in 1999. The case concerned the implementation by the Swedish authorities of EC Regulation 3295/94, designed to prevent trade in counterfeit goods. Under the regulation, implementation was left expressly to the national authorities. Following the seizure of counterfeit goods by the Swedish customs the owner of the original product sought to take action to enforce his rights against the consignee of these goods. The Swedish authorities, bound by their national confidentiality rules, refused to reveal his identity. In a reference for interpretation of the regulation under Article 234 the Court found that the system laid down by the regulation depended directly for its effective application on the information supplied to the holder of the right. If the identity of the consignee could not be disclosed to him it was in practice impossible for him to proceed with his case. The regulation could not therefore be understood as precluding disclosure to the holder of the right of the information which he needs.

The result of the ECJ's approach is that there will be some differences in the ways and circumstances in which individuals may enforce their rights under EC law throughout the Union. The Court has been criticised for a piecemeal and reactive approach to the question of procedures and remedies, although given the sensitivity of the area such an incremental approach is hardly surprising. Indeed, there are those who, far from criticising the ECJ, have recognised that it has had to tread a difficult line between excessive judicial activism and the need to ensure that EC law rights are protected effectively. It seems clear that legislative action in this area is necessary should more thorough changes be introduced. Despite judicial suggestions that such action is desirable, if not necessary, there has been little response from the political institutions. It may be that the Member States have chosen not to legislate in this area; that agreement is difficult to reach because of the sensitivity and complexity of the issues involved; or, simply, that the question of harmonisation in this area has simply not had a sufficiently high priority to bring it on to the legislative agenda. For the time being, then, it seems that procedural matters will continue to be decided on the principle of national procedural autonomy balanced by concepts of equivalence and effectiveness.

FURTHER READING

Accetto, M and Zleptnig, S, 'The principle of effectiveness: Rethinking its role in Community law' (2005) 11 EPL 375.

Albors-Llorens, A, 'Changes in the jurisdiction of the European Court of Justice under the Treaty of Amsterdam' (1998) 35 CML Rev 1273.

Anagnostaras, G, 'The quest for an effective remedy and the measure of protection afforded to putative Community law rights' (2007) 32(5) EL Rev 727.

Betlem, G., 'Torts, A European Ius Commune And The Private Enforcement Of Community Law' (2004) 64 CLJ 126.

Biondi, A., 'The ECJ and certain national procedural limitations: Not such a tough relationship' (1999) 36 CML Rev 1271.

Cabral, P and Chaves, MC, 'Member State liability for decisions of national courts adjudicating at last instance' (2006) Maastricht Journal of European and Comparative Law 109–26.

Caranta, R, 'Judicial protection against Member States: A new *jus commune* takes shape' (1995) 32 CML Rev 679.

—— 'Learning from our neighbours: Public law remedies homogenization from bottom up' (1997) MJ 220.

Case notes on C–224/01 *Köbler v Republik Österreich* [2005] ERPL 419.

Coppell, J, 'Domestic limitations on recovery for breach of EC law' (1998) ILJ 259.

Craig, P, '*Francovich*, remedies and the scope of damages liability' (1993) 109 LQR 595.

—— 'Once more unto the breach: The Community, the state and damages liability' (1997) 113 LQR 67.

Dougan, M, 'Cutting your Losses in the enforcement deficit: A Community right to the recovery of unlawfully levied charges?' (1998) 1 CYELS 233.

Drake, S, 'Scope of courage and the principle of 'individual liability' for damages: Further development of the principle of effective judicial protection by the Court of Justice' (2006) EL Rev 841.

Fennelly, N, 'The area of freedom, security and justice and the European Court of Justice' (2000) 46 ICLQ 941.

Gravells, N, 'Disapplying an Act of Parliament: Constitutional enormity or community law right?' [1989] PL 568.

Himsworth, C., 'Things fall apart: The harmonisation of Community judicial protection revisited' (1997) 22 EL Rev 291.

Hoskins, M, 'Tilting the balance: Supremacy and national procedural rules' (1996) 21 EL Rev 365.

Kilpatrick, C, Novitz, T, and Skidmore, P (eds), *The future of remedies in Europe* (Hart Publishing, 2000).

Lang, JT, 'The duties of national courts under Community constitutional law' (1997) 22 EL Rev 3.

—— 'The duties of national authorities under Community law' (1998) 23 EL Rev 109.

Nebbia, P, 'Damages actions for the infringement of EC competition law: Compensation or deterrence?' (2008) 33(1) EL Rev 23.

Oliver, P, 'Enforcing Community rights in English courts' (1987) 50 MLR 881.

Prechal, S, 'Community law in national courts: The lessons from *Van Schijndel*' (1998) 35 CML Rev 681.

—— 'Member State liability and direct effect: What's the difference after all?' (2006) 17 EBL Rev 299–316.

Ross, M, 'Refining effective enjoyment' (1990) 15 EL Rev 476.

—— 'Beyond *Francovich*' (1993) 56 MLR 55.

—— 'Effectiveness in the European legal order(s): Beyond supremacy to constitutional proportionality?' (2006) 31(4) EL Rev 476

Snyder, F, 'The effectiveness of European Community law' (1993) 56 MLR 19.

Steiner, J, 'How to make the action fit the case: Domestic remedies for breach of EEC Law' (1987) 12 EL Rev 102.

—— 'From direct effects to *Francovich*: Shifting means of enforcement of Community law' (1993) 18 EL Rev 3.

—— 'The limits of state liability for breach of European Community law' [1998] EPL 69.

Vajda, C, 'Liability for breach of Community law: A survey of the ECJ cases post *Factortame*' (2006) 17 EBL Rev 257–68.

Van den Berg, R and Schafer, HB, 'State liability for infringements of the EC Treaty' (1998) 23 EL Rev 552.

Van Gerven, W, 'Bridging the gap between Community and national law: Towards a principle of homogeneity of legal remedies' (1995) 32 CML Rev 679.

Woods, L and Smith, F, 'Causation in *Francovich*: The neglected problem' (1997) 46 ICLQ 925.

9

State liability

9.1 Introduction

The preceding chapters have identified that the ECJ, relying to a significant extent on the need to make EC law effective, extended the possible mechanisms by which individuals could seek access to rights derived from EC law in their national courts. Giving individuals incentives through the possibility of financial redress to bring legal action not only protects their rights but ensures enforcement of Community law. Whether these two objectives are equally weighted has been the subject of some debate. Perhaps the most significant development in this area over the past 25 years has been the creation and development of the principle of state liability under *Francovich* (cases C–6 and & 9/90). A logical development of the notion of direct effect, it can enable an individual, before his national court, to seek a remedy for losses suffered as a result of the failure by a Member State to implement, or apply correctly, provisions of EC law. While the national courts may have accepted this development, despite it potential impact on the autonomy of the national legal systems, there are still questions about the scope of the doctrine. This chapter will outline the development of the state liability doctrine and, in doing so, will examine its scope and the conditions for liability, as well identifying its relationship with other provisions. In all this, we question what the doctrine's underlying rationale is and, consequently, whether state liability can be extended beyond Community law to other pillars.

9.2 Principle of state liability under *Francovich v Italy*

9.2.1 The *Francovich* ruling

The shortcomings of the principles of direct and indirect effects, particularly in the context of enforcement of directives, as outlined in Chapter 5, led the European Court of Justice (ECJ) to develop a third and separate principle in *Francovich v Italy* (cases C–6 and 9/90), the principle of state liability. Here the claimants, a group of ex-employees, were seeking arrears of wages following their employers' insolvency. Their claim (like that in the subsequent case of *Wagner Miret* (case C–334/92)) was based on Directive 80/987, which required Member States, inter alia, to provide for a guarantee fund to ensure the payment of employees' arrears of wages in the event of their employers' insolvency. Since a claim against their former employers would have been fruitless (they being insolvent and 'private' parties), they brought their claim for compensation against the state. There were two aspects to their claim. The first was based on the state's breach of the claimants' (alleged) substantive rights contained in the directive, which they claimed were directly effective. The second was based on the state's primary failure to implement the directive, as required under Article 249 and Article 10 EC (post Lisbon Articles 288 TFEU and Art 4 TEU). The Court had already held, in Article 226 EC post Lisbon Article 258 TFEU proceedings, that Italy was in breach of its Community obligations in failing to implement the directive (*Commission v Italy* (case 22/87)).

With regard to the first claim, the Court found that the provisions in question were not sufficiently clear, precise, and unconditional to be directly effective. Although the content of the right, and the class of intended beneficiaries, was clear, the state had a discretion as to the appointment of the guarantee institution; it would not necessarily itself be liable under the directive. The claimants were, however, entitled in principle to succeed in their second claim. The Court held that where, as here, a state had failed to implement an EC directive it would be obliged to compensate individuals for damage suffered as a result of its failure to implement the directive if certain conditions were satisfied—that is, where:

(a) the directive involved rights conferred on individuals

(b) the content of those rights could be identified on the basis of the provisions of the directive and

(c) there was a causal link between the state's failure and the damage suffered by the persons affected.

The Court's reasoning was based on (i) the Member States' obligation to implement directives under Article 249 and their general obligation under Article 10 EC to 'take all appropriate measures . . . to ensure fulfilment of' their obligations under Community law; (ii) on its jurisprudence in *Van Gend en Loos* (case 26/62) and *Costa v ENEL* (case 6/64) that certain provisions of EC law are intended to give rise to rights for individuals; and (iii) that national courts are obliged to provide effective protection for those rights, as established in *Amministrazione delle Finanze dello Stato v Simmenthal SpA* (case 106/77) and *Factortame* (case C–213/89)—see further Chapter 4). It concluded that 'a principle of state liability for damage to individuals caused by a breach of Community law for which it is responsible is inherent in the scheme of the Treaty'.

Thus, where the three conditions of *Francovich* are fulfilled, individuals seeking compensation as a result of activities and practices which are inconsistent with EC directives may proceed directly against the state. There will be no need to rely on the principles of direct or indirect effects. Responsibility for the non-implementation of the directive will be placed not on the employer, 'public' or 'private', but squarely on the shoulders of the state, arguably, where it should always have been. Rather than changing the law, it provides compensation for a Member State's failure to do so and, as well as providing protection for individuals' rights, creates an indirect mechanism for enforcement of Community law.

9.2.2 Scope of the principle

The reasoning in *Francovich* is compelling; its implications for Member States, however, remained unclear. Although expressed in terms of a state's liability for the non-implementation of a directive, *Francovich* appeared to lay down a wider principle of liability for all breaches of Community law 'for which the state is responsible'. Would it then apply to legislative or administrative acts and omissions in breach of treaty articles or other provisions of EC law? Would it be an additional remedy, or available only in the absence of other remedies based on direct or indirect effects? Apart from the three conditions for liability, which are themselves open to interpretation, what other conditions would have to be fulfilled? Would liability be strict or dependent on culpability, even serious culpability, as was the case with actions for damages against Community institutions under Article 288 (2) (ex 215(2) EC, post Lisbon 340 TFEU) (see Chapter 14)? In the case of non-implementation of directives, as in *Francovich* itself, the state's failure is clear; *a fortiori* when established by the Court under Article 226. But in cases of faulty or inadequate implementation it is not. The state's 'failure' may only become apparent following an interpretation of the directive by the Court (see, eg, the sex-discrimination cases such as *Marshall* and *Barber*—see Chapter 27). Here the case for imposing liability in damages on the state is less convincing.

9.2.2.1 *Type of action*

Many of these questions were referred to the Court of Justice for interpretation in *Brasserie du Pêcheur SA v Germany* and *R v Secretary of State for Transport, ex parte Factortame* (cases C–46 and 48/93). The Court held that the principle of state liability is not confined to a failure to implement EC directives; rather, *all* domestic acts and omissions, legislative, executive, and judicial, in breach of Community law, can give rise to liability. Provided the conditions for liability are fulfilled it applies to breaches of *all* Community law, whether or not directly effective. However, arguing from the principles applicable to the Community's non-contractual liability under Article 288(2), the Court held that where a state is faced with situations involving choices comparable to those made by Community institutions when they adopt measures pursuant to a Community policy it will be liable only where three conditions are met (see paras 50 and 51 of the judgment):

(a) the rule of law infringed must be intended to confer rights on individuals

(b) the breach must be sufficiently serious

(c) there must be a direct causal link between the breach of the obligation resting on the state and the damage sustained by the injured parties.

The 'decisive test' for whether a breach is sufficiently serious is whether the institution concerned has 'manifestly and gravely exceeded the limits of its discretion' (para 55). The factors to be taken into account in assessing this question included:

> the clarity and precision of the rule breached, the measure of discretion left by that rule to the national or Community authorities, whether the infringement and the damage caused was intentional or voluntary, whether any error of law was excusable or inexcusable, the fact that the position taken by a Community institution may have contributed towards the omission, and the adoption or retention of national measures or practices contrary to Community law. [Para 56.]

9.2.2.2 *For whose actions is the state liable?*

One question left open by *Brasserie de Pêcheur* is for whose action a Member State can be liable. There can be little doubt as to the state's liability for actions taken by the government itself in the context of the obligation to implement EC measures. But what about other parts of the state? In *Haim v Kassenzahnartzliche Vereinigung Nordrhein* (case C–424/97) it was established that a legally independent body may be liable under *Francovich*, as well as the Member State itself.

In *AGM-COS MET Srl v Suomen Valtio and Tarmo Lehtinen* (case C–470/03), the Court held, without exploring the point fully, that an individual official may be liable in addition to a Member State for any damage caused by that individual's actions which are in breach of Community law. Article 4(1) of Directive 98/37/EC on machinery requires that Member States do not restrict the marketing and use of machinery which complies with the Directive. Lehtinen was an official who had been involved in safety inspections of vehicle lifts in respect of which he had doubts as to their safety. His actions included making various public statements about his concerns, although Finland did nothing to arrange for the machinery to be withdrawn from the market. The manufacturer's sales plummeted in the wake of this, and an action was brought for state liability. The Court held that statements such as the ones made by Lehtinen, if attributable to the state as giving the impression of reflecting official rather than personal opinions (which was for the national court to determine), could give rise to liability. It went on to say that Lehtinen's statements could be a breach of Article 4(1) of the Directive and could not be justified on the basis of public health or freedom of expression. As the provision conferred rights on individuals and left no discretion to the Member States, the conditions for liability were satisfied. Crucially, as well as the Member State itself, the individual official could also be held liable under national law. The Court appears to treat this (cf para 98 of the judgment) as the corollary of its ruling in *Haim* that a public body may also be liable under the state liability principle. However, the prospect of individual officials being held liable for actions carried out in their official capacity is a worrying one. The Court has tempered its ruling on this point by adding the proviso that Community law does not *require* such liability, although it does not preclude it.

Of course, the argument that the Member State is the appropriate body to sue because it is at fault, is also challenged in these circumstances, as the behaviour complained of is hardly within the control of the Member State. A similar argument could be made about the actions of regional and local government. In these scenarios, it seems state liability is more about compensating individuals than enforcing EC law. The key point is that the liability—which remains with the state at central government level—is then decoupled from the body actually in breach. From the perspective of the individual claiming compensation, this matters not.

Brasserie de Pêcheur also suggested that there may be liability for judicial failures, which was controversial. However, in *Köbler v Austria* (case C–224/01), the ECJ confirmed that such liability may arise in particular circumstances. The case concerned the refusal by the Austrian Administrative Supreme Court (Verwaltungsgerichtshof) to grant Mr Köbler a 'length of service' increment on the basis that the payment would be a loyalty bonus, for which time spent in similar positions in other Member States could not be taken into account. This was a wrong interpretation of EC law and in direct conflict with an earlier ruling by the ECJ (*Schöning-Kougebetopoulou* (case C–15/96)), and Mr Köbler therefore brought a new claim under *Francovich* for the failure of the Verwaltungsgerichtshof to apply EC law correctly.

The ECJ stated that, in international law, state liability can arise on the basis of acts by the legislature, executive and judiciary, and that the same must be true of EC law (para 32). In addition, the principle of effectiveness (see 8.3) requires that there must be instances when a state will incur liability for actions by its courts which are in breach of EC law (para 33). However, the ECJ limited this to instances where courts are adjudicating at the last instance (para 33) and emphasised the mandatory jurisdiction of such a court under Article 234 to request a preliminary ruling on the interpretation of EC law (see Chapter 10). In order to ensure the effective protection of individual's rights under Community law, there has to be a possibility of claiming compensation for damage caused by an infringement of these rights by a court adjudicating at last instance (para 36). Such an infringement must be manifest, and it is for the national legal system to designate the courts that would hear such claims. This ruling, it is submitted, follows logically from the basic justification for state liability, and its restrictions to courts of last instance is entirely appropriate because at that point there would be no possibility of an appeal against a ruling which infringes an individual's Community rights. In order to avoid opening the floodgates to claims of state liability or Article 234 references in such circumstances, the ECJ is at pains to emphasise that 'state liability for an infringement of Community law by a decision of a national court adjudicating at last instance can be incurred only in the exceptional case where the court has manifestly infringed the applicable law' (para 53), although this is not limited to intentional fault or serious misconduct by the national court (*Traghetti del Mediterraneo SpA v Italy* (case C–173/03)). Whether this will serve as an appropriate brake to such actions remains to be seen.

In coming to its conclusion, the Court had to deal with several fundamental objections. The first was that the principle of *res judicata* (finality of judgments) might be undermined by imposing liability on the state for a serious infringement of EC law. The Court, somewhat optimistically, stated that state liability in such circumstances would not affect the finality of the judgment at issue, especially because the parties to the state liability action would be different, and a finding of liability would not result in a revision of the original decision (para 39). At a technical level, that may be correct, although it cannot be denied that the authority of the ruling in the original case would be undermined. Secondly, there was concern that the independence of the judiciary may be affected, and the authority of the court undermined, by the possibility of a state liability claim. This, too, was given short shrift by the Court, simply denying that there would be 'any particular risk to the independence' of the court concerned (para 42), and that the possibility of a state liability action might be 'regarded as enhancing the quality of a legal system and . . . the authority of the judiciary' (para 43). However, the Court did not expand on this in any detail, and its assertion remains somewhat unconvincing. Finally, there was concern as to whether there would be an appropriate domestic court which might hear a claim for state liability. In this regard, the ECJ referred back to established principles according to which it is for national legal systems to determine the appropriate court to hear such claims. That, however, does not solve the difficulties that may arise in practice. Presumably, a Member State found liable before a domestic court has a right of appeal. In the UK, this might produce the rather strange situation whereby the House of Lords might eventually be called upon to hear a case in state liability based on one of its own judgments. Whilst the basic outcome in *Köbler* therefore can be defended at a purely logical level, there are many practical difficulties which remain unresolved by this decision. As a final point, it may be noted that in *Köbler* itself, the ECJ thought that the breach by the Austrian Verwaltungsgerichtshof was not sufficiently serious for a claim in state liability to succeed.

9.2.2.3 *Liability only where measure confers rights*

One of the key requirements of liability under *Francovich/Brasserie de Pêcheur* is that the rule of law infringed must be intended to confer rights on individuals. Consequently, where a directive in issue does not confer rights on individuals, then there can be no claim under *Francovich*. Thus, in *Peter Paul v Germany* (case C–222/02), the failure of the German banking supervisory authority correctly to supervise a bank, which subsequently failed, in accordance with the relevant directive (94/19/EC), did not permit depositors to maintain an action for compensation for lost deposits beyond the maximum threshold of 20,000 provided for in the directive. This was because the obligation to ensure supervision was not combined with an independent right to compensation for the consequences of any failure in that regard, and the individual rights under this directive were limited to a specified amount of compensation (which had been paid already).

9.2.3 **Conditions of liability**

For liability to arise it is not necessary for the infringement of Community law to have been established by the Court under Article 226 or 234; nor is it necessary to prove fault on the part of the national institution concerned *going beyond that of a sufficiently serious breach of Community law*. In *Brasserie du Pêcheur* the Court rephrased the three conditions laid down in *Francovich* and incorporated a requirement that the breach be sufficiently serious. Condition (b) of *Francovich* (the content of the right infringed must be sufficiently clear) may now be regarded as contained within the definition of 'sufficiently serious'.

The Court based its decision on its past case law, particularly its reasoning in *Francovich*: states are obliged under Articles 249 and 10 to provide effective protection for individuals' Community rights and ensure the full effect of Community law. As regards its own jurisdiction to rule on the matter of states' liability in damages, challenged by the German government, it reasoned that, since the EC Treaty had failed to provide expressly for the consequences of breaches of Community law, it fell to the Court, pursuant to its duty under Article 220 EC (ex 164, post Lisbon Article 19 TEU), to ensure that 'in the interpretation and application of this treaty the law is observed'. The application of the Court's ruling and questions of damages and causation are discussed further below.

Despite the hostility with which this decision was greeted in anti-European quarters, it is submitted that the Court's ruling on the question of, and conditions for, liability is *prima facie* consistent with existing principles and, provided that the multiple test in para 56 of what will constitute a 'sufficiently serious' breach is rigorously applied, strikes a fair balance between the interests of the Community in enforcing Community law and the interests of Member States in restricting liability to culpable breaches of Community law.

9.2.3.1 *Meaning of 'sufficiently serious'*

For liability to arise, the institution concerned must have 'manifestly and gravely exceeded the limits of its discretion': the breach must be 'inexcusable'. If there is to be equality of *responsibility* as between the liability of the Community under Article 288(2) EC and Member States under *Francovich*, the criterion of a 'sufficiently serious' breach laid down in *Brasserie du Pêcheur* should be interpreted strictly. The question remaining was whether the Court would apply the 'sufficiently serious' test to *all* claims based on *Francovich*, including claims for damage resulting from breaches of Community law which do *not* involve legislative 'choices' analogous to those made by Community institutions when implementing policy. Alternatively it might continue to 'interpret' Member States' actions as involving such choices, as it did, surprisingly, in *Brasserie du Pêcheur*. To limit the application of the sufficiently serious test to situations in which Member States are involved in 'legislative choices', by analogy with the position of Community institutions under Article 288(2) (see Chapter 14), as was suggested in *Brasserie du Pêcheur*, would be to ignore the essential difference between the position of Member States, when *implementing* Community law, and that of Community institutions when *making* Community law. Since liability depends on the breach by a Member State of a Community obligation, liability should in all cases depend on whether the breach is sufficiently serious. This is reflected in the multiple test laid down in para 56.

Given the lack of clarity of much EC law, and that Member States have no 'choice' to act in breach of Community law, it is submitted that the crucial element in para 56 will often be the clarity and precision of the rule breached, as suggested by Advocate-General Tesauro in *Brasserie du Pêcheur*.

This view obtained some support in *R v Her Majesty's Treasury, ex parte British Telecommunications plc* (case C–392/93), a case decided shortly after *Brasserie du Pêcheur*. The case, brought by BT, concerned the alleged improper implementation of Council Directive 90/351 on public procurement in the water, energy, transport, and telecommunication sectors ([1990] OJ L297/1). BT, which claimed to have been financially disadvantaged as a result of this wrongful implementation, was claiming damages based on *Francovich*. The Court, appearing to presume that the other conditions for liability were met, focused on the question whether the alleged breach was sufficiently serious. It applied the test of para 56 of *Brasserie du Pêcheur*. Although it found that the UK implementing regulations were contrary to the requirements of the directive, it suggested that the relevant provisions of the directive were sufficiently unclear as to render the UK's error excusable. At para 43 of its judgment the Court said that the article in question (Article 8(1)) was:

> imprecisely worded and was reasonably capable of bearing, as well as the construction applied to it [by the ECJ] the interpretation given to it by the United Kingdom in good faith and on the basis of arguments which are not entirely void of substance. The interpretation, which was also shared by other Member States, was not manifestly contrary to the wording of the Directive or to the objective pursued by it.

This interpretation was, it is submitted, generous to the UK. The Court held that in the context of the transposition of directives, 'a restrictive approach to state liability is justified' for the same reasons as apply to Community liability in respect of legislative measures, namely:

> to ensure that the exercise of legislative functions is not hindered by the prospect of actions for damages whenever the general interest requires the institutions or Member States to adopt measures which may adversely affect individual interests. [Para 40.]

The Court adopted a rather different approach in *R v Ministry of Agriculture, Fisheries and Food*, ex parte *Hedley Lomas (Ireland) Ltd* (case C–5/94). This case concerned a claim for damages by an exporter, Hedley Lomas, for losses suffered as a result of a UK ban on the export of live sheep to Spain. The ban was imposed following complaints from animal welfare groups that Spanish slaughterhouses did not comply with the requirements of Council Directive 74/577 on the stunning of animals before slaughter ([1974] OJ L316/10). The Spanish authorities had implemented the directive, but had made no provision for monitoring compliance or providing sanctions for non-compliance. The UK raised the matter with the Commission, which, following discussion with the Spanish authorities, decided not to take action against Spain under Article 226. Although the UK ban was clearly in breach of Article 29 of the EC Treaty, the UK argued that it was justified on the grounds of the protection of health of animals under Article 30 (for further discussion of the substantive issues see Chapter 20). However, the UK provided no evidence that the directive had in fact been breached, either by particular slaughterhouses or generally.

The Court found that the ban was in breach of Article 29, and was not justified under Article 30. The fact that the Spanish authorities had not provided procedures for monitoring compliance with the directive or penalties for non-compliance was irrelevant. 'Member States must rely on trust in each other to carry out inspections in their respective territories' (para 19). Furthermore, the breach was 'sufficiently serious' to give rise to liability under *Francovich*. The Court suggested (at para 28) that:

> where, at the time when it committed the infringement, the Member State in question was not called upon to make any legislative choices and had only considerably reduced, or even no, discretion, the mere infringement of Community law may be sufficient to establish the existence of a sufficiently serious breach.

This ruling, delivered two months after *R v Her Majesty's Treasury, ex parte British Telecommunications plc*, was surprising. While a finding that the UK would in principle be liable in damages was justified on the facts, the UK having produced no evidence of breach of the directive constituting a threat to animal health to justify the ban under Article 30, the suggestion that a 'mere infringement' of Community law might be sufficient to create liability where the state is not 'called upon to make any legislative choices' or has 'considerably reduced, or no, discretion' is questionable. While a state may have a choice as to the 'form and method of implementation' of directives, and some discretion under the treaty to derogate from basic treaty rules, its discretion is strictly circumscribed, and it has no discretion to act in breach of Community law. The UK had no more 'legislative' discretion in implementing Directive 90/531 in *BT*, indeed possibly less, than it had under Article 30 in *Hedley Lomas*. Indeed, prior to the Court's decision in *Hedley Lomas*, it was thought that a Member State *would* have a discretion to derogate from the prohibition of Article 29 where this was necessary to protect a genuine public interest (see Chapter 20). To pursue the analogy between the Community's liability for 'legislative choices involving choices of economic policy' and Member States' liability under *Francovich*, as the Court has done in all these cases, is to disguise the fact that *the two situations are not similar*. The principal reason for limiting liability under *Francovich* is not because Member States' 'discretion' in implementing Community law must not be fettered, but because the rules of Community law are often not clear. To hold them liable in damages for 'mere infringements' of such rules, thereby introducing a principle akin to strict liability, would not only be politically dangerous, it would be contrary to the principle of legal certainty, itself a respected principle of Community law (for further analysis see Chapter 14).

Nevertheless the principle of liability for a 'mere infringement' of Community law in situations in which Member States are not required to make legislative choices was invoked by the ECJ in *Dillenkofer v Germany* (cases C–178, 179, 188, 189 and 190/94). That case Germany's failure fully to implement Directive 90/314, designed to protect consumers in the event of travel organisers' insolvency, was on all fours with that of the Italian government in *Francovich*, was clearly 'inexcusable', and therefore, as the Court acknowledged, 'sufficiently serious' to warrant liability. Similarly, in *Rechberger and Greindle v Austria* (case C–140/97), concerning the same directive, the ECJ found that the implementing measures set the period for the commencement of claims at a date some months later than the time limit for implementation of the directive, which was 'manifestly' incompatible with the directive, and sufficiently serious to attract liability. In neither *Hedley Lomas* nor *Dillenkofer* did the Court attempt to apply the multiple test laid down in para 56 of *Brasserie du Pêcheur*.

However, in *Denkavit International BV v Bundesamt für Finanzen* (cases C–283, 291 and 292/94), which were cases involving claims for damages resulting from the faulty implementation of a directive decided shortly after *Dillenkofer*, the Court followed its approach in *BT*. On the basis of a strong submission from Advocate-General Jacobs, it applied the criteria of para 56 of *Brasserie du Pêcheur* and concluded that, as a result of the lack of clarity and precision of the relevant provisions of the directive, and the lack of clear guidance from the Court's previous case law, Germany's breach of Community law could not be regarded as sufficiently serious to justify liability. Significantly, the Court did not draw a distinction, for the purposes of liability, between acts of Member States involving 'choices of economic policy' and 'mere infringements' of Community law.

In an attempt to rationalise this aspect of state liability, Advocate-General Jacobs in *Sweden v Stockholm Lindöpark AB* (case C–150/99) commented on the origins of the phrase 'sufficiently serious breach'. At para 59 of his opinion, he noted that:

In French, the Court has always used—originally with regard to liability incurred by the Community—the term 'violation suffisamment caractérisée'. This is now normally translated into English as 'sufficiently serious breach'. However, the underlying meaning of 'caractérisé', which gives rise to its inherent implication of seriousness, includes the notion that the breach (or other conduct) has been clearly established in accordance with its legal definition, in other words, that it is a definite, clear-cut breach. This may help to explain why the term was previously translated as 'sufficiently flagrant violation' and may throw additional light on the choice of factors which the Court has indicated should be taken into consideration when deciding whether a breach is 'sufficiently serious'.

On this reasoning, in order to be sufficiently serious, the breach of Community law would have to be definite and clear-cut. Nevertheless, establishing whether a breach is of that nature can be a difficult issue, and the approach by the ECJ to the assessment of the matter of a 'sufficiently serious' breach has not been fully consistent. In *Lindöpark* itself, the Court effectively followed *Hedley Lomas*. Lindöpak had not been entitled to deduct VAT on goods and services used for the purposes of its business activities in breach of the sixth VAT directive (91/680/EEC, [1991] OJ L376/1). Sweden had amended its VAT legislation with effect from 1 January 1997, following which Lindöpak was entitled to deduct VAT. It claimed for a return of VAT payments made between Sweden's accession to the Community on 1 January 1995 and 1 January 1997. The ECJ observed that the right to deduct VAT was capable of being directly effective. Although the question of Member State liability did not strictly speaking arise, the ECJ was nevertheless prepared to indicate whether Sweden had committed a sufficiently serious breach. It noted that 'given the clear wording of [the directive], the Member State concerned was not in a position to make any legislative choices and had only a considerably reduced, or even no, discretion'. The mere infringement of the directive was therefore enough to create liability.

Although the ECJ has, in some cases, concluded whether a breach was sufficiently serious to give rise to liability, that assessment is properly left to the national courts, with the ECJ only able to provide general guidance (which is correct, in principle, given the nature of the ECJ's jurisdiction under Article 234). Thus, in *Norbrook Laboratories Ltd v Minister of Agriculture, Fisheries and Food* (case C–127/95), a case involving a claim for damages for wrongful implementation of EC directives on the authorisation of veterinary products, the ECJ, following an extensive examination of the provisions of the directive allegedly breached, which revealed a number of clear breaches, invoked the *Hedley Lomas/Dillenkofer* mantra:

Where . . . the Member State was not called upon to make legislative choices, and had considerably reduced, if no discretion, the mere infringement of Community law may be sufficient to establish the existence of a sufficiently serious breach.

The ECJ then left it to the national court to assess whether the conditions for the award of damages were fulfilled. Similarly, in *Klaus Konle v Austria* (case C–302/97), in a claim for damages for losses suffered as a result of laws of the Tyrol governing land transactions, allegedly contrary to Article 46 EC (ex 56) post Lisbon Article 52 TEFU and Article 70 of the Act of Accession, the Court examined these provisions for their compatibility with Community law. and finding some (but not all) of the laws to be 'precluded' by Community law, left it to the national court 'to apply the criteria to establish the liability of Member States for damage caused to individuals by breaches of Community law in accordance with the guidelines laid down by the Court of Justice' (see also *Haim v KLV* (case C–424/97)).

If national courts are to assess this crucial question of the seriousness of the breach, it is essential that these guidelines are clear. The multiple criteria laid down in para 56 of *Brasserie du Pêcheur* are clear and comprehensive. The *Hedley Lomas* requirement, that in some circumstances a 'mere infringement' of Community law will suffice to establish liability, clouds the issue. It is submitted that if it is to be invoked, it will be applicable only *following* an examination of the Community law allegedly breached under the multiple test in para 56; for only then will the issue of whether the state has any 'discretion' in the exercise of its legislative powers be resolved. If the aim, and the substance, of the Community obligation allegedly infringed is 'manifest', the state will have no discretion to act in its breach. If it is not, the breach will not be sufficiently serious. The *Hedley Lomas* mantra is, it is submitted, superfluous. Nevertheless, it was invoked in *Haim v KLV* alongside the multiple test of para 56 and has been referred to since, though in cases in which the ECJ seems to suggest that the clarity and precision of the rule are key (*The Queen, on the application of: Synthon BV v Licensing Authority of the Department of Health* (case C–452/06), para 39).

One factor which may assist the national court is the rulings by the ECJ on the interpretation of the measure in issue. Indeed, it seems that even if there is some ambiguity in the text of the relevant measure, the *ex parte BT* approach will not be followed where the ECJ has interpreted a particular provision of Community law and a Member State has subsequently failed to apply that provision in accordance with the ECJ's interpretation (*Gervais Larsy v Institut national d'assurances sociales pour travailleurs indépendants (Inasti)* (case C–118/00)). In that case, it can no longer be said that the Member State has a legislative choice. However, where the exact position only emerges gradually through several rulings by the Court, the national court can take this into account when considering the clarity of the rule in question and whether any errors of law were excusable or inexcusable (*Test Claimants in the FTI Group Litigation v Commissioners of Inland Revenue* (case C–446/04)). By way of contrast, see *Robins v SoS for Work and Pensions* (case C–278/05), where the ECJ held that the UK had incorrectly implemented Article 8 of Directive 80/987/EEC on protecting employees in the event of insolvency of their employer by not ensuring that a sufficient proportion of expected pension benefits were protected. The UK's liability turned on the interpretation of 'protect' in Article 8, and as its meaning had been unclear prior to the interpretation given in this case, it seemed unlikely that the UK's breach would be sufficiently serious, although it was for the national court to come to a final decision.

9.2.3.2 *The claimant must prove that damage has been suffered*

It is also important that the claimant is able to establish that he has suffered loss or damage. In *Schmidberger v Austria* (case C–112/00), Austria had allowed a public protest to take place on the main motorway across the Alps which closed the motorway for 28 hours. Schmidberger claimed damages for delay to his business of transporting goods from Germany to Italy on the basis that this amounted to a breach of Articles 28–30 EC (post Lisbon Articles 34–36 TFEU) (see Chapter 19). Advocate-General Jacobs noted that it was necessary for the claimant to establish loss or damage which is attributable, by a direct causal link, to a sufficiently serious breach of Community law. Importantly, this included a right to claim for lost profit. However, if the claimant is unable to establish the existence of any loss or damage, then there cannot be a claim for state liability. The Advocate-General was willing to accept that it may not be possible to quantify exactly the loss suffered, in which case this may be calculated on an appropriate flat-rate basis. On the facts, the Advocate-General thought that the breach of Articles 28–30 in that case was not sufficiently serious. Austria had authorised a 28-hour demonstration which blocked the main transit route across the Alps, which was technically a breach of Articles 28–30, but this had to be balanced against the freedom of expression of the demonstrators (see further Chapter 6). This and the short duration of the disruption would not be a sufficiently serious breach of Community law. The ECJ, having decided that there was no breach of Articles 28–30, did not address the question of state liability in its judgment. As far as the requirement that damage be proven is concerned, it is submitted that the reasoning of this Advocate-General is sound.

9.2.3.3 *The damage must have been caused by the breach*

It is also necessary that the claimant can demonstrate that any damage suffered was caused by the Member State's breach of EU law. In *Brinkmann Tabakfabriken GmbH v Skatteministeriet* (case C–319/96), a case along the more moderate line in *BT* (case C–392/93), the Court found that the Danish authorities' failure properly to implement Directive 79/30 on taxes other than turnover taxes affecting the consumption of manufactured tobacco was not sufficiently serious to incur liability. The classification adopted by the authorities, which resulted in the applicant having to pay the higher rates of taxes, was not 'manifestly contrary' to the wording and aim of the directive. It was not clear from the directive whether the tobacco rolls imported by the applicant, which had to be wrapped in paper to be smoked, constituted 'cigarette tobacco' or 'cigarettes'. Significantly, both the Commission and the Finnish government supported the classification adopted by the Danish authorities. The question of liability turned on the question of causation. The directive in question had not been implemented in Denmark by legislative decree, although the authorities had given immediate (albeit imperfect) effect to its provisions. There was no direct causal link between that former (legislative) failure and the damage suffered by the applicant. It is implicit in the decisions that, contrary to the view of some commentators, provided that the requirements of a directive are complied with in practice, a failure to implement a directive by legislative means will not necessarily constitute a sufficiently serious breach to warrant liability.

9.2.4 *Brasserie du Pêcheur* in the English courts

In 1997 the ECJ's ruling in *Brasserie du Pêcheur* and *R v Secretary of State for Transport, ex parte Factortame Ltd* (cases C–46 and 48/93) was applied in the English High Court with a view to ascertaining whether the UK's action in introducing the Merchant Shipping Act 1988 in fact constituted a sufficiently serious breach of Community law (*R v Secretary of State for Transport, ex parte Factortame Ltd (No 5)* [1998] 1 CMLR 1353). Hobhouse LJ considered the ECJ's case law on state liability and concluded that whether or not a Member State's action involved the exercise of discretion (ie, 'legislative choices') the same test, requiring proof of a sufficiently serious breach of Community law, applied. That test, requiring a 'manifest and grave disregard of whatever discretion the Member State might possess', was based on the same principles as applied to Community liability under Article 288(2), and was a relatively difficult one to meet. Having reasoned impeccably thus far he concluded that the UK's breach as regards the Merchant Shipping Act 1988 was sufficiently serious to warrant liability and referred the case back to the Divisional Court to decide the question of causation. Two factors in particular were cited by Hobhouse LJ as rendering the breach of Community law (Article 43 (ex 52) EC) sufficiently serious:

(a) The UK had introduced the measures in question in primary legislation in order to ensure that the implementation would not be delayed by legal challenge (at the time it was thought that primary legislation could not be challenged, but see now *R v Secretary of State for Transport, ex parte Factortame Ltd* (case C–213/89), noted in Chapter 4).

(b) The Commission had from the start been opposed to the legislation on the grounds that it was (in its opinion) contrary to Community law.

Both the Court of Appeal and the House of Lords agreed with Hobhouse LJ that the UK's breach of Community law was sufficiently serious to warrant liability. Both courts applied the multiple test laid down in para 56 of *Brasserie du Pêcheur* (cases C–46 and 48/93) (although they suggested that the list was 'not exhaustive') and found that the balance tipped in favour of the respondents. In pressing ahead with its legislation, against the advice of the Commission, despite its clear adverse impact on the respondents, and in a form (statute) which it was thought could not be challenged, the UK Government was clearly taking a 'calculated risk'. Lord Slynn did, however, express the opinion, contrary to the view of Hobhouse LJ and the Court of Appeal, that the considered views of the Commission, although of importance, could not be regarded as conclusive proof as to:

(a) whether there had been a breach of Community law

(b) whether the breach (if any) was sufficiently serious to justify an award of damages.

Lords Hoffmann and Clyde expressed a similar view; the position taken by the Commission was 'a relevant factor to be taken into account' in deciding whether a breach was sufficiently serious, but it was not conclusive.

Following the House of Lords' decision in *Factortame*, Sullivan J in the English High Court, in assessing the seriousness of the Department of Social Security's breach of Article 7(1) of the Sex Discrimination Directive 79/7 in *R v Department of Social Security, ex parte Scullion* ([1999] 3 CMLR 798), also applied the multiple test of para 56 of *Brasserie du Pêcheur*, which he described as the 'global' or 'basket' approach, and decided that, since there the scope of Article 7(1) was not clear at the relevant time, and there was no evidence that the Department had sought legal advice on the matter either from the Commission or from its own legal advisers, the breach was sufficiently serious.

9.2.5 Relationship of the principle of state liability with direct effect

The principle of state liability is an important complement to the principles of direct and indirect effect, particularly in the context of enforcement of directives. Of course, liability under the principles of both direct and indirect effect has been strict (this was confirmed in *Draehmpaehl v Urania Immobilienservice OHG* (case C–180/95)); there has been no need to consider whether the alleged breach of Community law is 'sufficiently serious'. For direct effects, the criteria have in the past been loosely applied; sometimes, in the case of indirect effects (and sometimes in the case of direct effects), they have not been applied at all. On the other hand, national courts' reluctance to apply these principles in some cases (eg, *Duke v GEC Reliance Ltd*; *Rolls-Royce plc v Doughty*) appears to have stemmed in part from the perceived injustice of imposing liability, retrospectively, on parties, public or private, when the precise nature of their obligations under Community law at the relevant time was not clear. The existence of a remedy under *Francovich* effectively completes the picture of ensuring the effective protection of individual rights under EU law. A good example is *Francovich* itself, following the ECJ's denial of the direct effects of the relevant provisions of Directive 80/987.

One question that arises is whether state liability can be used in preference to direct effect and indirect effect, or whether it can only be used if neither of these two mechanisms are available. In many decisions (eg, *Faccini Dori*), the ECJ has pointed out a gap in protection—in particular due to the fact that directives do not have horizontal effect—can be remedied through the use of state liability. The doctrine on this view has a fallback role. In *Brasserie du Pêcheur* the ECJ viewed state liability in a slightly different light, seeing it as a corollary of direct effect (para 22). Nonetheless, the preferred approach seems to see state liability as the approach of last resort. It was suggested in *Lindöpark* that a damages claim is unnecessary where the applicant can obtain relief by instituting an alternative course of action set down in national law. Some commentators have suggested that *Bonifaci v INPS* (case C–94 and 95/95) implies it is possible to make admissibility of such proceedings dependent on the exhaustion of other domestic remedies which offer full reinstatement of rights. None of this however requires such an approach before an action in state liability may be brought.

9.2.6 State liability and the other pillars

The original judgment in *Francovich* refers to remedies for a breach of Community law. Does this mean that the remedy is not available for a failure to comply with Union law under the JHA and CFSP pillars? Member States certainly sought to exclude direct effect (but not other doctrines such as indirect effect and state liability), and the ECJ's jurisdiction is limited in both these pillars. Nonetheless, as we have seen in Chapter 5, the boundary between the pillars is porous and, in *Pupino* (case C–105/03), the ECJ held that the duty of cooperation which gave rise to the doctrine of indirect effect applied to Union law just as much as to Community law. This is a significant judgment. Of particular importance here is the fact that the doctrine of state liability is likewise based on Article 10 EC, which could imply that state liability—like indirect effects—applies to Union law. This is a contentious issue, but the removal of the pillar structure, should the Lisbon Treaty come into force, would reinforce this argument. For the time being, the question remains open.

9.2.7 Classifying state liability in national law

The principle of state liability remains a hybrid, part national, part Community law, with national courts ultimately responsible for applying the conditions to a particular case. This has created problems for national courts. Prior to *Brasserie du Pêcheur* it was assumed, following *Francovich*, that a claim for damages against the state must be brought on the same basis, and according to the same rules, as the 'equivalent' claim based on national law.

However, regrettably, as noted above, the rules governing state liability laid down in *Brasserie du Pêcheur* were not comprehensive. It was left to national courts to decide, according to the principles applicable to equivalent claims based on national law, whether the Community law breached was intended to benefit persons such as the applicant (condition (a)); whether there existed the appropriate direct causal link between the state's breach and the applicant's damage (condition (c), which was raised, but not decided, in *Schmidberger* (case C–112/00)); and whether the damage suffered was of a kind in respect of which damages might be awarded.

Although a principle of state liability for executive acts, and judicial remedies in respect of such acts, already exists in all Member States, these claims will now also be subject to the rules laid down in *Brasserie du Pêcheur*. As with legislative acts, existing national remedies may need to be modified to ensure that they are effective in protecting individuals' rights; alternatively (and preferably) claims may be brought under a new *Francovich* tort.

A principle of liability for judicial acts in breach of Community law, as laid down in *Brasserie du Pêcheur*, clearly breaks new constitutional ground in most if not all Member States. If available in theory, it is unlikely to be applied freely in practice. If only for reasons of polity, neither the ECJ nor a national court is likely to find a judicial breach of Community law sufficiently serious to warrant liability.

There is a degree of freedom for the Member States to specify the circumstances in which Member State liability may arise, provided that these are not stricter than those laid down in Community law. Thus, in *Traghetti del Mediterraneo SpA v Italy* (case C–173/03), Italian legislation excluded state liability for judicial functions involving the interpretation of legal provisions or the assessment of facts and evidence. Following on from its ruling in *Köbler* (case C–224/01), the Court observed that whilst the interpretation of the law is part of the essence of judicial activity, it is possible that a manifest breach of Community law might occur during the process of interpretation (paragraph 35). Consequently, excluding liability for damages caused by interpretation of law or assessment of facts is incompatible with national law, as is a limitation of liability to instances of intentional fault or serious misconduct by the national court, especially where this would narrow the criteria laid down in *Köbler*. In *AGM-COS MET Srl v Suomen Valtio and Tarmo Lehtinen* (case C–470/03), the Court held that national law may lay down specific conditions, provided that they do not make it impossible or excessively difficult in practice to obtain compensation caused by a Member State's breach of Community law. The Finnish limitation to damage caused by a criminal offence, the exercise of public authority, or on the basis that there are other especially serious reasons for awarding compensation were too restrictive because there may be conduct otherwise giving rise to liability not covered by these factors.

9.3 Conclusions

The principle of state liability provides individuals with a strong tool before their national courts to secure the enforcement of their rights under Community law. Although controversial, the decision in *Köbler v Austria* strengthens this further.

However, as the case law on state liability has shown, *Francovich* is not a universal panacea. To succeed in a claim for damages the applicant must establish that the law infringed was intended to confer rights on individuals and that the breach is sufficiently serious (as well as the requisite damage and causation). In cases of non-implementation of directives, as in *Francovich* or *Dillenkofer*, where there is no doubt about the nature of the Community obligation, the breach is likely to be sufficiently serious. However, where the Community obligation allegedly breached is less clear, the breach may well be found to be excusable. This then is a limitation on the ability of the doctrine to provide an effective remedy—or an effective enforcement mechanism—in every circumstance. Nonetheless, the introduction of state liability was a significant moment in the jurisprudence of the ECJ as it undermined the principle found in the legal systems of many Member States: that the state would not be liable for legislative (in)action. At a systemic level, the introduction of the doctrine emphasises that in the field of Community (if not Union) law, Member States play a subordinate role. It is surprising perhaps, that the doctrine has been so well accepted in the legal systems of the Member States.

FURTHER READING

Anagnostaras, G, 'The principle of state liability for judicial breaches: The impact of European Community law' (2001) EPL 281.

Cabral, P and Chaves, MC, 'Member State liability for decisions of national courts adjudicating at last instance' (2006) Maastricht Journal of European and Comparative Law 109–26.

Case notes on C–224/01 *Köbler v Republik Österreich* [2005] ERPL 419.

Coppell, J, 'Domestic limitations on recovery for breach of EC law' (1998) ILJ 259.

Craig, P, '*Francovich*, remedies and the scope of damages liability' (1993) 109 LQR 595.

—— 'Once more unto the breach: The Community, the state and damages liability' (1997) 113 LQR 67.

Gravells, N, 'Disapplying an Act of Parliament: Constitutional Enormity or Community law right?' [1989] PL 568.

Prechal, S, 'Member State liability and direct effect: What's the difference after all?' (2006) 17 EBL Rev 299–316.

Ross, M, 'Refining effective enjoyment' (1990) 15 EL Rev 476.

—— 'Beyond *Francovich*' (1993) 56 MLR 55.

Steiner, J, 'From direct effects to *Francovich*: Shifting means of enforcement of Community law' (1993) 18 EL Rev 3.

—— 'The limits of state liability for breach of European Community law' [1998] EPL 69.

Vajda, C, 'Liability for breach of Community law: A survey of the ECJ cases post *Factortame*' (2006) 17 EBL Rev 257–68.

Van den Berg, R and Schafer, HB, 'state liability for infringements of the EC Treaty' (1998) 23 EL Rev 552.

Van Gerven, W, 'Bridging the gap between Community and national law: Towards a principle of homogeneity of legal remedies' (1995) 32 CML Rev 679.

Woods, L and Smith, F, 'Causation in *Francovich*: The neglected problem' (1997) 46 ICLQ 925.

10

The preliminary rulings procedure

10.1 Introduction

The European legal system has several enforcement mechanisms. The most obvious is the possibility for the Commission or Member States to begin actions against Member States for breaching the EC Treaty. As we have seen however (and will see again in Part III), the role of individuals in the enforcement and development of EC law has been vital. This has been possible through private actions begun in the national courts where private litigants assert their directly effective rights derived from EC law against the state or, in some cases, other private persons. In practice this private enforcement has been critical to the success of the European legal order. Given the need to accord EC law priority, it is perhaps surprising, that the system created by the EC Treaty was not, however, one based upon an appellate structure whereby cases begun in national courts could be appealed to the European Court of Justice (ECJ) for final disposal. Rather the system is one of reference whereby national courts conduct the proceedings throughout but may (and sometimes must) ask the ECJ for its view on the interpretation of any point of EC law relevant to the case before the national court. The national court is described as making a 'reference' to the ECJ to obtain a 'preliminary ruling'. After the ECJ has given its view on the point of EC law, the case is finally resolved by the national court in light of the legal opinion received. The ECJ does not have the power to make final orders or enforce its judgments in the Member States national legal systems. As a result, the willingness of the national courts to refer cases to the ECJ and follow its interpretations of the EC law in good faith has been critical to the whole evolution of the European legal system.

This chapter seeks to consider the relationship between the national courts and the ECJ in the context of preliminary rulings. In particular we consider the following key issues:

(a) the relative importance of the Article 234 preliminary reference procedure to the development of EC law and European integration, and the role of individuals in that process;

(b) the extent to which the national courts are willing and able to gain access to the ECJ in order to resolve questions of EC law before them;

(c) how far the Article 234 system has ensured that EC law is interpreted uniformly throughout the Member States;

(d) the nature of the relationship between the national courts and the ECJ, and whether that remains one of cooperation between equal partners or whether it has evolved into something more hierarchical, with the ECJ effectively acting as a supreme court for the Union;

(e) the extent to which the Article 234 procedures adequately protect funda-
     mental rights and give effective remedies to private litigants; and

(f) the problems raised by the special procedures laid down in the amended
     treaties which restrict references from national courts to the ECJ in cases
     involving justice and home affairs.

10.2 The text of Article 234 and an overview of the procedure

Article 234 EC (EX 177) provides that:

(1) The Court of Justice shall have jurisdiction to give preliminary rulings concerning:
   (a) the interpretation of this Treaty;
   (b) the validity and interpretation of acts of the institutions of the Community;
   (c) the interpretation of the statutes of bodies established by an act of the Council,
       where those statutes so provide.

(2) Where such a question is raised before any court or tribunal of a Member State, that
    court or tribunal may, if it considers that a decision on the question is necessary to
    enable it to give judgment, request the Court of Justice to give a ruling thereon.

(3) Where any such question is raised in a case pending before a court or tribunal of a
    Member State, against whose decisions there is no judicial remedy under national
    law, that court or tribunal shall bring the matter before the Court of Justice.

Lisbon makes some textual changes and renumbers the provision Article 267 TFEU

10.2.1 The historical importance of the Article 234 procedure

It is not clear that the framers of the EC Treaty realised the full significance that the
Article 234 procedure, linking national courts to the ECJ, would come to have on
the development of EC law. The text is fairly humble, suggesting that the ECJ might
be called upon to adjudicate to avoid conflicting interpretations of EC law by the
national courts. Thus its original purpose was to ensure, by authoritative rulings on
the interpretation and validity of EC law, the correct and uniform application of
EC law by the courts of Member States. By contrast, it is likely that the framers saw
enforcement action by the Commission in cases brought directly before the ECJ
(under Article 226 EC; post Lisbon, Article 258 TFEU) as the key to the effectiveness
of Community law. The role of citizens and legal persons as enforcers was less obvious. In its early case law however the ECJ suggested that the possibility of individuals bringing cases to it through the national court reference procedure under Article
234 indicated that the treaty was more than simply an 'ordinary' international
agreement between states. Citizens too could use Article 234 to gain access to the
ECJ and this was one factor that inspired the development of the doctrines of direct
effect and supremacy in *Van Gend en Loos* (case 26/62), *Costa v ENEL* (case 6/64) (see
Chapter 5). The ECJ jurisprudence giving powerful rights to individuals has in turn
encouraged more litigation and thus more Article 234 references to be made.

10.2.1.1 *Impact on claimant*

The reference procedure has thus been very valuable to the individual, since it has provided him or her with the primary means of access to the ECJ to challenge Member State actions alleged to breach EC law. It will be recalled that there is no possibility for individuals themselves to begin enforcement action against a Member State under Article 226 EC Treaty. This is reserved to the Commission. In this way the individual has been able indirectly to challenge action by Member States (eg, *Van Gend en Loos*). Similarly, individuals have found it difficult to begin direct actions before the ECJ under Article 230 against the acts and legislation of Community institutions under because of the restrictive rules on standing (see Chapter 12). By bringing a case in the national courts to challenge domestic measures implementing EC law a reference can be made to the ECJ which can rule that the Community legislation is invalid. Using this 'indirect' action, the individual can then obtain an appropriate remedy from his national court, following the decision by the ECJ to declare a Community measure null and void (see Chapter 6 and, eg, *Royal Scholten-Honig*—EC regulation invalid for breach of principle of equality).

10.2.1.2 *Impact on development of Community law*

The importance of the Article 234 procedure has been greatly increased by the development by the ECJ of the concept of direct effects. Where originally only 'directly applicable' regulations might have been expected to be invoked before national courts, these courts may now be required to apply treaty articles, decisions, and even directives. Even where EC law is not directly effective it may be invoked before national courts on the principles of indirect effects or state liability under *Francovich*. As a result, national courts now play a major role in the enforcement of EC law. As we will see, the cooperative relationship between the ECJ and the national courts has been a key factor in the success of the preliminary-rulings procedure.

The ECJ has also used the preliminary rulings to pronounce many new legal doctrines vital for the substantive development of EC law. A glance through the preceding chapters of this book will reveal that the majority of cases cited, and almost all the major principles established by the ECJ, were decided in the context of a reference to that court for a preliminary ruling under Article 234. Cases such as *Van Gend en Loos* (case 26/62), *Costa v ENEL* (case 6/64) and *Defrenne v Sabena (No 2)* (case 43/75), concerned with questions of interpretation of EC law, enabled the ECJ to develop the crucial concepts of direct effects and the supremacy of EC law. *Internationale Handelsgesellschaft mbH* (case 11/70); *Stauder v City of Ulm* (case 29/69) and *Royal Scholten-Honig (Holdings) Ltd* (cases 103 and 145/77) (see Chapter 6), which raised questions of the validity of EC law, led the way to the incorporation of general principles of law into EC law. The principle of state liability in damages was laid down in *Francovich* (cases C–6 and 9/90) in preliminary ruling proceedings. In all areas of EU law, the Article 234 procedure has played a major role in developing the substantive law. The procedure accounts for over 50 per cent of all cases heard by the ECJ. This percentage has of course increased as the Court of First Instance (CFI) has taken over responsibility for judicial review actions (Chapters 12 and 13) and actions for damages (Chapter 14). Nonetheless, the preliminary rulings procedure plays a central part in the development and enforcement of EC law.

10.2.2 **Nature of the preliminary rulings procedure**

The preliminary-rulings procedure is not an appeals procedure. An appeals procedure implies a hierarchy between the different types of court, some courts being higher and having more authority than those lower down the judicial architecture. Typically, appeal courts can overrule the decisions of lower courts. The decision whether or not to appeal lies, in the first place, in the hands of the parties, although in some instances leave to appeal from certain courts is required. In contrast, the preliminary-rulings procedure merely provides a means whereby national courts, when questions of EC law arise, may apply to the ECJ for a preliminary ruling on matters of interpretation or validity prior to themselves applying the law. In principle, it is a matter for the national courts to decide whether or not to make a reference. It is an example of shared jurisdiction, depending for its success on mutual cooperation. As Advocate-General Lagrange said in *De Geus en Uitdenbogerd v Robert Bosch GmbH* (case 13/61), the first case to reach the ECJ on an application under the preliminary-rulings procedure:

> Applied judiciously—one is tempted to say loyally—the provisions of Article 177 [now 234] must lead to a real and fruitful collaboration between the municipal courts and the Court of Justice of the Communities with mutual regard for their respective jurisdiction.

We shall consider how far the ECJ has attempted to go beyond this view and impose itself on the national courts in ways that may have departed from the original text and purpose of the treaty.

10.3 **The generous approach of the ECJ to Article 234 references**

We have noted above that the ECJ has relied heavily upon Article 234 references to develop the jurisprudence of EC law. It has adopted a purposive approach in its rulings on the meaning of EC law aiming to strengthen the effectiveness of EC law and build the single market. Article 234 has thus been crucial to the ECJ securing its own vision of European law. For this reason we can see that, for a long time, the ECJ adopted an open-door approach to national courts and tribunals seeking to refer questions to it. Certainly until fairly recently, the ECJ encouraged wide use of preliminary rulings in order to both secure uniformity of EC law throughout Member States but seemingly also to have more opportunity to develop new principles giving greater rights to individuals. As a result, the ECJ has followed a generous approach to the interpretation of Article 234 whenever parties or Member States sought to prevent a reference from being ruled upon by the court, by arguing that the reference was in some way inadmissible. This can be seen by the ECJ's willingness to accept reference from a wide range of bodies (see 10.3.1 and 10.3.2 below) but also by its lack of formality and flexibility in giving rulings on references from national courts in as many situations as possible (see 10.3.6 below).

We can however detect some changes in the outlook of the ECJ over time. One concern is that the ECJ has become overloaded with cases. This has caused delay, extra cost, and uncertainty for parties and the EC legal system overall. Consequently the ECJ has adopted certain decisions to limit the number of cases brought before it. Here, we can see the ECJ is becoming more like a superior court for Europe in that it wishes to be more than a passive recipient of whatever national courts send it. The ECJ has developed jurisprudence aimed at controlling the types of cases it will hear and a doctrine similar to precedent. Thus whilst the early period of the reference procedure saw the ECJ largely allow any reference to proceed to a hearing with a full premlinary ruling being given, this has changed over time. The relationship between the ECJ and national courts has shifted to some extent from one of cooperation amongst equal partners towards a hierarchy with the ECJ attempting to postion itself at the apex of the European legal system. This is, however, always subject to the important reality that the ECJ has no means of ensuring that national courts actually follow its rulings or make references when required to do so under Article 234 (but see *Köbler* (case C-244/01) 10.5.3).

10.3.1 What is a 'court or tribunal'?

Jurisdiction to refer to the ECJ under Article 234 is conferred on 'any court or tribunal'. With rare exceptions (eg, *Nordsee Deutsche Hochseefischerei GmbH* (case 102/81) to be discussed below; *Corbiau v Administration des Contributions* (case C–24/92) (a fiscal authority is not a court or tribunal); *Victoria Film A/S v Riksskattenverkert* (case C–134/97) (a court exercising its administrative duties is not a court or tribunal)) this has been interpreted in the widest sense. Whether a particular body qualifies as a court or tribunal within Article 234 is a matter of *Community* law. National-law classifications are not determinative. Arguably, this facilitates equality of access across the Union. A broad interpretation reduces the risk of rulings which are inconsistent with EC law coming into being.

The ECJ is generally accepted as having set down a number of criteria by which a 'court or tribunal' might be identified. The early case law identified five criteria:

(a) statutory origin

(b) permanence

(c) *inter partes* procedure

(d) compulsory jurisdiction

(e) the application of rules of law.

(See also *Dorsch Consult v Bundesbaugesellschaft Berlin* (case C–54/96), para 23). Subsequent decisions, such as *Preto di Salo v Persons Unknown* (case 14/86), made it clear than the independence of the body would also be a factor.

In *Broekmeulen* (case 246/80) the Court was faced with a reference from the appeal committee of the Dutch professional medical body. One of the questions referred was whether the appeal committee was a 'court or tribunal' within what is now Article 234. The Court held that it was:

> in the practical absence of an effective means of redress before the ordinary courts, in a matter concerning the application of Community law, the appeal committee, which performs its duties with the approval of the public authorities and operates with their assistance, and whose decisions are accepted following contentious proceedings and are in fact recognised as final, must be deemed to be a court of a Member State for the purpose of Article 177 [now 234].

It was held that it was imperative, to ensure the proper functioning of Community law, that the ECJ should have the opportunity of ruling on issues of interpretation and validity raised before such a body.

More recently, the ECJ has held that a person appointed to hear appeals against home affairs ministry decisions in immigration cases, an Immigration Adjudicator, could make a reference (*El-Yassini v Secretary of State for the Home Department* (case C–416/96)). In this case, the office of Immigration Adjudicator was a permanent office, established by statute which gives the officer in question the power to hear and determine disputes in accordance with rules set down by statute. The ECJ further agreed with the Advocate-General, who had emphasised the *inter partes* nature of the procedure (para 20) and the fact that the adjudicators are required to give reasons for their decisions.

The ECJ has since been criticised by the Advocate-General in *de Coster* (case C–17/00) for an approach to the interpretation of a 'court or tribunal' that is confused, especially as regards the criteria of whether the body is established by law, the independent nature of the body and the need for *inter partes* procedure, as well as the requirement that the body's decision be of a judicial nature. Although in cases such as *Criminal Proceedings against X* (cases C–74 and 129/95), in which the ECJ declared it did not have jurisdiction because the prosecutor making the reference was not independent, and *Dorsch Consult* (case C–54/96), in which the Court emphasised the need for the referring body to carry out its responsibilities 'independently' (para 35), in other instances, such as *El-Yassini*, the ECJ has not stringently assessed the requirement of independence. Another such example is *Gabalfrisa v AEAT* (cases C–110–47/98). There the ECJ held that the Spanish Economic-Administrative Courts, which do not form part of the judiciary but are part of the Ministry of Economic Affairs and Finance, fell within Article 234. The ECJ accepted that the separation of functions between the departments of the Ministry responsible for tax collection and the Economic–Administrative Courts, which ruled on complaints lodged against the collection departments, was sufficient to ensure independence, despite the Opinion of Advocate-General Saggio in that case to the contrary.

In *de Coster*, the Court, contrary to the view of the Advocate-General, accepted the reference. It noted that the body in question was 'a permanent body, established by law, that it gives legal rulings and that the jurisdiction thereby invested in it concerning local tax proceedings is compulsory' (para 12). In the subsequent *Schmid* case (case C–516/99), however, the ECJ went to great lengths to distinguish the Fifth Appeal Chamber for the Regional Finance Authority, the referring body in *Schmid*, from the bodies found to fall within the definition of a 'court or tribunal' in *Dorsch Consult* and *Gabalfrisa*, which the Advocate-General in *de Coster* had criticised. Like the bodies in those cases, the appeal chamber was linked in organisational terms to the body whose decisions it reviewed. The ECJ held that the appeal chamber was not independent. In *Synetairismos Farmakopoion Aitolias & Akarnanias v GlaxoSmithKline plc* (Case C–53/03), the ECJ held that the Greek competition tribunal was subject to control by the relevant government department and therefore not sufficiently independent to be regarded as a 'court or tribunal' for the purposes of Article 234. Whether these cases indicate that the ECJ has taken the comments of the Advocate-General in *de Coster* into account, or rather reflects the fact that some administrative bodies simply cannot be seen as independent is debatable.

Moreover, the ECJ has sometimes emphasised the importance of the *inter partes* nature of proceedings (see, eg, *El Yassini* (case C–416/96)), although there have been cases, such as *Dorsch Consult* which concerned undefended proceedings, where this criterion has seemed less central to the determination of the question as to whether a body constitutes a 'court or tribunal'. In a more recent case, *Roda Golf and Beach Resort* (C-14/08) Advocate-General Ruiz Jarabo Colomer gave an opinion allowing a reference from a court where proceedings had not yet commenced and a single party was seeking to require the court to effect service a notice cancelling a contract on counterparties to the contract. He sought to argue that the *inter partes* rule should not be rigidly applied and it is suggested that this is right. Where there is a genuine issue of EC law that affects legal rights or remedies then a reference should be possible even in the absence of *inter partes* proceedings being on foot.

10.3.2 Can arbitrators be a 'court or tribunal'?

The position of arbitrators has always given rise to problems in this context. The Court took a narrow view of a 'court or tribunal' in the early case of *Nordsee Deutsche Hochseefischerei GmbH* (case 102/81). The case arose from a joint shipbuilding project which involved the pooling of EC aid. The parties agreed that in the event of a dispute they would refer their differences to an independent arbitrator. Their agreement excluded the possibility of recourse to the ordinary courts. They fell into disagreement and a number of questions involving the interpretation of certain EC regulations were raised before the arbitrator. He sought a ruling from the ECJ as to, inter alia, whether he was a 'court or tribunal' within the meaning of Article 234. The Court held that he was not. According to the Court, the key issue was the nature of the arbitration. Here the public authorities of Member States were not involved in the decision to opt for arbitration, nor were they called upon to intervene automatically before the arbitrator. If questions of Community law were raised before such a body, the ordinary courts might be called upon to give them assistance, or to review the decision; it would be for *them* to refer questions of interpretation or validity of Community law to the ECJ.

The Court's decision in *Nordsee* ignored the fact that in this case recourse to the courts was excluded, and the arbitrator was thus required to interpret a difficult point of Community law, of central importance in the proceedings, unaided. Since in *Nordsee Deutsche Hochseefischerei GmbH* there was no effective means of redress before the ordinary courts and the decisions of the arbitrator were accepted following contentious proceedings and recognised as final it seems that the only factor distinguishing it from *Broekmeulen* was the element of *public* participation or control. This, it seems, will be essential. Certainly, in subsequent cases, such as *Danfoss* (case 109/88), the ECJ has focused on the compulsory nature of an arbitrator's jurisdiction, by contrast to the position in *Nordsee*, when the parties agreed to refer their dispute to arbitration.

The position was confirmed in *Denuit v Transorient* (C–125/04) involving a dispute under the Package Travel Directive (90/314/EEC) before the arbitration panel of the Belgian Travel Dispute Committee. Having confirmed its case law, the ECJ rejected the reference on the basis that the panel was not a 'court or tribunal', because the parties were 'under no obligation, in law or in fact, to refer their disputes to arbitration' (at para 16). No regard was had to the fact that, in a consumer situation, arbitration may be the only formal procedure which may practically be available to a consumer because of the comparatively high cost of court action; a matter which surprises in view of the increasing emphasis on out-of-court procedures in consumer cases.

10.3.3 'Court or tribunal': Evaluation

In general, the ECJ's approach to the definition of 'court or tribunal' for the purposes of Article 234 has been generous. This approach would seem to have been driven by the need to ensure correct and uniform interpretation of the treaty. One might argue that access to justice from the perspective of the parties would also argue in favour of such a broad definition, especially when the referring body did not meet the criterion of independence. Against this, however, a number of other factors should be weighed. One of the significant problems in the current jurisprudence is a lack of certainty as to where the ECJ will draw the line between a 'court or tribunal' for the purposes of the EC Treaty and other bodies. The current approach, which (usually) takes a broad view of the bodies permitted to refer, means that the ECJ receives more references. An approach which encourages references was understandable during the early years of the Community when both the substantive law and the relationship between the ECJ and national courts needed to be consolidated, but what of the position now? It has been suggested that although there is much to be said for encouraging national courts, now more experienced in the application of EC law, to decide matters for themselves, there is no justification for a position whereby access to the ECJ is totally excluded. The Advocate-General in *de Coster*, however, commented that '[o]ne well thought out and well-founded decision resolves more problems that a large number of hasty judgments which do not go deeply into the reasoning and do not address the questions submitted to them'.

Essentially, it seems that the ECJ is a victim of its own success, with longer delays in dealing with references, delays themselves that do not assist in the proper administration of justice. The Advocate-General suggested that the ECJ should tighten its definition of 'court or tribunal', with the likely consequence that the relationship between the national courts and the ECJ would change. The national courts from this perspective would need to take greater responsibility for Community law.

10.3.4 The question must be a matter of Community law

The Court is only empowered to give rulings on matters of Community law (and, as noted below, limited aspects of the second pillar on justice and home affairs (JHA)). It has no jurisdiction to interpret domestic law, nor to pass judgment on the compatibility of domestic law with EC law. The Court has frequently been asked such questions (eg, *Van Gend en Loos* (case 26/62); *Costa v ENEL* (case 6/64); *Netherlands v Ten Kate Holding BV* (case C–511/03)), since it is often the central problem before the national court. But as the Court said in *Costa v ENEL*:

> a decision should be given by the Court not upon the validity of an Italian law in relation to the Treaty, but only upon the interpretation of the above-mentioned [Treaty] Articles in the context of the points of law stated by the Giudice Conciliatore.

Where the Court is asked to rule on such a matter it will merely reformulate the question and return an abstract interpretation on the point of EC law involved. This respects the division of competences laid down in the treaty and avoids the ECJ becoming involved in national law issues over which it has no jurisdiction.

10.3.5 The Court's role is one of interpretation of EC law not application to the facts

The Court maintains a dividing line in principle between interpretation and application. It has no jurisdiction to rule on the application of Community law by national courts. However, since the application of Community law often raises problems for national courts, the Court, in its concern to provide national courts with 'practical' or 'worthwhile' rulings, will sometimes, when interpreting Community law, also offer unequivocal guidance as to its application (see eg, *Stoke-on-Trent City Council v B&Q* (case C–169/91); *R v Her Majesty's Treasury, ex parte British Telecommunications plc* (case C–392/93); *Arsenal Football Club v Reed* (case C–206/01)).

10.3.6 The Court must not interfere with the matters within national court discretion

The Court maintains a strict policy of non-interference over matters of what to refer, when to refer, and how to refer. Such matters are left entirely to the discretion of the national judge. As the Court said in *De Geus en Uitdenbogerd v Robert Bosch GmbH* (case 13/61), its jurisdiction depends 'solely on the existence of a request from the national court'. However, it has no jurisdiction to give a ruling when, at the time when it is made, the procedure before the court making it has already been terminated (*Pardini* (case 338/85); *Grogan* (case C–159/90)). In contrast, the Court does have jurisdiction where a court is involved in preparatory inquiries in criminal proceedings which may or may not lead to a formal prosecution, where the question of EC law may determine whether the inquiries will continue (case C–60/02, *Criminal proceedings against X ('Rolex')*).

No formal requirements are imposed on the framing of the questions. Where the questions are inappropriately phrased the Court will merely reformulate the questions, answering what it sees as the relevant issues. It may interpret what it regards as the relevant issues even if they are not raised by the referring court (eg, *OTO SpA v Ministero delle Finanze* (case C–130/92)). Nor will it question the timing of a reference. However, since 'it is necessary for the national court to define the legal context in which the interpretation requested should be placed', the Court has suggested that it might be convenient for the facts of the case to be established and for questions of purely national law to be settled at the time when the reference is made, in order to enable the Court to take cognisance of all the features of fact and law which may be relevant to the interpretation of Community law which it is called upon to give (*Irish Creamery Milk Suppliers Association v Ireland* (cases 36 and 71/80); approved in *Pretore di Salò* (case 14/86)). In *Telemarsicabruzzo SpA v Circostel* (cases C–320, 321, 322/90) it rejected an application for a ruling from an Italian magistrates' court on the grounds that the reference had provided no background factual information and only fragmentary observations on the case. The ECJ has since reaffirmed this approach in several cases (eg, *Pretore di Genova v Banchero* (case

C–157/92); *Monin Automobiles v France* (case C–386/92)). The ECJ has held, however, that the need for detailed factual background to a case is less pressing when the questions referred by the national court relate to technical points (*Vaneetveld v Le Foyer SA* (case C316/93)) or where the facts are clear, for example, because of a previous reference (*Crispoltoni v Fattoria Autonoma Tabacchi* (cases C–133, 300 and 362/92)). The concern seems to be that not only must the ECJ know enough to give a useful ruling in the context, but that there is also enough information for affected parties to be able to make representations. This, according to the ECJ, is especially relevant in competition cases (*Deliege* (case C–191/97), paras 30 and 36 (see further Chapter 29). The Court has issued an 'Information Note on references from national courts for a preliminary ruling' ([2005] OJ C143/1, replacing guidance issued in 1996), consolidating its rulings in these cases. The circumstances in which the ECJ will decline jurisdiction are discussed further below.

10.3.7 The national courts may refer cases on the validity of EC measures

As confirmed in Article 234 itself, the validity EC measures may be called into question within national proceedings. Thus for example a regulation or directive passed by the Council and Parliament may be said to be ultra vires the EC Treaty. If an individual is adversely affected by the measure, they may begin proceedings in the national courts to challenge it. The national courts have often made references to the ECJ in such cases. The ECJ has been receptive to such cases (subject to 10.4.4 below) and is willing to rule that EC measures are invalid in responding to Article 234 references. The only limit placed upon national courts is that they themselves do not have the power to declare EC measures invalid (see *Foto-Frost v Hauptzollamt Lübeck-Ost* (case 314/85)). The ECJ has been keen to maintain a monopoly over this power because of the danger that national courts may undermine the effectiveness of EC law if they were unilaterally to declare measures invalid. The ECJ did however confirm that national courts can grant interim relief suspending the implementation of EC measures that they believe to be invalid in *Zuckerfabrik Süderdithmarschen AG v Hauptzollamt Itzehoe* (cases C–143/88 and C–92/89). The national courts must use this power with great care and make an urgent reference to the ECJ. This is a good example of the cooperative nature of the relationship between the ECJ and the national courts. The ECJ sought to balance the concerns of national courts about invalid EC legislation affecting individuals with its own concerns about the effectiveness and uniform application of EC law.

10.3.8 The practical reality of the ECJ's jurisdiction

Some of the above limitations of the Court's jurisdiction are more apparent than real. The line between matters of Community law and matters of national law, between interpretation and application are more easily drawn in theory than in practice. An interpretation of EC law may leave little room for doubt as to the legality of a national law and little choice to the national judge in matters of application if he is to comply with his duty to give priority to EC law. The Court has on occasions, albeit in abstract terms, suggested that a particular national law is incompatible with EC law (eg, *R v Secretary of State for Transport, ex parte Factortame*

Ltd (case C–221/89); *Johnston v RUC* (case 222/84)). The Court may even offer specific guidance as to the application of its ruling. In the *BT* case (case C–392/93), for example, the ECJ commented:

> Whilst it is in principle for the national courts to verify whether or not the conditions of State liability for a breach of Community law are fulfilled, in the present case the Court has all the necessary information to assess whether the facts amount to a sufficiently serious breach of Community law.

The Court then went on to hold that there had been no breach. Further, in re-phrasing and regrouping the questions the Court is able to select the issues which it regards as significant, without apparently interfering with the discretion of the national judge.

It may be argued that some encroachment by the ECJ on to the territory of national courts' jurisdiction is necessary to ensure the correct and uniform application of Community law. However, its very freedom of manoeuvre in preliminary rulings proceedings, combined with its teleological approach to interpretation, have resulted on occasions in the Court overstepping the line, laying down broad general (and sometimes unexpected) principles, with far-reaching consequences, in response to *particular* questions from national courts (eg, *Barber* (case 262/88); *Marshall (No 2)* (case C–271/91)). This has not been conducive to legal certainty. Such activism has not gone without criticism, as calculated to invite 'rebellion', even 'defiance' by national courts.

The potential difficulties arising from the ECJ overstepping the boundary between its role of interpreting EC law and the national courts' role of applying that ruling to the facts can be seen in the case of *Arsenal Football Club v Reed* ([2002] All ER (D) 180 (Dec)). The case before the national court concerned the action commenced by Arsenal to prevent Reed from continuing to sell souvenirs which carried its name and logos. The national court referred a number of questions to the ECJ on the interpretation of the Trade Mark Directive (see case C–206/01). The main issue was whether trade mark protection extended only to the circumstances in which the sign was used as a trade mark or whether an infringement would occur irrespective of how the marks were used. The ECJ handed down a judgment in the following terms:

> In a situation which is not covered by Article 6(1) of the First Council Directive 89/104/EEC of 21 December 1988 to approximate the laws of the Member States relating to trade marks, where a third party uses in the course of trade a sign which is identical to a validly registered trade mark on goods which are identical to those for which it is registered, the trade mark proprietor of the mark is entitled, in circumstances such as those in the present case, to rely on Article 5(1)(a) of that directive to prevent that use. It is immaterial that, in the context of that use, the sign is perceived as a badge of support for or loyalty or affiliation to the trade mark proprietor.

The phrase 'in circumstances such as those in the present case' would seem to give the national court little freedom in its determination of the case for which the preliminary ruling was originally made. In the *Arsenal* case, however, the referring court accepted the argument of the defendant's counsel to the effect that in the course of its judgment and in particular by tying the operative part of its judgment to the facts of the case, the ECJ had made a determination of fact which in some aspects was inconsistent with the finding of fact made by the national court. On this basis, the national court commented: 'If this is so, the ECJ has exceeded its jurisdiction and I am not bound by its final conclusion. I must apply its guidance on the law to the facts as found at the trial' (para 27).

It further remarked:

> The courts of this country cannot challenge rulings of the ECJ within its areas of competence. There is no advantage to be gained by appearing to do so. Furthermore national courts do not make references to the ECJ with the intention of ignoring the result. On the other hand, no matter how tempting it may be to find an easy way out, the High Court has no power to cede to the ECJ a jurisdiction it does not have. [Para 28.]

Although the court has phrased this in terms of the limits of jurisdiction, rather than an overt defiance, the assertion by the national court of the limits of the ECJ's jurisdiction was itself a form of rebellion because the trial judge refused to follow the application of law to the facts that had been suggested by the ECJ. The High Court before which the *Arsenal case* was heard did point out that there was the possibility of an appeal to the Court of Appeal, which might make a different application of the law to the facts but in the absence of this, he declined to accept the ECJ's, as he saw it, improper ruling on factual matters. This is what happened subsequently (see [2003] 2 CMLR 25), when the Court of Appeal held that the ECJ's reference to the facts was *not* at variance with those of the trial judge, but that there was a difference in legal reasoning. The trial judge had therefore been wrong to disagree with the ECJ in this case, although the Court of Appeal did confirm the principle on which the first-instance decision was based. We can see in *Reed* a good example of a case where the ECJ was perceived to have exceeded its proper jurisdiction as a court of reference by taking the final decision on the case away from the national court. The nature of cooperation requires that both national courts and ECJ respect each others jurisdictions.

10.4 The ECJ's refusal to give rulings in some cases

As was noted above, for many years, the ECJ generally encouraged national courts to refer and did not seek to limit the kinds of cases sent to it. There have however been important limitations upon the ECJ's policy of being willing to provide rulings in all cases referred to it. These limitations are controversial because some of them go against the text of Article 234 which seems to require the ECJ to give a ruling whenever this is 'necessary' to resolve an issue of EC law. There appears to be no inherent jurisdiction in the ECJ to refuse to give a ruling. Furthermore, refusal to answer may lead to uncertainty in national courts about when to refer and this may damage the uniform application of EC law. One practical, thus justifiable, limitation that we have already seen is that the ECJ will refuse jurisdiction when the referring court has not included enough information to enable the ECJ to give a ruling on the question referred (see eg, *Telemarsicabruzzo SpA v Circostel* (cases C–320, 321, 322/90)).

We now consider some more important limitations developed by the court. These show the ECJ developing the idea that, as a kind of supreme court for the EU, it should have the inherent power to decide which kinds of cases it will hear. This is sometimes referred to as the compentence to determine its own jurisdiction (Kompetenz-Kompetenz is the German phrase).

10.4.1 The ECJ can decline to hear cases brought in artificial proceedings

The most important limitation was first laid down by the ECJ in the cases of *Foglia v Novello (No 1)* (case 104/79) and *Foglia v Novello (No 2)* (case 244/80). Here for the first time the Court refused its jurisdiction to give a ruling on a question of EC law. The questions, which were referred by an Italian judge, concerned the legality under EC law of an import duty imposed by the French on the import of wine from Italy. It arose in the context of litigation between two Italian parties. Foglia, a wine producer, had agreed to sell wine to Mrs Novello, an exporter. In making their contract the parties agreed that Foglia should not bear the cost of any duties levied by the French in breach of EC law. When duties were charged and eventually paid by Foglia, he sought to recover the money from Mrs Novello. In his action before the Italian court for recovery of the money that court sought a preliminary ruling on the legality under EC law of the duties imposed by the French. The ECJ refused its jurisdiction. The proceedings, it claimed, had been artificially created in order to question the legality of the French law; they were not 'genuine'. The parties were no more successful the second time when the judge referred the case back to the ECJ having not received a satisfactory answer to his previous reference. In a somewhat peremptory judgment the Court declared that the function of Article 234 was to contribute to the administration of justice in the Member States; not to give advisory opinions on general or hypothetical questions.

The ECJ's decision has been criticised. Although the parties had contrived their contractual arrangements so as to bring a claim in their own national court, rather than challenging the French duty in the French courts, they did genuinely think the duty was in breach of EC law and the Italian judge called upon to decide the case was faced with a genuine problem, central to which was the issue of EC law. If, in his discretion, he sought guidance from the ECJ in this matter, surely it was not for that Court to deny it. The principles expressed in *Foglia v Novello* were, however, applied in *Meilicke v ADV/ORGA AG* (case C–83/91). Here the Court refused to answer a lengthy and complex series of questions relating, inter alia, to the interpretation of the second Company Law Directive. The dispute between the parties centred on a disagreement as to the interpretation of certain provisions of German company law. It appeared that the EC directive was being invoked in order to prove the theories of one of the parties (a legal scholar). The Court held that it had no jurisdiction to give advisory opinions on hypothetical questions submitted by national courts (contrast *Mangold* (case C–144/04, discussed in Chapter 5), which also appeared to have been raised to prove an argument made by one of the parties (cf para 32), but a contract forming the basis of the dispute and the Article 234 reference had been performed—thereby causing the ECJ to reject the German government's claim that the case was artificial). It is not unusual for supreme courts to limit cases to those where parties really are in dispute with each other. The reasons are partly those of docket control but also to prevent the courts becoming the forum for political rather than legal disputes.

It has also been suggested that political considerations and national rivalries played their part in the *Foglia* decision (the Court held it 'must display special vigilance when . . . a question is referred to it with a view to permitting the national court to decide whether the legislation of another Member State is in accordance with Community law': *Foglia v Novello (No 2)*). This assessment is supported by the more recent case of *Bacardi-Martini SAS v Newcastle United Football Company Ltd* (case C–318/00). Bacardi entered into a contract for advertising time on an electronic revolving display system during a match between Newcastle and Metz, a French football club. The match was to be televised live in the United Kingdom and France. Although the advertising deal was in compliance with English law, it contravened French law and Newcastle therefore pulled out of the advertising agreement. Bacardi brought an action against Newcastle, claiming that it could not rely on the French law to justify its actions, as the French law was incompatible with Article 49 EC (ex 59; post Lisbon 56 TFEU) on the freedom to provide services. The High Court made a reference on this point. When discussing the question of admissibility, the ECJ referred to *Foglia* and the special need for vigilance when the law of another Member State was in issue; it then reviewed whether the national court had made it clear why an answer was necessary. The ECJ concluded:

> In those circumstances, the conclusion must be that the Court does not have the material before it to show that it is necessary to rule on the compatibility with the Treaty of legislation of a Member State other than that of the court making the reference. [Para 53.]

From this case, it seems that although a national court is not precluded from referring questions relating to the national laws of other Member States, the ECJ will review the justification for the reference more stringently than it would otherwise do.

10.4.2 The case must relate to a cross-border issue and not a purely internal situation

Another area in which the ECJ has sometimes limited references has been when the subject matter of the case is 'internal' and does not involve Community law directly. Internal law issues are governed by national not EC law. The ECJ has generally been careful not to rule on cases which appear to concern internal situations because to do so would be to assume a power not conferred upon it by the EC Treaty. This issue came before the Court in *Dzodzi v Belgium* (cases C–297/88 and C–197/89). Here the Court was prepared to provide a ruling on the interpretation of EC social security law in a purely 'internal' matter, for the purpose of clarifying provisions of Belgian law invoked by a Togolese national. The Court held that it was 'exclusively for national courts which were dealing with a case to assess, with regard to the specific features of each case, both the need for a preliminary ruling in order to enable it to give judgment, and the relevance of the question'. Following *Dzodzi*, in *Leur Bloem* (case C–28/95), the ECJ held that it has jurisdiction to interpret provisions of Community law where the facts of the case lie outside these provisions but are applicable to the case because the national law governing the main dispute has transposed the Community rule to a non-Community context ('spontaneous harmonisation'). This is subject to the proviso that national law does not expressly prohibit it (*Kleinwort Benson* (case C–346/93)). Similarly, the ECJ has accepted references for a preliminary ruling in circumstances where a national provision is tied into a Community rule in order to avoid non-discrimination even in purely internal situations (case C–300/01, *Salzmann*—internal situation affected by rules on free movement of capital in Article 56 (ex 73b) EC; post Lisbon 63 TFEU).

10.4.3 A preliminary ruling must be 'objectively required'

Another potential limitation on the ECJ's willingness to accept references can be seen in *Monin Automobiles—Maison du Deux-Roues* (case C–428/93). There the ECJ suggested that the questions referred must be 'objectively required' by the national court as 'necessary to enable that court to give judgment' in the proceedings before it as required under Article 234(2). This case concerned a company which was in the process of being wound up. The company argued that it should not be finally wound up until certain questions relating to EC law had been answered. Conversely, the company's creditors thought that the company had been artificially kept in existence for too long already and should be wound up immediately. The national court referred the EC-law questions to determine the strength of the company's argument. The ECJ held that, although there was a connection between the questions and the dispute, answers to the question would not be *applied* in the case. The ECJ therefore declined jurisdiction.

10.4.4 The parties must challenge EC measures directly under Article 230 if they have standing

Another limitation on the ECJ's willingness to give premilinary rulings relates to cases where a party is seeking to challenge an EC measure indirectly using proceedings in the national courts. Whilst we saw that often the ECJ will rule on such issues where national courts refer questions to the ECJ under Article 234 (see 10.3.7 above), there are some limits to this open-door policy. The Court has been concerned to prevent parties using Article 234 to get round the rules on direct challenges under Article 230. This was the situation in *TWD Textilwerke GmbH v Germany* (case C–188/92) where the Court refused to give a ruling on the validity of a Commission decision, addressed to the German government, demanding the recovery from the applicants of state aid granted by the government in breach of EC law. Its refusal was based on the fact that the applicants, having been informed by the government of the Commission's decision, and advised of their right to challenge it under Article 230, had failed to do so within the two-month limitation period. Having allowed this period to expire the Court held that the applicants could not, in the interests of legal certainty, be permitted to attack the decision under Article 234. This would defeat the restrictions on challenging Community acts imposed by Article 230 because a party could wait many months or years before attempting to invalidate long-standing EC decisions or legislation.

This decision, wholly out of line with its previous jurisprudence, which has been to encourage challenges to validity under Article 234 rather than (the more restrictive) Article 230, has caused concern, as calculated to drive parties, perhaps prematurely, into action under Article 230, for fear of being denied a later opportunity to challenge Community legislation under Article 234 (see further, Chapter 12). However, the ECJ has since mitigated some of the effects of its judgment in *TWD*. In *R v Intervention Board for Agriculture, ex parte Accrington Beef Co Ltd* (case C–241/95), the parties had not sought to bring an action for annulment within the time limits set out in the then Article 230. Nonetheless, the ECJ was prepared to hear the preliminary ruling reference because it was not clear, as the parties were seeking to challenge a regulation, that they would have had standing to bring an action under Article 230 (see also *Atzeni and others* (cases C–346 and 529/03), discussed at 11.4.3.4). It seems therefore that Article 234 can be used in such cases as long as it is not obvious that the party would have had standing to challenge the EC measure directly under Article 230.

10.5 National courts and the reference procedure

We should note at the outset the position of the national courts is in some ways more powerful than that of the ECJ. Because there is no right of appeal to the ECJ, it is up to the national-court judge whether to decide to refer matters to Luxembourg. As will be seen, in some cases Article 234 imposes a duty to refer cases but there is no method of compelling this if a national court declines to do so. The ECJ has thus relied very much upon judges cooperating with it in order to develop European law and to ensure uniform application throughout the Member States. In this sense, national courts are also part of the Union legal order.

10.5.1 When must a national court refer and when does it have choice?

Although any court or tribunal may refer questions to the ECJ under Article 234, a distinction must be drawn between those courts or tribunals which have a discretion to refer ('permissive' jurisdiction) and those for which referral is mandatory ('mandatory' jurisdiction). Under Article 234(3), where a question concerning interpretation is raised 'in a case pending before a court or tribunal of a Member State, *against whose decisions there is no judicial remedy under national law*, that court or tribunal *shall* bring the matter before the Court of Justice' (emphasis added). For all courts other than those within Article 234(3) referral is discretionary. The treaty therefore created a system whereby most of the time the national courts would have a choice about when to refer questions to the ECJ. Decisions of national courts which are disputed (including on points of EC law) could be appealed internally (subject to the national law regarding appeals of the particular Member State). Only when a case could go no further within the domestic legal system does the treaty require a reference to the ECJ.

10.5.2 Article 234(3): The mandatory obligation to refer for courts against whom no appeal lies

The purpose of Article 234(3) must be seen in the light of the function of Article 234 as a whole, which is to prevent a body of national case law not in accordance with the rules of Community law from coming into existence in any Member State (*Hoffman-La Roche AG v Centrafarm Vertiebsgesellschaft Pharmazeutischer Erzeugnisse mbH* (case 107/76)). To this end Article 234(3) seeks to ensure that, when matters of EC law arise, there is an obligation to refer to the ECJ if the proceedings can go no further in the domestic court system. This purpose should be kept in mind when questions of interpretation of Article 234(3) arise.

The scope of Article 234(3) is not entirely clear. While it obviously applies to courts or tribunals at the apex of the legal system whose decisions are *never* subject to appeal (the 'abstract theory'), such as the House of Lords in England, or the Conseil d'État in France, it is less clear whether it applies also to courts whose decisions *in the case in question* are not subject to appeal (the 'concrete theory'), such as the Italian magistrates' court (*giudice conciliatore*) in *Costa v ENEL* (case 6/64) (no right of appeal because sum of money involved too small). Furthermore, if leave to appeal is required to go to a higher court and this is refused, does this mean the lower court becomes a court 'against whose decisions there is no judicial remedy under national law'? In the UK we see this in appeals from the Court of Appeal where leave to the House of Lords is refused, or when the High Court refuses leave for judicial review from a tribunal decision. These cases all involve courts not at the apex of the system but whose decision has effectively concluded the domestic proceedings. If a point of EC law remained in dispute, the parties would not have had the benefit of a ruling from the ECJ and so their fundamental rights might have been impaired. Furthermore, the interpretation and application of EC law in that Member State might be wrong thus threatening the uniformity of the EC law system across the Member States.

The judgment of the ECJ in *Costa v ENEL* was seen, albeit *obiter*, to support the wider, 'concrete' theory. In that case, in the context of a reference from the Italian magistrates' court, from which there was no appeal due to the small amount of money involved, the Court said, with reference to the then Article 177(3) (now 234(3)): 'By the terms of this Article . . . national courts against whose decisions, *as in the present case*, there is no judicial remedy, *must* refer the matter to the Court of Justice' (emphasis added). Taking into account the function of Article 234(3) and particularly its importance for the individual, this would have seemed to be the better view.

The issue has finally been resolved by the ECJ in favour of the concrete theory in the *Lyckeshog* (case C–99/00). The ECJ ruled that where there was a right for a party to seek to appeal against the decision under challenge, that was not a final court. It followed that if there was no right to appeal against the decision then that court was a 'final court' regardless of its status in the judicial hierarchy.

In *Lyckeshog* case the ECJ was also referred the question of whether national courts are 'final' courts for the purposes of Article 234(3) if an appeal against their decision is possible but only with leave to appeal having been granted by a higher court (or the lower court itself). The ECJ noted that the function of the obligation on courts against whose decisions there was no judicial remedy to refer questions to the ECJ was to prevent a body of national case law coming into being that was inconsistent with the requirements of Community law. The ECJ argued that 'the fact that examination of the merits of such appeals is subject to a prior declaration of admissibility by the supreme court does not have the effect of depriving the parties of a judicial remedy' (para 16). In coming to this conclusion, the ECJ noted that 'uncertainty as to the interpretation of the law applicable, including Community law, may give rise to review, at last instance, by the supreme court' (para 17). In this light, the ECJ concluded that, where leave depends on permission from a superior 'final' court, that latter court is obliged to grant the requested leave and make a reference to the ECJ when a question of EC law arises. Any other course would frustrate the purpose of Article 234 and amount to a denial of the individual's Community law rights.

10.5.3 When does a 'question' of EC law arise?

Whether a national court is a final court or merely one that has a discretion to refer cases to the ECJ, the national judge must consider if a case raises a 'question' of Community law such that a ruling from the ECJ is *necessary* to enable it to give judgment'. If the case does raise such a question then, if the court is a final court, the judge must, in principle, refer the case to the ECJ. Of course, not every case where a party relies on Community law may be said to involve a 'question' of EC law. Only those cases where the point of EC law concerned is in doubt really involve a question of law requiring the ECJ's interpretation.

Guidelines on these matters have been supplied by the ECJ and by national courts. It is submitted that as the ultimate arbiter on matters of Community law the ECJ must decide whether a 'question' of EC law arises. We can see a tension in relation to this issue. On the one hand the ECJ has been keen to encourage references to be made to ensure uniformity of application of EC law. On the other hand, there has been the concern that overloading the ECJ with references diminishes the effectiveness of judicial protection for parties because of delay this produces. The ECJ has also been mindful of national courts being reluctant to refer cases that are too 'obvious' seriously to raise EC law issues. It has sought to find a rule that allows national courts not to refer cases where there clearly is no danger that they will misinterpret the issue of EC concerned.

The ECJ considered a number of relevant matters in this context in the important case of *CILFIT Srl* (case 283/81). The reference was from the Italian Supreme Court, the Cassazione, and concerned national courts' mandatory jurisdiction under Article 234(3). On a literal reading of Article 234(2) and (3) it would appear that the question of whether 'a decision on a matter of Community law if necessary' only applies to the national courts' discretionary jurisdiction under Article 234(2). Thus in principle the highest national court would have to refer all questions of EC law to the ECJ even if not strictly necessary to resolve the case before it. This would have been an absurd result whereby the lower courts had more discretion than the supreme court. However, in *CILFIT* the ECJ held that:

> it followed from the relationship between Article 177(2) and (3) [now 234(2) and (3)] that the courts or tribunals referred to in Article 177(3) [now 234(3)] have the same discretion as any other national court or tribunal to ascertain whether a decision on a question of Community law is necessary to enable them to give judgment.

Thus both final courts and other courts have the power to consider if the 'question' of EC law that requires resolution through a ruling from the ECJ is actually material to deciding the case before them. While it is clearly not necessary for 'final' courts to refer questions of Community law in every case, a lax approach by such courts towards their need to refer, resulting in non-referral, may lead to an incorrect application of Community law and, for the individual concerned, a denial of justice. Since *Köbler* (case C–224/01), 'final' courts choosing not to make a reference run the risk of incurring liability under *Francovich* should they get the point of EC law significantly wrong (see 9.2.2.2).

10.5.3.1 *A doctrine of precedent in EC law*

One way in which the ECJ has allowed national courts to avoid referring cases was the early development of a form of principle of precedent. The doctrine was first invoked in the sphere of EC law by Advocate-General Lagrange in *Da Costa en Schaake NV* (cases 28–30/62), in the context of a reference on a question of interpretation almost identical to a matter already decided by the Court in *Van Gend en Loos* (case 26/62). Like *CILFIT Srl*, it arose in a case concerning the court's mandatory jurisdiction under Article 234(3). While asserting that Article 234(3) 'unqualifiedly' required national courts to submit to the ECJ 'every question of interpretation raised before the court', the Court added that this would not be necessary if the question was materially identical with a question which had already been the subject of a preliminary ruling in a similar case. This was an important step because it established the ECJ as laying down general interpretations that could and should be followed by all the national courts rather than individual rulings only addressed to the particular court that made the reference.

However, the *Da Costa* criteria are not foolproof and have been criticised as providing national courts with an excuse not to refer, undermining the very purpose of Article 234(3). In *R v Secretary of State for the Home Department, ex parte Sandhu* (*The Times*, 10 May 1985), the House of Lords was faced with a request for a ruling on the interpretation of certain provisions of Regulation 1612/68 (concerning rights of residence of members of the family of workers), in the context of a claim by an Indian, the divorced husband of an EC national, threatened with deportation from the UK as a result of his divorce. The *Da Costa* criteria were cited, as was *Diatta v Land Berlin* (case 267/83), a case dealing with the rights of residence of a *separated* wife living apart from her husband, which was decided in the wife's favour. The House of Lords found that the matter had already been interpreted in *Diatta*, and, on the basis of certain statements delivered *obiter* in *Diatta*, decided not to refer. On their Lordships' interpretation Mr Sandhu was not entitled to remain in the UK.

The existence of a previous decision may not negate a national court's obligation to refer under Article 234(3) where the matter involves the legality of an *EC measure* (as opposed to a challenge to Member State measures). The ECJ has always been very concerned to ensure that it has a monopoly on declaring EC measures invalid rather than see national courts do so. Thus it made clear in *Gaston Schul v Minister van Landbouw* (case C–461/03) that invalidity cases should always be referred by final courts. This case involved a question as to the validity of Article 4(1)–(2) of Commission Regulation 1423/95 on import rules for products in the sugar sector ([1995] OJ L141/16). The provisions corresponded with those in another regulation (1484/95) which had been declared invalid by the ECJ in an earlier decision (*Kloosterbooer Rotterdam*, case C–317/99). The Dutch court in *Gaston* therefore asked whether it was still subject to the mandatory obligation to refer the question of validity to the ECJ under Article 234(3). The ECJ held that questions of *validity* of EC law differed from questions of *interpretation*, and a reference should always be made, even where there is an earlier ruling dealing with corresponding provisions in another measure (para 25). The possible time delay was not a justification for changing the position that questions of invalidity are only for the ECJ to decide upon (para 23).

10.5.3.2 *Acte clair*

For some time, it seemed that once a relevant 'question' of EC law had arisen before a final court, so long as the point had not been previously ruled upon by ECJ, the national court must make a reference. This was so even if the point of law was very simple and incapable of more than one interpretation. The ECJ was under some pressure from the highest courts within the Member States to allow them a means of not referring such cases which they felt they could safely rule upon themselves. The ECJ had no means to compel referral and faced the embarrassing prospect of final courts in Member States declining to pass cases on to it according to a variety of different national principles of interpretation. The solution fashioned by the ECJ was to create an EC law exception to Article 234(3) allowing final courts not to refer cases where the issue of law is particularly obvious. This is known as *acte clair*.

Acte clair is a doctrine originating in French administrative law whereby, if the meaning of a provision is clear, no 'question' of interpretation arises. The ECJ eventually accepted a very limited version of *acte clair* in *CILFIT Srl* (case 283/81) in the context of a question from the Italian Cassazione (Supreme Court) concerning its obligation under Article 234(3). The national court asked if Article 234 created an absolute obligation to refer, or was referral conditional on a prior finding of a reasonable interpretative doubt in relation to the question of EC law? The ECJ summarised its case law thus far saying that there was no need to refer if the matter was (a) irrelevant, (b) materially identical to a question already the subject of a preliminary ruling, or (c) so obvious as to leave 'no scope for reasonable doubt'. This third criteria may be taken as endorsing a version, albeit a narrow one, of *acte clair*. Of particular importance to its third criterion is the Court's rider that, in deciding whether a matter was free from doubt, account must be taken of the specific characteristics of Community law, its particular difficulties, and the risk of divergence in judicial interpretation. The ECJ also required the national court to consider each of the different language versions of the EC law measure under consideration. Thus, if *acte clair* is to be invoked by a final court so as not to refer a case to the ECJ, the issue of EC law must meet the *CILFIT* criteria. This will be rare. As such, the ECJ did not actually cede much power to national courts through the *acte clair* doctrine. It set the benchmark so high that, whilst theoretically possible, in practice final courts will find it difficult to safely conclude that there is no 'question' of EC law requiring resolution. This means that whilst formally paying deference to the expertise of the national courts, the ECJ has maintained its monopoly over interpretation. The ECJ has however been urged by some commentators to relax the *CILFIT* criteria in recent years to help reduce the burden of its caseload.

The ECJ's caution is probably justified as there is some danger that national courts acting in accordance with their own views without seeking a reference may make errors of interpretation even in relation to matters they consider to be 'obvious'. This was revealed in the Court of Appeal in the case of *R v Henn* ([1978] 1 WLR 1031). There Lord Widgery suggested that it was clear from the case law of the Court of Justice that a ban on the import of pornographic books was not a quantitative restriction within Article 28 (ex 30) of the EC Treaty (post Lisbon, Article 34 TFEU). A subsequent referral on this matter by the House of Lords revealed that it undoubtedly was. Lord Diplock, giving judgment in the House of Lords ([1981] AC 850), warned English judges not to be too ready to hold that because the meaning of an English text seemed plain to them no question of interpretation was involved: the ECJ and the English courts have very different styles of interpretation and may ascribe different meanings to the same provision. He did, however, approve a version of *acte clair* consistent with that of the ECJ in *Da Costa en Schaake NV* and *CILFIT Srl* in *Garland v British Rail Engineering Ltd* ([1983] 2 AC 751) when he suggested that where there was a 'considerable and consistent line of case law' from the ECJ the answer would be 'too obvious and inevitable' to be capable of giving rise to what could properly be called a question within the meaning of Article 234.

Moreover, the doctrine, depending as it does on a subjective assessment as to what is clear, can all too easily be used as a means of avoiding referral. This appears to have occurred in *Minister of the Interior v Cohn-Bendit* ([1980] 1 CMLR 543). In this case, heard by the French Conseil d'État, the supreme administrative court, Cohn-Bendit sought to invoke an EC directive to challenge a deportation order made by the French authorities. Certain provisions of the directive had already been declared by the ECJ to be directly effective (*Van Duyn v Home Office* (case 41/74); see Chapter 5). Despite urgings from the Commissaire du Gouvernement, M Genevois, that in such a situation the Conseil d'État must either follow *Van Duyn* and apply the directive or seek a ruling from the Court under Article 234(3), the Conseil d'État declined to do either. In its opinion, the law was clear. The directive was not directly effective.

10.5.3.3 *The question may not be relevant to the case*

The ECJ had confirmed in *CILFIT* that there was no obligation to refer questions relating to EC law that were not relevant to the case before the national court. This is in one sense obvious but there is potential for final national courts to misuse this discretion so as to decline to refer cases that should be referred. A court may avoid its obligations under Article 234(3) by deciding the case before it without considering the possibility of referral (see, eg, *Mees v Belgium* [1988] 3 CMLR 137, Belgian Conseil d'État). In *Wellcome Foundation Ltd v Secretary of State for Social Services* ([1988] 1 WLR 635) the House of Lords, in considering the factors to be taken into account by a licensing authority in issuing a licence to parallel import a trade-mark medicine, thought it 'highly undesirable to embark on considerations of Community law which might have necessitated a referral to the Court of Justice under Article 177 [now 234]'. This suggests the national court did not consider closely enough the relevance of EC law to the case in question.

In contrast, the German federal constitutional court has emphasised national courts' duty to refer under Article 234(3), according to the *CILFIT* criteria, in the strongest terms. In quashing the German Bundesfinanzhof's decision on the direct effects of directives in *Re VAT Directives* ([1982] 1 CMLR 527), *Kloppenburg v Finanzamt Leer* ([1989] 1 CMLR 873), it held that a court subject to Article 234(3) which deliberately departs from the case law of the ECJ and fails to make a reference under that article is acting in breach of Article 101 of the German constitution. The principle of *acte clair* could not operate where there existed a ruling from the ECJ to the contrary (*Re VAT exemption* [1989] 1 CMLR 113). In *Re Patented Feedingstuffs* ([1989] 2 CMLR 902), the same court declared that it would review an 'arbitrary' refusal by a court subject to Article 234(3) to refer to the ECJ. A refusal would be arbitrary:

(a) where the national court gave no consideration at all to a reference in spite of the accepted relevance of Community law to the judgment and the court's doubt as to the correct answer

(b) where the law consciously departs in its judgment from the case law of the ECJ on the relevant questions, and nevertheless does not make a reference or a fresh reference

(c) where there is not yet a decisive judgment of the ECJ on point, or such judgments may not have provided an exhaustive answer to the relevant questions or there is a more than remote possibility of the ECJ developing its case law further, and the national court exceeds to an indefensible extent the scope of its necessary judicial discretion, as where there may be contrary views of the relevant question of Community law which should obviously be given preference over the view of the national court.

It is suggested that these principles, applied in good faith, would ensure that a reference to the ECJ will be made in the appropriate case. Although a decision of a domestic court rather than of the ECJ, these principles should prove useful to the courts from all the Member States.

10.5.4 Article 234(2): Courts that have a discretion whether to refer or not

Courts or tribunals which do not fall within Article 234(3) enjoy, according to the ECJ, an unfettered discretion in the matter of referrals. This reflects the importance of the cooperative nature of the relationship between the ECJ and national courts. The ECJ has sought to respect the unfettered jurisdiction of national courts, where a case falls under Article 234(2), by refraining from being prescriptive about when cases should be referred to it. A court or tribunal at any level is free, 'if it considers that a decision on the question is necessary to enable it to give judgment', to refer to the ECJ in any kind of proceedings, including interim proceedings (*Hoffman-La Roche AG v Centrafarm Vertriebsgesellschaft Pharmazeutischer Erzeugnisse mbH* (case 107/76)), at any stage in the proceedings. In *De Geus en Uitdenbogerd v Robert Bosch GmbH* (case 13/61) the Court held that national courts have jurisdiction to refer whether or not an appeal is pending; the ECJ is not even concerned to discover whether the decision of the national judge has acquired the force of *res judicata*. However, following *Pardini* (case 338/85) and *Grogan* (case C–159/90), if proceedings have been terminated and the Court is aware of this fact, it may refuse jurisdiction on the grounds that its ruling is not necessary to enable the national court to give judgment.

10.5.4.1 *Courts may make a referral even where there is a previous ECJ ruling on the issue*

Even if the ECJ has already ruled on a similar question, national courts are not precluded from requesting a further ruling. This point was made in *Da Costa en Schaake NV* (cases 28–30/62). There the Court held, in the context of a reference for interpretation of a question substantially the same as that referred in *Van Gend en Loos*, that the Court should retain a legal right to depart from its previous judgments. It may recognise its errors in the light of new facts. It ruled in similar terms in the context of a request concerning the effect of a prior ruling of validity in *International Chemical Corporation SpA v Amministrazione delle Finanze dello Stato* (case 66/80). Here it held that while national courts could assume from a prior declaration of invalidity that the regulation was invalid, they should not be deprived of an opportunity to refer the same issue if they have a 'real interest' in making a further reference.

10.5.4.2 *National Courts can ignore national rules of precedent in order to refer cases*

This discretion to refer is in no way affected by national rules of precedent within the Member State. This important principle was established in the case of *Rheinmühlen-Düsseldorf* (case 146/73). In this case, which concerned an attempt by a German cereal exporter to obtain an export rebate under Community law, the German federal tax court (the Bundesfinanzhof), hearing the case on appeal from the Hessian tax court (Hessische Finanzgericht), had quashed the Hessian court's judgment and remitted the case to that court for a decision on certain issues of fact. The Hessian court was not satisfied with the Bundesfinanzhof's ruling since questions of Community law were involved. It sought a ruling from the ECJ on the interpretation of the Community law, and also on the question of whether it was permissible for a lower court to refer in this way when its own superior court had already set aside its earlier judgment on appeal. On an appeal by Rheinmühlen-Düsseldorf to the Bundesfinanzhof challenging the Hessian court's right to refer to the ECJ, the Bundesfinanzhof itself referred certain questions to the Court of Justice. The principal question, raised in both cases, was whether Article 234 gave national courts an unfettered right to refer or whether that right is subject to national provisions whereby lower courts are bound by the judgments of superior courts.

The Court's reply was in the strongest terms. The object of the preliminary rulings procedure, the Court held, was to ensure that in all circumstances the law was the same in all Member States. No provision of domestic law can take away the power provided by Article 234. The lower court must be free to make a reference if it considers that the superior court's ruling could lead it to give judgment contrary to Community law. It would only be otherwise if the question put by the lower court were substantially the same. The ECJ's view may be compared with that of Wood J in the Employment Appeal Tribunal in *Enderby v Frenchay Health Authority* ([1991] ICR 382). Here he suggested that lower English Courts were bound even in matters of Community law by decisions of their superior courts; thus they should not make references to the ECJ but should leave it to the House of Lords, a fortiori when the House has decided on a particular issue that British law does not conflict with EC law. Wood J's observations are clearly at odds with Community law. It appears that *Rheinmühlen-Düsseldorf* was not cited before the tribunal. A reference to the ECJ was subsequently made in this case by the Court of Appeal ([1992] IRLR 15) resulting in a ruling (case C–127/92) and a decision on an important issue of equal pay for work of equal value contrary to that of Wood J and in the claimant's favour.

10.5.4.3 *How should non-final courts exercise their discretion to refer?*

When the national court hears a case in which there arises a question of EC law a number of factors will obviously have to be taken into account in deciding whether or not to refer. These are largely questions for domestic courts according to the particular features of the domestic legal system. They have not been subject to detailed scrutiny by the ECJ because they are largely outside its jurisdiction.

There has been some interesting discussion in the lower courts of the UK on this question. In an early opinion, Lord Denning in *HP Bulmer Ltd v J Bollinger SA* ([1974] Ch 401) sitting in the Court of Appeal adopted a broad approach which required the national judge to consider a wide range of factors before making a reference. He suggested that a decision would only be 'necessary' if it was 'conclusive' to the judgment. Even then it would not be necessary if:

(a) the ECJ had already given judgment on the question or

(b) the matter was reasonably clear and free from doubt.

Although the criteria in both cases are similar, the first and third *CILFIT Srl* criteria are clearly stricter; it would be easier under Lord Denning's guidelines to decide that a decision was not 'necessary'.

If courts within the area of discretionary jurisdiction consider, applying the *CILFIT* criteria, that a decision from the ECJ is necessary, how should they exercise their discretion? With regard to other factors, Lord Denning suggested in *HP Bulmer Ltd v J Bollinger SA* that time, cost, workload of the ECJ, and the wishes of the parties should be taken into account by national courts in the exercise of their discretion. In a contrasting view, however, Bingham J in *Commissioners of Customs and Excise v Samex ApS* ([1983] 3 CMLR 194) said that factors such as time and cost need to be treated with care, weighing the fact that deferring a referral may in the end increase the time and cost to the parties: there may be cases where it is appropriate to refer at an early stage. He also stressed the ECJ's 'panoramic' view of the Community law system that a national judge would find it impossible to match. The more difficult and uncertain the issue of EC law, the greater the likelihood of appeal, requiring, in the end, a referral to the ECJ under Article 234(3). The workload of the ECJ is an increasing problem and no doubt a reason for some modification in recent years of its open-door policy. However, whereas it may justify non-referral in a straightforward case, it should not prevent referral where the point of EC law is difficult or novel. The *CILFIT* criteria should operate to prevent unnecessary referrals.

On the question of timing, the ECJ has suggested that the facts of the case should be established and questions of purely national law settled before a reference is made (*Irish Creamery Milk Suppliers Association v Ireland* (cases 36 and 71/80)). This would avoid referrals being made too early, and enable the Court to take cognisance of all the features of fact and law which may be relevant to the issue of Community law on which it is asked to rule. A similar point was made by Lord Denning MR in *HP Bulmer Ltd v J Bollinger SA* ([1974] Ch 401) ('decide the facts first') and approved by the House of Lords in *R v Henn* ([1981] AC 850). However, Lord Diplock did concede in *R v Henn* that in an urgent, eg interim, matter, where important financial interests are concerned, it might be necessary to refer *before* all the facts were found.

The wishes of the parties also need to be treated with caution. If the point of EC law is relevant (which under *CILFIT* it must be) and difficult or uncertain, clearly *one* of the parties' interests will be better served by a referral. As Templeman LJ said in the Court of Appeal in *Polydor Ltd v Harlequin Record Shops Ltd* ([1980] 2 CMLR 413) when he chose to refer a difficult point of EC law in proceedings for an interim injunction, 'it is the right of the plaintiff [claimant] to go to the European Court'. Furthermore, the ECJ has held that the question of referral is one for the national court and that a party to the proceedings in the context of which the reference is made cannot challenge a decision to refer, even if that party thinks that the national court's findings of fact are inaccurate (*SAT Fluggesellschaft mbH v European Organization for the Safety of Air Navigation* (case C–364/92)).

Another factor which might point to an early referral, advanced by Ormrod LJ in *Polydor Ltd v Harlequin Record Shops Ltd* is the wider implications of the ruling. In *Polydor Ltd v Harlequin Record Shops Ltd* there were a number of similar cases pending. The issue, which was a difficult one, concerned the protection of British copyright law in the context of an international agreement between the EC and Portugal, and affected not merely the parties to the case but the record industry as a whole.

Finally, in *R v Henn* Lord Diplock suggested that in a criminal trial on indictment it might be better for the question to be decided by the national judge and reviewed if necessary through the hierarchy of the national courts. Although this statement could be invoked to counter spurious defences based on EC law, and unnecessary referrals, it is submitted that where a claim is genuinely based on EC law, and a ruling from the ECJ would be conclusive of the case, delay would serve no purpose. The time and cost of the proceedings would only be increased.

10.6 What is the temporal effect of a ruling from the ECJ?

There are a number of issues concerning the effect of a preliminary ruling by the ECJ. These ramifications can often go well beyond the particular proceedings that led to the reference. Particularly because of development of what is effectively a doctrine of precedent discussed earlier, important rulings from the ECJ can affect legal relations across all the Member States and lead to wide economic and social impacts. There have therefore been some cases in which the ECJ has limited the effects of its rulings so that they are only 'prospective' and do not affect prior legal relations. More narrowly, clearly a ruling from the ECJ under Article 234 is binding in the individual case and will govern the legal effects between the parties. Given Member States' obligation under Article 10 (ex 5) EC to 'take all appropriate measures . . . to ensure fulfilment of the obligations arising out of this treaty or resulting from action taken by the institutions of the Community' the ruling should also be applied in all subsequent cases. This does not preclude national courts from seeking a further ruling on the same issue should they have a 'real interest' in making a reference (*Da Costa en Schaake* (cases 28–30/62)—interpretation; *International Chemical Corporation SpA* (case 66/80)—validity).

10.6.1 Rulings involving interpretation are generally retrospective in effect

The question of the temporal effect of a ruling on persons not party to the case, namely whether it should take effect retroactively (*ex tunc*, ie from the moment of entry into force of the provision subject to the ruling) or only from the date of judgment (*ex nunc*) is less clear. In *Defrenne v Sabena (No 2)* (case 43/75) the

Court was prepared to limit the effect of the then Article 119 (now 141) to future cases (including *Defrenne* itself) and claims lodged prior to the date of judgment. 'Important considerations of legal certainty', the Court held, 'affecting all the interests involved, both public and private, make it impossible to reopen the question as regards the past'. The Court was clearly swayed by the arguments of the British and Irish governments that a retrospective application of the equal pay principle would have serious economic repercussions on parties (ie, employers) who had been led to believe they were acting within the law.

However, in *Ariete SpA* (case 811/79) and *Salumi Srl* (cases 66, 127 and128/79) the Court made it clear that *Defrenne* was to be an exceptional case. As a general rule an interpretation under Article 234 of a rule of Community law 'clarifies and defines where necessary the meaning and scope of that rule as it must be or ought to be understood and applied *from the time of its coming into force*' (emphasis added). A ruling under that article must therefore be applied to legal relationships arising prior to the date of the judgment provided that the conditions for its application by the national court are satisfied. The court said:

> It is only exceptionally that the Court may, in the application of the principle of legal certainty inherent in the Community legal order and in taking into account the serious effects which its judgments might have as regards the past, on legal relationships established in good faith, be moved to restrict for any person concerned the opportunity of relying on the provision as thus interpreted with a view to calling into question those legal relationships.

Moreover, 'such a restriction may be allowed *only* in the actual judgment ruling upon the interpretation sought' and 'it is for the Court of Justice *alone* to decide on the temporal restrictions as regards the effects of the interpretation which it gives'.

These principles were applied in *Blaizot* (case 24/86) and *Barra* (case 309/85). Both cases involved a claim for reimbursement of the Belgian minerval, based on *Gravier* (case 293/83, see Chapter 23). In both cases the claims were in respect of periods prior to the ECJ's ruling in *Gravier*. In *Barra* it was not disputed that the course for which the minerval had been charged was vocational; but Blaizot's university course in veterinary medicine was, the defendant university argued, not vocational, not being within the scope of the *Gravier* ruling.

Since *Barra's* case fell squarely within *Gravier* and the Court had imposed no temporal limits on the effect of its judgment in *Gravier* itself, that ruling was held to apply retrospectively in *Barra's* favour. *Blaizot*, on the other hand, raised new issues. In deciding that university education could, and a course in veterinary science did, constitute vocational training the Court, clearly conscious of the impact of such a ruling on Belgian universities if applied retroactively, decided that 'important considerations of legal certainty' required that the effects of its ruling should be limited on the same lines as *Defrenne*—that is, to future cases and those lodged prior to judgment.

Unless the Court can be persuaded to change its mind and reconsider the question of the temporal effect of a prior ruling in a subsequent case when *no* new issues are raised, the question of the temporal effect will need to be considered in every case in which a retrospective application may give rise to serious repercussions as regards the past. Yet it is in the nature of this kind of ruling that it and, therefore, its consequences are unpredictable. Should a party wish, subsequently, to limit the effects of an earlier ruling, it will be necessary to ensure, as in *Blaizot*, that some new issue of EC law is raised.

In *Barber v Guardian Royal Exchange Assurance Group* (case C–262/88) the Court was again persuaded by 'overriding considerations of legal certainty' to limit the effects of its ruling that employers' contracted-out pension schemes fell within the then Article 119 (now 141) EC. Unfortunately the precise scope of the non-retroactivity principle that 'Article 119 [now 141] may not be relied upon in order to *claim entitlement* to a pension with effect prior to that of this judgment (except in the case of workers . . . who have initiated proceedings before this date or raised an equivalent claim under the applicable national law)' was disputed as being unclear. This lack of specificity, a characteristic of the Court's style of judgment, can create problems in the context of rulings on interpretation under Article 234. The Court's judgments can on occasions be too Delphic, leaving too much to be decided by national courts. It has taken a protocol to the Maastricht Treaty and further cases to spell out the precise scope of the *Barber* ruling (see Chapter 27). Only now are the *full* implications of the Court's rulings in *Francovich* (cases C–6, 9/90) and *Marshall (No 2)* (case C–271/91) being revealed.

Despite its commitment to the principle of legal certainty the Court has chosen not to limit the effect of its rulings in a number of cases in which it has introduced new and unexpected principles with significant consequences for Member States and even (in the case of treaty articles) for individuals. It did not limit the effects of its judgment in *Francovich* despite Advocate-General Mischo's warnings as to the 'extremely serious' financial consequences for Member States if the judgment were not so limited: nor did it do so when it laid down a principle of full compensation for breach of a directly effective directive in *Marshall (No 2)*. Where a ruling is likely to result in serious consequences, whether for states or 'public' or private bodies, for example employers, Member States would be advised to take advantage of their opportunity to intervene in Article 234 proceedings as they are entitled to do, to argue against retroactivity, as they did successfully in *Defrenne* and *Barber*. Other 'interested parties' may also apply to intervene.

The effects of the ECJ's strict approach to retroactivity may be mitigated by its more recent approach to Member States' procedural rules. In a number of cases (*IN CO GE '90* (cases C–10 and 22/97) and *EDIS* (case C–231/96)), it has held that the principle of retroactivity should not prevent the application of detailed procedural rules (in these cases relating to limitation of actions) governing legal proceedings under national law, provided that these national rules do not make it 'impossible or excessively difficult' for individuals to exercise their Community rights (see further Chapter 8).

The impact of an interpretation on previous rulings by domestic administrative authorities which conflict with the ECJ's ruling was considered in *Kühne & Heitz NV v Productschap voor Pluimvee en Eieren* (case C–453/00). The case involved a claim for reimbursement of export refunds made by a Dutch administrative authority against Kühne. The latter's objection had been rejected by a court and the claim had therefore become a final decision by the administrative authority. The ECJ then delivered a ruling (*Voogd Vleesimport en-export* (case C–151/93)) which rendered the previous Dutch decision incorrect. Kühne therefore requested a reopening of the administrative procedure. The ECJ held that there was an obligation on administrative authorities to comply with an interpretation given by the Court in respect of all legal relationships, because the effect of a ruling is to clarify and define the meaning of a European rule 'as it ought to have been understood and applied from the time of its coming into force' (para 21). This was subject to the principle of legal certainty, requiring finality of administrative decisions once a reasonable time-limit for legal remedies had expired or those remedies had been exhausted (para 24); in such circumstances, there was no obligation to reopen previous decisions which had become final. However, on the facts of the case, the Dutch authority could reopen its decision, and the ECJ held that in such a situation, where a decision had become final and was based on a misinterpretation of EC law adopted without a preliminary ruling, and the matter had been raised without delay after the ECJ's intepretation, the administrative authority should review its decision.

10.6.2 Rulings as to the validity of EC measures: More flexible temporal effects

The cases considered above relate to rulings on interpretation. Where matters of validity of EC measures are concerned, the Court's approach is more flexible. This is logical because where a prima facie valid EC measure has been in place for some time, the finding that it is invalid may cause serious disruption to those that relied upon it. On grounds of legal certainty there are good arguments to decide in each case what effect the finding of invalidity should have. The ECJ has adopted the same approach to the effects of a ruling of invalidity to those of a successful annulment action, as a result of which the illegal act is declared void. However, arguing from Article 231(2) (ex 174(2)), which enables the Court, in a successful annulment action, to limit the effects of a regulation which it has declared void (see Chapter 12), the Court has limited the effects of a finding of invalidity in a number of cases, sometimes holding the ruling to be purely prospective (ie, for the future only, *excluding* the present case, eg, *Roquette Frères v France* (case 145/79); policy doubted in *Roquette Frères SA v Hauptzollamt Geldern* (case C–228/92), see Chapter 12). The Court has not so far insisted that the effect of a ruling of invalidity can only be limited in the case in which the ruling itself is given. The Court is more likely to be prepared to limit the effects of a ruling on validity than one on interpretation. Where matters of validity are concerned parties will have relied legitimately on the provision in question. A retrospective application of a ruling of invalidity may produce serious economic repercussions: thus it may not be desirable to reopen matters as regards the past. On the other hand too free a use of prospective rulings in matters of interpretation would seriously threaten the objectivity of the law, its application to all persons and all situations. Moreover, as the Court no doubt appreciates, a knowledge on the part of Member States and individuals that the law as interpreted may not be applied retrospectively could foster a dangerous spirit of non-compliance.

10.7 Special limits on references in JHA

Thus far we have discussed the system that operates for references under Article 234. This constitutes the vast majority of cases. There is one notable exception to this system—that of home affairs. When the EC (and EU) came to have powers in the field of JHA, some of the Member States were reluctant to allow easy access to the ECJ from the national courts. This was partly because of concerns that the broad purposive approach to interpretation taken by the ECJ might lead to greater obligations being placed upon Member States than they anticipated. On the other hand, it was clear that there had to be some judicial means of resolving questions of interpretation relating to EC justice and home affairs legislation. The result was a compromise which created special, more restrictive, arrangements in relation to references in this field such that not all national courts can make references to the ECJ.

The first instance of this was in the Maastricht Treaty, more properly known as the Treaty of the European Union (TEU), which introduced the possibility for preliminary references within the JHA second pillar by virtue of Article 35 TEU which relates to police and judicial cooperation issues in criminal and civil cases. Following this, the Treaty of Amsterdam (ToA) led to the introduction of the new Title IV into the EC Treaty relating to asylum and immigration cases. This created a separate preliminary-rulings mechanism in Article 68 EC for questions relating to that title. Thus we have two separate systems for different aspects of JHA. As we shall see below, each has restrictions not found in Article 234.

The ECJ only has jurisdiction in relation to certain limited JHA provisions of the TEU comprising 'framework decisions and decisions' and conventions established under the JHA. Thus, cases regarding certain measures simply cannot be brought before the ECJ for a preliminary ruling. Furthermore, the ECJ only has jurisdiction to hear any references insofar as each Member State accepts its jurisdiction (Article 35 TEU). There is no compulsory jurisdiction. Even then, each Member State has the option of limiting the rights of the national courts to refer a question to the ECJ to courts against whose decision there is no judicial remedy under national law. So far, most Member States have accepted the ECJ's jurisdiction at least as regards 'final' courts and around half have conferred jurisdiction upon all national courts. This 'flexible' approach to jurisdiction has led to confusion, but may also be criticised for the uncertainties and inequalities it introduces into the system: individuals' rights of access to the ECJ will vary depending on the Member State in which the action is brought. There is real danger that there will be a failure of effective legal protection, which is particularly significant because JHA measures touch upon individual liberty. This still may be better than the previous position under the TEU, where there was no such access. The courts of some Member States are availing themselves of the possibility to refer questions in the field of JHA (see Chapter 26).

The Article 68 provisions relating to asylum and immigration in Title IV of the EC Treaty create a different regime as regards the jurisdiction of the ECJ in respect of the provisions in Title IV. Although a preliminary ruling procedure will apply in all Member States to all these provisions, there are certain differences from Article 234. Most notably, only the courts against whose decisions there is no judicial remedy are required to ('shall') make a reference 'if they consider it necessary' to do so. Furthermore, the ECJ will not have jurisdiction in relation to measures taken under new Article 62(1) EC (concerning the crossing of external borders) relating to 'the maintenance of law and order and safeguarding of internal security'. These provisions create holes in the judicial protection offered; unlike the JHA Pillar of the TEU, the ECJ's jurisdiction under Article 234 prior to the ToA applied to the whole of the EC Treaty. The ToA amendments undermine the homogeneity and generality of access to the ECJ. Many important references under Article 234 came from the lower courts: now these courts are, in this new area, precluded from making references. Consequently, individuals seeking a European ruling will be forced to litigate through their national appeal structure. The provision also creates uncertainty: when will circumstances necessitating the maintenance of law and order or safeguarding internal security arise? Indeed, who decides this question? It affects those most in need of protection: an asylum seeker, for example, may not be in a position to exhaust national remedies. Even if he does, he may find he falls outside the ECJ's jurisdiction. This approach, accepted with reluctance by the Commission on the insistence of Member States, hardly matches up with a Union which claims to be based on the rule of law and respect for human rights. The position will be improved if the Lisbon Treaty comes into force because this provides for the normal preliminary rulings procedure to apply to justice and home affairs issues subject to limitations relating to validity of law enforcement and national security (Article 276 TFEU). CFSP, which remains in the TEU, continues by Article 275 TFEU to fall outside the preliminary rulings procedure contained in what will, should the Lisbon Treaty come into force, become Article 267 TFEU.

10.8 The increasing workload of the ECJ: The need for reform

The current system governing preliminary rulings is under stress as, despite the *acte clair* doctrine, the number of references made to the ECJ remains high. With enlargement, the backlog can only get worse. There will probably be an increased number of referrals as an enlarged geographic jurisdiction will lead to a greater number of people (and courts) covered by EU law. The very fact that the new Member States are still new to the EU legal system could mean that they are likely to create initially a disproportionate number of references. This arises from two linked points. The first is that there are more likely to be questions arising in the new Member States as their legal systems adjust to the Union legal order. Further, their courts are less likely to have the experience and confidence to deal with many EU law questions without guidance from the ECJ, especially given that many of the new Member States are relatively new to democracy and a market economy.

There are many proposals to reform the current system to ensure that the ECJ can better provide effective judicial protection by removing the delays in the reference system. The difficulty remains one of how to reduce the number of references without damaging the uniform interpretation of EU law. The easy access of national courts to the ECJ has been the key to the relationship between domestic and EU legal systems. Some have suggested that the ECJ should become a true appeal court which decides for itself which cases to hear by granting or refusing leave to appeal from the national courts. This would require treaty amendments and would be controversial because it would more openly establish the ECJ as the supreme court in the Union legal order. This would look rather too much like a federal state to be politically acceptable to the Member States. Other suggestions have been to create Union Courts located in the Member States (rather like the federal Circuit Courts in the United States of America).

The Treaty of Nice attempted to address the problem by providing in Article 225(3) that the CFI is to have jurisdiction to hear preliminary references in areas specified in the Statute of the Court. As a safety mechanism, the same paragraph further provides that where a 'case requires a decision of principle likely to affect the unity or consistency of Community law' the CFI 'may refer the case to the Court of Justice for a ruling'. Additionally, decisions of the CFI on preliminary references may be subject to review by the ECJ. This possibility is stated to be available 'exceptionally' and 'where there is a serious risk of the unity or consistency of Community law being affected'. In the November 2005 version of the Statute, no areas were allocated to the CFI under Article 225(3).

Once the power in Article 225(3) is exercised, the restriction of access to the ECJ may cut down that Court's workload and, subject to the CFI not being swamped by the cases diverted to it, may reduce the backlog in cases—especially the preliminary references. In any event, this would constitute a significant change in the judicial architecture within the European Union.

More modestly the ECJ itself has introduced new rules into its Rules of Procedures and Statute that allow for expedited procedures to be used in some cases which are simple or raise no new issues. Thus the ECJ is taking steps to devote less resources to cases that do not merit them because they are legally straightforward. This change emphasises the importance of the ECJ in the Union's court system, suggesting a more hierarchical structure to the system than that found in the early days. Unlike the power in Article 225(3) EC, these steps are actually being put into practice. Thus Article 104a provides for an accelerated procedure where the case involves a matter of 'execeptional urgency'. This provision is particularly important in cases involving persons in detention, those facing deportation or children. The court can fix a hearing date within weeks in these cases. Article 104(3) allows the ECJ to dispense with oral hearings and proceed simply by issuing a 'reasoned order' where the case referred raises identical issues upon which the ECJ has already ruled or is free from reasonable doubt. Thus if a national court refers a case that meets the *CILFIT* rules, the ECJ can deal swiftly with the matter. The Statute was also amended by the Nice Treaty so that where no new point of law arises, the ECJ can dispense with the requirement for an Advocate-General's opinion. These procedural steps have helped to focus the ECJ's resources upon cases that really need them because they raise new issues of EU law but they have preserved the crucial right of access that national courts have to refer any question that they wish to.

10.9 Conclusions

The success of the preliminary rulings procedure depends on a fruitful collaboration between the ECJ (and, at some point, the CFI) and the courts of Member States. Generally speaking both sides have played their part in this collaboration. The ECJ has rarely refused its jurisdiction or attempted to interfere with national courts' discretion in matters of referral and application of EC law. National courts have generally been ready to refer; cases in which they have unreasonably refused to do so are rare. Equally rare are the cases in which the ECJ has exceeded the bounds of its jurisdiction without justification. However, this very separation of powers, the principal strength of Article 234, is responsible for some of its weaknesses. The decision whether to refer and what to refer rests entirely with the national judge. No matter how important referral may be to the individual concerned (eg, *Sandhu*) he cannot compel referral; he can only seek to persuade. And although the ECJ will extract the essential matters of EC law from the questions referred it can only give judgment in the context of the questions referred (see *Hessische Knappschaft v Maison Singer et Fils* (case 44/65)). Thus, it is essential for national courts to ask the right questions. As the relevance of the questions can only be assessed in the light of the factual and legal circumstances of the case in hand, these details must also be supplied. A failure to fulfil both these requirements may result in a wasted referral or a misapplication of EC law. Given the increasing pressures on the ECJ, wasted references and the drafting of sloppy questions can also be seen as a waste of the limited judicial resources at the Union level.

As the body of case law from the ECJ has developed and national courts have acquired greater confidence and expertise in applying EC law and ascertaining its relevance to the case before them, there should be less need to resort to Article 234. The initial issue, of whether a decision on a 'question' of EC law arises during the proceedings, has become crucial. As we have seen *CILFIT Srl* (case 283/81) has supplied guidelines to enable national courts to answer this question. Where a lower court is in doubt as to whether a referral is necessary the matter may be left to be decided on appeal. On the other hand, where a final court has the slightest doubt as to whether a decision is necessary, it should always refer—bearing in mind the purpose of Article 234(3) and its particular importance for the individual litigant. The danger that final courts will fail to refer seems to have been one of the factors that influenced the ECJ in its ruling in *Köbler* (Case C–224/01) which allows individuals to sue for damages where a reference was not made when it should have been. This case, along with others like *CILFIT* and *Foglia v Novello* is illustrative of the trend that we have noted whereby the ECJ has been positioning itself not as an equal partner in a horizontally structured relationship, but as a superior court. Some might even say it sees itself as the supreme court for the Union. In so doing, it has sought to put itself firmly in control of the development of European law and not simply to act as the servant of the national courts.

The historical significance of the ECJ's rulings and the Article 234 procedure has been well recognised by courts, commentators and Member States. The current issue of importance for the procedure is the delay inherent in the legal system of the expanded European Union which is jeopardising effective judicial proctection and uniform application of EC law. The solutions to these problems are not clear but the procedural steps taken by the ECJ so far have had some effect in limiting any increase in the length of references if not actually reducing it. Further steps would require serious changes to reduce the number of cases heard by the ECJ which would entail a system of prioritising cases. This would remove the ease of access to the ECJ that has hitherto been so successful. Nevertheless, such a change is probably justified given the growing maturity of the EC law system and the increased familiarity of judges with it. The alternative of increasing delay is just as unattractive as that of some risk of 'wrong' decisions being made by national courts.

FURTHER READING

Alexander, W, 'The temporal effects of preliminary rulings' (1988) 8 YEL 11.

Anagnostaras, G, 'Preliminary problems and jurisdiction uncertainties: The admissibility of questions referred by bodies performing quasi-judicial functions' (2005) 30 EL Rev 878–90.

Anderson, D, 'The admissibility of preliminary references' (1994) 14 YEL 179.

Barnard, C and Sharpston, E, 'The changing face of Article 177 references' (1997) 34 CML Rev 1113.

Bebr, G, 'Arbitration tribunals and Article 177' (1985) 22 CML Rev 498.

—— 'The reinforcement of the constitutional review of Community acts under Article 177 EEC' (1988) 25 CML Rev 684.

Gray, C, 'Advisory opinions and the European Court of Justice' (1983) 8 EL Rev 24.

Koopmans, T, 'The future of the Court of Justice of the European Communities' (1991) 11 YEL 15.

Maher, I, 'National courts as European Community courts' (1994) 14 LS 226.

Nascimbene, B, 'Community Courts in the area of judicial cooperation' (2005) 54 ICLQ 489–97.

O'Keeffe, D, 'Appeals against an order to refer under Article 177 of the EEC Treaty' (1984) 9 EL Rev 87.

—— 'Is the spirit of Article 177 under attack? Preliminary references and admissibility' (1998) 23 ELR 509.

'Quis custodiet the European Court of Justice?' Editorial (1993) 30 CML Rev 905.

Rasmussen, H, 'The European Court's acte clair strategy in CILFIT (1984) 9 CML Rev 242.

—— 'Between self-restraint and activism: A judicial policy for the European Court' (1988) 13 EL Rev 28.

Toth, A, 'The authority of judgments of the European Court of Justice: Binding force and legal effects' (1984) 4 YEL 1.

Tridimas, T, 'The Court of Justice and judicial activism' (1996) 21 EL Rev 199.

Waelbroeck, M, 'May the Court of Justice limit the retrospective operation of its judgments?' (1981) 1 YEL 115.

Watson, J, 'Experience and problems in applying Article 177 EEC' (1986) 23 CML Rev 207.

11

Enforcement actions

11.1 Introduction

We have already seen that it is vital for the success of the Union that Member States comply with their obligations under the EC Treaty (Article 10 (ex 5) EC; post Lisbon, Article 4 TEU). Member States should ensure not only that they implement Community legislation by the due date, but also that they comply with decisions made by the Commission (eg, in the field of state aid), and judgments of the Court of Justice made under Article 234 EC (ex 177; post Lisbon, Article 267 TFEU). There is a danger that this obligation would be ineffective were there no mechanism by which Member States that infringe Community law could be pursued. Indeed, the Commission would find it much more difficult to fulfil one of its main objectives, which is to ensure compliance with treaty obligations (Article 211 EC (ex 155); post Lisbon, Article 19(1) TEU), if it did not have strong tools to support it in this task. Whilst Article 234 relies heavily on the involvement of individuals and allows them to enforce their rights, enforcement actions are not aimed at providing redress for individuals. The focus is enforcement of EC law. The key provision in this context is Article 226 (ex 169; post Lisbon, Article 258 TFEU). Article 226 EC is also a centralised system, which—certainly in its early approach—seemed based on a traditional intergovernmental approach on roles and relationships; which has seemed more political than judicial on the way it developed. By contrast with the Article 234 procedure, it has seemed ineffective. Looking at the development of Article 226, we can, however, identify a shift through the inclusion of the possibility of imposing fines for non-compliant Member States. The inclusion of provisions whereby a Member State may be brought before the European Court of Justice (ECJ) for non-compliance and may be fined for continued non-compliance, is important not just in terms of the effective implementation of EC law. It also illustrates certain supranational elements in the Union structure. As we shall see, this has been reinforced by the Commission's and the ECJ's approach to the imposition of fines.

11.2 Outline of enforcement mechanism

The principal mechanism provided by the treaty to pursue infringements of EC law by Member States is the direct action before the ECJ under Article 226 EC, which provides:

> If the Commission considers that a Member State has failed to fulfil an obligation under this Treaty, it shall deliver a reasoned opinion on the matter after giving the state concerned the opportunity to submit its observations.
>
> If the state concerned does not comply with the opinion within the period laid down by the Commission the latter may bring the matter before the Court of Justice.

A second procedure, in similar terms, provides for action by Member States under Article 227 EC (ex 170; post Lisbon, Article 259 TFEU).

Also, 'in derogation from the provisions of Articles 226 and 227', the Commission is empowered to bring a Member State before the Court under Article 88(2) (ex 93(2); post Lisbon, Article 108 TFEU) (infringement of Community rules on state-aid provision, see Chapter 31), Article 95(9) (ex 100a(4); post Lisbon, Article 114 TFEU), para 3 (improper use of derogation procedure provided by Article 95(4), para 1, see Chapter 16) and Article 298 (ex 225; post Lisbon, Article 248 TFEU) (measures taken to protect essential security interests or to prevent serious internal disturbances, see Chapter 20).

11.2.1 Substantive areas covered by Article 226

The Commission's power under Article 226 applies to the whole of the EC Treaty (Article 46 of the Treaty of the European Union (TEU)). In contrast to the position as regards the preliminary reference procedure (see Chapter 10), this power, bringing with it the possibility of the ECJ's jurisdiction, has not been limited in regard to the new Title IV in the EC Treaty introduced by the ToA. The Commission has identified ensuring the proper application of this area as one of its priorities. Conversely, although the ECJ's jurisdiction to interpret the provisions of justice and home affairs (JHA) remaining within the TEU has been introduced by the ToA, the Commission has not been given the power to bring a Member State which has failed in its obligations under these provisions before the ECJ. The impact of the Treaty of Lisbon will be discussed at 11.9 below.

11.2.2 Development of enforcement procedure

Article 226 was not designed as a punitive measure. Until the passing of the TEU (1992) no sanction was provided against Member States found by the ECJ in breach of their obligations; they were merely required 'to take the necessary measures to comply with the judgment of the Court of Justice' (original Article 171 EC). Although normally no time limit was prescribed for Member States' compliance the Court had held (*Commission v Italy* (case 69/86)) that implementation of a judgment must be undertaken immediately and must be completed within the shortest possible time. Where a state failed to comply with these obligations the Commission could only seek to enforce the judgment by further proceedings for breach of original Article 171 (now 228(1) EC; post Lisbon, Article 260 TFEU). While few such actions were taken in the early days of the Community, their number increased alarmingly in the course of the 1980s. As a result Article 228 was amended by the TEU to allow the Commission, subject to the Court's approval, to impose fines and penalties on Member States which had failed to comply with a judgment against them in Article

226 proceedings. The Commission now takes decisions under this provision, and while most of these have not necessitated a fine being imposed by the ECJ, there have been a number of high-profile cases (see 11.7 below) which have.

11.3 Purpose of enforcement actions

The purpose of Article 226 EC is threefold. First, and primarily, it seeks to *ensure compliance* by Member States with their Community obligations. Secondly, it provides a valuable non-contentious *procedure for the resolution of disputes* between the Commission and Member States over matters of Community law: at least one-third of all Article 226 EC proceedings are settled at the preliminary informal stage. Finally, where cases do reach the ECJ they serve not only to bring particular breaches of EC law to light but also to *clarify* the law for the benefit of all Member States. The enforcement procedure is not intended to provide redress to individuals, a fact certainly reinforced by the limited approach taken to allowing involvement of individuals in the process, as we shall see.

It is no doubt on account of the latter function that the Court has held that even if a state has complied with its obligations prior to the hearing before the Court, the Commission is entitled to judgment; it is not necessary for the Commission to show the existence of a 'legal interest' (*Commission v Italy (Re Ban on Pork Imports)* (case 7/61)). It is in the general interest of the Community to obtain a declaration of any failure to fulfil obligations under the treaty, because this may assist other Member States in ensuring that they comply with Community law (*Commission v France* (case C–333/99), para 23).

11.4 Member States' failure to fulfil an obligation

11.4.1 Member States as defendants

Although national governments appear before the Court as defendants in an Article 226 action, proceedings are brought against the *state*. Thus they may be brought in respect of a failure on the part of *any* agency of that state, executive, legislative, or judicial. The responsibility of the state is engaged 'whatever the organ of the state whose action or inaction constitutes a failure, even if it concerns an institution which is constitutionally independent' (*Commission v Belgium* (case 77/69)).

The Commission, on the basis of the *Lyckeskog* case (Case C–99/00) regarding the obligation on the courts of member states to refer questions to the ECJ (discussed in Chapter 10) and the fact that the Swedish Supreme Court referred very few questions, sent a reasoned opinion to Sweden (see Bernitz, in Further Reading below). It seems that the Swedish authorities have sought to negotiate a conclusion to this matter, and proposed an amendment to the Swedish system, so the matter has not come before the ECJ. Nonetheless, it suggests that the Commission is moving on from its hitherto preferred approach of publicising the national courts' failures in its annual reports on the monitoring and application of Union law and is prepared to take action against Member States for the failures of their courts, judicial independence notwithstanding. In this, the Commission is in line with the ECJ's approach with regard to the doctrine of state liability in *Köbler v Austria* (case C–224/01) (see Chapter 9). Note, though, that a failure by domestic courts or administrative authorities may be based on a problem with the legislation which these bodies have to apply. In *Commission v Italy* (case C–129/00), Italian legislation on the repayment of tax levied in breach of Community law was ambiguous with regard to the burden of proof in establishing whether the costs incurred as a result of having paid such a tax had been passed on to third parties. Some court judgments imposed that burden on the person who had paid the tax in a manner contrary to Community law. The ECJ confirmed that an action could be brought under Article 226 EC in these circumstances, and noted that a provision open to judicial constructions which could be interpreted both in line with, and contrary to, Community law was not sufficiently clear. The ECJ concluded that Italy had been in breach for failing to amend the legislation to remove the ambiguity. An issue not raised before the Court was the obligation of the domestic courts to interpret legislation in accordance with Community law under the doctrine of indirect effect (see Chapter 5), which would have made it necessary to consider the availability of an Article 226 action for incorrect judicial application of Community law head on. It seems that in a situation such as this, the non-compliance will be found in the legislation itself, rather than the domestic courts' failure to interpret this correctly. It remains to be seen what would happen if a domestic court were to make an error of law in applying a directly applicable provision of Community law.

11.4.2 Meaning of 'failure'

A state's 'failure' may be in respect of any binding obligation arising from Community law. This would cover obligations arising from the EC Treaty and its amending and supplementing treaties; from international agreements entered into by the Community and third countries where the obligation lies within the sphere of Community competence; from EC regulations, directives and decisions; and even from general principles of law recognised as part of Community law where the breach of these principles occurs within the context of an obligation of EC law (see Chapter 6). 'Failure' can include any wrongful act or omission, ranging from a failure to notify an implementation measure, to partial implementation, to faulty implementation, to non-implementation of Community law, or simple maintaining in force national laws or practices incompatible with EC law. The Commission has brought action in the case of relatively minor breaches when this seems to be part of a consistent practice and will also bring actions where the breach is caused by a general administrative practice. In *Commission v Ireland* (case C–494/01), the ECJ accepted that separate individual breaches could together constitute a general and persistent breach, though the Commission will each time have to prove its case on the facts (cf *Commission v Germany* (case C–441/02)).

As the case of *Commission v France* (case C–265/95) also makes clear, the failure to fulfil an obligation may also arise in circumstances where the state has failed to take action to prevent other bodies from breaching EC law. In this case, the French authorities' failure to take action in the face of blockades of imported products was found, following an Article 226 action by the Commission, to be a breach of Article

28 (ex 30) in conjunction with Article 10 (see further Chapter 19, and discussion at 11.6.2 below). Thus failure can include the Member States' positive obligations too.

11.5 Procedure

Notices of Member States' failures may come as a result of the Commission's own enquiries, from (increasing) complaints from the public, or from the European Parliament. The Commission's 25th Annual Report on Monitoring the Application of Community Law for 2007 (COM (2008) 777, 18 November 2008) showed that the number of files increased by 5.9 per cent from the 2006 figure to 3,400. Complaints accounted for 35.9 per cent of the total number of cases, or two-thirds of all cases on issues other than late transposition, an 8.7 per cent decrease from 2006. The Commission itself detected a smaller number of complaints showing a decrease of 9.4 per cent. A major group is that concerning Member States' failure to notify transposition measures: from 2006 to 2007, there was a 32.3 per cent increase.

The sensitive nature of an action under Article 226 is reflected in its procedure. It follows a number of stages. The initial stages, both formal and informal, between the Commission and the Member State, are designed to achieve compliance by persuasion. Only if this fails is it necessary to proceed to the final, judicial stage before the ECJ. The procedure notoriously excludes the involvement of third parties, even if affected by Member States' non-compliance. To some extent the Commission has become aware of this, as it issued a Communication on Relations with Complainants (COM (2002) 141). Despite this, it is important to remember that a complainant does not have a right that the Commission should bring an action; this decision lies within the Commission's broad discretion. Article 226 EC is an elite and exclusive process, and has been described as reflecting an earlier conception of the EU as being part of international law based on intergovernmental relations. Certainly, the informal and pre-judicial stages allow for flexibility and for political considerations to have an impact. The Commission in its Annual Report acknowledges that it has enforcement priorities, and that it will choose to bring cases in areas with the greatest impact on the general good. The Commission's motivation for bringing an action is, in the ECJ's view, irrelevant to the question of whether the case (if it eventually ends up before the ECJ) is admissible.

11.5.1 Informal proceedings

The Commission begins informally with a notification to the state concerned of its alleged failure, to which the state will respond. Interestingly, the Commission notes in its 2007 Annual Report that 70 per cent of complaints are resolved before this preliminary stage. Commentators have noted that the Commission has a broad discretion in terms of the cases it chooses to bring, and even when to conclude them. In some ways, this seems more like a negotiation than the beginning of a judicial process. Where they are not so concluded, the Commission may proceed to the next, formal stage.

11.5.2 **Formal proceedings: First stage**

11.5.2.1 *Formal notice*

The Commission opens proceedings by letters of formal notice, inviting the Member State concerned to submit its observations. In order that the state has a full opportunity to put its case, the Commission must first inform the state of its grounds of complaint. The complaint need not at this stage be fully reasoned, but the state must be informed of *all* the charges which may be raised in an action before the Court. In *Commission v Italy (Re Payment of Export Rebates)* (case 31/69) the Commission alleged that Italy was in breach of its EC obligations in failing to pay certain export rebates to its farmers, required under EC regulations; in opening the proceedings the Commission charged Italy with breaches up to 1967, but failed to mention a number of breaches committed after that date. When the matter came before the Court, the Court refused to consider the later breaches. The Court said that the Member States must be given an adequate and realistic opportunity to make observations on the alleged breach of treaty obligations. In deciding whether a state has had such an opportunity the Court may take into account communications made by the Commission during the informal stage.

The Commission must send a letter of formal notice which is identified as relating to Article 226 proceedings. It seems that a formal letter sent under a different measure will not suffice. In *Commission v France* (case C–230/99), France had notified the Commission under Directive 83/189/EEC (see 16.3.6) of a draft order concerning rubber materials. The Commission felt that, if implemented, the order would affect the free movement of goods and delivered a detailed opinion under the directive, setting out its objections to the proposed French order. France rejected the Commission's opinion and adopted the order. The Commission subsequently sent a reasoned opinion pursuant to Article 226 (see 11.5.2.2 below). The Court ruled that the enforcement action was inadmissible because the Commission had failed to follow the correct procedure by not sending a formal notice before submitting its reasoned opinion. Moreover, a formal notice must allege a prior failure by the Member State to whom it is addressed to comply with Community law, which could not be the case here as the opinion sent under Directive 83/189/EEC related to a draft measure. The ECJ took the view that it would violate the principle of legal certainty should the function of the opinion change, ie, from notification under Directive 83/189/EEC to a letter of formal notice, depending on whether the Member State amended its proposed legislation in accordance with the opinion.

11.5.2.2 *Reasoned opinion*

Following the submission of the state's observations to the Commission, the Commission issues a 'reasoned opinion'. In its 2007 Annual Report, the Commission stated that 85 per cent of the cases are resolved without the need for the Commission to issue this 'opinion'. The reasoned opinion will record the infringement and require the state to take action to end it, normally within a specified time limit. Although it cannot introduce issues not mentioned in the formal notice, this does not mean that the reasoned opinion and the formal notice have to be exactly the same. In particular, the Commission may limit the scope of the enquiry (*Commission v Italy* (case C–279/94)). Further, although the opinion must be 'reasoned' it need not set out the Commission's case in full. In the case of *Commisson v Italy (Re Ban on Pork Imports)* (case 7/61) the Court held, in response to the Italian government's claim that the Commission's reasoned opinion was inadequate, that the reasoned opinion need only contain a coherent statement of the reasons which had convinced the Commission that the Italian government had failed to fulfil its obligations. No formalism was required. The only purpose of the reasoned opinion was to specify the point of view of the Commission in order to inform the government concerned, and, possibly, the Court. The reasoning behind the decision is clear. If the state refuses to accept the Commission's opinion, it may proceed to the second stage before the Court. It will then be for the Court to weigh in detail the merits of the case on both sides.

11.5.2.3 *Challenging a reasoned opinion*

In *Commission v Germany* (case C–191/95) Germany challenged the admissibility of Article 226 proceedings on a number of grounds. The first of these related to the Commission's decision to issue the reasoned opinion for breach of the principle of collegiality. Germany argued that the Commissioners themselves at the time did not have all the facts to enable them to make such a decision; furthermore they had not seen the draft reasoned opinion. The ECJ held that the decision to issue a reasoned opinion could not be described as a measure of administration or management and could not be delegated by the Commissioners themselves to their officers. Nonetheless, this does not mean that the Commissioners have to agree the wording of the reasoned opinion; it is sufficient if they have the information on which the decision to send a reasoned opinion is based.

The ECJ has held (*Alfons Lütticke GmbH v Commission* (case 48/65)) that the reasoned opinion is merely a step in the proceedings; it is not a binding act capable of annulment under Article 230 (ex 173; post Lisbon, Article 263 TFEU) (see Chapter 12). While the defendant state may choose to impugn the Commission's opinion in proceedings under Article 226 before the Court, where the Member State complies with the opinion, a third party, possibly adversely affected by the Commission's opinion, has no equivalent right. However, in *Amministrazione della Finanze dello Stato v Essevi SpA* (cases 142 and 143/80) the Court held that the Commission has no power in Article 226 proceedings to determine conclusively the rights and duties of a Member State. These may only be determined, and their conduct appraised, by a judgment of the Court. The Commission may not, in the opinion which it is obliged to deliver under Article 226, exempt a Member State from compliance with its obligations under the treaty or prevent individuals from relying, in legal proceedings, on the rights conferred on them by the treaty to contest any legislative or administrative measure of a Member State which may be incompatible with Community law. Thus, a third party, dissatisfied with the Commission's opinion, could raise the issue of the legality of the Member State's action indirectly before his national court and seek a referral on the relevant questions of interpretation to the ECJ under Article 234. This was done in *Essevi SpA* in a domestic action for the recovery of taxes levied allegedly in breach of Article 90 (ex 95; post Lisbon, Article 110 TFEU).

The same principle would apply where the Commission has decided in its discretion not to institute or pursue Article 226 proceedings. In *Alfons Lütticke GmbH v Commission* (case 48/65), Alfons Lütticke GmbH had complained to the Commission that its own (German) government was acting in breach of EC law by introducing a levy on imported powdered milk. As an importer of powdered milk the levy affected it adversely. It asked the Commission to take action under Article 226 against Germany. The Commission refused. Germany had since withdrawn the levy and the Commission decided in its discretion not to take action. It was a political compromise. Lütticke, on the other hand, wished to establish the infringement in order to recover for losses suffered while the German law was in force. Since Article 226 gave the Commission a discretion in the matter, there was no way in which its refusal to bring proceedings could be challenged either under Article 230 (annulment action) or Article 232 (ex 175; post Lisbon, Article 265 TFEU) (failure to act) (see Chapters 12 and 13). However, in a parallel action before its national courts in *Alfons Lütticke GmbH v Hauptzollamt Saarlouis* (case 57/65), it succeeded in obtaining a ruling under Article 234 from the ECJ on the direct effects of what is currently Article 90, the article which it alleged the German government had breached. Since the article was found directly effective, it could be applied in the company's favour.

11.5.2.4 *Time limits*

While there are no time limits in respect of the stages leading up to the reasoned opinion, thereby giving both parties time for negotiation, the Commission will normally impose in its reasoned opinion a time limit for compliance. A Member State will not be deemed in breach of its obligations until that time limit has expired. Where the Commission does not impose a time limit the Court has held that a reasonable time must be allowed. A state cannot be relieved of its obligations merely because no time limit has been imposed (*Commission v Italy (Re Premiums for Reducing Dairy Production)* (case 39/72)). The Commission has a complete discretion in the matter of time limits, subject to the possibility of review by the Court. The Court may dismiss an action under Article 226 on the grounds of inadequate time limit. An action by the Commission against Belgium for its failure adequately to implement the *Gravier* Decision (case 293/83) was dismissed on the grounds that the compliance period of 15 days prescribed by the Commission in its reasoned opinion did not give Belgium sufficient time to respond to its complaints, either before or after the issuing of its reasoned opinion (*Commission v Belgium (Re University Fees)* (case 293/85)). On the other hand, in *Commission v Belgium* (case 85/85) a compliance period of 15 days was held to be reasonable in the light of the extensive information provided by the Commission at the informal stage.

11.5.3 **Formal proceedings: Second stage**

If a Member State fails to comply with the Commission's reasoned opinion within the specified time limit, proceedings move to the final, judicial stage before the Court. The Court will examine the situation as it prevailed when the time limit set in the reasoned opinion expired and will not take account of any subsequent changes (*Commission v France* (case C–147/00)). However, the action taken before the Court must be based on the same grounds as stated in the reasoned opinion and may not introduce new grounds (*Commission v Italy* (case C–35/96) and *Commission v Italy* (case C–439/99)). It is possible to limit the subject matter of the proceedings (*Commission v Austria* (case C–203/03)), or to rephrase the grounds for complaint as long as this does not change its substance (*Commission v UK* (case C–305/03)). Moreover, if the Member State concerned amends its legislation in order to comply with EC law, but does so incompletely, the Commission may withdraw its action in part but continue it with regard to the domestic provisions that are not in compliance (*Commission v France* (case C–177/04)).

Again, the initiative rests with the Commission, which '*may* bring the matter before the Court of Justice' (Article 226). No time limits are imposed on the Commission in commencing the second stage; however, this position seems to be qualified by a requirement that the length of the pre-litigation procedure must not have adversely affected the rights of defence of the Member State concerned (*Commission v France* (case C–333/99), para 25). Here the Commission is obliged to set out the subject matter of the dispute, the submissions and a brief statement of the grounds on which the application is based. With regard to the latter it is not enough simply to refer to all the reasons set out in the letter of formal notice and the reasoned opinion (*Commission v Germany* (case C–43/90)).

The judicial stage is not a review procedure, although at this stage the legality of the Commission's reasoned opinion may be reviewed (*Commission v Belgium* (case 293/85)). Here the ECJ, exercising plenary jurisdiction in contentious proceedings, conducts a full enquiry into the merits of the case and decides the matter *de novo*. Interested Member States (but not individuals: *Commission v Italy (Re Import of Foreign Motor Vehicles)* (case 154/85R)) are entitled to intervene in the proceedings. The Commission is entitled to request, and the Court to order, interim measures (eg, *Commission v UK (Re Merchant Shipping Rules)* (case 246/89R); *Commission v Ireland (Re Dundalk Water Scheme)* (case 45/87R)). Application for interim relief may, however, only be made 'by a party to the case before the Court' and where it 'relates to' that case.

11.6 Defences

Many defences to an action under Article 226 have been attempted; few have succeeded. The best defence is clearly to deny the obligation. It may be conditional, for example, on a time limit that has not expired. The Commission is also under an obligation to prove that the breach exists and in doing so the Commission may not rely on any presumption (*Commission v Ireland* (case C–532/03), regarding ambulance services). Member States may also argue about the substantive scope of the obligation they are alleged to have breached, suggesting that their actions fall within the proper scope of the relevant obligation. Where a breach of secondary legislation is alleged, the legislation may be attacked for illegality. Otherwise, the traditional defences of international law offer little hope of success.

11.6.1 Reciprocity

The defence of *reciprocity*, an accepted principle of international law, even entrenched in some Member States' constitutions (eg, France, Article 55), whereby in the event of a breach of his obligations by one party the other party is likewise relieved of his, was rejected by the Court in *Commission v Luxembourg and Belgium (Re Import of Powdered Milk Products)* (cases 90 and 91/63). Here the governments argued that their alleged breach of Article 25 (ex 12) of the EC Treaty would have been legal but for the Commission's failure to introduce certain measures which they were authorised to enact. This argument, based on reciprocity, the Court held, was not applicable in the context of Community law. The Community was a new legal order; it was not limited to creating reciprocal obligations. Community law governed not only the powers, rights and obligations of Member States, but also the *procedures* necessary for finding and sanctioning all violations that might occur.

The defence of reciprocity was also rejected in the context of a failure by another Member State to comply with a similar obligation; it made no difference that Article 226 proceedings had not been instituted against that state in respect of a similar breach (*Commission v France (Re Restrictions on Imports of Lamb)* (case 232/78); *Steinike und Weinlig* (case 78/76)).

11.6.2 Necessity and *force majeure*

Similar reasoning to that advanced in *Commission v Luxembourg and Belgium* led to the rejection of a defence of *necessity* in *Commission v Italy (re ban on pork imports)* (case 7/61). The treaty provided, in Article 226 for procedures to be followed in cases of emergency. This precluded unilateral action on the part of Member States.

A defence based on *force majeure* was rejected in *Commission v Italy (re transport statistics)* (case 101/84). Here Italy was charged with non-implementation of a Community directive; the reason for its non-implementation was that the data-processing centre involved in the implementation of the directive had been bombed. The Court held that while this might amount to *force majeure*, which could provide an excuse for non-implementation, a delay of four and a half years, as in this case, was inexcusable. As the Court said, 'time will erode the validity of the excuse'.

The concept of *force majeure* was considered in the case of *McNicholl v Ministry of Agriculture* (case 296/86), not in Article 226 proceedings, but in order to challenge via the preliminary rulings procedure the forfeiture of a deposit for failing to comply with an export undertaking as required by Community law. The Court held that:

> whilst the concept of *force majeure* does not presuppose an absolute impossibility of performance, it nevertheless requires that non-performance of the act in question be due to circumstances beyond the control of persons pleading *force majeure*, that the circumstances be abnormal and unforeseeable and that the consequences could not have been avoided through the exercise of all due care.

This definition should be equally applicable in Article 226 proceedings. Where it is clear that the fulfilment of a Community obligation will be impossible, a Member State should alert the Commission at the earliest opportunity in order to ascertain whether a compromise arrangement can be made (*Commission v Italy* (case C–349/93)).

The ECJ faced a situation of civil disorder, by French farmers blocking imports of agricultural produce, contrary to Article 28 EC, in *Commission v France* (case C–265/95). Here, despite complaints by the Commission, the French authorities had failed to take any significant action to prevent the demonstrations, arguing that more determined action might lead to more serious breaches of public order or even to social conflict. The ECJ refused to accept these arguments:

> Apprehension of internal difficulties could not justify a failure by a Member State to apply Community law correctly . . . It was for a Member State to guarantee the full scope and effect of that law, to ensure its proper implementation, unless the state could show that action by it could have consequences for public order with which it could not cope.

The government had failed to adduce any evidence of the latter. Although a serious threat to public order might justify non-intervention by the police, that argument could only be adduced with regard to a specific incident, and not, as in the case in question, in a general way, covering all the incidents cited.

11.6.3 Constitutional difficulties

Another defence, frequently raised and consistently rejected by the Court, is based on *constitutional, institutional or administrative difficulties* within a Member State. As the Court held in *Commission v Italy* (case 28/81), a Member State cannot plead the provisions, practices, or circumstances existing in its own legal system in order to justify a failure to comply with obligations resulting from Community directives. The same reasoning would apply to a failure to comply with any other Community obligations (eg, *Commission v Italy (Re Premiums for Reducing Dairy Production)* (case 39/72—regulation)).

Similarly in *Commission v United Kingdom (Re Tachographs)* (case 128/78) the Court refused to accept an argument based on *political* (ie, trade union) difficulties, submitted as justification for a failure to implement a Community regulation on the installation of tachographs.

11.6.4 Factual application

Another popular but equally unsuccessful defence rests on the argument that while Community law may not be applied *de jure*, administrative practices ensure that EC law is in fact applied. This argument was advanced in *Commission v France (Re French Merchant Seamen)* (case 167/73), in an action based on the French Code Maritime. The code was clearly discriminatory, since it required a ratio of three Frenchmen to one foreigner in certain jobs. The French government's argument that the code was not enforced in practice was unsuccessful. Enforcement by administrative practices, the Court held, is not enough. The maintenance of national laws contrary to Union law gives rise to an ambiguous state of affairs, and leaves citizens of a Member State in a state of uncertainty (see also *Commission v Ireland* (case C–381/92)).

Similar reasons led to the rejection of another argument in the same case based on the *direct effects* of Community law. If the Community law in question, in this case what was then Article 7 of the EEC Treaty (now Article 12 (ex 6) EC), were directly effective, argued the French, this would be enough to ensure that the state fulfilled its obligations. The Court did not agree (see also *Commission v Belgium (Re Type Approval Directives)* (case 102/79)).

The Court took a (seemingly) more moderate line in *Commission v Germany (Re Nursing Directives)* (case 29/84). Here it conceded that a defence based on direct effects might succeed if the state's administrative practices guaranteed that the directives would be applied fully and ensured that the legal position was clear and that all persons concerned were fully aware of their rights. These requirements were not, however, found to be satisfied in this case. It is submitted that they will rarely be satisfied. This seems to be borne out in the case of *Commission v Italy* (case 168/85), in which the Court held that the right of citizens to plead directly applicable provisions of the treaty before national courts is only a minimum guarantee and insufficient in itself to ensure full and complete application of the treaty.

11.6.5 Domestic law is in compliance

A variation on the defence of 'factual application' is either that existing domestic law already adequately implements the corresponding European rule, or that the legislation that has been adopted to give effect to such a rule will be interpreted by the courts in accordance with it (in line with the principle of 'indirect effect'; see Chapter 5). The ECJ has accepted that existing domestic law can be sufficient to give effect to an EC directive, even where the words of the domestic measure depart from the text of the directive itself. Provided that the general legal context ensures the full application of a directive in a sufficiently clear and precise manner, a Member State will be deemed to have fulfilled its obligations (see, eg, *Commission v Germany* (case 29/84), para 23; and *Commission v Spain* (case C–58/02), para 26). In *Commission v Spain* (case C–58/02), Spain sought to rely on its existing criminal code provisions on the violation of intellectual property rights as being equivalent to the requirements of the directive on conditional access services (98/84/EC, [1998] OJ L320/54), but this was rejected by the court (see also *Commission v Italy* (case C–372/99) and *Commission v Netherlands* (case C–144/99), discussed in Chapter 16).

Where legislation has been adopted to give effect to an EC obligation, but the wording of that legislation differs from the European text, there is an obvious risk that domestic law may not comply with EC law. However, the mere fact that a different wording has been chosen may not be conclusive evidence of a failure to comply with EC law if there is no corroborating evidence such as court judgments (see, in particular, *Commission v United Kingdom* (case C–300/95), discussed further in Chapter 16).

11.6.6 Treaty derogation

Where there is a derogation from a treaty obligation in the treaty itself, provided the terms of that derogation are satisfied then it goes without saying that an Article 226 EC action would be unsuccessful. In *R v Chief Constable of Sussex, ex parte International Trader's Ferry Ltd* ([1999] 1 CMLR 1320) the House of Lords was asked to consider whether a failure by the Sussex constabulary adequately to police animal-rights protestors seeking to obstruct the export of live cattle from local ports was in breach of Community law. Faced with mounting and unsustainable costs, the chief constable had decided to reduce policing from five to three days per week. Although that failure might constitute a barrier to exports, in breach of Article 29 (ex 34), it was argued that the breach was justified under Article 30 (ex 36), on public-policy grounds. Given that there was no likelihood of obtaining funds from the government, and that the police had a continuing obligation to protect the general public against crime and disorder, the restrictions on policing were neither unreasonable nor disproportionate. This argument was accepted by the House of Lords. The question is, would it have been accepted by the ECJ?

In *Commission v France* (case C–265/95), the Court conceded in principle, it is submitted correctly, that the need to preserve public order is, in an appropriate situation, a valid defence. Given the competing demands of public order in *R v Chief Constable of Sussex* and the necessity, in the face of finite public funds, to strike a balance between them, it may be argued that the House of Lords was right in concluding that the chief constable's decision, taken conscientiously, to reduce policing at the ports was justified, albeit on public-policy or public-order grounds rather than simply on the grounds of cost, and was not disproportionate.

More recently, in *Commission v Italy* (motorbike trailers) (case C–110/05), the ECJ accepted that the Italian rules regarding the use of trailers might constitute a measure having equivalent effect contrary to Article 28 EC, but that the measures was as justified by reasons relating to the protection of road safety . This case makes the point that a Member State may rely on 'imperative requirements' to justify such measures under Article 226 as much as Article 28 (see Chapter 19).

11.7 Consequences of a ruling and of a failure to comply

11.7.1 Obligations following a ruling under Article 226 EC

If the Court finds that the Member State has failed to fulfil its obligations under the EC Treaty, the Member State is 'required to take the necessary measures to comply with the judgment of the Court of Justice' (Article 228 EC). Until the Maastricht Treaty (TEU) the only sanction against a state which had failed to comply with a ruling from the Court under Article 226 was a second action under that Article for failure to comply with its obligations under Article 228. The number of such repeat actions had been steadily increasing. Although the ECJ had provided individuals with a means of enforcement of their Community rights via the principles of direct and indirect effects and state liability under *Francovich* (cases C–6 and 9/90), these remedies were uncertain and unequal in their application, and provided a remedy only in the individual case. Following its clarification in *Brasserie du Pêcheur* (cases C–46 and 48/93), a remedy under *Francovich* will only be available in circumstances where the state has 'manifestly and gravely' acted or failed to act in breach of EC law. A state will not be liable in damages for 'excusable' failures. Although excusable failures may be established in actions based on direct effects or indirect effects, in which liability has hitherto been strict, or under Articles 226–7, success in such actions will not *of itself* guarantee that states rectify their breaches of Community law.

11.7.2 Penalty payments for continuing failure to comply

At Maastricht a further weapon was added to the Court's armoury. Article 228(2) now provides as follows:

If the Commission considers that the Member State concerned has not taken such measures [to comply with the Court's judgment under Article 226] it shall, after giving the state an opportunity to submit its observations, issue a reasoned opinion specifying the points on which the Member State concerned has not complied with the judgment of the Court of Justice.

If the Member State concerned fails to take the necessary measures to comply with the Court's judgment within the time limit laid down by the Commission, the latter may bring the case before the Court of Justice. In so doing it shall specify the amount of the lump sum or penalty payment to be paid by the Member State concerned which it considers appropriate in the circumstances.

If the Court of Justice finds that the Member State concerned has not complied with its judgment it may impose a lump sum or penalty payment on it.

Article 228 is significant: it shows a shift from a diplomatic approach, in the preliminary stages in the Article 226 procedure, to a legal framework. It also suggests a shift from the intergovernmental approach, where breach of obligations could be negotiated, to a supranational one, in which the need to enforce Union law takes priority. For the first few years after Maastricht, there were no actions involving the imposition of fines. In 1996 and 1997, the first fines were proposed, and the first case in which a penalty was imposed was *Commission v Greece* (case C–387/97). In this case, Greece was found to have failed to comply with an earlier judgment in Article 226 proceedings (case C–45/91). The Court therefore exercised its powers under Article 228(2) and imposed a penalty of 20,000 for each day of delay in ensuring compliance with the earlier judgment. Ultimately, Greece paid 5.4 million in penalties before it finally complied with the judgment in March 2001 (19th Annual Report on Monitoring the Application of Community Law (COM (2002) 324 final, p 14). In its 2004 Report, the Commission stated that a there were 73 cases under consideration for which the Article 228 procedure had been opened. The worst offender was France, with 17 cases under consideration, followed by Italy (12 cases). In its report for 2007, the Commission noted that the number of cases relating to a *second* reference under Article 228, was down from ten in 2006, to seven in 2007.

There is no treaty limit to the level of fines that may be imposed by the Court, although the Commission is required to propose a fine when it commences proceedings. Initially it was not clear how the Commission was going to calculate the fines, and it was only in November 1997 (four years after this provision came into effect) that the Commission published guidance on calculating the penalty payments (COM (97) 299). A new notice was issued in December 2005 (SEC (2005) 1658), which applies to all Article 228 cases started after 1 January 2006 and which consolidates the practice and ECJ rulings to date.

In the past, the Commission requested periodic penalty payments rather than a lump sum. This may have been the result of an ambiguity in Article 228(2) authorising the ECJ to impose 'a lump sum *or* penalty payment' (emphasis added). In *Commission v France* (case C–304/02), the ECJ held that the word 'or' should be understood in a cumulative rather than an alternative sense, and that it would be possible to impose both a lump sum and penalty payment. The lump sum would reflect the failure of the Member State to comply with the earlier judgment (particularly where there has been a long delay), whereas the penalty payment would act as an incentive to the Member State to bring the infringement to an end as soon as possible (para 81) (see further below). Consequently, the Commission has changed its practice and will now request a lump-sum penalty as well as a periodic payment (SEC (2005) 1658). The lump sum is intended to penalise the continuation of the infringement between the dates of the judgment in the Article 226 proceedings and of the Article 228 proceedings, whereas the penalty payment is to cover each day of delay after the judgment under Article 228 EC.

In considering what sort of financial penalty to ask for, the Commission will take into account the seriousness of the infringement, its duration and the need for deterrence to prevent future infringements (para 6). The notice then spells out the approach the Commission adopts in calculating the penalty payment. It starts from a standard flat rate amount currently set at 600 per day. This amount is multiplied by a 'seriousness coefficient' ranging from 1 to 20. This is followed by a 'duration coefficient' which increases that sum by a multiplier of between 1 and 3 (at a rate of 0.10 per month from the date of the Article 226 judgment). That sum is then multiplied by a further factor specific to each Member State based on its GDP and number of votes in Council.

As far as the lump sum is concerned, a minimum sum for each Member State is specified in the notice. This will be requested unless a sum calculated by multiplying a daily amount by the number of days the infringement persists exceeds that amount. The 'daily amount' is calculated in the same way as the daily penalty payment. The number of days will be the period between the first judgment (under Article 226 EC) and the judgment under Article 228 EC. In this regard, it should be noted that the Commission does have a degree of discretion as to the timing of launching Article 228 proceedings, which may affect the duration of the period on the basis of which the lump sum is calculated. It remains to be seen whether this fact could form the basis for a claim of discriminatory treatment by the Commission against a particular Member State, or whether the time it takes the Commission to take action under Article 228 reflects the nature and seriousness of the infringement.

The combination of lump sum and penalty payments could therefore result in the imposition of considerable fines, which may act as a strong deterrent. The Court of Justice has made it clear that it is not bound by the Commission guidance, although it regards it as 'a useful point of reference' (*Commission v Greece* (case C–387/97), paras 89–90; *Commission v Spain* (case C–278/01), para 41; *Commission v France* (case C–304/02), para 103), and it has, so far, calculated the penalty on the basis of the criteria specified by the Commission (although not always applying the same factors). It has made it clear that the Commission can propose a penalty, but that the ultimate decision is for the Court, and that the Court may depart from the criteria stated in the notice, eg by adopting a duration coefficient that exceeds the maximum of 3 (*Commission v France* (case C–177/04), para 71). As regards to the French infringement which was the original case in which the double approach was taken, the French government is seeking to challenge the Commission's assessment that the breach continues and the amount of fines claimed (*France v Commission* (case T-139/06)). This case is still pending.

In *Commission v Spain*, Spain had failed to comply with the Bathing Water Directive (76/160/EEC [1976] OJ L31/1) even after an adverse judgment under Article 226 (see *Commission v Spain* (case C–92/96)). Having found that Spain continued to be in breach, the ECJ addressed the question of penalty payments. A difficulty with imposing a daily payment was that the nature the obligation imposed by the directive (improvements to the quality of bathing waters) meant that compliance could only be established on an annual basis once the water had been analysed and a report submitted. The ECJ accepted that it would be unfair to impose a daily fine at the same level up to the point when a report confirming compliance was received, because Spain may in fact have complied sooner. The Court therefore imposed a penalty payment which would only be payable annually, and be calculated on the basis of the percentage of Spanish bathing waters not in compliance with the directive. This decision is important in that it creates a balance between ensuring that the fine achieves its objective of securing compliance and the need to avoid penalising a Member State which has already complied.

The more recent decision, *Commission v France* (case C–304/02), seems to herald a much stricter approach by the ECJ in dealing with Article 228 EC cases, at least in circumstances where the infringement in question has persisted for a significant time after the initial judgment in Article 226 proceedings. The case involved the failure by France fully to comply with control measures for fishing activities, in respect of which the ECJ had given judgment in 1991 (*Commission v France* (case C–64/88)). Despite repeated inspections, a reasoned opinion by the Commission in April 1996, and a supplementary opinion in June 2000, France still failed to comply fully with the earlier judgment. The ECJ therefore held that France had failed to fulfil its obligations under Article 228 EC. The Commission had suggested the imposition of penalty payments rather than a lump sum. The ECJ, clearly irritated by the fact that France had not complied more than a decade after the first judgment, raised of its own motion the possibility of imposing a lump sum in addition to penalty payments (para 75). Having concluded that it would be possible to impose both penalty payments and a lump sum (paras 76–86), the Court then had to consider whether it was appropriate for it to depart from the Commission's suggestions as to penalty. Some Member States expressed concerns that the Court, exercising a discretion of this kind, would conflict with the principles of legal certainty, predictability, transparency, and equal treatment. Moreover, it was argued that the ECJ could not go beyond the parties' claims, and the defaulting Member State would need to be able adequately to defend itself. The ECJ rejected those concerns, primarily because of the special nature of Article 228 proceedings to bring about a cessation of an infringement. The ECJ thereby reserved the right to determine the type of penalty and level of payment that it regards as the most appropriate to the infringement at issue. In this case, it held that a penalty payment, to be imposed on a half-year basis, was appropriate; however, because France had remained in default for a long period since the judgment in Article 226 proceedings, it was 'essential to order payment of a lump sum' (para 114). There can be little doubt that the imposition of a lump sum as well as penalty payments reflected the ECJ's view that the degree of non-compliance in the particular case was severe, and the failure of France to put matters right sooner bordered on contempt. This judgment sends a strong message to the Member State to respond more rapidly to a finding of non-compliance in Article 226 proceedings, and it also sees the ECJ flexing its muscles in an area where, hitherto, a finding of non-compliance may have been little more than a minor embarrassment.

As noted above, in the wake of *Commission v France* (case C–304/02), the Commission has amended its guidelines and will now always ask for a lump sum to cover the continuation of the infringement, as well as a penalty payment to bring the Member State into line. It remains to be seen how the ECJ will handle subsequent cases. In *Commission v Italy* (case C–119/04), which involves an infringement which started in 1995 and in respect of which the court passed judgment against Italy in 2001 (*Commission v Italy* (case C–212/99)), Advocate-General Mauduro proposed that the Court should not exercise its discretion to impose a lump sum in addition to the penalty payments suggested by the Commission because whilst the period since the Article 226 judgment was 'substantial', it was 'not in the same league as the exceedingly long period' (para 49) in *Commission v France* (case C–304/02). In *Commission v France* (case C–177/04), the infringement that remained following amendments made after the Article 226 proceedings (*Commission v France* (case C–52/00), see Chapter 16) was not particularly serious, which may have influenced the ECJ in deciding not to impose a lump sum, despite the fact that the infringement had carried on for over 17 years.

11.8 Action by Member States (Article 227 EC)

In addition to enforcement actions brought by the Commission, there may be situations in which one Member State has reason to complain about an infringement of Community law by another Member State. In such circumstances, if the Commission fails to act, then a Member State may wish to bring infringement proceedings itself. This possibility is provided for in Article 227 (ex 170) EC (post Lisbon, 259 TFEU), which states:

> A Member State which considers that another Member State has failed to fulfil an obligation under this Treaty may bring the matter before the Court of Justice.
>
> Before a Member State brings an action against another Member State for an alleged infringement of an obligation under this Treaty, it shall bring the matter before the Commission.
>
> The Commission shall deliver a reasoned opinion after each of the states concerned has been given the opportunity to submit its own case and its observations on the other party's case both orally and in writing.
>
> If the Commission has not delivered an opinion within three months of the date on which the matter was brought before it, the absence of such opinion shall not prevent the matter from being brought before the Court of Justice.

The procedure is thus similar to that of Article 226 EC save that it is initiated by a Member State which, if the Commission fails to deliver a reasoned opinion within three months, is entitled to bring the matter before the ECJ. In addition, both parties are entitled to state their case and comment on the other's case both orally and in writing.

It has been suggested that since Article 227(1) gives Member States a general right to bring proceedings, the issuing of a reasoned opinion cannot preclude the complainant state from bringing proceedings before the Court if it is dissatisfied with the opinion or if it wishes to obtain a final judgment from the Court. This latter occurred in *France v United Kingdom (Re Fishing Net Mesh Sizes)* (case 141/78).

The procedure provided under Article 227 has rarely been used; Member States seem cautious about bringing an action under this provision because, since no Member State has a perfect record for the implementation of Community law, there is a danger that a defendant state might bring a retaliatory action against its prosecutor. It is likely to be deemed more politic to bring the alleged infringement to the attention of the Commission, leaving the Commission to act under Article 226. Nonetheless, the Article 227 procedure was used in *Belgium v Spain* (case C–388/95), concerning the rules regarding the application of the wine denomination, Rioja. It is interesting to note that the dispute brought in other Member States, which intervened in favour of one side or the other, revealed a split in opinion between the main wine-growing states and others. The ECJ found in favour of Spain. More recently, Spain used the procedure against the UK in respect of voting rights for commonwealth citizens in Gibraltar and lost (*Spain v UK* (case C–145/04)). In contrast to *Belgium v Spain*, no other Member States intervened, perhaps reflecting the politically sensitive, bilateral nature of the dispute.

In case of dispute between Member States, the treaty also provides a further, voluntary procedure. Under Article 239 EC (ex 182; post Lisbon, 273 TFEU), states may agree to submit to the ECJ any dispute relating to the subject matter of the treaty.

11.9 Impact of the treaty amendment

Although the future of the Treaty of Lisbon is uncertain at this time (see Chapter 1), the changes that were proposed merit brief consideration. Articles 226–8 EC would become Articles 258–60 of the Treaty on the Functioning of the European Union (TFEU). Although reworded, they would be identical in substance to the current provisions, with one addition: a new subparagraph would be added to current 228 EC, to become Article 260(3) TFEU. This provision would permit the Commission to ask for a fine in proceedings under Article 258 TFEU (current 226 EC) in which it was alleged that a Member State had failed to notify the measure transposing a directive to the Commission. Should the ECJ decide that a fine should be paid, it may not exceed the amount specified by the Commission. In this, the Lisbon Treaty tracks the amendments that were proposed under the Constitution.

This provision is remarkable, because it would enable the Commission to request a fine (lump sum or penalty payment) in the context of what are currently Article 226 EC proceedings. This would change the purely declaratory nature of these proceedings. However, it must be emphasised that this procedure could only be used for a failure to *notify*. If a Member State has notified transposition measures, but has incorrectly implemented a directive, then the Commission can only request a fine after having first obtained judgment under Article 258 TFEU (current 226 EC) and having taken further action under Article 260 TFEU (current 228 EC).

The Treaty of Lisbon would abolish the current three-pillar structure, and the ECJ's powers under Articles 258–60 TFEU would cover all of the material in TFEU, that is the current EC and JHA. What is currently the common foreign and security policy (CFSP) will remain in the EU Treaty and therefore outside the reference to 'this Treaty' in Article 258 TFEU.

11.10 Special enforcement procedures: State aid, breach of Article 95(4) procedures, and measures to prevent serious internal disturbances

These procedures, which apply only within the areas specified, operate 'in derogation from the provisions of Articles 226 and 227'. There are certain essential differences between these procedures and Articles 226–7. In the case of Article 88(2) the Commission, after giving the parties concerned an opportunity to submit their comments, issues a *decision* requiring the Member State concerned to alter or abolish the disputed aid within a specified time limit. If the state concerned does not comply with the decision within the prescribed time, the Commission or any other interested state may bring the matter to the ECJ. Since a *decision*, unlike a reasoned opinion, is a binding act it will be subject to challenge under Article 230 EC (*Commission v Belgium* (case 156/77), see Chapter 12).

Article 298 EC provides an accelerated procedure whereby the Commission can, without preliminaries, bring a Member State directly before the ECJ if it considers that that state is making improper use of its powers provided under Articles 296–7 EC (ex 223–4; post Lisbon, 346–7 TFEU). Under these provisions Member States are empowered to take emergency measures to protect essential security interests (Article 296) or in the event of serious internal disturbances, war or threat of war, or for the purposes of maintaining peace and international security (Article 297). A ruling of the Court under Article 298 is given in camera.

Article 95(9) also provides for an accelerated procedure whereby the Commission and any Member State may bring a state before the Court if it considers that a Member State has made improper use of the powers of derogation provided for in Article 95(4) in deciding 'to maintain national provisions on grounds of major needs referred to in Article 30, or relating to the protection of the environment or the working environment', or in Article 95(5) (see also Chapter 16).

11.11 Conclusions

The compliance of the Member States with their Community obligations is crucial in ensuring the success of the Community. Without the enforcement procedure provided in Article 226 EC, and crucially that in Article 228 EC, it seems that there would be a much lower level of compliance. The procedure itself seems to work tolerably well, although the Commission has, on occasion, been slow to proceed to the second stage of the formal procedure, and the exclusion of parties affected by Member States' non-compliance has given rise to adverse comment. The possibility of imposing penalty payments appears to have encouraged Member States to put a stop to continuous infringements more quickly than would otherwise have been the case. Yet, there is still a general problem with most Member States as far as complying with Community law is concerned, and there is a steady stream of cases under Article 226.

The case law which is developing under Article 228 EC seems to be marking the start of a new period of activism by the ECJ, at least with regard to persistent failures to comply with EC law. The Court appears to have lost its patience with countries that disregard judgments under Article 226 EC and has given a very strong indication that penalties under Article 228 should be punitive, as well as remedial. The Commission has responded by changing its practice, as confirmed in the 2005 Guidelines.

The recent enlargement of the Community may increase the Commission's workload in this area significantly if it is to fulfil its role as 'guardian of the treaties' adequately. Early indications are that the countries which joined in 2004 generally managed to ensure that their national legal systems had implemented the *acquis communautaire*, although there have already been some instances of inconsistent application, and failures to comply outright.

FURTHER READING

Berntiz, U, 'Controlling Member State courts under EU Law: The duty to refer cases to the ECJ and the Köbler doctrine on Member State liability', paper presented to Harvard Law School.

Commission's Annual Reports on the Monitoring and Application of Community Law (published at <http://ec.europa.eu/dgs/secretariat_general/publications/laws_procedures/index_en.htm>).

Hilson, C, 'Legality review of Member State discretion and directives' in T Tridimas and P Nebbia (eds), *European Law for the 21st Century* (Hart Publishing, 2004).

Timmermans, C, 'Use of the infringement procedure in cases of judicial errors', in JW de Zwaan, JH Jans, and FA Nelissen (eds), *The European Union: An ongoing process of integration* (The Hague: TMC Asser Press, 2004).

Wenneras, P, 'A new dawn for Commission enforcement under Articles 226 and 228 EC: General and persistent (GAP) infringements, lump sums and penalty payments' (2006) 43 CML Rev 31–62.

12

Direct action for annulment

Introduction

One of the fundamental means by which the actions of any legislature can be controlled is the process of judicial review. This enables a court to consider whether a legally binding measure violates procedural or substantive rules of law and should therefore be rendered inapplicable. Binding acts of the Union institutions are subject to review through a number of routes (see Chapter 7), and the most direct way of review is to challenge the legality of a particular measure. Article 230 EC (ex 173; post Lisbon, Article 263 TFEU) provides the mechanism for a direct challenge to the legality of Community acts. A further means of challenge is provided by Article 241 EC (ex 184; post Lisbon, 277 TFEU), which permits a claim *incidental* to a main action that a regulation should not be applicable.

This chapter examines the operation of the Article 230 procedure in detail. There are four main elements:

- the types of act that are subject to review
- the bodies that may bring an action for review
- the time within which an action may be brought
- the grounds on which such an action may be based.

We will consider each of these aspects in turn.

It will be seen that the most controversial aspect of this provision concerns the limited extent to which individuals are able to bring a challenge under Article 230. There have been many calls for reform, and recent case law of the Court of First Instance (CFI) and the Court of Justice (ECJ) revealed the existence of conflicting views as to the extent to which individuals can rely on the procedure in Article 230 to have a measure annulled, although, as will be seen, the ECJ has reasserted the established, restrictive, view. We will return to this point in detail below, having examined the basic framework in Article 230. Despite many calls for European institutions and lawmaking to come closer to the citizen, it seems that the limitations in this area currently remain. Another limiting aspect of the judicial review procedure is the strict time limit. The interrelationships between Article 230 and other mechanisms for review are thus important. We shall see how the ECJ has limited the scope of avoiding time limits in Article 230 by recourse to Article 234 (ex 177; post Lisbon, Article 267 TFEU) and examine the operation of the indirect review mechanism found in Article 241.

12.2 **Overview of provisions**

12.2.1 **Judicial review**

Article 230 EC provides:

> The Court of Justice shall review the legality of acts adopted jointly by the European Parliament and the Council, of acts of the Council, of the Commission and of the [European Central Bank], other than recommendations and opinions, and of acts of the European Parliament intended to produce legal effects *vis-à-vis* third parties.
>
> It shall for this purpose have jurisdiction in actions brought by a Member State, the European Parliament, the Council or the Commission on grounds of lack of competence, infringement of an essential procedural requirement, infringement of this Treaty or of any rule of law relating to its application, or misuse of powers.
>
> The Court shall have jurisdiction under the same conditions in actions brought by the Court of Auditors and by the European Central Bank for the purpose of protecting their prerogatives.
>
> Any natural or legal person may, under the same conditions, institute proceedings against a decision addressed to that person or against a decision which, although in the form of a regulation or a decision addressed to another person, is of direct and individual concern to the former.
>
> The proceedings provided for in this Article shall be instituted within two months of the publication of the measure, or of its notification to the plaintiff, or, in the absence thereof, of the day on which it came to the knowledge of the latter, as the case may be.

The equivalent provision in the Treaty on the Functioning of the European Union (TFEU), should Lisbon come into force, is found at Article 263 TFEU. With the exception of a couple of amendments, this provision, on its entry into force, would not change the current position much, save to extend the scope of review to acts of 'bodies, offices or agencies of the Union intended to produce legal effects vis-à-vis third parties' (see 12.3.3 below). The changes are more in the way of updating and reflecting the existing practice than anything else. The crucial exception to note is the change to the wording of the position of individuals seeking to challenge acts not addressed to them (see 12.4.3.5 below). Many of the changes are proposals that would have been introduced had the Constitution come into force; in this context, there are parallels between Lisbon and the Constitution.

12.2.2 **Indirect challenge**

Article 241 (ex 184) EC provides:

> Notwithstanding the expiry of the period laid down in the fifth paragraph of Article 230, any party may, in proceedings in which a Regulation adopted jointly by the European Parliament and the Council, or a Regulation of the Council or of the Commission is in issue, plead the grounds specified in the second paragraph of Article 230, in order to invoke before the Court of Justice the inapplicability of that Regulation.

As with the other judicial-review actions, Article 241 has been amended to reflect the ability of the European Parliament and the European Central Bank to adopt binding acts. Lisbon, were it to come into force, would reword this provision but leave the substance unchanged. The provision would also be renumbered as Article 277 TFEU.

12.3 Judicial review: Reviewable acts

12.3.1 Acts that may be challenged

Reviewable acts, defined as acts 'other than recommendations and opinions', are not confined—as they might appear to be—to regulations, directives, or decisions. The Court has held that they include all measures taken by the institutions designed to have legal effect, whatever their nature or form (*Commission v Council (Re European Road Transport Agreement)* (case 22/70)). The measure in this case was a Council resolution setting out the position to be taken by the Council in the preparation of the road-transport agreement. The Commission sought to challenge this resolution, since it considered that the matter lay outside the Council's sphere of competence. Applying the above test, the action was declared admissible.

Similarly in *Re Noordwijk's Cement Accord* (cases 8–11/66), the act challenged was a registered letter sent by the Commission to the applicant in the context of EC competition policy, to the effect that the companies' immunity from fines was at an end. The letter was not called a 'decision'. Nevertheless it was held that since it produced legal effects for the companies concerned and brought about a change in their legal position it was an act capable of annulment under Article 230 (see also *BEUC v Commission* (case T–37/92)). A similar approach can be seen with regard to a decision not to investigate an alleged case of state aid (*Athinaiki Techniki AE v Commission* (case C–521/06 P)). Indeed, the fact that the Commission had not followed formal procedures for making such a decision, does not affect this assessment. To do so, would have allowed the Commission a route to evade review. In *France v Commission (Re Pension Funds Communication)* (case C–57/95) the ECJ held that a communication, which was phrased in imperative language, was intended to have legal effects and could be challenged. In *Infront WM AG v Commission* (case T–33/01), the applicant sought to challenge a Commission letter to the UK government, indicating that the Commission had no objection to measures taken, in accordance with Article 3a Television without Frontiers Directive (Directive 89/552/EEC, as amended), by the UK to ensure the broadcast of football World Cup finals on free-to-air television. In defence, it was argued that the letter was not a decision, but was analogous to a definition of position of intention not to take action under Article 226 proceedings, which is not susceptible of review (see, eg, *Dumez v Commission* (case T–126/95)). Further, the legal effects stemmed from the underlying national law, not the Commission letter, which did not change the legal position. The CFI disagreed and held the letter was susceptible of review as it concluded the verification procedure which the Commission is obliged to carry out under the Television without Frontiers Directive. It therefore triggers the mutual recognition system in the Directive, according to which other Member States are obliged to prevent broadcasters established under their respective jurisdictions from avoiding national regulation about access to television content. The matter was appealed (case C–125/06 P) where the ECJ agreed that the action was admissible.

Not all letters issued by the Commission will necessarily be capable of challenge. The *max.mobil* case (case T–54/99, *max.mobil v Commission*, on appeal case C–141/02P) illustrates the difficulty of determining whether a decision by an institution is capable of being reviewed. The underlying complaint concerned the telecommunications market in Austria. Max.mobil complained to the Commission, asking it to take action under Article 86. The Commission, referring to its existing policy in this area, declined to do so and wrote to max.mobil to this effect. Max.mobil sought to challenge this letter; the Commission argued that it was of an informative nature only. The CFI agreed with max.mobil, suggesting that on the basis of previous case law (notably case C–107/95P *Bilanzbuchhalter*, discussed in Chapter 13), an individual had the right to have a diligent and impartial treatment of the complaint; thus the Commission must consider the matter before coming to its decision. The letter, in the view of the CFI, was therefore a decision on this basis which was subject to review. The ECJ disagreed. It argued that 'The fact that max.mobil has a direct and individual interest in the annulment of the Commission's decision to refuse to act on its complaint is not such as to confer on it the right to challenge that decision' (para 70).

It concluded that the letter to max.mobil was of an informative nature only. Such an approach does limit the protection awarded by Article 230, and is particularly worrying given the ease with which a challenge to inaction can be ended. It is equally difficult to reconcile the approach here with that taken by the CFI in *Air France* (case T–3/93).

In *Air France v Commission* (case T–3/93) a mere statement by a Commission spokesman, not published but reported by the press agencies, that a proposed acquisition of Dan-Air by British Airways lay outside the scope of the Commission's competence under Regulation 4064/89, was held to be capable of annulment, since it confirmed the Commission's position 'beyond all doubt'. The fact that the statement was not addressed to a particular person and was given orally was not relevant: it was the content and legal effect of the measure which were crucial. (See also cases regarding the European Parliament at 12.3.2 below.) It may be that one way of reconciling these cases is to note that the broader approach to the notion of a decision is taken by the CFI, the ECJ seemingly taking a narrower approach.

Both courts have held, in contrast to the case law discussed above, that preliminary measures, designed simply to pave the way for a final decision, are not reviewable (see *Nashua Corporation v Commission* (cases C–133 and 150/87)). In *Dysan Magnetics Ltd v Commission* (case T–134/95), the opening by the Commission of a dumping investigation, a purely preparatory measure which preceded the adoption of definitive anti-dumping duties, and which did not have an immediate and irreversible effect on the legal situation of concerned undertakings, was held not to be open to challenge under Article 230. In *Philip Morris International and others v Commission* (cases T–377/00, T–379/00, T–380/00, T–260/01, and T–272/01), the Commission's decision to commence proceedings against various tobacco manufacturers in an American court was challenged by the defendants to that action, but the CFI held that the action was inadmissible because the decision to commence proceedings had no binding legal effects on the applicants. The legal effects, if any, would derive from the decision of the American court.

This principle, that it is the true nature and effect of a measure rather than its label which determines whether it may be reviewed under Article 230, is very important, since this provision is subject to a strict two-month time limit. If the measure is not recognised as a binding act and challenged in time, the action will be declared inadmissible, whatever its merits (eg, *Commission v Belgium* (case 156/77)—no success under Article 241 because the original act (a letter) was not challenged in time; see below).

The Lisbon Treaty amends this provision to give the ECJ power to review the legality of 'acts adopted jointly by the European Parliament and the Council', the phrase replacing the words, 'legislative acts'.

12.3.2 Acts of Parliament

Although only acts of the Council and the Commission were expressed to be capable of challenge under the original Article 173, the Court had, prior to the passing of the Treaty of the European Union (TEU), admitted challenges to acts of the European Parliament having legal force with regard to third parties (see *Luxembourg v Parliament* (case 230/81); *Partie Ecologiste ('Les Verts') v Parliament* (case 294/83)). This was justified on the grounds that Parliament had, over the years, acquired powers to issue such acts. In *Luxembourg v Parliament*, Luxembourg was seeking to challenge Parliament's resolution to move its seat from Luxembourg to Strasbourg and Brussels. In *'Les Verts' v Parliament*, the Green Party sought to challenge a decision of the Bureau of Parliament on the allocation of campaign funds for the 1984 European elections. Clearly Parliament's acts in these cases produced significant legal effects for both applicants (cf *Les Verts v Parliament* (case 190/84)).

Contrast these cases with *Le Pen* (case T–353/00, under appeal, case C–208/03 P). It concerned the question of a declaration of the president of the Parliament, and turned on the issue of whether the declaration had legal effects. In earlier cases (*Council v Parliament* (case 34/86) and *Council v European Parliament* (case C–284/90)), the ECJ had held that a declaration could have legal effects. The *Le Pen case* was different. The declaration here consisted of recognition of the legal position in France, rather than creating legal effects of its own. Thus, when looking at acts giving rise to legal effects, it is not sufficient that the act be of the type that could give rise to legal effects, but it must itself give rise to such effects.

The principles established in cases such as *'Les Verts'* have now been incorporated into Article 230 EC. Also, reflecting Parliament's powers of co-decision granted under the TEU, Article 230 now provides for challenge to acts adopted 'jointly by Parliament and the Council' under Article 251 (ex 189(b)) EC.

In general terms, the courts have accepted that internal rules of organisation for the Parliament do not have legal effects on third parties (ie externally) and are therefore not capable of being reviewed (*Weber v Parliament* (case C–314/91)). A declaration of the European Parliament waiving the rights and immunities of one of its members went beyond the 'internal' and therefore was capable of being subject to review (*Mote v Parliament* (case T–345/05)).

12.3.3 Acts of other bodies

Article 230 also now specifies that acts of the European Central Bank (ECB) may be challenged. It seems that the acts of other bodies may also be challenged though, in order to be capable of challenge, the measure must proceed from a Community institution empowered under the treaty to enact binding measures. Thus in

Commission v Council (case C–25/94), a decision by the Committee of Permanent Representatives (COREPER), and in *Parliament v Council* (case C–181/91), a decision of the Member States meeting in Council (but not of the *Council* as such), could not be challenged. The Treaty of Lisbon recognises this. As noted above, should it come into force, the amended provision would provide that the Court may review 'the legality of acts of bodies, offices or agencies of the Union intended to produce legal effects *vis-à-vis* third parties'. Note also that Article 263 TFEU refers to acts of the European Council intended to have binding effects. Presumably this phrase will be interpreted in the same way as for the European Parliament.

12.3.4 Review under TEU

The ECJ's jurisdiction under Article 230 EC is, of course, currently limited to Community acts. This does not mean that the actions of the Union will completely escape the ECJ's review. The ECJ has already held that it has the power to review actions taken under the justice and home affairs (JHA) pillar of the TEU to ensure that such measures have been properly adopted thereunder and are not diluting the Community *acquis* (*Commission v Council (Air Transport Arrangements)* (case C–170/96)).

Following the Treaty of Amsterdam (ToA), Article 35 TEU provides for judicial review of actions taken under the JHA pillar, albeit limited in terms of the measures which may be challenged (framework decisions and decisions) and the grounds of challenge. Furthermore, only the Commission and the Council can bring an action under these provisions. Parliament and 'natural or legal persons' have no *locus standi* to challenge action in this area.

The Treaty of Lisbon, should it come into force, would abolish the three-pillar structure bringing JHA, subject to limitations relating to law enforcement and national security within review (Aricle 276 TFEU). The common foreign and security policy (CFSP) provisions, even post Lisbon, will remain in the TEU, and the terms of Article 230 refer to 'this Treaty', that is the EC Treaty (after Lisbon Article 263 referring to TFEU). This would seem to exclude such provisions from review, but Article 275 TFEU specifies that the ECJ may review the legality of restrictive measures against natural or legal persons under Chapter 2, Title V TEU and the ECJ will continue to have the power to review the boundary between the different areas of jurisdiction, as it does now (see Chapter 3).

12.4 *Locus standi:* Who may bring an action?

The question of *locus standi* (or standing)—that is, of who should be entitled to challenge the legality of a particular measure—is controversial. On the one hand, it may be desirable to provide for broad *locus standi* to ensure that the legislature is subjected to adequate control. On the other hand, it is equally desirable to ensure that somebody who is wholly unconnected with the adoption or effects of a legally binding act is not in a position to challenge its validity, as this would otherwise admit too many challenges, with an adverse effect on legal certainty, as well as the Court's workload. There are strict *locus standi* requirements in Article 230. Applicants are divided into privileged and non-privileged applicants, with the Court of Auditors and the Central Bank occupying a semi-privileged position. The main controversy in recent years has been over the restricted interpretation given by the Court to the *locus standi* rules on non-privileged applicants. This part examines these rules in more detail.

12.4.1 Privileged applicants

Member States, the Parliament, the Council and the Commission are entitled to challenge *any* binding act under Article 230. A 'Member State' for the purposes of this article does not include governments of regions or of autonomous communities (*Region Wallonne v Commission* (case C–95/97)). However, regional authorities may intervene, if they have legal personality under their domestic law, as a non-privileged applicant. As such, they must satisfy the requirements of direct and individual concern (*Comunidad Autonoma de Cantabria v Council* (case T–238/97)) (see further below). It is arguable that regional authorities should have semi-privileged status to protect their prerogatives, but this has not been given serious consideration by the Member States or the Union.

12.4.1.1 *The changing nature of Parliament's standing*

Although Parliament is now a privileged applicant, this was not always so, despite the fact that Parliament has always had *locus standi* to bring an action against another institution for a failure to act (Article 232 (ex 175), post Lisbon, 265 TFEU see Chapter 13). It had sometimes been suggested that, because of the parallels between Articles 232 and 230 EC, the Parliament's standing under Article 230 should match that under Article 232 EC. In *Parliament v Council (Comitology)* (case 302/87), however, the Court held that there was 'no necessary link' between the actions under Article 230 and 232, respectively. This seemed to rule out any right of Parliament to challenge the validity of measures adopted by the Commission and Council. Nonetheless, in *Parliament v Council (Chernobyl)* (case C–70/88), the Court held that Parliament *did* have standing to challenge acts of the Commission or the Council under the precursor of Article 230 where this was necessary to protect its prerogative powers. Parliament was therefore entitled to challenge a Council decision which had allegedly been taken in breach of an obligation to consult Parliament (see also *Parliament v Council* (case C–65/90)).

At the intergovernmental conference (IGC) in Maastricht in 1992, the heads of state decided not to grant Parliament a *general* right to challenge acts of the Council or the Commission, and, despite suggestions that it should, the position did not change at Amsterdam either. Article 230 was revised by the TEU to include Parliament's right of challenge to the extent that this was necessary to protect its prerogatives, reflecting the approach in the Court's jurisprudence. The Court had adopted a strict interpretation of this requirement. In *Parliament v Council (Re aid to Bangladesh)* (cases C–181 and 248/91), Parliament could not challenge the Commission's handling of aid to Bangladesh because no prerogative power of Parliament had been infringed. (See also *Parliament v Commission (Re legislation on organic production)* (case C–156/93)). Moreover, where Parliament's prerogatives were in issue, the Court insisted on strict compliance with form. In *Parliament v Council (Re European Development Fund)* (case C–316/91), Parliament challenged an act of Council as enacted on the wrong legal basis, not requiring consultation with

Parliament. The allegedly correct basis required consultation, but the Court held that there had been no breach of Parliament's prerogatives because Parliament had, in fact, been consulted.

It was not until the Treaty of Nice came into force in early 2003 that Parliament finally assumed the full status of privileged applicant. Arguably, as the only democratically elected EC institution, with an express role in *supervising* Community activities, this is a welcome development. However, as commentators have noted, parliamentary procedure is not designed for litigation and it may seem a little strange that Parliament has the power of challenge, particularly in view of the diverse political interests it represents. It is submitted that the rather unique legislative procedure in Community law and the nature of the Union itself merit this form of control.

12.4.1.2 *Other bodies*

Should the Lisbon Treaty come into force in its current form, Article 263(3) TFEU extends the semi-privileged position noted in relation to the Court of Auditors and the ECB to include the Committee of the Regions.

12.4.2 **Non-privileged applicants**

Compared with Member States and Community institutions, the *locus standi* of individuals under Article 230 is much more limited. A 'natural or legal person' is entitled only to challenge:

(a) a decision addressed to *himself or herself*, or

(b) a decision, in the form of a regulation or a decision addressed to another person, which is of direct and individual concern to himself or herself.

A 'natural or legal person' includes a state which is not a Member State of the EC (*Gibraltar v Council* (case C–298/89)) as well as autonomous regions of a Member State (see 12.4.1 above).

All claims by natural or legal persons are now brought before the CFI with a right of appeal to the ECJ on points of law only (see Chapter 7).

No problem exists where the decision is addressed to the applicant, with one minor exception (to be discussed in Chapter 13). Provided the applicant brings the action within the two-month time limit his or her claim will be admissible. Many such decisions have been successfully challenged (eg, in competition law).

Where the decision is addressed to another person, problems arise. 'Another person' has been held to include a Member State (*Plaumann & Co v Commission* (case 25/62)). Despite dicta by the ECJ in *Plaumann*, that the provisions of the treaty concerning the right to seek a legal remedy ought not to be interpreted strictly, the Court, and now the CFI, has adopted a very restrictive approach towards the individual seeking to challenge acts addressed to another person, although there has been some relaxation of the rules in recent years.

12.4.2.1 *Trade associations*

Although the Court has been unwilling to entertain actions by trade or other associations under Article 230, maintaining that 'defence of a common interest is not enough to establish admissibility', the CFI held in *Associazione Italiana Tecnico*

Economica del Cemento (AITEC) v Commission (cases T–447–9/93) that a trade association would be permitted to bring an action against a decision addressed to 'another person' where it represented the individual interests of some of its members whilst at the same time protecting the interests of the section as a whole. The CFI noted that 'in these circumstances collective action brings procedural advantages'. As a result, Italian and British associations of cement producers were able to challenge a Commission decision addressed to the Greek government approving the grant of state aid to a Greek producer, Heracles, and succeeded in obtaining its annulment. Likewise a trade union and a works council, as 'recognised representatives' of employees affected by a proposed merger under Merger Regulation 4064/89, were held entitled to challenge a Commission decision approving Nestlé's takeover of Perrier SA (see *Comité Central d'Entreprise de la Société Générale des Grandes Sources v Commission* (case T–96/92) and *Aktionsgemeinschaft Recht und Eigentum eV v Commission* (case T–114/00)—association formed to protect the collective interests of its members had *locus standi* to challenge a Commission decision not to instigate the formal procedure under Article 88(2) EC, on behalf of those members who would have been parties concerned within the meaning of Article 88(2) EC (see Chapter 30)). In *Federolio v Commission* (case T–122/96), the CFI identified three situations when an association would be granted *locus standi*:

(a) the trade association has been expressly granted procedural rights

(b) it represents the individuals or undertakings which themselves have standing

(c) the trade association itself is affected—for example if its right to negotiate is affected.

This will still leave many associations or pressure groups without *locus standi* (see, for example, *Stichtling Greenpeace Council v Commission* (case C–585/93), the subject of an unsuccessful appeal (case C–321/95 P)). Perhaps this is not surprising, given the stringency of the test applied to individuals.

12.4.3 Challenging decisions addressed to another person

For a claim by a 'natural or legal person' against a decision addressed to 'another person' to be admissible, three criteria must be satisfied:

(a) the measure must be equivalent to a decision

(b) it must be of direct concern to himself or herself

(c) it must be of individual concern to himself or herself.

Since *all* of these criteria must be fulfilled the question of admissibility may be decided, and the application rejected, on the basis of any one of them. In the order in which it examines the above requirements, and in its approach to all three criteria, the Court has not been consistent. Further, it now seems that the CFI is requiring an individual seeking to challenge a decision to show a legal interest in bringing the proceedings as an additional test. In *Schmitz-GothaFahrzeugwerke v Commission* (case T–167/01), the CFI held that showing a legal interest in bringing the challenge is an essential and fundamental prerequisite for any legal proceedings and without it, the Court will not proceed to examine the questions of whether the decision is of direct and individual concern (*Olivieri v Commission* (case T–326/99)). The ECJ has apparently accepted this extra requirement (*Rendo and Others v Commission* (case C–19/93 P), para 13). It seems in this regard that the burden of proof lies on the applicant (*Sniace SA* (case T–141/03), paras 31–2). Given the strictness with which both courts have interpreted these requirements, the extent to which this makes it more difficult for individuals to challenge acts, or whether the difficulty is merely being rephrased is questionable. In *Infront* (case T–33/01), the applicant was found to have an interest by the CFI but was then also found to satisfy the test for standing. In *Flaherty and others v Commission* (C–373/06 P, C–379/06 P, and C–382/06 P), the CFI held that individuals who were intending on building a boat, the name of which was listed in the Annex to the contested decision, did not have an interest as the boat was 'fictional', that is, it did not at the time of the decision, exist. It further held the applicants were not individually concerned. The ECJ overturned the ruling as regards the applicants' interest, arguing that they were listed in the relevant annex because they had applied for support under a particular scheme and the contested decision denied them that support. The fact that they had not yet built the boat (for which they needed the support) did not change this assessment. The ECJ then overturned the CFI on the question of whether the applicants were individually concerned. At the least, there are strong links between these two tests.

12.4.3.1 *The measure must be, as far as the applicant is concerned, a decision*

Since many of the Commission's policies, for example in the highly regulated field of agriculture, are implemented by directly applicable regulations, often with wide-ranging and adverse effects on individuals (eg, withdrawal of subsidies, imposition of levies), many cases have arisen in which individual applicants have sought to challenge regulations. Although it would have been open to the Court to interpret Article 230(2) to enable them to do so provided that the applicant could prove 'direct and individual concern', the Court was originally insistent that a natural or legal person could not challenge a 'true' regulation. For this reason in *Koninklijke Scholten-Honig NV v Council and Commission* (case 101/76) the applicant glucose producers' attempt to challenge certain regulations requiring glucose producers to pay levies on the production of glucose, for the benefit of sugar producers, was held, despite the merits of the case, to be inadmissible. (See also *Calpak SpA v Commission* (cases 789 and 790/79)—attempt (failed) by Italian pear processors to challenge a regulation fixing production aids for pear processors; *Alusuisse* (case 307/81).)

However, whether a measure is, as far as the applicant is concerned, a 'true' regulation or not involves a very subtle enquiry, a fact underlying the decision of the ECJ in *R v Intervention Board for Agricultural Produce, ex parte Accrington Beef Co Ltd* (case C–241/95). There, the ECJ acknowledged that an individual seeking to challenge a regulation could not be sure whether or not he would have *locus standi* under Article 230. In *Confédération Nationale des Producteurs de Fruits et Légumes v Council* (cases 16 and 17/62) the Court held that to determine the legal nature of an act it is necessary to consider the nature and content of an act rather than its form. It is the substance, not the label, which is crucial. A true regulation is a measure of general application, ie normative; it applies to objectively determined situations and produces legal effects on categories of persons viewed abstractly and in their entirety. On the other hand the essential feature of a decision, which is defined as 'binding upon those to whom it is addressed' (Article 249 (ex 189)) arises from the limitation of the persons to whom it is addressed; a decision concerns designated persons individually.

In *International Fruit NV v Commission (No 1)* (cases 41–4/70) the applicants, a group of fruit importers, were held entitled to challenge a Community 'regulation' laying down the quantity of import licences to be issued for a certain period. The quantity of licences was calculated on the basis of applications from, inter alia, the applicants, received during the preceding week; thus it applied to a finite number of people and was issued in response to their applications. Although it appeared to be a general measure it was found in fact to be a disguised bundle of decisions addressed to each applicant (see also *Roquette Frères SA v Council* (case 138/79)).

The ECJ has also suggested that a measure may be 'hybrid' in nature, ie, it may be a measure of general application which is, nonetheless, in the nature of a decision for certain 'designated individuals'. In the *Japanese ball-bearings* cases (cases 113 and 118–21/77) four major Japanese producers of ball bearings were held entitled to challenge an EC anti-dumping regulation. Although the measure was of general application some of its articles specifically referred to the applicants. For them, it was in the nature of a decision. In *Allied Corporation v Commission* (cases 239 and 275/82) some of the applicant companies seeking to annul an anti-dumping regulation were charged with illegal dumping in the regulation itself. The ECJ held that although measures involving anti-dumping duties were:

> as regards their nature and scope, of a legislative character, inasmuch as they apply to all traders concerned taken as a whole, the provision may nonetheless be of direct and individual concern to those producers and exporters who are charged with practising dumping.

On this basis the applicant producers' and exporters' claims were held to be admissible.

In *Timex Corporation v Council* (case 264/82) the applicant company, which succeeded in establishing *locus standi* to challenge another anti-dumping regulation, was this time a complainant which, through its national trade association, had brought certain illegal dumping practices (concerning Russian watches and watch movements) to the Commission's attention. The regulation had been issued as a result of enquiries following Timex's complaints. The ECJ held that although the measure was legislative (ie, normative) in nature, it was a decision of direct and individual concern to Timex since it had been issued in response to Timex's complaint and the company had given evidence to the Commission during the anti-dumping proceedings.

It may be noted that in *Allied*, in admitting that the measures challenged were legislative in character, ie 'true' regulations, the ECJ did not consider the question whether they were in the nature of a decision to the applicants. It appeared to be sufficient that the applicants had established direct and individual concern. This approach, although not followed in *Timex*, has since been adopted in a number of cases, principally, but not exclusively, in the context of challenge to regulations imposing anti-dumping duties. Under EC anti-dumping rules such duties, which are normally levied on importation of the product concerned, can only be imposed by regulation. Such regulations may adversely affect undertakings such as producers and exporters situated outside the Union who have no opportunity to challenge the measures in an action before the courts of Member States. The Court has admitted a number of challenges to regulations by producers or exporters who were able to establish that they were identified in the measures adopted by the Commission or the Council (as in *Timex*) or were concerned in the Commission's preliminary investigations (see *Nashua Corporation v Commission* (cases C–133 and 150/87), *Neotype v Commission* (case C–305/86)): also by importers whose retail prices for the goods in question or whose business dealings with the manufacturer of those goods played a part in establishing the existence of dumping (*Enital v Commission* (case C–304/86); *Gestetner Holdings plc v Commission* (case C–156/87)). Such claims were admissible because (as well as the applicants being directly concerned) the factors cited above were deemed to constitute individual concern. In *Extramet Industrie SA v Council* (case C–358/89), the ECJ went further and admitted a challenge to a 'true' regulation by an *independent* importer whose retail prices and business dealings in the goods in question were *not* taken into account in establishing the existence of dumping, simply because he was able to establish individual (as well as direct) concern.

Also, outside the area of anti-dumping, in *Sofrimport v Commission* (case C–152/88), the ECJ allowed an applicant importer to challenge a regulation suspending imports into the EC of apples from certain third countries solely on the basis of direct and individual concern; the Court did not avert to the question of whether the measure was in the nature of a decision as regards the applicant.

In *Codorniu SA v Council* (case C–309/89) the principal producer of quality sparkling wine in Spain, and holder of graphic trade-mark rights in the title 'Gran Cremant di Codorniu' was allowed to challenge EC regulations on the description of sparkling wines in which the word 'cremant' was to be reserved for certain quality sparkling wines produced in France and Luxembourg. Although the measures in question were legislative measures applicable to traders in general they were of individual concern to the applicant.

These cases suggest that in the context of a challenge to a regulation, where the applicant can prove direct and (particularly) individual concern, the Court may no longer require proof that the measure constitutes a decision as far as he is concerned. This approach, although prima facie contrary to the literal wording of Article 230 EC and the Court's earlier case law is, as Advocate-General Jacobs pointed out in *Extramet*, consistent with the general scheme and purpose of the article and necessary to ensure effective judicial protection for those (such as manufacturers and exporters in countries outside the EC) who may be seriously affected by regulations but who lack alternative or adequate means by which to challenge them. Since the concept of individual concern is very strictly interpreted by the Court, it may be argued that it is sufficient in itself (together with the concept of direct concern) to restrict access to judicial review of regulations by natural or legal persons. Moreover, since, as will be seen, the two questions of (a) whether a measure, although called a regulation, is in fact in the nature of a decision to the applicant and (b) whether it is of individual concern to the applicant often involve the same enquiry: thus where the latter criterion is met, the need to prove the former becomes superfluous.

There have been few examples of challenge by natural or legal persons to directives. Since directives are addressed to Member States it might have been thought that they are closer to a decision than to a regulation, and as such, more likely to be challengeable. However in *Gibraltar v Council* (case C–298/89) the Court refused to admit a challenge to an EC directive by the government of Gibraltar (found to be a natural or legal person) on the grounds that directives, being 'normally a form of indirect regulatory or legislative measure' were not open to challenge by such persons. Since the directive in question, although affecting the applicants by excluding them from its territorial scope, applied to 'objectively determined situations' the applicants' claim was inadmissible. Here, however, unlike the applicants mentioned above who succeeded in establishing *locus standi* to challenge regulations, the applicants were unable to prove individual concern. In *Salamander and ors v European Parliament and Council* (joined cases T–172 and T–175–7/98), concerning a challenge to the Tobacco Advertising Directive (Directive 98/43/EC), the CFI seemed to suggest that a directive could in principle be capable of challenge by individuals provided they could show direct and individual concern. In this case, however, the applicants were unable to show direct concern.

By contrast to the position taken in *Gibraltar v Council* in relation to directives, where the measure in question is described as a decision, provided it has a specific addressee, the Court presumes it to be a decision, even though, as in the case of a decision addressed to a Member State, it may lay down normative rules.

12.4.3.2 *The measure must be of direct concern to the applicant*

A measure will be of direct concern to the applicant if it leaves the Member State no real discretion in implementation. Often the Commission will issue a decision to a state requiring, or authorising, the state to act in a particular manner. Whether the individual affected by such action may challenge the Community decision will depend on whether the action affecting the applicant was within the area of the Member State's discretion or not. In *Eridania v Commission* (cases 10 and 18/68) an Italian sugar-refining company sought to challenge three Commission decisions granting aid to its competitors. Its action under Article 230 was declared inadmissible. Although the Commission's decisions had authorised the granting of aid, and indeed named the companies concerned, those decisions were not of direct concern to the applicants, since the decision regarding the *allocation* of the aid had been made by the Italian government. This was a matter within the government's discretion. Where the matter of which the applicant complains lies within the discretion of the state the appropriate challenge is to the national authority responsible for the relevant decision.

The question of whether a particular Community decision leaves room for discretion on the part of a Member State is susceptible to different interpretations. Interpreted broadly, as in *Plaumann & Co v Commission* (case 25/62) and *SA Alcan Aluminium Raeren v Commission* (case 69/69), it could mean that where the Commission merely *permits* or *authorises* a Member State to act the state still retains a discretion as to whether to act or not. In *Alcan* the Court agreed with Advocate-General Roemer's suggestion in *Plaumann* that even where the Commission *refuses* permission to act, the state, in its discretion, may choose to act in disregard of this refusal and face the consequences of an action under Article 226 (ex 169). On the other hand, interpreting the question of discretion narrowly, as in the *Japanese ball-bearings* case (cases 113 and 118–21/77), it could be said that where implementation of a Community decision is *automatic* or a *foregone conclusion*, as can be presumed where permission or authorisation is sought, no real discretion exists on the part of the state, and the measure will be of direct concern to the applicant.

A number of cases in which the applicant has succeeded in establishing *locus standi*, such as *Alfred Toepfer KG v Commission* (cases 106 and 107/63) and *Werner A Bock KG v Commission* (case 62/70) have involved decisions of confirmation (*Toepfer*) or authorisation (*Bock*). In these cases it seems to have been presumed that the measures were of direct concern to the applicants. In the case of *AE Piraiki-Patraiki v Commission* (case 11/82), in the context of a Commission decision authorising the French to impose a quota system on imports of Greek yarn, Advocate-General VerLoren van Themaat suggested that a Community measure would be of direct concern if its legal effects on interested parties and their identity could 'with certainty or with a high degree of probability be inferred'. The Court considered that the possibility that the French government would not take advantage of the Commission's decision was 'purely theoretical'. In the more recent cases the ECJ and CFI seem to have returned to the language of 'no discretion' and 'automatic'. Thus in *Infront*, the ECJ held the test:

> requires the contested Community measure to affect directly the legal situation of the individual and leave no discretion to its addressees, who are entrusted with the task of implementing it, such implementation being purely automatic and resulting from Community rules without the application of other intermediate rules. [Para 47.]

Nonetheless, here the ECJ was referring to the term of the Television without Frontiers Directive which required Member States to recognise other Member States' systems for ensuring certain content was available on free-to-air television, once the Commission had approved the content to be so provided, and it found the test to be satisfied. In *Commission v Ente per Le Ville vesuviane* and *Ente per le Ville vesuviance v Commission* (joined cases C–444 and 455/07 P), the ECJ took a less favourable stance, although it relied on exactly the same test. The case concerned the closure of financial assistance from the European Regional Development Fund (EDRF) for some projects in Ente. Although Ente was named as the beneficiary, the application was made by the Italian state. Requests to the Commission by the Italian state for the payments to be made to Ente had not been made by the due deadline. Representatives of Ente sought to challenge the Commission's decision. The ECJ determined that because the grants were applied for through the Italian state and it was still possible that the Italian government could have changed its mind, Ente was not directly concerned. This indicates that, although *Infront* suggests that the courts no longer assume that Member States may choose to disregard their Community law obligations, there is still a risk that Member States may be deemed to have exercised choice.

Decisions need not, of course, be addressed to Member States. Where decisions have been addressed to natural or legal persons, the CFI has often taken a narrow view of when these decisions could be said to affect other persons directly. The Commission's decision to approve Nestlé's takeover of Perrier in *Comité Central d'Entreprise de la Société Générale des Grandes Sources v Commission* (case T–96/92) was found not to be of direct concern to the applicant employee representative bodies. Any disadvantage suffered by employees following the merger would result from action by the merged undertaking itself, subject to the protection provided for employees in these circumstances under national and Community law. It did not result directly from the Commission's decision. The applicants were only directly concerned by the decision to the extent that their procedural rights, granted to 'recognised representatives' under the Merger Regulation, might have been infringed. More recently, a supplier under a contract with the Ukraine, which received financial aid from the Community, was held not to be directly affected by a Commission decision that its contracts did not satisfy the Community's criteria for release of payments to the Ukraine (*Richco Commodities Ltd v Commission* (case T–509/93)). The CFI pointed out that there was no legal relationship between the supplier and the Commission. The fact that the contract was expressed to be conditional on payment of the aid was irrelevant; standing under Article 230 cannot be dependent on decisions made in commercial negotiations. This ruling may now be open to question. In a series of cases on appeal from the CFI regarding the same point, the ECJ has held the individual to be directly concerned (see, eg, *Glencore Grain Ltd v Commission* (case C–403 and 404/96)).

12.4.3.3 *The measure must be of individual concern to the applicant*

The concept of individual concern has been construed very restrictively by the ECJ (and CFI). Because it operates to exclude so many cases it is often the first criterion to be examined, as it was in *Plaumann & Co v Commission* (case 25/62). Plaumann & Co were importers of clementines who sought to annul a Commission decision, addressed to the German government, refusing the government permission to reduce its customs duties on clementines imported from outside the EC. Plaumann & Co claimed that, as a large-scale importer of such clementines, they were 'individually concerned'. The Court disagreed. The importing of clementines, the Court held, was an activity which could be carried out by anyone at any time. There was nothing in the decision to distinguish Plaumann & Co from any other importer of clementines. In order to establish individual concern, the applicant must prove that the decision affects him or her because of 'certain characteristics which are peculiarly relevant to him, or by reason of circumstances in which he is differentiated from all other persons, and not by the mere fact that he belongs to a class of persons who are affected'.

The '*Plaumann*' test has become the classic test for individual concern. It was crucially confirmed in *Union de Pequenos Agricultores v Council* (case C–50/00; see 12.4.3.5 below). It is, however, more easily stated than applied, since it does not specify *what* characteristics 'peculiarly relevant to him' the applicant must prove to establish individual concern or what circumstances will differentiate him from all other persons.

It will *not* be sufficient to prove that his business interests have been adversely affected, as was clearly the case in *Plaumann & Co v Commission. Nor* is it sufficient that they were affected in a different way, or more seriously, than other similar traders. These arguments were rejected in *Eridania* (cases 10 and 18/68), and in *Calpak* (cases 789 and 790/79), in which the applicant pear processors claimed that the Commission's mode of calculation of pear-processing aids operated particularly unfairly on itself as a private company as compared with other pear producers such as public companies and cooperatives.

Equally is it not sufficient that the applicant's identity is known to, or ascertainable by, the Commission when the measure is passed. In *UNICME v Council* (case 123/77) an association of Italian motorcycle importers was seeking to annul a Commission regulation, authorising the Italian government to impose temporary quotas on motorcycles imported from Japan. The measure was in retaliation for the imposition by the Japanese of a quota on the import of Italian ski boots. Members of the association were the only persons concerned and they were all concerned. They were ascertainable and many had already applied for import licences. Their application was held inadmissable. The Court found it unnecessary to consider whether the contested measure was a true regulation, as it was not of direct or individual concern to the applicants. It 'would only affect the interests of the applicants when their request for a licence was refused'. 'The possibility of determining more or less precisely the number or even the identity of the persons to whom the measure applies by no means implies that it must be regarded as being of individual concern to them'. While the former statement may be open to question as a ground for denying direct and individual concern, since it could be applied to *any* act addressed to a third party, such as the decisions in *Bock* and *International Fruit Co NV*, which were found to be of individual concern, the latter recurs consistently in the Court's case law on individual concern.

Will a measure be deemed of individual concern if a causal connection can be proved between a particular measure and the applicant's own case? This was not found to be the case in *Spijker Kwasten BV v Commission* (case 231/82). Here the Commission issued a decision, at the request of the Dutch government, enabling the government to ban the import of Chinese brushes for a six-month period, from July to 31 December 1982. Prior to the above request being made the applicant had applied for a licence to import such brushes. There was no doubt a causal link between its application and the Dutch government's request. The request and the Commission's decision were prompted by its application. Moreover the company was the only importer of these brushes in Holland, and the only one likely to want to import them during the six-month period in question. Yet it was held not to be individually concerned. The measure, the Court held, was of general application. There was nothing to stop others applying for licences during that same period.

This case also confirmed a point established earlier in *Glucoseries Réunies v Commission* (case 1/64), that the fact that the applicant (in this case the sole producer of glucose in Belgium and the principal exporter of glucose in France) is the *only* person likely to be affected by the measure is not a characteristic peculiarly relevant to him such as to give rise to individual concern, as long as there is a theoretical possibility that others can enter the field and be affected by the same measure.

What characteristic peculiarly relevant to him must the applicant then prove in order to establish individual concern?

(a) *Measure referable specifically to applicant's situation and affecting a closed class*

Although there is no single satisfactory test a common thread runs through most of the cases in which individual concern has been held to exist. In almost every case the measure which the applicant seeks to challenge, although addressed to another person, is referable specifically to his situation. Moreover, not only does it affect him as though he were the person addressed, but it affects him either *alone* or as a member of a fixed and *closed* class; no one else is capable of entering the field and being affected by the same measure.

For example, the measure may have been issued in response to a licence or tender application. In *Alfred Toepfer KG v Commission* (cases 106 and 107/63) Toepfer had, amongst others, requested a licence from the German government to import cereals from France. The Commission's decision, made at the request of the German government, was a confirmation of the government's measure refusing to grant the import certificate. The only persons affected by the decision were those who had already applied for licences. They were individually concerned.

Similarly in *Werner A Bock KG v Commission* (case 62/70), the firm of Bock had applied for a permit to import a consignment of Chinese mushrooms, for which it already had a firm offer. As Chinese mushrooms, at the time, were in free circulation in the EC, the German government, if it wished to prohibit their import into Germany, needed authority from the Commission to do so. Following Bock's application, the German government, on 11 September, applied to the Commission for that authority, which the Commission granted by a decision on 15 September. The Court held that Bock was individually concerned; the decision was passed in response to its application. (See also *Simmenthal SpA v Commission* (case 92/78)—decision issued in response to claimant's tender.)

A similar connection existed in *Philip Morris Holland BV v Commission* (case 730/79). Here the decision in question, which was addressed to the Dutch government, requested the government to refrain from granting state aid to the applicant tobacco company, Philip Morris. The Court assumed without argument that the company was individually concerned. In *Consorzio Gruppo di Azione Locale 'Murgia Messapica' v Commission* (case T–465/93) the applicant consortium had applied for grants from the Community Leader programme: they were found to be individually concerned by the Commission's decision addressed to the Italian authorities rejecting their application for aid.

International Fruit Co. NV v Commission (No 1) (cases 41–4/70) concerned a Commission 'regulation', controlling the issue of import licences for apples from non-Member States. The regulation was issued by the Commission on the basis of applications received during the preceding week, following an assessment of the overall situation. It applied *only* to those who had applied for licences during that week. It was held to be of individual concern to the applicants. On the same reasoning the measure was found not to be a true regulation at all, but a bundle of decisions.

The courts have noted that an individual will be individually concerned should their existing rights be affected by the decision. This can be seen clearly in the *Infront* case, which concerned the exclusive rights to broadcast certain football matches, which were acquired by Infront before the UK (acting under the Television without Frontiers Directive) determined that those matches should be broadcast free to air. Being the holder of an intellectual property right may give a strong claim to be individually concerned by a measure affecting those rights (see also *Codorniu SA v Council* (case C–309/89) below).

However, even a 'true' regulation can be of individual concern to *some* individuals, as it can be in the nature of a decision to some individuals, if it is referable expressly or impliedly to their particular situation, either alone or as a member of a known and *closed* class (*Japanese ball-bearing case* (cases 113 and 118–21/77); *Allied Corporation v Commission* (cases 239 and 275/82); *CAM SA v Commission* (case 100/74), overruling *Compagnie Française Commerciale et Financière SA v Commission* (case 64/69)). Likewise in *Codorniu SA v Council* (case C–309/89) the applicant producers of sparkling wine were differentiated from all other producers of sparkling wine because they were prevented by the regulation from exercising their registered trade-mark right in 'Gran Cremant di Codorniu'. *Sofrimport SARL v Commission* (case C–152/88) also concerned a successful challenge of this nature. The applicants, who were fruit importers, were seeking to annul a number of Commission regulations suspending the issue of import licences for apples from Chile and fixing quantities of such imports from third countries. Under one of the regulations (2702/72) the Commission was required under Article 3 to take into account, when exercising its powers under the regulations, the 'special position of products in transit' when the regulations come into force. The applicants had goods in transit when the contested regulations came into force. The ECJ held that they were individually concerned. 'Such persons constituted a restricted group *which could not be extended* after the contested measure took effect'.

The reason why the applicant in *Spijker Kwasten* (case 231/82) failed to establish individual concern was that, although there was a causal link between its licence application and the Commission's decision, the latter measure allowing the Dutch authorities to introduce a quota was deliberately designed to take effect for the period *subsequent* to that for which the applicant had applied for licences. The applications it had already lodged were not affected by the measure: it applied only to future transactions: thus there was a theoretical possibility that other traders could be equally affected.

(b) *Measure issued as a result of proceedings initiated by applicant or in which the applicant has played a legitimate part*

A rather different situation in which the necessary link has been held to exist between the applicant and the challenged act to constitute individual concern, is when the act is not 'directed at' him but issued as a result of proceedings in which the applicant has played a legitimate part. In *Metro-SB-Grossmärkte GmbH & Co KG v Commission* (case 26/76) the applicant was seeking to challenge a decision issued to another firm, SABA, in the context of EC competition policy. The decision was issued following a complaint by Metro under Article 3 of Regulation 17/62 (now repealed, see Chapter 29) that SABA was acting in breach of Article 81 (ex 85; post Lisbon 101 TFEU). The Court held, on the question of admissibility, that since persons with a legitimate interest were entitled, under Article 3 of Regulation 17/62, to request the Commission to investigate the infringement they should be allowed to institute Article 230 proceedings in order to protect that interest. Thus Metro was individually concerned. A similar approach has been taken with regard to involvement in state aid proceedings (see Chapter 31).

On similar reasoning, in *Timex Corporation v Council* (case 264/82), Timex was deemed to be individually concerned and permitted to challenge an anti-dumping regulation; the company had initiated the complaint (as it was entitled to do under a further anti-dumping regulation) and had given evidence in the proceedings. (See also *COFAZ v Commission* (case 169/84)—applicants individually concerned in Commission decision concerning state aids; they had initiated the complaint and taken part in the proceedings; see also *FEDIOL v Commission* (case 191/82); *Associazione Italiana Tecnico Economica del Cemento v Commission* (cases T–447–9/93); *Comité Central d'Entreprise de la Société Générale des Grandes Sources v Commission* (case T–96/92)—applicants were 'recognised representatives of employers' under Regulation 4064/89).)

(c) Anti-dumping cases

It has been noted above that in considering whether the measure challenged is in the nature of a decision to the applicant, the Court appears to have moved towards a more liberal approach, particularly in the context of a challenge to anti-dumping duties, even when they are imposed in 'true' regulations. It has also relaxed its approach to the question of individual concern in this area. Where the applicant is a complainant or has been concerned in the preliminary investigations he will be individually concerned on the principles outlined above. But he will also be deemed to be individually concerned where his retail prices or business dealings have been used as a basis for establishing the existence of dumping (see *Enital* (case C–304/86)). However, in the absence of these factors the ECJ was not in its earlier case law prepared to find individual concern. In *Allied*, independent importers (as opposed to manufacturers and exporters) who had not been involved in the preliminary proceedings and who were affected simply as members of a class failed to establish individual concern. However, in *Extramet* (case C–358/89) the ECJ, departing from its previous case law, was prepared to concede that an independent importer, who was not involved in the original proceedings and whose retail prices or dealings with manufacturers or exporters of the goods in question were not taken into account by the Commission in establishing the existence of dumping was individually concerned in a regulation imposing definitive anti-dumping duties on imports of calcium metal from the People's Republic of China and the Soviet Union. The ECJ held that:

> the recognition of the right of certain categories of traders to bring an action for the annulment of certain anti-dumping Regulations cannot prevent other traders from also claiming to be individually concerned by reason of certain attributes which are peculiar to them and which differentiate them from all other persons.

The relevant attributes, satisfied in *Extramet*, were:

(a) They were the largest importer of the product forming the subject-matter of the anti-dumping measure and were the end users of the product.

(b) Their business activities depended to a very large extent on the imports in question and were seriously affected by the contested regulation.

(c) There was a limited number of manufacturers of the product concerned and the importers had difficulty in obtaining supplies from the sole Community producer, who was its main competitor for the processed product (pure calcium for use in the metallurgy industry).

The judgment in *Extramet* extended, but did little to clarify, the law in this difficult area; it did however indicate a possible trend towards a more liberal approach to the question of individual concern where the number of affected applicants is limited and the effect of the measure on the applicant severe. The principles stated were not expressly confined to anti-dumping cases.

(d) *Other situations*

In addition to the categories of cases outlined above in which individual concern may be found two further exceptional cases must be mentioned. In *Partie Ecologiste 'Les Verts' v Parliament* (case 294/83) the ECJ found that the Green Party was individually concerned in Parliament's decision, taken in 1983, allocating funds for the European election campaign of 1984, even though the decision affected all the political parties, actual and potential, seeking election in 1984. The Green Party was only affected as a member of an indeterminate class. However, the Court's decision on this matter was clearly (and expressly) based on policy. It reasoned that the political parties represented on the Bureau making the decision on the allocation of funds had themselves benefited from the allocation, and there was no way in which rival groupings might challenge this allocation in advance of the elections. The case was admissible and the applicants succeeded in their claim for annulment. As has been noted, the Court took a more restrictive view in the subsequent case of *Les Verts v Parliament* (case 190/84).

AE Piraiki-Patraiki v Commission (case 11/82) concerned rather different facts. The applicants were a group of Greek manufacturers and exporters of cotton yarn, who sought to challenge a Commission decision addressed to the French government authorising the latter to impose a quota system on the import of Greek cotton yarn. As the decision applied generally and there were no factors linking it directly with the applicants' particular situation, one might have imagined that individual concern would be lacking. This was not found to be the case. The Court found that for those who, prior to the decision, had entered into contracts to be performed subsequently, the decision was of individual concern. The Court's decision was firmly based on Article 13(3) of the Act of Accession 1979, which imposes a duty on the Commission to consider those whose contracts may be affected by their measures. The Commission's decision was held not to be of individual concern to manufacturers and exporters whose existing contracts were not affected by the measure.

In that the Act of Accession expressly required the Commission to take into account those manufacturers and exporters whose contracts might be affected by its measures, the decision is consistent with *Sofrimport* (case C–152/88). Nevertheless, while such a class is closed it is potentially very wide. Thus *AE Piraiki-Patraiki* must be seen as a case resting on its own special facts, and not as giving rise to a general claim for individual concern based on interference with the applicants' existing contracts. EC legislation will frequently interfere with existing business contracts: this will not, of itself, be sufficient to constitute individual concern.

12.4.3.4 *Can the restrictive interpretation of* locus standi *for individuals still be justified?*

There is no doubt that it is fear of opening floodgates, together with a desire not unduly to hamper the institutions in their task of implementing Community policies, problems common to all administrative law systems, which has led the courts to a strict interpretation of Article 230, particularly Article 230(2) concerning the *locus standi* of individuals. In closing the door to an application under this article the courts have often adverted to the possibility of alternative means of challenge to the validity of Community law under Article 234, in an action before the applicant's national court (eg, *Spijker Kwasten BV v Commission* (case 231/82); *UNICME* (case 123/77)). Any binding Community act can be challenged in preliminary rulings proceedings (see Chapter 10). It has been suggested that this roundabout approach to matters of validity (which can only be decided authoritatively by the ECJ) is prompted by a desire to filter out unnecessary claims and ensure that only the claims of genuine merit reach the ECJ. One such claim was *Royal Scholten-Honig (Holdings) Ltd v Intervention Board for Agricultural Produce* (cases 103 and 145/77) in which the claimant finally succeeded in obtaining a declaration of invalidity on a reference under Article 234 having failed to establish *locus standi* in an action under Article 230 (*Koninklijke Scholten-Honig NV v Council and Commission* (case 101/76)) on the grounds that the disputed measure was a true regulation. Thus where there is an appropriate issue of national law which a 'natural or legal person' may raise before his national court, to which he may attach a challenge to the validity of Community law, a fortiori where there may be difficulty in establishing individual concern, the safer course would be to raise the issue of invalidity before his national court and press for an early reference to the ECJ under Article 234. Where he has no claim under national law, and thus no alternative remedy, and is able to establish direct and individual concern, the courts' recent case law suggests that an application under Article 230 may be admissible even if the applicant seeks to challenge a true regulation.

The above comments, based on the ECJ's past jurisprudence, have now to be considered in the light of *TWD Textilwerke Deggendorf GmbH v Germany* (case C–188/92), decided in 1994. Here the ECJ refused to exercise its jurisdiction under Article 234 to declare on the validity of a Commission decision, addressed to the German government, requiring the government to recover state aids paid to the applicant in breach of the then Articles 92–3 (now 87–8) EC. The German government had informed the applicants of the existence of the decision and of their right to challenge it under Article 230, but the applicants took no action under this article. Instead they sought to challenge the decision later, in the context of domestic proceedings for recovery of the aid wrongfully paid. When the German judge referred to the ECJ for a ruling on the validity of the Commission's decision the ECJ refused its jurisdiction on the grounds that the applicants could and should have challenged the decision directly under Article 230. Since they had been informed of the decision and of their right to challenge it they could not circumvent the two-month limitation period of that article by resorting to action under Article 234.

The implications of this decision are disturbing. Although the applicants were aware of the decision as soon as it was received and clearly would have had *locus standi* to challenge it under Article 230, as being directly and individually concerned, it was not addressed to them. Nor had they been informed of its existence officially, by the Commission. Can and should a notification and advice to act by a national government be deemed sufficient notice of a party's rights and obligations, when he is not the addressee of the decision, such as to require that he move immediately to action under Article 230, or forfeit his right of challenge? Can this be deemed effective judicial protection for individuals' Community rights? Although the *TWD* ruling has been applied subsequently (for example, *Wiljo NV v Belgium* (case C–178/95)), the ECJ has also recognised the difficulties for an applicant unsure of his *locus standi*. In *R v Intervention Board for Agricultural Produce, ex parte Accrington Beef Co Ltd* (case C–241/95) the ECJ held that a preliminary rulings reference challenging the validity of a regulation was admissible despite the applicant's failure to bring a claim under Article 230 within the time limit, since it was not clear that the applicants would have had standing for a judicial-review application. More recently, an Article 234 reference which came before the ECJ in a case based on the same facts as those in which a judicial review action had been summarily dismissed by the CFI was held to be admissible (*Atzeni and ors* (joined cases C–346 and 529/03)). The CFI had dismissed the judicial review action for being out of time without considering the *locus standi* of Atzeni et al. When the matter came before the ECJ via Article 234, the ECJ had to consider whether *TWD* applied. It emphasised that the *locus standi* of the applicants was not clear: they had not been mentioned in the decision addressed, in this case, to the Italian government; nor had the government informed them of the decision and of the possibility of reviewing it.

Given the difficulties of establishing clear rules in relation to *locus standi* for Article 230, the extent of this ruling is not clear, although it seems that the ECJ is limiting *TWD* to its facts. Nonetheless, the approach in *TWD* will undoubtedly continue to create uncertainty, and encourage pre-emptive and possibly inappropriate action under that article by parties fearing rejection in preliminary rulings.

12.4.3.5 *A false dawn:* Jego-Quere (case T–177/01) v Union de Pequenos Agricultores (case C–50/00)

Despite the frequent criticism of the restrictive interpretation given to direct and individual concern, the ECJ has adhered to the view originally taken in *Plaumann*. However, a strong Advocate-General's opinion in *Union de Pequenos Agricultores (UPA) v Council* (case C–50/00) and the judgment by the CFI in *Jego-Quere et Cie v Commission* (case T–177/01) appeared to herald a more liberal attitude to the interpretation of individual concern.

In *UPA*, a trade association challenged a Commission regulation (1638/98), but this application had been dismissed by the CFI because UPA could not demonstrate individual concern. Moreover, the CFI pointed out that UPA could have brought an action under national law and then asked for a reference to be made under Article 234 to question the legality of the regulation in question. UPA's argument that the restrictive interpretation of individual concern meant that there was no effective legal protection for individuals was rejected. On appeal, Advocate-General Jacobs was unconvinced by the CFI's reasons for dismissing the application and reviewed extensively the arguments put forward for the restrictive interpretation of individual concern. He observed that a direct challenge under Article 230 would be more appropriate than the procedure under Article 234, and that the restrictive approach taken to individual applicants was 'anomalous' in the light of the Court's case law on other aspects of judicial review (para 37). The difficulty with the Article 234 route is that it requires an action before a national court which is not itself entitled to annul the contested measure. Instead, the national court has to consider whether there is sufficient doubt as to its legality for a reference for a preliminary ruling to be made under Article 234. Moreover, not all Community measures could give rise to an action before a national court; consequently, such measures could not be challenged through the Article 234 route at all.

In relation to the test for individual concern itself, Jacobs argued that there was no reason why this should entail a requirement that an individual applicant was differentiated in some way for all others affected by the measure. If a measure adversely affects a large number of individuals and causes widespread harm, then this is a strong reason for accepting challenges by one or more of those individuals (para 59). Accordingly, the test of individual concern should be satisfied if a Community measure, by reason of an individual's particular circumstances, has, or is liable to have, a substantial adverse effect on his interests (para 60, and see paras 61–99 for a detailed justification).

The Advocate-General's opinion in *UPA* found favour with the CFI in *Jego-Quere* (case T–177/01), which was decided between the delivery of the Advocate-General's opinion and the judgment in *UPA*. In *Jego-Quere*, the applicant was found not to have individual concern within the meaning of the established *Plaumann* line of reasoning. In *Jego-Quere* the only possibility for the claimant to challenge the contested regulation was by violating the rules it laid down and then claiming their illegality by way of defence in national proceedings. Nonetheless, the CFI held (rightly, it is submitted), that individuals cannot be required to breach the law to gain access to justice (para 45). Accordingly, and largely in line with Advocate-General Jacob's opinion in *UPA*, the CFI proposed a revised test for individual concern. According to this:

> [a] person is to be regarded as individually concerned by a Community measure of general application that concerns him directly if the measure in question affects his legal position in a manner which is both definite and immediate, by restricting his rights or imposing obligations on him. [Para 51.]

Although this judgment was welcomed by commentators throughout the Union, it appears to have been rather short-lived. When the ECJ handed down its judgment in *UPA*, it reaffirmed the *Plaumann* jurisprudence on individual concern, and emphasised that there was a complete system of judicial protection in place at the Union level. It was for the Member States to ensure that they provide a system which ensures respect for the right to effective judicial protection and which would allow individuals to use the Article 234 route to challenge the validity of Community measures. The Court barely mentioned the Advocate-General's opinion, and completely ignored the decision in *Jego-Quere*. When it heard the appeal from the CFI's decision in *Jego-Quere* (case C–263/02), the ECJ reiterated this reasoning. Despite the continued concerns of Advocate-General Jacobs, the ECJ overturned the decision of the CFI. The ECJ has since reiterated this approach (see, eg, *PKK and KNK* (case C–299/05P)) and has, for example in *Ente per le Ville vesuviane*, rejected claims that such an approach infringed the claimant's right to to a fair trial.

These judgments are a serious blow to those who favoured a more liberal interpretation of the test for individual concern, in particular because *UPA* was decided by an extended Court. It seems that, for the time being, the established interpretation of individual concern will continue to apply. It is now unlikely that there will be a change, and an amendment to the treaty will be required to counter the effects of the *Plaumann* judgment.

This point has been evident for some time. In a report issued in May 1995 for the IGC in 1996 on possible revisions of the provisions relating to the judicial system, the ECJ pointed out the limitations of direct action for annulment for natural or legal persons. It questioned whether the right to bring an action under this provision, which individuals enjoy only with regard to acts of direct and individual concern to them, was sufficient to guarantee for them effective protection against infringements of their fundamental rights from the legislative activity of the Community. No action was taken at Amsterdam, nor at Nice, to guarantee that protection. The Treaty of Lisbon does change the position, though it does not adopt the solution proposed by Advocate-General Jacobs. Instead following the approach proposed in the Constitution, the amended Article 263(4) TFEU would provide that:

> Any natural or legal person may . . . institute proceedings against an act addressed to that person or which is of direct and individual concern to him or her, and against a regulatory act which is of direct concern to him or her and does not entail implementing measures.

Note that this provision changes, and potentially enlarges, the categories of acts which might be challenged by an individual. Crucially, as far as regulatory acts are concerned, the requirement of individual concern has been deleted, though the meaning of 'regulatory acts' in unclear.

12.4.3.6 *Admissibility and interim relief*

In an action for interim relief in a claim based on invalidity of a Community measure, the court will not usually examine the question of admissibility, so as not to prejudice the substance of the case. However, where there is a contention that the claim is 'manifestly inadmissible', the judges hearing the application for interim relief must investigate whether there is a prima facie case for finding that the main application is inadmissible.

12.5 Time limits

An applicant, whether an individual, a Member State or a Community institution, must bring a claim for annulment within two months of:

(a) the publication of the measure, or

(b) its notification to the claimant, or, in the absence thereof,

(c) the day on which it came to the knowledge of the latter, as the case may be (Article 230(3)).

The Rules of Procedure of the Court of Justice, as amended, provide that time runs from receipt by the person concerned of notification of the measure or, where the measure is published, from the end of the fourteenth day after its publication in the *Official Journal*.

Since regulations and, following the TEU, directives, and decisions adopted under the co-decision procedure of Article 251 EC and directives of the Council and the Commission addressed to all Member States are required to be published, time will run for them from the date of their entry into force, which will be either the date specified in the provisions or on the twentieth day following that of their publication (Article 254(1)–(2) EC (ex 191(1)–(2); post Lisbon, Article 297 TFEU). Other directives and decisions 'shall be notified to those to whom they are addressed and shall take effect upon such notification' (Article 254 (ex 191(3)). In the case of a measure addressed to a person other than the applicant, time will run from the date of the applicant's knowledge. This has been held to require 'precise knowledge' of both the contents of the measure in question and the grounds on which it is based. This is necessary to ensure that the applicant is able to exercise his right to initiate proceedings. Thus a summary of the measure will not suffice (*Commission v Socurte* (case C–143/95 P)). Once he is aware of the existence of the measure he must, however, ask for a full text within a reasonable period (*Consorzio Gruppo di Azione Locale 'Murgia Messapica' v Commission* (case T–465/93)).

The 'date of knowledge' is the date on which the applicant became aware of the precise content of the measure. It is not the date on which he realised it could be challenged. Hence the importance of recognising an act as a measure capable of annulment.

The limitation period may be extended to take into account the distance between the ECJ at Luxembourg and the applicant's place of residence. In the UK ten days are allowed. It may also be extended if the party concerned proves the existence of unforeseeable circumstances or *force majeure*. In *Bayer AG v Commission* (case C–195/91 P) the ECJ held that in order to establish such grounds the applicant must show 'abnormal difficulties, independent of the will of the person concerned, and apparently inevitable, even if all due care is taken'. Likewise, the concept of 'excusable error', justifying derogation from time limits, can concern only 'exceptional circumstances' in which the conduct of the EC institution has given rise to a pardonable confusion on the part of the party concerned. The applicant cannot rely on his or her own organisation's internal malfunctioning as an excuse for an error.

12.5.1 Expiry of time limit

Once the two-month time limit has expired a claimant cannot seek to challenge a measure by the back door, either by invoking Article 241 (*exception d'illégalité*, see *Commission v Belgium* (case 156/77)) or by alleging a failure to act when the institution concerned refuses by decision to amend or withdraw the disputed measure (see *Eridania v Commission* (cases 10 and 18/68)) or take the requested action (*Irish Cement Ltd v Commission* (cases 166/86 and 220/86), see Chapter 13). Time limits will not be allowed to run afresh when the addressee objects to the EC institution's initial reasoning and that institution (normally the Commission) merely confirms its original decision (*Control Union Gesellschaft für Warenkontrolle mbH v Commission* (case C–250/90)).

An indirect challenge using the preliminary rulings procedure before the applicant's national court will not be subject to the two-month limit. In actions before national courts national rules of limitation apply, provided they are adequate to ensure the effective protection of individuals' Community rights (see Chapter 8). However, following *TWD Textilwerke Deggendorf GmbH v Germany* (case C–188/92) it is possible that an individual who has *locus standi* under Article 230 will not be allowed to circumvent the time limit imposed by that Article by challenging legislation outside those limits under Article 234. If this is the case, access to the Court under Article 234 should only be denied when the applicant's *locus standi* under Article 230 is unequivocally clear. As suggested above this seems to have been the approach adopted and, for example, in *Eurotunnel* (case C–408/95), the challenge via Article 234 was allowed as it was not clear that the claim under Article 230 would have been admissible.

12.6 The merits

Once the Court has decided that the claim is admissible, the case will be decided on the merits. Article 230 provides four grounds for annulment, drawn directly from French administrative law. These are:

(a) lack of competence

(b) infringement of an essential procedural requirement

(c) infringement of the treaty or any rule of law relating to its application

(d) misuse of powers.

These categories are not mutually exclusive, and often more than one ground is cited in a given case. Nonetheless, in making an application, the applicant must identify clearly the facts and basic legal arguments of the case. In particular, the applicant should not rely on 'catch-all' references to documents annexed to the application. The CFI has held that it is not for the Court to seek out and identify the grounds in which the application is based (see, eg, *Cipeke–Comércio e Indústria de Papel Lda v Commission* (case T–84/96), paras 29–4). However, it is not clear how this statement relates to the idea that the Court can consider an infringement of an essential procedural requirement of its own motion (see *Socurte–Sociedade de Curtumes a Sul do Tejo Lda v Commission* (case T–432–4/93), para 63). It seems, however, that the principle has gained acceptance. More recently, in *Laboratoires Servier v Commission* (case T–147/00, on appeal case C–156/03P), the CFI annulled a Commission decision withdrawing marketing authorisation for certain medicinal products. It did so on its own motion, observing that the lack of competence of an institution which has adopted an act constitutes a ground of annulment for reasons of public policy, which must be raised by the court. The ECJ confirmed this approach in the appeal against the CFI's decision. (See also *Strabag Benelux v Council* (case T–183/00, under appeal case C–186/030; and *Henkel v OHIM-LHS (UK)* (case T–308/01).)

12.6.1 Lack of competence

This is the equivalent to the English doctrine of substantive ultra vires. The institution responsible for adopting the measure in question must have the legal authority to do so. This may derive from the EC Treaty or from secondary legislation. In the *ERTA* case (case 22/70) the Commission challenged the Council's power to participate in the shaping of the road transport agreement, since under the treaty (Article 300 (ex 228); post Lisbon, Article 218 TFEU) it is the Commission which is empowered to negotiate international agreements and the Council whose duty it is to conclude them. On the facts the Court found that the Council had not exceeded its powers. On a number of occasions Community law has been challenged as having been enacted under the wrong legal basis (see *Parliament v Council* (case C–295/90)). Clearly the choice of legal basis will be important, as it will determine the appropriate procedure to be followed and the vote required for the adoption of legislation (see Chapters 2 and 3).

The Court allows the institutions some latitude in their choice of legal base and their scope for action under that base. In *Germany v Commission* (case C–359/92) it held that Article 95 (ex 100a; post Lisbon, Article 114 TFEU), which provides for the approximation of the provisions laid down by law, regulation or administrative action in Member States which have as their object the establishing and functioning of the internal market (see Chapter 16) was to be interpreted as 'encompassing the Council's power to lay down measures relating to a specific class of products and, if necessary, individual measures concerning those products'. Germany's challenge to Article 9 of Council Directive 92/59 on product safety, based on former Article 100a (new 95), which empowered the Commission to adopt decisions requiring Member States to take temporary measures in the event of a serious and immediate risk to the health and safety of consumers, failed. In *Portugal v Council* (case C–268/94), the Portuguese government sought the annulment of a decision on the basis that the wrong treaty base had been used. The decision referred to what were then Articles 113 and 130y EC (now 120 and 181 EC; post Lisbon, Articles 144 and 211 TFEU respectively), dealing with commercial policy, which only required that the decision be adopted by qualified majority vote. The Portuguese government claimed that the agreement to which the decision related contained provisions aimed at protecting democracy and human rights in India, and should have been made under former Article 235 EC (now 308; post Lisbon, Article 352 TFEU), which would have required unanimity. The ECJ held that on the facts of the case the provisions of the then Article 130y (now 181) were broad enough to encompass the complained-of clauses, and that to rule otherwise would be to deprive the specific clauses of their substance.

We have seen that similar issues arise in relation to determining the allocation of powers between the pillars of the Union, and that the ECJ has tended to favour an approach which gives the *acquis communautaire* the maximum protection (see, eg, *Kadi v Council* (joined cases C–402 and 415/02P), discussed Chapter 3).

The Court is stricter in its approach to questions concerning the allocation of competence between the Union institutions (see, eg, *France, Netherlands and Spain v Commission* (case C–327/91)), and, as noted earlier, the ECJ's decisions have protected the procedural rights of the European Parliament (see, eg, *Parliament v Council (Re European Development Fund)* (case C–316/91)).

12.6.2 Infringement of an essential procedural requirement

This is equivalent to procedural ultra vires in English law. Institutions, when enacting binding measures, must follow the correct procedures. These procedures may be laid down in the EC Treaty or secondary legislation. For example, Article 253 EC (ex 190; post Lisbon, 296 TFEU) requires that all secondary legislation must state the reasons on which it is based, and must refer to proposals and opinions which were required to be obtained. The Court has held that reasons must not be too vague or inconsistent; they must be coherent; they must mention figures and essential facts on which they rely. They must be adequate to indicate the conscientiousness of the decision, and detailed enough to be scrutinised by the Court (*Germany v Commission (Re Tariff Quotas on Wine)* (case 24/62)—Commission decision annulled; too vague, no facts and figures). The purpose of the requirement to give reasons is to enable those concerned to defend their rights and to enable the Court to exercise its supervisory jurisdiction. However, the Court will not annul an act for an insignificant defect. Nor will it annul an act on this ground unless the claimant can prove that, but for this defect, the result would have been different (*Distillers Co Ltd v Commission* (case 30/78)).

In *Roquette Frères SA v Council* (case 138/79) and *Maizena GmbH v Council* (case 139/79) a Council regulation was annulled on the grounds of the Council's failure to consult Parliament, as it was required to do under Article 37 EC (ex 43(2); post Lisbon, Article 43 TFEU). Although the Council had consulted Parliament, it was held not to have given Parliament sufficient time to express an opinion on the measure in question. Where no time limit is imposed it is presumed that Parliament must be given a reasonable time in which to express its opinion. In *Infront* (case T–33/01), the letter to the UK government was signed by a director-general of the Commission who had not consulted the College of Commissioners. The letter was therefore annulled for failure to follow proper procedures.

12.6.3 Infringement of the treaty or any rule of law relating to its application

Clearly, when an act is invalid for lack of competence or for an infringement of an essential procedural requirement, this may involve an infringement of the treaty, but this ground of annulment is wider since it extends to *any* treaty provision. In *Adams v Commission (No 1)* (case 145/83), an action for non-contractual liability (see Chapter 13), the Commission was found to have acted in breach of its duty of confidentiality under Article 287 (ex 214; post Lisbon, 339 TFEU).

Infringement of any rule of law relating to the treaty's application is wider again, and certainly wider than any comparable rule of English law. This is where general principles of law, discussed at length in Chapter 6, are relevant. A measure can be annulled if it is in breach not only of any general principle of law approved by the Court (eg, equality, proportionality) but of any principle common to the constitutions of Member States (*Internationale Handelsgesellschaft mbH* (case 11/70)) and even principles of international treaties in the field of human rights on which Member States have collaborated (*J Nold KG v Commission* (case 4/73)). In *Royal Scholten-Honig (Holdings) Ltd v Intervention Board for Agricultural Produce* (cases 103 and 145/77) a Community regulation was held invalid for breach of the principle of equality. In *Transocean Marine Paint Association v Commission* (case 17/74) (see Chapter 6) part of a decision was annulled for breach of the principle of natural justice. In *August Töpfer & Co GmbH v Commission* (case 112/77) a decision was annulled for breach of the principle of legal certainty, for infringement of the applicant's legitimate expectations. Although the Court will not lightly set aside legislation for breach of this principle and will expect businessmen to anticipate and guard against foreseeable developments, within the bounds of 'normal' economic risks, this is a ground of some potential (see *Amylum v Council* (case 108/81); *Mulder v Council* (case C–104/89)). Note, however, that a trader is unlikely to have legitimate expectations that do not accord with existing Community rules (see, for example, *Efisol SA* (case T–336/94)). Thus, it is difficult to argue that a requirement to pay back illegally granted state aid would be in breach of legitimate expectations. In *Opel Austria GmbH v Council* (case T–115/94), the CFI held that the principle of legitimate expectations within the EC was the corollary of the principle of good faith in public international law. Where Community institutions have deposited their instruments of approval of an international agreement and the date of the entry into force of that agreement is known, any measures contrary to provisions of such agreements having direct effect will be in breach of legitimate expectations. In *Racke* (case C–162/96), the ECJ held that the ECJ's jurisdiction to review the validity of a Community act could not be limited as regards the grounds on which it could find a measure invalid. In this case, it held that a Community measure, a regulation, could be held to be invalid were it contrary to international law (c.f. *Kadi* (joined cases C–402 and 415/05P)).

Although it has not yet been done successfully, legislation could in principle be challenged for breach of the principle of subsidiarity, either as a general principle or as now expressed in Article 5 (ex 3b) EC (see Chapters 3 and 6). The German government raised the question of subsidiarity, albeit in a different context, in *Germany v Parliament* (case C–233/94). It sought to challenge Directive 94/19, arguing that there had been a breach of the duty to state reasons for the legislation as required by the then Article 190, in that the directive did not explain how it complied with the principle of subsidiarity set out in Article 5 EC. The ECJ rejected this argument, stating that the necessary information could be inferred from the recitals to the directive.

Because of the breadth of the concept of 'any rule of law relating to the [treaty's] application', the acts of the EC institutions are vulnerable to attack on this ground. Thus the ECJ has held that where the Community legislature has a discretion to act in a complex economic situation, such as the implementation of the Community's agricultural policy, both as regards the nature and scope of the measures to be taken and the finding of basic facts, the Court, in reviewing the exercise of such a power:

> must confine itself to examining whether it contains a manifest error or constitutes a misuse of power or whether the authority in question did not clearly exceed the bounds of its discretion. [*Commission v Council* (case C–122/94).]

The ECJ's approach to the Community's liability in damages for legislative measures involving choices of economic policy, which the CFI adopts also, reflects a similar concern not to fetter the discretion of the EC institutions when they are implementing Community policy. In this context the Court may be accused of occasionally going too far to protect the Community institutions (see *Germany v Council* (case C–280/93), see Chapters 6 and 14).

12.6.4 Misuse of power

This concept stems from the French *détournement de pouvoir*. It means, broadly, the use of a power for purposes other than those for which it was granted—for example, where powers granted to help one group (eg, producers) are used to benefit another (eg, distributors) (see *Simmenthal SpA v Commission* (case 92/78)). It has been defined by the ECJ as:

> the adoption by a Community institution of a measure with the exclusive or main purpose of achieving an end other than that stated or evading a procedure specifically prescribed by the Treaty for dealing with the circumstances of the case. [*Parliament v Commission* (case C–156/93).]

The concept is not confined to abuses of power, nor is an ulterior or improper motive essential; an improper or illegitimate use of power is all that is required. However, this provision has been narrowly interpreted. In *Fédération Charbonnière de Belgique v High Authority* (case 8/55), in interpreting the comparable provision (Article 33) of the ECSC Treaty, the Court held that a measure will not be annulled for misuse of power if the improper use had no effect on its substance; nor will it be annulled if the authority had acted from mixed motives, proper and improper, as long as the proper purpose was dominant. It is thus a difficult ground to establish.

The case of *Werner A Bock KG v Commission* (case 62/70) was considered, but not decided, on this ground. Although there was no clear collusion between the German government and the Commission over the issuing of the decision, there were definite signs of collaboration. The case was eventually decided, and the decision annulled, for breach of the principle of proportionality. The Commission's action was more than was necessary in the circumstances, since the quantities of mushrooms at stake were so small as to be insignificant.

There is much overlap between the above grounds. The Court rarely examines each one precisely and is often vague as to which ground forms the basis of its decision. *BEUC v Commission* (case T–37/92) concerned the Commission's decision not to investigate the agreement between the British Society of Motor Manufacturers and the Japanese government limiting imports of Japanese cars to 11 per cent of total UK sales. This decision was prima facie contrary to Article 81, but was justified by the Commission, inter alia, because the agreement was permitted as a matter of UK policy. The CFI annulled the decision simply on the ground that it constituted an 'error of law'. Despite the Court's lack of precision in these matters it is wise to plead as many grounds as seem applicable.

The grounds apply equally to an examination of the validity of a measure on reference from national courts under Article 234. They also apply to an enquiry into the validity of regulations under Article 241 (12.8) and to an application for damages under Article 288(2) (ex 215(2)) (Chapter 14) where the action is based on an illegal act of the institutions.

12.7 Consequences of a successful action

If an annulment action under Article 230 is successful the act will be declared void under Article 231 (ex 174; post Lisbon 264 TFEU). A measure may be declared void in part only, provided that the offending part can be effectively severed. Under

Article 231(2), however, the Court may, following a successful action for annulment, 'state which of the effects of the Regulation which it has declared void shall be considered as definitive'. This has been done in the interests of legal certainty, to avoid upsetting past transactions based on a regulation, a normative act. In *Roquette Frères SA v France* (case 145/79) a declaration of invalidity of a Community regulation was held to be purely prospective in its effects. The wisdom of such a ruling has since been doubted, on the grounds that such a limitation would deprive the applicant of his right to effective judicial protection (*Roquette Frères SA v Hauptzollamt Geldern* (case C–228/92)). However, in *Parliament v Council* (case C–360/93) the ECJ annulled two Council decisions and, on the basis of Article 231(2) ordered that *all* the effects of the annulled decisions must be maintained in force. In *R v Ministry of Agriculture, Fisheries and Food, ex parte H and R Ecroyd Holdings Ltd* (case C–127/94) the ECJ held that, in a complex field, an individual may not rely on a ruling of invalidity, even in a situation arising *after* that ruling, until replacement legislation has been introduced. Nonetheless, it should be noted that in a subsequent case involving Ecroyd (*Ecroyd v Commission* (case T–220/97)), the CFI held that should a court find a measure invalid, it is not enough to repeal that measure; the position of the complainants must also be addressed so that they do not continue to suffer loss. A successful action for damages under Article 288(2) could arise in these circumstances, as indeed it did in this case.

A slightly different point arose in *Commission v AssiDoman Kraft Products AB* (case C–310/97P). The case concerned certain fines imposed on a number of undertakings for breach of the competition rules. Some of the undertakings appealed against the Commission's decisions, resulting in the partial annulment of the Commission's decision and the reduction of the fines imposed on the appellant undertakings. Several other companies, which had also been fined but which had not been party to the appeal, then requested that the Commission reconsider their position in the light of the annulment ruling. The Commission refused, as it argued that the companies involved in the competition proceedings had each been addressed individually and therefore a finding of invalidity as regards a decision addressed to one company did not affect a similar decision addressed to another. The applicant companies sought to challenge before the European courts on the basis that the Commission was obliged to reconsider by virtue of Article 233 (ex 176; post Lisbon 266 TFEU). The matter finally came before the ECJ, the CFI having found in the companies' favour. The ECJ overturned the CFI's ruling, holding that the scope of Article 233 was limited in two ways. First, a ruling for annulment could not go further than the applicant requested, and thus the matter tried by the Community courts could relate only to aspects of the decision which affected the applicants. The ECJ then held that although the operative part of the judgment and its reasoning were binding *erga omnes*, '[this] cannot entail annulment of an act not challenged before the Community judicature but alleged to be vitiated by the same illegality' (para 54).

The applicants in this case could not of course challenge the original Commission decision to fine them because the time limits for bringing a challenge had long expired. Although one might argue that the companies in this case could have challenged the Commission's decision earlier, the ruling in this case does lead to the anomalous position that some companies are treated less favourably than others in an equivalent situation.

12.8 Scope of indirect review under Article 241 EC

12.8.1 Scope

Although Article 241 entitles 'any party' to attack a regulation 'notwithstanding the expiry' of the time limit laid down in Article 230, it is not designed to provide a means of escaping the restrictions either of time or *locus standi* laid down in Article 230. No action can be brought *directly* against a regulation under Article 241. As the Court held in *Milchwerke Heinz Wöhrmann & Sohn KG v Commission* (cases 31 and 33/62), in the context of an action brought under Article 241 to annul three Commission decisions, a plea under Article 241 can be raised as an *incidental* matter *only* in the course of legal proceedings based on other provisions of the treaty. In *Wöhrmann* the action was brought *solely* under Article 241, since the time limit within which the decisions should have been challenged under Article 230 had elapsed. Thus, the application was rejected. (See also *Commission v Belgium* (case 156/77) and, more recently, *Comité des Salines de France v Commission* (case T–154/94).)

The purpose of Article 241 is to allow a party to question the legality of a general act on which a subsequent act (eg, a decision), or failure to act, is based. A decision is often, indeed normally, based on some general authorising act. Although a decision, in principle subject to challenge under Article 230, may in itself be unimpeachable, it may be based on a general act that is not. A non-privileged applicant has no *locus standi* to challenge a general act under Article 230. Even a privileged applicant under Article 230 may not be aware of the illegality of the general act until affected by some subsequent act issuing from that 'tainted' source. By this time the two months within which the original act should have been challenged may have elapsed. Article 241 provides a means whereby this underlying act may be challenged *indirectly*, free of time limit, before the ECJ in proceedings in which it is 'in issue', in much the same way as questions concerning the validity of EC law may be raised indirectly in the context of domestic proceedings before national courts.

12.8.2 Proceedings in which Article 241 may be invoked

In theory Article 241 may be invoked in the context of any proceedings brought directly before the ECJ in which it is relevant. This interpretation should be treated with caution. In *Hessische Knappschaft v Maison Singer et Fils* (case 44/65) the Court was not prepared to consider a claim under Article 241 in the context of a reference from a national court under Article 234. However, in that case the parties had attempted to raise the plea of illegality as a new issue; it had not been raised in the reference by the national court. Their attempt to raise it before the ECJ was thus seen by the Court as an interference with the national court's discretion, and, as such, unacceptable. Nevertheless, it would not be necessary to invoke Article 241 before a national court since these courts are free to refer to the ECJ under Article 234 questions of validity of *any* Community act, and are not constrained by the time limit applicable to a direct challenge under Article 230, subject, of course to the impact of *TWD*. This point seems to have been made in *Nachi Europe GmBH v Hauptzollamt Krefeld* (case C–239/99). The Court held that

Article 241 could not be invoked in the context of a preliminary reference under Article 234, because this is not regarded as a main action before the ECJ (para 34). To hold otherwise would be to provide a duplicate means of challenge as Article 234 already provides for a challenge to the validity of the measure on which a domestic court has requested a ruling.

The main context in which Article 241 is likely to be invoked is to support a challenge under Article 230 to the validity of a measure based on the original, allegedly invalid, act. If the underlying act, challenged under Article 241, is found invalid, it will be declared 'inapplicable' and the subsequent act, affecting the claimant, will be void. Thus the principal object of the exercise will be achieved.

Article 241 may also be relevant to an action under Article 232 for failure to act, where the failure (eg, to issue a decision to the claimant) is based on an invalid general act (see *SNUPAT v High Authority* (cases 32 and 33/58), action under the equivalent provision of the former ECSC Treaty, Article 35). It may also, in theory, be invoked to support an action for damages under Articles 235 and 288(2) EC, or arising out of contract under Article 238 (which gives the court 'jurisdiction to give judgment pursuant to any arbitration clause contained in a contract concluded by or on behalf of the Community') or in appeals against penalties under Article 229 EC. It is submitted that Article 241 may also be invoked as a defence to an action against a Member State under Article 226 (but see *Commission v Belgium* (case 156/77)).

A legitimate challenge under Article 241 may be brought by the applicant or the defendant. There must, however, always be a 'direct judicial link' between the act (or failure to act) affecting the applicant and the general underlying measure subject to challenge (*Italy v Council* (case 32/65)).

As Article 241 is only a complementary remedy it is essential to its success that the time limit and *locus standi* requirements imposed in the principal action before the Court are observed. Article 241 does not provide a means of evading these limits (see *Wöhrmann* (cases 31 and 33/62); *Commission v Belgium* (case 156/77)). Indeed, the Court ruled that a private claimant could not rely on Article 241 EC where it would have been able to bring a challenge under Article 230 EC but failed to do so within the time limit (*Nachi Europe GmBH v Hauptzollamt Krefeld* (case C–239/99)). In this we might see parallels with the ECJ's approach under *TWD*.

12.8.3 Reviewable acts

Although Article 241 is expressed to apply only to regulations, the Court, in keeping with its approach in Article 230, has held that Article 241 applies to any general act having binding force. In *Simmenthal SpA v Commission* (case 92/78) the claimant, a meat processing company, was seeking to annul, under Article 230, a decision addressed to the Italian government, in which the company was directly and individually concerned. The basis of its claim for annulment was that the 'parent' measure, a general notice of invitation to tender, on which the decision was based, was invalid. The Court held that since the notice was a general act, which, although not in the form of a regulation, produced similar effects, it could be challenged under Article 241. The challenge was successful and resulted in the annulment of the decision affecting the claimant.

12.8.3.1 *Is the scope for challenge under Article 241 limited to general measures?*

The principal reason for making an 'exception' for regulations would appear to be to enable individuals, who are unable to challenge general acts under Article 230, to do so when they seek, legitimately, to rely on their invalidity in the context of other proceedings before the Court. A secondary reason would be that, since a regulation is 'of general application' and is not addressed to anyone, its invalidity may not be apparent to the claimant until a subsequent individual measure, based on the general measure, brings it to his attention. Both reasons, ie, lack of opportunity to challenge and absence of notification, would justify extending the scope of Article 241 to enable an individual to challenge, indirectly, any 'parent' act which was not addressed to him or in which he was not directly and individually concerned. The second reason would provide grounds for allowing a privileged applicant to challenge indirectly any 'parent' act which was not addressed to the applicant. This matter has yet to be decided by the Court.

12.8.4 *Locus standi*

Although *locus standi* under Article 241 appears to apply to 'any party', doubts have been expressed as to whether it extends to privileged applicants. It is argued that since Member States and institutions are entitled to seek annulment of *any* act under Article 230, to allow them to invoke Article 241 would be to enable them to challenge acts which they should have challenged, within the time limit, under Article 230. However, Advocate-General Roemer in *Italy v Council* (case 32/65) took the view that a Member State *should* have *locus standi* under Article 241, since the wording of the provision was in no way restrictive, and the illegality of the general provision might not become apparent until it was applied subsequently in a particular case. The Court did not comment on the matter, since it found that the regulations in issue were not relevant to the case, but its silence could be read as consent. Advocate-General Roemer's reasoning is persuasive. Moreover, Article 241 can never be used *merely* to circumvent a time limit; it can only be invoked as an incidental issue, when the claimant is affected by some subsequent act (or failure) arising from the original general act. This provides ample safeguard against abuse.

This point is illustrated by *Commission v Belgium* (case 156/77). Here Article 241 was raised as a defence to an enforcement action against Belgium for infringement of Community law relating to state aids. The Belgians had failed to comply with a Commission decision of May 1976, addressed to the Belgian government, requiring the Belgians to abolish certain state aids within a three-month period; nor had they attempted to challenge that decision. In proceedings brought by the Commission in December 1977 for non-compliance with the decision the Belgian government argued, invoking Article 241, that the decision was invalid. The claim was held inadmissible. The Court found that the Belgians' claim was, in essence, a claim for the annulment of the decision of May 1976. They had been free to contest this decision under Article 230, but had failed to do so within the time limit. They could not allow this limit to elapse and then challenge the decision's legality under Article 241.

This case, it is submitted, does not decide that Article 241 can never be raised in enforcement proceedings against Member States. The Belgians' claim under the then Article 184 was rejected on different and wholly legitimate grounds. They were not invoking the article as a collateral issue; their defence was based *solely* on the legality of a decision addressed to them which they had failed to challenge in time.

12.8.5 Grounds of review

The grounds on which regulations may be challenged under Article 241 are the same as those provided under Article 230 (see *Simmenthal SpA v Commission* (case 92/78), and discussion at 12.6).

12.8.6 Consequences of a successful challenge

Where an action under Article 241 is successful, the regulation is declared 'inapplicable'. Since there is no time limit within which acts may be challenged under the article, it is not, for reasons of legal certainty, void, but voidable. However, a declaration of inapplicability will render a subsequent act, based on that act, void. Thus, although action under Article 241 is an 'incidental matter', it will be conclusive of the principal action before the Court. A declaration of inapplicability under this article may also be invoked to prevent the application of the invalid act in a subsequent case.

12.9 Conclusions

The procedure in Article 230 is an important cog of the judicial-review machinery, but it is not without shortcomings. The time limits can impose significant constraints and we have seen that other possible routes to challenge Community acts have been interpreted so as not to undermine this limitation. The greatest criticism has been of the restrictive test for individual concern, and the attitude to trade associations and pressure groups is also rather restrictive. Although there have been attempts to broaden the test to provide for more effective judicial protection, it seems that, for the time being, the status quo will prevail. It is arguable that too broad a rule could open the floodgates, but that does not have to be the inevitable consequence of a more relaxed approach to non-privileged standing. Moreover, if a particular measure has adversely affected a large number of people, then fairness demands that they be given the opportunity to challenge the measure in question. In any event, it must be remembered that to be given *locus standi* is not tantamount to succeeding on the substance, and an individual who may have standing could still lose on the merits. Although the Treaty of Lisbon could ease the situation somewhat, its scope will still be subject to interpretation by the CFI and ECJ, which could transfer the interpretation of direct concern into the requirements for standing under the Treaty of Lisbon. Nonetheless, the change in itself could be seen as a signal that the political institutions feel that the current test for standing is too restrictive.

FURTHER READING

Arnull, A, 'Private applicants and the action for annulment under Article 173 of the EC Treaty' (1995) 32 CMLR 7.

—— 'Private applicants and the action for annulment since *Cordoniu*' (2001) 38 CML Rev 7.

Bradley, K St Clair, 'Sense and sensibility: *Parliament v Council* continuing' (1991) 16 EL Rev 245.

Craig, P, 'Legality, standing and substantive review in Community law' (1994) 14 Oxford J Legal Stud 507.

Enchelmeier, S, 'No-one slips through the net? Latest developments, and non-developments, in the European Court of Justice's jurisprudence on Art 230(4) EC' (2005) 24 YEL 173.

Greaves, R, '*Locus Standi* under Article 173 EEC when seeking annulment of a regulation' (1986) 11 EL Rev 119.

Harding, C, 'The private interest in challenging Community action' (1980) 5 EL Rev 345.

Harlow, C, 'Towards a theory of access for the European Court of Justice' (1992) 12 YEL 213.

Neuwahl, NAEM, 'Article 173 Paragraph 4 EC: Past, present and possible future' (1996) 21 EL Rev 17.

Ragolle, F, 'Access to justice for private applicants in the Community legal order: Recent (r)evolutions' (2003) 40 CML Rev 90.

Rasmussen, H, 'Why is Article 173 interpreted against private plaintiffs?' (1980) 5 EL Rev 112.

Van Nuffel, P 'What's in a Member State? Central and decentralised authorities before the Community courts' (2001) 38 CML Rev 871.

Vogt, M, 'Indirect judicial protection in EC law: The case of the plea of illegality' (2006) 31 ELRev 364.

13

Action for failure to act

13.1 Introduction

If the institutions of the Community are to operate according to the rule of law, as they are obliged to do under Article 7 (ex 4) of the EC Treaty, they must be answerable not only for their actions but for their failure to act in breach of EC law. In this, the provision is a mirror of that action for judicial review of actions of the institutions. As with that provision, concern focuses on the extent to which non-privileged applicants are adequately protected by the Union legal order, in particular as regards the rules relating to *locus standi* and—consequently—the right of access to a court. Whilst much has been written about the scope of Article 230 EC, there has been much less attention paid to this provision; perhaps because it is relatively easy for an institution to bring itself outside the scope of the provision. Here the concept of an institution 'defining its position' is key. This chapter, after outlining the scope of the provision, will consider who can bring an action, and what sorts of omissions are capable of being the subject of review. Finally, this chapter will consider the relationship of this provision with Article 230, and consider the effects of a successful claim.

13.2 Overview of the provisions

The relevant provision is Article 232 (ex 175), which provides as follows:

Should the European Parliament, the Council or the Commission, in infringement of this Treaty, fail to act, the Member States and the other institutions of the Community may bring an action before the Court of Justice to have the infringement established.

The action shall be admissible only if the institution concerned has first been called upon to act. If, within two months of being so called upon, the institution concerned has not defined its position, the action may be brought within a further period of two months.

Any natural or legal person may, under the conditions laid down in the preceding paragraphs, complain to the Court of Justice that an institution of the Community has failed to address to that person any act other than a recommendation or an opinion.

The Court of Justice shall have jurisdiction under the same conditions in actions or proceedings brought by the European Central Bank in the areas falling within the latter's field of competence and in actions or proceedings brought against the latter.

Actions brought by a natural or legal person under Article 232 EC now fall within the jurisdiction of the Court of First Instance (CFI), although appeal on points of law may be made to the European Court of Justice (ECJ) (see Chapter 7).

Articles 232 and 230 (ex 173; post Lisbon 263 TFEU) are essentially complementary remedies. As the ECJ held in *Chevalley v Commission* (case 15/70) when confronted with the applicant's uncertainty as to whether Articles 232 or 230 was the appropriate form of action, it is not necessary to characterise the proceedings as being under one or the other article, since both prescribe one and the same method of recourse. They represent two aspects of the same legal remedy. For this reason, any inconsistency between the two provisions should be resolved by applying the same principles to both. This is known as the 'unity principle'. This is all the more important in the light of the Court's interpretation of Article 232, which may result in an action, begun under that article, being concluded under Article 230. It should be noted that this principle will not extend to the more limited provisions for annulment of measures taken under the justice and home affairs (JHA) pillar of the Treaty of the European Union (TEU) (Article 35 TEU); moreover, the latter does not provide for an action for failure to act in respect of measures in this area. Nonetheless, in cases arising under the EC Treaty, the unity principle, or the coherence between the two provisions, remains a relevant factor referred to by the CFI (see, eg, *Gestevision Telecinco v Commission* (case T–95/96)).

Should the Lisbon Treaty come into force, this provision will be renumbered Article 265 TFEU in similar terms, save that the failure to act of the European Council and the European Central Bank (ECB) would also be included within its scope. The scope of review will be enlarged by virtue of the abolition of the pillar structure and the incorporation of JHA matters within the Treaty on the Functioning of the European Union (TFEU) subject to limitations noted at 12.3.4.

13.3 Reviewable omissions

The institution's failure to act must, first and foremost, be 'in infringement of this Treaty'. Since this would include legislation enacted under the treaty it would apply to any failure on the part of the institution to act when it was under a legal duty to do so. In *Parliament v Council* (case 13/83), in an action by Parliament under Article 232 alleging the Council's failure to implement a Community transport policy, the Court held that 'failure' can cover a failure to take a number of decisions; the nature of the acts which may be requested need not be clearly circumscribed as long as they are sufficiently identified. The failures alleged by Parliament in this case were:

(a) failure to introduce a common transport policy, as required by the then Article 74

(b) failure to introduce measures to secure freedom to provide transport services, as required by the then Articles 75, 59, 60, and 61.

The Court held that Parliament was entitled to succeed on the second allegation but not on the first. While the second obligation was complete and legally perfect, and should have been implemented by the Council within the transitional period, the former obligation was insufficiently precise to constitute an enforceable obligation. Prior to the TEU, action under the then Article 175 (now 232) could be brought only against the Council or the Commission, but now, action may also be brought against the European Parliament. Omissions of the ECB are also subject to review under Article 232. Although the Court of Auditors was awarded the power to bring actions under Article 230 by the Treaty of Amsterdam (ToA), its inaction is not subject to review under Article 232. This is probably a consequence of their limited and non-binding status. It has now been established that the actions of the Ombudsman may give rise to liability under Article 288 EC (ex 215; post Lisbon 340 TFEU) (see case C–234/02P, *European Ombudsman v Lamberts*), and it may therefore also be possible for an individual to complain under Article 232 EC, should the Ombudsman fail to act in response to a complaint.

Although only non-binding acts in the form of recommendations and opinions are expressly excluded in the context of individual action under Article 232, third paragraph, the unity principle would suggest that a failure under Article 232 would only cover a failure to issue a binding act.

13.4 *Locus standi*

13.4.1 **Privileged applicants**

Parliament, is, along with Member States and the other institutions, a 'privileged applicant' under Article 232. Privileged applicants enjoy a right to challenge *any* failure on the part of the Council and the Commission, ie an omission to adopt *any* binding act which these institutions have a duty to adopt. Under the TEU, the ECB was given *locus standi* to bring proceedings under Article 232 'in the areas falling within [its] field of competence'.

It should be noted that there is no obligation on a Member State to bring an action under Article 232. This was confirmed by the ECJ in *Netherlands v Ten Kate Holding BV* (C–511/03), where a Dutch manufacturer sought to bring an action against the government for failing to take action under Articles 230 and 232 EC. The Court held that neither provision imposed an obligation on a Member State to bring an action, and not doing so would not constitute an infringement of that state's obligations under EC law (and therefore not give rise to a claim in state liability under *Francovich*). However, the ECJ emphasised that EC law did not preclude a domestic rule that would impose liability on the government of a Member State which could have brought an action under Articles 230 or 232 EC, but did not do so. This would be a matter entirely for domestic law on which the ECJ could not express an opinion.

13.4.2 **Individuals**

13.4.2.1 *Measures subject to challenge by individuals*

In comparison with Member States and Community institutions, individuals, as under Article 230, have a limited *locus standi* under Article 232(3). Natural or legal persons may bring proceedings only where the institution complained of has failed to address to that person any act other than a recommendation or an opinion. Since an act which is addressed to a designated person is in substance a decision, this seems to mean that an individual's *locus standi* is limited to a failure on the part of the Council or Commission to adopt what is in essence a *decision* addressed to *himself or herself*. The individual has no express *locus standi* to challenge an omission to address to *another person* a decision of direct and individual concern to himself or herself.

This apparent deficiency has been remedied by the Court. In *Nordgetreide GmbH & Co. KG v Commission* (case 42/71), Advocate-General Roemer, invoking the unity principle, suggested that since Articles 230 and 232 constituted part of a coherent system, an individual should have a right to demand a decision vis-à-vis a third party in which the individual was directly and individually concerned. In *Bethell v Commission* (case 246/81) this right was implied when the Court, in rejecting Lord Bethell's claim as inadmissible, held that he had failed to show that the Commission had failed to adopt, in relation to him, a measure *which he was legally entitled to claim*. In the context of Article 232, the equivalent to a decision of direct and individual concern under Article 230, it was a decision which the applicant is *legally entitled to claim*.

This test was relaxed in *T Port GmbH & Co KG v Bundesanstalt für Landeswirtschaft und Ernährung* (case C–68/95)). Reasoning from the unity principle and the test of direct and individual concern used for Article 230 actions, the ECJ stated that Article 232(3) could be invoked where an institution has failed to act in respect of a measure which would have concerned the applicant in the same way (para 59). The CFI has subsequently followed the *T Port* case in the more recent cases involving challenges to the funding of public service broadcasters (eg, *Gestevision Telecinco SA v Commission* (case T–95/96)), thus suggesting that this approach has now been consolidated into the courts' case law.

Many of the claims under Article 232 EC prior to *T Port GmbH* (case C–68/95) failed because the applicant was seeking the adoption of an act which he was not entitled to claim. For example, in *Ladbroke Racing Ltd v Commission* (case T–32/93), an individual complainant was held not to have a right to demand action by the Commission under the state aid provisions of the then Article 90(3) (now Article 86(3); post Lisbon 106 TFEU). This may be compared with the more recent case of *Bundesverband der Bilanzbuchhalter eV v Commission* (case C–107/95 P) in which the ECJ accepted that in limited circumstances, details of which it did not elaborate, an applicant could demand action under Article 86(3) (ex 90(3)) EC, although in *Commission v T-Mobile Austria* (case C–141/02P), the ECJ appeared to move away from that view (see paras 68–9). In *Gestevision Telecinco SA v Commission* (case T–95/96), the CFI held that an individual could demand that the Commission make a decision at the end of the initial investigatory phase of state aid proceedings under Article 88(3) post Lisbon 108 TFEU. Further, where the Commission has difficulty in determining whether the funding in issue constitutes state aid or whether it is compatible with the common market 'the institution has a duty to gather all necessary views and to that end initiate the procedure under 93(2)' (now 88(3)).

In both of these circumstances, Article 232 proceedings could be brought against a failure on the Commission's part to act. It may be that the easing of the test here and in *T Port* (case C–68/95) will result in an increase in the number of successful actions brought by non-privileged applicants. Arguably, a more generous approach to individuals' *locus standi* under Article 232 EC is justified if individuals are to be denied access to the ECJ to challenge an institution's failure to act under Article 234 EC.

On rather different reasoning in another failed claim in the earlier case of *Eridania v Commission* (cases 10 and 18/68), the Court held that the applicants could not invoke Article 232 to obtain a revocation by the Commission of a decision addressed to third parties, as other methods of recourse, namely, Article 230, were provided by the treaty; to allow parallel recourse via Article 232 would enable applicants to avoid the conditions (ie, time limit) laid down by the treaty.

13.4.2.2 *Challenges with regard to regulations*

It is clear that the act demanded must be in substance a decision. In *Nordgetreide GmbH & Co KG v Commission* (case 42/71) the applicant company was seeking the amendment by the Commission of a regulation. When the Commission rejected its request the company instituted two actions, one for failure to act, under Article 232, and one under Article 230 for annulment of the Commission's decision refusing to act. The action under Article 232 would in any case have failed because, as Advocate-General Roemer pointed out, the company was seeking from the Commission what would have amounted to a normative act; in fact the Court found its claim inadmissible on different grounds (to be discussed below). The claim under Article 230 was also held inadmissible. Although the contested decision was addressed to the applicant, the Court held that a decision refusing to act (a 'negative' decision) would only be open to attack under Article 230 if the *positive* measure being sought were open to attack (see also Advocate-General Gand in *Alfons Lütticke GmbH v Commission* (case 48/65)). Since the company was seeking to amend a regulation, this would not be the case. This same reasoning would apply to a refusal by the Commission to issue a decision to another person which the applicants were not entitled to claim. Thus, even though a decision may have been addressed to the applicant, Article 230 cannot be invoked as an adjunct to Article 232 to annul a decision not to act, in order to compel an institution to act *when it has no duty to do so at the behest of the applicant*. Although this has been attempted on a number of occasions, it has always failed (eg, *Alfons Lütticke GmbH v Commission* (case 48/65); *Star Fruit Company SA v Commission*; *J v Commission* (case T–5/94)—applicants demanding action by the Commission under Article 226 (ex 169) against a Member State; *Bethell v Commission* (case 246/81)—applicant seeking to force Commission to take action under Article 85 (ex 89) against Member States' airlines).

13.4.2.3 *Procedural rights*

A case in which the applicant was entitled to demand action from the Commission, but in which its claim was surprisingly held inadmissible, was *Deutscher Komponistenverband v Commission* (case 8/71). Here the applicant alleged that the Commission had failed in its obligation under EC competition law (Regulation 17/62, now repealed) to grant it, as a complainant under Article 3 of that regulation, a hearing. Advocate-General Roemer suggested that acts susceptible of action under Article 232 should cover any measures which give rise to legal effects for the applicant; they should then include measures of a procedural nature. The Court disagreed, holding that Article 232(3) only applied to a failure to adopt a decision; it did not cover the promulgation of a formal act. Nevertheless the Court did examine the merits and concluded that since the applicant had had an opportunity to make its submissions in writing there had been no failure on the part of the Commission.

It is submitted that Advocate-General Roemer's view is to be preferred to that of the Court. Since there was no doubt that the applicant was entitled to a hearing any failure to grant it that hearing should have been actionable under Article 232. And if it was refused such a hearing, as it was, it should have been entitled to challenge that refusal under Article 230, as the positive measure requested was one which it was entitled to demand.

This view seems to have been taken by the Court in *FEDIOL v Commission* (case 191/82). In this case an EC federation of seed crushers and oil processors was seeking to compel the Commission to take action against alleged dumping practices on the part of Brazil. As undertakings which considered themselves injured or threatened by subsidised imports, the applicants were entitled under Regulation 3017/79 (the principal anti-dumping regulation) to lodge a complaint (Article 5), to be consulted (Article 6), and to receive information (Article 9). In April 1980 they lodged a complaint with the Commission. Following enquiries and negotiations with the Brazilian government the Commission decided to take no further action. In September 1981 FEDIOL instituted Article 232 proceedings. Following further correspondence between FEDIOL and the Commission the Commission informed FEDIOL by letter in May 1982 that it intended to take no further action against Brazil. FEDIOL then brought Article 230 proceedings to annul that letter. The Court held that since the regulation under which they complained recognised specific rights on the applicants' part they were entitled to a review by the Court of any exercise of power by the Community institutions which might affect these rights. Thus the action was held admissible. Although the applicants could not compel the Commission to take action against Brazil, that being a matter within the Commission's discretion, they were entitled to a review by the Court of the Commission's letter of May 1982 to ensure that their procedural rights were respected.

This case may be contrasted with the earlier case of *GEMA v Commission* (case 125/78). Here GEMA initiated a complaint to the Commission under Article 3 of Regulation 17/62, alleging a breach by Radio Luxembourg what is now of Articles 81–2. In March 1978 the Commission wrote to GEMA saying that it had decided not to pursue the matter. In May 1978 GEMA instituted Article 232 proceedings against this refusal to act. Subsequently, in March 1979, GEMA brought proceedings under Article 230 to annul the letter of March 1978. The action under Article 232 failed because the Commission was held to have defined its position in the letter of March 1978. The action under Article 230 failed on the grounds that, assuming that the letter could be contested, this did not entitle the applicants to a *final decision* on the existence of an infringement under Article 82. In any case the letter had not been challenged in time and the parties' attempts to extend the limit on the grounds of fresh issues based on matters of fact and law failed. In the appeal in *Guérin Automobiles v Commission* (case C–282/95 P), the ECJ confirmed that a letter to a complainant was a definition of a position for the purposes of Article 232, but that it could not be challenged because the letter was a preparatory stage in proceedings. The applicants were entitled under competition procedural rules to make representations, after which the Commission must make a decision which would have legally binding effects. It would be at this stage that an applicant could challenge a failure to act although it still could not force the Commission to take a decision that was favourable to the applicants.

Thus, in all of these cases the parties were only entitled in law to protection by way of review under Articles 232 and 230 to protect their procedural rights. They had no right to compel the Commission to institute proceedings against third parties; that was a matter within the Commission's discretion (see also *Ladbroke Racing Ltd v Commission* (case T–32/93)). Even in *Gestevision*, where the Commission seemed to be under an obligation to investigate the funding to state broadcasters further, this obligation arose out of the need to protect the procedural rights of all involved and did not entitle Gestevision to any particular finding on the question of state aid.

Where an individual does have a right to complain and to request action, as in *FEDIOL*, *GEMA*, and *Guérin*, should the Commission take action and issue a decision to a third party, the complainant will be deemed to be directly and individually concerned and will be entitled to a full review of the decision under Article 230 EC (*Metro-SB-Grossmärkte GmbH & Co KG v Commission* (case 26/76); *Timex Corporation v Council* (case 264/82), see Chapter 12; *COFAZ* (case 169/84); *British American Tobacco Co. Ltd v Commission* (cases 142 and 156/84)).

13.5 Procedure

Where the applicant has a right to require an institution to act, and the institution is under a corresponding duty, the applicant must first call upon the institution to act. No time limit is imposed for the institution's alleged failure, but the Court has held that proceedings must be brought within a reasonable time of the institution's having demonstrated its intention not to act (*Netherlands v Commission* (case 59/70)—case brought under Article 35 of the ECSC Treaty).

The institution then has two months within which it may either act in accordance with the request, or 'define its position'.

If the institution fails to act or to define its position the claimant has two months within which to bring his case before the ECJ, running from the date on which the institution should have defined its position. These limits are strictly enforced. In *Guérin Automobiles v Commission* (case T–195/95) the Commission, responding to a complaint by Guérin concerning an alleged breach by Nissan of Article 81(1) (ex 85(1) post Lisbon, 101 TFEU), merely sent them a copy of Nissan's response to the complaint. When Guérin subsequently submitted their observations to the Commission in February 1995, the Commission failed to respond. In October 1995 they brought an action before the CFI under Article 232. The Court found the action inadmissible. Even supposing that the letter sent by the applicants in February 1995 could be regarded as an invitation to act in the sense of Article 232, to which the Commission had failed to respond, the application to the CFI should have been introduced within four months of the date on which the letter was sent, as required by that article. Guérin wrote to the Commission again, and then brought another action under Article 232, this time within four months from the date of this letter. Again, the company was unsuccessful, as the Commission had, by the time the matter came before the CFI, defined its position.

It may sometimes be difficult to establish the point at which the institution can be said to have defined its position. In *CEVA and Pharmacia v Commission* (cases T–344 and T–345/00), a letter which merely stated that the questions submitted by the applicants were still under consideration by the Commission was not a definition of position, whereas the subsequent adoption of a draft regulation was. The action under Article 232 could not proceed. However, a delay by a Community institution in defining its position which results in loss to an applicant may give rise to liability under Article 288 EC (see Chapter 14).

13.5.1 Effect of definition of position

Article 232 is silent as to what happens if the institution concerned defines its position. Although it was not necessary so to construe this article, the Court held in *Alfons Lütticke GmbH v Commission* (case 48/65) that a definition of position brought proceedings under Article 232 to an end. The claimant in this case, it will be remembered, was attempting to persuade the Commission to bring an action under Article 226 against the German government for its alleged infringement of Article 90. When the Commission refused to act Alfons Lütticke GmbH brought proceedings under Article 232 for failure to act. The Commission defined its position in a letter to Lütticke, again refusing to act, and Lütticke brought proceedings under Article 230 to annul that refusal. The Court, in the briefest of judgments, held that the Commission's refusal was a 'definition of position' which ended its failure to act. The action under Article 232 was therefore inadmissible.

With regard to the action under Article 230, Advocate-General Gand's submissions were again convincing. The applicant would only be entitled to challenge the Commission's refusal to act (the 'negative decision'), he suggested, if it had been entitled to challenge the positive act requested. This it would not, since it had no right to demand action from the Commission vis-à-vis the German government. The Court, on the other hand, chose to treat the Commission's refusal not as a definition of position but as a 'reasoned opinion' under Article 226, which, as a purely preliminary act, was not, the Court held, capable of annulment.

The Court did adopt reasoning similar to that of Advocate-General Gand in *Lütticke* in *Star Fruit Company SA v Commission* (case 247/87). Here, as in *Lütticke*, the applicants, a firm of banana importers, were seeking to compel the Commission to institute Article 226 proceedings, this time against France in respect of the French regime regulating banana imports, which they considered was in breach of Article 28 EC (ex 30 EC post Lisbon 34 TFEU). They had complained to the Commission and the Commission had acknowledged their request. The applicants subsequently brought Article 232 proceedings against the Commission for their failure to take action against France, and Article 230 proceedings for the annulment of the Commission's letter of acknowledgment. On the claim for failure to act, the Court held that since the Commission was not required to instigate proceedings under Article 226, but on the contrary had a discretionary power, 'individuals were not entitled to require that the institution adopt a particular position'.

On the claim under Article 230, the Court pointed out that by requesting the Commission to set in motion a procedure under Article 226 the applicant was 'in reality requesting the adoption of acts which were not of direct and individual concern to it within the meaning of Article [230], and which in any event it could not challenge by means of an action for annulment'.

13.5.2 Definition of position and Article 230

The Court has, however, consistently followed its position in *Lütticke* and held that, in Article 232 proceedings, a definition of position by the defendant institution ends its failure to act. It is not surprising that so few cases have reached the ECJ and now the CFI under that provision. However, this is not necessarily the end of the road for the applicant. In a *legitimate* case, *where he is entitled to demand action* from the institution concerned, he may challenge the definition of position, as a decision addressed to himself, under Article 230, and provided that he does so in time, his application should be admissible. It is submitted that *Lütticke*, with its special facts (applicant not entitled to demand action), and its judgment cast in terms of Article 226, cannot be invoked to prevent such a challenge. *FEDIOL* (case 191/82) supports this view. Although not described as such, the Commission's letter of May 1982, in which the Commission informed FEDIOL of its decision not to act, and which FEDIOL were held entitled to challenge under Article 230, was undoubtedly a 'definition of position' within Article 232 (see *GEMA* (case 125/78)).

Where an institution defines its position and refuses to act, an applicant who is not entitled to demand that action cannot challenge that refusal under Article 230; and even a legitimate claim under Article 232 is likely to result in an action to review that refusal under Article 230. In the latter case it is therefore essential that a definition of position be recognised as a decision capable of challenge under Article 230, and that it be challenged in time (cf *GEMA; Irish Cement Ltd*). The extent of the review conducted by the Court under Article 230 will depend on the extent of the applicant's rights. Since the institutions have wide discretionary powers in the pursuit of economic policy objectives, individuals' rights, at least where action vis-à-vis third parties are concerned, are likely to be limited and mainly of a procedural nature. However, as has been demonstrated in *Parliament v Council* (case 13/83), Article 232 offers considerable scope for privileged applicants.

In *Parliament v Council* (case 13/83) Parliament's case was heard before the ECJ under Article 232, as the Council's 'definition of position' was found to be inadequate. As it neither confirmed nor denied the alleged failure (implementation of transport policy), and failed to reveal the Council's position with regard to the measure which the Council intended to adopt, it was held not to amount to a definition of position at all.

13.6 Consequences of a successful action

Whether the action is admitted before the Court under Article 232, as a failure to act, or under Article 230, as a claim for annulment of a decision not to act, the consequences of a successful action are the same. Under Article 233 (ex 176; post Lisbon 266 TFEU): 'The institution whose act has been declared void or whose failure to act has been declared contrary to this Treaty shall be required to take the necessary measures to comply with the judgment of the Court of Justice'.

The institution will be required by the Court to take action to remedy its failure. It will not necessarily be the action required by the applicant. Should he wish to challenge the institution's implementation of the judgment he could do so under Article 230.

No sanctions beyond the possibility of further action under Article 232 are provided for non-compliance with the Court's judgment. Unlike Article 228, which was amended by the TEU to provide for the imposition of fines and penalties on Member States which fail to comply with a judgment of the Court under Article 226 (see Chapter 11), Article 233 was not amended to provide for similar penalties against EC institutions in respect of their failures established under Article 232. Also, although Article 233(2) provides that the obligation imposed by Article 233(1) 'shall not affect any obligations which may result from the application of the second paragraph of Article 288' (governing the Community's non-contractual liability) the opportunity for individuals to obtain damages from the Community is, as will be seen, extremely limited (see Chapter 14).

13.7 Conclusions

It has been seen that the procedure under Article 232 complements the Article 230 procedure for directly challenging the validity of acts adopted by the institutions because it seeks to ensure that the institutions act on their powers whenever required. It is just as important to challenge legislation adopted by the institutions where this exceeds their powers as it is to challenge inaction when a positive step was required. Once Article 232 is invoked, the institution concerned must at least define its position. This, in turn, can then be reviewed under Article 230, subject to the requirements on *locus standi* (see Chapter 12). Although a successful Article 232 claim may persuade the institution concerned to take action, this does not mean that the claimant will receive the decision he might prefer. Nevertheless, action by the Community institution would remove the uncertainty that could otherwise prevail if no action were taken at all.

14

Community liability in tort: Action for damages

14.1 Introduction

We have already seen that there are various mechanisms in the treaty by which the acts of the Union institutions can be reviewed. In addition to challenging acts directly and, if the challenge is successful, having these declared inapplicable, it may also be necessary to make good any loss that has been caused as a result of the adoption of a measure which is unlawful. The treaty contains provisions that provide for the non-contractual liability of the Community in Articles 235 (ex 178) and 288 (ex 215). Although Article 288 is potentially of great utility, in practice its application has been limited by the Courts. Whilst the approach to *locus standi*, has been less stringent than that taken in relation to judicial review, the Courts have taken a restrictive approach to the question of the test to show a violation of the Community's obligations. In assessing the scope and effectiveness of this action, we should, however, bear in mind the role of the institutions, and the circumstances in which actions are likely to be brought. Problem areas include liability for legislative action and the question of whether liability arises for lawful action. These points are contentious or, at best, narrowly viewed in that national legal systems. One final issue relates to the parallels between this action and the action for state liability against the Member States. As we shall see, the European Court of Justice (ECJ) has attempted to develop the case law in both fields in the light of the jurisprudence of the other and in this the case of *Bergaderm* seems to have marked a significant shift in the courts' approach.

14.2 Scope of non-contractual liability

14.2.1 The treaty provisions

According to Article 235 (post Lisbon, Article 268 TFEU), 'The Court of Justice shall have jurisdiction in disputes relating to the compensation for damage provided for in the second paragraph of Article 288'.

Article 288(2) provides that:

> In the case of non-contractual liability, the Community shall, in accordance with the general principles common to the laws of the Member States, make good any damage caused by its institutions or by its servants in the performance of their duties.

Thus, the Community may be liable for both *fautes de service*, ie, wrongful acts on the part of one of its institutions, and *fautes personelles*, wrongful acts on the part of its servants. Provided in both cases that the wrongful acts are committed in the performance of the perpetrator's Community functions, the responsible institution may be sued. Where more than one institution is concerned, or where there is doubt as to which institution is responsible, both (or all) may be sued. In the case of *faute personelle*, the Community is liable on the principle of vicarious liability, albeit interpreted in a slightly narrower sense than that in which it is understood under English law (see *Sayag v Leduc* (case 9/69), proceedings under Article 188(2) of the Euratom Treaty, in which it was held that the Community is only liable for those acts of its servants which, by virtue of an internal relationship, are the *necessary* extension of the tasks entrusted to the institutions). One question which remains to be addressed is the extent to which the institutions will be liable for action which is not unlawful. This is discussed below.

In applying Article 288(2) the Court is required to determine liability 'in accordance with the general principles common to the laws of Member States'. Where the principles of non-contractual liability, which embrace principles concerning the basis of liability (ie, fault or non-fault), causation and damages are not 'common' to all Member States, the Court has drawn on the principles governing tortious liability in the Member States in order to develop its own specific principles of Community law. The process is thus different from its approach to the incorporation of general principles of law for the purposes of judicial review of Community law (see Chapter 6).

14.2.2 Liability under the second and third pillars

As was the case with actions for failure to act under Article 232 (ex 175), the Treaty of Amsterdam (ToA) failed to provide for an action for damages in respect of measures taken under the justice and home affairs (JHA) pillar of the Treaty of the European Union (TEU) (Article 35 TEU). In *Gestoras Pro Amnistía and ors v Council* (case C–354/04 P), Gestoras Pro Amnistía concerned an action or damages for the harm allegedly sustained by it due to the inclusion of Gestoras Pro Amnistía in the list of persons, groups, or entities referred to in Article 1 of Council Common Position 2001/931/CFSP of 27 December 2001 on the application of specific measures to combat terrorism. This claim had been rejected at first instance by the Court of First Instance (CFI) and this case was an appeal against that decision. The CFI had held that it clearly had no jurisdiction, in the legal system of the European Union, to hear and determine the appellants' claim for damages, as the acts in issue had as their legal basis Article 34 EU. The only remedies permissible were those referred to in Article 35 EU were the reference for a preliminary ruling, the action for annulment, and the procedure for settling disputes between Member States. The applicants argued that the Union is a community governed by the rule of law, guaranteeing by virtue of Article 6(2) TEU the right to an effective remedy laid down in Article 13 of the ECHR and the right to a tribunal provided by Article 6 of that convention. It would be impossible to bring an action in the courts of a Member State for an action of the Member States acting jointly. The ECJ upheld the CFI's interpretation of Article 35 TEU and although it agreed that the system of protection was incomplete, it held that that was a matter for the Member States to reform. Further, it held that it was not correct to hold that the applicants were entirely without remedy as the institutions were subject to review of their actions under Article 35 EU.

14.2.3 Impact of treaty revision

Should the Lisbon Treaty enter into force, Article 235 EC would be re-enacted as Article 268 of the Treaty on the Functioning of the European Union (TFEU), and Article 288 EC as Article 340 TFEU. As part of the abolition of the pillar structure should Lisbon come in to force, the reference to 'Community' in this provision would be changed to 'Union', arguably rendering the distinctions made by Gestoras of less significance. There would be no substantive difference, although the third paragraph of what is currently Article 288 would be clarified by imposing liability on the European Central Bank for damage caused by it or its servants. In this, the Lisbon Treaty would introduce changes that track those that would have been introduced by the Constitution.

14.3 *Locus standi*

14.3.1 Personal limitations

Unlike the position in the area of judicial review, there are no personal limitations on the right to bring an action under Article 288(2). There is no distinction between privileged and non-privileged applicants.

14.3.2 Time limits

Moreover, a specific and generous limitation period of five years is provided (Article 46 Statute of the Court of Justice), running from the occurrence of the event giving rise to liability. The Court has held that the limitation period cannot begin until all the requirements for liability, particularly damage, have materialised (*Birra Wührer SpA v Council* (cases 256, 257, 265, and 267/80, and 5/81)). Where the damage results from a legislative measure, time runs not necessarily from the date of enactment but from the date on which the injury occurs, or at least when the applicant becomes aware of it (see, eg, *Buhring v Council* (case T–246/93)).

14.3.3 Relationship with Articles 230 and 232 EC

These *locus standi* provisions are important, since, as will be seen, it may be possible to obtain a declaration of invalidity in the context of a claim for damages, thereby circumventing the *locus standi* limitations of Article 230 (ex 173; post Lisbon 263 TFEU) (see *Aktien-Zuckerfabrik Schöppenstedt v Council* (case 5/71)). The action for damages is a separate action from the judicial review action as can be inferred from the wording of the treaty. Article 233(2) (ex 176(2)) provides that the obligation to remedy a failure to act 'shall not affect any obligation which may result from the application of the second paragraph of Article 288'. This was the view taken in

Alfons Lütticke GmbH v Commission (case 4/69). In this case, Lütticke, having failed to establish the Commission's failure to act under Article 232 (see Chapter 13), sought damages from the Commission in a separate action under Article 288(2). The action was held admissible. The Court said that the action for damages provided for under Articles 235 and 288(2) was established as *an independent form of action with a particular purpose to fulfil*. It would be contrary to the independent nature of this action, as well as to the efficacy of the general system of forms of action created by the treaty, to regard as a ground of inadmissibility the fact that, in certain circumstances, an action for damages might lead to a result similar to that of an action for failure to act under Article 232. Although *Lütticke* failed on the merits (there being no wrongful failure), an important principle was established.

Similarly, *Aktien-Zuckerfabrik Schöppenstedt v Council* (case 5/71), the Court held that the claimant company could sue the Council for damages on the basis of an allegedly illegal regulation even though as a 'natural or legal person' they would have no *locus standi* to seek its annulment under Article 230. This point has been reiterated recently in *Holcim (Deutschland) v Commission* (Case C–282/05 P), where the ECJ held that standing under Article 230 was not a relevant criterion for determining whether there had been a violation of Article 228. In *Krohn & Co Import-Export GmbH & Co KG v Commission* (case 175/84), the Court held that since an action for non-contractual liability was an autonomous form of action, the expiry of the time-limit for challenge under Article 230 did not render an action for damages inadmissible.

The ECJ did, however, make the point in *Krohn & Co Import-Export GmbH & Co KG* that a claim might not be admissible if the purpose of the Article 288(2) action was purely to attain by another route the remedy provided by Article 230, an approach reaffirmed by the CFI in declaring an action inadmissible in *Cobrecaf SA v Commission* (case T–514/93) and reflecting that taken by the ECJ regarding time limits on Article 234 (ex 177) references on the validity of Community acts (*TWD Textilwerk Deggendorf GmbH v Germany* (case C–188/92)) (see Chapters 10 and 12).

14.4 Elements of non-contractual liability

The basic elements of non-contractual liability are familiar. They embrace:

(a) unlawful conduct on the part of the institutions

(b) damage to the claimant

(c) a causative link between the two.

(See eg, recently, *Medici Grimm KG v Council* (case T–364/03), para 59.)

For liability to arise, all three elements must be proved. The CFI has noted that it is not necessary to deal with these elements in any particular order. If it seems likely that one of them will not be satisfied, the Court can deal with it first and, if appropriate, dismiss the application without discussing the remaining elements (*Elliniki Viomichania Oplon AE (EVO) v Council and Commission* (case T–220/96)).

The ECJ and the CFI were somewhat shy of endorsing a principle of liability without fault in EC law, despite the opportunity to rule specifically on this matter in *Atlanta* (case T–521/93) and *Édouard Dubois et Fils SA v Council* (case T–113/96).

The ECJ had not, however, ruled out that possibility (see *Compagnie d'Approvisionnement v Commission* (cases 9 and 11/71); *Biovilac v Commission* (case 59/83)). In *Dorsch Consult* (case T–184/95), the CFI commented, without specifically ruling on the point of whether liability could arise for a lawful act, that a precondition for such liability would in any event be the existence of 'unusual' and 'special' damage, which in this case was not satisfied. The matter has been discussed again, in the recent case of *FIAMM and FIAMM Technologies v Council and Commission* (case C–120/06P), discussed below.

14.5 Wrongful acts or omissions

Although, following continental traditions, non-contractual liability is not divided up into specific 'torts', wrongful acts and omissions may be grouped under three broad categories:

(a) Failures of administration. Community institutions are under a duty of good administration. Failures of administration would include, for example, a failure to adopt satisfactory procedures, a failure to obtain the relevant facts before making the decision, the giving of misleading information, a failure to give the necessary information (eg, *Odigitria AAE v Council* (case T–572/93)—but no liability because of lack of causal link), or a significant delay in acting (*CEVA and Pharmacia v Commission* (case T–344 and T–345 /00)—failure to act for a period of 19 months constituted a clear and serious breach of the principle of sound administration). As with negligence, the decision taken or advice offered need not be right as long as it is adopted according to the correct procedures and the conclusions reached are reasonable in the light of the information to hand.

(b) Negligent acts by a servant in the performance of his duties. This category would also include a single negligent act. For example, in *Grifoni v Euratom* (case C–308/87), a case concerning the Euratom Treaty, Euratom contracted with Mr Grifoni to have the roof of a building repaired. While inspecting the roof, Grifoni fell off. The ECJ held that Euratom was at fault in not providing the necessary guard rails.

(c) The adoption of wrongful (ie, illegal or invalid) acts having legal effect, or the wrongful failure to adopt a binding act when under a duty to do so.

This chapter focuses principally on the last issue, because this is most closely linked with the remedies considered so far relating to judicial review. However, it is also important to appreciate that, following *Bergaderm* (case C–352/98) (discussed below), the administrative or legislative nature of the act complained about is no longer central (paras 46–7).

14.5.1 Action taken under the EC Treaty

It is perhaps self-evident that liability cannot arise from action taken under primary legislation, that is, pursuant to the EC treaties themselves. This was confirmed in *Édouard Dubois et Fils SA v Council* (case T–113/96). Here the applicant, a customs agent, was seeking damages for losses arising from the completion of the single internal market. Following its completion on 1 January 1993 his business suffered 'an almost total and definitive cessation of its activities as a customs agent', resulting in material damage. He claimed compensation on the basis of strict liability or, alternatively, fault. The CFI held that the agreement to complete the single internal market contained in the Single European Act (SEA), as an agreement between Member States, could not give rise to non-contractual liability on the part of the Community. Articles 235 and 288(2), being also primary Community law, cannot be brought to bear on instruments of an equivalent level where this is not expressly provided for. It was thus unnecessary to answer the question concerning strict liability.

14.6 Establishing an unlawful act

The problem with an action for non-contractual liability lies not in establishing admissibility but in succeeding on the merits of the case. Originally, the ECJ adopted a very restrictive approach towards Community liability in tort, particularly towards liability resulting from the adoption of wrongful acts (or the wrongful failure to adopt an act). Indeed, there are strong policy reasons for limiting the non-contractual liability of public authorities. These bodies are charged by law to take decisions in the general interest over a wide range of activities. These decisions often involve the exercise of discretion and affect a substantial section of the public. Sometimes the decisions are unlawful. Whilst it is right that such decisions be subject to judicial review, it may be argued that to expose public bodies to liability in damages for unlawful acts in the absence of bad faith or an improper motive or (quaere) 'gross' negligence would unduly hamper the administrative process and impose an excessive burden on the public purse, a fortiori in a community as large as the EU.

Thus, it is not sufficient for Community liability to arise that the measure in question is unlawful, nor that the institution has unlawfully failed to act. For some time, the test to establish whether there was an unlawful act was the so-called *Schöppenstedt* formula (from *Aktien-Zuckerfabrik Schöppenstedt v Council* (case 5/71)): where the action concerns a legislative measure which involves choices of economic policy, the Community incurs no liability unless a sufficiently serious breach of a superior rule of law for the protection of the individual has occurred. A significant body of case law has built up under this formula. However, there had been concern that the approach to Community liability under Article 288 and the development of state liability (see Chapter 9) ought to be following the same principles. This nettle was grasped in *Brasserie du Pêcheur and Factortame* (joined cases C–46/93 and C–48/93; see Chapter 9), where the Court, in the context of a state-liability case, stated that the basis of liability under Article 288 and under the state-liability principle should be the same, because the protection of individuals' rights cannot vary depending on whether a national authority or a Community authority is responsible for the act or omission which is the subject of complaint. This was firmly established in *Laboratoires Pharmaceutiques Bergaderm SA and Goupil v Commission* (case C–352/98 P), a case decided under Article 288.

Before we set out the current position, it will be helpful to examine the approach adopted in this area prior to *Bergaderm*. As was noted above, the *Schöppenstedt* formula contains three essential elements. It requires a legislative measure involving choices of economic policy, a breach of a superior rule of law for the protection of individuals and that the breach is 'sufficiently serious'. These will now be examined in turn.

14.6.1 Development of the *Schöppenstedt* formula: A brief overview

14.6.1.1 *A legislative measure involving choices of economic policy*

Although the term 'legislative act' relates primarily to regulations, it will apply to any binding act which purports to lay down general rules. In *Gibraltar v Council* (case C–298/89) the Court suggested, albeit in the context of proceedings under Article 230, that directives 'normally' constitute 'a form of indirect regulatory or legislative measure'. It was accepted in *Odigitria AAE v Council* (case T–572/93) that an international agreement dealing with fishing rights would be a legislative act involving economic policy because of its impact on the Community's fisheries policy. The majority of legislative measures will involve choices of economic policy, since the institutions enjoy wide discretionary powers in all areas of activity, and it is possible to construe many measures even of a social nature as economic in the context of the EC Treaty.

Following the ECJ's judgment in *Laboratoires Pharmaceutiques Bergaderm SA and Goupil v Commission* (case C–352/98P) (discussed below), for wrongful acts it is no longer crucial whether the measure is legislative or individual. Now, the important consideration for determining whether there was a wrongful act giving rise to liability is whether the institution concerned was involved in the exercise of any form of discretion.

14.6.1.2 *A breach of a superior rule of law for the protection of individuals*

Any general principle, such as equality or proportionality, accepted as part of Union law (see Chapter 6) would constitute a superior law for the protection of individuals. Thus, a breach of the principle of legitimate expectations was argued successfully in a claim for damages in *Sofrimport SARL v Commission* (case C–152/88, see Chapter 12). Most fundamental principles of *Community* law (eg, freedom of movement for workers; non-discrimination between producers and consumers (Article 34(2)), agriculture) whether expressed in the EC Treaty or in secondary legislation could likewise form the basis of a claim for damages. In *Firma E Kampffmeyer v Commission* (cases 5, 7, and 13–24/66) a provision in an EC regulation directed at ensuring 'appropriate support for agricultural markets' was construed as intending to benefit, inter alia, the interests of individual undertakings such as importers. The claimants, as importers, were thus entitled to claim damages as a result of the Commission's action in breach of these provisions. It seems therefore that, as long as the rule of law can be construed as designed in part to benefit a particular class of people, it may be deemed to be 'for the protection of individuals'.

The original formulation of the test in *Schöppenstedt* refers to a 'superior rule of law', but the word 'superior' was dropped in more recent cases, referring to general principles such as proportionality simply as a 'rule of law' (see, eg, *Etablissements*

Biret v Council (case T–210/00), para 53). Following *Bergaderm*, the focus is now on a rule intended to confer rights on individuals, in parallel with the rules on state liability and the CFI has expressly stated that there is no distinction to be made (arguments of the Council) between a 'superior rule of law' and a rule of law (*Sison v Council* (case T–47/03), para 234).

14.6.1.3 *The breach must be 'sufficiently serious'*

Even under the old formula, a breach of a superior rule of law, including a fundamental rule such as the principle of equality, was not in itself sufficient to give rise to a claim in damages. The claimant must prove that the breach is 'sufficiently serious'. This principle has been very narrowly construed. In *Bayerische HNL Vermehrungsbetriebe GmbH & Co KG v Council* (cases 83 and 94/76, and 4, 15, and 40/77), the Court suggested that in a legislative field in which one of the chief features is the exercise of a wide discretion, the Community does not incur liability unless the institution concerned has *manifestly and gravely disregarded the limits on the exercise of its power*.

When interpreting this requirement, the Court adopted two broad approaches:

(a) the *effect* of the measure on the applicant, at the nature and extent of the harm to his interests

(b) the nature of the breach.

An example of the first approach can be seen in *HNL v Council* an action had been brought by a number of animal-feed producers for damages for loss suffered as a result of an EC regulation requiring animal-feed producers to purchase skimmed-milk powder instead of the cheaper and equally effective soya, as a means of disposing of surplus stocks of milk. This regulation had been found by the Court in a prior preliminary ruling proceeding (*Bela-Mühle Josef Bergmann KG v Grows-Farm GmbH & Co KG* (case 114/76); *Granaria BV v Hoofdproduktschap voor Akkerbouwprodukten (No 1)* (case 116/76)) to be in breach of the principles of non-discrimination and proportionality. In deciding whether the breach was sufficiently serious, ie whether the Commission had manifestly and gravely disregarded the limits on the exercise of its powers, the Court looked at the effect of the breach. It had affected a wide group of persons (all buyers of protein for the production of animal feed); the difference in price between the skimmed milk and soya had only a limited effect on production costs, insignificant beside other factors such as world prices; and the effect of the regulation on their profits did not exceed the normal level of risk inherent in such activities. The breach was not sufficiently serious (cf *P Dumortier Frères SA v Council* (cases 64 and 113/76; 167 and 239/78; 27, 28, and 45/79), where the claimants were a small, clearly defined group, and their loss went beyond the risks normally inherent in their business).

In looking at the nature of the breach, the Court was effectively asking in what way, and to what extent, is the institution *culpable*?

It seems from the case law that both enquiries are relevant. The breach must be both serious as regards its effect on the applicant *and* inexcusable. Thus, in the 'Isoglucose' cases (*Koninklijke Scholten-Honig NV v Council* (case 143/77); *GR Amylum NV v Council* (cases 116 and 124/77)), the claimant glucose producers were seeking damages for losses suffered as a result of a Community regulation which imposed levies on the production of glucose in order to increase consumption of Community sugar. Clearly glucose and sugar were to some extent in competition for a market. The regulation had been found invalid, in breach of the principle of equality, in a prior preliminary ruling reference in *Royal Scholten-Honig (Holdings) Ltd v Intervention Board for Agricultural Produce* (cases 103 and 145/77). The claimants were a small and closed group, and the damage which they suffered as a result of the regulation was described as 'catastrophic'. One firm, the Dutch firm Koninklijke Scholten-Honig NV had been forced into liquidation. Yet they failed to obtain damages. Although the treatment of the glucose producers as compared with that of the sugar producers was 'manifestly unequal', the Court held that the defendants' errors were not of such gravity that their conduct could be regarded as 'verging on the arbitrary'.

Whether a particular risk is regarded as foreseeable will be determined according to the standard of the prudent and discriminating trader (see, eg, *EFISOL SA v Commission* (case T–336/94)).

14.6.2 **The modern approach:** *Bergaderm* **and beyond**

In view of the stringent nature of the *Schöppenstedt* formula it is not surprising that very few claimants succeed. The Court had justified its strict approach on the basis of its:

> concern to ensure that the legislative function is not hindered by the prospect of actions for damages whenever the general interest requires the institutions . . . to adopt measures which may adversely affect individual interests. [*R v HM Treasury,* ex parte *BT* (case C–392/93), para 40.]

In its anxiety to protect the Union institutions it has applied the restrictive *Schöppenstedt* test in a seemingly indiscriminate manner to claims arising from actions which do not involve legislative choices. For this it has been rightly criticised. As Advocate-General Tesauro pointed out in *Brasserie du Pêcheur* (cases C–46 and 48/93) on the date on which the opinion was approved (26 November 1995), only eight awards of damages against Union institutions had been made. Although there have been a number of successful cases since then, these have tended to arise in the context of administrative failures rather than in circumstances involving economic policy (eg, *New Europe Consulting and Brown v Commission* (case T–231/97) and *Embassy Limousines v European Parliament* (case T–203/96)).

The emergence of the principle of state liability served to highlight the limitations of Article 288(2) and pointed to the need for a broader and more flexible test for liability capable of taking into account the different types of breach and the different situations of EC institutions and Member States.

In relation to state liability, this was provided in *Brasserie du Pêcheur*. Here the Court confirmed the concept of the 'sufficiently serious' breach as the basis for liability, but introduced, in para 56, a wide range of criteria by which the question of whether the breach was sufficiently serious might be judged. These included:

the clarity and precision of the EC rule breached, the measure of discretion left by that rule to the national or Community authorities, whether the infringement and the damage caused was intentional or voluntary, whether [the] error of law was excusable or inexcusable. [See further Chapter 9.]

Subsequently, this test has been applied to all breaches of Community law, whether by EU institutions or by Member States. It enabled the Court to decide, in a whole variety of circumstances, whether a breach of Community law, whether committed by an EU institution or by a Member State, was sufficiently serious to attract liability. The ECJ clearly intended this approach to be used in all these circumstances, although it was not until *Bergaderm* that the application to Community liability was confirmed.

The action in *Laboratoires Pharmaceutiques Bergaderm SA and Goupil v Commission* (case C–352/98 P) arose out of an amendment to Directive 76/768/EEC ([1976] OJ L262, p 169) to limit the level of psolaren molecules in sun oils. Bergaderm was no longer able to sell its sun oil and the company was put into liquidation. It brought an action under Article 288(2) EC, claiming that the Commission had committed various wrongful acts (procedural errors, breach of the principle of proportionality, and misuse of powers) during the adoption of the Adaptation Directive (which amended Directive 76/768/EEC), which had caused significant financial damages to Bergaderm. The claim was rejected by the CFI (*Laboratoires Pharmaceutiques Bergaderm SA and Goupil v Commission* (case T–199/96)). On appeal, the ECJ brought Article 288 and state liability full circle. Having considered the test for state liability in *Brasserie du Pêcheur* (see Chapter 9), the Court held that there would be liability under Article 288 where a rule of law intended to confer rights on individuals had been infringed; the breach had to be sufficiently serious, and there had to be a direct causal link between the breach and the damage caused. With regard to establishing whether a breach was 'sufficiently serious', the Court said that:

as regards both Community liability under [Article 288] of the Treaty and Member State liability for breaches of Community law, the decisive test for finding that a breach of Community law is sufficiently serious is whether the Member State or the Community institution concerned manifestly and gravely disregarded the limits on its discretion. [C–352/98P, para 43.]

This meant that the crucial factor in establishing whether there had been an unlawful act was the degree of discretion available to the institution concerned. The Court also noted that where there is no exercise of discretion, the *Hedley Lomas* (case C–5/94) principle developed in the context of Member State breaches of Community law (see Chapter 9) applies, according to which, if there is considerably reduced, or no, discretion, the mere infringement of Community law may be a sufficiently serious breach.

The new approach, in the wake of *Bergaderm*, therefore marks a departure from *Schöppenstedt* in three main aspects: first, it is no longer necessary to consider whether the rule infringed was a 'superior rule of law'; instead, the rule infringed has to be one intended to confer rights on individuals. Secondly, in establishing whether a breach is sufficiently serious, the criteria listed in para 56 of *Brasserie de Pêcheur* are now applied, rather than the cases on the effects of the breach and harm to the claimaint. In *MyTravel Group plc v Commission*, (case T–212/03), in the case of a third party affected by a Commission decision on the acceptability of a merger, which decision was subsequently annulled, the CFI elaborated that:

> the right to compensation for damage resulting from the conduct of the institution becomes available where such conduct takes the form of action manifestly contrary to the rule of law and seriously detrimental to the interests of persons outside the institution and cannot be justified or accounted for by the particular constraints to which the staff of the institution, operating normally, are objectively subject. [Para 43.]

Finally, the focus has also shifted away from the question of whether the act complained about was administrative or legislative; instead, what matters now is the degree of discretion for the Community institution. In *Holcim (Deutschland) v Commission* (Case C–282/05 P) the ECJ also reaffirmed that in determining discretion, this issue was not determined by whether the measure was general or individualised.

It seems therefore that the test for the application of Article 288(2) can still be reduced to a list of three elements, but these vary from those previously used. They can be summarised as follows:

(a) unlawful action

(b) damage

(c) causal link between the action and the damage.

Although the vast majority of cases involving Article 288 decided after *Bergaderm* have followed this new approach (eg, *Beamglow Ltd v Parliament, Council and Commission* (case T–383/00) *Medici Grimm KG v Council* (case T–364/03); *Holcim (Deutschland) v Commission* (Case C–282/05 P)), there are some decisions which have been decided squarely on the basis of *Schöppenstedt*. Thus, in *CEVA v Commission* (T–344/00), an instance of Commission inaction under Regulation 1308/99, the CFI regarded this as a breach of the principle of sound administration (a higher-ranking rule of law), and imposed liability on that basis. In *Commission v Fresh Marine* (case C–472/00), the claimant's case that there had been a breach referred to *Schöppenstedt*, but the ECJ considered the claim purely on the basis of *Bergaderm* (see also, eg, *Comafrica and Dole Fresh Fruit v Commission* (joined cases T–230/97, T–171, 174, and 198/95 and T–225/99)).

13.6.3 Individual acts

It was assumed that the *Bergaderm* approach, as did the *Schöppenstedt* formula, would not apply to individual acts which do not involve the exercise of discretion. Since such acts affect only their addressees they do not raise the same floodgate problems, thus it is not necessary to subject them to such stringent criteria. The ECJ has now expressly stated in *Holcim (Deutschland) v Commission* (Case C–282/05 P) that:

the applicant is not justified in submitting that the criterion of a sufficiently serious breach of a rule of law applies only where a legislative act of the Community is at issue and is excluded when, as in the present case, an individual act is at issue. Contrary to what is argued, the Court of First Instance could not limit itself to making a finding of unlawfulness, but had to apply, as it correctly did, the criterion of the existence of a sufficiently serious breach. [Para 49.]

(Contrast Advocate-General Tesauro's criticism of the Court's application of Article 288(2) in *Brasserie du Pêcheur* (cases C–46 and 48/93)).

Where an individual act is prima facie unlawful and threatens to cause damage to its addressee, it may be challenged under Article 230. Where he fails to challenge the measure in time he may still bring an independent action under Article 288(2) where damage has occurred as a result of its application (*Krohn* (case 175/84)). To succeed, however, it may not be enough to establish the illegality of the measure. Although there is little authority on this point it is thought that fault must be proved, although what may be deemed to constitute fault in this context remains unclear. In *Grifoni v Euratom* (case C–308/87), for example, a failure to provide a guard rail despite clear guidelines requiring their provision provided the basis for community liability.

14.7 Liability for lawful acts

As was suggested earlier, there was some confusion as to the position regarding lawful acts. This matter has recently been addressed by the ECJ in *FIAMM and FIAMM Technologies v Council and Commission* (case C–120/06 P), which concerned compensation claimed for the damage suffered by the applicants after the United States was authorised under the World Trade Organisation (WTO) rules to implement retaliatory measures following the EU failure to change its banana regime. The retaliatory measures were felt by other sectors. The CFI had ruled against the applicants, although it suggested that liability could in principle arise whether there was no wrongful act. This case was an appeal on points of law. The ECJ agreed with the CFI that there was no wrongful act and further remarked that whilst the conditions for liability for wrongful acts were clear, the position was not so clear for liability for lawful acts. In so doing, it seems to suggest that liability could arise for such acts. It then noted the suggestion, referring to *Dorsch Consult* (para 18) and *Biovilac* ((case 59/83), para 28) that in addition to the underlying action, there were at least three conditions of liability:

(a) damage

(b) causal link

(c) unusual and special nature of the damage.

The ECJ then went on to re-emphasise that liability for legislative activity arose only in limited circumstances, as set down in *Bergaderm*. It concluded:

that, as Community law currently stands, no liability regime exists under which the Community can incur liability for conduct falling within the sphere of its legislative competence in a situation where any failure of such conduct to comply with the WTO agreements cannot be relied upon before the Community courts.[Para 176.]

The outcome of this judgment—beyond the facts in the case—is not clear, as the reasoning can be read three ways. First as affirming the principle of liability for lawful acts but not in this case; as affirming the principle, but not for legislative acts; or, as overturning the CFI's view that liability could arise for lawful acts, though presumably if the ECJ had intended the latter interpretation, it would have said so and not discussed the particular difficulties of legislative acts.

14.8 Damage

Once it has been established that there was an unlawful act, it is necessary to consider if damage has been caused. This requirement will be considered in this section.

14.8.1 Only specific losses are recoverable

The ECJ (and now the CFI) is as restrictive in its approach to damages as it is to fault. Clearly the Court will award compensation for damage to person or property provided the damage is sufficiently direct. Although it will in principle award damages for economic loss, such losses must be specific, not speculative. Only actual, certain and concrete damages are recoverable (*Société Roquette Frères v Commission* (case 26/74). Thus in *Firma E Kampffmeyer v Commission* (cases 5, 7, and 13–24/66) the Court was prepared to award damages for lost profits on contracts which had already been concluded, which applicants had had to cancel as a result of the illegal decision, although these damages were reduced to only 10 per cent of the profits they might have expected to make, on account of the risks involved in the transactions in question. Applicants who had not concluded contracts prior to applying for import permits were awarded no damages at all. In *CNTA SA v Commission* (case 74/74) the Court found that the Commission had breached the principle of legitimate expectations when it introduced a regulation, suddenly and without warning, which deprived the claimant of export refunds at a particular rate, fixed in advance. Although the regulation was not in itself invalid, the Commission's mode of introduction of the measure was wrongful. Thus the Commission was liable in principle. However, although CNTA had entered into export contracts on the basis of its legitimate expectations, the Court held that it was only entitled to recover for losses actually suffered, not anticipated profits, and, since currency fluctuations at the time of import had resulted in its suffering no loss on the refunds themselves, it recovered no damages (see also *Firma Gebrüder Dietz v Commission* (case 126/76)).

The ECJ has held that the applicant must specify the amount of damages (*Camar and Tico v Commission* (joined cases T–79/96; 260/97, and 117/98)), save in limited circumstances (*Sinara Handel v Council and Commission* (case T-91/05), para 110) and those circumstances must be indicated (*Goldstein v Commission* (case T–262/97), para 25). In *CEVA v Commission* (T–344/00), the CFI decided to rule that the Community was liable in damages even though it was not, at the time of judgment, possible to quantify the loss suffered by the applicant. In *Coldiretti and ors v Council and Commission* (Case T–149/96) the applicants specified the different types of damage suffered and provided detailed estimates of the loss of profits suffered.

14.8.2 Loss and third parties

Where the loss has been passed on to third parties, or could have been passed on in higher prices, no damages will be recoverable (*Interquell Stärke-Chemie GmbH & Co KG v Council* (cases 261 and 262/78), 'quellmehl' case). In *P Dumortier Frères SA v Council* (cases 64 and 113/76; 167 and 239/78; 27, 28, and 45/79) the claimants satisfied the Court that the losses could not have been passed on without risk of losing valuable markets. An injured party is expected to show reasonable diligence in limiting the extent of his loss; otherwise he must bear the damage himself (*Mulder* (case C–104/89)). In *Antillean Rice Mills NV v Commission* (cases T–480 and 483/93), the CFI suggested that since the damage to the applicants was foreseeable they could have taken precautions against it. Since they did not, 'neither the fault nor the damage alleged by the applicants are such as to cause the Community to incur non-contractual liability'.

In *Dorsch Consult* (case T–184/95), the CFI held that the applicant had not shown actual and certain damage. The case concerned a contract for the provision of services in Iraq. The applicants had not been paid for the work done when the UN Security Council imposed a trade embargo on Iraq, which the European Community implemented within the EC. As a response to this, the Iraqi government froze all property, assets, and income from them, held at the material time by the governments, undertakings, companies, and banks of those states which had adopted 'arbitrary decisions' against Iraq. The applicants claimed that the Community was liable for the damage it had suffered from not being able to obtain payment from Iraq. The CFI pointed out that the applicants had not tried to press for payment, even when the relevant Iraqi law was repealed.

14.8.3 Loss of a chance

In *Farrugia* (case T–230/94) the CFI considered a claim for compensation for the loss of a chance. The applicant claimed that an error on the part of the Commission concerning his nationality had deprived him of the opportunity of a fellowship in the field of research and technological development in the UK. The CFI found that although the Commission had made a mistake the applicant had failed to prove that, in the absence of that mistake, he would have had a 'strong chance' of being awarded the fellowship he sought. This implies that the Court would consider a claim for loss of a chance of success provided that the chance was proved to be sufficiently strong. The Court did not indicate what standard of proof would be necessary to establish a 'strong chance' of success.

14.8.4 Payment of damages in national currency

Damages are payable in the applicant's national currency at the exchange rate applicable on the date of the judgment under Article 288(2). Interest on that sum is payable from the date of judgment (*Dumortier*).

14.9 **Causation**

The Court is similarly restrictive in its approach to matters of causation. In *Dumortier* it said that the principles common to the laws of Member States cannot be relied on to deduce an obligation to make good every harmful consequence, even a remote one, of unlawful legislation. The damage must be a *sufficiently direct* consequence of the unlawful conduct of the institution concerned.

Thus in *Dumortier*, the parties were entitled to recover the refunds which had been unlawfully withheld as a result of the invalid regulation, but not for further alleged losses in the form of reduced sales or for general financial difficulties resulting in the closing of some factories. Even though these difficulties might have been exacerbated by the illegal regulation they were not a sufficiently direct consequence of the unlawful act to render the Community liable (see also *Blackspur DIY Ltd v Council* (case T–168/94)). Other factors such as obsolescence and financial stringency were responsible. Similarly, where a party engages in activities designed to replace activities denied or restricted as a result of Community law any operating losses incurred as a result of these activities will be deemed too remote, and not attributed to the Community (*Mulder* (cases C–104/89 and C 37/90)).

Elliniki Viomichania Oplon AE (EVO) v Council and Commission (case T–220/96), concerned the trade embargo imposed on Iraq following its invasion of Kuwait. The Community had adopted Regulation 2340/90 ([1990] OJ L213, p 1) to implement the embargo. EVO had supplied ammunition to Iraq, but Iraq failed to pay sums due. It claimed that it could not pay because of two United Nations resolutions which also imposed an embargo on the country. EVO brought an action under Article 288 EC to recover the payment due from Iraq by way of a damages claim against the Community. The CFI rejected the claim both because Iraq had not refused payment because of Regulation 2340/90 but because of the UN resolutions and because the regulation itself did not apply to the particular contracts for which EVO was still owed payment. There was no causal link between the loss suffered and the Community act complained about (see 14.8.2 and 14.9.2 for a further claim based on the Iraq embargo in *Dorsch Consult*).

14.9.1 **Break in the chain of causation**

The ECJ (and now the CFI) has taken the view that the acts of the applicants, and sometimes even their failure to act, will break the chain of causation. Traders are expected to act as prudent business people. For example, in a claim based on misleading information the required causal link will be established only if the information would have caused an error in the mind of a reasonable person (*Compagnie Continentale France v Council* (case 169/73); see also *SA Oleifici Mediterranei v EEC* (case 26/81) and *Antillean Rice Mills NV v Commission* (cases T–480 and 483/93)). In *EFISOL SA v Commission* (case T–336/94) the CFI suggested that a legitimate expectation (as to a certain state of affairs) could not arise from conduct on the part of the (Community) administration which was inconsistent with Community rules. Thus it seems that the prudent trader is expected to know if a Community institution misapplies Community rules!

In *International Procurement Services SA v Commission* (case T–175/94) the applicant tenderer suffered loss in a contract with the Mozambique government. Following advice from the Commission the government reduced the payment originally agreed for the supply of steel billets by the applicant. Although the Commission was found to have indirectly influenced the Mozambique government's decision to pay the lower price, the applicant's damage was held by the CFI to derive from two factors: the Mozambique government's refusal to pay the originally agreed price, and the applicant's failure to challenge that refusal in arbitration proceedings, as it was entitled to do. The fact that IPS had taken that course of action because it was 'in urgent need of liquid funds' would not have the effect of attaching responsibility for the damage to the defendants.

14.9.2 Loss must be foreseeable

Where other factors can be seen as contributing to the claimant's loss the damage is normally seen as too remote. The CFI considered the nature of the causal link in *Dorsch Consult* (case T–184/95). There, it commented that the applicant had not succeeded in showing that the adoption by the Iraqi government of a law freezing the applicants' assets in retaliation for the trade embargo imposed on Iraq was 'an objectively foreseeable consequence, in the normal course of events, of the adoption' of that Community's regulation implementing the embargo. A requirement of foreseeability seems to have been introduced as a precondition to the finding of a causal link.

14.9.3 Contributory negligence

The Court does not as a general rule attempt to apportion blame on the basis of contributory negligence. It appears that apportionment is reserved for claims of particular merit. In *Adams v Commission* (*No 1*) (case 145/83) Adams's damages for the Commission's breach of confidence, which had caused him irreparable financial and emotional damage, were reduced by 50 per cent to take into account Adams's contribution in failing to protect his own interests. Similarly, in *Grifoni v Euratom* (case C–308/87), although Euratom was clearly at fault in not providing guard rails, equally Grifoni, an experienced contractor, should have known that he had to take some precautions himself. His damages were reduced, also by 50 per cent.

14.10 Impact of other possible causes of action

Where the Court rejects a claim for damages, as in the isoglucose cases, it often points out that applicants are not without a remedy. The action must be assessed having regard to the whole system of legal protection of individuals set up by the treaty. Where a person suffers, or is likely to suffer, damage as a result of an unlawful act he may challenge that measure before his national courts and seek a ruling under Article 234 on its validity. The Court has said that the existence of such an action is by itself of such a nature as to ensure the effective protection of the individuals concerned. Not all would agree with this view. There may be no issue of national law in which to raise questions of EC law. As is borne out in *Koninklijke Scholten-Honig NV v Council* (case 143/77), heavy, even irreparable losses may be incurred while proceedings before the national courts are pending. An action before a national court may be successful in obtaining interim relief (see, eg, *Zuckerfabrik Süderdithmarschen AG v Hauptzollamt Itzehoe* (cases C–143/88 and 92/89); *Antonissen v Council* (case C–393/96 P/R), noted in Chapter 7), or, in time, a declaration of invalidity, but where damage has occurred a national court cannot award compensation for wrongs attributable to the Community (see *Krohn* (case 175/84), discussed below).

Surely the most appropriate forum in which to challenge Community action (or inaction) would be before the European Courts under Article 230 EC (or Article 232 EC), alongside, or prior to, a claim for damages under Article 228(2). Yet, as has been seen in Chapter 12, the individual has no *locus standi* to challenge or demand genuine legislative measures under these articles. Since the European courts are understandably reluctant to expose the Community to unlimited claims, and, where the exercise of discretion by a Community institution is concerned, to fetter that discretion by the prospect of such exposure, arguably the most effective protection for applicants would be speedy interim relief from the European courts to forestall the application of unlawful measures and prevent damage occurring. Although this may be obtained in an action under Article 288(2) (see *Kampffmeyer* (cases 56–60/74), considered at 14.11), it would seem more logical, in the absence of damage, to proceed under Article 230. Where damage is suffered as a result of lawful action on the part of the Community, perhaps the courts could be persuaded, in exceptional cases, to accept some form of strict liability on the principle of *égalité devant les charges publiques*. It cannot be right that a few should bear a disproportionate burden as a result of measures enacted in the interest of the many.

14.11 Relationship between Article 288(2) and other remedies

If a claim for damages for non-contractual liability, particularly a claim based on an unlawful legislative act, is unlikely to succeed for the many reasons outlined above, its value in the overall scheme of remedies available against the Community should not be underrated. Since an action under Article 288(2) is an independent form of action (*Lütticke* (case 4/69); *Schöppenstedt* (case 5/71); *Krohn* (case 175/84)), an action for damages based on invalidity or wrongful failure may be effective in obtaining a declaration of invalidity or failure to act notwithstanding that the applicant has no *locus standi*, either personal or temporal, to challenge that same act (or inaction) in proceedings under Article 230 or Article 232. Moreover, the Court has held (*Kurt Kampffmeyer Mühlenvereinigung KG v Council* (cases 56–60/74)) that where the damage to the claimant is imminent, or likely with a high degree of certainty to occur, the claimant may bring proceedings under Article 288(2)) *before* the damage has occurred. Although he may not be found entitled in principle to damages, he may obtain a declaration of invalidity or unlawful failure to act, including interim relief, in time to prevent the damage occurring.

It is submitted that the Court will admit such actions under Article 288(2) only where a claim for damages is genuine; it will not allow this provision to be used solely as a means of evading the *locus standi* limitations of Articles 230 and 232 (see *Krohn* (case 175/84) and *Cobrecaf SA v Commission* (case T–514/93)).

14.12 Concurrent liability

As Community law is, to a large extent, implemented by national authorities, there may be cases in which it is unclear whether the cause of action—for example, for the return of money paid under an invalid regulation, or for a wrongful failure on the part of a national body to pay a subsidy to which the applicant feels he is entitled—lies against the national authority, in national courts, according to national law; or against a Community institution, before the CFI; or against both. Motivated no doubt by a desire to reduce its workload and/or its potential liability, the Court, as illustrated by *Koninklijke Scholten-Honig NV* (case 143/77) (and countless other cases), prefers to direct applicants to seek a remedy before their national courts, leaving questions of validity to be referred to the ECJ, if necessary, under Article 234.

It is submitted that, largely as a result of this preference, the case law on what might loosely be termed concurrent liability is both confusing and contradictory.

Initially, in cases such as *Firma E. Kampffmeyer v Commission* (cases 5, 7, and 13–24/66) and *R & V Haegeman Sprl v Commission* (case 96/71), the ECJ espoused a doctrine of 'exhaustion of national law remedies'. In *Kampffmeyer* the applicant grain dealers were seeking, before the ECJ, as a result of an invalid EC regulation:

(a) the return of levies paid to the German authorities

(b) compensation for contracts cancelled.

They had already begun parallel proceedings before the German courts, but those proceedings had been stayed pending the outcome of the Community proceedings. The ECJ held that the German court should first be given the opportunity to decide whether the German authorities were liable. The proceedings were stayed accordingly.

In *Haegeman* the applicant was seeking the annulment of a Commission decision refusing to return levies paid to the German authorities by the applicant as a result of an allegedly invalid regulation. This time, unlike *Kampffmeyer*, the levies had been paid into Community funds, and Haegeman had not instituted parallel proceedings before its national courts. Again the Court refused to admit the action. Haegeman's claim should have been made against the national authorities to whom the refunds were originally paid.

There followed a series of cases in which claims before the ECJ were made:

(a) for the return of *sums unlawfully levied* (eg, *Société Roquette Frères v Commission* (case 26/74))

(b) seeking payment of *sums unlawfully withheld* (*IBC v Commission* (case 46/75); *Lesieur Costelle et Associés SA v Commission* (cases 67–85/75)).

These were held to be inadmissible on the grounds that the applicants should have brought their actions before their national courts.

On the other hand in *Compagnie d'Approvisionnement de Transport et de Crédit SA v Commission* (cases 9 and 11/71); *Merkur-Aussenhandels GmbH v Commission* (case 43/72); *Holtz & Willemsen GmbH v Council* (case 153/73); and *CNTA SA v Commission* (case 74/74) the ECJ was prepared to admit claims seeking payment of *sums unlawfully withheld* without requiring claimants to proceed first before their national courts.

In *Firma Gebrüder Dietz v Commission* (case 126/76), and *CNTA* (case 74/74) the applicants were seeking damages for losses suffered as a result of the sudden introduction by the Commission of monetary compensatory amounts in agriculture; they had not brought actions before their national courts. Their claims under Article 288(2) were held admissible.

In the second 'grits' and 'quellmehl' cases, and the 'isoglucose' cases, admitted under Article 288(2), proceedings had already been brought and the invalidity of the measures in question decided, before the applicants' national courts.

From the above cases the following tentative conclusions may be drawn:

(a) A claim for the return of sums unlawfully paid to the relevant national authorities should always be brought before a national court, even though those sums may have been paid into Community funds (*Kampffmeyer, Haegeman; Roquette*; see also more recently *Industrie-en Handelsonderneming Vreugdenhil BV v Commission* (case C–282/90)).

(b) A claim for sums unlawfully withheld, even when withheld by a national authority, may be brought *either* before national courts or the CFI. The weight of authority (*Compagnie d'Approvisionnement; Merkur; Holtz & Willemsen; CNTA*) leans towards this view. However, the existence of *IBC* and *Costelle* render it advisable to bring such a claim before a national court, *provided* that no further damages are required from the Community *and* payment of the sums involved was required to be channelled through the national authority.

(c) A claim for unliquidated damages for losses suffered as a result of illegal Community action (eg, financial losses in *Dietz*; *CNTA*; *Dumortier*) can *only* be brought before the European Courts under Article 288(2). In this respect it is submitted that *Kampffmeyer* was wrong. Therefore, if these losses result from sums unlawfully withheld, the appropriate forum for recovery of *both* sums would be at the European level.

Further support for principles (b) and (c) above may also be derived from *Krohn & Co Import-Export GmbH & Co KG v Commission* (case 175/84). Krohn & Co was seeking compensation for financial losses suffered as a result of its national (German) authority's refusal to grant it licences to import manioc from Thailand. In rejecting its application the authorities were acting on mandatory instructions from the Commission. Krohn brought an action before the German courts seeking an annulment of the national authority's decision and an injunction requiring it to issue the licences, and a parallel action before the ECJ for compensation for losses suffered as a result of its action in denying him the licences. The Commission argued that the action under Article 288(2) was inadmissible, since:

(a) the refusal of the licence came from the national authority

(b) the applicant should have exhausted its remedies before its national court

(c) to admit liability would be equivalent to nullifying the Commission's decision, which the applicant had failed to challenge in time.

All three arguments were rejected by the Court. With regard to (a) the Court found that although the refusal emanated from the national authority, the unlawful conduct was to be attributed not to the German authorities but to the Community itself. The Commission was the 'true author' of the decision.

With regard to (b) the Court held that while admissibility may be dependent on national rights available to obtain the annulment of a national authority's decision, that would only be the case where national rights of action provide an *effective means of protection* for the individual concerned and are capable of resulting in compensation for the damage alleged.

Clearly, since the alleged 'tort' had been committed by the Community, only the Community would be liable to pay compensation.

The Court's response to (c) has already been noted. An action under Article 288(2) was an autonomous form of action with a particular purpose to fulfil (*Lütticke* (case 4/69)).

Thus, in deciding whether action should be brought before a national court or before the European Courts, the appropriate question is whether action before a national court can provide an *effective means of protection* for the claimant's interests. Where he merely seeks the return of money paid, or payment of money unlawfully withheld, or a declaration of invalidity or an injunction to prevent the application of the unlawful act, a fortiori when the wrongful act can be laid at the door of the national authorities (see *Société des Grands Moulins des Antilles v Commission* (case 99/74), and *Krohn*, in which it was held that national courts retain sole jurisdiction to order compensation for damage caused by national institutions), he should proceed before his national courts. Where he seeks damage from the Community for injury suffered as a result of wrongful acts attributable to the Community, his action must be before the CFI (or ECJ). This is a right which cannot be 'exhausted' before a national court. Where remedies are required of both national authorities and the Community, it will be necessary to proceed against both. Clearly he cannot recover twice for the same loss.

14.13 Conclusions

In dealing with claims under Article 288, the European Courts have to balance the conflicting interests of permitting flexibility in decision-making and protecting individuals who may suffer as a result of such action. For a long time, the Court had taken a very restrictive approach to claims brought under Article 288, but it is questionable whether this approach was entirely justified. The alignment of Community liability and state liability through *Brasserie de Pêcheur* and *Bergaderm* has improved this position to an extent, but it remains difficult for individuals seeking damages against the Community to succeed with their claim. Following *Brasserie du Pêcheur*, claims for damages under Article 288(2) should now be approached in the same way as claims under the state-liability principle. In situations where the defendant institution is acting pursuant to a wide discretion (which will often be the case in action taken under Article 288), the list of factors to be taken into account in establishing whether a breach is sufficiently serious set out in para 56 of *Brasserie du Pêcheur* is now relevant. Moreover, it also appears that, following *Bergaderm*, it seems less relevant whether the measure complained of is of general or individual application. But although the applicant may succeed in establishing the existence of a sufficiently serious breach, he may still fail to establish that damage and causation. Although restrictive rules in relation to damage and causation may be justified to protect the Community against extensive liability to commercial undertakings for pure economic loss, it is questionable whether the rules as they currently are offer effective judicial protection for individuals. This has not changed to any significant extent in the wake of recent developments. Further, the position of the courts regarding liability for lawful acts still remains to be clarified fully. Despite these somewhat tentative extensions of the scope of Article 288, it remains of limited use.

FURTHER READING

Hartley, TC, *The Foundations of European Community Law*, 5th edn (OUP, 2003).

Hilson, C, 'The role of discretion in EC law on non-contractual liability' (2005) 42 CML Rev 677.

Kuijper, PJ and Bronckers, M, 'WTO law in the European Court of Justice' (2005) 42 CML Rev 1313–55.

Schermers, H, Heukels, T, and Mead, P (eds), *Non-contractual Liability of the European Communities* (Nijhoff Publications,1988).

Steiner, J, 'The limits of state liability for breach of European Community Law' (1998) EPL 69.

Wils, W, 'Concurrent liability of the Community and a Member State' (1992) 17 EL Rev 191.

PART III

15

Introduction to the internal market

15.1 Introduction

The creation of the common market—or, post Lisbon, the internal market—is one of the central purposes of the European Community, and, after Lisbon, the Union (see Article 3(3) of the Treaty of the European Union (TEU) as amended by Lisbon). The specific activities to fulfil this task can currently be found in Article 3 EC. Article 3(1)(a) refers to the prohibition of customs duties while Article 3(1)(b) refers to the Community's common commercial policy, as well as common policies in certain areas, such as agriculture, fisheries, and transport. Article 3(1)(g) specifies that the Community shall introduce a system to ensure that 'competition in the internal market is not distorted', and Article 3(1)(h) provides for 'the approximation of laws of the Member States to the extent required for the functioning of the common market'.

Following the Single European Act (SEA), another term was introduced, that of an 'internal market'. Article 14 (ex 7a) describes the internal market as 'an area without internal frontiers in which the free movement of goods, persons, services and capital is ensured in accordance with the provisions of the Treaty'.

These are referred to together as the 'four freedoms'. The common market, in addition to the four freedoms, also deals with common commercial policy—commercial relations with third countries—and competition policy. On this basis, it could be argued that the term 'common market' is slightly wider than 'internal market'. The European Court of Justice (ECJ) has, in practice, not tended to distinguish between the terms. It seems that should the Lisbon Treaty come into force, the blurring of boundaries between the two concepts would continue. In addition to introducing the phrase 'internal market' to the Union's objectives, all references in the current EC Treaty to the 'common market' would be replaced with the words 'internal market' (see Article 2(2)(g) of the Lisbon Treaty). This then would remove the concept of the common market from the Union. Additionally, Article 14 would be renumbered Article 26 of the Treaty on the Functioning of the European Union (TFEU). It would thus no longer form part of the general principles in Pt 1 of the EC Treaty, but be found in Pt 3 of the TFEU, which identifies Union policies. Pending that time, it is probably still sensible to view the two terms as having the same scope. In any event, the 'four freedoms' remain central as one of the shared areas of competence. This chapter identifies certain common themes affecting those of the four freedoms treated in this book: subsequent chapters look at the detail of these provisions.

15.2 Overview of the four freedoms

15.2.1 Free movement of goods

The principle of freedom of movement of goods has been described as a fundamental freedom, the 'cornerstone' of the internal market. For many Member States the opportunity of access for their goods to a single, European-wide market was, and remains, a primary reason for membership. The free play of market forces within that larger market would increase economic efficiency, widen consumer choice, and enhance the Union's competitiveness in world markets. However, since the principle of freedom of movement was intended to apply to all goods, including goods imported from outside the Union, it was necessary to eliminate distortions of competition resulting from different national rules regulating trade with third countries by presenting a common commercial front to the outside world. To achieve these goals:

(a) The EC Treaty sought to establish a *customs union* which shall involve (Article 23 (ex 9) EC):

   (i) 'the prohibition between Member States of customs duties on imports and exports and of all charges having equivalent effect' (Article 25 EC), and

   (ii) 'the adoption of a common customs tariff in their relations with third countries'.

   Should Lisbon come into force, these provisions will remain unaltered save that they will be renumbered Articles 28 and 30 TFEU respectively. Note that this aspect of the free movement of goods will be expressed to fall within exclusive Union competence, post Lisbon (Article 3 TFEU).

(b) The EC Treaty sought the elimination of quantitative restrictions on imports and exports and all measures having equivalent effect (Articles 28–9 (ex 30 and 34) EC). Post Lisbon these provisions will be referred to as Articles 34–5 TFEU.

(c) In addition states were required to adjust any state monopolies of a commercial character so as 'to ensure that . . . no discrimination regarding the conditions under which goods are procured and marketed exists between nationals of Member States' (Article 31 (ex 37) EC). This provision will be renumbered by Lisbon; it will become, should Lisbon come into force, Article 37 TFEU (thus returning to its original number under the EEC Treaty).

The provisions relating to the free movement of goods apply to both industrial and agricultural products—save, where agriculture is concerned, as otherwise provided in Articles 33–8 EC (ex 39–46; post Lisbon Articles 39–44 TFEU) (Article 32(2) (ex 38(2); post Lisbon, Article 38 TFEU)—whether originating in Member States or coming from third countries which are in free circulation in Member States, even where, in the latter case, the goods have been admitted to the original state of import under special dispensation from the Commission under Article 134 (ex 115) EC (*Levy* (case 212/88)) (repealed by Lisbon). Products coming from third countries are regarded as in free circulation in a Member State:

if the import formalities have been complied with and any customs duties or charges
having equivalent effect which are payable have been levied in that Member State, and
if they have not benefited from a total or partial drawback of such duties or charges.
[Article 24 EC (ex 10(1); post Lisbon, Article 29 TFEU).]

15.2.2 **Free movement of people**

The basic principles relating to the free movement of persons are contained in
Articles 39–42 (ex 48–51) EC (workers), and Articles 43–8 (ex 52–8) EC (freedom of
establishment) (post Lisbon 45-8 and 49-54 TFEU respectively). The freedom to provide services is often seen as providing for the free movement of people although it
is identified separately within the four freedoms (see 15.2.3 below). These freedoms
have been further substantiated by secondary legislation. The rules apply throughout the territories of the Member States of the Union.

The basic rights enshrined in these provisions, granted to EU nationals (defined
according to the law of each Member State) and companies and firms formed
in accordance with the law of one of the Member States (Article 48 (ex 58; post
Lisbon, Article 54 TFEU)), comprise the right freely to leave, or enter and reside in
a Member State for the purposes of work or establishment (or the provision of services) and the right to be treated in the host Member State free from discrimination
on the grounds of nationality. As we shall see below, the ECJ has—at least as regards
individuals—interpreted these provisions to a large extent in parallel, a process
which has been reinforced by the introduction of European citizenship. The fact
that there is a large degree of similarity has lead to the restructuring of the chapters
on free movement of people. Whereas previous editions dealt with this topic by
looking at the treaty articles individually, this edition takes a horizontal approach,
looking at each of the rights accorded to migrant EU nationals, so commonalities
and differences can be more easily seen, and duplication avoided.

These rights are not absolute; not even citizenship rights are absolute. Rights of
entry and residence are subject to derogation on the grounds of public policy, public
security, and public health (Articles 39(3) and 46 (post Lisbon, Articles 45 and 52
TFEU respectively); Directive 2004/38/EC). Exceptions from the non-discrimination
principle are provided for 'employment in the public service' (Article 39(4)) and
'activities connected with the exercise of official authority' (Article 45; post Lisbon,
Article 51 TFEU).

15.2.2.1 *Who benefits from the free movement of workers?*

One of the key questions to be asked, in relation to free movement of people, is
whether the individuals claiming the rights fall within the scope of the treaty. In
this, we can see a broadening of protection in two ways: judicial and legislative.
As regards the judicial activity, although the rights contained in the treaty were
originally expressed to be limited to those who are economically active—that is,
workers or persons, natural or legal, exercising rights of establishment or providing
services in the host state—broad definitions of the relevant terms, in particular the
definition of worker, and generous interpretation on the part of the Court, have extended the scope of their protection. Furthermore, secondary legislation, originally
enacted in 1968 and 1970, extended these rights to the families of economically

active EU migrants, irrespective of their nationality. Legislative action also extend-ed similar rights to a wider category of persons, by the enactment of three directives (90/364, 90/365, 90/366 (amended and re-enacted as Directive 93/96) [1990] OJ L180) granting rights of entry and residence to retired persons, to persons of inde-pendent means and to students (provided they are EU nationals) 'insofar as they do not enjoy these rights under other provisions of Community law'. This trend was then given treaty recognition by the introduction of citizenship rights under Articles 18 *et seq* (ex 8a–e; post Lisbon, 21-5 TFEU), introduced by the TEU. Most recently, these rights have been consolidated and updated by the introduction of another directive, sometimes called the 'Citizenship Directive' (Directive 2004/38/EC). In the light of these developments, as regards EU citizens, falling within the scope of the treaties is now relatively easy to show. The questions arise with regard to third-country nationals, but even as regard this group of individuals, a greater degree of protection is now shown (see Chapters 21 and 26).

15.2.2.2 *Scope of rights*

A second central question relates to the scope of the rights granted. The early legis-lation provided more detail on the scope of rights, as can be seen particularly in re-lation to Regulation 1612/68 regarding workers. The rights under these provisions have been supported by an extensive interpretation by the ECJ. The ECJ developed in many cases a discrimination based argument so that with the expanded inter-pretation as to when free movement rights had been affected, and a broader scope to the treaties themselves, post Maastricht, the scope of rights available are broad, covering rights to education, the rights to war compensation, and even the right to name your child in a certain way.

15.2.2.3 *Infringement and justification*

With an expansive interpretation to the coming into existence of claims, the focus shifts to questions of infringement and justification. In many cases involving social and ancillary rights in particular, infringement is clear to see on the basis of indirect discrimination (eg residency clauses, and see further 15.3.3 below). Where meas-ures do not directly discriminate, they may be justified and an increasingly com-mon argument being used by the Member States is that the migrant claiming the right does not have sufficient connection with the host Member State; that there is no 'real link'. In principle it seems this argument can be used in relation to cases brought under an economic free movement right (eg, Article 39; see, eg, *Collins*) or under the citizenship provisions (*Bidar* (case C-209/03)), although whether it means the same thing in all circumstances is not yet clear. It does now seem to be the key concept to be used for balancing the rights of free movement against the need for Member States to protect themselves against social tourism.

15.2.2.4 *Citizenship rights*

Citizenship rights, set out in Articles 18–21 EC, comprise the right 'to move and reside freely within the territory of the Member States', the right to stand and vote in municipal and European Parliament elections, and the right to petition the om-budsman and the European Parliament. We have noted that as regards the right of free movement, the ECJ has interpreted the rights of citizens in line with the other free-movement rights. The introduction of the concept of citizenship, however, also raised questions as to what rights citizens should expect, and has fuelled the debate on whether the Community should do more to protect the individual citizen. This question, for example, was addressed by the Commission in *Modernising and Improving Social Protection in the EU* (COM (97) 102 of 13 March 1997). Despite the opportunity to amend the citizenship provisions that the ToA (1997) provided, nothing was done expressly to expand the rights attaching to citizenship, although it did introduce the so-called area of freedom, security, and justice (Article 62(1) EC). More recently, as we have already noted, rights have been given an express form, not only in the Citizenship Directive, but also as regards non-citizens in the Family Reunion Directive (Directive 2003/86/EC, [2003] OJ L251/12) and the Directive on Third-Country Nationals Who Are Long-term Residents (Directive 2003/109/EC). Lisbon again rejects the possibility of adding to citizenship, though the provisions are more explicitly linked to the principle of non-discrimination. Thus, when considering the provisions relating to the free movement of persons and to provisions on social policy in general, it is important to remember the dual imperatives, economic and social, affecting the development of these provisions and their interpretation.

15.2.3 Freedom to provide services

The freedom to provide services is found in Articles 49–55 EC; if Lisbon comes in to force, these provision will become Articles 56–62 TFEU. In this book the freedom to provide services is treated as part of the free movement of people. When someone provides a service, it may also involve that person moving, even if temporarily, to the Member State where the service is received. However, it should be noted that services themselves can move, without necessarily requiring that a person also moves to provide the service. Examples of this principle can be seen in sectors such as broadcasting or insurance. Nonetheless, the same provisions of Article 49 EC *et seq* apply in this context as apply in relation to the provision of services where a person moves, although it may be that a difference in the way the provisions are interpreted can be seen in the two types of circumstance. The fundamental right comprises the freedom to access both the territory and market of other Member States and to be treated on the same basis as the nationals of the host Member State. A further significant development can be seen in relation to the right to receive services, especially as regards public service provided by the individual Member States. Jurisprudence of the ECJ is eroding Member States' ability to control individuals' access to public services in other Member States. This area is discussed in Chapter 24 but has given rise to debate as to whether this case law allows for the most efficient use of such services across Europe or merely constitutes an unjustified erosion of national solidarity.

15.2.4 Free movement of capital

The provisions on capital and payments, substantially amended by the TEU, are found in Articles 56–60 (ex 73b–g). In its post-Maastricht form, the central provision bears a resemblance to the approach taken in relation to the free movement of goods. Recent case law suggests that the ECJ's approach has paralleled that taken in respect of the other three freedoms. These provisions, with some alterations, will be renumbered as Articles 63–6 TFEU, should the Lisbon Treaty come into force.

There are nonetheless, distinctive features relating to the provisions on capital. It should be noted that the treaty distinguishes between payments and capital movements between Member States themselves and between Member States and third countries. In the latter situation the Council may, in limited circumstances, take measures limiting the movement of capital and payments from third countries (Article 57(2)), Article 59, and Article 60 (ex 73g); post-Lisbon Article 75 TFEU).

Article 58 deals with tax, and permitted distinctions based on place of residence, as well as public-policy exceptions to the free movement of capital. Despite these provisions, it will be seen in the chapter on economic rights (Chapter 22) that Member States' freedom in the field of taxation has been curtailed. Article 58(2) provides that the provisions relating to capital are to operate without prejudice to the operation of restrictions on the freedom of establishment that are compatible with the treaty. Effectively, this means that a person cannot seek to evade a legitimate restriction on establishment via the capital provisions. It seems, however, that the reverse might be true. The relationship between capital and the other provisions as discussed at 17.5.

Finally, Article 58(3) provides that any national measures taken on the basis of Article 58(1) are 'not to constitute a means of arbitrary discrimination or a disguised restriction on the free movement of capital'. This wording parallels that used in relation to the derogation from the free movement of goods found in Article 30 (see further Chapter 17).

15.3 Common themes in the free movement provisions

Although the terms of the freedoms are each worded slightly differently, certain common elements must be shown before a case for the application of one of the freedoms can be made. In all cases it seems that there must be both an economic element and an interstate factor to bring the situation within the scope of any of the freedoms. Note also that, although citizenship does not require an economic element, it does require some connection with another Member State to be shown. It has also been argued that a convergence can be seen in the approach taken to identifying the trigger for a finding of breach of the freedoms.

15.3.1 Economic activity

In the earlier years of the Community, to invoke the non-discrimination principle it was necessary for the migrant claimant to be or have been engaged in some form of economic activity in the host state. In *Walrave v Association Union Cycliste Internationale* (case 36/74), in the context of a challenge to the cycling association's rules relating to 'pacemaker' cyclists, which were clearly discriminatory, it was held that the prohibition of discrimination on the grounds of nationality contained in former Article 7 EEC (currently Article 12 (ex 6) EC; post Lisbon, 18 TEU) does not apply to sports teams that have nothing to do with economic activity. The practice of sport is subject to Community law *only insofar as it constitutes an economic activity* within Article 2 of the EC Treaty (see further, eg, *Deliege* (joined cases C–51/96 and C–191/97), discussed in Chapter 21). Just as the rights of free movement are only granted to workers and the self-employed and their families (albeit, as will be seen, very liberally interpreted), to invoke the principle of non-discrimination of Article 12 EC in this context, there must be some economic nexus.

This principle has been considerably eroded over the past three decades, as the European Economic Community has been transformed into the European Union. In *Gravier v City of Liège* (case 293/83) and *Cowan v French Treasury* (case 186/87) the Court held that students (*Gravier*) and tourists (*Cowan*), temporarily resident in a Member State as recipients of services, were entitled to invoke the then Article 7 EEC (now 12 EC) to claim equality of treatment for certain financial benefits available under national law only to nationals of the host State (see also *Commission v Spain* (case C–45/93)) .

Similarly the directives extending free-movement rights to persons of independent means, retired persons, and students, now consolidated into the Citizenship Directive, also appeared to dilute the need for an economic link. Persons claiming under these directives must be covered by medical insurance and must have sufficient financial resources to avoid becoming a burden on the Member State. This requirement suggests that such persons may not be able to claim publicly funded welfare benefits on a basis of equality with nationals of the host state. Although European citizenship is not limited to the economically active, it is 'subject to the limitations and conditions laid down in this treaty and by the measures adopted to give it effect' (Article 18(1) EC). Nonetheless, more recent decisions of the ECJ now suggest that Union citizens who are not economically active but who enjoy or acquire rights to enter and reside in another Member State may invoke the non-discrimination principle to claim rights currently accorded to that state's nationals or to migrant workers and their families, although the precise extent to which they may do so remains unclear (eg, *Martinez Sala v Freistaat Bayern* (case C–85/96); *Trojani v Le Centre Public d'Aide Sociale de Bruxelles* (case C–456/02); *Collins* (case C–138/02); *Bidar* (case C–209/03)). Important questions regarding the scope of application of the non-discrimination principle remain to be resolved, either by secondary legislation or by the Court. On the Court's past record it is unlikely that it would tolerate discriminatory treatment of EU migrants and their families or deny *settled* immigrants the right of residence when their resources are exhausted (see, eg, *Baumbast* (case C–413/99) and Chapter 23). As noted, however, in determining the scope of such rights it seems that the key element will be the demonstration of a 'real link'.

Although goods are not usually considered in this light, economic considerations can be seen in the definition attributed to them in the ECJ's jurisprudence. Though the terms are used interchangeably, 'goods' and 'products' are not defined in the treaty. They were interpreted by the ECJ in *Commission v Italy (re Export Tax on Art Treasures)* (case 7/68) as anything capable of money valuation and of being the object of commercial transactions. It does not matter whether the individuals are moving goods as part of their business or in their private capacity, provided the items satisfy the definition of goods.

15.3.2 **Internal situations and migration**

An individual who has never sought to exercise his or her right to freedom of movement will not be able to rely on EC-law rights. The matter will be regarded as 'wholly internal' (see, eg, *R v Saunders* (case 175/78); *Ministère Public v Gauchard* (case 20/87)). This principle, that EC law has no application to purely internal matters, can operate harshly. In *Morson v Netherlands* (cases 35 and 36/82), two mothers from Surinam wished to join their children in The Netherlands. Since they were not entitled to do so under Dutch law they sought to rely on EC law, which permits family members to join EC migrants. In this case the applicants were unsuccessful: since their children had never exercised their right to freedom of movement in the Union there was no factor connecting them with Union law. Equally in *Sloman* (cases C–72 and 73/91) the ECJ held that it was not contrary to Union law to discriminate against migrant workers from third countries (that is, countries outside the EU) in the absence of factors connecting them with Community law. Even in the context of citizenship, some transnational element must be identified (joined cases C–64 and 65/96, *Hecker* and *Jacquet*).

Once again, the impact of this rule has been limited. Once a connecting factor has been established, however, migrants will be able to rely on EU rights on returning to their own Member State (*R v Immigration Appeal Tribunal, ex parte Secretary of State for the Home Department* (case C–370/90); see further Chapter 20). Further, in more recent cases involving citizenship, no cross-border movement was involved. The Community link was shown by citizens of one Member State challenging the rules in another Member State (*Garcia Avello* (case C–148/02); *Chen* (case C–200/02); see further Chapter 21).

A similar approach is taken in relation to goods. Again the Court has limited the circumstances in which an internal situation will be found through the width of the test used to determine when there is an impact on trade. The famous test in *Dassonville* (case 8/74) refers to a measure 'directly or indirectly, actually or potentially' hindering trade being sufficient to trigger Article 28, suggesting that an actual interstate element is not necessary in a particular case provided the possibility of such an effect can be shown. From the case law it seems possible that cases where a national trader selling or distributing national goods seeking to challenge a rule of the same Member State could fall within Article 28, as happened in *Pistre* (case C–321–4/94, discussed in Chapter 19). Similar approaches can be seen in relation to capital, services, and establishment.

15.3.3 Discrimination or access to the market?

Because of the fundamental importance of the principle of free movement of goods the treaty rules in this area have been strictly enforced, and exceptions, where provided, have been given the narrowest scope. In interpreting the rules the ECJ looks not to the name of a particular national measure, nor to the motive for its introduction, but to its *effect* in the light of the aims of the treaty; does it create an obstacle to the free movement of goods within the single internal market? Article 28 is not limited to circumstances in which a Member State has discriminated against imported goods. The provision, as seen by the ECJ, is far wider than that. Interpreted in this way, many national measures, not overtly or intentionally protectionist, designed to achieve the most worthy objectives, have been found to be capable of hindering trade between Member States, prima facie in breach of Union law. Such measures, as will be seen, have nevertheless been permitted by the Court on an ad hoc basis where they could be proved to be 'objectively justified' as necessary to safeguard vital interests ('mandatory requirements'), such as the protection of health, the environment, or the consumer.

A move away from an interpretation based on the need to show discrimination, whether direct or indirect, to one that focuses on the removal of obstacles to free movement can be seen in the context of persons too. The basic right contained in Articles 39, 43, and 49 is that migrant workers should not be discriminated against on grounds of nationality. This is reinforced by Article 12 EC which provides that 'Within the scope of application of this Treaty, and without prejudice to any special provisions contained therein, any discrimination on grounds of nationality shall be prohibited'.

This provision has been important in ensuring that the migrant individual and his family, once legally resident in the host Member State, receives parity of treatment with nationals of the host state in respect not only of employment rights but of social rights in general.

The prohibition of discrimination on the grounds of nationality applies to all forms of discrimination, both overt and covert. It will often take the form of a residence or length-of-residence requirement. In *Sotgiu v Deutsche Bundespost* (case 152/73) the claimant was an Italian national employed by the German post office in Germany. His family lived in Italy. Following the issue of a circular, post-office workers separated from their families in Germany were to be paid an increased 'separation' allowance while workers who were living abroad at the time of recruitment would continue to be paid at the same rate. The rule was not overtly discriminatory, since it applied to all workers, regardless of nationality. But clearly its effects could fall more heavily on foreigners. The Court, on a reference from the Bundesarbeitsgericht held that the prohibition of discrimination (expressed here in Article 7(1) of Regulation 1612/68, but equally applicable to Article 12 EC) prohibited all covert forms of discrimination which, by the application of criteria other than nationality nevertheless led to the same result. A residence criterion *could* have a discriminatory effect, prohibited by the treaty and the regulation. In the *O'Flynn* case (case C–237/94), the ECJ characterised four groups of conditions as potentially discriminatory, even if phrased in nationality-neutral terms. The conditions are:

(a) those which affect essentially migrant workers

(b) those where the great majority of those affected are migrant workers

(c) those which can be more easily satisfied by national workers than by migrant workers

(d) those where there is a risk that they might operate to the particular detriment of migrant workers.

Thus, in the context of the provision of services and establishment (as well as to workers), certain professional rules and codes of practices or even professional qualifications have been found to be indirectly discriminatory. By imposing conditions additional to those required in the worker's home state, and which may be more difficult or burdensome for the migrant worker to satisfy, they create obstacles to the free movement of persons in the same way as indistinctly applicable rules applied to goods (see Chapter 22).

More-recent case law such as *Bosman* (case C–415/98) in respect of workers; *Säger v Dennemeyer* (case C–76/90) in respect of services; and *Gebhard* (case C–55/94) in respect of establishment, has developed this category of indirectly discriminatory measures. Indeed, they suggest that the Court is phrasing its arguments in terms of obstacles to trade and movement rather than as species of discrimination. In this again, we see parallels to the approach taken in relation to goods, and which can now also be found in the context of capital.

As in the case of goods, such measures may be permitted if they are objectively justified—that is, if they are not disproportionate and pursue legitimate ends. The extent to which these principles applicable to goods can be applied in the context of workers, establishment, and services has been raised in a number of cases. (See, for example, the comments of the Advocates-General in *Bosman* (case C–415/93) and *Volker Graf* (case C–190/98); see Chapter 22). Certain differences in approach remain, as illustrated by the case of *Alpine Investments* (case C–384/93) (see further Chapter 22).

15.3.4 **Direct effect**

Although the free-movement provisions are addressed to Member States, all the main articles have been found to be directly effective (see Chapter 5) and thus may be invoked by individuals. Whether *all* the treaty freedoms are horizontally effective is less clear; contrast the position regarding goods and persons.

15.3.5 **Need for harmonisation**

The Treaty derogations and the grounds for justification accepted by the Court, described as mandatory requirements or reasons of overriding public interest, clearly jeopardised the functioning of the single market. Nor was the problem confined to goods; it also applied to the other elements of the internal market. It became clear that if important public interests were to be protected without impairing the functioning of the internal market, action would have to be taken at Community level. Following the publication by the Commission in 1985 of a White Paper on the Completion of the Internal Market, Member States agreed to embark on a massive harmonisation programme, designed to provide common standards of protection, to be completed by 31 December 1992. This was enshrined in the SEA 1996 (Article 14 EC). To speed up the legislative process, a new Article 95 (ex 100a; post Lisbon, 114 TFEU) was introduced into the EC Treaty, providing for the 'approximation' (ie, harmonisation) of the 'provisions laid down by law, regulation or administrative action in Member States which have as their object the establishing and functioning of the internal market' (subject to some exceptions in Article 95(2)) by measures to be enacted by qualified majority vote, instead of as heretofore, under Article 94 (ex 100; post Lisbon 115 TFEU), by unanimity (see Chapter 16.) This programme, an example of 'positive integration' (as opposed to the 'negative integration' achieved by decisions of the ECJ rendering 'inapplicable' domestic measures contrary to EU law), has been largely successful. Although not all of the Commission's proposals were approved within the deadline, the vast majority of measures, particularly those relating to the free movement of goods, are now in place. By the end of 1994, 89 per cent of Community legislation relating to the internal market had been transposed into national law. Legislative activity has, of course, not ceased with the passing of 1992. Not only has Community competence extended since then, but legislation also needs to be reviewed and updated in the light of changing circumstances. For example, the development of electronic commerce has generated directives on electronic signatures and on contracts concluded via electronic means. The more recent emphasis in the internal-market programme is that of simplifying legislation (SLIM), with the aim of increasing transparency and making cross-border transactions easier. The so-called open method of coordination (OMC) (discussed in Chapters 3 and 16) can also be seen as part of the attempt to lessen the regulatory burden on businesses.

15.4 Relationship between the freedoms

The Court has held that the freedoms are mutually exclusive. This approach is supported by the terms of the treaty itself. As noted above, the provisions on capital are expressed to apply without prejudice to the operation of the principles on establishment, and the service provisions are expressed to apply to situations 'insofar as they are not governed by the provisions relating to freedom of movement for goods, capital and persons'. Despite the similarity in approach between the freedoms identified above, it remains necessary to identify the scope of particular freedoms. It seems easy to identify where the boundary between goods and persons might arise, but other circumstances are less clear-cut. The boundary between services and establishment seems in some instances to be one of degree, rather than there being any qualitative difference between the subject matter of the two freedoms, though the introduction of the Services Directive may make it more important to make a distinction. (See further Chapter 22) It is also important, as we have noted (see 15.2.4 above), to distinguish between capital and establishment. Given that the provisions relating to capital may be relied upon by those in third countries, the classification of a measure as affecting establishment or capital has consequences for the group of persons who may rely on free movement rights in a given set of circumstances. More difficulties arise in relation to the boundary between goods and capital, on the one hand, and goods and services on the other.

In *R v Thompson* (case 7/78) goods were held to include collectors' coins in gold and silver, provided they were not coins in circulation as legal tender. The latter are covered by the provisions of the treaty relating to capital (Article 56 EC, see *Bordessa* (cases C–358 and 416/93)). In *Commission v Ireland Re Dundalk Water Supply* (case 45/87) the concept of goods was held to apply not only to the sale of goods per se but to goods and materials supplied in the context of the provision of services. However, where goods are supplied in the context of the provision of services, to fall within the goods provisions of the treaty, the importation or exportation of the goods in question must be an end in itself. Materials such as advertisements or tickets, supplied simply as an adjunct to a service—for example, a lottery—will fall within the provisions governing services, namely Articles 49 and 50 EC (*Her Majesty's Customs and Excise v Schindler* (case C 275/92); see Chapter 20). The cases involving advertising of goods, especially those concerning broadcast advertising, illustrate the narrow boundary between goods and services (see, eg, *de Agostini* (joined cases C–34–6/95), discussed further in Chapters 19). In cases of doubt it is advisable to invoke both goods and services provisions.

15.5 **The social dimension**

In addition to the rights conferred on those seeking to exercise their right to free movement, the treaty seeks to increase social protection in areas such as employment and education. Where not already included, these goals were explicitly incorporated into the EU Treaty by the TEU (see Article 3(i), (o), and (p)). The purpose of EU *employment* legislation is to harmonise national laws, normally by directive, to provide common standards of protection throughout the Union in the interest both of the worker and the more effective functioning of the single market. Harmonised standards are intended to create a level playing field, and avoid social dumping. It is thought that disparity between the laws of Member States as regards standards of employment protection will give a competitive advantage to states with lower standards. EU action in the field of *social rights* aims to promote and encourage the well-being of Union citizens, by action in the fields of public health or education, or to benefit the disabled, the deprived ('victims of social exclusion'), the elderly, or victims of disaster. Measures here are designed to stimulate and complement rather than replace national provision, according to the principle of subsidiarity.

Although the TEU re-emphasised the need for increased social protection, both by extending the Community's goals and by introducing a more rounded conception of the individual in the Community, the Member States were by no means in agreement about the extent of the rights to be granted by Community law, particularly in relation to employment legislation. In the field of employment rights 11 of the then 12 Member States (the UK, then under John Major's Conservative government, excepted) signed an Agreement on Social Policy in a protocol attached to the Maastricht Treaty, with a view to 'continuing along the path laid down in the 1989 Social Charter'. The agreement had as its objectives:

> the promotion of employment, improved living and working conditions, proper social protection, dialogue between management and labour, the development of human resources with a view to lasting high employment and the combating of exclusion. [Article 1.]

The signatory states were required to take implementing measures in respect of these policy areas, but this has turned out to be problematic. Difficult questions arose as to where the boundary between the protocol and the EC Treaty's pre-existing social provisions lay. These difficulties are now, as far as social policy is concerned, at an end. Following the change in UK government after Labour's election victory in 1997, the UK agreed to have the provisions of the Agreement on Social Policy incorporated into the EC Treaty by the ToA, replacing the social chapter provisions currently there, to give a more extensive set of rights to workers. The few measures agreed under the agreement were extended to the UK in advance of the ratification of the ToA. However, the new social-protection provisions introduced by the ToA (Articles 136–41 EC; post Lisbon 151-7 TFEU) were, in keeping with the spirit of the ToA, extremely cautious and unanimous voting will continue to be required in the more sensitive areas (eg, Article 137(3)). Under Lisbon, Article 137 would be amended so that the 'ordinary legislative procedure' involving co-decision and unanimity in Council, would be the default procedure here. Although there might not have been much direct action under the social policy provisions, workers' protection is also ensured by the general non-discrimination provisions (discussed in Chapter 23).

15.6 Completion of the internal market and the position of third-country nationals

The EC Treaty has always envisaged the possibility of a frontier-free Europe. This was re-emphasised by the insertion by the SEA of Article 14 EC, which provides for 'an area without internal frontiers in which the free movement of goods, persons, services and capital is ensured'. Progress on achieving an internal market in persons, by abolishing the barriers existing at the frontiers of Member States, was slow, partly because of the sensitivity of the area and partly because Member States were not agreed on whether the internal market in persons should include third-country nationals (TCNs) or be limited to EU nationals. The result was that certain Member States concluded an agreement outside the framework of the EC/EU to achieve such an area. Under an agreement signed at Schengen in 1990, five Member States (Germany, France, and the Benelux countries, later joined by Italy, Spain, Portugal, and Greece) agreed to remove all checks on the movement of people across their borders.

With the changes introduced by the TEU, the Union began to develop, under the JHA pillar of the TEU, the foundations for a policy on TCNs. Although some decisions were made under JHA, progress in this area was slow. The need to reform the JHA was an important issue considered at Amsterdam.

Prior to the ToA, the majority of Member States had signed, if not ratified, the Schengen Agreement. The majority thus agreed at the 1996 intergovernmental conference (IGC) in effect to incorporate the terms of the Schengen Agreement into the EC Treaty (the UK and Ireland opting out, and the Danish being undecided). The result was a new Title IV in Pt 3 of the EC Treaty. Individuals lawfully resident within the EU will be able to travel between Member States which have agreed to Title IV without being stopped at internal borders. Member States are also to develop common immigration and visa policies under these new provisions (see Chapter 26 for further detail). These changes, especially the ability to move freely between Member States, will benefit TCNs as well as EU citizens although, as noted, the relationship between these provisions and the right to free movement of persons as part of the four freedoms might raise some questions.

With the advent of the concept of European citizenship and the development of common immigration and asylum policies, as now envisaged following the ToA, there will be further pressure to extend the rights currently granted to EU workers and their families to all persons legitimately resident in the European Union. Although the concept of citizenship under Article 17 EC comprises only limited political rights, it provides for the granting of rights 'to move and reside freely within the territory of the Member States'. These provisions are already leading to social rights which apply to a more extensive group of EU citizens. It remains to be seen how far TCNs (who are not members of the family of EU nationals) legitimately resident in the Union will be able to claim equality of treatment with EU nationals. So far, the emphasis under JHA as regards TCNs seems to have been directed more at keeping them out of the EU, rather than integrating them into the Union.

Nonetheless recent legislative activity (discussed in Chapter 27) does seem to have improved the position somewhat, even if the position of TCNs is not on a par with migrant EU citizens. Thus, even where they are legitimately resident, or indeed have been born in the European Union, TCNs cannot claim the same rights of EU citizenship as EU nationals: nor are they entitled to rights granted to them under the Citizenship Directive.

This point has been raised as particularly problematic for some individuals in the new Member States who have not been granted nationality of those states due to political sensitivities (see discussion in Chapter 1). This point is not unique to these states; many of the EU 15 Member States have established minority communities who escape the full protection of Union law. As Weiler comments:

> It would be ironic that an ethos which rejected the nationalism of the Member States gave birth to a new European nation and European nationalism . . . We have made little progress if the Us becomes European (instead of German or French or British) and the Them becomes those outside the Community or those inside who do not enjoy the privileges of citizenship.

The following chapters deal with the four freedoms. This part of the book also considers certain provisions relating to citizenship and the free movement of TCNs as part of the free movement of persons before we look at sex discrimination, one of the treaty's key objectives and which was central to the early development of Community law. Finally we consider competition policy, including state aids.

FURTHER READING

Barnard, C, 'Fitting the remaining pieces into the goods and persons jigsaw?' (2001) 26 EL Rev 35.

Closa, C, 'The concept of citizenship in the Treaty on European Union' (1992) 29 CML Rev 1137.

Commission's Annual Report on the Internal Market: from 1993.

Curtin, D and Meijers, H, 'The principle of open government in Schengen and the European Union: Democratic retrogression?' (1995) 32 CML Rev 391.

Curtin, D and O'Keeffe, D (eds), *Constitutional Adjudication in European Community and National Law* (1992), p 67.

Dougan, M, 'The constitutional dimension to the case law on Union citizenship' (2006) 31 EL Rev 613.

d'Oliveira, H, 'Expanding external and shrinking internal borders: Europe's defence mechanism in the areas of free movement, immigration and asylum' in D O'Keeffe and P Twomey (eds), *Legal Issues of the Maastricht Treaty* (Wiley Chancery Law, 1994), p 261.

—— 'Nationality and the European Union after Amsterdam' in D O'Keeffe and P Twomey (eds), *Legal Issues of the Amsterdam Treaty* (Hart Publishing, 1999).

Fitzpatrick, B, 'Community social law after Maastricht' (1992) 21 ILJ 199.

Mortelmans, K, 'The Common Market, the internal market and the single market: What's in a market?' (1998) 35 CML Rev 101.

O'Higgins, TF, 'The family and European law' (1990) 140 NLJ 1643.

O'Keeffe, D, 'The free movement of persons and the single market' (1992) 17 EL Rev 3.

—— 'Union citizenship' in D O'Keeffe and P Twomey (eds), *Legal Issues of the Maastricht Treaty* (Wiley Chancery Law, 1994).

O'Brien, C, 'Real links, abstract rights and false alarms: The relationship between the ECJ's "real link" case law and national solidarity' (2008) EL Rev 643.

Peers, S, 'Towards equality: Actual and potential rights of third-country nationals in the European Union' (1996) 33 CML Rev 7.

Pickup, D, 'Reverse discrimination and freedom of movement for workers' (1989) 23 CML Rev 135.

Shaw, J, 'Twin-track social Europe: The inside track' in D O'Keeffe and P Twomey (eds), *Legal Issues of the Maastricht Treaty* (1994, Wiley Chancery Law).

Snell, J, 'And then there were two: Products and citizens in Community law' in Tridimas and Nebbia (eds), *European Union Law for the Twenty-First Century: Rethinking the new legal order* (Hart Publishing, 2004).

Van den Bogaert, S, 'Horizontality: The Court attacks?' in Barnard and Scott (eds) *The Law of the Single Market: Unpacking the premises* (Hart Publishing, 2002).

Watson, P, 'The Community social charter' (1991) 28 CML Rev 37.

—— 'Social policy after Maastricht' (1993) 30 CML Rev 481.

Weiler, JHH, 'The transformation of Europe' (1991) 100 Yale LJ 2403.

16

Harmonisation

16.1 Introduction

The objective of creating the internal market requires the removal of barriers to the four freedoms. It will be seen how Articles 28–9 (ex 30–1; post Lisbon, Articles 34–5 TFEU) strike down domestic rules which could constitute barriers to trade between the Member States. However, these articles do not strike down all such rules because both the treaty itself (Article 30 (ex 36; post Lisbon, Article 36 TFEU)) and the jurisprudence developed under Article 28 (*Cassis de Dijon, Keck*) recognise that there are public interests that may need to be protected by such domestic rules. A similar approach can be seen with regard to workers, services, and establishment, as well as capital. Barriers to trade will therefore remain, as significant differences in the laws of the various Member States still exist, in particular where national laws are aimed at protecting interests recognised by the Union. Although the removal of barriers would undoubtedly improve the workings of the internal market, it would not be enough simply to remove those national rules which affect the free movement of goods, services, persons, and capital. Positive steps towards creating standards throughout the Union to protect such interests are also necessary. The creation of such standards would also reduce the potential threat of a 'downward spiral' in standards arising from producers and service providers seeking to move their base to the Member State with the lowest regulatory burden. This process, by which the Union sets down a standard in a particular field that all the domestic legal systems must meet, is known as harmonisation.

This chapter considers the nature of harmonisation, as opposed to other forms of Union action, as well as discussing the different approaches taken by the Union to harmonisation itself. In this discussion, key issues concern the relationship between harmonising measures and underlying treaty provisions, indirectly concerning the freedom of Member States to take individual action in harmonised fields. This discussion links in to questions about the degree to which we require uniformity at Union level and the extent to which the Union can tolerate diversity. Given the impact of harmonising legislation, the legitimacy and effectiveness of the techniques adopted must also be considered (though see also Chapter 3). This chapter also reviews the scope of the Community's power to enact harmonising measures in the context of the internal market and the extent to which the Community effectively has a general power to regulate. In this discussion the scope of Article 95 is central, and its relationship not only to Member States' competence, but also to the other pillars. Rather than being a technical question of appropriate treaty base, the scope of Article 95 has a constitutional aspect relating to the balance of powers within the Union and between the Community and the Member States. In this chapter, much of the discussion will relate to measures dealing with trade in goods; similar principles, however, also apply to the other freedoms.

16.2 The nature of harmonisation

16.2.1 Positive and negative harmonisation

The form of harmonisation by which a common standard is introduced throughout the Union is sometimes referred to as 'positive' harmonisation, because new standards are introduced. The removal of existing barriers by the striking down of national laws (eg, under Articles 28 (ex 30), 39 (ex 48; post Lisbon, Article 45 TFEU), 43 (ex 52; post Lisbon, Article 49 TFEU), and 49 (ex 59; post Lisbon, Article 56 TFEU) EC) is known as 'negative' harmonisation. This chapter focuses on positive harmonisation.

From the beginning, the EC Treaty provided for the creation of common Community rules, not only in the areas marked out for common organisation, such as agriculture, but in all the areas of activity outlined in the treaty, or falling within the broader objectives of the Community (see Article 308 (ex 235; post Lisbon, Article 352 TFEU) EC and Chapter 3). A huge body of rules is now in place. Many of these rules, particularly, but not exclusively, those enacted under Articles 94–5 (ex 100 and 100a) EC, seek to harmonise national laws, normally by means of directives. Should the Treaty of Lisbon come into force, they will be renumbered Art 115 and 114 of the Treaty on the Functioning of the European Union (TFEU) respectively. Although directives require implementation at national level, and leave national authorities some choice as to 'the form and method of implementation' (Article 249 (ex 189; post Lisbon, Article 288 TFEU) EC; see Chapter 3), once the period allowed for implementation has expired, Member States are not free to enact or maintain domestic measures inconsistent with their obligations under the directive or with the general purposes of the directive. Where there is a conflict between provisions of national and Community law, Community law must prevail (see Chapter 4). A question that arises once harmonisation has taken place is the extent to which the Member States are free to derogate from their obligations under the treaty either under the *Cassis* rule of reason or Article 30 EC, or to enact more stringent rules. These issues will be considered at 16.3 below.

Positive harmonisation may be seen to have a number of advantages over negative harmonisation. It seems possible at least in principle, to attain two objectives through the use of harmonising measures: the protection of the public interest; and the creation of the internal market. By contrast, where negative harmonisation is used, there seems to be a trade-off between the need to protect the public interest (letting the national rule stand) and the creation of the internal market (striking down the national rule). As will be seen, although mutual recognition facilitates the free movement of goods, disparities in national systems remain where 'mandatory requirements' and treaty derogations operate to save national rules that prima facie constitute a barrier to interstate trade, thus the barriers to trade remain with adverse consequences for the creation of the single market. Subsequent chapters indicate a similar process in relation to the other freedoms.

There are other possible advantages to positive harmonisation too—one of these can be seen if we consider the way negative and positive harmonisation operate. Negative harmonisation, through a finding that a treaty freedom has been violated and the national measure cannot be justified, means that the national rule will be struck down; the ECJ cannot create an alternative acceptable rule to replace the offending national measure. It is for this reason that negative harmonisation is said to be deregulatory, as it can only remove rules. In contrast, positive harmonisation re-regulates at the Union level. Although inconsistent national measures will no longer be good law, they will be replaced by the Union standards, reducing the risk of creating a regulatory gap, and in the case of an action against a public body, potentially may be relied on in national courts (see Chapter 5). Further, as noted at 16.1, positive harmonisation could counter the threat of a downward spiral in standards. Positive harmonisation might also be said to respect the division of powers within the Union. Laws and standards are properly made through the democratic process—that is by the involvement of political institutions, rather than by the judicial process. Finally, in theory, the use of directives allows the various Member States to take account of legal principles already in existence within their individual legal systems and to ensure that the requirements of Union law blend in with that system, though the reality may leave Member States with little choice (see 16.5 below).

The difficulty with harmonisation is that, even with qualified majority voting (QMV) (see Chapter 2), it can be difficult for Member States to come to an agreement, especially where total harmonisation, discussed below, is concerned. Thus, not only is legislative action difficult in the first place, but it can be problematic to amend a directive, with the result that standards become outdated. The difficulties of achieving consensus can be illustrated by reference to the rules harmonising the marketing of chocolate. A directive on the marketing of chocolate was agreed in 1973 ([1973] OJ L 228/23). The area was contentious because some Member States allowed the addition of vegetable fats to the cocoa butter used in chocolate, but other Member States, such as Italy, did not. The compromise position found in the directive was not clear. An ECJ ruling clarified that the effect of the directive was that the inclusion of vegetable fats could be permitted by individual Member States, but that 'chocolate' produced in this way could not claim the benefit of the free movement under the directive. Some Member States retained stringent rules, effectively protecting their domestic market from chocolate with vegetable fat in it. It was not until 2000, approximately quarter of a century later, with the enactment of Directive 2000/36 ([2000] OJ L 197/19) that the matter was resolved: chocolate made with vegetable fats was now generally permissible but must be labelled as containing vegetable fats.

16.2.2 Harmonisation and unification

Harmonisation may be contrasted with 'unification'. A process of unification would result in the complete replacement of particular aspects of the legal orders of the Member State with a new order adopted at the European level. For example, although it has not pursued this idea, in its Communication on European Contract Law (COM (2001) 398 final), the Commission considered among other things whether the entire system of contract law of the Member States might be replaced with a new European contract code. Unification would mean that existing legal principles would be replaced with new principles applicable throughout all the Member States. In contrast, although harmonisation may result in the creation of a common set of rules which have the same substantive scope, the implementation of these rules utilises the legal principles and concepts familiar to each particular Member State.

16.2.3 Other forms of Union action

It needs to be remembered that the Union does not focus exclusively on harmonisation. In some fields, such as public health, harmonisation is expressly precluded (see further 16.1). Harmonisation is clearly an important aspect of the Union's activities, but there are other means by which Union objectives can be supported, for example through the coordination of national measures—this is the approach taken in relation to social-security arrangements. There, Regulation 1408/71 provides the framework for the transfer of social-security arrangements between Member States' social-security schemes, but does not provide Union standards.

A further form of Union action, which operates independently, but may also be a precursor to a harmonising measure, is the open method of policy coordination. This has a legal basis in Article 137(2)(a) EC in respect of social rights, but the approach was extended by the Lisbon European Council in March 2000 to other policy areas. It does not result in legislation at the European level. The White Paper on European Governance (COM (2001) 428 final) states that this method of coordination can be used to encourage cooperation, exchange best practice and agree common targets and guidelines for the Member States. Progress by the Member States towards reaching these targets is monitored regularly. The Commission generally assumes a coordinating role, and the White Paper emphasised the need to keep the European Parliament informed. This form of Union action may complement legislative action, but can also be used where 'there is little scope for legislative solutions' (p 22) (see also, eg, *Strengthening the Social Dimension of the Lisbon strategy: Streamlining open coordination in the field of social protection* (COM (2003) 261 final)).

16.3 Types of harmonisation

There are several forms of harmonisation. These may be classed according to the degree of freedom left to the Member States to adopt measures that differ from the harmonised rules, either by setting a higher standard, or by maintaining existing lower standards. There is a certain lack of consensus about the number and types of categories of harmonisation; the types discussed in this section are the main forms of harmonisation usually found in EU law.

16.3.1 Total harmonisation

Total harmonisation leaves the Member States with no scope for further independent action in the field covered by the harmonising measure. In other words, Member States' competence to act has been pre-empted by Union action. As far as the area covered by a total harmonisation directive is concerned, Member States must ensure that their domestic system provides exactly what is required by that directive. It is not possible to introduce a stricter standard. In *Commission v United Kingdom*, (*Dim-Dip Lights*) (case 60/86), the compatibility of a requirement introduced by the UK that all new cars should be equipped with dim-dip lights with the relevant directive, Directive 76/759, was decided against the UK because the directive specified exhaustively the types of lights which could be fitted to cars. In its earlier decision in *Prantl* (case 16/83), the ECJ stated that 'once rules on the common organisation of the market may be regarded as forming a complete system, the Member States no longer have competence in that field unless Community law expressly provides otherwise' (para 6).

Thus if a measure is a total harmonisation measure, Member States will not be free to adopt additional provisions covering the same sector even in relation to purely internal situations. These principles are not limited to technical rules relating to goods, but apply to all aspects of EC law. Thus, in *Inspire Art* (case C–167/01), Dutch legislation imposing disclosure obligations on branches of foreign companies exceeded the requirements of the Eleventh Company Law Directive (89/666/EC), and was therefore not permitted. That directive was exhaustive and a branch could not be required to disclose information beyond that required by the directive.

The exclusion of higher domestic standards applies even where this might be of benefit to individuals, such as consumers. In *Commission v France* (case C–52/00), the ECJ held that France had incorrectly implemented several provisions of Directive 85/374/EEC (Product Liability Directive [1985] OJ L210/29). Article 9 specifies that liability for property damage would only arise if the damage caused were to exceed 500 ECU. France chose not to implement this threshold and put forward two arguments to justify its position. It claimed first that the directive should be interpreted in the light of Article 153 (ex 129a) EC (post Lisbon 169 TFEU) which permits a higher national level of protection than specified in relevant consumer protection directives. Moreover, the Product Liability Directive allowed the Member States to depart from several of the rules it laid down and permission to do likewise in relation to other areas covered by the directive could be inferred. The ECJ rejected France's contention and held that 'The margin of discretion available to the Member States . . . is *entirely determined by the directive itself* and must be inferred from its wording, purpose and structure' (para 16).

Member States may only derogate from the provisions of a total harmonisation directive in so far as the directive expressly permits. The fact that a directive permits derogation for particular aspects falling within the scope of the directive or leaves certain matters for domestic law does not change its character as a total harmonisation measure (*Commission v France* case C–52/00, para 19).

This position was also adopted in *Sanchez v Medicina Asturiana SA* (case C–183/00), again involving Directive 85/374/EEC. The Product Liability Directive establishes a system of strict liability for injury or property damage caused by defective products. Article 13 of the directive preserves the application of other systems of contractual or non-contractual liability *based on other grounds*. Prior to the introduction of the directive, Spain had adopted a system of strict liability which it did not repeal when it implemented the directive. The earlier system was more favourable to the claimant. The ECJ held that although Article 13 did not prevent the maintenance of a fault-based system of product liability, it precluded the retention of a more extensive system of liability which uses the same basis as that in the directive (ie, strict liability).

Both cases illustrate the impact of a total harmonisation measure. Such a directive precludes Member States from adopting or retaining rules which cover the same ground as the directive and which are based on the same legal principles. This had led to fears about the impact on the Member States' diversity from the threat of homogenised 'Euro-products'. To some extent, this fear is overstated as total harmonisation directives have contained a range of provisions variously allowing specific derogations, opt-out clauses and phased introduction of the obligations. While the resulting directives may be complex, these approaches allow some account to be taken of national differences. Thus, a total harmonisation measure may permit specific derogations by giving Member States the option whether to implement particular provisions in the directive.

In all cases, it will be necessary to identify exactly what the directive provides, and the scope of any opt-outs, and which aspects of the relevant field it regulates—ie, it is necessary to identify the 'occupied field', as areas which lie outside the field of a total harmonisation directive can still be regulated by the Member States. Member States' competence will always be subject to the requirement to comply with the treaty, which, in practice, means the provisions on the four freedoms. For example, in *Inspire Art* (case C–167/01), mentioned above, the Dutch legislation on branches of foreign companies also introduced several obligations on such branches that went beyond disclosure obligations, including the requirement to have a minimum share capital. The directive on branches (Directive 89/666/EEC) only dealt with disclosure obligations, and any additional requirements which had to be met by branches of foreign companies were within the domain of the Member States. The minimum capital requirement could therefore be imposed unless it conflicted with the freedom of establishment (Article 43 EC; post Lisbon 49 TFEU). The ECJ first considered whether this requirement was caught by Article 43, and having found that it was, considered whether it could be justified on objective grounds, applying the *Säger v Dennemeyer* (case C–76/90) test. On the facts, the minimum capital requirement was not justified and therefore incompatible with the treaty.

16.3.2 Derogation from a total harmonisation measure

The general rule is that once a common Union organisation for a particular product has been set up, Member States are no longer entitled to maintain in force provisions or adopt practices which are incompatible with the scheme of common organisation or which jeopardise its aims or functioning (see also *Tasca* (case 65/75)). In each case it is necessary to examine the harmonising measure to ascertain whether the field is occupied. If so, any national measure conflicting with the common provision will be illegal. If not, national measures are permissible provided they do not impair the effective functioning of the common organisation or run counter to Article 28 EC. In this case derogation may still be permissible under Article 30 EC.

It was originally thought that, once the Union had legislated in a particular field, states were no longer free to enact legislation in that field or resort to Article 30 EC (the 'strict', 'total', or 'classic' pre-emption theory). This view derived support from the Court's ruling in *Tedeschi v Denkavit Commerciale Srl* (case 5/77). Here in the context of a dispute concerning a Community directive regulating the use of food additives, the Court held that where in the application of the then Article 100 (now 94) Community directives provide for harmonisation of the measures necessary to the free movement of goods, recourse to Article 30 was no longer justified. The Court appeared to take the same view in a case involving the Solvents Directive (73/173) in *Ratti* (case 148/78). However, in both cases, the directives contained 'market access' clauses, expressly prohibiting domestic restrictions on imports which complied with the requirements of the directives, and, more importantly, provided safeguard procedures (requiring notification to, and approval by, the Commission) should Member States need to adopt 'protective measures' in the public interest.

Where EC legislation did not provide such procedures, it subsequently appeared to be possible for states to take emergency action based on what is now Article 30, provided a genuine justification could be proved. In *van Bennekom* (case 227/82) the Court held (at para 35):

> It is only when Community directives . . . make provision for the *full* harmonisation of all the measures needed to ensure the protection of [in this case] human and animal life and *institute Community procedures to monitor compliance therewith* that recourse to Article 36 [now 30] ceases to be justified. [Emphasis added.]

See also *van der Veldt* (case C–17/93). *Van Bennekom* seems to have suggested a double test for the exclusion of Member State competence. Not only must there be total harmonisation in the field, but monitoring procedures should be included in the relevant EU legislation.

This view was modified in *R v Ministry of Agriculture, Fisheries and Food, ex parte Hedley Lomas (Ireland) Ltd* (case C–5/94), in a move towards a narrower view of Member State competence. The case concerned a claim for damages against the UK for losses resulting from a ban on the export of live sheep to Spain on the grounds that Spain had failed to comply with Council Directive 74/557. The directive, an animal welfare measure, required Member States to provide for the stunning of animals before slaughter. It did not expressly require Member States to monitor its implementation or provide penalties for non-compliance. The directive was implemented by the Spanish authorities but without providing for monitoring procedures or penalties for non-compliance. Although the ban was clearly contrary to Article 29, the UK argued that it was justified under Article 30 as a measure designed for the protection of the health of animals. The Court found that it was not. The UK had failed to adduce any evidence that Spanish slaughterhouses were not fulfilling their obligations under the directive.

This finding was no doubt correct on the facts: the necessity for a ban was not proved, and it was in any case disproportionate. Also, to the extent that the directive provided for harmonisation of the measures necessary to achieve the *specific objective* required by the UK government (ie, the stunning of animals before slaughter), the matter was covered by the directive. However, since the directive failed to prescribe procedures to monitor compliance, Member States might have thought they were entitled to resort to Article 30 EC when there was evidence that the directive had been breached, as had been suggested in *van Bennekom* (case 227/82). In *Hedley Lomas* the Court found otherwise:

> recourse to Article 36 [now 30] is no longer possible where Community directives provide for harmonisation of the measures necessary to achieve the *specific objective which would be furthered by reliance upon this provision*.
>
> This exclusion of recourse to Article 36 [now 30] cannot be affected by the fact that . . . the directive does not lay down any Community procedure for monitoring compliance nor any penalties in the event of breach of its provisions . . . Member States are obliged, in accordance with the first paragraph of Article 5 [now 10] and the third paragraph of Article 189 [now 249] of the Treaty, to take all measures necessary to guarantee the application and effectiveness of Community law . . . In this regard, the Member States must rely on trust in each other to carry out inspections on their respective territories. [Paras 18 and 19; emphasis added.]

This ruling was clearly designed to prevent Member States from taking reciprocal action contrary to the treaty in the face of alleged breaches of Union law *to protect an interest which is already protected by Union rules*. However, it does not mean that states are powerless to protect such an interest in the face of a breach of those rules. They may persuade the Commission to act under Article 226 (ex 169) EC. If the Commission refuses to act, they may themselves take action under Article 227 (ex 170) EC (post Lisbon 258 and 260 TFEU), if necessary seeking interim relief. Arguably they may now claim damages on the basis of *Francovich v Italy* (cases 6 and 9/90) (see Chapter 9). But they will not be allowed to act unilaterally in breach of Articles 28–9 EC on the basis of Article 30. This is consistent with the Court's rejection of the defence of reciprocity in actions under Article 226 EC (see Chapter 11).

16.3.3 The Union's power to re-legislate

Although it is clear that Member States have no power of action once a total harmonisation measure has been adopted, the Union itself is able to amend existing harmonisation measures and thereby to re-legislate in an area in which it has previously adopted harmonising measures. In *R v Secretary of State for Health, ex parte British American Tobacco and ors* (case C–491/01), it was argued that Directive 2001/37/EC ([2001] OJ L194/26) on the manufacture, presentation and sale of tobacco products was void because, inter alia, it amended Directive 90/239/EEC ([1990] OJ L137/36) on the maximum yield of tar of cigarettes. Both directives had been adopted on the basis of Article 95. The applicants' contention was that Directive 90/239/EEC had already established a fully harmonised regime on the yield of tar of cigarettes and that the Community could therefore not legislate afresh, at least not in the absence of new scientific evidence. The ECJ held (at para 77) that although the *Member States* were no longer able to introduce a rule in this area, the *Community* was nevertheless able to amend earlier legislation to safeguard the general interests recognised by the treaty. The Court went on to hold that:

> It follows that, even where a provision of Community law guarantees the removal of all obstacles to trade in the area it harmonises, that fact cannot make it impossible for the Community legislature to adapt that provision in step with other considerations. [Para 78.]

Such adaptation may be the result of new developments based on scientific facts (para 79), but may also follow from 'other considerations, such as the increased importance given to the social and political aspects of the anti-smoking campaign' (para 80). The Union has a general power to re-legislate, but can only exercise this power if there are scientific or other reasons for doing so.

16.3.4 Minimum harmonisation

There was a trend, commencing with the Single European Act (SEA), and particularly since Maastricht, towards minimum harmonisation and some provisions of the treaty, post SEA, specifically refer to minimum harmonisation. It has the advantage of allowing flexibility and diversity in the regulatory system. The main harmonising provisions (such as Articles 94–5 EC) make no express reference to minimum harmonisation and in more recent times, the focus seems to be turning away from this form of harmonisation in favour of maximum harmonisation (see, eg, Directive 2005/29/EC on Unfair Commercial Practices).

In a minimum harmonisation measure, the EU will set down a minimum standard with which all the Member States must comply. Beyond this minimum level, Member States are free to set their own standards, subject to the requirements of the EC Treaty. The main objective of minimum harmonisation is not to specify an absolute standard which must be met by all the Member States, but rather to reduce the differences that exist by narrowing the freedom given to the Member States to regulate particular aspects within their territory. Importantly, minimum harmonisation:

> does not limit Community action to the lowest common denominator, or even to the lowest level of protection established by the various Member States. [*Commission v UK* (case C–84/94), para 56.]

It simply indicates that there is a degree of freedom left to the Member States to exceed the standard set by such a measure.

Minimum harmonisation can only be of limited assistance in creating a level playing field. It may be useful to the extent that it sets a minimum standard below which none of the Member States may fall, but it still leaves room for divergence in standards between Member States. Minimum harmonisation does no more than to shift the boundaries of what is permissible, in that Member States are no longer free to maintain standards lower than those in a minimum harmonisation directive, but standards higher than those in such a directive can be maintained. Sometimes, the level of protection contained in a minimum harmonisation directive is high, in which case there would be only very limited scope for the Member States to adopt additional rules. In many instances, however, there will still be a considerable degree of variation between the Member States in respect of the area subject to minimum harmonisation because, with lower standards identifying the base level of protection, Member States will enjoy relative freedom to impose stricter standards. An added dimension to this problem is introduced when directives include optional provisions which Member States are permitted, but not obliged to, implement.

Arguably, minimum harmonisation and optional provisions undermine the purpose of harmonisation, because the continuing freedom to set standards above the baseline identified by the harmonising measure still subjects individuals and businesses to the possibility of divergent rules throughout the Union. These differences may impose extra burdens on producers, if applied to imported as well as domestic products, and are likely to create barriers to the internal market. If they do so, actually or potentially, will they be permitted to apply only to domestically produced goods, or may they be applied to all goods? If applicable only to domestic production, domestic producers will be disadvantaged. If applicable to all goods, when, and in what circumstances, will they be permitted?

16.3.5 Minimum harmonisation and reverse discrimination

In the case of a minimum harmonisation measure, it may be easier for the Member States to derogate from the harmonised standard than it is in the case of total harmonisation. Indeed, it is inherent in the concept of minimum harmonisation that Member States *will* introduce or retain rules which go beyond what is required of such a directive. However, it is clear that Member States cannot fall below the minimum standard introduced by a directive, and even where national legislation sets a higher standard than the relevant directive, the national measure has to comply with the treaty. Thus, the final boundary is set by the four freedoms.

Confusingly, harmonisation measures do not follow a single pattern. Some minimum harmonisation directives contain a 'market access' clause, whereas others do not. A market-access clause specifies that Member States may not prevent the import of products which comply with the minimum standard, but do not meet the higher standard imposed by the particular Member State. Such a provision was at issue in *R v Secretary of State for Health*, ex parte *Gallaher Ltd* (case C–11/92). The question was whether domestic producers could invoke a market access clause to challenge national rules which applied only to domestic production (reverse discrimination). The case concerned a challenge by three leading UK cigarette producers to UK regulations implementing Tobacco Directive 89/622. The directive required Member States to provide, inter alia, for health warnings on cigarettes to cover 'at least' four per cent of the packet (Article 4(4)). It also contained a market-access clause. Member States were not to prohibit or restrict the sale of products which complied with the directive (Article 8(1)). The UK regulations provided for more extensive health warnings than required by the terms of the directive, to cover six per cent of the packet, but these requirements were applicable only to domestic production. The ECJ held that this was permitted.

If *Gallaher* is followed (and always depending on the wording of the directive), where there is minimum harmonisation and a market access clause EU law will permit reverse discrimination, as it has done in other areas. Such a proposition was confirmed in *R v Minister of Agriculture, Fisheries and Food, ex parte Compassion in World Farming Ltd* (case C–1/96). Here a British animal-welfare group was seeking to prevent the export of live calves to other Member States which permitted the rearing of calves in crates, a practice prohibited by the UK (and a Council of Europe Convention). EC Directive 91/629, a harmonisation measure relating to the health of animals, laid down minimum common standards for the protection of live calves, but specifically allowed Member States to apply, within their own territory, stricter rules. In this way, as the ECJ pointed out, the directive aimed to strike a balance between the interests of animal protection and the smooth functioning of the organisation of the market in calves and derived products. It followed that:

> a Member State cannot rely on Article 36 [now 30] of the Treaty in order to restrict the export of calves to other Member States for reasons relating to the protection of the health of animals, which constitutes the specific objective of the harmonisation undertaken by the directive.

In reaching this conclusion, paras 18 and 19 of *Hedley Lomas*, quoted above, which referred to a total harmonisation directive, were invoked. Although there might be questions in a given case as to the specific objective of the harmonisation, it can be seen that the ECJ has unequivocally held that where a directive providing for minimum standards of harmonisation allows Member States to maintain stricter standards these can only be applied in their own territory to the State's own products. A similar approach is now being taken in the fields of services and establishment (see Chapter 22).

Gallaher has been criticised as tending to undermine competition in the internal market and discourage experiment and diversity. It is argued that Member States are unlikely to enact legislation in the interest of higher standards where this will result in a competitive disadvantage for domestic products. However, in the light of the principle of subsidiarity, a system permitting reverse discrimination may be a more practical way of regulating Member States' freedom to supplement Union provision than ad hoc assessment by the Court under Article 30 EC or the rule of reason. Higher standards may even prove more attractive to consumers.

As noted, some other directives contain no market access clause. In such a case, domestic measures over and above those required by the directive which restrict interstate trade will be permissible provided they are justified under the rule of reason or Article 30. Where the directive provides procedures for derogation, or, in the case of measures enacted under Article 95 EC, under Article 95(4), those procedures must be followed (see below).

16.3.6 Technical harmonisation and the 'new approach'

Originally, Member States had the power to lay down the performance objectives and design specifications, or 'technical standards', for goods manufactured and sold in their territory. Goods which did not comply with such technical standards could not be sold in that Member State. As seen in other chapters dealing with the four freedoms, some of these rules could be struck down as barriers to trade under Articles 28–9 (see also mutual recognition below), but others would be accepted as necessary by the ECJ. Such a divergence in technical standards can lead to competitive distortions in much the same way as differences between national measures in other fields. That is why the Union has had a specific programme for the harmonisation of such technical standards, often referred to as 'technical harmonisation'.

In the field of technical harmonisation, the Union initially adopted a sector-by-sector approach to adopt very detailed technical specifications. In 1985, when it had become apparent that the slow progress would make it very difficult to complete the internal market, the Council adopted a resolution on the 'New Approach to Technical Harmonisation' ([1985] OJ C136). The Institutions will now lay down so-called 'essential safety requirements' for a particular sector, but leave it to the European standardisation bodies, such as CEN, to work out the detailed technical rules by which compliance with the requirements can be demonstrated. Compliance with a European standard is voluntary and producers can choose to meet the safety requirements another way. Compliance with the standard has the advantage that it creates a presumption that products comply with the essential safety requirements and should therefore be allowed to be marketed in all Member States. Compliance with European standards is indicated by the CE marking on the product. Producers can opt to comply with other standards (such as those created the International Standards Organisation (ISO)) or not to comply with a technical standard at all, but they must nevertheless satisfy the procedures for assessing conformity which will be set out in the relevant directive which specifies the essential safety requirements for a particular sector.

In addition to sector-specific measures, the Institutions also adopted the Directive on General Product Safety (Directive 2001/95) which imposes a general requirement that all goods put on the internal market must be safe. Compliance with this general safety requirement can be demonstrated in the same manner as with sector-specific measures by complying with relevant European or national standards.

In addition, Directive 98/34/EC (which replaces Directive 83/189) lays down a procedure for the provision of information in the field of technical standards and regulations which applies when a Member States adopts a new technical regulation. Such a measure must be notified to the Commission before it is adopted to ensure that its impact on the free movement of goods is minimised and that both the Commission and the other Member States are aware of the measure and given an opportunity to propose amendments to it. Given the fact that non-notified national measures may not be relied on (see the discussion in Chapter 5), the scope of the directive—particularly the meaning of 'technical standards'—has gained in significance.

The advantage of the 'new approach' is seen to be threefold. First there is the flexibility the new approach allows for manufacturer in that they identify the hazards to be dealt with, but do not predict the technological solutions for doing so. Secondly, this in theory leaves room for innovation, especially as standards can be updated more quickly than legislative responses. Finally, this provides advantages for the legislator, as new approach frameworks are easier to maintain. Of course, no system is perfect and the new approach sometimes does not leave manufacturers much freedom of choice as to how they meet essential requirements. Given its significance, the standard agreeing process can be long and unwieldy, and commentators have noted that the membership of such committees is not representative. Nor is a technology-driven approach necessarily politically neutral; it limits regulatory choices, which has consequences for the social and cultural sphere. In this, it is possible to see a change of emphasis with the Community, as the Lisbon Agenda, and subsequent action plans, focus on the modernisation of the European social model.

Although the system has remained in place for more than 20 years, a number of Commission Communications have identified that the system could be improved in terms of transparency, enforcement, and recognition of the system by consumers and small- and medium-sized enterprises. As a result it put forward a package of measures aimed at facilitating the marketing of products (Regulation

765/2008 setting out the requirements for accreditation and market surveillance relating to the marketing of products and repealing Regulation (EEC) No 339/93 (OJ [2008] L 218/30); Regulation 764/2008 laying down procedures relating to the application of certain national technical rules to products lawfully marketed in another Member State and repealing Decision 3052/95/EC (OJ [2008] L 218/21); and Decision 768/2008/EC on a common framework for the marketing of products and repealing Council Decision 93/465/EEC (OJ [2008] L 218/82)). In particular, it suggested that bodies which assess goods for their compatibility with national technical measures should themselves meet some common standards for accreditation and coordination. Further, it also proposed a common framework to ensure an equivalent level of market surveillance to prevent non-compliant and potentially dangerous products being marketed. The Commission also noted the need to improve understanding and recognition of the 'CE' mark. Finally, the Commission noted the need to change the legal framework with regard to individual, sectoral measures, and it therefore proposed the introduction of a horizontal framework comprising all the common elements of the product legislation such as definitions and conformity assessment procedures. A new regulation also changed the burden of proof, so that it is no longer the case that importers or producers have to prove compliance with a Member State's legislation but rather the Member State of import has to justify the application of the national rule to the imported product.

At the same time as the Commission has sought to reinforce the 'new' approach to technical harmonisation, it also recognises, as part of the drive to 'better regulation', that measures in addition to binding legal measures may be used, such as guidelines, interpretative communications, and other 'soft-law' measures, as well as using co-regulation and self-regulation (see, eg, COM (2007) 724 and 725 final). While these measures may be flexible, they do give rise to questions about the legitimacy and democratic credentials of the resulting standards (see further Chapter 3).

16.3.7 Other types of harmonisation

Some harmonisation measures are limited to the cross-border context. If goods are sold across borders, the goods must comply with the harmonised standards used. For those who operate exclusively within the territory of one Member State, there is no need to comply with the Union standard. Sometimes, producers who do not operate across borders may be given the option of whether to comply with the Union or domestic standards. This may be of benefit to a producer who may intend to trade across borders in the future. Slot (see Further Reading below) describes these two related forms as 'optional' and 'partial' harmonisation, respectively. Optional harmonisation allows a producer to select whether to follow the harmonised or the national rules. Partial harmonisation requires a producer to adopt the Union standard if he wishes to engage in cross-border trade. These forms of harmonisation may be less intrusive than other types but seem to be less frequently used.

16.3.8 The 'country of origin' principle and mutual recognition

First espoused by the Court of Justice in *Cassis de Dijon* (case 120/78) in the context of 'negative harmonisation', the 'mutual recognition' principle has become a stalwart of EU law. In essence, the principle requires any Member State to admit onto its territory goods or services which are marketed lawfully in the originating Member State. It will thus rarely be possible to prevent the free circulation of goods within the internal market once these are sold lawfully in one Member State, although derogations remain possible (see further Chapter 19).

A variation of the 'country of origin' principle is occasionally used in legislation which also harmonises some parts of the relevant laws of the Member States (see, eg, Article 2 of the Television without Frontiers Directive (89/552/EEC [1989] OJ L298/23; also Article 3(1) of the Electronic Commerce Directive (2000/31/EC [2000] OJ L178/1). Under this principle, an operator in the internal market is only subject to regulation in his home Member State, and another Member State may not restrict that operator's activities in the host territory. Crucially, no derogations seem permissible, except where expressly provided for (see Article 2a Television without Frontiers Directive). For a trader seeking to sell goods or services in another Member State, this approach can be attractive, because it is only necessary to comply with the specific requirements imposed in the home country. However, it also gives rise to concerns about a 'race to the bottom', particularly where there is a significant variation in the level of regulation between the Member States (see further discussion in Chapter 22). Such concerns could be met by combining this principle with a maximum harmonisation measure, as all Member States' standards would then be the same. Even then the principle may be rejected (see, eg, the recent Directive on Unfair Commercial Practices (2005/29/EC), the first proposal of which included a country of origin clause which was removed during the legislative process; see also the debate about a directive on services (see Chapter 22), especially where there are concerns about the level of protection conferred by the directive in question).

It is clear, however, that the country-of-origin principle has a role to play in the harmonisation landscape in that it can complement measures harmonising some aspects of domestic law. It may also be a bargaining tool in the legislative process to secure agreement on a harmonising measure, although, as more recent examples show, it can also have the opposite effect.

16.4 Article 95 and harmonisation

Much of the EC's harmonising legislation centres on the internal market, and it is therefore appropriate to consider the key provision in this regard, Article 95 EC, in some detail. This is particularly important because the ECJ has attempted to lay down clear limits within which this provision may be utilised for the adoption of legislation.

Before the adoption of the SEA, harmonisation measures were often adopted on the basis of Article 94. This provision enables the adoption of harmonising directives which directly affect the establishment or functioning of the common market. Article 94 requires unanimity within the Council, and requires only that the Parliament be consulted. The unanimity requirement was blamed for the slow progress in completing the common market.

The SEA introduced what has become the most significant provision for the EC's harmonisation programme: Article 95. Article 95(1) states that:

> By way of derogation from Article 94 and save where otherwise provided in this Treaty, the following provisions shall apply for the achievement of the objectives set out in Article 14. The Council shall, acting in accordance with the procedure referred to in Article 251 and after consulting the Economic and Social Committee, adopt the measures for the approximation of the provisions laid down by law, regulation or administrative action in Member States which have as their object the establishment and functioning of the internal market.

In contrast to Article 94, there is no requirement for unanimity. Moreover, since the Treaty of the European Union (TEU), Parliament is actively involved in the legislative process through the use of the co-decision procedure. Whilst the wording of Article 95 suggests that it is subordinate to Article 94, practice has proved otherwise. Should Lisbon come into force, the order of the articles will be reversed to reflect this reality and the phrase 'by way of derogation from Article 94 and' will be removed from Article 95.

Article 95 can form the basis for two types of measures: those which have the object of establishing the internal market, and those which relate to the functioning of the internal market. The objective of Article 95 is to reduce or remove altogether competitive disadvantages caused by the higher cost of having to comply with rules which are stricter in some Member States than in others. In addition, it may extend to cover harmonising measures which affect goods irrespective of their ultimate destination, including goods manufactured exclusively for export, if there is a risk that their reimport could undermine the harmonising measure (in *R v Secretary of State for Health, ex parte British American Tobacco and others* (case C–491/01) at para 82, and see para 166 of Advocate-General Geelhoed's opinion in the same case).

It must be noted that not all measures which may be significant for the internal market will be based on this provision. For example, the directives in the company-law field are generally adopted on the basis of Article 44, especially Article 44(2)(g), although they are clearly of relevance to the internal market (eg, Directive 2005/56/EC on cross-border mergers of limited-liability companies [2005] OJ L310/1). However, such measures pursue a different objective and are not necessarily concerned with the establishment or functioning of the internal market as such, although sometimes the dividing line can be a fine one (cf Directive 68/151/EEC, adopted before Article 95 was introduced, and concerned, inter alia, with the protection of third parties dealing with companies, which seeks to introduce equivalent safeguards throughout the EC).

16.4.1 The extent of the Union's power to legislate under Article 95

Article 95 has formed the basis of numerous directives. The Union has used its powers under Article 95 extensively. It seemed that the scope of legislation on the basis of this article was very broad; some commentators have suggested that it had been interpreted as a general power to regulate (see, eg, Wyatt). The extent of the Union's powers under this article was clarified in *Germany v Parliament and Council* (case C–376/98), but it is questionable the extent to which this case provided a new line of authority which limits Union competence, or was an anomaly in the otherwise broad interpretation of Article 95. The case concerned the Tobacco Advertising Directive (Directive 98/43/EC) which prohibited the advertising and sponsorship of tobacco products. In a challenge to the legality of the measures which were essentially based on health concerns, the ECJ annulled the directive. The Court emphasised that Article 95 could form the basis only for measures which are intended to improve the conditions for the establishment and functioning of the internal market, but that it did not give a general power to the Union legislature to regulate the internal market (para 83). Such a general power would conflict with Article 5 EC, which provides that the Community must act within its powers (see further Chapter 3). The Court went on to say that:

> a measure adopted on the basis of Article 100a [now 95] of the Treaty must *genuinely* have as its object the improvement of the conditions for the establishment and functioning of the internal market. [Para 84; emphasis added.]

It has often been the case that Article 95 was used not only to harmonise existing divergences to facilitate the functioning of the internal market, but also to prevent the emergence of *future* obstacles to trade which could be caused by the diffuse development of the national legal systems. The Court confirmed that Article 95 could still be used for that purpose provided that 'the emergence of such obstacles [is] likely and the measure in question [is] designed to prevent them' (para 86; see also *R v Secretary of State for Health*, ex parte *Swedish Match* (case C–210/03), para 31). However, a 'mere finding of disparities between national rules and of the abstract risk of obstacles to the exercise of fundamental freedoms or of distortions of competition' (para 84) would be insufficient to justify Union action. If a particular measure is aimed at eliminating distortions of competition, the Court has to be satisfied that this distortion is 'appreciable', because the powers of the Union legislature would otherwise be 'practically unlimited' (para 107, and see also *Commission v Council*, (Titanium Dioxide) (case C–300/89) and *R v Secretary of State for Health, ex parte Alliance for Natural Health* (joined cases C–154/04 and 155/04). The holding in *Tobacco Advertising* confirms the views of Advocate-General Fennelly, who observed that:

> the pursuit of equal conditions of competition does not give *carte blanche* to the Community legislator to harmonise any national rules that meet the eye . . . it would risk transferring general Member State regulatory competence to the Community if recourse to Article 100a [now 95] . . . were not subject to some *test of the reality of the link between such measures and internal market objectives*. [Opinion, case C–376/98, para 89.]

A measure could not be justified on the basis of Article 95 if its effect on the harmonisation of competitive conditions was 'merely incidental' (para 91). In *Germany v Parliament and Council* (case C–376/98), the directive prohibited outright advertising of, and sponsorship by, tobacco products. The ECJ held that Article 95 was an inappropriate legal basis for the directive because it not only failed to improve competition but sought to eliminate it altogether.

There is therefore a burden on the Union legislator to identify obstacles to the functioning of the internal market before adopting harmonising legislation on the basis of Article 95. It is necessary to establish first of all that disparate national laws actually constitute a barrier to free movement or distort competition, and then that Union action contributes to the establishment and functioning of the internal market and goes no further. It seemed that this could have required a detailed analysis of the competitive conditions prevailing in a particular sector to establish whether an identified obstacle to free movement or competition is appreciable such as to justify Union action. It is debatable, however, whether the Court has consistently carried out such an assessment in subsequent case law: in some cases—and contrary to its reasoning in *Tobacco Advertising*—it assumes that the existence of different regulatory approaches justify Community action (see eg *The Queen, on the application of Alliance for Natural Health and Others v Secretary of State for Health and National Assembly for Wales* (joined cases C–154 and 155/04)). In the second *Tobacco Advertising Directive case* (*Germany v European Parliament and Council* (case C–380/03)), the ECJ argued that:

> where there are obstacles to trade, or it is likely that such obstacles will emerge in the future, because the member States have taken, or are about to take, divergent measures with respect to a product or a class of products, which bring about different levels of protection and thereby prevent the product or products concerned moving freely within the Community, Article 95 authorises the Community legislature to intervene by adopting appropriate measures . . . [Para 41.]

16.4.2 Article 95 and 'flanking policies'

A further question is to what extent Article 95 can be used as a legal basis to harmonise areas in which the Union does not have a direct competence to harmonise, or where there is more than one potential legal basis for a particular measure. In *Germany v Parliament and Council*, it was argued that the directive sought to harmonise public health legislation. Under Article 152(4) (ex 129(4); post Lisbon 168 TFEU), the Union is expressly precluded from harmonising legislation in this area. The ECJ emphasised that other treaty articles may not be used to circumvent an express exclusion of harmonisation such as the one laid down in Article 152(4), but this did not rule out the possibility that harmonising measures adopted on the basis of other treaty provisions could have an impact on the protection of human health (para 78). In *R v Secretary of State for Health, ex parte British American Tobacco and others* (C–491/01), Advocate-General Geelhoed emphasised that it must be possible to adopt harmonising measures under Article 95 to the extent that national measures within the field of public health create barriers to trade, but it is also clear that there is no independent power to harmonise public health legislation (see paras 112–14). The ECJ confirmed that as long as a directive 'genuinely has as its object the improvement of the conditions for the functioning of the internal market', it would be possible to adopt it on the basis of Article 95 'and it is no bar that the protection of public health was a decisive factor in the choices involved in the harmonising measures' (para 76).

On this basis, the Union has a degree of competence to harmonise all areas in which divergent national laws may adversely affect the operation of the internal market, but cannot adopt measures that have the effect of harmonising excluded areas beyond what is necessary to eliminate distortions of competition. This seems to be a very fine distinction to make and will require the Union legislator to be even more careful in adopting legislation on the basis of Article 95.

An additional problem with 'flanking policies' may arise where a measure could be adopted on the basis of two or more treaty provisions. For example, in *ex parte BAT*, the directive had been adopted on the basis of both Article 95 and Article 133. It was argued that this combined legal basis was inappropriate. The ECJ observed that if a measure simultaneously pursues a number of objectives without one or more being secondary to a main objective, multiple legal bases may be acceptable. However, the Court regarded this as 'exceptional' and the general position is:

> If examination of a Community act shows that it has a twofold purpose . . . and if one of these if identifiable as main or predominant, whereas the other is merely incidental, the act must be founded on a sole legal basis, that is, the one required by the main or predominant purpose. [Para 94.]

In the case, all the relevant provisions could have been adopted on the basis of Article 95, and the additional use of Article 133 was not permissible. This in itself did not mean that the directive was invalid, however, because it only formed a 'purely formal defect' (see also *R v Secretary of State for Health, ex parte Swedish Match* (case C–210/03), para 44). However, if the use of multiple legal bases gives rise to an irregularity in the procedure used for the adoption of the directive concerned, the position would be different (see also *Titanium Dioxide*, case C–300/89, paras 17–21). In *ex parte BAT*, the relevant legal bases were Articles 95 and 133. In contrast to Article 95, which requires use of the co-decision procedure, Article 133 simply requires a decision by qualified majority in the Council, without any involvement by Parliament. The ECJ did not regard this as a procedural irregularity, because both articles required a decision by qualified majority and the co-decision procedure had, in fact, been followed. That case differed from *Titanium Dioxide*, where one of the conflicting legal bases required a unanimous decision. Although this view appears attractive, the ECJ sidestepped the argument that use of the co-decision procedure under Article 133 was contrary to the separation of powers in the treaty by holding that Article 133 was not required for the adoption of the directive.

16.4.3 Article 95 and the other pillars

A similar question arises in relation to Article 95 and matters falling within either the justice and home affairs (JHA) or common foreign and security policy (CFSP) pillars. The ECJ has of recent years had the opportunity to consider the relationship between the EC and the other pillars of the EU, and in doing so it has emphasised its responsibility to ensure that EU competence does not encroach upon the EC as required by Article 47 EU (see, eg, *Commission v Council* (case C–176/03), environmental crimes; *Commission v Council* (Case C–91/05), moratorium on small arms sales in West Africa).

In the *PNR* case (*Parliament v Council and Commission* (case C–317 and C–318/04)), the Parliament challenged a Council decision concluding an agreement between the EU and the USA on the transfer of passenger data. The Parliament argued that, since the objective was combating terrorism, Article 95 could not be used as the basis of the decision. The ECJ based its decision of Article 95 in conjunction with the Data-Protection Directive, holding that the decision was not justified. The Advocate-General was clearer: in his view the decision was not primarily concerned with the internal market and Article 95 should not therefore have been used (see Opinion of Advocate-General, paras 140–52). Recently, the ECJ has had to consider the scope of Article 95 EC in the context of a challenge by Ireland (*Ireland v Parliament and Council* (case C–301/06), decision of the Grand Chamber) to Directive 2006/24/EC on data retention by public telecommunications companies and which sought to amend Directive 2002/58/EC (which had been enacted on the basis of Article 95). Ireland argued—following the line of reasoning of the Advocate-General in the *PNR* case—that the purpose of the directive was the fight against terrorism, and it should not therefore be based on Article 95 EC, but rather Articles 30, 31(1)(c), and 34(2)(b) TEU. Whilst the Irish government argued that the ECJ should verify whether the measure's centre of gravity fell with Article 95 as in *Titanium Dioxide*, the ECJ adopted the test found in *Tobacco Advertising*, where there was no possible alternate treaty base. It concluded that Member States were adopting, in an attempt to combat terrorism, different rules on data retention and that these were liable to have a direct impact on the functioning of the internal market (though it did not explain precisely how). It then stated:

> insofar as the amendment of Directive 2002/58 effected by Directive 2006/24 comes within the scope of Community powers, Directive 2006/24 could not be based on a provision of the EU Treaty without infringing Article 47 thereof.

It is not clear what the ECJ is saying here. It could be interpreted as meaning that if an amending directive falls within the scope of the EC Treaty then basing such a directive on provisions in the other pillars would contravene Article 47. This is self-evident. Alternatively, the ECJ could be suggesting that the amendments of a directive validly based on Article 95 bring the amending directives within the scope of the EC Treaty, presumably irrespective of its content. Perhaps to mitigate the potential consequences of that statement, the ECJ then went on to argue that the main focus of the directive were the activities of the service providers and not those of the police and judicial authorities.

16.4.4 Derogation under Article 95

Where derogation may legitimately be sought from harmonisation measures enacted under Article 95(1), this will now be governed by Article 95(4)–(5). Article 95(4), first introduced by the SEA in 1986, provides that where harmonising legislation has been passed by qualified majority, Member States who deem it necessary to *maintain* national provisions on grounds of major needs referred to in Article 30, or relating to the protection of the environment or the working environment' must notify the Commission and state the grounds for maintaining these rules. Similarly, Article 95(5) requires notification to the Commission if a Member State deems it necessary, after the adoption of a harmonising measure, to *introduce* national measures based on new scientific evidence relating to the protection of the environment or the working environment on grounds of a problem specific to that Member State (note that Article 95(5) does not refer to Article 30 as a ground for introducing new measures). These conditions are cumulative. It is implicit in the system that the Member State accepts that the national rule in issue is incompatible with the relevant directive.

Whether the Member State relies on Article 95(4) or (5), the Commission may then approve or reject the national provisions after having verified that they do not constitute a means of 'arbitrary discrimination or disguised restriction on trade between Member States', nor an obstacle to the functioning of the internal market (Article 95(6)). In making this assessment, the ECJ has held that the Commission has a wide discretion (*Commission v Netherlands* (C–405/07 P)), though this does not mean it is not amenable to review. There is no obligation on the Commission to give the Member State who made the notification, nor any other Member State, the right to make representations (*Denmark v Commission* (case C–3/00)). In the light of this, and given the width of its discretion, the procedural guarantees, such as the duty to give reasons, are particularly important.

The Commission must decide within six months, although this period may be extended by a further six months if the matter is complex and there is no danger to human health. If the Commission fails to act within that time, the national measure is deemed to have been approved (for an example, see *Germany v Commission* (case C–512/99)). The Commission has issued guidelines setting out the procedures for submitting notifications under Article 95(4)–(5) by the Member States and explaining how the Commission will handle such notifications (COM (2002) 760 final). The Commission or any other Member State may bring the matter before the ECJ if it considers that a state is making improper use of these powers.

Although expressed to apply only where harmonisation measures have been enacted by qualified majority, it has been suggested that the same procedure should be available where legislation has been passed unanimously; the Article 95(4) or (5) procedure is not in terms limited to states that have not agreed to the measure in question, and some scope for derogation should be available to meet emergencies not foreseen at the time when the legislation was passed. Moreover, in an emergency, arguably, it should not be necessary for a state to obtain *prior* approval for its actions from the Commission, provided that the need for action is genuine and urgent and the Commission is notified at the earliest possible time (for a recent example, see *Land Oberösterreich v Commission* (case T–366/03)).

16.5 The impact of harmonisation on domestic law

The general obligation of the Member States to ensure compliance with EU law has already been discussed. Generally, it is necessary to implement directives and to ensure that they are fully given effect in domestic legislation. For some Member States, the adoption of a directive, even a minimum harmonisation measure, may result in significant changes to domestic law whereas the same measure may have a very limited impact in others. An example is Directive 99/44/EC on the sale of consumer goods, which triggered a complete reform to the German law of obligations and significantly improved the position of German consumers. In contrast, the directive's impact in the UK was far less severe and resulted in few changes to the substance of English law.

It is, however, appropriate to highlight particular aspects of this obligation which arise in the context of harmonisation. It is usually the case that harmonisation is to be achieved through the adoption of directives. These need to be implemented into the legal orders of the Member States. Directives are 'binding as to the result to be achieved' (Article 249 EC), but the Member States are free to choose how to implement the rules in a directive. It seems, therefore, that a Member State is not required to reproduce the text of a directive verbatim in the implementing legislation, as long as it can demonstrate that national law complies with the directive. However, the more detailed and technical the provisions of a directive, the narrower will be the scope for a Member State to depart from its wording. Moreover, a directive which takes a total harmonisation approach may have to be transposed by closely following its wording to avoid the risk of incorrectly implementing it (see, eg, the difficulties caused by Directive 2005/29/EC on Unfair Commercial Practices, a total harmonisation measure with, potentially, a very wide reach into domestic consumer laws).

If a directive is not transposed at all, or only incompletely, someone seeking to rely on the directive may be able to use on the doctrine of direct effect (see Chapter 5). Similarly, if domestic legislation is worded differently from the corresponding provisions in a directive, the doctrine of indirect effect requires that domestic legislation should be interpreted to conform to the directive (see Chapter 5). However, recent cases suggest that the Commission and the ECJ distinguish between two different types of domestic legislation. Where a Member State introduces specific legislation to implement a directive, the use of a (slightly) different wording may be acceptable, provided that the domestic courts would interpret such legislation in accordance with the directive. In contrast, it does not seem acceptable for a Member State to rely on existing legislation and argue that it could be interpreted in line with the directive (and, indeed, should be so interpreted: see *Ratti*), particularly where direct rights are at stake and where the retention of existing rules could conflict with the principle of effectiveness (see also Chapter 8). This position is reflected in a number of cases involving consumer-protection measures.

In *Commission v United Kingdom* (case C–300/95), the Commission brought infringement proceedings against the UK for a failure correctly to implement Article 4(1)(e) of Directive 85/374/EEC (Product Liability Directive). The UK government had chosen a wording that differed from that in the directive, although it did not conflict directly with it. The ECJ rejected the Commission's application, because there was insufficient evidence that the UK had failed to give full effect to the requirements of Article 4(1)(e). In particular, there was no case law at the time on the application of the directive and therefore no evidence that the implementing legislation would lead to results different from those required by the directive. There was nothing to suggest that the domestic courts would fail to interpret the implementing legislation in accordance with the directive. *Commission v UK* suggests that Member States have some leeway in implementing the provisions of a directive and that greater evidence, such as court decisions, is required before it is possible to say that there is a failure correctly to implement a directive. As a result, the courts in the UK have adopted an approach whereby cases brought under the relevant domestic legislation are, in effect, dealt with by applying the corresponding directive itself (see *A and ors v The National Blood Authority* [2001] 3 All ER 289 (High Court); also *Director-General of Fair Trading v First National Bank* [2002] 1 AC 481 (House of Lords)).

The principle in *Commission v UK* was accepted in *Commission v Italy* (C–372/99). The Commission claimed that Italy had failed to ensure that terms recommended by trade association in standard contracts could be challenged when the term had not actually been used in a consumer contract (as per Article 7(3) of the Unfair Contract

Terms Directive 93/13/EEC). The Italian implementing legislation was ambiguous and capable of interpretation contrary to the objective pursued by the directive. The ECJ noted that the possibility of ensuring compliance with a directive through case law, even where there is case law in line with the directive, did not suffice where the legislation itself was insufficiently clear, or contradictory. Accepting compliance through case law would not be in accordance with the principle of legal certainty. Moreover, Italian case law was neither unanimous nor sufficiently well established to guarantee an interpretation in line with the Unfair Contract Terms Directive.

Therefore, this approach may not be sufficient to satisfy the Member States' obligations where the domestic legislation does not clearly and precisely reflect the position under the relevant directive. In *Commission v Netherlands* (case C–144/99), the ECJ held that the Netherlands had failed fully to implement Directive 93/13/EEC on Unfair Contract Terms. The Commission was particularly concerned about the implementation of Article 4(2) (an exception from the fairness requirement for core contract terms) and Article 5 (a 'plain and intelligible language' requirement) of the directive. The Netherlands argued that there was no need expressly to implement particular parts of a directive if existing national rules already fulfilled the requirements of that directive. Moreover, taking the lead from *Commission v United Kingdom* (case C–300/95), compliance with the directive would be ensured by the courts which would interpret existing legislation in accordance with the directive, as required by the ECJ's case law on indirect effect. The ECJ disagreed. It held that the legal position under national law must be sufficiently clear and precise so that individuals are made fully aware of their rights (para 17). It had not been demonstrated that the Dutch courts consistently interpreted the legislation in line with the directive (para 20). Finally, even where it is settled in the case law of a Member State that provisions of national law *are* interpreted in line with a directive, this does not ensure the clarity and precision to meet the requirement of legal certainty. This is particularly relevant in the context of consumer protection (para 21).

Commission v Netherlands appears to mark a significant tightening of the requirement to implement directives into domestic law. It seems to depart from the position accepted in *Commission v United Kingdom* and could be seen as throwing some doubt on whether that ruling remains good law. It may be possible to distinguish the two decisions on the basis that the conflict in *Commission v Netherlands* was between a directive and a national provision already in place, whereas in *Commission v United Kingdom* the national measure had been adopted to comply with the directive. Moreover, in *Commission v UK*, there were no cases under the national measure. However, in *Commission v Italy*, the implementing measures were ambiguous and case law interpreting these was not unanimous. In those circumstances even new national measures may not be treated as correctly implementing a directive.

Member States may not enjoy as great a choice as suggested by Article 249 in implementing harmonisation directives. In particular, where individual rights are affected, it now seems that domestic legislation must be clear and precise to allow individuals to ascertain the scope of their rights from the legislation. A significant factor underlying this development may be the greater involvement of the Parliament in the legislative process. It has become a common feature of the co-decision procedure that Parliament and the Council will disagree over details in the wording of particular provisions in a draft directive (see for example, the legislative history to Directive 99/44/EC on the sale of consumer goods), and the actual text of the directive has political significance. To permit Member States to deviate from the text of directives which have resulted may be regarded as side-stepping, or even undermining, the legislative procedure.

However, it also seems that, in practice, the fact that a directive is a minimum harmonisation measure may cause a Member State to be less systematic in transposing it into domestic law. A maximum harmonisation measure may necessitate a thorough review of the affected area of domestic law, and a high degree of care in ensuring that the implementing legislation fits into the wider legal framework. This may be less important where a directive permits variations, and domestic rules are often retained on the basis of a minimum clause.

The Commission has become concerned about the long delays in transposing many directives, particularly those affecting the internal market. It has therefore issued a Recommendation to the Member States about procedural matters to be adopted at the national level to ensure a speedy and accurate transposition of these directives ([2005] OJ L98/47). Unfortunately, this document does not contain any substantive guidance on how to transpose directives. The Commission, now, habitually includes a provision in proposals requiring Member States to provide a table of transposition, showing how each article has been implemented in to national law. More positively, the Commission Staff Working Document (COM [2007] 724 final) accompanying the Communication on a Single Market for the 21st Century (COM [2007] 725 final) notes some of the difficulties Member States face, as well as some of the steps taken to facilitate transposition of particular directives, such as the holding of transposition workshops, or the drafting of detailed guides to the meaning of directives. It also suggests the Union legislation should be drafted so as to minimise difficulties for Member States, though how the Commission is supposed to do this is unclear. The Commission also suggests a move to the use of regulations over directives, to avoid the risk of 'gold plating'—namely, the imposition of additional regulatory burdens as part of the transposition process. If such an approach is adopted, it would herald a move to greater uniformity, allowing less flexibility and diversity for Member States. It also raises more significant drafting questions at Union level, as provisions would have to be drafted in such a way that they were clear enough to need no implementation.

Of course, the question of how Member States choose to implement directives and, in particular whether they choose to adopt the 'copy out' technique or to reword the provision can be seen from the domestic perspective, and in particular the position of the courts which have to interpret the resulting legislation. Views are split on this. Jacob LJ in the English Court of Appeal had, however, the following to say about the changes to the Copyright, Designs and Patents Act to implement the Software Directive in *Nova Games v Mazooma* ([2007] EWCA Civ 219):

> The UK Act, drafted with the traditional, but wholly unhelpful way of re-wording a Directive, sets out 'a computer program' and 'preparatory design work for a computer program' as though they are entirely different types of work in which literary copyright can subsist. What the Directive actually says is: 'the term "computer programs" shall include their preparatory design material'. That may not be quite the same thing—the EU legislation appears to contemplate just one copyright in a computer program, not two, one in the preparatory work and the other in the program itself. . . . The re-wording, as it nearly always does, throws up room for wholly unnecessary uncertainty and argument. [Para 28.]

16.6 **Conclusions**

It has been seen that harmonisation is a fundamental, and perhaps the most significant, aspect of EU law. It is not without problems, however. One of the central difficulties relates to the fact that there is no one type of harmonisation: different approaches leave Member States varying degrees of legislative freedom. Although total harmonisation is necessary in some areas, there has been a minimum-harmonisation approach in some areas (such as consumer protection) to create at least a 'lowest common denominator' in the Member States. Nevertheless, as Weatherill comments (see Further Reading below), the process of minimum harmonisation 'does not solve the specific problem of which market-partitioning national measures are justified and which are not'. National measures which set a standard that exceeds a minimum-harmonisation measure are always potentially liable to challenge under provisions guaranteeing free movement. A second problem concerns the scope of the EU's power to enact harmonising measures, especially in relation to Article 95 EC. Despite the fact that harmonisation might seem to solve a number of problems with the operation of the internal market, the EU does not have a general power to regulate trade. The precise scope of Member States' power to legislate and the impact of the four freedoms on that competence will continue to be relevant.

FURTHER READING

Cross, ED, 'Pre-emption of Member State law in the European Economic Community: A framework for analysis' (1992) 29 CMLR 447–72.

Davies, G, 'Can selling arrangements be harmonised?' (2005) 30 EL Rev 370.

De Sadeleer, N, 'Procedures for derogations from the principle of approximation of laws under Article 95 EC' (2003) 40 CMLR 889–915.

Dimitrakapoulos, DG, 'The transposition of EU law: Post-decisional politics and institutional autonomy' [2001] 7 ELJ 4.

Dougan, M, 'Minimum harmonisation and the internal market' (2000) 37 CMLR 853–85.

Howells, G, 'Federalism in USA and EC: The scope for harmonised legislative activity compared' (2002) ERPL 601–22.

Kurcz, MB, 'Harmonisation by means of directives: Never-ending story?' [2001] EBLR 287.

Radeideh, M, *Fair Trading in EC Law* (Groningen: Europa Law Publishing, 2005).

Ramsey, 'The copy out technique: More of a 'cop out' than a solution?' [1996] 17 Statute Law Review 3.

Slot, PJ, 'Harmonisation' (1996) 21 EL Rev 378–97.

Schutze, R, 'Co-operative federalism constitutionalised: The emergence of complementary competences in the EC legal order' (2006) 31 EL Rev 167.

Waelbroek, M, 'The emergent doctrine of community pre-emption', in T Sandalow and E Stein (eds), *Courts and Free Markets* (Clarendon Press, 1982).

Weatherill, S, *Law and Integration in the European Union* (Clarendon Press, 1995), Ch 5.

—— 'Why harmonise?' in T Tridimas and P Nebbia (eds), *European Union Law for the Twenty-first Century: Rethinking the new legal order* (Hart Publishing, 2004).

—— 'Harmonisation: How much, how little' [2005] EBLR 533.

—— 'Free movement of goods' (2006) 55 ICLQ 457–67.

—— 'Recent Developments in the law governing the free movement of goods in the EC's internal market' (2006) 2 ERCL 90–111.

—— 'European private law and the constitutional dimension' in F Cafaggi (ed), *The Institutional Framework of European Private Law* (Oxford University Press, 2006).

Woods, L, *Free Movement of Goods and Services within the European Community* (Ashgate, 2004), Ch 13.

Wyatt, D, 'Community competence to regulate the internal market' University of Oxford, Faculty of Law, Legal Studies Research Paper Series, Working paper 9/2007, available at <http://papers.ssrn.com/Abstract=997863>.

17

Free movement of payments and capital

17.1 Introduction

Originally the free movement of capital was governed by Articles 67–73 EEC and by secondary legislation made under those provisions. Although one of the four freedoms listed in Article 14 EC, its treatment had been somewhat different from the liberal approach taken both in the secondary legislation and by the European Court of Justice (ECJ) regarding the free movement of persons, services, and goods. Indeed, by striking contrast to its approach to these freedoms, the ECJ ruled that the original pre-Treaty of the European Union (TEU) capital provisions did not have direct effect (*Casati* (case 203/80)) and could therefore not be relied on before the domestic courts (see Chapter 5). As noted in the chapter on the preliminary reference procedure (Chapter 10), the fact that individuals can rely on EC rights in national courts has been a significant factor in the development of Community law. The capital provisions, quite apart from being more cautiously drafted, therefore lacked this mechanism for development. The area was sensitive, linked to monetary policy, a fact that was reflected in the drafting of the original provisions dealing with free movement of capital.

The TEU changed the position significantly, as it introduced the provisions for the development of Economic and Monetary Union (EMU) (consideration of which lies outside the scope of this book), and included changes in the provisions relating to capital and payments. What was then Article 73a EC replaced the original system with the then Articles 73b–g EC. Following the Treaty of Amsterdam (ToA), these articles were renumbered Articles 56–60 EC. There are also a number of pieces of secondary legislation aimed at facilitating the free movement of capital. With these changes, the ECJ's approach has also changed, moving towards the approach taken with regard to the other freedoms on the back of an increasing number of references on the subject. As Leo Flynn commented in 2002, 'free movement of capital has ceased to be the runt of the litter amongst the market freedoms'. Nonetheless, differences remain; and some concerns have been raised about the approach of the ECJ to third-country nationals (TCNs) (including companies) who seek to rely on these provisions.

17.2 Outline of provisions relating to the free movement of capital

The 'fourth' freedom, capital, can be broken down into two linked elements:

(a) capital

(b) payments.

Article 56 prohibits all restrictions on the free movement of capital (Article 56(1) EC) and payments (Article 56(2) EC) whether between Member States or between Member States and third countries. In this, there is a change from the scope of the prohibition contained in the original Article 67 EEC: that provision referred not only to restrictions on the movement of capital but also to 'discrimination based on the nationality or on the place of residence of the parties or on the place where such capital is invested'. Whether this has had any significant impact on the way the ECJ has interpreted the capital provision is debatable (see 17.3.4 below). Article 56 will be renumbered 63 of the Treaty on the Functioning on the European Union (TFEU) should the Lisbon Treaty come into force. Likewise, Articles 57–9 would be renumbered 64–6 TFEU respectively. Article 60 EC would be renumbered Article 75 TFEU and, in the process, it would be amended.

Articles 57–60 EC contain the exceptions to the general rule. These can be divided into two categories: those that relate to capital movement between Member States (Article 58; see also Articles 119–20 (ex 109h–i), post Lisbon, Articles 143–4 TFEU respectively); and those that relate to movement to third countries (Articles 57 and 59–60). Article 58 is the provision containing the express exceptions to the free movement of capital. It can be seen as analogous to Articles 30 (goods), 40(3) (workers), and 46 (establishment/services). Nonetheless, there are also some differences, as Article 58 contains some exceptions that are unique to capital: Article 58(1)(a) contains provisions specific to Member States' individual tax regimes. Article 58 also expressly raises the question of the relationship of the free movement of capital with the freedom of establishment (Article 58(2) and (3)). This issue, as well as the relationship between capital and services, which has significance for the rights of those in third countries, is discussed at 17.5 below.

17.3 Scope of the free movement of capital

17.3.1 Who can rely on the free movement of capital?

Community nationals may rely on this freedom, as may legal persons. The original Article 67 EEC merely required residence in the Union for a body to be able to rely on the freedom of capital (contrast the nationality requirements for services and establishment, see Chapter 21). The situation is now wider still, Article 56 EC making no reference to such a requirement. Like the provisions relating to the free movement of goods, and in contrast to those relating to services and people, the capital provisions may be relied on by TCNs. The situation is the same whether the capital movement is intra-Community, or between a third country and the Union. The ECJ has in some circumstances ruled that a matter fell to be considered under Article 49 or 43 EC; in those circumstances the TCN or company could not rely on the free movement of capital provisions (see below).

17.3.2 Direct effect

In contrast to the position prior to the amendments made by the Maastricht Treaty noted above, the current prohibition *has* been held to be directly effective:

see *Bordessa* (cases C–358 and 416/93) and *Sanz de Lera and others* (cases C–163, 165 and 250/94). This is the case whether we are considering prohibitions on restrictions on capital movements between Member States or between Member States and third countries and irrespective of the type of capital in issue. There is no jurisprudence as yet on whether Article 56 will have horizontal effect (see Chapter 5).

17.3.3 Types of act caught

The ECJ has taken a broad approach to the types of act caught by the prohibition in Article 56 EC. This was the case even before the Maastricht amendments to the capital provisions. In *Brugnoni and Ruffinengo* (case 157/85), decided in 1986, the ECJ accepted that 'restriction' covered more than just legislative acts, and also covered administrative obstacles to free movement. Equally, it seems not to matter in which capacity a government is acting when a potential restriction under Article 56 is in issue. In *Eurobonds* (case C–478/98), a case involving a prohibition on Belgian residents subscribing to securities issued abroad (Eurobonds), the Belgian government argued that it was acting not in its capacity as public authority but on the same terms as a private borrower when it adopted the restriction. The ECJ rejected this argument on the facts of the case, although the status of measures not dependent on public powers remains open.

Finally, a regulation which implements economic sanctions as part of the fight against terrorism and prohibits the transfer of economic resources to individuals in third countries, does not fall within the ambit of the provisions on free movement of capital and payments (*Kadi* (joined cases C–402 and C–415/05 P), para 188).

17.3.4 Meaning of capital

The prohibition operates on both capital movements and those relating to payments. This could suggest that the two concepts are different, and indeed early case law, *Luisi and Carbone* (case 286/82), distinguished between the two, since the prohibition operates on both in the same terms. More recently, the need to distinguish between the two has effectively been removed. Neither term is defined in Article 56, although Article 57 lists some types of capital, such as direct investments and the provision of financial services. This provision has not, however, been referred to by the ECJ in determining the scope of 'capital'. In terms of defining capital, the ECJ held in *Trummer* (case C–222/97) that Directive 88/361, passed before the changes brought in by TEU, remains relevant in terms of identifying what constitutes capital (see para 21 of the judgment). An annex to this directive contains an indicative 'nomenclature' (a list of categories), listed under 13 headings (eg, property investment). As the ECJ made clear, this list is not exhaustive. In *Verkooijen* (case C–35/98), the ECJ ruled that the receipt of dividends from investments abroad, a category not listed in the nomenclature, was inextricable from a capital movement and therefore fell within the scope of Article 56. Further, it has also held that an inheritance, whether of money, or immovable or movable property, is a movement of capital for the purposes of Article 56 EC (*Arens-Sikken v Staatssecretaris van Financiën* (case C–43/07), rules concerning inheritance duties and transfer duties where there is no convention on double taxation). Potentially the scope of Article 56 *et seq* is wide, especially as the nomenclature in Directive 88/361 includes not only the capital movement itself but also the underlying transaction (see, eg, heading VIII 'Financial Loans and Credits'). This approach opens up the possibility of overlap between the free movement of capital and the freedom to provide services (see further 17.5 below).

17.3.5 Test for application of free movement of capital

The concept of a 'restriction on the free movement of capital' has been interpreted broadly, as with the other freedoms. Where additional protection is required, vis-à-vis relations with third countries, this is provided by specific safeguard and derogation clauses, not by differential interpretation of the prohibition contained in Article 56 EC. The prohibition operates to eliminate measures which effectively prevent an individual being able to use a currency of another Member State, such as in *Trummer* (case C–222/97) (prohibition on mortgages in a foreign currency). It also applies to less stringent measures, such as requirements for prior authorisation of currency transactions. The prohibition does not apply just to absolute barriers to free movement, but also to those measures which hinder or dissuade people from exercising free-movement rights.

In the other freedoms we have seen a move from a discrimination-based approach to one that looks at hindrances. The change in emphasis in wording, noted in 17.2, between Article 67 EEC and Article 56(1) EC reflects this trend. Nonetheless, the ECJ has not always distinguished clearly between restrictions and discrimination when handing down its judgments. Thus in the *Portuguese Golden Shares* case (case C–367/98), it was accepted that the Portuguese national rules precluding investors from other states from acquiring more than a specified number of shares in certain newly privatised companies constituted 'unequal treatment of nationals of other Member States and restricts the free movement of capital' (para 40). This is a case of direct discrimination. Similarly, in *Konle* (case C–302/97), an Austrian rule, which in the interests of planning control exempted Austrian nationals only from having to obtain authorisation before acquiring a plot of land was seen as creating a discriminatory restriction against nationals of other Member States. Even in this case, however, the ECJ linked the existence of discrimination to the creation of a restriction. In other cases the ECJ has used terms such as 'obstacles' or 'liable to dissuade' (*Trummer*). These phrases seem similar to the approach taken in relation to the freedom to provide services (see Chapter 22). In the British *Golden Shares* case, the ECJ noted that even rules which apply without distinction to non-nationals and nationals alike can 'deter investors from other Member States from making such investments and, consequently, affect access to the market' (*Commission v UK (Golden Shares)* (case C–98/01), para 47).

This phraseology has been repeated: *Van Hilten-van der Heijden v Inspecteur van de Belastingdienst/Particulieren/Ondernemingen buitenland te Heerlen* (case C–513/03, para 44; national rules creating the legal fiction that a national of a Member State who dies within ten years of ceasing to reside in that Member State is deemed to have been resident there at the time of his death—not contrary to Article 56 EC); *Festersen* (case C–370/05, para 24, requirement that someone who acquires agricultural property must take up residence there—contrary to Article 56); and

Skatteverkert v A (case C–101/05), decision of Grand Chamber, para 40, exemption from income tax in respect of dividends conditional on the company making the distribution being established in a state within the EEA or a state with which a taxation convention providing for the exchange of information had been concluded— not contrary to Art 56 EC) and it is irrelevant whether the restriction affects the movement of capital between Member States themselves, or between a Member State and a third country. It seems the ECJ here is moving away from a discrimination-based approach and looking at the impact on the market. Certainly, in the *Portuguese Golden Shares* case, the ECJ commented that Article 56 'goes beyond the mere elimination of unequal treatment, on grounds of nationality, as between operators on the financial markets' (para 44).

17.3.5.1 *Requisite impact on the market*

The UK government in the *Golden Shares* case (case C–98/01) suggested that the principle in *Keck* should apply to Article 56. It argued that the rules in issue had an impact on the market which was too indirect to fall within the scope of the prohibition. The ECJ did not address this point directly. Nonetheless, the implication of the wording in the UK *Golden Shares* case, with its emphasis on access to the market, is that rules that have an impact which is too indirect will not fall within Article 56. This approach indeed had been suggested by the Advocate-General in the earlier case of *ED Srl* (case C–412/97), but again the ECJ did not address the point. Instead, it dealt with the matter under a different provision of the treaty, as one concerning goods (see further Chapter 19).

17.3.5.2 *Effects-based test*

The purpose behind the national rule is not relevant, although the ECJ will sometimes highlight when there is a protectionist motive (see, eg, *Verkooijen* (case C–35/98), para 34, *Reisch* (joined cases C–515, 519–40/99), para 32). It is the effect that is crucial and, as with the other freedoms, there is no *de minimis* exception.

17.3.6 **Internal situations**

Like the other freedoms, Article 56 may not be relied on in internal situations. It cannot therefore be used to challenge Member States rules regarding, for example, the acquisition of property. It should be noted, however, that the ECJ has given a generous interpretation of when there is no such internal situation. In the case of *Reisch and ors* (cases C–515, 519–40/99), the ECJ held:

> A reference for a preliminary ruling from a national court may be rejected by the Court only if it is quite obvious that the interpretation of Community law sought by that court bears no relation to the actual nature of the case or the subject-matter of the main action. [Para 25.]

This is potentially a very broad test and one that is uncertain in the scope of its application. It seems that few rules would fall within the 'internal situation'.

17.4 Exceptions to the free movement of capital

17.4.1 Express treaty derogation

Member States can restrict free movement of capital and payments on the grounds set out in Article 58.

17.4.1.1 *National taxation systems*

Member States may distinguish between taxpayers who are not in the same situation with regard to their place of residence or with regard to the place where their capital is invested (Article 58(1)(a)).

As noted earlier, this is a specific exception, unique to the free movement of capital provisions. This is restrictively interpreted: although taxation remains within Member States' competence, this power must be exercised within the scope of Union law. In *Petri Manninen* (case C–319/02), the ECJ commented that Article 58(1)(a) 'cannot be interpreted as meaning that any tax legislation making a distinction between taxpayers by reference to the place where they invest their capital is automatically compatible with the Treaty' (para 28), and in particular noted that Article 58(1)(a) is limited by Article 58(3) (see below). In *Verkooijen* (case C–35/98), the ECJ commented that this provision effectively codified the approach that it had taken in *Schumacker* and *Bachmann* (discussed in Chapter 23), which permits Member States to protect the coherence of their internal taxation system. However, an argument based on the need to safeguard the cohesion of a tax system must be examined in the light of the objective pursued by the tax legislation in question (*De Lasteyrie du Saillant* (case C–9/02), para 67) to see if such rules are actually necessary. In particular, the ECJ has held that there must be a direct link between the tax advantage concerned and the offsetting of that advantage by a particular tax levy (see *Deutsche Shell* (case C–293/06) taxation of losses incurred through exchange rates on start up capital for subsidiary in another Member State, decided under Article 43 EC). Indeed, the ECJ has consistently held that reduction in tax revenue cannot be regarded as an overriding reason in the public interest which may be relied on to justify a measure which is in principle contrary to a fundamental freedom (see, eg, *Verkooijen*, para 59; *X and Y* (case C–436/00), para 50). Laws may also be justified where the difference in treatment concerns situations which are not objectively comparable or in the interests of the fight against tax avoidance and the effectiveness of fiscal supervision. These will be similarly strictly reviewed.

Note, however, that Member States still have a certain degree of fiscal autonomy. Thus, where a disadvantage arises from two Member States choosing to exercise their fiscal sovereignty in such a way as to result in double taxation, neither Member State is obliged to amend their taxation system so as to eradicate the double taxation (*Block v Finanzamt Kaufbeuren* (case C–57/08)). The ECJ has noted that the treaty offers no guarantee to a citizen of the Union that transferring his residence to a Member State other than that in which he previously resided will be neutral as regards taxation. Given the disparities in the tax legislation of the Member States, such a transfer may be to the citizen's advantage or not, according to circumstances (*Lindfors* (Case C–365/02), tax levied on car registration consequent on relocation from one Member State to another).

17.4.1.2 *Anti-avoidance and public policy*

Member States may take action to prevent the avoidance of national regulation; to lay down procedures for the declaration of capital movements for the purposes of administrative or statistical information; or in the interests of public policy or public security (Article 58(1)(b)).

This is a three-pronged exception, which is a mixture of concern for fiscal supervision and a standard public-policy exception. The concern for fiscal supervision has links with the issues discussed at 17.4.1.1 above. In the *Eurobonds* case (case C–478/98), the prohibition on the acquisition by Belgian residents of securities of a loan issued abroad was not justified. The ECJ commented that 'a general presumption of tax evasion or tax fraud cannot justify a fiscal measure', especially where the national measure constituted 'an outright prohibition of a fundamental freedom' (para 45). Note that the reference to 'national regulation' is not necessarily limited to concerns listed in Article 58(1)(b): taxation and the prudential supervision of financial institutions. In *Bordessa* (joined cases C–358/93 and C–416/93), the ECJ held that other types of measure would be permitted where they were aimed at preventing 'illegal activities of comparable seriousness, such as money laundering, drug trafficking or terrorism' (para 21). The ECJ recognises, however, that the approach to assessing fiscal supervision is different depending on whether we are looking at movement between Member States or a Member State and a third country. In *A* (case C–101/05), the ECJ noted that 'such movements take place in a different legal context' (para 60) and that:

> it is, in principle, legitimate for that Member State to refuse to grant that advantage if, in particular, because that third country is not under any contractual obligation to provide information, it proves impossible to obtain such information from that country. [Para 63.]

Note that the second element of Article 58(1)(b) is potentially a broad category, although the ECJ will construe all exceptions to treaty freedoms narrowly. There is also no equivalent provision to this provision in the articles derogating from the other treaty freedoms. In this instance, therefore, jurisprudence developed in relation to the other treaty freedoms can probably not be used to derive guidance on the likely scope of this derogation. It seems that some prior *notification* requirements for statistical purposes or to prevent money laundering, for example, may be acceptable, but not prior *authorisation* (see *Sanz de Lera* (cases C–163, 165 and 250/94)).

Looking at the third aspect of Article 58(1)(b), note that a similar wording is used here to the exception to the free movement of goods and the exceptions relating to services, workers, and establishment (see Chapters 20 and 25). Likewise, the test adopted is that a sufficiently serious threat to fundamental interest exists and is similar to that used in regard to the other freedoms. (See for example *Association Eglise de Scientology de Paris and Scientology International Reserves Trust v the Prime Minister* (case C–54/99); *Commission v Belgium* (case C–503/99); *Commission v France* (case C–483/99); and the *Golden Shares* cases: *Commission v UK* (case C–98/01) and *Commission v Spain* (case C–436/00)). See also the prohibition on buying property near military sites, which would be acceptable only if military interests of the Member State would be exposed to real, specific and serious risks which could not be countered by less restrictive means (*Albore* (case C–423/98)).

17.4.1.3 *Impact on establishment*

Restrictions may result in restrictions on the right of establishment and must therefore be compatible with those provisions (Article 58(2)). (See, eg, *Algemene Maatschappij voor Investering* (case C–141/99).) The relationship between establishment and capital is discussed at 17.5 below.

17.4.1.4 *Interpreting the derogations*

As the ECJ noted in the *Church of Scientology* case (case C–54/99) derogations from the fundamental principle of the free movement of capital must be interpreted strictly. Their scope cannot be determined unilaterally by individual Member States without any supervision by Community institutions. Note, however, that should the Lisbon Treaty come into force Article 58 (Article 65 TFEU) will have a new paragraph added to it, the effect of which is to give the Council the power to adopt a decision stating that restrictive tax measures adopted by a Member State concerning one or more third countries are to be considered compatible with the treaties in so far as they are justified by one of the objectives of the Union and compatible with the proper functioning of the internal market. This is limited in that, the Council may only make such a decision in the absence of action on the matter by the Commission and the Council must act unanimously. Nonetheless, it seems indicative of a tightening-up of the approach towards third countries. In any event, any rule falling within any of the above exceptions cannot constitute a means of arbitrary discrimination or disguised restriction on the free movement of capital or payments (Article 58(3)). The ECJ has reaffirmed that derogations cannot be applied so as to serve purely economic ends (see also *Portuguese Golden Shares* case (case C–367/98)). As with the other exceptions to treaty freedoms, it would seem that the crucial question will be proportionality of the Member State's measure, whether the Member State is seeking to justify its measure under express treaty derogations or in relation to a rule of reason-style argument. More unusually, the ECJ in the *Church of Scientology* case made two more points about the use of derogations. Any person affected by such a restrictive measure had to have access to legal redress: in this, the ECJ is reflecting the general approach to right to a remedy found in Union law (see further Chapters 6 and 8). Additionally, such a person had to be 'apprised of the extent of their rights and obligations deriving from Article [56] of the Treaty' (para 22).

Again, this reflects a general principle of Union law. What is interesting is that it is only in respect of the free movement of capital that this point is made express.

17.4.1.5 *Non-Euro Member States*

For Member States which have not joined up to the Euro, there are two further provisions which may be relied on where there are balance of payment difficulties—Articles 119–20 EC. Although these empower such Member States to take unilateral action (subject only to veto or amendment by the Council acting by qualified majority), the protective measures must cause the least possible disturbance to the common market and must not be wider in scope than is strictly necessary.

17.4.2 **Rule of reason?**

There are more similarities with the other freedoms: Article 56 does not just catch those rules which discriminate directly against capital movements, it also catches rules which indirectly restrict capital movements. With a restriction-based test, it seems that Member States may be able to rely on grounds of overriding public interest to justify a national measure. In *Reisch* (joined cases C–515, 519–40/99), the Court, referring to its previous case law in *Konle* (case C–302/97), summarised the position as follows:

> It is not in dispute that those measures, by laying down a procedure of prior notification/ authorisation for the acquisition of immovable property, restrict, by their very purpose, the free movement of capital. [See, to that effect, *Konle*, cited above, para 39.]
>
> Such restrictions may nevertheless be permitted if the national rules pursue, in a non-discriminatory way, an objective in the public interest and if they observe the principle of proportionality, that is if the same result could not be achieved by other less restrictive measures. [Paras 32–3.]

This point was re-emphasised in the *Golden Shares* cases (*Commission v UK* (C–98/01), and *Commission v Spain* (C–436/00); see also *Communication of the Commission on Certain Legal Aspect Concerning intra-EU Investment* ([1997] OJ C220/15)). As with the other freedoms, the list of possible public interest justifications, by contrast with the exceptions in Article 58, is open-ended. Thus in *Konle*, town-and-country planning was accepted as an appropriate overriding requirement in the general interest; similarly, environmental protection and land management concerns have been recognised (*Reisch* (joined cases C–515, 519–40/99)); and the *Golden Shares* cases (*Commission v UK* (case C–98/01), and *Commission v Spain* (case C–436/06)) recognised the importance of undertakings which are involved in the provision of services in the public interest.

There is some lack of clarity around the consequence of whether a national rule is discriminatory or not. In the *Portuguese Golden Shares* case (case C–367/98), the ECJ reiterated the position that overriding requirements of the general interest may be used in relation to rules 'which are applicable to all persons and undertakings pursuing an activity in the territory of the host Member State'; in this it is following the approach already identified in *Reisch* (joined cases C–515, 519–40/99). Nonetheless, in some cases the ECJ has accepted the principle on an overriding reason in the general interest although the rule has been characterised as discriminatory. See, for example, *Svensson and Gustavvson* (case C–484/93), which, at paras 16–19, contains a discussion of overriding reasons in the general interest despite the fact that the ECJ had held, in para 15 of the same judgment, that there had been discrimination because the rule was based on the place of establishment and that the rule could therefore only be justified by reference to the grounds of derogation set out expressly in the treaty.

As with the express treaty derogation, and in common with the other freedoms, any Member State measure must satisfy the test of proportionality. As the ECJ phrased this in *Reisch* (joined cases C–515, 519–40/99), proportionality requires that 'the same result could not be achieved by other less restrictive measures'. In practice it seems that this is a hard test to satisfy: in many cases the requirement of prior authorisation has not been found to be proportionate. It seems that the ECJ is more likely to find a requirement to make a declaration acceptable (see, eg, *Bordessa* (cases C–358 and 416/93). The ECJ did accept in the Portuguese *Golden Shares* case (case C–367/98) that in some instances prior authorisation might be necessary (here the provision of services in the public interest or strategic services), but even then any such system must be proportionate and use non-discriminatory criteria which would be known in advance to the relevant undertakings. Further, all persons affected by a restrictive measure had to have a legal remedy available to them. On the facts of the case, the Portuguese government was unsuccessful.

17.5 Relationship with other freedoms

The precise scope of these provisions is not clear: some have suggested that the free movement of capital is ancillary to the other freedoms, for example goods or establishment. Certainly, those provisions may be seen as dependent on the freedom of payments—there would be little incentive to export goods, for example, were it not possible to repatriate the value of those costs. Equally clearly, there is a potential for overlap between the provisions, as the provisions relating to tax harmonisation and the harmonisation of the market for financial services illustrate (see directives on insurance and banking). See also the discussion in cases such as *Trummer v Mayer* (case C–222/97) (national prohibition on the creation of a mortgage in a foreign currency), *Svensson and Gustavvson* (case C–484/98), *Safir v Skattemyndigheten i Dalamas Lan* (case C–118/96) (taxation of savings where a different tax regime applied according to where the insurance company providing savings scheme was established) and *Konle v Austria* (case C–302/97) (authorisation required for acquiring immovable property).

It is not entirely clear whether the capital provisions may be applied in tandem with the provisions relating to establishment or those concerning services. The wording of the treaty with regard to Article 49 would suggest that it, at least, applies when other freedoms do not. It would seem, however, that in some cases the ECJ has not clearly differentiated the different fields of application for the two provisions, as can be seen, for example, in, *Safir* (case C–118/96). The Advocates-General in *Svensson and Gustavsson* (case C–484/93) and in *Safir* expressed unease with an approach which conflates services and capital. In *Safir*, the Advocate-General suggested that the boundary lay between a direct restriction on capital, which would fall to be considered under Article 56, and the situation where the restriction was indirect, which would be considered as affecting services. In its judgment, the ECJ merely remarked that it was unnecessary to consider the free movement of capital provisions; it is unclear whether this silence on the reasoning of the Advocate-General connotes agreement with his reasoning or not. More recently, in *Fidium Finanz v Bundesanstalt für Finanzdienstleistungsaufsicht* (case C–452/04, Grand Chamber), which involved a Swiss institution granting credit to people in Germany (via an Internet site), the ECJ state that Articles 49 and 56 EC 'were designed to regulate different situations and they each have their own field of application' (para 28). The ECJ then had to tackle the argument that the free movement of services would only apply when the other freedoms were inapplicable. It rejected that argument, holding:

Although in the definition of the notion of 'services' laid down in the first paragraph of Article 50 EC it is specified that the services 'are not governed by the provisions relating to freedom of movement for goods, capital and persons', that relates to the definition of that notion and does not establish any order of priority between the freedom to provide services and the other fundamental freedoms. The notion of 'services' covers services which are not governed by other freedoms, in order to ensure that all economic activity falls within the scope of the fundamental freedoms. [Para 32.]

The ECJ is here suggesting that there is a distinction between the definition of subject matter (services or establishment) and the decision whether or not to apply a particular rule., though it is unclear from the reasoning in the case how the definitional hierarchy was being applied. If a situation can be assessed by reference to services and capital, the ECJ held that in principle, only one provision should apply. It is then necessary to determine which provision, Article 49 or 56 EC, is relevant. In determining this question, the ECJ borrowed from its case law regarding the boundaries between other freedoms and suggested that where one freedom is secondary to the other, the ECJ would consider the primary freedom. Here, the ECJ held that the rules were primarily concerned with the freedom to provide services and that the impact on the free movement of capital was 'merely an inevitable consequence of the restriction imposed on the provision of services' (para 49).

It is implicit in *Fidium Finanz* that, potentially, both freedoms could apply at the same time. Indeed, this question had already arisen. In the *Italian Recruitment Agencies* case (case C–279/00), the Commission brought an action against Italy in respect of a requirement that undertakings providing temporary workers must lodge a guarantee with a credit establishment having its seat or a branch in Italy. The Commission argued that this rule violated both the freedom to provide services and the free movement of capital. The ECJ analysed this rule both from the perspective of the employment agencies and from that of the banks. The ECJ ruled that the provision was a restriction on capital movement as far as the employment agencies were concerned and a violation of the banks' freedom to provide services within Article 49. It has been suggested that given that there are two sets of circumstances arising from the same rule, there is not a concurrent application of the two freedoms—though arguably the real effect is the same as the concurrent application of such rules.

The ECJ had cause to consider the relationship between Article 43 and 56 in *Européenne et Luxembourgeoise d'investissements SA* (ELISA) *v Directeur général des impôts, Ministère public* (case C–451/05). The case concerned the imposition of a tax on immovable property in France held by a company in Luxembourg, although its effective centre of management was in France. The referring court was unsure whether the provision on establishment in Article 43 EC or those on capital in Article 56 EC relevant. It pointed out the link between Article 43 in that the right to establish oneself causes capital movements. The ECJ held that the purchase of immovable property constituted a capital movement within the scope of Article 56 EC. Whilst Article 43 implies the existence of a stable and continuous basis in the economic life of the host Member State, in order for Article 43 EC, 'it is generally necessary to have secured a permanent presence in the host Member State and, where immovable property is purchased and held, that that property should be actively managed' (para 64). Here, there was no evidence that the property was acquired as part of its business, nor that it was actively managed. Article 43 did not therefore apply.

17.6 Restrictions on free movement of capital between Member States and third countries

Although in principle free movement of capital between Member States and third countries is secured by Article 56 EC, the restrictions on free movement of capital set out in Article 58 apply equally to free movement as regards third countries. This is a less liberalised framework, however, than that relating to intra-Community movements as we have seen in relation to the interpretation of the derogation found in Article 58 EC. Additional restrictions may also apply:

(a) Article 56 does not apply to national measures existing on 31 December 1993—although the Council may act to remove such measures (Article 57; see 17.7 below). For recent Member States, a different date applies.

(b) In limited circumstances where serious difficulties in the operation of EMU arise, the Council may take short-term measures restricting capital movements to third countries (Article 59).

(c) In urgent cases, restrictions which form part of economic sanctions may be introduced (Article 60). Post Lisbon, these provisions will be moved, and reworded, to tie them in more clearly to the fight against terrorism. Note the scope of Union competence under Article 60 EC has been discussed in Chapter 3.

17.7 Power to legislate in the field of free movement of capital

Article 57(2) EC provides that the Council may, by qualified majority and following a proposal by the Commission, legislate on the free movement of capital to or from third countries. It identifies the categories of measure which can be taken. In *Kadi* (joined cases C–402 and C–415/05 P) which concerned measures implementing UN economic sanctions aimed at individuals by freezing their assets, the ECJ held that the restrictive measures imposed by the contested regulation did not fall within one of the categories of measures listed in that provision and that Article 57(2) could not therefore be the legal basis for that regulation. This indicates that the categories of measure listed in Article 57(2) EC are closed.

There appears to be some tension in this provision. On the one hand, the objective of such action has to be to endeavour to achieve the free movement of capital between Member States and third countries 'to the greatest extent possible'. Nonetheless, the same provision envisages the possibility of a 'step back in Community law' regarding the liberalisation of capital to or from third countries, although this is tempered somewhat by the requirement that any measure constituting a 'step back' must be adopted unanimously. Should Lisbon come in to force, the last sentence of current Art. 57(2) will be reworked and renumbered as Article 64(3) TFEU. It makes clear that unanimity is required in Council for a 'step back', but that the Parliament need only be consulted.

In contrast to the other freedoms, therefore, there is no all-encompassing competence to adopt legislation to facilitate the free movement of capital (and payments) between Member States. However, where the European legislator has deemed it necessary to adopt legislation dealing with the movement of capital between Member States, it has achieved this by relying on Article 95 EC (eg, Directive 97/5/EC on cross-border credit transfers [1997] OJ L43/25). For a discussion of the limits of Article 95, see Chapter 16.

17.8 Conclusions

Since 1992 and the TEU, the number of cases decided under the free movement of capital provisions has increased significantly, and the jurisprudence on this freedom has developed correspondingly. The ECJ seems to have been willing to borrow principles from the other freedoms and apply them to the capital case law, resulting in certain parallels between all the freedoms. The result is that the approach to the free movement of capital has been liberalised, with potentially far-reaching effects on Member States' internal policies, particularly their taxation systems, as recent cases show. Problem areas do remain, particularly with regard to the ECJ's approach to the relationship between the different freedoms. Despite the increasing parallelism, it must be recognised that certain provisions remain unique to the free movement of capital, and that there may be circumstances in which the difference between the freedoms remains important. Furthermore, the imposed liberalisation via the ECJ's interpretation of Article 56 EC with regard to the relationship of Member States with third countries seems to have given rise to concern in some Member States and it is, perhaps, as a response to this that we see Lisbon seeking to clarify some aspects of the Council's freedom to 'step back'. In any event, the current financial climate adds to the tension in this area.

FURTHER READING

Flynn, L, 'Coming of age: The Free Movement of Capital Case Law 1993–2002' (2002) 39 CML Rev 773–805.

Mitroyanni, J., 'Exploring the free movement of capital in direct taxation' (2005) 8(1) EC Tax Journal 1.

O'Brien, M, 'Company taxation, state aid and fundamental freedoms: Is the next step enhanced cooperation?' (2005) 30(2) EL Rev 209.

Oliver, P and Bache, J-P, 'Free movement of capital between the Member States: Recent developments' (1989) 26 CML Rev 61.

Peers, S, 'Free movement of capital: Learning lessons or slipping on spilt milk' in Barnard and Scott (eds) *The Law of the Single Market: Unpacking the premises* (Hart Publishing, 2002).

Usher, J, 'Capital movements and the treaty on European Union' (1992) 12 YEL 35.

Wattel, PJ, 'Red herrings in direct tax cases before the ECJ' (2004) 31(2), Legal Issues of Economic Integration 81–95.

18

Customs union

18.1 Introduction

As we have seen in Chapters 3 and 15, the main mechanism for attaining the Union's goals is through the creation of both the common market and the internal market. Central to the common market is the free movement of goods, which aims to ensure that imported goods are not disadvantaged by extra costs of whatever nature. The most obvious way in which extra costs can be imposed on imports is by subjecting them to additional duties, such as customs duties, or by imposing a separate (and disadvantageous) taxation system on them. There are a number of relevant provisions in the treaty to deal with this problem: notably Articles 23, 25, and 90 (post Lisbon, Articles 28, 30, and 110 TFEU respectively). The articles in the EC Treaty go further than prohibiting such charges; they aim to create a customs union, which requires all Member States take a common approach to the import of goods from third countries. The EC Treaty, therefore, contains provisions for a common customs tariff (CCT) (Articles 26–7 (ex 18–29; post Lisbon, Articles 31–2 TFEU)). Allied to these provisions are Articles 3(b) and 131–4 (ex 110–15; post Lisbon, Articles 206–7 TFEU) EC, which provide for the establishment of a common commercial policy towards third countries.

This chapter briefly discusses the provisions establishing the CCT, before considering the prohibition on customs duties and on discriminatory taxation. In doing so, several key points should be noted. First the prohibition on customs duties is one of the central features of the customs union. It has been interpreted broadly as a result, and any exceptions to the prohibition are strictly limited. The provisions on customs duties are linked to those on discriminatory taxation—the prohibition on discriminatory taxation serves to prevent Member States from circumventing the prohibition on customs duties by discriminating against imports via their internal taxation system. It is because of this link that the discriminatory taxation provisions are dealt with here, as part of the free movement of goods, despite the fact that within the treaty they are located in a separate section dealing with taxation. Despite their common function, in some ways the taxation provisions are more problematic than those relating to customs duties. Taxation in general still remains part of the Member States' competence; further, in determining the scope of 'similar' products, the European Court of Justice (ECJ) has a certain degree of interpretive freedom. Although Article 90 does not require Member States to adopt any particular system of taxation, the rulings of the ECJ under Article 90 have had an impact on Member States' policy choices. Article 90 jurisprudence is, to some degree, therefore contentious.

18.2 **Common customs tariff**

As part of its common commercial policy, and to ensure equal treatment in all Member States for goods imported into the EC from third countries, thereby enabling *all* goods in circulation within the Community to benefit equally from the free movement provisions, the treaty provided for the introduction of the CCT, sometimes known as the common external tariff (CET). The CCT applies to all products imported into the Community from outside the EC, erecting a single tariff wall which no individual State is free to breach. Lisbon describes this area as falling within exclusive Union competence.

The operation of the CCT is governed by Articles 26–7 EC and is enacted by directly applicable regulations. Should Lisbon comes into force, these articles will be renumbered as Articles 31–2 of the Treaty on the Functioning of the European Union (TFEU). Under the CCT, goods are classified according to a common nomenclature, and are subject to common Community rules as to value and origin. Products are divided into lists, the classifications being derived from the Brussels Convention on Nomenclature for the Classification of Goods. The lists, and the applicable tariff rates, are set out in Annex I to the EC Treaty. The CCT is published by the Commission and is regularly updated. The Council is empowered to alter or suspend duties within certain limits (Article 26 (ex 28)). Once goods are imported into the Union—that is, when they have complied with import formalities and paid the relevant customs duties, the free movement provisions of the treaty apply. Even where goods are imported into a Member State under a special tariff quota the ECJ has held that a state cannot deny the application of the free movement provisions to the import and export of such goods within the Union unless the Commission has, under Article 134 (ex 115) EC, authorised derogation in order to avoid a deflection of trade or economic difficulties in one or more Member States (see *Criel, nee Donckerwolcke* (case 41/76)). This provision would be deleted by Lisbon.

The Commission, subject to the Council's approval, has a central role in establishing and administering the CCT. In carrying out its task it is required to balance a number of (often conflicting) economic needs set out in Article 27 (ex 29), in the light of the general aims of the Union. Although the Commission has an important role in the administration of the CCT, there is no such body as a Union customs service. The Union is dependent on the customs officers of the various Member States to implement the CCT. Duties raised under the CCT are payable to the Community and form part of its 'own resources'. Under Article 135 EC, the institutions may enact measures to strengthen the cooperation between Member States in this regard and between the Member States and the Commission; should Lisbon come into force this provision will be Article 33 TFEU.

18.3 **Prohibition between Member States of customs duties on imports and exports and of all charges of equivalent effect**

This area is governed by Articles 23 and 25 EC. Article 23 establishes the customs union and Article 25 is the mechanism whereby this is achieved, as it prohibits between Member States any customs duties.

Article 23 states:

> 1. The Community shall be based upon a customs union which shall cover all trade in goods and which shall involve the prohibition between Member States of customs duties on imports and exports and of all charges having equivalent effect, and the adoption of a common customs tariff in the relations with third countries.
> 2. The provisions of Article 25 and of Chapter 2 of the Title shall apply to products originating in Member States and to products coming from third countries which are in free circulation in Member States.

Article 25 specifies:

> Customs duties on imports and exports and charges having equivalent effect shall be prohibited between Member States. This prohibition shall also apply to customs duties of a fiscal nature.

If Lisbon comes into force Articles 23 and 25 EC shall be renumbered (somewhat confusingly) Articles 28 and 30 TFEU.

18.3.1 Scope of the prohibition

The prohibition applies to all duties, whether applied directly or indirectly. In *Van Gend en Loos* (case 26/62) the product in question had been reclassified under Dutch law, with the result that it became subject to a higher rate of duty. The ECJ held that this would constitute a breach of what is now Article 25.

Article 25 has also been held to apply to a charge on imports and exports into a *region* of a Member State, not only insofar as it is levied on goods entering that region from other Member States, but also when it is levied on goods entering that region from another part of the same state (*Simitzi v Kos* (cases C–485 and 86/93), *ad valorem* municipality tax imposed on imports into and exports from the Dodecanese (Greece)). This obligation was held to derive from the 'absolute nature' of the prohibition of all customs duties applicable to goods moving between Member States and emphasises the single nature of the European market. This approach also applies to additional charges levied on goods imported into a region which originated from a third country (*Société Cadi Surgélés v Ministre des Finances* (case C–126/94)), and to charges levied on goods *exported* from a region, irrespective of whether their final destination is within the same Member State, or abroad (*Carbonati Apuani Srol v Comune di Carrara* (case C–72/03)).

If the meaning of 'custom duties' is clear, what are 'charges having equivalent effect' to a customs duty? It was held by the ECJ in the case of *Sociaal Fonds voor de Diamantarbeiders* (cases 2 and 3/69), in the context of a challenge to a 'tax' imposed on imported diamonds, that it included any pecuniary charge, however slight, imposed on goods by reason of the fact that they cross frontiers. The charge need not be levied at the frontier; it can be imposed at any stage of production or marketing; but provided it is levied *by reason of importation* it will breach Article 25 (*Steinike und Weinlig v Germany* (case 78/76)). This then is a key element to determine a charge falling within Article 25: the question of whether the charge is triggered by the crossing of a frontier.

18.3.2 **Distinction between customs duties and taxes**

A charge of equivalent effect to a customs duty may come in many guises, and is often disguised as a 'tax'. Since genuine taxes fall to be considered under Article 90 EC, it is necessary at the outset to distinguish between a charge, falling within Article 25, and a genuine tax. A genuine tax was defined in *Commission v France (Re Levy on Reprographic Machines)* (case 90/79) as one relating 'to a general system of internal dues applied systematically to categories of products in accordance with objective criteria irrespective of the origin of the products'.

To ascertain whether a 'tax' is genuine it must be examined to see whether it fits into an overall system of taxation or whether it has been superimposed on the system with a particular purpose in mind. Provided the tax is genuine, it may be imposed on imports even where the importing state produces no identical or similar product (*Commission v France*). In such a case it will not breach Article 25 but may be examined for its compatibility with Article 90 (see further below).

18.3.3 **An effects-based test**

To breach Article 25, a charge need not be introduced for protectionist reasons. It was pointed out in the *Sociaal Fonds* case that no diamond-mining industry existed in Belgium, and the proceeds of the charge were used for a most worthy purpose, to provide a social fund for workers in the diamond industry. These factors were held by the ECJ to be irrelevant. Such duties are forbidden independently of the purpose for which they are levied and the destination of the charge. In reaching its decision the Court looked at the effect of the measure: any pecuniary charge imposed on goods by reason of the fact that they cross frontiers is an obstacle to the free movement of goods.

A similar conclusion was reached by the ECJ in *Commission v Luxembourg (Re Import on Gingerbread)* (cases 2 and 3/62) in the context of a compensatory 'tax' on imported gingerbread. The governments claimed the 'tax' was introduced merely to compensate for the competitive disadvantage resulting from a high rate of domestic tax on rye, an ingredient of gingerbread. The purpose of the prohibition on measures of equivalent effect to customs duties, the Court held, was to prohibit not only measures ostensibly clothed with the classic nature of a customs duty but also those which, presented under other names or introduced by the indirect means of other procedures, would lead to the same discriminatory or protective *results* as customs duties. If compensatory 'taxes' of this type were allowed, states would be able to make up for all sorts of taxes at home by imposing a so-called balancing charge on imports. This would ensure that imported goods would lose any competitive advantage they might have as against the equivalent domestic product and thereby frustrate the objectives of the single market.

18.3.4 **Limitations on the prohibition**

Even when the charge is levied to benefit the importer, it may still breach Article 25. In *Commission v Italy (Re Statistical Levy)* (case 24/68) a levy, applied to all imports and exports, regardless of source, the proceeds of which were used to finance an export statistical service for the benefit of importers and exporters, was found to be in breach of Articles 23–5 EC. The ECJ held that the advantage to importers was so general and uncertain that it could not be considered a payment for service rendered (see also *W Cadsky SpA* (case 63/74), in relation to charges on the *export* of goods).

This implies that a charge levied for a service rendered to the importer and which is *not* too general and uncertain would be permissible. This principle has, however, been given the narrowest possible scope. The ECJ has held that where an inspection service is imposed in the general interest, for example for health or safety purposes or quality control, this cannot be regarded as a service rendered to the importer or exporter to justify the imposition of a charge (*Rewe-Zentralfinanz eGmbH v Landwirtschaftskammer Westfalen-Lippe* (case 39/73)). This principle applies regardless of the nature of the agency, public or private, providing the service, and whether or not the charge is borne by virtue of a unilateral measure adopted by the authorities or as a result of a series of private contracts (*Édouard Dubois et Fils SA v Garonor Exploitation SA* (case C–16/94)). Even when such inspections are expressly *permitted* under EU law, as in *Commission v Belgium (Re Health Inspection Service)* (case 314/82), the Court held that a charge for such a service cannot be regarded as a service rendered for the benefit of the importer. It is only when such services are mandatory, as part of a common Union regime, or arising from an international agreement into which the EU has entered (*Bakker Hillegom* (case C–111/89)), that Member States are entitled to recover the cost, and no more than the cost, of the service (*Bauhuis v Netherlands* (case 46/76)).

Unless a service is required under Union law, it appears that only a service which gives a tangible benefit to the importer, or the imported goods, for example a finishing or packaging service, will be regarded as sufficient to justify a charge, and even then it will not be permissible if the 'service' is one imposed on the importer in the general interest. Where a genuine service is provided for the benefit of the importer the ECJ has held that the charge must not exceed the value or the cost of the service (*Rewe-Zentralfinanz eGmbH* (case 39/73)), or a sum proportionate to the service provided (*Commission v Denmark* (case 158/82)). A charge based on the value of the goods is not permissible (*Ford España SA v Spain* (case 170/88)). In *Donner* (case 39/82) the Court suggested that a charge by the Dutch Post Office for dealing with the payment of VAT on imported books on behalf of the claimant might be regarded as a payment for services rendered but left the national court to decide whether on the facts it was and, if so, whether it was proportionate.

Where a charge is imposed only upon domestically produced goods, the ECJ appears to take a more lenient view. In *Apple & Pear Development Council v KJ Lewis Ltd* (case 222/82) a number of growers challenged a compulsory levy imposed on growers of apples and pears in the UK. The proceeds of the levy went to finance the Apple and Pear Development Council, a semi-public body whose functions included research, the compilation of statistics, provision of information, publicity, and promotion. The ECJ held that since the levy did not apply to imported products there was no breach of Articles 23–5. The charge would only be illegal if it served to finance activities which were incompatible with EU law.

18.3.5 Non-discriminatory charges

All the cases considered so far have concerned unilateral charges, charges imposed only upon imported or exported products and not on the comparable domestic product (or vice versa). Clearly such charges undermine the principle of free trade and free competition within the common market and discriminate against imported products. What about a non-discriminatory charge, applied to a particular product regardless of source? Will this be capable of infringing Article 25 EC? This calls for a more subtle enquiry into:

(a) the nature of the charge and its mode of calculation

(b) the destination of the charge, ie, who receives the benefit.

Three situations may be considered:

(a) If the charge is identical in every respect and levied as part of a general system of taxation it will not fall within Article 25 and will be treated as a fiscal measure, and examined for its compatibility with Article 90 (prohibition on discriminatory taxation).

(b) If the same charge is levied on a particular product, regardless of source, it will nonetheless breach Article 25 if the charge on the imported or exported product is not imposed in the same way and determined according to the same criteria as apply to the domestic product. This point was made by the ECJ in *Marimex SpA v Italian Minister of Finance (No 2)* (case 29/72) in the context of a challenge to a 'veterinary inspection tax' imposed on imported meat, live and dead, to ensure that it conformed to Italian health standards. Similar domestic products were subject to corresponding inspections which were also 'taxed', but they were conducted by different bodies according to different criteria. The ECJ held that such a tax on imports would be in breach of the then Article 9 (now 23).

(c) Even if the charge is levied at the same rate and according to identical criteria it may still breach Articles 23 and 25 if the proceeds of the charge are applied to benefit the domestic product *exclusively*. This point was first made in *Capolongo v Azienda Agricola Maya* (case 77/72). In this case the Italians had introduced a charge on imported egg boxes, as part of an overall charge on cellulose products, the aim being to finance the production of paper and cardboard in Italy. Although the charge was imposed on all egg boxes, domestic and imported, the Court held it was in breach of the then Article 13 (deleted by the Treaty of Amsterdsam (ToA)). Although applied to domestic and imported goods alike, it was discriminatory if it was intended exclusively to support activities which specifically benefited the domestic product.

The scope of *Capolongo* was restricted in the subsequent case of *Fratelli Cucchi v Avez SpA* (case 77/76). Here a dispute arose concerning the legality of a levy on imported sugar. Domestically produced sugar was subject to the same levy. The proceeds of the levy went to finance the sugar industry, to benefit two groups: the beet producers and the sugar-processing industry. The ECJ held that such a charge would be of equivalent effect to a customs duty if three conditions were fulfilled:

(a) if it has the *sole* purpose of financing activities for the specific advantage of the domestic product

(b) if the taxed domestic product and the domestic product to benefit are the same

(c) if the charges imposed on the domestic product are made up *in full*.

If these conditions are not fulfilled the charge will not breach Article 25 EC. However, where the same tax, levied on domestic and imported products alike, gives only *partial* benefit to the domestic product, it may be deemed a discriminatory tax, in breach of Article 90 EC (*Commission v Italy* (*Re Reimbursement of Sugar Storage Costs*) (case 73/79); *Cooperative Co-Frutta* (case 193/85)). A grant to a particular industry may be adjudged a state aid in breach of Article 87 (ex 92) EC (see chapter 31).

18.3.6 Derogation from prohibition on customs duties

The rules concerning charges of equivalent effect to a customs duty are strictly applied by the ECJ. Indeed, in its anxiety to ensure that no pecuniary restriction, however small, shall create obstacles to trade, particularly to imports, the Court is even prepared to countenance a degree of reverse discrimination, since Member States are required themselves to finance measures such as health inspections which may be fully justified in the public interest (see *Rewe-Zentralfinanz eGmbH* (case 39/73)). Nor does the treaty or the Court provide for any derogation in this field. In *Commission v Italy (Re Export Tax on Art Treasures)* (case 7/68) the Italians argued that the tax was justified to protect their artistic heritage. Under Article 30 (ex 36) states are entitled to derogate from the prohibition on imposing quantitative restrictions on imports (Article 28 EC) or exports (Article 29 EC), or measures of equivalent effect, on the grounds of inter alia, 'the protection of national treasures possessing artistic, historic or archaeological value'. The Court held that the then Article 36 (now 30) could never be invoked to justify a charge (see also *Marimex SpA* (case 29/72)).

The only way for a Member State to defend a charge is to argue that:

(a) it does not fall within the definition of customs duty by virtue of it being part of an internal system of taxation, in which case it will be assessed by reference to Article 90

(b) it is required by Community law in accordance with the principles in *Bauhuis* (case 46/76) (see 18.3.4 above)

(c) it is actually a service for payment rendered (see *Statistical Levy case* and 18.3.4 above).

18.3.7 Enforcing Article 25

Since Article 25 is directly effective, any sums paid under an illegal charge are recoverable. This might, in certain circumstances, require the relevant domestic bodies to reconsider a previous decision once it has become clear that charges should not have been made (*Kühne & Heitz NV v Productschap voor Pluimvee and Eieren* (case C–453/00)). Although repayment must be sought within the framework, and according to the rules, of national law, conditions must not be so framed as to render it excessively difficult or impossible in practice to exercise the rights conferred by Community law (*SpA San Giorgio* (case 199/82), see further Chapter 8). The principle of unjust enrichment may be invoked to deny a claim for repayment where the charge has been incorporated into the price of goods and passed on to purchasers (*SpA San Giorgio, Weber's Wine World* (case C–147/01)). However, national authorities may not impose the burden of proving that a charge has *not* been passed on to those persons seeking reimbursement, nor may restrictive or onerous evidential requirements (such as documentary evidence alone) be imposed. Member States are not entitled to presume that illegal taxes have been passed on (*Commission v Italy Re Repayment of Illegal Taxes* (case 104/86)). In *Just v Danish Ministry for Fiscal Affairs* (case 68/79), in a claim based on Article 90, the Court held that national courts may take into account damage suffered by the person liable to pay the charge by reason of the restrictive effect of the charge on imports from other Member States. This principle should also apply to damage suffered as a result of a charge in breach of Article 25 EC.

18.4 Prohibition of discriminatory taxation

18.4.1 Meaning of taxation

As noted above, the Court draws a distinction between a charge having equivalent effect to a customs duty and a genuine tax. A genuine tax is a measure relating to a system of internal dues applied systematically to categories of products in accordance with objective criteria irrespective of the origin of the products (*Commission v France (Re Levy on Reprographic Machines)* (case 90/79)). Even what may appear a genuine tax may be treated as a charge if it is earmarked to benefit only the domestic product subject to the tax (see *Fratelli Cucchi v Avez SpA* (case 77/76)). However, the fact that it is levied by a body other than the state, or is collected for its own benefit and is a charge which is special or appropriate for a specific purpose, cannot prevent it from falling within the field of application of Article 90 (*Ianelli & Volpi v Meroni* (case 74/76)).

The line between a charge and a genuine tax may be hard to draw and may turn on slight differences in the facts. In *Essent* (case C–206/06), charges imposed on both domestic and imported products were offset as regard the domestic product. The ECJ noted that if the entire burden was offset, the matter fell to be determined under Article 25 whereas if the burden was only partially offset, then the case fell within Article 90 EC. The Court has held (*Fratelli Cucchi v Avez SpA*) that the prohibition of customs duties and charges having equivalent effect and of discriminatory internal taxation are mutually exclusive, it is safer in case of doubt to invoke both Article 25 and Article 90 and leave the Court to define the boundaries.

18.4.2 Scope of Article 90

A 'genuine' tax must comply with Article 90. This provision will be renumbered Article 110 TFEU should the Lisbon Treaty come into force, but will otherwise remain unchanged. It provides that:

> No Member State shall impose, directly or indirectly, on the products of other Member States any internal taxation of any kind in excess of that imposed directly or indirectly on similar domestic products.
>
> Furthermore, no Member State shall impose on the products of other Member States any internal taxation of such a nature as to afford indirect protection to other products.

While states are free to decide on the rate of taxation to be applied to a particular product and discriminate between different types of product (for example
Outokumpu Oy (case C–213/96), different sources of fuel), subject to certain overriding provisions of EU law (see further below), they are not free to apply rates which
discriminate, directly or indirectly, as between domestic and imported products
which are similar or which afford indirect protection to the former. To do so would
give a competitive advantage to the less highly taxed product and thereby distort
competition within the single market. As the Court has held in a number of cases, a
Member State's internal taxation system will be compatible with the requirements
of Article 90 only if it is shown to be structured so as to exclude any possibility of
having a discriminatory effect (see, eg, *Haahr Petroleum Ltd v Åbenrå Havn* (case
C–90/94), para 34).

There are a number of aspects to Article 90. First, the issue of discriminatory
taxation is clearly central to any discussion (see 17.4.3). Secondly, the meaning of
'products from other Member States' must be understood. This is discussed in more
detail at 17.4.4. Finally, note also that Article 90 contains two prohibitions:

(a) Article 90(1) which deals with 'similar' products
(b) Article 90(2) which concerns goods which, although not exactly similar,
     are still in competition with each other.

The difference between the two provisions may be slight and therefore difficult to
identify with precision. Indeed, in early case law the ECJ did not always bother to
distinguish between Article 90(1) and (2), holding that Article 90 could be applied
as a whole (see, eg, *Commission v France (Spirits)* (case 168/78), para 13). The problem
of adopting a 'global' approach to Article 90 is that it blurs the distinction between
paragraphs (1) and (2) in terms of the consequences of a finding of a violation for
Member States. A Member State is obliged to *equalise* the taxes on domestic and
imported products when the Court has found a violation of Article 90(1). In contrast, when there has been a violation of Article 90(2), the Member State is required
to remove the protective effect of the offending national rules. Such a requirement
does not necessarily entail equalisation of the tax burdens on the goods in question;
ie, the tax on imported products need not be identical to that on domestic products.
It seems that in later cases the ECJ has made greater efforts to distinguish between
Article 90(1) and (2). In the *John Walker* case (case 243/84), concerning whether liqueur fruit wine was comparable to whisky, the ECJ found that the two products
were not 'similar' for the purposes of Article 90(1), therefore the national rules
would be assessed by reference to Article 90(2). The notion of similarity is discussed
further at 18.4.5 below.

18.4.3 Discriminatory measures

A measure will be indirectly discriminatory if, although applicable to all goods,
regardless of origin, it falls more heavily on the imported product. For example
in *Humblot v Directeur des Services Fiscaux* (case 112/84) a French car tax, calculated according to the power rating of the car, which imposed a disproportionately
heavy burden on the more powerful cars, *all of which were imported*, was found to
breach Article 90. There was no apparent justification for the excessive difference
between the rates charged on the different categories of car. It should be noted that

a taxation system should not be discriminatory '*solely* because *only* imported products, in particular those from other Member States, come within the most highly taxed category' (Case 132/88 *Commission v Greece*, para 18, emphasis added).

Differentiating between products on objective grounds, which is permissible, can lead to imports and domestic products being treated differently because of the specific characteristics of the two categories of goods. Objective grounds for differentiation in treatment are considered at 18.4.6 below.

The Court has held that internal tax may be imposed on imported products even if there is no domestic production of a similar or competing product as long as it applies to the product as a class, irrespective of origin (*Fink-Frucht GmbH* (case 27/67), applied in *Commission v France* (case 90/79)). The Court has suggested that if in such a case the 'tax' is set at such a level as to compromise the free circulation of trade within the Union, it cannot be deemed part of a general system of taxation (*Commission v Denmark* (case 47/88)). It may, however, fall within other provisions of the treaty.

In assessing the question of discrimination, it is necessary to take into account not only the rate of direct and indirect internal taxation on domestic and imported products, but also the basis of assessment and the detailed rules for its collection. Where differences result in the imported product being taxed, *at the same stage of production or marketing*, more heavily than the similar domestic product, Article 90 is infringed (*Ianelli & Volpi v Meroni*). It may also be necessary to have regard to taxation levied at earlier stages of manufacture and marketing, particularly to ensure that goods are not taxed twice (*FOR v VKS* (case 54/72)). The Court insists on strict equality, rather than broad equivalence, to ensure 'transparency'. It has even applied Article 90 to penalties. In *Commission v France* (case 276/91) a provision of the French customs code, which provided for more severe penalties for VAT offences in relation to imported goods than for similar offences related to domestic transactions, was found to breach Article 90. Although some difference in treatment might be justified for administrative reasons, in that VAT offences committed outside the importing state were not as easily discoverable as those committed in the home state, this could not justify a manifest disproportion in the severity of the two categories of offences. It has been suggested that this decision, no doubt correct as to its result, would have been better based on Article 28, or Article 12, the general prohibition of discrimination on the grounds of nationality.

18.4.4 Products from other Member States

Although Article 90 is expressed as applying to the 'products of other Member States', the Court has held (*Cooperative Co-Frutta SLR v Amministrazione delle Finanze dello Stato* (case 193/85)), arguing from *Criel, nee Donckerwolcke v Procureur de la République* (case 41/76), that the prohibition of discriminatory taxation must apply, by analogy with the free movement of goods provisions, to goods from third countries in free circulation within the Member States. Similarly, although the reference to 'products of other Member States' would seem to imply that Article 90 only applies to taxes which discriminate against imports, the Court has held that in order to guarantee the neutrality of national systems of taxation, Article 90 will also apply to exports (*Statenskontrol v Larsen* (case 142/77)).

In *Stadtgemeinde Frohnleiten, Gemeindebetriebe Frohnleiten GmbH v Bundesminister für Land und Forstwirtschaft, Umwelt und Wasserwirtschaft* (case C–221/06), the

Austrian government tried to argue that the charge on the tipping of waste products did not fall within Article 90 because the charge imposed pertained to a service. The ECJ rejected this argument: Article 90 applies to internal taxation which is imposed on the use of imported products where those products are essentially intended for such use and have been imported solely for that purpose. Further, if the levy is imposed on the only use to which the items can be put, then charges on that activity fall within Article 90 EC.

18.4.5 'Similar' products

It is clear that products need not be identical to fall within Article 90. What then is a 'similar' product? In the course of a number of judgments, mostly infringement proceedings against Member States under Article 226 (ex 169) EC (post Lisbon 263 TFEU) (see Chapter 11), in respect of allegedly discriminatory taxation of alcoholic drinks (eg, *Commission v France (Spirits)* (case 168/78)), the Court has held that 'similar' must be interpreted widely. In assessing the question of similarity, classification of the product under the same heading in the CCT will weigh heavily, but it is not conclusive. The important factor is whether the products:

> have similar characteristics and meet the same needs from the point of view of consumers . . . not according to whether they are strictly identical but whether their use is similar or comparable. [*Commission v Denmark* (case 106/84).]

The concept of similarity is thus analogous to that of the relevant product market in EC competition law (see Chapter 29).

To decide if the products meet the same consumer needs the Court has held (*Commission v UK (Re Excise Duties on Wine)* (case 170/78)) that it is necessary to look not only at the present state of the market but also at possible developments—ie, the possibility of substituting one product for another. Taxation policy must not be allowed to crystallise consumer habits. In *Commission v Italy (Bananas)* (case 184/85), the ECJ had to determine whether bananas were 'similar' fruit for the purposes of Article 90(1). In making its assessment, the Court took into account the objective characteristics of bananas and other fruit, including the extent to which they could satisfy the same consumer need. In this case, the ECJ held that bananas were not similar to other fruit (although the national rules in the issue might fall within Article 90(2)).

18.4.6 Objective grounds for differentiation

Different rates of taxation may, however, be applied to what appear to be 'similar' products provided they are based on objective criteria, designed to achieve economic policy objectives which are compatible with EC law, and are applied in such a way as to avoid discrimination against imports or afford indirect protection to domestic products. This reasoning was applied in *Commission v France* (case 196/85) in the context of infringement proceedings for a system of differential taxation in which certain wines known as natural sweet wines or liqueur wines, production of which is 'traditional or customary', attracted more favourable tax rates than ordinary wine. The purpose of the special rate was to bolster the economy in areas largely dependent on the production of these wines, to compensate for the relatively rigorous conditions under which they are produced. The Court found the economic policy objectives pursued by the French to be justified. Such rules, it said, may not be regarded as contrary to Union law merely because they may be applied in a discriminatory manner if it is not proved that they have in fact been applied in such a manner. Clearly in this case it felt that neither discrimination nor protectionist motives had been proved (see also *Chemial Farmaceutici SpA v DAF SpA* (case 140/79)). Where a system involving different rates of taxation, although prima facie objectively justified, in effect discriminates against the imported product or affords indirect protection to domestic products, it will not be permissible (*Bobie v HZA Aachen Nord* (case 127/75)). This principle can be seen in operation in *Commission v Greece* (case C–375/95), which concerned a Greek rule which provided that a reduced rate of tax would apply to cars using 'anti-pollution' technology. According to the Greek government, this reduced rate was not available to imports because the testing of each import to verify that it satisfied the relevant criteria was not practicable. The ECJ responded that such consideration could not justify discriminatory taxation (see also *Outokumpu Oy* (case C–213/96) and *Stadtgemeinde Frohnleiten, Gemeinde betriebe Frohnleiten GmbH v Bundesminister für Land und Forstwirtschaft, Umwelt und Wasserwirtschaft* (case C–221/06)). Reverse discrimination on the other hand will be permitted (*Peureux v Directeur des Services Fiscaux* (case 86/78)).

18.4.7 Taxation affording indirect protection to domestic products

Internal taxation will be contrary to Article 90 if it affords indirect protection to domestic products. Article 90(2) is intended to cover 'all forms of indirect tax protection in the case of products which, without being similar within the meaning of Article 95(1) (now 90(1)), are nevertheless in competition, even partial, indirect or potential competition, with each other' (*Cooperative Co-Frutta SRL* (case 193/85)). It is wider than Article 90(1), and wider than the concept of the relevant product market in EC competition law. This may be demonstrated by comparing *Cooperative Co-Frutta* with the case of *United Brands v Commission* (case 27/76, see Chapter 29). In *Co-Frutta* a consumer tax, imposed on both domestic and imported bananas but which in practice applied almost exclusively to imported products (domestic production being extremely small), and which was not applied to other fresh (principally home-produced) fruit was found to afford indirect protection to domestic production, in breach of Article 90(2). In *United Brands*, on the other hand, bananas were found to constitute a separate product market; the relevant product market did not include other fresh fruit. Clearly a more generous approach to the question of competition is justified in the context of Article 90(2), to safeguard the Community against fiscal protectionism on the part of Member States.

Since Article 90(2) does not depend on 'similarity' between the domestic and imported products, it will be necessary, in a claim based on this article, to demonstrate that the domestic and imported products, while not being similar, are in fact in competition with each other, and that the effect of the impugned tax regime is to afford indirect protection to the domestic product (*Commission v UK* (case 170/78)). This is the case concerning British rules which subjected some wines to a rate of taxation approximately five times that applied to beer. In determining whether wine and beer were in fact in competition with each other, the Court held that 'to a certain extent at least, the two beverages were capable of meeting identical needs' (para 8). It would seem that product substitutability is the basis on which the ECJ will determine whether products are in competition. Further, as seems to be the case for determining similarity, consumer preferences will not be determinative because they are 'essentially variable in time and space' (para 8).

Once it has been determined that certain products are in competition, the next question is whether there is a 'protective effect'. In *Commission v Belgium* (case 356/85), national rules were in issue. Wine, an imported product, was taxed at 25 per cent, whereas beer, a domestic product, was taxed at 19 per cent. The ECJ rejected the argument that the legislation provided a protective effect in favour of beer. The Court based its reasoning on the insignificant impact of the difference in tax rates on price. The Court's approach in this case did not require complex market analysis but seems, rather, to have depended on a common-sense assessment of the impact of the tax differential. On the other side of the coin, the Court has taken an equally common-sense view of whether there is likely to be an impact, rather than requiring a detailed statistical analysis of the point. Statistics have, however, been used to show that apparently neutral rules do in fact discriminate.

18.5 Harmonisation of indirect taxation

Although the Community has the power to harmonise laws relating to indirect taxation to the extent that it is necessary to ensure the establishment and functioning of the internal market (Articles 93–4 (ex 99–100)) and has made considerable progress in this area in the case of VAT, excise duties and corporation tax, Member States have understandably been reluctant to cede competence to the Union outside these areas. Proposals to approximate rates of indirect taxation within broad tax bands, introduced under the internal market programme, have not so far met with success. Since different tax regimes clearly have an adverse impact on the functioning of the internal market by distorting the 'normal' flow of trade and competition within the Union the Commission has expressed its intention to continue to seek progress in this area. However, since fiscal measures remain subject to a requirement of unanimity, as an exception to the principle of qualified majority voting introduced by Article 95 EC, which remains even after Nice, it is likely that progress will be slow; a position unlikely to change under the Lisbon Treaty. This position may, of course, now change with the advent of the Euro. Indeed, a communication from the Commission to the Council European Parliament and ECOSOC on Tax Policy (COM (2001) 260 final) suggests that the Commission is attempting to move matters forward in this area. This can be seen in the consolidation of the existing regimes dealing with, for example, VAT (see Regulation 1777/2005). More contentions issues arise where direct taxation has an impact on other policies, as has been seen in cases involving the free movement of persons and the freedom to provide services. Taxation also has an impact in the context of other areas, such as employment, the environment, public health, not to mention monetary union, for all of which the Union has competence. Nonetheless, legislative progress may well be slow, given the sensitivity of the issues involved and the fact that the need for unanimity remains.

18.6 Conclusions

The creation of the customs union is one of the fundamental elements of the Union project. In view of this, the Court's broad interpretation of the relevant prohibitions is not surprising. Given the international-law trade context, in which overt protectionism is frowned on, the ECJ's approach to customs duties and measures having equivalence caused, in general, little comment. The provisions relating to taxation are the subject of greater discussion, touching as they do on an area of competence central to Member States' sovereignty. The breadth of some of the judgments has impinged on Member States' freedom to pursue other policy objectives, such as protection of the environment. It is somewhat ironic that increasingly, these objectives are recognised as worthy of a high level of protection by the treaty. A further irony for the Member States lies in the fact that, in failing to agree to harmonising legislation in all but limited fields of indirect taxation, they have effectively put the development of taxation policy in the hands of the ECJ. This may result in decisions that have a greater impact on national taxation policies than any harmonised legislation.

FURTHER READING

Barents, R, 'Recent case law on the prohibition of fiscal discrimination under Article 95' (1986) 23 CML Rev 641.

Danusso, M and Denton, R, 'Does the European Court of Justice look for a protectionist motive under Article 95?' (1991) 1 LIEI 67.

Easson, A, 'Fiscal discrimination: New perspectives on Article 95 of the EC Treaty' (1981) 18 CML Rev 521.

Grabitz, E and Zacher, C, 'Scope for action by Member States for the improvement of environmental protection under EEC law: The example of environmental taxes and subsidies' (1989) 26 CML Rev 423.

Schwartze, J, 'The Member States' discretionary powers under the tax provisions of the EEC Treaty' in J Schwartze (ed), *Discretionary Powers of the Member States in the Field of Economic Policies and their Limits under the EEC Treaty* (Baden-Baden: Nomos, 1988).

Tryfonidou, A, '*Carbonati Apuani Srl v Comune di Carrara*: Should we reverse "reverse discrimination"?' (2005) 16 King's College Law Journal 373–81.

19

Free movement of goods

19.1 Introduction

The rules relating to the abolition of measures having equivalent effect to quantitative restrictions have been central to the development of the single market. The abolition of customs duties and charges of equivalent effect and prohibition on discriminatory taxation would not have been sufficient to guarantee the free movement of goods within the common market. In addition to pecuniary restrictions, there are other barriers to trade of a non-pecuniary nature, usually in the form of administrative rules and practices, protectionist and otherwise, equally capable of hindering the free flow of goods from state to state. Articles 28–9 (ex 30–4) EC are designed to eliminate these barriers.

The significance of these rules is based on the breadth of the circumstances in which they can come into play. The prohibition on measures having equivalent effect do not apply just to rules that apply at the border, or which intend to discriminate against imports (or exports). They apply in a much wider ranger of circumstances, catching national rules that may have been enacted for legitimate, non-trade-related reasons, such as worker protection, consumer protection, or protection of the environment, and which apply to domestic goods as well as to imports or exports. Given the interplay between trade objectives and other policy aims, the central question is, 'Where does the proper scope of Article 28 end?' As we shall see below, this question has given rise to a considerable amount of case law and academic criticism. The issue is important as the scope of Articles 28–9 may limit the powers of each of the Member States to regulate matters that are not just trade-related. As a result, there is a tension between integration, driven by the Union institutions, and national regulatory competence.

Running parallel to this issue is another concern: that of the de-regulatory effect of the treaty freedoms. The effect of using Articles 28–9 is to strike down national legislation, thereby removing the rules regulating trade. This is sometimes called negative harmonisation. The difficulty is that a national rule may have been enacted for good reason. The European Court of Justice (ECJ) is therefore left with the task of balancing trade concerns with other concerns, as permitted by the treaty derogation (Article 30, discussed in Chapter 20) and through the rule of reason (see 19.6.2.1). Given that the ECJ may not be the best body to assess such questions, it is sometimes suggested that the use of positive harmonisation, which involves the political institutions in the determination of agreed standards (see Chapter 17) is a better approach.

A further obstacle to the free movement of goods may be caused by the existence of what is referred to in the EC Treaty as a 'State monopoly of a commercial character'. Such monopolies exist where a Member State has restricted the right to sell particular goods to one body. State monopolies are clearly capable of obstructing the free movement of goods as their position in a particular market enables such monopolies to control the flow of goods in and out of the Member State, as well as the conditions under which trade in such goods takes place. Although a separate provision, Article 31 (ex 37), deals with state monopolies, it is dealt with here because of the broad similarity of the potential effect on trade. When considering Article 31 and state monopolies, the relationship between this provision and competition provisions, notably state aid (see Chapter 31) as well as Article 86 EC, should also be borne in mind. All these provisions seek to deal with state behaviour which has the effect of distorting, or reinforcing the distortion of, competition.

This chapter starts by looking at the elements common to the articles. Then, after considering the meaning of quantitative restriction, the chapter focuses on the development of the jurisprudence relating to measures having equivalent effect to quantitative restrictions. As we shall see, the case law has not been entirely consistent and the state of the law is still not completely clear. We will look at the jurisprudence as falling broadly into three phases: the early years; the expansion of Article 28 following the case of *Cassis de Dijon* and the consequent problems; and finally *Keck* and the question of whether the ECJ is now following a consistent policy. The chapter concludes with a consideration of Articles 29 (exports) and 31.

19.2 Outline of provisions

19.2.1 Quantitative restrictions

As will be apparent, Articles 28–9 EC cover a much wider range of measures than Articles 23 (ex 9) and 25 (ex 12) (post Lisbon, 28 and 30 TFEU), but unlike these latter articles provision is made for derogation under Article 30 (ex 36).

The principal provisions are:

(a) Article 28 (ex 30), which prohibits quantitative restrictions, and all measures having equivalent effect, on *imports*

(b) Article 29 (ex 34), which contains a similar prohibition on *exports*.

The prohibition is twofold, embracing:

(a) quantitative restrictions

(b) measures of equivalent effect to quantitative restrictions (MEQR).

Original Articles 31–3, which provided for the gradual abolition of import restrictions during the transitional period, were deleted by the Treaty of Amsterdam (ToA). Should the Lisbon Treaty come into force, Articles 28–9 EC shall be renumbered Articles 34–5 of the Treaty on the Functioning of the European Union (TFEU) respectively, but they otherwise remain substantively the same.

Article 30 (ex 36) provides that the prohibitions in Articles 28 and 30 will not apply to restrictions on imports and exports which are *justified* on a number of specified grounds (see Chapter 20). Should Lisbon come into force, Article 30 EC will be renumbered Article 36 TFEU, which may be slightly confusing given its number in the original Treaty of Rome was Article 36 EEC.

Even where a particular activity falls within other provisions of the treaty, such as the 'services' provisions, it may still fall foul of Article 28 (*Commission v Ireland (Re Dundalk Water Supply)* (case 45/87), requirement that pipes required under a contract for the supply of services must comply with Irish specifications held in breach of Article 28 (ex 30)). The relationship between the four freedoms, together with the definition of 'goods', is discussed further in Chapter 15.

19.2.2 State monopolies

Article 31(1) (ex 37) EC states that 'Member States shall adjust any State monopolies of a commercial character so as to ensure that no discrimination regarding the conditions under which goods are procured and marketed exists between nationals of Member States'.

Lisbon does not alter the substance of this provision; should Lisbon come into force it will be renumbered Article 37 TFEU, thus returning it, too, to its original number under the 1957 version of the EC Treaty. Member States must also refrain from introducing any new measure which is contrary to Article 31(1) or which restricts the scope of Articles 25, 28, or 29 EC (Article 31(2)). This does not mean that no new monopolies may be created, but rather that if such monopolies are formed, they must be compatible with the provisions on the free movement of goods.

There is no specific provision derogating from Article 31; Article 30 cannot be used in this context.

There is special emphasis, in respect of state monopolies designed to make it easier to dispose of agricultural products, on safeguarding the employment and standard of living of the agricultural producers (Article 31(3)).

19.3   Whose actions are caught?

To engage the articles, the actions challenged must be capable of being traced back by the categories of persons covered by the relevant article. These articles are addressed to, and relate to, measures taken by Member States but, despite their wording, there are three ways in which to the meaning of 'Member States' has been expanded.

19.3.1 Application to the institutions

First, the institutions are bound by the terms of the treaty generally, including these provisions. Union institutions may derogate from the provisions of Articles 28–9 where they are expressly authorised to do so by other provisions of the treaty, for example in implementing the common agricultural policy (Articles 33–8 (ex 39–46, post Lisbon, Articles 39–44 TFEU) EC) (*Rewe Zentrale AG v Direktor der Landwirtschaftskammer Rheinland* (case 37/83)).

19.3.2 **Public bodies**

Secondly, 'measures taken by Member States' have been interpreted in the widest sense. They include the actions of all forms of government, whether central, regional, or local and extend to the activities of any public body, legislative, executive, or judicial, or even semi-public body, such as a quango, exercising powers derived from public law (eg, *Apple & Pear Development Council v KJ Lewis Ltd* (case 222/82)). In *R v Royal Pharmaceutical Society of Great Britain* (cases 266 and 267/87) the ECJ held that measures adopted by professional bodies, such as the Royal Pharmaceutical Society, on which national legislation has conferred regulatory or disciplinary powers were 'measures taken by Member States' subject to what is now Article 28. In determining whether the actions of a body fall within the scope of Article 28, the ECJ will consider the body's functions, statutory basis, management, and funding; its legal form will not be determinative. In the *Quality Labels* case (*Commission v Germany* (case C–325/00)), the fact that a body which awarded quality labels to German products was established as a private limited company did not take its actions outside Article 28, despite the fact that the German government could not directly influence its actions. The ECJ noted that the company was financed by a public body itself financed by compulsory contributions, its functions were determined, albeit broadly, by statute and it was subject to the supervision of the public body from which it derived its funding. More recently, the ECJ has held that, in principle, the opinions of a public official (expressed via interviews with the media) were sufficient to implicate the state provided the persons to whom the statements were addressed could reasonably suppose that the statements were given by the official with the authority of his office (*AGM-COS MET Srl v Finland* (case C–470/03)). This issue would be one for the national court to assess on the facts in a given case.

19.3.3 **Horizontal direct effect**

One question is whether these provisions have horizontal direct effect, a question that gained importance with the ECJ's ruling in *Angonese* (case C–281/98), see Chapter 21). Given the nature of Article 31, it is unlikely that this is a question that has much relevance for this provision. Although there had been some debate on the whether Articles 28–9 had horizontal effect, it seems that these provisions are limited to the actions of public bodies, however broadly seen (see, eg, *Sapod-Audic* (case C–159/00)). In principle then, these articles do not have horizontal direct effect.

This does not mean that the actions of individuals are completely beyond the reach of these articles. It now seems that the actions of individuals can be challenged indirectly by imposing positive obligations upon Member States. The starting point is *Commission v France* (*Angry Farmers*) (case C–265/95). The problem here did not concern actions by the French state but rather its failure to take action to prevent private individuals from impeding the cross-border flow of goods. According to the Commission, the French government should have taken action to stop the blockade of imported agricultural produce and demonstrations in which property was damaged. The ECJ agreed, stressing the fundamental nature of Article 28 and then referring to Article 10 (ex 5; post Lisbon,

Article 4(3) TEU), which puts Member States under an obligation 'to take all nec-essary and appropriate measures' to ensure that Union fundamental freedoms are respected in their territory. This ruling makes it clear that Member States' obligations extend to positive measures as well as refraining from taking action incompatible with the EC Treaty. The precise extent of this obligation remains uncertain, although *Schmidberger* (case C–112/00) (discussed below) provides fur-ther guidance. In the *Angry Farmers* case, the ECJ emphasised the duration and severity of the incidents in France and the passivity of the French authorities in this case. Note also that a Member State is only obliged to take 'necessary and proportionate' measures. Member States thus still retain some discretion in determining, for example, their policing policy, and would certainly not be obliged to quell every public demonstration. The question then is when does the Member State's obligation arise?

After the *Angry Farmers* case, a regulation, the so-called 'rapid intervention mech-anism', was enacted to deal with obstacles to trade which originate in the action or inaction of the Member States (Regulation 2679/98 ([1998] OJ L337/8)). In defining 'inaction' the regulation tracks the wording of the *Angry Farmers* case. The regula-tion gives the Commission the power to intervene in such circumstances, provid-ing the Commission with the possibility of taking a Member State before the ECJ should obstacles covered by the regulation continue in existence. The regulation defines in Article 1 the notion of an 'obstacle' requiring action. It lists three cumu-lative requirements:

(a) the serious disruption of the free movement of goods

(b) serious loss to individuals affected

(c) the necessity of immediate state action.

This definition would seem to take one-off actions outside the scope of the regu-lation. Such an approach would seem in line with the *Angry Farmers* case, which emphasised the severity and duration of the French farmers' action. In the more recent *Schmidberger* case (case C–112/00), the Advocate-General suggested that a one-day motorway blockade held in accordance with the relevant Member State's laws should trigger the application of Articles 28–9 where relevant, a view the Court followed. In the ECJ's reasoning, the severity of the disruption would be relevant for justification for failure to act rather than the application of Article 28–9 in the first place. Seemingly, there is now a divergence between the treaty jurisprudence and specific secondary legislation. In a report commissioned by the European Commission in 2007 on the functioning of the rapid intervention mech-anism, the problems arising from the lack of clarity as to the regulation's scope were noted. The question of the extent of Member States' obligations to take measures becomes ever more important in the light of the possibility of a claim for damages under the doctrine of state liability in respect of public authorities' liability for omissions (see Chapter 9), an issue that was raised but not decided in *Schmidberger* (case C–112/00). In addition to the problems relating to scope, and the practical problems of reacting to obstacles notified at short notice, the report highlighted some other weaknesses, in particular the lack of a financial penalty under the regu-lation where Member States do not comply, together with an absence of a monitor-ing mechanism of state compliance.

19.4 Types of act caught by Articles 28–9

We need also to consider whether the types of act challenged fall within the terms of the relevant articles. Articles 28–9 refer to measures, a term which clearly includes national legislative acts. The ECJ will assess national legislation as it has been interpreted by national practice. According to the ECJ's case law, 'measure' for the purpose of Article 28 is wider than legislation. It includes administrative acts, as the *Franking Machine* case (case 21/84) shows. There, although a discriminatory law had been repealed, the administrative practice had not changed, the authorities showing a 'systematically unfavourable' attitude towards the approval of imported products. A measure does not need to be a binding act to fall within the prohibition as can be seen in the preamble to the Commission's Directive 70/50, and confirmed by the ECJ in *Commission v Ireland* ('Buy Irish' campaign) (case 249/81). In this case certain activities of the Irish Goods Council, a government-sponsored body charged with promoting Irish goods by, inter alia, advertising, principally on the basis of their Irish origin, were held to be in breach of the then Article 30 (now 28). Even though no binding measures were involved, the Board's actions were capable of influencing the behaviour of traders and thereby frustrating the aims of the Community. This approach was reasserted more recently in *AGM-COS MET* (case C–470/03), where the views of an official were held to fall within Article 28 EC, provided that they appear to be official position taken by the state and not the personal opinions of the individual. As we have already seen from the *Angry Farmers* case, omissions can also constitute 'measures'.

19.5 Prohibition on quantitative restrictions

Quantitative restrictions were interpreted in *Riseria Luigi Geddo v Ente Nazionale Risi* (case 2/73) as any measures which amount to a total or partial restraint on imports, exports or goods in transit. They would clearly include a ban, as was found to be the case in *Commission v Italy (Re Ban on Pork Imports)* (case 7/61) and *R v Henn* (case 34/79) (ban on import of pornographic materials). They would also include a quota system, as in *Salgoil SpA v Italian Ministry for Foreign Trade* (case 13/68). The *Ditlev Bluhme* case (case C–67/97) confirms that a ban on imports operates as a quantitative restriction even if the prohibition extends to part only of a Member State's territory. This case concerned the Danish prohibition on the import onto the island of Læsø of live domestic bees or reproductive material for them, the aim of which was to protect the Læsø brown bee. This, the ECJ held, was a quantitative restriction although it applied only to a small part of Denmark.

A covert quota system might operate by means of an import (or export) licence requirement. A licensing system might in itself amount to a quantitative restriction, or, alternatively, a measure of equivalent effect to a quantitative restriction. It was held in *International Fruit Co NV v Produktschap voor Groenten en Fruit* (cases 51–4/71) that even if the granting of a licence were a pure formality, the requirement of such a licence to import would amount to a breach of Article 28. In that case it was deemed to be a measure of equivalent effect to a quantitative restriction.

Although Articles 28–9 identify two types of prohibited behaviour, quantitative restrictions and MEQR, it seems as though the case law no longer maintains a firm and consistent distinction between the two, many cases which could be viewed as a quantitative measure now being considered as MEQR.

19.6 Prohibition on measures having equivalent effect to quantitative restrictions

The concept of MEQR is altogether wider in scope than that of quantitative restrictions. Perhaps to the surprise of Member States, it has been interpreted very generously by both the Commission and the ECJ, to include not merely overtly protective measures or measures applicable only to imports or exports ('distinctly applicable' measures), but measures applicable to imports (or exports) and domestic goods alike ('indistinctly applicable' measures), often introduced (seemingly) for the most worthy purpose. The precise scope of Article 28 has therefore been the subject of much discussion, and central to the debate is the question of whether Article 28 is about discrimination, whether direct (distinctly applicable measures) or indirect (indistinctly applicable measures), or instead about ensuring that individual national markets are opened up to goods from other Member States. It is questionable the degree to which the ECJ has developed a consistent policy. There are three key cases: *Dassonville* (case 8/74), *Cassis de Dijon*, and *Keck*, which may serve as landmarks as we navigate the development of the Article 28 jurisprudence. While the main elements of the jurisprudence are clear, there are a number of grey areas near the boundaries.

19.6.1 *Dassonville* and the early years

It was generally accepted in the early years of the EC, that Article 28 caught measures that discriminated against imports, that is were directly discriminatory by treating imports differently. The question was whether Article 28 could also catch indirectly discriminatory measures, which appeared on the face to treat imports and domestic products alike, but which in effect discriminated against imports. The Commission, in Directive 70/50 (which is no longer of legal effect), suggested that both direct and indirect discrimination should be caught. It was not until 1974 that the ECJ, in the case of *Procureur du Roi v Dassonville* (case 8/74), introduced its own definition of measures having equivalent effect to quantitative restrictions. *Dassonville* concerned Belgian rules which required imported goods bearing certain designations of origin to have a certificate of authenticity from the authorities in the country of origin. Criminal proceedings were instituted against traders who acquired a consignment of Scotch whisky in free circulation in France and imported it into Belgium without being in possession of a certificate of origin from the British customs authorities. The ECJ determined that such a measure, which focused on imported goods, would fall within Article 28, arguing thus 'All trading rules enacted by Member States which are capable of hindering, directly or indirectly, actually or potentially, intra-Community trade are to be considered as measures having an effect equivalent to quantitative restrictions'.

This definition, now known as the '*Dassonville* formula', has since been applied consistently, almost verbatim, by the ECJ in subsequent cases. It is a broad, effects-based test. As became apparent, it is not necessary to show an actual hindrance to trade between Member States as long as the measure is capable of such effects. Unlike the competition provisions of Articles 81–2 (ex 85–6; post Lisbon, Articles 101–2 TFEU), which require an 'appreciable effect' on trade and competition between Member States, the ECJ has in the past held that Article 28 is not subject to a *de minimis* rule (*van de Haar* (case 177/82)).

19.6.1.1 *Internal situations*

Although *Dassonville*, as we shall see, is a broad test, there are some limitations. A measure which is not capable of hindering trade between Member States, which merely affects the flow of trade *within* a Member State, will not breach Article 28 (ex 30). In *Oebel* (case 155/80) a Belgian law banning the production and delivery to consumers and retail outlets of bakery products during the night hours, designed to protect workers in small and medium-sized bakeries, was held not to breach Article 28 because, although delivery of imported products through some outlets was precluded, 'trade within the Community remained possible at all times' (see also *Blesgen* (case 75/81)). In *Quietlynn Ltd v Southend Borough Council* (case C–23/89) a licensing requirement for the sale of sex appliances by sex shops was held not to breach Article 28, since the goods in question, which included imported goods, 'could be marketed through other channels'.

The case law of the Court has not been consistent on this point. In *Torfaen Borough Council v B & Q plc* (case 145/88) the Court found that a ban on Sunday trading in England and Wales under the Shops Act 1950, the effect of which was to restrict the volume of imports to the shops trading in breach of the rules, was prima facie contrary to Article 28, even though alternative outlets for the sale of these goods existed during the working week (see also *Conforma* (case C–312/89) and *Marchandise* (case C–332/89)). Following a change in the Court's approach, these latter cases involving Sunday trading would be decided on a different basis today (see *Keck* (cases C–267 and 268/91) and subsequent cases to be discussed below). The ECJ discussed the question of whether a national measure had an effect on inter-state trade in *Pistre* (joined cases C–321–4/94) which concerned a French rule limiting the marketing of products with the designation of 'montagne' to those originating in certain areas in France. The ECJ held that this rule had a Community dimension. In the ECJ's view, it did not matter that all the relevant facts arose in France; it was sufficient that the rule could affect inter-state trade. It would seem clear from this case, and other similar cases, that the question of internal situation is very closely linked to the question of whether there is hindrance to inter-state trade (see also 19.6.5). This connection can be seen from the ECJ's more recent restatement of the position in *Karner* (case C–71/02):

> That principle has been upheld by the Court not only in cases where the national rule in question gave rise to direct discrimination against goods imported from other Member States (*Pistre and ors*, paragraph 44), but also in situations where the national rule applied without distinction to national and imported products and was thus likely to constitute a potential impediment to intra-Community trade covered by Article 28 EC (see, to that effect, case C–448/98, *Guimont*, paras 21 and 22). [Para 20.]

19.6.1.2 *Reverse discrimination*

A measure falling within the *Dassonville* formula but which operates solely to the disadvantage of domestic production will not fall foul of Union law. The ban in *Oebel* on the production of bakery products during the night, which prevented Belgian bakers from benefiting from the early morning trade in adjacent Member States, was found not to breach what are currently Articles 12 (post Lisbon, Article 18 TEU), 28, and 29 EC. The Court held that it was not contrary to the principle of non-discrimination on grounds of nationality for states to apply national rules where other states apply less strict rules to similar products. The ECJ took the same view of a Dutch regulation concerning the permitted ingredients of cheese, which was only applicable to cheese produced in Holland (*Jongeneel Kaas BV v Netherlands* (case 237/82), see also approach to interpretation of Article 29 EC) and of a French law requiring French retailers to adhere to a minimum selling price for books, provided it was not applied to books which, having been exported, were reimported into France (*Association des Centres Distributeurs Edouard Leclerc v 'Au Blé Vert' Sàrl* (case 229/83)).

In this respect, as in other areas (eg, free movement of workers), the Court is prepared to accept a measure of reverse discrimination. While Member States must be compelled, in the interests of the single market, not to discriminate against, or in any way prejudice, imports, it seems that they may be safely left to act themselves in order to protect their own interests. There is now a consistent line of authority from the ECJ to this effect.

19.6.1.3 *Early application of Dassonville*

In the cases of *Tasca* (case 65/75) and *van Tiggele* (case 82/77) the *Dassonville* test was applied in the context of a domestic law imposing maximum and minimum selling prices, respectively. The laws were indistinctly applicable, that is they applied to both domestic and imported goods. In both cases the issue of Article 28 arose in criminal proceedings against the defendants for breach of these laws. Tasca was accused in Italy of selling sugar above the permitted national maximum price; van Tiggele in Holland of selling gin below the national minimum price. Both pleaded that the measures were in breach of EC law. Applying the *Dassonville* test the ECJ found that both measures were capable of breaching Article 28. Regarding the maximum price, the Court held a maximum price does not in itself constitute a measure equivalent in effect to a quantitative restriction. It becomes so when fixed at a level such that the sale of imported products becomes, if not impossible, more difficult. The maximum price in *Tasca* could have that effect, in that importers of more highly priced goods might have to cut their profit margins or even be forced to sell at a loss. In *van Tiggele* the minimum price also acted as a hindrance to imports, since it would prevent the (possibly) lower price of imported goods from being reflected in the retail selling price. The Court suggested, however, that a prohibition on selling below cost price, or a minimum profit margin, would be acceptable, since it would have no adverse effect on trade between Member States (principle applied in *Commission v Italy (Re Fixing of Trading Margins)* (case 78/82)).

In applying the *Dassonville* formula in these three cases, the Court did not distinguish between distinctly (or directly discriminatory) and indistinctly applicable (or indirectly discriminatory) measures. The breadth of the formula, especially when applied 'mechanically', looking to the *effect* of the measure on inter-state trade rather than to the question of *hindrance*, despite the fact that a hindrance seems to be required by the terms of the *Dassonville* formula, bore harshly on Member States, particularly where the measure was indistinctly applicable and might be justified as in the public interest.

19.6.2 Indistinctly applicable measures: *Cassis de Dijon*

Perhaps taking heed of criticisms arising from its application of the *Dassonville* formula in these last three cases discussed above, the Court took a decisive step in the case of *'Cassis de Dijon' (Rewe-Zentral AG v Bundesmonopolverwaltung für Branntwein* (case 120/78)) and paved the way for a distinction between distinctly and indistinctly applicable measures. The question before the ECJ in *Cassis* concerned the legality under EC law of a German law laying down a minimum alcohol level of 25 per cent for certain spirits, which included cassis, a blackcurrant-flavoured liqueur. German cassis complied with this minimum, but French cassis, with an alcohol content of 15–20 per cent, did not. Thus although the German regulation was indistinctly applicable, the result of the measure was effectively to ban French cassis from the German market. A number of German importers contested the measure, and the German court referred a number of questions to the ECJ.

19.6.2.1 *Rule of reason*

The ECJ applied the *Dassonville* formula, thus confirming should there have been any doubt, that Article 28 could apply to measures which, on their face, appeared to apply both to domestic products and imports. Crucially, it developed a suggestion in its earlier *Dassonville* judgment that state measures falling within the formula might be acceptable where the restrictions on inter-state trade were 'reasonable', stating that:

> Obstacles to movement within the Community resulting from disparities between the national laws relating to the marketing of the products in question must be accepted insofar as those provisions may be recognised as being necessary in order to satisfy mandatory requirements relating in particular to the effectiveness of fiscal supervision, the protection of public health, the fairness of commercial transactions and the defence of the consumer.

This principle ('the first *Cassis* principle'), that certain measures, though within the *Dassonville* formula, will not breach Article 28 if they are necessary to satisfy 'mandatory requirements' (now often referred to as matters of overriding public interest), has come to be known as the 'rule of reason', a concept borrowed from American anti-trust law, which also occasionally appears in the context of EU competition law (see Chapter 29).

Prior to *Cassis*, it was assumed that any measure falling within the *Dassonville* formula would breach Article 28 and could be justified only on the grounds provided by Article 30. Since *Cassis*, at least where indistinctly applicable measures are concerned, courts may apply a rule of reason to Article 28. If the measure is necessary in order to protect 'mandatory requirements', it will not breach Article 28 at all. Distinctly applicable measures on the other hand will normally breach Article 28, but may be justified under Article 30. This distinction is significant, since the mandatory requirements permitted under *Cassis* are wider than the grounds provided under Article 30, and, unlike Article 30, are non-exhaustive. The ECJ refuses to contemplate a justification based on purely economic grounds (see, eg, *Duphar BV v Netherlands* (case 238/82) and, more recently, *Decker* (case C–120/95)).

Box 19.1 Examples of matters of Overriding Public Interest

Oebel (case 155/80)—working conditions
Cinéthèque SA (cases 60 and 61/84)—culture
Commission v Denmark (Re disposable Beer Cans) (case 302/86) environment
Torfaen Borough Council v B & Q plc (case 145/88)—socio-cultural characteristics
Vereinigte Familiapress case (case C–368/95)—diversity of the press
Dynamic Medien (C–44/06)—protection of young people

It should be noted that the rule of reason as laid down in *Cassis* was not in terms confined to indistinctly applicable measures. Shortly after *Cassis*, in *Gilli* (Italian cider-vinegar case) (case 788/79), the Court suggested (para 14) that the principle applied only where national rules apply *without discrimination* to both domestic and imported products, a distinction that it has reiterated (*Aragonesa de Publicidad Exterior and Publivía Cases* (cases C–1/90 and C–176/90), para 13). The distinction between indistinctly and distinctly applicable measures therefore assumes a significance in terms of the justifications on which Member States may rely when national measures have been found to constitute MEQR. Problematically, the ECJ has not consistently insisted on this distinction, and, has also been inconsistent as to where the boundary between distinctly and indistinctly applicable measures lie (*Commission v Belgium (Walloon Waste)* (case C–2/90); *Aher-Waggon v Germany* (case C–389/96); *Commission v Austria (prohibition of heavy lorries)* (case C–320/03), all concerning environmental justifications). In many cases concerning indistinctly applicable measures, the ECJ has not considered the issue and, perhaps because the line between the two is not always clear, has dealt the question of justification of indistinctly applicable measures not on *Cassis* principles but under Article 30 (see *Sandoz BV* (case 174/82); more recently, *Commission v Germany (hospital pharmacy supply)* (case C–141/07)). There appear to be two possible reasons for this approach: in some cases the Court is merely responding to questions submitted by national courts under Article 234 (ex 177; post Lisbon, 267 TFEU); in others, where the 'mandatory requirement' falls under one of the specific heads of derogation provided by Article 30, the Court may prefer to rely on the express provisions of that article (see, eg, *Commission v Germany (re German sausages)* (case 274/87) (health justification) and *Ditlev Bluhme* (case C–67/97) (protection of biodiversity and the environment/health and life of animals)).

19.6.2.2 *Proportionality*

In applying the rule of reason to the facts in *Cassis* the Court found that the German law was in breach of Article 28. Although the measure fell within the categories suggested, being allegedly enacted in the interests of public health (to prevent increased consumption resulting from lowering the alcoholic content of cassis) and the fairness of commercial transactions (to avoid giving the weak imported cassis an unfair advantage over its stronger, hence more expensive, German rival), the measure was not *necessary* to achieve these ends. Other means, such as labelling, which would have been less of a hindrance to trade, could have been used to achieve the same ends. Thus the word 'necessary' has been interpreted to mean no more than is necessary—ie, subject to the principle of proportionality. This is the case, even if the public objective aimed at is the protection of fundamental human rights although it is an open question as to whether the ECJ uses, or should use, exactly the same test in this regard (*Dynamic Medien* (C–244/06) (protection of young people/rights of the child)). In this, there are parallels to the approach taken by the ECJ with respect to the heads of derogation in Article 30 (see 20.3 and 20.4.2).

Although, where a domestic measure is challenged before a national court it is for the national court to apply the proportionality principle, the ECJ has often, in interpreting Union law at the request of national courts, offered guidance as to the specific application of that principle. In doing so it has applied the principle rigorously, excluding all measures that go beyond what is strictly necessary to achieve the desired end. In *Walter Rau Lebensmittelwerke v De Smedt PVBA* (case 261/81) a Belgian law requiring margarine to be packed in cube-shaped boxes, allegedly introduced in the interests of consumers, to enable them to distinguish margarine from butter, was held to be in breach of Article 28. The same objective could have been achieved by other means, such as labelling, which would be less of a hindrance to trade. Similar arguments have been used successfully to challenge national rules, allegedly in the interest of public health and consumer protection, concerning the permitted ingredients of pasta (*Drei Glöcken* (case 407/85)) and sausages (*Commission v Germany* (case 274/87)). In *Schutzverband gegen Unwesen in der Wirtschaft v Rocher* (case C–126/91) a German law prohibiting 'eye-catching' price comparisons in advertisements, designed to prevent consumers from being misled, was held to be disproportionate on the grounds that such advertisements were forbidden *whether they misled the public or not*. It was implied that a ban on *misleading* price comparisons would have been acceptable. Falling on the other side of the line is the case of *Dynamic Medien* (C–244/06). There, the ECJ held that rules which prohibit the mail-order sale of image storage media which have not been examined and classified by the competent national authority for the purposes of protecting young persons and which do not bear a label from that authority indicating the age from which they may be viewed, would be proportionate, unless the procedure for examination, classification and labelling is not readily accessible or cannot be completed within a reasonable period, or that a decision of refusal is not open to challenge before the courts. Nonetheless, while the rule of reason has, in principle, an unlimited list of possible justifications for national measures, proportionality has operated to limit when a national rule will be found to be justified, even under the rule of reason.

The requirement that national measures be proportionate is significant in the context of Article 30 also (see Chapter 20).

19.6.2.3 *Mutual recognition and the home country principle*

The Court established a second important principle in *Cassis*. It suggested that there was no valid reason why 'provided that [goods] have been lawfully produced and marketed in one of the Member States, [they] should not be introduced into any other Member State' (para 14).

Thus, national provisions making a product which was lawfully manufactured and marketed in another Member State subject to additional controls, save in the case of exceptions provided for or allowed by Union law, will constitute a MEQR. Is this principle, known as the principle of 'mutual recognition', not in conflict with the rule of reason? It is submitted that it is not. It merely gives rise to a presumption that goods which have been lawfully marketed in another state will comply with the 'mandatory requirements' of the importing state. This can be rebutted by evidence that further measures are *necessary* to protect the interest concerned. Given the requirement of proportionality, that presumption will be hard to rebut; the burden of proving that a measure is necessary is a heavy one, particularly when, although justifiable in principle, it clearly operates as a hindrance to intra-Community trade. Note that mutual recognition is now a central plank of the Union approach to the internal market and directives have been enacted to ensure that when Member States enact measures to protect a matter of public interest, those measures are notified to the Commission and reviewed to ensure that the measure is necessary and that mutual recognition is insufficient to protect the public interest at issue; it is this system which has given rise to the incidental direct effect cases (see 5.2.5.8). A similar notification approach is found with respect to designations of origin (see below).

19.6.2.4 *Impact of Cassis on rules of origin and quality*

The extent to which Member States are now limited, in the interests of the single market, in their ability to introduce indistinctly applicable and seemingly justifiable measures is illustrated by the case of *Commission v UK (origin marking of retail goods)* (case 207/83). Here the Commission claimed that a British regulation requiring certain goods (eg, clothing, textiles) sold retail to indicate their country of origin was in breach of Article 28. The British government argued that the measure was justified on *Cassis* principles in the interest of consumers, who regarded the origin of goods as an indication of their quality. The Court refused to accept this argument. It held that the regulation merely enabled consumers to assert their prejudices, thereby slowing down the economic interpenetration of the Union. The quality of goods could as well be indicated on the goods themselves or their packaging, and the protection of consumers sufficiently guaranteed by rules which enabled the use of false indications of origin to be prohibited. Whilst manufacturers remained free to indicate their own national origin it was not necessary to compel them to do so. The regulation was in breach of Article 28.

This judgment, initially surprising, demonstrates the Commission's and the Court's overriding concern to promote market integration by striking down national rules which tend to compartmentalise the market, particularly along national lines. In a single market, based on free competition, products must be allowed to compete on their merits, not on the basis of national origin. (See also *Apple & Pear Development Council v Lewis* (case 222/82); *Commission v Ireland (re 'Buy Irish' campaign)* (case 249/81) and Chapter 29 on competition law.) There has, however, more recently been some softening of the rules in respect of local or regional designations of origin of goods.

In *Exportur SA v LOR SA et Confiserie du Tech* (case C–3/91) the Court held that rules protecting indications of provenance and designations of origin laid down by a bilateral Convention between Member States were permissible under Union law provided that the protected designations had not acquired a generic connotation in their country of origin. The institutions have now established a register (Regulation 510/2006 (OJ [2006] L 93/12), replacing Regulation 2081/92 dealing with food products for human consumption; a separate system exists for wines and spirits) providing for the protection of designations of origin and geographic indications for in excess of 300 named products, such as Stilton cheese and Hereford beef. This regulation protects registered designations of origin against all use, including 'evocations'. An evocation is a designation so evocative of the protected designation that, when a consumer is confronted with the product, the image that is triggered in the consumer's mind is that of the product the designation of which is protected. Thus, a soft cheese manufactured in Germany and called 'Cambozola' is an evocation of 'Gorgonzola' (*Conzorzio per la Tutela del Formaggio Gorgonzola v Käserei Champignon Hormeister GmbH & Co KG, Eduard Bracharz GmbH* (case C–87/97)). There are limitations to the protection granted. For example, since Cambozola had been made and registered as a trademark long before the introduction of the regulation, the ECJ also held that notwithstanding the prima facie prohibition of the use of the evocation, the trade mark 'Cambozola' could still be used were its initial registration to have been made in good faith and its continued use not likely to deceive the public. Union law will not, however, allow Member States to protect generic names, such as Cheddar cheese, which are not tied to a particular geographical area.

19.6.2.5 *Over-extension of Article 28*

Although the rule of reason has allowed states some latitude to enact or maintain indistinctly applicable measures that are capable of hindering trade between Member States to protect important national interests, while ensuring that such measures are subject to judicial control as to their proportionality, the rule has not been without its problems. These arose from a tendency to a lax, 'mechanical' application of the *Dassonville* formula, requiring measures which might affect the volume of imports overall, but with little potential to *hinder* imports, to be justified under the rule of reason. Certainly the idea of discrimination, or even indirect discrimination, seems to disappear in this body of cases where rules which equally affect domestic products were held to fall within Article 28 and following which Article 28 began to look like a 'right to trade' without any connection with the creation of the single market (for a similar trend with regard to the right to regulate at Union level, see the scope of Article 95 EC discussed in Chapter 16).

Defence lawyers in Member States were quick to exploit the 'Eurodefence' of Article 28 to charges involving a wide range of regulatory offences. Examples of such defences include challenges to Dutch laws restricting the use of free gifts for promotional purposes (*Oosthoek's Uitgeversmaatschappij BV* (case 286/81)); to French laws prohibiting the door-to-door selling of educational materials (*Buet v Ministère Public* (case 382/87)); to English laws requiring the licensing of sex shops for the sale of sexual appliances (*Quietlynn Ltd v Southend Borough Council* (case C–23/89)); to laws prohibiting 'eye-catching' price comparisons as in *Rocher* (case C–126/91); and a number of cases such as *Torfaen Borough Council v B&Q plc* (case 145/88) pleading the illegality under Article 28 of national rules limiting Sunday trading. In all of these cases the legality of these measures under EC law was ultimately upheld, sometimes (eg, *Quietlynn*), on the grounds that Article 28 was not applicable at all, more often following the application of the rule of reason. Given the result, the cases might be thought unproblematic but there are difficulties relating to the approach of the ECJ in determining the connection with Article 28. Including a rule within the scope of Article 28 means that, in principle, the rule is unlawful and the burden of justification falls upon the state, not an easy task given the ECJ's approach to proportionality. Further, not only was Article 28's scope very widely drawn, but the case law has not been consistent here as to whether Article 28 applied in the first place or whether the national rule would be justified by a rule of reason. Moreover, as the Sunday-trading cases demonstrate, national courts face great difficulties in applying a rule of reason, particularly when there exist a number of possible justifications for the measure challenged and its harmful effect on trade between *Member States* (as opposed to between particular undertakings) is minimal. In these circumstances a national judge may be reluctant to entertain a challenge to domestic legislation, duly enacted by the national legislature, based on its lack of proportionality (see, eg, Hoffmann J in *Stoke-on-Trent City Council v B&Q plc* [1991] Ch 48).

These problems surfaced in the Sunday trading cases. In *Torfaen Borough Council v B&Q plc*, the ECJ had held that the rules in question, which prohibited large multiple shops such as the defendant's from opening on Sunday, might be justified to ensure that working hours be arranged to accord with 'national or regional socio-cultural characteristics', and directed the referring magistrates' court to examine the rules in the light of their proportionality. Unfortunately the precise grounds of justification permitted to protect such socio-cultural characteristics were not spelt out; nor was any guidance offered on the question of proportionality. Different British courts in different cases came to different conclusions. Courts which concluded that the socio-cultural purpose of the rules was to protect workers who did not want to work on Sunday not surprisingly concluded that the rules were disproportionate (eg, *B&Q Ltd v Shrewsbury & Atcham Borough Council* [1990] 3 CMLR 535); those which saw the rules as designed to 'preserve the traditional character of the British Sunday' legitimately concluded otherwise: the rules were not more than was necessary to achieve that end (eg, *Wellingborough Borough Council v Payless DIY Ltd* [1990] 1 CMLR 773). Despite a clear ruling from the Court in two cases subsequent to *Torfaen Borough Council v B&Q plc* (*Conforama* (case C–312/89) and *Marchandise* (case C–332/89)) that similar rules would be permissible under the rule of reason, the question of the legality of the English Sunday trading rules was only decided conclusively when the ECJ, following a reference from the House of Lords in *Stoke-on-Trent City Council v B&Q plc* (case C–169/91), applying the rule of reason in *Cassis*, found that the rules were justified and not disproportionate.

Whether as a result of these problems and the uncertainty surrounding the scope of Article 28 in the case of non-discriminatory national rules with a minimal impact (in terms of hindrance) on intra-Community trade, resulting in some exploitation of Union rules, or of a new post-Maastricht commitment to the principle of subsidiarity, the Court, in *Keck and Mithouard* (cases C–267 and 268/91), signalled an important change of direction.

19.6.3 *Keck* and *Mithouard*

19.6.3.1 *Possible approaches to Article 28*

The approach to Article 28 drew a significant amount of academic comment, most of it critical. A range of suggestions were put forward to correct the perceived defects. One suggestion was that the ECJ should return to the wording of *Dassonville* and look for a hindrance to interstate trade to trigger the application of Article 28. This is similar to the approach taken with regard to competition rules (see Chapter 29). Another was to draw a distinction between dual-burden and equal-burden rules. The former category places an additional burden on imports, and can therefore be seen as being akin to indirectly discriminatory rules. The rules in *Cassis* could be seen as falling in this category. Equal burden rules are rules which do not have a greater impact on imports though they may have an impact on trade. The Sunday trading rules could be an example of an equal-burden rule. The suggestion is that the boundary of Article 28 properly falls between the two categories. Another suggestion, focuses on the distinction between rules which relate to the characteristics of the goods, as in *Cassis*, and rules which relate to the conditions of sale, such as the *Sunday Trading* cases. A further distinction may be made as regards this latter category between conditions of sale which apply generally, such as opening hours (sometimes called static conditions of sale) and those which relate to the marketing of the product itself, for example a ban on advertising a particular product (sometimes called dynamic conditions of sale).

19.6.3.2 *Keck:* The judgment

These cases concerned the legality under EC law of a French law prohibiting the resale of goods in an unaltered state at prices lower than their actual purchase price, in the interests of fair trading, to prevent 'predatory pricing' (see Chapter 29). Keck and Mithouard, who had been prosecuted for breach of this law, claimed that it was incompatible with EC law. Although Article 28 was not expressly invoked, the reference being made for interpretation of Articles 3 and 12, the Court, to provide the French court with a 'useful' reply, focused on Article 28, which was clearly the relevant article. It cited the *Dassonville* test. It pointed out that legislation such as the French law in question:

> may restrict the volume of sales, and hence the volume of sales of products from other Member States, insofar as it deprives traders of a method of sales promotion. But the question remains whether such a possibility is sufficient to characterise the legislation in question as a measure having equivalent effect to a quantitative restriction on imports.

It went on to suggest:

> in view of the increasing tendency of traders to invoke Article 30 [now 28] of the Treaty as a means of challenging any rules whose effect is to limit their commercial freedom even where such rules are not aimed at products of other Member States, the Court considers it necessary to re-examine and clarify its case law on this matter.

Citing the rule of reason from *Cassis de Dijon* it drew a distinction between rules which lay down 'requirements to be met' by goods, such as those relating to designation, size, weight, composition, presentation, labelling and packaging, and rules relating to 'selling arrangements'. Rules governing 'requirements to be met' falling within the *Dassonville* formula remained subject to the rule of reason in *Cassis*. However, 'contrary to what [had] previously been decided':

> the application to products from other Member States of national provisions restricting or prohibiting certain selling arrangements is not such as to hinder, directly or indirectly, actually or potentially, trade between Member States within the meaning of the *Dassonville* judgment, provided that those provisions apply to all affected traders operating within the national territory and provided that they affect in the same manner, in law and in fact, the marketing of domestic products and of those from other Member States.
>
> Where these conditions are fulfilled, the application of such rules to the sale of products from another Member State meeting the requirements laid down by that State is not by nature such as to prevent their access to the market or to impede access any more than it impedes the access of domestic products. Such rules therefore fall outside the scope of Article 30 [now 28] of the Treaty.

Keck thus seemed to suggest that where a selling arrangement was in issue, the *Dassonville* test would not be satisfied. The impact of such rules was likely to be too indirect or insignificant to constitute a MEQR. In this, traces of similarity with the approach of the Commission towards indistinctly applicable measures in Directive 70/50 can be seen. There the Commission accepted indistinctly applicable measures might have some impact on trade provided 'the restrictive effect of such measures on the free movement of goods exceeds the effects intrinsic to trade rules' (Article 3). We can also see similarities with the distinction between characteristics of the goods and their conditions of sale. *Keck* did not seem to distinguish between static and dynamic rules. In *Keck*, however, the ECJ emphasised that the selling arrangement must apply equally in law and in fact, and it is this proviso that was to prove to be significant in determining the direction of post-*Keck* case law. For the time being, the new approach to Article 28 was affirmed in a number of cases.

Box 19.2 Examples of the application of *Keck*: Selling arrangements

Hünermund (case C–292/92)—prohibition on pharmacists advertising, outside pharmacy premises, pharmaceutical products which they are authorised to sell.

Commission v *Greece* (case C–391/92)—requirement for processed milk for infants to be sold only in pharmacies.

Belgapom (case C–63/94)—rules prohibiting sales yielding very low profit margins.

Banchero (case C–387/93)—rules reserving the retail sale of tobacco to authorised distributors.

By contrast with these cases involving 'selling arrangements', measures constituting 'requirements to be met', such as a Dutch law prohibiting dealings in gold and silver products not bearing a Dutch, Belgian, or Luxembourg hallmark (*Houtwipper* (case C–293/93)) and German rules requiring the labelling of the contents of certain foods additional to that which was required under Union law

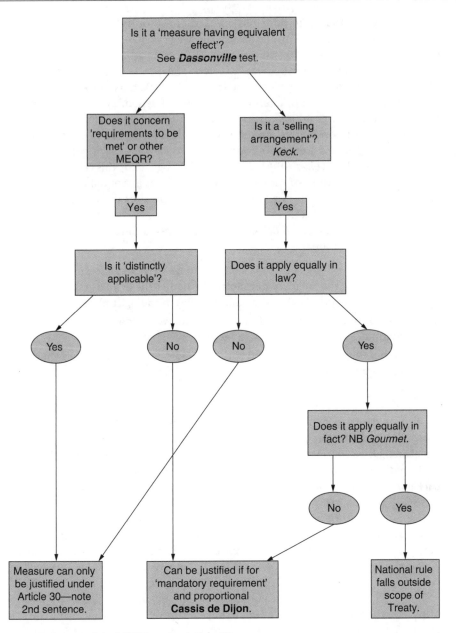

Fig 19.1 Approach to MEQR under Article 28

(*Commission v Germany* (case C–51/94) were examined, as *Keck* suggested, under the rule of reason and found not to be justified. Thus the approach to determining whether there is an MEQR can be rendered in diagrammatic form as seen in Fig 19.1.

19.6.4 **Weaknesses of the *Keck* approach**

Keck can be viewed as a return to an approach based on discrimination. The move towards a more 'formalistic' approach towards Article 28 initiated in *Keck* has been both criticised as 'lacking in principle' and acclaimed for its 'tendency to cut back on unnecessary intrusions into the laws of the Member States in cases where access to the relevant national market is not at stake' (see the articles by Reich and Roth respectively, listed in the further reading). Roth argues, persuasively, that the focus of Article 28 should be on access to the (national) market, its purpose to promote interstate trade in goods, not to ensure commercial freedom as such. It is arguable that the more recent post-*Keck* cases see the ECJ responding to some of these criticisms and, at least, considering questions such as the impact of a measure on access to the market. Perhaps a more appropriate way to view *Keck* is to consider, as the Advocate-General in *Volker Graf* (case C–190/98) suggested, the view that selling arrangements are harmless in internal market terms as a rebuttable presumption rather than as a rule. Even now, more than a decade after the decision, the jury seems still to be out on *Keck*.

There are two main areas of difficulty, together with a third issue which has not received much attention:

1. where the boundary between a selling arrangement and a requirement to be met lies, with the ancillary questions of whether the ECJ has taken a consistent approach and whether the boundary lies in the right place

2. the scope of the 'discrimination proviso' and whether a broad interpretation undermines the value of the *Keck* 'exception'

3. whether there are only two categories of trading rule: selling arrangements and product requirements.

19.6.4.1 *Meaning of 'selling arrangement'*

There is no doubt that the 'formalistic' approach introduced in *Keck* creates uncertainty. The ambit of the phrase 'certain selling arrangements' is unclear and ultimately remains a Union concept the scope of which is controlled by the ECJ. We can see from the cases above that some aspects of marketing (eg, advertising claims on packaging) (*Mars: Verein gegen Unwesen In Handel und Gewerbe Köln eV v Mars GmbH* (case C–470/93); and *Clinique: Verband Sozialer Wettbewerb eV v Clinique Laboratoires SNC et Estee Lauder Cosmetics GmbH* (case C–315/92)) can fall within the notion of a product requirement as can the incorporation in a product of material for the purpose of increasing sales. One example of this occurred in *Vereinigte Familiapress Zeitungsverlags- und Vertriebs GmbH v Heinrich Bauer Verlag* (case C–368/95), which concerned the Austrian prohibition on prize draws or competitions in periodicals. Although the ECJ accepted that publishers would include such games in publications with the hope of increasing circulation, this was not enough to bring the rule within *Keck*: the prohibition concerned the content of a magazine and therefore was a requirement to be met. Since it was an indistinctly applicable measure, it could, however, be justified under the *Cassis* rule of reason. The common theme in these cases is that the rules in question impose a dual burden on the manufacturer or importer; product requirements seem implicitly to involve de facto discrimination through the imposition of extra costs.

The ECJ summed the position up in *Morellato* (case C–416/00), that 'the need to alter packaging or the labelling of imported products prevents such requirements from constituting selling arrangements' (para 29). This case concerned the requirement to package bread made from partially baked dough, but finished off on-site, before sale, such packaging to contain certain information. Here the ECJ held that the prior-packaging requirement did not mean it was necessary to alter the product. The rules therefore concerned selling arrangements and would be acceptable provided they applied equally in law and in fact (see 19.6.4.2). The approach in this case does hint at difficulties with the boundary between a product requirement and a rule relating to selling arrangements. What would the classification of a rule be, for example, if certain information was required but not included on the label, but national law would be satisfied by additional packaging? The question of a packaging requirement arose in *Schwarz* (case C–366/04). Austrian law required chewing gum to be packaged if it was to be dispensed via certain types of vending machine, whereas other Member States, specifically Germany, did not impose this requirement. Those manufacturers of gum established in a state where there was no such requirement would therefore have to go to the extra expense of packaging the gum to distribute in Austria. Without considering the question of a selling arrangement, the ECJ assumed that Article 28 was triggered and went on to assess and accept the question of justification under Article 30. This suggests that the ECJ thought that the rule could not benefit from the selling arrangement 'exception'. This implication is supported by the reasoning of the Advocate-General in *Schwarz*, who adopted the same test as the ECJ had in *Morellato*. Applying it in *Schwarz* however, the requirement was found to be a product requirement (para 29) even though the national laws did not require the alteration of the packaging (the boundary suggested by *Morellato*) but the *addition* of packaging. There is clearly a fine line to be drawn here and perhaps one distinction between *Morellato* and *Schwarz* is that the obligation in *Schwarz* could fall on the producer rather than the retailer. Whereas retailers can be seen as supplying goods from multiple origins in one place, manufacturers deal with one product, but subject to potentially many regimes. The problem in *Schwarz* again seems to be the concern about a dual burden.

One particular problem area in this context is that of advertising. One might argue that it falls within the ambit of 'selling arrangement' rather than 'requirements to be met'; indeed in *Leclerc-Siplec* (case C–412/93) the ECJ held that legislation which prohibits television advertising in a particular sector concerns selling arrangements for the products in that particular sector. Therefore, as the ECJ suggested in *Komsummentombudsmannen v De Agostini* (joined cases C–34–6/95), even an outright ban on the advertising of certain products—here toys—will not fall within the then Article 30 (now 28 EC) provided always that such measures apply to domestically produced and imported products equally in law and in fact. Sales promotions forming part of the packaging, as the *Mars* case illustrates, will conversely constitute a product requirement. The boundary between the two situations—sales promotion/advertising constituting a 'selling arrangement' on the one hand and product characteristics (including packaging) on the other—will not always be easy to identify. With the development of new television services, such as television shopping and 'infomercials', it will become increasingly difficult to identify where broadcasting (a service) ends and selling arrangements start. There is another risk here: that if a measure is found to constitute a selling arrangement, and therefore non-problematic in terms of Article 28, the ECJ may nonetheless return for a second 'bite of the cherry' and find there is a barrier to trade under Article 49 as far as advertising services are concerned.

Some commentators suggested that a clearer distinction than that between product requirements and selling arrangements can be found in the distinction between rules aimed at static and dynamic selling arrangements (see 19.6.3.1 above). The ECJ has not adopted such an approach, however, as can be seen from cases such as *Hünermund*, *Infant Milk*, *Banchero* and *TK Heimdienst* (Case C–254/98). Much more recently, the ECJ in *Schmidt* (Case C–441/04) held that a prohibition on the doorstep sale of silver jewellery was a selling arrangement and compatible with Article 28. In the *Hospital Pharmaceutical Supply case* (*Commission v Germany* (Case C–141/07)) rules imposed on pharmacists supplying products to hospitals were selling arrangements, albeit rules which might not operate equally. From this list, it seems rules relating to place of sale of particular products, as well as limitations as to who can sell them, should be seen as selling arrangements.

Contrast *Banchero*, concerning limitation on who could sell tobacco, with *Rosengren* (Case C–170/04, decision of the Grand Chamber). *Rosengren* concerned the Swedish alcohol monopoly and the consequent restriction on private individuals importing alcohol directly from overseas suppliers. Whilst the alcohol monopoly might seem to be a restriction on who can sell the product, the ECJ categorised it as a MEQR.

Another difficult case to fit in this framework is *Alfa Vita Vassilopoulos and Carrefour-Marinopoulos* (cases C–158–9/04 and C–82/05) which concerned town planning rules imposing construction restrictions with regard to bakeries and the machinery that they must have and which affected shops baking, partially pre-baked bread supplied to those shops in frozen form. This, the ECJ considered to be a product requirement, although the rules related to the place such bread was sold and not the bread itself. The reason given for the decision is that the rules affect the process of production of the product; other cases concerning planning or licensing rules have not had an impact on such a process. We can suggest that this approach is in line with the concern noted in relation to *Morellato* and *Schwarz* about where in the production process the impact of the rule is felt: the earlier in the production process, the more likely it is to affect the nature of the product. Whether this is convincing or not, is another question. Here, it is arguable that the rules should not have been considered to be a product requirement as they had no direct link with the content of the product itself; and the dual burden justification normally found with regard to product requirements is not easily found here. Further, the boundary between production and retail becomes blurred in this context. Although the Advocate-General notes that the effect of the rules is that only bakeries can sell 'bake-off' bread, it is still hard to distinguish a limitation such as this one and a rule which limits the sale of infant-formula milk to pharmacies; the rules here do not require the nature of the product itself to be changed. In this context, *Alfa Vita* could be seen as evidence of a contraction of the selling arrangement 'exception' found in *Keck*. Interestingly, the Advocate-General in *Alfa Vita* notes the difficulties in this area, and while retaining support for the *Keck* approach, makes a plea for greater clarity in this area; he suggested that the key factor is whether there is discrimination against the exercise of free movement, but the ECJ did not address the point.

19.6.4.2 *Non-discrimination in* Keck

It is not clear the extent to which the *Keck* assumption that selling arrangements should fall outside Article 28 is undercut by the requirement that any such selling arrangements should apply equally in law and, crucially, in fact. This point was raised in *De Agostini* (joined cases C–34–6/95). There, the prohibition applied to all adverts, whether they related to imported products or not. It therefore operated equally in law. The difficult question of whether it operated equally in fact was left by the ECJ to the national court, although the ECJ did note that in some circumstances the only practicable way to break into a new market will be through such advertising. Implicitly, this suggests that it would be difficult for such a rule to apply equally in practice. The ECJ has left the question of assessment of whether there is equal application in fact to the national courts (see, eg, *Burmanjer and ors* (Case C–20/03)).

The ECJ itself undertook the assessment of the equal operation of the selling arrangement in law and in fact in *Schutzverband gegen unlauteren Wettbewerb v TK-Heimdienst Sass GmbH* (case C–254/98). Under Austrian legislation bakers, butchers, and grocers may offer goods for sale on rounds from door to door, provided such sales are made by traders who have a permanent establishment in that district or in a municipality adjacent to it and the sales relate to the type of goods sold at that establishment. This rule became the subject of proceedings and the question as to whether the rule was compatible with Article 28 was referred. The ECJ found that the rules constituted a selling arrangement; it then went on to consider whether the rules applied equally in law and in fact. The fact that traders established in one part of Austria would also be affected in respect of home delivery services in other areas of Austria does not change this assessment. What was important is that 'the national legislation impedes access to the market of the Member State of importation for products from other Member States more than it impedes access for domestic products'. Whereas the application of equality in law seems to be based on the notion of discrimination, the approach to equality in fact seems to bring us back to questions about access to the market, characteristic of pre-*Keck* jurisprudence.

The problem of the equal application of selling arrangements arose again in the context of Swedish rules limiting the advertising of alcoholic beverages to publications directed to point of sale and the trade press. In *Gourmet International Products* (case C–405/98), a publisher challenged these rules on the basis that they were contrary to Articles 28 and 49 EC. In its judgment, the ECJ restated the test in *Keck*, and following *TK-Heimdienst* closely, reiterated a test based on access to the market (para 18).

It then noted that *De Agostini* accepted the possibility that a prohibition might have a greater impact on imports than on domestic products. The Court concluded:

> Even without its being necessary to carry out a precise analysis of the facts characteristic of the Swedish situation, which it is for the national court to do, the Court is able to conclude that, in the case of products like alcoholic beverages, the consumption of which is linked to traditional social practices and to local habits and customs, a prohibition of all advertising directed at consumers in the form of advertisements in the press, on the radio and on television, the direct mailing of unsolicited material or the placing of posters on the public highway is liable to impede access to the market by products from other Member States more than it impedes access by domestic products, with which consumers are instantly more familiar. [Para 21.]

The ECJ in this case seems to give the national court very little scope but to follow the ECJ's view that the national rules here do not apply equally in fact. The consequence is that the rule will fall to be assessed under the rule of reason and Article 28, as it would have been pre-*Keck*. It should be noted that the ECJ is not stating that all advertising will necessarily fall within Article 28; it clearly seeks to limit the impact of its judgment by linking the type of product to 'traditional social practices'. Nonetheless, both *Gourmet International Products* and *TK Heimdienst* suggest that the selling-arrangement/product-requirement distinction proposed in *Keck* will not always answer the question of whether a measure falls outside the scope of Article 28 or not. The problem, as the ECJ seems to be recognising, is that even selling arrangements may have an impact on trade.

The current problem is what degree of impact, actual or potential, is required before a selling arrangement does not operate equally in fact—note that *Keck* seemed to imply that a trading rule might have an inherently restrictive effect. In *Deutscher Apothekerverband eV v 0800 DocMorris* (case C–322/01), the ECJ noted in respect of a prohibition on the mail order sale of medicinal products that, despite the fact that it limited the ability of German pharmacies to gain access to the entire German market:

> [a] prohibition which has greater impact on pharmacies established outside the German territory could impede access to the market for products from other Member States more than it impedes access for domestic products. [Para 74.]

On this basis, the selling arrangement did not apply equally in fact and therefore triggered an analysis under Article 28. The wording the ECJ uses in this case is broad. Although very similar to the test used in *TK-Heimdienst* and *Gourmet*, it seems not to require an actual impact, but suggests that a potential effect would suffice. The ECJ has repeated its broad approach in *Hospital Pharmaceutical Supply case* (*Commission v Germany* (Case C–141/07)). There it held:

> For a national measure to be characterised as discriminatory or protective within the meaning of the rules on the free movement of goods, it is not necessary for it to have the effect of favouring national products as a whole or of placing only imported products at a disadvantage and not national products. [Para 39.]

This approach seems to suggest that the test for the equal application of selling arrangements is the same as the test used to identify an MEQR in the first place. If this is the case, it renders the Keck 'exception' nothing but a detour to come to the same place as an assessment of all rules would have done prior to *Keck*. It is hard to square this approach—or, indeed, that in *TK-Heimdienst* and *Gourmet*—with that in the *Greek Pharmacies* case (*Commission v Greece* (case C–391/92)), handed down shortly after *Keck*. The boundary of Article 28 seems to have moved, becoming more broadly drawn again.

Despite this line of cases, there still seems some uncertainty as to where the actual boundary of discrimination does now lie. *Karner* concerned the Austrian prohibition on misleading advertising in relation to the sale of goods via auction. In this case, the auction catalogue, including the (misleading) statement that the goods in issue were from an insolvent estate, was advertised on the Internet. By contrast to *de Agostini*, in the Court's opinion, the national provision in this case did not constitute a total prohibition on all forms of advertising.

Consequently, although the Court accepted that the prohibition could affect the total number of sales, it did not affect the marketing of products originating from other Member States more than it affects the marketing of products from the host Member State (para 42) (see also *Dynamic Medien Vertriebs GmbH v Avides Media AG* (Case C–244/06)). Crucially, the ECJ pointed to lack of evidence from those seeking to benefit from Article 28 as to the impact of the national rule. This approach, which implicitly requires an actual impact, does not seem entirely on all fours with the approach in *DocMorris*. It may well be that the different rules did have a differential impact on the facts, justifying a difference in treatment. Nonetheless, any unifying principles on which these judgments are based remain unclear.

19.6.4.3 *Other categories of trading rule*

As we noted earlier, *Dassonville* was very broad and covered many areas of law. *Keck* identifies two subcategories: product requirements and selling arrangements and tells us how to treat them. The question is, are all rules found within these two categories, or are there others? Part of the difficulties with *Alfa Vita* seems to be the underlying assumption that the measure must fall into one or other of the categories. Presumably, there is scope for viewing rules as satisfying the *Dassonville* test without having to ascribe them either to a category of product requirement or selling arrangement. We might then question whether all rules falling in this third category are equally inimical to trade. This question could arise in relation to rules relating to the use of a product. If the use of a product is prohibited, we can see that such a rule would deter consumers from buying such products with a potential impact on trade. Equally, a rule limiting the circumstances in which a product can be use (eg, a push bike not being allowed on a motorway) would have little impact on trade. It has been suggested, by the Advocate-General in *Åklagaren v Mickelsson and Roos* (case C–142/05), that such rules should be treated as analogous to selling arrangements and that the crucial factor would be whether they applied equally in law and in fact. This case has not yet been decided, so it remains to be seen what approach the ECJ will take. The issue of a ban on the use of a product, that of tinted film for car windows, has more recently come before the ECJ (*Commission v Portugal* (tinted window film) (case C–265/06)). In that case, the ECJ concluded that the rules were MEQR, and proceeded to determine if they were justified; neither it nor the Advocate-General considered the issue of whether such rules should be treated akin to selling arrangements. This omission is perhaps not surprising: a total ban on a product's use has a direct impact on its marketing and sales.

19.6.5 **Alternative solutions**

Over the years other tests have been suggested. A test of 'substantial' hindrance was suggested by Advocate-General Jacobs in *Leclerc-Siplec* (case C–412/93), although the Court chose to apply *Keck*. An approach which considers the impact of a measure, however, seems to have been favoured by the ECJ in a number of cases. We have seen that in cases such as *TK-Heimdienst* and *Gourmet International Products*, the ECJ has focused on the importers' ease of access to the markets of other Member States, rather than on the issue of whether a rule is a selling arrangement or not. In *DocMorris*, we also find references to ease of access to the market in the context of assessing whether the selling arrangement applies equally in fact. Indeed, in *Gourmet International Products*, the phrasing of the judgment is not in terms of discrimination but of access to the market. On one analysis, these rulings might not be too far from the *Keck* approach, in that *Keck* can be seen as distinguishing between measures which impact directly on the producer/importer and those which have an impact on consumers and thus only an indirect impact on the free movement rights.

On the other side of the coin the ECJ has also emphasised that the impact of national rules must not be too remote from interstate trade. In *BASF AG v Präsident des Deutschen Patentamts* (case C–44/98), BASF tried to challenge a German law which, as permitted by the European Patent Convention, required patents that were granted by the European Patent Office in respect of Germany to be translated, at the patent proprietor's cost, into German. BASF argued that because of high translation costs, patent proprietors would be forced into choosing the countries in which to have patent protection as they would not be able to afford the translation costs for the entire Union. This, in turn, would affect patent proprietors' decisions about the Member States in which the patented product would be marketed, thus partitioning the internal market, contrary to Article 28. In *ED Srl v Fenocchio* (case C–412/97), ED argued that Italian rules which precluded the obtaining of summary judgments against debtors who resided outside Italy would dissuade those resident in Italy from contracting with those who resided elsewhere, as debt recovery would be more difficult in respect of non-Italian residents. On this basis, it was argued that the rule should be regarded as incompatible with Article 29 as it would discourage exports. In both cases the ECJ gave these convoluted arguments short shrift, holding in both instances that the effect on Union law was too uncertain and indirect to constitute a measure having equivalent effect. A similar approach has also been used in the context of freedom of establishment (see Chapter 22). These cases are unlikely to constitute a significant shift in the ECJ's approach to the scope of Article 28 in which access to markets is clearly impeded. (Contrast *Schutzverband gegen unlauteren Wettbewerb v TK-Heimdienst Sass GmbH* (case C–254/98) in which the Austrian government unsuccessfully tried to argue that the impact of the legislation there would be too uncertain.)

The ECJ's approach in *BASF* and *ED Srl* was similar to that in the earlier case of *DIP SpA* (cases C–140–2/94), although with a different result. *DIP SpA* concerned a challenge to an Italian law permitting the opening of new shops in particular areas only on receipt of a licence, to be issued by municipal authorities on the recommendation of a local committee. The committee, which represented a variety of interest groups, made its recommendations according to specific criteria. Perhaps because the rule did not fall clearly within the category of either 'requirements to be met' or 'selling arrangements' the Court did not apply the *Keck* formulae. Instead it looked at the effect of the measure, and found its restrictive effect 'too uncertain and too indirect' for the obligation which it imposed to be regarded as hindering trade between Member States. It was thus compatible with Article 28.

19.7 Prohibition, as between Member States, of quantitative restrictions on exports and of all measures having equivalent effect (Article 29)

All the principles relating to imports under Article 28 will also apply to exports under Article 29, including, as seems to have been accepted by the English courts in *R v Chief Constable of Sussex, ex parte International Trader's Ferry Limited* ([1996] QB 197 (QBD), [1997] 3 WLR 132 (CA), [1999] 1 CMLR 1320), the possibility of Member States being under positive obligations by virtue of Article 29 in conjunction with Article 10, with one important exception.

It seemed that there was a difference in approach between the scope of Articles 28–9 and that measures which are *indistinctly applicable* would not breach Article 29 merely because they are capable of hindering, directly or indirectly, actually or potentially, intra-Community trade. The *Dassonville* test does not apply, but rather a test set down in *PB Groenveld BV* (case 15/79). Here, a national law prohibiting the large-scale manufacture of horsemeat sausages and limiting the sale of such sausages by small specialist butchers to consumers only, designed to safeguard exports of such products to countries which prohibit the sale of horseflesh, was found, applying the above test, not to breach Article 29, although, as Advocate-General Capotorti pointed out, it presented an almost insuperable obstacle to exports. The ECJ held that to breach Article 29 such measures must have as their specific object or effect the restriction of patterns of exports and thereby the establishment of a difference in treatment between the domestic trade of a Member State and its export trade in such a way as to provide a particular advantage for national production or for the domestic market of the state in question, at the expense of the production or of the trade of other Member States. Thus there is a double test: not only must there be a measure but it must benefit the domestic market. In other words, they must be overtly or covertly protectionist. The Court's judgment represented a clear departure from the opinion of the Advocate-General. He had approached the matter along the lines of Article 28; he applied the *Dassonville* test, and *Cassis*, and found that the measure was not justified since other, less restrictive measures, such as labelling, could have been used to achieve the same ends.

In *Oebel* (case 155/80) the restriction on night working and delivery hours for bakery products, although undoubtedly a barrier to exports, since it precluded Belgian bakers from selling bread in adjacent Member States in time for breakfast, was found, following *PB Groenveld BV*, not to breach Article 29.

On the other hand measures which are *distinctly applicable* and which discriminate against exports *will* normally breach Article 29. In *Bouhelier* (case 53/76) the requirement in France of an export licence, following a quality inspection, for watches destined for export was held to breach Article 29 since the same inspection and licences were not required for watches sold on the domestic market.

The principles of both *PB Groenveld BV* and *Bouhelier* were applied in *Jongeneel Kaas BV* (case 237/82). Here Dutch rules, indistinctly applicable, regulating the quality and content of cheese produced in The Netherlands were found not to breach Article 29, even though domestic producers were thereby at a competitive disadvantage vis-à-vis producers from other states not bound by the same standard of quality, since they did not fall within the *PB Groenveld BV* criteria, whereas a distinctly applicable rule requiring inspection documents for exports alone was, following *Bouhelier*, in breach of Article 29. This approach has been reiterated more recently, for example in *Ravil* (case C–469/00).

The Court's tolerance towards indistinctly applicable, non-protective restrictions on exports introduced in *PB Groenveld BV* is in line with the Court's attitude, noted above, towards reverse discrimination. Clearly where there is no danger of protectionism the Court can afford to take a more lenient view. Restrictions on imports, on the other hand, will always raise a suspicion of protectionism. Nonetheless, it seems that there has been a move away from the 'double' test, even if *Groenveld* is the ECJ's starting point for cases concerning exports. This can be seen in the Grand Chamber decision in *Lodewijk Gysbrechts* (case C–205/07). The case concerned a Belgian rule, which prohibited vendors from asking for customers' credit card details before the expiry of a cooling off period, even if the vendor undertook not to take payment prior to the end of that period. The ECJ accepted that this could constitute a measure having equivalent effect to a quantitative restriction on exports as it deprives traders of an efficient tool with which to guard against the risk of non-payment. The ECJ noted a discriminatory effect as such a rule would fall particularly on those who sold direct consumers in other member states where transactions were of a small pecuniary value. Thus even if the prohibition on asking for credit-card numbers applies to all, it has a greater impact on exports. The ECJ then concluded that there was a prohibited MEQR within the scope of Article 29, without considering whether there had been an advantage to the domestic market. It is hard to spot such an advantage in the facts of this case, suggesting that Article 29 is now being interpreted more broadly.

Since only protective or discriminatory measures were thought to breach Article 29, it was usually also thought that a rule of reason will not be applied and justification can only be sought under Article 30. The beginnings of a change in approach can be seen in *Schmidberger* (case C–112/00), where the ECJ discussed the justification for a 'measure' within Article 29 in conjunction with that for a MEQR within Article 28. This suggests that similar principles should be used in assessing derogations from Article 28 and 29. The ECJ did not, however, address the point directly. In *Lodewijk Gysbrechts*, however, it stated unequivocally that:

[a] national measure contrary to Article 29 EC may be justified on one of the grounds stated in Article 30 EC, and by overriding requirements of public interest, provided that the measure is proportionate to the legitimate objective pursued. [Para 45.]

Article 29 now seems to be being interpreted much more in parallel with Article 28, though there is still not equivalent of the *Keck* approach here.

19.8 State monopolies

19.8.1 Meaning of 'monopoly'

The bodies subject to Article 31 are those through which 'a Member State, in law or in fact, either directly or indirectly, supervises, determines or appreciably influences imports or exports between Member States' (Article 31(1), para 2).

To qualify as a monopoly it is not necessary to exert total control of the market in particular goods. It is sufficient if the bodies concerned have as their object transactions regarding a commercial product which could be traded between Member States, if they play an *effective* part in such trade (*Costa v ENEL* (case 6/64)).

It seems that state monopolies must be used for the pursuit of a public-interest aim; therefore, the object of Article 31 EC is to reconcile the desire of a Member State to do so with the need to maintain the common market (*Harry Franzen* (case C–189/95)). It is not clear whether monopolies which do not pursue a public-interest aim are compatible with the provisions on the free movement of goods, although it is arguable that state restrictions on granting a monopoly to a body could be characterised as 'selling arrangements' under *Keck* and *Mithouard* (contrast the approach in the *Infant Milk case* and *DocMorris*).

A state monopoly within the scope of Article 31 may also exist where an exclusive right to export or import particular goods is given to one body (*Manghera* (case C–59/75)). However, Article 31 does not apply where retailers in a Member State need to be authorised to sell a product, such as tobacco (*Banchero* (case C–387/93)). This is subject to the proviso that the state does not interfere with the *supply* of the goods to be sold and leaves the retailers free to choose the source of the product.

19.8.2 Prohibition on discrimination on grounds of nationality

Article 31 prohibits discrimination on the grounds of nationality in the operation of the state monopoly. The aim of Article 31 is not to abolish monopolies per se, but rather to ensure that they do not operate in a discriminatory manner. The overriding objective is to ensure that obstructions to the free movement of goods and distortions of competition within the Union as a result of such a monopoly are kept to a minimum. In *SA des Grandes Distilleries Peureux* (case 119/78), rules regarding the French monopoly for the distillation of raw materials were held to be discriminatory and contrary to Article 31(1) EC because they prohibited the use of raw materials imported from another Member State. In contrast, in *Harry Franzen* (case C–189/95), Swedish provisions on the existence and operation of the monopoly retailer of alcoholic beverages were found to be compatible with Article 31. The existence of this monopoly was not of concern, provided that it was set up in such a way that it was not more difficult for suppliers from other Member States to sell alcohol in Sweden.

More recently another Swedish monopoly, one concerning the retail sale of medicinal preparations, has been successfully challenged (*Hanner* (case C–438/02)). The Court reiterated its position that Article 31 does not require the abolition of state monopolies; it controls the way they operate. In this instance, the contract establishing the monopoly did not provide for either a purchasing plan or a system of calls for tender which would provide an opportunity for producers of products that are not selected by the monopoly to find out why and, possibly, to challenge the decision. Here, the state monopoly had absolutely free choice as to the products it would stock. The ECJ held that the agreement did not therefore ensure that discrimination was ruled out. On this basis the state monopoly's system for selecting the products to stock is liable to place products from other Member States at a disadvantage. It was therefore, in principle, contrary to Union law.

19.9 Relationship with other treaty provisions

19.9.1 Article 28

Article 31 is part of Title I, Chapter 2 of the EC Treaty on prohibitions of quantitative restrictions between Member States. It is as noted complementary to Articles 28–9 EC. However, in contrast to Articles 28–9, Article 31 does not benefit from the equivalent of the Article 30 derogation (see Chapter 20), and it may therefore be important to identify whether a particular provision is subject to the free movement provisions or the state monopoly provision.

It has been held that Article 31 only applies to activities that are intrinsically connected with the specific business of the monopoly (*SA des Grandes Distilleries Peureux* (case 119/78)). However, related activities may be subject to Article 28 EC. In *Franzen*, it was argued that the Swedish alcohol monopoly was contrary to both Articles 28 and 31. The ECJ drew a distinction between those provisions which related to the existence and operation of the monopoly itself, which would be subject to Article 31, and provisions which were separable from the operation of the monopoly but which had a bearing on it. The latter would be subject to assessment under Article 28 EC. The provisions at issue in *Franzen* concerned both the monopoly itself and the requirement for importers of alcohol to hold a licence. The monopoly itself was not contrary to Article 31, but the requirement of an import licence fell foul of Article 28 and could not be justified under Article 30.

19.9.2 Other provisions

Article 31 only applies to state monopolies in the provision of goods. It does not apply to services. However, if a state monopoly exists in the provision of services, and operates in a discriminatory manner, then it may be caught by the general prohibition against discrimination on grounds of nationality in Article 12 (ex 6) EC. It may also be subject to the provisions on the free movement of services (Articles 49–55 EC (ex 59–66)), or Article 82 (ex 86) EC (post Lisbon, 56–62 and 102 TFEU), which prohibits the abuse of a dominant position. To the extent that there is a comparable provision regarding services, this is Article 86(2) (post Lisbon, 106 TFEU), which deals with the provision of services of general economic interest (see also Chapter 28).

19.10 Conclusions

This chapter illustrates the importance of the jurisprudence defining the scope of the prohibition on measures having an equivalent effect to quantitative restriction. The key question is the relationship between free movement and national regulatory competence. This question is affected by the scope of the derogation principles (Chapter 20) and by positive harmonisation measures (Chapter 16). In addition to these provisions, there is also Article 31. Although there is very little jurisprudence on Article 31, it nevertheless fulfils an important function in ensuring that the free movement of goods in the common market is not restricted any more than is justifiable.

As far as this chapter is concerned, the central problem relates to how to determine the scope of Article 28. The ECJ's case law has not always been consistent and it seems that during the development of the Community different approaches have been taken ranging from tests based on discrimination, access to the market and the more formalistic approach under *Keck*. Behind all of these runs the underlying questions of how much regulation of trade (and trade-related matters) is desirable and who gets to choose the form of that regulation. With the single market, if not actually completed, being in a more developed phase than when *Dassonville*, *Cassis de Dijon*, and even *Keck*, were handed down, one remaining question is whether the internal market should tolerate more regulation and greater divergence or less.

FURTHER READING

Arnull, A, 'What shall we do on Sunday?' (1991) 16 EL Rev 112.

Barents, R, 'New developments in measures having equivalent effect' (1981) 18 CML Rev 271.

Gormley, L, 'Actually or potentially, directly or indirectly? Obstacles to the free movement of goods' (1989) 9 YEL 197.

Krämer, L, 'Environmental protection and Article 30 EEC Treaty' (1993) 30 CML Rev 111.

Mortelmans, K, 'Article 30 of the EEC Treaty and legislation relating to market circumstances: Time to consider a new definition?' (1991) 28 CML Rev 115.

Oliver, P, 'Measures of equivalent effect: A reappraisal' (1982) 19 CML Rev 217.

Prete, L, 'Of motorcycle trailers and personal watercrafts: The battle over *Keck*' (2008) 35(2) LIEI 133.

Quinn, M and McGowan, N, 'Can Article 30 impose obligations on individuals?' (1987) 12 EL Rev 163.

Reich, N, 'The November revolution: *Keck, Meng, Audi* revisited' (1994) 31 CML Rev 459.

Roth, WH, Casenote on *Keck* and *Hünermund* (1994) 31 CML Rev 845.

—— 'Export of goods and services within the single market: Reflections on the scope of Articles 29 and 49 EC' in Tridimas and Nebbia (eds), *European Union Law for the Twenty-First Century: Rethinking the new legal order* (Hart Publishing, 2004).

Steiner, J, 'Drawing the line: Uses and abuses of Article 30 EEC' (1992) 29 CML Rev 749.

Weatherill, S, 'After *Keck*: Some thoughts on how to clarify the clarification' (1996) 33 CML Rev 885.

Weatherill, S, 'Recent developments in the law governing the free movement of goods in the EC's internal market' (2006) 2 ERCL 90.

White, E, 'In search of limits to Article 30 of the EEC Treaty' (1989) 26 CML Rev 235.

Wils, WPJ, 'The search for the rule in Article 30: Much ado about nothing?' (1993) 18 EL Rev 475.

Woods, L, *Free Movement of Goods and Services in the European Community* (Ashgate, 2004), Chs 4–6.

20

Derogation from the free movement of goods

20.1 Introduction

The previous chapter has explored and emphasised the width of the fundamental principle of the free movement of goods. Article 30 (ex 36) EC contains the treaty exception to this principle. The balance between principle and exception reveals tensions at two, linked, points. The first is substantive: the balancing of different policy interests, which can be characterised as trade versus non-trade interests. The second relates to competence, that is the freedom of Member States to put into place policies and the extent to which the EU policy of free movement of goods constrains that freedom. It will be seen that, although to some degree the scope of Article 30 will be affected by the arguments brought by the Member States to justify specific national rules in sets of circumstances pertaining to individual Member States, for example national conceptions of morality, the European Court of Justice (ECJ) has ensured that final review of the scope of Article 30 remains at the Union level. Two general points can be made about the ECJ's approach. As with other freedoms, the ECJ has held that any derogation from a treaty freedom must be interpreted narrowly. This has an effect not only on the substantive scope of the heads of derogation found in Article 30, but also in terms of the application of those grounds to the national rules. The ECJ has developed the notion of proportionality, found in other areas of EU law (see Chapter 6), to ensure that where a legitimate interest exists, Member States do not try to use it to hide measures that are essentially restrictions on trade.

20.2 Outline of Article 30

The principal provision for derogation from Articles 28 and 29 (ex 30–4) EC (post Lisbon 34–5 TFEU) is Article 30 EC, which provides:

> The provisions of Articles 28 and 29 shall not preclude prohibitions or restrictions on imports, exports or goods in transit justified on grounds of public morality, public policy or public security; the protection of health and life of humans, animals or plants; the protection of national treasures possessing artistic, historic or archaeological value; or the protection of industrial and commercial property. Such prohibitions or restrictions shall not, however, constitute a means of arbitrary discrimination or a disguised restriction on trade between Member States.

If the Lisbon Treaty comes in to force, Article 30 EC will be renumbered Article 36 of the Treaty on the Functioning of the European Union (TFEU).

20.2.1 Relationship with the 'rule of reason' under *Cassis de Dijon*

Since indistinctly applicable measures restricting imports from Member States will now be subject to the rule of reason under *Cassis* (case 120/78) (Chapter 19), it will normally only be necessary to apply Article 30 EC to distinctly applicable measures in breach of Articles 28–9 EC. However, where indistinctly applicable measures are clearly discriminatory in their effect on imports, or fall within one of the heads of derogation of Article 30 EC, the Court may consider the question of justification under Article 30 EC. (See *R v Royal Pharmaceutical Society of Great Britain* (cases 266– 7/87); *Commission v UK* (Re UHT Milk) (case 124/81) to be discussed later.) Distinctly applicable measures, on the other hand, can never be justified under *Cassis*.

Justification of a distinctly applicable measure by reference to *Cassis* style reasoning was tried in *Commission v Ireland (re restrictions on importation of souvenirs)* (case 113/80). Here the Irish government sought to justify, on *Cassis* principles, an order requiring that imported souvenirs be marked 'foreign', or with their country of origin, arguing that the measure was necessary in the interests of consumers and fair trading—to enable consumers to distinguish the 'genuine' (home-produced) souvenirs from the (imported) 'fakes'. The Court held that since the measure applied only to imported souvenirs it could not be judged on *Cassis* principles. It could only be justified on the grounds provided by the then Article 36 (now 30). Since that article created an exception to the principle of free movement of goods it could not be extended to situations other than those specifically laid down. The measure could not be justified in the interests of consumer protection.

The ECJ has on occasion seemed to bend the definition of what might be seen as a discriminatory measure to allow a national measure, particularly those aimed at environmental protection, to be justified following *Cassis* on grounds not set out in Article 30 (see eg, *Commission v Belgium (Walloon Waste)* (case C–2/90)). Advocate-General Jacobs in the case of *PreussenElektra* (*PreussenElektra AG v Schleswag AG* (case C–379/98)) criticised the *Walloon Waste* case and suggested that the ECJ should abandon the distinction between distinctly and indistinctly applicable measures and allow even discriminatory measures to be capable of justification by reference to mandatory requirements, at least where environmental protection is concerned. The ECJ, however, disregarded the suggestions of the Advocate-General, and came to the conclusion that the national rules, which were aimed at encouraging the use of electricity produced from renewable energy sources, did not contravene Article 28 in the first place. As a consequence, not only has the ECJ's approach to determining whether there is a discriminatory or indistinctly applicable measure not been consistent, but it seems reluctant to address the issue of whether the distinction should stay.

20.3 Proportionality and disguised restriction on trade

Although the grounds listed in Article 30 EC appear extensive they have been narrowly construed. The Court has held on many occasions that the purpose of this article is not to reserve certain matters to the exclusive jurisdiction of the Member

States; it merely allows national legislation to derogate from the principle of free movement of goods to the extent to which this is and remains justified to achieve the objectives set out there (*Commission v Germany (re health control on imported meat)* (case 153/78)). A measure is 'justified' if it is necessary, and no more than is necessary, to achieve the desired result (the proportionality principle). There are two elements to satisfy:

- a suitability test
- a necessity test.

Both must be satisfied. Thus if measure is not appropriate to attain the objective or the same objective can be achieved by less restrictive measures, then the national measure will be found to be disproportionate. It is sometimes argued that if another Member State has chosen a different mechanism then the measure of the first Member State will be disproportionate. Differences between Member States do not, however, automatically mean that a measure is disproportionate. As Member States may choose the level of protection that they wish to award to a public interest objective, legitimate differences can arise from this fact. Thus the assessment of national provisions is provisions assessed solely by reference to the objective pursued and the level of protection which the Member State in question intends to provide.

Moreover, Article 30 EC cannot be relied on to justify rules or practices which, though beneficial, are designed primarily to lighten the administrative burden or reduce public expenditure, unless in the absence of such rules or practices the burden or expenditure would exceed the limits of what can reasonably be required (*Officier van Justitie v de Peijper* (case 104/75)).

As well as being necessary, measures must comply with the second sentence of Article 30; they must not 'constitute a means of arbitrary discrimination or a disguised restriction on trade between Member States'. Discrimination will be regarded as arbitrary if it is not justified on objective grounds. Even where a legitimate purpose can be identified, should the manner in which the Member State implements its rules benefit domestic producers, the ECJ may view this as a disguised restriction on trade. The enquiry under Article 30 is very similar to that conducted in applying the rule of reason (see Chapter 19) and, as with the application of that rule, the presumption in favour of goods lawfully marketed in one of the Member States of the Union means that a state seeking to rebut that presumption must itself prove that the conditions for the application of Article 30 are satisfied.

20.4 Grounds for derogation

20.4.1 Public morality

The public morality ground was considered in two English cases, *R v Henn* (case 34/79) and *Conegate Ltd v Customs and Excise Commissioners* (case 121/85). In *R v Henn*, the then Article 36 (now 30) was invoked to justify a ban on the import of pornographic materials. To a certain extent the ban was discriminatory, since not all pornographic material of the kind subject to the ban was illegal in the UK. In the UK it was illegal only if likely to 'deprave or corrupt', whereas under UK customs legislation, import was prohibited if the goods were 'indecent or obscene'. On a reference from the House of Lords, the ECJ found that the ban was in breach of the then Article 30 (now Article 28) but was justified under former Article 36 (now 30). Although it was discriminatory, the discrimination was not arbitrary; nor was it a disguised restriction on trade between Member States; there was no lawful trade in such goods in the UK. The measure was genuinely applied for the protection of public morality, not for the protection of national products. It was for each state to determine in accordance with its own scale of values the requirements of public morality in its territory.

The ECJ took a stricter view in *Conegate Ltd v Customs and Excise Commissioners*. Here Article 30 was invoked to justify the seizure by HM Customs and Excise of a number of inflatable rubber dolls euphemistically described as 'love dolls', together with other exotic and erotic articles imported from Germany, on the grounds that they were 'indecent and obscene'. The importers claimed the seizure was in breach of Article 28, and, since there was no ban on the manufacture and sale of such items in the UK (the sale was merely restricted), it was discriminatory. Their argument succeeded before the ECJ. The Court held that the seizure was not justified under Article 30, since, unlike *R v Henn*, there was no general prohibition on the manufacture and marketing of such goods in the UK; nor had the state adopted serious and effective measures to prevent the distribution of such goods in its territory. (Similar reasoning has been applied in the sphere of free movement of persons, see Chapter 25.) Thus, while Member States retain the freedom to regulate in the area of public morality, in cases such as this, the implication that the national measure is in fact a disguised restriction on trade will preclude the Member State from successfully relying on the derogation in Article 30 EC.

20.4.2 Public policy

This ground, potentially wide, has been strictly construed, and has rarely succeeded as a basis for derogation under Article 30 EC. However, in *R v Thompson* (case 7/78) a restriction on the import and export of gold collectors' coins was held to be justified on the grounds of public policy, since the need to protect the right to mint coinage was one of the fundamental interests of the state. More recently, it seems that the test developed under the free movement of people in the case of *Bouchereau* is being used across the four freedoms. Thus the ECJ will seek to identify if there is a sufficiently serious threat to one of the fundamental interests of society in issue. The ECJ has accepted that the need to prevent or detect crime may also fall within public policy. Examples include the need to prevent dealing in stolen cars (*Boscher* (Case C–239/90)) or to combat fraud in connection with export funds (*Deutsche Milchkontor* (case C–426/92)). Thus, Member States, retain the discretion to determine the issues which as a matter of public policy need tackling, but it is important to note that public order (and public security) cannot be defined solely by reference to the national legal system; it is certainly not enough to state that a matter is a criminal offence in a particular Member State to justify a restrictive national measure. Public policy cannot be invoked solely on the grounds that the activity which the impugned national measure seeks to curb carries criminal sanctions (*Prantl* (case 16/83)). Indeed, in many cases, as in *Prantl* itself, Article 28 EC has proved a valid defence to a criminal charge.

Unsurprisingly, the Court has repeatedly stated that public policy cannot provide a clause of general safeguard (*Commission v Italy (re ban on pork imports)* (case 7/61)) and can never be invoked to serve purely economic ends (*Commission v Italy* (case 95/81)). In *R v Secretary of State for the Home Department, ex parte Evans Medical Ltd* (case C–324/93) it found that a prohibition against the importation into the UK without a licence of the drug diamorphine could not be justified by the need to maintain the economic viability of the sole licensed manufacturer of the drug in the UK, although it might be permitted on public-health grounds to ensure that a country has reliable supplies for essential medical purposes. *Evans* indicates that financial consideration may affect legitimate public policy concerns, although the precise circumstances in which the ECJ would accept this sort of argument are unclear.

The interrelationship between public funding, in which economic considerations might play a part, and public policy underlay the debate in *R v Chief Constable of Sussex, ex parte International Trader's Ferry Ltd* ([1997] 3 WLR 132, CA, [1999] 1 CMLR 1320 HL). The case arose in the context of widespread demonstrations by animal-rights supporters against the transporting of live animals for slaughter. Demonstrations were centred in docks and airports around the UK. Extensive and expensive policing had been in force to ensure that the traffic in these animals, which was lawful, might not be prevented. The action arose from the chief constable's decision to restrict his force's services in policing demonstrations at particular ports to three days a week, in order to save resources. As a result, International Trader's Ferry Ltd was prevented by the protesters from transporting loads on the days on which policing had been withdrawn. The company sued the chief constable for the resultant losses under both English and EU law. The House of Lords' decision, confirming the legality of the chief constable's decision to withdraw policing of animal rights demonstrators on public-policy grounds, was firmly based on the need to protect public order. Financial factors, such as the need to balance scarce resources, were relevant only to the reasonableness and proportionality of the chief constable's decision.

This case which, it is submitted, is on its facts correct, may be compared with *Commission v France* (case C–265/95). Here, in the context of widespread public demonstrations in France to prevent foreign produce from reaching local markets, the ECJ found that the French authorities, in failing to take any significant action against these demonstrations, despite repeated requests from the Commission, had failed in their obligations under the EC Treaty. Since they had adduced no evidence justifying this failure, they could not rely on the public-policy derogation under Article 30.

The cases about public protest illustrate another aspect of the public-policy exception. In *Schmidberger* (case C–112/00), which concerned protests about the environmental impact of excessive road transport, the ECJ accepted that the need to protect human rights fell within public policy, an approach which the ECJ implicitly took in *Dynamic Medien Vertriebs GmbH v Avides Media AG* (case C–244/06). *Dynamic Medien* concerned a challenge to German rules which precluded the direct sale by mail order of DVDs and similar products to children if the product had not been examined and classified by the competent German authority. The ECJ noted that the objective of the measure was the protection of children, an objective recognised by international human rights law in the UN Convention on the Rights of the Child. Whilst the ECJ did not expressly state that the rights of the child formed part of public policy (and indeed, the UK suggested this might be a matter of public morality), it was discussed in that context and including human rights protection within public policy seems to be common to the other freedoms also (see eg *Omega Spielhallen* (Case C–36/02)). Whether the standard proportionality text would be applied in such a case, or whether the ECJ would adopt a balancing test as it did in the case of *Schmidberger*, seems uncertain. Whilst the proportionality test requires the national measure to be no more than necessary to achieve the objective, it is submitted that a balancing test gives greater emphasis to the value of fundamental rights and is therefore to be preferred.

Even where a public-policy justification appears to be legitimate, as in *Campus Oil Ltd* (case 72/83) (see below) in which Advocate-General Slynn was prepared to accept a public-policy justification, the Court has in the past preferred to base its judgment on other grounds. It seems that public policy will be an exception of last resort.

20.4.3 Public security

The boundary between the concept of public policy and public security is not completely clear. The ECJ has held that they are independent concepts, but this does not help us identify the nature of the boundary. In *Commission v Portugal* (Tinted Window Film) (case C– 265/06), the Advocate General suggested that the distinction used in some national systems between crime prevention (public security) and punishment (public policy) need not be transferred to the Union level. It would seem that in most cases where there is doubt, argument is made on both grounds and, again, any derogation is interpreted narrowly.

This ground was successfully invoked in *Campus Oil Ltd* (case 72/83) to justify an Irish order requiring importers of petroleum oils to buy up to 35 per cent of their requirements of petroleum products from the Irish National Petroleum Co (INPC), at prices to be fixed by the minister. The measure was clearly discriminatory and protective. The Irish government argued that it was justified, on public-policy and public-security grounds, to maintain a viable national refinery that would meet essential needs in times of crisis. The Court found it in breach of Article 28 but, contrary to the view of the Commission, justifiable on public-security grounds, since its purpose was to maintain the continuity of essential oil supplies. Petroleum products, the Court held, are of fundamental importance to the country's existence, since they are needed not only for the economy, but for the country's institutions, its vital services, and the survival of its inhabitants. The Court stressed that purely economic objectives would not provide justification under Article 30, but provided the measure was justified on other grounds the fact that it might secure economic objectives did not exclude the application of that article. As to whether the measures were necessary, the Court held that a compulsory purchase requirement would be justified only if the output of the INPC refinery could not be freely disposed of at competitive prices, and the compulsory prices only if they were competitive in the market concerned; if not, the financial loss must be borne by the state, subject to the prohibition on state aids (see Chapter 31).

The reasoning in *Campus Oil* (case 72/83) was much criticised and has not been successfully argued since. In *Cullet* (case 231/83), which concerned similar rules, the Advocate-General went to some lengths to distinguish the case from *Campus Oil*.

In another case involving oil refineries, the ECJ found the national rules in issue disproportionate (*Commission v Greece* (case 347/88)). Given the increasing possibility that fuel supplies may run low, it may be that the issue of fuel security will arise more frequently and as a more pressing matter.

20.4.4 Protection of the health and life of humans, animals, and plants

This is a potentially broad head of derogation containing three separate groups of interests: those of humans, those of animals and those of plants and covering a range of concerns. In some respects there are links between these issues and environmental considerations (eg, the *Danish bee* case: *Ditlev Bluhme* (case C–67/97), see further below). The ECJ has repeatedly held that the health and life of humans rank foremost among the assets or interests protected by Article 30 EC. The ECJ has noted the importance of this ground of derogation beyond the confines of human health—including, for example, some aspects of animal or environmental protection. In *Nationale Raad van Dierenkwekers en Liefhebbers VZW, Andibel VZW v Belgium* (case C–219/07 (prohibition on holding mammals of certain species)), the ECJ stated 'the protection of the health and life of animals constitutes a fundamental requirement recognised by Community law'. The ECJ has also recognised that 'more often than not, damage to the environment or to health cannot, by reason of its nature, be eliminated retroactively'. (See, eg, *Commission v Germany* (Case C–114/04) concerning pharmaceutical products).

It is for the Member States, within the limits imposed by the treaty, to decide on the degree of protection which they wish to afford to public health and on the way in which that degree of protection is to be achieved. Although this seems to afford Member States considerable discretion, and variance between the levels of protection chosen by the various Member States is permitted, in practice there are limitations on this discretion. So, while discriminatory measures for which justification may be sought on health grounds may include bans, tests, and inspections of imports to ensure that domestic standards are met, and licensing or documentary requirements to provide evidence of this fact, to succeed on this ground it is necessary to prove a real health risk (see also *Duphar BV* (case 238/82)) and the burden of proof falls on the Member State (see, eg, *Ahokainen and Leppik* (case C–434/04), national legislation prohibiting, without prior authorisation, the importation of undenatured ethyl alcohol of an alcoholic strength of more than 80 per cent).

A Member State will not succeed where the exporting state maintains equivalent standards and those standards are adequate to meet that risk. In *Commission v UK (re UHT milk)* (case 124/81) the Court found that a requirement that UHT milk should be marketed only by approved dairies or distributors (allegedly to ensure that milk was free from bacterial or viral infections), which necessitated the repacking and re-treating of imported milk, was not justified, since there was evidence that milk in all Member States was of similar quality and subject to equivalent controls. Although the measure was prima facie indistinctly applicable, the Court considered it to be discriminatory in effect and examined it for its compatibility with Article 30. (See also *Decker* (case C–120/95) regarding the need to maintain the quality of medical products.)

In contrast, in *Rewe-Zentralfinanz eGmbH* (case 4/75) a plant health inspection applied only to imported apples, designed to control a pest called San José scale, which was clearly in breach of Article 28, was found to be justified on health grounds, since the imported apples constituted a real risk which was not present in domestic apples. Although discriminatory, the discrimination was not arbitrary. (Although the inspection was justified, it will be remembered from Chapter 17 that the charge for the inspection was not, since Article 30 is not available to justify a charge: *Rewe-Zentralfinanze GmbH* (case 39/73).)

More recently in *Ditlev Bluhme* (case C–67/97), a prohibition on the import onto the island of Læsø of Danish domestic bees and reproductive material for them was held to be justified under Article 30. The aim of the measure was to protect an indigenous population that was in danger of disappearance as a result of cross-breeding with other bee species. The ECJ held that by seeking to protect biodiversity through ensuring the survival of a distinct indigenous species, the measures protect the life of those animals.

The health justification has often failed on proportionality grounds, or because it constitutes 'arbitrary discrimination or a disguised restriction on trade between Member States'. In the *UHT Milk* case (case 124/81), in addition to the marketing restrictions, UHT milk coming into the UK required a specific import licence. The Court found both requirements disproportionate; it was not necessary to market the products in that way, and the information gleaned from processing the licensing applications could have been obtained by other less restrictive means, for example, by declarations from importers, accompanied if necessary by the appropriate certificates. For similar reasons in *Commission v UK (re imports of poultry meat)* (case 40/82) a specific import licence requirement for poultry and eggs, allegedly designed to prevent the spread of Newcastle disease, was found not to be justified. Yet in *Commission v Ireland (re protection of animal health)* (case 74/82), which also concerned Newcastle disease, a similar import-licence requirement was permitted under Article 30 on account of the exceptionally high health standards of Irish poultry, a standard which was not matched by British flocks. The Court said it was necessary in each case to weigh the inconvenience caused by the administrative and financial burden against the dangers and risks to animal health. Thus it may be difficult to predict when a specific import licence requirement will or will not be justified. In *Ahokainen and Leppik* (case C–434/04) the ECJ left it to the national court to assess whether the national rules were such as to combat effectively abuse arising from the consumption of spirits as a drink, or whether less restrictive measures could ensure a similar result. In the view of the ECJ, the national court was in a better position to assess the facts that were pertinent to such a decision.

In the first Newcastle disease case, *Commission v UK* (case 40/82) the same licensing system was found to result in a total ban on imports from six Member States. The Court found that the measure did not form part of a seriously considered health policy and operated as a disguised restriction on trade between Member States.

Similar protectionist motives were discovered in *Commission v France (re Italian table wines)* (case 42/82). Here the Court found excessive delays in customs clearance of wine imported from Italy into France, pending analysis of the wine to ensure it complied with French quality standards. While it conceded that some analysis in the form of random checks, resulting in minor delays, might be justified, the measures taken by the French, which involved systematic checks greatly in excess of those made on domestically produced wine, were both discriminatory and disproportionate.

Cases concerning pharmaceuticals and other medicinal products have shown a greater leniency on the part of the Court, especially when there is no evidence of a protectionist motive, perhaps because of the particularly high value accorded to human health. In *R v Royal Pharmaceutical Society of Great Britain* (cases 266, 267/87) the Court found that the rules of the Society prohibiting the substitution by pharmacists of other equivalent drugs for proprietary brands prescribed by doctors, although clearly discriminatory in the effect on imports, were justified to maintain patients' confidence and to avoid the 'anxiety factor' associated with product substitution (see also *Lucien Ortscheit GmbH v Eurim-Pharm Arzneimittel GmbH* (case C–320/93)).

Although there have been a number of harmonising directives in the field of pharmaceuticals and similar products, the area is not exhaustively regulated at EU level. There is still then room for the treaty derogation (see *DocMorris* (case C–322/01), discussed in Chapter 19), which concerned, inter alia, the sale via mail order of prescription goods. The ECJ accepted that Article 30 could apply to such a restriction given the risks attaching to such products, the need to ensure the patient understands how to use them, and the need to ensure that prescriptions reach their intended recipient (para 119).

Another argument was put forward in *DocMorris* (case C–322/01), that the German system to which the Dutch mail-order suppliers were not subject, obliged pharmacies to stock a range of drugs at certain prices. The control of prices was necessary to ensure the functioning of part of the German health system. This is a different kind of public-health argument, one that is linked to the provision of a public service (see also Chapters 24 and 28). Nonetheless the ECJ has accepted the argument, at least in principle, here and in other cases. Thus, in *DocMorris*, the ECJ held:

> Although aims of a purely economic nature cannot justify restricting the fundamental freedom to provide services, it is not impossible that the risk of seriously undermining the financial balance of the social security system may constitute an overriding general-interest reason capable of justifying a restriction of that kind (see *Kohll*, para. 41; *Vanbraekel*, para. 47; *Smits and Peerbooms*, para. 72; and case C–358/99 *Müller-Fauré and Van Riet* [2003] ECR I–4509, paras 72 and 73). Moreover, a national market for prescription medicines could be characterised by non-commercial factors, with the result that national legislation fixing the prices at which certain medicinal products are sold should, in so far as it forms an integral part of the national health system, be maintained. [Para 122.]

Crucially in *DocMorris*, the German government had not put forward any arguments on this point and so the ECJ dismissed the point for that reason.

In cases where it is unclear whether a product or additive is safe (and there is no Union legislation on the point), it is possible for individual Member States to restrict the sales of such products, provided that there is a swift and accessible authorisation procedure available.

The prohibition in the *Danish bee* case (*Ditlev Bluhme* (case C–67/97)) was also found to be proportionate. In that case, as well as there being no protectionist motive, the ECJ highlighted the fact that the measures formed the basis of a mechanism recognised in international law for the protection of species—the establishment of a conservation area.

20.4.5 **Protection of national treasures possessing artistic, historic, or archaeological value**

So far these grounds have not been used successfully to provide a basis for derogation under Article 30, but it was suggested in *Commission v Italy (re export tax on art treasures)* (case 7/68) that a desire to prevent art treasures leaving the country would have justified a quantitative restriction, even though it could not justify a charge. It is thought that it would normally apply to restrictions on exports. There is also now a directive governing the export of cultural property (Directive 93/7/EC) to complement the already existing regulation (Regulation 3911/92/EEC), which deals with the export of cultural goods from Member States to third countries.

The ECJ has, on a number of occasions, held that cultural diversity does not fall within this heading, but rather must be considered as a mandatory requirement under the rule of reason (*Leclerc v Au blé vert* (case 229/83) concerning minimum book prices, approved by the Advocate-General in *Fachverband der Buch-und Medienwirtschaft* (case C–531/07)). Since Maastricht, Article 151(4) has provided 'The Community shall take cultural aspects into account in its action under other provisions of this Treaty, in particular in order to respect and to promote the diversity of its cultures' (post Lisbon, 167 TFEU).

The inclusion of this provision, and the protection awarded to cultural and linguistic diversity by Article 22 of the Charter of the Fundamental Rights of the European Union does not seem to have extended the scope of the derogation under Article 30.

20.4.6 **Protection of industrial and commercial property**

The exception provided by Article 30 for industrial and commercial property has perhaps been one of the most litigated heads of derogation. It is noteworthy in three main respects. First it constitutes the grant of a derogation in respect of actions of private individuals, the intellectual-property rights holders; the national law granting the intellectual-property rights is not under challenge as a result of Article 295 (ex 222) EC (post Lisbon 345 TFEU). It provides that 'This Treaty shall in no way prejudice the rules in Member States governing the system of property ownership'. Given this basis, it should not be surprising that a number of challenges to the rights of intellectual-property rights holders have also arisen under competition law. The ECJ has attempted to develop a parallel approach.

Secondly, the nature of intellectual-property rights is such that they often operate (or can be used) to partition the market; they thus run counter to the basic notion of the internal market. The ECJ has thus had to reconcile these competing notions. It has done so by developing two main doctrines. The first of these is the idea that there is a difference between the existence of the right and its exercise. Whilst the former is protected, the latter is subject to review to ensure that protection claimed by holders of property rights does not exceed the central area protected by the property rights, its 'specific subject matter'. Further, the Court has applied the doctrine of exhaustion to limit the scope of intellectual-property rights. The owner of the right can control the first marketing of the product, but cannot control its marketing and distribution thereafter.

The third significant point is that the doctrine of proportionality, which is central in the assessment of the acceptability of derogations under other grounds and, indeed, in respect of the rule of reason, does not tend to arise here, or at least not expressly. It may be that the limitations imposed by the specific subject matter of the right operate to fulfil the same function, or that the exercise of rights beyond those limitations implicitly constitutes a disguised restriction on trade.

In the light of the vast body of cases, the parallels with intellectual-property rights cases under the competition provisions, and the dissimilarities with those under Article 30, this chapter will not deal with the case law on intellectual-property rights. Instead, they will be discussed together with the relevant competition law cases in a separate chapter, Chapter 30.

20.5 Derogation provisions other than Article 30 EC

In addition to the rule of reason and Article 30 EC there are further specific provisions of the treaty allowing for derogation from the principles of Articles 28 and 29 EC, mainly in the field of economic and commercial policy; hence the Court's refusal to allow Article 30 to justify purely economic measures. These comprise:

(a) measures to meet *short-term economic difficulties* ('conjunctural policy') (Article 99 EC (ex 103; post Lisbon, Article 121 of the TFEU))

(b) measures to meet *balance of payment difficulties* (Articles 108–11 EC (ex 107–9; post Lisbon, Articles 130–2 and Article 219 TFEU)

and most important of all:

(c) measures to meet:

  (i) *deflections of trade* which might obstruct the execution of EU commercial policy or

  (ii) *economic difficulties in any Member State* resulting from the implementation of commercial policy (Article 134 (ex 115) (see *Criel, nee Donckerwolcke v Procureur de la République* (case 41/76)).

  This last provision would be repealed by the Treaty of Lisbon should it come in to force.

Article 134 EC applies only in the context of the common commercial policy—ie, to goods originating from third countries that are in free circulation within the EU—and is necessary, since deflections of trade or economic difficulties may well arise as a result of differences in regimes between Member States, permitted under the Unions's common commercial policy.

Measures taken under the above articles are required to be taken either by the Commission or the Council (on a proposal from the Commission), or, if taken by Member States, subject to authorisation or approval by the Commission. They are subject to strict EU control. As with measures taken under Article 30, they must comply with the proportionality principle.

Derogation is also permitted *in the interests of national security* (Articles 296–7 EC (ex 223–4; post Lisbon, Articles 346–7 TFEU)). Under Article 296, a state 'may take such measures as it considers necessary for the protection of the essential interests of its security which are connected with the production of or trade in arms, munitions and war material', provided that such measures do not adversely affect competition within the common market regarding products which are not intended for military purposes. Under Article 297 EC, states may consult with each other and take steps to counteract measures taken by a Member State in the event of war or the threat of war or serious internal disturbances, or to carry out obligations undertaken for the purpose of maintaining peace or international security. Should the Commission or a Member State consider that a state is making improper use of its powers under Articles 296–7 they may bring that state before the Court under Article 298 EC. It would seem that for these provisions, as for Article 30, where there is an EU measure covering the specific subject, a Member State cannot rely on the derogation provided in the treaty itself. In *R v HM Treasury, ex parte Centro-Com Srl* (case C–124/5), for example, the UK sought, on the basis of the UN sanctions against Serbia and Montenegro, to prevent the payments of sums held in a London bank account by a Montenegrin to an Italian company. The ECJ, however, pointed out that this issue was dealt with by an EC regulation and that the UK could thus not rely on the national security exception in the then Article 224 (now 297) EC.

20.6 Conclusions

In the area of the derogation from free movement, the ECJ has sought to reconcile the tension between the needs of the internal market and those of the individual Member States, a task that is not always easy to accomplish. The approach of the ECJ has interpreted the scope of the derogation provisions narrowly. Although the ECJ has shown some willingness to accept a Member State's assessment of when a public-interest issue arises, as can be seen in the sphere of public policy, public health, and even as regards the existence of intellectual-property rights, it has stringently assessed whether any national measures are necessary or whether such measures constitute a disguised restriction on trade. In this context the principle of proportionality has been central. Some relatively recent case law, such as *PreussenElektra* in the environmental field, suggests that in policy areas in which the EU itself has interests—such as the protection of the environment (see Article 6 EC, discussed in Chapter 2)—then the ECJ may be prepared to more generous. This case law is as yet tentative and may well be limited to environmental concerns. For the rest, it seems that the internal market and trade concerns continue to be high priorities, a state of affairs which means that the protection offered through harmonising legislation (Chapter 16) remains important.

FURTHER READING

Alexander, W, 'IP and the free movement of goods: 1996 caselaw of the ECJ' [1998] 29 IIC 16.

Castillo de la Torre, F, 'Trade marks and free movement of pharmaceuticals in the European Community: To partition or not to partition' [1997] 6 EIPR 304.

Roberts, G, Casenote on *Gallaher* (1994) 31 CML Rev 165.

Weatherill, S, 'Regulating the internal market: Result orientation in the House of Lords' (1992) 17 EL Rev 299.

Weatherill, S, Casenote on *Gallaher* (1994) 19 EL Rev 55.

Woods, L, *Free Movement of Goods and Services in the EC* (Ashgate, 2004), Ch 7.

Ludwig, R, and O'Gorman, R, 'A cock and bull story? Problems with the protection of animal welfare in EU law and some proposed solutions' (2008) 20(3) J Env L 363–90.

21

Citizenship: Rights of free movement and residence

21.1 Introduction

The rights relating to free movement of individuals have changed dramatically over the EU's existence. Originally, these rights formed part of the rules creating the single market and had a primarily economic focus. With the jurisprudence of the European Court of Justice (ECJ), we see a broad interpretation being given to these rights. As well as having an economic function, allowing the movement of factors of production, the free-movement provisions have also been interpreted in the light of the fact that economic actors are people, not just inanimate objects, allowing them social and ancillary rights. This approach has been given political recognition through the introduction of European citizenship and reinforced through the ECJ's interpretation, not just of the citizenship provision itself, but of the original free-movement provisions in the light of citizenship.

The free-movement right can be seen to comprise three elements. The first is the right to move to another Member State and to live there (including the right to remain). This is a prerequisite to the second right, which is to access the job market in the host Member State. Finally, but importantly in terms of removing disadvantages to the migrant arising from the exercise of the right of free movement, there are ancillary rights. This chapter is the first of three dealing with free-movement rights and will deal with the first of these aspects: access and residence, as well as the question of who benefits from the free-movement rights. The succeeding chapters will deal with economic and social aspects respectively. Limitations will be dealt with thereafter.

When considering this area, it is important to note the layering of different provisions: the citizenship provisions are broad, underpinning the system; the original free-movement rights (Articles 39, 43, and 49 EC) accord some groups additional rights. Their rights are all implemented through Union legislation. None of these provisions replaces the other and their relationship gives rise to some quirks in the level of protection awarded in different circumstances. Thus, although citizenship provides a broad framework of rights diminishing the need for an economic nexus found in the original treaty freedoms, it is important still to understand the varying scope of categories of beneficiary under Articles 39 (ex 48) (workers), 43 (ex 52) (establishment), and 49 (ex 59) (services) to recognise of the different level and scope of protection so awarded. In this discussion two themes recur. The first concerns the link between migration and the rights claimed; the second, the underlying concern about abuse of Union-law rights. It seems that questions about the appropriate scope of rights are now being dealt with by a test focusing on the degree of integration for the immigrant into society in the host Member State. Furthermore, while some rights may be exercised by citizens, others may be exercised by citizens and legal persons, raising the question of the extent to which the same interpretation should be given to the provisions when they are exercised by individuals or inanimate bodies.

21.2 Overview of provisions

21.2.1 Citizenship: Article 18 EC

Article 18 (ex 8a) EC provides:

> (1) Every citizen of the Union shall have the right to move and reside freely within the territory of the Member States, subject to the limitations and conditions laid down in this Treaty and by the measures adopted to give it effect.

A second paragraph gives the Union institutions the power to enact legislation to facilitate the exercise of the rights granted using the co-decision procedure. The Treaty of Nice added a further paragraph:

> (3) Paragraph 2 shall not apply to provisions on passports, identity cards, residence permits or any other such document or to provisions on social security or social protection.

Article 18 will be renumbered should Lisbon come into force: Article 21 of the Treaty on the Functioning of the European Union (TFEU). The right to move and to reside will also be contained in Article 20 TFEU post Lisbon; the significance (if any) of this duplication is not clear. Note that Article 18 grants two rights: the right to move and the right to reside. Although the ECJ's jurisprudence has long recognised that the corollary of the right to move and to work (whether as an employed or self-employed person) implied the right to reside in the host Member State (see below), Article 18 constitutes the first express treaty recognition of this right.

21.2.2 Workers: Article 39 EC

The principal treaty provision governing the free movement of workers is Article 39 (ex 48) EC:

> 1. Freedom of movement for workers shall be secured within the Community.
>   It elaborates the aspects of this freedom and in particular:
>
>   . . .
>
> 3. It shall entail the right, subject to limitations justified on grounds of public policy, public security or public health:
>
>   . . .
>
>   (b)   to move freely within the territory of Member States for this purpose; . . .

(c) to stay in a Member State for the purpose of employment in accordance with the provisions governing the employment of nationals of that State laid down by law, regulation or administrative action;

(d) to remain in the territory of a Member State after having been employed in that State, subject to conditions which shall be embodied in implementing regulations to be drawn up by the Commission.

Should the Lisbon Treaty come into force, this provision will be renumbered Article 45 TFEU, and the reference to 'Community' shall be changed to 'Union'.

21.2.3 Establishment: Article 43 EC

Article 43 (ex 52), paragraph 1 provides:

Within the framework of the provisions set out below, restrictions on the freedom of establishment of nationals of a Member State in the territory of another Member State shall be prohibited. Such prohibition shall also apply to restrictions on the setting up of agencies, branches or subsidiaries by nationals of any Member State established in the territory of any Member State.

The Lisbon Treaty would somewhat unhelpfully renumber this provision Art. 49 TFEU, as this means the provision dealing with establishment after Lisbon comes into force will have the same treaty number as the provisions dealing with services do under the current system.

21.2.4 Services: Article 49 EC

Article 49 paragraph one provides:

Within the framework of the provisions set out below, restrictions on freedom to provide services within the Community shall be prohibited in respect of nationals of Member States who are established in a State of the Community other than that of the person for whom the services are intended.

Again, this provision would be renumbered should the Lisbon Treaty come into force, as Article 56 TFEU. The reference to 'Community' will be amended to refer to 'Union' and 'Member State' inserted for 'State of the Community'. These are not changes of significance.

21.2.5 Implementing legislation

As required under Articles 39(3)(d) (ex 43(3)(d)) and 40 (ex 49), secondary legislation was introduced to give further substance to the above principles. Notably, the Residence Directives extended rights of movement to the non-economically active, provided those individuals were not a burden on the social assistance schemes of the host Member State. The resulting legislation was updated and consolidated by Directive 2004/38/EC, the Citizenship Directive, which was additionally based on

Article 18 EC. Whilst one of the regulations, Regulation 1612/68, was amended by this directive, Articles 10–11 being repealed and the rest of the regulation remaining, the remainder of the existing legislation was repealed by the Citizenship Directive.

21.3 Enforcement

As we have seen in Chapter 3, there are different legal consequences from the choice of type of legal measure, regulations being directly applicable and directives being binding on those to whom they are addressed. The fact that the doctrine of direct effect (Chapter 5) cannot be relied on in horizontal situations in respect of directives may have consequences for the enforceability of the rights contained in the Citizenship Directive, should they need to be relied on against private individuals (eg refusal to give employment to a migrant worker's family member of grounds of nationality—see former Article 11 Regulation 1612/68). Rights of access to the territory will only be relied on against public bodies and should not therefore cause problems in this regard.

These implementing measures, as the Court held in *Procureur du Roi v Royer* (case 48/75), merely determine the scope and detailed rules for the exercise of rights conferred directly by the treaty. Implementing measures are not necessary to give effect to the treaty articles. Article 39 may thus be relied on by individuals in their national courts. Likewise, Articles 43 (*Reyners v Belgium* (case 2/74)) and 49 (*van Binsbergen* (case 33/74)) have direct effect. Clearly, an individual may enforce the rights contained in these articles against public bodies (*Steinhauser v City of Biarritz* (case 197/84) see Chapter 24), but do they have horizontal effect? The implication from early case law was that they should. In *Walrave v Association Union Cycliste Internationale* (case 36/74), the Association, a legally recognised professional body, was found to be bound by the terms of what is now Article 49. To put an end to any doubt, the ECJ, drawing on its previous case law (*Walrave* (case 36/74), and *Bosman* (case C–415/93, discussed Chapter 23), stated in its judgment in *Angonese v Cassa di Risparmio di Bolzano SpA* (case C–281/98), in relation to workers, that 'limiting application of the prohibition of discrimination based on nationality to acts of a public authority risks creating inequality in its application' (para 33). Therefore the prohibition on discrimination set out in Article 39 applies to private persons as well as to public bodies (para 36). It seems likely that the *Angonese* style reasoning will apply to both establishment and the provision of services.

One question which has not been addressed directly is that of whether the horizontal nature of Articles 39, 43, and 49 will also apply where the acts in question are not directly discriminatory on grounds of nationality but which nonetheless impede access to the market. It is nonetheless clear that some private bodies—such as sporting bodies—will be bound even in cases of indirect discrimination or access to the market, as *Bosman* illustrates. Two further cases (*Laval un Partneri v Svenska Byggnadsarbetareförbundet* (case C–341/05) and *International Transport Workers' Federation (ITF) and Finnish Seamen's Union (FSU) v Viking Line*, case C–438/05) concerning Articles 49 and 43 respectively confirm that industrial action will, in principle, be caught by the treaty. The logic of extension to all private bodies would be the same as for *Angonese*, but given the potential breadth of circumstances in which the provision could be applied, it may be very difficult to police. This is one reason which has been given for limiting the scope of Article 28 in relation to goods to public bodies.

Originally, it was not clear whether Article 18 had direct effect. Many Member States, such as the UK, suggested it did not, whereas the Commission took the contrary view. As we have just seen, the mere fact that secondary legislation is envisaged in a policy area, as here, does not preclude the treaty provision itself from having direct effect (see, eg, *Procureur du Roi v Royer* (case 48/75); *Reyners* (case 2/74); *Van Binsbergen* (case 33/74)). For some time the ECJ avoided ruling on whether Article 18 has direct effect, despite a number of references on this point, dealing instead with the references on other grounds (eg, *Wijsenbeek* (case C–378/97)). Eventually, however, the ECJ confirmed that Article 18 does have direct effect (see, eg, *D'Hoop* (case C–224/98)).

21.4 Personal scope: Who benefits?

21.4.1 General

'Who benefits' is the first question we need to ask when considering the scope of the free movement provisions. It is possible to identify some common themes running through the jurisprudence relating to Articles 18, 39, 43 and 49 EC:

(a) nationality

(b) migration *v* internal situation.

An additional requirement arises in relation to Articles 39, 43, and 49—that there is an economic nexus, though this requirement has been phrased in slightly different language in the case of each article. This essentially comes down to the question of who are workers; what are establishment and services? These questions are discussed at, respectively, 21.4.5, 21.4.6, and 21.4.7 below. Crucially, the requirement of an economic nexus does not arise in the context of Article 18, though the extent to which the distinction in treatment, between those who are economically self-sufficient and those who are not, has been entirely removed is questionable (see 21.5.2 below and Chapter 23).

21.4.2 Nationality

The rights in Article 18 EC are granted to all European citizens. Article 17 (ex 8) EC defines European citizens as: 'Every person holding the nationality of a Member State'. Although not expressly required by the wording of Article 39 EC itself, a worker must be a national of one of the Member States. The right of establishment and the right to provide services is accorded under the treaty to EU nationals and to companies formed according to the law of one of the Member States (on companies, see further 21.4.3 below). To benefit from the freedom to provide services, an EU national (or company) must be established in a Member State. Thus in *Fidium Finanz AG v Bundesanstalt* (case C–452/04) a Swiss company providing credit services could not rely on Article 49 to challenge German rules requiring authorisation by the relevant German authorities of companies providing such services in Germany. There is here a double requirement of nationality (of one of the Member States of the Union) and residence, and both must be satisfied. *FKP Scorpio Konzertproduktionen GmbH v Finanzamt Hamburg-Eimsbüttel* (case C–290/04) concerned the case of a recipient of services, who was contracting with a party in another Member State. Normally this situation would be covered by Article 49, but in this case, the contracting party—although established in another Member State—did not have the nationality of one of the Member States. Article 49 did not therefore apply. As the ECJ commented, the treaty 'does not extend the benefit of those provisions to providers of services who are nationals of non-member countries, even if they are established within the Community and an intra-Community provision of services is concerned' (para 68).

Nationality is determined according to the domestic law of the Member State concerned. As a protocol to the Treaty of the European Union (TEU) made clear, it is for each Member State to decide for itself who is to be considered a national of that Member State. Thus, Member States may only require that an individual provide appropriate identity documents and may not criticise the decision of another Member State to recognise an individual as having the nationality of that Member State. Although the protocol relates to the introduction of citizenship, this approach pre-dates it. In *Micheletti* (case C–369/90), for example, the ECJ held that the Spanish could not challenge the claim of Micheletti—who had the nationality of both Italy and Argentina—to be Italian on the grounds that the Spanish did not recognise the concept of dual nationality. According to the ECJ, the important point was whether the Italians recognised his claim (see also *Stephen Saldanha and MTS Securities Corporation v Hiross Holding AG* (case C–122/96)). The viewpoint of the Member State is determinative, as can be seen in *Kaur* (case C–192/99). The English High Court referred certain questions to the ECJ concerning the extent of the freedom of Member States to define citizenship and, in particular, the limitations imposed on this freedom by the need to respect individuals' fundamental rights (*R v Secretary of State for the Home Department, ex parte Manjit Kaur*, case C–192/99). The ECJ avoided answering the specific questions on the impact of fundamental human rights, but confirmed that the scope of European citizenship, as far as British subjects were concerned, was determined by the relevant British declarations on this subject.

Unusually, this important criterion for access to Union rights is not an EU concept and inequalities as to who may benefit from a range of rights may be apparent across the Union (contrast, for example, the definition of 'worker', which is a Union concept). As the *Chen* case ((case C–200/02), discussed at 21.4.5 below) illustrates, the patchwork of different national approaches to nationality, which gave a child of Chinese parentage born and resident in the UK Irish citizenship, can have some strange, unintended effects which can be manipulated to an individual's advantage. As *Chen* also illustrates, following the approach in *Micheletti* and other cases, Member States cannot challenge another Member State's choice about refusing or restricting citizenship/nationality (see *Rottmann v Freistaat Bayern* (case C–135/08) on the impact of the revocation of nationality, though at the time of writing not yet decided). This may have particular consequences for recent Member States, many of which have not granted citizenship on the Russian population who are nonetheless legally resident within their territory, and many of whom have been born in territory that now forms part of the EU. As a result of a national decision, these people are denied European citizenship, with consequences for free movement rights.

21.4.3 Companies

One final point to note concerns Articles 43 and 49. These two rights, unlike citizens' rights and workers' rights, are expressed as capable of being claimed by legal persons. Article 48 EC specifies:

> Companies formed in accordance with the law of a Member State and having their registered office, central administration or principal place of business within the Community shall be treated in the same way as natural persons who are nationals of Member States.

If Lisbon comes into force, Article 48 EC will become Article 54 TFEU.

A company's 'nationality' is determined by reference to the Member State in which it has its seat (*Commission v France (tax credits)* (case 270/83)). In the same way as a Member State may choose the conditions on which it grants nationality to individuals, it may choose the connecting factors for a company to acquire 'nationality', that is the conditions it must satisfy to be recognised by the law of the Member State as a company established under the laws of that Member State (*Cartesio Okató és Szolgàltató bt* (case C–210/06)). There are two main theories governing the formation of companies: that which posits that a company is established where it has its main administration (*siège réel*) or that which determines the question by reference to where the company has its formal head office (*siège statutaire*). The fact that Member States have not taken a common approach to this question has given rise to some problems. A brief overview of the position as regards companies and the particular difficulties arising in that context is given at Chapter 22 (at 22.9).

Where the central management or principal place of business lies outside the Union the company's activities must have:

> [an] effective and continuous link with the economy of a Member State, excluding the possibility that this link might depend on nationality, particularly the nationality of the partners or the members of the managing or supervisory bodies, or of persons holding the capital stock. ['General programme for the abolition of restrictions on freedom to provide services', *Common Market Reporter*, para 1546; JO 1962, 32.]

This link is the price exacted for valuable access to the Union market.

21.4.4 Transitional arrangements

Where a state has acceded to the EU but is still subject to transitional arrangements, a national of that state may claim rights as a 'favoured EU national' only insofar as that status ensues from the transitional provisions, unless he has been lawfully employed in the territory of one of the old Member States (*Lopes da Veiga* (case 9/88)).

Such arrangements have been criticised both as a matter of principle and for practical reasons. The restrictions run counter to the notion of free movement and equality of citizenship enshrined in the EU treaties. They are also complex, especially given the way different Member States have chosen to apply them.

21.4.5 Migration and the internal situation

The ECJ has long held that the freedoms constituting the common market do not apply to internal situations; there must be a cross-border element. This, then, constitutes the limit of Union competence. Thus, in *Nino* (joined cases C–54, 91/88 and 14/89), Italian law made it an offence to practise as a doctor without proper authorisation. Nino and others charged with her were Italian nationals who qualified as biotherapists and pranotherapists, activities which fell within the definition of doctor, while residing in Italy and who were charged as a result of treatment administered solely within the territory of that Member State. The ECJ held that Article 43 did not apply to this situation as it was purely internal (see in relation to Article 49 eg *Jägerskiöld* (case C–97/98) which concerned access to fishing rights; in respect of Article 39: *Hecker* and *Jacquet*(joined cases C–64 and 65/96)). In *D'Hoop* (case C–224/98), the would-be claimant of a job-seekers allowance, who had done her schooling in another Member State although her parents had not moved from their state of origin, was held not to fall within Article 39. The workers in this case were the parents and they had not moved; the person moving had not worked. Nonetheless, the ECJ held that she fell within Union law by virtue of Article 18. In this, the ECJ seemingly rejected the argument of the British government that to fall within Union law not only must an individual move but also pursue an activity which falls within the scope of the treaty, such as studying for a vocational course. This is a qualitative shift in approach: the consequence of citizenship is that movement in itself triggers Union law.

Although the rights conferred by Article 18 arise as a consequence of an individual holding the nationality of a Member State without further requirement (see eg, *Zablocka-Weyhermüller v Land Baden-Württemberg* (case C–221/07), para 26), the ECJ has nonetheless repeatedly held that internal situations fall outside the scope of Union law, even where citizenship is in issue. Internal situations have, however, been construed narrowly.

The migration requirement can be easy to satisfy, as *de Coster* (case C–17/00) illustrates. There the ECJ accepted the potential for movement as sufficient. *De Coster* concerned a tax on the installation of satellite dishes. Although the complainant had not exercised his right to free movement, nor were the satellite dishes necessarily imported, the ECJ assumed a cross-border element because the dishes could receive satellite television signals which, as they are inherently transnational, might be from another Member State. This case not only confirms that services themselves can move (as well as the person providing or receiving them), it suggests that where there is the possibility of cross-border movement, the test for migration will be satisfied (see similarly Chapter 19 regarding the free movement of goods). Two subsequent cases on municipal taxes reaffirm this point: *Mobistar* (case C–544/03) and *Viacom* (case C–134/03). *Mobistar* concerned a tax on mobile phone masts and *Viacom* concerned a tax on bill posting. Although in both these cases the national rules were found to be acceptable under Article 49, the ECJ's reasoning still assumed the possibility of a cross-border element, suggesting a desire on its part to have the jurisdiction to scrutinise national rules for compliance with free-movement rights.

The ECJ has stretched the idea of migration into other areas, where the argument for the link with Union law is not based on the potential for cross-border movement. This point is illustrated by the somewhat unusual facts in the case of *Chen* (case C–200/02). The case concerned a Chinese couple who travelled to the UK when Mrs Chen was six months' pregnant. She gave birth to a daughter, Catherine, in Belfast and both mother and daughter then moved to Cardiff. Catherine did not acquire British citizenship, as birth in the territory of the UK itself no longer confers British nationality. The operation of Irish nationality laws meant that Catherine did acquire Irish nationality, as any person born on the island of Ireland is an Irish citizen from birth if not entitled to citizenship of any other country. Catherine lost the right to Chinese nationality by virtue of being born in Northern Ireland. None of the parties was entitled to reside in the UK under British law, but Catherine was not entitled to reside in China. The parties were not dependent on the British state to survive and it was unlikely that they would be so dependent. Nonetheless, the Secretary of State refused Mrs Chen and Catherine long-term residence permits. The British and Irish governments argued that Catherine could not exercise free-movement rights because she had not moved from one Member State to another; she had only ever lived in the UK.

The ECJ rejected this argument. Relying on *Garcia Avello* (case C–148/02), the ECJ held that the situation of a national of one Member State who has only ever lived in the host Member State cannot be assimilated to a purely internal situation (para 19). Further, the ability to exercise free-movement rights is not circumscribed by the need to acquire legal capacity; children may exercise free-movement rights. These, and similar cases, raise the question of the longevity of migration status (see also *Grunkin and Paul* (case C–353/06)) or, put another way, if you have migrated once, are you always a migrant? On the basis of current case law, children whose parents exercised free-movement rights, or whose parents hold different EU nationalities, would seem destined to live their lives within the sphere of EU law. Another question then arises: what is the scope of the rights available in such circumstances?

Questions as to scope and longevity of rights are not new, though the impact of citizenship might be significant in terms of the circumstances in which rights can arise. In *Konstantinidis v Stadt Altensteig-Standesamt and Another* (Case C–168/91) a Greek national was established as a self-employed person in Germany. His claim was based on the fact that his name, χρήηστοζ Κωνσταντινίδηζ, was wrongly transliterated as 'Konstadinidis' on the marriage register there, instead of the correct 'Konstantinidis', as found on his passport. When he applied for rectification of the register, he was told that German rules required transliteration according to a particular standard, which resulted in the (incorrect) transposition. He challenged the rule as contrary to the then Article 52 (now Article 43). Note that the marriage register did not relate to his business activities; accepting his argument would have meant a broad scope being applied to the right, which was not necessarily tied to the initial exercise of the free-movement right or the continuing activity. The Advocate-General took the view that the rules constituted covert discrimination and the fact that this was not directly related to his business was irrelevant. He further considered the question of whether Konstantinidis was entitled to rely on the

ECHR (particularly Article 8 with regard to private life) as protected by Union law and concluded that he was. The ECJ, however, took a different approach. It held:

> Rules of this kind must only be considered incompatible with Article 52 EEC [now Article 43 EC] in so far as their application creates for the Greek national such a constraint that it actually interferes with the unfettered exercise of the right of establishment conferred upon him by that Article. [Para 15.]

This is a much narrower conception, making clear the link with the economic function of the provision, rather than the approach suggested by the Advocate-General, which would have had the impact of creating a class of favoured migrants. Whether Article 43 is still so limited as regards the rights of individuals in the light of the introduction of citizenship rights may, however, be questionable (contrast *D'Hoop* above). We return to the issue of the scope of rights, and particularly Union competence in Chapters 22 and 23.

A similar broad approach to the existence of the connection with Union law can be seen with regard to companies. Migration occurs not only when a company moves, but when it sets up a branch, agency, or subsidiary in another Member State. Establishment rights may be exercised against home and host Member State. In *Marks and Spencer* (case C–446/03) a British law precluded a parent company from deducting losses made by its subsidiaries in other Member States, though it could deduct losses made by subsidiaries in the UK. The effect of this rule was to deter companies established in the UK from establishing subsidiaries in other Member States. Thus a UK rule was challenged by a UK company; the cross-border element was provided by the impact on its choices about whether to set up subsidiaries in other Member States; actual movement—or relocation—by the company was not required. (See similarly *Cadbury Schweppes v Commissioners of Inland Revenue* (case C–196/04), which concerned a national tax rule which operated so as to dissuade companies from establishing themselves in Member States with a low-tax regime.)

A right may also be relied on when those who have exercised their rights of free movement seek to return to their state of origin. In *Knoors* (case 115/78), a Dutch national moved to Belgium where he worked as a plumber. He returned to the Netherlands and relied on his experience in Belgium when he sought to have his qualifications recognised by the Dutch authorities. A similar approach can be seen with relation to workers (eg *R v Immigration Appeal Tribunal, ex parte Secretary of State for Home Department* (case C–370/90)). Mr Singh was an Indian who had married a British national in 1982. He and his wife subsequently went to work in Germany, returning in 1985 to open a business in the UK. Their marriage broke down in 1988. Following the issue of a decree nisi but before the decree became absolute, that is before the divorce was finalised, the UK authorities sought to deport Mr Singh. His appeal against the deportation order was successful. Since the divorce was not yet a legal fact, the case still concerned the position of spouses and the rights that spouses could claim under EU law. The question of the effect of the subsequent divorce was not an issue before the Court (although the fact of divorce was known). The ECJ held that, as the spouse of an EU national who had exercised her rights to work in Germany, Singh was entitled on their return to claim his rights as a spouse under EU law. *Singh*, at the time, was considered significant for its approach regarding genuine marriages; the full significance of the right to return had yet to be recognised and the issue of longevity of rights was not raised (see further 21.5.1.1 below). Likewise in *Eind* (case C–291/05) (discussed at 25.5.1.1), the ECJ held that a worker would have such rights against his state of origin irrespective of whether he was going to engage in economic activity there.

Additionally, what is implicit in the company cases, such as *Marks and Spencer* and *Cadbury Schweppes* is that the right of exit allows beneficiaries of a free movement right to rely on that right not just against the host Member State, but also as against the state of origin.

21.4.6 Meaning of 'worker' for Article 39 EC

As the ECJ held in *Levin v Staatssecretaris van Justitie* (case 53/81), the concept of 'worker' is a Union concept, not dependent for its meaning on the laws of Member States. There are two aspects to the definition of worker:

- a formal aspect
- an economic aspect.

The formal aspect questions whether an individual is employed, rather than self-employed; while the economic test looks at the nature, duration, and quality of the work. These two elements can be seen in *Lawrie-Blum v Land Baden-Württemberg* (case 66/85), which concerned a trainee teacher. The German government contended that, as a trainee, Lawrie-Blum did not fall within the definition of 'worker'. The ECJ rejected this argument and in doing so laid down a three-stage test for a worker. It suggested that the 'essential characteristic' of a worker is that:

1. during a certain period of time
2. he performs services for and under the direction of another
3. in return for remuneration.

Note that remuneration need not be in the form of cash, but could also be benefits in kind (see *Steymann* (case 196/87), below).

As regards the economic element of the test for 'worker', in *Levin* (case 53/81) the ECJ held that the term 'worker' applied even to those who worked to a limited extent (ie, part-time), provided that the work was 'real' work, and not nominal or minimal. The rights only attach to those who perform or wish to perform an activity of an economic nature. The Court went on to say that this principle applied whether the worker was self-supporting or whether he wished to make do with less than the national minimum income. It was able to side-step the problem of the part-time worker who relies on public funds for his support.

This issue was squarely faced in *Kempf v Staatssecretaris van Justitie* (case 139/85). Kempf was a German, a part-time music teacher working in The Netherlands from 1981 to 1982. During this time he was in receipt of Dutch supplementary benefit, both sickness benefit and general assistance. In November 1981 he applied for a Dutch residence permit. He was refused on the grounds that he was not a 'favoured EC citizen', since his income from his work was not sufficient to meet his needs. He challenged that decision before the Dutch courts. The Raad van State referred to the ECJ the question whether a part-time worker such as Kempf, whose income was below subsistence level and who did not have sufficient means of support, was a 'worker' entitled to benefit under Union law. The Court replied that he was. Freedom of movement of workers was, it held, one of the fundamental freedoms and must, as such, be defined broadly; a person who pursued a genuine and effective activity as an employed person, even on a part-time basis, could not be excluded from the scope of Union rules merely because he sought to supplement his income, which was lower than the means of subsistence, by other lawful means of subsistence. It was irrelevant whether the income was supplemented out of a private income or from public funds.

The Court has, however, held that the duration of the activity concerned was a factor which might be taken into account in assessing whether the employment was effective and genuine or so limited as to be marginal or ancillary (*Raulin,* (case C–357/89), see further 21.4.6.1 below and note similarities with services and establishment case law).

Following *Kempf,* in *Steymann v Staatssecretaris van Justitie* (case 196/87) the Court held that the claimant's occupation as part of a religious community, entitling him to his 'keep' and pocket money, but not to formal wages, constituted a genuine and effective activity where commercial activity is an inherent part of membership of that community. In contrast, in *Bettray v Staatssecretaris van Justitie* (case 344/87) paid activity provided by the state as part of a drug rehabilitation programme under its social employment law was held by the Court not to represent 'real and genuine economic activity'. To give rise to the status of 'worker', the work performed must fulfil, or derive from, some *economic* purpose. It has been suggested, however, that the principle of *Bettray* does not apply to 'ordinary' sheltered employment. The undertaking in *Bettray* existed solely for the purpose of rehabilitation and re-education of the persons employed therein.

The question of whether an individual who works and receives benefits in kind at a minimal level was raised more recently in *Trojani* (*Trojani v Le Centre Public d'Aide Sociale de Bruxelles* (case C–402/05)). In this case, the ECJ reiterated the points made in its earlier case law. The determination of whether someone is a worker is a question of fact to be assessed by objective criteria. In this case, the applicant was carrying out jobs for approximately 30 hours per week for the Salvation Army as part of a personal reintegration programme. In return, he received benefits in kind. The ECJ made two points. The ECJ identified that the key question in determining whether Trojani was a worker or not was whether his activities formed part of the 'normal labour market'. Secondly, this was a question of fact over which the national court has exclusive jurisdiction. The ECJ consequently did not come to a determination on the facts. Although the final result in this case is consequently not clear, the principle remains that rehabilitation does not constitute work for the purposes of Article 39. It may well be, however, that this issue has lost much of its significance with the introduction of citizenship and the rights flowing from migrant citizen status (see Chapter 23).

Note finally that it is not just the employee who may rely on the right in Article 39, but the employer also.

21.4.6.1 *The position of students*

The position of people who migrate and then become students has given rise to difficulties. The status of students as workers was raised in *Brown* (case 197/86) and *Lair* (case 39/86). In both these cases the parties, having obtained a place at university, Brown at Cambridge to study engineering, and Lair at the University of Hanover to study languages, were claiming maintenance grants from the UK and German authorities respectively. Although Brown had dual French/English nationality, he and his family had for many years been domiciled in France; Lair was a Frenchwoman. Prior to taking up his place at Cambridge, Brown had obtained university sponsorship from, and worked for, Ferranti in Scotland. The job lasted for eight months. Lair had worked intermittently in Germany for over five years, with spells of involuntary unemployment. Both parties were refused a grant and sought to challenge that refusal on the basis of, inter alia, Regulation 1612/68, Article 7(2)–(3) (these provisions will be discussed in Chapter 23).

The crucial question was whether Brown and Lair were 'workers', and therefore entitled to claim the grants under Article 7, Regulation 1612/68; the ECJ excluded an argument that Brown and Lair could rely on the general principle of non-discrimination in Article 12 EC as education was not at that point within the scope of Community competence. Brown had come to the UK primarily to prepare for his engineering studies at Cambridge and his work experience formed part of this preparation; he had obtained his place at Cambridge prior to taking up work in the UK. Lair on the other hand had undoubtedly come to Germany many years before, intending to work. The Court, which delivered judgments in both cases on the same day, held that the concept of worker must have a Union meaning. Nevertheless, in Brown's case, although he might be regarded as a worker, he was not entitled to claim the grant as a social advantage because he had acquired the status of worker exclusively as a result of his having been accepted for admission to university. The employment was merely ancillary to the studies to be financed by the grant. With regard to Lair's claim, the Court draw a distinction between a claim by a migrant worker who was *involuntarily* unemployed, who, if legitimately resident, was entitled to the same treatment as regards reinstatement or re-employment as national workers, and one who gave up his work in order to undertake further training in the host Member State. In the latter case, he or she might only claim a grant for such a course if there was some link between the studies to be pursued and his previous work activity.

The Court chose to base its decision in both cases on fine factual distinctions rather than on the 'genuineness' of the claimant's status as a worker, although it did add in *Lair*, in response to the expressed worries of Member States as to the possibility of abuse, that:

> insofar as a worker has entered a Member State for the sole purpose of enjoying, after a very short period of work activity, the benefit of the student assistance system in that State, it should be observed that such abuses are not covered by the Community provisions [ie, Article 7(2)–(3)] in question. [Para 43.]

This reasoning, which is implicitly based on the possibility of 'abuse', is problematic. It suggests that motive is relevant for the acquisition of worker status, whereas in many cases, the ECJ has expressly stated that motive is irrelevant. Nonetheless, the tension between acceptable and unacceptable uses of Union law remains, and recurs periodically in the case law. Further, it is regrettable that in its concern to appease the anxiety of Member States, the ECJ chose in *Lair* to limit the scope of Article 7(2) by denying a right to 'social advantages' in the form of grants to migrant workers who have not become unemployed but who genuinely want to improve their prospects by retraining in a *new* field of activity. In an era of rapid technological and economic change, flexibility in the workforce is surely to be encouraged; nonetheless, a similar approach is found in the Citizenship Directive, Article 7(3)(d).

This area continued to give rise to litigation. In *Raulin* (case C–357/89), in a claim by a French national for a grant to pursue a full-time course in the plastic arts in the Netherlands, following 60 hours' work as a waitress there, the Court followed *Brown* and *Lair*, adding only that in assessing whether the work undertaken was 'effective and genuine' for the purpose of acquiring the status of worker, both the length of time of employment and all the activities undertaken in the host state might be taken into account, but not the activities conducted elsewhere in the Union. This assessment was left for the national courts to undertake. The approach might be criticised, not least because of its tendency to partition the national markets.

The situation of someone who works for a short period and then becomes student was considered again in *Ninni-Orache* (case C–413/01). The applicant was an Italian national who married an Austrian and moved to Austria. After about two years, she took up a fixed-term contract as a waitress and cashier, working for only a couple of months. She also completed a distance learning diploma in bookkeeping and commerce. She then tried to get a job relying on her diploma but was unsuccessful, so she started studying Romance languages at Klagenfurt University. The case concerned her claim for financial assistance from the Austrian government. The ECJ reiterated its approach in *Lair* and *Raulin*, that is, a worker who ceases to work retains some rights to social assistance provided there is continuity between the previous occupational activity and the studies pursued. Following its previous case law, the ECJ also noted that this limitation was not imposed on those who are involuntarily unemployed. In this case, the ECJ emphasised the determination of whether someone is a 'worker' is based on objective criteria and should take into account circumstances as a whole. The ECJ specifically rejected certain factors which the referring court had identified as potentially relevant to the assessment of her status—that is, the fact she did not start work immediately on her entry into Austria, the fact that she became eligible for study by virtue of her diploma, and her attempts to find work. These were not relevant as they preceded or were subsequent to the period of employment.

A fixed-term contract expiring does not necessarily mean a person has become voluntarily unemployed. This may vary on facts. Crucially, some of the factors the ECJ dismissed as not relevant to the determination of the economic aspect of 'worker' might be relevant in identifying if a worker has become of voluntarily unemployed are not. The ECJ has repeatedly held that motivation for moving is not a relevant factor in determining whether someone is a worker in the first place, but seems to become relevant where an individual stops work and seeks to rely on continuing rights. This assessment could be based on the implicit concern, already noted, that individuals who migrate and do minimum work for a short period before seeking to claim benefits in the host Member State are manipulating, if not abusing, the system. The rights granted to workers can be traced to an idea of solidarity, where the migrant has already contributed to the system on which he or she seeks to rely. Nonetheless, the approach here might seem to be taking a more generous line than that adopted in *Raulin*. (See also *Ioannidis* (case C–258/04), ECJ assumed migrant who had completed a paid training course in another Member State was a worker).

Summarising the position, it would seem as though the position of someone seeking host-state support for studies could be attributed to one of four categories:

1. the work undertaken was ancillary to another activity (In this case the individual is not a worker and cannot claim rights under Article 39 or Regulation 1612/68. Note the impact of citizenship in eg *Bidar* (case C–209/03) (discussed Chapter 24) on this sort of case.)

2. the work undertaken is marginal and therefore the individual is not a worker (Presumably this would be cases such as *Raulin*, though it it not possible to state this with certainty, as the ECJ has left national courts to assess the facts.)

3. a student was a worker and became voluntarily unemployed, in which case to be entitled to support there must be a link between the previous work and the study (*Bernini*).

4. a student was a worker and became involuntarily unemployed, in which case the individual retains his or her rights as a worker even if the study is unconnected with the previous work (*Lair; Ninni-Orasche*).

Individuals falling in each of these categories will also be EU citizens and claim rights as such, though the significance of this to such individuals would depend on which category each fell in, and consequently whether they could claim rights as workers and the scope of any such rights. The ECJ has not been consistent in this approach, however, as can be seen in a recent decision of the Grand Chamber, *Förster v Hoofddirectie van de Informatie Beheer Groep* (case C–158/07). Förster, a German national, moved to the Netherlands to be with her partner. She worked for a short while before commencing her studies. During this time she continued to work and received maintenance payments from the Dutch authorities which viewed her as a worker. She then stopped working part-time and the authorities tried to reclaim payments made. The Advocate-General noted that *Förster* fell in the same line of cases as *Lair, Raulin, Ninni-Orasche* etc, and that therefore, as the Dutch authorities had accepted she was a worker, Förster was entitled to the payments. The ECJ did not consider this possibility, suggesting that, in fact, it viewed Förster as falling outside the definition of 'worker'. In the end, the ECJ determined that Förster was a migrant EU national, but not entitled to payments as she was not sufficiently integrated in the Netherlands, despite her three years' residence there.

Förster is a somewhat surprising case. Although somewhat unclear, the trend of the cases had been to take a broad view of a worker, resulting in migrants being able to access social advantages in other Member States. This trend was re-emphasised with the citizenship case law, as we shall see in Chapter 23 (eg, *Grzelczyck* (case C–184/99)). *Förster*, however, seems to adapt the techniques previously used to extend rights, notably the concept of integration (and the 'real link' with the host Member State), to limit rights; in this there may be some similarities with the citizenship case law (*Bidar* (case C–209/03); *Collins* (case C–138/02)). This is the more surprising given that *Förster* seems to fit well within the previous worker/students case law; and worrying as the ECJ gives no reason to distinguish *Förster* from previous jurisprudence. It remains to see whether *Förster* is an isolated example.

Whilst the case law can be seen as a separate strand of cases relating specifically to students, the cases might also be seen as part of the case law on continuing rights. Continuing rights are rights to which someone is entitled after he stops working, by virtue of having been a worker (see also 21.5.2.2 below). The longevity of rights, especially when no longer directly connected with economic activity, is contentious. Whilst the ECJ has not come to a coherent theory for all circumstances, since continuing rights remain after a person ceases to be a worker, it could be argued that this justifies a slightly more restrictive view of the scope of the rights available to individuals in such circumstances.

21.4.7 Meaning of establishment for Article 43

21.4.7.1 *General*

A right of establishment is a right to install oneself, to 'set up shop' in another Member State, permanently or semi-permanently, whether as an individual, a partnership or a company, for the purpose of performing a particular economic activity there. The concept of establishment has been held to be 'a broad one, allowing a Community national to participate on a stable and continuous basis in the economic life of a Member State other than his own' (*Gebhard v Consiglio dell'Ordine degli Avvocati e Procuratori di Milano* (case C–55/94)). In the *German insurance case* (*Commission v Germany (insurance services)* (case 205/84)) the Court suggested that an enterprise would fall within the concept of 'establishment' even if its presence is not in the form of a branch or agency but consists merely of an office managed by the enterprise's own staff or by a person who is independent but is authorised to act on a permanent basis for the enterprise. Thus in the case of *Gambelli* (case C–243/01), the ECJ commented:

> Where a company established in a Member State . . . pursues the activity of collecting bets through the intermediary of an organisation of agencies established in another Member State (such as the defendants in the main proceedings), any restrictions on the activities of those agencies constitute obstacles to the freedom of establishment. [Para 46.]

21.4.7.2 *Elements of establishment*

Certain elements need to be shown to bring the freedom of establishment into play. We have noted the requirement for migration and for economic activity above. The ECJ has borrowed the test for economic activity from both the workers and services spheres to determine that work or service performed is genuine and effective and not such as to be regarded as purely marginal and ancillary (*Jany* (case C–268/99), para 33). As regards companies, Article 48(2) expressly excludes those companies which are non-profit making. This does not mean that the business must make a profit but that it is intended so to do. Charitable work seems to be excluded.

The final element is self-employed activity; this is a formal criterion. The cases on workers (at 21.4.6 below) discuss the definition of employment. We can therefore identify self-employment by a process of elimination. The ECJ identified the criteria for self-employed activity in *Jany* starting from this premise. Although the case concerned the Europe Agreements, the principles can nonetheless be applied here, as the same concepts as found in Article 43 EC were under consideration. The question before the ECJ was whether women working as window prostitutes in Amsterdam could claim the benefit of the freedom of establishment. The question was crucial for the women in *Jany*, as the association agreements did not give the right to take up employment although it permitted establishment. The ECJ held that establishment required:

- the provision of a service
- outside any relationship of subordination concerning the choice of that activity, working conditions and conditions of remuneration
- under that person's own responsibility
- in return for remuneration paid to that person directly and in full (para 71).

The ECJ rejected the Dutch government's argument that, given the subordinate relationship of a prostitute to her pimp, she was in an employment relationship; the ECJ pointed out the Dutch government had adduced no evidence on the point and furthermore disagreed with the assumption that a relationship of dependency could be equated to an employment relationship. In assessing whether a person is carrying out such activities, it does not matter that he or she is undergoing professional training (*Morgenbesser* (case C–313/01), recognition of French legal qualifications in Italy, requirement for further training).

21.4.8 **Meaning of Services for Article 49 EC**

21.4.8.1 *General*

'Services' are defined as those 'normally provided for remuneration, insofar as they are not governed by the provisions relating to freedom of movement for goods, capital and persons' (Article 50(1) (ex 60(1)) EC). Services in the field of transport are 'governed by the provisions of the Title [Part Two, Title IV] relating to transport' (Article 51 (ex 61) EC). The liberalisation of banking and insurance services connected with movements of capital was to be effected 'step by step with the progressive liberalisation of movement of capital' although the Treaty of Amsterdam (ToA) removed the word 'progressive' from this article. Article 50 EC provides a non-exhaustive list of examples of services. There are a number of key elements in identifying a service for the purposes of Article 49 EC.

21.4.8.2 *Types of Activity Caught*

Although Article 50 provides a list of services that are definitely caught by Article 49, *Society for the Protection of Unborn Children Ltd v Grogan* (case C–159/90), discussed below, illustrates that no area of economic activity in principle falls outside the treaty, no matter what its moral, cultural, or ethical status. Article 49 will, in theory, only apply if none of the other freedoms do—that is, it is a catch-all or fall-back provision—and provided the service does not fall within the treaty provisions dealing with transport.

Because of the special nature of services, lending themselves to promotion and even provision via modern 'distance' methods of communication, a service can be deemed to 'move' within the Union without either the provider or the recipient moving across national borders. Thus, Article 49 can be used to regulate either the provider, or the service itself. In *Alpine Investments BV v Minister van Financiën* (case C–384/93) a Dutch prohibition on 'cold calling' (the soliciting of business by telephone), by providers of financial advice established in the Netherlands, was held to constitute a barrier to the free provision of services contrary to the then Article 59 (now 49) EC (although it was found on the facts to be justified). Restrictions on cross-border advertising relating to the distribution of goods will be dealt with under the free movement of goods provisions of Article 28 (ex 30) (*Leclerc-Siplec v TF1 Publicité SA* (case C–412/93), decided on *Keck* principles, see Chapter 19, but contrast *Karner* (case C–71/02)). The broad scope of the right means that it can be relied on against both host and home Member State and, as *Alpine Investments* shows, in an 'export' situation as well as when the services are being imported.

Finally, the right to provide services includes the right to receive (*Luisi and Carbonne* (cases 286/82 and 26/83)). This aspect of the rights is discussed in Chapter 24.

As with establishment and workers, there must be an economic element. The test derived is that the services performed must be genuine and effective and not marginal and ancillary. In *Deliège*, we can see that the ECJ has found this requirement to be satisfied quite easily. *Deliège* concerned the case of an amateur athlete. In considering whether or not economic activity was involved, the ECJ argued:

> that sporting activities and, in particular, a high-ranking athlete's participation in an international competition are capable of involving the provision of a number of separate, but closely related, services which may fall within the scope of Article 59 [now 49] of the Treaty even if some of those services are not paid for by those for whom they are performed.

In developing its earlier jurisprudence on television broadcasting (see *Bond van Adverteerders and ors v Netherlands State* (case 352/85), paragraph 16) the ECJ suggested that the fact that activities can form the basis of commerce means Article 49 must be engaged. Note it also seems that it does not matter whether remuneration is found in the particular case under consideration, provided the type of service is such that it is usually provided for remuneration (see, eg, *Freskot* (case C–355/00), para 54; but note difficulties with public services, eg *Commission v Ireland (emergency ambulance services)* (case C–532/03), the existence of funding arrangements between public bodies does not imply provision of services for the purposes of Article 49 EC; and see further Chapter 24). Further, it does not matter whether an activity is profitable or not if there is an intention to 'make a cash profit' (*ANOMAR* (case C–6/01), para 47).

Although the ECJ has repeatedly held that the basic treaty freedoms must be interpreted widely, there are limits. In *Society for the Protection of Unborn Children Ltd v Grogan* (case C–159/90), the provision of information, contrary to the Irish constitution, about abortion clinics in other Member States by officers of a students' union was held not to receive the protection of Article 49. Although abortion (when legal in the Member State in which the procedure took place) could constitute a service within the treaty, the link between the provision of an information service about the clinics and the clinics themselves was too tenuous to be considered a restriction on the freedom to provide services; specifically it lacked an economic aspect as the SU was providing this as a free service and did not receive payment from the clinics. Some have suggested that this judgment is an isolated decision and that the ECJ's reasoning in this case was motivated by a desire to avoid a sensitive political issue. The Irish position as regards abortion was formalised by a Protocol annexed to the TEU.

21.4.9 Distinction between the provisions

The relationship between the freedoms is dealt with in general terms in Chapter 15. Nonetheless, given the similarities in circumstances in which these rights may be exercised, some further consideration is due here. There are two aspects to consider: one may be considered vertical, which permits overlap between the freedoms and citizenship (eg, *Collins* and *Grzlczyk*); the second, where the freedoms are mutually exclusive, can be considered horizontal. The relationship may be rendered diagrammatically as seen in Fig 21.1.

The circle represents citizenship, which incorporates all of workers and non-economic individuals (protected by Union legislation), but only those aspects of establishment and services pertaining to individuals. There is no overlap between the freedoms, though the boundary between them may be fine. In terms of application, the ECJ has determined that the freedoms are specific examples of the rights accruing to citizens and applies those freedoms of relevant; citizenship is then used as a fall-back position to fill in the gaps, but also as an aid to interpretation of the freedoms. It has also held that where the more specific provisions apply, for example Article 39, there is no need to interpret Article 18 (see *Stylianakis v Elliniko Dimosio* (case C–92/01), regarding the relationship between Article 18 and Article 49 EC; *Skanavi and Chryssanthakopoulos* (case C–193/94), regarding establishment; and *Oteiza Olazabal* (case C–100/01), regarding workers).

Some lack of clarity remains. In some of these cases where free movement provisions could apply, the ECJ does not refer to citizenship at all (see, eg, *Stylianakis v Elliniko Dimosio* (case C–92/01)). In others, although the questions is determined on the basis of one of the four freedoms, the interpretation of that freedom is affected by the notion of citizenship (see eg, *Oteiza Olazabal* (case C–100/01); *Bickel and Franz* (case C–274/96)), which the ECJ has held to be a fundamental status of EU nationals (see, eg, *Grzelczyck* (case C–184/99), para 31) (see further Chapter 23). The ECJ has, in some cases, referred to one of the economic freedoms and citizenship (see eg *Schwarz and Gootjes-Schwarz* (case C–76/05) concerning the right to tax deductions against private school fees).

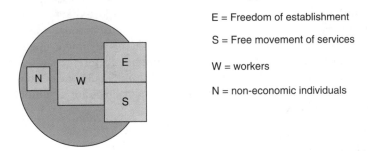

E = Freedom of establishment

S = Free movement of services

W = workers

N = non-economic individuals

Fig 21.1 Relationship between citizenship, freedom of establishment, free movement of services, and free movement of workers

We have noted the difference between workers and establishment at 21.4.7.2 above. The relationship between establishment and services should, however, be considered further. The difference between the right of establishment and the right to provide services is, in many instances, one of degree rather than of kind, though with the introduction of the Services Directive (see Chapter 22 at 22.7.3) the distinction may acquire a new significance. The key distinction seems to be the strength of the connection between the right holder and the host Member State. Whereas establishment suggests some degree of continuity or permanence, the right to provide services connotes the provision of services in one Member State, on a temporary or spasmodic basis, by a person established in another Member State. In the latter case it is not necessary to reside, even temporarily, in the Member State in which the service is provided. The temporary nature of the activities in question should be determined in the light not only of the duration of the service but of its regularity, periodicity, and continuity (*Gebhard* (case C–55/94)). Applying these principles in *Gebhard* the Court found that the setting up of chambers in Italy by a German barrister, a practising member of the Stuttgart Bar, fell within the concept of establishment. A person could be established, within the meaning of the treaty, in more than one Member State, in particular, in the case of companies, through the setting up of branches or subsidiaries, and, in the case of members of the professions, by establishing a second professional base.

The relationship between the secondary implementing legislation and the underlying treaty articles deserves further comment. As we see in Chapter 16, the ECJ, in the context of harmonisation under Article 95, has repeatedly held that in such circumstances it will rely on the directive as delineating more precisely the treaty rights in that context, rather than interpreting the underlying treaty provisions. This approach could be seen as a judicial deference to the political choices made by the Union legislative process evidenced in the terms of the directive. In the context of the free movement of people, however, the ECJ has continued to look, in some cases, to the interpretation of underlying treaty articles, to avoid limitation on free movement imposed by the implementing directives, or to limit discretion allowed to Member States by the terms of the directives (see eg *Collins* (case C–138/02) re Article 39 and 18, *Baumbast* (case C–413/99), and *Grzelczyck* (case C–184/99) regarding Article 18). One might question the legitimacy of this approach, as it seems to ignore political choices about the scope of rights. There are a number of possible reasons for this. First, the Citizenship Directive is different in scope and purpose from harmonising directives, though the ECJ has not used this argument to distinguish its different approaches. It has also been argued that the introduction of citizenship is an instruction to the court, incorporated through treaty amendment, which legitimises such an approach. Whilst this argument might succeed with regard to Article 18, it is more difficult to run in circumstances where the ECJ has relied on the economic free movement provisions. Finally, the ECJ has consistently justified this approach on the basis that secondary legislation cannot limit the scope of the treaty provisions.

21.4.10 Families

It is in the context of determining family rights that the changes introduced by Directive 2004/38/EC can be seen. In some respects, the fundamental position has not changed. The rights of family members are parasitic on those of the EU national, if they are not an EU national themselves. As noted in 21.4.5 above, the citizen must satisfy the migration test before he or she, or any family members can benefit from the rights granted. In this respect Directive 2004/38 does not change the position. The changes introduced by Directive 2004/38/EC can, however, be seen in the definition of family member, as Directive 2004/38 not only incorporates judicial developments in this area, but fills in lacunae in protection left by the ECJ's jurisprudence.

Much of the jurisprudence relating to families arose in the context of the free movement of workers. Families were defined in Regulation 1612/68 (Article 10(1)) as a worker's 'spouse and their descendants who are under the age of 21 years or are dependants', and 'dependent relatives in the ascending line of the worker and his spouse'. Under Directive 2004/38/EC, Article 10 (as well as Article 11) of Regulation 1612/68 are repealed (as well as legislation dealing similarly with establishment and services). Article 10(1) is replaced by Article 2(1)(2) Citizenship Directive, which states:

'Family member' means:

(a) the spouse;

(b) the partner with whom the Union citizen has contracted a registered partnership, on the basis of the legislation of a Member State, if the legislation of the host Member States treats registered partnerships as equivalent to marriage and in accordance with the conditions laid down in the relevant legislation of the host Member State;

(c) the direct descendants who are under the age of 21 or are dependants and those of the spouse or partner as defined in point (b);

(d) the dependent direct relatives in the ascending line as defined in point (b).

Article 3 identifies the beneficiaries of the rights specified in the directive. In addition to Union citizens and their family members, Article 3(2) recommends that Member States facilitate the entry of two other groups of people:

(a) any other family members, irrespective of their nationality, not falling under the definition in point 2 of Article 2 who, in the country from which they have come, are dependants or members of the household of the Union citizen having the primary right of residence, or where serious health grounds strictly require the personal care of the family member by the Union citizen

(b) the partner with whom the citizen has a durable relationship, duly attested.

21.4.10.1 *'Spouse' and 'partner'*

The definition in Article 2(2) includes both the category of a worker's spouse and that of a worker's partner. In this, the article is broader than the drafting of Article 10 Regulation 1612/68, but in fact reflects the jurisprudence of the ECJ, based on the principle of non-discrimination. In *Netherlands v Reed* (case 59/85) the ECJ was asked whether the term 'spouse' included a cohabitee. The case concerned Ms Reed's right to reside in Holland with her English cohabitee of five years' standing, who was working in Holland. Ms Reed, who was also English, was not herself a worker. The Court held that in the then state of Community law the term spouse referred to marital relationships only. This did not mean that Ms Reed was not entitled to remain in Holland. As her cohabitee was a worker in Holland, and since aliens with stable relationships with *Dutch* nationals were entitled in similar circumstances to reside in Holland, it would be discriminatory, in breach of what is now Article 12 EC and 39 (also Article 7(2), Regulation 1612/68), not to accord him the same treatment as national workers. Ms Reed was not entitled to remain as a 'spouse', but she was entitled to remain on account of her cohabitee's rights not to be discriminated against under the EC Treaty.

'Cohabitee' in the *Reed* sense seems to equate to 'partner' in the context of Article 2(1). There are two points to note. First, non-marital partnerships within the meaning of Article 2 are limited to those which are registered; other partnerships are dealt with under Article 3(2). Secondly, the directive is based on the principle of non-discrimination with how a registered partnership is treated under the national regime of the host Member State, as was *Reed*. The approach in *Reed* was criticised because it did not introduce equality across the Union; different Member States could treat non-married couples differently. The Citizenship Directive has not addressed this point. Nonetheless, this line of reasoning may have the benefit of assisting same-sex couples in Member States where they may register their unions.

Since the rights of partners are to some degree limited, the precise extent of the notion of spouse still has meaning; the case law from Regulation 1612/68 is probably still good law in this regard. Another question which arises, is whether a divorced spouse is entitled to claim rights as a 'spouse' under EU law. This can be seen as a question about the meaning of the term 'spouse', or as a question of whether someone who was a spouse has residual rights after he or she ceases to be a spouse. In *Diatta v Land Berlin* (case 267/83) the Court held that a separated spouse (in this case a Senegalese national), who intended to obtain a divorce and who was living apart from her husband, a worker in Germany, did not lose her rights of residence in Germany merely because she did not live under the same roof as her husband. The marital relationship is not dissolved, the Court held, when spouses live separately. As the matter came before the Court on a reference for interpretation it was not necessary for the Court to decide on the effect of divorce on a spouse's rights.

The problem for a divorced spouse is particularly acute where the spouse is not a national of a Member State, as in *Diatta*. A spouse who has EU nationality can always become a worker in her own right, and, after *Kempf* (case 139/85), even for a spouse with family responsibilities this should not prove too daunting a prospect as it does not require self-sufficiency. The position of the divorced spouse where there are children was addressed by the ECJ in *Baumbast and R* (case C–413/99), concerning two separate cases referred by the British Immigration Appeal Tribunal. In one of the cases, *R*, a migrant EU national divorced a United States citizen but remained in the host Member State. The non-EU national, the mother, was the principal carer for the children who had the right to remain (see below). On this basis the ECJ determined that the mother also had the right to remain as a corollary of the children's rights. The fact that she was not an EU national and was divorced from the migrant EU worker made no difference.

It is important to note, however, that this case did not address the position of the divorced spouse in her own right; her position was considered as an adjunct of her children's rights. The position of the divorced spouse without children remained unclear. The matter has now, somewhat inelegantly, been addressed by Directive 2004/38/EC. Article 13 provides both EU nationals and TCNs with some protection in the event of divorce, annulment or termination of registered partnerships. The precise phraseology and scope of Article 13 should be noted. There is a drafting point: the right is granted to family members. This approach assumes that for the purposes of EU law, family members remain family members even after divorce or termination of a civil partnership, otherwise the protection would have no force whatsoever being granted only to family members. The position for family members who are not EU nationals is more limited. To claim the benefit of the continuing rights under Article 13, the TCN must satisfy one of four tests. The four possibilities are:

(a) prior to initiation of the divorce or annulment proceedings or termination of the registered partnership, the marriage or registered partnership has lasted at least three years, including one in the host Member State

(b) by agreement between the spouses or partners or by court order, the person who is not an EU national has custody of the Union citizen's children

(c) this is warranted by particularly difficult circumstances, such as having been the victim of domestic violence during the subsistence of the marriage or registered partnership

(d) by agreement between the parties or by court order, the spouse or partner who is not an EU national has the right of access to a minor child, provided that the court has ruled that the access must be in the host Member State, for as long is required.

A similar question to *Baumbast* has been referred to the ECJ from the English courts, asking whether the right to remain for a non-EU national spouse and her EU national children accompanied an EU national who came to the UK as a worker, but then the EU national then ceased to be a worker and subsequently left the UK, and the non-EU national spouse and children are not self-sufficient and are dependent upon social assistance in the UK exists, and if so whether it is based on the terms of Directive 38/2004 or on the children's right to education guaranteed by Regulation 1612/68 (see Chapter 23) (*London Borough of Harrow v Hassan Ibrahim and Secretary of State for the Home Department* (case C–310/08); *Teixeira v LBC Lambeth, Secretary of State for the Home Department* (case C–480/08)). At the time of writing these cases are still pending.

Note that the protection granted by Article 13 does not appear to extend to partnerships which are not registered, nor does it apply to other family members falling within Article 3(2)(a). Presumably a *Reed* style argument could be used to gain equivalence of protection where the host Member State granted rights to remain to those who have not registered their partnership or who were family members within the sense of Article 3(2)(a).

One final area of concern regarding the definition of family members concerns the meaning of 'durable relationship' for the purposes of Article 3(2)(b), which is not defined in the Citizenship Directive. This question is presumably one for each of the Member States. Although there might be differences in approach between the Member States, the prohibition on discrimination should prevent authorities from discriminating between their nationals and migrants when assessing 'durable relationship'.

21.4.10.2 *Dependants and descendants*

For the children of the marriage, or the worker's dependent relatives, problems would not have arisen. Even after divorce they will remain members of the worker's family. They will now benefit from the rights granted by Article 13 (see above). Problems may have arisen for a spouse's dependent relatives. If they, like the spouse, are not EU nationals, they too risk losing their status as 'favoured Union citizens' on the separation or divorce of their relative.

Although families are expressed in terms of 'descendants' it would be in keeping with the ECJ's approach to take a broad view of the rights of children of the family. It would not be likely to deny favoured EU citizen status to children who had been treated as children of the family (ie, children of the Union citizen and the TCN) even though they were not, strictly speaking, descendants of the Union citizen. In *Baumbast and R* (case C–413/99), the ECJ confirmed that descendants within Article 10(1) Regulation 1612/68 extended:

> both to the descendants of that worker and to those of his spouse. To give a restrictive meaning to that provision to the effect that only the children common to the migrant worker and his spouse have the right to install themselves with them would run counter to the aim of Regulation 1612/68. [Para 57.]

This ruling now finds its expression in Article 2(2)(c) Directive 2004/38/EC and the same approach has been taken with respect to relatives in the ascending line. All such persons would be able, in principle, to claim the continuing rights granted under Article 13 Citizenship Directive (2004/38/EC).

A family member threatened with loss of EU rights, perhaps because he or she did not satisfy the tests in Article 13(2) could invoke the principle of respect for the right to family life expressed in Article 8 of the European Convention of Human Rights, which in the context of the application of Union law must be respected by the authorities of Member States (see also *Commission v Germany* (case 249/86)). The impact of Article 8 can also be seen in *Carpenter* (case C–60/00) which concerned the scope of the family rights of a service provider (see 21.5.1.1 below).

Note also that third-country nationals (TCNs) may benefit from the family re-unification directive and the directive concerning long-term residents (Directive 2003/109) (see Chapter 26).

21.5 Material Scope: Rights of access of the host Member State (Directive 2004/38/EC)

21.5.1 Rights of entry

Rights of movement are granted by the economic rights: Articles 39, 43, and 49 EC and the Citizenship Right in Article 18 EC. There were questions as to the relationship between these rights. The rights granted under Articles 39, 43, and 49 are not unlimited; the question was whether Article 18 was so limited. As we shall see, the rights are not free from formality as illustrated by the case of *Wijsenbeek* (case C–378/97) in which the ECJ held that the right of free movement is different from the obligation to prove one's identity as an EU national. Equally, the right to free movement is subject to the derogations laid down in the treaty, as can been seen in *ex parte Yiadom* (case C–357/98). In this case, the UK authorities were able to refuse a suspected Dutch people smuggler the right to enter the UK on grounds of public policy. Thus all rights may be limited on the grounds of public policy, public security, or public health, though in interpreting the derogation regard must be had to the existence and nature of citizenship and limit any action to what is strictly necessary and proportional.

These rights are now regulated by Directive 2004/38/EC as part of the citizenship package, replacing Directive 68/360. They comprise, for the EU migrant citizen and his family (as defined above: Directive 2004/38/EC Article 2(2)), the right:

(a) to leave their home state for another Member State (Directive 2004/38/EC, Article 4)

(b) of entry to that other Member State.

Note that the right of entry, is subject to derogation on grounds of public policy, public security, and public health. In *Jipa* (case C–33/07), the ECJ confirmed that Member States could derogate from the right of exit on the basis of these interests also, though they would be construed narrowly, as they would in the context of the right of entry (see Chapter 25).

Although not exactly the same, we have already noted that Article 49 applies to rules on the export of services as well as imports; and rules which dissuade companies from setting up branches or subsidiaries in other Member States. In one sense, these rights also provide a right of exit too.

21.5.1.1 *TCN family members*

The provisions on the right of migrant EU nationals to bring their existing families with them when they exercise their free movement rights, and as *Singh* (case C–370/90) shows, that applies on their return. The right in this context is non-contentious: there is a clear link between the right to bring a family member with you and the exercise of the right. As an individual, I would clearly be dissuaded from exercising those rights if I could not take my family members with me. What, however, of the position where the family members are not moving from one Member State to another, but are using EU rights to enter the EU (or claim residence there) for the first time? What also of the position where the exercise of free movement rights pre-dates the existence of the family relationship and where there is, therefore, no connection between the decision of whether to exercise the right, and the right of the family member to enter the Member State? These are difficult issues which the ECJ has dealt with in a number of much discussed and in some instances, highly criticised, cases.

The first case of which we need to be aware is *Carpenter* (case C–60/00). Under the Union legislation then in force, a service provider moving to another Member State to provide services was permitted to take family members with him for the duration of the provision of services. *Carpenter*, however, concerned the right of an individual established in his state of origin, who provided occasional, temporary services in other Member States, to rely on these rights as against the state of origin so as to ensure that his wife, who was a TCN who had outstayed her rights of entry under national law, could nonetheless remain in the EU. She did not seek to move from one EU state to another and, indeed, nor did he. This was a new departure in the case law. The rationale underlying the right for migrants to have their family members accompany them is the removal of a disincentive to free movement. This argument does not apply in the Carpenters' situation: the exercise of the right to have family members with the service provider did not coincide with the exercise of the right to provide services. On the contrary, the right to provide services actually operates to split the family unit, albeit temporarily. Nonetheless, the ECJ held that Mr Carpenter could rely on his EU-law rights as against his state of origin, and that any derogation from these rights must be assessed in the light of the right to family life contained in Article 8 ECHR. The question of abuse was not discussed; perhaps because the Carpenters had not manipulated their circumstances to fall within Union law. The ECJ did not face directly the question of whether EU law should cover the position where a TCN seeks to use EU law to access the territory for the first time: Mrs Carpenter had been legally resident in the UK before her visa expired.

MRAX (Case C–459/99), handed down just two weeks later suggested the answer to that question. It concerned the Belgian rules regarding the proof to be supplied to gain access to Belgian territory where the marriage had occurred overseas. The ECJ considered the question only from the perspective of an EU migrant worker; as this challenge was abstract (concerning the existence of the rules rather than their application to a particular case), there was no need for the ECJ to consider the problem of disassociation of the free movement right from the reunification right. The ECJ, basing its reasoning on the requirement on Member States to facilitate entry, and the emphasis given to Article 8 ECHR, concluded:

> it is in any event disproportionate and, therefore, prohibited to send back a TCN married to a national of a Member State where he is able to prove his identity and the conjugal ties and there is no evidence to establish that he represents a risk to the requirements of public policy, public security or public health. [Para 61.]

Furthermore, in the case of a TCN who had entered the host Member State illegally, it would be disproportionate to deport for failure to have a visa; other sanctions may be appropriate. There is no consideration of the question of whether this constitutes the granting of a right of access to EU territory, nor recognition of the fact that the 'administrative formality' is actually the Member State's right to control entry of TCNs to its territory. While *MRAX* may be seen as challenging mere formalities, it was a potentially far-reaching decision.

The next case, *Akrich* (case C–109/01) another referral from the British Immigration Appeals Tribunal, had been referred before the judgment in *MRAX* was handed down, and also fits into the development of the jurisprudence relating to returners' rights. *Singh* (case C–370/90) had illustrated that migrant workers could rely on at least some rights as against their Member State on return but the scope of this right, and its longevity, was somewhat uncertain though potentially far-reaching. *Akrich* concerned a Moroccan who was refused entry into the UK. He subsequently married a UK national. She moved to Ireland to work for a short period and he entered Ireland, relying on EU-law-derived rights. The couple then tried to return to the UK on the basis of *Singh*. It transpired that the purpose of the sojourn in Ireland had been for the purpose of bringing the couple within Union law, so seeking to evade British immigration controls. Whilst the exercise of free movement is clearly tied to the reunification right, this case raises concerns about the abuse of Union law. Were this line of reasoning to be accepted, it would introduce the possibility that no Member State would have any control over immigration into the EU in such cases. Whilst this issue had been elided in the reasoning in *MRAX*, in *Akrich* it was centre stage.

The Advocate-General in *Akrich* noted that the situation in *Singh* was different from that in issue in a number of respects. Crucially, Akrich had not been permitted to enter any Member State under national law. The Advocate-General commented that '*Singh* does not create a right in favour of that national of a non-Member State to enter the territory of the European Union' (para 134). The ECJ also found in favour of the UK government, addressing the both the issues about the scope of the reunification right. First, it seemed to link the right of family reunification with the right of free movement. It argued that, as Akrich could not lawfully reside with his wife in the UK, there was no disincentive in her not having her husband with her if she moved to another Member State, that is the prohibition could not 'constitute less favourable treatment than that which they enjoyed before the citizen made use of the opportunities afforded by the Treaty as regards free movement of persons' (para 53).

Nonetheless, the ECJ confirmed the point it had made in earlier jurisprudence, that the motives of persons seeking to exercise their rights of free movement are not relevant when assessing whether or not they benefit from those rights (paras 55–6), though the position might be different in the context of marriages of convenience. Secondly, the ECJ held that Regulation 1612/68 concerned only movement within the Union and not initial access to the territory of the Union. The ECJ then added that to benefit from the rights granted, the spouse of a citizen had to be 'lawfully resident in a Member State when he moves to another Member State to which the citizen of the Union is migrating or has migrated' (para 49).

Although it is submitted that some limits to the reasoning in *Singh* should be found, the reasoning of both the ECJ and the Advocate-General in *Akrich* is problematic. The precise scope of the ruling is not clear and does not sit easily with *MRAX* (case C–459/99). As noted, *MRAX* did not distinguish between the role of national and Union law in determining the right of access to Union territory, nor did it distinguish between legal and illegal immigrants, a distinction central in *Akrich*. It was suggested that the solution which best reconciles the case law is one which sees *Akrich* as confined to similar factual situations, where a TCN has been illegally resident in a Member State and is using Union law to avoid attempts to deport him and does not affect all TCNs wishing to enter directly into the host Member State.

We have already discussed the case of *Chen* (at 21.4.5 above). Although the parents of the child had not resided lawfully within the EU prior to the birth of the child and admitted manipulating the national rules to obtain residency as family members of an EU national, the question of abuse was not raised in this case. *Chen* is nonetheless another case in which the Member States' right to control the first entry of non EU nationals into the EU is compromised.

Our analysis of *Akrich* would be consistent with that taken in *Jia* (case C–01/05) which concerned an EU worker who had married a non-EU national. She subsequently moved to another Member State with her husband. Thereafter, she sought to rely on her EU law rights to allow her mother-in-law, also a non-EU national, residency in the host Member State although her mother-in-law had never resided in the EU. Here, the ECJ was prepared to allow a TCN access to the EU territory without that person having entered the EU territory on the basis of one of the Member State's immigration systems. *Jia* can be distinguished from *Akrich* on the basis that there is no suggestion of manipulation of the system in the same way as in *Akrich*, since in *Jia* the migrant EU national had been resident in the host Member State for approximately eight years before her mother-in-law sought to enter the state. The issue that is not discussed in *Jia* is the link—or rather the lack of one—between the exercise of free movement rights and the family reunification rights. Despite the ECJ's argument in *Mettock and ors* (case C–127/08) (see further below) that the competence of the Member States regarding immigration are respected, as the EU rules relate only to the circumstances of free movement rights, this assessment is contestable. Where an EU national exercises the free movement rights and then subsequently gets married or seeks to have dependent family members join him or her, intra-EU movement rights are not in issue. There is no connection between the decision to move and the circumstances in which the family member's right is subsequently deployed. A different argument in favour of *Jia*, however, is that the migrant had formed a 'real link' with the host Member State. We can see this argument deployed in cases involving rights to social benefits (chapter 23). There is a difference between the two sets of facts, though. In the social rights cases, immigrants are essentially asking to be treated on a par with nationals of the host Member States; in *Jia* the argument results in preferential treatment for the migrant. The ECJ is clearly stepping into a sensitive area here, with the possible consequence of reverse discrimination for nationals who do not seek to exercise their free movement rights.

Following *Jia*, it seemed that *Akrich* was restricted to cases of abuse; whether it is still possible to rely on *Akrich* at all is now highly doubtful. In *Akrich*, the ECJ suggested that it was no disincentive to free movement to prohibit the entry of Akrich to another Member State as the couple could not live together anyway in the state of origin. A variant of this argument was raised in *Eind* (case C–291/05). The case concerned a Dutch migrant worker seeking to return to his state of origin with his daughter, a TCN. His daughter did not have the right of residence in the Netherlands prior to the exercise of the free movement right, but by contrast to the position in *Akrich*, her entry to the EU was not illegal. The ECJ held that the fact that she had not right of residence was irrelevant to the determination of whether she had a right to reside with her father (at least until she was 21). The ECJ gave 2 reasons:

1. such a requirement is not laid down in Union law, and Union law on free movement should not be interpreted restrictively
2. such a requirement would run counter to the objectives of the Union legislature in protecting family life.

Eind is interesting for a number of reasons. It seems inconsistent with *Akrich*, but there is no specific reference to that case and, although the ECJ refers to *MRAX* and *Carpenter*, it does not expressly state that it is following the lines of reasoning in those cases. Significantly, the ECJ in its first reason, concerning Union law, is ignoring the limits on Union competence regarding first access to the EU territory, a division of competence it has elsewhere stated that it respected.

Mettock and ors (case C–127/08),a decision of the Grand Chamber on a reference from Ireland, deals directly with the family rights in Citizenship Directive for the first time. *Mettock* concerns four cases based on a similar-fact pattern. In each case, a TCN was refused asylum in Ireland and subsequently married a migrant EU national lawfully resident in Ireland. Each couple sought to challenge refusal or residency or deportation on the basis of EU-law rights. With the exception of the *Mettock* case, the couples met in Ireland and married within a comparatively short timescale, though the national court accepted that none of the cases concerned a marriage of convenience. In this, the facts are more similar to *Jia*, where the migrant was still residing in the host member state, than *Akrich*, which concerned the right of return to the home Member State. Nonetheless, our two themes can be seen: (a) the disassociation between free movement and reunification; and (b) the question of access to EU territory. The Irish authorities referred to *Akrich* and sought to rely on the requirement that the spouses must have been lawfully resident within the EU. The ECJ dismissed this argument, stating that the conclusion in *Akrich* must be 'reconsidered' (para 58), effectively overruling its decision in that case. It argued that the Union institutions have consistently widened the rights available to individuals, and that those rights are not dependent on preconditions such as the prior lawful residence of such a spouse in another Member State. Perhaps because it was not raised by the Irish authorities, the ECJ did not address the issue of the link between the right of free movement and the reunification right. Whilst the decision in *Mettock* may be applauded on humanitarian grounds, it is still problematic. As noted above, the issue of longevity of the rights consequent on migration have not been addressed by the ECJ, but it is submitted that this is an issue that needs addressing as, depending on the scope of the rights awarded by migration, the ECJ could create a privileged class of individuals in circumstances which have little to do with integration in a host Member State.

The ECJ suggested in *Mettock* that its ruling was not effectively opening the floodgates to uncontrolled immigration from third countries, as Member States were still entitled to exclude family members on the basis of Article 27 Citizenship Directive (if appropriate—see Chapter 25), and that Article 35 Citizenship Directive entitles Member States to 'adopt the necessary measures to refuse, terminate or withdraw any right conferred by this Directive in the case of abuse of rights or fraud, such as marriages of convenience'. There have been no cases on the scope of this provision, though any such measures would have to comply with the principle of proportionality, suggesting it will be narrowly construed.

21.5.2 **Right of residence**

With the right of entry comes the right of residence, a necessary precursor for an individual to engage in activities in the host member state. The original provisions relating to workers were generously interpreted by ECJ. In *Procureur du Roi v Royer* (case 48/75) the Court held that the right of entry granted by Article 3 of Directive 68/360 included the right to enter *in search of work*. In *R v Immigration Appeal Tribunal, ex parte Antonissen* (case C–292/89), the ECJ was asked to rule on the legality of English immigration rules which permit the deportation of migrants after six months if they have failed to find employment. The Court held that there was 'no necessary link' between the right to unemployment benefit under Regulation 1408/71, discussed Chapter 23, and the right to stay in a Member State for the purpose of seeking work. A Member State could, however, deport an EU migrant if he had not found employment after six months unless he provided evidence that he was continuing to seek employment and that he has a genuine chance of being engaged. Significantly the Court chose not to impose a specific time limit. Subsequently, it was held that Belgian legislation, which in effect excluded those seeking work after three months, was in contravention of Union law (*Commission v Belgium* (case C–344/95)). Thus, it seems that at the least those genuinely seeking work were entitled to stay in the host Member State for longer than three months.

Likewise, those providing services or seeking to establish themselves had the right of residence, though that of the service provider would be coterminous with the provision of services. Right of residence was extended again with directives dealing with retired, the self-sufficient and students; these directives have been replaced by the Citizenship Directive. The rights of residence contained within Article 18 remain, though as with the rights under Article s 39, 43, and 49, they are given greater detail by the implementing legislation. Significantly, the right of residence is available to all, a point the ECJ recognised in *Baumbast* (case C–413/99), when it held that the right was conferred on every citizen of the Union irrespective of whether he or she was engaged in an economic activity. In *Baumbast*, the migrant Union citizen did not comply with the formal requirements of the residence directive—to be insured against medical emergencies—but was not a financial burden on the host Member State. According to the ECJ, Article 18(1) had to be read in accordance with the limitations imposed by the residence directives, but that these limits themselves had to be understood in the light of the principle of proportionality, and the UK's refusal to renew his residence permit on the facts of this case was disproportionate. *Baumbast* can thus also be seen as authority for the proposition, seen in other cases (see eg *Kaba* (case C–356/98) and *Chen* (case C–200/02)), that Article 18(1) residence rights are not unconditional. In *Trojani* (case C–456/02), the ECJ held that, contrary to the position in *Baumbast*, a claimant who is carrying out minimal economic activities and is dependent on the host state, does not derive a right to reside on the territory for want of sufficient resources (para 36). As we shall see in Chapter 23, a 'real link' with the host Member State has become key.

The rights are now found in Directive 2004/38/EC, but it is important to note that the directive does not reflect the case law precisely, so it may still be necessary to refer to the underlying treaty provision. Further, not all citizens have the same rights as is shown in Table 21.1.

21.5.2.1 *Temporary residence*

Article 6 provides temporary residence of up to three months to all migrant EU citizens, without any requirement that they be self-sufficient or even looking for work.

Table 21.1 Rights of residence available to citizens

	Right of Entry (Art 5)	Right of Temporary Residence (Art 6)— 3 months	Right of settled residence (Art 7)—more than 3 months	Right of Permanent Residence (Art 16)
Economically active	Yes	Yes	Yes	Provided legally resident for 5 years
Non-economically active	Yes	Yes	If they have sufficient resources and sickness insurance	Provided legally resident for 5 years – that is satisfy conditions in Art 7(b) and (c)
Family members	Yes	Yes	Yes if EU national satisfies conditions; note limitations on family members of students (Art 7(4))	Provided legally resident for 5 years

Note, however, EU citizens will retain this right only as long as they do not become an unreasonable burden on the social assistance system of the host Member State (Article 14(1)). In one sense, this is wider than *Antonissen* (case C–292/89) because it is not limited to work-seekers; should the Union citizen be a work-seeker then in derogation of Article 14(1), provided he or she can provide evidence that he or she is continuing to seek work and have a reasonable chance of being employed, a Member State may not deport that person (unless there are grounds under Article 27). It is more limited that the existing jurisprudence because the right is expressed to be for three months only. Note that secondary legislation cannot limit treaty freedoms, so for those seeking work it will remain possible to rely on *Antonissen* (case C–292/89) and *Commission v Belgium* (case C–344/95), which are ultimately based on Article 39 (for a similar approach in a different context, see *Collins* (case C–138/02), discussed in Chapter 23 at 23.2.11). Such individuals may be able to rely on Article 7 after the three month period has expired. Note, family members have matching rights of residence.

21.5.2.2 *Settled residence*

Union citizens have the right to reside for as long as they satisfy the conditions in Article 7, that is if they fall into one of three categories. These are that they:

- are workers or self-employed
- have sufficient resources for themselves and their family members not to become a burden on the social assistance system of the host Member State
- are enrolled at a private or public establishment for the principal purpose of following a course of study, including vocational training with sufficient resources.

This may be described as the right to 'settled' or 'lawful' residence. As noted above, a worker may retain his or her status in certain circumstances. Article 7(3) reflects this position and clarifies the position for the self-employed. Under Article 7(3) a Union citizen retains their economic status (and consequently does not have to show sufficient resources) in the following situations:

(a) he/she is temporarily unable to work as the result of an illness or accident

(b) he/she is in duly recorded involuntary unemployment after having been employed for more than one year and has registered as a job-seeker with the relevant employment office

(c) he/she is in duly recorded involuntary unemployment after completing a fixed-term employment contract of less than a year or after having become involuntarily unemployed during the first twelve months and has registered as a jobseeker with the relevant employment office (in this case, the status of worker shall be retained for no less than six months)

(d) he/she embarks on vocational training. Unless he/she is involuntarily unemployed, the retention of the status of worker shall require the training to be related to the previous employment.

Although the directive specifically provides that a right of residence does not end if the worker becomes incapable of work through illness or accident or involuntary unemployment, Article 7(3)(b) implies that that right will be lost if he is *voluntarily* unemployed, where the worker has only been working for a period of less than a year. Note that in this case there may also be implications for the individual's right to social rights (Article 24(2)).

21.5.2.3 *Permanent residence*

Unusually, Chapter IV provides for a right of permanent residence. Article 16 specifies that 'Union citizens who have resided legally for a continuous period of five years in the host Member State shall have the right of permanent residence there'. Crucially, this right is not subject to the same conditions as the temporary and settled rights of residence (eg terms of Article 14). This right is extended to family members, who must each complete their own period of five years' legal residence (Article 16(2)). The directive defines continuous residence, allowing the migrant to be absent for periods totalling no more than six months in a year, with special exceptions for circumstances such as military service, and pregnancy and childbirth. Once acquired, the right may be lost, but only through a period of absence exceeding two consecutive years. Given this right is dependent on legal residence, an EU national must either be economically active or self-sufficient for the five-year period. Special provisions apply to protect the position of those who retire or become incapacitated (Article 17).

21.5.3 **Formalities**

Under Directive 2004/38/EC migrant EU citizens need only produce a valid identity card or passport' (Article 5(1)) to enter a host Member State. Entry visas (or their equivalent) may not be demanded except for members of the family who are not nationals of a Member State in accordance with Regulation 539/2001 or, in some instances, national law. In *Wijsenbeek* (case C–378/97), the ECJ had to consider whether the introduction of European citizenship rendered border controls illegal. In this case the ECJ held that Member States were still entitled to check the identity documents (in this case the passport) of EU nationals travelling between Member States, despite the fact the all EU nationals are now European citizens. The ECJ then went on to hold, however, that any penalties for failure to comply with such rules must be proportionate in the light of European citizenship and the right to move from one Member State to another. In this, the ECJ made a distinction between the right to move between Member States and the ability to do so without having to prove one's identity or nationality. Thus, this ruling would suggest that citizenship on its own is not enough to create an area without internal frontiers even if it is a lot easier, as an EU national, to cross those borders.

Where a person has a residence card within the meaning of Article 10 Directive 2004/38/EC, they are exempt from any visa requirement. Member States are required to accord to such persons every facility for obtaining the necessary visas (Article 5(2)). According to *MRAX* (case C–459/99), although Article 3(2) Directive 68/360 made the right of entry conditional on the holding of the visa, the rights of the Member State in respect of this condition are limited indeed. Such a visa should be issued without delay and, as far as possible, at the place of entry into the Member State. These requirements are now found in Article 5(2) Directive 2004/38/EC.

The ECJ further held in *MRAX* that, where a TCN is able to prove his or her identity and provide evidence of a marriage, it would be disproportionate to send a TCN back to his or her state of origin in the absence of evidence that he or she represents a risk to public policy, public security, or public health. Article 5(4) Directive 2004/38/EC incorporates these requirements, additionally specifying that a Member State must give such persons a reasonable opportunity of obtaining the necessary documents or of having them sent or otherwise proving that they are covered by the right of free movement and residence.

An economically active migrant need only register when he or she is resident for more than three months; in such cases the obligation to apply occurs only when the Member State runs a registration scheme. To obtain a registration certificate a worker needs to provide:

(i) a valid identity card or passport, and

(ii) a confirmation of engagement from the employer or a certificate of employment (Article 8(3)).

The requirements for members of the family who are Union citizens (Article 9(5)) are:

(i) their documents of entry

(ii) a document proving their relationship with the worker, and where relevant documents testifying to their dependent status (Article 3(2)(a)) or proof of a durable relationship (see Article 3(2)(b)).

For family members who are not Union citizens, Article 9 provides for a separate procedure. Member States are required to issue such family members a residence card within six months of the date of application. To obtain a residence card a family member must show:

(a) a valid passport

(b) documentary evidence of their relationship with the worker and

(c) in the case of relatives identified in Article 2(2)(c) or (d), and Article 3(2)(a) and (b) proof that the conditions specified in the respective provisions are satisfied (see 21.4.10).

The residence permit must be valid throughout the territory of the Member State which issued it; it must be valid for at least five years from the date of issue or for the envisaged of residence of the Union citizen; and it must be automatically renewable (Article 11). Temporary absences, as detailed in Article 11(2) do not affect the validity of the residence card. A worker's right to reside in the state where he is employed is not dependent on his possession of a certificate of registration. Neither a migrant nor his family can be deported because the identity card or passport on which they entered the host Member State has expired (Article 15(2), Directive 2004/38/EC). As long as the migrant is economically active, he will be entitled to reside in the host Member State without formalities. And as long as he is entitled to stay, his family will also be entitled to stay. In *MRAX* (case C–459/99) the ECJ confirmed that a Member State is not permitted to refuse a residence permit to a family member, who is able to prove his or her identity and the existence of a marriage to a migrant EU worker, purely on the grounds that he or she entered the host Member State illegally (see also *Commission v Spain* (case C–503/03) on the relationship between Union law and the Schengen system with regard to TCNs who are family members, discussed Chapters 26). Nor can that Member State expel such a TCN on the grounds that his or her visa expired before he or she applied for a residence permit. A residence permit may not be refused on these grounds either.

A Member State is, however, entitled to demand that migrant workers and their families comply with its administrative formalities on immigration, as is recognised in Directive 2004/38/EC, Articles 8–9, and can even impose penalties in the form of fines for non-compliance, provided that the penalties are not disproportionate. In *Messner* (case C–265/88) a time limit of three days from crossing the frontier in which aliens were required to register their presence with the Italian police, sanctioned by criminal penalties, was found to be unreasonable. A failure to comply with such formalities can never be a ground for deportation (see also *Watson* (case 118/75); *Commission v Belgium* (case 321/87)).

The maintenance of a database of non-nationals so registering has been challenged for constituting discrimination contrary to Articles 12, 18, and 43 EC, as well as raising questions about compliance with the Data Protection Directive (Directive 95/46) (*Huber v Germany* (case C–524/06)). Although Germany registers the basic details of its citizens in municipal registers, it does not have a centralised system for them. The details of non-nationals are additionally registered on a centralised system, which is more extensive in terms of the information so entered. The German government argued that this difference in treatment is acceptable because of the different residence rights of the two groups. The Advocate-General was not convinced:

> this is no more than stating the obvious; it says nothing about how this difference in residence status should relate to the collection and processing of the personal data of German citizens and citizens of other Member States . . . For a finding of non-discrimination, it is not sufficient to point out that German citizens and foreign nationals are not in the same situation. It is also necessary to demonstrate that the difference in their respective situations is capable of justifying the difference in treatment. In other words, the difference in treatment must relate and be proportionate to the difference in their respective situations. [Para 7.]

Whilst the case law of the ECJ and the terms of Directive 2004/38 envisage the collection of some data, it does not mean that the Member States are entirely unfettered in this regard. The Advocate-General emphasised the fundamental status of citizenship, arguing that a system would be discriminatory in so far as it includes data beyond those specified in Article 8(3) of Directive 2004/38/EC and allowed access by authorities other than the immigration service. The ECJ, while recognising the need for some data to be held, determined that such data must be limited to that necessary for the purpose and that the storage and processing of personal data containing any individualised (as opposed to anonymised) data cannot under any circumstances be considered necessary. Furthermore, Member States cannot put in place a data processing system which focusses on the personal data of non-nationals for the purposes of fighting crime. Member States' ability to keep data on particular population groups has clearly been limited.

21.6 Conclusions

This chapter has looked first at the scope of the free movement provisions *ratione personae*, that is in terms of who benefits from Union-law rights in this area; and secondly, at the scope of one aspect of the rights (*ratione materiae*), the right of access to the territory of the host Member State. The conditions governing *ratione personae* operate to determine the circumstances in which Union law may be invoked. They thus delimit the scope of Union competence, and the circumstances in which Member State freedom is limited. In general terms, we can say that the ECJ has interpreted these matters broadly, as can be seen from its approach, for example, to internal situations. It has also generally adopted a Union approach to key terms. This, of course, is beneficial to the individuals seeking to rely on those rights. Within this framework, two key strands of case law can be determined: that relating to students as workers; and the case law on TCNs entering the territory of the EU as family members of migrant EU nationals. Here the sensitivity of the issue is not just which EU nationals can claim rights, but the scope of those rights and whether they are necessarily connected with enhancing free movement. It is arguable that we see here the beginnings of a qualitative shift from a focus on facilitating free movement of economic factors, to creating a community of individuals. This, however, is problematic. The case law creates a favoured class of individuals; although the ECJ has consistently accepted reverse discrimination, it hardly matches a view of the Union where there is no discrimination. Further, there is a constant concern about abuse of Union law rights, so as to allow social benefit tourism or to evade immigration controls into the EU itself. Perhaps as a reflection of the sensitivity of these areas, the jurisprudence of the ECJ is not wholly consistent. Nonetheless, it is still true to say that the freedom to move is available to a broad class (individual and legal body alike), a fact which has had, and will continue to have, a huge impact the freedom of Member States to regulate, and which has had particular impact on the acceptability of distinguishing between nationals and migrant EU nationals.

FURTHER READING

Daniele, L, 'Restrictions to the free movement of persons' (1997) 22 EL Rev 191.

Dougan, M, 'The constitutional dimension to the case law on Union citizenship' (2006) 31(5) EL Rev 613–41.

Hartley, T, 'Free movement of students in European Community law' (1989) Cahiers de Droit Européen.

Kocharov, A, 'What intra-Community mobility for third-country workers?' (2008) 33(6) EL Rev 913–26.

Kostakopoulou, D, 'Ideas, norms and European citizenship: Explaining institutional change' (2005) 68(2) MLR 233–67.

Kunoy, B, 'A union of national citizens: The origins of the Court's lack of avant-gardisme in the *Chen* case' (2006) 43(1) CML Rev 179–90.

Reich, N and Harbacevica, S, 'Citizenship and family on trial: A fairly optimistic overview of recent Court practice with regard to free movement of persons' (2003) 40(3) CML Rev 615–38.

Stalford, H, 'Concepts of family under EU law: Lessons from the ECHR' (2002) International Journal of Law, Policy and the Family 410.

Tryfonidou, A, '*Jia* or "*Carpenter II*": The edge of reason' (2007) 32(6) El Rev 908–18.

Watson, P, 'Free movement of workers: A one way ticket?' (1993) 22 ILJ 68.

White, R, 'Conflicting competences: Free movement rules and immigration laws' (2004) 29(3), EL Rev 385–96.

White, R, 'Free movement, equal treatment, and citizenship of the Union' (2005) 54(4) ICLQ 885–905.

Woods, L, 'Family rights in the EU: Disadvantaging the disadvantaged?' (1999) 11 Child & Family Law Quarterly 17.

Woods, L, 'Scope of services I: Definitions' in *Free Movement of Goods and Service within the European Community* (Ashgate, 2004).

22

Economic Rights: Workers, establishment, and services

22.1 Introduction

The four freedoms are fundamental to the creation of the common market and as such have been interpreted broadly. We have noted that the rights granted by the freedoms relating to people and legal entities have different aspects: a territorial aspect (discussed in Chapter 21); an economic aspect; and a social aspect (discussed in Chapter 23). This chapter will focus on the second aspect: the right to the job market or the right to trade as self-employed. In their economic aspects, the free movement of workers, the right of establishment, and the freedom to provide services, probably show the greatest similarity to the other freedoms (goods and capital). Similar themes can be identified in these freedoms, in particular a broad interpretation of the rights. Furthermore, there has been a move from a discrimination based test for the application of the article to one based on the notion of an obstacle to the exercise of the right. When we look at economic rights, however, there might be different policy issues in play in different circumstances. To what extent should there be a difference in approach with regard to rules which operate to deter individuals and companies from moving in the first place, those that affect access to the market, and the rules that come into play when running a business? Equally, we might consider whether the same approach is desirable with regard to individuals (who might benefit from citizenship rights) and legal entities which will not have the same social needs. (The issue of who benefits from these rights is discussed in Chapter 23.)

This chapter begins be reviewing the relevant provisions and, crucially, the changing approach to the European Court of Justice (ECJ)'s interpretation of the treaty freedoms and the consequent impact on Member States' ability to regulate within their own territory. The case law considered in this chapter raises the issues about regulatory competition and the deregulatory impact of the freedom to provide services, as with the other freedoms. This chapter focuses in particular on certain problem areas, such as qualifications and the abuse of Union-law rights to evade national regulation, as well as the position regarding companies. We also consider the position of services, where services are provided cross-border without anyone physically moving (eg broadcasting). Services in this context may be provided in more than one Member State simultaneously, raising questions not only about which Member State should have the right or responsibility to regulate the service provider, but also about the dangers of abuse of Union-law rights to avoid national regulation. These questions have a greater significance with the introduction of the Services Directive.

22.2 Treaty provisions

Chapter 21 discusses the meaning of workers, establishment, and services and the conditions in which the rights are triggered (that is the requirements for a cross-border element and an economic element that is not marginal or ancillary). As noted there, these provisions have direct effect. We now focus on the conditions relating to the right to trade and to work.

22.2.1 The free movement of workers

As noted in Chapter 21, the principal treaty provision governing the free movement of workers is Article 39 (ex 48) EC. As regards the economic aspect of the workers' rights it provides:

1. Such freedom of movement shall entail the abolition of any discrimination based on nationality between workers of the Member States as regards employment, remuneration and other conditions of work and employment.
2. It shall entail the right, subject to limitations justified on grounds of public policy, public security or public health:

    (a) to accept offers of employment actually made; . . . .

Lisbon will renumber Article 39 EC as Article 45 of the Treaty on the Functioning of the European Union (TFEU), but there are no changes of significance to the substance of the provision.

22.2.2 Freedom of establishment

Article 43 (ex 52) now provides:

Within the framework of the provisions set out below, restrictions on the freedom of establishment of nationals of a Member State in the territory of another Member State shall be abolished. Such abolition shall also apply to restrictions on the setting up of agencies, branches or subsidiaries by nationals of any Member State established in the territory of any Member State.

Freedom of establishment shall include the right to take up and pursue activities as self-employed persons and to set up and manage undertakings, in particular companies and firms within the meaning of the second paragraph of Article 48, under the conditions laid down for its own nationals by the law of the country where such establishment is effected, subject to the provisions of the Chapter relating to capital.

Article 43 EC will become Article 49 TFEU, should the Lisbon Treaty come into force.

22.2.3 The freedom to provide services

Articles 49 (and 50(3)) as amended now provide:

Within the framework of the provisions set out below, restrictions on freedom to provide services within the Community shall be prohibited in respect of nationals of Member States who are established in a State of the Community other than that of the person for whom the services are intended. [Article 49.]

> Without prejudice to the provisions of the Chapter relating to the right of establish-
> ment, the person providing a service may, in order to do so, temporarily pursue his activ-
> ity in the State where the service is provided, under the same conditions as are imposed
> by that State on its own nationals. [Article 50(3).]

Lisbon would renumber these provisions as Articles 56 and 57 TFEU respectively.

22.2.4 Public service

The treaty limits the right of access to jobs in the public sector. Article 39(4) specifies that 'The provisions of this Article shall not apply to employment in the public
service'. Similar provision apply to establishment and services. Article 45 provides
that 'The provisions of this Chapter [establishment] shall not apply, so far as any
given Member State is concerned, to activities which in that State are connected,
even occasionally, with the exercise of official authority'. According to Article 55,
the terms of Article 45 also apply to services. Articles 45 and 55 EC would become
Articles 51 and 62 TFEU respectively, should Lisbon come into force.

22.3 Right of access to the market

22.3.1 Workers

Regulation 1612/68 was passed to implement Articles 39(2) and 39(3)(a) and (b) of
the EC Treaty. As stated in the preamble to Regulation 1612/68, the attainment of
the objective of freedom of movement for workers requires, in addition to rights
of entry and residence, 'the abolition of any discrimination based on nationality
between workers of the Member States as regards employment, remuneration and
other conditions of work and employment' (first recital).

It also requires, in order that the right of freedom of movement may be exercised
'in freedom and dignity', equality of treatment in 'all matters relating to the actual
pursuit of activities as employed persons'. Regulation 1612/68 contains specific provisions dealing with eligibility for employment and terms of employment and has
been interpreted broadly. It is essentially a restatement of Article 39(2) EC and that
the ECJ when considering cases relating to terms of employment can consider them
under Article 39(2) rather than Regulation 1612/68 (see eg *Delay* (case C–276/07)),
although this practice has been viewed as problematic (see 22.4.9 below). Article 39
was expressed in terms of a prohibition on discrimination, whether direct or indirect.
In *Hartmann v Freistaat Bayern* (case C–212/05) (Grand Chamber), the ECJ restated
that the prohibition relates not only to discrimination on grounds of nationality but
to the 'application of other criteria of differentiation' which would have the same
effect. These principles are reflected in the terms of Regulation 1612/68.

Any national of a Member State has the right to take up activity as an employed
person, and pursue such activity, in the territory of another Member State under the
same conditions as nationals of that state (Article 1).

A Member State may not discriminate, overtly or covertly, against non-nationals,
by limiting applications and offers of employment (Article 3(1)), or by prescribing

special recruitment procedures or limiting advertising or in any other way impeding recruitment of non-resident workers (Article 3(2)). Member States must not restrict by number or percentage the number of foreign nationals to be employed in
any activity or area of activity (Article 4; see *Commission v France (French merchant
seamen)* (case 167/73), ratio of three French to one non-French imposed under
Code du Travail Maritime 1926 on crew of French merchant ships held in breach
of EU law).

Member States must offer non-national applicants the same assistance in seeking
employment as are available to nationals (Article 5). A worker who is a national of
a Member State may not, in the territory of another Member State, be treated differently from national workers by reason of his nationality in respect of any conditions of employment and work, in particular as regards remuneration, dismissal
and, should he become unemployed, reinstatement or re-employment.

In *Ugliola* (case 15/69) a condition whereby a German employer took into account, for the purposes of calculating seniority, employees' periods of national
service *in Germany,* thereby prejudicing an employee such as Ugliola, who was required to perform his national service in Italy, was held unlawful under this article. Similarly in *Sotgiu v Deutsche Bundespost* (case 152/73) the German post office's
decision to pay increased separation allowances only to workers living away from
home in Germany, was held to be *capable* of breaching Article 7(1). In *Schöning-
Kougebetopoulou v Freie und Hansestadt Hamburg* (case C–15/96), the ECJ held that a
collective wage agreement which provided for promotion on grounds of seniority
after eight years' employment in any given group, excluding periods of comparable employment in the public service of another Member State, was contrary to
the treaty. The terms of the agreement manifestly worked to the disadvantage of
migrant workers as they are less likely, or it is harder for them, to satisfy the eight-
year rule.

Workers are also entitled to social and tax advantages; these are discussed in
Chapter 23.

Regulation 1612/68, Article 7(4) deals with collective and individual agreements
relating to eligibility for work, as well as terms and conditions of work, remuneration and conditions of dismissal. Any such conditions shall be null and void insofar as they are discriminatory in respect of workers from other Member States. In
Merida (case C–400/02), a collective agreement applicable to civilians employed by
foreign armed forces in Germany was in issue. It provided for 'interim assistance'
to workers where their contract were terminated. The payment was subject to the
deduction of the German income tax. Merida was a French national. Due to a taxation treaty between France and Germany, Merida's tax should have been calculated
on the basis of his country of residence, at that time France, rather than in Germany
at the German rate. He brought an action arguing that this was contrary to Article
39 EC and Article 7(4) Regulation 1612/68. Although the terms of Article 7(4) do
not refer to the possibility of justification, the ECJ did note the possibility that
indirectly discriminatory measures (such as this one) could be justified in the public interest provided it was proportionate to its aim. The ECJ rejected the German
government's justifications based on simplified administration and limitation of
financial charges.

Under Article 8 of Regulation 1612/68 a migrant worker is entitled to equality of treatment as regards 'membership of trade unions and the exercise of rights

attaching thereto, including the right to vote and to be eligible for the administration and management of bodies governed by public law and from holding office governed by public law'.

The precise relationship between trades union and collective action rights and free movement rights is not clear, especially when the exercise of collective action rights operates to limit employers' rights under Article 43 or 49. In *Laval un Partneri v Svenska Byggnadsarbetareförbundet*, (case C–341/05), the blockade of a building site to prevent the construction company using foreign labour who were not covered by a collective agreement and were not therefore entitled to the same level of pay as Swedish workers fell in principle within Article 49. (Re Article 43, see *International Transport Workers' Federation (ITF) and Finnish Seamen's Union (FSU) v Viking Line* (case C–438/05), concerning an attempt to reflag a ship to take the seaman outside the protection of a collective agreement.) *Laval* has been criticised for failing to give adequate protection to social rights and is a marked contrast to the ECJ's opinion in a competition case, where it held:

> It is beyond question that certain restrictions of competition are inherent in collective agreements between organisations representing employers and workers. However, the social policy objectives pursued by such agreements would be seriously undermined if management and labour were subject to Article 85(1) [now 81(1)] of the Treaty when seeking jointly to adopt measures to improve conditions of work and employment. [Para 59.]

22.3.2 Establishment

Central to the rights in Articles 43 is the right to carry on business in another Member State, whether as a primary business (that is, moving and setting up your business entirely within the host Member State), or as a secondary establishment (that is, maintaining an establishment in one Member State and having other offices, whatever their legal form, in other Member States). Article 43 EC applies not just to the market, but also to the terms under which business may be carried on. For example, the recognition of qualifications might be seen as affecting the right to enter a profession or business, codes of conduct tend to control the way businesses are run. The central element of these rights is to be subject to the same conditions as apply to nationals of the host Member State.

Article 43 EC, together with Article 12 (ex 6) EC (post Lisbon, 18 TFEU), may be invoked to challenge a national rule which is discriminatory. For example, in an enforcement case against Italy (*Commission v Italy (freedom of establishment)* (case 168/85)), the ECJ confirmed that rules which required Italian nationality as a precondition for the exercise of certain activities—operation of pharmacies and journalism—were contrary to Article 43. As with Article 39, this prohibition applies to both direct and indirect discrimination; indeed the ECJ has held that Articles 39 and 43 should afford the same legal protection (*Roux* (case C–363/89)).

The scope of carrying on business for the purposes of Article 43 is broad, as can be seen in *Steinhauser v City of Biarritz* (case 197/84). Steinhauser, a German, was a professional artist resident in Biarritz. He applied to the Biarritz authorities to rent a *crampotte*, a fisherman's hut of a type used locally for the exhibition and sale of works of art. He was refused on the grounds of his nationality; under the city's regulations *crampottes* could only be rented by persons of French nationality.

He challenged that decision, and the ECJ held that freedom of establishment provided under the then Article 52 (now 43) related not only to the taking up of an
activity as a self-employed person but also the pursuit of that activity in the widest
sense to include, inter alia, the right to rent premises, to tender, and to qualify for
licences and concessions. The breadth of the potential scope of Article 43 was reiterated recently in *Sevic Systems* (case C–411/03). There, the ECJ held that 'the right
of establishment covers all measures which permit or even merely facilitate access
to another Member State and the pursuit of an economic activity in that State . . . '
(para 18). Clearly, this approach will have relevance for social rights, discussed further in Chapter 23. It also suggests that Article 43 is likely to cover similar issues as
are dealt with by Regulation 1612/68 with regard to workers; for example, arrangements for the payment of taxes or the right to join a trade association.

Box 22.1 Examples of rules falling with Article 43

Rules relating to treatment of company following cross border merger:
Sevic Systems (case C–411/03).

Prohibition on more than one place of establishment:
Ordre des Avocats v Klopp (case 107/83).

Tax treatment of losses incurred by a permanent establishment situated in
a Member State of the EEA and belonging to a company having its seat in a
Member State of the European Union:
*Finanzamt für Körperschaften III in Berlin v Krankenheim Ruhesitz am Wannsee-
Seniorenheimstatt GmbH* (case C–157/07).

Advance on costs for registration of company documents:
Innoventif Limited (case C–453/04).

Rules restricting profession of architect to possession of a diploma or professional qualification:
Conseil National de l'Ordre des Architectes v Dreessen (case C–31/00).

Renewal of 329 horse-race betting licences without inviting competing bids:
Commission v Italy (case C–260/04).

Finally, note that Article 43 will catch rules which prevent persons from seeking
to exercise their rights, whether those rules are imposed by the host or the home
Member State.

22.3.3 Services

As with Article 43, Article 49 grants the right to carry on business in another Member
State. Again, the core element is equal treatment, that is to be subject to the same
conditions as apply to nationals of the host Member State.

Article 49 EC, together with Article 12 EC, may be invoked to challenge a national rule which is in some way discriminatory, whether directly or indirectly. Article
49 addresses discrimination arising not only to the taking up of an activity (access
to the profession), but to pursuit of that activity (rules relating to the running of
a business). Cases concerning the recognition of qualifications (discussed in more

detail below) relate to the taking up of an activity. By contrast, *Van Binsbergen* was a case relating to the Dutch rule which required representatives before tribunals to be resident in the Netherlands. *Gouda* concerned Dutch rules limiting the carrying of advertising on television channels. Both these cases dealt with regulations on the running of a business. This latter category of restrictions must be viewed in the widest sense. It has caught prohibitions on lotteries, access to museums, and rules regulating broadcasting, to name but a few.

Box 22.2 Examples of Article 49

Prohibition and limitation of gambling:

Läärä, Cotswold Microsystems Ltd, Oy Transatlantic Software Ltd v Kihlakunnansyyttäjä (Jyväskylä) (case C–124/97); *Her Majesty's Customs and Excise* v *Schindler* (Case C–275/92).

Requirement to comply with collective agreement for minimum wage:

Rüffert v Land Niedersachsen (case C–346/06).

Rules relating to broadcasters offering entry to competition via phone:

Kommunikationsbehörde Austria v Österreichischer Rundfunk (ORF) (case C–195/06).

Tax deductibility of school fees:

Schwarz, Gootjes-Schwarz v Finanzamt Bergisch Gladbach (case C–76/05).

As well as including restrictions on those providing services, Article 49 catches those measures designed to discourage those who want to travel to receive services. In *Bent Vestergaard* (case C–55/98), for example, Danish tax rules discriminated between professional training courses held in Denmark and those held abroad. The Danish tax authorities allowed the expenses incurred in respect of Danish courses to be deducted from the tax bill, those incurred in respect of overseas trips were not so deductible.

The case law in both instances now needs to be considered in the light of the Services Directive and, in particular, the country of origin rule in Article 16 of the directive (see 22.7.3.4 below).

22.3.4 Linguistic concerns

Under Regulation 1612/68 Member States are entitled to permit the imposition on non-nationals of conditions 'relating to linguistic knowledge required by reason of the nature of the post to be filled' (Article 3(1)). In *Groener v Minister for Education* (case 379/87) the ECJ held that a requirement of Irish law that teachers in vocational schools in Ireland should be proficient in the Irish language would be permissible under Article 3(1) in view of the clear policy of national law to maintain and promote the use of the Irish language as a means of expressing national identity and culture. The Irish language was the national language and the first official language of Ireland. Such a requirement must not, however, be disproportionate to the objectives pursued. A similar approach to the non-discrimination treaty provision of Article 39(2) was taken, albeit with a different result, in *Spotti v Freistaat Bayern* (case C–272/92), in the context of a challenge to a German law permitting contracts of limited duration for foreign language teaching assistants. The Court held that such contracts, prima facie in breach of Article 39(2), would only be permitted if they were objectively justified. Since the principal justification for the rules was that they ensured up-to-date tuition, it is not surprising that the Court found them not to be justified (see also *Alluè v Università degli Studi di Venezia* (cases C–259, 331, and 332/91) and *Commission v Luxembourg* (case C–111/91)). Likewise in *Angonese v Cassa di Risparmio di Bolzano SpA* (case C–281/98), a requirement to take a specific language test, rather than proving linguistic capabilities by other means, was held to constitute indirect discrimination contrary to Article 39. The burden of proving justification for discriminatory rules will always be heavy: the rules must be designed to achieve legitimate ends, and must be both appropriate and necessary to achieve those ends.

Note that linguistic concerns do not affect just workers; they may be relevant to those seeking to provide services or establish themselves. Thus Directive 2005/36 on the recognition of qualifications recognises the need for knowledge of the language of the host Member State (Article 53). Again, caution must be exercised about the circumstances in which such provisions may be relied upon. In *Wilson* (case C–506/04), a number of questions were referred to the ECJ concerning the circumstances in which Union law allows a host Member State to make the right of a lawyer to practise on a permanent basis in that Member State under his home-country professional title subject to a test of his proficiency in the languages of that Member State. Directive 98/5 allows a lawyer to so practise, provided he submits a certificate attesting to his registration with the competent authorities in his home Member State. Given that the directive requires such lawyers to comply with the relevant ethical standards of the bar councils, which include requirements as to linguistic knowledge, a Member State could not make registration under Directive 98/5 subject to a prior examination of his proficiency in the languages of the host Member State.

22.3.5 Public service

In the field of employment rights, Member States are entitled under Article 39(4) EC to deny or restrict access to 'employment in the public service' on the basis of a worker's nationality. Given the potential breadth of this provision, it is not surprising that it has been exploited by Member States nor that the ECJ has given it the narrowest scope. Freedom of establishment and the freedom to provide services are expressed not to apply to 'activities which in that state are connected, even occasionally, with the exercise of official authority' (Article 45 and Article 55 EC applying Article 45 to services). Although phrased in slightly different language from Article 39(4), the principles applicable to workers will apply equally to the establishment and services provisions. As in the case of workers, the derogation has been given the narrowest scope.

The German post office sought to rely on this exclusion in *Sotgiu v Deutsche Bundespost* (case 152/73) to counter Sotgiu's allegations that the post office's rules granting extra allowances to workers living apart from their families in Germany were discriminatory. On a reference from the Bundesarbeitsgericht the ECJ held that the exception provided by the then Article 48(4) (now 39(4)) did not apply to all employment in the public service. It applied only to 'certain activities' in the public service, connected with the exercise of official authority. Moreover, it applied only to conditions of *access*; it did not permit discriminatory conditions of employment once access had been granted.

The matter was further clarified in *Commission v Belgium* (Public Employees) (case 149/79). This was an infringement action against Belgium for breach of the then Article 48 (now 39). Under Belgian law, posts in the 'public service' could be limited to Belgian nationals. This was applied to all kinds of posts: unskilled workers, railwaymen, nurses, plumbers, electricians, and architects, employed by both central and local government. The city of Brussels (seat of the European Commission!) was one of the chief offenders. The Belgian government (supported by France and Germany intervening) argued that all these jobs were 'in the public service' within Article 39(4). The ECJ disagreed. The concept of public service was a Union concept; it applied only to the exercise of official authority, and was intended to apply only to employees *safeguarding the general interests of the state*. The fact that higher levels of a post might involve the exercise of official authority would not justify assimilating the junior levels to that status. Belgium was in breach of EU law.

Similar proceedings were brought, and upheld, against France in *Commission v France (French nurses)* (case 307/84) against a French law limiting the appointment of nurses in public hospitals to French nationals.

When a particular job will involve 'the exercise of official authority' is not altogether clear. It certainly does not apply to civil servants generally. In *Lawrie-Blum v Land Baden-Württemberg* (case 66/85) the Court held that access to certain posts could not be limited by reason of the fact that in a given Member State persons appointed to such posts have the status of civil servants. To make the application of Article 39(4) dependent on the legal nature of the relationship between the employer and the administration would enable Member States to determine at will the posts covered by the exception laid down in that provision. To constitute employment in the public service, employees must be charged with the exercise of powers conferred by public law or must be responsible for *safeguarding the general interests of the state*. In *Bleis v Ministère de l'Education Nationale* (case C–4/91) the Court held that the concept of public service 'presumes on the part of those occupying such posts the existence of a special relationship of allegiance to the State and reciprocity of rights and duties which form the foundation of the bond of nationality'. This approach by the ECJ might be termed a 'functional' approach to the determination of whether the 'exercise of official authority' is involved, as it considers the responsibilities of each job individually.

On these criteria, it seems that the derogation provided by Article 39(4) will be of limited use, confined to occupations such as the judiciary and the higher echelons of the civil service, the armed forces, and the police. Identical principles will apply to the interpretation of Article 45 in relation to services and establishment.

Since most of the posts in the above cases may not be denied to non-nationals, access to these posts by way of examination or training must be open, on equal terms, to workers (or their families) who are non-nationals. Thus in *Lawrie-Blum* (case 66/85) a practical training scheme for teachers, organised in Baden-Württemberg within the framework of the civil service, was not within Article 39(4) and could not be confined to German nationals.

In view of the widespread practice among Member States of excluding non-nationals from a wide range of occupations in the public service on the basis of Article 39(4) the Commission published a Notice in 1988 (OJ No C 72/2) identifying certain sectors of employment which it considered to be for the most part 'sufficiently remote from the specific activities of the public sphere as defined by the European Court that they would only in rare cases be covered by the exception of Article 48(4)' (now 39(4)).

These comprise:

(a) public health-care services

(b) teaching in State educational establishments

(c) research for non-military purposes in public establishments

(d) public bodies responsible for administering commercial services.

The Commission has brought enforcement actions against certain Member States for failure to take action following the communication (eg, *Commission v Belgium* (case C–173/94); *Commission v Greece* (case C–290/94); *Commission v Luxembourg* (case C–473/93)). In its judgments given on the same day, the ECJ confirmed the Commission's approach of identifying types of work which would rarely fall within Article 39(4) EC. In these circumstances, it is still open to the national authorities to show, on a functional basis, that specified jobs within such sections do fall within the public service exception. It has been suggested that the review should result in the opening up of many posts which in many Member States are currently reserved for nationals, representing a 'tremendous leap forward in the attainment of a true community-wide labour market' (see Watson, noted below). More than a decade later, it seems that this has yet to happen.

22.4 Test for the application of Articles 39, 43, and 49 EC

22.4.1 Discrimination

The jurisprudence of the early years shows a test based on discrimination. This is not surprising as the terms of Article 39(2) refer expressly to the abolition of discrimination on the grounds of nationality, whether arising from legislation, regulation or administrative practice. Article 39 is in this context a specific form of the general prohibition on discrimination on the grounds of nationality found in Article 12 EC. Although the wording in Articles 43 and 49 do not refer expressly to a prohibition on discrimination, the ECJ took a similar approach in respect of these two provisions. In *Reyners* (case 2/74), the applicant was a Dutch national residing in Belgium. He had the necessary Belgian qualification in law for admission as an *avocat*, but was refused admission purely because he did not have Belgian nationality. This constituted discrimination contrary to Article 43.

Discrimination, as we have seen above, includes those rules which although not distinguishing on the face of it are harder to satisfy for non-nationals (eg, language requirements), disadvantage them (eg, rules about length of service in the host Member State), or put them under a dual burden (ie, non-recognition of qualifications). In *O'Flynn v Adjudication Officer* (case C–237/94) (see Chapter 15) the ECJ made clear that it was not necessary to prove that a national measure in practice affected a higher proportion of foreign workers, but that the measure was intrinsically liable to affect migrants more than nationals of the host Member State.

As in relation to the free movement of goods (and now capital), indirect discrimination is capable of being 'objectively justified' (*Sotgiu* (case 152/73)). Direct discrimination as, for example, established in relation to Article 49 in *Bond van Adverteerders v Netherlands* (case 352/85), could only be justified under Article 46 EC, which was strictly construed. (See further 22.6 below.)

22.4.2 Beyond discrimination

As with the free movement of goods, the ECJ has moved to an approach which moved beyond a discrimination based test. It was thought initially that national regulatory rules and professional practices which were not discriminatory, which applied 'without distinction' to all persons providing services or established in a particular Member State, and which clearly served a useful purpose, could not be challenged under the treaty (eg, *Koestler* (case 15/78)). The rights granted to EU nationals under Articles 49 and 50 EC were to provide services in other Member States 'under the same conditions' as applied to the state's own nationals. Although national regulatory rules might create barriers to the free movement of services and freedom of establishment they could only be removed by harmonisation, as provided under Articles 46–7 (ex 56–7) EC (post Lisbon, 52–3 TFEU).

Since harmonisation proved slow to achieve, some of these measures came to be challenged as 'discriminatory' in that they were harder to satisfy for non-nationals or imposed a dual burden upon migrants. As this category of rule would apply without distinction, it was suggested that they would be permissible provided they could be objectively justified (see, eg, *van Binsbergen* (case 33/74) and *Commission v Germany, (insurance services)* (case 205/84)).

For example, in *Commission v Germany*, the rules required, inter alia, that a person providing direct insurance must be established and authorised to practise in the state in which the service is provided. The Court held that the then Articles 59–60 (now 49–50) require the removal not only of all discrimination based on nationality but also all restrictions on his freedom to provide services imposed by reason of the fact that he is established in a Member State other than that in which the services are provided.

So while the *van Binsbergen* analysis was based on finding discrimination, it seemed that the ECJ was suggesting a test which focussed not so much on the position of the individual but on the impact on the activity (whether work, establishment or services). The case law was, however, slow to develop and the principles were unclear. It was not until 1991 with *Säger v Dennemeyer and Co Ltd* (case C–76/90) that the Court established a coherent approach to indistinctly applicable rules in the field of services parallel to that pioneered in the sphere of goods in the 1970s in *Dassonville* (case 8/74) and *Cassis de Dijon* (case 120/78). In doing so it undoubtedly opened up the possibility for further claims under Article 49, and with it, as with any easing of the rules, some abuse (see, eg, *TV 10 SA v Commissariaat voor de Media* (case C–23/93), see 22.9.3).

22.4.2.1 *Services*

Säger v Dennemeyer concerned a specialist in patent renewal services, Dennemeyer, who based in the UK. He provided these services in Germany, without the licence which German law requires for persons attending to the legal affairs of third parties. Such licences were not normally granted to patent renewal agents. Dennemeyer's right to provide such services in Germany was challenged by Säger, a German patent agent operating in Germany. Dennemeyer argued that the German rules, which limited access to the relevant profession were a hindrance to the freedom of movement of services, contrary to Articles 49 and 50(3). A number of questions were referred to the Court. As Advocate-General Jacobs pointed out, while it was clear that Article 49 applied to discriminatory rules, it was not yet clear whether it applied to rules which were applicable to all providers of services, whether established in the Member State in which the service was provided or not. As noted, the principles laid down in *van Binsbergen* and the insurance cases had proceeded on the basis that the rules in question were discriminatory. While it was not unreasonable to expect compliance with the rules of the Member State by any person established in that state, there was less justification for demanding compliance by those providing services there but who were based elsewhere. In these circumstances he suggested an approach based on the Court's jurisprudence on Article 28 (ex 30) in relation to indistinctly applicable rules.

The Court endorsed his suggestion. While asserting that:

> Article 59 [now 49] requires not only the abolition of all discrimination against a person providing services on the ground of his nationality but also the abolition of any restriction, even if applied without distinction to national providers of services and to those of other Member States, when it is liable to prohibit or otherwise impede the activities of a provider of services established in another Member State where he lawfully provides similar services [para 12]

it held that:

> Having regard to the particular characteristics of certain specific provisions of services, specific requirements imposed on the provider cannot be regarded as incompatible with the Treaty.

However:

> The freedom to provide services may be limited only by rules which are justified by imperative reasons relating to the public interest and which apply to all persons and undertakings pursuing an activity in the State of destination insofar as that interest is not protected by rules to which the person providing the service is subject in the State in which he is established. In particular, these requirements must be objectively necessary in order to ensure compliance with professional rules and must not exceed what is necessary to attain those objectives.

It may be noted that, to establish a prima facie breach of Article 49, the rule challenged must be 'liable to prohibit or otherwise impede' the provision of services. On the face of it, this is a stricter test than the *Dassonville* test applied to goods. On the other hand, the criteria relating to justification, embracing the principles of proportionality and mutual recognition, are substantially the same as the twin principles laid down in *Cassis*, albeit lacking examples as to what will constitute 'imperative reasons relating to the public interest'.

The principles laid down in *Säger v Dennemeyer and Co Ltd* have been followed in a succession of cases in which national or professional rules likely to 'prohibit or otherwise impede' the free provision of services have been tested for their compatibility with Article 49. Thus in *Commission v France* (case C–154/89) a requirement of French law that tourist guides must obtain a licence by examination, although justifiable in principle in the interest of consumers as contributing to a 'proper appreciation of places and things of interest', was found to be disproportionate. The licence requirement went further than was necessary in order to protect this interest. In *Vander Elst v Office des Migrations Internationales* (case C–43/93) the requirement of a French work permit for third-country nationals (TCNs) seeking to work in France was held not to be justified by 'overriding reasons in the general interest' (to regulate access to the national labour market), since these workers were already in possession of a work permit obtained in Belgium. On the other hand, in *Ramrath v Ministre de la Justice* (case C–106/91) rules governing the conditions for the provision of auditing services in Luxembourg were found on the facts to be justified and not disproportionate. Similarly in *Alpine Investments BV v Minister van Financiën* (case C–384/93) a Dutch prohibition on 'cold calling' by providers of financial advice established in the Netherlands was found to be justified in order to protect consumers and the reputation of the Netherlands' security market and was not disproportionate. In each case the measure in question and its alleged justification were tested on their merits.

A couple of further points should be noted. Some, such as Advocate-General Lenz in *Union royale belge des sociétés de football association ASBL v Bosman* (case C–415/93), had suggested that there should be a distinction between rules relating to access to a profession and those concerning the operation of a business, as the former would be more damaging to the internal market. This view has not been universally accepted, as can be seen from the comments of Advocate-General Alber in *Lehtonen and Castors Canada Dry Namur-Braine ASBL v Fédération royale belge des sociétés de basket-ball ASBL (FRBSB)* (case C–176/96). It seems in general that there is no such distinction made in the ECJ's approach and that in some circumstances the ECJ has conflated the two issues (eg, *Kraus v Land Baden-Württemberg* (case C–19/92), para 23). It may still be that the latter group of restrictions could be more easily justified.

The second point to note is that Article 49, as with Articles 39 and 43, applies to 'export' situations, as we can see from *Alpine Investments BV*. It is open to debate whether the ECJ has (or should) take a more lenient approach to export cases, as it has done in the context of the export of goods. Interestingly, in *Alpine Investments BV* the national rules were found to be justified and proportionate.

22.4.2.2 *Establishment*

Arguably, the principles established in *Säger v Dennemeyer* appeared to apply only to the provision of services. Paragraph 13, suggested that 'a Member State may not make the provision of services in its territory subject to the conditions required for establishment . . . and thereby deprive of all practical effectiveness the provisions of the Treaty whose object is, primarily, to provide services'.

Clearly, the ECJ notes a difference between services and establishment, a difference which also shows when considering justification for restrictive national measures, as services will be regulated by the home Member State. This reasoning also implied that persons who established themselves in a Member State must comply with the conditions laid down in that state for its own nationals. *Gebhard v Consiglio dell'Ordine degli Avvocati e Procuratori di Milano* (case C–55/94) changed our understanding of Article 43. *Gebhard* involved a challenge by a German lawyer, a member of the Stuttgart Bar, to a decision by the Milan Bar Council prohibiting him from practising from chambers set up in Italy under the title *avvocato*. He claimed the rules of the Milan Bar breached the then Articles 59 and/or 52 (now 49 and 43).

The Court held that the possibility for a national of a Member State to exercise his right of establishment, and the conditions for the exercise of that right, had to be determined in the light of the activities which he intended to pursue on the territory of the host Member State. Where an activity was not subject to any rules in the host state, a national of another Member State was entitled to establish himself on the territory of the first state and pursue his activities there. On the other hand, 'Where the taking up and pursuit of a particular activity was subject to certain conditions in the host State a national of another Member State intending to pursue that activity must in principle comply with them'. However, national measures which hinder or make less attractive the exercise of fundamental freedoms guaranteed by the treaty must fulfil four conditions: they must be applied in a non-discriminatory manner; they must be justified by imperative requirements in the general interest; they must be suitable for securing the attainment of the objective which they pursue; and they must not go beyond what is necessary in order to attain it.

Member States must take into account the equivalence of diplomas and if necessary proceed to a comparison of the knowledge and qualifications required by their national rules and those of the person concerned. It was left to the national court to decide whether the rules in question were in fact justified. (On qualifications see further 22.8 below.)

Gebhard can thus be seen as a recognition of an approach to national measures parallel to that taken in respect of services (and goods), which is not to analyse the issues by reference to discrimination but to the existence of a hindrance. As with *Säger v Dennemeyer* for services, *Gebhard* widened the potential scope of Article 43.

22.4.2.3 *Workers*

Whether the same approach would be taken as regards workers was clarified in the *Bosman* case (case C–415/93). It concerned rules that were not overtly discriminatory but which still had an adverse impact on individuals' ability to exercise their free-movement rights.

The case centred on Belgian football transfer rules, which accorded with international football rules. These rules provided that a club which sought to engage a player must pay a specified, sometimes considerable, sum to the player's existing club. The rules applied irrespective of the nationality of the player and whether the player was going to be playing for a Belgian team or not. Further, there were limits on how many non-nationals a club could employ. In Bosman's case, he was signed up to play for a Belgian team and the rules effectively stopped him from moving to play for a French team. After a lengthy legal dispute, the matter was referred to the ECJ. Bosman argued that the rules were, inter alia, contrary to Article 39. The ECJ held that, although the rules were not discriminatory, they still 'directly affect[ed] players' access to the employment market in other Member States and are thus capable of impeding freedom of movement of workers'.

In principle, the rules were incompatible with Article 39 unless they pursued a legitimate aim compatible with the treaty, were justified by pressing reasons of public interest and were proportionate. In *Bosman*, therefore, the ECJ was not concerned with discrimination but with the question of whether cross-border access to the job market of each Member State was safeguarded. In this approach we clearly see parallels to that taken by the ECJ in relation to the free movement of goods and 'indistinctly applicable' measures. Indeed in *Bosman*, we see perhaps the strongest statement of the scope of these rights as it is stated clearly to be concerned with 'access to the market' and the level of impact required to trigger Article 39 is low: 'directly affecting'.

22.4.2.4 *A distinction between personal discrimination and restrictions on professional activity?*

It had been thought that a distinction could be discerned between the approach towards personal matters and those relating to professional rules. Rules distinguishing on the basis of nationality, for example, would be dealt with on a discrimination-based analysis, whilst rules which concerned professional matters, would be analysed from an access to the market-style approach. It seems that the ECJ has not continued to make this distinction. Whether this means that the distinction between personal and professional rights has been eradicated entirely is not certain. In some instances the ECJ seems to use both concepts (eg, *Payroll Data Services (Italy) Srl v ADP Europe and ADP GSI SA* (case C–79/01), concerning rules requiring small enterprises to have their payslips produced by bodies registered with specified bodies). If we look to the case law concerning workers and their social and ancillary rights, the ECJ still uses a test based on discrimination (see, eg, *Ioannidis* (case C–258/04) see Chapter 23) and the Italian rules relating to exchange assistants for languages were likewise held to be indirectly discriminatory (*Delay v Universita degli studi di Firenze* (case C–276/07)). Nonetheless, in the majority of cases concerning the economic-rights, a test which focused on the restriction of an activity rather than individual discrimination seems to be more common.

22.4.2.5 *A common approach, a consistent approach?*

A general trend can be identified in all three provisions towards the use of a test based on access to the market irrespective of whether the right is being relied on by an individual or a legal person and irrespective of whether the right is exercised by an employer or employee; recipient or provider of service. Nonetheless, the ECJ has not used the same test in respect of the three articles. Thus, the test used in *Gebhard* is, on a strict interpretation of the wording, less demanding than the 'prohibit or otherwise impede' threshold introduced in *Säger v Dennemeyer*. Whether this test is now to be applied to both establishment and services is not clear. In *Gebhard* the ECJ noted that both constitute 'fundamental freedoms provided by the Treaty'. It would thus make sense that the same test is applied to both articles, and indeed to Article 39. The wording used in *Bosman* is again different. In the more recent *CaixaBank France* (case C–442/02), the ECJ adopted yet another test in respect of the freedom of establishment, stating that measures which 'prohibit, impede or render less attractive' the exercise of freedom of establishment are restrictions for the purposes of Article 43. This seems to blend the *Säger* and *Gebhard* tests, arguably requiring very little in the way of an impediment to freedom of establishment.

Whilst in subsequent case law on Article 49 EC the ECJ has, in the main, applied the *Säger* test, there are inconsistencies here too. In the more recent case of *Kohll* (case C–158/96, prior authorisation of medical expenses by home state required), the ECJ citing *Commission v France* (case C–381/93) applied a slightly different test from that used in *Säger*. It held that what is now Article 49 (ex 59) 'precludes the application of any national rules which have the effect of making the provision of services between Member States *more difficult* than the provision of services purely within one Member State' (para 33; authors' emphasis). It is not clear whether the use of this test will become generalised within Article 49 case law: although this version of the test was found in cases involving transport, it seems to be coming more widely used (see, eg, *Leichtle* (case C–8/02), reimbursement of expenditure for health cure). In some cases the ECJ seems to be avoiding the issue entirely, using neither of these formulations. For example, in *Gambelli* (case C–243/01) the ECJ merely remarked, 'It is appropriate to inquire whether Article 49 precludes legislation such as that in issue in the main proceedings which, although it does not discriminate on grounds of nationality, restricts the freedom to provide services' (para 69). This is a yet more stringent approach than *Säger* or *Kohll*.

It is, in the final analysis, not obvious what difference in practice the use of the different tests would make. In any event, the measure in question must be examined to identify if it is objectively justified: the emphasis in all the cases is on justification for the rules in terms of the *activity undertaken* rather than on the burden imposed on the 'guest' undertaking or worker.

In sum, it seems that these provisions will be easy to trigger, raising the spectre of the problems in the goods case law following the *Sunday Trading cases*, and the question of whether the appropriate balance between the competence of the EU and of the Member States has been appropriately drawn. This is illustrated by *Caixa Bank* (case C–442/02), a French rule prohibited a certain type of account from being marketed in France. The ECJ argued that the rule hindered subsidiaries of foreign banks by depriving them of the possibility of 'competing more effectively' against established banks because the established banks 'have an extensive network of branches and therefore greater opportunities . . . for raising capital from the public' (para 13).

Implicitly the ECJ suggests that the incoming companies need to be allowed to provide a greater range of services to give them a competitive edge. In this, the ECJ departed from the opinion of the Advocate-General who noted that the effect of the national measures in question would merely be to 'reduce the economic attractiveness' of carrying on the activity regulated. According to the Advocate-General, such an interpretation would upset the balance of powers between the regulatory powers of the Members States and the Union. He noted that the Union does not have general regulatory powers, such power falling to the Member States subject to the overriding prohibition on discrimination and obstacles to establishment. Further, the impact of such an approach would be de-regulatory as it would enable economic operators to oppose any national measure because that measure could 'in the final analysis narrow profit margins'. As the Advocate-General suggested, this would result in a view of the treaty freedoms which operated 'not in order to create an internal market in which conditions are similar to those of a single market and where operators can move freely, but in order to establish a market without rules' (*CaixaBank*, Opinion, paras 58–63). Nonetheless, this is precisely the route the ECJ has seemed to take, and which has been recognised in subsequent case law on Article 49, as well as Article 43 (*Corporación Dermoestética SA v To Me Group Advertising Media* (case C–500/06), rule limiting advertising of services to local television). As, in the final analysis, any regulatory rule has the effect of making a business less desirable or profitable than if those rules were not in place, the consequence seems to be that any attempt at regulation is capable of being challenged on this approach.

22.5 Limitations on the application of Articles 39, 43, and 49

We have noted the breadth of circumstances in which Articles 39, 43, and 49 can be triggered. Following *Bosman*, it seemed that the ECJ was providing limits to these circumstances. The ECJ took the opportunity to refine the scope of *Bosman*, and consequently the scope of Article 39 as regards non-discriminatory rules which nonetheless might affect the functioning of the internal market, in *Volker Graf v Filzmoser Maschinenbau* (case C–190/98). The rules challenged in this case concerned Austrian employment legislation which required employers to make certain payments to employees on the termination of an employment contract, when the employee was not leaving the job voluntarily. Graf handed in his notice to go to work in Germany. He claimed the payments, but Filzmoser Maschinenbau refused to make the payments as Graf was leaving voluntarily. He argued that the rules that excluded him from receiving the payments were likely adversely to affect those who sought to move from Austria to another Member State more than those who were leaving employment but staying in Austria. Arguing from the ECJ's approach in *Bosman*, Graf claimed that the Austrian rules were incompatible with what is now Article 39 EC. The question as to whether this was incompatible with the requirements of the free movement of workers was referred. The ECJ confirmed that Article 39 not only applies to discriminatory rules but also to rules which, although they are expressed to apply without distinction, impede the exercise of free-movement rights. It went on to say, however, that for such rules to constitute an obstacle prohibited under Article 39, the provisions 'must affect access of the workers to the labour market'. In this case, the entitlement was only contingent on certain events happening—basically the unfair dismissal of an employee—and therefore any effect on the internal market of this sort of rule was too uncertain and indirect to fall within the prohibition. Thus, although the ECJ's test of measures affecting access to the host market would seem on the face of it to be very broad, the latter part of the judgment clearly focuses on the need for an obstacle to accessing that market to exist. A similar approach can be seen, as regards goods, in *Dip Spa* (cases C–140–2/94) (discussed in Chapter 19).

The ECJ in relation to goods adopted another limitation mechanism, that found in *Keck* (cases C–267 and 268/91), which allows certain types of rule to be treated more leniently (known as 'selling arrangements') (see *De Agostini* (cases C–34–6/95) and Chapter 19). This has similarities to the approach adopted in *Graf* and in *Dip Spa*, as measures which have an effect which is too uncertain and indirect are not be caught by the prohibition. Indeed, the Advocate-General in *CaixaBank* considered the possibility of limiting Article 43 in a similar way, suggesting that those measures which have an effect which is too uncertain and indirect should not be caught by Article 43. It is striking that the ECJ did not even consider this possibility, thus opening a rift between the case law in this regard on establishment not only with that concerning goods but also the workers jurisprudence. Although the *Graf* question does not seem to have been raised before the ECJ with regard to services, it seemed to reject the need for a *Keck*-style approach to services in *Alpine Investments* (case C–384/93), turning its back on the suggestion of Advocate-General Jacobs that the Court adopt a *de minimis* rule, and that only rules which 'substantially impede' the freedom to provide services should be deemed prima facie in breach of Union law (see also in relation to goods *Leclerc–Siplec* (case C–412/93)). Although the precise scope of the ruling *Alpine Investments* in that context has been the subject of some debate, it seems that where the advertising of services is concerned, the ECJ does not even consider the question of whether there is a distinction between 'selling arrangements' and 'product requirements'. Thus, in *Corporación Dermoestética SA v To Me Group Advertising Media* (case C–500/06), which concerned a limitation on the advertising of advertisements for medical and surgical treatments (the adverts were prohibited on national television but permitted on local television), the ECJ merely assessed the national rules as a hindrance to cross-border trade (contrast approach in relation to goods where the ECJ has distinguished between total and partial bans on advertising: see Chapter 19).

22.6 A Rule of reason?

As we have seen in the field of goods, the ECJ seems to have felt the need to balance a broad Union competence to review national legislation with the possibility for Member States to justify their national rules. This is particularly important with regard to the training and educational backgrounds of those seeking employment or to trade in another Member States, as the requirements in the Member States are not uniform. Both Article 43 and Article 49 recognised the need for Member States to limit the right of individuals and legal persons to trade. The right to equality of opportunity provided by Articles 43(2) can only be exercised 'under the conditions laid down for its own nationals by the law of the country where such establishment is effected' (Article 43(2) EC). Article 50(3) EC likewise provides in relation to services that it can only be exercised 'under the same conditions as are imposed by that State on its own nationals'. Even within Regulation 1612/68 we can find recognition of this point: an employer may require a non-national to undergo a vocational test provided he expressly requests this when making his offer of employment (Article 6(2)). This provision may not however be used as a means of covert discrimination.

These types of rule are likely to be caught by Articles 43 and 49, even prior to *Säger v Dennemeyer*. Equally, striking such measures down would be unlikely to be in the public interest. The ECJ seemed aware of the problem even in the relatively early jurisprudence. In *van Binsbergen* (case 33/74) it was acknowledged, in the context of a challenge to a residence requirement imposed by the Dutch Bar on those seeking to provide certain legal services in Holland, that specific requirements imposed on a person providing services would not infringe Articles 49–50 where they have as their purpose the application of professional rules justified by the general good—in particular, rules relating to organisation, ethics, qualifications, supervision and liability, which are binding on any person established in the territory of the Member State in which the service is provided. The person providing the service cannot take advantage of his right to provide services to avoid the professional rules of conduct which would be applied to him if he were established in that state.

Professional rules which inhibit the free provision of services would only be permissible if they were:

(a) non-discriminatory

(b) objectively justified

(c) not disproportionate.

These principles were subsequently applied in *Webb* (case 279/80) in the context of the provision of manpower services. The Court added in *Webb* that, in ascertaining whether its own rules are justified, the host Member State must take into account the justifications and safeguards already provided by the applicant in order to pursue the activity in question in his state of establishment (approved in *Commission v Germany (lawyers' services)* (case 427/85)).

The principles expressed in *van Binsbergen* and *Webb* were refined and developed in 1986 in the 'insurance' cases (*Commission v Germany (insurance services)* (case 205/84); *Commission v Ireland (co-insurance services)* (case 206/84); *Commission v France* (case 220/83); *Commission v Denmark (insurance services)* (case 252/83)). These actions were based on alleged infringements of Articles 49–50 (ex 59–60) and Insurance Directive 78/473 by the defendant Member States in their rules regulating the provision of insurance services. The rules and the breaches alleged in each state were similar.

Effectively, the imposition of the rules of the host Member State meant that cross-border service providers were subject to regulation more than once. Because of this, the Court held that not *all* the legislation applicable to nationals or those engaged in permanent activities could be applied to the *temporary* activities of enterprises established in another Member State. It could be applied only if three criteria were satisfied:

(a) it is justified by imperative reasons relating to the public interest

(b) the public interest is not already protected by the rules of the state of establishment

(c) the same result cannot be obtained by less restrictive means.

Thus, in the field of services, the Court moved towards a test for professional rules not unlike the *Cassis de Dijon* (case 120/78) test applied to goods (see Chapter 19). As with that test, it is likely that the criteria will be strictly applied to ensure that each rule is necessary and genuinely justified. If not, it will breach Articles 49–50. In *Commission v Germany* the Court found that the establishment requirement was not justified; indeed, it was the very negation of the freedom to provide services and would only be permissible if indispensable. The authorisation requirement, on the other hand, at least as related to the rules concerning technical reserves, might be justified for the protection of policyholders and insured persons.

The Commission's action failed in this respect. Applying the same approach in *Commission v Luxembourg* (case C–351/90) the Court found that a 'single surgery' rule applied in Luxembourg, the effect of which was to prohibit doctors, dentists, and veterinary surgeons established outside Luxembourg from opening surgeries in Luxembourg, was not justified, as was argued, in the interest of good professional practice (to ensure proximity to patients). Such a general prohibition (which in any case was applied more strictly to professionals established in other Member States) was found to be 'unduly restrictive', 'too absolute and too general'.

A similar approach can be seen with regard to establishment. As we have seen *Gebhard*, discussed above, introduced what might be called a 'rule of reason'. Thus, national rules which aim at a legitimate objective will not be struck down under Article 43 if they satisfy a four stage test:

(1) they apply in a non-discriminatory manner

(2) they are justified by overriding reasons in the general interest

(3) they are suitable for obtaining that objective

(4) they do not go beyond what is necessary to attain that objective.

This test, or the last three elements of it, is sometimes referred to as a proportionality test. It is important to emphasis that it is a cumulative test; all elements must be satisfied for a national rule which falls within the *Gebhard* test to be protected. Although the possible categories of justification are not closed (by contrast to those listed in the treaty), the scope of this rule is, as in other areas, limited in practice by the rigour of the proportionality review.

It should be noted that there seems to be a necessary distinction between the necessity and proportionality assessments under services by comparison with establishment (and possibly workers), as the presumption of home Member State control is greater in the context of the provision of services, which are often seen as temporary; double regulation is less easily justified. Note now, however, the impact of the Article 16 Services Directive, which introduces the principle of country-of-origin regulation, with very limited grounds for derogation. These latter are narrower than the public-interest grounds recognised under the rule of reason by the ECJ. Whilst the case law with regard to workers is more often focused on personal rights, there is no reason to suppose that in terms of measures applying without distinction the ECJ would not take a similar approach. In this context, there would be a similar distinction between the considerations taken into account in the proportionality assessment between workers and services as with establishment and services.

22.6.1 Boundary between discriminatory measures and those that apply without distinction

The case law so far suggests that we have a model which distinguishes between (directly) discriminatory rules on the one hand and those that apply without distinction (including indirectly discriminatory rules) on the other. The consequence of this distinction is felt in the way the rules may be justified: discriminatory rules may only be justified by grounds specified in the treaty; the others may be justified on broader grounds of public interest under a 'rule of reason'. The situation can be seen in Fig 22.1.

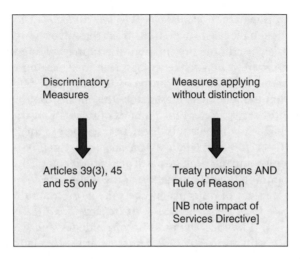

Fig 22.1 Impact of boundary between discriminatory measures and those that apply without distinction

One problem in this area is the distinction between discriminatory measures and those which apply without distinction. There are two elements to this problem. Firstly, it has been suggested that the ECJ has not always been clear as to whether measures are discriminatory or not. Secondly, this problem may be exacerbated by the use of an obstacle-based test rather than one that looks at the notion of discrimination, whether direct or indirect, as the ECJ no longer has to consider the distinction in its analysis.

We can seen this problem with regard to residence requirements. As the ECJ has argued, a residence requirement is indirectly discriminatory because 'is liable to operate mainly to the detriment of nationals of other Member States, since non-residents are in the majority of cases foreigners' (see, eg, *Commission v Italy (museum entry)* (case C–388/01), para 14). This approach has been taken in other cases too (eg *Sotgiu* (case 152/73)). In the earlier case of *Gouda* (case C–288/89), however, the ECJ held that Article 49 catches 'discrimination against a person providing services on the grounds of his nationality or the fact that he is established in a Member State other than one in which the service is provided' (para 10). The distinction is significant because direct discrimination, as the residence requirement was seen to be in *Gouda*, can be justified only under the terms of the express treaty derogation (*Gouda*, para 11).

To take an example, should single-surgery rules be viewed as discriminatory? In *Commission v Luxembourg* (case C–351/90), such a rule was treated as applying without distinction though it would make cross border establishment impossible. More recently in *Marks and Spencer* (case C–446/03), the measure in issue could be categorised as discriminatory, as different rules applied depending on the place of establishment. Nonetheless, the ECJ went on to consider the possible justifications for the rule and did not limit itself to the grounds set out in the express treaty provisions derogating from the right of free movement. In this, we can see reflections of the difficulties encountered by the ECJ in a number of cases concerning the free movement of goods, specifically in relation to rules designed to protect the environment (eg *Commission v Belgium (Walloon Waste)* (case C–2/90)). In both cases, there have been suggestions from the Advocates-General that the distinction between discriminatory and non-discriminatory rules should be abandoned, but to no avail. A new reference has been made asking whether nationality discrimination can be justified on the basis of the public interest; although it is not clear from the reference, presumably this means the rule-of-reason version of public interest rather than the grounds of treaty derogation. If this is the case, then the chance to dissolve this distinction lies before the ECJ (see *Sjöberg v Åklagaren* (case C–447/08) and *Gerdin v Åklagaren* (case C448/08)). Of course, the tax cases involving companies can be particularly problematic because of the uncertainties surrounding the determination of the seat of the company (see 23.9). Analyses based on place of residence has become more complex in this context (contrast *RBS* (case C–311/97) and *Lankhorst-Hohorst GmbH* (case C–324/00); see also *Danner* (case C–136/00)). The problem of residency and whether it should be viewed as indirectly or directly discriminatory arises in relation to social and ancillary rights too.

22.7 Harmonisation

Some national rules, particularly those relating to conduct of professions and qualifications, might survive the application of Article 43 in the interests of protecting the public from unqualified practitioners. The disadvantage is, of course, that the European market could remain segmented. The answer to this particular problem, as we have seen in Chapter 16, is to replace national regulations with European rules, otherwise known as harmonisation.

22.7.1 The early period

The treaty provided for the abolition of existing restrictions on freedom of establishment and freedom to provide services to be achieved in progressive stages during a transitional period. During the first stage the Council, acting on a proposal from the Commission, was to draw up a general programme on the abolition of restrictions on freedom of establishment (former Article 53, which was deleted by the Treaty of Amsterdam (ToA)) and on the freedom to provide services (Article 52 (ex 63) EC; post Lisbon, 59 TFEU). In addition these institutions were required, during the first stage, to 'issue Directives for the mutual recognition of diplomas, certificates and other evidence of formal qualifications' (Article 47(1) EC) and to 'issue Directives for the coordination of the provisions laid down by law, regulation or administrative action in Member States concerning the taking up and pursuit of activities as self-employed persons' (Article 47(2) EC). Article 55 EC extends this provision to services.

The general programmes were adopted in 1961 (JO 1962, 36, 32). The agreeing of directives under Article 47(1)–(2) proved more difficult. Although many directives were eventually passed in areas ranging from wholesaling to hairdressing to medicine, progress was slow. Notably, the Architects' Directive alone took 17 years to pass.

It should be noted that the area of qualifications and access to professions are not the only ones resulting in Union measures. In the *Tobacco Advertising case* (*Germany v Parliament and Council* (case C–376/98)), the Advocate-General likened the scope of Article 47(2) to that of Article 95, albeit more limited in scope (para 63). A broad range of directives have been enacted under this provision, such as the Television without Frontiers Directive (Directive 89/552/EEC (OJ [1989] L 298/23), as amended, now Audiovisual Media Services Directive).

22.7.2 Mutual recognition and the home-country principle

Because of the problems outlined above, and because progress on harmonisation for the purpose of mutual recognition of qualifications had been so slow, the Union decided on a new approach. Instead of attempting to harmonise by profession, known as the sectoral or 'vertical' approach, the Commission adopted a general or 'horizontal' approach, based not on harmonisation but on the mutual recognition of qualifications. This applied not just to individual professions but to all areas of activity for which a higher education diploma was required. Directive 89/48 (OJ [1989] L 19/16), based on these principles, was approved in December 1988. The Council then agreed a second directive dealing with secondary education (Council Directive 92/51/EEC (OJ [1992] L 209/25) and also based on the principle of mutual recognition. Both directives were repeatedly amended and the whole system has now been replaced by Directive 2005/36/EC (OJ [2005] L 255/22), which came into force 20 October 2007. The basic systems remain, however, and are discussed at 22.8.2.

Mutual recognition is not limited to the recognition of qualifications, but is an approach used in many directives (and, indeed, underpins much of the ECJ's approach to necessity and proportionality of host state regulations). The approach is based on the following principles:

(a) the harmonisation of *essential* safeguards and standards applicable to activities as a whole

(b) within that framework, acceptance of the standards of other Member States on a basis of mutual trust and recognition, on the principle of home country control and supervision.

Essential to the effective functioning of these principles would be the concept of the single licence known as home-country regulation. This would allow an institution licensed in one Member State to offer its services to another Member State, either by establishing a branch or agency in that state or by supplying its services there. The Television without Frontiers Directive, for example, is a minimum-harmonisation directive which operates on the country of origin principle. Although television signals may be received in more than one Member State, only one Member State has responsibility for regulation, the Member State in which the broadcaster is established. (The problems with this approach are discussed at 22.9.3).

22.7.3 The Services Directive

Despite the efforts of the ECJ in developing a broad-based test for the application of Article 49 and the harmonising directives already existing, the Commission concluded that there still existed significant barriers to entry for the cross border provision of services. To this end, it proposed that a general services directive be enacted, based on the principle of home country regulation, administrative co-operation and administrative simplification. The directive also contained a number of specific derogation principles to temper the potentially deregulatory impact of the directive, as well as excluding some sectors of the service industry, such as gambling and gas and water supply, from its scope. The Services Directive has proved to be controversial; discontent with its potential impact on the provision of public services has been suggested to have had an influence on the French 'no' vote. The European Parliament, in expressing concern about the relationship between the directive and services of general economic interest (that is, services that are in the public interest), commented that within the EU legal order trade liberalisation is not an end in itself, nor was it to be benefited at the expense of other tasks of the Union. Others considered the interrelationship between the general services directive and the subject specific directives had been dealt with inadequately. Nonetheless, the Services Directive (Directive 2006/123/EC, OJ [2006] L376/36) was adopted on 12 December 2006 and will have to be implemented by Member States three years after its publication, by 28 December 2009, at the latest. Given the scope of the directive and its impact, implementation may prove a challenge for the Member States.

22.7.3.1 *Scope of the directive*

The directive applies to all services which are not explicitly excluded from its scope and in principle the definition of services matches that taken under the treaty. Given that the case law of the ECJ has not automatically excluded public services from the scope of the treaty, in principle some services provided by the state may also be caught by the directive. The directive explicitly excludes, however, 'non-economic services of general interest' (Article 2(2)(a)). The Commission has suggested that national primary and secondary education, which is not provided for remuneration, would fall within the excluded category, whereas services in the utilities (such as electricity and gas) would be caught by the directive. Financial services are excluded (Article 2(2)(b)), as are electronic communication services and networks, and associated facilities and services as defined in Article 2 of the Electronic Communication Framework Directive (Article 2(2)(c)). Transport (Article 2(2)(d)), the service of hiring out workers provided by temporary work agencies (Article 2(2)(e)), health care (Article 2(2)(f)), broadcasting (Article 2(2)(g)), gambling (Article 2(2)(h)), and some social services (Article 2(2)(j)) are likewise excluded—though in each case the definition ascribed to the relevant category of service should be checked. Additionally, the exercise of public authority (Article 2(2)(i)), private security services (Article 2(2)(k)) and bailiffs appointed by an official act of government (Article 2(2)(l)) are excluded. Finally, Article 2(3) states that the Services Directive does not apply to the field of taxation. Although this may seem to constitute a broad range of exclusions, the Services Directive covers many activities, including those in which small- and medium-sized enterprises are active, a group which may have found wrestling with 'red tape' particularly challenging.

The directive covers the activities of those who have the nationality of a Member State or by a legal person under the laws of a Member State and established in a Member State. These reflect the terms of the treaty provisions. By contrast, services provided by natural persons who are not nationals of a Member State or by entities which are established outside the Union or are not incorporated in accordance with the laws of a Member State are not covered by the directive.

The directive concerns 'requirements' relating to the provision of services. According to Article 4(7), the concept of requirement covers any obligation, prohibition, condition, or any other limitation imposed on service providers (or recipients of services), such as an obligation to obtain an authorisation or to make a declaration to competent authorities. It does not cover general rules, such as those relating to town planning. The extent to which the Services Directive would cover social and ancillary rights is not clear; it seems principally aimed at restrictions on professional activity. It has also been noted that it is not clear whether the Services Directive will take a discrimination based or a restriction based approach to defining 'requirements' and recitals can be found which support either interpretation.

22.7.3.2 *Administration*

The directive envisages the simplification of administrative requirements, the provisions attaining this are set out in Chapter II of the directive. Article 5(1) requires Member States to undertake a process of administrative simplification, to assess whether all procedures are necessary. The directive also envisages that Member States should introduce 'points of single contact' through which service providers can complete all procedures and formalities needed for access to and exercise of their service activities. Interestingly, the directive requires the introduction of fully functioning and interoperable electronic procedures to make administrative requirements less burdensome.

22.7.3.3 *Freedom of establishment*

The Services Directive also contains provisions relating to the freedom of establishment (Articles 9–15). They apply to all cases where a business seeks to establish in a Member State, and covers both the situation where a service provider seeks to establish in another Member State and the situation where a provider seeks to establish in his own Member State: this, then, is wider than merely removing boundaries between Member States. Member States must review authorisation schemes, which—according to the case law of the ECJ (eg, *Analir* (case C–205/99)) and Article 9 of the directive—they may only maintain if the schemes are non-discriminatory, justified by an overriding reason relating to the public interest and proportionate—ie, satisfy a rule of reason test. The term, 'overriding reason relating to the public interest' is defined in Article 4(8) as reasons recognised by the ECJ. Although Article 4(8) gives examples of such reasons, the class is not closed as the definition will continue to reflect any developments in the ECJ's case law. Article 10 contains the criteria against which the process for granting authorisations must be judged. In particular, authorisations must not duplicate controls in the home Member State, a requirement which again follows the jurisprudence of the ECJ (eg, *Canal Satélite* (case C–390/99)). All decisions must be fully reasoned and subject to a right of appeal. Article 14 establishes a list of requirements which Member States cannot impose for access to or exercise of a service activity, which reflect the existing case law. An example would be a nationality requirement or a limitation on the number of establishments. By contrast, Article 15 lists the sorts of requirements which usually constitute a restriction but which in some circumstances may be justified, such as territorial or quantitative restrictions (eg, no more than one petrol station per 30 kilometres). It does not, however, does not cover limits imposed on input, output or emissions, for example regarding CO_2 emissions or emissions of other gases.

22.7.3.4 *The cross-border provision of services*

Articles 16–21 deal with cross-border provision of services, which are subject to a different regime than that applicable to establishment. It is therefore important to distinguish between the two. The directive follows the distinction made in *Gebhard* (case C–55/94) (see 22.4.7.1 above). According to *Schnitzer* (case C–215/01) establishment requires integration into the economy in the Member State involving the acquisition of customers in that Member State from the basis of a stable professional domicile (para 29). (See also *Gebhard*, discussed above and Chapter 21.)

The cornerstone of the system is Article 16 which applies the country of origin principle. This means that, save in limited circumstances, Member States may not impose host country requirements on cross-border service providers. This is a development of the ECJ's case law on the rule of reason which required Member States to take into account country of origin regulation. According to Article 16(b), application of national requirements can only be justified if necessary for the protection of public policy, public security, public health or the environment. This excludes Member States from invoking other public interest objectives. It is the narrow scope of these grounds that has made scope of the directive so significant.

Some further derogation are found in Article 17, such as services of general economic interest, matters relating to the posting of workers and matters covered by Directive 77/249 on legal services. Article 17(6) ensures the full application of Title II of the Professional Qualifications Directive (Directive 2005/36 (OJ [2005] L 255) discussed at 22.8.2) in the case of cross-border service provision, as by virtue of this provision Article 16 will not apply to matters relating to professional qualifications.

Recipients of services are also covered by the directive (Articles 19–21).

22.7.3.5 *Administrative cooperation*

The Commission's Report on 'The State of the Internal Market for Services' highlighted lack of trust between the Member States as a reason for multiplicity of regulation and control. It is this issue which the administrative cooperation provisions aim to address. Articles 28–36 legally oblige Member States to give each other mutual assistance, in particular to reply to information requests and to carry out, if necessary, factual checks, inspections, and investigations.

To facilitate this process, Member States are required to identify 'liaison points', which have the responsibility for coordinating or supervising cooperation within a given state. The directive also envisages the establishment of the Internal Market Information System (IMI) to make the exchange of information by electronic means possible. In addition, to the provision of information on request, Article 32 lays down a mechanism aiming to ensure that Member States inform all other Member States concerned and the Commission within the shortest possible time if they become aware of acts of a service provider or specific circumstances relating to a service activity that could cause serious damage to the health or safety of persons or to the environment.

22.7.4 **Relationship between directives and other provisions**

Where directives have been passed harmonising or recognising national rules the provisions of the directive will be conclusive on the matter. However, in each case it will be necessary to decide whether the rule in question has been covered by the directive. This is not always as simple as it might seem. For example, the Television without Frontiers Directive (89/552/EEC, as amended by 97/36/EC), currently under revision for a second time, covers only television broadcasting. In these days of 'web-casting' and watching TV on mobile phones, the question does arise, 'what is broadcasting'? The scope of the Television without Frontiers was considered in *de Agostini* (joined cases C–34-36/95, discussed in Chapter 19), in which the Advocate-General and the ECJ came to different conclusions about the scope of the directive in relation to television advertising. In *Commission v Germany* (case 205/84) the insurance directive was found to be designed to ensure that undertakings were solvent; it did not attempt to harmonise national rules concerning technical reserves. Given the potential impact of the Services Directive, the precise boundaries between directives might become of more significance.

Harmonisation is discussed in more detail in Chapter 16 and the points made in relation to directives made under Article 95 can, in general, be transposed to those made under Article 47(2).

22.8 **Professional qualifications**

22.8.1 **Jurisprudence of the ECJ**

We have seen that professional qualifications in particular have given rise to barriers to the free movement of self-employed persons and that the legislative process for directives in this area was initially slow. It fell to the ECJ to cover the gap in protection offered. A starting point was holding that both Articles 43 and 49 had direct effect. Further, the ECJ has repeatedly held that it is discriminatory, in breach of Articles 43, as well as Articles 49–50, together with Article 12 EC to refuse permission to practise to a person whose qualifications have been recognised as equivalent to those required in the state in which he seeks to practise.

In *Thieffry v Conseil de l'Ordre des Advocats à la Cour de Paris* (case 71/76) the Court held that the French Bar Council could not refuse to allow Thieffry, a Belgian national with a Belgian law degree, to undertake practical training for the French bar, as his Belgian degree had been recognised by the University of Paris and he had acquired a qualifying certificate in France for the profession of *avocat*. (See also *Patrick v Ministre des Affaires Culturelles* (case 11/77), recognition of architecture qualification in the absence of express recognition by French law.)

Where a directive has been issued for the mutual recognition or harmonization of qualifications in a particular profession that profession may no longer insist on compliance with its own requirements by persons who have qualified in another Member State according to the terms of the directive. In *Broekmeulen* (case 246/80) the Dutch General Practitioners' Committee was unable to refuse Broekmeulen permission to practise as a GP in Holland even though he had qualified as a GP in Belgium, where it was not necessary to complete the three years' specialised training required for GPs in Holland. The relevant directive (75/362) did not require GPs to undergo training additional to their original qualification. Parties may not, however, claim freedom of establishment or freedom to provide services in reliance on a directive until the period provided for its implementation has expired (*Auer* (case 136/78)), or where they do not fall within the terms of the directive (*Dreessen v Conseil National de l'Ordre des Architectes* (case C–447/93)).

In *Arantis v Land Berlin* (case C–164/94), the ECJ held that where a profession was not regulated by an EC directive, the then Articles 6 and 52 (now 12 and 43) EC required the authorities in a host Member State to take into account an individual's qualifications and other relevant experience acquired in the home state. In doing so, the ECJ extended its ruling in *Vlassopoulou* (case C–340/89), which is discussed below in relation to regulated professions, to unregulated professions. In both *Arantis* and *Vlassapoulou* (and arguably *Thieffry*), we can see the ECJ adopting an approach that is based on the idea of mutual recognition—that is, a recognition that, in principle, the training and experience gained throughout all Member States should be acceptable in other Member States and should therefore be taken into account when assessing an individual's qualifications and experience. What is acceptable in one Member State, broadly speaking, is acceptable in all. This will have a significant effect in blocking any remaining gaps in the protection afforded to those with qualifications awarded by a Member State which are not covered by a directive.

22.8.2 **The directives**

The Recognition of Professional Qualifications Directive (Directive 2005/36) (PQD) replaces the previous system, but it broadly adopts the same principles as the previous directives. The case law on the previous directives would therefore seem relevant to the understanding on the new directive. There are some key differences. Unlike the previous general directives, the PQD deals with both the general system and some of the sectorally regulated professions (eg, medicine). The PQD introduces the idea of 'common platforms' of training. Procedures, including time frames within which decisions must be made, are more closely regulated. A separate part of the PQD provides for collaboration between the competent administrative authorities of both home and host Member State. The PQD also seeks to clarify the criteria for distinguishing between the cross-border provision of services on a temporary and occasional basis on the one hand, and for establishment on the other; different systems apply to the two situations.

Like the previous directives, the PQD applies only to regulated professional activities (Article 2), although it is sufficient if they are regulated in only one state in the Union. It will apply to workers as well as the self-employed (Article 2(1)). Although the concept of a regulated activity might seem clear, it has not been unproblematic. In *Arantis* (case C–164/94), the ECJ defined the term as meaning that the professional activity in question is governed by laws, regulations, or administrative provisions that create a system under which that professional activity is expressly reserved for those who fulfil certain conditions and access is prohibited to those who do not fulfil them. It now seems that the profession must be a separate activity from other professions. This can be seen in *Morgenbesser* (case C–313/01), who sought to rely on her French diploma in law to be registered as a *practicante* in Italy. Although the ECJ accepted that there was a system which denied precluded persons not fulfilling certain criteria from acting as *practicante*, the ECJ also noted that the activities carried out as a *practicante* formed the practical part of the training to become an *avvocato*. The activity of *practicante* could not therefore be considered as a separate regulated activity within Directive 89/48, one of the PQD's predecessor directives.

The starting point for the principle of mutual recognition is that a Member State 'shall recognise professional qualifications obtained in one or more other Member States' so as to allow the migrant 'to gain access in that Member State to the same profession as that for which he is qualified in the home Member State and to pursue it in the host Member State under the same conditions as its nationals' (Article 4). For establishment (or employment), the PQD consolidates the approaches taken with regard to the mutual recognition of a higher education diplomas and to diplomas and certificates awarded after a post-secondary education course of at least one year's duration, though the mechanism of recognition established by Directives 89/48/EEC and 92/51/EEC remains unchanged. The PQD recognises that there are different levels of qualification, which are identified in Article 11 (reflecting for example the difference between secondary education and higher education). The conditions for recognition are set out in Article 13, which specifies that access to the profession in the host Member State shall be given to 'applicants possessing the attestation of competence or evidence of formal qualifications required by another Member State in order to gain access to and pursue that profession on its territory'.

The PQD recognises that the various Member States have different training systems, and therefore provides that the attestation of competence 'shall attest a level of professional qualification at least equivalent to the level immediately prior to that which is required in the host Member State, as described in Article 11'. Furthermore, those who have practised the relevant profession for at least two years in the previous ten in a Member State that does not regulate the profession may benefit from mutual recognition, providing a certain level of qualification may be proven. The PQD, like its predecessors, permits the requirement of 'compensatory measures', such as an adaptation test, in specified circumstances. As noted above, the PQD envisages 'common platforms', which are defined in Article 15 'as a set of criteria of professional qualifications which are suitable for compensating for substantial differences which have been identified between the training requirements existing in the various Member States for a given profession'. Recital 16 gives examples: requirements such as additional training, an adaptation period under supervised practice, an aptitude test, a prescribed minimum level of professional practice, or combinations thereof. Common platforms are to be submitted by professional bodies or associations so as to facilitate the mutual recognition of qualifications. Where common platforms have been agreed, and where the applicant's qualifications satisfy the criteria, the host Member State is obliged to waive any compensation measures it would normally impose under Article 14 PQD.

It was noted with regard to the Mutual Recognition of Diplomas Directive that, although the directive gave an individual holding a diploma certain rights, the operation of mutual recognition is not automatic (*Morgenbesser* (case C–313/01), para 44); Member States may review the qualifications. Although the new system is aimed at facilitating free movement, the system is still based on the idea that the host Member State may set standards for the exercise of a given profession and that it must go through the process of recognising the qualifications and individuals may be required to satisfy compensatory measures. Note, however, that the PQD also covers professions that were subject to sectoral regulation (eg, doctors and vets). Individuals satisfying the coordinated requirements of minimum training shall benefit from automatic recognition of their qualifications (Article 21). The PQD also specifies, in Recital 11, that it is not to be used as a mechanism whereby nationals may evade enforcement of regulation of professions.

Note also the existence of Decision 2241/2004 which provides a framework for individuals to describe qualifications and competence. Additionally, the European Qualifications Framework provides a system whereby qualifications can be 'translated' across different systems. Neither of these two developments provide for recognition of the qualification.

Directive 98/5/EC (OJ [1998] L 77) gives all qualified lawyers the right to practise in another Member State on a permanent basis, using the professional title gained in the home Member State. They must comply with the professional and ethical rules of both the host Member State and their home state. Article 10 specifies that lawyers who have effectively and regularly pursued, for a period of at least three years, an activity in the host Member State under the home-country professional title are exempted from the aptitude test. For those who have practised for a shorter period, the competent authority of the host Member State must take into account all knowledge and professional experience of the law of the host Member State, as well as any attendance at lectures or seminars on the law of that state. In both instances, the lawyer's experience may be subject to verification. The conditions governing the provision of services on an occasional basis by lawyers established in another Member State, under the home-country professional title, without prior recognition of their qualification, are set out in Directive 77/249 (OJ [1977] L 78). Those lawyers who have not completed their professional training are not covered by the directives, though they may receive some protection through the operation of the jurisprudence of the ECJ under Articles 39 and 43 (*Morgenbesser* (case C–313/01)).

Even in areas not covered, or not yet covered, by these directives, the Court has held that professional bodies of a Member State, in deciding whether to allow persons who do not satisfy their own state's professional requirements, must take into account the applicant's qualification and compare them with the 'home' requirements, in order to assess whether they are in fact equivalent. Applicants are entitled to be given reasons for decisions, and must have an opportunity to challenge them in judicial proceedings (*Vlassopoulou v Ministerium für Justiz* (case C–340/89)). There is now a consistent line of authority to this effect.

A person who has qualified in a non-Member State cannot invoke either the directives or the Union principle of mutual recognition even though the qualification is recognised in a *particular* Member State and the person has been practising the profession *within that state*: the only entitlement is to practise *in that state* (*Tawil-Albertini v Ministre des Affaires Sociales* (case C–154/93)). However, if a Member State chooses to recognise such a qualification, it must take into account practical training or professional experience obtained in other Member States in order to determine whether the requisite national training period has been fulfilled (*Haim v Kassenzahnärtzliche Vereinigung Nordrhein* (cases C–319/92 and C–424/97)). *Haim* can be seen as imposing on Member States the obligation to undertake a *Vlassapoulou* style comparison of experience in such circumstances. *Hocsman* (case C–238/98) extended the scope of this obligation. Crucially in *Hocsman*, the ECJ stated that Member States were under an obligation to take into account the qualifications obtained elsewhere, as well as any practical experience. This means that the conditional nature of the obligation found in *Haim*—that the obligation only arose where a Member State had recognised a qualification—has effectively been removed.

22.9 Establishment, services, and companies

22.9.1 General

Despite the apparent simplicity of Article 48, in practice it has been rather difficult for companies to move around the Union. Companies are entities created by domestic law and only have legal capacity in accordance with these rules. Moving into another jurisdiction might therefore require a company to be wound up in its state of origin, and re-formed in the host Member State. Although Article 293 EC provides a legal basis for the Member States to agree a mechanism for the transfer of companies between them, the only attempt to do so (in 1968) was unsuccessful. Note therefore the potential impact that Article 43 might have on the rules of the Member States regarding company formation.

The main problem in this area is that the Member States apply different rules for identifying which legal system is applicable to a company (*lex societas*). As we noted in Chapter 21, there are two approaches to this issue. One possibility is to use the 'incorporation' doctrine (sometimes called *siège statutaire*), according to which the location of the company's registered office determines the applicable law. On this theory, the applicable law will be that of the country of incorporation. The second theory is the 'real seat' doctrine (or *siège réel*). Applying the real-seat doctrine, a company is subject to the law of the jurisdiction where its head office or central management is based, and this requires that the company's registered office needs to be located in the same jurisdiction. Quite clearly, the different theories will have an impact on the company law applicable, and therefore will affect the procedures and regulations with which a company will need to comply when running its business. The ECJ has been given a number of opportunities to consider the compatibility of these doctrines with EU law, but has not been consistent.

The starting point is *R v HM Treasury and Commissioners of Inland Revenue ex parte Daily Mail and General Trust PLC* (case 81/87). There, a company incorporated under the laws of England and Wales sought to move its central management to the Netherlands, whilst retaining its status as a British company. The Treasury demanded that certain transactions had to occur before it would permit the move. The company argued that this was a restriction on its right of establishment under Article 43. The ECJ held that there was no right for under Article 43 for a company to move its head office to another Member State, and the home Member State could impose conditions on a company seeking to leave its jurisdiction.

Daily Mail would seem to suggest that, contrary to the position as regards individuals, some restrictions on the movements of companies would not be affected by Article 43 EC. *Daily Mail* has been criticised and it now seems that while Article 43 does not give a company the unrestricted right to maintain its head office in one Member State whilst remaining incorporated under the laws of another, obstacles to its freedom to move aspects of its business through the establishment of a branch, subsidiary or agency will be prohibited by Article 43 unless justified. According to the ECJ in *Cartesio Okató és Szolgáltató bt* (case C–210/06) (Grand Chamber) there is in fact a distinction to be made between the nationality of the company (determined under Article 48) and a the right of a company established in one of the Member States to establish itself in another Member State, under Article 43 EC. So, the ECJ in *Cartesio* reaffirmed the approach in *Daily Mail* (and in *Überseering BV v Nordic Construction Company Baumanagement GmBH* (case C–208/00), see further below) as to a Member State's right to identify the connecting factor between companies established under its laws and its territories, whether this be by virtue of the doctrine of *siège statutaire* or *siège réel*. This, according to the Court, is the consequence of Article 48. The right of the Member State includes the right to remove the status of a company being incorporated under the laws of that Member State if the company ceases to comply with the requirements of national law. This does not mean that the company must be wound up; the company may acquire the status of a company under the laws of another Member State and the original Member State has no right to stop that happening.

22.9.2 Regulatory competition

We have seen that there are significant differences in the Member States' individual approaches to company formation and regulation, quite apart from the issue of the rules relating to *siège statutaire* or *siège réel*. It might be easier for someone (whether natural or legal) who wishes to trade in one Member State to establish a company in another Member State and rely on the right to secondary establishment contained in Article 43 to set up business in the original, target Member State. The question is, is this a legitimate use of freedom of establishment, or does it constitute an abuse of Union law?

Early case law on the question of abuse arose in relation to services. Sometimes the service providers were formally established in one member state but provided services to another Member State, and relied on Article 49 so as to avoid compliance with the host Member State's regulation for that sector. At one stage, the ECJ sought to avoid difficult questions by recharacterising the provision of services as a question of establishment. In *TV10 v Commissariaat voor de Media* (case C–23/93), a company established itself in one Member State and broadcast into another Member State, the Netherlands, hoping to avoid the Dutch limitations on broadcast advertising. Here the ECJ adopted a broad interpretation of the concept of establishment and decided that the company involved was actually established in the Netherlands. On this basis, the Dutch rules were applicable to the broadcaster. The ECJ here seems to be identifying establishment by reference to a form of the real-seat doctrine. Should the same principles be applied to the establishment of a business as to the regulation of its business activities?

In *Centros v Erhvervs- og Selskabsstyrelsen* (case C–212/97), a private limited company registered in the UK but with two Danish shareholders sought to establish a branch in Denmark. At the time, the company had not traded in the UK. In the light of the Danish connection (and the lack of any British business activity), the Danish registrar refused to register the branch because he regarded Centros as a Danish company. Crucially, Centros had failed to comply with a minimum capital rule imposed under Danish law but with no equivalent under the English system. The ECJ held that this was a breach of Article 43 EC which could not be justified. The ECJ held:

> the fact that a national of a Member State who wishes to set up a company chooses to form it in the Member State whose rules of company law seem to him the least restrictive and to set up branches in other Member States cannot, in itself, constitute an abuse of the right of establishment. The right to form a company in accordance with the law of a Member State and to set up branches in other Member States is inherent in the exercise, in a single market, of the freedom of establishment guaranteed by the Treaty. [Para 27.]

Setting up a company in one Member State and then exercising the right to set up a secondary establishment was not an abuse of the right of establishment, even though it had the effect of circumventing incorporation requirements in the host Member State. The decision was interpreted as holding that in EU law, the jurisdiction where the registered office was based would be the law applicable to the company. Of course, this leaves a potential problem where Member States take a different view about the 'connecting factor' with its territory. If a Member State takes the connecting factor to be the real seat rather than the formal place of establishment, there is the possibility of 'double nationality' if the place of formal incorporation by contrast looks to the *siège statutaire*, as arguably was the case in *Centros*. The analysis of the ECJ in *Centros* seems to favour the *siège statutaire* over the *siège réel*.

A similar issue arose in *Überseering BV v Nordic Construction Company Baumanagement GmBH* (case C–208/00). There, a Dutch company owned by German shareholders sought to take legal action in the German courts. German law determined a company's legal capacity by reference to its real seat. Since the company had moved its centre of administration to Germany the German courts found its real seat to be in Germany. Überseering was formally incorporated in the Netherlands, and so complied with that state's rules of incorporation rather than German rules. As the company did not comply with German rules, the German court held that it was not properly incorporated and therefore did not have the capacity to take legal action. The ECJ held that because the company had been validly incorporated in the Netherlands, and had not lost this status, the German court's refusal to recognise its legal capacity fell within Article 43 and was not on the facts justified. We might suggest that there are similarities here with the *Daily Mail* case. The ECJ distinguished the two cases on the facts (implicitly reaffirming *Daily Mail*). Whilst the Daily Mail had sought to rely on Article 43 against its state of incorporation when it sought to emigrate, *Überseering* concerned the rights of an immigrating company against the host Member State. According to the ECJ, '[t]he requirement of reincorporation of the same company in Germany is therefore tantamount to outright negation of freedom of establishment' (paras 80–1). In its consideration of justification, the ECJ also seemed to suggest that although restrictions on establishment might be open to justification and outright prohibition on secondary establishment never could. Articles 43 and 48 EC therefore require a host Member State to recognise the legal capacity of a company under the law of its Member State of incorporation. This seems to be yet another blow to the real-seat doctrine.

Slightly different issues arose in *Chamber of Commerce Amsterdam v Inspire Art Ltd* (case C–167/01), where Dutch law sought to impose a number of restrictions on companies incorporated in a Member State other than the Netherlands, but which were predominantly or exclusively active in the Netherlands. Inspire Art was incorporated under the laws of England and Wales, but had a Dutch sole director. It established a branch in Amsterdam without complying with the Dutch formalities for 'formally foreign' companies and the competent Dutch authorities brought an action against Inspire Art as a consequence. The ECJ held that insofar as Dutch law gave effect to certain company-law directives, the rules were compatible with Article 43 EC, unless foreign companies were treated differently with regard to penalties for non-compliance. Any rules going beyond the directives had to be compatible with the EC Treaty. The additional Dutch rules were caught by Article 43 EC and not justifiable on the facts, and therefore infringed EU law. Once again, the ECJ seems to have favoured the incorporation doctrine over the real-seat theory.

It should be noted that in these cases the ECJ has refrained from addressing the question directly. It thus remains unclear whether the ECJ intends to eradicate the real seat doctrine in favour of the incorporation theory or not; most recently in *Cartesio*, the ECJ has re-emphasised that the question of a company's 'nationality' is one for the Member States. Nonetheless, what remains clear is that Member States will not be able to impose restrictions on companies formed elsewhere, even 'pseudo-foreign' companies without very good (and proportionate) reason. (See also *SEVIC Systems* (case C–411/03) concerning the impact of a cross-border merger and its relationship with national rules on company formation found to be incompatible with Article 43.)

22.9.2.1 *Taxation: Are anti-avoidance measures permissible?*

One area where Member States are concerned about the impact of the use of freedom of establishment is in the area of taxation, as in many Member States different rules apply depending on residency. With freedom of establishment, it is no longer clear that such distinctions are acceptable. With the right legal advice, freedom of establishment can be used to minimise a tax bill, for example by locating profits through a group company to a Member State with a low rate of taxation. The ECJ has had to face a series of cases which deal with the boundary between Member State competence and the right of establishment. In *Halifax plc and ors v Customs and Excise* (case C–255/02) the case concerned a corporate structure where payments were made specifically to minimise VAT payments. The ECJ distinguished between artificial transactions, which would constitute abuse, and taking advantage of Union law which would be acceptable. The same year another tax case from the UK was decided, this time concerning direct taxation: *Cadbury Schweppes plc v Inland Revenue* (case C–196/04), where Cadbury sought to channel profits through an Irish subsidiary formed to reduce the rate of tax payable. Again the ECJ distinguished between artificial transactions, and the right of establishment; the mere setting up of a subsidiary of itself cannot set up a presumption of tax evasion justifying the limitation of a fundamental freedom. So where is the boundary between the two? The ECJ noted that the purpose of Article 43 was to allow an individual or a company 'to set up a secondary establishment in another Member State to carry on his activities there and thus assist economic and social interpenetration within the Community'. Abuse, which seems here to be equated to the notion of an artificial transaction, is found where, in addition to there being a subjective element consisting in the intention to obtain a tax advantage, there are objective circumstances showing that, despite formal observance of the conditions laid down by Union law, the objective pursued by freedom of establishment has not been achieved. On the facts of this case, this double element was not sufficiently proven. It has been suggested that the approach here is not consistent with that taken with regard to company law in *Centros*. (See also *Thin Cap Group Litigation* (case C–524/04) concerning a rule prohibiting the characterisation of loan interest owed by subsidiary to parent as a dividend, here found disproportionate and contrast *Columbus Container Services* (case C–298/05) where similar rules found not to constitute a restriction.)

22.9.3 Regulatory competition: The position of services—home-country control and abuse

As we can see from *TV10 v Commissariaat voor de Media* (case C–23/93), there has been a concern that the exercise of free movement rights in certain contexts may give rise to a dilution of national standards as businesses establish themselves in the Member State with a lighter regulatory regime and then rely on Article 49 to trade in Member States with more stringent regulatory regimes. In this there are certain commonalities with the problems arising in the field of establishment, particularly with regard to companies setting up branch offices or subsidiaries, discussed above. The difficulty felt in services, however, is in some ways more acute, as Member States' freedom to regulate incoming services is constrained by the need to take into account home-country regulation; such host Member State regulation is more likely to be assessed as unnecessary or disproportionate. The Services Directive may exacerbate this tendency as it limits the public-interest grounds on which Member States may rely.

   As with the other freedoms, the ECJ made it clear that Union law may not be used (or abused) in order to undermine the legitimate rules and standards of Member States. Thus the ECJ has held that establishing oneself in one member state for the purposes of evading host member state rules is unacceptable (see, eg, *van Binsbergen* (case 33/74)). In *Vereniging Veronica Omroep Organisatie v Commisariaat voor de Media* (case C–148/91), which again concerned a media company broadcasting from one Member State to another to avoid the recipient Member State's regulation on broadcast content, the ECJ held that the recipient Member State could rely on its regulations as against the broadcaster (see also *TV10 v Commissariaat voor de Media* (case C–23/93)). A similar approach can be seen in respect of services regulated by harmonising legislation. For example, in *van de Bijl v Staatssecretaris van Economische Zaken* (case 130/88), the Court was asked to rule on a claim by a Dutch decorator, based on EC Directive 64/427, which provides, inter alia, for the mutual recognition of qualifications for self-employed persons in small craft industries. Under Directive 64/427 states were required to accept a certification of competence and work experience provided by the appropriate authorities of another Member State in respect of work performed in that state. It was suggested in van de Bijl's case that the certificate issued by the UK authorities, which the Dutch authorities had refused to accept as a basis for registration in Holland, was based on questionable evidence. The Court held that the host (ie, Dutch) state was entitled to take steps (eg, verification of evidence) to prevent the relevant Union rules being used for the purpose of circumventing the rules relating to particular occupations applicable to its national.

This line of case law does raise difficult questions of what is considered to be abuse. Are we concerned with the intentions of the parties seeking to rely on the right to provide services, or merely with its impact on the host Member State? If we are looking at intention, is it required that the parties sought to rely on the freedom to provide services always with the view to exploit the treaty freedoms, or is it sufficient that the rights holders start at some point intending to evade Union law? The case law in this area has not been clear or consistent. Even apart from this difficult question, how is such intention to be proved? Advocate-General Lenz highlighted this problem in the context of broadcasting. If we argue that a broadcaster established in Luxembourg but staffed in the main by Dutch people, broadcasting in Dutch, to the Netherlands is intending to evade national law and thus abuse Union-law rights purely by reference to nationality and language criteria, we are not only undermining the right of those people to exercise rights under Article 39 and 43 to go to Luxembourg in the first place, but arguably we are indulging in a form of nationality discrimination. The precise scope of this 'exception' to the free-movement rights was not clear and subsequent cases interpreted it narrowly (*VT4 Limited v Vlaamse Gemeenschap* (case C–56/96) and see *Konsumentombudsmannen v De Agostini* (joined cases C–34–6/95) below).

Problems with a perceived downward spiral of standards may also arise when policy areas have been harmonised by directive. Minimum harmonisation (discussed Chapter 16, and see also 22.7.3 regarding the Services Directive) allows Member States to set different standards, higher than those set out in the directive in question. These rules must of course be compatible with general treaty objectives. The difficulty in this context arises when there is a market-access clause, which means that a Member State may require those established within its jurisdiction to comply with the higher standards but cannot impose these requirements on those established elsewhere in the Union. Minimum harmonisation therefore introduces the possibility of differing approaches to regulation being taken by the various Member States which is a situation which is open to abuse. The same general rules apply here as they do to the treaty articles; companies and individuals are entitled to take advantage of the internal market and the 'abuse' argument will only be accepted in very limited circumstances. Member States must rely on mutual recognition—that is, an acceptance that standards in other Member States are sufficient.

It is clear that in some instances the ECJ has difficulty accepting flagrant behaviour by service providers. In addition to the re-characterisation of services as establishment in *TV 10*, the ECJ has also re-characterised the legal issue in a different way by referring to Article 28, again to allow the host Member State some control. In *Konsumentombudsmannen v De Agostini* (joined cases C–34–6/95), the question of broadcasting aimed at children in Sweden would seem to fall under the Television without Frontiers Directive (89/552, as subsequently amended by 97/36), which contained a market-access clause. The broadcaster was established in the UK, which does not prohibit such broadcasts. On this assessment, given the market-access clause and the rules of the Member State in which the broadcaster was established, the Swedish could do nothing to stop the broadcasts. The ECJ, however, took the view that the advertisements should be seen as relating to the sale of the goods they were advertising rather than the service of broadcasting, thereby removing regulation away from the British and allowing the Swedes to maintain their rules (provided such rules operate equally in law and in fact). (See also Chapter 19.) The difficulty here is that is impossible to predict when the ECJ will choose to re-characterise Article 49; the certainty is that the ECJ will do so only rarely. Interestingly, when the Television without Frontiers Directive was revised by the Audiovisual Media Services Directive (2007/65/EC) (OJ [2007] L 332/27) an anti-abuse clause was inserted in the directive.

This area of law is problematic. It highlights the ever-present tension between the need to create and to facilitate the functioning of the internal market and the competence of the Member States and their legitimate concerns. As with the pre-*Keck* case law on the scope of Article 28, the Court seems to be encountering some difficulty in distinguishing between legitimate exploitation of rules and their abuse. It is indeed unfortunate that the ECJ has not developed a unified principle to deal with cases in this area.

22.10 Conclusions

This chapter has looked at the ways national rules can impede the exercise of free movement as far as access to the job market or the right to trade is concerned. We have looked at ways in which the EU institutions have responded, whether through legislation or through the judgments of the ECJ. In this, there are three themes. First, the move from a discrimination-based test, so as to catch measures that are applicable to nationals of the host Member State as to migrants, is clear. In this we see parallels with the free movement of goods, and now the free movement of capital. The precise scope of the test, and consequently the freedoms, is not clear. The ECJ has used different language, emphasising different concerns in the various cases before it. The question is, where is the outer boundary of the freedoms, and consequently the boundary of acceptable Member State regulation. As we have seen, in some cases the ECJ has adopted a very broad approach indeed. Against this background, we come to the second theme and note the changing political climate and the desire to implement the Lisbon Agenda. Whilst in the early days of the Union harmonising legislation was sectoral, detailed, and hard to agree, recent legislative activity shows that the Union (and the Member States) now adopts a horizontal approach, which is based strongly on mutual recognition and limited spheres, particularly as regards services, in which a Member State may legitimately mistrust its fellow Member States. A new emphasis is on the focus on administrative cooperation and on the removal of 'red tape'. The third theme is a familiar one: that of the concern about the legitimate uses of Union-law rights and the problems of abuse. Despite the agreement of the Services Directive, there are still concerns about abuse and a downward pressure on standards, with a desire to retain control over individuals who are, in reality, targeting the host Member State, as are evidenced in the anti-abuse statements in the PQD, the Services Directive, and even sectoral directives such as the Audiovisual Media Services Directive. The EU has some way to go before it truly is a single market in services and employment.

FURTHER READING

Art J, 'Legislative lacunae: The Court of Justice and freedom to provide services' in D Curtin and D O'Keeffe (eds), *Constitutional Adjudication in European Community Law and National Law* (Dublin: Butterworths, 1992), p 121.

Daniele, L, 'Non-discriminatory restrictions to the free movement of persons' (1997) *22 EL Rev* 191.

Davies, G, 'The Services Directive: Extending the country of origin principle, and reforming public administration' (2007) 32(2) EL Rev 232–45.

De la Feria, R, 'Prohibition of abuse of (Community) law: The creation of a new general principle of EC law through tax' (2008) 45(2) CML Rev 395–441.

Drury, R, 'The "Delaware syndrome": European fears and reactions' (2005) Nov JBL 709.

Edward, D, 'Establishment and services: An analysis of the insurance cases' (1987) 12 EL Rev 231.

Looijestijn-Clearie, A, '*Centros Ltd*: A complete u-turn in the right of establishment for companies?' (2000) 49 ICLQ 621.

Meulman, J and de Waele, HCFJA, 'A retreat from *Säger*? Servicing or fine tuning the application of Article 49 EC' (2006) EL Rev 207.

Pelkmans, J, 'Deepening services market integration: A critical assessment' (2007), available on SSRN.

O'Brien, M, 'Company taxation, state aid and fundamental freedoms: Is the next step enhanced co-operation?' (2005) 30(2) EL Rev 209.

Syrpis, P and Novitz, T, 'Economic and social rights in conflict: Political and judicial approaches to their reconciliation' (2008) 33(3) EL Rev 411–26.

23

Free movement: Social rights

23.1 Introduction

We have noted that the free-movement rights granted by Articles 18 (citizenship), 39 (workers), 43 (establishment), and 49 (services) comprise three elements. The first is the right to move to another Member State and to live there. This is a prerequisite to the second right, which is to access the job market in the host Member State. Finally, but importantly in terms of removing disadvantages to the migrant arising from the exercise of the right of free movement, there are ancillary rights. These are a broad range of social rights which aim to ensure that the migrant and his or her family integrate into the host Member State and are normally claimed from that host Member State. While the preceding two chapters have focused on access to the territory of the host Member State (including family rights, sometimes seen as a form of ancillary right) and access to the labour market, this chapter will focus on social rights.

The granting of social rights has had a long history. As well as having an economic function, allowing the movement of factors of production, the free movement of workers has also been interpreted in the light of the fact that workers are people, not just inanimate objects. The personal aspect to the freedom of movement has lead to a particularly broad interpretation of the social rights available. This is a key element of the Article 39 EC jurisprudence, in particular, though the impact of citizenship has been significant. As with the right to enter and reside, citizenship has not obliterated all distinctions, and the categories from the original economic freedoms may still have an impact on the scope of rights available in particular circumstances. The distinctions are also key to the reasoning of the European Court of Justice (ECJ)—that is, the issue of how we justify the protection offered.

When looking at this area there are a number of recurring themes. As we have noted in earlier chapters, one particular question relates to who obtains the benefit of Union-law rights. In this context, we return to the issue of Member State competence, and the limits placed on it through Union law. While the economic rights were broadly interpreted and relied heavily on a wide conception of the circumstances in which the prohibition on discrimination could operate, there had—for the rights to come into play—to be some level of migration and some contribution to the host Member State economy. Expansion, both of the groups entitled to the rights and the types of rights themselves, is challenging, especially in the light of concerns about 'social dumping' and 'benefit tourism'. Social justice and schemes for the redistribution of wealth commonly assume either a contribution to the system or some common ground justifying support. Is citizenship at the EU level enough to ground broad-ranging citizenship rights based on individual Member States' social systems? Here we return to questions identified earlier about the link with migration, with economic contributions, or, more recently, the question of whether there is a 'real link' with the host Member State.

In looking at the scope of the rights, this chapter will take a somewhat historical approach in that will look at the development of the social-rights jurisprudence in the economic context with the main focus being on the cases relating to workers, before looking at the contribution based on citizenship. In this way we may be able to assess the extent to which it is possible to say that citizenship is something new, rather than the same level of protection expressed in different words.

23.2 Economic migrants

23.2.1 Equality of treatment Article 39(2) EC and Regulation 1612/68

As we noted earlier, Article 39(2) EC (ex 48; post Lisbon Treaty, Article 45 TFEU) prohibits discrimination as regards employment, remuneration, and other conditions of work and employment. Regulation 1612/68 was enacted to flesh out the detail of this right, but does not replace it. As we shall see, it continues to be possible to rely on the underlying treaty right (see, eg, *Collins* (case C–138/02); see also 21.4.9). Of particular relevance here is Article 7(2) which entitles the migrant worker to 'the same social and tax advantages as national workers'. The term 'social advantages' has been interpreted in the widest sense and it is here that we begin to understand that while we might initially think these rights were linked to the employment context, in practice they have a much broader ambit. Also relevant are the provisions relating to training and education.

23.2.1.1 *Social advantages*

In *Fiorini v SNCF* (case 32/75) the Court was faced with a claim by an Italian lady living in France, the widow of an Italian who had worked in France, for a special fare reduction card issued by the French railways to parents of large families. Her husband had claimed it while he was alive. She had been refused the card on the grounds that she was not of French nationality. She claimed discrimination in breach of Article 12 and Article 7(2) of Regulation 1612/68. The French tribunal took the view that Article 7(2) was not applicable, since it was concerned only with advantages granted to citizens within the ambit of work or by virtue of work as employed persons. This would limit the advantages that could be claimed by a worker to those directly linked to his or her employment. The ECJ took a different view. It held that, although certain provisions of Article 7(1) refer to relationships deriving from the contract of employment, there are others which have nothing to do with such relationships. Article 7(2) covers all social and tax advantages, whether or not attached to contracts of employment. Moreover, these rights continue even if the advantages are sought after the worker's death to benefit the family remaining. Since the family had a right under Community law (what was then Regulation 1251/70) to remain in France, they were entitled under Article 7(2) to equal 'social advantages'.

Subsequently, in *Even* (case 207/78), the Court held, following *Fiorini*, that the social advantages covered by Article 7(2) were 'those which, whether or not linked to a contract of employment, are generally granted to national workers primarily because of their objective status as workers *or by virtue of the mere fact of their residence on national territory*' (emphasis added). This formula, the '*Even*' formula, has since been applied in a number of cases in the context of claims by both workers and the members of their families to a wide range of social benefits and continues to define the scope of benefits to which migrants may lay claim.

In *Reina v Landeskreditbank Baden-Württemberg* (case 65/81) an Italian couple living in Germany, the husband being a worker in Germany, invoked Article 7(2) to claim a special childbirth loan, state-financed, from the defendant bank. The loan was payable under German law only to German nationals living in Germany. The bank argued that the loan was not a 'social advantage' within Article 7(2), since the loan was granted not as a social right, but rather in the field of political rights, for demographic purposes—ie, to increase the birth rate in Germany. Granting of the loan was, moreover, discretionary. It argued also that the difference in treatment was justified on account of the practical difficulties of recovering loans from workers who return to their own countries. Despite these persuasive arguments the ECJ found that, since the loan was granted by reason of the claimant's objective status as a worker or by virtue of the mere fact of residence, it was a 'social advantage' within Article 7(2). Social advantages covered not only benefits granted as of right but also those granted on a discretionary basis.

In *Castelli v ONPTS* (case 261/83), on similar reasoning, an Italian mother, who, on being widowed, went to live with her son in Belgium (the son having been a worker and retired there), was held entitled to claim a guaranteed income (not a social security benefit) paid to all old people in Belgium. Since she had a right under Article 10 of Regulation 1612/68 to install herself with her son, she was entitled to the same social and tax advantages as Belgian workers and ex-workers. The Court again applied the *Even* formula; the old-age benefit was one granted to national workers primarily because of their objective status as workers or by virtue of their residence of national territory. The reasoning seems to be that if dependants were not paid benefits, this could constitute an obstacle to the free movement of workers (see, eg, *Deak* (case 94/84))

The same reasoning was applied in *Hoeckx* (case 249/83), and *Scrivner* (case 122/84), to claims in Belgium for a minimum income allowance, the 'minimex', by a member of the family of a worker and an unemployed worker respectively. (See also *Frascogna* (case 256/86); *Deak* (case 94/84), 'tiding over' allowance paid to young job-seekers a 'social advantage'; *Schmid* (case 310/91), allowance for handicapped child of a retired worker; *Commission v Luxembourg* (case 111/91), childbirth allowance.) Famously the ECJ's judgment in *Lair* opened the door for student grants and loans to be considered as social rights, although as we have noted in Chapter 21, there are limits to this possibility. Similarly in *Matteucci v Communauté Française de Belgique* (case 235/87) a scholarship to study abroad arising under a reciprocal arrangement between Belgium and Germany was held to constitute a social advantage to which the child of an Italian, established as a worker in Belgium, was entitled. (See also *Meeusen* (case C–337/97), note this form of right can also be claimed under the citizenship provisions: *Morgan v Bezirksregierung Köln* and *Bucher v Landrat des Kreises Düren* (joined cases C–11/06 and C–12/06).)

There are limits to the possibility of treating migrant workers exactly the same as nationals of the host state. The ECJ recognised in *Kaba* (case C–466/00) that the worker's status is conditional upon that individual continuing to satisfy the test of being a worker. In *Kaba* this conditionality justified a difference between the period that must elapse before the spouse of a person present and settled in the UK under English could apply for indefinite leave to remain (12 months) and that in respect of the spouse of a migrant EC national (four years).

Further, the benefit claimed must constitute a social advantage for the state's own nationals. In *Belgium v Taghavi* (case C–243/91) the Iranian wife of an Italian national residing as a worker in Belgium was held not to be entitled to a benefit for handicapped persons, described as a 'personal' right and not a social-security benefit, on the grounds that the benefit was not available to spouses of *Belgian* nationals who were not themselves EC nationals.

In this area, as with discrimination in other areas, indirect discrimination may be permitted as 'objectively justified' if the legislation pursues a legitimate end and the measure is no more than is necessary to achieve that end. (For an example of the ECJ's reasoning see *O'Flynn v Adjudication Officer* (case C–237/94), discussed Chapter 15.) In this area, as in others, the ECJ is moving to a test based on a 'real link' with or integration into the host Member State to determine whether re-strictions on rights are acceptable. *Geven* (case C–213/05, judgment of the Grand Chamber) concerned a claim for the German child-rearing allowance. Geven was a Dutch national living in the Netherlands but working, after the end of the statutory maternity period, in Germany for between 3 and 14 hours per week. The national authorities rejected the claim on the basis that she was neither resident in Germany nor satisfy a test based on a minimum amount of work. The ECJ accepted that Geven was a worker for the purposes of Article 39 EC and therefore in principle entitled to the social advantage the allowance constituted. The German government argued that the allowance was an instrument of family policy aimed at benefitting those with a real link to Germany, whether through residence of by a contribution to the national labour market. This argument the ECJ accepted as being appropriate and proportionate to the German government's aim.

Despite the breadth of the *Even* test, not all state support falls within Article 7(2). We shall see below that social security is excluded. Even outside the field of social security there are still some limitations on the *Even* test. In *Baldinger* (case C–386/02) the payment in issue was a monthly grant to former prisoners of war, subject to the condition that the recipient is an Austrian national. The applicant was a former Austrian national, who had been a prisoner of war in the former USSR from 1945–7, but who had become a Swedish national, losing his Austrian nationality, in 1967. He sought to claim equality of treatment. The ECJ rejected his argument. The payment was made to compensate citizens for the hardships they had endured for their country. It was not granted to individuals either because of their status as a worker or because of their lawful residence in a Member State and therefore did not fall within Article 7(2). The payment also had nothing to do with conditions of employment, remuneration or working conditions. It therefore could not fall within Article 39(2) EC either. Such rights may be claimed as a matter of citizenship rights, see below.

The right to equal social advantages cannot be claimed by all EU nationals and their families who are lawfully resident in the host state. An important limitation was placed on Article 7(2) in *Centre Public d'Aide Sociale de Courcelles v Lebon* (case 316/85), in the context of a claim by a French national, Ms Lebon, for the Belgian minimex. She was living in Belgium and her claim was based, inter alia, on the fact that she was looking for work in Belgium. The ECJ held that the right to equality of treatment in the field of social and tax advantages granted by Article 7(2) enured for the benefit only of workers and not for nationals of Member States who migrate in search of employment.

In *Lebon*, for the first time, the Court drew a distinction between those who are lawfully entitled to 'settled' residence as a result of obtaining employment, and those who are permitted temporary rights of residence in order to search for work. Only the former will be entitled to equality of treatment in respect of all social advantages. Likewise, EU nationals (and their families) who move within the Union to receive services will not be entitled to full equality of treatment as regards social benefits provided by the host state. Collins (*Collins v Secretary of State for Work and Pensions* (case C–138/02)) sought to challenge the distinction between those seeking work and those actually working on the basis of the ECJ's ruling in *Martinez Sala* (case C–85/96) (see further 23.4 below) in which the court held that a person seeking work should be considered a worker for the purposes of Regulation 1612/68 (para 32). The ECJ reiterated its previous jurisprudence to the effect that the notion of 'worker' for the purposes of the treaty must be interpreted broadly. Nonetheless the ECJ has consistently drawn a distinction between the situation where a person has entered a Member State but not yet worked and a person who is not currently working but has worked (see, eg, *Lair* (case 39/86), paras 32–3). The former group enjoy equality of treatment as regards access to work whilst the second group may claim the same social and tax advantages. In confirming that '[t]he concept of "worker" is thus not used in a uniform manner', the ECJ reaffirmed its approach in *Lebon* as to workers. Nonetheless, the ECJ accepted in *Collins* that discrimination within the scope of the treaty was not permissible unless justified, which has the effect of undermining the *Lebon* distinction it seemed to have started off by accepting.

As we have seen (at 22.4.6.1), a second important limitation was placed on Article 7(2) in the cases of *Brown* (case 197/86), and *Lair* (case 39/86), also as a result of the claimants' status. It could be that these cases on students can be understood as part of the case law on continuing rights.

23.2.1.2 *Continuing rights*

In some circumstances, a former migrant worker who ceases to be a worker will continue to retain the benefit of his or her former status, without any condition that he or she resides in the competent Member State. In a number of cases, the ECJ has held that such benefits are those 'the payment of which is dependent on the prior existence of an employment relationship which has come to an end and is intrinsically linked to the recipients' objective status as workers' (case C–43/99 *Leclere and Deaconescu v Caisse nationale des prestations familiales*, para 57; see also case C–57/96 *Meints*, para 41). This means that a person who is no longer a worker, even if he still receives some benefits, such as invalidity pension, by virtue of his former worker status, can claim new rights, such as childbirth rights for his family members, which have no links with his former employment (*Leclere and Deaconescu*).

This reasoning was relied on in *Collins* (case C–138/02). Collins was born in the United States of America and as well as possessing American nationality, had Irish nationality. He spent ten months working in the UK in 1980–1, before returning to the USA. He did not return to the UK until 1998, when he tried to find employment in the social services sector. During his job search, he tried to claim jobseeker's allowance, based on the fact that he had been a worker and migrant workers are entitled to certain rights linked to that status even when no longer employed. Even accepting that the level of work carried out by Collins made him a worker, he was not entitled to jobseeker's allowance as no link could be established between that work and the search for another job 17 years later (para 28). Given the length of Collins' absence, his position was comparable with that of someone searching for work for the first time. The consequences of the reasoning in *Collins* are not clear; it seems to be introducing (or clarifying) a limitation on the circumstances in which a worker can claim continuing rights, in that the ECJ required that there be a link between the original work and the search for another job, though the nature of that link is uncertain. As with *Geven* (case C213/05) above), this seems to be a variant of the 'real link' test we find being introduced in the citizenship cases; it is unclear whether a worker claiming a social right has to show the same sort (or length) or 'real link' as someone who has no connection with the job market of the host Member State (contrast *Bidar* (case C–209/03), below). Note, however, that in *Collins*, the ECJ also held that migrant EU nationals enjoy equality of treatment in their search for a job (see below). The implications of *Collins* are raised in *Vatsouras and Koupatantze v Arbeitsgemeinschaft (ARGE) Nürnberg 900* (case C–22 and 23/08, not yet decided).

23.2.1.3 *Tax advantages*

The starting point for matters relating to direct taxation is that this area falls within the competence of the Member State, but that competence must be exercised within the framework of the treaty. Specifically, migrant workers are entitled under Article 7(2) of Regulation 1612/68 to the same tax advantages as nationals of the host state and some cases have been considered under the general rules on non-discrimination in Article 12 EC (eg, *Turpeinen* (case C–520/04)). Nonetheless, this is an area where a measure such as a residence requirement, which is covertly discretionary, may be objectively justified, or where the situations of the national worker and the migrant worker will not be regarded as comparable. Such may be the case, as was conceded in *Schumacker* (case C–279/93) where the worker's residence and principal place of work (and therefore of income) is in another Member State, in which the taxing authorities are better able to take into account his personal and family circumstances (see also *Wielockx v Inspector der Directe Belstingen* (case C–80/94), person with main income in a Member State effectively in the same position as a resident there). In *Bachmann v Belgium* (case C–204/90) the Court found that a Belgian rule, which allowed the deduction from income tax of contributions to health and life insurance policies only if they were paid in Belgium, although indirectly indiscriminatory, was justified as necessary to ensure the coherence of the tax system. Under this system, tax deductions in respect of insurance contributions could be offset by taxes levied from insurers in Belgium. This would not be possible where insurance was effected in another Member State. This case may be contrasted with *Asscher* (case C–107/94), a case involving the right of establishment where differential taxation rates were found to be indirectly discriminatory but unjustified. This case can be seen as an example of the ECJ seeking to limit the circumstances in which a Member State may rely on the coherence of the tax system justification found in *Bachmann*. (See also eg, *Verkooijen* (case C–35/98), rebates for income tax limited to residents found to be unjustified.) As in other areas involving indirect discrimination, the Court will in each case scrutinise the justification offered and ensure that the measures adopted are not disproportionate, though it seems to be accept arguments based on administrative need more readily than perhaps in other areas (*Pusa* (case C–224/02); *Turpeinen* (case C–520/04)).

23.2.1.4 *Access to training in vocational schools and retraining centres*

Article 7(3) entitles workers to access, under the same conditions as national workers, to training in vocational schools and retraining centres.

Although Article 7(3) is expressed in terms of access, it seems likely that the ECJ will take a broad view of what is meant by access. In *Casagrande v Landeshauptstadt München* (case 9/74) the Court held, in the context of a claim by a child under Article 12 of Regulation 1612/68, that the right to be *admitted* to the host state's educational, apprenticeship, and vocational training courses included not only admission but 'general measures to facilitate attendance', which in Casagrande's case, included a grant.

More broadly, differential fees cannot be imposed on migrant EU nationals, as can be seen in the case of *Gravier v City of Liège* (case 293/83). There the Belgian authorities sought to charge a special fee levied only on non-nationals, for attendance on a four-year course in the art of strip cartoons. Access to vocational training was a matter covered by Community law, and to charge fees would constitute discrimination contrary to what is now Article 12 EC; *Gravier* was not determined on the basis of Article 7(3) Regulation 1612/68. It sparked a number of cases some of which determined the scope of 'vocational training'. In *Gravier*, the definition was wide. It was held to include all forms of teaching which prepares for and leads directly to a particular profession, trade or employment, or which provides the necessary skills for such profession, trade or employment, even if the programme of instruction includes an element of general education. In *Blaizot v University of Liège* (case 24/86), in the context of a claim by university students of veterinary science for reimbursement of the *minerval*, based on *Gravier*, the Court applied the *Gravier* definition of vocational training and held that university education could constitute vocational training:

> not only where the final exam directly provides the required qualification but also insofar as the studies provide specific training (ie, where the student needs the knowledge so acquired for the pursuit of his trade or profession), even if no legislative or administrative provisions make the acquisition of such knowledge a prerequisite.

In general, university courses would meet these criteria. The only exception would be courses designed for persons seeking to 'improve their general knowledge rather than prepare themselves for an occupation'. Even where, as in veterinary or medical science, the training comprises two stages, the second representing the practical stage, the first, academic stage must be regarded as vocational. The two stages must be viewed as a single unit.

Similar reasoning informed the Court's decision in *Belgium v Humbel* (case 263/86). This case concerned a claim by the Belgian authorities for the payment of the *minerval* in respect of *secondary* education received in Belgium by the son of a French national living in Luxembourg. Although the course as a whole appeared to be vocational, the fees giving rise to the dispute concerned one year within that course of general education. The Court held that such a course of general education must nonetheless be treated as 'vocational' if it forms an integral part of an overall programme of vocational education.

Finally, on the same day as the decision in *Humbel*, the Court, in a case brought by the Commission against Belgium (*Commission v Belgium* (case 42/87)) challenging its rules on access to higher education, revised in the light of *Gravier*, allowing access, inter alia, to only 2 per cent of 'outsiders', held that inasmuch as the rules related to vocational training they were in breach of what is now Article 12 EC.

On the basis of these cases, where educational courses are concerned, provided they are found *overall* to be vocational, according to the generous interpretation provided by the Court, EU nationals who are neither migrant workers nor the children of migrant workers living in the state in which the education is provided may claim equal access under equal conditions to nationals of the home state, even if the courses are financed or subsidised by the state as a matter of social policy.

Since grants and loans would now appear to be included in the category of 'social advantages' under Article 7(2) there is perhaps no need for special pleading for their inclusion in Article 7(3) (see *Brown* and *Lair*). Article 7(2) and (3) were not mutually exclusive and any distinction may be undermined by the impact of the non-discrimination principle in conjunction with the citizenship provisions.

23.2.1.5 Housing

A migrant worker is entitled to enjoy 'all the rights and benefits accorded to national workers in matters of housing, including ownership of the housing he needs' (Article 9; see *Commission v Greece* (case 305/87), restrictions on foreigners' right to acquire property held unlawful). The right extends to public and private housing. It is submitted that all statutory protection in this field must apply equally to 'favoured EC citizens'—ie, those who are lawfully resident. These rights would also constitute 'social advantages' under Article 7(2).

More broadly, indirectly discriminatory rules providing for tax rebates for the acquisition of real property were held to be contrary to the principle of non-discrimination in Article 12 in conjunction with Articles 39, 43, and 18 EC (*Commission v Germany* (case C–152/05)).

23.2.1.6 The rights of workers' families

We have discussed the right of entry of workers' family members at 21.4.10. Once admitted and installed it is submitted that such members effectively attain the status of favoured EU citizens. In *Lebon* (case 316/85) the Court held, in the context of a claim for the Belgian minimex by the adult child of a retired French worker living in Belgium, that the status of dependency resulted from a purely factual situation—ie, support provided by the worker; it did not depend on objective factors indicative of a need for support. Certainly, Article 24 Directive 2004/38/EC extends the principle of equality of treatment to family members who are not nationals of a Member State and who have the right of residence or permanent residence (see 23.5 below).

Family members who are nationals of a Member State are covered by the directive in their own right, as migrant EU nationals.

Article 10(3) Regulation 1612/68 required that, in order that the family may install themselves with the worker, the worker must have available for his family 'housing considered as normal for national workers in the region where he is employed'. The Court interpreted this requirement narrowly (*Commission v Germany* (case 249/86)) and the terms of Article 10(3) have not been carried over into Directive 2004/38/EC.

Insofar as the rights acquired by family members in their capacity as such should be considered ancillary to the worker's rights on free movement, we should note that family members acquire the right to work in the host Member State. Originally, this right was found in Article 11 of Regulation 1612/68, which has been repealed by the Citizenship Directive. It has been replaced by Article 23 Citizenship Directive which provides, in somewhat broader terms, 'Irrespective of nationality, the family members of a Union citizen who have the right of residence or the right of permanent residence in a Member State shall be entitled to take up employment or self-employment there'.

The jurisprudence in relation to old Article 11 (*Gül* (case 131/85)), held that as long as the family member has the qualifications and diplomas necessary for the pursuit of the occupation in question in accordance with the legislation of the host state, and observed the specific rules governing the pursuit of that occupation, he was entitled under Article 11 (and now under Article 23), as the spouse of an EU worker, to practise his profession in that Member State, even though he did not have EU nationality. In the case of a spouse seeking to practise a profession it will be necessary to establish whether the spouse's qualifications are recognised as equivalent, which in Gül's case they were. (For a fuller discussion of this matter see Chapter 22.) It might be of significance in this context that the provisions are now contained in a directive rather than a regulation should a Member State fail to transpose the provisions. A private employer might discriminate against a third-country national (TCN) either directly on grounds of nationality, or on grounds of qualification. Directives do not have horizontal direct effect and it might be difficult therefore to enforce rights in such a case (though note possibility of indirect effect—see further Chapter 5 and the possibility of rights under Article 39 itself).

23.2.1.7 *Children: Access to educational apprenticeship or vocational training courses*

The case of *Casagrande* (case 9/74) established that Article 12 entitled children not merely to admission to such courses but also to general measures to facilitate attendance, including grants. This right has been held to extend to a grant to study abroad provided it is available to nationals of the host state (case C–308/89) and see further now as a citizenship right). In *Commission v Belgium* (case 42/87) the Court held that the children of migrant EU workers are entitled to full national treatment as regards *all* forms of state education, even if the working parent has retired or died in that state. The Court went further in *Moritz v Netherlands Minister for Education* (case 390/87). This case involved a claim for an educational allowance from the Dutch authorities by the child of a migrant worker, a German, who had left Holland and returned to his native country. His son sought to return to Holland to complete his studies there since he could not do so in Germany, there being no coordination of school-leaving certification as between the two countries.

The Court held that in such a case, having regard to the need to ensure the integration of migrant workers in the host state, and the need for continuity in their children's education, a child was not to be regarded as having lost its status as a 'child of the family' benefiting from the provisions of Regulation 1612/68 merely because his family had moved back to its state of origin. It may be presumed that his rights under Regulation 1612/68 would cease when the course was concluded. A similarly generous approach was taken in *Gaal* (case C–7/94). Here it held that a child of a (deceased) migrant worker, a Belgian national (legitimately) living in Germany, who was over the age of 21 and not dependent on his remaining parent, was entitled to claim equality with nationals under Article 12 in order to obtain finance for studies in Scotland from the German authorities. The Court held that the definition of family in Article 10 could not be invoked to limit financial assistance to students by age or dependency.

The generous interpretation of Article 12 of Regulation 1612/68 has continued. In *Baumbast and R* (case C–413/99), Article 12 was interpreted not just to give the children of a migrant worker the right to stay in the host Member State to study, but also to give the parent with responsibility for their care the right to remain also, irrespective of their nationality or whether the responsible parent was married to a resident migrant worker.

Despite the fact that Article 12 does not give a spouse the right to equal access to educational, apprenticeship, or vocational training courses, a spouse was successful in claiming such a right in *Forcheri v Belgium* (case 152/82). Mrs Forcheri was the wife of an Italian working as a Community official in Brussels. She applied for admission to a social-work training course in Brussels. She was accepted, but required to pay a special fee, the *minerval*, required of all students who were not Belgian nationals. She claimed that the fee was discriminatory, in breach of then Articles 7 (now 12 EC) and 48 EEC (now 39 EC) and Article 12 of Regulation 1612/68. The ECJ drawing support from the fifth recital in the preamble to Regulation 1612/68, held that to require of a national of another Member State, *lawfully established* in the first Member State, an enrolment fee which is not required of its own nationals constitutes discrimination by reason of nationality which is prohibited by what is now Article 12 EC.

In Mrs Forcheri's case, the right was deemed to arise not from Article 12 of Regulation 1612/68, from which she was clearly excluded, but from the general prohibition on discrimination in the treaty (now Article 12 EC). Her position as a favoured EU citizen, as the spouse of a worker, brought her 'within the scope of application of this Treaty'.

In the light of subsequent developments in the ECJ's jurisprudence, it would now be permitted to base such a claim for fees levied at the lower, Belgian rate on Article 7(2), as a social advantage.

It should always be borne in mind, as was made clear in *Lebon* (case 316/85), that members of the worker's family are only *indirect* beneficiaries of the right to equal treatment accorded to the worker under Article 7(2) of Regulation 1612/68; social advantages can only be granted to members of the family under Article 7(2) as advantages to the *worker*. This is a subtle distinction, but an important one. Even though Article 24 Directive 2004/38/EC also gives family members rights to equal treatment (see below), this right is dependent on the status of being a family member of a migrant EU national.

23.2.1.8 *Article 39 and workers' rights*

As noted above, the rights contained in Regulation 1612/68 are an expression of the rights granted to workers by Article 39 and do not replace them. It is possible to bring an action under Article 39, as Collins did (*Collins* (case C–138/02)). Despite being unsuccessful in his claims under Article 7(2) Regulation 1612/68, the ECJ accepted that he could argue that there had been discrimination under Article 39(2). The UK government had rejected his application for jobseeker's allowance as he was not habitually resident in the UK. This constituted indirect discrimination in the context of access to employment but was, in the circumstances, justified. Although unsuccessful on the facts, the fact that the ECJ accepted the principle might apply to jobseekers could have the effect of undermining the significance of the distinction in *Lebon* between those who move for work and those who move to seek work (see discussion at 23.2.1). The *Collins* style of reasoning was applied in *Ioannidis* (case C–258/04), in which the ECJ re-emphasised that nationals of a Member State seeking employment in another Member State fall within the scope of the EC Treaty and therefore enjoy the right to equal treatment. (Note position under Citizenship Directive, Article 24(2).)

23.2.2 Establishment

We have noted the huge significance of the ECJ's jurisprudence relating to social rights under Regulation 1612/68 both for the worker and the worker's family was discussed. Regulation 1612/68 (now amended by Directive 2004/38/EC), being expressed in terms of the situation of employment, had no parallel for the self-employed which resulted in the special importance in this area of the principle of non-discrimination on the grounds of nationality for those that were self-employed. Where the self-employed or their families are 'lawfully resident' in a Member State, Article 12 (ex 6, originally 7) may, in certain circumstances, be invoked to ensure that they receive equal treatment in the form of 'social' or any other advantages with nationals of the host Member State. For example, in *Commission v Italy (re housing aid)* (case 63/86) the ECJ held that a cheap mortgage facility, available under Italian law only to Italian nationals, was in breach of the then Article 7 EEC (now Article 12 EC), even where such provision was an aspect of social law, and thus (it was implied) should be available on a basis of equality in Italy to EU nationals providing services *as long as the nature of the services provided was such as to require a permanent dwelling there.* (See similarly *Commission v Germany* (case C–152/05), tax rebates for real property.) To a certain extent the significance of the distinction between workers and the self-employed has diminished with the entry into force of Directive 2004/38/EC (see below).

23.2.3 Services

Whilst the self-employed or their families are 'lawfully resident' in a Member State, Article 12 EC may be invoked to ensure equal treatment with nationals of the host Member State, in the case of the provider of services, the matter is less clear. While he or she is undoubtedly able to claim full equality as regards access to, and conditions of, work within the host Member State it is unlikely that he or she can claim for himself and his family benefits in the form of social assistance, especially when they are ongoing, such as may be claimed as social advantages under Article 7(2) of Regulation 1612/68. It could be argued that these should be claimed from the Member State in which the applicant is permanently established. An analogy could perhaps be drawn here with the person migrating in search of employment, who, according to *Lebon* (case 316/85) has no entitlement to the social advantages provided by the host Member State. Again, the impact of citizenship rights may be felt here, as well as the impact of fundamental rights, as we can see in the case of *Carpenter* (case C–60/00), which concerned the right of a service provider to have his wife, who was a TCN, remain in the EU although she had outstayed her visa. Interestingly, Carpenter's claim was against his country or origin, not the states in which he provided cross border services.

Note also the impact of the right to receive services on both the rights of the individual who migrates and on the provision on public services by Member States (see Chapter 24).

23.3 **Social security**

In addition to 'social advantages' in Regulation 1612/68 Article 7(2), the treaty also makes provision for the coordination of social security. Under the laws of Member States, both eligibility for benefit and the amount of benefit paid may depend on the number and extent of contributions made to the institution responsible for social security in the relevant state. Eligibility may also be conditional on the claimant's residence in the state responsible for payment and benefits.

It was to meet these problems that Article 42 (ex 51) of the EC Treaty provided for measures to be adopted in the field of social security to secure for migrant workers and their dependants the implementation of two fundamental principles:

(a) aggregation, for the purpose of acquiring and retaining the right to benefit and of calculating the amount of benefit, of all periods taken into account under the laws of the several countries

(b) payment of benefits to persons resident in the territories of Member States.

To this end, Regulation 1408/71 was passed, replacing the earlier Regulation 3/58. Regulation 1408/71 was implemented and supplemented by Regulation 574/72. Initially applying only to workers and their families these Regulations were amended to include the self-employed by Regulations 1390/81 and 3795/81. These regulations were amended by Regulation 883/2004, which came into force at the end of 2006 (see 23.3.4 below). Note that should Lisbon come into force, Article 42 EC—renumbered as Article 48 TFEU—will allow legislation to be made using the 'ordinary legislative procedure', thus removing the need for unanimity, but subject to an 'emergency brake system', whereby a Member State may require a proposal to be discussed by the European Council.

The aim of EU legislation on social security is not to harmonise Member States' social security legislation but to *coordinate* their provision to secure the objectives of Article 42 EC, and to ensure that claimants' contributions in different Member States are *aggregated* for the purpose outlined in Article 42(a) of the EC Treaty and that persons entitled to benefits may *collect* them wherever they are resident in the EU. The system is designed to abolish, as far as possible, the territorial limitations on the application of the different social security schemes within the Union (*Hessische Knappschaft v Maison Singer et Fils* (case 44/65)). However, in securing these objectives, clearly Member States' social-security laws will be modified. Arguably, the ECJ's interpretation of these provisions have resulted in maximum modification, and there is an uneasy relationship between these provisions, and the approach to social rights found in the free-movement provision, including the right to receive services.

Regulation 1408/71, as amended is long and complex. It is not possible in a book of this nature to examine each substantive provision in detail. Instead it is proposed to examine its general scope, both in terms of the *persons* and the *kind of benefits* covered, and the *principles* on which the detailed provisions are based.

23.3.1 Personal scope

Regulation 1408/71 covers the same groups as are covered by the other legislation relating to free movement of persons: workers, the self-employed and their families and survivors. The workers and self-employed must be nationals of one of the Member States. It also covers survivors who are EU nationals irrespective of the nationality of the worker, and stateless persons and refugees (Article 2). However, the definition of the employed and self-employed is different, being the fact of being or having been insured under any form of social-security scheme. As long as the employed or self-employed person is covered by some national scheme for insured persons in one of the Member States he will be covered by the regulation, even, it seems, if he is or has been working outside the Union (see *Laborero* (cases 82 and 103/86), claimants working in Belgian Congo). By contrast, payments, such as pensions, do not have to be made to a person who moves and resides outside the EU (*Chuck v Raad van bestuur van de Sociale Vezekeringsbank* (case C–331/06)).

Also, in contrast with other legislation relating to workers, these provisions may apply to persons who move as recipients of services (eg, *Kohll* (case C–158/96)). In *Hessische Knappschaft v Maison Singer et Fils* (case 44/65) a German worker was killed in a road accident while on holiday in France. His dependants were paid by the German social-security authorities who then sought to sue the driver of the vehicle responsible for the accident in France. To do so, they needed to rely on their rights of subrogation under Regulation 3/58 (now Regulation 1408/71, Article 93(1)). It was argued that the rights arising under the then Article 51 (now 42) of the EC Treaty were such as to promote freedom of movement for workers *as* workers, not *qua* holidaymakers. The Court disagreed, holding that nothing in the then Article 51 required that the concept of worker be limited solely to migrant workers *sensu stricto*, or to workers required to move for the purpose of their employment.

The definition of family member is also different, being defined in Article 1(f) as:

> any person defined or recognised as a member of the family or designated as a member of the household by the legislation under which benefits are provided [and] where . . . the said legislations regard as a member of the family or a member of the household only a person living under the same roof as the worker, this condition shall be considered satisfied if the worker in question is mainly dependent on that worker.

Both families' and survivors' benefits under EU social security legislation derive from the worker's insurance, unless they are or have been themselves insured under the appropriate scheme. In its earlier case law, the ECJ distinguished between social security benefits which were granted as a personal right and those acquired solely through the claimant's status as a member of the family of a worker. Only the latter could be claimed, on a basis of equality with national claimants, under Regulation 1408/71 (*Kermaschek* (case 40/76)). However, in *Bestuur van de Sociale Verzekeringsbank v Cabanis-Issarte* (case C–308/93), the ECJ departed from *Kermaschek*. Here it held that the claimant, a French woman who had lived with her French husband in Holland while he worked there, and who had never herself been a worker, could, on their return to France following his retirement, invoke the non-discrimination principle of Article 3 of Regulation 1408/71 in order to claim equality of contribution to a Dutch voluntary personal pension scheme to which she had contributed while she was living in the Netherlands. To maintain a distinction between rights in person and derived rights would, the Court held:

> undermine the fundamental Community law requirement that its rules should be applied uniformly, by making their applicability to individuals depend on whether the national law relating to the benefits question treats the rights concerned as rights in person or derived rights, in the light of the specific features of the domestic social security scheme.

Where an individual does not fall within Regulation 1408/71, it is still possible to bring an action under other provisions, such as Article 39 and Regulation 1612/68 or Article 43 (see, eg, *Geven* (case C–213/05)). Indeed, in some cases, it seems as though the ECJ has deliberately chosen not to determine whether a situation falls within Article 39 EC or Regulation 1408/71, instead referring to the citizenship provisions (see eg, *Gaumain-Cerri and Barth* (joined cases C–502/01 and C–31/02), paras 32–3, regarding a residence requirement for a carer's benefit). In this, the ECJ has not followed its normal approach, where the more specific provision should be relied on in preference to the general provision.

23.3.2 Material scope

Article 4(1) of Regulation 1408/71 provides that:

> This Regulation shall apply to all legislation concerning the following branches of social security, reflecting the nine official categories recognised by the ILO:
>
> (a) sickness and maternity benefits;
> (b) invalidity benefits, including those intended for the maintenance or improvement of working capacity;
> (c) old-age benefits;
> (d) survivors' benefits;
> (e) benefits in respect of accidents at work and occupational diseases;
> (f) death grants;
> (g) unemployment benefits;
> (h) family benefits.

Article 4(2) provides that the regulation shall apply 'to all general and special social security schemes, whether contributory or non-contributory'. According to consistent case law of the ECJ, a benefit will be a social-security benefit 'if, first, it is granted, without any individual and discretionary assessment of personal needs, to recipients on the basis of a legally defined position and, second, if it related to one of the risks expressly listed in Article 4(1)' (*Hoeckx* (case 249/83), paras 12–14).

However, the regulation does *not* apply to 'social and medical assistance, to benefit schemes for victims of war or its consequences, or to special schemes for civil servants and persons treated as such' (Article 4(4)).

As the term 'social assistance' is not a term of art, it is not defined in Regulation 1408/71, and will be subject to different interpretations in different Member States. Interpretation has been left to the ECJ, largely on reference from national courts seised with the problem. Not surprisingly, the Court has given the term the narrowest scope.

In a series of cases, starting with *Frilli v Belgium* (case 1/72), the Court, in assessing whether a particular benefit, which may look like social assistance, qualifies as social security, has applied a 'double function' test. Some kinds of benefit, the Court reasons, perform a double function; they are akin to social assistance, since need is the essential criterion, and eligibility is not dependent on employment; yet they are akin to social security since they confer on the beneficiary a legally defined position. Since such difficulties must not be allowed to prejudice the rights of workers, such benefits must be deemed to be social security benefits, and assimilated where possible to the social security benefits listed in Article 4(1). Applying this test in *Frilli*, a non-contributory guaranteed minimum income, unrelated to insurance, payable in Belgium to Belgian citizens or those resident for a minimum period of five years, was assimilated to the old-age pension and deemed to be social security; as such it could not be denied to Frilli in breach of Regulation 1408/71, Article 3.

In *F v Belgium* (case 7/75) the claimant was the 14-year old handicapped son of an Italian worker in Belgium. He had been refused a special grant for handicapped persons, again because he could not fulfil the (Belgian) nationality or (15-year) residence requirement. Prima facie the benefit was social assistance; it was not a 'family' benefit, nor a workers' invalidity benefit; it was not related to contributions and was available to the whole (handicapped) population. Nevertheless, applying the double-function test the Court found it to be social security within Regulation 1408/71. Further a dependent person such as Mr and Mrs F's son was entitled to equality of treatment as long as his parents were resident in a Member State. Even when he ceased to be a minor his right to equality of treatment would not cease. The migrant worker, as Advocate-General Trabucchi suggested, must be treated not just as a source of labour but as a human being.

As suggested in the test in *Hoeckx*, the only criterion by which a claim might still be excluded as constituting 'social assistance' was if the benefit involved a discretionary assessment of need or personal circumstances (eg, *Fossi* (case 79/76) and *Tinelli* (case 144/78)). Needless to say this test did not serve to exclude many claims (*Fossi* and *Tinelli* were claiming as 'victims of war' and thus fell within Regulation 1408/71, Article 4(4); on victims of war see further 23.4.3 below).

The Court switched its approach in the 1980s. Instead of stretching Regulation 1408/71 to encompass social-assistance-type claims, the Court chose an alternative route, treating the benefits as 'social advantages' under Article 7(2) of Regulation

1612/68, the scope of which was expanded following the introduction of the 'lawful residence' test in *Even* (case 207/78); and it now seems that a benefit can fall within Regulation 1408/71 and be a 'social advantage' for Article 7(2) Regulation 1612/68. Likewise with the advent of citizenship, the ECJ has another route by which it may protect the interests of EU nationals (see 23.4 below).

Regulation 1408/71 will, of course, continue to apply, and apply alone, to 'genuine' social-security benefits, and, if a claimant wishes to 'export' a benefit, this can only be achieved under the specific provisions of that regulation. A claimant who wishes to invoke the aggregation principle will likewise have to show that his claim falls within Regulation 1408/71.

From the above cases it is clear that the ECJ will use all the means at its disposal to ensure that migrant workers and their families are in no way disadvantaged as a result of moving within the Union. To achieve its ends the Court will not be deterred by apparent shortcomings in EU legislation.

23.3.3 Principles

The general principles underlying Regulation 1408/71 are stated in the preamble; they are laid down in more detailed form in the regulation itself. Most of these principles are designed to secure one further overriding goal: that the migrant worker and his family should suffer no disadvantage as a result of moving within the Union.

23.3.3.1 *Non-discrimination on grounds of nationality*

This is perhaps the most important principle. It has certainly been the most frequently invoked. Article 3(1) of Regulation 1408/71 provides that:

> Subject to the special provisions of this Regulation, persons resident in the territory of one of the Member States to whom this Regulation applies shall be subject to the same obligations and enjoy the same benefits under the legislation of any Member State as the nationals of that State.

Article 3(1) applies to all forms of discrimination, direct and indirect. Discrimination will often take the form of a residence or length of residence requirement. A benefit covered by the regulation cannot be refused in breach of Article 3. Unlike other areas of EU law it appears that in its social security rules reverse discrimination is not permitted. The Court held in *Kenny v Insurance Officer* (case 1/78):

> it is for the national legislation to lay down the conditions for the acquisition, retention, loss or suspension of the right to social security benefits so long as those conditions apply without discrimination to *the nationals of the Member State concerned* and to those of other Member States. [Para 16, emphasis added.]

23.3.3.2 *Payment regardless of residence*

This principle derives from Article 42(b) of the EC Treaty. Article 10(1) of Regulation 1408/71 provides that certain types of benefit are payable even if the recipient no longer resides in the competent Member State. It will be noted that this principle, known as the 'exportability' principle, is not expressed to apply to *all* social-security benefits; sickness benefits and family benefits, for example, are subject to special provision in Regulation 1408/71 and Regulation 574/72. Unemployment benefits can be claimed elsewhere if certain conditions set down in Articles 69–71 are satisfied (see, eg, *de Cuyper v ONEM* (case C–406/04)). Article 10 is expressed to apply only 'save as otherwise provided'.

Note however the potential impact of the case law regarding the right not to be discriminated against on grounds of residence for rights falling within the scope of free movement or citizenship rights. *De Cuyper* concerned an unemployment benefit the payment of which was conditional on residence. This condition was found to be a restriction, as it could dissuade individuals from exercising free-movement rights. The national measure was justified, however, because of the difficulty in monitoring compliance. The ECJ held, however, that such benefits continue not to be exportable within the scope of Regulation 1408/71. In *Hendrix v Raad van Bestuur van het Uitvoeringsinstituut Werknemersverzekeringen* (case C–287/05), a benefit was classified by the ECJ as special non-contributory benefits referred to in the provisions of Article 4(2a) in conjunction with Article 10a of Regulation 1408/71, receipt of which could lawfully be reserved to persons who are resident in the territory of the Member State whose legislation provides for such a benefit. The ECJ also noted that Regulation 1408/71 dealt specifically with the question of coordination of social security schemes, and that Regulation 1612/68 gives Regulation 1408/71 priority. Nonetheless, the ECJ held that the benefit could also be considered a social advantage under Article 7(2) Regulation 1612/68 and that the ECJ has repeatedly held that a Member State may not make payment of a social advantage within the meaning of Article 7 of Regulation 1612/68 dependent on the condition that recipients are resident in the national territory of that Member State unless it is objectively justified and proportionate to the objective pursued. This interpretation seems to undermine the limitations on exportability imposed by Regulation 1408/71 (see further 23.4 below).

23.3.3.3 *No overlapping of benefits*

Article 12(1) of Regulation 1408/71 provides that 'This Regulation can neither confer nor maintain the right to several benefits of the same kind for one and the same period of compulsory insurance'.

In *Schmidt v Rijksdienst voor Pensioenen* (case C–98/94) the Court held that benefits will be of the 'same kind' when the purpose and object as well as the basis on which they are calculated and the conditions for granting them are identical. On the other hand, characteristics which are purely formal are not relevant criteria for the classification of benefits. Thus, in *Schmidt* a retirement pension for a divorcee, designed to ensure for that person adequate means of support, was not of the same kind as a personal retirement pension.

Where a worker has contributed to social-security schemes in two or more Member States, he may have become entitled to benefit in respect of the same contingency from more than one state. Article 12 operates to prevent him receiving double benefit. However, since entitlement is subject to the single-state principle (see below), and the 'competent' state is determined according to Union law, Article 12 could result in the claimant receiving a lesser sum from the competent state than that to which he would be entitled under the law of another state. Where this occurs the Court has held he is entitled to receive the difference between the smaller and the larger sum, the difference payable by the competent institution in the more 'generous' state. 'A worker cannot be deprived of more favourable allowances by substituting the benefits available from one Member State for the benefits due from another Member State' (see, eg, *Baldi* (case 1/88), family allowances; *Di Felice* (case 128/88), retirement pension; *Georges* (case 24/88), family allowances).

Article 12(1) does not apply to benefits in respect of invalidity, old age, death (pensions) or occupational disease.

23.3.3.4 *Aggregation*

This principle, derived from Article 42(a) EC, is spelt out specifically with regard to each type of benefit covered. It means that the competent Member State, when calculating the right to benefits, is obliged to take into account insurance periods or periods of residence spent in other Member States.

23.3.3.5 *The single-state principle*

This is provided by Article 13, which states as a general rule that 'A worker to whom this Regulation applies shall be subject to the legislation of a single Member State only'.

23.3.3.6 *No disadvantage*

As noted above, the Court has held that a worker may not be allowed to suffer disadvantage as a result of the application of EU rules. Rules against overlapping cannot result in a loss of advantages for a migrant worker. Where the worker is doubly entitled, he or she may choose the more advantageous benefit (*Iacobelli v INAMI* (case C–275/91)). The worker cannot as a result of moving from one Member State to another be put in a worse position than workers who have not availed themselves of their right of free movement (*Masgio* (case C–10/90)).

The Court has been forced to acknowledge that some disadvantage to migrant workers cannot be cured by the application of this principle. This is the inevitable result of the fact that Article 42 is not designed to create a common social-security scheme but simply to coordinate national social-security schemes (see *McLachlan v CNAVTS* (case C–146/93)).

23.3.4 **Regulation 883/2004**

Despite the ECJ's extensive interpretation, there were lacunae in protection awarded to migrant individuals such as those who were not economically active. The institutions agreed a regulation to amend the current system, updating and streamlining it, but also filling in some of these gaps in protection. At the forefront of the changes was a concern to ensure that migration should be made easier by removing the risk of loss of benefits. From a starting point of European citizenship, Regulation 883/2004 applies to non-economically active persons. Health-care benefits have been aligned; restrictions on the export of special, non-contributory benefits are to be based on transparent and objective criteria; and the possibility of exporting a jobseeker's allowance has been increased from three months to six months.

23.4 **Citizenship**

23.4.1 **A discrimination-based approach**

While Article 18 EC provides specific rights to move to another Member State and to reside there, the real impact of citizenship can be seen when considered in conjunction with the concept of discrimination. In *Martinez Sala* (case C–85/96), the ECJ held that a national of one Member State resident in another could rely on the non-discrimination principle in Article 12 EC on matters falling within the scope of the EC Treaty. There are two aspects to consider. The first concerns the scope of the EC Treaty. As we have seen, areas covered by the EC Treaty have been increased with successive treaty amendments, thus increasing the areas in which individuals can bring claims on the basis of discriminatory treatment (contrast *Lair* and *Brown* with *Bidar*). The second area concerns the issue of who can bring a claim. As we have seen, the idea of relying on Article 12 EC in conjunction with other treaty articles is not new: it has been relied on in the context of Articles 39, 43 and 49 EC, but in such case the individuals would have been economically active. On one reading *Martinez Sala* can be seen narrowly; Martinez Sala had been a migrant worker and was claiming rights coordinated by the treaty and therefore came within the scope of Union law on that basis. Alternatively, we could see *Martinez Sala* as the basis of the argument that a lawfully resident migrant European citizen may not be discriminated against by the host Member State on matters falling within the scope of EU law. *Martinez Sala* therefore starts the process of decoupling the acquisition of rights from the requirement to be economically active. The ECJ affirmed this approach in *Baumbast*. There it held that 'The Treaty on European Union does not require that citizens of the Union pursue a professional or trade activity, whether as an employed or self-employed person, in order to enjoy the rights provided in Part Two of the EC Treaty, on citizenship of the Union'.

The scope of this ruling has been elaborated in subsequent judgments, perhaps one of the most noteworthy of which is *Grzelczyk* (case C–184/99). It will be remembered that the position of students seeking maintenance grants had caused concern in the Member States. The ECJ ruled in *Brown* (case 197/86, para 18) that assistance given to students for maintenance and training fell outside the non-discrimination principle currently found in Article 12 EC. *Grzelczyk* concerned a migrant student who, in his third year of studies, applied for such social assistance and was turned down as permitted by *Brown* on the basis of his nationality. The ECJ expressly noted that the nature of the Community has changed since *Brown*, notably with the introduction of citizenship. The ECJ therefore reasoned that:

> the fact that a Union citizen pursues university studies in a Member State other than the State of which he is a national cannot, of itself, deprive him of the possibility of relying on the prohibition of all discrimination on grounds of nationality laid down in Article 6 [now 12] of the Treaty. [Para 36.]

This judgment effectively overruled the principle in *Brown*: where a Member State does not require its own nationals to be workers to claim certain benefits, it cannot require that a migrant EU national fall within the scope of Regulation

1612/68 to claim the same benefit. Central to the ECJ's approach is the prohibition on discrimination. There is, however, a change here in the reasoning of the ECJ. Whereas in *Martinez Sala* the benefit did fall within the scope of Regulation 1612/68, here the right to claim equality is based on the fact the claimant has moved; no economic activity was required.

On another level, the consequences of *Grzlczyk* may be more limited, given the terms of Article 1 of the Students Directive (now replaced by Directive 2004/38/EC), which requires students to be self-supporting. *Grzlczyk* did not overrule this requirement. Nonetheless, although Member States may withdraw the right of residence where a student does not have sufficient resources, such a withdrawal may not be automatic. The reasoning in *Grzelczyk* seems to create a circular position; although lawfully resident migrants are entitled to claim some benefits on the basis of non-discrimination, actually claiming those benefits might be proof that they are an unreasonably burden on the host state. The difficulties can be seen in *Trojani v Le Centre Public d'Aide Sociale de Bruxelles* (case C–456/02). Where the migrant is lawfully resident, and Trojani had been issued with a residence permit, the fact that the migrant could not claim the right of residence under Article 18 or Directive 90/364 (now replaced by Citizenship Directive), as was the position here, does not affect the migrant's right to equality of treatment within the scope of the treaty (para 40). Lawful residence thus entitles the migrant to social assistance on the same terms as the national of the host Member State. The ECJ, however, expressly pointed out that a Member State could withdraw the residence permit. Critics have noted that this might leave Member States in the position of being able to require a migrant to leave, but not able to impose a lesser restriction of not granting a benefit. Article 14 of the Citizenship Directive does make the point that 'an expulsion measure shall not be the automatic consequence of a Union citizen's or his or her family member's recourse to the social assistance system of the host Member State', which limits Member States' freedom. Member States can justify discrimination and in this regard the issue of integration into or a real link with the host Member State is key.

One further point about the ECJ's reasoning in these cases should be noted, as we can see from the case of *Collins* (case C–138/02). Collins entered the UK to try to find a job and claimed jobseeker's allowance, which he was refused. The ECJ stated that:

> citizens lawfully resident in the territory of a host Member State can rely on Article [12] of the Treaty in all situations which fall within the scope *ratione materiae* of Community law. Citizenship of the Union is destined to be the fundamental status of nationals of the Member States, enabling those who find themselves in the same situation to enjoy the same treatment in law irrespective of their nationality, subject to such exceptions as are expressly provided for. [Para 61.]

The reasoning reveals a tension. On the one hand, citizenship is a fundamental status but, on the other hand, the rights that come with it can seemingly be exercised only by those who are lawfully resident (or, as in *Trojani*, have a residence permit), whether the right is claimed under EU law or national law. This suggests that, despite the grand terminology, the ECJ has not adopted a full citizenship model where Union migrants are placed on a completely equal footing unless Union law expressly provides otherwise.

An alternative view of the case law is that the ECJ has adopted a graduated approach which is expressed through the test of requiring a real link with the host Member State. The longer a migrant has been in the host Member State, the more integrated he or she is, the greater his or her rights. Martinez Sala had been resident in Germany for a considerable period and had contributed to host-state funds; Grzelczyck, with a relatively short stay in the host Member State is entitled to limited social assistance. In *Collins*, the ECJ accepted the principle that Collins could be entitled to claim jobseeker's allowance, but then also held that the right could be restricted if objectively justified, inter alia, by a wish on the part of the host Member State to ensure that there is a genuine link between an applicant and a social advantage (para 67). In *Bidar* (case C–209/03), which concerned a legally resident student's claim for state support, the ECJ emphasised the link between the host Member State and the migrant, making it possible for a Member State to impose prerequisites on the right of a claimant. In coming to its conclusion in *Bidar*, the ECJ seems implicitly—or effectively—to have overruled some aspects of *Lair* (case 39/86) regarding the non-availability of the non-discrimination argument to maintenance for University studies. Conversely, *Ioannidis* (case C–258/04) concerned a claim for a jobseeker's allowance (the same allowance as in *D'Hoop*) by a Greek person who had studied in Belgium but then moved to France for a relatively short period and then returned to Belgium. Here, the ECJ reaffirmed that a Member State may wish to ensure that there is a real link between the applicant and the geographic employment market concerned. The condition imposed in this case, that the applicant must have completed his secondary education in the Member State was not acceptable. It was not necessarily representative of a real and effective degree of connection, and therefore went beyond what was necessary to obtain the objective.

The case law is not entirely consistent but, in general, it might be argued that those with a stronger temporal link have greater rights. One might suggest that a graduated approach, or one which seeks a 'real link' with the host Member State, is in line with that adopted in the Citizenship Directive, discussed below at 23.5. There we can see that the longer an individual remains in a host Member State, the greater his or her entitlements (see restrictions on rights for temporary residents; preconditions for acquisition of permanent residence). Of course, there are some questions here. As an approach, it may fit with a view which seeks to integrate migrants; it does not fit with a test which looks at the question of whether the migrant is dissuaded from exercising their rights, that is indirect discrimination and, particularly, rules which apply without distinction. (See further Chapter 21 on access to the territory.) As we see at 23.4.2 below, there are some suggestions that the ECJ is moving towards a restriction-based test.

The prohibition of discrimination is not limited to claims concerning financial assistance. *Bickel and Franz* (case C–274/96), an early citizenship case, concerned the right to have court proceedings carried out in a language the migrant can understand. In *Garcia Avello* (case C–148/02), the issue under discussion was the right of a family to register their children's names in Belgium in the Spanish manner. *Chen*, discussed above, gave a dependent child the right to have her mother reside with her. *Pusa* (case C–224/02) concerned a tax prepayment scheme in one Member State of origin to ensure repayment of a debt, which did not take account of the tax paid on the income in another Member State.

In this context, note that we have been considering discrimination based on nationality. Since the enactment of Directive 2000/43 on Discrimination Based on Ethnic Origin (OJ [2000] L 180/22), discrimination based on ethnic origin is also prohibited (see Chapter 27).

23.4.2 Discrimination, obstacles to free movement, and justification

It seems that, as with other areas, the discrimination prohibited by citizenship applies to both direct discrimination and indirect discrimination. *Garcia Avello* can be seen as concerning rules discriminating against those who had a second nationality. In *Collins*, for example, the jobseeker's allowance was refused because the UK had not been Collins's habitual residence, a condition which is harder for nationals to satisfy than non-nationals. As *Collins* also illustrates, such rules may be permissible if objectively justified in addition to the express treaty derogations and those provisions found in Directive 2004/38/EC (replacing Directive 64/221/EEC).

Given the developments in the context of Articles 39, 43, and 49 towards a restriction-based test, an obvious question would be whether the ECJ will adopt such an approach in relation to citizenship. Although the case law is not entirely clear, it seems that there are suggestions that the ECJ is moving in this direction. In *D'Hoop* (case C–224/98), the Belgian rules, which required an individual to have completed his or her secondary education in Belgian to claim the 'tide-over' allowance whilst finding employment, are likely to affect non-nationals more than nationals. They could thus be viewed as indirectly discriminatory. The ECJ did not expressly phrase its judgment in terms of indirect discrimination, however. It referred to rules which placed those who exercised their right of free movement 'at a disadvantage'. A similar approach can be seen in *Pusa*, in which the ECJ based its reasoning on *D'Hoop*. Both these two cases are unusual in the sense that they concern the rights of returning migrants against their state of origin (see also *Tas–Hagen*, 23.4.3 below). Should this approach become more general, the potential scope of the non-discrimination principle is wide indeed, even taking into account that the rules in *Pusa* and *D'Hoop* were capable in principle of being objectively justified.

23.4.3 Rights against state of origin

Much of the case law in this field concerned claims against the host Member State rather than the Member State of origin. Indeed, in the area of social policy, a certain amount of territoriality is accepted. After all, if a person leaves a Member State, he or she no longer shares in that community or contributes to it. Thus the exportability principle found in Regulation 1408/71 was exceptional. Now, however, the ECJ has developed its jurisprudence to that a migrant can bring a claim based on Article 18 against his or her state of origin, even in fields where the subject matter falls within the competence of Member States. Even such rules must be exercised within the scope of EU law, and not restrict the right of free movement.

Tas-Hagen, Tas v Raadskamer WUBO van de Pensioen- en Uitkeringsraad (Case C–192/05) concerned an award to civilian war victims by the Netherlands. Both applicants were recognised as civilian war victims, but were refused the payments on the basis that, although they had lived in the Netherlands, they now lived in Spain. The ECJ held that national legislation which places at a disadvantage certain of the nationals of the Member State concerned simply because they have exercised their freedom to move and to reside in another Member State is a restriction on the freedoms conferred by Article 18(1) EC; this reasoning did not distinguish between restrictions imposed by the host state or the state of origin. Such an approach has been used in a number of other cases concerning war pensions (eg, *Nerkowska v Zaklad Ubezpiezen Spotecznych* (case C–499/06); *Zablocka-Weyhermüller v Land Baden-Württemberg* (case C–221/07)) and has been used in relation to other benefits, such as grants to study abroad (*Morgan v Bezirksregierung Köln* and *Bucher v Landrat des Kreises Düren* (Joined Cases C–11/06 and C–12/06)).

It could be argued that this development in the jurisprudence constitutes a qualitative shift in approach. Rather than the exceptional grant of exportability as a form of privilege, territoriality of national social security systems, despite the flexibility the ECJ claims the Member States enjoy in this field, now becomes a restriction on free movement which must be justified. It has been suggested, however, that we can see this obligation on the state of origin as the reverse side of the control given to host Member States through the operation of the real link test.

23.5 Citizenship directive

Article 24 provides a general right of equal treatment. It specifies:

> Subject to such specific provisions as are expressly provided for in the Treaty and secondary law, all Union citizens residing on the basis of this directive in the territory of the host member State shall enjoy equal treatment with the nationals of that Member State within the scope of the Treaty. The benefit of this right shall be extended to family members who are not nationals of a Member State and who have the right of residence or permanent residence.

Article 24 reflects in some ways the approach adopted in Even in relation to Article 7(2) Regulation 1612/68 in that the crucial factor is lawful residence. It also reflects previous case law in that the no-discrimination principle is extended to TCNs who are family members. The right is not unlimited: it is expressed to be subject to contrary provision in the treaty and in other secondary law (such as the social security regulation, perhaps). The article also contains a crucial second paragraph. It states:

> By way of derogation from paragraph 1, the host Member State shall not be obliged to confer entitlement to social assistance during the first three months of residence or, where appropriate, the longer period provided for in Article 14(4)(b), nor shall it be obliged, prior to the acquisition of the right of permanent residence, to grant maintenance aid for studies, including vocational training, that consist in student grants or student loans to persons other than workers, self-employed persons, persons who retain such status and members of their families.

There are thus two categories of exceptions. Temporary residents or those seeking work are not entitled to social assistance. Secondly, maintenance for students is limited to the economically active and their families. It seems that this provision relates only to the rights of incoming migrants against the host Member State; it does not deal with exportability rights against the Member State of origin.

23.6 Conclusions

The Union has long recognised that migrants are not just factors of economic production, and the institutions have enacted over the course of the last five decades a range of legislative instruments to define the rights of individuals who migrate so as to facilitate the creation of the internal market. The ECJ has likewise been active, interpreting these acts and the treaty provisions broadly. While we might commend the humanitarian spirit, such interpretations have stretched the meaning of provisions and seem to ignore the specified relationship between the various acts, and the general relationship between treaty provisions and secondary measures. The case law here has a constitutional significance as it impacts on Member States' control of their social security systems and rewrites the attribution of competence within the Union. The case law has significance in a second way, as it creates substantive rights particularly as regards citizenship and creating a community which is more than just purely economic. According to the US Supreme Court, the American constitution was 'framed upon the theory that the peoples of the several states must sink or swim together, and that in the long run prosperity and salvation are in union and not division' (Cardozo J in *Baldwin v GAF Seelig* 294 US 522, 523 (1935)). The question is whether, in eroding the edges of Member State competence, extending rights to a greater range of people and circumstances, the ECJ has adopted this framework for the EU, or whether the requirement of a 'real link', seen to operate even against citizenship rights, undermines any such project.

FURTHER READING

Dougan, M, 'The constitutional dimension to the case law on Union citizenship' (2006) 31 El Rev 613.

Hailbronner, K, 'Union citizenship and access to social benefits' (2005) 42 CML Rev 1245.

Peers, S, 'Social advantages and discrimination in employment caselaw confirmed' (1997) 22 EL Rev 157.

Spaventa, E, 'Seeing the woods despite the trees? On the scope of Union citizenship and its constitutional effects' (2008) 45 CML Rev 40.

Steiner, J, 'The Right to Welfare: Equality and Equity under Community Law' (1985) 10 EL Rev 21.

White, R, 'Free movement, equal treatment, and citizenship of the Union' (2005) 54 ICLQ 885.

24

Right to receive services

24.1 Introduction

So far we have discussed the economic rights mainly from the perspective of the provider. Article 49 has been broadly interpreted to include the right to receive services. While this clearly covers the economic arena, the right is broader than that. In particular, it raises the possibility of the right to travel and to receive services which are provided as public services. It is here that the significance of the case law can be seen in two ways. First, an extension to Article 49 now opens the possibility of supporting a broader non-economic conception of the Union; one that provides or at least facilitates access to public services. Secondly, and as a consequence, this jurisprudence challenges the boundary between Union and market-led provision of services and the idea of the state as provider of certain fundamental services which fall within the competence of the Member States. Arguably, the expansion of the rights facilitated by the EU, which may add substance to the legally based relationship between EU and citizen, has the potential to undermine the link between national citizenship and Member State.

In the light of the potential constitutional and political significance of the case law, we will investigate the scope of the right to receive services. In doing so, we will track three main lines of approach that the European Court of Justice (ECJ) has adopted to facilitate the expansion of individuals' rights of access: the use of the non-discrimination argument for matters falling within the scope of the EC Treaty; the broad interpretation given to services and related benefits; and the use of remuneration as the boundary between EU and state competence. As regards this latter point, the chapter will trace the development of the jurisprudence, with particular emphasis on the health-care cases to assess the impact of the ECJ's decisions on the ability of Member States to provide public services before questioning whether the early protection for the role of the state remains. Finally, we will identify the scope of relevant EU legislation in this field.

24.2 General

The freedom provided by Articles 49–50 (post Lisbon, Articles 56–7 of the Treaty on the Functioning of the European Union (TFEU) respectively) is expressed in terms of the freedom to *provide* services. It was subsequently extended by the ECJ to embrace the freedom to *receive* services.

The point was originally raised in *Watson* (case 118/75), where the Commission suggested that the freedom to move within the Community to receive services was the necessary corollary to the freedom to provide services. This was approved by the Court in *Luisi v Ministero del Tesoro* (case 286/82) in the context of criminal proceedings in Italy against Luisi and Carbone for breach of Italian currency regulations. They were accused of taking foreign currency out of the country in excess of the maximum permitted under Italian law. They had taken the money out for the purposes of tourism and medical treatment. The question referred to the ECJ was whether payment for such services represented movements of capital, within the then Articles 67–73 of the EC Treaty (provisions deleted by the Treaty of Amsterdam (ToA)), or payments for the provision of services; if the latter, was it governed by the then Articles 59–66 (now 49–55)?

Advocate-General Mancini, arguing from *Watson* (case 118/75) suggested that Article 49 was concerned with the receipt of services as well as their provision. In support of this view he cited the general programme for the abolition of restrictions on the freedom to provide services (*Common Market Reporter*, para 1545, JO 1962, 32), Directive 64/221, which expressly referred in Article 1(1) to 'freedom of movement for employed or self-employed persons or the *recipients* of services' and Directive 73/148, Article 1(1)(b), which required Member States to abolish restrictions on the movement and residence of 'nationals of Member States wishing to go to another Member State as *recipients* of services'.

The Court, following Advocate-General Mancini, found the money to be payment for services and held that freedom to provide services, as provided by Article 49, includes the freedom, for recipients of services, to go to another Member State, without restriction, in order to receive a service there. Recipients of services were held to include tourists, persons receiving medical treatment and persons travelling for the purposes of education and business.

Thus, the right to enter and remain in another Member State for the purpose of receiving services has been established. In *Commission v Netherlands (re entry into Dutch territory)* (case C–68/89) the Court held that nationals of one EC state were entitled to enter another Member State simply on production of a valid identity card or passport. National immigration authorities were not entitled to question EU nationals seeking to enter a Member State except in order to query the validity of the identity card or passport. On the other hand, when applying for a residence permit national authorities may require proof of the applicant's status as a provider or recipient of services. Recipients of services are entitled to residence for the period during which the service is provided. Any restrictions on these freedoms will prima facie breach Articles 49–50, subject to limitation on the grounds of public policy, public security, and public health (Articles 46 and 55 EC). The question remains whether the recipient of services, by reason of his status or his right of residence, can invoke these provisions, together with Article 12 (ex 6) EC (post Lisbon, 18 TFEU), to claim equality of treatment with nationals of the host state. A number of services, such as education and medicine, are publicly funded and provided not so much as a commercial activity but as a public service. Are these to be available to nationals of the Member States on the same basis as to the states' own citizens?

24.3 Non-discrimination and Union competence

24.3.1 Fees and access to courses

Vocational training was considered in the context of educational services in *Gravier v City of Liège* (case 293/83). The applicant was a young French woman who had applied to and been accepted by the Liège Académie des Beaux-Arts for a four-year course in the art of strip cartoons. As a foreign student she was charged a special fee, known as a *minerval*, for the course. This was not payable by Belgian citizens, whether or not they lived or paid taxes in Belgium, nor by EU nationals working in Belgium, or members of their families. She brought an action before the Belgian courts, claiming the fee was discriminatory. Her case rested on two arguments.

First, she suggested that the *minerval* constituted an obstacle to her freedom of movement to receive services as established in *Luisi v Ministero del Tesoro* (case 286/82) in breach of Article 49. Her second argument was based on the vocational nature of the course. Vocational education fell within the scope of the treaty; as a matter covered by EC law it was discriminatory, in breach of Article 12, to charge higher prices to EC nationals who were not Belgian citizens or resident in Belgium. The ECJ, following the opinion of the Advocate-General, found in Ms Gravier's favour on this second ground. Access to vocational training was a matter covered by Community law; moreover, it was an essential element in promoting freedom of movement for persons throughout the Union. The Court expressly dissociated itself from the wider issues involved, discussed at length by the Advocate-General, concerning the organisation and financing of such courses, and confined its judgment merely to conditions of access to a course affecting foreign students alone, and relating to a particular kind of course, namely vocational education. (See further 23.2.1.4 on scope of 'vocational training')

The decision in *Gravier* caused considerable concern amongst Member States. This decision, with its wide definition of vocational training, meant that many courses, including perhaps university courses, often entailing substantial contributions from public funds (the Belgians pointed out that the *minerval* itself only covered 50 per cent of the cost of the education provided), would have to be offered on equal terms to all EU nationals. Underlying this discussion is a more general concern about the right of migrant EU nationals to receive public services on equal terms, although in *Gravier* the matter was not discussed in these terms.

Gravier was indeed a landmark case, an example of the Court in activist mood. The legal basis for the decision, resting on (what was at the time) Article 128 EEC, is slender. While Article 128 EEC may have provided a sufficient legal basis for the issuing of directives in the field of vocational training (as the Court found in *UK v Commission* (case 56/88)), it may be doubted that it was sufficiently clear, precise, and unconditional to give rise to direct effects. In any event, Article 128 EEC was replaced in the Maastricht Treaty (TEU) by Article 127 (now 150) EC, which requires the Union to implement a vocational training policy which will 'support and supplement the action of Member States while fully respecting the responsibility of the Member States for the content and organisation of vocational training'. This article represents one of several specific examples of the subsidiarity principle introduced by the TEU. The TEU also introduced a specific provision relating to education, Article 149 EC (ex 126), although the precise relationship between Article 149 and Article 150 is not clear. Despite the limitation of the Union to a supporting role in action under Articles 149–50 and the change in wording of the relevant provisions compared to the text in cases such *Gravier*, the ECJ has applied these cases in the context of equal access to Austrian higher-education institutions (*Commission v Austria (recognition of qualifications)* (case C–147/03)). Imposing discriminatory treatment, in this case the requirement on those who did not do their secondary education in Austria to undertake extra tests to prove their academic status, is contrary to Articles 12, 149 and 150 EC. In coming to this conclusion, the ECJ relied not only on the terms of Article 149(2) EC, which seeks to encourage student mobility, but, significantly, on European citizenship. The ECJ reaffirmed the fundamental nature of European citizenship which enables 'those who find themselves in the same situation to enjoy the same treatment irrespective of their nationality' (*Commission v Austria (recognition of qualifications)*, para 45 (See also 23.4)).

24.3.2 Scholarships and grants

The Court in *Gravier* (case 293/83) refrained from considering whether the right of EU nationals to vocational training carried with it a right to grants and scholarships from the host state to enable them to take up these courses. Advocate-General Sir Gordon Slynn was clearly of the opinion that such a right was not included in the right to receive services. In this same context the Belgian, Danish, and British governments regarded such a result as unthinkable in view of the differences which exist between the number of students moving, for educational purposes, into different Member States. The matter was resolved in *Brown* and *Lair* (cases 197/86 and 39/86; for detailed discussion of these cases see Chapters 21 and 23). Both *Brown* and *Lair* involved claims for maintenance grants for university courses. In both cases their entitlement to the grants as 'workers', or the 'children of migrant workers', was doubtful. So they sought also to rely on *Gravier*, arguing that the course in question constituted vocational training, to which the then Article 7 EEC (now Article 12 EC) applied. Thus they were entitled to be treated on a footing of equality with nationals.

The Court, no doubt anxious to quell the anxieties of Member States on this issue, disagreed. Although university courses were capable of constituting vocational training, to which they were entitled to equal access in respect of fees, Article 12 EC did not apply to maintenance grants. Assistance in the form of maintenance grants, the Court held, fell outside the scope of the EC Treaty. It was a matter of educational policy, and, as such, had not been entrusted to the Community institutions; it was also a matter of social policy, which fell within the competence of Member States insofar as it was not covered by the provisions of the EC Treaty.

Whilst there is little logic in the distinction between fees, which relate to conditions of access to vocational training, and maintenance grants, which do not, it is clear that the judgments in *Brown* and *Lair* reflected the Court's desire, on grounds of policy, to call a halt to the development of an EU educational policy by means of judicial decision. The judgments were greeted with relief by Member States. *Grzelczyck* (case C–184/99) and other cases in this area suggest that issue may have to be revisited in the light of changes to the treaty, notably the introduction of European citizenship. As a migrant student, Grzelczyck was not entitled to state assistance under Article 7(2) Regulation 1612/68. As a migrant European citizen however, he might be so entitled. The impact of citizenship and the inclusion of education within the scope of EU law can also be seen in *Bidar* (case C–209/03), in which an individual could not be subjected to different conditions for eligibility for preferential rate student loans (see 23.4.1). EU competence has expanded to include other areas too, such as public health (see 24.5.2).

24.4 Scope of services: Corollary to the right to receive

In a number of successful cases, the discrimination principle was used in conjunction with the recipient being in the host Member State for business or for tourist purposes: in either situation contributing to the host Member State's economy. We can see such an extension of the equality principle in *Cowan v French Treasury* (case 186/87). The claimant, an English citizen on holiday in Paris, was claiming compensation for personal injuries sustained as a result of a mugging in the Paris Metro. Under French law compensation was provided out of public funds and payable only to French nationals. Cowan claimed that since he was exercising his freedom to receive services, this rule was in breach of Article 12 EC. The ECJ held that he was entitled to equal protection against, and compensation for, the risks of assault. This right was a corollary of his right to receive services. Since the judgment was expressed in narrow, specific terms, it remains to be seen what rights are to be regarded as a 'corollary' to the right to receive services.

In *Commission v Spain* (case C–45/93) the Court found that in charging discriminatory entrance fees to national museums (lower fees being charged for Spanish citizens and residents and EU nationals under 21 years) Spain was acting in breach of Article 12 EC and Article 49 EC. The freedom to provide services recognised by Article 49 included the freedom for recipients of services, including tourists, to go to another Member State to enjoy those services under the same conditions as nationals. As visiting museums was one of the determining reasons why tourists decide to go to another Member State, any discrimination with regard to admission would influence some persons' decisions to visit the country. The fact that a museum service was a public service financed by the state was not raised by the Spanish government and was not considered by the Court. In subsequent cases concerning discriminatory terms of access to facilities such as museums, the ECJ has not addressed the point wither, relying instead on its reasoning in *Commission v Spain* (see, eg, *Commission v Italy* (case C–388/01)).

In a rather different context, in *Hubbard v Hamburger* (case C–20/92), a provision of German law requiring a national of another Member State who, in the capacity of executor of a will, had brought proceedings before one of its courts, to lodge security for costs—something which was not required of German nationals— was held to constitute discrimination on grounds of nationality, prohibited by Articles 49–50 EC. Although in this case both the provider (the executor) and the recipient (the beneficiary) of services were established outside German territory (in the UK), the rule was clearly a barrier to the free provision (or receipt) of services.

24.5 Remuneration and the role of the state

24.5.1 Education

One further question, raised but not answered in *Gravier* (case 293/83), was whether the equality principle could be applied as an adjunct to the right, established in *Luisi* (case 286/82) to move within the Community to *receive* services under what was then Article 59 (now 49). The right to receive educational services was more plainly seen in *Belgium v Humbel* (case 263/86), which concerned the imposition of fees for secondary education which concerned the right to receive services. As we have seen, to fall within Article 49, services must have an economic element, no matter how slight (see, eg, *Deliège* (case C—51/96 and C–191/97), discussed Chapter 21). The question facing the ECJ in *Humbel* was whether this element of remuneration was present. The ECJ held:

> The essential characteristic of remuneration thus lies in the fact that it constitutes consideration for the service in question, and is normally agreed upon between the provider and the recipient of the service.
>
> That characteristic is, however, absent in the case of courses provided under the national education system. First of all, the state, in establishing and maintaining such a system, is not seeking to engage in gainful activity but is fulfilling its duties towards its own population in the social, cultural and educational fields. Secondly, the system in question is, as a general rule, funded from the public purse and not by pupils or their parents.
>
> The nature of the activity is not affected by the fact that pupils or their parents must sometimes pay teaching or enrolment fees in order to make a certain contribution to the operating expenses of the system. [Paras 17–19.]

It is important to note that in addition to looking at how the system of education was funded, the ECJ emphasised the purpose of the activity and recognised that the state is acting in its capacity as political unit, with ties to its citizens. This case could be seen as providing an exception to the scope of Article 49 and free movement logic.

Wirth (case C–109/92) arguably changed the emphasis, by focusing on the nature of the funding mechanism. The case concerned higher education rather than secondary education, but the ECJ still recognised that higher education can be provided as a state activity. Crucially, however, it held that, although most higher education institutions would be funded by the state and therefore would fall within the *Humbel* 'exception', those which were funded privately or which sought to make a profit would fall within Articles 49.

We have seen that in the context of education the ECJ distinguished between education which was provided by private finance, with a view to profit, and education as a public service, financed wholly or partly by the state, as an aspect of social policy. The position therefore seemed to be that—apart from the area of vocational training (access and fees), which is governed by *Gravier*—public services such as health and education provided by the state for the benefit of its citizens, and not for commercial reasons with a view to profit, cannot be claimed on a basis of equality by EU nationals who have temporary residence as recipients of services but do not enjoy 'lawful residence' on a 'settled' or permanent basis as 'favoured Community citizens'—that is, those who are, or have been, employed and self-employed migrants and their families (see Chapter 23) in the state providing the services. Whether the *Humbel* 'exception' remains is debatable, as we shall see below in the cases on the right to health care and some more recent cases on education.

24.5.2 Cross-border health care

Kohll (case C–158/96) concerned the Luxembourgoise requirement that, if an individual wanted to be able to reclaim the cost of medical treatment outside Luxembourg from the medical insurance company, then prior authorisation granted only in limited circumstances would be required. Kohll sought to challenge this rule on the basis of what was then Article 59 (now 49). The Luxembourg government argued that the rule complied with Article 22 of Regulation 1408/71 concerning social security. The ECJ agreed that, in principle, it is for Member States to organise their own social-security systems, including the right or duty to be insured with a social-security scheme and the benefits available under any such scheme, it held that in doing so Member States must comply with EU law, including the right to provide and receive services. The ECJ held that the orthodontist's treatment in Germany in issue in this case was to be considered 'services' for the purposes of the EC Treaty as the treatment was provided for remuneration and constituted a professional activity. Thus the Luxembourg social-security rules regarding medical treatment had to be considered in the light of Article 49. They were found to constitute a barrier to the freedom to provide services and were not objectively justified either for the protection of the financial equilibrium of the social-security system or for reasons of national health.

This judgment (and *Decker* (case C–120/95), handed down the same day concerning the provision of spectacles and therefore considered under Article 28 (ex 30); (see Chapter 19), which caused some concern among many Member States, raised many questions about the scope of the treaty freedoms in the context of public health care and the congruence between the case law regarding medical care and the existing case law on public services.

In this context it should be noted that the *Kohll* situation is different from the cases on education. In those cases, the host Member State bore the cost the individuals moving to receive services; here, the cost is repatriated. Concern arose as to whether the *Kohll* approach would be adopted in regard to health-care systems which operate by providing the service free rather than by reimbursing the cost. This question was referred to the ECJ in the cases of *Geraets-Smits v Stichting Ziekenfonds* and *HTM Peerbooms v Stichting CZ Groep Zorgverzekeringen* (case C–157/99), which concerned a system based on social insurance whereby the funding was derived from a mix of individual premiums, state funding, and funding from other private insurance funds. Each of the applicants had obtained treatment without obtaining prior authorization. The Advocate-General in this case adopted the reasoning in *Humbel* and *Wirth* (discussed at 24.5.1 above) to suggest that the provision of health care in such systems does not fall within Article 50 EC, constituting instead part of the Member State's obligation towards its population (para 47). The ECJ, however, followed its approach in *Kohll* and held that medical care fell within the scope of Article 49, although certain restrictions could be justified on public-policy grounds, such as the need to protect public health by ensuring an appropriate distribution of hospitals, adequately equipped and staffed, so as to meet the needs of the population. The ECJ first noted that although the Dutch system (the ZFW) may have provided benefits in kind, the treatment the patients actually did receive was paid for by them. As a separate argument, the ECJ held:

> Furthermore, the fact that hospital medical treatment is financed directly by the sickness insurance funds on the basis of agreements and pre-set scales of fess is not in any even such as to remove such treatment from the sphere of services within the meaning of Article [50] of the Treaty.
>
> First it should be borne in mind that Article [50] of the Treaty does not require that the service should be paid for by those for whom it is performed . . .
>
> Second, Article [50] of the Treaty states that it applies to services normally provided for remuneration and it has been held that, for the purposes of the that provision, the essential characteristic of remuneration lies in the fact that it constitutes consideration for the service in question. In the present cases, the payments made by the sickness insurance funds under the contractual arrangements provided for by the ZFW, albeit set at a flat rate, are indeed the consideration for the hospital services and unquestionably represent remuneration for the hospital which receives them and which is engaged in an activity of an economic character. [Paras 56–8.]

While on a superficial level the ECJ has followed the approach in *Humbel* by focussing on remuneration, its approach to identifying when there is remuneration owes more to the general case law on services which has adopted a broad approach to finding payment. Crucially, it makes no reference to the point made in *Humbel* about the intention of the system, nor to the role of the state in providing public services.

On one level, it can be said that the judgment avoids distinguishing between the health-care systems of the different Member States as to whether they fall within Article 49 or not on the basis of how they are funded. This judgment does, however, mean that there is a split in the jurisprudence between education and health, which seems hard to justify. Furthermore, this is a different approach from that adopted in the context of competition law, where the ECJ has looked at purpose to limit the scope of bodies caught as undertakings by Articles 81–2 (see, eg, *FENIN*; see Chapter 29). The alternative interpretation would be that the *Humbel* and *Wirth* line of cases should no longer be viewed as good law. Certainly the ECJ does not seem to be changing its approach to health care, as an increasingly long line of cases illustrates (see, eg, *Leichtle* (case C–8/02); *Müller-Fauré* (case C–385/99)). Indeed, the ECJ may be pushing its reasoning still further, as the case of *Watts v Bedford Primary Care Trust* (case C–372/04)) illustrates.

Watts concerned the NHS which operates a system whereby health care is provided free at point of provision; furthermore it does not envisage the possibility or reimbursement for treatment elsewhere whether private treatment within the UK, or treatment outside the UK (although this latter possibility is envisaged for limited cases under Regulation 1408/71, see further Chapter 23), and the trusts operating health care in the UK have no funds available for this purpose. Mrs Watts had arthritis and was in pain, but medical authorities put her in a standard category as far as her need for treatment was concerned and she was consequently placed on a waiting list for an operation. She went to France for the operation, returned to the UK and demanded reimbursement, as well as post-operative physiotherapy. On being refused payment by the Trust, Watts brought an action for judicial review which resulted in a reference to the ECJ.

In the arguments before the ECJ, much was made of the fact that the NHS was in a parallel situation to the educational system in *Humbel*, in being state funded. The ECJ avoided considering whether the provision of health care in the UK was a commercial activity, but focused—as it had done in *Geraets-Smits*—on the fact that Watts paid directly for her treatment and the status of the NHS was irrelevant to that assessment (para 89). The fact that the UK had, as a political matter, chosen a system which, effectively, involves rationing and waiting lists was ignored. Whilst the ECJ does recognise the possibility of managing public health-care systems as a derogation from this right, in *Watts* it conducted a review of the way the system worked to find that the system did not meet the ECJ's standards. This decision has been much criticised. While the ECJ may state that there is scope for Member State choices about the level of health-care provision and the way that care is provided, in practice the ECJ is undermining that freedom. Legal choices at the European level are superceding national political choices and medical assessment. It is now difficult, for example, for the UK to have a system that is not based to some degree on reimbursement, limiting the political choices about how to structure and fund the NHS. The decision in *Watts* seemingly overruled a medical decision about the comparative urgency of the surgery in this case and, as the ECJ does not distinguish between the different aspects of care involved in the procedure, allowed the patient to queue-jump with regard to post-operative care, again replacing a medical assessment as to comparative need. While it has been suggested that the ECJ is supporting individuals' rights to prompt health care, it seems that this will benefit a particular class of well-informed patient at the expense of national solidarity.

24.6 Assessment of the position of public services under Article 49

Whilst *Humbel* has not been expressly overruled, it seems difficult to believe that, following cases such as *Watts*, the exception for state-funded education holds good. There is no logical distinction between the two categories of provision. Indeed, there is a private education system requiring payment just as much as health-care services and therefore forms part of an economic sector. This view is supported by the case of *Schwarz and Gootjes-Schwarz v Finanzamt Bergisch Gladbach* (case C–76/05), which concerned rules permitted tax deductions in respect of private school fees paid to certain institutions. Here, the parents had chosen to send their children to private school in Scotland rather than one of the approved schools in Germany. The German government sought to argue that this matter fell within the *Humbel* 'exception'. Whilst the ECJ reiterated its approach with regard to remuneration that it adopted in *Humbel*; it then went on to state that 'All that matters is that the private school established in another Member State may be regarded as supplying services for remuneration' (para 44). In doing so, the ECJ relied on *Watts*. While we might argue that this case changes nothing, in that it follows the ideas in *Wirth* that private education would be a service within Article 50, the reliance on *Watts* and the breadth of the ECJ's reasoning here, suggest that the boundaries between the two areas are blurring.

The approach of the ECJ is worrying. It seems to result in an erosion of Member States' competence, limiting their political choices and social solidarity in favour of provision by the market (see similarly criticisms of *Laval* at 22.3.1). These judgments are therefore hugely significant, as public service has been at the heart of Member States' relationship with their citizens. It is also questionable whether the direction of these cases is in line with political signals provided by the terms of EU legislation and even treaty amendment.

24.7 Legislation

The impact of the Services Directive was discussed in Chapter 22. There we noted that one of the concerns surrounding the enactment of the directive was its impact on public services. Thus, although the directive covers the right to receive, it should be noted that the directive excluded some sectors from its ambit. Significantly, the recitals to the Services Directive state:

> This Directive covers only services which are performed for an economic consideration. Services of general interest are not covered by the definition in Article 50 of the Treaty and therefore do not fall within the scope of this Directive. Services of general economic interest are services that are performed for an economic consideration and therefore do fall within the scope of this Directive. [Recital 17.]

This does not clarify the difficulties arising from the case law: presumably state-funded education is a service of 'general interest', as referred to in Recital 17, whilst health is a service of general economic interest. In fact the recitals effectively restate the case law from *Humbel*, and whilst cases are to be assessed on their individual facts, Recital 34 specifies that the ECJ:

> has recognised that the characteristic of remuneration is absent in the case of activities performed, for no consideration, by the State or on behalf of the State in the context of its duties in the social, cultural, educational and judicial fields, such as courses provided under the national education system, or the management of social security schemes which do not engage in economic activity.

Whilst health care is, following the ECJ's approach, of necessity not included in this list, the directive states that the reimbursement of health-care fees should be dealt with in a separate legal instrument and not under the Services Directive (Recital 23). These exclusions from the scope of the directive are found in Article 2.

Following the suggestion that cross border provision of healthcare be dealt with in a separate legal instrument, the Commission, after much internal disagreement, produced a communication on an EU framework on the application of patients' rights in cross-border healthcare (COM (2008) 415) together with a draft directive (COM (2008) 414), the aim of which is ensuring a clear and transparent framework for the provision of cross-border health care within the EU, for those occasions where the care patients seek is provided in another Member State than in their home country. The aim of the directive is not to change the Member States' freedom in this area (that has already been eroded by the ECJ) but to facilitate cooperation. It is therefore interesting to note that this proposal was put forward on the basis of Article 95, although the Commission states that it respects the division of responsibilities in Article 152, which excludes harmonisation in public health. Apparently, the German government has already expressed concerns about the directive's treaty base. (On the scope of Article 95, see Chapter 16.) The directive has not yet been enacted, but has been discussed by the Council and put forward amendments to the Commission proposal. Whilst it is not certain what form the directive will take, the Council 'recommended that the Regulation on the coordination of social security systems (1408/71) should be supplemented by the Directive on cross-border healthcare and that a "third method" of reimbursement should be avoided', a reference to the ECJ's jurisprudence, and 'the ministers asked that Member States should be able to make the use of cross-border healthcare subject to prior authorisation or to apply the "gatekeeping" principle, for example by the attending physician' (PRES/08/358). It seems that whilst Member States accept that patients moving to receive medical care cannot be avoided, they are seeking to control the circumstances in which this may occur. Whether they will be successful is another matter, as within the Council there is much disagreement about the appropriate approach to take.

24.8 Conclusions

The general theme of the case law is that the ECJ has developed a number of mechanisms to extend rights for those who have moved to receive services, particularly public services, whether the purpose of the move was to receive those services or not. On one level we can commend this, as it supports the rights of individuals, either by making host states provide services without discrimination, as in *Cowan*, or by repatriating the cost, as in *Watts*. The case law is problematic in a number of respects. The distinction in treatment between education and health rests on uncertain foundations, as we have noted. Where the host Member State ends up paying for the service, arguably this is on the basis of European solidarity, though this does seem to be an incursion into an area of Member State competence. Perhaps in this field we will see, as we have seen elsewhere, the use of the 'real link test' to limit unfair advantage being taken of Member States where social provision is comparatively generous. It is the second situation which calls for more comment. Superficially, repatriation of costs might seem appropriate, as it is the state with which the beneficiary has the most connection (and presumably where the beneficiary has contributed in economic terms) which pays. There is a problem with this analysis. Essentially, the ECJ's approach favours individualistic choices which disturb systems based on scarcity, resource allocation, and solidarity. Further, as the level of competence, the ECJ's decision represents a considerable incursion in to sensitive Member State territory.

FURTHER READING

Cygan, A, 'Public healthcare in the European Union: Still a service of general interest?' (2008) 57(3) ICLQ 529.

Davies, G, 'Welfare as a service' (2002) 29 LIEI 27.

Woods, L, 'Scope of services I: Definitions' in *Free Movement of Goods and Services within the European Community* (Ashgate, 2004).

25

Free movement of persons: Limitations on grounds of public policy, public security, or public health

25.1 Introduction

The last few chapters have shown that the European Court of Justice (ECJ) has interpreted the treaty freedoms applying to persons widely. Nonetheless, as is the case with goods, there are some circumstances where other interests must be balanced against the right to free movement and non-discrimination on the grounds of nationality. We have seen that non-discriminatory measures may be justified on public-interest grounds during the application of the treaty freedom itself. There are specific exceptions to the non-discrimination principle in terms of access to jobs and to professions, as regards linguistic capability (see Article 2(2), Regulation 1612/68) and as regards public services (Article 39(4) as regards workers and Article 45 as regards services and establishment). Beyond these specific and limited provisions, the treaty permits a Member State to derogate from the treaty freedoms on the grounds of public policy, public security, and public health (Articles 39(3) and 46 EC). It is these latter provisions on which this chapter focuses. As with other derogation provisions, these articles have been interpreted narrowly.

One distinctive feature in this area is that the institutions enacted a directive, Directive 64/221, to delineate the scope of the derogation more clearly in relation to individuals. This directive has now been repealed and replaced by Chapter VI of the Citizenship Directive (Directive 2004/38/EC). Most of the case law relates to Directive 64/221, rather than the underlying treaty provisions, even though the directive does not apply in all circumstances. The Citizenship Directive, although not phrased in exactly the same terms as Directive 64/221, draws on it and the relevant jurisprudence heavily. It seems likely that the Citizenship Directive will be interpreted along the same lines as Directive 64/221.

A further significant feature is that any derogation needs to be interpreted in the light of individuals' fundamental rights. The ECJ even in its early jurisprudence recognised this. Over the years, the ECJ has, when considering the basis for exceptions to free movement and assessing their proportionality, taken into account the impact of human rights; not only the right to family life but also procedural rights. Additionally, the law in this area increasingly seems to be affected by the notion of European citizenship, as is most recently emphasised by the enactment of the Citizenship Directive, which is based on the concept of citizens' rights.

25.2 Scope of Directive 2004/38/EC and its relationship with treaty provisions

The exception provided by Articles 39(3) and 46 (ex 48(3) and 56) EC was originally implemented in Directive 64/221 to give substance to the rather vague and potentially catch-all provisions of the treaty. These provisions, should Lisbon come in to force, will be renumbered Articles 45(3), 52, and 63 of the Treaty on the Functioning of the European Union (TFEU) respectively. Directive 64/221 allowed for 'special measures concerning the movement and residence of foreign nationals which are justified on the grounds of public policy, public security and public health'. This general principle has been restated in Directive 2004/38/EC. Article 27(1) provides that 'Member States may restrict the freedom of movement and residence of Union citizens and their family members, irrespective of nationality, on grounds of public policy, public security or public health'.

Although the focal point of the provision remains the same, two points could be made about the changed wording. First, it is more honest, identifying that we are talking about the limitation of individuals' rights (contrast 'special measures concerning'). Secondly, the reference to 'foreign nationals', which distinguished between the nationals of one Member State and another, has been replaced by the reference to 'European citizens', as defined in the Citizenship Directive.

There are two aspects contained in this section of Directive 2004/38/EC. First it lays down the principles on which a state may refuse entry or residence to those who would otherwise be eligible, on the grounds of public policy, public security, or public health; and secondly, it lays down procedural safeguards which must be followed by the relevant authorities when they are seeking to exclude non-nationals on one of the permitted grounds.

25.2.1 'Restrictions'

Directive 64/221 applied to 'measures' taken by Member States. 'Measures' taken on the grounds of public policy, public security or public health were defined in *R v Bouchereau* (case 30/77) as any action affecting the rights of persons coming within the field of application of Article 39 EC to enter and reside freely in a Member State on the same conditions as apply to nationals of the host state. This description would still seem to be good law despite the change in terminology to 'restriction'.

25.2.2 Who benefits?

The directive applies to European citizens and their family members; their status as employed or self-employed or otherwise satisfying tests of economic sufficiency is irrelevant. It applies, however, only to restrictions on the *movement* and *residence* of *natural* persons. The general exceptions on the basis of public policy, public security, and public health do not allow for discrimination as regards access to or conditions of employment. Access to employment and social rights will be subject to the derogation provided under Article 2(2) of Regulation 1612/68 (linguistic knowledge) or Articles 39(4) (public services) or 45 (activities connected with official authority) or non-discriminatory rules in the public interest. Whilst the underlying treaty provisions may be relied on by legal persons, Directive 2004/38, as it covers citizens and their family members, does not apply to legal persons.

Interpretations of the concept of public policy delivered under Directive 64/221, and now Directive 2004/38/EC, which relate to the personal factors justifying discrimination, will not necessarily be appropriate to the public-policy exception applicable to undertakings under Article 46 EC. This has not always been recognised by the Court, which has tended to interpret Article 46 by reference to cases decided under Directive 64/221 (see, eg, Advocate-General Mancini's opinion and the Court's judgment in *Bond van Adverteerders* (case 352/85) noted in Chapter 22). Similar problems have arisen in the context of individuals' rights to receive health care in other Member States in which the Member State has sought to raise public health—that is, the provision of a public health-care system—as a justification. This is a different aspect of public health from that envisaged in ether Directive 64/221 or Directive 2004/38/EC. Nonetheless, it is possible for the underlying treaty provisions to be relied on where the situation falls outside the scope of the directive, as cross-border medical-care cases illustrate (*Geraets-Smits and Peerboom* (case C–157/99), discussed in Chapter 24; *DocMorris* (case C–322/01), discussed in Chapter 19).

Directive 64/221 did not apply to third-country nationals (TCNs) (save those of European Economic Area (EEA) countries), except to the extent that they formed part of a migrant EC national's family. In principle this has not changed with the introduction of Directive 2004/38/EC. We will see in Chapter 26 the steps that the institutions have taken to protect the rights of TCNs, especially those that are long-term residents in the EU.

25.2.3 Enforcement

Directive 64/221 provided a source of substantive and procedural rights for individuals, since all its main provisions were directly effective. It seems safe to assume that the relevant provisions in Directive 2004/38/EC will also be directly effective. The underlying treaty provisions are also capable of being relied on directly.

25.3 Substantive grounds for derogation

25.3.1 Public policy

The meaning and scope of the public-policy derogation was originally not clear but nonetheless potentially broad. In *Van Duyn v Home Office* (case 41/74) the Court held, on a reference from the English High Court, that the concept of public policy must be interpreted strictly; its scope cannot be determined unilaterally by Member States without being subject to control by the institutions of the Union. However, the Court conceded that the concept of public policy must vary from state to state; states must have an area of discretion within the limits defined by the treaty.

As the European integration project progressed, Member States' individual areas of discretion became narrower, a process which seems to have continued in the terms of the Citizenship Directive. This narrowing process can be seen even quite early on in the ECJ's jurisprudence in the rather stricter view in *Rutili v Ministre de l'Intérieur* (case 36/75), which arose in the context of an action by Rutili, an Italian and a noted political agitator, to annul a decision from the minister which restricted his activities to certain regions of France. The Court held that restrictions cannot be imposed on the right of a national of a Member State to enter the territory of another Member State, to stay there, and to move within it unless his presence constitutes a *genuine and sufficiently serious threat to public policy* ('une menace réelle et suffisamment grave pour l'ordre public'). This principle, the Court added, was an embodiment of the principles contained in the European Convention on Human Rights (ECHR) that no restrictions in the interests of national security or public safety shall be placed on the rights secured by Articles 8–11 of the Convention other than such as are *necessary* for the protection of those interests in a democratic society. All restrictions are subject to the proportionality principle.

The concept was narrowed even further in *R v Bouchereau* (case 30/77) where the Court added that the concept of public policy must always presuppose a genuine and sufficiently serious threat to the requirements of public policy *affecting one of the fundamental interests of society*. This case law has now been embodied in Directive 2004/38/EC. Article 27(2) states that the conduct of the individual which forms the basis of a public-policy derogation 'must represent a genuine, present and sufficiently serious threat affecting one of the fundamental interests of society'. This test introduces the requirement that there must be a present, or current threat, rather than a threat that has ceased to be (see, eg, *Calfa*, discussed below) or that might arise in the future. This temporal element resurfaces in the case law on spent convictions and in the discussion of 'personal conduct'. The threat must arise in addition to the perturbation of the social order that any infringement of the law involves.

In the early case law, it seemed that behaviour did not have to be illegal to be considered as falling within the public-policy derogation. Thus, in *Van Duyn v Home Office* (case 41/74) the claimant, Ms Van Duyn, a Dutch national, was refused entry into the UK on the grounds of public policy. She was seeking to enter the UK to take up employment with the Church of Scientology. The practice of scientology was not illegal in the UK but it was regarded as socially undesirable. The refusal was claimed to be on the basis of her personal conduct. Two questions were referred to the ECJ. First, can membership of an organisation count as 'personal conduct' within the meaning of Article 3(1) Directive 64/221? This point is discussed at 25.4 below. Secondly, if it can, must such conduct be illegal in order to provide grounds for exclusion on public policy grounds? With regard to the second question, the Court held that the conduct does not have to be illegal to justify exclusion of non-nationals, as long as the state has made it clear that it considers the activities in question to be 'socially harmful', and has taken administrative measures to counteract the activities. *Van Duyn* must now be read in the light of the more restrictive test advanced in *R v Bouchereau* (case 30/77); the activities in question must be sufficiently socially harmful to pose a genuine and sufficiently serious threat to the requirements of public policy affecting one of the fundamental interests of society.

The kind of evidence needed to prove that a particular activity is considered by the state to be sufficiently harmful to justify exclusion on the grounds of public policy was considered by the ECJ, in the context of many questions referred by the Liège District Court, in the case of *Adoui and Cornuaille v Belgium* (cases 115 and 116/81). Here two prostitutes were appealing against the Belgian authorities' refusal to grant them a residence permit in Belgium, where they were seeking to practise their arts. The Court held that Member States could not deny residence to non-nationals by reason of conduct that, when attributable to a state's own nationals, did not give rise to repressive measures or other genuine and effective measures to combat such conduct. Evidence of measures of this nature will have to be adduced to prove that the public-policy justification is genuine.

Directive 2004/38/EC, like Directive 64/221, lays down a number of circumstances in which measures taken on the grounds of public policy or public security will *not* be justified:

(a) They 'shall not be invoked to serve economic ends' (Article 27(1)). Here the directive makes explicit what was found to be implicit in cases under the derogating treaty provisions, such as Article 30 (ex 36) EC (post Lisbon Art 36 TFEU), in the context of goods. To allow an economic justification would clearly run counter to the fundamental aims of the treaty.

(b) 'Previous criminal convictions shall not *in themselves* constitute grounds for the taking of such measures' (Article 27(2), emphasis added). Thus under certain circumstances past criminal convictions may constitute sufficient grounds, but they will not necessarily do so. (See *R v Bouchereau* (case 30/77) and *Donatella Calfa* (case C–348/96), discussed below.) Certainly automatic deportation would seem unacceptable (see opinion of Advocate-General in *Commission v Germany* (case C–441/02)). Article 27(3) allows a host Member State to check the criminal record of a migrant EU citizen for the purposes of assessing whether an individual might constitute a threat, but the provision specifically states that a Member State cannot make such checks automatically.

(c) The expiry of the identity card or passport used by the person concerned to enter the host country and to obtain a residence permit does not justify expulsion from the host Member State (Article 15(2)). As was noted in *Procureur du Roi v Royer* (case 48/75), the right of residence does not depend on the possession of a residence permit, it merely provides proof of such a right, which derives from the Treaty itself. The same principle applies to identity cards and passports. As was established in *Watson* (case 118/75), a state may impose penalties for failure to comply with administrative formalities, provided the penalties are not disproportionate, but a failure to comply with such formalities can never provide grounds for deportation. (See also *Wijsenbeek* (case C–378/97), discussed in Chapter 21.)

It seems that the test for the use of the public-policy derogation used in respect of cases under the directive has also been applied in the context of Article 46 EC (post Lisbon, Art 52 TFEU) with regard to legal persons. For example, in *Commission v UK (Open Skies)* (case C–466/98), concerning the refusal to grant an operating licence to an airline on the basis that it constituted a threat to public policy, the ECJ applied the *Bouchereau* test. A similar tendency can be seen in relation to the other freedoms.

25.3.2 Public security

Although public security has long been identified as a separate head of derogation, there has been little specific discussion of this term; it tends to be considered with public policy. According to Article 27(2), and in the same way as for public policy, measures to protect public security must be based on the individual conduct of the person concerned. Individual conduct is discussed at 25.4 below. The limitations identified at 23.3.1(a)–(c) in relation to public policy apply also to public security in terms of the procedural guarantees available. It would seem also that the personal conduct test would also have to be satisfied. As we shall see (at 25.5.2.3 below), Directive 2004/38/EC has introduced a distinction between public policy and public security, but has given no guidance on determining the boundaries between the two categories. It seems that public security implies rather more serious conduct than that comprising public policy; presumably it would include, for example, terrorism.

25.3.3 Public health

Article 29(1) specifies that the only diseases justifying measures restricting freedom of movement are those 'with epidemic potential as defined by the relevant instruments of the World Health Organisation', as well as other infectious diseases or contagious parasitic diseases provided they are the subject of protection provisions applying to nationals of the host Member State. This is a narrower list than applied under the previous directive. In its earlier communication (COM (1999) 372), the Commission made the point that all the institutions have clearly stated that the free movement of persons with HIV/AIDS must be safeguarded. Further diseases occurring after a three-month period from the date of arrival cannot constitute grounds for expulsion. There is therefore a distinction between the public-health justification for expulsion and those based on public policy or public security, in that the latter two categories can be relied on at any point during the migrant's stay in the host Member State; whilst reliance on the public-health derogation is limited in time. Again, the host Member State has the right to investigate migrants, this time by requesting an individual to undergo a free medical examination. Such an examination cannot be required as a matter of course.

Note that the scope of public health under the treaty provisions is somewhat broader than the terms of Directive 2004/38/EC, being developed in parallel with the derogation in relation to goods, Article 30 (see, eg, *Kohll* (case C–158/96)). In addition to personal health, it includes protection against risks to public health and also arguments based on the need to provide a functioning health service (see Chapter 24).

25.4 Personal conduct

Measures taken on the grounds of public policy or public security must be based *exclusively* on the *personal conduct* of the individual concerned (Article 27(2)). This provision reflects the terms of Directive 64/221, Article 3(1), which it replaced; the case law under the old provision would seem to be relevant to our understanding of Article 27(2).

The ECJ distinguished between past and present association; past association cannot count as personal conduct; present association, being a voluntary act of the person concerned, can. Thus, resignation from a group considered undesirable or illegal would, in the absence of other evidence, suggest that such membership can no longer be taken into account by the relevant authorities. This approach would match the approach taken with regard to criminal convictions. As we have already seen, Article 27(2) Directive 2004/38/EC, replicating Article 3(2) Directive 64/221/EEC, expressly provides that previous criminal convictions shall not in themselves constitute grounds for measures taken on public-policy grounds. The same principle applies to current criminal convictions. In *Bonsignore v Oberstadtdirektor of the City of Cologne* (case 67/74), Bonsignore, an Italian worker living in Germany, bought a pistol in breach of German firearms law, and accidentally shot his brother. The action against his brother carried no punishment, but he was fined for unlawful possession of a firearm, and his deportation was ordered. The German authorities argued that his deportation was necessary as a general preventive measure to deter other immigrants from committing similar offences. The ECJ rejected this argument, holding that the concept of personal conduct expresses the requirement that a deportation order may only be made for breaches of the peace and public security that might be committed by the individual concerned. Thus deportation could not be based on reasons of a general preventive nature. This principle now finds expression in Directive 2004/38/EC. The second paragraph of Article 27(2) provides that justifications which 'are isolated from the particulars of the case or that rely on considerations of general prevention shall not be accepted'.

It should be noted that certain circumstances do permit Member States to take general preventative measures, notably measures connected with gatherings attended by large numbers of people, especially when the people come from different Member States. In its communication, the Commission suggests examples of such events: large sports events, rock concerts, and political demonstrations.

The conduct in *R v Bouchereau* (case 30/77) was more serious than in *Bonsignore*. Mr Bouchereau was a French national who took up employment in the UK in 1975. In June 1976 he was found guilty of unlawful possession of drugs. He had already pleaded guilty to a similar offence in January 1976, and had received a 12-month conditional discharge. In June 1976 the court (Marlborough Street Magistrates) wished to make a deportation order against him. He claimed this was contrary to what was then Article 48 (now Article 39) and Directive 64/221. One of the questions referred to the ECJ concerned Article 3(2) of Directive 64/221 and 'previous criminal convictions'. If they could not 'in themselves' constitute grounds for exclusion, when could they be taken into account? Were they relevant only insofar as they manifested a propensity to act in such a manner, contrary to public policy or public security? The Court held that the existence of previous convictions could only be taken into account as evidence of personal conduct constituting a *present* threat to the requirements of public policy, as showing a propensity to act in the same way again. However, past conduct alone *could* constitute a threat to the requirements of public policy. Thus, it would depend on the gravity of the conduct, past or present, whether it would in fact constitute a present threat to the requirements of public policy.

This point was re-emphasised in *Donatella Calfa* (case C–348/96), concerning a Greek rule which automatically required the expulsion—for life—of non-nationals who had been convicted of certain offences. Calfa was an Italian tourist who was convicted of offences relating to the possession of drugs. She appealed against her sentence on the basis that it was incompatible with her right to receive services under what is now Article 49 (ex 59). The ECJ held that her expulsion could only be based on personal conduct *besides* the commission of the offence. It seems that national authorities must thus look at the individual's conduct in addition to that which gave rise to the criminal offence. In any event, all rules must be proportionate, which an automatic life ban is not. Given the wording of Directive 2004/38/EC, it would seem this approach still applies.

The ECJ has also more recently held that Article 3 of Directive 64/221 precludes a national practice whereby national courts cannot take into account changes in factual circumstances when reviewing a decision to deport, especially where there has been a lengthy delay. The requirements of personal conduct and 'present threat' are not satisfied (*Oliveri* (case C–493/01)). Interestingly, this case was brought as a matter of interpretation of Article 3 of Directive 64/221, rather than under the procedural provisions (discussed at 25.6.3 below). Given the new directive also refers to personal conduct and incorporates the test of a present threat, a similar interpretation would apply to that provision too.

The requirement of 'personal conduct' has implications for the Schengen implementation system (see further Chapter 26). The Commission brought an action against Spain (*Commission v Spain* (case C–503/03)) for refusing entry to two TCNs, both of whom were married to migrant EU nationals. Spain refused entry automatically on the basis of information in the Schengen Information System entered by the German authorities. The ECJ held that, in the case of a migrant EU national's family member, a Member State must check the threat posed by the individual in the light of the *Bouchereau* test.

Since a denial of residence must be based exclusively on personal conduct, it follows that a worker who is entitled to residence cannot be refused entry or deported merely because the worker is involuntarily unemployed or unable to work through incapacity, even if the worker becomes a charge on public funds (see *Lubbersen v Secretary of state for the Home Department* [1984] 3 CMLR 77, Immigration Appeal Tribunal). The same applies to the worker's family. This accords with what was Directive 68/360 (see now Article 7(3) Directive 2004/38/EC and discussion in Chapter 21).

25.5 Types of measure

The original directive was silent as to the type of 'measure' that individual Member States would be permitted to take against foreign nationals. There are a range of options, for example registration requirements, though it would seem the most likely would be refusal of entry or expulsion. Case law has developed limitations in respect of both geographical and temporal considerations, driven by the concept of proportionality and, more recently, citizenship.

25.5.1 Partial restrictions

It was originally thought, following the *Rutili* decision (case 36/75), that the derogation operated only to justify a total ban on residence in a Member State rather than partial restrictions on the right of residence. Unsurprisingly, this ruling came in for a certain amount of criticism as an unnecessary restriction on Articles 39(3) and 46 of the EC Treaty. The derogation exists precisely in order to enable Member States to discriminate against non-nationals on limited and specific grounds. As the ECJ pointed out in *Van Duyn* (case 41/74), it is a principle of international law that states cannot deny rights of residence to their own nationals. To require a total ban where a partial ban would suffice is surely to impose on non-nationals greater restrictions than are necessary to protect the particular interest concerned. This issue was revisited in *Olazabal* (case C–100/01) in which the ECJ reviewed its ruling in *Rutili*. In contrast to Olazabal, who had been convicted of offences related to terrorism, Rutili was subject to restrictions because of political and trades-union activities. In *Rutili*, the national referring court had not been sure that national law allowed the adoption of the national measure in question. In *Olazabal*, the national court was clear that Olazabal's activities were of such a serious nature that they justified his deportation. The ECJ concluded that a Member State would not be precluded from imposing limitations on the right to residence within the territory of that Member State provided that:

(a) such action is justified by reasons of public order or public security based on the individual's conduct

(b) the only alternative course of action, given the seriousness of that conduct, would consist of a measure prohibiting the individual from residing in the whole of the national territory

(c) the conduct which the Member State concerned wishes to prevent gives rise, in the case of its own nationals, to genuine and effective measures designed to combat it (para 45).

This approach is reflected in Article 22 of the Citizenship Directive which provides that limitations may only be imposed on migrants where the same restrictions apply to the Member State's own nationals.

25.5.2 Expulsion

There are two main problems in this area: expulsion in addition to a criminal penalty; and life-long bans. Case law has sought to limit the Member States' power in such circumstances by use of the doctrine of proportionality and by reading the relevant provisions in the light of the requirements of citizenship. Directive 2004/38/EC incorporates this approach.

25.5.2.1 *Expulsion in addition to a criminal penalty*

Bonsignore indicates that deportation cannot be required in addition to a criminal penalty as a matter of course; this would offend against the requirement of personal conduct and, as in the case of *Calfa*, proportionality. Additionally, there are procedural rights concerning the requirement of temporal proximity between the decision to deport and the deportation itself (see 25.4). These concerns now find their expression in Article 33.

25.5.2.2 *Permanent exclusion*

If a Member State has grounds for restricting the right of free movement, this does not mean that it can permanently exclude someone. Such an approach could, as we have seen in *Calfa*, be disproportionate. Article 27(2) now specifies that any measures shall be proportionate. Article 32 now gives the right to apply for the lifting of an exclusion order where there has been a material change in circumstances.

25.5.2.3 *Protection against expulsion*

An innovation introduced by Directive 2004/38/EC is Article 28 which imposes limitations on a Member State's freedom to expel an EU national. Article 28(1) provides that in deciding whether or not to expel an individual, a Member State must take into account factors such as how long the individual has resided on its territory, the age of the person concerned, state of health, family and economic situation, as well as the links with the country of origin. These conditions are the types of consideration that the ECJ has highlighted as being required by respect for family life under Article 8 ECHR (see case C–482/01, *Orfanopoulos*, citing *Boultif v Switzerland*). Many of these factors reflect a graduated level of protection awarded to migrants, based on their level of integration into the host Member State, which we will also see in Chapter 24 regarding citizenship rights.

Article 28 then goes on to identify three specific circumstances: the position of those who have a right of permanent residence (Article 28(2)); those who have resided in the host Member State for the previous ten years (Article 28(3)(a)); and minors (Article 28(3)(b)). For those falling within the scope of Article 28(2), Member States may only take an expulsion decision on serious grounds of public policy or public security. For the other two categories, an expulsion decision may only be made on 'imperative grounds of public security'; seemingly public policy will not justify such a decision.

25.6 **Procedural rights**

Directive 2004/38/EC provides extensive procedural safeguards for parties seeking to assert rights of entry or residence in Member States, based on the provisions in Directive 64/221. The rights in Directive 64/221 were directly effective, and it is highly likely that the equivalent provisions in Directive 2004/38/EC are also directly effective. In the light of this, any decision issued in violation of these rights may be challenged as contrary to EU law.

25.6.1 **Temporary residence**

Directive 64/221 specified that:

> a person awaiting a decision to grant or refuse a first residence permit in a Member State must be allowed to remain temporarily in that state pending that decision. The decision must be taken as soon as possible and not more than six months from the date of application. [Article 5(1).]

Given that Union citizens no longer have to apply for a residence permit, there is no equivalent provision in Directive 2004/38/EC. Instead, Article 30(3) requires the Member State to specify the time limit within which a person must leave the territory, which save in cases of emergency (duly substantiated) may not be less than one month, and Article 31(2) provides that, where an individual appeals and applies for a suspension of the removal order, such a person will not be required to remove themselves from the territory whilst the matter is pending, save in limited, specified circumstances. By contrast to Directive 64/221 (Article 7), there are no specific time limits contained in Directive 2004/38/EC.

25.6.2 Reasons for decisions

The person concerned shall be informed in writing of any decision made under Article 27, in a manner so that he or she is able to understand not only the decision but its implications. Further, the person must be informed, precisely and in full, of the grounds of public policy, public security, or public health upon which the decision taken in his or her case is based, unless this is contrary to the interests of the security of the state (Article 30). Any notification must inform the person of where, when, and how an appeal may be lodged (Article 30(3)).

In developing the provisions of Directive 64/221, Directive 2004/38/EC seems to be incorporating the jurisprudence of the ECJ in cases such as *Rutili*. The Court held in *Rutili* (case 36/75) that the authority making the decision must give the applicant a precise and comprehensive statement of the ground for the decision, to enable the applicant to take effective steps to prepare his or her defence. The Commission in its communication made the point that the duty to give reasons applies also to decisions regarding the applications for visas by family members who are TCNs.

25.6.3 Remedies: Rights of defence

Directive 2004/38/EC amends the format of the rights of the defence. Directive 94/221 provided for a right of access to remedies by comparison with the position of nationals of the host Member State (Article 8), but then also provided a minimum guarantee that a decision to deport must be reviewed by a competent authority (Article 9). A certain amount of case law arose about the scope and inter-relationship of the two provisions, which may be of historic interest only given the changes introduced by the Citizenship Directive. Article 31 of the Citizenship Directive provides:

> The persons concerned shall have access to judicial and, where appropriate, administrative redress procedures in the host Member State to appeal against or seek review of any decision taken against them on the grounds of public policy, public security or public health.

Interestingly, the phraseology represents a change in that individuals under the new system are given a right of access to a judicial remedy and possibly an administrative remedy. The matter is not one of comparison, as under former Article 8, nor of merely showing that a competent authority has reviewed the decision.

Although the terms of the two sets of provisions are different, a number of points from the case law on the old system might well be applicable to the new. Note that neither system specified the precise nature of the remedies to be available; this is consonant with the principle of national procedural autonomy (see Chapter 8). The ECJ noted, in relation to Article 9, Directive 64/221, that the provisions incorporated the minimum requirements of natural justice. According to the ECJ, they therefore called for a broad interpretation. Whether a review of the case law truly reveals a high level of protection or not, this principle would seem to apply to Article 31, Directive 2004/38.

In *Royer* (case 48/75), the ECJ held that Member States could not execute a deportation order without giving the migrant the chance to avail himself of the right to the remedy granted under Article 8, Directive 64/221. The substance of Directive 2004/38/EC reflects this. Not only should a Member State not normally allow less than a month for an individual to leave (Article 30(3)), but Article 31(2) allows for an individual to remain on the territory pending the outcome of the appeal, subject to certain specified exceptions (see also Article 31(4)).

There were two aspects to the case law on Article 9, Directive 64/221: the class of people to whom it applied; and the scope of the rights granted.

The ECJ had to consider the question of the beneficiaries of procedural rights in *MRAX* (case C–459/99). In this case the Belgian government argued that Article 9 did not apply to the TCNs who were members of a migrant workers family, but who had entered the host Member State illegally. Given the importance of Directive 64/221, and particularly these procedural articles, for guaranteeing the rights set out in Article 6 and 13 ECHR, however, the ECJ held that the illegality of their original entry to the host Member State could not deprive these individuals of the protection granted by Article 9. As the ECJ pointed out, to require an individual to be in possession of a valid identity document or visa would rob the procedural guarantees of much of their effectiveness. A similar argument could be made in respect of the guarantees in Articles 30–1, Directive 2004/38.

As regards the scope of the rights, the ECJ seems also to have been influenced by the need to ensure a fair trial and the right to an effective remedy contained in the ECHR, which are surely still relevant under the new system. Under Article 9, Directive 64/221, as the Court pointed out in *Rutili* (case 36/75), the person concerned must at the very least be able to exercise his or her rights of defence before a competent authority, which must not be the same as that which adopted the measure which restricted the person's freedom. Principles of independence must inform an assessment of the appropriateness of bodies providing redress under Article 31, Directive 2004/38; see further below.

In *R v Secretary of state for the Home Department, ex parte Santillo* (case 131/79), Santillo, an Italian, had been convicted in the UK of a number of crimes of violence including rape, buggery, and indecent assault. He was sentenced to eight years in gaol, with a recommendation for deportation at the end of his sentence. Nearly five years later the Home Secretary made a deportation order against him. He applied for judicial review to quash this decision. Two issues were raised in the proceedings. First, whether the trial judge's recommendation was an 'opinion from a competent authority', as required by Article 9(1), Directive 64/221; and secondly, if so, whether a lapse of time between the issuing of this 'opinion' and the making of the order could deprive the judge's recommendation of its status as an 'opinion' under Article 9(1). The ECJ, on a reference for interpretation from the English High Court, held that the trial judge's recommendation did amount to an 'opinion' within

Article 9(1); but that the safeguard provided by Article 9 could only be a real one if that opinion were sufficiently proximate in time to the decision recommending deportation, to ensure that the factors justifying deportation still existed at the time when the order was made. A change of heart or political climate could mean that the public policy justification had ceased to exist. This safeguard has been enacted by Article 33(2), Directive 2004/38, which provides that where an expulsion order is enforced more than two years after it was issued, the Member State is under an obligation to check that the individual concerned is 'currently and genuinely a threat to public policy or public security' and to assess whether there has been any 'material change' in circumstances since the expulsion order was issued.

Like its predecessor, the Citizenship Directive gives no definition of what appropriate remedies might be. Jurisprudence in respect of Article 9(2), Directive 64/221 was considered in *R v Secretary of state for the Home Department, ex parte Gallagher* (case C–175/94), with particular reference to what could constitute a competent authority and the scope of the information regarding the appeal body that was required to be given to the applicant. Gallagher had been convicted in Ireland for the possession of rifles for unlawful purposes. He subsequently went to the UK and took up employment there. He was arrested and deported. On arrival in Ireland he challenged the deportation decision as unlawful, and was interviewed in Dublin. His interviewer gave no name and no information concerning the grounds for his expulsion. At his request his case was reconsidered by the Home Secretary, but the deportation decision was not reversed. The ECJ found that the matter fell within Article 9(2), but did not specify how the competent authority should be appointed, nor what its composition should be. It was nonetheless essential that it should be independent of the authority empowered to take the measure concerning deportation, and that the person concerned should be able to submit his or her defence. There was no need to notify the claimant of the identity of the authority as long as the national court was in a position to determine whether it was impartial. These questions were left to the national court to decide. Although one might suggest the level of protection awarded in *Gallagher* was low and perhaps driven by political sensitivities, the underlying principles regarding independence and impartiality as touchstones for determining whether procedural safeguards have been satisfied must remain. Article 31(3) further specifies the scope of the jurisdiction of the appeal bodies. It provides that:

> the redress procedures shall allow for an examination of the legality of the decision, as well as of the facts and circumstances on which the proposed measure is based. They shall ensure that the decision is not disproportionate, particularly in view of the requirements laid down in Article 28.

It seems, following *R v Secretary of state for the Home Department, ex parte Shingara* (cases C–65 and 111/95), that where an individual who has been refused admission to a Member State, reapplies for admission to a country after a reasonable length of time (in *Shingara* approximately three years), the procedural safeguards in Articles 8–9, Directive 64/221 would apply anew to that reapplication. Individuals expressly have the right to apply to have exclusion orders lifted under Article 32. It is submitted that following the *Shingara* reasoning, they too would benefit from procedural rights, although Article 32(2) states that such persons do not have the right of entry to the territory of a Member State while their application is being considered.

25.7 Conclusions

It can be seen that derogation from the free movement of people has common themes with the derogation from the free movement of goods. Both sets of derogation are interpreted narrowly, with Member States' actions being closely scrutinised. In this context the interpretation of personal conduct has been of great significance in limiting general actions by Member States against groups of EU migrants on the basis of their nationality. Another important aspect of the case law in this area has been the Court's interpretation of the procedural guarantees contained in the second part of the directive, which is clearly linked with the guarantees to a fair trial contained in the ECHR (on fundamental rights in the EU, see Chapter 6). Since *Donatella Calfa*, it now seems likely that the scope of the derogations will also have to be understood in the light of the impact of European citizenship, again constraining Member States' freedom in this area. In this respect the terms of the new directive do not represent a break with past practice, but rather constitute a codification of that jurisprudence.

FURTHER READING

Connor, TC, 'Migrant community nationals: Remedies for refusal of entry by Member States' (1998) 28 EL Rev 157.

Furse, M and Nash, S, 'Free movement, criminal law and fundamental rights in the European Community' [1997] JR 148.

Hall, S, 'The European Convention on Human Rights and public policy exceptions to the free movement of workers under the EEC Treaty' (1991) 16 EL Rev 466.

Handoll, J, *Free Movement of Persons in the European Union* (J Wiley and Son, 1995), Ch 7.

O'Keeffe, D, 'Practical difficulties in the application of Article 48 of the EEC Treaty' (1982) 19 CML Rev 35.

Van Overbeek, PM, 'Aids/HIV infection and the free movement of persons in the European Economic Community' (1990) 27 CML Rev 791.

Woods, L, *Free Movement of Goods and Services within the European Community* (Ashgate, 2004), Ch 12.

26

The area of freedom, security, and justice: EU home affairs law and policy

26.1 Introduction

The European Union's stated goal for its activities in relation to home affairs is the creation of an 'area of freedom, security and justice' in Europe. This chapter will seek to do the following: first, to set out the historical development of home affairs law in the Union; secondly, to give detailed consideration to the Union's laws on immigration and asylum; thirdly, to set out the legal framework and principles surrounding the Union's criminal-justice policies. There are also two underlying themes that will be considered. These are the assessment of the degree of protection given to fundamental rights by the Union in its home-affairs policies; and also the consideration of the extent to which the legal regime found in these more-sensitive fields is less supra-national (and hence affords the Member States more power) than that which operates in Community law.

26.2 Historical Development

26.2.1 The place of home affairs in EU law

As we have already seen, the European Union began life as a largely *economic* project. Despite the more ambitious political aims of achieving a unified Europe, the original EC Treaty focused upon the creation of the internal market. There were good pragmatic reasons for the narrow focus; achieving agreement on more controversial issues like policing, immigration, or the administration of justice would have been difficult. Member States were also reluctant to give up their sovereign powers in such areas. As the single-market project progressed, broader issues that were closely linked to economic development, such as environmental protection and social security for workers, began to be incorporated into the Union's policy–making. In the 1980s and 1990s governments became more concerned about non-economic issues with trans-European dimensions such as organised crime, terrorism, drug-trafficking, asylum, and immigration. There had been a growing degree of ad hoc collaboration between Member States in such areas, but it was only relatively recently that the Union began to acquire formal legal powers in these more politically sensitive fields.

26.2.2 The acquisition by the European Union of powers over home affairs

It was the Maastricht Treaty (TEU) in 1993 that created the first clear legal basis for the Union to act in relation to home affairs. Even then, Member States were careful to ensure that home affairs would not be subject to the same degree of integration and loss of sovereignty as they had experienced in relation to the internal market. As we shall see, this resulted in methods of decision-making in relation to home affairs which entail a reduced role for the more pan-European institutions of Commission, European Court of Justice and European Parliament. Power has remained concentrated in the Council of the European Union, the institution which reflects to a greater degree the perceived national interests of the governments of the Member States. Although this position is gradually shifting, home affairs has therefore remained a field typified by much looser intergovernmental methods than that of mainstream European law.

Even though the Member States until recently retained a veto over Union lawmaking, a considerable body of law has been developed in the field of home affairs. This is particularly the case in relation to the immigration and refugee status of non-citizens of the Union (whom we shall refer to as third-country nationals (TCNs)). For this group of persons we can say that the basic minimum standards governing their right to enter, stay and move within the Member States of the Union are now found in European Union law rather than national law. Furthermore, in 2004, immigration and asylum became incorporated into the first pillar and thereby powerful roles were assigned to the European Parliament and European Court of Justice (ECJ). By contrast, the other main area of home-affairs policy—policing and criminal justice—has produced less by way of concrete legislation. This is partly because policing cooperation tends to be more executive in nature rather than legislative. Police forces seek to coordinate their actions through Union institutions but not to pass laws as such. Furthermore the institutional architecture in relation to policing has remained more intergovernmental. Decisions are still taken under the second pillar of the TEU (see Chapters 1 and 3) and require unanimity. The proposed Lisbon Treaty reforms, if passed, will however bring policing and judicial matters into the mainstream of what is currently Community decision-making.

In this Chapter we shall thus focus upon the more substantial body of law in relation to immigration and asylum. We will however also mention some important issues of legal principle raised by Union lawmaking in relation to policing and criminal justice.

26.2.3 The need to respect fundamental rights

One crucial theme that runs throughout the whole field of European Union home affairs is that of legal accountability and protection of fundamental rights. Unlike the more economic focus of the internal market hitherto considered, the expulsion of vulnerable refugees or the arrest and prosecution of suspects puts Union law into more obvious potential conflict with fundamental human rights. There are clear dangers that, in moving away from national towards supra-national action, proper checks and balances on police and immigration officials may be neglected. This may be exacerbated through the Union lawmaking process itself which are unduly secretive and undemocratic. There may be few political incentives to protect the rights of 'outsiders' such as alleged criminals or non-EU citizens. There are thus dangers that standards of human rights protection fall to the level of the 'lowest' Member State. Information may be exchanged and action taken through remote executive agencies that are not open to scrutiny. The move to supra-nationalism may also make it harder to ensure that individuals have ready access to judicial remedies that previously were clearly located in the national legal order. In short, supra-nationalism in home affairs provides much greater dangers for individual rights than almost any other area of Union policy. This is particularly so given the lack of a binding Bill of Rights within EU law. We have already seen (Chapter 6) that the European Court of Justice has previously recognised the risk of a protection gap and developed general principles of EU law to fill it. Thus the Court has drawn upon the European Convention on Human Rights (ECHR), general international law norms, and national constitutional traditions to protect human rights where these are threatened by the Union institutions or the Member States. These principles will be of still greater importance in the new area of home affairs.

One further concern as regards judicial protection is the delay in obtaining decisions from the ECJ where references are made to it. In cases involving individual liberty or deportation, delay may have serious consequences. In 2008 the Rules of Procedure of the ECJ were amended to include Article 104b which permits an expedited urgent procedure to be used in matters arising in relation to justice and home affairs. As a result cases are heard within a few weeks. For an example see *Rinau* (C–195/08 PPU) in which child-custody proceedings were expedited so as avoid the child being wrongly kept from her parental guardian.

26.2.4 **The area of freedom, security, and justice**

The previous rather disparate home-affairs activities of the Union were eventually grouped together by the Treaty of Amsterdam (ToA) under the theme of the need to create an area of 'freedom, security and justice' within Europe. This label was an attempt to provide a grand positive vision (rather like the creation of the internal market) behind various initiatives that had been developed on a piecemeal and pragmatic basis. These ranged from common visa systems for TCNs to police cooperation in combating drug trafficking and organised crime; from mutual recognition of arrest warrants to enforcement of freezing orders. The range of matters covered is not totally logical or complete. It represents the topics over which Member States have felt able to agree to closer cooperation. The one common thread noted by the preamble to the Treaty on European Union (TEU) is the need for Member States to 'facilitate the free movement of persons, while ensuring the safety and security of their peoples'. This is a reference to the link between the removal of border controls inherent in the internal market and the need to provide alternative guarantees for Member States against a range of threats. This said, the Member States have given only limited powers to the Union to achieve these goals. There is in no sense a European Union interior ministry with comprehensive powers over policing, criminal procedure, sentencing, prisons, immigration control, and so forth. In fact, the legal and institutional structure relating to the area of freedom, security, and justice is confusing and ambiguous. As noted above, some elements of home affairs, particularly migration issues, have passed to the first pillar (the Community). This means the Commission (through the Director-General (DG) Justice, Freedom, and Security) proposes legislation and the co-decision system applies, thus giving equal power to the Parliament and Council. There is also now a European border-control agency called Frontex that supports Member State immigration control over the EU borders (see 26.3.5 below). By contrast, policing and criminal justice are largely the preserve of the Council of the Union in its justice and home affairs (JHA) incarnation. Here the various interior Ministers make laws under the more opaque and less democratic second-pillar procedures (those in the JHA). These laws are declared by Article 34 TEU not to be directly effective. Implementation of these measures thus remains largely a matter at the discretion of the Member States free from the normal enforcement mechanisms of EC law (see Chapters 5 and 9).

26.3 The migration of TCNs and the need for European Union powers

TCNs are relatively new as subjects of mainstream EC law. Apart from the family members of EU citizen migrants who are permitted to move and reside in other Member States under Directive 2004/38 (see Chapter 21) and certain country-specific agreements, EU law had very little to say about the immigration of such persons. They did not feature in the original EEC Treaty and still do not have treaty rights as such (all their rights stem from secondary legislation). In fact, for many years, there were no powers to legislate in relation to immigration and asylum of non-EU citizens. Immigration powers over such persons, a powerful symbol of national sovereignty, were essentially reserved to Member States. However pressure for completion of a borderless internal market had been growing since the 1980s. This required a common approach to the migration of TCNs in order to allow removal of internal border controls between Member States. In effect, there had to be a system of deemed permission to enter set up for all migrants.

The politically sensitive nature of the issue initially meant the Union did not act but rather separate intergovernmental action led to the Schengen Treaty of 1985. Britain, Ireland, and Denmark did not participate in this treaty which created a framework outside the EU system for most continental Member States to collaborate on migration issues. The treaty was followed in 1990 by the Schengen Convention that created a common short-stay-visa system and permitted internal movement of TCNs across borders between participating states. As a quid pro quo, the Convention also better facilitated participating states' policing of the external border through establishing both a common database of persons who should be excluded on security grounds and agreed standards on policing the external borders so as to reduce the numbers of irregular migrants. Security was therefore a key feature of European supra-national policy on migration even before the Union itself acquired powers in this field. A very detailed body of rules, institutions and procedures forming the Schengen *acquis* was set up during the 1990s.

The ToA finally gave the Union legislative power over migration from 1999 but the Member States were sensitive to loss of control and initially conceded only a consultative role to the European Parliament. Since 2004, the Parliament has had an equal role in legislation in these fields under the co-decision procedure. In addition, under Article 68 EC Treaty, the ECJ can only receive references from national courts against which there is no judicial remedy. This is in contrast to the standard procedure under Article 234 EC Treaty under which *any* national court or tribunal can make a reference (see Chapter 10). Furthermore, Article 68(2) excludes the Court's jurisdiction to rule on certain border measures taken by the Union to protect law and order or internal security. As a result there have been few cases heard by the Court in the immigration and asylum field. There is also considerable concern that this unique prohibition on references by lower courts means that the rule of law and fundamental rights may be imperilled because the ECJ is unable to give rulings on questions involving vulnerable groups such as refugees. Only cases that are taken all the way up the judicial hierarchy, which take time and money, will result in a reference and ruling from the ECJ.

Alongside completion of the internal market through incorporating the Schengen *acquis* in the Union system, the main pragmatic reason for the Union taking these powers has been to gain a higher degree of control over TCNs' migration than was possible with national regulation. The immigration policy of each Member State bears upon the others, particularly, because of the removal of internal EU borders. Geography also permits legal or illegal migration across Europe once a foothold has been obtained in any Member State. The framework set out in Title IV Articles 61–4 EC Treaty required minimum standards in respect of asylum and measures in respect of immigration but said little about the substantive content and direction of the new EU powers over migration.

26.3.1 The Tampere programme

The meeting of the heads of state at the Tampere European Council in 1999 proved to be a crucial occasion for the setting of the Union's objectives in the field of migration control. The programme agreed at Tampere required the adoption of common policies in relation to refugee protection based upon the 1951 Refugee Convention, strong measures to prevent irregular migration through the Union external border and a clear commitment to better integration of long-term residents based upon approximation of their status to that of EU citizens. The years since have however seen a political climate that has been antagonistic towards immigration and asylum. Concern has been heightened by concerns over foreign links to terrorism following the 11 September 2001 attacks in the United States and then later atrocities in Madrid and London. Security and exclusion have thus been key features of the Union agenda on migration. By the same token, there has been ongoing concern that segregation, racism, and xenophobia have fuelled extremism within migrant communities in Europe. The legislative programme that has emerged since Tampere has thus reflected a complex set of, sometimes contradictory, political objectives: humanitarianism; policing and public order concerns; economic self-interest; and social or cultural integration.

Any assessment of the Union's lawmaking in this area is complex. We can identify four reasons for this complexity. First, there were already diverging national migration laws governing most of the topics that have now become part of EU law. Thus the extent to which EU law has improved on the previous position depends upon the country of comparison. Secondly, there are important international human rights conventions by which Member States are bound by in this area. The most important are the 1951 Refugee Convention and 1950 ECHR. Because these were signed before the EEC Treaty, they override any contrary obligation. This is as a result of Article 307 EC Treaty which states that 'rights and obligations arising from agreements concluded between one or more Member States . . . and one or more third countries shall not be affected by this Treaty'. EU migration law has attempted to comply with and implement these treaties but there are areas of possible conflict. Thirdly, EU migration policy has been to harmonise national laws completely, but in several areas Member States resisted this. Thus, much of the Union's legislation sets minimum standards only. These reflect the lowest standards amongst the Member States' previous laws. Therefore we have three overlapping sets of rules; national, international, and European. This means it is not always clear which rule applies in any particular case. Finally, Ireland, Denmark, and the UK are only bound by measures that they opt into, pursuant to protocols annexed to the ToA. In broad terms, these three countries have opted in to measures on asylum and illegal immigration but not those giving immigration rights.

26.3.2 Immigration rights and integration

One clear message from Tampere was the moral and political need to ensure that established resident migrants were given strong immigration rights to promote their integration into their host communities. There remained however disagreement about how far such migrants should be given exactly equal rights to nationals and/or EU-citizen migrants. Nevertheless European states had concluded that insecure 'guest worker' statuses (as practised, for example, in Germany during the 1960s toward millions of Turkish workers) should not be allowed. Such workers were only ever given temporary permits and were thus always vulnerable to expulsion however long they had remained in their host state. Their status was viewed in purely economic terms as a reserve of labour to be tapped or shut off as required by the economy rather than as human beings with possibly deep attachments to their host nation. Also, in terms of the internal market in labour, the Member States accepted that there should be a more level playing field with each state providing similar levels of immigration status to long-term residents. This would render each Member State equally attractive as a destination for migrant workers. The Union has, however, no power to alter sometimes very restrictive national citizenship laws regarding who can become a citizen of a Member State. Thus there was no possibility of requiring Member States to naturalise long-term residents. This would, after all, have been the simplest and most direct route for giving them equal status. The status of citizen of the EU is itself dependent upon acquiring citizenship of a Member State. This left long-term resident TCNs in a vulnerable position.

26.3.2.1 *The Long-term Residents Directive*

One way forward was a more secure immigration status derived from EU law. This led to the passing of Directive 2003/109/EC on the Status of Long-term Residents (OJ [2004] L 16/44) based on Article 63 EC, which is the key measure in this field. It provides permanent residence for persons who have resided legally in a Member State for five years (Article 4). This is however made conditional upon proving that they have stable and regular resources sufficient to maintain themselves and their family members without social assistance from the state and also sickness insurance to cover all risks normally covered in the Member State concerned (Article 5). There are thus important differences between EU citizens (and their families) and TCNs. We note four main differences in particular. It will be recalled that, under Directive 2004/38 EU citizens acquire the right of permanent residence after five years without, once they have satisfied this criterion, having to show they will be self-sufficient (Article 16 Citizenship Directive, see Chapter 21). Furthermore, Member States are entitled to impose 'integration conditions' on TCNs as a condition of acquiring permanent residence status (Article 5(2) Long Term Residents Directive). The nature of these conditions is not spelled out in the directive but would include matters like passing tests in the native language or cultural knowledge. Furthermore, TCNs who have been residing as students or under humanitarian/refugee protection cannot gain rights under the directive (Article 3(2)). Finally, family members of long-term residents are only allowed to acquire permanent residence if the TCN has sufficient resources to support them. This is not the case for the family of EU citizens under Directive 2004/38.

Granting a right of permanent residence in the first instance may also be denied on the grounds of public policy or public security but, importantly, not due to economic considerations such as the level of unemployment (Article 6). In such cases Member States must weigh up the threat posed by the person as against their length of residence and other links with the country of residence but there are no further constraints on their discretion to refuse. Thus before a long-term resident is formally given permanent residence they are more vulnerable to expulsion. By contrast, after a permanent residence permit has been issued Article 12 gives only a more restricted power to withdraw such a resident permit when the migrant is an 'actual and sufficiently serious threat to public policy or public security'. In this case the proportionality exercise requires weighing up matters such as duration of residence, age, consequences for the person and family members, and links with other countries. There must be judicial redress and legal aid must be given on the same terms as for nationals. These provisions reflect standards found in the case law of the European Court of Justice in relation to expulsion of EU citizens (see, eg, example *Bouchereau* (C–30/77), and Chapter 25). In this sense the directive provides a high level of security of immigration status for long-term resident TCNs.

Apart from permanent residence in the host Member State, the directive confers other important rights. Article 11 requires Member States to grant equal treatment with nationals as regards a broad range of matters: access to employment and self-employment, along with remuneration and conditions; education and training, including study grants; social security, social assistance, and social protection; tax benefits; and freedom of association and free access to the entire territory of the host state. This is an important and extensive package of rights, close to that given to EU citizens under Directive 2004/38 Article 24 (see Chapter 24). It does, however, mean that in principle only the entitlements listed are subject to equal treatment. Other benefits may be denied such as those found to fall within the broad concept of 'social advantages' developed by the ECJ in relation to Article 7(2) of Regulation 1612/68. Article 11(4) also allows Member States a power to restrict equal treatment in relation to social assistance and protection (but not social security) to 'core benefits'. This term is not defined but the preamble to the directive says that these must include income support, and assistance for persons who are ill, pregnant, in need of long-term care or require parental assistance. Such a restriction to core benefits again suggests that the equal treatment principle is not as strongly protected for TCNs as for EU citizens.

In keeping with the idea of creating a internal market, permanent resident TCNs are given a right to reside in another Member State other than their host for work, studies, or any other purpose (Article 14). This is a significant mobility right but again it is not unconditional. The migrant must show they and their family are self-sufficient (Article 15). The directive also importantly allows the second Member State power to derogate completely from the right by maintaining systems of quotas on TCNs. This could render the right illusory for some Member States if the quota was set at zero or at a very low level. In times of unemployment, this seems likely to be a serious issue. Thus again, free movement rights are less extensive for TCNs than EU citizens, for whom economic factors cannot justify exclusion. Furthermore, preference can be given to EU citizens and other residents over TCNs in access to employment (Article 14(3)). This is despite the fact that the Article 11 equal treatment right generally applies in the second Member State. Finally, a more limited range of family members (compared to EU citizens under Directive 2004/38) of the permanent resident can accompany them to the second Member State (Article 16).

Thus we can see the directive goes a good way to meeting the Tampere objective of providing nearly equal rights for aliens who are highly integrated but there are significantly less expansive rights in some key areas. Some important rights, like the right to migrate to a second Member State, are conditional upon the labour market or social policies of Member States. It is not obvious why this should be so for persons who may have lived within the Union for many decades contributing to society, taxation, and national income. The shortage of persons of working age within Europe suggests that attracting migration will remain an issue for years to come. The directive provides some incentives for migrants to remain in Europe but is not equivalent to the full status of EU citizenship. Nevertheless, for the many millions of long-term migrant workers who have been unable or chosen not to naturalise, the directive is a significant step towards their greater security and integration. It removes the ability of the Member States to withdraw residence on economic grounds and effectively ends the possibility of guest-worker systems being reintroduced. It is thus important both as a practical measure for immigrants and as a political expression of a positive European commitment towards resident foreigners.

26.3.2.2 *The Family Reunification Directive*

We should also note the other key immigration instrument, the Family Reunification Directive 2003/86 (OJ [2003] L 251/12), based on Article 63(3)(a) EC, which gives rights to non-EU citizens to join their family in the Union. The sponsor must hold a residence permit of at least one year validity (Article 3) but does not need to be a long-term resident. The range of family members that have the right to be admitted is more limited than for EU citizens under Directive 2004/38 (which permits adult children, grandparents and certain other dependents to accompany the migrant). For TCNs, by contrast, only the spouse and minor children must be admitted (Article 4(1)). The directive unsurprisingly confirms that the Member States have powers to refuse entry and residence on public policy, security, or health grounds (Article 6). More problematically, the directive permits derogation in the case of children aged over 12 who have spent some time living apart from the rest of the family. In these cases, some Member States were concerned that such children might be difficult to integrate, being older and thus, allegedly, less adaptable to a new culture. The directive therefore permits Member States to subject such children to tests, such as language examinations, to see if they meet integration conditions. It also allows Member States to require applications from minor children to be submitted before they reach the age of 15 (Article 4(6)). Finally, Member States were also permitted to require a sponsor to have been resident for two years before allowing family re-union (Article 8). Thus the Family Reunification Directive illustrated the limited extent to which some Member States were prepared exhaustively to harmonise this field. The Council agreed to pass the directive in this form, which potentially allows Member States to keep older children separated from their families.

These provisions restricting family reunion were challenged by the European Parliament on human rights grounds in a case before the Grand Chamber of the Court, *Parliament v Council of the European Union* (case C–540/03). It will be recalled that the ECJ can judicially review European legislation to see that it accords with the ECHR (see *Bosphorus Airways v Ireland* (No 45036/98) discussed Chapter 6). Here the Parliament was concerned about the concessions made to Member States by the Council. It wished to see EU immigration legislation adopt high standards of protection for the family life of migrants. It argued that the directive breached Article 8 ECHR, the right to respect for family life. In fact the ECJ held that the directive did not in itself breach Article 8. Rather, the Member States must ensure that each individual decision involving children respected the right to respect for family life. In doing this, Member States were entitled to consider the degree to which older children had close links to their own country and how far they could adapt if admitted to that Member State. It is suggested that the case was correctly decided because Article 8 ECHR does give a wide discretion to states to apply im-migration control, particularly when deciding whether to admit a TCN who has not lived there before. However the fact that the directive does not breach human rights standards does not mean that it is wise or humane to restrict family reuni-fication in this way. The Tampere objective of achieving near equal treatment for TCNs is important as a measure of respect and equal worth. The directive fails to achieve this and instead suggests that TCN families are not as worthy of respect as those of migrant EU nationals. The justification for this lower level of rights is said to be the need to ensure that family members of TCNs demonstrate that they can integrate into their host Member State. This concern is not raised in the context of migrant EU nationals, a contrast made stronger by the fact that the families of migrant EU nationals may also include TCNs. It is moreover not clear that immigration policy is the only or even the best way of achieving this objec-tive of integration.

26.3.2.3 *Other EU immigration measures*

The most important EU general immigration measure is the common-visa system that was first set up under the Schengen Convention and incorporated in to the EC system by Regulation 562/2006. This provides for a common-visa format which is recognised by all Member States. Migrants who are issued with these visas can use them to move between Member States without the need for further visas or border controls.

As to further areas of Union migration policy, it is worth noting that there is now Student Directive 2004/114 which creates common rules to permit TCNs to enter a Member State for study purposes. They must be self-sufficient and have health insurance. This mirrors the equivalent rules for EU citizens. However unlike EU citizens, TCNs can be discriminated against in terms of being charged higher fees. There is no equivalent to Article 24 Directive 2004/38 which forbids this.

One area where there has been no progress towards harmonisation is the crucial one of economic migrants to Union. Each Member State currently decides on which criteria to use when deciding on which classes of workers should be allowed in. The demand for workers from outside the Union to supplement the ageing workforce of the Member States has been strong since the 1980s. The European Commission has encouraged this because inward migration has generally been viewed as good for the EU economy overall. Creating common rules regarding which types of skilled workers and professionals the Union particularly needs is an attractive idea. This is particularly so if such workers can move freely across the Union once they attain long-term residence status or citizenship. They would be important additions to the whole European economy, not simply the Member State where they first arrive. Nevertheless, Member States have fiercely resisted any attempt to set European rules on this question for fear of losing the ability to control the volume of economic migration into their countries. This issue remains therefore still governed by national law.

26.3.3 The regulation of asylum: Harmonisation or exclusion?

The duty to provide asylum to persons fleeing persecution is one of the oldest human-rights obligations known to international law. It was formally incorporated into a multilateral treaty in 1951—the Refugee Convention. All Member States of the European Union had signed the Convention and were operating it before their accession to the Treaty of Rome. It may be wondered therefore why the European Union began to develop asylum policies given that refugee protection was already a legal obligation upon the individual Member States. The answer lies in the rapid growth in the numbers of asylum seekers entering Europe in the 1980s and 1990s. Many hundreds of thousands of persons sought protection, but the pattern of applications for asylum varied. Some northern states such as Germany and Holland received many of the refugees whilst others, particularly in southern Europe took very few per capita. There was a perception that 'burden-sharing' was not equitable between different Member States. This was partly ascribed to divergent practices between different states. Although they were all applying the same Refugee Convention, interpretations differed on many questions. Examples include: who qualifies as a refugee; whether social support should be available during the application process; and what appeal rights should be given upon refusal. It was said that some states were thus more attractive as asylum destinations, although the extent to which individuals 'shopped' around for their preferred country of refuge was never really established.

The first attempt to solve this was through an intergovernmental system, the Dublin Convention 1990, for allocating asylum seekers to particular Member States so that they were not able to choose where to go. This employed a formula based upon the degree to which individuals had connections with a Member State through, for example, prior residence there, family members, having made a previous asylum claim, or being the place of first arrival in the Union. Those claiming asylum in one Member State when their tie to another Member State was greater could be removed to the other Member State without further consideration of their claim. This came to be known as the 'safe third country' principle—the asylum seeker could be expelled safely to a country other than that where they feared persecution. It was hoped that this would stop people moving across Europe in search of the most generous Member States. The Dublin Convention was eventually incorporated into European Union law as Council Regulation 343/2003. In fact, its impact has been fairly small because very few persons either had or could be shown to have connections with other Member States. In addition, courts sometimes declared other Member States unsafe as destinations because they did not provide adequate protection for refugees. We shall consider this at 26.3.4.1 below. As a result, few asylum seekers could be sent back to other Member States and so some countries continued to handle many more cases than others.

A more ambitious attempt to solve the problem of disparate distribution of asylum claims lay in harmonising substantive asylum law and practice at EU level. The 1999 Tampere programme laid down objectives to achieve common standards in these three key areas; definition of a refugee, reception conditions, and asylum procedures. These objectives were met through completion of a legislative programme in 2005, the target date set at Tampere. However the degree of harmonisation has been disappointing in many respects. Furthermore, the standards adopted have in some cases lowered protection levels below those pre-existing in individual Member States and even gone below those recommended by the United Nations High Commissioner for Refugees. In addition to the harmonisation issue, asylum came to be viewed partly as border security issue. Because of European government restrictions on the migration of persons from poorer refugee-producing countries, asylum seekers often entered the European Union illegally. There were well-established smuggling routes through parts of Europe for such persons. Of those entering illegally, sometimes significant numbers were ultimately refused asylum. These persons fell to be expelled from the Union but this was far from straightforward in practice. In this sense, the Union began to perceive that its external borders should be more secure to prevent illegal entry (including of asylum seekers) and to ensure swift expulsion in such cases. The goal of high levels of refugee protection was therefore not always consistent with the political pressure to better police border controls. Joint action in European border security could in itself more readily lead to genuine refugees being expelled or denied entry.

26.3.4 The three Refugee Directives

There are three principal directives impinging upon asylum seekers and refugees. They each relate to different issues namely: definition of refugees and rights of recognised refugees; reception and support for asylum seekers; and finally, asylum-law procedures and appeals. Together they provide a nearly comprehensive framework of law regulating the Member States' treatment of this very important group of migrants. In this area, European law has effectively replaced the divergent laws and practices of the Member States. The directives have been incorporated into national law and policy but remain the overriding source of law under the doctrines of supremacy and direct effect.

26.3.4.1 *The Refugee Definition Directive*

The most important measure is undoubtedly the Refugee Definition Directive (Council Directive 2004/83/EC OJ [2004] L 304/12), based on Article 63 EC which provides for a common definition of who is a refugee. This had been a source of serious difficulty, as illustrated by conflicts between Member States' national courts on the meaning of core aspects of the term 'refugee'. Thus, despite the fact that national courts were all interpreting the same 1951 Refugee Convention, there were irreconcilable differences of opinion. The starkest illustration in this respect was that of whether a person who faced persecution from non-governmental actors such a private citizens or paramilitaries could be a refugee. The UK courts held that such a person should be considered a refugee if there was a failure of protection by the asylum seekers' own government (see *R v Secretary of state, ex parte Aidan and Aitseguir* [2000] UKHL 4). By contrast, the German jurisprudence held that only if the state itself had condoned or tolerated the persecution could such a person be a refugee (see Appn No 43844/98 *TI v UK*, 7 March 2000). The French courts adopted a similar approach (see the discussion of French law in *R v Secretary of state, ex parte Aidan and Aitseguir* [2000] UKHL 4). These divergences meant that when asylum seekers in the UK were due to be returned to Germany or France, because of having passed through there or having other connections there, under the safe-third-country principle, they were able to successfully challenge their expulsion from the UK in British courts. This meant that the UK had to process their asylum claim even if another Member State should have been responsible for their case. The Refugee Definition Directive solved this problem by providing that 'actors of persecution' can include non-state actors where the authorities are unable or unwilling to provide protection against them (Article 6). This accords with the view of the British courts (and more generally with academic scholarly opinion and that of the United Nations High Commissioner for Refugees).

Furthermore the directive provides a broad inclusive definition of the 'persecution' that a refugee must demonstrate in Article 9 to be offered protection. Thus, rather requiring refugees to show a fear of death or torture only, any sufficiently serious human rights violations will now be enough to constitute 'persecution'. Another element of the 1951 Refugee Convention is the requirement that a person face persecution 'for reasons of political opinion, race, nationality, religion or membership of a particular social group'. The directive provides harmonising standards on who is a member of a social group. Additionally, the directive provides a definition of when a person who might be a refugee is excluded from protection on the grounds that they have committed serious offences, such as war crimes, before seeking asylum. It also provides for a common approach for when Member States may withdraw of refugee status in cases where a person presents a threat to public security after they have been given refugee status.

The Refugee Definition Directive also provides for a right to 'humanitarian protection' for persons not qualifying under the 1951 Refugee Convention. When a person faces 'serious harm' in their own country but this threat is not on account of their political opinion or other personal characteristics they will not be a 'refugee'. They might, for example, be threatened with death because of a personal argument with someone. There was however a doubt about the level and type of threat they must face in order to qualify under directive. This was due to a drafting ambiguity in the directive arising from disagreement between the Member States.

Article 15(a)–(b) says that persons facing the death penalty, torture of inhuman and degrading treatment in their country merit humanitarian status. It also refers at 15(c) to a 'serious and individual threat to a civilian's life or person by reason of indiscriminate violence in situations of international of internal armed conflict'. This suggested that persons fleeing the dangers of civil war might be fall within the humanitarian-protection obligation. However some thought this interpretation was too wide and that the reference to 'serious and individual threat' meant the person had to show they were likely to be singled out for torture or inhuman or degrading treatment beyond the risk felt by the population at large. Member States had argued that their obligation should be no greater than that under Article 3 of the ECHR. In the important case of *Elgafaji v Staatssecretaris van Justitie* (Case C–465/07) the Grand Chamber of the ECJ rejected this argument and confirmed that humanitarian protection is available to those who can show that indiscriminate violence has reached such a high level that substantial grounds exist for believing that a civilian returned there would face a real risk of death or serious harm to their person. They do not need to show they are individually being targeted. This decision means that the directive goes beyond existing refugee law and that of the ECHR in affording protection to those fleeing civil war and internal armed conflict.

For persons who are recognised as refugees or given humanitarian protection, the directive sets out a list of social, economic, and cultural rights that are derived from the 1951 Refugee Convention. These aim to provide for a status for refugees and those granted humanitarian protection equal to that of lawfully resident TCNs in the Member States. We can conclude that the Refugee Definition Directive is a largely successful attempt to harmonise the protection given to refugees across the Member States of the Union in a manner compatible with human-rights standards.

26.3.4.2 *The Reception Conditions Directive*

Turning to the second important measure, the Reception Conditions Directive (Directive 2003/9 OJ [2003] L 31/18) seeks to provide common housing, educational, medical, and material support to asylum seekers. The aim of this was to ensure that each Member States offered sufficiently similar support to asylum seekers such that the perceived forum-shopping was reduced. Prior to the directive, there were clearly different approaches, with some southern European Member States recording very few asylum applications and having minimal reception facilities. Some northern European states, by contrast, had to spend large sums supporting asylum applicants. Importantly, the trend across the Union was to reduce social support to asylum seekers on the basis that too many unfounded claims were being made. This meant that the directive aimed to harmonise but in the context of a political environment that looked towards dissuading asylum seekers from coming to Europe.

The directive is successful in providing an important set of minimum guarantees that did not clearly exist before in all Member States. Thus asylum seekers and their dependents must be provided with material reception conditions to ensure a standard of living adequate for the health of applicants and capable of ensuring their subsistence (Article 13). This may take the form of accommodation in centres or border camps (Article 14). They may be provided with vouchers or cash to support themselves (Article 13(5)). They also have a right to necessary health care which must at least include emergency care and essential treatment of illness (Article 15).

For minors, there must be education provided under similar condition to that of nationals, although this may be in accommodation centres (Article 10). This is an important set of key entitlements. Access to employment proved more controversial. On the one hand, allowing asylum seekers to work reduces the burden on the state, on the other it may result in jobs being given to foreigners over nationals. As a result, Member States retained the right to set an embargo on access to the labour market for asylum seekers. However access to employment must be granted within one year of the application for asylum (Article 11(2)).

As noted above, the directive provides that asylum seekers must be given accommodation during the processing of their claim. However, the UK insisted upon a provision in the directive allowing such support to be denied to those who did not seek asylum on their arrival at the border. A great many asylum seekers apply for asylum after arrival and so could be caught by this. They could also be denied access to work for 12 months. These provisions combine to mean that a person could be denied support and also denied the right to earn money themselves. This raised the prospect of large-scale destitution for asylum seekers. This was held to be a breach of Article 3 of the ECHR by the UK House of Lords in the case of *R (on the application of Adam, Limbuela and Tesema) v Secretary of state for the Home Department* ([2005] UKHL 66) because allowing persons to starve or suffer other ill-health due to destitution amounted to 'inhuman or degrading treatment'.

A further human-rights issue raised by the directive is the detention of asylum seekers. Many Member States had already begun to receive asylum applicants in closed reception facilities that did not allow them to leave. These prison-like conditions raise concerns about the right to liberty protected under the Article 5 ECHR. On this point the directive is distinctly weak as far as the protection of liberty and the rule of law is concerned. Thus Article 7 confirms that 'asylum seekers may move freely with the territory of the host Member State or within an area assigned to them'. But it also says that Member States may, 'when it proves necessary, for example for legal reasons or reasons of public order . . . confine an applicant to a particular place in accordance with their national law'.

This confinement includes detention behind fences or in prisons. The grounds to detain are very opaque: 'legal reasons' are not specified and 'public order' could be viewed quite broadly. There is also no requirement for judicial authorisation of detention nor any rule requiring bail to be considered. There are no time limits on the period of detention either. Whilst a detainee must have access to judicial review if they seek it, this may be difficult for practical reasons of cost and availability of lawyers. The directive therefore accommodates Member States that seek to process asylum claims by using administrative detention in ways that are at variance with some principles of the rule of law.

26.3.4.3 *The Asylum Procedures Directive*

The final measure, the Asylum Procedures Directive 2005/85 (OJ [2005] L 326/13), proved the most difficult to agree and provided the least degree of harmonisation. The aim was to ensure that asylum claims were processed according to common minimum standards on issues like legal aid, interpreting, interviewing, medical evidence, standards of proof, and appeals so that stark differences could be removed. In this area again, as in refugee definition cases, there had been conflicts between national courts on what the 1951 Refugee Convention required. There was thus a possibility that the directive could, in harmonising these matters, raise refugee protection standards to those of the better Member States. In practice, Member States each came to the negotiation to ensure that they could maintain the growing number of restrictions on asylum claims that had developed during the 1990s. The final directive mutated from its early draft containing common standards into a receptacle permitting each Member State to maintain their own restrictions on asylum procedures. The result is a complex and difficult to interpret piece of law-making that neither achieves harmony nor raises standards of refugee protection in Europe.

As to the key positive obligations on Member States, we can say as follows. The decision-making authority must have up-to-date information relating to the asylum applicant's country and must decide each case individually, objectively and impartially (Article 8). A reasoned decision must be given in writing to the applicant (Article 9). Applicants must be given information, including the decision, in a language they understand and the services of an interpreter to submit their case, at least during any interview (Article 10).

Turning to rights that are less secure, we must consider the personal interview which should be at the heart of any asylum application in accordance with guidance. The directive says that an interview shall be offered but then significantly undermines this by saying it is not required in a wide variety of significant cases (Article 12(2)(b)). Thus where the authorities conclude a person has only raised issues in their application of 'minimal relevance' to an asylum claim they can refuse to interview them. Similarly if the applicant comes for a country deemed to be a 'safe country of origin' or a 'safe third country' that they can be returned to, there is no obligation to interview. Where an applicant has made 'inconsistent, contradictory, improbable or insufficient representations' again they do not need to be interviewed. Additionally, persons whose application is believed to have been made 'merely in order to delay or frustrate' their removal, need not be interviewed. These restrictions are very significant because they open up the risk that the authorities may expel someone with a valid refugee claim without gathering all the relevant information. This would breach both the Refugee Convention and the ECHR (see *Hatami v Sweden* (Appn 32448/6) European Human Rights Commission, Decision of 23 April 1998).

There is a right to consult a lawyer at the applicant's expense (Article 15(1)). In practice, many refugees have few resources and legal aid is important in such cases. The directive says Member States shall provide free legal assistance and/or representation following a decision to refuse refugee status (Article 15(2)). This does not however apply to the pre-decision stage which means an applicant cannot get free help to prepare their application. Furthermore, Article 15(3) allows Member States to restrict free legal advice to those appearing before courts or tribunals and then only if the proceedings are deemed by the authorities as likely to succeed. The scope of legal aid is therefore limited and it may be denied to applicants who do in fact have meritorious claims. This may result in denial of access to an effective remedy against deportation to a country where the person may be tortured. This may in turn breach Article 13 ECHR (for example see *Airey v Ireland* (1979-80) 2 EHRR 305 where denial of legal aid led to a breach of the right to a fair trial).

In relation to the crucial issue of rights of appeal, the directive does not give a full right to appeal on the merits against a refusal but only a right to an 'effective remedy' (Article 39). The case law from the ECHR does however require that persons whose deportation would expose them to torture in breach of Article 3 ECHR have a right to quite rigorous scrutiny by an independent Court (see Appn No 51564/99, *Conka v Belgium*, 5 February 2001 (2002) 34 EHRR 54). This obligation is binding on Member States. However, in practice, it will be difficult to succeed in many cases because the reviewing court will not interfere with the initial decision unless it is clearly wrong. A further problem is the directive does not require any judicial review to suspend the execution of the expulsion order. Thus, in principle, an asylum seeker may be expelled before the court or tribunal has had a chance to consider the matter (Article 39(3)). Again, this may violate the case law established in relation to Article 3 and 13 ECHR. A full suspensive appeal on the merits is an essential safeguard that the directive failed to provide to refugees who are often faced with poorly reasoned and formulaic decisions from the relevant executive agency of the government.

The directive also endorses the 'safe third country' and 'safe country of origin' principles which means that refugee applicants can find their individual circumstances are not considered by the asylum authorities. Thus the directive permits Member States to refuse to consider an application at all when a person has passed through another country en route to the European Union (Article 25(2)((c)). This third country has to meet certain really minimal conditions such as being a signatory to the 1951 Refugee Convention and that the 'possibility exists to request refugee status' (Article 27(1)). There is however no requirement that this third country actually has adequate procedures for protecting refugees. Such an application may be declared inadmissible and the person summarily removed under the directive. This may expose them to a chain of deportations leading to persecution in their home country without ever having had proper consideration of their refugee claim. As a result, there may be a breach of Article 3 of the ECHR because the European Court of Human Rights has said that states must ensure that conditions in the third country really are adequate to provide protection before deportation occurs (see Appn No 43844/98 *TI v UK*, 7 March 2000). The directive goes further towards harmonising this issue by requiring the Council to adopt a common list of safe European third countries relating to those on the borders of the EU (Article 36). Again the standard set for the third country is low. It must merely have signed the 1951 Refugee Convention, the 1950 ECHR, and have in place 'an asylum procedure prescribed by law' (Article 36(2)(b)).

The clear intention of these provisions is to facilitate the return of applicants to nearby non-EU transit countries like Ukraine, Albania, and Turkey through which asylum seekers often pass before arriving in Europe. It is clear that asylum seekers would find it difficult to secure refugee status in such places because the safeguards and procedures operated there are far below those in the EU. This illustrates a key element of EU policy on asylum—the desire to restrict access to formal asylum processes in the Union by shifting responsibility to neighbouring states whenever possible. There is a real danger that some persons passed back in this way may ultimately be returned to their countries to face persecution. Such shifting of responsibility may conflict with the expressed Tampere Council goal of providing refugees with protection in accordance with the Refugee Convention. The positive elements of the EU's refugee package, including reception conditions and legal, interpreting, and other assistance may be side-stepped by simply expelling applicants to neighbouring countries that do not have these facilities.

Turning to the issue of safe country of origin, this is something many Member States had already introduced in national law in order to reject applications or provide only limited rights to applicants by reference to nationality alone. The directive says that where an application is made by such a national, Member States may declare it manifestly unfounded (Article 28). As noted above, they may also dispense with an interview in such cases. The directive requires that the Council adopt common lists of such countries based upon them being places where there is 'generally and consistently no persecution . . . no torture . . . and no threat of indiscriminate violence in situations of international or internal armed conflict' (Annex II). There are great dangers in such procedures because the designation of a country as 'safe' is fraught with difficulty. It may be safe for some groups and not others. Asylum authorities must consider the individual applicant's case to avoid the possibility of error.

26.3.4.4 *Assessment of refugee directives*

In summary, the refugee package passed by the European Union must be viewed as reflecting very mixed motives. On the one hand, there was a desire to fix a common set of standards to limit the possibility of more 'generous' Member States attracting unfair numbers of asylum seekers. This is the idea of burden-sharing. It could have been used to set a common high standard of refugee protection for all Member States. On the other hand, Member States were keen to limit the numbers of refugees they recognised. As a result, the package allows Member States to continue with their own previous practices because the minimum standards set were quite low. Indeed the directives perhaps invite 'high-standard' Member States to move toward 'low-standard' states. There were no 'stand-still clauses' in the package to prevent a 'race to the bottom'. More importantly, the minimum standards set open up the possibility of breaches of the 1951 Refugee Convention because they authorise Member States to engage in no or only cursory examination of significant numbers of asylum claims.

26.3.5 **Irregular migration and policing the EU border**

Another area where the Union has been very active is in attempting to combat illegal migration. There was long-standing concern about people-smuggling routes through southern Europe from Africa. With eastern enlargement, the Union's borders were more exposed to smuggling from Asia through Russia and Turkey. Migrants entering this way could gain access to any of the Member States. The opening of internal borders within the Union was seen as requiring the strengthening of these weak external borders. This has resulted in joint policies to secure the external borders of the Union and also action against illegal migrants found within the Union. Thus the policies are both preventive and remedial. These policies can also be linked to traditional EU social and employment polices, particularly those aimed at preventing exploitation of irregular migrants by undercutting EU citizens and other lawful residents. There is also a growing emphasis on security rationales for controlling migration by non-EU citizens. In this respect the Union is beginning to assume state-like aspirations to control territory. This has led the Union to seek to confirm powers of coercion and detention upon the Member States as agents of the Union.

26.3.5.1 *Border-control measures and irregular migration*

The earliest measure in this field was Directive 2001/40/EC on the Mutual Recognition of Decisions on the Expulsion of Third Country Nationals. This allows a Member State to expel a person present on its territory who has been subject to an expulsion order issued in another Member State. The aim is clearly to better facilitate expulsions from the Union of persons who are illegally present by sharing the responsibility between Member States. This means that fresh expulsion proceedings are not required in the second Member State nor does the person have to be extradited back to the first Member State. There are however obvious dangers in such automatic reliance upon decisions taken in other Member States. In the end, each Member State is responsible under international law for ensuring it does not expel someone in breach of their fundamental rights. It cannot and should not automatically defer to another Member State or to European Union law (see the European Court of Human Rights in Appn No 43844/98 *TI v UK*, 7 March 2000).

A variety of other measures have been passed to deter illegal migration. Thus there is harmonising measure that requires certain minimum penalties for persons found guilty of facilitating illegal entry, for example, by smuggling migrants. There are currently proposals to require Member States to impose criminal penalties upon employers who employ migrants without work permission or proper immigration status. This is one increasingly popular policy adopted by several Member States. As noted at 26.2.4 above, the Union has established its own external border agency, Frontex, that has responsibility to assist national border police in preventing illegal entry. There are also measures to enable Member States arrange joint flights to effect the expulsion of illegal immigrants. Furthermore, there is a vast database, Eurodac, which contains personal identity data for persons expelled or refused entry or visas for any Member State. This information is shared with all the Member States and is used to justify refusing further visas or entry into the Union to persons on the database. The data base presents serious risks for both the privacy of data and the fairness of decisions. As with mutual recognition of expulsion, a migrant may find all Member States rely upon erroneous data or decisions made by one Member State. This is where we can see how the desire to cooperate between Member States in the interests of efficiency immigration control can seriously undermine fundamental human rights. This position is also in stark contrast to the position of migrant EU nationals and their families (see, e.g, *Commission v Spain* (case C–503/03) concerning reliance on data entered into the Schengen Implementation System, discussed 25.4).

26.3.5.2 *The Returns Directive*

The most significant and controversial measure in relation to illegal entry is the Returns Directive (Directive 2008/115, OJ [2008] L 348/98). This measure seeks to bolster the policing role of the Union both in relation to external borders and also internally to ensure that migrants not entitled under national law to be present are removed. It creates a harmonised system for the expulsion of non-EU citizens found illegally present in any of the Member States. The clear aim is to require each Member State to contribute towards tackling the issue of illegal immigration rather than to simply allow such migrants to remain when detected. Thus, Article 6 requires Member States to issue a 'return decision' in respect of such persons.

Furthermore they must then take 'all necessary measures to enforce' this decision, including coercive methods such as arrest (Article 8). This must not however involve more than reasonable and proportionate force (Article 8(4)). Member States are however still allowed to grant a residence permit on humanitarian or compassionate grounds (Article 6(4)). Thus it is clear that the directive does allow Member States to be more generous but the tone and purpose is clearly to exclude illegal immigrants. The directive does require the possibility of an effective remedy be granted to challenge the return decision itself before an impartial body (Article 13). There is no obligation on the review body to engage with the merits of the case. Where a person raises issues of fundamental human rights then the ECHR requires an independent tribunal to review the merits carefully (see Appn No 51564/99, *Conka v Belgium*, 5 February 2001 (2002) 34 EHRR 54). The directive also suggests an exclusionary bias in EU policy by requiring Member States to impose a ban on re-entry for migrants returned other than voluntarily (Article 11(1)). This operates to prevent the migrant from coming back to *any* Member State. There is a discretion as to the period for which the ban is imposed, but the directive suggests five years or longer in more serious cases (Article 11(2)). Such re-entry bans may lead to breaches of Article 8 of the ECHR if they disproportionately deny such migrants access to family members in the Union (see *Abdulaziz, Cabales and Balkandali v UK* (1985) 7 EHRR 47).

Very significantly the directive authorises detention of persons subject to return decisions pending their expulsion where the authorities (a) have objective reasons to believe that a person may abscond or (b) where the detainee 'hampers' the effort to remove them (Article 15). There is a dangerous lack of clarity in what constitutes 'hampering' and this power suggests that detainees are open to punishment for non-cooperation. The directive requires that detention should be for shortest possible period but six months is permitted (Article 15(5)). Even then, this can be extended to eighteen months in certain cases (Article 15(6)). There is no requirement that judicial approval be obtained for any of this detention unless it is 'prolonged' (a term which is not defined). To comply with the ECHR (Article 5(1)(f)) the Member State must act with 'due diligence' to effect expulsion (see *Chahal v United Kingdom* [1996] 23 EHRR 413). This requires that states show that they are taking reasonably active steps to expel a detainee. The European Convention also requires however that there be mandatory judicial review of detention that extends beyond a few days (see *Shamsa v Poland*, Applications nos 45355/99 and 45357/99, Judgment of 27 November 2003). The very lengthy administrative detention periods without mandatory judicial review may lead to arbitrary imprisonment and abuse of power. This is a serious question that the ECJ will have to consider in accordance with its fundamental rights case law.

26.4 EU criminal justice policy

This chapter does not seek to set out in comprehensive form all the policies relating to criminal law. Indeed, the European Union has not developed a complete set of criminal justice policies. Policy regarding what conduct to make criminal, sentencing, prison policy and court procedures remains largely concentrated at Member

State level. The Union only has limited powers to act. This is in contrast to the position in relation to asylum and immigration where EU legislation is now central to the law in all Member States. Nevertheless there has been growing cooperation in a number of areas, despite great reluctance by Member States to accept the Union institutions of Commission, Parliament and Court having a prominent role in criminal justice. This has led to conflict between Member States and European institutions over how far 'normal' principles of law developed under the EC Treaty, direct effect and supremacy in particular (see Chapters 4 and 5), should apply in relation to criminal-law measures taken under the TEU. There has been a renewal of the same dissent, previously shown by national constitutional courts concerned about the lack of fundamental rights protection in the EC Treaty, toward criminal measures that arguably infringe their citizens' constitutional rights. We shall set out here some of the main issues of legal principle that have arisen rather than attempting to summarise the content of the actual legislation passed.

26.4.1 Criminal liability arising ancillary to legislation passed under the main EC Treaty

We need to make clear here the distinction between the EC Treaty (which covers the main economic, environmental, and social policies of the Union) and the TEU, which covers, among other things, cooperation in judicial and policing matters under the so-called 'third pillar' (see also Chapter 3). The EC Treaty gives powers to the institutions to pass legislation to regulate the internal market (see Chapter 16). In practice, such legislation sometimes includes criminal sanctions to give effect to its goals or it may require Member States to pass criminal laws to do so. By contrast, the TEU gives powers to the Council of Ministers to pass criminal-law measures in relation to cross-border crime such as cybercrime, human trafficking, terrorism, internet pornography, and so forth. In the latter case, the powers are specifically designed to pass criminal-law measures rather than to regulate markets. Importantly they are subject to national veto because unanimity is required under the third pillar. The existence of criminal-lawmaking powers under the third pillar gave rise to the question of whether the EC Treaty could lawfully be used to make criminal law in relation to the internal market. This has been a controversial issue because such a power challenges the reservation of competence to Member States in the field criminal law.

To explain this further we can consider an example. When the institutions act to pass laws under the EC Treaty, say a directive on financial services regulation, they may wish to impose a penalty upon natural or legal persons for a breach of the market regulations. The directive may create criminal offences to ensure compliance by those to whom it is directed. Thus, in harmonising regulation in financial markets, it might require criminal sanctions for 'insider trading'. This would ensure that there is a level playing field in terms of economic activity in that market. There would be no possibility for traders or firms to set up in a 'light regulation' Member State because they would be equivalence in criminal law standards across the Union. In this scenario, criminal sanctions are simply a tool to use to regulate activities falling within the EC Treaty internal market goals.

The Member States were however very reluctant to accept that the EC Treaty gave a power to enact criminal sanctions. They saw this as reserved to the Member

States or falling only under the more limited intergovernmental negotiations outside the EC Treaty framework. Even prior to the TEU, however, the ECJ had held in *Commission v Greece (Greek maize)* (case 68/88, [1989] ECR 2685), however, that some EC legislation might impliedly require Member States to impose criminal penalties in order to ensure its effectiveness. These penalties must be 'effective, proportionate and dissuasive'. They must also be set at a level equivalent to those imposed on similar offences in national law. The Commission took this as a sign that criminal sanctions could be included directly in EC legislation and began to draft measures in those terms. This became an important issue of political and legal principle for the European Union. The Member States felt that criminal law should remain largely up to national law or be decided within the more intergovernmental third pillar under the TEU. The Commission wanted the EU institutions to have power to criminalise conduct harmful to the internal market under the EC Treaty.

The ECJ again sided with the Commission in the important case of *Commission v Council* (Case C–176/03). Here the Commission had proposed a directive on environmental damage liability which included criminal sanctions for serious polluters. The Member States refused to accept that the Commission could propose criminal sanctions. Instead they had decided in the Council to pass their own framework directive on environmental crime under the third pillar of the TEU and thus without the involvement of the Commission or Parliament. They thus maintained their monopoly of power over criminal law and argued the directive was really a measure on criminal law, not the environment. The Commission challenged the power of the Council to pass the measure by arguing that as an environmental protection law, it should have been passed under the EC Treaty procedure. The European Court agreed ruling that although criminal law did not generally fall within the competence of the institutions under the EC treaty, this did not prevent criminal sanctions being imposed where these were necessary to ensure that the environmental protection rules were fully effective.

The conclusion from this case is that legislation relating to matters such as regulation of the internal market under the EC Treaty can include criminal sanctions. Furthermore, Member States cannot try to exclude the Commission or Parliament's involvement by attempting to argue that any criminal sanctions associated with such legislation fall within the intergovernmental third pillar. This is a very significant development in expanding the potential for European criminal laws to be passed because they will be considered under the qualified majority voting procedure of the EC Treaty rather than be subject to national veto under the third pillar. There have been a large number of criminal sanctions passed in single-market areas as a result. Two examples are crimes relating to employee workplace safety and internet piracy. In addition, such laws are subject to the full jurisdiction of the European Court and national courts are able to refer questions under the Article 234 procedure. They also have direct effect and supremacy over national law. It is important to note however that the European Court has held that criminal liability cannot be created or aggravated by an unimplemented directive (see *Arcaro* (C–168/95)). This is in order to comply with the principle of legal certainty embodied in Article 5 of the ECHR. Only where the Member State has provided the public with clear knowledge of the offence by implementing criminal sanctions into national law will a directive lead to criminal liability.

26.4.2 Pure criminal law arising under the third pillar of the TEU

Outside the EC Treaty framework, there are specific powers to pass measures relating to criminal law contained in the third pillar of the TEU. These are contained in Title VI Articles 29–42. The main thrust of these powers was supposed to be directed at providing 'citizens with a high level of safety within an area of freedom, security and justice' (Article 29). The institutional methods under Title VI here are completely different from those of the EC Treaty being largely intergovernmental with the Member States acting in the Council (though Lisbon would change this, see 26.4.3.2 below). There is no Commission monopoly on proposing measures and the European Parliament has only a right to be consulted in relation to binding legislation (Article 39(1)). Similarly the ECJ currently only has jurisdiction to references brought by national courts where their Member State has chosen to allow this (Article 35(3)(b)). Even then, Member States have can choose to only allow cases to be referred from a final court (Article 35(3)(a)). This is completely unlike the generous access to the European Court enjoyed by national courts under Article 234 EC Treaty (see Chapter 10). Around half the Member States have opted-in to allow the Court to hear references but this means that uniformity of interpretation and application is not achieved as between Member States.

As we saw above, the Council cannot try to avoid the involvement of the Commission or Parliament required under the EC Treaty by passing criminal laws under the third pillar if they relate to first pillar subject matter. Leaving this limitation aside, the TEU does not expressly limit the issues over which criminal law can be passed under the third pillar. There is no agreed list, although Article 29 TEU (post Lisbon, Article 67 TFEU) refers to 'preventing and combating crime, organised or otherwise, in particular terrorism, trafficking in persons and offences against children, illicit drug trafficking and illicit arms trafficking, corruption and fraud . . . '. Legislation and cooperation have thus developed over an ad hoc set of issues generally comprising matters with a cross-border element.

We will not consider here the details of the measures passed save to say that they attempt to provide common definitions and minimum sentences for such crimes. They also require Member States to have common criminal procedures regarding, for example, the gathering and use of evidence in relation to certain cross-border crimes.

There have also been significant attempts to increase information-sharing between police forces across the Union. The Hague European Council in 2004 went so far as to say law enforcement officers should in general make available to law enforcement officers in other Member States information needed to perform their duties. These measures raise important questions about respect for the right to privacy and the protection of personal data. The Hague Council also gave great prominence to combating terrorism through pooling intelligence and freezing assets. Perhaps most importantly, there have been efforts to secure the 'mutual recognition' of criminal judgments and orders by the courts of each of the Member States. The aim has been to render borders irrelevant in terms of criminal enforcement. As we shall see below, this has raised serious constitutional issues for the courts of the Member States anxious to maintain national safeguards for criminal suspects.

26.4.3 The status of criminal law measures taken under the third pillar in the Member States

As well as the institutional mechanism for passing these laws being largely inter-governmental, the laws themselves appear to have a less significant impact by comparison to those passed under the EC Treaty. The reluctance of the Member States to accept loss of sovereignty over criminal law led them to insert Article 34(2)(b) in the TEU, which expressly declares that decisions and framework decisions, the only binding types of measures possible under that treaty, shall not have direct effect (see Chapter 5 on the nature of direct effect). This appeared to mean that such provisions could not be invoked within national courts which rather had to look only at implementing national law, if any had been passed. This situation suggested that third-pillar measures would have little impact in the internal legal orders of the Member States. There are close links between direct effect and the doctrine of supremacy. Indeed, the supremacy of the EC Treaty had been developed alongside direct effect in the early cases of *Van Gend en Loos* and *COSTA v ENEL*, on the basis of similar, teleological reasoning. Some have suggested that, if there were no direct effect of third-pillar measures, there would be no supremacy either, although the TEU was silent on this particular issue.

In an important and controversial case, however, the ECJ in *Criminal Proceedings Against Maria Pupino* (Case C–105/03) [2005] ECR I-5285 held that the prohibition on direct effect in Article 34(2)(b) TEU did not exclude *indirect effect* of framework decisions. This principle of indirect effect, it will be recalled, requires national courts to interpret national law as far as possible in accordance with applicable European law rules. This case concerned criminal proceedings in Italy against a schoolteacher for assaulting a child. The prosecution wished to allow the child to give evidence prior to the trial in order to spare them distress. The national law appeared to allow this only in cases of sexual crimes. However there was an applicable framework directive on witness protection that required vulnerable witnesses be given sensitive treatment allowing for evidence to be given outside of the full trial hearing. The ECJ held that the duty of loyal cooperation incumbent on the Member States required that framework directives should be followed as far as possible. The Court thus required the national court to read down the national law as far as possible to protect the witness. As noted (at 26.4.1 above), indirect effect cannot create or aggravate liability but the Court here found that removing a procedural safeguard for the defendant did neither of those things.

This radical case showed that the Member States had not fully succeeded in their efforts to prevent the legal effect of criminal law measures passed under the third pillar. It also raised questions about how far the principle of supremacy might also apply to third-pillar measures (see Chapter 4). If national law must be interpreted so as to conform to third-pillar law, such measures provide the framework within which national law operates. On this basis it is arguable that national courts are under an obligation to set aside any incompatible national law, effectively suggesting supremacy extends beyond EC law to EU law. This would be extremely controversial because the TEU creates a very different system of law by comparison to the EC Treaty. The special features of the latter, including the powerful role of the supranational institutions of Commission, Court, and Parliament and the enforcement action system under Article 226 (see

Chapter 11), were among those that the ECJ had first used to justify supremacy in the *COSTA v ENEL* judgment. Whilst some commentators have suggested that the absence of these features from the TEU, in favour of looser intergovernmental decision-making, points towards this treaty not having supremacy over national law, it is also arguable that the effectiveness arguments which underpin supremacy, as well as many other EC law doctrines, could justify supremacy in the other pillars (see Chapter 4). The ECJ has yet to give its view on this problem but it can be argued that the national courts have already effectively rejected supremacy of third-pillar measures, as we shall see below.

26.4.3.1 *European arrest warrant*

The problem of supremacy of third-pillar measures has been most pronounced in relation to the European arrest warrant created by Framework Directive 2002/548. This is perhaps the most controversial measure ever passed by the European Union. Its purpose was clearly to reduce the complexity and delay involved in arresting and extraditing criminal suspects between Member States. This was previously governed by extradition treaties between Member States which laid down certain safeguards for suspects. The most important of these was the rule of 'double criminality' which meant that in simple terms a person could not be extradited unless they faced prosecution for conduct that was criminal in both the requesting and the requested states. Furthermore, the extradition treaties only applied to foreign nationals not citizens of the state receiving the request. The European arrest-warrant system is entirely different. It is largely automatic and removes most of the power from the courts of the requested state to block extradition. The procedures are bureaucratic rather than judicial. The double criminality rule is largely abolished in relation to 32 types of criminal conduct. Thus if the suspect is facing prosecution in relation to one of these areas, they can be returned to the requesting state regardless of the whether the conduct would be criminal in the state receiving the request. Most controversially, there is no exception made to prevent citizens of the requested state being arrested and sent to the requesting state. The effect of this is to require national courts to authorise the arrest, return and prosecution of persons of whatever nationality and regardless of the fairness of trial procedures in the requesting Member State.

This removal of crucial restrictions on extradition was unacceptable to many constitutional courts in the Member States. Most obviously it conflicted with the constitutional guarantee in many Member States against the expulsion of nationals. Thus the German, Polish, and Cypriot courts held that the implementation of the European arrest warrant by national law was unconstitutional on the ground that it required nationals of these states to be expelled in the same way as foreigners. We see here a direct clash between the fundamental idea of the special obligation of each Member State towards its own nationals set against the mutual obligation to assist other Member States in punishing crime. Ultimately this situation sets national constitutional guarantees against the obligations imposed by the European arrest-warrant system. To the extent that national constitutions prevail then there can be no supremacy of law made under the TEU. This recalls the *Solange I* ruling of the German constitutional court in 1972 which rejected supremacy of EC Treaty law over the guarantees of the German Constitution (see Chapters 4 and 6).

The ECJ has heard a challenge to the European arrest-warrant system brought by a Belgian lawyers' association in *Advocaten voor de Wereld VZW v Leden van de Ministerrad* (case 303/05). This case was however brought on the basis that the framework directive had been passed in breach of general principles of European law recognised by the ECJ itself. The argument put was that the removal of the double criminality rule was in itself a breach of the principle of the rule of law. This was said to be because suspects could be arrested and sent back to Member States without the sending national court assessing in any way the crime with which they were charged. Thus it was said that return could occur even though the suspect would be charged with a vague crime which perhaps did not meet the requirements of legal certainty imposed by the ECHR, national constitutional law, and EU general principles. The court rejected this argument saying that the Member State receiving the suspect must always abide by these principles and that the sending Member State court had no need to consider such matters for itself. This suggests that Member States' courts must trust each other to uphold important principles of fundamental rights rather than seek to evaluate these in each case.

The decision in *Advocaten voor de Wereld* did not however, on its facts, raise issues of conflict between national constitutional law and the European arrest warrant system. This is precisely the issue that had led to the decisions of the German constitutional court to annul implementation of the system. There is likely to be further litigation to determine how to resolve this conflict. National courts may find further cause to challenge arrest warrants issued by Member States where the trial procedures, legal aid, access to lawyers, or other matters are considered to be deficient as compared with the national law of the requested Member State. To accede to a request in such a case may breach the national constitution and/or the ECHR. The European Commission has even proposed a common code on criminal procedure to allay the concerns of national courts, but this is limited in the rights conferred and unlikely to be passed (see COM 2004/328). The ECJ may therefore find further instances of national courts defying the principle of supremacy in relation to third pillar measures. It is not clear that the European Court can resolve all these issues by recourse to its own fundamental rights jurisprudence. The Member States' courts will be keen to ensure that national constitutional standards are upheld in relation to criminal suspects, particularly in the case of their own nationals. The lack of an enforceable code of fundamental rights within the TEU continues to be an additional obstacle to reassuring national courts (see Chapter 6 on fundamental rights in the EU and note limits on the European court's jurisdiction as far as judicial review is concerned, Chapter 12).

26.4.3.2 *Assessment*

In conclusion we can see that criminal law raises serious problems of a complex nature for European law. There have already been real conflicts between the Member States and the EU institutions over how far sovereignty in relation to criminal law has or should be transferred to the those institutions. Furthermore, there have been conflicts between national courts and the ECJ over the extent to which criminal law measures can take effect in national law, particularly if they conflict with constitutional safeguards. This issue has not been resolved yet and it may be that the ECJ will have to reassure national courts that fundamental rights are not being compromised by criminal measures taken under the third pillar. Despite these difficulties, the European Union has passed a significant number of measures relating to criminal law under both the EC Treaty and the TEU. The number of cross-border criminal issues concerning Member States points towards this trend continuing. The important issue is how to protect fundamental rights in the face of attempts to harmonise criminal law.

In this context, we should note the impact of the Lisbon Treaty, should it come in to force. In particular, the structural changes (discussed in Chapter 1) that abolish the pillar system and transfer much of the the substance of JHA in to what is currently the EC Treaty (after Lisbon, the TFEU), may mitigate some of these tensions. There are three points to note:

(1) the change in law-making procedures, which, in particular, may allow a greater role for the European Parliament;

(2) the greater possibility of review by the European courts, in particular for compliance with human rights standards, though the ECJ's jurisdiction is limited as regards validity and proportionality of police operations or with regard to law and order and internal security (Article 276 TFEU, see Chapters 10 and 12);

(3) the greater emphasis given to human rights through the according of legal status to the Charter and the stated intention to accede to the ECHR (post Lisbon, Article 6 TEU, discussed in Chapter 6).

Nonetheless, the German constitutional court, in its Lisbon judgment, emphasised the cultural specificity of criminal law in particular. Union competence in this field must be interpreted narrowly and any extension of competence (Articles 82(3), 83(3) and 48(7)(3) TFEU must be done within a system of national democratic review, rather than executive action. Further action in this area may be contentious.

26.5 Conclusions

Union law has now begun to exert consideration influence on home affairs policy. This is most clear in relation to asylum and immigration where there are quite comprehensive systems of legislation that provide the main rules governing migration into the Union. There are however no measures yet on migration for purely economic purposes which thus remain under national control. Furthermore several Member States have not opted-in to some of the measures passed, particularly in relation to immigration. The legislation passed so far does not provide a comprehensive set of minimum standards for migrants because there are areas where Member States can opt to provide lower standards than the basic ones set. Particularly in relation to asylum procedures, Member States fought hard to keep national standards and the directive therefore reads less like a harmonising measure and more like a collection of national favourite rules. When looking at the package from the perspective of international human-rights standards, there are some encouraging aspects. The refugee definition is broad and inclusive and largely accords with international law. The humanitarian-protection provision is generous as interpreted by the ECJ in *Elgafaji*. As against this, we must conclude that the procedures directive may breach international standards in allowing widespread expulsion without consideration of the merits of the individual case. Turning to immigration the picture is more positive because the Family Reunion and Long-term Residents Directives do provide enhanced standards of respect for migrants within the Union. These approach the protection offered to EU migrant citizens although do not fully mirror them.

Regarding judicial and policing matters under the third pillar the picture is rather different. There has not been the same degree of harmonisation of substantive law here, although financial crime and terrorism are exceptions. There has been a great deal of cooperation between police forces. The main legislative emphasis has been upon mutual recognition of criminal court orders and judgments. The European arrest warrant has been the centrepiece of this process. The possible conflict between this measure and national and international fundamental rights protection has not yet been resolved by the ECJ and the supreme courts of the Member States. The contentious question of whether criminal measures under the third pillar have primacy over national law has not yet been resolved. The area of policing and criminal justice does therefore present the potential for serious clashes over the effectiveness and legitimacy of EU law. Despite these difficulties, the Lisbon Treaty would move judicial and policing matters from the third pillar into the first pillar, thus removing many of the distinctions. Whilst we might suggest that this could lead to an improvement in legitimacy, transparency and human rights protection, the possible increase in Union activity in this sensitive field could give rise to greater conflict.

FURTHER READING

Peers, S, 'Implementing equality? The Directive on Long-term Resident Third Country Nationals' [2004] 29 EL Rev 437.

Peers, S, *EU Justice and Home Affairs Law*, 2nd edn (Oxford University Press, 2006).

Douglas-Scott, S, 'The rule of law in the European Union: Putting security into "the area of freedom security and justice"' [2004] 29 EL Rev 219.

Gilbert, G, 'Is Europe living up to its obligations to refugees?' [2004] 14(5) European J International Law 963.

Lambert, H, 'The EU asylum qualification directive, its impact on the jurisprudence of the United Kingdom and international law' [2006] 55 ICLQ 161.

Baker, E and Harding, C, 'From past imperfect to future imperfect? A longitudinal study of the third pillar' [2009] 34 EL Rev 25.

27

Discrimination

27.1 Introduction

The general principle of non-discrimination on the ground of nationality underpins much of EU law, as we have seen in the discussion of workers (see Chapters 22 and 23). This chapter will examine the many attempts that have been made to combat discrimination. Central to this discussion is the extensive body of legislation and the European Court of Justice (ECJ) jurisprudence in the field of equal treatment between men and women. More recently, however, the EU has broadened its focus to deal with discrimination in other areas, including age, race, religious belief, and sexual orientation. A brief discussion of these aspects of EU policy lie within this chapter, though it remains to be seen if these provisions will have the impact of the sex discrimination provisions. The main focus of this chapter remains the law on sex discrimination.

Provisions on sex discrimination, or gender discrimination (as it is now called by the EU), have been part of the EC Treaty since its beginning. They are significant for three main reasons. The prohibition of discrimination on grounds of nationality has been central to the development of the law in a number of areas (see Chapter 6). The prohibition on sex discrimination was of similar importance, and has seemingly increased in significance. Article 2 EC now includes the promotion of equality between men and women as one of the tasks of the Community, and Article 13 EC includes a general power for the Community to act to combat discrimination on various grounds, including sex. Recent years have also seen the Union attempt to integrate sex equality issues into all its policies and actions (see, eg, Report on Equal Opportunities for Women and Men (COM (2003) 98 final)).

Additionally, it constitutes an illustration of the interplay, and even conflict, between policy areas. It has been described as one of the 'foundations of the Community', designed, according to the ECJ in *Defrenne v Sabena (No 2)* (case 43/75), apropos the then Article 119 (now 141), to achieve a 'double objective', economic and social. Its social goal is to achieve 'social progress', the 'improvement of the living and working conditions of their peoples', as required by the treaty (preamble, 2nd and 3rd recitals). It can also be seen as ensuring there are no distortions in competition throughout the Union. Businesses in a Member State which had legislation aimed at ensuring equal treatment could be at a disadvantage in terms of, for example, wage costs compared with businesses established in another Member State without similar legislation. It was, indeed, on this basis that the sex-discrimination provisions were included in the original treaty. It now seems, however, that the economic aim is secondary to the social aim of these provisions. This emphasis on the value of non-discrimination has been underscored by treaty amendments, notably the changes introduced by the Treaty of Amsterdam (ToA). Since the ToA, an objective of the Community is to combat discrimination of all types. Furthermore, if the Lisbon Treaty comes into force, equality between men and women would be recognised as a fundamental value of the Union.

Finally, the law in this area is significant because it shows the interrelationship between judicial and political actions. The *Barber* case (case C–262/88) was a broad and unexpected ruling; it led to the Member States seeking to clarify (and limit) its scope in a protocol to the treaty. Equally, some judgments which have shown the limits of sex equality, such as *P v S* and *D v Council* (C–125/99P) regarding sexual orientation and *Kalanke* concerning positive discrimination (discussed below), may have provided the spur for Community legislative action.

The first part of this chapter considers sex (or gender) discrimination. The chapter concludes by looking at Directives 2004/43 and 2000/78 regarding equal treatment irrespective of race or ethnic origin, and religion, respectively. There is little case law on these directives and the discussion is therefore, at this stage, brief.

27.2 Overview of provisions on gender equality

27.2.1 Sphere of application

EU law on sex discrimination, unlike the fundamental EC Treaty provisions relating to goods and workers, is not limited in its application to migrant workers. Its application may be, and invariably is, 'wholly internal'. It is, however, confined strictly within the economic context; it was not designed to settle questions concerned with the organisation of the family, or to alter the division of responsibility between parents.

27.2.2 Provisions Concerning Gender Discrimination

Even before the Treaty of Amsterdam (ToA), EC law on sex discrimination was extensive and comprised:

  (a) Article 119 of the EC Treaty, which laid down a general principle of *equal pay for equal work* for men and women (now, after amendment, Article 141)
  (b) Directive 75/117, which implements the principle of equal pay in more specific terms, to include equal pay for work of *equal value*
  (c) Directive 76/207 (as amended by Directive 2002/73/EC), which provides for *equal treatment* for men and women in the context of employment
  (d) Directive 79/7, which applies the equal treatment principle to matters of social security
  (e) Directive 86/378, which extends the equal treatment principle to occupational pension schemes
  (f) Directive 86/613, which provides for equal treatment in self-employment.

The ToA incorporated into the main body of the EC Treaty, as Chapter 1 of new Title XI of the Treaty, the provisions of the Protocol on the Social Chapter, which had been annexed by the TEU to the EC Treaty, some of which also have a bearing on sex discrimination. The incorporation of the terms of the Protocol on the Social Chapter not only means that legislation enacted under these provisions now extends to the UK (which had hitherto opted out of the extended social policy provisions) as well as to the other Member States, but that the social protection provisions contained within the EC Treaty will be extended significantly. The prohibition on sex discrimination, now amended and renumbered as Article 141 EC (ex 119, post Lisbon Article 157 TFEU), remains central.

Linked closely to the question of sex discrimination are a number of issues: the position of part-time workers, the majority of whom are women, and the impact of pregnancy and maternity on the working woman. The Union has enacted certain directives in these areas (Directive 96/34 on pregnancy and 92/85 on parental leave). Despite this legislative activity, the case law of the ECJ in this area remains important. Less directly connected with employment but still concerned with sex discrimination is Directive 2004/113 on equal treatment in access to goods and services.

In view of the extensive jurisprudence that has evolved in this area, the Commission put forward a proposal to adopt a consolidating directive (COM (2004) 279 final).

On July 2006 Directive 2006/54 on the implementation of the principle of equal opportunities and equal treatment of men and women in matters of employment and occupation (recast) was adopted ('recast Equal Treatment Directive'). The directive systematises existing provisions, incorporates principles on equal treatment and prohibition of discrimination established in the Court's case law, and repeals a number of separate directives; but it does not make any significant new additions to the current legal framework. It was criticised for being unambitious and, indeed, for not 'recasting' all the directives. The approach seems to have been driven by the need to fit the directive within the treaty base of Article 141 EC, rather than using social policy provisions, such as Article 137 EC, which are more onerous (see Chapter 3). This process of recasting reflects the approach adopted elsewhere (eg, the Citizenship Directive)—ie, the updating and revising of older legislation in light of ECJ case law and subsequent developments—and is generally to be welcomed.

The recast Equal Treatment Directive repeals Directive 75/117 on equal pay for men and women; Directive 76/207 on the principle of equal treatment for men and women as regards access to employment, vocational training, and promotion and working conditions; and Directive 86/378 on the principle of equal treatment in occupational social-security schemes, which are examined in detail below. It also repeals the Burden of Proof Directive (Directive 97/80). Whilst references to specific directives have changed, the substantive rules remain the same. Indeed, Article 34(2) of the recast directive (Directive 2006/54) specifies that 'References to the repealed Directives shall be construed as to this Directive' and a table of equivalence is contained in an annex to the directive. Thus, this chapter retains its existing structure.

27.2.3 Overview of Recast Equal Treatment Directive

The directive covers access to employment (including promotion) and vocational training; working conditions (including pay); and occupational social-security schemes (Article 1). It prohibits direct or indirect discrimination on grounds of sex in the public or private sectors (Article 14). Discrimination includes harassment and sexual harassment, instructions to discriminate against persons on grounds of sex, and any less favourable treatment of a woman related to pregnancy or maternity leave (Article 2). As the use of the term 'includes' implies, this list is not exhaustive, so other forms of adverse treatment may also come within the scope of the directive. Since the latter's aim is to establish a minimum standard of protection, Member States may introduce or maintain more favourable provisions (Article 27). The directive also provides that Member States shall ensure that those who claim that they have been discriminated against have at their disposal adequate enforcement procedures and remedies (Articles 17–18) and that once a claimant has established facts from which it may be presumed that there has been direct or indirect discrimination it is for the defendant employer to prove that he complied with the principle of equal treatment (Article 19). Member States were under an obligation to transpose the directive into their domestic legal systems by 15 August 2009 at the latest.

27.2.4 Equality law in the national legal system

Since Article 141 EC and, to a more limited extent, the directives on sex discrimination have been declared directly effective (see Chapter 5), EC law has been invoked on a number of occasions by individuals seeking to challenge allegedly discriminatory practices which are nonetheless permissible under domestic law. Domestic implementation of EU law has frequently been found inadequate. Furthermore, the case law in this area has had a significant impact on each Member State's national procedures and remedies (discussed in Chapter 8).

27.3 Equal pay for equal work: Article 141 EC

Prior to the ToA, the then Article 119 provided:

> Each Member State shall during the first stage ensure and subsequently maintain the application of the principle that men and women should receive equal pay for equal work.
>
> For the purpose of this Article, 'pay' means the ordinary basic or minimum wage or salary and any other consideration, whether in cash or in kind, which the worker receives, directly or indirectly, in respect of his employment from his employer.

This Article, now Article 141, was amended by the ToA. Article 141(1) now provides that:

> Each Member State shall ensure that the principle of equal pay for male and female workers for equal work or work of equal value is applied.

The remaining paragraphs provide that:

1. For the purpose of this Article, 'pay' means the ordinary basic or minimum wage or salary and any other consideration, whether in cash or in kind, which the worker receives directly or indirectly, in respect of his employment, from his employer.
2. Equal pay without discrimination based on sex means:
   (a) that pay for the same work at piece rates shall be calculated on the basis of the same unit of measurement;
   (b) that pay for work at time rates shall be the same for the same job.
3. The Council, acting in accordance with the procedure referred to in Article 251, and after consulting the Economic and Social Committee, shall adopt measures to ensure the application of the principle of equal opportunities and equal treatment of men and women in matters of employment and occupation, including the principle of equal pay for equal work or work of equal value.
4. With a view to ensuring full equality in practice between men and women in working life, the principle of equal treatment shall not prevent any Member State from maintaining or adopting measures providing for specific advantages in order to make it easier for the underrepresented sex to pursue a vocational activity or to prevent or compensate for disadvantages in professional careers.

Article 141(3) EC provides a specific legal basis for the adoption of measures to give effect to the principle of equal opportunities and equal treatment.

The fourth paragraph, which permits positive discrimination, was introduced by the ToA, and was given further effect in amending Directive 76/207/EEC by inserting a new Article 2(6). This will be discussed further at 27.9.7.3 below.

Whilst the text of the Treaty establishing a Constitution for Europe proposed small changes to the text of the provision, the Lisbon Treaty makes no such proposals. Should Lisbon come into force, Article 141 EC will be renumbered Article 157 TFEU, but continue in its current form.

27.3.1 Reach of the basic principle

The principle enshrined in Article 141, and reflected in the secondary legislation noted above, is of fundamental importance. Consequently, EU legislation which conflicts with this principle could be struck down on grounds of illegality, except where there is an objective justification for the measure (*Rinke v Ärztekammer Hamburg* (case C–25/02)).

27.3.2 Meaning of 'worker'

Article 141 refers to male and female 'workers'. In *Allonby* (case C–256/01), the ECJ noted that there was no single definition of this concept in Union law, but that this varied according to the context in which it was used. At the same time, the concept must be given a Union meaning. The Court chose to adopt the *Lawrie-Blum* (case 66/85) definition of 'a person who, for a certain period of time, performs services under the direction of another person in return for which he receives remuneration', which included a person who was self-employed where the status as self-employed was notional and disguised an employment relationship. In *Allonby*, the claimant was a part-time lecturer at Accrington and Rossendale College who had been made redundant and then immediately re-employed through ELS, an agency supplying lecturing staff. If her self-employed status was regarded as notional, she would be able to rely on Article 141 to challenge the validity of a domestic requirement of being under a contract of employment as a condition for access to a pension scheme for teachers (see also 27.4.2 below). A person will also be regarded as a worker where she is a part-time employee working to need, ie only the hours requested by her employer (*Wippel v Peek & Cloppenburg* (case C–313/02)).

27.4 Pay

27.4.1 What constitutes pay?

If the concept of pay is generously defined in Article 141, it has been even more generously construed. It was applied in *Garland v British Rail Engineering Ltd* (case 12/81) to cover the grant of special travel facilities to ex-employees after retirement, even though the benefit was received following termination of employment and was not granted pursuant to any contractual entitlement. The Court held that the argument that the facilities are not related to a contractual obligation is immaterial. The legal nature of the facilities is not important for the purposes of the application of Article 141 provided that they are granted in respect of the applicant's employment. On similar reasoning in *Worringham v Lloyds Bank Ltd* (case 69/80) a supplementary payment made by employers to male employees under the age of 25, for the purpose of contribution to the employees' occupational pension scheme, was held to be pay. Sums which are included in the calculation of the gross salary payable to the employee and which directly determine the calculation of other advantages linked to the salary, such as redundancy payments, unemployment benefits, family allowances, and credit facilities, form part of the worker's pay. Since the payment was not made to female employees under the age of 25 the scheme was in breach of Article 141.

Questions about the scope of 'pay' for the purposes of Article 141 continue to arise. In *Hill and Stapleton* (case C–143/95), a pay scale which discriminated between full- and part-time workers regarding the calculation of annual pay increments was considered to fall within Article 141, as the scale determined the progression of the workers' pay. *Abdoulage v Regie Nationale des Usines Renault* (case C–218/98) concerned a measure which provided that women going on maternity leave, as well as continuing to receive full pay, should also receive a lump sum of FFR7,500. The ECJ agreed that the lump sum could be considered to fall within pay for the purposes of Article 141. In *R v Secretary of State for Employment, ex parte Seymour-Smith* (case C–167/99) the ECJ held that redundancy payments also constituted pay.

However, in *Wippel v Peek & Cloppenburg* (case C–313/02), the Court noted that a framework contract within which the actual hours worked could be varied was not within the scope of Article 141 (or Directive 75/117), as the fact that the contract might have financial consequences was insufficient for it to give rise to questions about 'pay'. It was, however, within Directive 76/207 (see further below).

27.4.2 Pensions and social security benefits

The precise extent to which employers' contributions to pensions and other social security benefits fall within the scope of Article 141 has been much litigated.

Worringham v Lloyds Bank Ltd (above) was followed in *Bilka-Kaufhaus GmbH v Weber von Hartz* (case 170/84) in the context of a claim by a female part-time worker, Ms Weber, who was seeking to challenge her employer's occupational pension scheme. The scheme was non-contributory, financed solely by the employer. Under the scheme part-timers were entitled to benefit only if they had worked with the firm for at least 15 out of a total of 20 years. No such limitation was imposed on full-timers. Ms Weber alleged that the scheme was indirectly discriminatory, in breach of Article 141, since the majority of part-time workers were women. The Court agreed that it was *capable* of falling within the provision, as the scheme was contractual, not statutory, in origin; it originated from an agreement made between Bilka and the works council representing the employees, and the benefits were financed solely by the employer as a supplement to existing social-security schemes. The benefit constituted consideration paid by the employer to the employee for his employment.

The reasoning in *Bilka-Kaufhaus GmbH* (case 170/84) seemed to imply that benefits paid by an employer pursuant to or in lieu of a *statutory* scheme might not constitute pay. In *Defrenne v Belgium (No 1)* (case 80/70) the Court had held that although payment in the nature of social security benefits was not excluded in principle from the concept of pay, it was not possible to include in this concept, as defined in Article 141, social-security schemes and benefits, especially retirement pensions, which were directly settled by law without reference to any element of consultation within the undertaking or industry concerned, and which covered without exception all workers in general. Thus although Ms Defrenne (an air hostess) was entitled to invoke the then Article 119 (now, after amendment, 141) against her employer to claim equal pay to that of her male counterparts (cabin stewards) (*Defrenne v Sabena (No 2)* (case 43/75)), she was unable to challenge a Belgian law requiring different contributions for male and female employees, made by the employer, to a social-security scheme directly imposed by law. Such benefits are, the Court held, 'no more emoluments paid directly by the employer than are roads, canals, or water drains'.

However, the ambit of statutory social security schemes excluded from Article 141 in *Defrenne* has been whittled down by subsequent decisions of the Court. In *Liefting* (case 23/83) a statutory pension scheme applicable to a *particular group* of workers, namely civil servants, was found to be within its scope. The Court held that sums which public authorities are required to pay, though not in themselves pay, become pay if they are included in calculating their employees' gross pay used in the calculation of other salary benefits. If, as a result, the salary-related benefits are not the same for men as for women, Article 141 is infringed.

Article 141 was again held applicable to a statutory social security benefit in *Rinner-Kühn v FWW Spezial Gebäudereinigung GmbH & Co KG* (case 171/88). The case concerned a claim by a part-time worker, an office cleaner, against her employer, involving a challenge to German legislation permitting employers to exclude part-time workers (defined as persons working ten hours or less a week) from entitlement to sick pay. Prima facie the claim appeared analogous to the statutory social security scheme held in *Defrenne* to be outside the scope of the then Article 119 (now, after amendment, 141). Nevertheless, the Court found that the continued payment of wages to a worker in the event of illness fell within the definition of pay; therefore national legislation such as the legislation in question, which *allowed* employers to maintain a global difference in pay between the two categories of workers (one of which was predominantly female), must be regarded as contrary to the objectives pursued in Article 141. Being indirectly discriminatory, it would be acceptable only if objectively justified.

27.4.3 'A benefit received by reason of the existence of the employment relationship' (*Barber*)

In *Barber v Guardian Royal Exchange Assurance Group* (case C–262/88), the Court found, in a claim by a group of male employees who were seeking to challenge payments made by their employer under a contracted-out pension scheme, which operated as a substitute for the statutory social-security scheme, and under a statutory redundancy scheme, both of which were payable at different ages for men (65) and women (60), that such payments also constituted 'pay' since the worker received these benefits, albeit indirectly, from his employer for his employment:

> Although it is true that many advantages granted by an employer also reflect considerations of social policy, the fact that a benefit is in the nature of pay cannot be called into question where the worker is entitled to receive the benefit in question from his employer *by reason of the existence of the employment relationship*. [Para 18.]

This point was re-emphasised in *Beune* (case C–7/93), which concerned civil service pensions. The Court held that, even where the pension scheme was affected by considerations of social policy, state organisation, ethics, or budgetary concerns (factors usually indicative of a social-security scheme), the pension scheme of a public employer would still constitute pay where (a) it concerned only a certain category of workers rather than general categories; (b) it was directly related to the period of service; and (c) it was calculated by reference to the employee's last salary (para 45; see also *Schönheit v Stadt Frankfurt* (case C–4/02); *Commission v Greece* (case C–46/07)).

As was suggested in *Barber*, the only statutory social-security schemes which appear now to fall outside Article 141 are statutory social-security pension schemes provided for workers in general as a matter of social policy and funded from the public purse. The precise ambit of the statutory social schemes outside Article 141 is, despite numerous cases on this issue, still unclear.

While the application of Article 141 in a clear case of discrimination in respect of employers' *contribution* to an occupational pension scheme, as in *Worringham v Lloyds Bank Ltd* (case 69/80), causes few problems, its extension in *Barber* to the *award* of pensions hitherto tied to a permitted difference in pension age for men and women, in which actuarial factors also play a part, has created problems and led to great complexity.

Because the ruling in *Barber* was likely seriously to affect the financial balance of contracted-out pension schemes, the contributions and the calculations for which had been based on different retirement ages for men and women; and because, as the Court conceded, both Member States and the parties concerned were reasonably entitled to consider that this provision did not apply to pensions paid under contracted-out pension schemes, the Court held that its ruling as regards such schemes could not be applied retrospectively. Article 141 might not be relied on to claim entitlement to a pension with effect prior to the date of judgment, except in the case of workers, or those claiming under them, who had before that date initiated legal proceedings or raised an equivalent claim under the applicable national law (para 45). Following dispute over the scope of this ruling, as to whether Article 141 applies to all claims for *pensions arising* after the date of judgment or only to claims based on *benefits earned* after this date, the matter was finally resolved by a protocol issued at Maastricht in favour of the latter, more restrictive view. According to the protocol:

> For the purposes of Article 119 [now 141] of [the Treaty establishing the European Community], benefits under occupational social security schemes shall not be considered as remuneration if and insofar as they are attributable to periods of employment prior to 17 May 1990, except in the case of workers or those claiming under them who have before that date initiated legal proceedings or introduced an equivalent claim under the applicable national law.

This interpretation of *Barber* has since been applied by the Court in many cases including *Ten Oever* (case C–109/91, survivors' benefit); *Coloroll Pension Trustees Ltd v Russell* (case C–200/91); *Moroni* (case C–110/91, supplementary pension scheme, early retirement); *Neath v Hugh Steeper Ltd* (case C–152/91, supplementary pension scheme, early retirement); and *Defreyn* (case C–166/99, additional pre-retirement payment). However, in *Vroege* (case C–57/93), and *Fisscher* (case C–128/93) the Court held that the limit on retrospectivity of its ruling in *Barber* did not apply where it should have been clear to the employer that the terms fell within Article 141. In these cases, the provisions related to *access* to pension schemes, which, following *Bilka-Kaufhaus* (case 170/84), should be considered pay. Provided the female employees were prepared to pay the requisite contributions to a pension scheme for any period between *Defrenne* and *Barber*, employers were also obliged to make the relevant employer's contributions to such schemes retrospectively. This principle was affirmed in *Preston* and *Fletcher* (case C–78/98), and the non-retroactivity in *Barber*, as reinforced by the protocol, was affirmed in *Schönheit v Stadt Frankfurt* (joined cases C–4 and 5/02)).

Further problems arising from the application of Article 141 to the award of occupational pensions are illustrated in *Neath v Hugh Steeper Ltd* (case C–152/91). The case concerned a contracted-out pension scheme in which men were treated less favourably than women in respect of early retirement and lump-sum payments in lieu of pension payments. Neath claimed that, following *Barber*, this was contrary to Article 141. The Court, however, distinguished between the *accrual of the right* to receive benefits and the *funding* of those benefits. Both the pension payments themselves and the employees' contributions to a pension scheme fell within 'pay' and, therefore, neither should distinguish between the sexes. The funding arrangements established by the employer, however, fall outside the scope of Article 141 because the purpose of those arrangements is to ensure that there are adequate resources to make the pension payments when due. An employer, when calculating its contribution to funding, may therefore rely on actuarial factors which, for example, take into account differing average life expectancies of the sexes and thus may make different payments in respect of men and women (para 22). A corollary to this argument is that capital sum or transfer benefits such as lump-sum payments that are based on the method and amount of funding also do not fall within Article 141 (para 33). *Neath* was a retreat from the position in *Barber*, and has made the boundaries between pay and pensions even less certain than they seemed before.

The Court's judgment in *Neath* does not affect a further principle established in *Barber*, that, in order to comply with Article 141, it is not enough that the overall package of remuneration received by men and women be equal. Each element of the consideration paid to both sexes must be equal. The system of pay must be 'transparent', in order that clear comparisons as between men and women may be made.

27.4.4 Significance of a broad definition of pay

This broad interpretation of pay to include benefits relating in the widest sense to retirement or even death (provided they are not social-security benefits *sensu stricto*) is important, since it provides an opportunity for individuals to challenge rules as an issue of 'pay' matters, for example those relating to different retirement ages for men and women, which might otherwise have fallen under the various directives (discussed in greater detail below) In doing so, the Court could often sidestep the limitations of these directives, as well as the problems of horizontal direct effect.

The recast Equal Treatment Directive adopts the broad notion of pay, which is defined as 'the ordinary basic or minimum wage or salary and any other consideration whether in cash or in kind, which the worker receives directly or indirectly, in respect of his/her employment from his/her employer' (Article 2(1)(e)).

27.5 Discrimination

Discrimination, in breach of Article 141, can be direct or indirect.

27.5.1 Direct discrimination

Direct discrimination occurs when men and women are treated differently by virtue of their sex. In these cases, a difference in pay can never be justified. However, a difference in treatment as between men and women, even doing the same work or of equal value, will not necessarily constitute discrimination. In *Birds Eye Walls Ltd v Roberts* (case C–132/92) the Court found that a bridging pension, paid *ex gratia* to employees compelled on the grounds of ill-health to take early retirement and calculated to bridge the gap between the sum received under their occupational pension scheme and the state pension they would receive on reaching the statutory age of retirement, although less for the applicant woman than it would have been for a man, was not discriminatory on the grounds of sex. The mechanisms used for calculating the bridging pension were sexually neutral; the applicant's lower bridging pension corresponded to her lower input into the state pension scheme, *for which she had freely opted*. The applicant and the men with whom she sought to compare herself were not in comparable situations. For similar reasons different rates of pay may be awarded according to employees' qualifications, provided they are relevant to the job undertaken.

In *Hlozek v Roche Austria* (case C–19/02), a social plan to deal with the impact of a merger included provision of a bridging allowance for employees whose employment was terminated, provided they had reached the age of 55 (men) or

50 (women) and were not yet entitled to a pension. Mr Hlozek was made redundant at the age of 54 and was therefore unable to benefit. The Court held that the bridging allowance was 'pay' for the purposes of Article 141, but that there was no breach of that provision because the allowance was linked to the different retirement ages.

In *Commission v Greece* (case C–46/07) the Court ruled that the provisions of the Greek code of pensions which provided that women are entitled to a retirement pension at a different age from men and under different conditions regarding the minimum period of service required violated Article 141. The difference in treatment could not be saved under Article 141(4) as the provisions did not help to correct the problems which women may face in their professional career but merely allowed them to retire earlier than men.

The Court has also accepted that when Member States seek to amend national laws to achieve parity between the sexes, economic considerations may result in both sexes being treated at the level of the disadvantaged group, rather than improving the position of the disadvantaged group to the level of the advantaged group. In *de Weerd* (case C–343/92, discussed below), the Court commented that Member States, in order to control public spending, may remove benefits from certain categories of persons, provided that this was not done in a discriminatory manner. In *Smith v Avdel Systems Ltd* (case C–408/92) the ECJ was faced with a claim based on the changes made to pension schemes following *Barber*. The Court held that where discrimination is found, the disadvantaged class should, in the absence of domestic measures rectifying the position, be treated in the same way as the advantaged class. This did not, however, prevent the Member State from introducing measures which 'levelled down' benefits—in this case, raising the statutory retirement age to 65. Sex equality, it would seem, does not always benefit women.

In view of the central importance of the notion of 'direct discrimination', the EC has started to incorporate a definition in its most recent directives. The recast Equal Treatment Directive will define this as 'where one person is treated less favourably on grounds of sex than another is, has been, or would be treated in a comparable situation' (Article 2(1)(a)).

27.5.2 Indirect discrimination

27.5.2.1 *Definition of indirect discrimination*

Indirect discrimination occurs where rules which seemingly apply to both sexes, adversely affect a significant proportion of one sex more than the other. Unlike direct discrimination, indirect discrimination may be 'objectively justified'. The recast Equal Treatment Directive incorporates a definition of 'indirect discrimination' as:

> where an apparently neutral provision, criterion, or practice would put persons of one sex at a particular disadvantage compared with persons of the other sex, unless that provision, criterion or practice is objectively justified by a legitimate aim, and the means of achieving that aim are appropriate and necessary. [Article 2(2)(b).]

This definition presents, in very general terms, the substance of the indirect discrimination concept as it has been developed by the ECJ, and a discussion of this case law will help to flesh out the meaning further.

In *Jenkins v Kingsgate (Clothing Productions) Ltd* (case 96/80) the ECJ was asked whether a difference in pay (in this case 10 per cent) between part-time and full-time workers could constitute discrimination when the category of part-time workers was exclusively or predominantly female (only one, exceptional male was employed part-time). The Court held that such a difference would not infringe Article 141 provided that the difference in pay was 'objectively justified' and in no way related to discrimination based on sex. However, such inequality of pay would breach this provision where, having regard to the difficulties encountered by women in arranging to work the minimum (full-time) number of hours a week, the pay policy of the undertaking cannot be explained by factors other than discrimination based on sex.

In *Bilka-Kaufhaus GmbH v Weber von Harz* (case 170/84) the Court was faced again with a claim by a part-time worker, this time challenging her employer's occupational pension scheme, which discriminated overtly against part-time workers. Here both full- and part-time workforces comprised both men and women, but of the men employed (28 per cent of the total workforce), only 10 per cent worked part-time, as against 27.7 per cent of the female workforce. Overall, male part-time workers comprised only 2.8 per cent of the total workforce. The disadvantage suffered by part-timers thus fell disproportionately on the women. The ECJ was asked whether such a scheme might breach Article 141. Citing paragraph 13 of the judgment in *Jenkins v Kingsgate (Clothing Productions) Ltd* almost verbatim, the Court held (at para 29) that if it was found that a considerably smaller percentage of men than of women worked part-time, and if the difference in treatment could not be explained by any other factor than sex, the exclusion of part-time workers from the occupational scheme would be contrary to Article 141. The difference in treatment would, however, be permissible if it were explained by objectively justified factors which were unrelated to discrimination based on sex. It would be for the employer to prove, and for national courts to decide, on the facts, whether the difference in treatment was in fact objectively justified.

27.5.2.2 *Part-timers and overtime*

Although many circumstances where part-time employees have been disadvantaged have been found to constitute indirect discrimination by virtue of the larger number of female part-time workers, not all claims succeed: there is a boundary between being paid less because of working less and being discriminated against. In *Stadt Lengerich v Helmig* (cases C–399/92 et al) part-time workers alleged indirect discrimination because they did not receive overtime payments for working in excess of their normal working hours. Overtime only became payable when they worked longer than the full-time workers' normal hours. The ECJ held that this was not discrimination because part-timers and those who worked full-time received payment on the same basis for the hours worked. By contrast, *Kuratorium für Dialyse und Nierentransplantation eV v Lewark* (case C–457/93) dealt with a part-time worker who took part in a training course arranged within full-time working hours but in excess of her normal working hours. She was compensated for the loss of her normal part-time wages but did not receive payment for all the hours she spent at the course. The Court held that this was discrimination because the overall pay she received for the course was less per hour than that received by her full-time colleagues. Further the Court has held that a rule providing that both full-time and part-time workers will not receive any remuneration for additional hours worked when the additional work does not exceed three hours per calendar month is incompatible with Article 141 (and Directive 75/117) if it affects considerably more women than men and cannot be objectively justified by reasons unrelated to gender (*Elsner-Lakeberg* (case C–285/02)).

In *Voβ* (case C–300/06) the Court examined the compatibility with Article 141 of a payment scheme for civil servants which paid less for overtime work performed by part-timers than overtime work performed by full-time employees. The claimant was a part-time teacher who argued that since 88 per cent of part-time teachers in the Berlin area were women the scheme constituted discrimination based on gender. The Court distinguished the case from *Helmig* because here part-time employees did not receive the same pay with full-time employees who had worked for the same number of hours per week. It held that the scheme was indirectly discriminatory and could be justified only by objective reasons wholly unrelated to any discrimination based on sex, that being for the national court to assess.

The position of part-time workers is now dealt with by Directive 97/81 ([1998] OJ L14/9), which aims to implement the Framework Agreement reached between general cross-industry organisations (Article 1). . In particular, the directive provides that part-time workers are not to be treated in a less favourable manner than comparable full-time workers, save where differences in treatment are justified on objective grounds. The directive specifically notes that the principle of *pro rata temporis* may be applied, but this would not generally justify paying a part-time worker a lesser hourly rate than that paid to a comparable full-time worker. In this, there seems to be a convergence between the case law and the approach taken by the legislation.

27.5.3 Discrimination and difference in treatment

Having identified a difference in treatment, is the difference automatically discriminatory? In *Enderby v Frenchay Health Authority* (case 127/92) the ECJ commented that a difference in treatment between men and women would give rise to a presumption that discrimination existed. It would then fall to the employer to try to justify the difference in treatment. In the *Royal Copenhagen* case (case C–400/93), however, both men and women worked on a piecework basis under which their wages consisted of a fixed-base payment plus a variable amount determined by reference to the work produced. The Court held that here a difference in pay between groups did not necessarily raise an inference of discrimination: the difference in pay might reflect differences in output. The national court must decide if the difference results from differences in output, or from unacceptable differences in the amount the worker is paid per item. The Court's approach in this case is clearly more cautious than in *Enderby* as it moves away from the position that a purely statistical difference between groups of men and women creates a presumption of discrimination. It is arguable that in *Royal Copenhagen* the Court is mixing together questions which should be asked when determining justification of indirect discrimination with those that determine discrimination in the first place.

A similarly cautious approach can be discerned in *Angestellten Betriebsrat der Wiener Gebietskrankenkasse v Wiener Gebietskrankenkasse* (case C–309/97). The case concerned the difference in pay between two groups of psychotherapists. One group had been trained as doctors; the other, predominantly female group, which received lower pay, comprised graduate psychologists. This group argued, following *Enderby*, that as they were involved in the same work as the doctors they should be on the same pay scale.

The ECJ rejected this argument, accepting instead the argument that the difference in training could mean that the two groups of psychotherapists would be required to perform different duties and therefore could not be said to be performing the same work. Thus the approach in *Enderby* was not so much overruled as sidestepped in this case, the ECJ turning the issue into one of equal work rather than discrimination.

It is clear, however, from both *Jenkins* and *Bilka-Kaufhaus GmbH* that the fact that the group adversely affected by a particular measure comprises both sexes does not prevent that measure being discriminatory on the grounds of sex, as long as it affects one sex to *a disproportionate extent*. If this were not so, as Nicholls LJ pointed out in the Court of Appeal in *Pickstone v Freemans plc* ([1989] AC 66), as long as there is a man there doing the same work, 'which in some cases might be wholly fortuitous or even, possibly, a situation contrived by an unscrupulous employer', the woman cannot make the comparison, even if the difference in pay is attributable solely to grounds of sex. The criteria to identify when disproportionate discrimination occurs have not been precisely delineated. Further, the question of whether discrimination exists might vary over time as statistical evidence and working patterns changed (*R v Secretary of State for Employment, ex parte Seymour-Smith* ([1995] ICR 889)). Thus a regulation which disadvantages part-time workers will be discriminatory only for as long as a disproportionate number of workers are of one sex. Ultimately, unless one sex is disproportionately affected, a claim under Article 141 of discrimination *based on sex* will not succeed.

27.5.4 Pregnancy

Clearly, pregnancy may have an adverse impact on a woman's pay which, since only women become pregnant, is not easily categorised as direct or indirect discrimination. The difficulties pregnant women encounter have given rise to a specific jurisprudence on pregnancy (discussed later at 27.9.2).

27.6 Objective justification

27.6.1 General criteria

As noted above, differences in pay (or treatment) which discriminate indirectly against women or men will be permissible if they are objectively justified. Guidelines as to what might constitute objective justification were laid down in *Bilka-Kaufhaus GmbH v Weber von Harz* (case 170/84). There the Court held that in order to prove that a measure is objectively justified the employer must prove that the measures giving rise to the difference in treatment:

(a) correspond to a 'genuine need of the enterprise'

(b) are suitable for obtaining the objective pursued by the enterprise and

(c) are necessary for that purpose.

These principles, reminiscent of *Cassis de Dijon* (see Chapter 19), have been consistently applied by the Court. Requirements (b) and (c) together represent the familiar proportionality principle. What factors, then, will be regarded by the Court as providing 'objective justification' meeting a 'genuine need of the enterprise'?

27.6.2 Justifications based on economic factors, job performance, and market forces

Jenkins v Kingsgate (Clothing Productions) Ltd (case 96/80) and *Bilka-Kaufhaus GmbH* (case 170/84) suggest that economic factors would prove acceptable justification. In *Bilka-Kaufhaus GmbH* the defendants argued that part-time workers were less economic; they were less ready to work on Saturdays and in the evening; that it was necessary to pay more to attract full-timers. Justification on these grounds was not disputed in principle. Whether it would in fact be accepted would depend on whether the need for the difference in pay could be proved, and if so whether the proportionality principle were satisfied. In applying this ruling the German court found that it was not.

In *Cadman* (case C–17/05) the Court examined indirect discrimination against women resulting from the fact that one of the criteria taken into account for the assessment of pay was length of service. It held that rewarding an employee who has acquired experience enabling him to perform better constitutes a legitimate objective of pay policy, 'As a general rule, recourse to the criterion of length of service is appropriate to attain that objective. Length of service goes hand in hand with experience, and experience generally enables the worker to perform his duties better'.

Article 141 does not require employers to explain, every time they decide to reward experienced workers, why experience is important for a specific job. If, however, an employee provides evidence that the use of length of service to determine pay is, in the circumstances, inappropriate for attaining the legitimate objective of encouraging better job performance the employer may be required to prove that experience is necessary for the performance of specific duties.

While taking into account length of service in order to determine a worker's remuneration is lawful, the total exclusion of part-time employment from the calculation of length of service will violate the Equal Treatment Directive if it affects a much higher percentage of female workers than male workers unless it can be attributed to objective factors unrelated to sex (*Nikoloudi* (case C–196/02)) (on criteria for the determination of pay see also *Danfoss* (case 109/88), discussed below).

Although the Court has been sympathetic to the Member States' concern to control budgetary expenditure (eg, limitations imposed in *Barber* (case C–262/88); *Steenhorst-Neerings* (case C–338/91)), a *purely* economic justification of discrimination is unlikely to be successful. In *de Weerd* (case C–343/92) concerning Directive 79/7, the Court stated that to allow budgetary considerations to justify discrimination between men and women would be tantamount to agreeing that the fundamental principle of equality could vary over time and throughout the Union depending on the state of the Member States' public finances (paras 35–6) (see also *R v Secretary of State for Health, ex parte Richardson* (case C–137/94), and *Schönheit v Stadt Frankfurt* (case C–4/02)).

27.6.3 Administrative convenience

In *Kirsammer-Hack v Sidal* (case C–189/91), in a claim based on Equal Treatment Directive (76/207), the Court was prepared to concede that an exclusion from employment protection provided under German legislation for employees of firms comprising fewer than five employees, excluding employees working less than 10 hours a week or 45 hours per month, even if indirectly discriminatory against women, would be objectively justified on the grounds of the need to lighten the administrative, financial and legal burdens on small enterprises, acknowledged by the Community in the then Article 118a EC and its directives on health and safety of workers.

27.6.4 Social-policy objectives

In *Rinner-Kühn* (case 171/88) the Court suggested that a justification based on a "genuine objective of social policy" might be acceptable, provided that the means selected were appropriate and necessary to the attainment of that objective. However, it firmly rejected an argument that the difference in treatment as regards sick pay between part- and full-time workers was justified on the grounds that part-timers were not integrated into the business in the same way as full-time workers. "These considerations", the Court said, "only represent generalised statements concerning certain categories of workers and do not admit the conclusion of objective justification unrelated to any discrimination on the grounds of sex." Since women form the majority of the part-time workforce, it is they, as the Commission pointed out in *Rinner-Kuhn*, who are most vulnerable and in need of protection; thus a social policy objective resulting in discrimination against part-time workers is unlikely to be seen as valid justification. A justification on the grounds of social policy has, however, been accepted in a number of social security cases not involving part-time workers (eg, *Teuling* (case 30/85) and; *Commission v Belgium* (case C–229/89))).

27.6.5 Proportionality

It is likely that, as with the *Cassis de Dijon* principle applied to the free movement of goods (see Chapter 19), the Court will seek to ensure that the proportionality principle is rigorously applied, and will not hesitate to pass judgment on whether a purported 'objective justification' is suitable and necessary to achieve its desired and legitimate end. This can be seen in many decisions, such as *Schönheit v Stadt Frankfurt* (cases C–4 and 5/02), where a restriction on public expenditure was rejected as a possible justification.

27.7 Equal work

Equal work has been defined in Directive 75/117 as the 'same work' or 'work to which equal value has been attributed'. As noted above, this directive has been repealed and replaced by directive 2006/54 which consolidates the legislation in the light of legal developments.

27.7.1 Same work

In *Macarthys Ltd v Smith* (case 129/79) Advocate-General Capotorti suggested that 'same work' is not confined to identical work; it should include jobs which display a high degree of similarity the one to the other, even if there is not total identity between them. Since 'similar' work will shade into work 'of equal value', which is also subject to the equality principle, a precise definition of 'same' work is unnecessary.

27.7.2 **Work of equal value**

This concept was introduced by Directive 75/117. However, since the Court has held (*Jenkins v Kingsgate (Clothing Productions) Ltd* (case 96/80)) that Directive 75/117 is merely confined to restating the principle of equal pay as set out in Article 141, and in no way alters its content and scope, a claim for equal pay for work of equal value may be brought under Article 141 as well as under the relevant directive. Article 141, as amended by ToA, specifically refers to work of equal value. Indeed, a claim under Article 141 is advisable since it avoids possible problems over the direct effects of the directive. The concept of work of equal value will be further discussed below.

Any comparisons made for the purpose of deciding whether a man and a woman are engaged on the same work, or work of equal value, must be confined to parallels which may be drawn on the basis of concrete appraisals of the work actually performed by employees of different sex within the same establishment or service (*Macarthys Ltd v Smith* (case 129/79)). Comparisons cannot be made with the 'hypothetical male'. Further, comparisons must be made with groups picked on an objective basis and not those chosen solely with the aim of maximising the final amount received by the complainants. For example, in *Royal Copenhagen* (case C–400/93) the applicants sought to compare three groups each with different average pay. The lowest-paid group (female) sought to be upgraded first to the pay rate of the middle, male group and then to argue that the discrimination between the middle group (still mainly male) and the highest group (female) was also unjustified sex discrimination, thus raising all workers in the compared groups to that of the highest-paid group. The ECJ took the view that choosing comparator groups to allow 'leapfrogging' was not acceptable. In *Wippel v Peek and Cloppenburg* (case C–313/02), a part-time employee working only when needed by her employer could not compare her position with that of a full-time employee working regular hours.

Comparisons are, however, not necessarily limited to the same establishment or service. In *Defrenne v Sabena (No 2)* (case 43/75), the ECJ held that the then Article 119 (now, after amendment, 141) applied to discrimination which has its origin in legislative provisions ('general' social security provision excepted) or in collective labour agreements and which may be detected on a purely legal analysis of the situation. Moreover, where the employer is the same the fact that the pay of different groups of workers has been determined under separate collective bargaining agreements does not necessarily prevent the application of Article 141 (see *Enderby v Frenchay Health Authority* (case C–127/92); cf *Royal Copenhagen* (case C–400/93) and *Angestellten Betriebsrat der Wiener Gebietskrankenkasse v Wiener Gebietskrankenkasse* (case C–309/97)).

In the absence of collective agreements or job evaluation schemes affecting undertakings or industries at a national level, it is submitted that comparisons cannot be made *across* undertakings or industries. In *Lawrence* (case C–320/00), the local council, which had employed people directly to carry out cleaning and catering jobs, put these services out to competitive tender. During the tendering period, the women involved in these jobs won a case against the council arguing that their work was equal to work carried out by men for jobs such as gardening, refuse collection and sewage treatment. Thereafter, the women still employed by the council had their wages increased. The contractor who obtained the contract with the council for the cleaning and catering services then re-employed some of the former council workers, but paid them less than they had been paid by the council. The women employed by the contractor then brought a claim on the basis of Article 141 arguing that they were entitled to equal pay with male comparators employed by the council, regardless of whether the appellants had been originally employed by the council or were so employed at present. The ECJ, however, held that where the differences identified in the pay conditions of workers of different sex performing equal work or work of equal value cannot be attributed to a single source, Article 141(1) does not apply. In *Allonby* (case C–256/01), decided under Article 141, the ECJ held that a female lecturer whose contract had not been renewed, but who had been re-employed by the college through an agency, could not compare her situation to that of a male lecturer directly employed by the college.

As is clear from *Macarthys Ltd v Smith* comparisons are not limited to men and women engaged in contemporaneous employment. Nor is it necessary that the employment should be in the same Member State.

27.8 Equal pay for work of equal value

27.8.1 Scope of the directive

As has been noted, Directive 75/117, which was based on Article 119 (now 141), was introduced merely to implement and supplement that Article. In turn it has been replaced by Directive 2006/54. Article 4 Directive 2006/54 specifies that the principle of equal pay means:

> for the same work or for work to which equal value is attributed, the elimination of all discrimination on grounds of sex with regard to all aspects and conditions of remuneration.
>
> In particular, where a job classification system is used for determining pay, it must be based on the same criteria for both men and women and so drawn up as to exclude any discrimination on grounds of sex.

This tracks the wording of Article 1, Directive 75/117. Directive 75/117 also contained provisions regarding remedies. These provisions have been extended in Directive 2006/54. (On enforcement and remedies in national courts, see Chapter 8.)

27.8.2 Assessment comparability

In *Commission v United Kingdom (re equal pay for equal work)* (case 61/81) the UK was found to have failed, in breach of Directive 75/117 (Articles 1 and 6), to provide a means whereby claims of equal value might be assessed in the absence of a job evaluation scheme having been implemented by the employer.

Neither Articles 1 or 6 of Directive 75/117 nor *Commission v United Kingdom* (case 61/81) require that a claim to equal value must be assessed pursuant to a job evaluation study; indeed, the Court pointed out in *Commission v United Kingdom* that a system of job classification is only one of several possible methods for determining pay for work to which equal value is attributed. All that seems to be required under EU law is that where a prima facie claim to equal value exists, either as a result of a job evaluation study, as in *O'Brien v Sim-Chem Ltd* ([1980] ICR 573, House of Lords), or otherwise, an assessment must be made, if necessary in adversarial proceedings, by a body with the requisite power to decide whether work has the same value, after obtaining such information as may be needed.

It is regrettable that the Court in *Commission v United Kingdom* did not spell out in greater detail the scope of Member States' obligations in this field. Clearly some comparability must exist before a legitimate claim to equal value can arise. But how 'like' must two different jobs be for them to be deemed to be comparable? And if they are 'broadly' comparable, how, and in what detail, are they to be assessed in order to decide whether they are equal value? Will a 'felt fair' order of jobs, depending on the general level of expectation as to the value of the job, be adequate, as the Employment Appeal Tribunal suggested in *Bromley v H & J Quick Ltd* ([1987] IRLR 456), or should not, as the Court of Appeal decided, a full analytical study be made? If such a study is undertaken, what criteria are to be applied? Clearly the answers to all these questions, and the solutions adopted, will vary from state to state, as will their cost to the state. Moreover, a finding of equal value will have serious repercussions on costs, both for the individual concerned and possibly for an entire industry. This in turn will affect its competitiveness within the common market. Unless the rules relating to the application of the principle of equal value are determined and applied in a uniform manner throughout the Union they are likely to defeat the very 'economic objectives' which they were designed, in part, to achieve.

Where a job classification scheme is devised as a means of determining comparability, some general guidance as to its content was provided by the ECJ in *Rummler v Dato-Druck GmbH* (case 237/85). Here a woman packer, classified under wage group III under a job evaluation scheme implemented by her employers, and not, as she considered appropriate, under group IV, was seeking to challenge the criteria on which the scheme was based. These criteria included the muscular effort, fatigue and physical hardship attached to the job. She claimed this was discriminatory. The ECJ held that a job classification scheme based on the strength required to carry out the work or the degree of physical hardship which the work entailed was not in breach of Directive 75/117 as long as:

(a) the system as a whole precluded discrimination on grounds of sex and
(b) the criteria employed were objectively justified. To be objectively justified they must:
   (i) be appropriate to the tasks to be carried out, and
   (ii) correspond to a genuine need of the undertaking.

In addition, the classification scheme as a whole, if not to be discriminatory, must take into account the criteria for which each sex has a particular aptitude. Criteria based exclusively on the values of one sex contain, the Court suggested, 'a risk of discrimination'.

The principles of *Rummler v Dato-Druck* were extended significantly in *Handels- og Kontorfunktion ærernes Forbund i Danmark v Dansk Arbejdsgiverforening for Danfoss* (case 109/88), in the context of a challenge by the Danish Employees' Union to the criteria agreed by the Danish Employers Association and applied by the firm of Danfoss. These included, inter alia, the criteria of 'flexibility' and 'seniority'. While the minimum pay for each grade was the same for men and women, it was found that the average pay *within* each grade was lower for women than for men. The applicants alleged that the criteria were indirectly discriminatory. The ECJ held that where the application of neutral criteria, such as the criterion of quality (one element of 'flexibility'), was shown to *result* in systematic discrimination against female workers, this could only be because the employer applied it in an abusive manner. The criteria applied must be 'of importance for the specific duties entrusted to the workers concerned'. In *Brunnhofer* (case C–381/99) a female employee claimed she was being discriminated against in comparison to a male employee who was classified as being in the same job category. Although the basic wages were the same, both were paid, as part of their original contractual arrangements, a monthly allowance. Brunnhofer was paid a smaller allowance than her male counterpart. The ECJ held the fact that both employees were in the same job classification was not conclusive as to whether they were doing equal jobs: instead, the national court should look for more precise evidence regarding the activities the employees actually carry out. The ECJ continued, however, to state that the personal qualities of individual employees and the way in which they carried out their work could not be used to justify a pay differential which existed in the original contractual arrangements. This holding does not mean that such factors cannot be taken into account to justify differences in employees' career development, with a consequent effect on future pay.

27.8.3 Burden of proof

Where a pay system is characterised by a 'total lack of "transparency"', that is when the criteria for determining pay increments are not explicit, and where a female worker establishes, by comparison with a relatively large number of employees, that the average pay of female workers is lower than that of male workers—the onus is on the employer to prove that the criteria employed are justified. Moreover, in view of the greater difficulties faced by women in organising their time in a flexible manner, the criterion of adaptability (another element of 'flexibility'), which was prima facie capable of justification, would also require proof of justification from the employer. The criterion of seniority was found by the Court to be sufficiently transparent not to require justification by the employer. Thus, where the criteria employed are not transparent, or where they operate to the patent disadvantage of women, the employer must carry the burden of justification. The issue was discussed in *Brunnhofer* (case C–381/99). Citing *Danfoss* (109/88, para 54), the ECJ held that the burden of proof would shift to the employer to show there was no discrimination where the employer's system of payment was not transparent. In *Brunnhofer*, the inequality applied to a specific element of the total pay, an additional monthly allowance. In these circumstances the burden of proof remains with the claimant. Note that the question of burden of proof in sex discrimination cases was subsequently dealt with under the Burden of Proof Directive (Directive

97/80), which has also been repealed and recast as Article 19 of Directive 2006/54. (For a more recent application of *Brunnhofer* in the UK context, see *Sharp v Caledonia Group Services Ltd* [2006] ICR 218.)

27.8.4 Compliance

Finally, under Article 4 of Directive 75/117, states are required to ensure that provisions of collective agreements, wage scales, wage agreements or individual contracts of employment contrary to the principle of equal value 'shall be, or may be declared, null and void or may be amended'. (Now Article 23b Recast Equal Treatment Directive.)

States must also, under Article 5, ensure full protection for employees against dismissal as a reaction to a complaint or to legal proceedings 'aimed at enforcing compliance with the principle of equal pay'. (Now Article 24 Recast Equal Treatment Directive.)

Since the provisions of Directive 75/117 merely define the scope and substance of Article 141 EC they may be invoked, vertically or horizontally, in the context of a claim under that Article. As *Defrenne v Sabena (No 2)* (case 43/75) established, Article 141 is effective against *all* parties. Following *Marshall v Southampton and South West Hampshire Area Health Authority (Teaching)* (case 152/84), Directive 75/117 and now Directive 2006/54, as a directive, will not *in itself* be horizontally effective (see Chapter 5).

27.9 Principle of equal treatment for men and women

27.9.1 Scope of the directive

Directive 76/207, which was based not on Article 141 of the EC Treaty but on the institutions' general powers under Article 308 (ex 235), laid down the principle of equal treatment for men and women in Article 1(1) 'as regards access to employment, including promotion, and to vocational training and as regards working conditions and, on the conditions referred to in paragraph 2, social security'. The equivalent provisions are now found at Article 1 Recast Equal Treatment Directive.'Working conditions' are defined to include 'conditions governing dismissal' .

Article 1, para 2, provides for further action to implement the principle of equal treatment in matters of social security. This has now been achieved with Directives 79/7 (statutory schemes) and 86/378 (occupational schemes).

The directive was amended by Directive 2002/73/EC ([2002] OJ L269/15), adopted on the basis of the new Article 141(3) EC. The amendment introduced definitions of 'direct discrimination', 'indirect discrimination', 'harassment' and 'sexual harassment' (now found in Article 2 Directive 2006/54).

According to these changes, 'direct discrimination' as a situation 'where one person is treated less favourably on grounds of sex than another is, has been or would be treated in a comparable situation', and 'indirect discrimination' as 'where an apparently neutral provision, criterion or practice would put persons of one sex at a particular disadvantage compared with person of the other sex' unless objectively justified.

Furthermore, harassment and sexual harassment, as defined in Article 2(1), are to be regarded as discrimination within the scope of the directive, as is an instruction to discriminate against persons on the ground of sex (Article 2(2)). Examples of such discrimination are found at Article 9.

27.9.2 Meaning of 'sex'

For the purposes of this directive, 'sex' has been held to have a wide meaning, not limited to issues of gender discrimination. In *P v S* (case C–13/94), P's contract of employment was terminated because of P's proposed sex change. The question referred to the ECJ related to Article 5 of the directive: did Directive 76/207 preclude dismissal of a transsexual for a reason related to his or her gender reassignment? The Court held that the meaning of the directive, in view of the fundamental principle of equality which it represented, could not be interpreted so as to limit the protection to discrimination on grounds of gender. In the light of the broad terms of this judgment, the ECJ's more recent ruling in *Grant v South-West Trains Ltd* (case C–249/96) seems a somewhat surprising retreat. The case concerned a claim by a female employee with a female partner for rail benefits to which married couples were entitled. The ECJ rejected this, stating that the reference to 'sex discrimination' was not a reference to gender orientation. This limited view of sex discrimination was confirmed in *D v Council* (case C–125/99P). Discrimination in employment on the basis of sexual orientation is now covered by Directive 2000/78 (see below).

The meaning of 'sex' has, however, been raised again. *KB v The National Health Service Pensions Agency and the Secretary of State for Health* (case C–117/01) concerns the right of transsexuals to marry and consequently to claim a survivor's pension. The argument was that a rule which precluded transsexuals from marrying was discriminatory contrary to the Equal Treatment Directive. The case directly focuses on the tension between the approach in *P v S* and that in *Grant*. The ECJ noted that the domestic rule that prevented a transsexual from marrying had been found incompatible with Article 12 of the ECHR (in *Goodwin v United Kingdom*), and that, in such circumstances, Article 141 precludes domestic legislation which prevents a couple of whom one partner is a transsexual from marrying. In so holding, the ECJ managed to find in favour of the claimant, but it side-stepped the question whether the principle established in *P v S* applied in circumstances such as these. It may be noted that the approach adopted by the ECJ in *P v S* is reflected in Recital 3 to the recast Equal Treatment Directive which reads as follows:

> The Court of Justice has held that the scope of the principle of equal treatment for men and women cannot be confined to the prohibition of discrimination based on the fact that a person is of one or other sex. In view of its purpose and the nature of the rights which it seeks to safeguard, it also applies to discrimination arising from the gender reassignment of a person.

27.9.3 Retirement and pensions

The principal context in which the Equal Treatment Directive has been invoked in the UK has been to challenge different retirement ages as between men and women, since both the Equal Pay Act 1970 and the Sex Discrimination Act 1975 excluded from their scope 'provisions in relation to death or retirement'. Directive 76/207 contained no such exclusion, but Directive 79/7, Article 7(1), governing equal treatment in matters of social security, allows Member States to exclude from the scope of the equal treatment principle 'the determination of pensionable age for the purposes of granting old-age and retirement pensions and the possible consequences thereof for other benefits'. Directive 86/378 (Article 9) provided a parallel exclusion in respect of occupational pension schemes. It was therefore thought, it is submitted with some justification, that different retirement ages for men and women were permissible under EU law, especially since they were tied to the statutory pensionable age, which in the UK was 60 for women and 65 for men.

The scope of these provisions was considered by the Court in *Burton v British Railways Board* (case 19/81) in the context of a challenge by a railway worker, Mr Burton, to a voluntary redundancy scheme operated by British Rail. Under the scheme women were entitled to apply for voluntary redundancy at 55, and men at 60. Mr Burton, who, at 58, wished to take early retirement, alleged that the scheme was discriminatory. On reference from the Employment Appeal Tribunal for an interpretation on the scope and application of Directive 76/207 the ECJ held that the directive applied in principle to conditions of access to voluntary redundancy schemes. Moreover, the word 'dismissal', brought within the equality principle by Article 5, must be widely construed to cover termination of the employment relationship, even as part of a redundancy scheme. However, since in this case the ages for voluntary retirement were calculated by reference to, and tied to, the statutory retirement age (60 for women, 65 for men), Article 7 of Directive 79/7, which permitted states to exclude from the equal treatment principle 'the determination of pensionable age', applied. His claim under Directive 76/207 failed.

Undeterred by *Burton v British Railways Board*, the applicant in *Marshall v Southampton and South West Hampshire Area Health Authority (Teaching)* (case 152/84) brought a similar claim under Directive 76/207. Ms Marshall, an employee of the AHA, was seeking to challenge its compulsory retirement policy, under which women employees were required to retire at 60, and men at 65. On a reference from the Employment Appeal Tribunal, the ECJ, following *Burton v British Railways Board*, interpreted the retirement scheme as a 'condition governing dismissal' within Article 5 of Directive 76/207. However, distinguishing *Burton*, on the slenderest grounds (benefits *tied to* a national scheme which lays down a different minimum pensionable age for men and women) the Court found that her case was *not* within the exclusion of Article 7 of Directive 79/7. This Article allowed Member States to exclude from the equal treatment principle the determination of pensionable age 'for the purposes of granting old-age and retirement pensions and the possible consequences thereof for other benefits'. Where pensionable age was being determined *for other purposes*—eg, as in *Marshall*, for the purpose of *retirement*—the equal treatment principle would apply.

The ECJ took the same line, on the same reasoning, in *Roberts v Tate & Lyle Industries Ltd* (case 151/84). This time the applicant failed in her challenge to her employer's compulsory early retirement scheme. Although the scheme entitled those retiring to an accelerated pension under the firm's occupational pension scheme, it was held to fall within the scope of Directive 76/207 as a condition governing dismissal, and not Directive 79/7. However, in this case it was not discriminatory, since the age for retirement was fixed at 55 for both men and women (see also *Beets-Proper v F van Landschot Bankiers NV* (case 262/84)).

Member States' power under Article 7 of Directive 79/7 to exclude from the equal treatment principle 'the determination of pensionable age' has, in view of the fundamental importance of the principle of equal treatment, been given the narrowest scope. It seems it will only apply where the difference in age is *for the purpose* of the granting of old-age and retirement *pensions* and the possible consequences thereof for other benefits 'falling within the statutory [or occupational] social security schemes' (*Marshall*, para 35, see further below). Moreover, the exclusion from the equal treatment principle only applies to the determination of pensionable age for the purposes of granting *statutory* social security pensions. Despite the express exclusion in respect of the 'determination of pensionable age for the purposes of granting old-age or retirement pensions' as regards *occupational* pension schemes, contained in Directive 86/378, the Court held in *Barber* (case C–262/88) that the setting of different retirement ages for men and women for the granting of such pensions was in breach of Article 119 (now 141), since the difference in age *resulted* in a difference in pay. On similar reasoning different ages of access to statutory redundancy benefit for men and women were also held in breach of the then Article 119. *Burton v British Railways Board* (case 19/81) appears to have been distinguished out of existence. As was noted above, a difference in the employer's contribution to funded, defined-benefit schemes, affecting the transfer of pension rights and lump sum payments to employees was held in *Neath v Hugh Steeper Ltd* (case C–152/91) to fall outside Article 119 (now 141); it may thus be presumed that it will also fall outside Directive 76/207. In *Vergani* (case 207/04), a provision to encourage voluntary redundancy by providing reduced tax on redundancy payments for men who retired after the age of 55 and women who retired after the age of 50 fell foul of Directive 76/207.

27.9.4 Social assistance

Although the main discussion about the scope of the Equal Treatment Directive has concerned equal retirement ages and pensions, that is not the only area where its boundaries are unclear. *Meyers v Adjudication Officer* (case C–116/94) concerned family credit, which, at first glance, might fall within social security, Directive 79/7. Ms Meyers, however, brought an action under the Equal Treatment Directive claiming that rules precluding her from deducting childminding expenses from her income and thus preventing her from claiming family credit were indirectly discriminatory because the rules had a disproportionate adverse effect on single mothers. The Court held that since family credit provided a top-up income to low-income workers and therefore provided both assistance and an incentive for them to accept work, the scheme fell within the Equal Treatment Directive as it concerned both 'access to employment' and 'conditions of employment'. It would seem that the case was not brought under Directive 79/7 following *Jackson v Chief Adjudication Officer* (cases C–63 and 64/91) (discussed in more detail below), which held that supplementary benefits did not fall within the terms of that directive.

27.9.5 Other cases

Article 2(1) of Directive 76/207 has been held, in the absence of objective justification, to preclude a domestic rule which authorised part-time work for older employees only where they have worked full-time for at least three out of the five years before applying for a change to part-time status, where the vast majority of part-time workers are women and therefore much more likely to fall outside the scope of this rule (*Steinicke v Bundesanstalt für Arbeit* (case C–77/02)).

In *Gomez*, a collective agreement between workforce and employer provided for a specific period of annual leave, which overlapped with Gomez's maternity leave. The Court held that an annual leave entitlement was within the scope of (now deleted) Article 5(1) of the directive, and that the claimant was entitled to take her annual leave at a different time (*Gomez v Contintental Industrias* (case C–342/01)). The Court noted that it would generally be the case that a claimant should be entitled to take annual leave at a time different from the maternity leave period.

In *Nikoloudi v OTE* (case C–196/02), the post of part-time cleaner was reserved to females, but this was not, in itself, discrimination against women. However, the fact that part-time workers were excluded from appointment to established staff was contrary to Directive 76/207 and meant that this arrangement did constitute direct discrimination.

27.9.6 Enforcement

Like Directive 75/117, Directive 76/207, as amended, required states to 'take the necessary measures to ensure that any laws, regulations and administrative provisions contrary to the principle of equal treatment be abolished' (Article 3(2)(a)).

As noted earlier, these provisions have been extended and strengthened by the Recast Equal treatment Directive. The detail of these provisions is presently beyond the scope of this book. It should be noted that the Recast Equal Treatment Directive was due to be implemented by the summer of 2009.

27.9.7 Derogation from the equal treatment principle

Article 2(6) permits Member States with regard to access to employment and related training, to provide that 'a difference of treatment which is based on a characteristic relating to sex' is not discriminatory where because of 'the nature of the particular occupational activities concerned or of the context in which they are carried out, such a characteristic constitutes a genuine and determining occupational requirement'. This is now found in Article 14(2) Recast Equal Treatment Directive. Article 2(7) makes Directive 76/207 without prejudice to provisions on the protection of women during pregnancy and maternity leave (see now Article 15 Recast Equal Treatment Directive). In addition, Article 2(8) provides some scope for positive discrimination, by allowing for 'measures within the meaning of Article 141(4) of the Treaty with a view to ensuring full equality in practice between men and women', now found in Article 3 Recast Equal Treatment Directive.

These articles provide for derogation from the equal treatment principle in the case of *direct* discrimination, based on the sex of the worker. The provisions replace earlier derogations contained in what was Articles 2(2)–(4) of Directive 76/207. They are designed to reflect both key developments in the ECJ's jurisprudence, and the changes made to Article 141 after the ToA. The provisions have only been in force for a short time, and little ECJ case law on these revised provisions was available at the time of writing. The discussion below is based on the case law that evolved under the previous exceptions, and this will continue to offer guidance on the interpretation of the recast derogation provisions.

27.9.7.1 *Sex as a determining factor*

The former Article 2(2) of the original Equal Treatment Directive provided for a derogation in respect of 'activities . . . for which . . . the sex of the worker constitutes a determining factor'. This was considered by the ECJ in the Commission's second action against the UK (*Commission v United Kingdom (re equal treatment for men and women)* (case 165/82)) for failure to comply with the Equal Treatment Directive. One of the failures alleged was the exemption from the equal treatment principle, provided under the Sex Discrimination Act 1975, for employment in a private household (s 6(3)(a)) and for firms employing less than six staff (s 6(3)(b)). The UK argued that these provisions were justifiable under the former Article 2(2) of Directive 76/207. The Court disagreed. Whilst exemption under the former Article 2(2) might be available in the *individual* case under such circumstances, where the sex of the worker was a determining factor, the former Article 2(2) did not justify a blanket exclusion. It did, however, provide a valid defence to a charge against the UK in respect of its restriction, under the Sex Discrimination Act 1975, s 20, on male access to the profession of midwifery. The Court found that this was an activity for which the sex of the worker was a determining factor.

In *Stoeckel* (case C–345/89) a general ban on night work for women, provided for under German law, allegedly to protect women, was held by the Court not permissible under the former Article 2(2). However, in *Ministère Public v Levy* (case C–158/91) faced with a question of the compatibility of *Stoeckel* with French law imposing restrictions on night work in industry for women, designed to give effect to a provision of the ILO 1948, the Court suggested that national courts must not apply provisions of national law contrary to Article 5 of Directive 76/207 (now deleted) 'unless the application of national law is necessary to ensure compliance with international obligations' resulting from a convention concluded with third countries 'before the entry into force of the EC Treaty'. (See also *Office Nationale de l'Emploi v Minne* (case C–13/93) and *Habermann-Beltermann* (case C–421/92).) The point came before the ECJ again in the case of *Commission v Italy* (case C–207/96). In this case, Italy prohibited women from working overnight in accordance with the ILO Convention. Italy had, however, following the ECJ's previous ruling, denounced the Convention. The ECJ thus held that it could not rely on the Convention and that the prohibition was contrary to EU law.

The former Article 2(2) was also raised as a defence in the case of *Johnston v Chief Constable of the Royal Ulster Constabulary* (case 222/84) (see Chapter 6). This action was brought by a female member of the Royal Ulster Constabulary (RUC) against a decision by the RUC refusing to renew her contract of employment. The RUC had decided as a matter of policy not to employ women as full-time members of the RUC reserve, since they were not trained in the use of firearms nor permitted to use them. In proceedings before the ECJ concerning the interpretation of Directive 76/207, and in particular the scope for derogation from the equal treatment principle available under EU law, the RUC argued, by analogy with what was Article 48(3) (now 39(3)) EC (see Chapter 22), that in view of the political situation in Northern Ireland derogation was justified on public safety or public security grounds; it was also justified under the former Article 2(2) of Directive

76/207. To allow women to carry and use firearms, the RUC claimed, increased the risk of their becoming targets for assassination. The Court held that there was no general public safety exception to the equal treatment principle available under the EC Treaty. A claim for exemption could *only* be examined in the light of the provisions of Directive 76/207. With regard to the former Article 2(2), the Court held that:

(a) The derogation provided under Article 2(2) could be applied only to specific *duties*, not to activities in general. Nonetheless, it was permissible to take into account the *context* in which the activity takes place.

(b) Where derogation is justified in the light of (a) the situation must be reviewed periodically to ensure that the justification still exists.

(c) Derogation must be subject to the principle of proportionality.

It was for national courts to decide whether these conditions are satisfied.

Similar principles were applied, if somewhat leniently, in *Commission v France* (case 318/86). The Commission's action was in respect of recruitment practices in the French civil service, in particular the prison service and the police. Under the system in force men and women were subject to different recruitment procedures, with a fixed percentage of posts being allocated according to sex. The complaint concerning the prison service centred on access to the post of head warder (in male prisons), which was not accessible to women. The complaint regarding the police concerned recruitment to certain police corps generally.

In the case of the prison service the Court found that it was justifiable to discriminate on the grounds of the former Article 2(2) in respect of the post of *warder*. Since professional experience acquired as a warder was desirable for the performance of the duties of a prison governor (a post for which head warders were eligible), and since it was desirable to provide promotion opportunities for those in the lower (warders') posts, it was acceptable to treat the *head* warder's post in the same way. The recruitment practices were justified under the former Article 2(2). The recruitment practices of the police, on the other hand, were not permissible under the former Article 2(2). The exclusion provided by the former Article 2(2), the Court held, allows exceptions to the non discrimination principle only in relation to specific *activities*, and these exceptions must be sufficiently transparent to permit effective scrutiny. The fact that certain police functions cannot be performed by men and women does not justify discriminatory treatment in admission to the police force in general.

The scope of the former Article 2(2) also came under consideration in *Sirdar v The Army Board* (case C–273/97). The army board refused to transfer a female chef (who would otherwise be made redundant) to the Royal Marines because of her sex. She argued that this was contrary to the approach set down in *Johnston*. The ECJ, however, took a different view. It confirmed that Member States have a discretion regarding measures necessary for ensuring public security, although it further noted that any derogation from fundamental treaty rights (such as equality) must be narrowly construed and be proportionate to its aims. In this case, the ECJ focused on the special nature of the Marines, who are, in effect, front-line troops and in respect of whom an absolute rule provides that *all* Marines must be combat ready, irrespective of their normal role. It seems that it was the particularly dangerous nature of the Marines' role that, according to the ECJ, justified the UK's decision that the Marines should remain exclusively male. By contrast, in *Kreil v Germany* (case C–285/98) a German rule of more general ambit which precluded women from occupying posts which would involve the use of firearms constituted sex discrimination, even taking into account Member States' discretion regarding the organisation of their armed forces. *Kreil* cannot be interpreted to mean that Member States cannot organise their compulsory national service to apply to men alone, provided women have access to the armed forces where they choose to enlist (case C–186/01, *Dory*). Arguably, then, these rulings continue the approach to the former Article 2(2) which requires a *specific* assessment of the *specific* duties to be performed in individual cases.

In the light of the above case law, the derogation was recast, and the new provision, set out above, reflects the very strict interpretation given to the former Article 2(2).

27.9.7.2 *Pregnancy and maternity*

Former Article 2(3) of Directive 76/207 permitted 'provisions concerning the protection of women, particularly as regards pregnancy and maternity'. Pregnancy and maternity leave can, potentially, have a detrimental impact on the pay and career progression of women, who will be away from work for a period of time. In *Herrero v Imsalud* (case C–294/04), Ms Herrero, who had already been employed by Imsalud, was successful in applying for a new post whilst she was on maternity leave. She was able to defer taking up that post, but she challenged a rule whereby her seniority would only be calculated from the date she took up her post, rather than the date of appointment. The Court held that this situation was within the scope of Directive 76/207, and that it precluded a rule which excluded maternity leave from calculating the period of seniority. It followed the earlier decision in *Land Brandenburg v Sass* (case C–284/02), a case involving a woman from the former East Germany who had taken the then statutory period of 20 weeks, of which only eight weeks were taken into account by way of allowance in calculating her length of service. This meant that she was moved to a higher pay grade 12 weeks later than a comparable male worker, which was held to fall outside the derogation in Article 2(3) of the directive.

In *Kiiski* (case C–116/06) the claimant had been granted 'childcare leave' to enable her to care for her child. On becoming pregnant again, she asked her employer, first, to alter the dates of her 'childcare leave' and, subsequently, to interrupt it, so that she could take maternity leave. Her employer refused because, under the relevant collective agreement and Finnish case law, 'child-care leave' could be interrupted only for an unforeseeable and justified ground, and pregnancy did not constitute such a ground. The Court held that the refusal was incompatible with the directive since it was capable of affecting negatively the claimant's right to obtain maternity leave and enjoy the relevant benefits.

In *Johnston v Chief Constable of the RUC*, the RUC also sought to justify its action under former Article 2(3), as 'concerning the protection of women, particularly as regards pregnancy and maternity'. The Court found that the risks to policewomen arising from the situation in Northern Ireland were not within the scope of Article 2(3). Article 2(3) was intended to protect women's biological condition.

This interpretation of Article 2(3) had been supplied in *Hofmann v Barmer Ersatzkasse* (case 184/83) in response to a claim by a father to six months' leave following the birth of his child to look after the child while the mother went back to work. German law, which granted such leave only to the mother, was, he claimed, discriminatory, in breach of Directive 76/207. The Court disagreed. Special provision for maternity leave was, the Court held, permissible under Article 2(3), which was concerned to protect two types of female need. It protected:

(a) the biological condition of women during and after pregnancy

(b) the relationship between mother and child during the period following pregnancy and birth.

Directive 76/207 was not intended to cover matters relating to the organisation of the family or to change the division of responsibility between parents.

A second case brought by the Commission against France (*Commission v France* (case 312/86)) related to special privileges in the form of, inter alia, extended maternity leave, lower retirement age, extra time off to allow for children's illness and holidays, and extra allowances to meet the cost of nursery schools and child minders, awarded under French law to married women. The French sought to justify these privileges under Article 2(3)–(4). The Court, citing *Hofmann*, found that such measures fell outside the limits of Article 2(3); nor was there any indication that the rights claimed corresponded to the situation envisaged under Article 2(4). If such privileges are to be justified, they can only be justified on objective grounds *unrelated to sex*, such as the need to assist persons who carry primary responsibility for the welfare of the family, and particularly of children. As the Court pointed out in *Commission v France*, such responsibility may be undertaken by men. (See also *Griesmar* (case C–366/99). As an example of the application of 'neutral' criteria, see *Teuling* (case 30/85), which is discussed later in this chapter.)

Contrast *Commission v France* with *Abdoulaye v Regie Nationale des Usines Renault* (case C–218/98), albeit a case based on Article 141 rather than the Equal Treatment Directive. In *Abdoulage* a group of men sought to challenge the payment of a lump sum, in addition to their maternity pay, to women going on pregnancy leave. The men argued that a recent father was not entitled to the same amount and that the measure discriminated against men. The ECJ held the payment of the lump sum to be compatible with Union law as it was intended to compensate woman for the problems inherent in having to take time off work for maternity leave, and which are consequently specific to women.

The precise extent to which, and circumstances in which, a dismissal or refusal to employ a woman for reasons connected with pregnancy and childbirth will breach Directive 76/207 remains unclear, although it seems that the ECJ has become increasingly unsympathetic to employers. In *Dekker v VJV-Centrum* (case C–177/88) the defendant employer had withdrawn his offer of employment to the claimant when he discovered she was pregnant. He argued that his action was justified; her absence during maternity leave would not on the facts be covered by insurance, and he could not afford to pay for a replacement worker. The ECJ held that a refusal to employ a woman on the grounds of pregnancy constituted direct discrimination on the grounds of sex; as such it could not be justified on the basis of financial detriment to the employer.

The effect of this ruling was undermined in the Court's judgment in *Handels- og Kontorfunktion ærernes Forbund i Danmark v Dansk Arbejdsgiverforening* (Hertz) (case C–179/88) delivered on the same day. This case concerned a claim by a female employee against dismissal on the grounds of her extended absence from work as a result of illness which, though connected with pregnancy and childbirth, was suffered some time *after* the end of her maternity leave. The Court held that in this case there was no need to distinguish between illness resulting from pregnancy and maternity and any other illness such as might be suffered by a man. The dismissal was thus not directly discriminatory and could be justified. The reason for the distinction between *Dekker* and *Hertz*, suggested in *Hertz*, lay in Article 2(3) of Directive 76/207 which provided for measures concerning the protection of women, particularly as regards pregnancy and maternity.

Hertz was seized upon by the English Court of Appeal in *Webb v EMO Air Cargo (UK) Ltd* ([1992] 2 All ER 43), in the context of a claim at first sight closer to *Dekker*, for discrimination on the grounds of pregnancy. The claimant had been engaged to replace another employee who had become pregnant. Two weeks after accepting the post she discovered she too was pregnant. When she informed the employer of this fact she was dismissed. Glidewell LJ, following counsel for the employer's advice, chose to read *Dekker* and *Hertz* together. Dismissal on the grounds of pregnancy might under *some* circumstances constitute direct discrimination. But on these facts, where the claimant had been employed specifically to replace another pregnant worker, the situation should rather be compared with that of a man in a similar situation, for example, a man with an arthritic hip, who found, shortly after taking up employment, that he was soon to be called for a hip replacement operation necessitating a long absence from work. Since an employer would have been justified in dismissing a man under these circumstances, the claimant's dismissal was not discriminatory on the grounds of sex.

Following the applicant's appeal to the House of Lords questions as to the legality of dismissal on the grounds of pregnancy in these particular circumstances were referred by that court to the ECJ ([1992] 4 All ER 929) and the dismissal was found to be illegal (case C–32/93). In this ruling, the Advocate-General and the ECJ rejected the idea that a pregnant woman should be compared with a sick man (see also *Habermann-Beltermann* (case C–421/92)).

The ECJ's judgment raises some questions, not the least of which concerns where the boundary lies between being dismissed for pregnancy, which is unacceptable, and being dismissed for being ill, albeit because of pregnancy, which—provided it occurs outside the normal maternity leave—is acceptable (see *Hertz*). In *Handels-og Kontorfunktion ærernes Forbund i Danmark acting on behalf of Larsson v Dansk Handel & Service acting on behalf of Føtex Supermarket A/S* (case C–400/95), the ECJ held that a woman could be dismissed for absences other than maternity leave caused by pregnancy-related illnesses occurring both prior to and after the birth of the child, and in *North Western Health Board v McKenna* (case C–191/03), the Court held that where a female worker had been absent due to pregnancy-related illness before her maternity leave, her pay could be reduced if a man who had been absent for the same period would be treated in the same way. The decision in *Larsson* should be contrasted with *Brown v Rentokil* (case C–394/96), where it was held that a woman could not be dismissed at any time during her pregnancy for absences arising from pregnancy-related illnesses. The Pregnancy Directive (Directive 92/85, [1992] OJ L348/1) prohibits the dismissal of workers during the period from the beginning of their pregnancy to the end of their maternity leave, save in exceptional circumstances unconnected with their pregnancy. Pregnancy-related illnesses would seem not to justify dismissal during this time. The position after the end of the woman's maternity leave as regards such illnesses is not, however, dealt with expressly and some uncertainty as to the level of protection in this context remains.

A worker's dismissal while she was at an advanced stage of *in vitro* fertilisation treatment came before the Court in *Mayr* (case C–506/06). It held that even if the claimant could not rely on Directive 92/85 on pregnant workers, her dismissal would violate Directive 76/207 if it could be established that it was based on the fact that she has undergone such treatment.

Further, if the reason for a worker's dismissal is her pregnancy or childbirth, the dismissal will violate the directive irrespective of the moment when that decision to dismiss is notified (*Paquay* (case C–460/06)).

Another question arising in *Webb* concerned whether availability for work constitutes a fundamental condition of the employment contract. The ECJ rejected this contention, but on the basis that the time that the woman would be unavailable for work constitutes only a small proportion of the contract time in an indefinite contract. This did, however, undermine the position of women on short-term contracts. Could they be dismissed on the basis that their pregnancy constitutes too large a proportion of the contract? These issues were clarified in the cases of *Teledenmark* (case C–109/00), *Jiménez Melgar* (case C–438/99), and *Busch* (case C–320/01). In *Teledenmark*, a woman was employed on a six months' fixed-term contract, two of which were spent on a training course. After commencing employment, she notified her employer that she was pregnant, whereupon she was dismissed. The employer argued that she could not perform a substantial part of her duties and further that, in not mentioning her pregnancy before she was employed, she had violated the principle of good faith. The ECJ rejected these arguments:

> Since the dismissal of a worker on account of pregnancy constitutes direct discrimination on grounds of sex, whatever the nature and extent of economic loss incurred by the company as a result of her absence, because of pregnancy, whether the contract was concluded for a fixed term of for an infinite period has no bearing on the discriminatory character of the dismissal. In either case, the employee's inability to perform her contract of employment is due to pregnancy. [Para 31.]

The ruling was applied in *Jiménez Melgar*, which concerned a refusal to renew a fixed-term contract. In *Busch*, the ECJ, basing its judgment on *Teledenmark*, confirmed that a woman was under no duty to tell an employer that she is pregnant prior to accepting a job offer or returning to work.

This case law seems to reflect, if not go further than, the terms of the Pregnancy Directive. The directive provides core maternity rights including periods of maternity leave and protection from dismissal during such leave, whether the worker is on a short-term or indefinite contract, and will thus protect workers in this position. The Pregnancy Directive does not, though, deal with the position of the woman who is not appointed because she is pregnant. Presumably, this could still fall within the Equal Treatment Directive following *Dekker*. Certainly, the ECJ held in *Mahlburg v Land Mecklenburg-Vorpommern* (case C–207/98), that a hospital could not refuse to appoint a pregnant woman to a permanent post as a theatre nurse on the basis that she would not be able to carry out her duties while she was pregnant. In this case German legislation prohibited expectant mothers from being exposed to chemicals with which the applicant would have come into contact as part of her job. This demonstrates that where a permanent post is in issue, temporary absence or incapacity (even from the commencement date of the appointment) will not be a legitimate ground for refusal of employment.

The Pregnancy Directive also specifies that women on maternity leave are entitled to an 'adequate allowance'. Ironically, this provision weakened the applicants' arguments in *Gillespie v Northern Health and Social Services Board* (case C–342/93) that equal pay requires full pay. The ECJ followed the directive (although the actual situation in *Gillespie* predated it) holding that maternity pay did not need to be full pay, provided it was adequate. The Court also held, however, that maternity pay must take account of any pay increases during the maternity leave or during the period with reference to which the maternity pay is calculated (see also *Alabaster v Woolwich plc* (case C–147/02)). The ECJ has also ruled on the impact of maternity leave (in conjunction with sick leave) on a woman's entitlement to be considered for a 'merit increase' (*Caisse Nationale D'Assurance Vieillesse des Travailleurs Salaries (NAVTS) v Thibault* (case C–136/95)). As far as the applicant was concerned, the difficulty arose because she did not satisfy the prerequisite of six months' work because of the time she had had off, and was therefore ineligible for the pay rise. The ECJ agreed that this was contrary to the requirements of the Equal Treatment Directive. It stated that if a woman continued to be bound by her contract of employment, she should not be deprived of benefits which apply to men and other women by virtue of the employment relationship. The ECJ, in so holding, emphasised that the Equal Treatment Directive was intended to promote substantive equality. (See also *Gillespie* (case C–342/93).) Whether this desire to safeguard substantive equality is respected in all the ECJ's judgments relating to pregnancy issues is, however, another matter. The precise scope of the rights under the Pregnancy Directive will no doubt continue to be the subject of further litigation.

Many of these decisions are now incorporated into the text of the recast Equal Treatment Directive. Thus, Article 15 provides that a woman is entitled to return to her job, or an equivalent post, after the end of her maternity leave, on no less favourable terms and conditions and to benefit from any improvement in working conditions to which she would have been entitled during her absence. The previous case law will continue to be relevant in interpreting this broad rule.

27.9.7.3 *Positive discrimination (Article 2(8))*

The third exception to the principle of equal treatment is that of positive discrimination, which permits schemes to enable women to compete equally with men. Article 2(8) of the Equal Treatment Directive provides that 'Member States may maintain or adopt measures within the meaning of Article 141(4) of the Treaty with a view to ensuring full equality in practice between men and women'. Article 2(8) therefore now corresponds with the new Article 141(4), inserted by the ToA. Article 3 of the recast Equal Treatment Directive provides for positive discrimination in almost identical terms—'Member States may maintain or adopt measures within the meaning of Article 141(4) of the Treaty with a view to ensuring full equality in practice between men and women in working life'.

The earlier version of this derogation in the former Article 2(4) expressed the directive to be without prejudice to measures 'to promote equal opportunity for men and women, in particular by removing existing inequalities which affect women's opportunities'.

In *Kalanke v Freie Hansestadt Bremen* (case C–450/93), the ECJ held that a rule requiring the appointment of the female candidate when applicants were equally qualified and there was an under-representation of women at the level of the position for which the applicants were applying did not fall within the former Article 2(4). The Court stated that the purpose of the provision was to allow measures intended to eliminate or reduce actual instances of inequality so as to allow women to compete equally. In giving women 'absolute and unconditional' priority, the system overstepped the limits in the former Article 2(4).

This somewhat harsh decision caused outcry in certain quarters, including suggestions that the former Article 2(4) be broadened to allow positive discrimination. As already noted, the ToA amended Article 141 so as to strengthen the provision for positive discrimination with the addition of a new para (4), which provides that:

> With a view to ensuring full equality in practice between men and women in working life, the principle of equal treatment shall not prevent any Member State from maintaining or adopting measures providing for specific advantages in order to make it easier for the under-represented sex to pursue a vocational activity or to prevent or compensate for disadvantages in professional careers.

The ECJ started to interpret the former Article 2(4) in the light of this change even prior to the entry into force of the ToA. In *Marschall* (case C–409/95), which was decided before the addition of para 4 to Article 141 of the EC Treaty, the Court held that a national provision which gave priority to women applicants was compatible with Union law because it included a qualification that the employer could appoint a male applicant if there were special reasons for such an appointment. Similarly in *Badeck* (case C–158/97), decided after the ToA came into force, the Court ruled in favour of several provisions which gave priority to women in the context of public service employment because they were not 'absolute and unconditional' in the sense of *Kalanke*, but aimed at affording qualified women additional opportunities to enter working life and advance their career.

It seems that the crucial difference between these two cases and *Kalanke* is the existence of what the ECJ has termed a 'saving clause'. This means that the legislation which provides for the preferential treatment of women is not automatic, instead containing a clause that permits the appointment of a man if other societal reasons specific to that man apply. One example of such a factor is a policy designed to ensure the appointment of appropriately qualified handicapped people.

Further, positive discrimination measures must respect the principle of proportionality, as can be seen by the judgment in *Lommers* (case C–476/99), where the ECJ had to consider whether right of access to subsidised nursery places to female employees was acceptable. The ECJ noted that the former Article 2(4) authorises measures relating to access to employment which give a specific advantage to women to allow them to compete on an equal footing with men. The Court noted that the absence of suitable and affordable nursery facilities leads to parents, mainly women, giving up their jobs. The ECJ concluded that such measures would fall within the scope of the former Article 2(4). Nonetheless, any such measure must be proportional. A measure which excludes fathers from all possibility of access to such facilities would be disproportionate. Rules that exceptionally permit fathers who take care of their children would, however, be permissible. The same general approach seems to be taken here as was taken in *Badeck* and *Marshall*.

Interestingly, the ECJ noted in *Lommers* that measures such as those in this case, 'might nevertheless also help to perpetuate a traditional division of roles between men and women' (para 41). While there is undoubtedly a risk of stereotyping arising from positive discrimination measures such as this, the alternative may perpetuate a real existing disadvantage. The existence of these conflicting concerns suggests that it is not appropriate to state that all positive discrimination should be viewed as 'good' or 'bad', but that such measures should be assessed individually.

Finally, even after the coming into force of the ToA, measures which give automatic priority to certain candidates will be incompatible with the principle of equal treatment. In *Abrahamson and Anderson v Fogelqvist* (case C–407/98) the Court examined a rule which provided that candidates of the underrepresented sex would be appointed despite the fact that their qualifications were inferior to those of other candidates if such an appointment could be objectively justified. The Court held that this rule was disproportionate to the aim pursued since it granted automatic preference to the members of the underrepresented group with the result that the selection was ultimately based on the mere fact of belonging to a certain sex.

The effect of the Court's case law on positive discrimination is that rules which grant automatic priority by reference to a candidate's sex will be incompatible with Union law. By contrast, measures which are designed to combat existing inequalities in the market place by affording additional employment opportunities to members of the underrepresented sex who are suitably qualified and allow other factors (ie, beyond the candidates' sex) to be taken into account are acceptable.

The above cases involving exemption from the equal treatment principle all concern direct discrimination. Where the discrimination is indirect the same principles apply as apply in the field of pay; a difference in treatment as between one group of workers and another which *affects* one sex disproportionately will require objective justification. Here the justification need not be brought within Article 2 of Directive 76/207, since the difference in treatment for which justification is required is not between men and women, but between one group of workers (eg, part-timers) and another (eg, full-timers). Following *Danfoss* (case 109/88) the onus of proving justification is likely to fall on the employer. *Kirsammer-Hack v Sidal* (case C–189/91) provides an example of a successful defence of objective justification to a claim of indirect discrimination, based on the need to protect small undertakings against excessive administrative, financial, and legal burdens.

27.10 Principle of equal treatment in matters of social security (Directive 79/7)

Directive 79/7, which implements the principle of equal treatment for men and women in matters of social security, became directly effective once the date for its implementation by Member States had expired, on 23 December 1984 (see

Netherlands v Federatie Nederlandse Vakbeweging (case 71/85); *McDermott v Minister for Social Welfare* (case 286/85); *Clarke v Chief Adjudication Officer* (case 384/85)). No extension of time is permitted for transitional arrangements (*Dik v College van Burgemeester en Wethouders* (case 80/87)). Since Directive 79/7 applies only to *statutory* social security schemes its effects must inevitably be vertical. Also, since Directive 79/7 merely implements the principle of equal treatment in the field of social security expressed in Directive 76/207 (Article 1(1)) there is, as *Burton v British Railways Board* (case 19/81) illustrates, some overlap between the two directives. There is also considerable uncertainty as to where the boundary between Article 141 EC and Directive 79/7 lies (*Beune* (case C–7/93)).

27.10.1 Personal and material scope

Directive 79/7 applies to the working population, defined broadly to include 'self-employed persons, workers and self-employed persons whose activity is interrupted by illness, accident or involuntary unemployment and persons seeking employment', and to 'retired or invalided workers and self-employed persons' (Article 2). In *Drake v Chief Adjudication Officer* (case 150/85) the Court held that the term 'working population' must be defined broadly, to include persons who have been working but whose work has been interrupted. Thus Mrs Drake, who had given up work to look after her invalid mother, was entitled to claim a right to equal treatment under Directive 79/7. Directive 79/7 may also be invoked by the spouse of a person falling within Article 2, provided that the benefit claimed is within the scope of the directive; 'others too may have an interest in seeing the principle of non-discrimination respected on behalf of the person protected' (*Verholen* (cases C–87–9/90)). However, Article 2 cannot be invoked by persons who have not been employed and are not seeking work, or by those who have worked but whose work has not been interrupted by one of the risks referred to in Article 3(1) (*Achterberg-te Riele and ors v Sociale Verzekeringsbank* (cases 48 and 106–7/88)). This approach was followed in *Johnson v Chief Adjudication Officer* (case C–31/90), in which the ECJ held that a woman who had voluntarily given up work to care for her children would not be within the scope of the directive unless she was looking for work when one of the risks outlined in the directive occurred.

The principle of equal treatment under Directive 79/7 applies to:

(a) statutory schemes providing protection against sickness, invalidity, old age, accidents at work or occupational diseases and unemployment

(b) social assistance, insofar as it is intended to supplement or replace these schemes (Article 3(1)).

In *Drake* the Court held that the benefits covered by the directive must constitute whole or part of a statutory scheme providing protection against one of the specified risks or a form of social assistance having the same objective. It appears that the statutory scheme must be one for workers in general, and not one, as in *Liefting* (case 23/83), relating to persons employed by the State. A contracted-out scheme operating as a substitute for the statutory scheme will be treated as an occupational pension scheme, within Directive 86/378 (*Newstead v Department of Transport* (case 192/85)).

In an uncharacteristically restrictive interpretation the Court, contrary to Advocate-General Tesauro's recommendations, in *R v Secretary of State for Social Security, ex parte Smithson* (case C–243/90), denied the claimant's right to equality of treatment in respect of housing benefit under Directive 79/7 on the grounds that it was not within the scope of the directive. Although eligibility for the benefit, and the amount of benefit, was ascertained, inter alia, by reference to a (discriminatory) invalidity pension, the benefit was not 'directly and effectively' linked to the protection provided against one of the risks specified in Article 3(1); a similarly restrictive approach was adopted in *Jackson v Chief Adjudication Officer* (cases C–63, 64/91). Here, in a claim by two single mothers, one engaged in vocational training, one in part-time work, in respect of supplementary allowance and income support, the Court held that these benefits, which might be granted in a variety of situations to persons whose means were insufficient to meet their needs, did not relate to any of the risks listed in Article 3(1). Nor did they fall within Directive 76/207. Although the benefits in question might affect the single parent's ability to undertake vocational training or part-time employment, they did not relate to the subject matter of the Directive, which was *access* to employment, including vocational training and promotion and working conditions.

The Court's attitude in these cases stands in stark contrast to its previous approach to the 'social assistance' exemption in Social Security Regulation 1408/71 and to the concept of 'social advantage' under Regulation 1612/68 (see Chapter 23). *Jackson v Chief Adjudication Officer* may also be contrasted with *Meyers v Adjudication Officer* (case C–116/94). In *Meyers*, the ECJ held that family credit, by enabling a single mother to go out to work, concerned access to employment and therefore fell within the ambit of the Equal Treatment Directive 76/207. *R v Secretary of State for Health, ex parte Richardson* (case C–137/94) concerned UK regulations dealing with exemptions from prescription charges which were linked to retirement age and were therefore discriminatory. The ECJ held that such rules fell within Article 3(1) because they formed part of the statutory scheme providing protection against one of the risks covered by the directive, namely, sickness. These cases indicate that the ECJ may have had second thoughts about its earlier case law. Nonetheless, there must still be some links with the risks listed in Article 3(1): in *Atkins v Wrekin District Council* (case C–228/94) concessionary travel passes awarded to old age pensioners were held not to fall within the terms of the directive.

Survivors' benefits, and family benefits not granted by way of increases to the benefits covered by the directive, are excluded from Directive 79/7 (Article 3(2)).

Provided that the benefit in question is covered by Directive 79/7, the fact that it may be payable under national legislation to a third party does not take it outside the scope of the directive. Otherwise, as the Court pointed out in *Drake*, it would be possible, by making formal changes to existing benefits covered by the directive, to remove them from its scope. On this reasoning Mrs Drake was held entitled herself to invoke Directive 79/7 in respect of an invalidity allowance payable on behalf of her mother.

27.10.2 Scope of the equal treatment principle

The principle of equal treatment means, according to Directive 79/7, Article 4(1), that:

> there shall be no discrimination whatsoever on grounds of sex either directly, or indirectly by reference in particular to marital or family status, in particular as concerns:
> — the scope of [social security] schemes and the conditions of access thereto,
> — the obligation to contribute and the calculation of contributions,
> — the calculation of benefits including increases due in respect of a spouse and for dependants, and
> — the conditions governing the duration and retention of entitlement to benefits.

In *Drake* an invalidity allowance payable to a married man, but not to a married woman, was found in breach of Article 4(1).

Where a provision is indirectly discriminatory, it may be found to be objectively justified (see the earlier discussion on objective justification). In *Teuling* (case 30/85) an invalidity benefit, the amount of which was determined by marital status and either the (low) income derived from the spouse's occupation or the existence of a dependent child, designed to compensate for the 'greater burden' borne by persons in these categories, although indirectly discriminatory against women, was held to be objectively justified (see also *Commission v Belgium* (case C–229/89)). Such benefits, sexually neutral and designed to meet objective needs such as the need to support dependants, happen to benefit men more than women because the former are still, if to a diminishing degree, more likely to be responsible for dependants. Similarly, benefits to aid the long-term unemployed are acceptable because they are designed for gender-neutral policy purposes which, although they may benefit men more than women, are still justified (*Posthuma-van Damme v Bestuur van de Bedrijfsverenigung voor Detailhandel, Ambachten en Huisvrouwen* (case C–280/94)). In this case the ECJ also emphasised the wide margin of discretion Member States have in choosing their social policies.

Supplementary benefits payable for a spouse or persons deemed to be dependent on the claimant are payable under Article 4(1) irrespective of the sex of the claimant. This applies even if it results in double payment, for example, payment to both spouses for the same dependants. In response to the Irish government's argument in *Cotter v Minister for Social Welfare* (case C–377/89) that this would result in unjust enrichment the Court held that a defence based on this principle would enable the authorities to use their own unlawful conduct as a ground for depriving Article 4(1) of the directive of its full effect.

Jonkman (joined cases C–231–3/06) concerned a special statutory social security scheme for civil aviation air crew. When that scheme was first established, female workers were excluded because, at that time, it was impossible for them to continue their career as members of an air crew beyond the age of 40. Since they could not complete a full career, they were not included in the special scheme. Subsequently, air hostesses were integrated into the scheme and were allowed to claim pensions under the same conditions as stewards provided that they paid, in a single sum, adjustment contributions representing the difference between the contributions they had paid in the past and the higher contributions paid by stewards together with interest at the annual rate of 10 per cent. The Court held that requiring air hostesses to pay adjustment contributions was compatible with Directive 79/7, since what equal treatment requires is to place the female worker who had suffered discrimination in the same position as that of male workers; air hostesses could not claim the same higher pensions that stewards received without paying the relevant contributions. However, the requirement to pay interest above what was necessary to compensate for inflation was incompatible with the directive. Similarly, the requirement to pay the additional contributions in a single sum would be a violation of the directive where the amount was so large as to make the adjustment impossible or excessively difficult in practice.

In *Richards* (case C–423/04) the Court held that an employee who had undergone male-to-female gender reassignment surgery could claim a retirement pension from the day on which she turned 60, the statutory retirement age for women. Referring to its judgment in *KB* (see above), the Court explained that the reason the claimant was denied the pension was that her new gender was not recognised for the purpose of applying the Pensions Act 1995, while, had she been held to be a woman as a matter of national law, she would have received it; thus, the refusal amounted to discrimination prohibited by Article 4(1) of the directive.

In *Ruzius-Wilbrink* (case 102/88) the ECJ held that the principle of equal treatment expressed in Article 4(1) was capable of being applied to part-time workers. The claim concerned invalidity benefits provided under the Dutch social security system. Under the scheme the amount payable to part-timers was linked to the claimant's previous income; full-time workers, regardless of the size of their previous income, were entitled to a guaranteed 'minimum subsistence income'. The claimant, who had been a part-time worker, claimed that the system was indirectly discriminatory against women, since the part-time workforce in the Netherlands contained a much smaller percentage of men than women. The Court held that in these circumstances the difference in treatment would breach Article 4(1) of Directive 79/7 unless it could be justified by objective factors unrelated to sex. The fact that it would be unfair, as was argued by the Netherlands Social Insurance Board, to grant part-time workers an allowance higher than the wages they had previously received in employment was held not to amount to objective justification, since in a substantial number of cases the amount granted to those entitled to a minimum subsistence income was also higher than their previous income.

The principle of equal treatment is 'without prejudice to the provisions relating to the protection of women on the grounds of maternity' (Article 4(2)). These provisions are likely to be interpreted according to the same principles as apply to Article 2(3) of Directive 76/207.

27.10.3 Exclusions

Article 7(1) expressly allows Member States to exclude certain matters from the scope of the equal treatment principle. These are:

(a) the determination of pensionable age for the purposes of old-age and retirement pensions and possible consequences thereof for other benefits

(b) benefits or entitlements granted to persons who have brought up children

(c) wives' derived old-age or invalidity benefits

(d) increases granted in respect of dependent wives related to long-term invalidity, old age, accidents at work and occupational disease benefits.

Article 7 must now be read in the light of the Court's case law under Directive 76/207, and in particular *Marshall* (case 152/84), *Roberts* (case 151/84), and *Beets-Proper* (case 262/84). The exemption for the determination of pensionable age will apply *only* for the purposes of old-age and retirement pensions and possible conse-quences thereof for other social-security benefits. In *R v Secretary of State for Social Security, ex parte Equal Opportunities Commission* (case C–9/91), in an action brought by the EOC for a declaration that the British Social Security Act 1965, in maintain-ing different periods of contribution by men and women towards social security benefits, the men's being longer, tied to the difference in pensionable age, was in breach of Directive 79/7, the Court held that the derogation provided by Article 7(1)(a) applied to any forms of discrimination 'necessarily linked' to the different statutory pensionable age. This would include the maintenance of different contri-bution periods for male and female workers. Such a scheme reflected the purpose of the derogation, which was to:

> allow Member States to maintain temporarily the advantages accorded to women with respect to retirement in order to enable them progressively to adapt their pension sys-tems . . . without disrupting the complex financial equilibrium of those systems, the importance of which could not be ignored.

The scope of Article 7(1)(a) was further tested in *Secretary of State for Social Security v Thomas* (case C–328/91) in a claim by a number of women for severe disablement allowances and invalid care allowances. Under British law these benefits were not payable to those who had reached pensionable age (60 for women, 65 for men) un-less at that age they were already in receipt of the benefits. The applicants had not received these benefits before attaining pensionable age, nor had they, on reaching that age, been in receipt of an old age pension. They argued that the tying of ben-efits to pensionable age (save in the case of those already in receipt of benefits) was discriminatory, particularly since they were entitled, following *Marshall*, to con-tinue working until the age of 65. The central question was whether the benefits in question fell within the exception provided by Article 7(1)(a).

Citing *R v Secretary of State for Social Security, ex parte Equal Opportunities Commission* (case C–9/91), that the permitted derogation of Article 7(1)(a), as regards the 'pos-sible consequences thereof for other benefits' was confined to 'forms of discrimina-tion existing under other benefit schemes which are *necessarily and objectively* linked to the difference in retirement age', the Court held that discrimination in respect of other benefits would only be necessary 'to avoid disrupting the complex financial equilibrium of the social security system or to ensure consistency between retire-ment pension schemes and other benefit schemes' (para 12). Since the benefits in question were non-contributory there was no question in this case of disruption of the financial equilibrium of the UK social security system; nor was discrimination necessary to avoid inconsistency between different benefit schemes. Since, as the UK had argued, the benefits were intended to replace income in the event of ma-terialisation of the risk, the principle of consistency required that they should be available in cases such as the applicants', where claimants were unable to work and were not in receipt of an old age pension. In any event, national rules against over-lapping would prevent double recovery by those in receipt of a pension.

By contrast, in *Secretary of State for Social Security v Graham* (case C–92/94), a case concerning discrimination in respect of contributory invalidity pensions, the ECJ held that the difference in treatment was necessarily and objectively linked to the permitted difference in retirement ages for men and women. To interfere with the ability to set retirement ages would encroach on the rights of the Member States under Article 7(1)(a) and would also introduce inconsistencies in the treatment of able-bodied women who had retired at 60 and their disabled counterparts. Although the Court identified the purpose of the provisions as replacing income from employment, it did not conclude that, as women are entitled to remain in employment until 65 (*Marshall* (case 152/84)), they should be entitled to a replacement income for that period should they be prevented by illness from being able to work. This somewhat circumspect decision may well have been driven, in part, by the need to allay Member States' fears about the reduced scope for exemption under Article 7(1)(a). The ECJ in general has taken a very restrictive view of Article 7(1)(a)'s scope, as it does of all derogations from fundamental Union rights. *Graham* therefore indicates a slightly broader approach, but whether it will constitute the basis of a new approach is another question. In *Taylor* (case C–382/98), which concerned winter fuel payments, the ECJ took an approach similar to that in the *Equal Opportunities* case (case C–9/91). (See also case C–104/98, *Buchner*.) By contrast, in *Hepple* (case C–196/98), which concerned a reduced earnings allowance, the ECJ held that the scheme fell within Article 7(1)(a), and therefore unequal age conditions linked to different pensionable ages for men and women could be imposed. Although the difference in treatment was not necessary to maintain the financial equilibrium of the scheme—as had been the case in *Thomas* and *Graham*—the ECJ accepted that the rules were designed to achieve a coherence between the allowance and the pension scheme and were objectively necessary for that purpose. It is equally uncertain whether the other exceptions will be narrowly or generously construed.

States are required under Article 7(2) periodically to examine matters excluded under Article 7(1) to ascertain whether they are still justified.

27.11 Principle of equal treatment in occupational pension schemes (Directive 86/378)

27.11.1 Relationship with equal pay

Directive 86/378, which is complementary to Directive 79/7, implements the equal treatment principle in the field of occupational, as opposed to statutory, pension schemes. It has, following *Barber*, been amended by Directive 96/97. The original directive was subject to a three-year implementation period, which expired on 31 July 1989 (Article 12). However, under Article 8, states were given until 1 January 1993 to take 'all necessary steps to ensure that the provisions of occupational [pension] schemes contrary to the principle of equal treatment are revised'. This implies that while states might be liable for failure to implement the directive from 1 August 1989, it did not become *fully* effective until January 1993. Although that point might be of historic interest only, it should be noted that where the difference in treatment arises from the employer's contribution, direct or indirect, to the pension scheme, by way of consideration paid by the employer to the employee in respect of his employment, as in *Worringham v Lloyds Bank Ltd* (case 69/80), *Bilka-Kaufhaus GmbH v Weber von Harz* (case 170/84), and *Barber* (case 262/88), it may fall to be treated under Article 141 as 'pay', subject to the temporal limitations of *Barber* and the substantive limits imposed by *Neath v Hugh Steeper Ltd* (case C–152/91). Following *Bilka-Kaufhaus* such benefits can even be claimed by part-time workers where the discriminatory effects fall disproportionately on one sex, provided that the difference in treatment is not objectively justified. Where the matter falls within Article 141 any problems concerning the direct effects of the directive will be avoided.

27.11.2 Scope of the directive

With a few important exceptions Directive 86/378 is enacted in near-identical terms to Directive 79/7. It applies to occupational schemes 'not governed by Directive 79/7 whose purpose is to provide workers . . . with benefits intended to supplement the benefits provided by statutory social security schemes or to replace them' (Article 2). It applies to the same categories of persons (Article 3) in respect of the same risks (Article 4). Directive 86/378, however, contains no exclusions for survivors' and family benefits parallel to that of Article 3(2) of Directive 79/7, *provided* these benefits form part of the consideration paid by the employer by reason of the employee's employment (Article 4).

Article 6(1) gives a list of examples of provisions contrary to the equal treatment principle. As noted above, it was amended to reflect the principles contained in *Coloroll* and *Neath*. Article 6(1)(f) prohibits the fixing of different retirement ages for men and women, and Article 6(1)(j) the laying down of different standards or standards applicable only to a specified sex. Article 6(1)(h) disallows 'suspending the retention or acquisition of rights during periods of maternity leave', which has been interpreted to require the continuation of payments to a supplementary occupational pension scheme based on taxable pay, even though maternity pay is not taxable (*Mayer v Versorgungsanstalt* (case C–356/03)). Article 6(1)(h) prohibits the setting of different levels of benefit 'except insofar as it may be necessary to take account of actuarial calculation factors which differ according to sex in the case of benefits designated as contribution-defined'. Similarly although different levels of employee contribution are prohibited in principle (Article 6(1)(i)) they *may* be set 'to take account of the different actuarial calculation factors' (Article 9(c)). Thus differences in treatment may be objectively justified. Different levels of employer contribution may also be permitted if they are set 'with a view to making the amount of [contribution-defined] benefits more equal' (Article 6(i)).

27.11.3 Exceptions and derogations

Article 9, like Article 7 of Directive 79/7, enables Member States to exempt from the equal treatment principle the 'determination of pensionable age for the purposes of granting old-age or retirement pensions, and the possible implications for other benefits'. This provision was construed seemingly out of existence in *Barber* (case C–262/88): hence the Court's decision that its ruling on this issue should not be retrospective.

Article 9(b) provides that 'survivors' pensions which do not constitute consideration paid by the employer are exempt from the equal treatment principle until the date on which equality is achieved in statutory schemes, or at the latest, until equality is required by a Directive'. Following *Barber* such benefits, being paid by the employer as a result of the employment relationship, are likely to be construed as consideration and thus will not be exempt under Article 9(b). *Newstead* (case 192/85), which had decided otherwise, thereby excluding the employer's provision for survivors from the equality principle under Article 9(b), is unlikely to be followed. Survivors' pensions which do *not* constitute consideration paid by the employer are also exempt from the equal treatment principle *either* until the date on which equality is achieved in statutory schemes, *or*, at the latest, until equality is required by a directive (Article 9(b)).

27.12 Equal treatment in self-employment (Directive 86/613)

Directive 86/613 is designed to ensure the application of the equal treatment principle 'as between men and women engaged in an activity in a self-employed capacity, or contributing to the pursuit of such an activity, as regards those aspects not covered by Directives 76/207 and 79/7' (Article 1). It is complementary to Directive 76/207.

The directive applies to 'all persons pursuing a gainful activity for their own account . . . including farmers and members of the liberal professions' and to 'their spouses, not being employees or partners, where they habitually . . . participate in the activities of the self-employed worker and perform the same tasks or ancillary tasks' (Article 2).

The principle of equal treatment implies 'the absence of discrimination on the grounds of sex, either directly or indirectly, by reference in particular to marital or family status' (Article 3). This is without prejudice to measures concerning the protection of women during pregnancy and motherhood (preamble, ninth recital).

Under Article 4 Member States are required to take all necessary measures to ensure the elimination of all provisions which are contrary to the principle of equal treatment as defined in Directive 76/207, especially in respect of the establishment, equipment or extension of a business or the launching or extension of any other form of self-employed activity, including financial facilities.

Member States are also required: 'Without prejudice to the specific conditions for access to certain activities which apply equally to both sexes' to take the measures necessary to ensure that the conditions for the formation of a company between spouses are not more restrictive than the conditions for the formation of a company between unmarried persons (Article 5).

Where a contributory social-security scheme exists for self-employed workers in a Member State, the states must take the necessary measures to enable those spouses who participate in the activities of the self-employed worker, and who are not protected under the self-employed worker's social security scheme, to join a contributory social-security scheme voluntarily (Article 6).

States are required to introduce 'such measures as are necessary to enable all persons who consider themselves wronged by failure to apply the principle of equal treatment in self-employed activities to pursue their claims by judicial process, possibly after recourse to other competent authorities' (Article 9).

Member States were required to bring into force the measures necessary to comply with the directives by 30 June 1989. The date for compliance was extended to 30 June 1991 for states which had to amend their legislation on matrimonial rights and obligations in order to secure the principle of equal treatment in the formation of companies (Article 12). The directive became directly effective as against the state on the expiry of the applicable time-limit. Since the date for implementation has passed it may now be invoked as an aid to interpretation against private parties (*von Colson* (case 14/83) and *Harz* (case 79/83)).

27.13 Remedies

Directive 76/207, Directive 75/117, and the Pregnancy Directive (92/85) all require states to:

> introduce into their national legal systems such measures as are necessary to enable all persons who consider themselves wronged by failure to apply the principle of equal treatment . . . to pursue their claims by judicial process after possible recourse to other competent authorities.

Given this obligation, it is unsurprising that the sex discrimination jurisprudence has been central to the development of principles relating to remedies for breach of Community law. These matters are discussed in Chapter 8.

27.14 Directive 2004/113/EC: Equal treatment of men and women in access to goods and services

The most recent measure to give effect to the principle of equal treatment between men and women is Directive 2004/113/EC on equal treatment between men and women in the access to and supply of goods and services ([2004] OJ L373/37). According to Article 3(1), the directive applies to all persons who provide goods or services to the public and offered outside the area of private and family life. It does not seek to prevent freedom of contract, although it does affect the choice of a contracting partner based on sex (Article 3(2)). The directive also does not deal with employment matters, for which there is, of course, already existing legislation.

Article 4 then gives effect to the general principle of equal treatment, prohibiting both direct and indirect discrimination in this context. A controversial provision during the legislative process was Article 5, which prohibits 'the use of sex as a factor in the calculation of premiums and benefits for the purposes of insurance and related financial services'. There was concern that this would, for example, outlaw the variations in insurance premiums for male and female drivers. To meet such concerns, Article 5(2) allows Member States to decide before December 2007 to permit 'proportionate differences in individuals' premiums and benefits where the use of sex is a determining factor in the assessment of risk based on relevant and accurate actuarial and statistical data'.

This directive is regarded as laying down a minimum standard, and Member States may introduce provisions which are more favourable then the equal treatment principle (Article 7; for minimum harmonisation generally, see Chapter 16).

The remainder of the directive contains provisions on enforcement (Articles 8–11), and on the setting up of a body responsible for promoting and monitoring the equal treatment of all persons (Article 12). The latter provision duplicates provisions found elsewhere, and it seems that entrusting this task to a body generally responsible for equal treatment matters would suffice.

It may be noted that the Recast Equal Treatment Directive, which would modernise and update the legislation discussed in the preceding sections, does not extend to this most recent directive, which will therefore operate alongside the new general directive.

27.15 Directive 2000/43/EC: Equal treatment irrespective of racial or ethnic origin

The ToA enhanced the provisions dealing with discrimination, giving the EU powers to adopt measures against discrimination on grounds of race, religion, sexual orientation, or disability (Article 13 EC). Directive 2000/43/EC (([2000] OJ L180, p 22) has been adopted, on the basis of Article 13 EC, to combat discrimination, both direct and indirect, on grounds of racial or ethnic origin, in relation to employment matters, social protection, education, and access to public goods and services. However, the directive allows difference of treatment based on racial or ethnic origin in the context of particular occupational activities, provided that this is legitimate and proportionate (Article 4). It also permits positive action (Article 5). The scope of this provision is somewhat open to doubt as the ECJ has handed down judgments prior to the ToA that limit the scope of Member States" ability to introduce such measures in the field of sex discrimination. Even after the ToA, Member States" freedom to take positive measures in the field of sex discrimination is not unlimited. (See further 27.9.7.)

Directive 2000/43/EC provides a minimum level of protection, and Member States may introduce more stringent standards, but should not use the directive as an excuse to lower existing standards (Article 6). The directive further provides for enforcement and remedies (Articles 7–12), and requires that a body is set up to promote equal treatment without discrimination on grounds of racial or ethnic origin.

The scope of the concept of direct discrimination was discussed in *Feryn* (case C–54/07), in which the Court was asked whether a statement made publicly by the director of a company that he did not wish to employ immigrants was discriminatory for the purposes of the directive. A body designated to promote equal treatment brought proceedings against the company asking the national court to find that its recruitment policy was discriminatory. The ECJ ruled that the lack of an identifiable complainant did not mean that there was no discrimination. The director's statement was likely to strongly dissuade certain candidates from applying for the job and, thus, hindered their access to the labour market. Therefore, the statement constituted direct discrimination within the meaning of the directive despite the fact that no one had submitted a complaint claiming to be a victim.

Then, the burden fell on the employer to prove before the national court that his actual recruitment practices were non-discriminatory and did not correspond to that statement.

27.16 Directive 2000/78/EC: Equal treatment in employment and occupation

Directive 2000/78/EC ([2000] OJ L303, p 16), which has been adopted, on the basis of Article 13 EC, lays down a general framework for combating discrimination on the grounds of religion or belief, disability, age, or sexual orientation with regard to employment and occupation. It prohibits direct and indirect discrimination; harassment and an instruction to discriminate are also deemed to be forms of discrimination (Article 2). Article 5 requires that disabled persons are given reasonable accommodation, which means that employers must take appropriate measures to enable a person with a disability to have access to or advance in employment, unless such measures would be disproportionately burdensome for the employer. As with Directive 2000/43/EC, differential treatment is permitted where this is required for the particular activity (Article 4(1)). Moreover, as far as employment with the church or other religious organisations is concerned, difference of treatment based on religious beliefs is also not to be treated as discrimination (Article 4(2)). There are similar enforcement provisions to those in Articles 7–12 of Directive 2000/43/EC. Article 15 recognises the need to achieve a balance of representation of the major religious communities in Northern Ireland both in the police service and in the employment of teachers.

The effect of the directive and its relationship with the general principle of equal treatment came before the ECJ in *Mangold* (case C–144/04), which concerned age discrimination. The Court stated that the source of that principle is not the directive itself but the constitutional traditions common to the Member States and various international instruments; what the directive does is to lay down the general framework for combating discrimination on the grounds listed therein. Then, the Court went on to hold that the principle of non-discrimination on grounds of age is a general principle of Union law. Accordingly, the fact that the employment contract at issue had been concluded before the period prescribed for the transposition of the directive into domestic law had expired did not relieve Member States from their non-discrimination obligations. National courts hearing a dispute concerning discrimination in respect of age must ensure that individuals enjoy the protection guaranteed by Union law and that the relevant rules are fully effective, setting aside any conflicting provisions of national law.

This broad ruling in *Mangold* attracted criticism not only from academics but also from some of the Court's Advocates-General. The case of *Lindorfer* (case C–277/04 P) was about an employee of the European Community who argued, among others, that she had suffered age discrimination because the actuarial values used for the calculation of her pension were increasingly less favourable for employees as their age on recruitment increased. Advocate-General Sharpston suggested that what flows from the constitutional traditions common to the Member States and international law is the *general* principle of equality, while the specific prohibition of age discrimination is 'too recent and uneven' to be considered as a general principle of law; rather, it is a particular expression of the general equality principle. The Court held that the claimant had suffered no age discrimination since her situation was not comparable to an employee who had started his career with the Community at an earlier age and, thus, did not discuss the effect of *Mangold*.

Palacios de la Villa (case C–411/05) concerned the dismissal of an employee who had reached the compulsory retirement age. Advocate-General Mazák also disagreed with the Court's conclusion in *Mangold* that there is a general principle of law prohibiting age discrimination stating that such a 'bold proposition' is 'far from compelling'. Although the Court followed his suggestion and held that the national provision was objectively and reasonably justified by the legitimate aim of facilitating the entry into the labour market of certain categories of workers (Article 6(1) of the directive), it did not exclude compulsory retirement rules from the scope of its review. In other words, Member States are free to set age limits such as that at issue in the case only if they can establish that there are objective and reasonable social-policy justifications for them, with the ECJ having the last word.

A more narrow approach was adopted by the Court in *Bartsch* (case C–427/06), in which the Court was asked whether the application of the prohibition under Union law of discrimination on the ground of age was mandatory where the allegedly discriminatory treatment contained no link with Union law. The claimant was a widow who, after the death of her husband, was refused a survivor's pension because the guidelines of the pension fund stated than no pension would be paid out if the survivor is more than 15 years younger than the deceased person. The Court held that the situation at issue was outside the scope of Union law. Firstly, the pension fund's guidelines did not constitute a measure implementing Directive 2000/78 and when the death of the claimant's husband occurred the period for the transposition of the directive had not expired. Secondly, Article 13 EU could not by itself bring within the scope of EU law situations which were not covered by specific measures adopted under it such as Directive 2000/78.

Retirement age was again the issue in *Age Concern England* (case C–388/07). The Employment Equality (Age) Regulations 2006, which transposed Directive 2000/78, provide that an employer may dismiss an employee who has reached retirement age if that measure constitutes 'a proportionate means of achieving a legitimate aim'. The case turned on the interpretation of Article 6(1) of the directive which empowers Member States to provide that certain differences in treatment on the basis of age shall not constitute discrimination if they are objectively and reasonably justified by a legitimate aim, and then gives examples of what could be considered as an objective and reasonable justification. The 2006 regulations do not provide for such examples. The claimants argued that the meaning of Article 6 of the directive is that Member States must set out in their instruments of transposition a specific list of the differences of treatment which may be justified by reference to a legitimate aim; thus, if the relevant national law provides only that a difference of treatment on grounds of age, of whatever kind, is lawful if it can be shown that it constitutes a proportionate means of achieving a legitimate aim it is incompatible with Article 6. The Court disagreed. It reiterated its earlier case law that Member States have wide discretion as to the choice of methods for the transposition of a directive, and that their obligation to ensure the effectiveness of a directive does not necessarily mean that its provisions must be incorporated formally in express, specific legislation.

Therefore, the lack in the regulations of a precise list of aims which can justify discrimination does not render them incompatible with the directive. However, the general content of the national measure should enable courts to identify what the legitimate aim is in each case and assess the proportionality of the means used to achieve it. The spirit of Article 6(1) of the directive, the Court continued, is that discriminatory measures may be justified by reference to social policy objectives such as those related to employment policy, the labour market, or vocational training; it for the national court to determine whether a particular measure can be justified by such an objective. The effect of the judgment is that Member States enjoy considerable discretion as to the way they design and implement their anti-discrimination legislation which gives effect to relevant rules. The limit of such discretion is the effectiveness of law: national legislation cannot provide for justifications of discriminatory treatment which are not objective and proportionate. This is a test which national courts should perform by applying the principles developed by the ECJ, and, if necessary, by making a preliminary reference.

The scope of the directive in relation to the forms discrimination may take was examined by the Court in *Coleman* (case C–303/06). The claimant was the mother of a disabled child who argued that, because of her child, she suffered adverse treatment in comparison to employees who did not have disabled children. The Employment Tribunal asked the ECJ whether Directive 2000/78 covered direct 'discrimination by association', ie discrimination suffered by an employee who, while not having himself one of the characteristics listed in the directive, is associated who a third person who does. Advocate-General Poiares Maduro noted that the directive operates 'at the level of grounds of discrimination', its aim being to prohibit completely the use of those characteristics as reasons to treat an employee less well than others. The Court followed the Attorney-General's opinion and held that the principle of equal treatment which the directive is designed to safeguard is not limited to people who themselves have a disability within the meaning of the directive, and that the prohibition of discrimination 'applies not to a particular category of person but by reference to the grounds mentioned in Article 1 [of the Directive]'. Thus, after *Coleman*, it is unlawful for an employer to treat adversely not only employees who themselves have one of the characteristics listed in Article 1 of the directive, but also employees who are associated with a third person having those characteristics, if the reason for the adverse treatment is that third person's religion, disability, age, or sexual orientation.

The directive's prohibition of discrimination on the basis of sexual orientation came before the Court in *Maruko* (C–267/06). The claimant had entered into a life partnership with another man, and when the latter died he applied for a survivor's pension. The state pension fund rejected his application on the ground that its regulations provided for such an entitlement only for surviving spouses but not for surviving life partners. Advocate-General Ruiz-Jarabo Colomer explained that the inequality at issue concerned the differential treatment of married couples and people who form partnerships covered by different legal arrangements, so the dispute turned on the effects of the two types of union. The national courts had already taken the view that a registered life partnership consists in a system of rights and obligations similar to that of marriage. Accordingly, the Advocate-General concluded, the refusal to grant a pension on the grounds that a couple has not married, where two persons of the same sex are unable to marry and have entered into a registered partnership, is incompatible with the directive. Similarly, the ECJ ruled that, since Germany had chosen to alter its legal system to allow persons of the same sex to enter into a registered life partnership, the conditions of which had been made equivalent to those applicable to marriage, it would constitute direct discrimination to withhold the pension from the surviving life partner while making it available to the surviving spouse of a married couple. *Maruko* neither prohibits all differences of treatment between married heterosexual couples and homosexual couples in a life partnership, nor does it impose on Member States an obligation to provide for civil partnerships in their domestic legal systems. However, if a Member State has chosen to introduce such partnerships in terms which make them similar to marriage it cannot withhold from those entering a civil partnership the benefits that married couples enjoy.

Finally, in *Chacón Navas* (case C–13/05) the Court held that 'disability' is a different concept from 'sickness', so a worker who is dismissed solely on account of sickness cannot rely on the directive, whose scope cannot be extended to include a prohibition of discrimination on the basis of reasons other than religion, age, disability and sexual orientation.

27.17 Conclusions

Recent years have seen an upsurge in the legislative activity in the area of discrimination. Not only has there been a widening in the substantive scope of the Union's activities, but there has also been a great deal of emphasis on enforcement, reflected initially in Directives 2000/43 and 2000/78, and then in the amendments to Directive 76/207 by Directive 2002/73. The Recast Equal Treatment Directive extends these new enforcement provisions into the remaining parts of the discrimination framework. It is to be welcomed that the legislation in this area is undergoing a major review, taking into account not only the various changes to the treaty since this legislation was first adopted, but also the jurisprudence by the Court.

In respect of the core area, sex discrimination, it can be seen that the ECJ has interpreted the provisions relating to equal pay and equal treatment broadly, emphasising the personal aspect of the rights over issues relating to distortion of competition. In so doing, the ECJ has not been afraid to make far-reaching decisions. Nonetheless, there are limitations to the scope of Article 141 and some secondary legislation has had its role in clarifying the mechanisms by which individuals' rights might be enforced. Given the development of the law in this area, sex discrimination is an area where the general principles might seem clear, but analysing the precise details of particular situations becomes the work of a specialist.

FURTHER READING

Ahtela, K, 'The revised provisions on sex discrimination in European law: A critical assessment' (2005) 11 ELJ 58–78.

Arnull, A, 'Out with the old . . . ' (Editorial) (2006) 31 EL Rev 1–2.

Besson, S, Never shall the twain Meet? Gender discrimination under EU and ECHR law', (2008) Human Rights Law Review 647.

Burrows, N and Robison, M, 'Positive action for women in employment: Time to align with Europe?' (2006) 33 J Law & Soc 24.

Curtin, D, 'Scalping the Community legislator: Occupational pensions and *Barber*' (1990) 27 CML Rev 475.

Docksey, C, 'The principle of equality between men and women: A fundamental right under Community law' (1991) 20 ILJ 258.

Hatzopoulos, V, 'A (more) social group: A political crossroad or a legal one-way? Dialogues between Luxembourg and Lisbon' (2005) 42 CML Rev 1599–635.

Hervey, T and O'Keeffe, D (eds), *Sex Equality Law in the European Union* (Wiley, 1996).

Honeyball, S, 'Pregnancy and sex discrimination' (2000) 29 ILJ 43.

Howard, E, 'Anti-race discrimination Measures in Europe: An attack on two fronts' (2005) 11 ELJ 468–86.

Masselot, A, The state of gender equality law in the European Union (2007) 13 ELJ 152.

Mancine, GF and O'Leary, S, 'The new frontiers of sex equality law in the European Union' (1999) 24 EL Rev 331.

Neuner, J, 'Protection against discrimination in European contract law' (2006) 2 ERCL 35–50.

Prechel, S, 'Remedies after *Marshall*' (1990) 21 CML Rev 451.

Shaw, J, 'European Community judicial method: Its application to sex discrimination law' (1990) 19 ILJ 228.

Whiteford, E, 'Social policy after Maastricht' (1993) 18 EL Rev 202.

28

Introduction to competition policy

28.1 The structure of EU competition provisions

The competition policy of the EU is based on Article 3(g) EC, requiring 'a system ensuring that competition in the common market is not distorted', and Articles 81–9 (ex 85–94; post Lisbon, 101–9 TFEU) EC. The competition provisions can, broadly speaking, be divided into those which focus primarily on the activities of governments and those which deal with the actions of private (and some public) undertakings.

The first group consist of the rules on State aid (Articles 87–9 (ex 92–4) EC), although the other competition rules may also affect governments' policies. The grant of state aid by a Member State to an undertaking based in its territory may have the effect of distorting competition in the internal market, because an undertaking which would otherwise struggle to compete may find itself in a better position to do so as a result of such financial support. The treaty provisions prohibit the grant of state aid, but there are several exceptions in recognition of the fact that such aid may be justified in particular circumstances. The rules on state aid are discussed in Chapter 31.

The second group of provisions consists of the rules concerning anticompetitive agreements or concerted practices between undertakings (Article 81 (ex 85)), the prohibition on abuse of a dominant position on the part of individual undertakings or groups of undertakings (Article 82 (ex 86)), and the rules relating to public undertakings granted special or exclusive rights (Article 86 (ex 90) EC).

In previous editions of this book, the chapters on competition law were extensive. Competition law was one of the first 'big' areas of EU law, and merited detailed consideration. This subject has become increasingly complex, and has now evolved to such an extent that it is a specialist area of study. In a general book on EU law, it is no longer possible to do full justice to this subject, and the discussion here has been curtailed to what may be regarded as the fundamental aspects of competition law. Articles 81–2 are therefore dealt with together in Chapter 29, together with an outline of the provisions related to their enforcement. Note, however, that with the decentralisation of enforcement, some aspects of enforcement will be affected by the rules on effectiveness (see Chapter 8). The interrelationship between competition rules and intellectual property rights will be considered in Chapter 30, which also examines the overlap with Article 28 (ex 30) in this regard. Although the rules in Article 86 are becoming increasingly important with the dismantling of state monopolies, especially regarding the provision of utilities and other services of general economic interest, this book will look at this provision only insofar as it affects the operation of state-aid rules or Article 82. The provisions concerned with the adverse effects on competition of dumping—the exporting of goods to the Union by third countries at prices that are less than the 'comparable' price of the like product on the domestic market—fall outside the scope of this book.

28.1.1 The significance of competition policy for the EU

Competition policy is an essential complement to the fundamental provisions of the treaty designed to create the single market. The obligations imposed on Member States to ensure the free movement of goods and services and freedom of establishment within the Union would be of little effect if parties were free to engage in restrictive practices such as concerted price fixing or market sharing which inhibit the free play of market forces within the single market, particularly when such practices tend to partition the market along national lines.

Broadly speaking, the purposes of EU competition policy, which is spelt out in detail in the Commission's annual reports on competition policy, is to encourage economic activity and maximise efficiency by enabling goods and resources to flow freely amongst Member States according to the operation of normal market forces. The concentration of resources resulting from such activity functioning on a Union, rather than a national, scale is intended to increase the competitiveness of European industry in a world market. In addition to this primary goal, and sometimes conflicting with it, European competition policy seeks to protect and encourage small and medium-sized enterprises so that they too may play their full part in the competitive process. Controversially, European competition policy has also been aware of the need to prevent the partitioning of markets along national lines, and this concern too, has affected the shape of the Union's approach to competition (see 28.3.2 below).

In order to understand and evaluate the policies pursued by the Commission it is necessary briefly to examine the economic theory underlying competition policy.

28.2 The theory of competition

28.2.1 Perfect competition

The original concept of competition, dating from the eighteenth century, and Adam Smith's *Wealth of Nations* (1776), merely meant the absence of legal restraints on trade. Modern economic theory, however, which stems from the late nineteenth century, and led to the first anti-trust legislation, the Sherman Act, in the USA in 1890, is based on the model of 'perfect competition'. This is an idealised concept, based on a number of assumptions. It assumes that there are in the market a large number of buyers and sellers, the latter all producing identical or homogeneous products; that consumers have perfect information, and always act in order to maximise utility; that resources flow freely from one area of economic activity to another, and that there are no impediments to the emergence of new competition ('barriers to entry'); and that business people always maximise profits. A system of 'pure' or 'perfect' competition guarantees the maximum efficiency, the optimum allocation of resources. It is the polar opposite to the monopoly.

28.2.2 **Market failures**

The 'traditional' view, adopted by the early economists, was that the real world did not correspond to this model of perfect competition. Rival undertakings might choose to cooperate rather than compete. Markets could be divided. Such practices which stood in the way of the achievement of perfect competition, which restricted the freedom of buyers and sellers, must therefore be curtailed. It was necessary to regulate the market in order to bring it closer to the ideal. Intervention was also seen as necessary to keep open opportunities for competitive activity, particularly for small and medium-sized firms, and to preserve real choice for consumers. Early anti-trust law, eg, the Sherman Act (1890, USA), was designed to make capitalism work more effectively.

28.2.3 **Social market economy**

Anti-trust law in Western Europe, which only became widespread after the Second World War, was based on this traditional view. The influence of this view was particularly strong in Germany, where concentrations of industrial power in pre-war Germany were seen as having contributed to a concentration of political power. This school of thought is sometimes referred to as the Freiburg School, or as ordoliberalism. The state was thus under an obligation to create a legal environment in which competition would exist and, in particular, to take action to prevent the creation of monopolies (or oligopolies) and cartels. As well as accruing political power, such entities undermine individual freedoms and autonomy. This view of competition is also linked to the concept of a social market economy, although this term was not used in the original EC Treaty. A social market economy implies the need for fairness because, whilst it is based on the idea of a market economy, it seeks to provide a system which does not just help the wealthy, but also care for those more in need of help, that is the combination of the principle of market freedom with that of social balance. A social market economy, to some extent implies the need for public service. It was this German inheritance, together with the appeal of the traditional view following the Second World War, which shaped EU competition law. French law too, though in much smaller degree, influenced EU law, particularly in its concern to protect the small trader.

28.2.4 **The Chicago school**

Opposed to the traditional view is the view of the Chicago school of economists. Although implicit in the laissez-faire view of the early nineteenth century, it has only relatively recently emerged and has been rapidly gaining ground over the traditional view, particularly in the USA. According to the Chicago school, the real world approximates quite well to the model of perfect competition; even monopolies are not in themselves anticompetitive as long as there are no barriers to entry, ie, as long as other business people are not prevented from entering the field as competitors. This will only occur if the minimum efficient scale of the operation is such as to make entry virtually impossible. The Chicago school believes that only the minimum intervention is needed, and then only to curb the most blatant forms of anticompetitive activity, as the market will regulate itself. Although a full review of the comparative case law under the EU and US systems lies well beyond the scope of this book, it is perhaps appropriate to note here that in some key cases the approach of the US has been noticeably different from that in the EU.

28.3 EU competition policy

28.3.1 A strict approach

The basic principles of EU competition policy, as adopted in the original EEC Treaty, were drafted in the broadest terms, leaving the Commission, subject to the supervision of the Court, to interpret these provisions and to develop detailed rules. In interpreting the treaty the Commission was heavily influenced by the traditional school. In the early years, it had been criticised as being excessively interventionist, although in more recent times, its approach has changed fundamentally.

In its concern to strike down all restrictions on competition it has been said that the Commission failed explicitly to distinguish between 'vertical' agreements (agreements between parties at different levels in the chain of distribution—eg, between manufacturer and his selected dealer, or between dealer and retailer) which carry many economic advantages, and 'horizontal' agreements (agreements between parties at the same level in the economic chain—eg, cartels between manufacturer and manufacturer, between dealer and dealer), which are potentially much more damaging to competition. Nor did it distinguish sufficiently between *ancillary restraints*—ie, restraints which are attached to some pro-competitive transaction, and *naked restrictions* on competition, clothed with no desirable transaction at all. While the latter are never justifiable, the former may be judged according to whether they are necessary to make the (desirable) transaction viable. The Commission has since changed its mind on all of these matters, although it has, perhaps, still not thrown off all the shackles of its previous approach and an increasing concern amongst the Member States may mean a resurgence of the social market economy (see further 28.3.4 below).

28.3.2 Market integration versus economic objectives

The Commission was also criticised for subordinating other goals, such as overall economic efficiency, to the supreme goal of market integration. Thus, to protect the single market, *intra-brand* competition (competition between undertakings dealing in the *same* brand—eg, between rival Ford car dealers) is protected at the expense of *inter-brand* competition (competition between undertakings dealing in *competing* brands—eg, between Ford dealers (or manufacturers) and Citroën dealers (or manufacturers)). The effect of this may be to reduce the competitiveness of the industry as a whole. These criticisms are less valid today, although the principal prohibition in Article 81(1) continues to be interpreted broadly. The Commission continues to issue exemption to whole categories of agreements which, although in themselves restrictive of competition and prima facie in breach of Article 81(1), are beneficial overall. Over the years, it has steadily extended the scope of these exemptions.

A similar relaxation of the rules is seen in the Commission's approach to Article 82 and merger control. Of late, with the change in economic conditions (slowdown in growth, increased unemployment, increased competition worldwide), mergers have been allowed to proceed which would have been unlikely to have been accepted earlier.

28.3.3 Relationship with other policies

It has also been suggested that by elevating the single market principle above all other considerations, the Commission and the Court (which rarely departs from the view of the Commission in broad matters of policy) have failed to take into account other Union objectives relevant to the application of competition law, such as the need to counter regional or structural imbalances and to safeguard employment and the environment. The increasing integration of the internal market will clearly have regional, social, and environmental repercussions which may necessitate the weighing of other wider policy considerations within the context of the application of EU competition rules.

This concern was recognised by the Commission as far back as 1993, in which it stressed the need:

> to ensure that the natural and logical linkages between the Community's competition, research, environmental and social policies are fully taken into account in the Commission's approach to competition policy. [(ISEC B 21/93.]

It was acknowledged by the Commission in its *23rd Report on Competition Policy* that the changes brought in by the Maastricht Treaty (TEU), such as the need to protect cultural diversity (Article 151 (ex 128) EC) and the environment (Article 174 (ex 130r(2)) EC), require the Commission to balance more and more competing interests. This factor has been recognised in the state aid provisions, in particular and as we shall see in Chapter 31, the Commission is now producing guidelines to as to better target state aid: recognition of the need for regional aid, aid for small enterprises and environmental aid are recognised. The approach of the European Court of Justice (ECJ) to allowing scope for public service seems to allow more freedom for Member States (see *Altmark*). Further, the Merger Regulation specifically requires the Commission, when considering whether to approve a merger, to take into account social factors such as the impact of the deal on employees' jobs (eg, *Comité Central d'Entreprise de la Société Générale des Grandes Sources v Commission* (case T–96/92); *Comité Central d'Entreprise de la SA Vittel v Commission* (case T–12/93)). Concern for the environment was a factor in the favourable Commission Decision on the *Philips/ Osram* joint venture ([1994] 5 CMLR 491), in which the Commission took note of the existence of equipment to reduce emissions at the factory in which the joint venture company was to operate. This change has perhaps been encouraged by the 'mainstreaming' of certain policies, such as protection of the environment, which requires such policies to be taken into account in all other EU policies. (see, eg, Article 6 EC). Article 16 EC, introduced by the Treaty of Amsterdam (ToA), which requires Member States providing 'services of general economic interest' to have regard to the 'shared values of the Union as well as their role in promoting social and territorial cohesion', illustrates Member States' concerns regarding the impact of privatisation on the provision of public services. (See also the Protocol on Public Service Broadcasting annexed to the ToA.) Other changes following the ToA, notably the emphasis on environmental policy and concern about high levels of unemployment, also reflect this trend. The Commission has, however, noted that environmental protection programmes could also be used to partition markets or to disguise other anticompetitive practices (see *23rd Report on Competition Policy*). No doubt other policy objectives could also be so used.

These factors and criticisms may be kept in mind when specific cases fall to be examined. Approval or disapproval of Union policies will ultimately depend on one's view of its economic, social, and political priorities. No doubt it was essential that market integration should come first during the Community's formative years. Equally, it is not surprising that, as the EU has become more closely integrated, there has been a greater recognition on the part of the Commission and the Court of the need to promote economic efficiency, to enable European industry to compete more effectively in the world market. Indeed the Commission has pointed out the necessity, in a climate of slow economic growth and fierce competition, for distinguishing, in the application of its competition policy, between behaviour that leads to the development and restructuring of European industry and behaviour that holds back that process by partitioning markets and strengthening domestic positions. This recognition of the need to give more weight to economic efficiency is clearly reflected in the Commission's changed attitude both to vertical agreements and horizontal cooperation agreements (see further Chapter 29). For decades, the Commission followed a strict legalistic approach, but in the late 1990s it changed towards an economics-based assessment. As a result, it regards fewer practices as problematic and now focuses on those agreements where the parties have significant market power. This approach, while more in tune with economic analysis, has been criticised by business for being more uncertain and difficult to apply. Nonetheless, the Commission has repeatedly stated that it needs to focus its limited resources where the real harm lies, and is therefore concentrating on significant abuse and major cartels, as well as the continuing problem of out-of-control state aids.

28.3.4 Competition and the Lisbon Treaty

Although the status of the Lisbon Treaty is somewhat uncertain, a couple of points regarding its potential impact on competition policy are worth noting. As noted in Chapter 1, the objectives of the Union will be found in the TEU, rather than in the EC Treaty. Article 3(3) TEU (post Lisbon) specifies that, inter alia, the Union shall establish an internal market based on 'a highly competitive social market economy'; this is the first time there has been an express reference to a social market economy. Further, the current Article 3(1), which includes at Article 3(1)(g) EC that the activities of the Community shall include a system ensuring that competition in the internal market is not distorted, will be deleted. As part of the treaty negotiations, the French government requested that the reference to competition as an objective of the Union be removed; it argued that competition was a means to an end, not an objective in its own right. These amendments could indicate a change of emphasis within the Union. It is, however, important not to overstate this possibility; the competition provisions themselves remain unchanged in the main body of the treaty and a protocol to the Lisbon Treaty emphasises that Article 2 TEU (post Lisbon) includes a system ensuring that competition is not distorted.

28.4 Enforcement of EU competition law

For four decades, enforcement of EU competition law had been entrusted to the Commission under Regulation 17/62, giving it exclusive enforcement powers. In view of the maturity of this area, and the increasing membership of the EU, the enforcement was largely devolved to national competition authorities in Regulation 1/2003, which came into force in May 2004. Any decisions still taken by the Commission may, however, be challenged under Article 230 (ex 173) EC (see Chapter 12) and a failure to take such a decision may be challenged under Article 232 (ex 175) EC (see Chapter 13). Challenges to Commission decisions regarding state aid may be likewise challenged. These matters are now dealt with by the Court of First Instance (CFI) subject to appeal on points of law to the ECJ. Articles 81–2 were declared directly effective (*BRT v SABAM* (case 127/73)) early in the development of competition policy, and Member States' courts have always been able to apply EU competition law, although they were not empowered to consider exemptions prior to the entry into force of Regulation 1/2003. Under the new enforcement scheme, there will be much more cooperation between both the Commission and national authorities, and the national authorities *inter se*. The decentralised approach is now also found in the application of state aid. To ensure consistent interpretation, the Commission has issued a number of block exemptions and guidance notices as to interpretation (see Chapters 29 and 31).

Unlike the provisions considered so far, a breach of Articles 81–2 may give rise to sanctions imposed by the Commission in the form of heavy fines and penalties. This is rare in EU law. Since companies in breach of competition rules may be subject to substantial fines, the European courts have been vigilant in ensuring that the companies' procedural rights are not infringed. For example, in *BASF AG v Commission* (cases T–80 et al/89), a decision was impugned because the decision was not properly adopted in all relevant official languages. In the *Soda Ash* cases, the CFI quashed Commission decisions because the companies' right of access to the file had been denied (*Solvay v Commission* (cases T–30–2/91); *ICI v Commission* (cases T–36–7/91)). (On procedural rights, see Chapter 6, on effectiveness of remedies, see Chapter 8.)

28.5 Role of the state

Although the obligations of Articles 81–2 are imposed on 'undertakings' and do not prima facie concern the activities of public authorities, Article 86(1) expressly provides that EU competition law applies to 'public undertakings and undertakings to which Member States grant special or exclusive rights', subject to exception for undertakings 'entrusted with the operation of services of general economic interest or having the character of a revenue-producing monopoly' insofar as the application of the rules may 'obstruct the performance of the particular tasks assigned to them' (Article 86(2)). This exception has been strictly construed. Derogation will be permitted only to the extent that it is necessary to the performance of the particular tasks assigned to such undertakings and to the economic equilibrium of the service operated in the general economic interest—eg by providing a set-off between profitable and unprofitable activities (*Corbeau* (case C–320/91), re Belgian postal monopoly). Outside these exempted areas:

> The legal framework within which agreements are made or decisions are taken and the classification (ie, public or private) given to that framework are irrelevant as far as the applicability of Community rules on competition are concerned. [*BNIC v Clair* (case 123/83) para 17.]

It is questionable the degree to which European control over the provision of national public services will be relaxed, especially with the current trend towards privatisation of 'services of general economic interest'. Even Article 16 EC, which emphasises the importance of public services, states that it operates 'without prejudice' to Articles 73 (public transport), 86 (public undertakings), and 87 (state aid, discussed in Chapter 31) and presumably therefore does not disturb the existing case law on these articles (see also the *Green Paper on Services of General Economic Interest* (COM (2003) 270 final, [2003] OJ C76)). Nonetheless, a greater emphasis seems to be being given to Member States' freedom in this regard (particularly in areas where there is no European action; cf, eg, telecommunications) as some cases post *Altmark* (discussed Chapter 31) suggest. Insofar as this is a trend, it can be seen to be supported by the changes introduced by Lisbon: not only the amendments to Article 2 TEU noted above, but the amendments to what is currently Article 16 EC (post Lisbon, Art 14 of the Treaty on the Functioning of the European Union (TFEU)).

Even where there is no agreement or behaviour on the part of a public (or semi-public) body such as to give rise to liability under Articles 81–2, a state may not adopt or maintain in force any measures which deprive these articles of their effectiveness. Any public measure that endorses or encourages action in breach of Articles 81–2 will be deemed unlawful (*GB-INNO v ATAB* (case 13/77)). Thus a public body, depending on its actions and the measures concerned, may, in the context of anticompetitive action, incur liability under other articles of the treaty (eg, Articles 10, 28, and 29 (goods), 49 (services)), *or* Articles 81–2. Where doubt exists as to which articles are appropriate, all relevant articles should be pleaded.

A number of areas, such as transport, were originally excluded from EU competition law. As has been noted, there has been scope under Article 86(2) for exemption for public undertakings. The scope of these exclusions has been considerably reduced in recent years, as the Commission has introduced liberalising measures in the field of communications, postal services, transport, energy, insurance and audiovisual media, with a view to further increasing competition in these spheres. Also, to achieve the benefits of free competition within the single market in the important field of public procurement, the Union has issued directives governing the award of public supply and public works contracts, laying down detailed procedures for the advertising (in the *Official Journal*) and award of such contracts, including the payment of damages by authorities acting in breach of these procedures (see Directive 89/665 [1989] OJ L395/33).

28.6 Competition and third countries

In the external sphere the Commission has stepped up its attempts to secure the acceptance and adoption of EU competition policy by the Union's main trading partners by means of bilateral or multilateral negotiation (for example, the revised form of the EU/US Cooperation Agreement has now been adopted ([1995] OJ L94/47 and [1995] OJ L13/38)), with a view to overcoming the adverse effects for EU traders of anticompetitive practices in non-EU markets.

FURTHER READING

Commission's Annual Reports on Competition Policy.

European Competition Law Review.

Flynn, L, 'Competition policy and public services in EC law after the Maastricht and Amsterdam Treaties' in D O'Keeffe and P Twomey (eds), *Legal Issues of the Amsterdam Treaties* (Hart, 1999).

Gerber, DJ, 'The transformation of European Community competition law?' (1994) 35 Harv Int'l LJ 97.

Goyder, D, *EC Competition Law*, 4th edn (Oxford: University Press, 2003).

Hancher, L, 'Community, state and market' in Craig, P and De Burca, G (eds), *The Evolution of EU Law* (Oxford University Press, 1999).

Hofmann, HCH, 'Negotiated and non-negotiated administrative rule making: The example of EC competition policy' (2006) 43 CML Rev 153–78.

Joerges, C, and Rödl, F, '"Social market economy" as Europe's social model?' *EUI Working Paper LAW*, No 2004/08.

Ross, M, 'Article 16 EC and services of general interest: From derogation to obligation?' (2000) 25 EL Rev 22.

Wesseling, R, 'Subsidiarity in Community antitrust law: Setting the right agenda' (1997) 22 EL Rev 35.

Whish, R, *Competition Law*, 5th edn (Butterworths/Oxford University Press, 2003).

29

Elements of competition law in the internal market

29.1 Introduction

Competition law was one of the areas where a complex body of law emerged from the early days of the European Economic Community. Over time, it has become a specialised area of law, evidenced by the fact that it is now frequently taught as a separate subject, rather than as part of a course on EU Law. Nevertheless, competition law remains crucial to an understanding of the internal market. Within the case law there are several recurrent issues. One such issue is the extent to which an economic analysis should be prioritised; the institutions have claimed to be moving towards such an approach. The Union has multiple objectives and sometimes it is claimed that competition policy is used in furtherance of those objectives, rather than taking a 'pure' competition based approach, and the institutions have sometimes been criticised for protecting the competition, rather than letting competition policy do its work. In previous editions of this book, there were several chapters on this topic, but in this edition, coverage has been adjusted to concentrate on the core elements of competition law and how this affects the internal market. In particular, the focus is on anticompetitive agreements, abuse of market power, and controls over concentrations.

29.2 Anticompetitive agreements, decisions, and concerted practices

A common form of anticompetitive behaviour is for businesses in a particular sector to come to an agreement on matters such as pricing, output, and the markets in which they will sell their respective goods. Price-fixing and market-sharing agreements, in particular, have been very common and, despite intense competition enforcement around the globe, businesses continue to come to such arrangements. In many cases, businesses that coordinate aspects such as price or output reduce the competitive pressures from other businesses in the same sector. As a result, competition is reduced, which may have the effect of increasing the price of goods or services, which is detrimental to buyers.

In the context of the common market, the danger of market-sharing is perhaps of particular significance. One of the objectives of the Community has been the creation of a market without barriers that transcends national lines. Consequently, businesses will face competition from businesses established in other Member States. It would undermine the aim of establishing the common market, or impede its operation, if businesses from the various Member States were to agree not to compete in each other's respective territories.

The Community was given a strong mandate to pursue anticompetitive practices in the original EC Treaty. Any form of coordination of commercial behaviour is dealt with under Article 81 EC (Ex 85). Traditionally the prohibition was applied on a broad basis. The Commission had a central role in enforcement, which brought with it problems in exempting agreements that were not harmful in competition terms, as well as the solutions to those problems. Since the modernisation process, which commenced in the late 1990s, there has been a shift, with the Commission now focusing its activities on serious cartels, and domestic competition authorities having a stronger role to play.

29.2.1 The general scheme

Article 81(1) prohibits:

> all agreements between undertakings, decisions by associations of undertakings and concerted practices which may affect trade between Member States and which have as their object or effect the prevention, restriction or distortion of competition within the common market.

Should the Lisbon Treaty comes into force, this provision will be renumbered Article 101 of the Treaty on the Functioning of the European Union (TFEU), and the references to the 'common market' will be replaced by 'internal market'. A number of examples of the types of agreements covered by this article are provided in para (1)(a)–(e). Article 81(2) provides that any agreement or decision in breach of Article 81(2) 'shall be automatically void'. Under Article 81(3), Article 81(1) may, however, be declared 'inapplicable' to agreements or decisions fulfilling a number of specified criteria.

Thus, Article 81(1) provides a very broad base of liability subject to the possibility of exemption under Article 81(3). Regulation 1/2003 provides that Article 81 is directly applicable in its entirety, and agreements which meet the criteria in Article 81(3) are automatically exempt. If required, national authorities and courts can consider whether a particular agreement or concerted practice satisfies the criteria in Article 81(3). Effectively, Article 81(3) is now a defence to a claim that Article 81(1) has been infringed.

The breadth of Article 81(1) and the severity of the consequences of breach historically caused a great deal of concern. There was a risk that many desirable, pro-competitive agreements would fall foul of its provisions, which would have required exemption under Article 81(3). In order to ease the operation of Article 81(3), the Commission has, over the years, issued a number of 'notices' and 'block exemptions'. The notices merely provide non-binding guidelines concerning the Commission's policy, principally as to the kinds of agreement which will *not* breach Article 81(1). The block exemptions, which are enacted by regulation, apply to agreements which *do* breach Article 81(1) but, because of their beneficial nature, are exempt en bloc on the grounds of Article 81(3). Under Regulation 1/2003, agreements falling outside a notice or block exemption will nevertheless benefit from automatic exemption, provided that the criteria in Article 81(3) are satisfied. However, notices, as non-binding measures, cannot guarantee immunity, and, to obtain the benefit of a block exemption, an agreement must not contain specific anticompetitive clauses listed in the relevant block exemption, even though they may seem to be justifiable. If this is not the case, the competition authorities of the Member States, or the Commission, can find that Article 81(1) has been infringed.

29.2.2 Elements of an infringement

Article 81(1) contains three essential elements. There must be:

(a) an agreement between undertakings, or a decision by an association of undertakings or a concerted practice

(b) which may affect trade between Member States and

(c) which must have as its object or effect the prevention, restriction or distortion of competition within the common market.

29.2.3 Agreements between undertakings, decisions by associations of undertakings and concerted practices

29.2.3.1 *Undertakings*

In the absence of a definition, the word 'undertaking' has been interpreted in the widest possible sense to include any legal or natural person engaged in some form of economic or commercial activity, whether in the provision of goods or services, including cultural or sporting activities (*Bosman* (case C–415/93)), banking (*Züchner v Bayerische Vereinsbank AG* (case 172/80)), insurance (*Verband der Sachversicherer eV v Commission* (case 45/85)) and transport (*Commission v Belgium* (case 156/77)). It is not necessary that the activity be pursued with a view to profit (eg, *Fédération Française des Sociétés d'Assurance v Ministère de l'Agriculture et de la Pêche* (case C–244/94). The Court of First Instance (CFI) reconsidered the meaning of 'undertaking' in *FENIN v Commission* (case T–319/99). FENIN was a Spanish association of the majority of undertakings marketing medical goods and equipment in Spain. Health bodies (hospitals etc) in Spain (SNS) purchase their requirements through FENIN. FENIN complained (under Article 82, see below) that the SNS bodies were abusing their dominant position by delaying payment for goods obtained through FENIN. This was rejected and FENIN appealed to the CFI, which also rejected the claim, as SNS could not be described as an undertaking. The CFI emphasised that an undertaking must carry on an economic activity, which is characterised by the business of offering goods or services in a particular market, rather than the simple fact of making purchases. Provided that the purpose for which goods purchased are subsequently used is part of an economic activity, then the purchase itself is an economic activity. SNS operated on the principle of solidarity financed by social security contributions and offered a free service to the general public, which is not an economic activity. SNS was therefore not an undertaking. Consequently, it is necessary to establish some economic activity, however marginal, for something to be regarded as an undertaking for the purposes of EU competition law (approach affirmed in the *German Sickness Fund* case; joined cases C–264/01, C–306/01, C–354/01, and C–355/01). (Contrast the approach in the case law on the right to receive services; Chapter 24.)

Article 81(1) applies to undertakings in the public as well as the private sphere (Article 86(1)) and *Italy v Commission* (case 41/83)) but, as regards undertakings falling within Article 86 EC, only insofar as the application of these rules 'does not obstruct the performance, in law or in fact, of the particular tasks assigned to them'.

29.2.3.2 *Agreements*

Agreements are not confined to binding agreements or to those which are written down. A 'gentleman's agreement' will suffice. Often, where competition authorities fail to show an agreement, they will be able to prove the existence of concerted practices. In view of the wide scope of 'concerted practices', the precise extent of the concept of 'agreement' is of less significance.

29.2.3.3 *Decisions by associations of undertakings*

The effect of decisions by trade associations may be to coordinate behaviour amongst undertakings with anticompetitive effects, without any need for actual agreement; hence their inclusion in Article 81(1).

This provision has been widely interpreted, and is not confined to binding decisions. It was held in *NV IAZ International Belgium v Commission* (case 96/82) that even a non-binding recommendation from a trade association which was normally followed by its members could constitute a decision within Article 81(1), as could a decision by an association of associations. In *Re the Application of the Publishers' Association* ([1989] 4 CMLR 825) the Association's Code of Conduct was found by the Commission to have the character of a recommendation to its members and customers, and as such was to be considered as a decision of an association of undertakings, despite its non-binding character. As well as the association itself, its members may be liable for fines if they comply, even unwillingly, with a decision in breach of Article 81(1). In *Wouters* (C–309/99), a regulation by the Dutch Bar Association on multi-disciplinary partnerships was held to be a decision by an association of undertakings because it related to the economic activity of its members (barristers) rather than to the public law function which the DBA also fulfilled.

29.2.3.4 *Concerted practices*

These are altogether wider than 'agreements' and 'decisions by associations of undertakings'. It was defined in *Imperial Chemical Industries Ltd v Commission (dye-stuffs)* (case 48/69) as a form of cooperation between undertakings which, without having reached the stage where an agreement properly so-called has been concluded, knowingly substitutes practical cooperation between them for the risks of competition.

To constitute a concerted practice, it is not necessary to have a concerted plan. It is enough that each party should have informed the other of the attitude they intended to take so that each could regulate his conduct safe in the knowledge that his competitors would act in the same way. Similarly, in a series of cases, the CFI has held that meeting to exchange information about pricing structures also constitutes a concerted practice as the participants cannot fail to take this information into account when devising their own market strategies (eg, *Shell International Chemical Co Ltd v Commission* (case T–11/89)). Clearly, such practices can be just as damaging to competition as agreements or decisions by associations, and are much harder to prove. *Imperial Chemical Industries Ltd v Commission* centred on three uniform price increases covering the same products introduced by a number of leading producers (including ICI) of aniline dyes, almost simultaneously, in 1964, 1965 and 1967. ICI unsuccessfully challenged a Commission decision that the producers were engaged in a concerted price fixing practice, arguing that such price increases were common in oligopolies (ie, where the market is dominated by a small number of large independent concerns). The Court held that whilst parallel behaviour does not in itself constitute a concerted practice, it provides strong evidence of such a practice if it leads to conditions of competition which do not correspond to the normal conditions of the market.

The latter aspect of the judgment is open to criticism, because a decision based solely on the 'normal conditions of the market' would be incapable of proof, and could render oligopolies highly vulnerable to a charge of concerted practices in the event of quite 'normal' parallel price increases. In *A Ahlström OY v Commission (re wood pulp)* (cases C–89, 104, 114, 116–7, and 125–9/85), the ECJ took a more cautious approach. In an action for the annulment of a Commission decision fining a number of the world's leading wood-pulp producers, which together held a two-thirds share of the Union market in wood pulp, for concerted practices in announcing quarterly simultaneous and identical price increases, the Court held that these factors did not provide evidence of concerted practices where the system of price announcements represented a 'rational response to the need to limit commercial risk in a long-term market'. It found that the similarity was the result of a high degree of market transparency, and the parallelism of the price increases could be satisfactorily explained by the oligopolistic tendencies of the market. On the other hand, the parties' agreement, at meetings within their trade association, to fix recommended prices and to notify members in advance of any proposed deviation from these prices was held to restrict competition within Article 81(1).

29.2.3.5 *Unilateral action: Refusal to supply*

Although Article 81(1) appears to require some form of agreement or concertation on the part of two or more undertakings, there are circumstances when what appears to be a unilateral act may be found to breach it.

In *AEG-Telefunken* (case 107/82) the parties had notified their distribution agreements for AEG products and obtained negative clearance from the Commission. AEG was subsequently found in breach of Article 81(1) for having *operated* the agreements in such a way as to restrict competition by systematically refusing to allow dealers into its network who did not comply with the (unofficial) pricing policy apparently observed by existing members. Moreover, since AEG had acted outside the framework of its agreement as notified, notification did not bring it immunity from fines.

Similarly, in *Ford Werke AG v Commission* (case 25/84) the Court approved the Commission's refusal to grant clearance for what appeared to be a perfectly acceptable standard distribution agreement because Ford was refusing to supply existing distributors in Germany with right-hand-drive cars for export in England, apparently to maintain an artificial partitioning of the market and thereby different price levels in different Member States. Although there was no clear evidence of concerted action, certainly none of any agreement, the Court held that Ford's decision to cease supplies formed part of the contractual relations between Ford Werke AG and its dealers. Admission to Ford's dealer network implied acceptance by the contracting parties of the policies pursued by Ford. This may be contrasted with the situation in *Volkswagen* (case T–208/01), where a circular issued by VW suggesting a certain level of pricing was held not to constitute an agreement between it and the members of its distribution network. In *Bayer* (joined cases C–2/01 and C–3/01), the ECJ noted that the fact that the practical effect of a unilateral decision by a supplier may be equivalent to an export ban does not mean that such a ban was imposed, nor that an agreement about such a ban could be inferred (para 88). These cases demonstrate that the Commission and the Court, in applying Article 81(1), will take into account the context in which a particular action operates, and will interpret the article against its literal meaning if that is necessary to suppress practices which are against the spirit, even if they seem to be within the letter, of European competition law.

29.2.3.6 *Public authorities*

Where public bodies are concerned, a distinction must be drawn between agreements or concerted practices entered into in the course of commercial activities, which are clearly capable of falling within Article 81(1), and executive measures which merely permit or encourage such action which, although illegal under other provisions of the treaty such as Articles 28–9 EC (see eg, *GB–INNO v ATAB* (case 13/77)), will not in themselves breach this article. In *Bodson v Pompes Funèbres* (case 30/87) a licensing arrangement, whereby the local authority granted exclusive rights in respect of certain funeral services to the Société des Pompes Funèbres, was held not to constitute an 'agreement between undertakings' within Article 81(1); but had the municipality imposed a certain level of prices on the licensees the Court suggested it would have been subject to EU competition rules.

In the *COAPI Decision* ([1995] 5 CMLR 468), the Commission determined that the Spanish official association of industrial agents fell within the ambit of Article 81, despite COAPI's argument that it was a public service body since it was established by government regulations, as was its scale of charges. The Commission, however, found that the agents were 'undertakings' and that the regulations constituted an agreement completely separate from the Spanish legislation. As the scale of charges, which set a minimum charge to be applied to foreign clients, affected trade between Member States COAPI was in breach of Article 81(1). This decision also makes it clear that associations offering international services with minimum or fixed rates of charges may be caught by Article 81, even if the association and its scale of charges is approved by a Member State.

29.2.4 **Field of application of Article 81(1) EC**

29.2.4.1 *Group companies*

Article 81(1) applies, in principle, to agreements or decisions of associations or concerted practices on a vertical level (eg, between manufacturer and dealer) as well as a horizontal level (eg, between manufacturer and manufacturer) (*Établissements Consten SA v Commission* (cases 56 and 58/64)). The undertakings must, however, be independent of each other. An agreement between a parent and its subsidiary will not breach Article 81(1) unless the subsidiary enjoys full independence of action, the reason being that competition between them cannot be restricted by the agreement, since they were never in competition with each other (eg, *Viho Europe BV v Commission* (case T–102/92)). However, a parent as well as its subsidiary may be liable for acts of the subsidiary vis-à-vis third parties in breach of Article 81(1) where the subsidiary has acted as a result of the parent's promptings; and an agreement between parent and (non-independent) subsidiary may fall within Article 82 if it constitutes an abuse of a dominant position (*Béguelin Import Co v GL Import-Export SA* (case 22/71)).

Similarly members of an 'economic unit' comprising bodies with identical interests and subject to common control may be liable under Article 81 or 82 (*Hydrotherm v Compact* (case 170/83)). This means that there may be an 'economic unit' where two companies are controlled by the same shareholder, although that fact is not, in itself, sufficient; there must be additional evidence to show that the companies were operated as an economic unit (*Preinsulated Pipes Cartel* (joined cases C–189/02 P, C–202/02 P, C–205–8/02 P, and C–213/02 P)).

But where a parent company holds all of the share capital in a subsidiary which has contravened Article 81(1), there is a rebuttable presumption that the parent exercises decisive influence on the subsidiary's conduct and that both therefore comprise an economic unit. The onus is on the parent company to rebut that presumption (*Akzo Nobel and others v Commission* (case T–112/05)).

The same principles as apply to parents and subsidiaries apply to agreements between principal and agent. However, the Commission will scrutinise the relationship between the parties to ascertain its true nature (see, eg, *Pittsburg Corning Europe* ([1973] CMLR D2); description of concession agreement as a commercial agency 'mere colouring').

29.2.4.2 *Undertakings outside the Union*

An undertaking situated outside the EU may be liable under Article 81(1) provided that the agreements or practices are implemented inside the common market. In *Imperial Chemical Industries Ltd v Commission* (case 48/69), ICI (UK) was held liable for the acts of its subsidiary in Holland although the UK was not yet a member of the Union. In the *Woodpulp* decision, ([1985] 3 CMLR 474), a number of firms, all from outside the EU, who were not acting through subsidiaries in the EU but who supplied two-thirds of the EU consumption of wood pulp, were fined for concerted practices in breach of Article 81(1) on the grounds that the *effects* of their practices were felt in the Union. Although the Court, in *A Ahlström & OY v Commission* (cases C–89, 104, 114, 116–7, 125–9/85), annulled the decision in part and reduced the fines, since not all the concerted practices were proved, it held that the applicant firms could be liable, even though they were situated outside the EU, as long as their agreement or practices were *implemented* in the Union.

29.2.5 'Which may affect trade between Member States'

The agreement or decision by associations of undertakings or concerted practice must be one which may affect trade between Member States to breach Article 81(1). In the absence of an effect on interstate trade any restriction on competition is a matter for national law alone. However, the question of whether trade between Member States may be affected has been broadly interpreted by the Commission and the Court. In *Société Technique Minière v Maschinenbau Ulm GmbH* (case 56/65), the Court held that an agreement was capable of affecting trade between Member States if, on the basis of objective legal or factual criteria, it allows one to expect that it will exercise a direct or indirect, actual or potential, effect on the flow of trade between Member States. The test is very similar to the *Dassonville* test applied in the context of Article 28 EC, but broader, since it requires simply an *effect* on, not a *hindrance* to, trade between Member States (see Chapter 19). Clearly the most obvious effect on trade between Member States occurs when parties attempt to partition the market along national lines by means of restrictions on 'parallel' imports or exports (ie, restrictions, usually agreed between manufacturers and appointed dealers, on dealers' powers to import or export goods across internal EU frontiers).

29.2.5.1 *Agreements within a Member State*

An effect on trade between Member States can occur even when an agreement takes place wholly within a Member State and appears to concern only trade within that state. This is so particularly in the case of decisions of associations of national agreements which are intended to operate across the whole national market. As the Court pointed out in *Vereeniging van Cementhandelaren v Commission* (case 8/72)—in the context of a challenge to a Commission decision that cement dealers' price-fixing scheme, limited to the Dutch market, infringed Article 81(1)—an agreement extending over the whole of the territory of a Member State by its very nature has the effect of reinforcing the compartmentalisation of markets on a national basis, thereby holding up the economic interpenetration which the treaty is designed to bring about and protecting domestic production.

The Court has on several occasions held that this provision applies to agreements between undertakings in the same state. For example in *Re Vacuum Interrupters Ltd* ([1977] 1 CMLR D67), a joint venture agreement between three UK manufacturers to design and develop switch-gear apparatus in the UK was held capable of affecting trade between Member States, since in the absence of such agreement they would have attempted to develop the apparatus independently and to market it in other Member States. (See also *Re Italian Flat Glass* [1982] 3 CMLR 366, agreement between Italian producers and wholesalers of glass representing more than half of the Italian market; *Salonia v Poidomani* (case 126/80), national selective distribution system for newspapers capable of affecting trade between Member States.)

29.2.5.2 *Combined effect of similar agreements*

In the case of a domestic agreement between individual traders, it may be necessary to examine the agreement in the context of other similar agreements, to ascertain whether, taken as a whole, they are capable of affecting trade between Member States (*Brasserie de Haecht SA v Wilkin (No 1)* (case 23/67), Belgian tied-house agreement part of a network of similar agreements). The question to be asked is whether the agreements taken as a whole make a significant contribution to the sealing-off of national markets from competition from undertakings situated in other Member States (*Delimitis v Henninger Bräu* (case C–234/89)).

29.2.5.3 *Actual or potential effect*

Since only a *potential* effect of trade need be proved the enquiry is not limited to existing patterns of trade; the Commission is prepared to speculate as to possible future patterns of trade. In *Pronuptia* (case 161/84) the Court accepted the Commission's finding that a franchising agreement between Pronuptia in France (the franchisor) and its franchisee in Germany, which restricted the franchisee's power to operate outside a particular territory, was capable of affecting interstate trade even though there was no evidence, and indeed it seemed highly unlikely, that the franchisee had any intention of extending its activities to other Member States.

The question of effect on trade between Member States is not concerned with the increase or decrease of trade which might result from an agreement; all that is required to be shown is a deviation (actual or potential) from the 'normal' pattern of trade which might exist between Member States (*Établissements Consten SA v Commission* (cases 56 and 58/64)). In assessing this question it is not necessary to examine every clause in the agreement as long as the agreement as a whole is capable of affecting trade between Member States (*Windsurfing International Inc v Commission* (case 193/83)).

29.2.6 'Which have as their object or effect the prevention, restriction or distortion of competition within the common market'

29.2.6.1 *Application to horizontal and vertical agreements*

As with the question of effect on trade between Member States, EU competition law is not concerned with the question of increase in trade between Member States but with whether there is a distortion of the 'normal' competition which should exist within the common market. Moreover, it is concerned not only with 'horizontal' agreements (ie, between competing manufacturers, or competing wholesalers—the 'classic' cartel), which clearly restrict competition, but also with 'vertical' agreements (ie, between manufacturer and distributor, between distributor and retailers, parties not competing with each other) which are often economically beneficial, since they streamline the distribution process and concentrate promotional activity, to the eventual benefit of consumers. These principles were established in *Établissements Consten SA v Commission* (cases 56 and 58/64), where the court established that competition law was concerned not only with agreements which restricted competition amongst competing manufacturers ('inter-brand competition'), but could also catch agreements with the object of eliminating competition in products by the same manufacturer (here, Grundig television sets) at the wholesale level ('intra-brand competition').

Although this view has been criticised, it must be acknowledged that restrictions on intra-brand competition, contained in vertical agreements, while they may carry economic benefits, can also be used to partition the market, usually along national lines, in order to insulate the distributor in each state from competition from parallel imports from states where price levels are low. Artificially high price levels may thus be maintained. Because of these dangers, Article 81(1) applies to these agreements, but they may often qualify for automatic exemption under Article 81(3), or fall within the relevant block exemption (Regulation 2790/1999) which is very broad indeed (see 29.2.12 below).

29.2.6.2 'Object or effect'

If the object of an agreement is to prevent or restrict or distort competition, for example, a naked price-fixing or market-sharing agreement between competing manufacturers, there is no need to prove its effect. Unless the agreement is clearly incapable of affecting competition, an anticompetitive effect will be presumed. Where the agreement is not designed to restrict competition, for example, a standard distribution agreement, a detailed economic analysis of its effects on the particular market will be necessary before a breach of Article 81(1) can be proved.

The scope of the analysis required was considered in *Société Technique Minière v Maschinenbau Ulm GmbH* (case 56/65). The case involved an exclusive distribution agreement between a German manufacturer of heavy earth-moving equipment, Maschinenbau Ulm GmbH (MU), and a French distributor, Société Technique Minière (STM), similar to the Consten–Grundig agreement, but without its undesirable features. It contained no restrictions on parallel imports or exports, and no abusive use of trade marks. STM sought to resile on its agreement, claiming it was in breach of Article 81(1). The ECJ held that in order to ascertain whether an agreement is capable of preventing, restricting or distorting competition a number of factors must be examined, ie:

(a) *The nature and quantity of the products concerned* (ie, the product market, and the parties' combined share in that market). The greater the market share held by the parties, the more damaging its impact on competition.

(b) *The position and size of the parties concerned* (ie, their position in the market). The bigger they are, in terms of turnover and *relative* market share, the more likely it is that competition will be restricted.

(c) *The isolated nature of the agreement or its position in a series* (see also *Brasserie de Haecht SA v Wilkin (No 1)* (case 23/67)). This is particularly relevant in the case of distribution agreements, which in themselves may appear insignificant, but which often form part of a network of similar agreements.

(d) *The severity of the clauses.* The more severe the clauses the more likely they will be deemed in breach of Article 81(1). However, any clause that is more than is necessary to achieve the desired (beneficial) result will risk infringing Article 81(1) (*L'Oréal NV v De Nieuwe AMCK PVBA* (case 31/80)).

(e) *The possibility of other commercial currents acting on the same products* by means of reimports and re-exports (ie, parallel imports or exports). Thus any agreement which attempts to ban or even limit parallel imports or exports will normally breach Article 81(1): *LC Nungesser KG v Commission* (case 258/78)).

The agreement between STM and MU was found on the facts not to breach Article 81(1).

The enquiry needed to ascertain whether an agreement has the potential to prevent, restrict, or distort competition within the common market is a wide-ranging one, often involving all the factors outlined above, *always* involving the first two. Such is the importance of the question of market definition that the Commission issued a Notice on the Definition of the Relevant Market for the purposes of Union competition law ([1997] OJ C372/5). In *European Night Services v Commission* (cases T–397/94 and T–375/94), the CFI emphasised that where an agreement does not contain obvious restrictions of competition, it is necessary to consider the actual context within which the agreement functions, with a particular focus on the economic context.

29.2.6.3 The de minimis principle

All agreements between business people curtail to some extent each other's freedom of action in the marketplace. Clearly not all such agreements are capable of preventing, restricting, or distorting competition to any noticeable extent. Always it is a question of size and scale whether in fact they do so. Hence the importance in competition law of the *de minimis* principle. The *de minimis* principle was developed by the court in *Völk v Établissements Vervaecke Sprl* (case 5/69), which concerned an exclusive distribution agreement between Völk, a small-scale manufacturer of washing machines in Germany, and Vervaecke, a Dutch distributor of electrical goods. Völk agreed, inter alia, to block all sales of his machines into Vervaecke's territory by third parties (ie, parallel imports). They were seeking absolute territorial protection for Vervaecke in relation to Völk's machines in Belgium and Luxembourg. The Court ruled that in order to come within Article 81(1), competition must be affected to a noticeable extent; there must be a sufficient degree of harmfulness. In this case, the effect of Völk–Vervaecke's agreement on the washing-machine market in Belgium and Luxembourg was insignificant. (In fact Völk's production of washing machines was between 0.2 and 0.5 per cent of the German market, and his share in the Belgian and Luxembourg market was minute.) The size of the parties, and even more important, their share in the relevant product market, will be an essential factor in determining liability. However, if the parties are powerful in a particular market, they cannot rely on the *de minimis* rule for any of their products within that market even though they may represent a negligible share of the market in other Member States (*Distillers Co Ltd v Commission* (case 30/78)).

If an agreement falls within the *de minimis* principle, even if it contains the most blatantly anticompetitive clauses (eg, price fixing), even if the parties *intend* to restrict competition (clearly the aim of the territorial protection clause in *Völk v Vervaecke*) there will be no breach of Article 81(1). Thus, in assessing the question of breach of Article 81(1), some economic and market assessment will have to be made in every case, although agreements which do not have the object of restricting competition will require a more thorough analysis to prove that they are capable of that effect.

Since 1986, the Commission has published a number of notices on agreements of minor importance ([1986] OJ C231/2, amended [1994] OJ C368/20; replaced in 1997 [1997] OJ C372/1). The current *de minimis* notice was issued in 2001 ([2001] OJ C368/13). The 2001 notice states that agreements between undertakings with a combined market share below a certain threshold will be regarded as *de minimis*. If the aggregate share of the parties to an agreement between competitors does not exceed 10 per cent of the relevant markets, it will not fall within Article 81(1). In the case of an agreement between non-competitors, the parties' market share must not exceed 15 per cent to fall within the *de minimis* principle. If it is not possible to classify the agreement as one involving competitors or non-competitors, the lower threshold will apply. However, if more than 30 per cent of the relevant market is covered by parallel agreements, then the market share of the parties to one such agreement must not exceed 5 per cent. However, the *de minimis* notice will not apply if the agreement contains clauses which amount to price fixing, territorial restrictions or output restrictions. The new notice reflects the new approach to competition law enforcement adopted at the EU level, which focuses on harmful anticompetitive agreements—ie, those involving price fixing and market sharing.

In *European Night Services*, the CFI observed that even where the thresholds in the notice have been exceeded, the agreement in question may still not be sufficiently appreciable as to give rise to a breach of Article 81(1). Where the threshold is exceeded only marginally, the Commission has to produce clear evidence that the agreement is caught by the prohibition in Article 81(1).

However, even though an agreement may be *de minimis* for the purposes of Article 81, this does not mean that there may not be a finding under corresponding *national* competition rules that there is a breach.

29.2.7 Agreements capable of preventing, restricting or distorting competition

Examples of agreements likely to breach Article 81(1) are provided in subparas (a)–(e). Any agreement falling within these categories will raise a prima facie case of breach of this article, provided that it does not fall within the *de minimis* principle and that competition within the common market is affected. The Union dimension is essential, but, since it is subject to the same principles as the question of 'effect on trade between Member States', not hard to prove.

Although it is always a question of size and scale whether or not a breach of Article 81(1) has occurred, it is possible from the approach of the Commission and the ECJ to the types of agreement listed in the article to distinguish between 'excusable' and 'inexcusable' restrictions. The inexcusable restrictions will breach the article and are unlikely to obtain exemption under Article 81(3). Excusable restrictions fall into one of two categories. *Either* they are found not to breach Article 81(1) at all, or they are found in breach of the article but eligible for exemption under Article 81(3).

29.2.7.1 *Article 81(1)(a): Agreements which directly or indirectly fix purchase or selling prices or other trading conditions*

29.2.7.1.1 *Price fixing*

Price-fixing agreements, because of their obvious anticompetitive effects, are almost always inexcusable. The ECJ was, in *Centres-Leclerc v 'Au Blé Vert' Sàrl* (case 229/83), prepared to accept that French legislation allowing a system of retail price maintenance for books, the prices to be fixed by publishers, was compatible with Article 81(1). The government had claimed that the measure was indispensable to protect books as a cultural medium against the negative effects of fierce price competition and to maintain the existence of specialist bookshops. However, in *Re the Application of the Publishers Association* ([1989] 4 CMLR 825) the Commission found that the Publishers Association's Code of Conduct, which laid down standard conditions for the sale of books at fixed prices ('net book' prices) and which applied to books sold throughout the UK as well as to exports and reimports, and which provided, inter alia, for a system of *collective* price maintenance, was in breach of Article 81(1) and not eligible for exemption under Article 81(3) (ex 85(3)). The CFI (case T–66/89) agreed with the Commission's decision because the agreement restricted competition within the single Community market, *even though it might produce beneficial effects within a national market.* The ECJ, however, overturned this ruling (*Publishers Association v Commission* (case C–360/92P)). The net book agreement was distinguished from the agreement in the Dutch books case (*VBVB v Commission* (cases 43 and 63/82)) to which the CFI had referred. That agreement was held to contravene Article 81(1) as it applied to all books and all publishers and was not capable of exemption under Article 81(3). The net book agreement, by contrast, applied only to some publishers and to those books which fell within the definition of a net book. Furthermore, the ECJ held that the Commission and CFI had failed to appreciate that the benefit to the book trade arising out of the agreement was not restricted to the UK but included the Irish market also, as both countries are primarily English speaking. Shortly after the ECJ's ruling the agreement collapsed.

Minimum prices are regarded in the same light as fixed prices. In *Hennessy/Henkell* ([1981] 1 CMLR 601, Commission Decision), a clause in an exclusive distribution agreement between Hennessy, the producer, in France, and Henkell, the distributor in Germany, setting maximum and minimum price limits for Hennessy's products, was found by the Commission to be in breach of Article 81(1) and not eligible for exemption under Article 81(3). In *Pronuptia v Schillgalis* (case 161/84) the Court ruled that recommended prices issued in the context of a distribution franchising system would not breach Article 81(1) as long as they did not lead to concerted practices and the franchisee remained free to fix his own selling prices. In this area parallel pricing will provide strong evidence of concerted practices, although following *A Ahlström OY* (cases C–89, 104, 116–17, 125–9/85), it will not be conclusive. In its subsequent decision on the *Pronuptia* Agreement ([1989] 4 CMLR 355) the Commission found the provision for recommended *maximum* prices to be acceptable.

29.2.7.1.2 *Other trading conditions*

A manufacturer will often seek to impose trading conditions on his distributors (or retailers) to ensure that the premises are suitable, or that adequate after-sales service is provided. He may insist that his distributor holds minimum stocks or that he engages in specific promotional activities. In return for his efforts, a distributor may seek to safeguard his investment through protection from competition within his particular territory. To what extent are these arrangements compatible with EU law?

The first principle, laid down in *Metro-SB-Grossmärkte GmbH & Co KG v Commission* (case 26/76), is that selective distribution systems will not breach Article 81(1) provided that dealers are chosen on the basis of objective criteria of a *qualitative* nature relating to the technical qualifications of the dealer and his staff and the suitability of his trading premises, and that such conditions are laid down uniformly and not applied in a discriminatory manner.

In *L'Oréal* (case 31/80) the ECJ followed *Metro*, adding that the qualitative criteria must not go beyond what is necessary. What is regarded as necessary will depend on the nature of the product. In *Re Ideal/Standard Agreement* ([1988] 4 CMLR 627) the Commission found that the characteristics of plumbing fittings were not sufficiently technically advanced to necessitate a selective distribution system in which wholesalers were required to be specialists in the sale of plumbing fittings and sanitary ware and to have a department specialising in the sale of such products. The products were too 'banal' to warrant such a system. With regard to *quantitative* criteria, such as, in *L'Oréal*, requirements that the distributor should guarantee a minimum turnover and hold minimum stocks, these were held to exceed the requirements of a selective distribution system, and were thus in breach of Article 81(1), although it was suggested that they might be capable of being exempted under Article 81(3).

However, in *Pronuptia v Schillgalis*, in addition to a number of qualitative restrictions relating to layout, shop fittings, advertising, and promotion, the Court did allow, as compatible with Article 81(1), a requirement that the franchisee should buy 80 per cent of its wedding dresses from Pronuptia and the remainder only from suppliers approved by Pronuptia. This requirement, like the qualitative requirements, was found essential in a franchising agreement to protect the know-how and reputation of the franchisor. The Commission confirmed in its decision on *Pronuptia* that certain quantitative restrictions, including an obligation to hold minimum stocks, were permissible as essential to a franchising agreement, at the same time stressing that retail franchising agreements were different in kind from distribution agreements. However, even if a quantitative restriction is not compatible with Article 81(1), it may nevertheless be exempt under Article 81(3), in particular where the block exemption on vertical agreements (Regulation 2790/1999), which does not prohibit quantitative restrictions, applies.

Conditions in the form of import and export restrictions, designed to partition the market and to protect the distributor from (intra-brand) competition within his particular territory, as in *Consten/Grundig*, will always breach Article 81(1) (unless it falls within the *de minimis* exceptions discussed above) and will rarely qualify for exemption under Article 81(3). The hard line taken by the Commission, with the qualified approval of the Court, is illustrated by its attitude to patent licensing agreements. In *LC Nungesser KG v Commission* (case 258/78), in the context of a licensing agreement assigning plant-breeder's rights, the Court drew a distinction between an 'open' exclusive licence (restricting the grantor's right to grant other licences to the licensee's territory or to compete there himself), which was compatible with Article 81(1), and a 'closed' exclusive licence (restricting the rights of third-party importers or licensees in other territories to import into the licensee's territory), which was not. Nor did the latter qualify for exemption under Article 81(3), since the condition was not regarded as indispensable to the agreement. In *Herlitz AG v Commission* (case T–66/92), the CFI held that the fact that an export ban had not been implemented did not remove its offensive qualities: the mere existence of such a provision would still have, 'visual and psychological' effect (see also *Parker Ltd v Commission* (case T–77/92)). However, in *Pronuptia* there was a suggestion by the Court that a restriction on franchisees' rights to open up on other franchisees' territory, although in breach of Article 81(1), might be justified to protect franchisees' investment in the business. This was confirmed in the *Pronuptia* Decision, and followed in a decision on the *Computerland Europe SA* franchising agreement ([1989] 4 CMLR 259). Thus a degree of territorial protection has been permitted in franchising agreements.

29.2.7.2 *Article 81(1)(b): Agreements which control production, markets, technical developments or investments*

These agreements, which are normally horizontal agreements, will invariably breach Article 81(1). 'Naked' restrictions of this nature will rarely, if ever, qualify for exemption. However, where the restriction is ancillary to some desirable, pro-competitive agreement, such as a specialisation agreement between small and medium-sized firms, or a research and development agreement, it is likely to qualify for exemption—either block exemption or automatic exemption under Article 81(3). In *Re Vacuum Interrupters Ltd* ([1977] 1 CMLR D67) the parties obtained individual exemption for such an agreement (research and development). (See also *Clima Chapée/Buderus* ([1970] CMLR D7); *ACEC/Berliet* ([1968] CMLR D35).) In *Wouters* (C–309/99), however, a prohibition on multi-disciplinary partnerships issued by the Dutch Bar Association, while capable of being caught by Article 81(1)(b) because it could limit production and technical development, was held not to fall within 81(1) at all because the restriction was necessary for the proper practice of the legal profession.

29.2.7.3 *Article 81(1)(c): Agreements to share markets or sources of supply*

These too will normally be horizontal agreements in breach of Article 81(1). A market-sharing agreement may qualify for exemption if ancillary to some beneficial agreement on the same principles as apply to Article 81(1)(b), provided it does not attempt to establish absolute territorial protection for the product in question in the markets concerned. An agreement to share sources of supply would require exemption, and would be difficult to justify.

29.2.7.4 *Article 81(1)(d): Agreements which apply dissimilar conditions to equivalent transactions with other trading parties, thereby placing them at a competitive disadvantage*

Concerted discriminatory treatment will always breach Article 81(1) and will rarely if ever be eligible for exemption. However, agreements imposing dissimilar conditions will only breach the Article 81(1) if the transactions are 'equivalent'; there will be no breach if the difference in treatment is objectively justified (see *Metro-SB-Grossmärkte GmbH & Co KG v Commission* (case 26/76)). Thus an agreement to charge different (but not fixed) prices to different customers would be permissible if the prices charged genuinely reflected different (eg, transport) costs; it would not if they were based on what the market would bear. Similarly, 'quantity' discounts (discounts for bulk purchases), if they genuinely reflect cost savings, are permissible, whilst 'fidelity' or 'loyalty' rebates, which are tied to the volume of business transacted, are not.

29.2.7.5 *Article 81(1)(e): Agreements which make the conclusion of contracts subject to acceptance by other parties of supplementary obligations which, by their nature and/ or according to commercial usage, have no connection with the subject matter of such contracts*

Such agreements, or, rather, such clauses in an agreement, will always breach Article 81(1) and will need to satisfy the criteria for exemption under Article 81(3). However, it is a matter of judgment whether an obligation is deemed to have the requisite connection with the subject matter of the contract. Agreements guaranteeing exclusivity, such as exclusive supply agreements (*Hennessy/Henkell*, *Pronuptia*) or exclusive licensing agreements (*Nungesser*) are seen as essential to the subject matter of the contract; attempts at territorial protection are not. Trading conditions based on necessary objective qualitative criteria are essential, those based on quantitative criteria are not *(Metro, L'Oréal)*, although certain 'essential' quantitative restrictions may be imposed in franchising agreements *(Pronuptia)* at least if expressed in percentage terms. In *Hennessy/Henkell*, a clause prohibiting Henkell & Co from dealing in products competing with Hennessy's was found acceptable as essential to the exclusive distribution agreement; a clause prohibiting them from dealing in any other products at all was not, nor was it justifiable under Article 81(3). 'Non-competition' clauses—ie, restraint-of-trade clauses attached on the sale of a business—have been found by the Commission to be essential to the main contract, since the know-how and goodwill of a business protected by a non-competition clause are seen to constitute a substantial part of the assets transferred *(Reuter/BASF AG* [1976] 2 CMLR D44; approved by the court in *Remia BV v Commission* (case 42/84)). However, the restraints must be no more than is necessary to preserve the value of the bargain. In *Reuter/BASF AG* a non-competition clause of eight years' duration and extending to non-commercial research was found excessive, and not justifiable under Article 81(3), and in *Remia BV* a ten-year restriction on competition was reduced to four.

29.2.8 Ancillary restrictions

Although neither the Commission nor the Court expressly distinguishes between naked and ancillary restrictions on competition, it is safe to say that naked restrictions in any of the above categories will breach Article 81(1) and will be unlikely to obtain exemption under Article 81(3).

Where ancillary restrictions are concerned, the approach of the Commission and the Court is not entirely consistent. Certain restrictions, contained in exclusive distribution agreements *(Metro-SB-Grossmärkte, L'Oréal, Hennessy/Henkell)*, or exclusive licensing agreements *(Nungesser)* or franchising agreements *(Pronuptia, Computerland)*, or attached to the sale of a business *(Reuter/BASF, Remia BV)*, although apparently falling within the wide words of Article 81(1), have been construed as essential to the main agreement, and as such not in breach of the article at all. Similarly, in *Bayer AG v Süllhöfer* (case 65/86) Advocate-General Darmon suggested that a no-challenge clause in a licensing agreement would be acceptable if it was *crucial* to the equilibrium of the licensing agreement, the object and effect of which is not shown to be specifically restrictive of competition. The Court confined itself to stating more narrowly that a no-challenge clause would not breach Article 81(1) where the licence was granted for no consideration or, although granted for consideration, it related to some outdated procedure. Other restrictions in these same types of agreement, although not blatantly anticompetitive, and arguably regarded by one, if not both, of the parties as necessary to the transaction as a whole, have been found in breach of Article 81(1) although possibly capable of being exempted under Article 81(3). In other kinds of agreement, for example, research and development or specialisation agreements, restrictions (eg, within Article 81(1)(b)) which are clearly justifiable in the context of the agreement as a whole have rarely been regarded by the Commission as acceptable per se; they must be capable of exemption under Article 81(3). However, in *Elopak/Metal Box-Odin* ([1990] OJ L209/15), the Commission was prepared to grant negative clearance to a joint venture between Elopak/Metal Box and Odin for the purposes of research and development.

The former approach, where clauses which are to a certain extent restrictive of competition are permitted under Article 81(1) as necessary to the agreement as a whole, is said to be an application of the rule of reason.

29.2.9 The rule of reason

The concept of 'rule of reason' originated in US antitrust law, where it was applied in interpreting s 1 of the Sherman Act 1890. This section, which condemns every contract in restraint of trade, does not contain any definition of restraint of trade or any provision for exemption for beneficial agreements on the lines of Article 81(3) EC. It was left to the courts to decide whether or not a restraint of trade had occurred. In 1911 the US Supreme Court held, in *United states v American Tobacco* ((1911) 221 US 106 at p 179) that not every contract in restraint of trade was illegal; it would only be illegal if it was unreasonable in that it operated to the prejudice of the public interest by *unduly* restricting competition. In applying this 'rule of reason', the US courts attempt to balance the pro-competitive and anticompetitive effects of an agreement to assess if a breach of s 1 has occurred.

The structure of Article 81 is quite different. It was clearly intended that this weighing of the pro-competitive and anticompetitive effects of an agreement was to take place not under Article 81(1) but under Article 81(3). Historically, this required an exemption decision by the Commission under Regulation 17/62. Alternatively, parties could rely on a block exemption. If parties structured their agreements to comply with the exemptions they would be free of risk. Another possible solution lay in the application of a rule of reason. Under the 'European' rule of reason, which is undoubtedly narrower than its US progenitor, only restrictions that constitute an *essential* element of the agreement, without which the agreement would be emptied of its substance, and which pose no real threat to competition or to the functioning of the single market, are deemed compatible with Article 81(1). Non-essential restrictions, or restrictions which might interfere with the functioning of the common market, are left to be decided under Article 81(3). Many of the agreements discussed above (eg, *Metro-SB-Grossmärkte, L'Oréal, Hennessy/Henkell, Nungesser, Pronuptia, Reuter/ BASF AG, Remia BV*) provide examples of both essential and non-essential restrictions. A similar two-tiered approach has already been noted in the Court's interpretation of quantitative restrictions under Articles 28 and 30, although in the case of Article 28 justification under the *Cassis* rule of reason is more explicit (see Chapter 19).

For some time, commentators argued that the Commission and, more particularly, the Court had been moving towards a rule of reason approach, although neither acknowledged the rule as such. Indeed, in *Metropole Television v Commission* (case T–112/99), the CFI emphasised that:

> the existence of such a rule has not, as such, been confirmed by the Community courts. Quite the contrary, in various judgments the Court of Justice and the Court of First Instance have been at pains to indicate that the existence of a rule of reason in Community law is doubtful . . . [Para 72.]

Perhaps the introduction of automatic exemption under Regulation 1/2003 will mean that the question of whether there is a rule of reason approach towards Article 81(1) has less practical relevance, because there will no longer be a need to notify the Commission for negative clearance exemption.

Although in its White Paper on the modernisation of the competition law enforcement mechanism ([1999] OJ C132/1), the Commission mooted the express adoption of a rule of reason approach, it did not proceed with this because of the risk of its unequal application by national courts. Instead, the Commission has sought to increase legal certainty and encourage agreements which are beneficial overall by issuing notices indicating the types of agreement which will be acceptable under Article 81(1) and introducing or extending block exemptions for those categories of agreement, which, although restrictive of competition, are clearly justified.

29.2.10 Consequences if agreement is within Article 81(1)

An agreement which is caught by Article 81(1), and not within a block exemption or the criteria in Article 81(3) (see 29.2.11 below), will be 'automatically void' (Article 81(2)). Moreover, parties to such an agreement or concerted practice may be fined for their anticompetitive conduct.

However, where undertakings in a particular Member State are subject to binding rules which require them to act in a manner which infringes Article 81(1) without any autonomy as to their ability to act, no sanctions may be imposed on them for such conduct. Instead, the national court must disapply the domestic law, and only if the undertakings do not subsequently change their conduct may they be found liable for infringements of Article 81(1) (*Consorzio Industrie Fiammiferi v Autorita Grante della Concorrenza e del Mercato* (case C–198/01)).

29.2.11 Article 81(3): Exemption

If an agreement satisfies the criteria in Article 81(3), Article 81(1) becomes inapplicable. The relevant criteria are that the agreement:

> contributes to improving the production or distribution of goods or to promoting technical or economic progress, while allowing consumers a fair share of the resulting benefit, and which does not:
>
> (a) impose on the undertakings concerned restrictions which are not indispensable to the attainment of these objectives;
> (b) afford such undertakings the possibility of eliminating competition in respect of a substantial part of the products in question.

In the past, the Commission had to grant an individual exemption under Article 81(3). This is no longer the case today, although the cases discussed below all arose under the old system. They are still relevant because they provide guidance as to the approach that might be taken by the domestic courts and authorities in applying this provision under the new enforcement system.

To qualify for an exemption under Article 81(3) the agreement or decision must satisfy four essential criteria discussed below. This paragraph is significant as it is the mechanism that allows the objectives of competition to be balanced against other, sometimes non-trade, concerns. Whether the Commission and the European courts have found the appropriate balance has been open to debate.

29.2.11.1 *It must contribute to improving the production or distribution of goods or to promoting technical or economic progress*

The agreement as a whole must show positive benefits. These are expressed in the alternative, although the more benefits that are proved the greater the likelihood of exemption. Different kinds of agreement will produce different benefits.

29.2.11.1.1 *Production*

Benefits in production are most likely to accrue from specialisation agreements. Specialisation enables each party to concentrate its efforts and achieve the benefits of scale; it avoids wasteful duplication. In *Clima Chappée/Buderus* ([1970] CMLR D7) the Commission granted exemption to a specialisation and reciprocal supply agreement between Clima Chappée in France and Buderus in Germany. Both were engaged in the manufacture of air-conditioning and ventilation systems and central-heating apparatus in their own countries. They agreed each to manufacture a certain range of products exclusively, and to supply the other exclusively with these products in the other's own country. Clearly there was some reduction in competition in the common market since they were potential competitors. Nonetheless the gains in production and distribution were clear, and the agreement contributed to both technical and economic progress. The other elements of Article 81(3) too were satisfied. The agreement would result in fair shares for consumers because there was sufficient inter-brand competition to ensure that the parties would pass on the benefit of their agreement to the consumers. Nor had they imposed on each other restrictions which were not indispensable; they were not obliged to purchase the other's products unless they were competitive. And there was no possibility of eliminating competition in respect of a substantial part of the products in question. Even combined, the parties were subject to strong inter-brand competition for the products in question.

29.2.11.1.2 *Distribution*

Benefits in distribution occur principally through vertical agreements in the form of exclusive supply or dealership or distribution agreements. The benefits result from the streamlining of the distribution process and the concentration of activity on the part of the distributor, whether it be in the provision of publicity, technical expertise, after-sales service, or simply the maintenance of adequate stocks. These factors were important in the *Transocean Marine Paint Association* Decision ([1967] CMLR D9). The agreement here was between a number of small and medium-sized manufacturers and distributors of marine paint from inside and outside the EU. The purpose of their collaboration was to produce and market marine paints to identical standards and to organise the sale of these products on a world-wide basis. They hoped thereby to compete with the giants of the paint world. The paints were sold under a single trade mark, though members were free to add their own name and mark. Markets were to be divided up on national lines, and members were free to sell in each other's territory only on payment of a commission. There was a degree of territorial protection. (Their original plan to prohibit sales on each other's territory was dropped at the request of the Commission.) The advantage claimed for the agreement was the achievement of a world-wide distribution network for the same interchangeable product. Alone, each manufacturer would be too small to offer adequate stocks and expertise.

Exemption was granted. The Commission agreed that the system did improve distribution; it streamlined the service to customers and led to a specialised knowledge of the market. Even the clauses granting limited territorial protection were permitted since they avoided fragmentation of the market, especially important during the launching period. While competition between members was restricted, on an international scale it was greatly increased. The use of the trade mark too was permitted, as it was used to identify the product, not to partition the market.

29.2.11.1.3 *Technical progress*

Technical progress is most likely to result from specialisation agreements, particularly those concerned with research and development. The *ACEC/Berliet* Decision ([1968] CMLR D35) concerned an agreement between ACEC, who were manufacturers, inter alia, of electrical transmission systems for commercial vehicles, and Berliet, who manufactured buses in France. They wished to collaborate to produce a new prototype bus. ACEC was to develop a new transmission system for the bus; Berliet agreed to buy the system only from ACEC; ACEC to supply only Berliet in France and not more than one outlet in any other Member State. ACEC also undertook to give Berliet 'most favoured treatment', and agreed not to reveal to any other manufacturer information acquired from Berliet. Despite these many restrictions the Commission granted them exemption. There were clear gains in production and technical progress.

In *Re Vacuum Interrupters (No 2)* ([1981] 2 CMLR 217) an agreement in the form of a joint venture between the three leading British companies engaged in the manufacture of switch gear for research and the development of vacuum interrupters was exempted. It was found to lead to benefits on all four fronts, but particularly technical progress (see also *ICI/BP* [1985] 2 CMLR 330).

29.2.11.1.4 *Economic progress*

Rather surprisingly, economic progress has received scant attention in decisions concerning exemption. It is normally presumed if improvements in production or distribution or technical progress are achieved. However, it did form the basis of a decision granting exemption to an agreement regulating the holding of trade fairs in *Cecimo* ([1969] CMLR D1) on the grounds that it tended to rationalise the operation and avoided wasteful duplication of time and effort.

29.2.11.2 *The agreement must allow consumers a fair share in the resulting benefit*

Provided there is sufficient (inter-brand) competition from other producers in the relevant market the improvements achieved will inevitably ensure to the benefit of consumers, either in the form of a better product, or a better service, or greater availability of supplies or lower prices. If the parties fail to pass on the benefits to consumers they risk losing out to their competitors. The parties' market share, both in absolute terms and in relation to their competitors, will be crucial. In all the cases considered above where exemption was granted the parties faced lively competition.

29.2.11.3 *The agreement must not impose on the undertakings concerning restrictions which are not indispensable*

This is the familiar proportionality principle, the downfall of many an agreement that would otherwise have been exempted. The Commission will examine each clause in an agreement to see if it is necessary to the agreement as a whole. Fixed prices, even fixed maximum and minimum price limits, as in *Hennessy/Henkell* will rarely be indispensable, nor will clauses seeking absolute territorial protection (*Consten/Grundig* (cases 56 and 58/64), *Hennessy/Henkell, Nungesser* (case 258/78)). Even these restrictions may occasionally be justified. In the *Transocean Marine Paint Association* decision some limited territorial protection in the form of a commission payable by the parallel importer to the appointed distributor in the territory in question was deemed to be necessary to avoid fragmentation of the market during the initial launching period. When the agreement was renewed five years later, when the product was launched and the parties had grown in size and strength, that clause was required to be dropped; it was no longer indispensable. In *Pronuptia* (case 161/84) there was a suggestion by the Court that some territorial protection for the franchisee might be justified. If the agreement is a desirable one, pro-competitive overall, even quite severe restrictions may be deemed indispensable. In *ACEC/Berliet*, ACEC's undertaking not to divulge to any other customer confidential information received from Berliet, even their agreement to give Berliet 'most favoured' (ie, discriminatory) treatment, was considered no more than was necessary to safeguard their investment in the light of the mutual confidence needed and the burden or risk involved in the enterprise.

In the *Carlsberg Beers* agreement ([1985] 1 CMLR 735) a cooperation agreement of 11 years' duration between Carlsberg Brewery Ltd (UK) and Grand Metropolitan plc, whereby Grand Metropolitan agreed to buy 50 per cent of its lager supplies from Carlsberg, was granted exemption. The agreement was necessary to enable Carlsberg to establish itself in the UK market and build up its own independent distribution network.

29.2.11.4 *The agreement must not afford such undertakings the possibility of eliminating competition in respect of a substantial part of the products in question*

In all the cases in which exemption has been granted, the parties have been subject to substantial inter-brand competition, whether from producers inside the common market or from outside (eg, *Re Vacuum Interrupters*, parties faced competition from the Americans and Japanese). It seems that, in the case of new products the market will not be too narrowly defined.

In *Metropole Television SA (M6) and ors v Commission* (cases T–185, 216, 99, and T–300/00), the CFI annulled a Commission decision exempting the Eurovision broadcasting agreement because the Commission had been wrong to determine that a sub-licensing scheme to competitors of European Broadcasting Union (EBU) avoided the elimination of competition in that market when the evidence demonstrated that this was not the case.

29.2.12 Block exemptions

29.2.12.1 *Background*

The old-style enforcement system was centralised and required action by the Commission. Because the Commission was unwilling, or felt unable, to apply a rule of reason to many restrictions on competition which were clearly justifiable on the principles outlined above, it chose to solve the twin problems of uncertainty (for business people) and workload (for itself) by means of block exemptions. If an agreement for which it might otherwise have been necessary to seek individual exemption fell within a block exemption, it would no longer need to be notified. Indeed, the block exemptions were passed in order to avoid the need for individual appraisal by the Commission, in the hope that parties would tailor their agreements to fit within their confines. In many cases this became standard practice. These block exemptions, being enacted by regulation, may, and where relevant *must*, be applied by national courts.

Most of the original regulations followed a similar pattern. First, they laid down the kinds of restrictions which were permitted, the 'white' list, the restrictions which are deemed 'essential' to the agreement in question; this was followed by the 'black' list—the kind of clauses which will not be permitted. With the Patent Licensing Regulation the Commission introduced a third category, the 'grey' restrictions. These were subject to a special procedure, known as the 'opposition' procedure. Under this procedure the grey restrictions must be notified to the Commission, but if they were not opposed within a specified period, they were deemed to be exempt. The Commission accepted that these 'old-style' block exemptions were too formalistic and generally failed to take into account the real economic impact of particular agreements. It therefore reviewed all of its block exemptions as they expired and adopted new exemptions which are based on a market-share threshold together with a list of prohibited 'hardcore' restrictions.

In addition the Commission has published detailed guidelines for the assessment of both vertical agreements ([2000] OJ C291/1) and (beneficial) horizontal cooperation agreements (OJ [2001] C3/2). These set out the approach the Commission will adopt when dealing with the types of agreement covered by these notices. Both guidelines reflect a more economics-based approach which focuses on market power (measured as a combination of market share and market concentration) of the parties to an agreement as a key criterion for assessing compatibility of that agreement with Article 81(1). As this is now a highly technical area of law it is not possible in a book of this nature to examine the guidelines and block exemptions in detail. Instead, the general scope of the exemptions, and their limitations, will be considered.

29.2.12.2 *Vertical agreements*

There is now a single block exemption (Regulation (EC) No 2790/1999 OJ[1999] L 336/21) applying to *vertical restraints* (although special rules continue to apply to some sectors such as petrol distribution). This new block exemption came into force on 1 June 2000. It applies to all agreements containing vertical restraints. It is wider than the previous block exemptions, as it will cover unfinished goods ('intermediate goods') and agreements between multiple parties.

The block exemption, unlike earlier block exemptions in the field, is based on a market-share test; where the parties to the agreement have a combined market share of up to 30 per cent, the agreement will enter a 'safe harbour' where the agreement will automatically be exempt from the Article 81(1) prohibition, unless it contains what are described as 'hard-core restrictions'. Market share will be determined by assessing the relevant geographical and product markets. The definition of these markets is discussed further at 29.3.4 below. Agreements which exceed the safe harbour limit are not necessarily contrary to Article 81 but may need further examination.

The block exemption identifies certain types of clauses which will not be permissible. These are non-compete clauses in excess of five years; clauses which prevent a buyer from manufacturing or selling certain goods after the agreement has terminated (save where innovative products are concerned, in which a one-year prohibition would be acceptable); and 'hard-core restrictions'. Hard-core restrictions include minimum and fixed resale price maintenance; restrictions on resale outside exclusive and selective distribution networks; and restrictions on active or passive selling by members of a selective distribution network.

The new regime, even before it came into practice, had been subject to criticism from industry. The legal certainty, which the earlier block exemptions provided, has been sacrificed. In particular, the determination of market share is not an exact science, and industry will be even more reliant on its legal and economic advisers (who are bound to take a cautious view) as to whether it satisfies the market test or not.

In addition to the general exemption for vertical agreements, the Commission recently adopted a new block exemption for vertical agreements in the motor vehicle sector (Regulation 1400/2002, [2002] OJ L203/30). This applies to vertical agreements for the sale or purchase of new cars, spare parts and repair and maintenance services. Generally, the conditions of this exemption are stricter than those in Regulation 2790/1999.

29.2.12.3 *Horizontal agreements*

A number of regulations have now been passed granting block exemption to certain categories of agreement, including:

(a) specialisation agreements (Regulation 2658/2000, [2000] OJ L304/3)

(b) research and development agreements (Regulation 2659/2000, [2000] OJ L304/7)

(c) technology transfer agreements (Regulation 772/2004, [2004] OJ L123/11; guidance notice published at [2004] OJ C101/2).

In addition to these general categories, further specific block exemptions have now been agreed (eg, shipping conferences, certain air transport agreements, insurance).

These block exemptions follow the new, economics-based approach first adopted by the Commission in the context of vertical agreements (see 29.2.12.2 above). In essence, the exemption applies provided that the combined market share of the parties does not exceed a specified threshold (20 per cent for specialisation and technology transfer agreements, 25 per cent for research, and development agreements) and the agreement does not include clauses which amount to price fixing, output limitation, or territorial allocation. In addition, each exemption contains additional provisions relating to the operation of the particular agreements. However, unlike earlier block exemptions, there is no longer a white list and a black list.

As the Commission's 1999 Report on Competition Policy noted, companies need to respond to increasing competitive pressure and changes in the marketplace driven by globalisation and the speed of technological progress. In this context, the Commission does not want to discourage horizontal cooperation as it can be a means of sharing risk, saving costs, pooling know-how, and consequently facilitating the launch of innovative products. The approach the Commission has adopted is similar to that adopted previously in respect of vertical agreements (see above), consisting as it does of a safe harbour clause for agreements under a certain market share. Although a market share approach for horizontal agreements is likely to run into similar criticisms to those encountered by the block exemption on vertical restraints, action by the Commission in this area must be seen as a positive step, as the reform of the regime for horizontal restraints had long been overdue.

29.2.13 Conclusions on Article 81

In recent years, the application of Article 81 has moved from a very rigid, formalistic approach to one that recognises the economic context within which particular agreements operate. The Commission now attempts to base its approach on considerations of market power and market concentration, rather than a simple application of the elements of Article 81(1). Both the new-style block exemptions on vertical agreements and on horizontal cooperation agreements reflect the general assumption that agreements involving parties who do not have a significant degree of market power will not normally be regarded as anticompetitive and can be exempted. At the same time, the *de minimis* threshold below which agreements are deemed not to fall within Article 81(1) at all has also been increased. The Commission's guidelines on vertical agreements and horizontal cooperation agreements, which reflect the experiences of four decades of centralised competition law enforcement, provide vital guidance on the types of agreements which are likely to be caught by Article 81 in future. In essence, only agreements in which the parties involved exercise market power and/or agreements which include hard-core restraints will fall foul of Article 81 and will be pursued vigorously both by the Commission and the national competition law authorities. Although this new approach may be criticised for lacking the legal certainty of the 'old-style' approach, it nevertheless offers a more targeted application of competition rules to agreements and concerted practices which pose a real threat to competition.

Overall, there is now a reasonably settled body of case law that lays down the general principles relating to Article 81, and although there is likely to be a continuous stream of litigation in relation to decisions adopted under this article, it seems that this will be more concerned with factual issues rather than fundamental aspects of the legal rules emanating from Article 81.

29.3 **Abuse of a dominant position**

The previous section examined how Article 81 deals with the dangers to competition which may arise when otherwise independent undertakings come together and coordinate their activities. Such collusion can have a serious effect on competition in that it may result in artificially high pricing levels and in limited supply of goods and services to the market. However, it is not always the coordinated action of several undertakings that give rise to concern. Some undertakings enjoy such a strong position in a particular market that they are able to act without any regard for any competitors—they are, to a large extent, immune from competition. Indeed, certain actions of such an undertaking may result in the elimination of competition altogether. It would, of course, be wrong to condemn an undertaking for being a strong player in a particular market in the absence of any anticompetitive practice, but where an undertaking in a strong position uses that position in an abusive manner, serious consequences for competition may follow. That is why Article 82 (ex 86) seeks to deal with such strong undertakings by prohibiting activities which could be regarded as an abuse of the undertaking's dominant position in a particular market.

In December 2005, the Commission issued a discussion paper to promote debate about the future priorities in the use of Article 82. In particular, the paper focuses on 'exclusionary abuses'—ie, behaviour which has the effect of keeping actual or potential competitors out of the market and which would therefore ultimately be detrimental to consumers. This document is not intended to lead to any specific legislative changes, but it may result in a change in enforcement practice, eg by concentrating resources on particular types of abuse. It also seems that the Commission may adopt a more economics-based approach to Article 82, as it has already done in the context of Article 81. At the time of writing, no concrete action had been proposed.

29.3.1 **Overview of prohibition**

Article 82 EC provides that 'Any abuse by one or more undertakings of a dominant position within the common market or in a substantial part of it shall be prohibited as incompatible with the common market insofar as it may affect trade between Member States.' Article 82 will be renumbered Article 102 TFEU, should the Lisbon Treaty come into force and remains unaltered save that the reference to 'common market' will be replaced by the words, 'internal market'.

The prohibition is followed by a list of examples of abuse considered later in this chapter. Article 82 is directly effective, and gives rise to rights and obligations for individuals. Provided the matter is seen to have the requisite Union dimension, an individual may challenge behaviour, and obtain remedies, in a situation in which he would have no remedy under national law.

Article 82 contains four essential ingredients. There must be:

(a) an undertaking

(b) a dominant position

(c) an abuse of that position

(d) abuse which affects trade between Member States.

29.3.2 **Undertakings**

The term 'undertakings' is subject to the same broad interpretation as is applied to Article 81 EC (see 29.2.3.1 above), and covers the same activities, both public and private. As its wording makes clear, the scope of Article 82 is not limited to monopolies or single organisations enjoying substantial market power. It applies also to undertakings within the same corporate or economic group which, when combined, together create a position of dominance. Where parent companies are acting in close conjunction with their subsidiaries they will often be treated as a single undertaking (see *Eurofix & Bauco v Hilti AG* [1989] 4 CMLR 677). The most vulnerable under Article 82 are the large multinationals. The Commission will not hesitate to take into account the economic strength of other members of a group or to fix them with liability if they are implicated in the abusive behaviour. The most obvious example is the case of *Europemballage Corp and Continental Can Co Inc v Commission* (case 6/72, discussed below). However, the scope of Article 82 is not limited, as will be seen, to very large undertakings.

29.3.3 **Joint dominance**

It was thought originally that Article 82 did not apply to undertakings which were independent of each other, and could not therefore be used to control oligopolies. This has not proved to be the case. In *Re Italian Flat Glass* ([1989] OJ L33/44), the Commission held that three Italian producers of flat glass, who between them held a 79 per cent to 95 per cent share of the Italian market in flat glass, had a *collective* dominant position in these markets and had abused that position. While the decision was annulled in part in *SIV v Commission* (cases T–68/89, T–77/89, and T–78/89) for lack of proof of dominance, the application of Article 82 to oligopolies was not disputed by the CFI. The potential application of Article 82 to oligopolies has since been affirmed, notably by the ECJ in *Municipality of Almelo v Energiededrifj IJsselmij NV* (case C–393/92). In that case, the ECJ stated that a collective dominant position would exist when 'the undertakings in question were linked in such a way that they adopt the same conduct on the market'. In *Irish Sugar* (case T–288/97), the CFI accepted the possibility that Irish Sugar, which produced sugar, and its distributor were together dominant, thus raising the possibility of vertical collective dominance as well as horizontal collective dominance. In *Compagnie Maritime Belge and ors v Commission* (case C–395–6/96P), the ECJ noted that it was not necessary to find contractual or other links in law. A finding of collective dominance could be based on 'other connecting factors and would depend on an economic assessment and, in particular, on an assessment of the structure of the market in question' (para 45).

In *Airtours* (case T–342/99), a case under the Merger Regulation, the CFI rejected a suggestion that the mere fact that the same institutional investors were found in three out of the four main tour operators was sufficient to give rise to collective dominance because it was not apparent that these shareholders directly influenced management decisions.

Nevertheless the implications of these decisions for oligopolies are not clear. It remains to be seen whether Article 82 could be invoked to control oligopolistic practices which are not in breach of Article 81(1), but which nevertheless undermine the competitive structure in a particular market. Nonetheless, it seems that Articles 81–2 are not mutually exclusive; where doubt exists as to which article is applicable, both should be pleaded.

29.3.4 **The principle of dominance**

Dominance was defined in *United Brands Co v Commission* (case 27/76), at para 65, as:

> a position of economic strength enjoyed by an undertaking which enables it to prevent effective competition being maintained on the relevant market by giving it the power to behave to an appreciable extent independently of its competitors, customers, and ultimately of its consumers.

To this the Commission added in *AKZO Chemie BV* ([1986] 3 CMLR 273) at para 67 that:

> The power to exclude effective competition is not . . . in all cases coterminous with in-dependence from competitive factors but may also involve the ability to eliminate or seriously weaken existing competitors or to prevent potential competitors from entering the market.

To assess if an undertaking has sufficient economic strength to behave independently of, or even exclude, competitors, it is necessary first to ascertain the relevant market in which competition is said to exist. As the Court pointed out in *Europemballage Corp and Continental Can Co Inc v Commission* (case 6/72), a position can be domi-nant within the meaning of Article 82 only if it is dominant in a relevant market. The definition of the relevant market requires consideration of three parameters: the relevant product market, the relevant geographical market and the temporal market. The determination of whether an undertaking is in a dominant position will depend on how those parameters are set. The following sections consider these aspects in turn, starting with the relevant product market, which is often the most complex aspect of establishing the relevant market. As a starting point in determin-ing the extent of the relevant market, both in respect of the product market and the geographic market, the Commission, in its Notice on the Definition of the Relevant Market ([1997] OJ C372), suggests a small, but significant and non-transitory in-crease in prices (SSNIP test) should be postulated and the likely reaction of custom-ers to that change evaluated. The question is, would the consumer switch to readily available substitutes? If such an increase were to result in a loss of profits as con-sumers switched to alternatives, there would clearly seem to be other suppliers or alternative products in the market. This test would then be reapplied, decreasing the relevant products or areas until there is no such change indicating no competitors.

29.3.4.1 *The relevant product market (RPM)*

This is defined by the Commission in its Notice on the Definition of the Relevant Market ([1997] OJ C372) and the Court in terms of product substitution. The rele-vant product market is one in which products are substantially interchangeable

(*Istituto Chemioterapico Italiano SpA v Commission* (cases 6 and 7/73)). It includes identical products, or products considered by consumers to be similar by reason of their characteristics, price or use. Two questions are central to this enquiry:

(a) To what extent is the customer, or importer, or wholesaler, able to buy goods *similar* to those supplied by the dominant firm, or *acceptable as substitutes?* This is known as cross-elasticity of demand, or 'demand-side' substitutability.

(b) To what extent are other firms *able to supply, or capable of producing* acceptable substitutes? This is known as cross-elasticity of supply, or 'supply-side' substitutability.

These questions may be assessed by reference to the characteristics of the product, its price, or the use to which it is to be put. Although the principles are expressed in terms of goods or products they apply equally in the context of services.

29.3.4.1.1 *End products*

Ascertaining the relevant product market is no easy matter. Its difficulties are illustrated in the case of *Europemballage Corp and Continental Can Co Inc* (case 6/72). This case involved the proposed takeover of a large Dutch packaging firm, Thomassen & Drijver-Vçerblifa NV (TDV) by Europemballage Corporation, a company registered in the USA, held and controlled by another US company, Continental Can Co Inc. Continental Can was a powerful organisation engaged in packaging operations throughout the world. It held an 86 per cent share in a German packaging company, Schmalbach–Lubeca-Werke AG (SLW), prominent in Germany in the manufacture of, inter alia, light metal containers for meat and fish and bottle-sealing machines. Continental Can proposed to transfer its interest in SLW to Europemballage. Thus the whole deal would result in Europemballage and, indirectly, Continental Can, holding significant market power in Europe. The Commission issued a decision that the takeover of TDV by Continental Can via Europemballage constituted a breach of Article 82.

Continental Can, through its holding in SLW, was alleged to be dominant in Germany in three separate product markets:

(a) light metal containers for meat products

(b) light metal containers for fish products

(c) metal closures for glass containers.

The acquisition of TDV by Europemballage would have further increased its dominance in these markets, since it would have removed an important potential competitor to SLW. Continental Can and Europemballage sought to annul the Commission's decision. Although the Court agreed with the Commission in principle that the takeover could constitute an abuse, it found that the Commission had failed to prove the claimants' dominance in the relevant product market. The Commission had failed to explore the question of product substitution. To be regarded as a distinct market, the Court held, the products in question must be individualised not only by the mere fact that they are used for packing certain products, but by particular characteristics of production which make them *specifically suitable for this purpose.* The Commission had also failed to consider the question of substitution on the supply side—ie, whether other potential competitors might not be able to enter the market by simple adaptation.

The Commission was more thorough in *United Brands Co v Commission* (case 27/76). In this case the Commission claimed that United Brands, one of the world's largest banana empires, producer of 'Chiquita' bananas, was abusing its dominant position in a number of ways. The question was whether the relevant product market was bananas, branded and unbranded, as the Commission claimed, or fresh fruit, as United Brands claimed. Clearly it was in the Commission's interest to define the market as narrowly, and in the interest of United Brands to define it as widely as possible. The Commission produced research from the Food and Agriculture Organisation which revealed that the existence of other fruit had very little influence on the price and consumption of bananas. Moreover, bananas occupied a special place in the diet of the very young, the sick, and the old. For them other fruits were not acceptable as substitutes. This time the Court accepted the Commission's view of the relevant product market.

It has been argued that the relevant product market could have been defined even more narrowly, either as branded bananas, or as bananas bought for the old, the sick or the very young, since there was evidence that customers continued to buy branded bananas even when they were considerably more expensive than unbranded bananas, showing little cross-elasticity of demand, while for the old, the sick, and the very young, there was practically no cross-elasticity at all.

On the question of cross-elasticity, both the Commission and the Court will scrutinise the evidence with care, and will not necessarily agree with the experts. In *Eurofix & Bauco v Hilti AG* ([1989] 4 CMLR 677), in the context of a finding of abuse against Hilti, a firm dominant in the market for cartridge strips and nails compatible with Hilti nail guns, the Commission rejected an econometric study produced by Hilti which purported to show significant cross-elasticity between nail guns and power drills, finding that the methodology of the study 'needed further refinement'. Moreover, the findings of the study were inconsistent with the way in which the market operated. The decision in *Hilti* was approved by the Court (*Hilti v Commission* (case 98/88)).

29.3.4.1.2 *Raw materials*

The relevant product market, and the question of substitutability, is not necessarily defined by reference to consumers. In *Istituto Chemioterapico Italiano SpA v Commission* (cases 6 and 7/73) the abuse alleged against Commercial Solvents Corporation (CSC)and its subsidiary, Istituto Chemicoterapico Italiano SpA (ICI), was a refusal to supply Zoja, with a particular chemical, aminobutanol, which CSC had supplied to Zoja in the past through ICI. The chemical was required for processing into ethambutol, a drug used for the treatment of tuberculosis. CSC had a near monopoly in aminobutanol, which was widely used as the best, and cheapest, for the manufacture of ethambutol. However, ethambutol was not the only drug suitable for treating tuberculosis. and ethambutol could be made from other raw materials. In an action before the Court for annulment of the Commission's decision, CSC argued that what mattered was whether consumers had a choice of drugs for tuberculosis as Article 82 was aimed at abuses which prejudiced the interests of consumers.

The Court disagreed. The article was concerned not only with abuses which prejudiced consumers directly. It was also aimed at abuses which prejudiced consumers indirectly by impairing the competitive structure. The effect of CSC's refusal to supply Zoja was to eliminate one of the principal manufacturers of ethambutol in the common market. Nor was the Court prepared to accept that Zoja could switch to other raw materials for the manufacture of ethambutol. The Court found that it was not feasible for Zoja to adapt its production in this way. Only if other raw materials could be substituted *without difficulty* for aminobutanol could they be regarded as acceptable substitutes. Since they could not the relevant product market was aminobutanol.

The hard line taken in this case illustrates that the Commission and the Court are not concerned merely with the immediate protection of the consumer; they are concerned to protect competition at the manufacturing level and in particular to prevent the smaller firm from suffering at the hands of its more powerful competitors. Similar thinking lay behind the Commission and the Court's approach in *Établissements Consten SA v Commission* (cases 56 and 58/64). Both reflect the influence of French and German competition policy on European law. (See Chapter 28.)

29.3.4.1.3 *Size of RPM*

In the above cases the relevant product market was a substantial one and the parties alleged to be dominant in that market wielded considerable power. But the relevant market, whether in goods or services, can be quite small, and provided an undertaking is dominant in that market it does not need to be generally powerful to fall foul of Article 82 EC. In *Hugin Kassaregister AB v Commission* (case 22/78) a Swedish firm, Hugin, which manufactured cash registers, supplying them to Liptons Cash Registers and Business Equipment Ltd in the UK through its British subsidiary, Hugin Cash Registers Ltd, was found to be dominant in the supply of spare parts for Hugin machines to independent repair businesses. (See also *AB Volvo v Erik Veng* (case 238/87).) In *British Brass Band Instruments v Boosey & Hawkes Interim measures* ([1988] 4 CMLR 67) the relevant product market, in which Boosey & Hawkes held a 90 per cent share, was held to be instruments for *British-style* brass bands. The fact that the market, or in this case the sub-market, was defined in narrow terms, did not, the Court said, exclude the application of Article 82. 'The essential question is whether the sub-market is sufficiently distinct in commercial reality.' Similarly, certain activities of a firm which seem quite insignificant may constitute a relevant market in which that firm may be dominant. In *General Motors Continental NV* ([1975] 1 CMLR D20) the issuing of test certificates for second-hand imports of Opel cars, carried out exclusively by General Motors in Belgium, constituted the relevant market, even though in one year (1973) only five cars were involved; and in *British Leyland plc* ([1984] 3 CMLR 92), BL was found to be dominant in the provision of national type-approval certificates for its vehicles since it alone had the right to issue these certificates. The decision was approved by the Court in *British Leyland plc v Commisson* (case 226/84).

29.3.4.2 *The relevant geographical market (RGM)*

29.3.4.2.1 *Determining the RGM*

To fall within Article 82 an undertaking must be dominant 'within the common market or in a substantial part of it'. Thus, the question of dominance must also be assessed in the context of the relevant geographical market. The relevant geographical market is the one in which the 'objective conditions of competition are the same for all traders' (*United Brands Co v Commission* (case 27/76)). It is the market in which available and acceptable substitutes exist, described, helpfully, by Overbury as 'the area in which consumers are willing to shop around for substitute supplies or in which manufacturers are willing to deliver'. This will depend on the cost and feasibility of transportation as well as consumer habits and preferences.

Where goods are homogeneous and easily and cheaply transportable, the relevant geographical market may be large. The Commission suggested in the *AKZO Chemie BV* decision ([1986] 3 CMLR 273) that in certain circumstances the whole of the common market may constitute the relevant geographical market. In *Eurofix & Hilti* the whole of the EC was found to constitute the relevant geographical market in the nail cartridge market. Where goods are differentiated, or where consumer tastes are inflexible, or where transportation is difficult or costly, a single state or even part of a state may constitute the relevant market. Where a service is only needed within one particular state, as in *British Leyland plc v Commission* (case 226/84), clearly that state will represent the relevant market. As the Court commented in *United Brands,* in order to ascertain whether a particular territory is large enough to amount to a substantial part of the market, the pattern and volume of the production and con-sumption of the products as well as the habits and economic opportunities of ven-dors and purchasers (and the users of services) must be considered. In *B&I/Sealink* ([1992] CMLR 255) the Commission decided that a port or airport, even if not itself a substantial part of the common market, may be considered such insofar as reason-able access to the facility is indispensable for the exploitation of a transport route which is substantial for the purposes of Article 82. Sealink's action as port authority in Holyhead in altering its own ferry times, thereby limiting access to the port by B&I's ships, was found to breach Article 82.

In determining the relevant geographical market, the cost of transport is particu-larly important. When deciding in *Hilti* that the relevant market was the whole of the EU, the Commission took into account the fact that nail cartridges could be transported throughout the Union at relatively little cost. Clearly, geographical markets have been growing and will continue to grow as the barriers to the single internal market are removed.

29.3.4.2.2 *Application beyond the EU*

In considering the relevant geographical market, the Commission has been criticised for failing adequately to take into account the possibility of countries outside the EU forming part of the relevant market, even though in the case of certain products (eg, vitamins) a world market may exist. For this reason a firm may be treated as domi-nant even though it is subject to substantial competition worldwide. However, in *SIV v Commission Re Italian Flat Glass* (cases T–68, 77, and 78/89) the Commission's decision was annulled in part on the grounds, inter alia, that the Commission had failed to take into account imports of flat glass from non-Member States.

29.3.4.3 *The temporal market*

In assessing the question of dominance the temporal aspect of the market should also be considered. It has been suggested that the Commission in *United Brands* should have defined the relevant product market by reference to the particular time of the year (eg, the winter months), when there was little opportunity for product substitution. The Commission did take the temporal element into account in *Re ABG Oil* ([1977] 2 CMLR D1) in limiting the market for oil to the period of crisis following the OPEC action in the early 1970s.

29.3.4.4 *Dominance in fact*

Once the relevant market is established, it is necessary to ascertain whether the parties concerned are dominant within that market. An undertaking can be dominant irrespective of whether it is a supplier or a purchaser (*British Airways v Commission* (case T–219/99), airline dominant in market for purchase of air travel agency services). When will an undertaking be regarded as dominant? The Commission suggested in *United Brands Co* ([1976] 1 CMLR D28) that:

> Undertakings are in a dominant position when they have the power to behave independently without taking into account, to any substantial extent, their competitors, purchasers and suppliers. Such is the case where an undertaking's market share, either in itself or when combined with its know-how, access to raw materials, capital or other major advantage such as trade-mark ownership, enables it to determine the prices or to control the production or distribution of a significant part of the relevant goods. It is not necessary for the undertaking to have total dominance such as would deprive all other market participants of their commercial freedom, as long as it is strong enough in general terms to devise its own strategy as it wishes, even if there are differences in the extent to which it dominates individual submarkets.

In *Michelin v Commission* (case 322/81), the ECJ adopted the test for dominance, which is now usually referred to as:

> A position of economic strength enjoyed by an undertaking which enables it to hinder the maintenance of effective competition on the relevant market by allowing it to *behave to an appreciable extent independently of its competitors and customers*, and ultimately of consumers. [Para 30, emphasis added.]

See also *Aéroports de Paris v Commission* (case T–128/98), para 47, which refers to 'the power to behave' rather than 'allowing', although there seems to be no significant difference in practice between the terms used).

Thus, the question of dominance requires a wide-ranging economic analysis of the undertaking concerned and of the market in which it operates. There are a range of relevant factors for establishing dominance which will now be considered in turn.

29.3.4.4.1 *Market share*

This will be of the first importance. In *Istituto Chemioterapico Italiano SpA* (cases 6 and 7/73), CSC (according to the Commisson; this was not found proved by the Court) held a virtual monopoly in aminobutanol. In *Europemballage Corp and Continental Can Co Inc* (case 6/72) SLW, owned by Continental Can, held a 70–80 per cent share in the RPM in Germany. In *Tetra Pak International SA v Commission* (case T–83/91) the CFI remarked that a market share of 90 per cent would be regarded as dominant save in exceptional circumstances. But such a high figure is not essential. United Brands held only a 40–45 per cent share in the banana market in a substantial part of Europe. Where the share is less than 50 per cent, the structure of the market will be important, particularly the market share held by the next largest competitor. In *United Brands* (case 27/76) the nearest competitors held 16 per cent and 10 per cent shares in the market. Where the market is highly fragmented the Commission has even suggested that a share of 20–40 per cent could constitute dominance (*10th Report on Competition Policy*). The Court has held that the existence of lively competition does not rule out a dominant position (*United Brands*).

A variation on the market share assessment can be seen in *British Airways v Commission* (T–219/99). In this case, BA's dominance as a purchaser in the market for air travel agency services was established on the basis of the number of seats which it was able to offer and therefore the number of tickets it might be able to sell through agencies. Its role was that of purchaser because it was 'buying' the service of the travel agencies for each ticket they sold on BA's behalf. It was irrelevant that there were competitors on some of the air routes, because the market for air transport services was different from that of air travel agency services. This, in turn, produced a market share calculation which demonstrated BA's dominance in the relevant market.

The ECJ, reflecting the view of the Commission, emphasised in *Hoffman La-Roche* (case 85/76) that although a high market share is clearly very important, it is not conclusive, and 'its importance varies from market to market according to the structure of the market'. It is therefore necessary to consider other factors, as well.

29.3.4.4.2 *The length of time during which a firm has held its position in the RPM*

This point was stressed in *Istituto Chemicoterapico Italiano* and *United Brands*. The firm cannot be dominant unless it is dominant *over time*. Clearly the longer a firm has been dominant, the greater the barriers to entry for potential competitors. Conversely, the greater the number of barriers to entry, the more likely it is that an undertaking may be in a dominant position.

A key factor, particularly in the so-called 'New Economy' (information technology), has been the fact that certain platforms (such as Microsoft) have become the norm and are widely adopted by consumers. This may permit an undertaking to maintain its dominance for a long period of time, and barriers to entry may be high.

29.3.4.4.3 *Financial and technological resources*

A firm with large financial and technological resources will be in a position to adapt its market strategy in order to meet and drive out competitors. It may indulge in predatory pricing, selling below cost if necessary to undercut rivals (see *AKZO Chemie BV* Decision [1986] 3 CMLR 273); it can maintain demand for its product by heavy advertising, thereby reducing cross-elasticity of demand, as was clearly the case in *United Brands*. Technological resources will enable a firm to keep ahead of potential competitors.

29.3.4.4.4 *Access to raw materials and outlets*

The greater the degree of vertical integration (ie, control over businesses up and downstream in the marketing process) the greater a firm's power to act independently. However powerful Zoja may have been as a manufacturer of ethambutol, it was dependent on CSC for its raw materials. CSC, on the other hand, controlled both raw materials and outlets via ICI. United Brands enjoyed an even greater degree of vertical integration. Its empire extended virtually from the plantation to the table. They owned plantations, fleets of refrigerated vessels and refrigerated warehouses in key ports throughout Europe.

29.3.4.4.5 *Behaviour*

The Commission suggested in *United Brands* that an undertaking's behaviour can in itself provide evidence of dominance. In *United Brands* the firm's discriminatory rebate system was taken, *inter alia*, as an indicium of independence. In *Eurofix & Bauco v Hilti* the Commission regarded Hilti's discriminatory treatment of its customers as 'witness to its ability to act independently and without due regard to other competitors or customers'.

Economists have questioned the validity in economic terms of some of these criteria, and even more so their application by the Commission in particular cases. For example, although United Brands had large financial and technological resources and enjoyed a high degree of vertical integration there was evidence that it faced fierce competition from time to time and its share of the market was falling. Moreover, its banana operations were not showing steady profits. These factors would not seem to indicate a power to behave independently of competitors. Such an approach may come close to blurring the line between determination of dominance and the finding of abuse.

29.3.4.4.6 *Barriers to entry*

In assessing dominance, it is not enough to examine the allegedly dominant undertaking's position in the existing state of the market; the question of *potential* competition must be assessed. This requires an examination into the whole range of barriers, geographical, financial, technical and temporal, to entry into that market. The Commission's decision in *Continental Can* was annulled for a failure to explore the possibility of product substitution. Both the Commission and the Court have been criticised for giving undue weight to such barriers, and particularly for failing to take a long-term view as to the prospects of market entry. This may result in a finding of dominance when the market is, in the longer term, contestable (see eg, *Michelin v Commission* (case 322/81)).

Common barriers to entry are things such as the superior technology and technical resources of the undertaking which could not be matched easily by others (eg, *Hoffmann-La Roche*, which was a market leader in innovation. Its ability to generate new technology was an important consideration in establishing dominance). Also, trademarks and brand names owned by the undertaking and its brand identity may make it more difficult for new brands to gain market share.

29.3.4.4.7 *Associated markets*

Proof of dominance in a particular market need not always be required. Where two markets are deemed to be associated, and a company is dominant on one of them, proof of dominance on the other does not need to be illustrated. In *Tetra Pak International SA v Commission* (case T–83/91) the CFI held that associative links between two product markets could be shown because the key products were the same in both markets and because many of the manufacturers and consumers in the two markets were also the same. Thus, for a company dominant in one market to be in breach of Article 82 EC in respect of an associated market, only abusive behaviour need be shown. The decision of the CFI has been confirmed by the ECJ (*Tetra Pak International SA v Commission* (case C–333/94P); see also *British Airways v Commission* (case T–219/99)).

29.3.5 Abuse

It is not dominance per se but the abuse of a dominant position that brings Article 82 into play and this must be understood bearing in mind the principle that dominant firms are under a special duty not to hinder competition (*Michelin v Commission* (case 322/81), at para 10). 'Abuse' is not defined in Article 82 itself. In *Hoffmann-la Roche*, the ECJ stated that abuse:

> is an objective concept relating to the *behaviour* of an undertaking in a dominant position which is such as to *influence the structure of a market* where, as a result of the very presence of the undertaking in question, *the degree of competition is weakened* and which, through recourse to *methods different from those which condition normal competition* in products or services on the basis of the transactions of commercial operators, has the effect of *hindering the maintenance of the degree of competition still existing* in the market or the growth of that competition. [Para 91, emphasis added.]

Examples of abuse are provided by the article. They comprise:

(a) directly or indirectly imposing unfair purchase or selling prices or unfair trading conditions

(b) limiting production, markets, or technical development to the prejudice of consumers

(c) applying dissimilar conditions to equivalent transactions with other trading parties, thereby placing them at a competitive disadvantage

(d) making the conclusion of contracts subject to acceptance by the other parties of supplementary obligations which, by their nature or commercial usage, have no connection with the subject of such contracts.

These are merely examples; the list is not exhaustive.

A glance back to Article 81 will reveal that the kinds of abuse prohibited under Article 82 run in close parallel to the examples of concerted behaviour likely to breach Article 81(1). As far as most forms of behaviour are concerned, the difference between Articles 81 and 82 is a difference in degree rather than in kind. The existence of a dominant position merely makes the conduct more dangerous; thus there is no possibility of exemption for a breach of Article 82.

Abuses prohibited under Article 82 have been divided into two categories: the exploitative abuses and the anticompetitive abuses. Exploitative abuses occur when an undertaking seeks to take advantage of its position of dominance by imposing oppressive or unfair conditions on its trading partners. Examples of these are provided under (a), (c), and (d) above, and some behaviour under (b). Anticompetitive abuses are those which, while not in themselves unfair or oppressive, are damaging because they reduce or eliminate competition. Such behaviour would arise under paragraph (b) above, and certain practices falling under para (d). Many kinds of behaviour fall into both categories (eg, *Istituto Chemioterapico Italiano SpA* (cases 6 and 7/73)). The Commission, in its 2005 Discussion Paper, has indicated its desire to focus on what it terms 'exclusionary abuses', ie anticompetitive abuses.

For the abusive behaviour to fall within Article 82, it is not necessary that the dominant undertaking reaps financial or commercial benefit from the behaviour the subject of complaint. In the *World Cup* case ([2000] OJ L5/55), the non-profit-making organisation with the responsibility for organising the distribution of tickets put forward the argument that it had not benefited from the limitation it had imposed on ticket sales, an argument the Commission dismissed as irrelevant.

29.3.5.1 *Exploitative abuses*

United Brands Co v Commission (case 27/76) provides examples of a number of such abuses.

29.3.5.1.1 *Unfair prices*

According to the Commission, United Brands Co was charging excessively high prices for its branded bananas. Although this point was not found proved by the Court, the Court agreed with the Commission on the matter of principle. An excessive price was defined by the Court as one which bears no reasonable relation to the economic value of the product. In *British Leyland plc v Commission* (case 226/84) the fees charged for the type-approval certificates for left-hand drive cars (when issued) were found to be excessive and discriminatory.

Problems arise over the question of 'economic value'. Deciding the economic value of a product or a service is a complex accounting exercise which leaves ample scope for differences of opinion. Economists would disagree as to what constituted the economic value of a product, and indeed, whether it can be accurately ascertained at all. What uniformity, then, can be hoped for from national courts when called upon to apply Article 82?

29.3.5.1.2 *Unfair trading conditions*

United Brands was found to be imposing unfair conditions by refusing to allow importers to resell bananas while they were still green. This meant that only wholesalers with the correct storage and ripening facilities were able to handle the bananas. The fact that the consumer might thereby be assured of obtaining a better, more standardised product did not prevent the Commission and the Court from finding that this requirement constituted an abuse. Again we find EU competition law protecting the 'middleman'.

29.3.5.1.3 *Discriminatory treatment*

United Brands was charging prices with a difference of, in some cases, more than 100 per cent in different common market countries, not, apparently, according to objective criteria, but according to what the market would bear. This constituted discriminatory treatment. Similarly, *British Leyland* (case 226/84) charged different prices for type-approval certificates for left-hand drive cars, without objective justification.

In *British Airways v Commission* (case T–219/99), BA held a dominant position as a purchaser of air travel-agency services. It had offered all UK travel agents a performance reward scheme if sales of BA tickets increased. Following a complaint by Virgin Atlantic, the Commission concluded that BA had abused a dominant position. The CFI upheld this finding. One element of the abuse was that it was possible under the scheme that two travel agents with identical sales would receive different rates of commission. BA's scheme therefore had discriminatory effects in the network of travel agents.

29.3.5.1.4 *Refusal to supply*

United Brands refused to supply one of its most important wholesalers, who had constructed special facilities to store and ripen the bananas, in retaliation for his taking part in an advertising campaign for a competitor. This was found to be an abuse. A refusal to supply which is not retaliatory would fall into the category of anticompetitive abuses, to be discussed at 29.3.5.2.3 below.

29.3.5.2 *Anticompetitive abuse*

This kind of abuse is less easy to detect than the exploitative abuse. Here the dominant firm uses its position in such a way as to undermine or even eliminate existing competitors, thereby reinforcing or increasing its dominance. A number of examples may be considered.

29.3.5.2.1 *Tying in*

A good example of tying-in practices is provided by the case of *Hoffman-La Roche & Co AG v Commission* (case 85/76). La Roche was the largest pharmaceutical company in the world, with a dominant position in seven separate vitamin markets. The alleged abuses lay in a number of tying-in practices. Customers undertook to buy all or most of their requirements from La Roche ('requirements contracts'); as a reward they were entitled to 'fidelity' rebates (discounts). The agreement also contained 'English' clauses. These provided that if customers found other suppliers offering similar products at cheaper prices they should ask La Roche to 'adjust' their prices. If La Roche failed to respond they were free to buy elsewhere. None of these clauses was oppressive as far as La Roche's customers were concerned. But the Commission (approved by the Court) found the practices to be abusive. The tying-in system limited their customers' freedom to buy from competing suppliers; the English clauses were unacceptable because they enabled La Roche to identify competitors and take pre-emptive action—eg, by dropping its prices to its competitors' levels, thereby nipping potential rivals in the bud.

The case law in this area, most recently confirmed in *Microsoft Corp v Commission* (case T–201/04) reveals a four-stage test:

(a) the tying and tied products are separate products

(b) the undertaking is dominant in the tying market

(c) consumers do not have the option to obtain tying product without the tied product and

(d) competition is foreclosed.

Nonetheless, if objective justification can be shown, there will be no infringement of Article 82 EC. (For more on *Microsoft*, see 29.3.5.2.4 below and Chapter 30.)

29.3.5.2.2 *Predatory pricing*

This is a strategy whereby prices are reduced, below cost if necessary, in order to drive potential competitors out of the market. In *AKZO Chemie BV* ([1986] 3 CMLR 273), AKZO, a firm dominant worldwide in the production of organic peroxides, was found to be engaged in such practices. However, as the Commission pointed out, it may be necessary to examine a firm's costs and motives in order to ascertain whether its low prices are predatory or merely the result of efficiency. Where low pricing is susceptible of several explanations evidence of an anticompetitive intent may be needed. Indeed, the lowering of prices may even be evidence of weakness. In *Hoffman-La Roche* the Court suggested that the fact that an undertaking is compelled by the pressure of its competitors' price reductions to lower its prices is in general incompatible with that independence which is the hallmark of dominance. The Court, in its first decision on predatory pricing (*AKZO Chemie v Commission* (case 62/86)), agreed with the Commission. There was a distinction, in competition-law terms, between lowering prices in order to win new customers and trying to eliminate a competitor. In the case of *AKZO* the firm's 'avowed intention' had been to eliminate one of its competitors.

In *Compagnie Maritime Belge Transports SA v Commission* (case T–24–6 and 28/93), the CFI emphasised the need to show intent. In this case, it was not clear that the dominant undertakings (this was a case involving collective dominance) had actually traded at a loss; certainly the Commission in its investigation did not carry out an analysis of costs and prices. There was, however, evidence to show that the motive behind the practice complained of was to drive the only existing competition out of the market. In this circumstance, the CFI seemed to place the burden on the dominant undertakings to show that their behaviour was not anticompetitive. Although the ECJ reduced the fines imposed in this case on appeal, the Court did confirm this aspect of the CFI's ruling (*Compagnie Maritime Belge Transports v Dafra Lines* (cases C–395–6/96P)). In the case of an allegation of abuse, though, how does the dominant undertaking show that its behaviour was normal in the circumstances? The danger is that normal price competition (for example, the reaction of a dominant undertaking to the news that one of its customers has been offered a lower price by a competitor) may be confused with predatory pricing.

29.3.5.2.3 *Refusal to supply*

While Article 82, in principle, respects the right of dominant firms to choose their contractual partners, in exceptional circumstances a refusal to supply may fall foul of Article 82 EC. Where supplies (or services) are refused to reduce or eliminate competition, such a refusal will constitute abuse. This appeared to be the case in *Istituto Chemioterapico Italiano SpA* (cases 6 and 7/73) where it was intended that CSC's subsidiary, ICI, would take over production of ethambutol previously undertaken by Zoja (see also *Hugin Kassaregister AB v Commission* (case 22/78)). Boosey & Hawkes' cessation of supplies to BBI was designed deliberately to prevent them entering into the market as competitors.

However, a refusal to supply either an existing or a new customer will not necessarily be abusive. Arguing from *Metro-SB-Grossmärkte GmbH & Co KG v Commission* (case 26/76), a refusal may be permissible if it is non-discriminatory and objectively justified. A refusal of supplies, particularly to an existing customer, will require cogent justification, and any signs of an anticompetitive motive will be fatal. In *Radio Telefis Eireann v Commission* (case T–69/89), *British Broadcasting Corporation v Commission* (case T–70/89) and *Independent Television Publications Ltd v Commission* (case T–76/89) the CFI upheld a decision of the Commission which condemned, for the first time, a refusal to supply a party with whom it had no pre-existing commercial relationship. Here the applicant television companies were seeking to exploit their copyright in television programme listings to prevent competitors from publishing television programme guides in competition with their own publications, to the detriment of consumers. The ECJ upheld this decision on appeal (*Radio Telefis Eireann v Commission* (cases C–241–2/91P) (*Magill* case)). The ECJ focused on the fact that the television companies were the sole source of the information which is needed to produce weekly listings guides for all channels, that there was a market for such a product and the product was not being produced because of the behaviour of the television companies, and that the television companies were therefore *without objective justification* seeking to reserve a secondary market (television guide publishing) to themselves. (See further 29.3.5.2.4 and Chapter 30.)

More recently, the ECJ has held that a refusal to supply, to protect the dominant company from the effects of parallel imports, constitutes abuse where it refuses to supply ordinary orders (*Sot Lélos-kai Sia EE v GSK* (joined cases C–468–78/06)). The key phrase is 'ordinary orders', as such an undertaking is permitted:

> to counter in a reasonable and proportionate way the threat to its own commercial interests potentially posed by the activities of an undertaking which wishes to be supplied in the first Member State with significant quantities of products that are essentially destined for parallel export. [Para 71.]

29.3.5.2.4 *An 'essential facilities' doctrine?*

The *Magill* case and subsequent developments have been interpreted as the development of an 'essential facilities' doctrine. The doctrine concerns undertakings which own or control a facility that is necessary to carry out a particular type of business, but which could not practically be reproduced by a competing entity or a potential competitor. The Commission Notice on access agreements in the telecommunications sector ([1988] OJ C265/3) described an essential facility as 'a facility or infrastructure which is essential for reaching customers and/or for enabling a competitor to carry on business, and which cannot be replicated by any reasonable means' (para 68).

In the absence of an objective justification, it seems that an essential facility must be made available to a competitor on reasonable terms. For example, in *Rødby Havn* ([1994] OJ L55/52), a Danish port was owned by DSB, a publicly owned port authority, which also operated the only ferry service between there and Germany. Two other companies were interested in running a ferry service on the same route. The Danish government refused permission to use the port or to build another facility close by. This decision was held to be an abuse within the terms of Article 82 because access to the port, a necessary prerequisite to the provision of the service, was prevented. Similarly, a ferry company controlling access to a port was not permitted to deny access or schedule departures to the detriment of rival companies providing ferry services out of that port without objective justification (*Sealink* [1992] 5 CMLR 255). Where there is no objective justification such behaviour is a prima facie breach of Article 82.

However, in *Oscar Bronner GmbH v Mediaprint* (case C–7/97), the ECJ sought to limit the scope of the doctrine. Bronner published a newspaper which had about 3.6 per cent of the daily market in Austria. Mediaprint's newspapers had a market share of around 44 per cent. Mediaprint had established a nationwide home-delivery scheme for its newspapers. Bronner wanted Mediaprint to include its newspaper within that system. Mediaprint did include another newspaper in its scheme, but refused to allow Bronner's newspaper into its network. Bronner claimed that Mediaprint was abusing its dominant position. The ECJ disagreed. It held that four factors were required for a refusal of access to constitute an abuse:

(a) refusal likely to eliminate all competition in the downstream market from the person requiring access

(b) refusal incapable of objective justification

(c) access must be indispensable for the other person for carrying on its business

(d) no actual or potential substitute for it.

These criteria had not been fulfilled, as Bronner could have set up his own distribution system, albeit at considerable cost.

The essential facilities doctrine must therefore be handled with caution. It poses particular challenges in the case of intellectual property rights (such as in *Magill*), where it could prove to operate against innovation and investment in research and development if companies were ultimately compelled to make available the results of their own efforts and expense. However, in *IMS Health* (C–418/01), the ECJ attempted to readjust the balance between protecting intellectual-property rights and innovation, when it held that a refusal to license the use of a particular system for collecting sales data to another undertaking would be an abuse where the undertaking requesting the licence intends to offer new products or services not offered by the IP owner for which there would be demand. The Commission, following a complaint from NDC, had taken the view that IMS Health has a dominant position in the German market for data services on sales and prescriptions of pharmaceuticals. IMS had developed a geographical model of analysis, called a 'brick structure', which is used for making available sales data to IMS customers and which constituted a de facto industry standard. The dominance arose because IMS customers had been heavily involved in the development of this 'brick structure' and were therefore dependent on it. Having concluded that IMS's refusal to license the use of their model of analysis meant that there existed a prima facie case for abuse of IMS's dominant position, the Commission ordered IMS to grant a licence by way of interim measure. This decision was suspended by the CFI and an appeal to the ECJ against the suspension failed. The CFI (case T–184/01 R) emphasised that:

> the respect for property rights in general and for intellectual property rights in particular is expressly reflected in Articles 30 and 295 EC. The mere fact that the applicant has invoked and sought to enforce its copyright . . . for economic reasons does not lessen its entitlement to rely upon the exclusive right granted by national law for the very purpose of rewarding innovation. [Para 143.]

The evidence suggested that the lack of competition which resulted from the refusal to license was not perceptible, but rather that the position of particular competitors had become difficult because they could not use similar technology. This, however, was not enough to find a prima facie infringement of Article 82 (note that the Commission subsequently withdrew its decision).

The decision in *IMS Health*, above, followed a complaint by NDC to the Commission. This had been prompted by a decision by a German court to grant an injunction in favour of IMS to prevent NDC from using a brick structure derived from IMS's structure. The German court referred a number of questions on the interpretation of Article 82 to the ECJ (see *IMS Health v NDC Health* (case C–418/01)). The Court confirmed that a refusal to license could not, in itself, be an abuse under Article 82, although the manner in which these rights are exercised could. It therefore held that it would be an abuse by a dominant undertaking which owned an intellectual property right in a brick structure indispensable to the presentation of regional sales data to refuse to grant a licence to another undertaking which also intends to provide such data in the same Member State. This was subject to a number of conditions: first, the undertaking requesting the licence intends to offer new products for which there is potential demand and which are not offered by the owner of the IP rights; secondly, there are no objective justifications for refusing to grant the licences; and finally, the refusal is such as to enable the owner of the IP rights to eliminate all competition on the relevant market.

The upshot of this ruling is that there may be circumstances where Article 82 *does* appear to require a degree of compulsory licensing, at least in circumstances where a refusal to do so would eliminate the possibility of innovation, and where there are no objective justifications for this refusal. The Court in *IMS* did not indicate what sort of objective justifications there might be, and it seems likely that future litigation will turn on this issue. In *Microsoft v Commission* (case T–201/04), Microsoft was unsuccessful in challenging the Commission's decision that it had breached Article 82 by refusing to supply interoperability information for its operating system because it had failed to demonstrate that disclosing this information would have a significant negative effect on its incentives to innovate. Some commentators have criticised the reasoning in Microsoft, because it takes a broad view of the criteria laid down in *IMS Health* and, arguably, operates to protect Microsoft's competitors rather then competition (see Chapter 30).

29.3.5.2.5 *Exclusive reservation of activities*

Similar principles to those applicable to a refusal to supply will apply where a dominant undertaking reserves certain activities to itself. This occurred in *Italy v Commission* (*Re British Telecommunications* (case 41/83)) where BT reserved for itself exclusive rights to its telex forwarding services, and in *Belgian Telemarketing* (case 311/84), in which a telephone marketing service was channelled exclusively through RTL's agent. The Court pointed out in *Belgian Telemarketing* that there was no 'objective necessity' for its so doing. This implies, in line with *Metro*, that the exclusive reservation of certain activities by a dominant undertaking, whether for itself or for an appointed agent, might be permissible if it were necessary and objectively justified. However the Court was not prepared to accept that the preservation of RTL's image constituted a 'necessity'.

29.3.5.2.6 *Import and export bans*

In view of the hard line of the Commission and the Court over such restrictions under Article 81 it is no surprise that import and export bans have been held to constitute abuse under Article 82 (*Suiker Unie v Commission* (case 40/73)). Apart from when industrial property rights are legitimately exercised to this end (see Chapter 30) it is hard to imagine a situation in which such a ban would not be deemed an abuse.

29.3.6 Trade between Member States

As with Article 81, there must be some effect on trade between Member States for Article 82 to apply, but such an effect is not hard to establish. The Court held in *British Leyland plc v Commission* (case 226/84) that it was not necessary to establish any specific effects, as long as there was evidence that a particular activity *might* affect trade between Member States. A theoretical possibility will be sufficient.

However, in *Hugin Kassaregister AB v Commission* (case 22/78) the Court annulled the Commission's decision ([1978] 1 CMLR D19) that Hugin had acted in breach of Article 82. Although it agreed with the Commission on the questions of the relevant product market and abuse, it found that Hugin's refusal to supply Liptons with spares did not affect trade between states. Hugin was a Swedish firm and at that time outside the common market, and Liptons was functioning in London on a purely local scale.

An effect on trade between Member States was held in *Istituto Chemioterapico Italiano SpA* (cases 6 and 7/73) to include repercussions on the competitive structure within the common market. This was approved and followed by the Court in *Bodson v Pompes Funèbres* (case 30/87) and an effect on trade between Member States found despite the Commission's view that a monopoly in funeral services granted to Pompes Funèbres by the municipality of Charleville-Mèziéres did not affect trade between Member States.

29.3.7 Relationship with Article 86(2) (ex 90(2)) EC

Some public undertakings (such as utility companies) defending a claim of alleged abuse under Article 82 may seek to rely on Article 86(2). This provides that undertakings entrusted with the operation of services of general economic interest or which have the character of a revenue-producing monopoly are subject to the rules in the treaty (including competition rules) unless the performance of the tasks assigned to them would be obstructed by the application of those rules. This exception is subject to the proviso that the 'development of trade must not be affected to such an extent as would be contrary to the interests of the Community'.

29.3.7.1 *When will Article 82 not apply?*

This is a three-stage test. To be able to rely on this exception, not only must the entity show, first, that it is the requisite type of undertaking, but, secondly, that it cannot perform the tasks assigned to it without relying on provisions or behaviour which would normally be in breach of competition provisions—in particular, Article 82. In *Corbeau* (case C–320/91), Corbeau was prevented from running a postal service because the Belgian postal service had a monopoly. Potentially this could have breached Article 82 unless the Belgian postal service could rely on Article 86(2). The ECJ accepted that the Belgian postal service was an undertaking within Article 86(2) and also that a certain amount of restriction of competition was necessary to enable it to remain economically viable. The postal service is required to perform some services which can only be carried out at a loss (for example, delivery to outlying areas) and it funds these activities from profit-making activities. Unrestricted competition would allow other companies to 'cream off' the profitable services without having to carry out the non-profitable activities, leaving the Belgian postal service with the obligation but not the means of paying for it. In *TNT Traco SpA v Poste Italiane SpA* (case C–340/99), therefore, a requirement that economic operators providing an express mail service that fell outside the scope of the universal postal service had to pay the equivalent of the normal postal charges to the universal service provider was compatible with Articles 82 and 86 if the proceeds of such payments were necessary to enable the universal service provider to operate in economically acceptable conditions. Moreover, the universal service provider must be under the same obligation when providing an express mail service which is not part of the universal service.

This does not mean, however, that all competition can be excluded: in deciding if a case falls within Article 86(2), the authorities must identify the extent of restriction necessary to enable the undertaking to perform its tasks, taking into account, 'the economic conditions in which the undertaking operates, the costs which it has to bear and the legislation, particularly concerning the environment, to which it is subject' (*Municipality of Almelo v Energiebedrijf IJsselmij NV* (case C–393/92), para 49).

29.3.7.2 *"Community interest"*

The interests of the Union must also be taken into account. Although it is not clear precisely what this element of Article 86(2) requires, it will clearly curtail the scope of the exception provided under this article. It has been suggested from the terms of the *Almelo* judgment that, broadly speaking, the same assessment will be made as is made under Article 81(1) (see above), entailing a balancing of the needs of the undertaking with other EU goals. It is not clear what impact Article 16 EC, which obliges Member States to ensure that services of general economic interest 'operate on the basis of principles and conditions which enable them to fulfil their missions', will have, as on the one hand both the Union and Member States are required to take into account the 'shared values of the Union as well as their role in promoting social and territorial cohesion' and, on the other hand, this provision is expressed to be without prejudice to certain treaty articles including Article 86.

29.4 **Enforcement of Articles 81 and 82**

Central to the effectiveness of the competition provisions are the rules on enforcement. Without proper enforcement, the substantive competition rules would lose much of their bite. For four decades, Regulation 17/62 gave the Commission a central role in enforcing the competition provisions within the EC Treaty, with significant powers of investigation and the right to impose penalties. During this time, two themes emerged in relation to competition enforcement by the Commission. The first concerned the scope of the Commission's powers. Although the decisions of the Commission may have been subject to judicial review, given their extent and their potential impact on undertakings, including individuals, the need to ensure procedural fairness became ever-more important. This point remains central today.

Secondly, the previously strongly centralised system meant that D-G Competition was subject to a very high workload, resulting in delays in the decision-making process. A thorough process of reform in a number of aspects of competition law in response to this second point was therefore undertaken. The replacement of the original system of enforcement with a new, decentralised system finally came into place when Regulation 1/2003 ([2003] OJ L1/1) entered into force in May 2004. It is supplemented by Regulation 773/2004 relating to the conduct of proceedings by the Commission pursuant to Articles 81–2 of the EC Treaty ([2004] OJ L123/18), as well as a 'Modernisation Package' of Commission notices which provide detailed guidance on the operation of the new system and the interpretation of key concepts (see [2004] OJ C101).

These regulations and notices replace the earlier Regulation 17/62, and this chapter will concentrate on the new system. It should be remembered that the bulk of the *acquis communautaire* in the field of competition law evolved through decisions and cases decided under the previous framework.

Article 1(1) of Regulation 1 states, rather boldly, that 'agreements, decisions and concerted practices caught by Article 81(1) of the Treaty which do not satisfy the conditions of Article 81(3) of the Treaty shall be prohibited, no prior decision to that effect being required' (Article 1(3) contains a similar statement in respect of Article 82 EC). The corollary of this basic prohibition is that an agreement caught by Article 81(1) which *does* satisfy the conditions of Article 81(3) is not prohibited, and no prior decision granting exemption is required (Article 1(2), Regulation 1). Unlike the previous system, it is not necessary to ask the Commission to examine individual agreements to establish whether the criteria for exemption are, in fact, satisfied. Rather, undertakings will have to examine for themselves whether any of their practices conflict with Article 81(1) but are exempt under Article 81(3), thus transferring the workload in making this assessment to the companies involved. This transfer also imposes a certain amount of risk on the companies making the assessment, should their advisors come to the 'wrong' conclusion about the acceptability of their agreements (and this fact comes to competition authorities' attention). Consequently, although the Commission is not involved in this assessment directly, it provides indirect support through its notices and block exemptions, as well as through formal decisions adopted previously and the case law of the courts. In particular, it has issued two documents containing guidelines on the notion of 'effect on trade' ([2004] OJ C101/81) and the application of Article 81(3) ([2004] OJ C101/97).

Although the Commission no longer deals with notifications, it retains the power to investigate specific anticompetitive practices on its own initiative or in response to complaints received from third parties. As the Commission's focus has now shifted towards investigating harmful anticompetitive practices, such as large price-fixing cartels, it seems likely that the Commission's involvement will be restricted (although it has encouraged complaints to be made). Instead, both national competition authorities (Article 3) and national courts (Article 6) now have the power to apply Articles 81–2 EC in full. However, this is subject to the requirement in Article 16 of Regulation 1 that national authorities and courts cannot adopt a decision running counter to a decision adopted by the Commission.

National authorities have the power to require that an infringement is brought to an end, to order interim measures, accept commitments and to impose fines, periodic penalty payments, or any other penalty provided by national law.

Where the Commission does investigate, it may similarly order the termination of an infringement and impose structural or behavioural remedies (Article 7). Under Article 9, where the Commission intends to adopt a formal decision that an infringement should be brought to an end, the undertakings concerned may offer commitments to meet the concerns expressed by the Commission. If these are accepted, the Commission may adopt a decision to that effect and thereby make the commitments binding on the parties. However, if there is a material change in the facts on the basis of which the commitments were accepted, or if the undertakings subsequently fail to honour their commitments, the Commission may reopen its investigation (Article 9(2)). Finally, the Commission retains the power to make a finding of inapplicability if it concludes that Article 81(1) EC or Article 82 EC does not apply at all, or, in the case of Article 81(1) EC, that the conditions of Article 81(3) EC are satisfied (Article 10). However, this power is only exercisable 'where the Community public interest' so requires and where the Commission acts on its own initiative.

The modernised enforcement system is based on the assumption that the relevant principles on the application of the competition rules are now well established, and that the Commission no longer needs to take a central role. However, it has been accepted that 'novel questions' regarding the scope and application of Articles 81–2 may still arise. Where undertakings are unable to assess whether a practice they are involved in constitutes an infringement because neither the various guidance notices, nor the *acquis communautaire*, provide an answer, they may seek informal guidance from the Commission in accordance with the Notice on informal guidance relating to novel questions concerning Articles 81–2 (2004/C 101/06, [2004] OJ C101/78). If appropriate, the Commission will issue an informal guidance letter, which is without prejudice to any subsequent formal investigation.

Earlier editions of this book devoted more space to the detail of the enforcement system, but for this edition, it was decided to curtail the discussion of the enforcement mechanism, as this is now more commonly taught in specialist modules on competition law. Readers seeking more detail on the enforcement system are advised to consult the previous edition of this book or specialist texts.

29.5 Mergers and concentrations

29.5.1 Background: From Articles 81 and 82 to the Merger Regulation

Perhaps the most surprising application of Article 82 came in the case of *Continental Can (Europemballage Corp and Continental Can Co Inc v Commission* (case 6/72)). Here the Commission had applied Article 82 in the context of a proposed merger, namely, the proposed takeover by Continental Can, which owned an 86 per cent share in SLW in Germany, of TDV in Holland, the entire package to be held by Continental Can's subsidiary Europemballage. The Commission issued a decision that the proposed takeover constituted an abuse of their dominant position within the common market (viz Germany). In annulment proceedings Continental Can argued that such action could not be regarded as an abuse. Article 82 was concerned only with behaviour detrimental to consumers. Moreover, it required some causative link between the position of dominance and abuse. Neither Continental Can nor Europemballage had used their power to effect the merger. The Court disagreed. Article 82 the Court said, cannot allow mergers which eliminate competition. Prejudice under that article does not mean affecting consumers directly but also prejudice through interference with the structure of competition itself. Nor was it necessary to prove a causal link between the dominance and the abuse. The mere fact of dominance rendered the proposed takeover an abuse. Although the Court annulled the Commission's decision on the grounds that the relevant product markets had not been fully proved, the principle was established. Following *Continental Can*, in *Tetra Pak* (case T–51/89), the takeover by Tetra Pak of a company holding an exclusive licence to new technology for sterilising milk cartons was held to constitute a breach of Article 82. Although the acquisition of an exclusive licence was not per se abusive, Tetra Pak's acquisition of that licence had the practical effect of precluding all competition in the relevant market. The existence of an exemption under the Exclusive Licence Block Exemption Regulation (2349/84) did not release a dominant undertaking from its obligation to comply with Article 82.

Continental Can and Article 82 remained the basis on which the Commission exercised control over mergers until the Court decided for the first time, in *BAT & Reynolds v Commission* (cases 142 and 156/84), that mergers could also fall within Article 81(1). The case arose from a proposed merger between Philip Morris Inc and Rembrandt Ltd, which would have given Philip Morris a controlling interest in one of its principal competitors, Rothmans Tobacco (Holding) Ltd, in the EU cigarette market. The Commission had been alerted to the proposed merger by the parties' competitors, BAT and Reynolds. Subsequently the agreement was modified by a decision from the Commission reducing Philip Morris's shareholding in Rothmans Ltd, and thereby ensuring that the relationship between them remained competitive. The decision was challenged by BAT and Reynolds. While the decision was upheld by the Court, the Court affirmed that Article 81(1) could apply in principle to mergers. Although the acquisition of an equity interest in a competitor did not in itself restrict competition, it might serve as an instrument to that end.

This decision paved the way for the acceptance by Member States of a regulation on merger control which had been languishing for many years. The final version of the regulation, Regulation 4064/89 (corrected version [1990] OJ L257/13), was adopted in December 1989, after much debate among Member States on the appropriate turnover and market-share thresholds required to bring the regulation into operation. It was replaced with a modernised regulation in 2004 (Regulation 139/2004 [2004] OJ L24/1). It requires notification to and approval by the Commission of proposed mergers above certain combined turnover thresholds. Moreover the Merger Regulation applies to 'full-function' joint ventures, which are joint ventures which perform, on a lasting basis, all the functions of an autonomous economic entity (Article 3(4)). Such joint ventures operate in the market in the same way as other undertakings and must have sufficient financial and other resources to be able to operate as a business on a lasting basis (see Commission Notice on Full-Function Joint Ventures, published at [1997] OJ C66 together with other notices on the notion of undertakings concerned, the notion of concentration and the calculation of turnover). However, a joint venture which does not fall within the definition of full-function joint venture will have to be assessed under Article 81, although a block exemption may then be available.

29.5.2 **The regulation**

Regulation 139/2004, which came into effect on 1 May 2004, applies to mergers, acquisitions, and certain joint ventures, known as 'concentrations' between firms with a combined worldwide turnover of more than 5,000 million, where at least two of the firms have a combined turnover of more than 250 million in the EU but do not earn more than two-thirds of their turnover in a single Member State (Article 1(2)). Article 1(3) provides that where a concentration does not meet these thresholds, it may still have a EU dimension if:

(a) the combined aggregate worldwide turnover of all the undertakings is more than 2,500 million

(b) in each of at least three Member States, the combined aggregate turnover of all the undertakings is more than 100 million

(c) in each of at least three Member States considered for (b) above, the aggregate turnover of each of at least two of the undertakings concerned is more than 25 million and

(d) the aggregate EU-wide turnover of each of at least two of the undertakings concerned is more than 100 million.

unless each of the undertakings concerned achieves more than two-thirds of its aggregate EU-wide turnover within one Member State.

A 'concentration' is defined in Article 3(1) as:

(a) a merger of two or more previously independent undertakings or

(b) the acquisition, by one or more persons already controlling at least one undertaking, or by one or more undertakings, whether by purchase of securities or assets, by contract or by any other means, of direct or indirect control of the whole or parts of one or more other undertakings.

'Control' confers the possibility of exercising 'decisive influence' on an undertaking. A joint venture will be concentrative if it performs on a lasting basis all the functions of an autonomous economic entity (Article 3(4)). The Commission issued guidance on the concept of a concentration, calculation of turnover and the definition of a full-function joint venture ([1997] OJ C66) under the old regulation; this had not been replaced at the time of writing.

The principle underlying the regulation is that of the 'one-stop shop'. Concentrations falling within the regulation will be subject to the exclusive jurisdiction of the Commission (Article 21(2)) and must be notified to the Commission (Article 4). A failure to notify may result in a fine of up to 10 per cent of the aggregate turnover of the undertaking(s) concerned (Article 14(2)), whereas supplying incorrect or misleading information may result in fines of up to 1 per cent of aggregate turnover (Article 14(1)). Concentrations falling outside the regulation's thresholds will be subject to control by the relevant national authority. However, a Member State or Member States jointly may ask the Commission to intervene in respect of a concentration falling outside the regulation which will 'significantly affect' competition within its own territory and have an effect on trade between Member States (Article 22(1)). Similarly, the Commission may refer a matter notified to it to the relevant national authority following receipt of notification by the Member State that a concentration may significantly affect competition in a market within that

Member State which has the characteristics of a separate market (Article 9). In this context, the Commission has provided guidance on how to deal with the allocation of cases in a Notice on Case Referral in respect of concentrations ([2005] OJ C56/2).

A concentration will be permitted if it would not 'significantly impede effective competition in the common market or in a substantial part of it, in particular as a result of the creation or strengthening of a dominant position' (Article 2(2)–(3)). It is, however, not clear if the test for 'dominance' would be the same as under Article 82. In the Green Paper (COM (2001) 745 final) leading to the reform, an altogether different test was proposed to avoid the links with Article 82, but this has not survived in the final version of the new regulation.

In making its decision, the Commission must take into account, inter alia, the 'need to preserve and develop effective competition within the common market', as well as 'the market position of the undertakings concerned and their economic and financial power' (Article 2(1)). The Commission has 25 days in which to decide whether to investigate the matter and four months from the date on which proceedings are initiated in which to reach a final decision (Article 10).

Procedures governing notification and detailed provision in respect of hearings and time limit are laid down in Regulation 802/2004 ([2004] OJ L133/1).

29.5.3 Residual role for Articles 81 and 82

Since Articles 81–2 are directly effective individuals remain free despite the regulation to raise questions concerning *any* concentration, whatever its dimensions, before their national courts. It cannot be guaranteed that concentrations falling outside the Merger Regulation will not be found to breach these articles. This problem apart, the Merger Regulation introduced a welcome degree of certainty in an area likely to be subject to ever-increasing activity as firms both within and outside the EU seek to take advantage of the opportunities offered by the single European market. In order to increase 'transparency' the Commission publishes a detailed analysis of its decisions under the Merger-control Regulation in its annual reports on Competition Policy.

29.6 Conclusions

This chapter demonstrates that competition law is a mature area of EU law, and one where there has been a move to decentralised enforcement and a use of more general block exemptions (at least as far as Article 81 is concerned). It is also a very complex one where law and economics interact ever-more closely. Difficulties may arise from the degree to which a court can properly be expected to make complex assessments of economics. There is also a tension between the different objectives of the EU— particularly the need to facilitate the internal market. Its contribution to the creation and functioning of the internal market has been immense, ensuring that undertakings do not undermine it by creating artificial barriers along national lines, or act in such a way as to undermine market integration. It is likely to continue to be a central area of law within the EU and is unlikely to be affected by the removal, should Lisbon come into force, of the reference to competition in the objectives of the EU.

FURTHER READING

Review of Article 82 at: <http://ec.europa.eu/competition/antitrust/art82/index.html>.

Andrews, P, 'Is meeting competition a defence to predatory pricing? The Irish sugar decision suggests a new approach' [1998] ECLR 49.

Camesasca, P, *European Merger Control: Getting efficiencies right* (Oxford: Hart Publishing, 2000).

De Jong, H, 'Unfair and discriminatory pricing under Article 86' [1980] ECLR 297.

Eilmansberger, T, 'How to distinguish good from bad competition under Article 82' (2005) 42 CML Rev 129.

Green, N, 'Article 85 in perspective: Stretching jurisdiction, narrowing the concept of a restriction and plugging a few gaps' [1988] ECLR 190.

Harrison, J and Woods, L, 'Media ownership: Impact on access and content' in *European Broadcasting Law and Policy* (Cambridge University Press, 2007).

Korah, V, 'Concept of a Dominant Position within the Meaning of Article 86' (1980) 17 CML Rev 395.

Lang, JT, 'Defining legitimate competition: Companies' duties to supply competitors and access to essential facilities' (1994) 18 Fordham Int'l LJ 437.

Mezzanotte 'Tacit collusion as economic links in article 82 EC revisited' (2009) 30(3) ECLR 137.

Monti, G, 'The scope of collective dominance under Article 82 EC' (2001) 38 CML Rev 131.

—— 'Article 81 and public policy', (2002) 35 CML Rev 1057.

Niels, G and Jenkins, H, 'Reform of Article 82: Where the link between dominance and effects breaks down' (2005) 26 ECLR 605–10.

Odudu, O, *The Boundaries of EC Competition Law: The scope of Article 81* (Oxford University Press, 2006).

Rodger, BJ, 'Market integration and the development of European competition policy to meet new demands: A study of oligopolistic markets and the concept of a collective dominant position under Article 86 of the Treaty' [1994] 2 LIEI 1.

Roitman, D, 'Legal uncertainty for vertical distribution agreements: The block exemption Regulation 2790/1999 (BER) and related aspects of the new Regulation 1/2003' (2006) 27 ECLR 261–8.

Soames, T, 'An analysis of the principles of concerted dominance: A distinction without a difference?' [1996] ECLR 24.

Stothers, C, 'Refusal to supply as abuse of a dominant position: The essential facilities doctrine in the European Union' (2001) 22(7) ECLR 256.

Tillotson, J and MacCulloch, A, 'EC competition rules, collective dominance and maritime transport' (1997) 21 World Competition (Law and Economics Review, Geneva) No 1, 57.

Vogelenganz, P, 'Abuse of a dominant position in Article 86: The problem of causality and some applications' (1976) 13 CML Rev 61.

Volcker, S, 'Developments in EC competition law in 2004: An overview' (2005) 42 CML Rev 1691.

Wesseling, R, 'The rule of reason and competition law: Various rules, various reasons' in Schrauwen (ed) *Rule of Reason: Rethinking another classic of European legal doctrine* (Hogenderp Papers 4) (Europe Law Publishing, 2005).

Whish, R and Sufrin, B, 'Article 85 and the rule of reason' (1987) 7 YEL 1.

30

Intellectual property rights and the internal market

30.1 Introduction

The exercise of intellectual property rights, or industrial and commercial property rights, such as trade marks, patents, and copyright, can have a negative impact on the operation of the internal market: it may be used to restrict the free movement of goods between Member States, and it can also result in restrictions of competition. As far as the latter is concerned, it is of course the very purpose of intellectual property rights to give their owner monopoly rights for a certain period of time as a reward for his creative endeavour or the acquired goodwill in his product. Intellectual-property rights are therefore necessary to encourage investment of time and money in creative endeavour. A balance has therefore to be struck between recognising intellectual-property rights and preventing their use from undermining the internal market objective (including competition policy).

In this chapter, we will consider to what extent it is possible to use intellectual-property rights to restrict the free movement of goods by analysing the case law that has developed under Article 30 (ex 36), which contains the derogations from the prohibition against quantitative restrictions or measures having an equivalent effect under Article 28 (ex 30; post Lisbon, 36 and 34 TFEU respectively) (see Chapters 19 and 20). We will then examine to what extent competition law under Articles 81–2 (ex 85–6; post Lisbon 101–2 TFEU, respectively) has been applied to control the use of their rights by the owners of intellectual property. It will become apparent that there is a degree of parallelism in the case law developed in these areas.

30.2 Derogation from Article 28: Protection of industrial and commercial property

As noted in Chapter 20, Article 30 permits a derogation from Article 28 where this is justified on grounds of the protection of industrial or commercial property. This exception must be read in conjunction with Article 295 (ex 222) EC, which provides that 'This Treaty shall in no way prejudice the rules in Member States governing the system of property ownership'. Should Lisbon come into force, this provision would be renumbered Article 252 of the Treaty on the Functioning of the European Union (TFEU).

Together these provisions would appear to ensure that national laws governing industrial property remain intact. However, since industrial property law by its very nature tends to contribute to a partitioning of the market, usually along national lines, its exercise inevitably restricts the free movement of goods and conflicts with the principle of market integration so fundamental to the EU. As we will see (at 30.3 below), the competition provisions of the treaty may be invoked to prevent this partitioning, but they are not in themselves sufficient to deal with all the situations in which industrial property law may be used to compartmentalise the market. So the Commission, and more particularly the Court, since the Commission has no power to enforce the free movement of goods provisions against individuals, have solved the problem by the application of Articles 28–30. As a result, despite the prima facie protection offered to industrial property rights by Articles 30 and 295 EC, these rights, protected under national law, have undoubtedly been curtailed.

30.2.1 'Specific subject matter' of the right

The scope of Article 30 was considered in *Deutsche Grammophon Gesellschaft mbH v Metro–SB–Grossmärkte GmbH & Co KG* (case 78/70). Here Deutsche Grammophon (DG) were seeking to invoke German copyright law to prevent the defendant wholesalers from selling DG's Polydor records, previously exported to France, in Germany. Since a prohibition on reimport would clearly breach Article 28, the matter fell to be decided under Article 30. Arguing from the second sentence of that Article, that 'prohibitions or restrictions shall not . . . constitute a means of arbitrary discrimination or a disguised restriction on trade between Member States' the Court concluded that the provision permitted prohibitions or restrictions on the free movement of goods only to the extent that they were justified for the protection of the rights that form the *specific subject matter of the property*. The Court drew a distinction between the *existence* of industrial-property rights which falls within the specific subject matter of the right and remains unaffected by EU law, and their *exercise*, which may come within the prohibition of the treaty. The specific subject matter (which overlaps with discussions of the purpose of an intellectual property right) will vary depending on the type of right in issue (eg, trade marks, see *Hag II*; on copyright see *Magill*, discussed at 30.3.2). If copyright protection is used to prohibit, in one Member State, the marketing of goods brought on to the market by the holder of the rights, or with his consent, in the territory of the other Member State (ie, to prevent what are known as 'parallel' imports) *solely* because the marketing has not occurred in the domestic market, such a prohibition, maintaining the isolation of the national markets, conflicts with the essential aim of the treaty, the integration of the national markets into one uniform market. Thus it would constitute an improper *exercise* of the property right in question and would not be justified under Article 30.

30.2.2 Exhaustion

The specific subject matter of the property, to protect which property rights may be legitimately exercised under EU law, was expressed in *Centrafarm BV v Sterling Drug Inc* (case 15/74) and *Centrafarm BV v Winthrop BV* (case 16/74), in the context of a claim for infringement of patents and trade marks respectively, as a guarantee that the owner of the trade mark or patent has the exclusive right to use that trade mark or patent, for the purposes of putting into circulation in the EU products protected by the trade mark or patent *for the first time*; either directly, or by the grant of licences to third parties. Once the protected product has been put on the market in a particular Member State by or with the consent of the owner, or by a person economically or legally dependent on him, such as a licensee, a subsidiary, a parent company or an exclusive distributor (but not an assignee of trade-mark rights, see further *IHT* (case C–9/93)), he can no longer rely on national property rights to prevent its import from that state into other Member States. His rights have been exhausted. The European Court of Justice (ECJ) has held that it is not permissible to rely on the right to place goods on the market for the first time to prevent the importation of goods lawfully manufactured in one Member State into the territory of another Member State where the goods have not yet been put into circulation but are in transit in order to be placed on the market of a non-Member State (in this instance, Poland prior to its accession) (*Rioglass* (case C–115/02)).

This doctrine of 'exhaustion of rights' has been applied by the Court to trade marks (*Centrafarm BV v Winthrop BV* (case 16/74)), patents (*Centrafarm BV v Sterling Drug Inc* (case 15/74)), industrial designs (*Keurkoop BV v Nancy Kean Gifts BV* (case 144/81)) and, subject to some qualification due to its special nature (see *Warner Brothers Inc v Cristiansen* (case 158/86); *Coditel v Cine Vog Films* (case 62/79)), copyright (*Musik-Vertrieb Membran GmbH v GEMA* (cases 55 and 57/80)). It is thought that plant breeders' rights too would be subject to the principle, since they were held in *LC Nungesser KG v Commission* (case 258/78) to fall within the concept of industrial and commercial property.

30.2.3 Consent

The underlying assumption in the exhaustion doctrine is that the owner has consented to the marketing of the products. Thus, in *Merck & Co Inc v Stephar BV* (case 187/80), the exhaustion principle was applied where the patent owner had sold his product in Italy, where there existed no system of patent protection. The Court held that having allowed the goods to be sold in Italy, he must accept the consequences as regards free circulation in the Community.

In contrast, where a product has been sold under a compulsory licence, without the consent of the owner, the latter is entitled under Article 30 EC to rely on his property right to prevent the marketing in a third Member State of that product resulting from the exploitation of the compulsory licence, since, not having consented to its use, he is still entitled to enjoy the substance of his exclusive licence (*Pharmon BV v Hoechst AG* (case 19/84). See also *Thetford Corp v Fiamma SpA* (case 35/87)). Similarly, where the manufacturing or marketing of a product is lawful in a Member State, *not* through the owner's consent but because of the expiry of the protection period provided for industrial-property rights under the law of that Member State, a person with exclusive rights in that product in another Member State may prevent the import of the protected product into the Member State in which he holds these rights (*EMI Electrola GmbH v Patricia* (case 341/87), which concerned rights of reproduction and distribution of musical works).

Where a product has been put lawfully on the market in a particular Member State with the owner's consent and the period of protection permitted under national law in that state has *not* expired, its import into another Member State may not be restrained, even though the purpose of an attempt to prevent importation is to prevent parties taking advantage of different price levels in different Member States, whether the reason for the price differences be government policy, legislation or ordinary market forces (*Centrafarm; GEMA*).

30.2.3.1 *Doctrine of common origin*

A particular case of where there was lack of consent can be seen in the cases involving the common origin doctrine, which initially concerned quite idiosyncratic facts. *Van Zuylen v Hag AG* ('*Hag I*') arose from an attempt by Van Zuylen Frères, who owned the trade mark for Hag coffee in Belgium and Luxembourg, to prevent the import into Luxembourg of 'Hag' decaffeinated coffee made by Hag AG in Germany. The trademark in both the Luxembourg and German had originally belonged to one group of companies, but the mark had been split after the Second World War as Hag Belgium was sequestrated and sold to a Belgian family. So both companies legitimately owned the mark. There was no question of exhaustion of rights, since Hag AG had clearly not consented to the original transfer of its trade mark. Thus the Belgian company could not stop the imported products as they were legitimately marketed in Germany.

The matter was reconsidered in Hag II (*SA CNL-SUCAL v Hag GF AG* (case C–10/89)), where the reverse fact situation applied; in this case the German company sought to stop imports of products bearing the other Hag trademark, and won. Following its ruling in *Pharmon BV v Hoechst AG* (case 19/84), the Court held that in the absence of an element of *consent* on the part of the trade-mark owner to the product being manufactured or marketed in another Member State, the owner was entitled to protect his product against imported goods which could be confused with his but for which he was not responsible. The decision, which was carefully reasoned, was based on the purpose of trade-mark protection, which is to guarantee the identity and origin of the marked products to the consumer and ultimate user, and avoid the possibility of confusion. The determining factor, as the Court pointed out (at para 15), was the absence of consent on the part of the proprietor to the putting into circulation in another Member State of similar products bearing an identical mark or one leading to confusion, manufactured by an undertaking which is legally and economically independent of the proprietor.

Hag II concerned a situation in which a trade-mark right, originally in common ownership, had been divided *involuntarily*, without the consent of the original owner. In *IHT Internationale Heiztechnik GmbH v Ideal-Standard GmbH* (case C–9/93), the Court had to decide whether a *voluntary* assignment to an independent undertaking of trade-mark rights in Ideal-Standard products in Germany, originating from a French subsidiary of IHT (USA), would exhaust the rights of the owner of the same trade-mark rights in Germany, which was also a subsidiary of IHT (USA). The ECJ held that the principle of exhaustion of rights only applied where the owner of the trade mark in the importing state and the owner of the trade mark in the exporting state were the same, or where, even if they are separate persons, they are economically linked, for example, as licensee, parent company, subsidiary, or exclusive distributor. It did not apply where trade-mark rights have been assigned to an unrelated enterprise such that the assignor and related enterprises no longer have control.

In the absence of consent, the essential concept for the purposes of exhaustion of rights, replacing the concept of common origin, is unitary control. In the absence of consent, or unitary control, guaranteeing uniform standards, there will be no exhaustion of rights.

30.2.4 **Special cases**

30.2.4.1 *Repackaging*

There have been a number of cases involving pharmaceuticals in which import-ers have sought to take advantage of these price differences and the exhaustion principle, but, because the same product has been marketed in different Member States under different guises, they have needed to repackage or relabel the goods to establish their identity in the Member State of import (see also Commission Communication on parallel imports of proprietary medicinal products for which marketing authorisations have already been granted (COM (2003) 839 final), pro-viding detailed guidance on the implications of the Court's jurisprudence).

The Court has held that persons may rely on trade-mark rights to prevent the im-port of such goods in order to avoid confusion as to the identity of the product, and to ensure that the consumer can be certain that the trade-marked product has not been subject to interference by a third party. However, it was decided in *Hoffman-La Roche & Co AG v Centrafarm* (case 102/77) that an attempt to prevent the import of the trade-marked goods would constitute a disguised restriction on trade between Member States (bringing it outside Article 30) where:

(a) the marketing system for the products adopted by the owner of the trade-mark rights involves an artificial partitioning of the market and where

(b) the repackaging cannot adversely affect the condition of the product

(c) the proprietor receives prior notice of the marketing of the repackaged product and

(d) it is stated on the new package that the product has been repackaged.

The Court added that these principles were not confined to medical products, a point confirmed by the ECJ in respect of the relabelling of alcoholic drinks in *Frits Loendersloot* (case C–349/95).

Similar reasoning underlay the decision in *Centrafarm BV v American Home Products Corporation* (AHPC) (case 3/78) about whether the importer, Centrafarm (again!), could change the name of the product it was seeking to import from the UK into Holland from Serenid D, under which it was marketed in the UK, to Seresta, the name under which a near-identical drug from the same manufacturer (AHPC) was marketed in Holland. The Court held that the proprietor of a trade mark was entitled to rely on his property rights to prevent the unauthorised fixing of trade marks on to the goods. However, while it might be lawful for a manufacturer to use different trade marks in different Member States, where a trade-mark system is used to partition the market along national lines a prohibition on the unauthorised fixing of labels would constitute a disguised restriction on trade between Member States, thereby falling outside Article 30.

The importer in *Pfizer Inc v Eurim-Pharm GmbH* (case 1/81) did its homework. Prior to importing Vibramycin tablets, manufactured by Pfizer Ltd in the UK, into Germany, Eurim-Pharm repackaged the tablets in packets resembling those used for Vibramycin tablets of German manufacture without tampering with the individual tablets; the new packages had windows through which the trade names 'Vibramycin' and 'Pfizer' could be seen. The pack stated that the tablets had been produced by Pfizer Ltd of Great Britain and had been repackaged and imported by Eurim-Pharm. And they had informed the claimant, Pfizer Inc (USA), the parent company which owned the Vibramycin and Pfizer trade marks in Europe, in advance of what they were intending to do. The Court held that the claimant could not rely on its trade-mark rights and Article 30 to prevent the import of the tablets into Germany under those circumstances. These rulings have been reaffirmed, in the context of the Trade Marks Directive (see further below), in *Merck and Co Inc v Primecrown Ltd* (cases C–267–8/95), *Bristol-Myers Squibb v Paranova A/S* (cases C–427, 429, and 436/93), *Pharmacia & Upjohn SA v Paranova A/S* (case C–379/97) *Merck, Sharp and Dohme* (case C–443/99) and *Aventis Pharma Deutschland* (case C–433/00). In *Merck, Sharp and Dohme*, however, the ECJ emphasised that the interference with the subject matter of the intellectual property right must be justified by the need to overcome barriers to trade within the European Economic Area (EEA), even if the repackaging did no harm to the reputation of the trade-mark owner.

30.2.4.2 'Similar' goods

Where goods have no common origin, but have been manufactured and marketed independently, it has always been possible to invoke trade-mark rights to prevent imports of goods with the same or similar trade marks where this might lead to the confusion of the customer, even though marketing of these goods under their respective marks may be quite lawful and even protected in their country of origin. In *Terrapin (Overseas) Ltd v Terranova Industrie CA Kapferer & Co* (case 119/75), a German firm, proprietors of the trade name Terranova, sought to prevent an English company from registering its trade name Terrapin in Germany, since the products of both firms (building materials) were similar, and would, the German company argued, lead to confusion amongst consumers. The ECJ held that Article 30 could be invoked to prevent the import of goods marketed under a name giving rise to confusion where these rights have been acquired by different proprietors under different national laws as long as they do not operate as a means of arbitrary discrimination or disguised restriction on trade between Member States.

A similar situation, involving a registered design, arose in *Keurkoop BV v Nancy Keane Gifts BV* (case 144/81). Here Keurkoop BV, the proprietor in Holland of a registered design for a particular style of handbag, sought to prevent the import into Holland of an identical bag, manufactured in France to a design registered in France by a different owner. The ECJ held that it would be entitled under Article 30 to exercise its property rights to prevent the bags being imported from France, since these bags had not been marketed in France by it or with its consent; the rights had arisen independently of each other. The Court did, however, suggest that the matter should be examined to ensure that there was no agreement or concerted practice between the parties concerned which might infringe Article 81.

In *Deutsche Renault AG v Audi AG* (case C–317/91), Audi was held entitled under Article 30, as the owner of a registered and protected trade mark in Germany, the 'Quattro' mark, to prohibit the use in Germany by a Renault subsidiary established in Germany of the designation 'Espace Quadra' for a four-wheel-drive vehicle marketed in France and elsewhere under that name, where the use of the name might cause confusion. It was left to the national court to decide whether the use of the name Espace Quadra would cause confusion, according to the meaning of the term in national (German) trade-mark law. The Court did, however, suggest that Union law 'did not lay down any strict interpretative criterion for the concept of the risk of confusion'. Following this judgment it may be doubted whether *Prantl* (case 16/83, see Chapter 19) remains good law.

The Trade Marks Directive and the Regulation on a Community Trade Mark now provide for the scope of a trade-mark proprietor's rights against infringement (see Trade Marks Directive Article 5, Regulation 40/94/EC Article 9), which includes protection as against similar goods. These provisions, which are central to the law relating to trade marks, have been the subject of judicial interpretation (see, eg, *Sabel v Puma* (case C–251/95); *General Motors* (case C–375/97); *Marca Mode v Adidas* (case C–425/98); *Hölterhoff v Freiesleben* (case C–2/00); *Davidoff* (case C–292/00); *Arsenal FC plc v Matthew Reed* (case C–206/01)). A consideration of this jurisprudence, however, lies outside the scope of this book.

30.2.4.3 *Intellectual-property rights and national origin*

In these cases, property rights were being invoked to protect the owner's legitimate property in his *product*. Where the owner seeks to invoke his rights to prevent the import of goods solely because the public *may be misled as to their national origin*, the Court has held (*Theodor Kohl KG v Ringelhan and Rennett SA* (case 177/83)) that national trade-mark law may not be relied upon in the absence of evidence of unfair competition. Similarly national measures which seek to employ industrial or commercial-property rights in order to encourage or protect domestic production at the expense of imports from other Member States will breach Article 28 and will not be permitted under Article 30 (eg, *Generics UK v Smith Kline* (case C–191/90), re licences of right; *Commission v UK* (case C–30/90), re compulsory patent licences).

30.2.4.4 *Copyright and lending rights*

Although in principle the doctrine of exhaustion applies to all forms of intellectual property, the ECJ accepted in *Warner Bros v Christiansen* (case C–158/86) that the doctrine of exhaustion was not appropriate where the specific subject matter of the right allows the copyright owner to control each use of the copyright work. This would cover the right to lend or rent, to perform, or show a copyright work in public. There is therefore a distinction between these sorts of rights and the right to control distribution (sale, import, and export).

30.2.5 **International exhaustion**

The principles outlined above will only apply to trade within the Union. Where parties seek to assert their property rights to prevent goods from third countries from entering the Union, the free movement provisions of Articles 28 and 30 do not apply (*EMI Records Ltd v CBS United Kingdom Ltd* (case 51/75), *Generics UK Ltd v Smith Kline and French* (case C–191/90), *Silhouette International Schmied GmbH & Co KG v Hartlaner Handelsgesellschaft mbH* (case C–355/96)—this last case concerned the Trade Marks Directive, discussed further below). In *Silhouette*, the ECJ held that national rules of an EU Member State providing for exhaustion of trade-mark rights for products put on the market outside the EEA with the consent of the trade-mark proprietor were incompatible with the terms of the Trade Marks Directive. From the wording of Article 7(1), exhaustion would take place only if the goods had been put on the market within the EEA. The Court took the opportunity to refine the scope of this ruling in *Sebago Inc. v GB-Unic* (case C–173/98). Sebago was the owner of trade marks for shoes, registered in Benelux. GB-Unic sold some Sebago shoes which had been manufactured in El Salvador and imported into the EU via a supplier in Belgium. Sebago claimed that this violated its rights, as it had not consented to the sale of those shoes in the Community. GB-Unic argued that it is sufficient for consent (thereby triggering the exhaustion doctrine) if the proprietor of the trade mark has consented to the marketing in the EU of similar goods bearing the same trade mark. Having reaffirmed its judgment in *Silhouette*, the ECJ then went on to take a narrow view of consent, stating that consent must relate to the specific goods in respect of which exhaustion was claimed. The question of consent arose again in *Zino Davidoff v A & G Imports Ltd* and *Levi Strauss & Co v Tesco* (joined cases C–414 to 416/99). The defendants in the case argued that, to fall within *Silhouette* and *Sebago*, a trade-mark proprietor must object to the import of trade-marked goods that had been lawfully marketed outside the EEA; failure to object implied consent. Although the ECJ accepted that consent in the context of international exhaustion could be implied from the circumstances, those circumstances must 'unequivocally demonstrate that the proprietor has renounced his right to oppose placing of the goods on the market within the EEA' (para 47). In particular, the defendant must prove that the trade-mark proprietor has consented to the marketing of the goods, it is not for the proprietor to prove that it has not so consented. As the ECJ pointed out, to have held otherwise would have meant that consent would have been deemed to be given in the absence of any proof (para 58), which is a different and more easily satisfied level of consent than implied consent.

The matter of proof came before the ECJ again, albeit in a different context, in the case of *van Doren + Q GmbH v lifestyle + sportswear Handelsgesellschaft mbH* (case C–244/00). The defendants in this case argued that they had obtained the goods (manufactured in the United States and subject to an exclusive distribution agreement in Germany) within the EEA and that the doctrine of exhaustion to prevent the trade-mark proprietor from stopping the parallel imports applied. Van Doren, however, alleged that the goods came directly from the United States. The question that was referred was: which party should be subject to the burden of proof and, in particular, whether Article 28 required that the burden of proof be removed from the defendant? The ECJ held that it is generally for the defendant to prove that the conditions for the application of the exhaustion principle exist, but this was qualified: if the defendant shows that there would be a risk of market partitioning if he had to bear the burden of proof, then it would be for the trade-mark owner to demonstrate that the goods in question were originally placed on the market outside the EEA by him or with his consent. A risk of market partitioning would arise because if the defendant had to prove that the goods were placed on the market within the EEA, the trade-mark owner might be able to identify the member of the exclusive or selective distribution network who supplied the defendant, and reduce supplies to that member to prevent further sales to the defendant. However, once the trade-mark owner has established that the goods were first marketed outside the EEA, then it would be for the defendant to prove, in turn, that the trade-mark owner consented to the subsequent marketing of the goods in the EEA.

30.2.6 Free movement of services

The case law discussed so far has been concerned with the free movement of goods, but the free movement of services may similarly be affected by the tension between protecting intellectual-property rights and ensuring free movement in the internal market. Although the derogation provision in Article 46 EC does not refer to the protection of industrial property, unlike Article 30, the Court has held that indistinctly applicable measures can justify intellectual-property rights that might otherwise conflict with the operation of Article 49 (*Coditel* (case 62/79), *Collins v Imtrat* (case C–92/92)). In *Coditel*, Belgian cable companies were picking up German terrestrial television transmissions of programmes and rebroadcasting them; the doctrine of exhaustion did not apply. However, in the absence of more specific case law on this point, it is difficult to predict the extent to which the Court would adopt a similar approach to that taken under Article 30 in the field of services. Certainly, the ruling in *Coditel* has been challenged in a recent reference to the ECJ, not yet decided. The case concerned the right of pub landlords in the UK to subscribe to Greek satellite-television services broadcasting English football matches despite the attempts of Sky (the company in the UK with the right to broadcast the matches) to prevent them (*Murphy v Media Protection Services Limited* (case C–429/08)). Questions have been referred not only on the scope of Article 49 EC, but also the competition provisions and, as far as the decoder boxes themselves are concerned, free movement of goods.

30.2.7 Harmonisation

Because of the wide disparity in national trade-mark rules and its resulting adverse impact on the internal market, harmonisation at EU level was clearly required. In the field of trade marks, Directive 89/104 was passed in 1989 ([1989] OJ L40/1). Its aim was to approximate those aspects of trade-mark law which most directly affect the functioning of the common market, to ensure that the conditions for obtaining and continuing to hold a registered trade-mark right are the same in all Member States. The directive defines trade-mark rights and the rights attached to trade-mark ownership, as well as its limitations. It provides common grounds for refusal of registration, invalidity and loss or exhaustion of rights. The effect of the measure is to broaden the scope of what may be registered as a trade mark and extend the rights conferred by trade-mark registration, thereby reducing the need for reliance on the unpredictable remedy of passing off. However, as the Court pointed out in *IHT* (case C–9/93), the directive does not change the essential character of national trade-mark law, which remains essentially territorial and independent.

The Trade Marks Directive has not been without its critics. One particular area of concern is the scope of the exhaustion doctrine in relation to goods from outside the EU, the case law on which parallels that in relation to similar cases brought under Article 30 (see 30.2.6). The narrow interpretation of the exhaustion rule in Article 7(c) of the Trade Marks Directive has been the subject of some adverse comment, as, by limiting the scope of the exhaustion doctrine, it allows companies to partition markets and maintain high prices. A report comparing prices between the EU and the USA showed that prices in the USA tend to be between 40–50 per cent of those in the EU.

In the absence of full harmonisation of national trade-mark law, Regulation 90/94 ([1994] OJ L11) was introduced. The regulation provided for the introduction of a Community trade mark, covering all the Member States, to be obtained by a single application. The Commission presented a proposal for amendments to the regulation (COM (2002) 767 final), which was subsequently adopted in Regulation 422/2004 ([2004] OJ L70/1).

The legal protection of designs is now covered by Directive 98/71/EC, which required Member States to harmonise the central elements of their design laws, was agreed in 1998 and came into force in 2001. The Regulation on Community Design was adopted in 2001 (Regulation 6/2002, [2002] OJ L3/1). It introduces Community registered designs and Community unregistered designs as other means of protection for designs. The Commission proposals on 'utility models' (COM (97) 691) have not progressed. The Commission has put forward proposals for a EU patent and a proposal for a directive on patent protection for inventions related to computer programs, both based on the Green Paper (COM (95) 382).

In the field of copyright, eight directives have been agreed. Directive 93/83 provided for the coordination of certain rules relating to copyright and rights relating to copyright applicable to satellite broadcasting ([1993] OJ L246), and Directive 93/98 provided for the harmonisation of the terms of protection of copyright and related rights ([1993] OJ L290). Specific directives apply to copyright in the broadcasting area (eg, the Lending Rights Directive 92/100/EEC ([1992] OJ L346/61) and the Satellite Broadcasting and Cable Retransmission Directive 93/83/EEC ([1993] OJ L248/15)) and there is a directive on the legal protection of topographies of semiconductor products (Directive 87/54/EEC) and on the legal protection of databases (Directive 96/9). More recently, directives on copyright and the information society (Directive 2001/29); and on the resale right for the benefit of the original author of a work of art (Directive 2001/84) have been agreed. Finally, a directive on measures and procedures to ensure the enforcement of intellectual property rights was adopted in 2004 (Directive 2004/48/EC [2004] OJ L195/16).

Should the Lisbon Treaty come in to force a new provision, Article 118 TFEU, gives the Union the power:

> to establish measures for the creation of European intellectual property rights to provide uniform protection of intellectual property rights throughout the Union and for the setting up of centralised Union-wide authorisation, coordination and supervision arrangements.

This power is expressed to operate 'in the context of the establishment and functioning of the internal market', though given how broadly similar provisions have been interpreted (see Chapter 16), it is questionable whether this requirement would constitute much limitation on the scope of the provision.

30.2.8 Discrimination

It may be noted that any discrimination, direct or indirect, in relation to industrial and commercial-property rights will fall foul of Article 12 (ex 6) EC (post Lisbon, 18 TFEU), which prohibits 'any discrimination on the grounds of nationality' (*Collins v Imtrat* (cases C–92 and 328/92)).

30.3 Intellectual-property rights and competition law

As the discussion above has demonstrated, the ECJ has drawn a distinction between the *existence* of industrial property rights and their *exercise*. The mere existence of industrial-property rights cannot infringe Articles 81 or 82 EC; an improper or abusive exercise of these rights, however, can. The exploitation of industrial or commercial-property rights will be improper if these rights are used to defeat EU law on restrictive practices (see, eg, *Consten* (cases 56 and 58/64; discussed below and in Chapter 29). Any concerted attempt or attempt by a dominant undertaking to use these rights to partition markets, or to maintain artificial price levels, or to impose discriminatory or unfair conditions on trading partners is liable to fall foul of Articles 81 or 82 EC.

30.3.1 Improper exercise of rights

In *Etablissements Consten SA v Commission* (cases 56 and 58/64) Consten could not rely on its trade-mark rights to prevent parallel imports of Grundig products from other Member States. The purpose of the GINT trade mark was not to protect the owner's legitimate rights in his product, eg to prevent other goods being passed off as Grundig's, but to partition the market and ensure absolute territorial protection for Grundig products in France. Thus its exercise in the context of Grundig's dealer agreement was in breach of Article 81(1).

The same principle has been applied to patents and copyright. In *Parke, Davis & Co v Probel* (case 24/67) the Court held that an 'improper exploitation' of patent rights in the context of agreements, decisions, and concerted practices of of undertakings in a dominant position could breach EU competition law.

In *Re GEMA* ([1971] CMLR D35) the Commission found that GEMA, an authors' rights society holding a dominant position in authors' copyright in Germany, was improperly exploiting its rights in breach of Article 82. GEMA was exploiting its copyrights by discriminatory practices; it was discriminating against nationals from other Member States, who could not become full members; it paid supplementary fees, 'loyalty bonuses', only to some of its members from a fund to which all had contributed, without objective justification. It was imposing unfair conditions on its members, by extending its contractual rights to non-copyright works, and claiming rights to future works. All these practices went beyond what was necessary to protect GEMA's legitimate property rights.

Similarly, in *Windsurfing International Inc v Commission* (case 193/83) WSI, the owner of patent licences in a special sail rig (comprising mast, mast foot, sail, and pair of curved booms) for use with windsurfing boards, was seeking in its licensing agreements to impose unnecessary restrictions on its licensees in breach of Article 81(1). For example, licensees were required to exploit the patents (for the rigs) *only* for the manufacture of sailboards using hulls which had been given WSI's prior approval; to pay royalties for rigs made under the patent on the basis of the selling price of the *complete* sailboard; to manufacture only in a specified manufacturing plant; and they were not permitted to challenge the licensed patents. These provisions were all found to constitute improper exploitation.

30.3.2 **The specific subject matter of intellectual-property rights**

In placing limitations on the exercise of industrial-property rights, the Commission, supported by the Court, has curtailed the very substance of these rights. These rights can now only be exercised to protect what the Commission regards as the 'specific subject matter' of the property concerned. In this, there are similarities to the approach adopted under Article 30 regarding goods, and under the ECJ's case law regarding services.

The specific subject matter of the property, to protect which industrial-property rights may legitimately be exercised, has been narrowly defined. For patents, it is to ensure, to the holder, so as to recompense the creative effort of the inventor, the exclusive right to use an invention (*Centrafarm BV v Sterling Drug Inc* (case 15/74)). Patent rights clearly merit protection if the EU wishes to encourage creative endeavour. Thus while patent licensing agreements have generally been held in breach of Article 81(1) the Commission has been prepared to grant exemption under Article 81(3) (eg, *Davidson Rubber Co* [1972] CMLR D52), and it is expected that this view will continue to be taken under the decentralised enforcement system now applicable.

The specific subject matter of a trade-mark right is to protect the owner from competitors who would profit, deliberately or accidentally, from the reputation and goodwill attached to the mark by selling goods with the same mark, or one which was sufficiently similar to cause confusion in the mind of the consumer (see, eg, *Deutsche Renault AG v Audi AG* (case C–317/91)). Thus, trade-mark rights cannot be used simply to prevent parallel imports within the EU of the trade-marked product, which may be cheaper than the same product sold in the importing state, even to protect a distributor's investment in a particular territory from 'free riders' (ie, parallel importers who seek to take advantage of the product's goodwill, built up by the promotional efforts of others). It is only rights *in the product* which are protected.

The specific subject matter or purpose of copyright protection was held in *Radio Telefis Eireann v Commission* (case T–69/89) to be to protect the owner's moral rights in the work and ensure a reward for creative endeavour, which entitles the holder to exclusive rights of performance and reproduction of the protected work (para 71). RTE could not take advantage of its legitimate monopoly in radio and TV broadcasts by refusing to grant licences for the reproduction of its advance programme listings to potential competitors, thereby retaining an 'unlawful monopoly downstream'. Such an exercise of copyright did not correspond to its essential function of copyright protection but pursued an aim 'manifestly contrary to Article [82]'. On appeal (*Radio Telefis Eireann v Commission* (cases C–241–2/91P)), the ECJ upheld the CFI's judgment, but without ruling explicitly on the purpose of copyright. In *Re GEMA*, the Commission suggested that any conditions embodied in an agreement or practice or imposed by a dominant undertaking which go beyond what is necessary to protect the owners' *existing* property, and certainly any discriminatory treatment, risk infringing Articles 81 or 82.

The possibility of requiring rights holders to license their works was picked up again in *NDC Health Corporation v IMS Health* (case C–481/01P(R)). There, the Court of First Instance (CFI) (upheld by the ECJ) emphasised that a refusal to licence intellectual property rights would only then constitute an abuse within Article 82 EC if there are exceptional circumstances in the public interest which required that a licence be granted. The facts are outlined in Chapter 29. The CFI (case T–184/01 R) emphasised that:

> the respect for property rights in general and for intellectual property rights in particular is expressly reflected in Articles 30 and 295 EC. The mere fact that the applicant has invoked and sought to enforce its copyright . . . for economic reasons does not lessen its entitlement to rely upon the exclusive right granted by national law for the very purpose of rewarding innovation. [Para 143.]

The case turned on the application of *Magill* (cases C 241–2/91) and *Bronner* (case C–7/97), discussed in Chapter 29) to the present situation. The Court confirmed that a refusal to license could not, in itself, be an abuse under Article 82, although the manner in which these rights are exercised could. It therefore held that it would be an abuse by a dominant undertaking that owned an intellectual property right in a brick structure indispensable to the presentation of regional sales data to refuse to grant a licence to another undertaking which also intends to provide such data in the same Member State. This was subject to a number of conditions:

1. the undertaking requesting the licence intends to offer new products for which there is potential demand and which are not offered by the owner of the intellectual property rights;

2. there are no objective justifications for refusing to grant the licences; and

3. the refusal is such as to enable the owner of the intellectual-property rights to eliminate all competition on the relevant market.

The extent of these three elements determine and dominate IPR-holder's intellectual property rights.

The matter has been raised again in *Microsoft v Commission* (case T–201/04, Grand Chamber) (discussed Chapter 29). Microsoft had not supplied interoperability information so competing companies could produce products that were interoperable with Windows operating system. The Commission found an abuse under Article 82 and Microsoft challenged that decision. The CFI returned to the criteria identified in *IMS Health* to uphold the Commission's decision; which can now be seen as comprising four elements:-

1. indispensibility;

2. likely to eliminate competition;

3. prevent appearance of new products; and

4. lack objective justification.

The CFI's ruling has been the subject of much comment. It is noteworthy that its approach seems to broaden the circumstances in which an abuse of Article 82 will be found. In particular, in *IMS* the possibility of abuse would only arise where the information was indispensable; in *Microsoft*, although Microsoft's failure to supply information to the degree requested by its competitors might have added to their costs, the information was not strictly indispensable. This then seems to be a softening in approach from that taken in other cases such as *Bronner*. The degree of innovation required to show a 'new' product was not addressed; it seemed sufficient that the competitors wanted to improve existing products. Finally, there was competition on the market. It is not necessary that all competition be eliminated, although the CFI also accepted the argument that it was better to act before it was too late because the effects would be hard to reverse.

The upshot of these rulings is that there may be circumstances where Article 82 *does* appear to require a degree of compulsory licensing, at least in circumstances where a refusal to do so would eliminate the possibility of innovation, and where there are no objective justifications for this refusal. The Court in *IMS* did not indicate what sort of objective justifications there might be, nor was this clear in *Microsoft*, and it seems likely that future litigation will turn on this issue. It seems that this will largely be a matter to be resolved before the domestic courts, because the ECJ emphasised that this decision would be for the national courts to take.

It must be emphasised that such protection as is offered to protect the specific subject matter of the property concerned has been significantly reduced by the doctrine of exhaustion of rights discussed above. Any rights claimed in the context of agreements or practices within Articles 81 or 82 EC that are not permitted under this doctrine will risk infringing EU competition law. Furthermore since *Radio Telefis Eireann v Commission* (cases C–241–2/91P), it is clear that, where exceptional circumstances exist, the holder of an intellectual-property right will not be permitted to refuse to license it. Whilst *Microsoft* may indicate a softening of the test for when such circumstances exist, it is not clear whether *Microsoft* is an exceptional case, based on the company's super-dominance and the particular nature of the market.

30.3.3 Block exemption and Article 82

The fact that an industrial-property right such as an exclusive licence falls within a block exemption cannot protect an undertaking from liability under Article 82 EC if that right is abused, even where the abuse consists only in increasing an already dominant position, thereby eliminating effective competition in a substantial part of the common market (*Tetra Pak* (case T–51/89)).

30.4 Conclusions

The case law of the ECJ, in the context of both the free movement of goods and competition law, represents an uneasy compromise between the single-market principle and the need to safeguard legitimate industrial- and commercial-property rights protected under national law. Other decisions indicate a greater willingness to safeguard the interests of creativity, originality, and goodwill protected by intellectual-property law, and to encourage and reward the taking of commercial risks. This is evidenced, eg, by a more generous approach to the question of the permitted *exercise* of property rights protected under national law (eg, *EMI Electrola v Patricia* (case 341/87); *Deutsche Renault AG v Audi AG* (case C–317/91)) and by limiting the scope of the exhaustion principle (*Hag II* (case C–10/89); *IHT* (case C–9/93); but cf *Silhouette* (case 355/96) and *Sebago* (case C–173/98)), although the difficulties with patents, especially pharmaceuticals, remain (eg, *Merck v Primecrown* (cases C–267–8/95)). In the area of copyright law the Court has refused to apply the exhaustion principle to the showing of films and hiring of video cassettes (as opposed to their sale), recognising the owners' legitimate claim to benefit from repeated use (*Coditel v SA, Ciné Vog Films* (case 62/79); *Warner Brothers Inc v Cristiansen* (case 158/86)).

EU legislation has supplemented the work of the Court and now provides a framework for the protection of industrial property rights in the Union, and steady progress has been made. Member States have clearly recognised industrial- and commercial-property law as an area in which, under the subsidiarity principle of Article 5 (ex 3b) EC, the objectives 'cannot be sufficiently achieved by the Member States' without endangering the single market and can be 'better achieved by the Community'.

Nevertheless, the Court's restrictive approach to intellectual-property rights under both the competition provisions and the doctrine of exhaustion may be criticised for curtailing rather too severely the rights of the owner of intellectual-property rights. The desire to promote market integration may have swung the balance too far away from protecting intellectual-property rights. The decisions in *IMS Health* and *Microsoft* may raise concerns in that they seem to weaken further the rights of intellectual-property holders. The challenge of finding the correct balance between protecting intellectual-property rights and promoting the internal market is one that has yet to be resolved in a satisfactory manner.

FURTHER READING

Anderman, S, *EC Competition Law and Intellectual Property Rights* (Oxford University Press, 1998).

Castillo de la Torre, F, 'Trade marks and free movement of pharmaceuticals in the European Community: To partition or not to partition' [1997] 6 EIPR 304.

Stothers, C, 'Who needs intellectual property? Competition law and restrictions on parallel trade within the European Economic Area' (2005) EIPR 458–66.

Woods, L, *Free Movement of Goods and Services in the EC* (Ashgate, 2004), Ch 8.

31

Restrictions on state aid

Introduction

State aid, like state monopolies, poses a threat to the free movement of goods, since by conferring a benefit on a particular (normally domestic) undertaking or industry, it distorts competition between Member States and interferes with the functioning of the single market. With the completion of the internal market, and the intensification of competition likely to result therefrom, it is even more important that state aid to industry be strictly controlled. Indeed, in a document produced prior to the Treaty of Amsterdam (ToA) (CSE (97) 1 final), the Commission identified the need to scrutinise aid as being one of the key actions for the future of the internal market, especially as levels of aid remained high. This concern to scrutinise and control granting of aid remains high, and the Commission embarked on a process to review, in the light of the Lisbon Agenda, and to streamline the state-aid process in the interests of effective implementation of the state-aid provisions (SAAP, 2005). In the light of the *Altmark* (case C–280/00) judgment, the Commission has also produced an action plan to ease the burden of and facilitate the notification procedure.

Even if it poses a threat to the Union interest, state aid represents for Member States a vital instrument of economic and social policy, necessary to the economic health of a region or to whole sectors of the economy, particularly in times of economic difficulty and high unemployment. The support across the EU to the banking sector in 2008 is an example of such action. The regulation of state aid is a sensitive area, requiring a balancing of the interests of Member States and of the Union and recent treaty amendments re-emphasise the tension between Member States' interests and the creation of the internal market. On the one hand, the industrial provision introduced by the Treaty of the European Union (TEU) highlights the importance of not distorting competition (Article 157 (ex 130) EC; post Lisbon, 173 TFEU). On the other hand, Article 16 EC (post Lisbon, 14 TFEU) highlights the importance of public services and the need to ensure that those who are entrusted with such public services are capable of carrying out their mission. This provision may thus imply that competition concerns are not the only factors to be taken into account but that other considerations, such as social cohesion, also have a value.

The line between state aid, discriminatory taxation, and measures equivalent to charges or quantitative restrictions is often a fine one (see eg *Essent Netwerk Noerd and ors v Aluminium Delfzijl BV* (case C–206/06), discussed in Chapter 18). Therefore, although included under the competition provisions of the treaty and logically belonging there, state aid should also be considered in conjunction with the provisions relating to the free movement of goods and services.

31.2 **Structure of state-aid provisions**

31.2.1 **The framework**

The EC Treaty attempts to achieve a balance between Member States and the Union by laying down a broad prohibition on the granting of state aid 'which distorts or threatens to distort competition by favouring certain undertakings or the production of certain goods' insofar as it affects trade between Member States (Article 87(1) (ex 92(1))), subject to express and extensive derogation to protect a number of legitimate economic and social goals (Article 87(2)–(3) (ex 92(2)–(3))). Should the Lisbon Treaty come into force, Article 87 shall be renumbered Article 107 of the Treaty on the Functioning of the European Union (TFEU) and subject to small amendments.

Article 87(2) lays down the categories of aid that '*shall* be compatible with the common market'. These comprise:

(a) aid having a social character, granted to individual consumers, provided that such aid is granted without discrimination related to the origin of the products concerned

(b) aid to make good the damage caused by natural disasters or exceptional occurrences

(c) aid granted to the economy of certain areas of the Federal Republic of Germany affected by the division of Germany, insofar as such aid is required in order to compensate for the economic disadvantages caused by that division.

The Lisbon Treaty would introduce a provision which would enable the removal of Article 87(2)(c) in future. References to the 'common market' in both current Article 87(2) and (3) EC would be replaced by the phrase 'internal market' but there is no indication that this change would constitute a change in meaning.

Article 87(3) lists those aids which *may* be compatible with the common market. These comprise:

(a) aid to promote the economic development of areas where the standard of living is abnormally low or where there is serious underemployment

(b) aid to promote the execution of an important project of common European interest or to remedy a serious disturbance in the economy of a Member State

(c) aid to facilitate the development of certain economic activities or of certain economic areas, where such aid does not adversely affect trading conditions to an extent contrary to the common interest

(d) aid to promote culture and heritage conservation where such aid does not affect trading conditions and competition in the Union to an extent that is contrary to the common interest

(e) such other categories of aid as may be specified by decision of the Council acting by a qualified majority on a proposal by the Commission.

Machinery for the application of Article 87 is provided by Articles 88–9 (ex 93–4). These provisions, with small amendments, would be renumbered by Lisbon as Articles 108–9 TFEU. Under Article 88(1) EC the Commission is required, 'in cooperation with Member States', to 'keep under constant review all systems of aid existing in those states ['existing aid']'. Under Article 88(3) EC, the Commission must 'be informed, in sufficient time to enable it to submit its comments, of any plans to grant or alter aid ['new aid']'. New aid may not be put into effect until the review procedure (described at 31.2.2 below) 'has resulted in a final decision' (Article 88(3) EC). It may sometimes be difficult to establish whether a particular payment is 'existing' or 'new' aid; for example when an existing scheme is re-enacted in the same terms. This may be particularly relevant where an existing Commission decision authorises aid and a subsequent payment is regarded as falling outside such authorisation. Following *Spain v Commission* (case C–36/00), such unauthorised aid should be treated as new aid and must be assessed accordingly. Further, a national amendment to existing aid will mean that that will also be considered as 'new' aid (see, eg, *Atzeni and Others* (joined cases C–346 and 529/03)).

31.2.2 Procedural aspects

Whether acting in relation to existing aids or in response to plans for new aids, where the Commission considers state aid to be incompatible with the common market, it must act according to the procedure laid down in Article 88(2):

> If, after giving notice to the parties concerned to submit their comments, the Commission finds that aid granted (or proposed) by a state or through state resources is not compatible with the common market having regard to Article 87, or that such aid is being misused, it shall decide that the state concerned shall abolish or alter such aid within a period of time to be determined by the Commission. [Para 1.]
>
> If the state concerned does not comply with this decision within the prescribed time, the Commission or any other interested state may, in derogation from the provisions of Articles 226 and 227 [ex 169 and 170], refer the matter to the Court of Justice direct. [Para 2.]

The investigation stage effectively has two stages. The first is a preliminary assessment of new aid under Article 88(3) during which the Commission identifies if there might be a problem with the proposed aid. In such a case the full investigation under Article 88(2) is required—the second stage. In *Commission v Germany* (case 84/82), the ECJ held that the Commission must act diligently when informed by a Member State of plans to grant aid under Article 88(3) and must open the Article 88(2) procedure within a reasonable time. If the Commission fails to act within that time, the aid can be put into effect and would then be subject to the rules on existing aid. In *Commission v Germany*, it was held that a reasonable period would be two months, drawing on the time limits in Articles 230 and 232 (see also *Austria v Commission* (case C–99/98), para 32)). Member States must provide sufficient information to the Commission for it to be able to carry out an initial assessment under Article 88(3) EC, and if the Commission requests further information, Member States must provide it. The two-month time period within which the Commission has to complete its initial assessment begins to run once sufficient information has been provided by the Member State to carry out the assessment, although the information provided need not be as exhaustive as would be required for a decision to be made under Article 88(2) EC. Whether the Commission has enough information for the purposes of Article 88(3) EC is determined objectively. In *Austria v Commission* (case C–99/98), the Commission made five separate requests for additional information, with some delays between each of the requests. The ECJ agreed with Austria's argument that sufficient information had been provided in response to the third request and that the time period had begun at that point. Consequently, the Commission had run out of time to commence a full investigation under Article 88(2) EC. The result of this was that the Austrian aid could no longer be considered as 'new' aid, which could not be implemented until the final decision on its compliance with the treaty had been made, but had become 'existing aid'. (See now Council Regulation 659/99, (Procedural Regulation) below.) The Commission has identified, as part of SAAP 2005, that it needs to identify swiftly cases which do give rise to concerns and to focus its resources on a full investigation of such cases, whereas other cases should be dealt with—and closed down—swiftly.

If the Commission decides that existing aid has to be abolished or amended, it may impose a time limit within which the Member State concerned must act. Where the Commission fails to impose a time limit for the abolition or amendment of existing aid the Court has held that a two-month time limit will normally be appropriate (*Gebrüder Lorenz GmbH v Germany* (case 120/73)).

The procedures laid down in Article 88(2) must be followed and procedural guarantees such as the duty to give reasons and the right to a hearing, as general principles of EU law (see Chapter 6), must be observed. The Commission's decision must contain sufficient facts and figures to support its conclusions. Decisions issued in breach of any of these requirements may be annulled (see, eg, *William Cook v Commission* (case C–198/91)). The Court may, however, refuse to annul a decision where the outcome would have been the same in the absence of the irregularity (*Commission v France* (case 259/85)).

In exceptional circumstances a Member State may apply to the Council for a decision, which must be unanimous, that in derogation from Article 87 or 89, an aid which it is granting (existing aid) or intends to grant (new aid) is compatible with the common market. In this case where proceedings have already been initiated by the Commission under Article 88(2) they will be suspended until the Council has made its attitude known (Article 88(2), paras 3 and 4). It may be noted that under Article 87(3)(d) the Council has the power to extend the categories of aid for which dispensation is allowed.

Finally, under Article 89 the Council, acting by qualified majority on a proposal from the Commission, is empowered to make regulations concerning the application of Articles 87–8. A regulation was adopted by the Council in May 1998 to facilitate the operation of the state aid system (994/98, [1998] OJ L142/1). It provides for the use of a block exemption system by the Commission for certain categories of aid. A number of exemptions have now been adopted by the Commission under Regulation 994/98; these are discussed at 31.3.7 below. A second regulation (Regulation 659/99, Procedural Regulation) has also been enacted which codifies the existing procedural practice of the Commission together with the rulings of the ECJ ([1999] OJ L83/1). It also provides for certain enforcement powers for the Commission. These provisions include a requirement on Member States to provide an annual report on all existing aid schemes. Regulation 794/2004 was enacted, (now, as amended) based on Article 27

Regulation 659/99. It covers the form and content of notifications, introducing a new compulsory notification form, as well as dealing with the form of annual reports. It also covers time limits and interest rates due on the repayment of illegal aid.

31.2.3 Consequences of aid being granted illegally

The Commission insists on strict compliance by Member States with their obligation under Article 88(3) to inform the Commission of plans to grant or alter aid. Since Member States not infrequently flouted this requirement, or, having notified the Commission, went ahead without giving the Commission time to respond, the Commission, in a practice note issued in November 1983 ([1983] OJ C318/3), expressed its intention to 'use all the measures at its disposal' to ensure compliance by Member States with Article 88(3). Henceforth Member States which had granted aid illegally, ie without informing the Commission, or precipitately, would be required to recover such aid from recipients, and, in the agricultural sector, would be refused advance payments from the European Agriculture Guidance and Guarantee Funds (EAGGF). Since then the Commission has taken many decisions requiring the repayment of aid. In July 1990 British Aerospace was required to repay £44.4 million worth of 'sweeteners' it received when acquiring the Rover car group in 1988 (decision successfully challenged on procedural grounds in January 1992: new decision issued in March 1993 (EC Bull 3 1993 1.2.50)). In the new 'General Block Exemption' (GBER)—see below—the Commission makes it plain that where a Member State fails to comply with the 'transparency requirements', the Commission has the discretion to withdraw the benefit of the GBER for the Member State concerned *for the future*. The Commission has also issue a Notice on the Implementation of Decisions to Recover Unlawful Aid (OJ [2007] C 272), to encourage Member States to take appropriate action quickly.

Recipient businesses are required to make repayments even if the business has changed hands and the new owners have never received aid from the state (*Re aid to ENI Lanerossi* (case C–303/88)). Repayment must be made even if it will cause the recipient of aid to be wound up (*Commission v Belgium* (case 52/84)). The Member State, under its duty of cooperation in Article 10 (ex 5) EC, on encountering difficulties in obtaining repayment should inform the Commission of them, together with suggestions for amendments to the decision requiring repayment so as to solve the problem. Further, in *TWD Textilwerke Deggendorf GmbH v Commission* (cases T–244 and 486/93), the Court of First Instance (CFI) approved the Commission's stance according to which implementation of a decision approving the payment of lawful aid was conditional on repayment of earlier illegal aid. This decision strengthens the Commission's hand, but weaknesses remain in the system for recovery of aid. Most notably, there is the problem that the recipient of unlawful aid retains the benefit of that aid until the decision is made requiring repayment. The decision-making process can take a considerable time and so the benefit illicitly obtained can be considerable. To counterbalance this benefit, however, the Commission may request the payment of interest running from the date the enterprise received the aid (eg, *Siemens SA v Commission* (case T–459/93)) (see now Regulation 794/2004, as amended by Regulation 271/2008 which provides for the calculation of interest on unrecovered aid).

Of course, where it is objectively impossible to recover aid, the Member States cannot be expected to do so (*Commission v Spain* (Case C–177/06), para 46). Even where the Member State argues that repayment is impossible, this argument cannot be raised without prior warning (*Commission v Italy* (case C–349/93)). Additionally, Article 14 of the Procedural Regulation identifies two exceptions to the rule that the Commission will require repayment of illegal aid:

(a) situations where ordering the recovery would be contrary to a general principle of law (Article 14(1))

(b) the expiry of the ten year limitation period under Article 15 of the Procedural Regulation.

In a number of cases a decision requiring repayment has been challenged on the grounds of breach of the claimant's legitimate expectations. In *RSV Maschinefabrieken & Scheepswerven NV v Commission* (case 223/85), a Commission decision ordering repayment of aid granted to RSV to write off financial losses was annulled at the suit of the recipient, since the decision was issued, without justification for the delay, some 26 months after the aid had been granted. However, in *Commission v Germany* (case C–5/89), the Court, endorsing its decision in *Commission v Germany* (case 94/87), held that save in exceptional circumstances firms in receipt of state aid could not have legitimate expectations concerning the lawfulness of aid unless it had been granted in accordance with the procedures of the then Article 93 (now 88). The diligent recipient of aid would make sure that these procedures had been complied with. This reasoning applies even if there has been significant delay between the granting of the (illegal) aid and the decision that the aid is illegal. Nor could the Member State plead the legitimate expectations of recipients in order to evade its obligation to comply with the Commission's decision requiring the recovery of aid. In *Commission v France* (case C–261/99), the ECJ emphasised that a Member State must inform the Commission if there are difficulties in recovering illegal aid. However, a Member State cannot bring an action for annulment of the relevant Commission decision to avoid the obligation to recover illegal aid and such aid must be recovered even if the annulment action is still pending.

To ensure 'transparency' the Commission now publishes an annual survey of its aid proceedings in the *Official Journal*, and warns potential recipients of the legal consequences of repayment decisions. It also publishes a section on state aids in its annual report on competition policy. In the light of these practices a defence based on legitimate expectations is only likely to succeed in exceptional circumstances (see, eg, *RSV* (case 223/85)).

Thus all aids granted by Member States are subject either to the dispensation of the Council, or, more normally, the strict supervision and control of the Commission, with ultimate recourse to the Court, either in annulment proceedings under Article 230 EC (see Chapter 12) or in proceedings under Article 88(2) (see 31.6 below). Note that in a review action, where the Commission has a wide discretion (such as in the assessment of the grounds of exception under Article 87(3)), the ECJ will not substitute its assessment for that of the Commission. It is limited to verifying whether the Commission's assessment of the case is 'vitiated by a manifest error or misuse of powers' (eg, *Atzeni* (joined cases C–346 and 529/03), para 84).

31.3 **Meaning of state aid**

No definition of state aid is given in the treaty but it has been broadly construed by the Commission and the European Courts. State aid has been held to comprise any advantages granted directly or indirectly through state resources. The Commission suggested in its Reports on Competition Policy that four cumulative elements must be shown to satisfy the test for state aid:

(a) the measure must be specific rather than general in nature

(b) it must grant an advantage to an undertaking

(c) the aid must come from state resources and

(d) the advantage must distort competition and have an effect on interstate trade.

These have been restated by the ECJ to be: intervention by the state or through state resources; the intervention must be liable to affect trade between Member States; it must confer an advantage on the recipient; and it must distort or threaten to distort competition (*Altmark* (case C–280/00), para 75; *Pearle and ors* (case C–345/02), para 32). These cover similar ground to the Commission's criteria, though the ECJ seems to see the requirements of distortion of competition and having an effect on interstate trade as separate issues. All elements must be shown for the state measure to fall within the definition of aid (see, eg, *Commission v Belgium* (Tubemeuse) (joined cases C–278–80/92)).

31.3.1 **Specificity**

For a measure to be classified as state aid, it must assist only certain firms or sectors: general economic policy remains a matter for the Member States. The concept does not include a system of minimum prices, as this is not an advantage granted to favour an undertaking or to benefit certain goods and will normally be applied to all goods irrespective of origin. (The latter will, however, be judged under Article 28 (ex 30)—see *van Tiggele* (case 82/77), discussed in Chapter 19.) State aid also does not include special treatment for small enterprises in the form of exemption from obligations arising from social protection (*Kirsammer-Hack v Nurhan Sidal* (case C–189/91)). It follows that, although certain measures of tax or social policy could give a competitive edge to undertakings established in a given Member State (for example, by lower employment costs), they do not fall within the state aid rules.

It is, however, sometimes difficult to identify the boundary between the two categories. In the *Maribel bis/ter case* (*Belgium v Commission* (case C–75/97)), for example, the Commission decided that a Belgian law which provided for additional reductions in social-security costs constituted aid because it benefited firms most exposed to international competition. Further, for a measure to be considered general, the Member State should have no discretionary power enabling it to vary the application of a measure depending on who was the beneficiary of the measure, even when the criteria to be taken into consideration were objective factors defined by law (*France v Commission (Kimberly Clark Sopalin)* (case C–241/94)). Thus, in the *DMT* case (case C–256/97), the ECJ held that the degree of discretion given to the body which had responsibility for chasing up social-security payments from employers and employees meant that, although the policy was phrased in general terms, in practice it turned into aid aimed at specific companies, in that they gained a benefit. Thus the same issue can be analysed from different perspectives (see discussion of 'advantage' at 31.3.2 below).

31.3.2 **Advantage to a firm**

To constitute state aid, a benefit must be conferred. Aid falling within the terms of Article 87(1) may be 'in any form whatsoever'. Thus aid can include, as well as actual payments, preferential tax treatment, preferential interest rates, grants to cover redundancy costs, investment grants and subsidies, financial incentives to privatisation (eg, British Aerospace), or special prices for land, plant or power (eg, *Kwekerij Gebroeders van der Kooy* (cases 67, 68, and 70/85), power company supplying natural gas at special reduced prices to the horticulture industry). In *Syndicat Français de l'Express International* (SFEI) *v La Poste* (case C–39/94), the ECJ defined a state aid as including not only benefits such as subsidies, but also interventions which might mitigate the charges normally included in the budgets of an undertaking and which are therefore of the same character and have the same effect as subsidies. When determining whether state aid exists, the question relates not to the causes or aims of state intervention; instead the test is an objective one, concerned with the effects of such an intervention (see, eg, *Italy v Commission (re aid to the textile industry)* (case 173/73), *Banco de Credito Industrial SA v Ayuntamiento de Valencia* (case C–387/92) and *Ladbroke Racing Ltd v Commission* (case T–67/94)).

To constitute state aid, the advantage must be granted for no consideration or countervailing benefit (*Denkavit* (case 61/79)). It will include injections of capital by a public investor which disregard any prospect of profitability (*Re aid to ENI Lanerosse* (case C–303/88)). The ECJ has held that aid exists where the recipient undertaking receives an economic advantage which it would not have obtained under normal market conditions (*SFEI and ors* (case C–39/94) para 60), The Court has also described aid as existing when state support has no objective commercial justification. The test of commercial justification is sometimes referred to as the hypothetical investor test. *Ryanair v Commission* (case T–196/04) concerned the agreement between the regional Walloon government and Ryanair, according to which Ryanair received a discount on the normal airport charges; this agreement was not notified. The Commission investigated and had first to assess whether this constituted aid. Rather than applying the market-investor test, the Commission took the view that in the fixing of landing charges, the Walloon government was exercising its legislative and regulatory competence and that this was not an economic activity that could be assessed by reference to the private-investor principle. Rather, the Walloon government exercised its public powers in a discriminatory manner. The CFI disagreed with this assessment. While the CFI agreed that application of the private-investor principle should not be used where the state acts as a public authority, here the Walloon government was operating in the economic sphere. The market-investor test should have been used. In the former situation, however, the conduct of the state should not be compared to that of an operator or private-investor in a market economy.

The use of the market-investor test is not entirely unproblematic, as it does raise the question of what normal investor behaviour would be. The ECJ has noted that this is a complex economic assessment in which the Commission has wide discretion (*DSG v Commission* (Case C–323/00P)) and the grounds of judicial review are therefore limited. In particular, the court cannot substitute its own economic decision for that of the Commission. If commercial justification does, however, exist then the fact that the support also fulfils a political purpose will not render it 'aid' within Article 87 (*Belgium v Commission* (case C–56/93)—special tariff rates to large Dutch industrial producers of ammonia by a company in which the Netherlands government had a 50 per cent holding justified on commercial grounds).

31.3.3 Public services and services of general economic interest

A controversial question which has occupied the ECJ—the Member States—is whether a financial advantage which could be characterised as compensation for a public-service obligation should be treated as state aid. Although Article 16 EC, introduced by the ToA, puts greater emphasis on ensuring that services of general economic interest can 'fulfil their missions', this is expressed to be without prejudice to Articles 73 and 86–7. Following Lisbon, should that treaty come into force, this provision will be renumbered Article 14 TFEU, but it will essentially stay the same, although it will permit the enactment of secondary legislation. The scope of this article remains uncertain, and, despite a number of protocols on the subject of public services, importantly, it does not suggest that public services cannot be subject to Article 87. The jurisprudence of the ECJ has been confused in this respect, as illustrated by two key cases.

In *Ferring SA v Agence centrale des organismes de securite sociale (ACOSS)* (case C–53/00), a pharmaceutical laboratory had been taxed on direct sales to pharmacies, whereas wholesale distributors were not taxed at all. Wholesalers were under a public-service obligation to ensure a sufficient supply of pharmaceuticals. Their relief from tax liability on direct sales to pharmacies by other suppliers could be regarded as compensation for the discharge of their public service obligation. Consequently, such differential treatment as regards taxation would not constitute state aid provided that the tax imposed on pharmaceutical laboratories corresponded to the cost actually incurred by wholesale distributors. However, to the extent that the financial advantage resulting from tax relief exceeds the cost incurred, it would constitute state aid within the scope of Article 87(1).

However, in *Altmark Trans GmBH v Nahverkehrsgesellschaft Altmark GmBH* (case C–280/00), Advocate-General Leger argued (in a rare second opinion given in the wake of the *Ferring* judgment) in the context of subsidies paid to public-transport providers, that the Court should not follow *Ferring*. He proposed that a distinction be drawn between the state as an economic operator who purchases goods or services on its own account and the state as an 'acquirer' of services that are made available directly to the public. In the former situation, there would only be state aid if the price paid exceeded the market price. In the context of public services, however, this approach should not be adopted, and any payments should be regarded as state aid. To do otherwise would result in conflating the question of whether aid is provided and whether the payment in question is compatible with the common market. Consequently, financial advantages granted by a Member State to compensate for the cost of a public service obligation *should* be regarded as state aid.

The argument that the advantage merely compensates for the additional cost incurred by the undertaking in providing the service should be taken into account in establishing whether the aid is compatible with the common market.

It seems that adopting Advocate-General Leger's approach would produce the same substantive outcome in *Ferring* that the tax advantage is not illegal. However, there is an important underlying issue of principle, which is the question of whether *any* form of state financial support to providers of public services should be subject to the state aid rules, or whether there are payments which should be regarded as falling outside the scope of Article 87(1) altogether. If Article 87(1) does apply, then it may be possible to rely either on Article 88, or on Article 86(2), which would enable the disapplication of the competition provisions (see Chapter 29), including Article 87, for services of general economic interest (telecommunications, postal, and certain transport services as well as public-service broadcasters) if their application would obstruct the performance, in law or in fact, of the particular task assigned to them. However, it is far from clear how exactly these various provisions interrelate, and clarification in this regard is now needed. The ECJ disagreed with A-G Leger, holding that where a financial measure is compensation for a public services obligation undertaken by the recipient, there is no advantage (and therefore no state aid), provided that:

(i)   the recipient has a clearly defined public service obligation to discharge
(ii) there is an objective and transparent system, established in advance, for calculating compensation
(iii) the compensation does not exceed the costs incurred in discharging the obligation, taking account of relevant receipts and a reasonable profit margin
(iv) where the provider is not chosen through public procurement procedures, the level of compensation is determined with reference to the costs which a typical undertaking would incur.

All four conditions must be satisfied to take the payment outside the state-aid provisions.

It might be argued that the adoption of the *Altmark* test gives the Member States greater scope for providing public services as they see fit, since *Altmark* constitutes a move away from the hypothetical investor test. At another level, as the Commission has noted, it is likely to result in an increased burden for Member States to notify, as few public services have been awarded via a public-tender process. Most public-service provision will not therefore satisfy the *Altmark* test and will be classified as aid. The *Altmark* case has been considered in a case concerning an Irish plan for the opening up of the Irish private medical-insurance market (*BUPA v Commission* (case T–289/03)). Central to the plan was a risk equalisation scheme according to which insurers which had a lower than average risk profile would pay a levy which would be redistributed to those insurers with a higher than average risk profile. Additionally, Irish regulations specified that insurers were not allowed to refuse applications and they had to provide lifetime cover. The effect of the plan was that the money went from new market entrants to the former incumbent operator. The Irish government notified the scheme and the Commission decided not to raise any objections on the basis that there was no state aid as the payment compensates for an obligation. BUPA challenged this decision before the CFI which upheld the Commission's decision in a ruling that seemed to take a very broad approach to the satisfaction of the criteria. In particular, the CFI noted that as the regards the third element of *Altmark*, parameters for compensation, a strict application of that test would undermine the Irish government's ability to set up the scheme at all and, in the view of the CFI, the compensation was not excessive. The CFI also dismissed the fourth test, arguing that the risk equalisation scheme was not intended to compensate for an identified cost, so that test could not be applied.

As a result of the judgment in *Altmark*, the Commission has adopted a state-aid action plan (see Commission Competition Policy Newsletter (2005) 2, p 4 *et seq*), which consists of three main strands: a Commission decision, a framework, and a proposed modification of the Transparency Directive (see further below). The Commission decision contains what is effectively a *de minimis* exception for small aid as well as excluding hospitals and social housing from the obligation to notify, in both cases provided there is no over-compensation. This is separate from the *de minimis* exception under the state-aid rules generally. The framework explains how the Commission will assess compatibility with the state-aid rules (Communication on Services of General Economic Interest (SGEIs)), which is effectively a codification of the Commission's existing practice under Article 86(2) EC (see further below and Chapter 28). The modification of the Transparency Directive is to ensure that the public service providers' accounts provide a clear separation of public service costs and costs for commercial services.

31.3.4 Origin of resources

To fall within the state-aid rules, the resources benefiting the undertaking must come from state resources, whether directly or indirectly. Aid may be granted through any central or local government body, or any agency subject to the control of the state. No distinction is made between aid granted directly by the state or by public or even private bodies established and operated by it to administer that aid (*Steinike und Weinleg* (case 78/76)). It is not necessary that the aid be paid directly out of public funds as long as the state plays a part in initiating or approving the aid. In *Kwekerij Gebroeders van der Kooy BV v Commission* (cases 67–8 and 70/85), a power company created under private law but controlled by the state through a 50 per cent shareholding, and whose prices were subject to government control, was held to be equivalent to the state for the purpose of establishing state aid. In *Syndicat Français de l'Express (SFEI) v La Poste* (case C–39/94), the ECJ held that the provision of logistical or commercial support by a public undertaking (La Poste) to a private subsidiary which was engaged in an activity open to free competition, when that subsidiary gave no counter consideration, constituted aid.

In contrast, in *Firma Sloman Neptun Schiffahrts AG v Seebetriebsrat Bodo Ziesemer of Sloman Neptun Schiffahrts AG* (cases C–72–3/91), the ECJ held that rules which permitted wages lower than the German minimum to be paid to foreign seamen did not constitute state aid. Although the lower wages costs resulting from the German rules benefited the boat companies, this was not aid for these purposes, as the advantage did not originate from state resources. In a similar vein, *Pearle* (case (C–345/02) clarifies the limits of *Steinike and Weileg*. *Pearle* concerned a trade association's right to raise levies from its members to pay for an advertising campaign.

The power to pass byelaws, including that on which the levy was based, was approved by the relevant ministry, as was its general power to organise and develop its sector of activity. *Pearle* challenged the levy on the basis of *Steinike and Weinleg*, arguing that the state's involvement constituted state aid, via its approval of the trade association and its byelaws. The ECJ rejected this argument, stating the requirement of state resources has two elements: direct or indirect use of state resources; and the aid is imputable to the state. Here the financing is not made available though state resources and, given that the advertising was funded by reference to the advantage each member of the association got from the advertising campaign, is no advantage. By contrast, *Steinicke and Weinleg* had involved state subsidy as well as members' contributions. *Steinicke and Weinleg* had also involved the implementation of government policy, thus going to the second element of the test. In *Pearle*, the trade association was implementing its own policy, not that of the government. There was thus no aid.

31.3.5 Distortion of competition

To constitute state aid in breach of Article 87, the benefit must distort or threaten competition by favouring certain undertakings or the production of certain goods. Given the tendency to use the hypothetical market-investor test—ie, identify whether a firm receives a benefit by reference to what a normal market operator would not do—if an advantage is found then it will, almost by definition, distort competition. Further, in *Vlaams Gewest v Commission* (case T–214/95), the CFI held that even small amounts of aid would distort competition for the purposes of this provision. It has been noted that even small amounts of aid can be significant in markets where there are a large number of competitors.

Although the courts have taken this stringent view, the Commission seems to have taken a more generous approach. The Commission, under its powers in Regulation 994/88, has adopted a *de minimis* exception for small amounts of aid, thus giving a legislative basis for its approach to small amounts of aid which is now found in Commission Regulation 1998/2006 ([2006] OJ L 379). This replaces a previous regulation. The 2006 *de minimis* regulation increases the ceiling for acceptable aid to 200,000 from the previous limit of 100,000 gross over any period of three years. In contrast to the previous regime, the 2006 *de minimis* regulation applies to the transport sector and to the processing and marketing of agricultural products, although the limit for the transport sector will be limited to 100 000. Aid is limited to types of aid where it is possible to determine the precise amount of aid in advance (transparent aid).

31.3.6 Impact on interstate trade

Aid must be capable of affecting trade between Member States. Many of the considerations under this heading are similar to those which relate to assessing distortion of competition. State aid will be deemed to affect trade between Member States if the beneficiary of aid competes with enterprises in other Member States, even if it does not export to those states. The argument is that where aid is given in a Member State to an undertaking, the aid might make it harder for a competitor in another Member State to break into the national market. Thus, the courts focus on the potential impact rather than any actual quantified impact. Even a small amount of aid may affect trade between Member States if there is strong competition in the relevant sector (*ENI Lanerossi* (case C–303/88); see also *Vlaams Gewest v Commission* (case T–214/95)).

31.3.7 Exemptions and guidelines

The Commission issued a number of guidelines regarding the application of the state-aid rules, for example:

- Aid for climate change and for other environmental protection
- Aid for research and development and innovation
- Aid for the rescue and restructuring of firms in difficulty
- Aid for small and medium-sized enterprises
- Aid to employment
- Training aid
- Aid for risk capital
- Aid for services of general economic interest.

The guidance took various forms: 'framework', 'guideline', or 'block exemption regulations' (BER). In order to simplify matters, in line with the better regulation initiative, the Commission has recently introduced a 'General Block Exemption' (GBER) which replaces the previous block exemptions (Article 1(3) GBER). GBER is divided into three parts: the first concerns procedures and common definitions; the second contains the substantive terms of the block exemptions; and the third deals with transitional matters. The objective was to introduce common definitions of standards concepts; uniform requirements for transparency and monitoring; and to avoid the need to cross-refer to other documents to understand the terms of the block exemptions. The terms of GBER are largely based on the terms of the previous BERs. Substantively the five block exemptions (small- and medium-sized enterprises, research and development for small and medium sized enterprises, employment aid, training aid, and regional aid) previously permitted are now contained in Part II of GBER, together with some new areas where block exemptions may be granted: environmental aid, aid in the form of risk capital, and research and development in favour of large enterprises. Previously this was limited to small- and medium-sized enterprises. GBER does not cover aid which is already subject to a recovery order, so as to avoid it being used to circumvent state aid rules. It does not apply to 'enterprises in difficulty'. This is in line with the Commission's long-standing policy concerning enterprises in difficulty, as defined in the rescue and restructuring guidelines. Likewise, it all does not apply to ad hoc aid to large enterprises. This is due to the fact that the 'incentive effect' (see below) of these types of measures is often difficult to establish.

As part of its simplification process, the cumulative notification criteria from previous BERs have been replaced with one figure, which is the maximum that the block exemption will permit in regard to a particular type of aid. The financial ceilings on the permissible amount of aid have also been substantially raised as compared to the previous BERs, meaning that larger amounts of individual aid may be provided without advance notification to the Commission. Where no ceiling is specified by Article 6 GBER, any amount of aid may be granted (provided it meets the other substantive requirements). For aid granted to large undertakings, the incentive effect of the aid must be demonstrated as, in the view of the Commission, if the aid does not change the behaviour of the recipient companies, the aid cannot contribute to the furthering of Union objectives, as set out in Article 87(3) of the treaty. In support of this approach, Recital 28 GBER states:

> In order to ensure that the aid is necessary and acts as an incentive to develop further activities or projects, this Regulation should not apply to aid for activities in which the beneficiary would already engage under market conditions alone.

31.4 **Policy of the Commission**

Whether aid is new or existing, whether it falls allegedly within Article 87(2)–(3), apart from the exceptional case under Articles 87(3)(d) and 88(2), which will be decided by the Council, it is the Commission, subject to final adjudication by the Court, which decides whether aid is in fact compatible with EU law. Applicants may thus challenge the Commission's decision that a particular payment or subsidy did (or did not) constitute state aid (see, eg, *Ladbroke Racing Ltd v Commission* (case T–67/94)); or whether it falls within any exception. Clearly if it falls squarely within Article 87(2), it must be allowed. If it falls within the permitted exceptions of Article 87(3)(a)–(c) the Commission has a discretion, both in permitting the exemption and in determining its scope (*Exécutif régional wallon v Commission* (case 67/87), modernisation aid granted to Glaverbel (Belgian glass manufacturers) not an important project of common European interest under the then Article 92(3)(b); to constitute the latter it must form part of a transnational European programme).

The exercise of this discretion, as the Court commented in *Philip Morris Holland BV v Commission* (case 730/79) involves economic, political, and social assessments which must be made in the EU context, the determining factor being the EU interest. The guiding principle that the Commission has emphasised since 2005, is less and better-targeted state aid, the acceptability of which will be assessed using an economic approach (both as to the existence of aid in the first place, and as regards whether it falls within one of the exemptions). As a general rule aid will only be allowed if it promotes recognised Union as opposed to national objectives and does not frustrate progress towards the single market (*20th Report on Competition Policy*). The Commission has restated that it will in future focus on the 'social welfare of the EU', which, it claims, is found in the references in Article 87 to the 'common interest'. As noted above, the Court will question the exercise of the Commission's discretion only in extreme cases.

In permitting *regional* aid under Article 87(3)(a) (to counter underemployment and to assist development), the Commission looks not to national levels of employment and income but to the standard of the Union as a whole. As a result eligibility for such benefit will depend on the state's position relative to the Union average. The Commission has also, in the interests of transparency, issued guidelines on national regional aid, in which it outlines circumstances in which aid will be considered to be in the Union interest. In so doing, it replaces a significant number of heterogeneous documents previously covering this area. This is part of a general trend to consolidate the guidance and block exemptions in the area of state aid generally.

In allowing *sectoral aid* (eg, to agriculture, transport, particular industries) under Article 87(3)(c), the Commission's main concern is to prevent the grant of state aid from exacerbating existing problems or from transferring them from one state to another. The Commission will not allow aid that strengthens the power of an undertaking compared with other undertakings competing in intra-Union trade. Thus, in *Philip Morris* the claimant failed to obtain the annulment of a Commission decision refusing to allow the Dutch government to grant aid to increase the production capacity of a Dutch cigarette manufacturer, who was in competition in Europe with a number of other manufacturers.

Nor will the Commission allow Member States to 'shore up obsolete structures' (*16th General Report*, 1982, p 104), to grant relief to rescue firms which are incapable of adjusting to conditions of competition (*15th Report on Competition Policy*, 1981, p 103). Aid will only be permitted which will lead to sound economic structures to enable an industry to become competitive, to resolve underlying problems, not to postpone or shift the solution. Thus the recent amendments to the guidelines on restructuring aid have operated to limit the circumstances in which restructuring aid may be granted.

The majority of aids, notably regional and sectoral aids—for example, aids to the textile industry, to shipbuilding and (prior to the TEU) to the film industry—have been granted under Article 87(3)(c) 'to facilitate the development of certain economic activities or of certain economic areas'. Regional aids, ie national as opposed to EU aid granted pursuant to its regional policy, have been subject to progressive coordination since the first formal guidelines were adopted in 1971 (First Resolution on Regional Aids, (1971) JO C111/1).

Exceptions under Article 87(3)(b) must relate to projects of common *European*, as opposed to national interest. Aid has been permitted under this head to enable firms to bring their plant into line with environmental standards (see Commission Guidelines on state Aid for Environmental Protection [2001] OJ C37/3). Most recently, the Commission has accepted temporary aid being granted to many banks across Europe to reassure the financial markets as to those banks' financial stability. The Commission determined that the particular circumstances applying to the financial sector in the context of the 'current exceptional crisis' could be considered to constitute a serious disturbance in the economy of a Member State within the meaning of the state-aid rules (Article 87(3)(b)). Article 87(3)(d) providing for the granting of aid to promote culture and heritage conservation, was introduced by the TEU in 1992. The film industry, a former beneficiary under subpara (3)(c), has been dealt with since the TEU under this provision. In addition, an amendment to Article 159 (ex 130b) EC (post Lisbon, 175 TFEU), also introduced by the TEU, will require decisions on state aid to take greater account of the need to strengthen economic and social cohesion (see Commission's Report on Competition Policy 1992 and ECOSOC resolution on 24th Report on Competition ([1996] OJ C39/79)).

Since German unification there is no longer any justification for continuing to subsidise areas of East Germany under Article 87(2)(c), although the Commission has recognised that some state aid will be necessary to ease East Germany's transition to a market economy. As noted, this provision may be removed should Lisbon come into force.

General aids as opposed to 'special' aids normally fall outside Article 87. General schemes may exceptionally be permitted for short periods to counter 'a serious disturbance in the economy of a Member State' (Article 87(3)(b)).

The Commission has taken the view that the provisions on state aids apply to aid granted to both private and public undertakings. It has issued directives on the transparency of relations between Member States and public undertakings (now codified as Commission Directive 2006/111/EC on the transparency of financial relations between Member States and public undertakings as well as on financial transparency within certain undertakings ([2006] OJ L 318/17)) requiring Member States to ensure that information regarding financial relations between public authorities and Member States be kept at the disposal of the Commission for a five-year period and to supply such information. In a communication based on the earlier version of this directive issued in 1991 ([1991] OJ C273/2), the Commission expressed its concern at the volume of aid granted by states to public undertakings which had not been notified under the then Article 93(3) (3.5 billion between 1985 and 1990). It stressed the need for the development of a policy for public undertakings, which had not hitherto been sufficiently subject to state-aid disciplines. Aid granted to public undertakings in the manufacturing sector *must* be notified in advance to the Commission. This communication was annulled on procedural grounds in 1993, but, the concerns remain. As a result, the Commission plans not only more-effective systems to direct state aid to the areas where it will do the most good (or the least harm) and the use of exemptions so that the Commission can focus on the more difficult cases, but to take steps to ensure that illegal aid is recovered promptly.

31.5 Relationship between state aid and other provisions of the treaty

31.5.1 Article 28 (ex 30) EC

State aid that is permitted under Article 87 cannot in itself fall within Article 28 (post Lisbon, 34 TFEU). To that extent the provisions are mutually exclusive. However, some aspects of state aid, not necessary for the attainment of its object, may be incompatible with other provisions of the treaty, even though they may not invalidate the aid as a whole (*Ianelli & Volpi SpA v Ditta Paola Meroni* (case 74/76)). Therefore, if the aid goes beyond what is necessary to achieve a particular legitimate objective it may infringe Article 28; similarly if it is applied to activities which are incompatible with Article 28 (eg, a 'Buy Irish' campaign sponsored by the Irish Goods Council: *Commission v Ireland* (case 249/81)).

31.5.2 Article 31 (ex 37) EC

On the same principle the operations of a state-owned monopoly are not exempt from Article 31 (post Lisbon, 37 TFEU) by reason of the fact that they may classify as aids. Even when the activities of a state monopoly are linked with a grant to producers subject to the monopoly they must still comply with the non-discrimination requirements of Article 31 (*Ianelli & Volpi SpA v Ditta Paolo Meroni* (case 74/76)).

31.5.3 **Article 81 (ex 85) EC**

Assessment under Article 88 EC to determine the compatibility of aid with the common market and the exemption from liability under the competition provisions of Article 81(1) provided by Article 81(3) are separate procedures. A favourable determination under one will therefore not preclude an unfavourable decision under the other.

31.5.4 **Article 86 (ex 90)**

As can be seen in Chapter 29, this provision prohibits rules contrary to the provisions of the treaty, especially the competition provisions, being maintained in force in respect of 'public undertakings and those to which Member States have granted special or exclusive rights' (Article 86(1)). Article 86(2), however, provides an exception to this general statement for 'Undertakings entrusted with the operation of services of general economic interest or having the character of a revenue-producing monopoly', which shall be subject to the treaty rules only insofar as their application 'does not obstruct the performance . . . of the particular tasks assigned to them'. The development of trade, however, must not be affected to such an extent as would be contrary to the interests of the EU (Article 86(2) EC). This exception in Article 86(2) could overlap with the state-aid rules thereby exempting those undertakings falling within Article 86(2) from state-aid rules. Although the question was raised in *Banco de Crédito Industrial SA v Ayuntamiento de Valencia* (case C–387/92), the ECJ did not address the issue. The Commission subsequently, made a couple of decisions exempting public-service broadcasters such as the BBC on this basis and has issued guidelines on public service broadcasting (see [2001] OJ C320/5). This indicated that Article 86(2) could be used in relation to state aid, thus providing an additional form of exemption for some cases of aid, and subsequent case law such as *Altmark* (case C–280/00) and *BUPA v Commission* (case T–289/03) reaffirms this approach. As we have seen (at 31.3.3 above), the Commission has issued a Communication on Services of General Economic Interest, setting out its approach in relation to state aid and Article 86(2) (C(2005) 2673). The Commission has also issued a communication on 'Services of general interest, including social services of general interest: a new European commitment' (COM (2007) 725 final).

31.6 **Enforcement by individuals**

Articles 87 and 89, both being dependent on the exercise of discretion by Union institutions, are not directly effective (*Ianelli & Volpi SpA v Ditta Paola Meroni* (case 74/76)). So, in the absence of a decision from the Commission or ECJ, a national court has no power to decide whether a state aid is compatible with Article 87. However, the procedural obligations of Article 88(3) are directly effective and, as such, as the Commission pointed out in its practice note of 1983, are amenable to assessment by national courts. The fact that the Commission is investigating the matter does not remove the obligation from the national courts. Thus an individual, provided he has *locus standi* under national law, may challenge in his domestic courts a grant of aid by national authorities in breach of Article 88(3). The Commission issued a Notice on Cooperation between National Courts and the Commission in the State Aid Field ([1995] OJ C312/7). This establishes machinery whereby national courts faced with a potential state aid may seek assistance from the Commission on whether it should be characterised as such. The Commission has recently updated this by a Commission Notice on Enforcement by National Courts (25 February 2009). Further, the Commission has also issued guidelines concerning aid in certain sectors, such as the environment ([2001] OJ C37/3) and employment ([1995] OJ C334). Also, as the ECJ noted in *Ianelli & Volpi SpA v Ditta Paolo Meroni*, if Article 87 is invoked before domestic courts in the context of directly effective provisions such as Article 28 and Article 31, questions relating to state aid may, along with other questions, be referred to the ECJ for preliminary ruling.

31.6.1 Challenge to aid granted

The case of *Syndicat Français de l'Express International v La Poste* (case C–39/94) illustrates the relationship between Articles 87 and 88(3). The case concerned a claim for compensation for losses suffered by the applicant, a competitor in the provision of postal services, resulting from alleged state aid granted to La Poste without notification to the Commission, in breach of Article 88(3). The matter had been under consideration by the Commission for two years, following a complaint by SFEI, during which time the Commission had neither adopted a position nor taken a final decision. Hence SFEI's action before the French courts seeking, inter alia, compensation in respect of the alleged breach. The French court sought clarification on a number of questions:

(a) whether the recovery of state aid was the only way of guaranteeing the effectiveness of Article 88(3) or whether parties such as the applicant who had suffered loss as a result of the alleged aid could recover compensation in their national court in respect of breaches of that article and

(b) whether, when the matter is under investigation by the Commission, a national court is under an obligation to declare its lack of jurisdiction or

(c) if it has declared jurisdiction, it is obliged to stay proceedings until the Commission takes a decision.

The ECJ's reply was unequivocal. The involvement of national courts is the result of the direct effects of Article 88(3). The initiation of procedures before the Commission cannot release national courts from their duty to safeguard the rights of individuals in the event of a breach of the notification requirement. Faced with an alleged breach a national court may have to interpret the concept of aid contained in Article 87 to determine whether a state measure introduced without notification ought to have been subject to that procedure. In doing so it may refer to the ECJ for an interpretation of that article. Where there is a lapse of time it will be for the national court to decide if it is necessary to order interim relief such as the suspension of measures to safeguard the interest of parties. Although the ECJ did not rule specifically on the question of damages, it is submitted that where it is necessary to award damages to safeguard individuals' rights under Article 88(3) a national court may do so (for example, the applicants in *Atzeni* (joined cases C–346 and 529/03), discussed above, claimed damages, but were unsuccessful—their claim failed on other grounds; see *CELF v Ministre de la Culture et de La Communication*)). Arguably, it may even, following *Antonissen* (case C–393/96 P(R)), order interim compensation (see further Chapter 8). The Commission has suggested that an action may lie against the Member State for state liability (Commission Notice on Enforcement), but EU law cannot be the basis of an action against a beneficiary.

In proceedings before national courts, actions by national authorities taken in breach of Article 88(3) cannot be legalised by a subsequent finding by the Commission that the aid is compatible with EU law (*Fédération Nationale du Commerce Extérieur des Produits Alimentaires v France* (case C–354/90)). However, a failure to notify the granting of aid does not automatically lead to nullity (*France v Commission* (case C–301/87)).

31.6.2 Review of Commission decisions on state aid

Once a decision about state aid has been issued, a recipient or potential recipient may challenge that decision before the ECJ under Article 230 EC; however, where a decision affects a whole industry, the Court has held that individual members have no standing to sue, although an organisation created to represent those members, if it took part in the proceedings relating to the granting of aid, may (*Kwekerij Gebruders van der Kooy* (cases 67–8 and 70/85)). In addition, any interested party who suspects that aid is being granted in breach of Article 87 may complain to the Commission and request the Commission to act, and, provided he acts in time, may challenge any action or inaction on the part of the Commission resulting from his complaint (*Irish Cement Ltd v Commission* (case 166/86), see Chapters 12 and 13). It is not just the originator of the complaint who can have standing to bring an action under these articles. The ECJ has held that, because of the lack of transparency and the lack of a role for third parties under Article 88(3), it is not necessary for third parties to show participation in the Commission investigation or to have been substantially effected by the measure to have standing to challenge a Commission decision concerning state aid. A competitor of the recipient of the aid could have standing (*William Cook plc v Commission* (case C–198/91) and *Matra SA v Commission* (case C–225/91R)). In *ASPEC v Commission* (case T–435/93), the CFI held that the impact of a decision on the competitive environment of a market together with the small number of producers in that market would give the competing producers sufficient standing to challenge that decision. Moreover, in *Aktionsgemeinschaft Recht und Eigentum eV v Commission* (case T–114/00), the CFI held that an association formed to protect the collective interests of its members had *locus standi* under Article 230 EC to bring an action for the annulment of a Commission decision not to instigate the formal procedure under Article 88(2) EC on behalf of those members who would have been parties concerned within the meaning of Article 88(2) EC and would be individually concerned within the meaning of Article 230 EC.

Any person seeking to challenge a decision concerning state aid, whether to himself or to another party, would be wise, where he has *locus standi*, to proceed quickly under Article 230 since following the decision of the Court in *TWD Textilwerke Deggendorf GmbH v Germany* (case C–188/92) there may be difficulties in obtaining relief under the alternative route to annulment provided by Article 234.

Where repayment of aid is ordered, recovery will be governed by the domestic law of the state in question, provided that the rules do not render recovery excessively difficult or impossible in practice (*Commission v Germany* (case 94/87)). As noted earlier, interest will be payable from the date on which the unlawful aid was paid. As the Court has decided that undertakings in receipt of state aid must be deemed to be aware of the rules regarding the recovery of illegally granted aid it is unlikely that a person in receipt of such aid can claim damages against the state, either on the basis of tort or under *Francovich v Italy* (cases C–6 and 9/90) (see Chapter 9); arguably, in a 'normal' case he could be seen as having caused his own loss.

31.7 Conclusions

State aid continues to result in distortions of the competitive conditions within the Union, especially with the entry of new Member States who are still in the process of adapting their economies to the internal market requirements. It should not be thought, however, that this is an issue just in relation to new Member States. As businesses within the Member States find it more difficult to cope with increased competition, national governments will seek to ensure that 'their' businesses do not fail. To a limited extent, the Commission recognises that aid given in this way may be beneficial for the competitiveness of the Union as a whole in the global marketplace and this is reflected in the various exemptions now adopted under Regulation 994/98. At the same time, however, it is necessary to ensure that the competitive balance between the various Member States is maintained. One important aspect for which clarification is required, especially in a Europe which emphasises social protection, is the extent to which payments to providers of public services are caught by the state-aid provisions. Although, following *Altmark* (case C–280/00), the Commission has issued a communication on this point, it should be noted that the tension between competition within the Union and the freedom of Member States to organise public-service provision as they see fit remains. Although the state-aid provisions seem to catch such activity, other provisions, such as Article 16 EC emphasise the importance of public services and the rights of Member States in this regard. This is a tension that will remain in the Lisbon Treaty, should it ever come into force, reflecting tensions in the objectives of the Union and differing views between Member States.

FURTHER READING

Abbamonte, GB, 'Competitors' right to challenge illegally granted aid and the problem of the conflicting decisions in the field of competition law' [1997] ECLR 87.

Bacon, KM, 'State aids and general measures' (1997) 17 YEL 269.

Braun, J-D and Kuhling, J, 'Article 87 EC and the Community courts: From revolution to evolution' (2008) 45(2) CML Rev 465.

Commission's Annual Reports on Competition Policy.

Gromnicka, E, 'Services of general economic interest in the state aids regime: Proceduralisation of political choices?' (2005) 11(3) EPL 429–61.

Harrison, J and Woods, LM, 'Defining European public service broadcasting' (2001) 16 European Journal of Communication 477.

Hellingman, K, 'State participation as state aid under Article 92 of the EEC Treaty: The Commission's guidelines' (1986) 23 CML Rev 111.

Kurcz, B, and Vallindas, D, 'Can general measures be selective? Some thoughts on the interpretation of a state aid definition' (2008) 45(1) CMLRev 159.

Prosser, T, 'Competition law and public services: From single market to citizenship rights?' 11(4) EPL 543.

Quigley, C, 'The notion of a state aid in the EEC' (1988) 13 EL Rev 242.

Renzulli, A, 'Services of general economic interest: The post-*Altmark* scenario' (2008) 14 EPL 399.

Rodger, BJ, 'State aid: A fully level playing field' [1999] ECLR 251.

Ross, M, 'State aids and national courts: Definitions and other problems—a case of premature emancipation?' (2000) 37 CMLR 401.

—— 'Article 16 EC and services of general interest: From derogation to obligation', (2000) 25 Eur LR 22.

Slot Piet, J, 'Procedural aspects of state aids: The guardians of competition versus the subsidy villains' (1990) 27 CML Rev 741.

Slotboom, MM, 'State aid in Community law: A broad or narrow definition?' (1995) 20 EL Rev 289.

Winter, JA, 'Supervision of state aid' (1993) 30 CML Rev 311.

—— 'Re(de)fining the notion of state aid in Article 87(1) of the EC Treaty' (2004) 41(2) CML Rev 475.

Woods, L, 'The application of competition rules to state aids for culture' in *Culture et Marché* (ERA Forum 1/2005).

FURTHER READING

PRINCIPAL SOURCES OF EC LAW

Official Journal (L series): Community secondary legislation.

Official Journal (C series): non-binding Community instruments; proposals, notices, opinions, resolutions, reports of proceedings in Parliament and the Court of Justice.

European Commercial Cases.

European Current Law.

European Court Reports: reports of cases from the Court of Justice.

Common Market Law Reports: reports of cases from the Court of Justice and national courts.

Bulletin of the European Union: reports on day-to-day activities of the Communities; supplements on specific topics.

Annual *General Report on the Activities of the European Communities.*

Annual *Report on Competition Policy.*

Halsbury's Laws of England, 4th ed., vols 51 and 52 (D. Vaughan, coordinating ed.) (London: Butterworths, 1986).

Encyclopedia of European Community Law, (London: Sweet & Maxwell, looseleaf). Constitutional Treaties, together with annexes and protocols. Secondary legislation.

Databases:

EUR-LEX – portal to European Union Law (full text)

URL – http://eur-lex.europa.eu/en/index.htm

Prelex – database on inter-institutional procedures allowing access to electronic texts available

URL – http://ec.europa.eu/prelex/apcnet.cfm?CL=en

LexisNexis – commercial database containing European Court reports, European commercial cases, and Commission competition decisions

General introductory

Szyszczak, E., and Cygan, A., *Understanding EU Law* 2nd ed. (London: Sweet & Maxwell, 2008)

Selected textbooks in specialised areas

(a) Introductory

Mathijsen, P., *A Guide to European Union Law*, 9th ed. (London: Sweet & Maxwell, 2007)

(b) General textbooks

Craig, P., and De Búrca, G., *EC Law: Text, Cases and Materials*, 4th ed. (Oxford: Oxford University Press, 2007)

Evans, A., *European Union Law* (Oxford: Hart Publishing, 1998)

Weatherill, S., *Cases and Materials on EU Law*, 8th ed. (Oxford: Oxford University Press, 2007)

Wyatt, D., and Dashwood, A., *European Union Law*, 5th ed. (London: Sweet & Maxwell, 2006)

(c) Constitutional, institutional and administrative law

Albi, A., *EU Enlargment and the Constitutions of Central and Eastern Europe* (Cambridge: Cambridge University Press, 2005)

Andenas, M., and Usher, W-H., (eds) *The Treaty of Nice and Beyond: Enlargement and Constitutional Reform* (Oxford: Hart Publishing, 2003)

Brown, N., and Jacobs, F., *The Court of Justice of the European Communities*, 5th ed. (London: Sweet & Maxwell, 2000)

Burrows, N., and Greaves, R., *The Advocate General and EU Law* (Oxford: Oxford University Press, 2007)

Craig, P., and De Búrca, G., (eds) *The Evolution of EU Law* (Oxford: Oxford University Press, 2002)

Curtin, D., (ed) *The EU Constitution: The Best Way Forward?* (The Hague: TMC Asser Press, 2005)

Hartley, T.C., *The Foundations of European Community Law*, 6th ed. (Oxford: Oxford University Press, 2007).

Hopkins, J., *Devolution in Context: Regional, Federal and Devolved Government in the EU* (London: Cavendish, 2002).

Lenaerts, K., Van Nuffel, P., and Bray, R., *Constitutional Law of the European Union*, 2nd ed. (London: Sweet & Maxwell, 2004)

Rittberger, B., *Building Europe's Parliament: Democratic Representation Beyond the Nation State* (Oxford: Oxford University Press, 2007)

Tridimas, T., *The General Principles of EU Law* (Oxford: Oxford University Press, 2007)

Ward, A., *Judicial Review and the Rights of Private Parties in EU Law* (Oxford: Oxford University Press, 2007)

Weiler, J.H.H., *The Constitution of Europe* (Cambridge: Cambridge University Press, 1999).

(d)   Substantive law

(i)   *Agriculture*

Barents, R., *The Agricultural Law of the EC* (Deventer: Kluwer Law & Taxation, 1994).

O'Rourke, R., *European Food Law*, 2nd ed. (London: Cavendish, 2001).

McMahon, J., *EU Agricultural Law* (Oxford: Oxford University Press, 2007)

(ii)   *Civil jurisdiction and enforcement of judgments*

Briggs, A., *Agreements on Jurisdiction and Choice of Law* (Oxford: Oxford University Press, 2008)

Plender, R., and Wilderspin, M., *European Contracts Convention: the Rome Convention on the Choice of Law for Contracts* (London: Sweet & Maxwell, 2nd ed., 2001)

(iii)   *Company law*

Andenas, M., and Kenyan Slade, S., *Financial Market Regulation and Company Law* (London: Sweet & Maxwell, 1993).

Dine, J., *EC Company Law* (Chichester: Jordans, looseleaf).

Edwards, V., *EC Company Law* (Oxford: Clarendon Press, 1999).

Maitland-Walker, J., *Guide to European Company Laws*, 2nd ed. (London: Sweet & Maxwell, 1997).

Rider, B., *European Financial Services Law* (The Hague: Kluwer, 1998).

Usher, J., *Law of Money & Financial Services in the EC*, 2nd ed. (Oxford: Oxford University Press, 2000).

(iv)   *Competition law*

Baquero Cruz J., *Between Competition and Free Movement* (Oxford: Hart Publishing, 2002).

Bellamy, C.W., and Child, G.D., *European Community Law of Competition*, 6th ed. (Oxford: Oxford University Press, 2008).

Cameron, P., *Competition in Energy Markets*, 2nd ed. (Oxford: Oxford University Press, 2007)

Gormley, L.W. (ed.), *Current and Future Perspectives on EC Competition Law* (The Hague: Kluwer Law International, 1997).

Goyder, J., and Albors-Llorens, A., *EC Competition Law*, 5th ed. (Oxford: Oxford University Press, 2009).

Grayston (ed) *European Economics and Law: Competition – Trade-Single Market* (London: Cavendish, 1999).

Hancher, L., *EC State Aids*, 2nd ed. (London: Sweet & Maxwell, 1999).

Jones, C., Van der Woude, M., and Lewis, X., *EC Competition Law Handbook* (London: Sweet & Maxwell, annual).

Korah, V., *An Introductory Guide to EC Competition Law and Practice* 7th edition (Oxford: Hart, 2000).

Lindsay, A. and Berridge, A., *EC Merger Regulation*, 3rd ed. (London: Sweet & Maxwell, 2009).

Stanbrook, C., and Bentley, P., *Dumping and Subsidies*, 3rd ed. (The Hague: Kluwer Law International, 1996).

Whish, R., *Competition Law*, 6th ed. (Oxford: Oxford University Press, 2008).

(v)   *Consumer*

Weatherill, S., *EU Consumer Law and Policy*, 2nd edition (Cheltenham: Edward Elgar, 2005)

(vi)   *Environment*

Krämer, L., *EC Treaty and Environmental Law*, 5th ed. (London: Sweet & Maxwell, 2003).

Scott, J., *Environmental Protection: European Law and Governance* (Oxford: Oxford University Press, 2009)

Wennerås, P., *The Enforcement of EC Environmental Law* (Oxford: Oxford University Press, 2007)

(vii)   *Free movement of goods and services*

Andenas, M., and Roth, W-H., (eds) *Services and Free Movement in EC Law* (Oxford: Oxford University Press, 2002)

Barnard, C., and Scott, J., (eds) *The Law of the Single European Market* (Oxford: Hart Publishing, 2002).

Lyons, T., *EC Customs Law* 2nd ed. (Oxford: Oxford University Press, 2008).

Oliver, P., *Free Movement of Goods in the EC*, 3rd ed. (London: European Law Centre, 1995).

Sauter, W. and Schepel, H., *State and Market in European Union Law* (Cambridge: Cambridge University Press, 2009).

Woods, L., *Free Movement of of Goods and services within the EC* (Aldershot: Ashgate, 2004).

(viii)   *Health*

Hervey, T., *Health Law and the European Union* (Cambridge: Cambridge University Press, 2004)

(ix)   *Remedies*

Heukels, T., and McDonnell, A., *The Action for Damages in Community Law* (The Hague: Kluwer Law International, 1997).

(x)   *Tax*

Farmer, P., and Lyal, R., *EC Tax Law* 2nd ed. (Oxford: Clarendon, 2003).

Gormley, L., *EU Taxation Law* (Oxford: Oxford University Press, 2005)

(xi)   *The social dimension*

Burcusson, B., *European Labour Law* 2nd ed. (Cambridge: Cambridge University Press, 2009)

Dashwood, A., and O'Leary, S., *The Principle of Equal Treatment in EC Law* (London: Sweet & Maxwell, 1997).

de Burca, G., de Witte, B., and Ogertschnig, L., *Social Rights in Europe* (Oxford: Oxford University Press, 2005)

Giubboni, S., *Social Rights and Market Freedom in the European Constitution* (Cambridge: Cambridge University Press, 2005)

Handoll, J., *Free Movement of Persons in the European Union* (J. Wiley & Son, 1995).

Hervey, T., and O'Keeffe, D., (eds), *Sex Equality Law in the European Union* (Wiley, 1996).

Hervey, T., *European Social Law and Policy* (London: Longmans, 1998).

Kenner, J., *EU Employment Law: From Rome to Amsterdam* (Oxford: Hart Publishing, 2002).

Nielsen, R., and Szyszczak, E., *The Social Dimension of the European Community*, 3rd ed. (Handelshøjskolens Forlag, 1997).

Prechal, S., and Burrows, N., *Gender Discrimination Law of the European Society* (Dartmouth: Gower, 1990).

van der Mei, P., *Free Movement of Persons within the European Community: Cross-Border Access to Public Benefits* (Oxford: Hart Publishing, 2002).

White, R., *Workers, Establishment and Services in the European Union* (Oxford: Oxford University Press, 2004)

(xii)   *Transport*

Balfour, J., *European Community Air Law* (London: Butterworths, 1995).

Greaves, R., *Transport Law of the European Community* (London: Athlone Press, 1991).

Articles, casenotes and reviews

American Journal of International Law.

Cahiers de Droit Européen.

Common Market Law Review.

European Business Law Review.

European Competition Law Review.

European Intellectual Property Review.

European Law Review.

European Public Law.

International and Comparative Law Quarterly.

Journal of Common Market Studies.

Journal of World Trade Law.

Legal Issues of European Integration.

Maastricht Journal.

Yearbook of European Law.

INFORMATION

Information Office of the European Commission, Jean Monnet House, 8 Storey's Gate, London SW1P 3AT. Tel: 0207 973 1992.

European Business Information (Small Firms' Service), 11 Belgrave Road, London SW1V 1RB. Tel: 0171-828 6201.

European Documentation Centres (in most major cities).

European Information Centres (in most major regional centres).

INDEX